American Slang

American Slang

FOURTH EDITION

BARBARA ANN KIPFER, Ph.D.
Editor

ROBERT L. CHAPMAN, Ph.D.
Founding Editor

COLLINS

A paperback edition of this book was published in 2001 by Quill/HarperResource. The first CollinsReference edition was published in 2005.

This work is based on the *Dictionary of American Slang* by Harold Wentworth and Stuart Berg Flexner.

This work is an abridgment of the *Dictionary of American Slang*, Fourth edition, published by HarperCollins Publishers.

AMERICAN SLANG *(fourth edition)*. Copyright © 2008 by HarperCollins Publishers. All rights reserved. Printed in the United States of America. No part of this book may be used or reproduced in any manner whatsoever without written permission except in the case of brief quotations embodied in critical articles and reviews. For information, address HarperCollins Publishers, 195 Broadway, New York, NY 10007.

HarperCollins books may be purchased for educational, business, or sales promotional use. For information, please e-mail the Special Markets Department at SPsales@harpercollins.com.

FOURTH EDITION

Designed by Walter Schwarz of Figaro

The Library of Congress has catalogued the previous edition as follows:

The Library of Congress Cataloging-in-Publication Data
  American slang / edited by Robert L. Chapman. 2nd ed.
     p. cm.
     Abridgement of Dictionary of American slang. 3rd ed. 1995.
  ISBN-10: 0-06-273293-5 (PB)   ISBN-13: 978-0-06-273293-4 (PB)
  1. English language—United States—Slang Dictionaries.   2. Americanisms—Dictionaries.
  I. Chapman. Robert L., 1920– Dictionary of American slang. II. Title.
  PE2346.C46 1993   98-22757
  427—dc21   CIP

ISBN : 978-0-06-117947-1 (4th ed.)

23 24 25 26 27 LBC 15 14 13 12 11

HB 12.27.2023 1110

CONTENTS

Considering Language then as some mighty potentate, into the majestic audience-hall of the monarch ever enters a personage like one of Shakespere's clowns, and takes position there, and plays a part even in the stateliest ceremonies. Such is Slang, or indirection, an attempt of common humanity to escape from bald literalism, and express itself illimitably.

WALT WHITMAN, *"Slang in America"*

PREFACE
To the Fourth Edition

THE EDITOR OF A DICTIONARY OF SLANG owes explanations to the general reader about why such a book is made, how it was made, and how to use it. Also, the editor must attempt to explain what slang is and the history of slang lexicography.

Why This Book Was Made

Why devote a book to this sort of uncouth language? Dictionaries are popularly thought to have strong influence, giving validity and authority to the entries and therefore having social and moral impact. A dictionary like this, which specializes in terms not to be lightly used in polite society, may therefore be thought of as teaching and advocating these terms.

Theoretically in linguistics, any corpus or body of vocabulary is worth recording. Lexicography is a science in that it values accuracy, completeness, and demonstrability. As a lexicographer, I collect and record slang because it is there—but this has been done carefully and responsibly. It is up to the reader to also be careful and responsible in using these powerful and provocative words.

Yes, children may sneak off into corners with this book and find dirty words—but the printed book is now challenged and often superseded as a source of these terms by films, television programs, and the Internet. These terms are no longer kept quietly in books, but at least in a book such as this, the words are explained, their usage offered, and histories described when available.

History of Slang Lexicography

In historical justification, this book joins itself to an Anglo-American tradition going back a little more than 200 years. Credit as founder of general slang lexicography (as distinct from those who dealt in specialized lexicons of the vocabularies of thieves and tramps) goes to the distinguished British antiquarian Francis Grose, who published *A Classical Dictionary of the Vulgar Tongue* in 1785. After two further editions, the book became the basis of an 1811 updating and expansion

vii

called *Lexicon Balatronicum: A Dictionary of Buckish Slang, University Wit, and Pickpocket Eloquence,* with nearly 5,000 defined entries. Grose's book and its successor include the slang of the so-called *balatrones,* "jesters, buffoons, contemptible persons; literally babblers," and of learned humorists, those of the universities, as well as of thieves.

Grose's work held on until it was superseded in 1859 by John C. Hotten's *A Dictionary of Modern Slang, Cant, and Vulgar Words,* which had new editions through 1874. Then, in 1887, Professor Albert M.V. Barrere published *Argot and Slang: A New French and English Dictionary* at his own expense until Ballantyne Press offered the 956 pages by subscription two years later as *A Dictionary of Slang, Jargon, & Cant.* Barrere's collaborator was Charles Godfrey Leland, the first American to figure prominently in general slang lexicography. The dictionary embraced "English, American, and Anglo-Indian slang, Pidgin English, tinkers' jargon and other irregular phraseology."

In 1890, the first volume of John Stephen Farmer and William Ernest Henley's *Slang and Its Analogues* was published; volume 2 came the following year and the subsequent five volumes through 1904. The total number of pages published was 2,736.

After Farmer and Henley, good general slang lexicography was not resumed until 1937, when Eric Partridge brought out the first edition of his masterwork, *A Dictionary of Slang and Unconventional English,* which was updated and enlarged in numerous editions and printings by Partridge himself through 1980, as well as posthumously to the present. Partridge was an important lexicographer and scholar, as well as a teacher, essayist, and novelist. He is credited with making slang lexicography more or less respectable.

The first full-scale dictionary of American slang appeared in 1960 when Harold Wentworth and Stuart Berg Flexner's *Dictionary of American Slang* was published by Thomas Y. Crowell (a company later incorporated into HarperCollins). Professor Wentworth had previously written the *American Dialect Dictionary,* portions of which were adapted for the slang dictionary. Flexner added thousands of slang definitions and wrote the invaluable preface, a wonderful treatment of the sociolinguistics of slang, last printed in the 1986 *New Dictionary of American Slang.* He also did the analytical work reflected in that book's appendix, which treated the processes of word-formation in slang. The 700-page Wentworth and Flexner was enlarged and updated in 1967 and 1975, and it is the basis of the present book.

The development of slang is swift and widespread. One may question how a print dictionary can hope to be accurate or up-to-date in the Internet age. The answer is, it cannot be; it is a snapshot in time. The analysis of what to include is much more important for a print dictionary, then, because it is essential to attempt to determine what words and meanings have lasting value versus ephemeral uses. Because of the enormity of the American slang vocabulary, no print or online dictionary is close to comprehensive despite the hard work of slang lexicographers.

The Internet is a dispenser, expediter, enhancer, and preserver of slang that must be entered into with a bit of caution. Any person or group can describe its slang vocabulary for the world to access, updated as often as daily. There are a growing number of glossaries and full-scale dictionaries online, spreading new slang.

Much of the material is raw, unfiltered, and untouched by professional linguists or lexicographers. It is interesting, possibly useful, but not comparable with well-researched books.

How This Book Was Made

The book has a primary utility for people who find slang terms in speech or writing and need help with their meaning. It also serves readers who just plain enjoy slang and are curious about the particulars, such as usage and etymology. This book is intended for the general reader and does not include some of the very specialized vocabulary of subcultures. The aim is to describe terms that have gained a kind of broad acceptance and use.

The previous edition was analyzed for its user-friendliness, and decisions were made to change some of the format of the entries, the order of the senses, etc. The basic policies of this new edition remain the same: that it is to be a general dictionary of current American slang rather than a collection of special vocabularies, a scholarly historical treatment, or a book with a regional or other bias.

The Wentworth and Flexner *Dictionary of American Slang* remains the "seed," and its wealth of material has been worked with over the years, retaining much, discarding some, and reviewing/revising all.

The new resource of the Internet/World Wide Web has certainly played a part in collecting and identifying new material, as well as standard lexicographic collection methods. Many Web sites describing slang terms exist, but almost none are authoritative in the sense that they have been assembled by trained lexicographers. However, that does not mean that they are not a great resource. Many Internet collections were examined, along with print collections of slang, in deciding what to include in this edition, as data for definition-writing, and for examples of usage.

The definitions, examples of usage, and etymologies of the third edition were examined and reedited for entries retained from the previous edition. Two appendices are in this edition: the various words for "drunk," "intoxicated," and "intoxicated by drugs," and a guide to text-messaging abbreviations. The vocabulary for drunk/drugged/intoxicated is large and ever-growing; the technical development of text messaging has added a new form of abbreviated communication to our culture.

Working through the various stages and having the advantage of using electronic files make dictionary work a less difficult task in the 21st century. The style and apparatus of this dictionary are explained in the "Guide to the Dictionary."

What Is Slang?

In linguistics, where definitions at best are often imprecise and leaky, that of slang is especially notorious. The problem is one of complexity, such that a definition satisfying to one person or authority would seem inadequate to another because the prime focus is different. Like the proverbial blind men describing the elephant, all correctly, none sufficiently, we tend to stress one aspect or another of slang. My own stress will be on the individual psychology of slang speakers.

Sociolinguistic Aspects of Slang

The external and quantitative aspects of slang, its sociolinguistics, have been very satisfactorily treated, nowhere more so than in Stuart Berg Flexner's masterful preface to the *Dictionary of American Slang*. Readers may also consult Eric Partridge's 1954 *Slang To-Day and Yesterday*, particularly parts III and IV. Here you will read an updated version of Flexner's discussion of the social milieu from which American slang emerges, largely credited to Dr. Robert L. Chapman.

Recorded slang emerged from the special languages of subcultures. The group studied longest and most persistently has been the criminal underworld and the prison population. Other subcultures contributing greatly have been those of athletes and their fans, cowboys, drug (narcotics) users, entertainers (show business), gamblers, gypsies, hoboes, immigrant or ethnic populations, jazz musicians and devotees, police, railroad and other transportation workers, sailors, soldiers, and, of course, students.

In the 21st century, we must note that some of these traditional spawning grounds for slang have lost or ceased productivity and other subcultures have emerged to replace them. The terminology from hoboes, railroads, gypsies, cowboys, and even the military has slowed to a trickle. Criminals and police still make contributions, and gamblers offer zesty coinages. Teenagers and students will reliably be innovative and shocking. The entertainment world is still a fertile source of slang. Railroad slang has been replaced, though on a lesser scale, by the terms of the airline and trucking industries. The jazz world offers less, now, than rock and roll and other musical genres like hip-hop and rap.

Terms from the drug world have multiplied astronomically, as has the slang vocabulary from sports. Among the immigrant-ethnic bestowals, Yiddish, Italian, and black American slang continue to add to our lexicon. In the matter of sex, our times have witnessed a great increase in the terms taken from or describing homosexuals. Some sources of slang are relatively new: the Internet/World Wide Web/computer milieu and the hospital/medical/nursing complex. Television is a driving force behind the spread of the latter, as well as disseminating the slang of law enforcement and crime and also the business world.

With the information explosion, people feel free to create slang, and its spread is more unpredictable than ever before. Slang comes from everywhere, and the wave of communication will carry it further and faster than in the previous century.

One further distinction can be pointed out, that of "primary" and "secondary" slang. Primary slang is the speech of subculture members, natural and pristine to them, but certainly only an alternative to the rest of us, something to be chosen rather than required. Much of teenage talk and the speech of urban street gangs are examples of primary slang. Secondary slang is chosen not so much to show one's part in a group as to express one's attitudes toward (agreement or disagreement) and resourcefulness in borrowing the verbiage of such a group. Secondary slang is a matter of stylistic choice rather than true identification. When a mom says to her child, "my bad" for throwing away his baseball-card collection, it is her attempt to use secondary slang to soften the blow of what she did.

Individual Psychology of Slang

Obviously, an individual in one of the groups or subcultures mentioned above, or any of many others, resorts to slang as a means of attesting membership in the group or otherwise separating or distinguishing himself or herself from mainstream culture. He or she merges both verbally and psychologically into the subculture that prides itself on being different from, in conflict with, and/or superior to the mainstream culture. Slang is an act of bracketing a smaller social group, one that can be verbally joined and understood. The act of using slang is an act of featuring and obtruding the self within the subculture—by cleverness, control, up-to-dateness, insolence, virtuosities of audacious or satirical wit, aggression, et cetera. All this happens in the psyche. It explains most of what we know and feel about slang.

Slang is a universal mode of speaking, as old as humankind. Slang actually has its roots in the deepest parts of the mind, in the unconscious itself. That territory is perilous ground for a lexicographer, but some conjectures and relationships can be proposed for consideration.

The deeper psychodynamics of slang may have to do with two things: (1) defense of the ego against the superego, and (2) our simultaneous eagerness and reluctance to be human. Surely wounded egos are the most common human (nonanatomic) possession. Slang might be seen as a remedy, a self-administered therapy. Slang is a remedy that denies weakness and brags about sinfulness. In this view, it would not be too much to claim that therapeutic slang is necessary for the development of the self: that society would not be able to exist without its slang. It is a curious linguistic phenomenon that seems fleeting and frivolous—yet we can acknowledge that it is deeply ingrained and vital to human growth and order. This is only one of the paradoxes of slang.

In this aspect, slang is similar to profanity. Like profanity, slang is a surrogate for destructive physical action. Freud once said that the founder of civilization was the first man who hurled a curse rather than a rock or spear at his enemy. Slang also has this usefulness, and profanity can actually be considered a subcategory of slang, the more elemental phenomenon.

Slang is language that has little to do with the main aim of language, the connection of sounds with ideas in order to communicate ideas—rather, it is an attitude, a feeling, a verbal action. To pose another paradox: Slang is the most nonlinguistic type of language.

What about "our simultaneous eagerness and reluctance to be human"—what has that to do with slang? The notion is that when you try to consider it deeply, slang seems to be joined with other phenomena such as Freud's "dream work," with comedy, and elements of myth. What slang shares with all of these is the salvational and therapeutic function of both divorcing us from and maintaining our connection with genetically being an animal. Dream work relieves us of the need to be reasonable and discharges the tension of the great burden with which our rationality charges us. Though we are uncomfortable with paradox in ordinary language, we easily tolerate it in slang, where it seems much at home.

Slang links itself to comedy in that it exploits and even celebrates human weakness (or animality) without working to destroy it completely. Slang makes room for our vileness, but only so much room. The great comics of the past have often come in pairs—Laurel and Hardy, Dean and Lewis, Huck Finn and Tom Sawyer—with each member having his/her legitimacy. In myth, there were many trickster figures with a fondness for sly jokes and malicious pranks—elements, too, of much slang vocabulary.

Slang is also the idiom of life force, with roots near those of sexuality, obscenity, and death. The "dirty" parts of slang we surely know, but what about the tendency to kid about being killed in various manners? Gallows humor is quite central to slang.

One change with obvious connections to sociolinguistics and psycholinguistics is the relation of slang to gender. Women use taboo and vulgar slang quite often now, something formerly thought of as a male preserve. Sociologically, this shows the determination of women to enter the power structure and shed the restrictions of being female. Psychologically, the implications are less clear, but it may be that women are determined to be aggressive and strong, once identified as a part of profound maleness.

Apologies

The aim of the editor was to make a dictionary of current general American slang, and I have done my best to weed out entries that are only of dubious current or general status. That which is not current or not general has been left in this dictionary so that those readers who come upon these words in early writings will be able to understand the terms. Some of these also aid in understanding the derivation of more current terms.

Slang is a gray area that shares boundaries with the relaxed vocabulary identified as "informal" or "colloquial," and inevitably this dictionary will include some of those terms deemed such by other books. Slang also shares a gray area with the "figurative idiom," in which inventive and poetic terms, especially metaphors, are used for novelty and spice, self-advertisement and cheekiness. Again, some of these terms will be found in this dictionary, and you may disagree with the choice to include them. Please do contact the publisher with corrections and suggestions for future editions.

I cannot possibly express my full debt to the late Dr. Robert L. Chapman, who was the editor of the second and third editions, the latter of which I assisted. I wish he had been here to consult with, and my hope is that I have made changes he would champion and additions he would delight in.

GUIDE
To the Dictionary

THE EDITOR HAS TRIED to make the apparatus of this book clear and self-explanatory, but a few guidelines may help the reader. These are given more or less in the order of the elements in the definition block itself.

The Main Entry

The main entry sometimes contains portions that do not appear in boldface and are not taken into account in alphabetization of the headwords. These include the articles *a, an,* and *the,* when they appear in the beginning of an entry, and the variable pronoun in a phrase, indicated by *someone, someone's, something, one's,* etc. Variant forms following *or* and variants found within parentheses appear in boldface but do not affect alphabetization.

Impact Symbols

Main entries considered to have strong social or emotional impact are indicated by delta symbols bracketing the entry itself or the separate definition numbers if the impact symbol does not apply to all senses of the term. The symbols are assigned on a two-level principle, corresponding to what have usually been called "taboo" and "vulgar." Taboo terms are *never* to be used, and vulgar terms are to be used only when one is aware of and desires their strong effect. In this book, terms of contempt and derision for racial or other groups have been included among the taboo terms.

Terms of strongest impact are marked with the symbols ◄► and those of lesser impact with the symbols ◁▷. The assignment of these is a matter of editorial judgment, and not everyone will agree with this judgment. In some places, it was difficult to assign impact symbols to terms that are acceptable within a group but are considered offensive when used by those outside the group. We have taken account of recent changes in the currency and acceptability of terms previously unspeakable.

Pronunciations

Words are respelled for pronunciation only when "normal" pronunciation cannot be readily ascertained or when pronunciation is crucial to the meaning of the term. The system of respelling is designedly very simple, depending on what we regard as a majority pronunciation of the respelled syllable and showing stressed syllables in capital letters.

Part-of-Speech Labels

Parts of speech and a few other grammatical particulars are indicated by rather self-explanatory abbreviations or labels:

adj	adjective	past part	past participle
adv	adverb	phr	phrase
affirmation		prefix	
combining form		prep	preposition
infix		pres part	present participle
interj	interjection	pron	pronoun
modifier		question	
n	noun	sentence	
negation		suffix	
		v	verb

Variant Forms

Variation is shown in three ways:

1. In the main entry itself, up to three variants are shown, separated by *or*.

2. Where there are more than three variants, or they apply to various parts of the main entry, they are shown in parentheses with the label *Variations*.

3. Where variant forms apply to particular numbered definitions, this is shown by printing the form or forms at the beginning of the sense, introduced by *also*.

Dating Labels

Even though this is not meant to be a full-fledged historical dictionary, the time of origin and/or special currency of the terms is shown by a dating label. These indicate the general time of origin when known. All labels are based upon evidence found in published scholarship or lexicography, and most are, of course, subject to correction where better evidence is found.

When an entry does not have a dating label, the inference is either that the date was undiscoverable or that the term is relatively recent.

Origin Labels

When the social group or milieu from which a term originated is known, it is indicated by an origin label that is often found with the dating label; for example, *late 1800s+ cowboys* or *1960s+ teenagers*.

Definitions

Definitions were written in what most users will accept as a normal form for dictionaries. A few added notes:

1. The usual distinction between transitive and intransitive verbs has not been used, in the belief that the definitions and the examples will make that distinction clear when useful.

2. After the label *sentence*, another sentence has been provided that translates the main entry.

3. Interjections, prefixes and suffixes, and combining forms have been explained "objectively," with no attempt made to provide a strictly substitutable definition.

4. When a word is defined in one part of speech but is often used in others, it may be defined by example in this book. The most common case is where a noun is often used as an attributive modifier, which in this book is indicated by the label *modifier* followed by a colon and by an example of the use. Definitions by example apply to part-of-speech shifts from the main definition, which may or may not precede them in the entry since the parts of speech are alphabetical in this book.

5. Definitions are not always given in chronological order, even when that is known. The order of the parts of speech is alphabetical, to make the book entirely consistent.

6. Occasionally when an example itself fully defines the term, it will stand as the definition without further ado.

Slang Synonyms

Often slang synonyms are provided at the ends of definitions in small caps. Slang synonyms are also provided as quick definitions when a full definition is given elsewhere at a synonymous entry, usually at a more frequently used or interesting term.

Editorial Notes

When certain information seems useful but does not fit into the normal format of the definition block, it is included as an editorial note. These are introduced by a large black dot.

Examples

In this book, usage examples are given either when they have been collected from the media or when an invented example seems to help in definition or in showing context and structure. Examples have a double function: to illustrate usage and to validate usage and the inclusion of the term.

Etymologies

Etymologies, or word histories, are given in square brackets at the end of the definition block, before the cross-references. Slang etymology is less certain and precise than standard etymology. Because of the moral and social dubiousness of slang, less of it has been printed over the years, yielding less evidence than the lexicographer needs.

Etymologies are not given here when they are deemed to be obvious, but when they are accepted and demonstrable, they are stated as fact. In cases where an etymology seems necessary but none has been discovered or surmised, the notation *origin unknown* is used.

A part of the fun of making a slang dictionary is the exercise of ingenuity and insight for etymologies through the lexicographer's research. Etymological research is ongoing, so the editor asks to be enlightened if an etymology has been improved upon by other scholars.

Cross-References

This book attempts to cross-reference nearly every important term in every phrase. Since this book defines a great number of phrasal entries, every attempt has been made to help the readers find the term being sought.

A

A *n* **1** Amphetamine **2** LSD; acid *(Narcotics)*

AA (pronounced as separate letters) *modifier* : *an AA barrage n* An antiaircraft weapon, or antiaircraft fire; ACK-ACK, FLAK *(WWI)*

abandominiums *n* Abandoned apartments or houses where addicts use drugs : *Abandominiums blighted the former middle-class neighborhood*

abbreviated piece of nothing *n* A worthless or insignificant person or thing : *Her unemployed neighbor is an abbreviated piece of nothing*

abc gum *n* Gum that has already been chewed : *There's abc gum under the desk*

abdabs (or **habdabs** or **screaming abdabs** or **screaming habdabs**) *n* Anxiety or nervous tension : *Starting any new project gives her the abdabs (1945+)*

Abe's cabe (or **abe**) *n phr* A five-dollar bill [Jive talk 1930s+ & rock and roll 1950s+; fr Lincoln's portrait on the bill, perhaps a shortening and repronouncing of "cabbage"]

abortion *n* Something of very poor quality; a messy failure; disaster : *That show is a real abortion*

about that *See* SORRY ABOUT THAT

about town *See* MAN-ABOUT-TOWN

above one's head *See* IN OVER ONE'S HEAD

abso-bloody-lutely *modifier* Absolutely : *He abso-bloody-lutely wanted to see her again*

absotively (posilutely) *modifier* Absolutely : *I absotively posilutely want to watch the basketball games*

Acapulco gold *n phr* Marijuana of high quality grown near Acapulco, Mexico, and having leaves with a golden hue *(Narcotics)*

accident *n* A person born from an unplanned pregnancy; an unplanned pregnancy : *At 50, this third one was an accident (1900+)*

accidentally on purpose *adv phr* As if by accident, but really by intention : *She missed the meeting accidentally on purpose*

account *See* NO-ACCOUNT

accounting *See* CREATIVE ACCOUNTING

AC-DC (Variations: **AC/DC** or **ac-dc** or **ac/dc**) *adj* Practicing both heterosexual and homosexual sex; bisexual *adv* : *I think she does it AC-DC* [fr the abbreviations for the two types of electrical current, alternating and direct; an appliance that can operate with either type is marked *AC-DC*]

ace *adv* : *He did it ace every time modifier* : *an ace mechanic/ the ace professor n* **1** A person of extraordinary skill, usu in a specified activity : *poker ace/ the ace of headwaiters* **2** A combat pilot who has shot down five or more enemy aircraft *(WWI)* **3** An unusually pleasant, generous, and decent person, esp a male; prince **4** A very close friend; BUDDY, PAL *(Black & street gang)* **5** A man who favors flamboyant, up-to-the-minute dress; DUDE *(Black)* **6** A marijuana cigarette; JOINT **7** A dollar bill **8** A hole scored in one stroke *(Golf)* **9** An unreturnable serve that scores a quick point *(Racquet games)* **10** A table for one; also, a single customer *(Restaurant)* **11** A grilled cheese sandwich *(Lunch counter);* v **1** To score by an ace : *He aced the fifth hole/ She aced him six times in one set (Sports)* **2** (also **ace out**) To make a perfect or nearly perfect score : *My sister aced the chemistry exam/ Ace the test and you go on to the next subject (College students)* [fr the name of the playing card] *See* COME WITHIN AN ACE

aced *modifier* Outscored; surpassed : *I was aced in the election runoff*

ace-high *adj* Of the best; first-rate : *His reputation is ace-high*

ace in *v phr* **1** To use strategy in getting oneself into a good or profitable position **2** To understand; DIG

ace in the hole *n phr* Something held privately in reserve until needed, esp for a winning stroke; a hidden reserve or advantage [fr poker term *in the hole* for a card dealt face down in a stud game]

ace it *v phr* To score an "A" on an exam

ace of spades *n phr* ◀1▶ A black person, esp a very dark one ◁2▷ The female genitals [fr the color and shape of the playing-card symbol]

ace out *See* ACE

aces *adj* Of the very best quality; superior; finest : *I said it in this very sincere voice. "You're aces."*

ace up one's sleeve *n phr* A hidden advantage, esp a tricky one [fr a common technique of magicians and cardsharps]

acey-deucey *adj* **1** Of mixed quality; having both good and bad, high and low; ambiguous : *an acey-deucey proposition* **2** So vague, generalized, or inclusive as to offend no one; satisfactory; mediocre; SO-SO [fr card games in which the ace is the highest and the deuce the lowest card in value]

acid freak or **acidhead** *n phr* or *n* A person who uses LSD, esp one who uses the drug heavily or habitually : *He has suggested that some of our recent Presidents were acidheads (Narcotics)*

ack-ack *modifier* : *ack-ack positions* n Antiaircraft gun or guns; antiaircraft fire; AA, FLAK *(WWI)*

across the board *adj phr* **1** Designating a bet in which the same amount of money is wagered on the horse to win, place, or show *(Horse racing)* **2** Designating an equal alteration to each member of a related set, esp an equal raising or lowering of related wages or salaries : *They got an across-the-board increase of a dollar an hour* **adv** **phr** **1** : *Marcus bet $2 across the board on Duck Giggle in the fifth* **2** : *The fees were lowered across the board* [fr the **totalizator board** that shows the odds at horse-racing tracks]

act *n* **1** A display of pretended feeling; an affected pretense : *His elaborate grief was just an act* **2** A dramatic mimicking; SHTICK, TAKEOFF : *You oughta see my Brando act See* a CLASS ACT, CLEAN UP one's ACT, GO INTO one's ACT, SISTER ACT

action *n* **1** Gambling activity; a crap game or other game of chance : *Most people now go to Atlantic City for the action* **2** Activity or entertainment : *looking for the local action* **3** The, or a, sex act : *He was ogling the girls, looking for a little action* **4** Illegal activity; criminal acts : *She's into some action in New York City See* a PIECE OF THE ACTION, WHERE THE ACTION IS

activated *adj* Intoxicated by alcohol; TIPSY : *They got a little activated after their team lost in the Elite 8*

◁**act like** one's **shit doesn't stink**▷ *v phr* To behave with self-assured haughtiness; show a sense of superiority

actor *n* An athlete who is good at pretending he has been hurt or fouled; esp, a baseball player who very convincingly mimes the pain of being hit by a pitch *See* BAD ACTOR

act up *v phr* To misbehave badly or improperly, esp to impress : *Her kids act up all the time* (1900+)

Ada from Decatur *See* EIGHTER FROM DECATUR

Adam *See* NOT KNOW someone FROM ADAM

add one's **two cents in** *See* PUT one's TWO CENTS IN

adjectival (or **adjective**) *adj* Euphemistic substitute for an expletive adjective : *You adjectival idiot!* (1850+)

adman *n* An advertising executive or copywriter (1900s+)

admin *adj* Pertaining to administrative duties; short for administrative or administration (1940s+) *n* **1** The administrative work of a department or company **2** An administrative worker, esp an assistant [short for administration]

adult *adj* Euphemistically meaning unsuitable for children : *adult entertainment* (1950s+)

advantage *See* HOME-COURT ADVANTAGE

Afro (or **fro**) *modifier* : *an Afro social club* n **1** A hairstyle worn by many blacks and some whites, usu with an exaggerated bouffant style of tightly curled hair **2** A black person

◁**Afro-Saxon**▷ *n* A black person who has assumed the behavior and values of the dominant white society; OREO, TOM *(Black)*

after *prep* In pursuit of; wanting, desiring : *He is after her job* (1775+)

afterparty *n* A celebration among intimates following another party : *When the block party ended, we went to their house for an afterparty*

ag (or **aggro**) *modifier* Aggravated or annoyed : *He got aggro when the interview took longer than he planned*

against the wall *See* UP AGAINST THE WALL

age out *v phr* To reach an age, usu in the 30s or 40s, when drugs no longer have the desired effect, whereupon the user gradually stops taking them voluntarily *(Narcotics)*

ager *See* GOLDEN-AGER

aggie *modifier* Agricultural : *We visited the dairy bar at the aggie school* n **1** An agricultural college, school, or university **2** A student at an agricultural school **3** An agate or imitation marble

agreement *See* SWEETHEART CONTRACT

agricultural *adj* Ungraceful or clumsy : *She took an agricultural swing at the ball* (1930s+)

ah *See* OOH AND AH

AH (pronounced as separate letters) *n* ASSHOLE : *You are such an AH*

ahead *See* COME OUT AHEAD

A-head *n* **1** A frequent user of amphetamines **2** ACID FREAK *(Narcotics)*

ahead of the game *adv phr* In a winning or advantageous position : *Hard as I try, I can't seem to get ahead of the game*

-aholic *suffix used to form nouns and adjectives* Addicted to and overengaging in what is indicated : *fuckaholic/ sleepaholic/ workaholic*

ain't, something or someone *negation* Something or someone emphatically is not ● Said as a wry and intensive negator in a comparative statement : *My joint? Buckingham palace it ain't/ Well, she sings OK, but Barbra Streisand she ain't* [perhaps fr a Yiddish syntactic pattern]

ain't hay *See* THAT AIN'T HAY

air *v* To broadcast by radio or television : *to air a new miniseries See* a BEAR IN THE AIR, FULL OF HOT AIR, GET THE AIR, GIVE someone THE AIR, GRAB A HANDFUL OF AIR, HOT AIR, SUCK AIR, UP IN THE AIR

air one's **dirty linen** *See* WASH one's DIRTY LINEN

airhead or **airbrain** *n* A stupid or silly person; BUBBLEHEAD, DITZ : *The airheads got in trouble on Spring Weekend*

airheaded or **airbrained** *adj* Stupid; silly; vapid; BUBBLEHEADED, DITZY : *the delightfully airbrained Mickie*

airmail *n* Garbage thrown out of a window

air out *v phr* 1 To stroll; saunter *(Black)* 2 To leave; SCRAM, SPLIT

air quotes *n phr* A twitching movement of the first and second fingers of each hand to quote another or emphasize or be sarcastic about a statement

airs *See* PUT ON AIRS

air time *n phr* The time a basketball player remains in the air while making a slam dunk

aisles *See* LAY THEM IN THE AISLES

◁**AK** or **ak**▷ (pronounced as separate letters) *n* 1 ALTER KOCKER 2 ASS-KISSER

aka (pronounced as separate letters) *prep phr* Also known as; alias : *He's an asshole, aka a big deal*

alike *See* LOOK-ALIKE

alkied or **alkeyed** (AL keed) *adj* Drunk

alky or **alki** (AL kee) *n* 1 Alcohol 2 Inferior or bootleg whiskey *(1920s+)* 3 A chronic alcoholic

all bases *See* TOUCH ALL BASES

all by one's **lonesome** *adv phr* Alone; solo : *She did it all by her lonesome*

all-clear *adv phr* Denoting authorization to proceed with something; a signal that there is no further danger *(1930s+)*

all ears *adj phr* Very eager to hear; acutely attentive : *Something juicy's coming, and they're all ears (1860s+)*

allergic *adv* Having a strong aversion to something or somebody ● Usu jocular : *Teachers have that effect on me. Quite frankly, I am allergic to them (1935+)*

alley *See* BACK ALLEY

alley cat *n phr* 1 A homeless cat; stray cat 2 A sexually promiscuous person, esp a woman

all-fired *adj* : *He's got an all-fired lot of nerve adv* To an extreme or extravagant degree : *Don't be so all-fired stupid* [1800s+; a euphemism for *hell-fired*]

all fired up *See* FIRED UP

all get out or **all get up** *n phr* The extreme or absolute case of what is indicated : *overwhelmingly white, and affluent as all get-out (late 1800s+)*

all good, it's *sentence* It's all right; everything is cool : *Are you worried about the game? It's all good, man*

all Greek to *adv phr* Unintelligible *(1600+)*

all hanging out *See* HAVE IT ALL HANGING OUT

all hang out *See* LET IT ALL HANG OUT

all hell broke loose *sentence* Things became very turbulent, dangerous, noisy, etc

all hollow *See* BEAT ALL HOLLOW

alligator *n* 1 An assertively masculine, flashily dressed, and up-to-the-minute male; DUDE,

SPORT *(Black)* 2 An active devotee of swing and jive music, dancing, and speech *(1930s+ Jive talk)* ● The salutation "See you later, alligator" is common 3 A white jazz musician or jazz enthusiast *(Black jazz musicians)*

alligators *See* UP TO one's ASS IN something

all in *adj phr* Tired; exhausted; BEAT, POOPED *(1900s+)*

all in one piece or **in one piece** *adv phr* Intact; unharmed : *She came out of it in one piece*

all (or **all stuff**) **like that there** *n phr* Other such things; etcetera : *They sold boots and shoes and all like that there*

all-nighter *See* PULL AN ALL-NIGHTER

all-out *adj* Holding nothing back; sparing nothing : *an all-out effort adv* : *He ran all-out for ten minutes*

all over *See* HAVE IT ALL OVER someone or something

all over someone *adj phr* 1 Very affectionate; eagerly amorous : *The wife went to get some popcorn and the husband was all over me* 2 Aggressively smothering or battering; assaulting : *They broke through the line and were all over the quarterback*

all-overish *adv* Denoting an indefinite overall malaise *(1830s+)*

all over it *adv phr* Taking care of something quickly and efficiently : *Did you contact him? I'm all over it.*

all over the map (or **the ballpark** or **the lot**) *adv phr* Very unfocused and inconsistent; confused : *His answers are all over the map/ But otherwise, you were all over the ballpark*

all-pro *adj* Of first quality; blue-ribbon; stellar : *an all-pro team of Washington super-lobbyists* [fr the annual designation of certain professional football players to the putative team of the best]

all quiet on the Western front *adj phr* Calm; peaceful; uneventful [WWI; fr the title of a WWI novel by Erich Maria Remarque reflecting the stagnation and stability of trench warfare]

all reet (or **reat** or **root**) *interj* An exclamation of approval : *"All reat" is the rug-cutters' way of saying "all right" (1930s+)*

all-right *adj* Good; commendable; of the proper sort ● Most often used of persons : *all-right guys trying to make a living*

all right (aw RĪT) *affirmation* Yes; I agree : *All right, I'll go when you want interj* An exclamation of strong approval, esp of something well done or successful; WAY TO GO

all right already *interj* A comment protesting that one has heard or had enough or a bit too much [fr Yiddish, translating *genuk shoyn*]

all righty *affirmation* (Variations: **rightie** or
rightee or **rightey** may replace **righty**) A
humorous or deliberately cute and childish
way of saying "all right"

all she wrote *See* THAT'S ALL SHE WROTE

all shook up or **all shook** *See* SHOOK UP

all six *See* HIT ON ALL SIX

all stuff like that there *See* ALL LIKE THAT THERE

all that *adj* Very cool : *Keir is all that*

all that jazz *n phr* Other such things; etcetera :
baseball, apple pie, Chevrolet, and all that jazz

◁**all that kind of crap**▷ *n phr* (Variations:
shit or **stuff** or **bull** may replace **crap**) Other
such stupid and boring things; the depress-
ing remainder : *they demand retractions, and
all that kind of crap*

all the marbles *See* GO FOR BROKE

all the moves *See* HAVE ALL THE MOVES

all the rage *adv phr* The current or latest
fashion : *Crop tops are all the rage* (1785+)

all there *adj phr* Intelligent; TOGETHER : *At least
Keir is all there See* NOT ALL THERE

all the way *adv phr* Without reservation; to
the end : *I'll back her all the way See* GO ALL
THE WAY

all thumbs *adj phr* Very awkward; inept : *I'm
all thumbs when it comes to drawing*

all together *See* GET IT TOGETHER, HAVE IT ALL
TOGETHER

all to hell *See* EXCUSE ME ALL TO HELL, PARDON ME
ALL TO HELL

all washed up *See* WASHED UP

all wet *adj phr* Incorrect; wrong : *Your idea is
all wet, I'm afraid* (1920s+)

almighty *adj* Enormous : *There was an almighty
fuss* (1820s+)

almost, the *n phr* Nearly the best or greatest
person or thing : *He's not top line, but he's
sure the almost* (1950s+ Beat & cool talk)

alone *See* GO IT ALONE

along for the ride *See* GO ALONG FOR THE RIDE

alphabet soup *n phr* An array of initialisms or
acronyms : *Their business-speak is alphabet
soup*

already *adv* **1** Without further ado; such being
the case : *Let's go already* **2** Right now; at
once : *Shut up already* **3** Very specifically;
precisely : *Drop dead already* • *Already* is used
chiefly for a humorous exasperated effect
and to suggest Yiddish speech patterns

also-ran *n* A person, competitive product, etc,
that does not succeed; a person of mediocre
talents; LOSER [fr the term for a racehorse
who runs fourth or worse]

◁**alter kocker** (or **cocker**)▷ (AL tə KAH kər)
n phr An old man, esp a disgusting and
querulous one; AK : *You young bloods have got
it all over us alter cockers* [fr Yiddish, literally
"old shitter"]

altogether, the *See* IN THE ALTOGETHER

am *See* PRO-AM

-ama *See* -RAMA

amateur night *n phr* **1** Any occasion on which
professionals do a bad or mediocre job : *After
the third inning it was strictly amateur night* **2**
A casual sex act done with a person who is
not a prostitute [fr the occasions when *am-
ateurs* are allowed to perform at venues or
on broadcasts]

ambidextrous *adj* Bisexual; AC-DC

ambisextrous *adj* Sexually attracted to both
sexes; bisexual • Used by or suitable for either sex. Jocular; a blend of ambidextrous
and sex : *introduced her ambisextrous friend*
(1926+)

ambulance chaser *n phr* **1** Any unethical
lawyer, or one who is too aggressive in
getting clients; SHYSTER (late 1800s+) **2** A
lawyer or lawyer's helper who urges accident victims to sue for damages, negligence,
etc (1900s+)

amidships *adv* Used to refer to the striking
of a blow in the abdomen [1937+; fr
earlier sense "in the middle of a ship,"
implying the most crucial or vulnerable
part]

Am I right? *question* Isn't that right? : *You
want a three-day weekend. Am I right?*

ammo (or **ammunition**) (AM oh) *modifier* : *The
fat ammo barge rocked up and down n* **1** Ammunition : *The platoon is out of ammo*
(1930+) **2** Information and other material that may be used in a debate, campaign, exposé, etc : *Your shabby personal life
gives lots of ammo to the opposition* **3** Toilet
paper

amp *n* **1** An ampere, the electrical unit of
measurement **2** An audio amplifier, esp one
used for electronic musical instruments **3**
An ampoule of a narcotic

amped *adj* **1** Excited, possibly angry : *I got so
amped, I almost started crying* **2** High on
methamphetamine

amscray *v* To leave at once; BEAT IT, SCRAM [Pig
Latin for *scram*]

anchorman *n phr* **1** The student having the
lowest academic standing in the class
(1920s+ College students) **2** (also **anchor**,
anchorperson) A television news broadcaster who has the principal and coordi-
nating role in the program

ancient history *n phr* Something or someone
from the past, esp an old romance : *Max is
ancient history*

and *n* The second of two items that normally
go together (Lunch counter) • "Coffee and"
means "coffee and doughnuts," "ham and"
means "ham and eggs," etc

and a half *n phr* Someone or something more than usual or expected : *Her bad timing is bad news and a half*

and change *n phr* An additional smaller amount : *It happened an hour and change before midnight/ That'll run the taxpayers $6 billion and change* [fr dollars plus *change*, "coins"]

and Co. *n phr* Used to denote the rest of a group [1757+; fr earlier use in the names of business companies]

and counting *adj phr* Plus more; gradually : *$840 million and counting* [1960s+; first used in the countdown to a rocket launching]

and how *interj* An exclamation of emphatic agreement or confirmation : *Are we happy? And how!* (1900s+)

and one *adv* Getting fouled while shooting the ball into the basket, qualifying for a free throw *(Basketball)*

angel *n* **1** A person who contributes to a politician's campaign fund (1920+) **2** A financial contributor to any enterprise, esp a stage production; BUTTER-AND-EGG MAN (1920s+ *Theater)* **3** A thief's or confidence man's victim; .MARK, PATSY *(Underworld)* **4** A homosexual male (1930s+ *Homosexuals)* **5** A vague and illusory image on a radar screen, often due to bird flights, rare atmospheric conditions, or electronic defects **6** A helicopter that hovers near an aircraft carrier to rescue aircrew who crash into the water *(Vietnam War Navy)* *v* : *My doctor angeled one of his friend's plays*

angel dust *n phr* **1** The powdered form of PCP, a tranquilizer used in veterinary medicine, which as a narcotic is either sniffed or smoked in a tightly rolled cigarette **2** A synthetic heroin

◁**Anglo**▷ *n* A white person; PADDY *(Hispanics)*

animal *n* A brutal or aggressive person, esp one given to excessive sexuality or violence (1940s+ *Army & students)*

ankle *v* To walk : *I ankled over to the bar* [perhaps in part from *angle*, cited fr 1890s in sense of "to walk"]

ankle-biter *n* A child [1980s+; fr children's height and sporadic outbursts of violence]

Ann *See* MARY ANN

Annie *See* BASEBALL ANNIE

annihilated *adj* Very drunk or drugged : *After such a bad week, she just wanted to get annihilated*

another country (or county or precinct) heard from *sentence* Still another voice makes itself heard • Usu an irritated and contemptuous response to a new or unwanted contribution of opinion

another peep (out of you) *n* More complaints, comments, or talk : *Sit there. Not another peep out of you!*

another pretty face *See* NOT JUST ANOTHER PRETTY FACE

ante *See* PENNY ANTE, UP THE ANTE

ante up *v phr* To contribute money one is responsible for or is expected to give : *On April 15 we all ante up to Uncle Sam* [1800s+; fr the poker term for an initial contribution to the pot as a game begins]

anti (AN tī) *n* A person opposed to a particular plan, position, action, etc : *The vote showed three pros and six antis*

ants or ants in one's **pants** *n* or *n phr* **1** An unrelaxed, disturbed condition; anxiety; acute restlessness : *After two days at sea she began to get ants* **2** Sexual excitement; the HOTS

antsy *adj* **1** In an anxious, disturbed state; nervous; jittery : *But when things are quiet, I get antsy* **2** Sexually aroused; lustful; HOT

A-number-1 or A-number-one *adj* Of the highest or best quality; first-class; excellent

anyhoo *adv* Anyhow • Mispronunciation used for presumed humorous effect

any old *adj phr* Having only ordinary or mediocre quality; of no special distinction : *Any old car will do me*

A-OK or A-Okay or A O-K *adj* Proceeding or functioning properly; giving no cause for worry; COPACETIC, GO : *Your X rays are A-OK adv* : *The plan's going A-OK (1960s+ Space travel)*

A–1 or A-one *adj* A-NUMBER-1

ape *adj* **1** (also **ape-shit**) Stupid and destructive; irrational; berserk : *You acted like you were ape, pounding the wall* **2** (also **ape-shit**) Very enthusiastic; highly excited; BANANAS : *He's ape about my new car n* ◀**1**▶ A black person **2** The best or greatest; the ultimate : *Her paintings are truly ape (Beat talk & rock and roll)* **3** An especially strong and pugnacious hoodlum; a strong-arm man or muscle man; GOON, GORILLA *See* GO APE, HOUSE APE, RUG RAT

◁**ape-shit**▷ *See* APE, GO APE

apple *n* **1** A ball, esp a baseball **2** A street or district where excitement may be found (1930s+ *Jazz musicians)* **3** Any large town or city (1930s+ *Jazz musicians)* ◁**4**▷ A Native American who has taken on the values and behavior of the white community; uncle tomahawk *See* the BIG APPLE, HORSE APPLE, SURE AS GOD MADE LITTLE GREEN APPLES, WISE GUY

Apple, the *See* the BIG APPLE

apple-pie order *n phr* A condition of neatness, correctness, and propriety : *Paul keeps the financial records in apple-pie order*

apple-polish *v* To flatter and pamper in order to gain personal advantage; curry favor; BROWN-NOSE, SUCK UP TO someone : *He started apple-polishing the captain as soon as he got on board*

apple-polisher *n* A person who apple-polishes [fr the traditional image of the pupil who brings the teacher a shiny red apple]

apples *See* HOW DO YOU LIKE THEM APPLES

applesauce *n* Nonsense; pretentious talk; BULLSHIT, BUNK : *"Ideologies" freely translated into American means "applesauce"* [1900s+; fr the fact that relatively cheap, hence worthless, **applesauce** would be served instead of choicer food in boardinghouses]

apples to oranges *n phr* An unfair comparison

appropriate *v* LIBERATE *(WWI Army)*

-arama *See* -RAMA

Archie Bunker *modifier* : *He has the support of the traditional Republican establishment, and is adding the Archie Bunker vote* *n phr* A bigoted lower-middle-class American; HARD HAT, REDNECK [fr the name of the leading character of the television comedy series *All in the Family*, who exhibited the traits indicated]

are we having fun yet? *sentence* Is this the fun you thought it would be? This is not the fun you thought it would be

-arino *See* -ERINO

arm *n* A police officer *v* highflag (Cabdrivers) [police sense fr **arm of the law**] *See* AS LONG AS YOUR ARM, CROOKED ARM, ONE-ARM BANDIT, STIFF, TWIST someone's ARM

arm, the *See* PUT THE ARM ON someone, a SHOT IN THE ARM

arm and a leg, an *n phr* An exorbitantly high price : *The trip cost an arm and a leg*

armchair general (or **strategist**) *n phr* A person who speaks authoritatively but not convincingly on matters where that person lacks practical experience; BLOWHARD, KNOW-IT-ALL

arm it *v phr* To convey a customer and collect the fare without using the meter; highflag, ride the arm [Cabdrivers; fr original vertical *arm* of the taxi meter, turned horizontal to start the meter]

armpit *n* A very undesirable place; geographical nadir; THE PITS; ASSHOLE : *My home town is the armpit of the universe* *See* PULL TEETH

arm-twisting *n* Extremely strong persuasion : *With some arm-twisting, she went to the party*

arm-waver *n* An excitable or emphatic person

army game, the (or **the old**) *n phr* Any swindle or confidence game; a dishonest gambling game; FLIMFLAM : *It's nothing but the army game*

-aroo *See* -EROO

-arooney or **-erooney** *suffix used to form nouns* A suffix added to imply familiarity or humor : *This little cararooney's got only 10,000 miles on her*

around or **around the block,** someone has been *sentence* The subject is not naive, but is experienced and clever : *He may look innocent, but he's been around/ Having been around the block, Sylvia not only writes stories but dispenses advice/ Oliver's been around the block and won't be seduced by money (first variant 1920s+, second variant 1990s+)*

around the bend *adj phr* Insane; BONKERS : *Around-the-bend views from the nation's top critics* *adv phr* With most or the hardest part done; OVER THE HILL : *Two more days and we'll be around the bend on this project* *See* ROUND THE BEND

around the bush *See* BEAT AROUND THE BUSH

around (or **round**) **the horn** *adj phr* Of throws from third base to second base to first base : *a brilliant round-the-horn double play* *adv phr* Legally detained on a minor charge but suspected and not yet charged for a more serious crime *(1930s+ Underworld)* [Baseball; fr the length and circuitousness of a voyage around Cape Horn at the southern tip of South America]

around the world *See* GO AROUND THE WORLD

arrive *v* To successfully establish one's position or reputation *(1880s+)*

arrow *See* STRAIGHT ARROW

arse *n* ASS *(1860+)*

article *n* A person, esp one considered to be clever, cute, or resourceful; NUMBER • Always preceded by an adjective or by the locution "Quite an" : *He is some slick article/ Your little sister's quite an article*

artillery *n* **1** A weapon or weapons, esp a handgun carried by a criminal; HEAT *(1900s+ Underworld)* **2** A drug user's hypodermic syringe *See* HEAVY ARTILLERY

artist *See* BULLSHIT ARTIST, BUNCO ARTIST, CLIP-ARTIST, GYP, MAKE-OUT ARTIST, PUT-ON, RIPOFF, SACK ARTIST

artsy-craftsy or **artsy** or **arty** *adj* Pretentiously and self-consciously artistic; straining for esthetic effect : *an artsy-craftsy little boutique on Nantucket (1940s+)*

artsy-fartsy or **artsy-smartsy** *adj* Pompously or blatantly esthetic • The superlative degree of *artsy-craftsy* : *The pianist veers toward the artsy-fartsy*

asap or **ASAP** (pronounced either as separate letters or as an acronym, AY sap) *adv* Right away; immediately : *Our job is simple—to liberate US POWs from Asia, ASAP* [Armed forces; fr *as soon as possible*]

as close as stink on shit *adv phr* Extremely close; intimate : *new lovers close as stink on shit*

ash can *n phr* An antisubmarine depth charge *(Navy fr WWI) See* KNOCK someone FOR A LOOP

ashes *See* GET one's ASHES HAULED

As if! *interj* That would be nice; I wish that were true! • Usu sarcastic : *Straight A's? As if!*

ask for it (or **trouble**) *v phr* To behave in a way that invites and deserves trouble; provoke : *I'm sorry you had that wreck, but with no brakes you were asking for it* (1900s+)

ask me another *sentence* Used to indicate that one does not know the answer to a question : *Am I ready? Ask me another. I am not in a position to say* (1910+)

asleep at the switch *adj phr* Not attending to one's duty and risking safety; unvigilant; inattentive *(Railroad)*

as long as your arm *adj phr* Very extensive; remarkably long : *The guy's a jailbird, a record as long as your arm*

as per usual *adv phr* As usual

asphalt jungle *n phr* A city's paved landscape; a big city

as right as rain *modifier* Completely correct

◁**ass**▷ *n* **1** The buttocks; posterior; BUTT : *a kick in the ass* **2** The anus; ASSHOLE : *You can take it and shove it up your ass* **3** A person regarded solely as a sex partner or target; TAIL : *She looks like good ass* **4** Sexual activity; sexual gratification : *He was out looking for ass* **5** The whole self; the person • Used for emphasis and euphony : *Get your ass out of here pronto/ I'm out in Kansas for the first time, my ass drafted See* one's ASS IS DRAGGING, someone's ASS IS ON THE LINE, BAG ASS, BET YOUR BOOTS, BURN someone's ASS, BUST one's ASS, CANDY ASS, CANDY-ASSED, CHEW someone's ASS, COLD AS HELL, COVER one's ASS, DEADASS, DRAG ASS, DRAG one's TAIL, DUMB-ASS, FALL ON one's ASS, FLAT-ASS, FLAT ON one's ASS, GET one's ASS IN GEAR, GET one's HEAD OUT OF one's ASS, GET OFF one's ASS, GET THE LEAD OUT, GIVE someone A PAIN, GRIPE one's ASS, one HAS HAD IT, HAUL ASS, HAVE A BUG UP one's ASS, HAVE someone's ASS, HAVE one's ASS IN A SLING, HAVE one's HEAD PULLED, HAVE one's HEAD UP one's ASS, HAVE LEAD IN one's PANTS, one's HEAD IS UP one's ASS, HORSE'S ASS, IN A PIG'S EYE, JUMP THROUGH one's ASS, KICK ASS, a KICK IN THE ASS, KISS MY ASS, KISS someone's ASS, MAN WITH A PAPER ASS, MY ASS, NO SKIN OFF MY ASS, NOT HAVE A HAIR ON one's ASS, NOT KNOW one's ASS FROM one's ELBOW, ON one's ASS, OUT ON one's ASS, a PAIN IN THE ASS, PIECE OF ASS, PISSY, PULL something OUT OF

one's ASS, PUT one's ASS ON THE LINE, RAGGEDY-ASS, a RAT'S ASS, RATTY, SHAG ASS, SHIT-ASS, SIT ON one's ASS, SIT THERE WITH one's FINGER UP one's ASS, SMART-ASS, STAND AROUND WITH one's FINGER UP one's ASS, STICK IT, SUCK ASS, TEAR OFF A PIECE, THROW someone OUT ON someone's ASS, TIRED-ASS, UP THE ASS, UP TO one's ASS IN something, WHAT'S-HIS-NAME, WILD-ASS, WORK one's ASS OFF

◁**-ass** or **-assed**▷ *suffix used to form adjectives* **1** Having buttocks of the specified sort : *big-ass/ fat-assed suffix used to form adjectives and nouns* **2** Having a specified character or nature to a high degree : *badass/ wildassed/ silly-ass*

◁**ass backwards**▷ *adj phr* : *The whole plan is ass backwards adv phr* In a reversed position or confused manner : *You installed it ass backwards/ She had it all ass backwards*

◁**assbite**▷ *n* A strong rebuke; reprimand : *I took the assbite without looking at him*

ass-chewing *n phr* A bawling out; verbal annihilation

◁**assed**▷ *See* HALF-ASSED, PUCKER-ASSED, RED-ASSED

◀**assfuck**▶ *n* An act of anal intercourse *v* To do anal intercourse; BUGGER[1], BUNGHOLE

◁**asshole** or **butthole**▷ *n* **1** The anus; rectum **2** A despised person; BASTARD, SHITHEAD : *Teenagers can be such assholes/ Better not, you butthole* (1930s+) **3** ASSHOLE BUDDY **4** The most despised and loathsome part; ARMPIT : *This town's the asshole of the North See* BLOW IT OUT, BREAK OUT INTO ASSHOLES, FLAMER, TANGLE ASSHOLES

◁**asshole** (or **buttfuck**) **buddy**▷ *n phr* A very close friend; best friend; PAL • Usu with only a humorous connotation of homosexuality : *He assumed the mail was going to be the friendly asshole buddy e-mail that one gets from colleagues*

◁**asshole deep**▷ *See* UP TO one's ASS IN something

as sin *modifier* To the extreme : *guilty as sin; ugly as sin* (1900+)

◁**ass in a sling**▷ *See* HAVE one's ASS IN A SLING

◁**ass is dragging,** one's▷ *sentence* The subject is very tired; one is exhausted and hence sluggish

◁**ass is grass,** one's▷ *sentence* The subject is in trouble; one will be ruined, undone, etc : *Give me a title, in short, or your ass is grass* (1940s+)

◁**ass is on the line,** someone's▷ *sentence* Someone is at risk; someone has taken a perilous responsibility : *A friend's ass is on the line and I promised I'd talk to you/ I better be right this time, because my ass is on the line* [fr the notion of a *line* separating hostile persons, such that encroaching on it is a challenge and a risk]

◁**asskicker**▷ *n* **1** An energetic person, esp an officer who harasses subordinates **2** Something that functions very well : *That little motor's a real asskicker* **3** An exhausting experience *(Army)*

◁**asskicking**▷ *adj* Functioning or performing well : *That's an asskicking little heater (Army)*

◁**ass-kisser**▷ *n* (Variations: **licker** or **sucker** may replace **kisser**) A person who flatters and serves obsequiously to gain favor with a superior; sycophant; AK, BROWN-NOSE, YES-MAN

◁**ass-kissing** or **ass-licking**▷ *n* Flattery; currying favor with superiors; BROWN-NOSING : *It's a short step from lip service to ass-kissing*

◁**ass man**▷ *n phr* **1** A man with an extraordinary and consuming interest in doing the sex act; lecher; satyr; COCKSMAN **2** A man whose favorite part of female anatomy is the buttocks

◁**ass** (or **buns** or **tail**) **off**, one's▷ *adv phr* Very hard; one's best; to one's utmost : *I worked my ass off for that ungrateful jerk/ listen to that drummer play his buns off*

◁**ass peddler**▷ *n phr* A prostitute, of either sex

as sure as hell *modifier* Absolutely certain; most certainly : *As sure as hell she called again (1970s+)*

◁**ass-wipe** or **ass-wiper** or **butt-wipe**▷ *n* **1** Toilet paper or something similarly used **2** Idiot, fool; ASSHOLE

◁**assy**▷ *adj* Malicious; nasty; mean; BITCHY *(Homosexuals)*

astronomical *adj* Inconceivably large : *an astronomical price for that car*

-ateria *suffix used to form nouns* (Variations: -teria or -eria or -eteria) Place or establishment where the indicated thing is done or sold : *bookateria/ caviarteria*

at liberty *adv phr* Unemployed

at loose ends *modifier* Discombobulated or without a clue : *at loose ends when they aren't around*

-atorium or **-torium** or **-orium** *suffix used to form nouns* Place where an indicated thing is done : *drinkatorium/ lubritorium/ printorium*

at sixes and sevens *modifier* In a state of confusion and disorder [1670+; fr the earlier phrase "set on six and seven," leave to chance, possibly a fanciful alteration of "set on cinque and sice" (= five and six), a gambling term denoting hazarding everything on throwing a five and a six at dice]

attaboy or **attagirl** *interj* An exclamation of approval or encouragement; WAY TO GO [fr *that's the boy*]

at the switch *See* ASLEEP AT THE SWITCH

attitude *n* A resentful and hostile manner; pugnacity *(Black & prison) See* HAVE AN ATTITUDE

attitude-adjuster *n phr* A police officer's club or stick

attract *v* To steal : *attracted some lumber and built a garage (1891+)*

aunt or **Aunt** *n* **1** The madame of a brothel **2** An elderly male homosexual

Aunt Flo *n* A woman's menstrual period : *my visit from Aunt Flo*

auntie[1] *n* Any elderly, esp black, woman *(1800s+)*

auntie[2] *n* An antimissile missile [Air Force; fr humorous mispronunciation of **anti**]

autopilot *n* Something done automatically, without much self-awareness : *She is on autopilot when driving them to school*

avoid like the plague *v phr* Evade or elude at any cost; shun : *avoid him like the plague (1936+)*

avoirdupois (AV ər də poyz) *n* Body weight; fat or fatness : *I have too much avoirdupois, so I'm dieting*

awash *adj* **1** Full of a liquid; full to surfeit : *Dr Johnson was awash in tea, drinking thirty cups each day* **2** Overwhelmed with; drowning in : *The dean was awash in niggling student complaints See* DECKS AWASH

away *adv* **1** Out : *Two away in the top of the eighth (Baseball)* **2** In prison *(Underworld)*

awesome *adj* Excellent; wonderful; outstanding; COOL, NEAT *(Teenagers) interj* Excellent! Great! : *You fixed it? Awesome!*

awful *adj* Extremely unpleasant or objectionable *adv* Very; intensely : *I feel awful bad about that See* GOD-AWFUL

awfully *adv* Very; very much : *It's awfully dark here*

AWOL or **awol** (pronounced either as separate letters or as an acronym, AY wawl) *adj* Absent without leave *n* A person who is absent without leave *(Armed forces fr WWI)*

aw right *See* ALL RIGHT

aw shucks *interj* An exclamation of embarrassment, self-abnegation, regret, and various other mildly uncomfortable feelings • Usu used in imitation of rural or extremely naive, boyish males *v phr* : *good-ole-boy aw shucksing* • Euph for *aw shit*

awshucksness *n phr* Modesty; self-abnegating embarrassment : *Young Crosby displayed all the easygoing awshucksness of his late father*

ax or **axe** *n* **1** Any musical instrument, esp the saxophone : *He played his ax at the casino (1950s+ Jazz musicians)* **2** A guitar *(Rock and roll) v* **1** To dismiss someone from a job, a team, a school, a relationship, etc; CAN, FIRE : *who suggested to Reagan that Deaver be axed* **2**

To eliminate; cut : *They axed a lot of useless stuff from the budget* [musical instrument sense fr the resemblance in shape between a saxophone and an ax, and possibly fr the rhyme with *sax*]

ax, the *See* GET THE AX, GIVE someone THE AX

axman *n* A guitarist, especially one who plays in a band or group : *learned guitar from Fats Domino's axman* [1976+ Jazz and rock music]

Aztec two-step *n phr* Diarrhea; MONTEZUMA'S REVENGE, TURISTA

B

b See SON OF A BITCH

B *n* **1** Benzedrine®; BENNY *(1950+)* **2** bee *(1970s+)* **3** The game of Frisbee *(1990s+ Students)*

babe *n* A girl or woman, esp a sexually desirable one; chick, DOLL • Used almost entirely by men and considered offensive by many women; strong resurgence of use in the 1990s *(1915+)*

babelicious *adj* Very sexually attractive : *Beyonce is connected with the word babelicious* [1992; coined in the film *Wayne's World*]

babe magnet or **chick magnet** *n* A male or one of his possessions that attracts females, esp beautiful ones : *The 350Z is definitely a babe magnet*

baboon *n* An uncouth or stupid person : *Outta my way, you baboon!*

baby *n* **1** A wife, girlfriend, or other cherished woman; also, less frequently, a husband, boyfriend, or cherished man : *My baby don't love me no more (1900s+)* **2** Any cherished or putatively cherished person • A shortening of earlier *warm baby (1900s+)* **3** A mean and dangerous man; TOUGH GUY • *Babe*, "a tough; a rowdy; blackguard," is attested in the 1860s : *I did not want them babies to think they had me under contract (1930s+)* **4** A term of address for a man or a woman; BUD, MAC, PAL • In stereotype, much used by show-business people : *And this is maximum security, baby (1910+)* **5** Anything regarded with special affection, admiration, pride, or awe : *Those babies'll turn on a dime/ What we had heard was the firing of those big babies a mile and a half from shore (1900+)* **6** A thing referred to, esp something one does not know the name of; GADGET, SUCKER : *What's this baby over here supposed to do? (1930s+)*

baby blues *n phr* Blue eyes : *lookin' up into the baby blues of some sweet-faced Army nurse (1970s+)*

baby boom *modifier : the millions of baby-boom couples who work for wages n phr* A significant rise in births, esp after 1945 *(1960s+, despite an isolated occurrence 1941+)*

baby boomer *n phr* A person born during the baby boom following World War II *(1970s+)*

babycakes or **honeycakes** *n* A sweetheart or other cherished person • A term of endearment : *Hey, babycakes, let's see those pecs/ "Ain't that right, baby?" "Sure is, honeycakes" (1960s+)*

baby doll *n phr* A pretty woman, esp one cherished by a man as his own *(1900s+)*

baby-kisser *n* A politician [fr the practice of candidates kissing babies, shaking hands, etc]

baby split *n phr* A split where two pins are left standing side by side *(Bowling)*

bach or **batch** *n* A bachelor *(1850s+) v* (also **bach it**) Of a man, to live alone *(1860s+)*

bachelor girl *modifier : a bachelor-girl apartment n phr* An unmarried young woman, usu with a career or a profession; career girl *(1890s+)*

back *adv* As a chaser : *She wants whiskey with water back (1980s+) n* (also **backup** or **backup for a beef**) Someone who will support and assist; a trusty ally *(1980s+ Teenagers) v* **1** To give one's support to some effort or person : *I'll back your application (1500s+)* **2** To bet on : *He backed Green Goo in the eighth (1600s+)* **3** To contribute money for; BANKROLL : *My cousin backed the rock show in the park (1880s+) See* GET one's or someone's BACK UP, GET OFF someone's BACK, GET THE MONKEY OFF, GIVE someone THE SHIRT OFF one's BACK, KNOCK BACK, MELLOWBACK, MOSSBACK, ON someone's BACK, PIGGYBACK, PIN someone's EARS BACK, YOU SCRATCH MY BACK, I SCRATCH YOURS

back alley *modifier : a back-alley saloon/ back-alley language n phr* An alley or street in a mean and disreputable neighborhood; slum street or area *(1860s+)*

backassed *modifier* In a backward or awkward manner : *Why would he attempt that in such a backassed way?*

backasswards *adv* ASS BACKWARDS

backbone *n* Integrity and courage; fortitude : *If you had any backbone, you would deal with him*

backbreaker *n* A very difficult job or task; BALL-BUSTER, BITCH, PISSER *(1900s+)*

back-burner *modifier : a back-burner project v* To put a project, idea, suggestion, etc, in reserve : *Shall we just back-burner that one? (1980s+)*

back burner See ON THE BACK BURNER

backchannel *n* A secret conduit for information : *Clinton's backchannel during the trouble was the Russian Embassy (1990s+)*

backchat *n* Impertinent and provocative replies, esp to a superior, elder, etc; BACK TALK, SASS *(1800s+ British military)*

back-door *adj* Dishonest; dubious • Earlier senses were "secret, clandestine" and "illegitimate, bastard" : *a sleazy little back-door business (1900s+)*

back door *n phr* **1** A devious, shady, and perhaps illegal means : *The US Government may*

11

be able to use a "back door" into Microsoft Windows to infiltrate computers worldwide (1581+) ◁2▷ The anus; ASSHOLE (1600s+)

backdoor man *n phr* A married woman's lover; jody (1960s+ *Black*)

backdoor trots *n phr* Diarrhea (1700s+ *British, now chiefly Canadian*)

back down *v phr* To retreat from one's position; surrender; retract : *He wouldn't back down even when they beat him up* (1850s+)

backhander *n* 1 A blow made with the back of a hand, esp to the face 2 Secret payment

back in the saddle *adj phr* Operational again; restored to function : *The economy is back in the saddle/ I have aspirations to get back in the saddle* [1940s+; fr a popular cowboy song *"Back in the Saddle Again"*]

back number *n phr* Someone or something out of date; HAS-BEEN : *Mr Stale is a back number* (1880s+)

back off *v phr* 1 To stop annoying or harassing someone ● Often a command or threat 2 To soften or moderate; relent : *The president backed off a little from his hardnosed line* 3 To slow down; go easier : *Hey, back off a little, I don't get you* (*primary sense "retreat"* 1930s+)

back someone off *v phr* To order someone to leave; eject someone : *The bouncer backed him off real quick*

back out *v phr* To cancel or renege on an arrangement; crawfish. FINK OUT : *We can't back out just because we're scared* (1800s+)

back passage *n phr* The rectum : *reached his back passage* (1960+)

back-pedal *v* To retreat, esp from a stated position; BACK OFF, BACK OUT : *This news caused the candidate to back-pedal hastily* (1900+)

backroom *adj* Having to do with political expediency; from the inner circles of party affairs : *a backroom decision/ backroom motives* [1940s+; fr *See what the boys in the back room will have*, suggesting a secret conclave in the rear of a saloon] *See* BOYS IN THE BACKROOM

backscratch or **backscratching** *n* A helping or accommodating of one by another : *It's got to be a mutual backscratch* (late 1800s+) *See* YOU SCRATCH MY BACK, I SCRATCH YOURS

back seat *See* TAKE A BACK SEAT

backseat driver *n phr* A person who gives unwanted and officious advice; KIBITZER (1920s+)

backside *n* The buttocks; rump : *slapped her on the backside*

back-slapper *n* A demonstratively friendly person : *Bob and Bill, they're back-slappers* (1924+)

back-slapping *adj* Demonstratively friendly : *the back-slapping jocosity that passes for humor here* (1777+)

back talk *n phr* Impudent response; impertinent comment; SASS (mid-1800s+)

back teeth are floating, one's *sentence* One needs very urgently to urinate (1890s+)

back to square one *adv phr* Returned to the starting point, usu having wasted a great deal of effort; no farther ahead : *Which means we're basically back to square one* [1960s+ British; origin uncertain, perhaps fr one of various board games] *See* GO BACK TO SQUARE ONE

back to the (old) **drawing board** *sentence* The matter must be reconsidered; it's time to start again : *So back to the drawing board. Find another way to go* [fr the caption of an early 1940s Peter Arno *New Yorker* cartoon showing a crashed airplane]

back to the salt mines *adv phr* Returned to hard work and unremitting discomfort after a period of relative ease and pleasure : *I had a week off, then back to the salt mines* [1920s+; fr the tradition of Russian penal servitude in Siberian salt mines]

back-track *See* BOOT

back someone up *v phr* 1 To confirm what someone says; support what someone does : *If you want to go in to complain, I'll back you up* (1860s+ *British*) 2 To be someone's substitute; be in reserve : *We've got three other drivers to back him up* (1950s+) 3 To play behind a fielder to retrieve balls that might be missed (1940s+ *Baseball*)

backwash *n* Something drunk that is regurgitated or spit back out *v* To regurgitate or spit back out liquid

bacon *See* BRING HOME THE BACON

bad *adj* Good; excellent; admirable : *real bad licks/ bad man on drums* ● The use is attested from slavery times, when this sense was marked by a lengthened vowel and a falling tone in pronunciation (1920s+ *esp black teenagers*) *See* SO BAD ONE CAN TASTE IT

ba da bing, ba da boom *interj* An exclamation describing something that happens quickly and easily : *went in to get a tattoo—ba da bing, ba da boom*

bad actor (or **actress**) *n phr* 1 A malicious or deceitful person 2 A habitual criminal 3 A vicious animal (1900+)

◁**badass**▷ *adj* 1 Difficult to deal with 2 Excellent; wonderful; RAD, SLAMMIN' (1980s+ *College*) *n* A belligerent and worthless person; BAD ACTOR, BAD EGG, BUM : *It's the badasses who don't want him back* (1950s+)

bad boy *n phr* An impressive and perhaps dangerous device; PUPPY, SUCKER : *You have written plenty of checks for your Harley, maybe even a few while right in the saddle of your bad boy* (1980s+)

bad business *n phr* 1 A morally questionable activity : *He has some bad business going on* *with the guys from the 'hood* **2** Poor business conduct : *That is just bad business to have ill-groomed servicepeople*

bad cop *See* GOOD COP BAD COP

bad day at Black Rock *n phr* An unhappy time : *It will be a bad day at Black Rock when the players gather for the last time* [fr the 1955 cowboy-suspense movie *Bad Day at Black Rock*]

baddie or **baddy** or **bad guy** *n* **1** Someone or something that is bad, esp a movie, television, or sports villain **2** A criminal or other habitually reprehensible person; bad man *(1930s+ Motion pictures)*

bad egg *n phr* A villain, criminal, or other deplorable person; BAD ACTOR, BADDIE *(1855+)*

badge *n* A police officer *(1920s+ Underworld)*

bad hair day *n phr* The sort of day when nothing goes right; the sort of day that is not one's day : *They had a bad hair day, a bad CD-ROM day, who knows?* [1990s+; fr the notion that one's well-being depends on whether one's hair looks good]

bad-mouth *n phr* : *If you can't say anything good, at least don't be a bad mouth* *v phr* To disparage; denigrate : *He bad-mouthed everybody (1930s+)*

bad news *n phr* **1** The bill for goods or services, esp a restaurant check; BEEF *(1920s+)* **2** Any unfortunate or regrettable situation or event : *That meeting was strictly bad news (1930s+)* **3** An ominous person; a menace : *Their big new linebacker is bad news (1960s+)* **4** An unpleasant or depressing person, esp a persistently annoying one : *Isn't she bad news since her old man left her?* [1970s+; all senses extended from the literal]

bad paper *n phr* **1** Worthless or counterfeit money, checks, etc : *They passed some bad paper (1940s+)* **2** A less-than-honorable discharge from military service *(1970s+ fr Vietnam veterans)*

bad patch *n phr* A period of difficulty, suffering, etc : *You went through a real bad patch, a shaky time (1920s+ British)*

bad rap *n phr* **1** An erroneous conviction or sentence; wrongful punishment; BUM RAP *(Underworld)* **2** Any unjustified condemnation : *Microsoft gets a bad rap for a reason*

bad scene *n phr* Something unpleasant, esp a displeasing and depressing experience or situation [1950s+ and popularized by the 1960s counterculture; fr the jazz sense of *scene*, "center of activity for musicians"]

◁**bad shit**▷ *n phr* **1** Something menacing and nasty : *A lot of bad shit goes down at the track, man (1950s+)* **2** Bad luck : *Breaking my leg was just bad shit (1950s+)* **3** A toxic or contaminated narcotic : *But it's bad shit, or too strong (1960s+)*

bad time *n phr* Time spent in the guardhouse and therefore not a part of one's required period of service *(Armed forces fr WWII)*

bad (or bum or down) trip *n phr* **1** A frightening or depressing drug experience, esp a nightmarish time with LSD *(1960s+ Narcotics)* **2** Any unpleasant occasion or experience; BUMMER, DOWNER : *The party was a real bad trip (1960s+ Counterculture)*

bag *n* ◁1▷ The scrotum *(1920s+)* ◁2▷ A condom; RUBBER, SCUMBAG *(1950s+)* **3** The cushionlike marker that serves as a base *(mid-1800s+ Baseball)* **4** A portion of narcotics, often wrapped in a paper or glassine envelope : *They found three nickel bags of marijuana on him (1960s+ Narcotics)* ◁5▷ A woman's breast • *Bag* has long meant an animal's udder *(mid-1600s+)* **6** An unattractive girl or woman; ugly woman *(1920s+)* **7** That which one prefers or is doing currently; KICK, THING • Said to be fr *bag of tricks (1950s+ Jazz musicians)* **8** One's preference; something suited to one's preferences or talents : *Archaeology is her bag, man* **9** An environment; milieu; SCENE : *That fox comes out of a very intellectual bag (1950s+ Jazz musicians)* *v* **1** To get or capture : *to bag a gold medal/ They bagged the mugger in the next block (1814+)* **2** To arrest; BUST, COLLAR : *You don't have to bag nuns (1800s+)* **3** To discharge; CAN, FIRE, SACK : *Just say the author was willing to bag an old friend (mid-1800s+)* **4** To suppress; get rid of; discard : *Let's bag the whole notion, okay? (1960s+)* **5** (also **bag it**) To avoid; not attend; SKIP : *We can bag gym class/ Like bag this movie, for sure (1892+ Students)* **6** (also **bag it**) To abandon; cease; give up : *I had to bag it. I had to give up all that stuff (1980s+ Students)* **7** To include; categorize; group with : *We're always bagged in England with bands like Iron Maiden (1960s+)* **8** To break into for a clandestine investigation; do a black-bag job on : *we picked up conversations by traveling execs, then "bagged" their hotel rooms to rummage through attaché cases (1990s+)* **9** BAG ON someone *(1990s+)* **10** To inhale fumes of an intoxicating substance : *the dangers of inhaling, sniffing, and "bagging" such chemicals (1960s+ Narcotics) See* BROWN-BAG, DIME BAG, DITTY BAG, DOGGY BAG, DOUCHE BAG, FAG BAG, FLEABAG, GRAB-BAG, HALF IN THE BAG, HAVE A BAG ON, IN THE BAG, LET THE CAT OUT OF THE BAG, NICKEL BAG, OLD BAG, RUM BAG, SANDBAG, SLEAZEBAG, SLIMEBAG, WINDBAG

bag and baggage *adv phr* Entirely; leaving nothing; with all one's possessions : *We threw her out bag and baggage/ It all went up in smoke, bag and baggage (1600+ British military)*

◁**bag ass**▷ *v phr* To leave quickly; get out; hurry; HAUL ASS (*1960s+ Navy*)

bagel *n* A tennis set won 6–0 • The term, said to have been coined by Eddie Gibbs, has spread to other sports, where it often means "zero, zip" [*1980s+*; fr the shape of a *bagel*, fr Yiddish *beygl*, of uncertain origin but attested fr the early 1600s]

baggage *See* EXCESS BAGGAGE

bagged *adj* 1 Drunk (*1950s+*) 2 Prearranged; FIXED 3 Exhausted; BEAT, POOPED : *I'm too bagged to breathe* [*1940s+*; fr the phrase *in the bag*] *See* HALF-BAGGED

bagger *See* BROWN BAGGER, DOUBLE-BAGGER, FOUR-BAGGER, ONE-BAGGER, THREE-BAGGER, TWO-BAGGER

baggies *n* 1 A pair of loose-cut boxer-type men's bathing trunks : *girls in bikinis and boys in baggies* (*1960s+ Surfers*) 2 A pair of full trousers with cuffs, resembling those of the 1930s : *Then comes a pair of "baggies," very baggy trousers* (*1970s+*)

bag it! *interj* Shut up! : *Bag it! I'm watching my show* v *phr* To bring one's lunch in a brown paper bag; bring lunch from home

bag job *n phr* A theft or burglary, esp of files, documents, etc • Became current during the early 1970s Watergate affair : *Someone had done a bag job on his precious files/ They're calling it a bag job* (*1970s+*)

bag lady or **shopping-bag lady** or **bag woman** *n phr* 1 A woman who goes about the streets collecting discarded objects and taking them home in shopping bags : *a bag lady whose tiny room was crammed with garbage* (*1970s+*) 2 A homeless woman, often elderly, who lives in public places and carries her possessions in shopping bags : *bag ladies, the Big Apple's discarded, homeless women*

bagman *n* 1 A person who collects money for bribers, extortionists, mobsters, etc : *And he was meeting the bagman and it went haywire* (*1920s+ Underworld*) 2 A person who peddles drugs; PUSHER (*1960s+ Narcotics*)

bag of worms *See* CAN OF WORMS

bag on someone *v phr* (also **bag**) To criticize someone; insult; DUMP ON, PUT DOWN : *He's not like smart. I'm not trying to bag on him/ Far be it from us to bag, but we must say Madonna's book leaves something to be desired* (*1980s+ College students*)

bags *n* 1 Trousers (*mid-1800s+ British*) ◁2▷ A woman's breasts; TITS (*mid-1600s+*) 3 A great quantity : *He's got bags of money* (*1920+*) *See* MONEYBAGS

bags of mystery *n phr* Sausages [*1860s+*; fr the uncertain nature of the ingredients]

bag some rays *v phr* To sunbathe (*1980s+*)

bag that *interj* Forget that! : *You want me to cook again? Bag that!*

bag your face *sentence* Conceal your face; you are repulsive • A generalized insult, perhaps related to *bag your head*, "shut up," attested fr the mid-1800s (*1980s+ High-school students*)

bag Zs *See* COP ZS

bail *v* To leave; CUT OUT, SPLIT : *Bruce has bailed from the scene entirely/ Most of my friends had bailed to stay with other relatives* [*1970s+* college students; fr *bail out*] *See* JUMP BAIL

bail on someone *v phr* 1 To break a date with someone; STAND someone UP 2 To tease someone; speak spitefully about someone; criticize someone (*1980s+ College students*)

bail out *v phr* To abandon an effort, project, relationship, etc, in order to minimize losses : *She has bailed out of doing more projects at this time* [*1940s+*; fr the 1920s aviation use, "to parachute from an aircraft"]

bail someone **out** *v phr* To get someone out of a difficult plight; relieve someone of debt, embarrassment, etc : *I'll bail you out this time, but next time bring enough money* [*1970s+*; fr paying someone's *bail* for release fr confinement]

bail out on *v phr* To leave someone behind or in the lurch : *bailed out on the book project*

bait money *n phr* Money given to a thief containing a device that will dye the money and the thief (*1990s+*)

baked *adj* 1 Intoxicated with narcotics; HIGH, STONED (*mid-1980s+*) 2 Sunburned : *I got baked on the deck today See* HALF-BAKED

baking *adj* Extremely warm and damp : *baking inside the laboratory with no windows* (*1786+*)

balderdash *interj* Nonsense! : *pure balderdash* [*1674+*; originally denoted a frothy liquid or an unappetizing mixture of drinks]

ball *n* ◁1▷ A testicle; NUT (*1300s+*) 2 A dollar, esp a silver dollar • Attested in the late 1980s as high-school student use (*1890s+ Underworld*) 3 The game of baseball (*1860s+*) *v* ◁1▷ To do the sex act; copulate with; SCREW (*1940s+ Jazz musicians*) 2 To have an especially good time; enjoy oneself in a relaxed and uninhibited way : *A good-time town, where everybody comes to ball* (*1940s+ Black*) *See* BALL UP, BEANBALL, BUTTERFLY BALL, CANNONBALL, CARRY THE LOAD, FIREBALL, FORKBALL, GET ON THE BALL, GO FOR THE LONG BALL, GOOFBALL, GOPHER BALL, GREASEBALL, HAVE A BALL, JUNK-BALL, KEEP one's EYE ON THE BALL, MEATBALL, NOT GET one's BALLS IN AN UPROAR, NUTBALL, ODDBALL, ON THE BALL, PLAY BALL, PLAY CATCH-UP, SLEAZEBAG, SLIMEBAG, SOFTBALL, THAT'S THE WAY THE BALL BOUNCES

-ball *combining word* 1 A person who is obnoxious or strange because of what is indicated : *oddball/ goofball/ dirtball/ dizzball/*

sleazeball **2** Baseball of a specified sort :
Billyball/ greedball [1970s+; first sense probably fr 1930s *screwball*, "eccentric person,"
fr late 1920s name of a baseball pitch, suggesting *screwy*, "crazy, eccentric"; second
sense fr the kind of baseball played by the
teams of the manager *Billy* Martin]

ball, a *n phr* An especially good time; a loud,
funny party : *The concert was a ball/ Man, we
had us a ball* (*1930s+ Black college students*)

◁**ball-and-chain**▷ *n* One's wife; OLD WOMAN
(*1920s+*)

◁**ball-buster**▷ (Variations: **breaker** or **wracker**
may replace **buster**) *n* **1** Something that is
very difficult to accomplish; a Herculean
task; KILLER (*1950+*) **2** Someone who assigns
and monitors extremely difficult tasks : *a real
ball-buster of a skipper* (*1970+*) **3** An intimidating man; ruffian; ENFORCER, GORILLA : *It
had been a mistake allowing these two ball-
breakers in* (*1970s+*) **4** A woman who saps
or negates a man's masculinity; castrating
female (*1970s+*)

◁**ball-busting**▷ *adj* : *thanks to all those ball-
busting fans out there n* The sapping or destruction of masculinity; NUT-CRUNCHING
(*1970s+*)

balled up *adj phr* In a thoroughly confused
and futile condition; erroneous and useless
because of perverse incompetence; FUCKED
UP, SCREWED UP : *Things were totally balled up
when the alarm went* [1880s+; probably fr
the helplessness of a horse on a slippery
street when its shoes have accumulated *balls*
of ice; somehow the term has come to be
associated with the testicles, as the related
term *bollixed up* shows]

ball game *n phr* **1** A given set of conditions;
complex of circumstances; situation : *What
we do and what they do isn't the same ball game*
(*1960s+*) **2** A competition; rivalry : *It's NBC
ahead in the network ratings ball game, NBC
says/ Goodbye, ball game, he said* (*late
1960s+*) **3** The decisive element or event,
esp in a competition or encounter; the NAME
OF THE GAME : *The third ward vote is the ball
game in this town* (*late 1960s+*) *See* THAT'S
THE BALL GAME, a WHOLE NEW BALL GAME

ball is in someone's **court,** the *sentence* The
next action, decision, response, etc, belongs
to the person or persons indicated : *That's my
offer. The ball is in your court* [1960s+; fr
tennis]

ballocks or **bollocks** *interj* Rubbish; nonsense
(*mid-1800s+*) *n* The testicles

ball of fire *n phr* A dazzling performer; spectacularly successful striver; overachiever;
GO-GETTER, HOT SHOT [1900+; perhaps fr earlier *ball of fire*, "a very fast train"]

ball of wax *See* the WHOLE BALL OF WAX

balloon *n* **1** A hobo's bedroll; bindle (*1920s+*)
2 A condom (*1960s+*) **3** A dollar bill; one
dollar : *It'll cost you six balloons* (*1970s+*) **4**
A platoon (*1970s+ Army*) **5** The floating
blob with a line to a speaker's mouth, used
to show speech in comic strips (*1840s+*) *v*
To lose one's lines completely during a performance; BLOW UP, go up (*1920s+ Theater*)
See LEAD BALLOON, TRIAL BALLOON

balloons *n* A woman's breasts, esp large
• Possibly offensive to women

ballot box *See* STUFF THE BALLOT BOX

ballpark or **park** *n* Claimed or designated
special territory; TURF : *Aren't you a little out
of your ballpark here?/ I've played mostly your
game. But now we're in my park* (*1963+*) *See*
ALL OVER THE MAP, IN THE BALLPARK

ballpark figure (or **estimate**) *n phr* A rough
numerical approximation : *I'd say forty, but
that's a ballpark figure* (*1960s+*)

balls *interj* An exclamation of incredulity,
disappointment, or disgust (*1940s+*) *n* ◁**1**▷
The testicles (*1300s+*) ◁**2**▷ Courage; nerve;
GUTS : *They have balls but not soul/ I admire a
woman with the balls to snowboard* (*1920s+*)
3 Nonsense; POPPYCOCK • Frequently an interj of disbelief, contempt, etc : *That story is
just such patent balls that I've written a letter/
He was talking high-minded balls. Twaddle!*
(*chiefly British 1880s+*) *See* BLUE BALLS, BUST
one's ASS, the CAT'S MEOW, FREEZE THE BALLS OFF
A BRASS MONKEY, GRIPE one's ASS, HAVE BRASS
(or CAST-IRON) BALLS, HAVE someone BY THE
BALLS, HAVE THE WORLD BY THE BALLS, NOT GET
one's BALLS IN AN UPROAR, PUT BALLS ON

◁**ballsiness** or **balliness**▷ *n* Courage; BALLS,
GUTS : *a dangerous ethic of ballsiness in international affairs* (*1950s+*)

balls-out *adj* Very great; extreme; total : *That
was more like a crazy, balls-out terrain, a
whack course* [1940s+; probably fr *balls to the
wall*]

balls to the wall *adj phr* : *They are not the cigar-
chomping "balls to the wall" warmongers of
popular perceptions adv phr* At or to the extreme; at full speed; ALL-OUT, FLAT OUT : *She is
driving balls to the wall in that Mini* [1960s+
Air Force; fr the thrusting of an aircraft
throttle, topped by a ball, to the bulkhead of
the cockpit to attain full speed]

balls-up *n* A confused and inept blunder;
FUCK-UP : *a world-class balls-up* (*late 1930s+
British*)

◁**ballsy**▷ *adj* Courageous; spunky; GUTSY :
Angelina Jolie's a very ballsy lady (*late
1950s+*)

ball the jack *v phr* **1** To move or work very
rapidly **2** To gamble or risk everything on
one stroke or try [fr railroad term meaning
"to go full speed"]

ball up *n* Confusion; blundering : *The ball-up abroad has been supervised by Harry's advisers* (*1900+*) *v phr* 1 To confuse; mix up; lead astray : *This guy has balled me up totally* • Attested fr 1856 in the sense "to fail an examination" 2 To wreck or ruin by incompetence; botch; BOLLIX UP, FUCK UP, SCREW UP : *I managed to ball up the whole project* (*1880s+*)

ball-wracker *See* BALL-BUSTER

ballyhooed *adj* Much publicized; HYPED : *two ballyhooed mergers between telephone companies and cable-TV outifts* (*1920s+*)

balmed or **balmy** *modifier* Intoxicated with alcohol

balmy *modifier* Crazy; insane *See* BARMY

baloney or **boloney** *n* 1 Nonsense; pretentious talk; bold and deceitful absurdities; APPLESAUCE, BULLSHIT, HOOEY : *No matter how you slice it, it's still baloney* 2 A stupid person : *You dumb baloney v* : *And don't try to baloney me, either* [late 1920s+, perhaps fr Irish *balonie*, "nonsense"; about 1920 the word meant "an unskilled boxer; palooka"]

Baltimore chop *n phr* A batted baseball that hits the plate or close in front of the plate and bounces high in the air *(Late 1890s+)*

bam[1] *interj* (also **bamm, bammo**) An exclamation imitating a hard blow : *I got tested and bammo! The bad news n* The sound of a hard blow : *It struck the desk with a resounding bam v* To strike or hit : *Heads may be biffed or bammed* (*1918+*) *See* WHAM-BAM THANK YOU MA'AM

bam[2] *n* A mixture of a depressant with a stimulant drug, esp of a barbiturate with an amphetamine [1970s+; fr barbiturate + *amphetamine*]

bambi *n* 1 A deer that appears out of nowhere, as on a highway 2 A person very new to something; newbie [fr being like a deer in the headlights]

bambino *n* 1 A baby or young child 2 A ruffian; an intimidating man; GORILLA, TORPEDO • In the mid-1800s *babe*, "rowdy, blackguard," is attested; the identification of infant and goon is durable [1920s+; fr Italian, "baby," literally "silly little one"]

bamboo curtain *n phr* The barrier of secrecy and exclusion that once cut the People's Republic of China and other Asian Communist countries off from the rest of the world [modeled on *iron curtain*]

bamboozle *v* To hoax; trick; swindle; FLIMFLAM : *My worthy opponent thrives by bamboozling the public* [Underworld 1700s+; origin unknown and much disputed; some claim a Romany source]

bamboozled *modifier* Confused; mystified (*1800s+*)

banana *n* 1 A comedian, esp in a burlesque show • These performers were ranked as "top banana," "second banana," etc (*1950s+ Show business*) 2 A sexually attractive light-skinned black woman • Consid-Considered offensive by the women to whom this term is applied (*1940s+ Black*) ◁3▷ The penis (*1916+*) ◁4▷ An Oriental sympathetic with and part of the white majority society • Because white on the inside though yellow on the outside (*1980s+*) 5 A patient with jaundice (*1980s+ Medical*) ◁6▷ A fool; an idiot • Attested as college slang in 1989, probably based on *bananas* (*1920+*) ◁7▷ A crazy person; LOONY (*1970s+*) *See* HAVE one's BANANA PEELED, TOP BANANA

banana ball *n phr* A hit or thrown ball that curves off to the right : *can go to a golf course and hit a banana ball supreme* [1960s+; fr the shape of a *banana*]

bananahead *n* A stupid person (*1950s+*)

banana oil *n* Nonsense, esp when used to flatter and mislead; BUNK [1910+; perhaps fr the oily smoothness and fruity odor of *banana oil*, amyl acetate]

◁**banana republic**▷ *n phr* A small country, esp Central American, dominated by foreign companies [1930s+; fr the fact that such places were typically under the control of the United Fruit Company and grew bananas]

bananas *adj* 1 Crazy; NUTS : *I could see that my calm was driving him bananas* (*1970s+*) 2 Very enthusiastic; highly excited; APE (*1960s+*) 3 Homosexual (*1930s+ Underworld*) *See* GO BANANAS

band *See* BIG BAND, TO BEAT THE BAND

Band-Aid *modifier* : *a Band-Aid expedient n* A temporary or stopgap remedy : *All they did to rectify the problem was to put a Band-Aid on it* [1960s+; fr *Band-Aid*, trademark for a brand of small adhesive bandages]

B and D *n phr* Bondage and discipline; sadomasochistic sexual practice; S AND M (*1960s+*)

bandit *n* 1 An enemy aircraft *(WWII)* 2 An aggressive homosexual who often resorts to violence (*1970s+ Prison*) *See* LIKE A BANDIT, MAKE OUT LIKE A BANDIT, ONE-ARM BANDIT

bandwagon, the *modifier* : *the bandwagon phenomenon n phr* The strong current popularity and impetus of a person, idea, party, etc : *the Reagan bandwagon/ the antinuke bandwagon* (*1890s+*) *See* GET ON THE BANDWAGON

bang *adv* Precisely; exactly : *bang on the hour* (*1820s+*) *n* 1 A very pleasurable sensation; surge of joy; thrill; KICK, RUSH : *This'll give you a big bang* (*1930+*) 2 An injection of a narcotic, esp an intravenous shot of heroin

(1910+ Narcotics) ◁3▷ The sex act : *The wedding night, you idiot. The first bang. How was it?* **4** An exclamation point; SHRIEK : *Let's stick a bang on it to dress it up (Printers 1930s+, computer 1980s+)* **5** A drink of liquor; SHOT : *Give me a bang of Jaeger Meister (1990s+)* ◁1▷ To do the sex act with or to; copulate with : *He banged her twice and left happy (1916+)* **2** To be in a youth gang; be a gangbanger [late 1980s+ Los Angeles gangs; from the rhyme, but influenced by *gang bang*, "serial sex act done by a group of males to one woman"] *See* BIG BANG, GANG BANG, GET A BANG OUT OF someone or something, GO OVER WITH A BANG, WHIZBANG

banger *n* **1** A cylinder in an automobile engine : *a souped-up four-banger (1950s+ Hot rodders)* **2** A car, esp an old and decrepit vehicle; HEAP, JALOPY : *this wonderful banger (1960s+)* **3** The front bumper of a vehicle **4** GANG-BANGER : *Lots of bangers living here (1980s+ Los Angeles gangs) See* FOUR-BANGER, WALL BANGER

bangers and mash *n phr* A minor car accident; BUMPER-THUMPER, FENDER-BENDER [1990s+; an adaptation of the British food phrase *bangers and mash,* "sausages and mashed potatoes," probably triggered by *banger,* "a car"]

bang for the buck *n phr* Value for what one pays : *You get the best bang for the buck right here/ Yet the bang we are getting for our buck is worth whimpering about* [late 1960s+; a frivolous way of referring to the national defense budget and the destructive power it produces]

banging *modifier* **1** Good and wonderful; exciting and energetic : *that banging chick at the bar* **2** Loud and relentless : *banging band at the fraternity*

bang on *adv* Precisely, exactly : *Her picks for the tournament came bang on* • Also used as adj.

bang out *v phr* To make or compose something, esp to write something, in a hurry; cobble up *(1940s+)*

bang people's heads together *v phr* Used to denote forcing a group of people to cooperate *(1957+)*

bang to rights *See* DEAD TO RIGHTS

bang-up *adj* Excellent; superior : *I have some bang-up gin/ You've done a bang-up job on that report, Smythe (1830s+ British)*

bank *n* Money *(late 1980s+ Teenagers)*

bankable *adj* Having a reputation or influence that ensures the success of a project : *after a decade when bankable stars have all but monopolized movies/ She had established herself as the most bankable female actress in Hollywood (1960s+)*

banker's hours *n phr* Short working hours, e.g., 9 AM to 3 PM : *kept banker's hours*

bank on *v phr* Depend or rely on : *You can bank on his word (1880s+)*

bankroll *v* To finance; put up the money for, esp for a theatrical production; ANGEL : *Whoever bankrolled this turkey will go broke (1920s+)*

bar *See* NUTBALL, SIDEBAR, SISSY BAR

Barbie Doll *modifier* : *Our Barbie Doll president with his Barbie Doll wife* *n phr* A mindless man or woman; a person lacking any but typical, bland, and neatly attractive traits : *a Barbie Doll programmed to sing, dance, and fall in love* [1970s+; fr the trademark of a very popular teenage doll for children]

barby or **barbie** *n* A barbecue : *Put a shrimp on the barby for me/ which is sure to have Aussies everywhere ducking under their barbies (1980s+ Australian)*

◁**bare-ass** or **bare-assed**▷ *adj* Naked; BUCK NAKED *(1930s+)*

bareback *adj* : *a bareback lay* *adv* Without using a condom *(1950s+)*

bareback rider *n phr* A man who does the sex act without using a condom *(1950s+)*

bare-bones *adj* Unadorned; spare; minimally accoutered : *as it attempts to upgrade its image from a bare-bones discounter* [1970s+; fr the phrase *bare bones,* "mere skeleton," which is attested fr the 1600s]

barefaced or **bareface** *adj* Bold; shameless; unscrupulous • Nearly always seen in *barefaced lie* or *barefaced liar,* attested from 1850 *(late 1600s+)*

barf *interj* An exclamation of strong disgust : *You want to know what I think of it? Barf! (1970s+)* *v* **1** To vomit *(1950s+ chiefly students)* **2** To respond strangely or with an error warning after unacceptable input : *This machine barfs when I ask for a simple sort* [Computer 1980s+; probably echoic]

barfaroni *n* Something or someone who makes one feel like vomiting : *That pre-cooked turkey breast is barfaroni*

barf bag *adj* Disgusting : *his barf-bag vocal stylings* *n phr* **1** A paper bag provided on airplanes, ambulances, etc, to catch and hold vomit *(1960s+)* ◁2▷ A disgusting person; something disgusting; DOUCHE BAG, SCUMBAG *(1980s+ Teenagers)*

Barf City *adj phr* Disgusting; loathsome; YUCKY *(chiefly 1980s+ Students)*

barfly *n* A heavy drinker; LUSH, SOUSE *(1910+)*

barf me out *interj* An exclamation of disgust; YUCK *(1980s+ High-school students)*

◁**barfola**▷ *n* An unattractive woman; DOG, DOUBLE-BAGGER *(1980s+ College students)*

barf-out *n* A very displeasing person or thing : *restaurant was a real barf-out*

bargain *See* NO BARGAIN

bargaining (or **gambling**) **chip** *n phr* Something to be offered, conceded, threatened, etc, in negotiations : *He is using his information like a bargaining chip/ The boy isn't just a gambling chip, Walter* [1960s+; fr the *chip* used in gambling]

bar-girl *n* B-GIRL

barhop *v* (also **bar crawl** or **pub crawl**) To go drinking from bar to bar (*first form 1940s+; third 1915+*)

barking dogs *n phr* Tired or sore feet (*1930s+*)

bark up the wrong tree *v phr* To be mistaken; be seeking in the wrong direction : *You're barking up the wrong tree if you think the cause is entirely economic* (*1830s+*)

barmy or **balmy** *adj* Mildly crazy; CRACKED : *One of your balmier notions* [first form chiefly British 1600+, second 1800s+; fr *barm*, "froth on fermenting beer," hence "flighty, ditsy"; fell in with *balmy*, said to be fr St Bartelemy, the patron of mad folk, perhaps because the words are homophones in British English]

barn *See* someone CAN'T HIT THE SIDE OF A BARN

barn-burner *n* Anything sensational or exciting; a great success : *They may have a barn burner of a natural gas well or a dry hole/ George's Bank has proved to be, in the words of one oil-company executive, "no barn-burner"* (*1940s+*)

barney *n* **1** A prizefight or race whose outcome has been prearranged; a fixed fight or race : *looked like a barney, as if there were some collusion* (*mid-1800s+*) **2** A despised person; NERD [1980s+ college students; second sense fr the name of a character in the TV show *The Flintstones*]

barracks bag *See* BLOW IT OUT

barracuda *n* A predator; a treacherous person : *barracudas at the casino*

barrel or **barrel along** *v* or *v phr* To speed, esp to drive a car very fast (*late 1920s+*) *See* CRACKER-BARREL, IN THE BARREL, LIKE SHOOTING FISH IN A BARREL, OVER A BARREL, SCRAPE THE BOTTOM OF THE BARREL

barrelhouse *modifier* : *barrelhouse jazz/ barrelhouse beat n* **1** A cheap saloon, esp one in combination with a brothel : *Barrelhouse kings, with feet unstable* (*1880s+*) **2** A jazz style marked by strong beat and ensemble improvisation; also, music in this style (*1920s+ Jazz musicians*)

barrel of fun *n phr* A great amount of fun; a person who is a lot of fun : *the hibachi chef is a barrel of fun*

bar the door *See* KATIE BAR THE DOOR

base *See* GET TO FIRST BASE, OFF BASE, TOUCH BASE WITH someone

baseball *See* OLDER THAN GOD

baseball Annie *n phr* A young female baseball fan, esp one who courts the players : *He was a big hit even with the Baseball Annies memo-*

rialized in Bull Durham/ the groupies known as Baseball Annies who hang around the players' hotels (*1960s+*)

basehead *n* A narcotics addict, esp one who uses freebase cocaine (*1980s+*)

bases *See* TOUCH ALL BASES

bash *n* **1** A party, esp a good, exciting one : *Her little soiree turned into a real bash* (*1940s+*) **2** An attempt; CRACK, WHACK : *Let's have a bash at moving this thing* (*1940s+ British*) *v* **1** To hit; CLOBBER, SOCK (*1860s+*) **2** To criticize, esp destructively : *bashing Google more than Microsoft now*

bashed *modifier* **1** Crushed **2** Intoxicated with alcohol : *went out and got bashed*

-basher *combining word* A person who harasses or beats the person or item indicated : *Japan-basher/ fag-basher/ honkybasher* (*1880s+ British*)

-bashing *combining word* Hating and attacking what or who is indicated : *Bush-bashing/ faggot-bashing/ geezer-bashing/ gringo-bashing/ Paki-bashing* (*esp since late 1950s+*)

basket *n* **1** The pit of the stomach; BREADBASKET : *a blow flush in the basket* (*late 1800s+*) **2** The male genitals, esp when prominently displayed in tight pants : *the yogis had baskets* (*1940s+ Homosexuals*)

basket case *n phr* **1** A helpless, hopeless, distraught person : *If I worried after a decision I'd be a basket case* **2** Anything ruined and hopeless : *Those are only the best-known corporate basket cases/ the reconstitution of the East Wing as an autonomous nation and international basket case* [1960s+; fr a 1919 term describing a person, usu a wounded soldier, without either arms or legs, who needed to be carried in a *basket*; use revived in 1939 by Dalton Trumbo's novel *Johnny Got His Gun*]

◁**bassackward** or **bassackwards**▷ *adj* Backwards; reverse; ASS BACKWARDS : *sort of bassackward hydraulic gimcrackery adv* : *He got it all bassackwards* (*1930s+*)

◁**bastard**▷ *n* **1** A man one dislikes or disapproves of, esp a mean, dishonest, self-serving man; PRICK, SON OF A BITCH (*late 1600s+*) **2** Anything unpleasant or arduous; BITCH : *Ain't it a bastard the way it keeps raining* (*1930s+*)

baste *v* To strike violently and repeatedly : *he basted the dog after it misbehaved* (*1530s+*)

basted *adj* Drunk (*1920s+*)

bat *n* ◁1▷ A prostitute; a loose woman • Probably so called because she works at night (*1600s+*) ◁2▷ OLD BAT ◁3▷ A woman, esp an ugly one (*1880s+*) **4** A spree; carousal; BINGE (*1840s+*) *See* GO TO BAT AGAINST, GO TO BAT FOR, HAVE BATS IN one's BELFRY, LIKE A BAT OUT OF HELL, RIGHT OFF THE BAT, TAKE OFF LIKE A BIGASS BIRD

bat an eye, not *See* NOT BAT AN EYE

bat around *v phr* To do nothing in particular; go about in idle pursuit of pleasure; FART AROUND, GOOF AROUND : *I want the kids home instead o' battin' around the street* [late 1800s+; perhaps fr the erratic movements of a *bat*]

bat something around *v phr* To discuss the pros and cons of an idea, project, etc; KICK something AROUND : *We batted around the notion of a sick-out* (*1940s+*)

bat boy *n phr* A person who beats homeless people [1990s+; fr the *bat boy* who looks after bats for a baseball team]

batch *See* BACH

ba(t)ch (it) *v phr* To enjoy the life of a bachelor : *With his wife on a trip, he bached it for a week*

bath *See* TAKE A BATH

bathroom humor *n phr* Very gross and puerile wit : *But bathroom humor, especially vile bathroom humor illustrated in full and graphic detail, has never appealed to me*

bat out *v phr* To write something more quickly than one ought; WHOMP UP : *He kept batting out scenes/ Bat me out a memo, please* (*1940s+*)

bats or **batty** *adj* Crazy; NUTS : *He was grinning like he was bats/ funnier than you'd expect, fairly batty* (first form *1920+*, second form *1900+*) *See* HAVE BATS IN one's BELFRY

bats in the belfry *n* Crazy : *she has bats in the belfry* (*1900+*)

batted *adj* Drunk : *got completely batted on light beer*

batten down the hatches *v phr* To get ready for trouble; take precautions; BUCKLE YOUR SEAT BELTS : *So we batten down the hatches and wait it out* [late 1800s+; fr the action of a ship's crew securing wooden *battens* over the hatches in anticipation of a gale]

battery acid *n phr* Coffee (*WWII armed forces*)

bat the breeze *v phr* To chat; converse, esp easily and idly; RAP, SHOOT THE BREEZE : *a couple of cops batting the breeze* (*WWII armed forces*)

battle-ax *n* An ill-tempered woman, esp a mean old woman; virago (*1890s+*)

Battle of the Bulge *n phr* The constant struggle to keep slim, to eliminate the bulge around one's waist [1960s+; fr the name of the Ardennes campaign of late 1944 in World War II]

battle royal *n phr* A general quarrel or fight; BRANNIGAN, DONNYBROOK : *What began as a mild disagreement escalated into a battle royal* (*1670s+*)

batty *See* BATS

bawl someone out *v phr* To reprimand severely; rebuke; CHEW someone OUT (*1900s+*)

bay window *n phr* A protuberant stomach; paunch; POTBELLY : *He's lean and mean, no bay window and no patience* (*1870s+*)

bazillion *n* A very large number; a zillion : *lavished bazillions of dollars* (*1980s+*)

◁**bazongas** or **bazoongies** or **bazookas**▷ (bə ZAHN gəz, bə ZOON geez) *n* A woman's breasts; BAZOOM, JUGS : *What difference would it make that her bazongas were twice the size of mine?* [1970s+; all based on *bazooms*]

bazoo (bə ZOO) *n* The mouth, esp regarded as a speech organ • The meaning shifted from "horn, trumpet" in phrases like "blow one's own bazoo" and "the silvery tinkle of his bazoo," attested in the mid-1800s : *if you would close that big bazoo* [1900s+; apparently fr Dutch *bazuin*, "trumpet"] *See* SHOOT OFF one's MOUTH

bazooka[1] (bə ZOO kə) *n* **1** A small antitank rocket launcher (*WWII Army*) **2** A very successful enterprise; BLOCKBUSTER : *its big bazooka, Home Improvement* [1990s+; first sense fr its resemblance to a tubular musical instrument played by the 1940s comedian Bob Burns, who invented and named it in 1905]

bazooka[2] *n* A marijuana cigarette impregnated with bazuco, a cheap cocaine paste [1980s+ Narcotics; fr Sp *bazuco*, "bazooka"]

◁**bazoom** or **bazooms**▷ (or **bazoongies** or **bawangos**) (bə ZOOM) *n* A woman's breast or breasts : *Whatever she wants to do with her bazooms is OK with me* [1950s+; fr comic mispronunciation of *bosom* and association with the excitement of *zoom*]

B-bag *See* BLOW IT OUT

B-ball *n* Basketball : *pickup b-ball*

b-boy *n* **1** A devotee of rap music • Originally applied to mid-1980s *break dancers* : *b-boys with business cards* **2** A stylish dresser [1980s+; perhaps abbreviation of *break boy*, perhaps of *beat boy* or *bad boy*]

beach blanket bingo *n phr* Sexual activity on the beach [1960s+; fr the title of a 1965 movie]

beach bum *n phr* A man who frequents beaches, esp one who is a surfer, who conspicuously shows his muscles, etc (*1960s+*)

beach bunny *n phr* A girl who, whether or not a surfer, spends time with surfers; GREMLIN (*1960s+*)

beached whale *n phr* A very obese person, esp one who cannot get out of bed or a chair without assistance (*1980s+ Medical*)

bead *See* GET A BEAD ON something or someone

beady eye *See* GIVE SOMEONE THE FISH-EYE

be a friend of Dorothy's *v phr* (also know Dorothy) To be homosexual [1990s+ Canadian students; fr *Dorothy*, the main character in *The Wizard of Oz*, played in the movie by Judy Garland; the actress is a great favorite of many homosexuals]

beak *n* **1** A mayor, magistrate, or trial judge • Still current in British slang

(1830s+) **2** The nose : *The beak-buster in the opening round was the first punch Moore had thrown*

be-all and end-all *n phr* Something regarded as the most important element : *the be-all and end-all of series finales* [1605; fr Shakespeare's *Macbeth*, "That but this blow Might be the be all, and the end all."]

be all over someone *v phr* To show great or excessive affection : *People magazine always describes celebrities as being all over each other (1912+)*

beam, the *See* OFF THE BEAM, ON THE BEAM

beam me aboard or **up** *v phr* (also **beam me up, Scotty**) *(1980s+ Students)* *v phr* **1** Tell me what is happening; BRING ME UP TO SPEED, clue me in *v phr* **2** Get me away from here [fr the TV series *Star Trek*, in which a character called *Scotty* teleported other characters by means of a "transporter *beam*"]

bean *n* **1** A five-dollar gold piece *(1850s+ Underworld)* **2** A dollar : *without a coat on his back or a bean in his pocket (1900+)* **3** A poker chip *(1900+ Gambling)* **4** The head, esp the human head and brain : *Whistling at a crook is not near as effective as to crack him on the bean with a hickory stick (1900+)* ◀**5**▶ A person of Spanish-American background, esp a Chicano *(1920+)* *v* To strike someone on the head, esp to hit a baseball batter on the head with a pitch : *Not the first time I've been beaned (1910+) See* FULL OF BEANS, SPILL THE BEANS, USE one's HEAD

beanball *n* A baseball pitch that hits or nearly hits the batter's head and is sometimes used to intimidate the batter : *Mr Bender places much reliance on the bean ball (1900+)*

bean counter *n phr* A statistician or arithmetical clerk in government or business; an accountant; GNOME, NUMBER CRUNCHER : *Even in Britain, the bean counters couldn't tolerate a negative cash flow forever/ The bean counters always spoil our fun* [1970s+; In the mid-1800s a popular comedian called Mose the Bowery Boy ordered pork and beans: "Say, a large piece of pork, and don't stop to count de beans," which became a much-quoted line]

bean-counting *modifier* Having to do with bureaucratic statistics and calculations : *We have our bean-counting ways; they have their bean-counting ways/ This bean-counting approach is an easy way to score debating points*

beanery *n* A restaurant or diner, esp a cheap one : *a beanery in Hell's Kitchen (1890s+)*

bean head or **beanhead** *n* A stupid person; an oaf : *You are such a beanhead*

beanpole *n* A tall, thin person; hatrack : *She was tall, but no beanpole (1830s+)*

beans *interj* An exclamation of disbelief or contempt *(1900s+)* *n* Nothing; a minimal amount; DIDDLY : *I wouldn't give you beans for that idea/ She would get all of her famous friends to appear and pay them beans* [1830s+; A *bean* in this sense is attested fr the 1200s. Semantically the same as *bubkes*] *See* FULL OF BEANS, a HILL OF BEANS, KNOW one's ONIONS, NOT KNOW BEANS

bean-shooter *n* A small-caliber pistol; POPGUN *(1940s+)*

bean time *n* Time for the evening meal; dinnertime

Bean Town *n phr* Boston, Massachusetts *(1900+)*

bear *n* **1** A capsule containing a narcotic *(1960s+ Narcotics)* **2** A difficult school or college course *(1960s+ Students)* **3** Anything arduous or very disagreeable; BITCH : *It's been a bear of a morning* • *Bear* is attested fr 1915 in a similar sense, "doozie, humdinger" *(1950s+)* **4** BEARCAT : *Stokovich was a bear for records* **5** A large, gruff man [1700s+; sense perhaps influenced by 1930s jazz musicians' use, "an unhappy state or condition; impoverishment," in which it was rhyming slang for "nowhere"] *See* DOES A BEAR SHIT IN THE WOODS

Bear *See* SMOKEY BEAR

bear cage *n* A police station : *town bear cage*

bearcat *n* **1** A durable and determined person; tough fighter or worker : *a bearcat for jobs like this* **2** Something remarkable, wonderful, superior, etc; BEAUT, HUMDINGER *(1916+)*

beard *n* **1** An up-to-the-minute, alert person; HIPSTER *(1950s+ Beat & cool talk)* **2** A person used as an agent to conceal the principal's identity : *Use him as a beard, is what Donny thought he'd do/ He's the beard. That's what they call the other man who pretends to be the lover (1980s+ Gambling)* **3** A bearded man, esp someone of apparent dignity and authority : *I can't believe the sainted beards would bang me with a manufactured case (1700s+)* ◀**4**▶ The pubic hair; BEAVER, BUSH *(late 1600s+)* *v* : *She says Rollins was supposed to beard for him*

◁**bearded clam**▷ *n phr* The vulva *(1960s+)*

bear hug *n phr* **1** A crushing embrace *(1930s+)* **2** A takeover bid so enticing that directors are forced to accept it *(1970s+ Business)*

bear in the air, a *n phr* A police officer in a helicopter [mid-1970s+; fr Smokey Bear]

bearish *adj* Showing a negative and unhopeful attitude; disheartening • Often used with "on" or "about" : *He's quite bearish on our chances/ She's not entirely discouraging but rather bearish* [fr the stock-market term *bear* *market*, "market in which price, sales, etc, tend to decrease"]

bear trap *n phr* A police radar trap for speeders [1970s+ Citizens band; related to Smokey Bear, "policeman"]

beast *n* ◁1▷ A cheap prostitute *(esp WWII Armed forces)* ◁2▷ (also **beastie, beasty**) An especially unattractive woman *(1940s+ Teenagers)* **3** Any woman whatever, but esp a young, attractive one *(1960s+ Jazz musicians)* **4** A crude or sexually aggressive male; animal **5** Anything regarded as difficult and misbegotten : *But that is part of the beast that was created* (1860s+)

beat *adj* **1** Very tired; ALL IN, POOPED : *You have been on the go right around the clock. You look beat* (1830s+) **2** Alienated from the general society and expressing this by a wandering life, the avoidance of work, the advocacy of sexual freedom, the use of narcotics, a distinctive style of dress and grooming, and the adoption of certain aspects of Far Eastern religions : *the beat generation/ beat poets* (1950s+ Beat talk) **3** Boring; stupid; LAME *(1980s+ Teenagers)* **modifier** : *anything I knew that I hadn't told the beat man at the news conference* n **1** A loafer; drifter; DEAD-BEAT, MOOCHER *(mid-1800s+)* **2** News printed or broadcast first, before one's competitors; SCOOP : *The News scored an important beat* (1900+ News media) **3** The area or subject matter that one is assigned to handle : *cop on his beat/ a reporter on the courthouse beat* (1700s+) **4** The basic meter of a piece of music, esp the insistent percussive rhythm of some jazz styles and rock and roll *(1930s+)* **5** BEATNIK **6** A short pause; heartbeat : *I waited a beat, then started for the garage/ It may take a couple of beats to absorb the shock of this new length* (1950s+ Theater) **v 1** To baffle; nonplus : *It beats me how she can do so much* (1830s+) **2** To avoid a fine or conviction : *He beat the burglary rap* (1920s+ Underworld) **3** To rob or defraud : *I sure got beat when I bought that old clunker* (1850+) See DOWN-BEAT, OFFBEAT, UPBEAT

beat a dead horse *v phr* To continue arguing, discussing, or broaching a matter that is settled or proved unavailing [mid-1800s+; *Dead horse* as something not revivable is attested fr the mid-1600s]

beat all *v phr* To surprise one; be a wonder : *Doesn't it beat all how Fred is always first in line?* (1830+)

beat all hollow *v phr* To defeat easily; surpass completely : *His story beats mine all hollow* [mid-1800s+; *Beat hollow*, "beat entirely, clobber" is attested fr 1769]

beat around (or **about**) **the bush** *v phr* To avoid speaking directly and precisely; evade; tergiversate *(mid-1500s+)*

beat one's brains out *v phr* **1** To labor strenuously with the mind, often with a sense of having failed : *I beat my brains out getting ready for it, but flunked anyway* (late 1500s+) **2** To beat someone severely : *threatened to beat my brains out*

beat someone or something **by a country mile** *v phr* To win or prevail by a comfortable margin : *Her cherry pie beats mine by a country mile/ He beat the throw by a country mile* (1940s+)

beat-down *n* **1** A quick body search for weapons, drugs, etc : *What you gonna do, give me a beat-down right here?* (1990s+) **2** A beating given to a member who decided to leave the gang : *So I didn't have to go through the beat-down or be jumped out* (1990s+ Street gang)

beaten-up See BEAT-UP

beater *n* A car, esp an old and junky one : *when he's stolen the beater off the streets* (1980s+) See EGGBEATER, GUM-BEATER, WORLD-BEATER

beat one's gums *v phr* To talk excessively : *she wastes all her time beating her gums*

beat someone **in** *v phr* To initiate someone into a gang by assaulting them : *"When you're getting 'beat in' or 'quoted' ",* one female *"G" explained* (1990s+ Street gang)

beating See GUM-BEATING, TAKE A BEATING

beat something **into** someone's **head** *v phr* To teach something persistently and rigorously : *How often must I beat it into your head that dragons are dangerous?* (1880+)

beat it *v phr* To go away; depart; SCRAM ● Often a command : *When the cop told us to beat it we didn't waste any time* (1900s+)

◁**beat one's meat**▷ *v phr* (Variations: **flog** or **pound** may replace **beat**; **dummy** or **log** may replace **meat**) To masturbate *(1960s+)*

beatnik *n* A person who is beat in the sense of alienation from society, etc [1950s+; See **beat** and *-nik*; coined by San Francisco newspaper columnist Herb Caen in 1958]

◁**beat off**▷ (also **ball off, jack off, jag off, jerk off, wack off, wank off, whack off**) *v* To masturbate *(1960s+)*

beat someone **out** *v phr* To surpass or best someone, esp by a narrow margin : *She just beat me out for the job, probably because she had more schooling* (1840s+)

beat something **out** *v phr* To play or use a keyboard : *she beat the manuscript out*

beat someone **out of** something *v phr* To take something away by cheating or fraud : *He was so simple they beat him out of his money before he knew it* (1880s+)

beats me *sentence* I don't know; I have no idea; I don't understand : *Why was he hired? Beats me/ Why don't they take the whole investigation? Beats the shit out of me* (*1880s+*)

be at square one *See* GO BACK TO SQUARE ONE

beat the band *v phr* To surpass everything : *if that doesn't beat the band* • often used in expressions of surprise (*1897+*)

beat the bushes *v phr* To search diligently; seek ardently : *You beat the bushes and beat the bushes for years* [1940s+; fr the practice of driving game out by *beating the bushes*]

beat the drum *v phr* To broadcast emphatically and constantly; insistently feature : *He's beating the drum for that pet idea* (*1600s+*)

◁**beat the hog**▷ *v phr* To masturbate (*1970s+*)

beat the rap *v phr* To go unpunished; be acquitted : *Every time they arrest him he beats the rap* (*1920s+ Underworld*)

◁**beat the shit out of** someone or something▷ *v phr* (Variations: **bejabbers** or **bejesus** or **daylights** or **hell** or **kishkes** or **living daylights** or **living shit** or **stuffing** or **tar** or **whey** may replace **shit**; **kick** or **knock** or another term denoting assault or punishment may replace **beat**) To defeat or thrash thoroughly; trounce; CLOBBER : *tried to blackmail him, he's beat the shit out of you/ He went up against palooka and they beat the stuffing out of him/ "I'll sue the shit out of her," vowed Professor Gold* (*entry form 1950+; others generally earlier*)

beat the socks off someone *v phr* To defeat decisively; trounce; CLOBBER : *In a surprising upset, Hart beat the socks off Mondale* (*1970s+*)

beat someone **to the draw** (or **to the punch**) *v phr* To act sooner or quicker than someone else; forestall : *If we beat 'em to the punch, they're not going to look too good*

beat to the ground *adj phr* (Variations: **a frazzle** or **the socks** may replace **the ground**) Totally exhausted; POOPED : *Frankie Machine, looking beat to the ground, brushed past* (*entry form 1940s+; second form 1900s+*)

beat-up *adj* Battered and damaged, esp by age and use : *He drove a beat-up Volvo/ an old beat-up dog* (*1930s+*)

beat up on *v phr* To attack and damage; criticize harshly; trounce; CLOBBER : *a message to people who beat up on the public programs* (*1900+*)

beat one's **way** *v phr* To travel without paying; travel in the cheapest possible way (*1870s+*)

beauhunk or **bohunk** *n* A handsome male : *I want to meet that beauhunk over there*

beaut (BYOOT) *n* A person or thing that is remarkable or extraordinary; HUMDINGER,

LOLLAPALOOZA : *While the president doesn't go off on these tangents often, when he does, they are beauts/ That black eye was a beaut* (*1860s+*)

beautiful *interj* An exclamation of approval and gratification (*mid-1800s+*) *n* A good-looking woman • Used in direct address : *Where've you been all my life, beautiful?* (*1920s+*)

beautiful people, the *n phr* People who are fashionable, wealthy, admired for style and opulence, etc; the JET SET (*1960s+*)

beauty *adj* Excellent; superior; GREAT : *I thought the guy was beauty* (*1970s+ Canadian*)

beauty contest *n phr* A canvass or occasion that reveals preference, without the force of an election : *the mini-convention billed as a beauty contest for those seeking the presidential nomination/ Today's primary is considered a beauty contest because no delegates to the convention will actually be chosen* (*1960s+*)

beauty sleep *n* Sleep required to feel refreshed : *Not tonight, honey. I need my beauty sleep*

beaver *n* **1** A bearded man (*1900s+ British*) **2** A full beard (*1900s+ British*) ◁**3**▷ The female genitals, esp with a display of pubic hair • First attested when the cry *Beaver!*, usu uttered at the sight of a bearded man, was uttered at the sight of a woman's pubic hair, seen through a keyhole (*1920s+ British*) ◁**4**▷ Pornography : *The editor lovingly runs his beaver one column over from his furious tirade* (*1960s+*) ◁**5**▷ (also **beaver movie** or **beaver flick**) A pornographic film; SKIN FLICK (*1960s+*) ◁**6**▷ A woman (*1970s+ Citizens band*) **7** A person who works hard and diligently (*mid-1800s+*) *See* SPLIT BEAVER

◁**beaver shot**▷ *n phr* A photograph showing the female genitals prominently, esp one focusing on the vulva (*1960s+*)

be big on someone or something *v phr* To be enthusiastic about or laudatory of someone or something : *The boss is very big on this guy, as of now* (*1960s+*)

bebop *See* BOP

be caught dead, not *See* NOT BE CAUGHT DEAD

be caught short *v phr* To not have enough : *was caught short at the ticket window*

bed *See* GO TO BED, GO TO BED WITH someone, HOTBED, MUSICAL BEDS

bedbug *See* CRAZY AS A LOON

bed-bunny *n* A promiscuous female; nymphomaniac : *After her, he wanted a bed-bunny*

beddy-bye *n* Sleep; time to go to sleep [1867+; fr earlier use as a sound to lull a child to sleep]

bed of roses *n phr* A luxurious situation; a highly agreeable position : *his life's a bed of roses* bedpan commando *n phr* A medical orderly *(WWII armed forces)*

bedrock *modifier* : *a bedrock discussion/ bedrock decision n* The basic facts; the crucial elements; the BOTTOM LINE, the NITTY-GRITTY [1870s+; fr *bedrock* "the solid rock underlying strata and detritus"]

bedroom or come-hither eyes *n phr* Seductive eyes : *I left them holding hands and gazing at each other with bedroom eyes (1940s+)*

beef *n* 1 A complaint; grievance : *Her mother called up to register a beef (1890s+)* 2 A criminal charge or indictment : *"What was your beef, Jim?" "Robbery" (1910+ Underworld)* 3 A quarrel; argument : *I've got no beef with you, buddy (1930s+)* 4 A customer's bill or check; BAD NEWS, DAMAGE *(1930s+)* 5 Muscle; strength; huskiness *(mid-1800s+)* 6 Bulkiness; fleshiness; mass : *The old chorus girls had lots of beef, not like now (mid-1800s+)* <7▷ The penis *(1890+) v* 1 : *The hospital beefed when the city announced plans (1880s+)* 2 To quarrel : *We started beefing with each other (1930s+)*

beef about someone or something *v phr* To complain about someone or something : *They beef about dinner constantly*

beefcake *n* A photograph or photographs of a muscular male body with little or no clothing; a muscular handsome man : *The actor has no objections to male cheesecake, or beefcake as it is called in Hollywood* [1940s+; based on *cheesecake*]

beefeater *n* An Englishman; LIMEY [1600s+; fr the preeminence of beef, esp roast beef, in the traditional English diet]

beefer *n* 1 A complainer; malcontent *(1930s+)* 2 A police informer; STOOL PIGEON *(1890s+)*

<▷beef injection▷ *n phr* (also hot beef injection) The sex act; penile penetration; BOP, SCREW : *Maybe she care to try my famous African beef injection/ He asked if my boyfriend had ever slipped me the hot beef injection* [1980s+; fr *beef*, "penis," and *injection*, attested in this sense by the 1740s]

beef up *v phr* To strengthen; reinforce • *Beef up!* is attested as an exhortation to use more strength by 1890 : *The Patriots beefed up their defense by adding an all-star lineman (WWII armed forces and industry)*

beefy *adj* Heavy-set; strong; bulky : *I tried to avoid the three beefy characters just ahead/ Reborn for a new calling, the beefy bikes came to be known as "clunkers" (mid-1700s+ British)*

bee in one's bonnet *n phr* A particular idea or notion, esp a fantastic or eccentric one; obsession : *He's got a bee in his bonnet about wheat germ curing all the world's ills* [mid-1800s+; attested as *bee in one's head* fr early 1500s]

beeline *n* A direct and speedy route [1830; fr the notion that bees take the most direct route in returning to their hives]

beely bopper *See* DEELY BOPPER

beemer *n* A BMW automobile

been around (the block) *adv phr* Sexually experienced : *She'd been around the block before he met her*

been (or was) had *adv phr* 1 Mistreated or cheated; outwitted : *been had by the neighbors* 2 Been bribed : *senator cannot be had*

been there, done that *sentence* That is nothing new; tell me something else; SO WHAT ELSE IS NEW [1990s+ College students; *Been there*, "experienced" is attested fr 1870]

been to hell and back *v phr* To have survived an ordeal or trouble : *been to hell and back with the kids*

beep *n* 1 : *The car gave a few hearty beeps (1920s+)* 2 A usu high-pitched short burst of sound emitted by an electronic device on a satellite, rocket, telephone answering machine, etc : *Please leave your message when you hear the beep (1950s+ Aerospace) v* 1 To sound the horn of a car *(1920s+)* 2 To notify someone by a beep that attention or action is needed : *So I called the doctor and they beeped him and he called me* [1970s+; echoic]

beeper *n* 1 A tiny radio receiver that gives a coded signal to a person being notified of a telephone call, a voice message, or other summons : *Beepers proliferate, tolling for many besides the doctor* 2 Any very small electronic device used to control garage doors, car doors, etc : *The gate was open, but I could see that one could close and open it with a beeper (1970s+)*

beer *See* CRY IN ONE'S BEER, SMALL POTATOES

beer and skittles *See* NOT ALL BEER AND SKITTLES

beer belly *n* 1 A protuberant paunch 2 A man with a prominent paunch *(1940s+)*

beerbong or beer bong *n* 1 A large funnel used to consume large amounts of an alcoholic beverage very quickly, the point being to increase and speed the intoxication process 2 A can of beer drunk in one gulp

beer bust (or blast) *n phr* A party where beer is the featured drink; BREWOUT : *It was supposed to be a party, a beer bust (1910+)*

Beer City or Beertown *n* Milwaukee, Wisconsin : *tiny minimum-security prisons right in the midst of Beertown (1940s+)*

beer goggles or beernoculars *n phr* Impaired vision and judgment due to drunkenness : *I must have had beer goggles on last night to think he was handsome (late 1980s+ College students)*

beer gut *n* Paunch created by drinking a lot of beer : *looks like a beer gut to me (1976)*

beer joint *n phr* A tavern or bar serving primarily beer *(1940s+)*

beer run *n phr* A venturing out to buy beer : *a proud holder of three drunk-driving convictions, really had to go on a beer run* (*1990s+*)

bees *See* the BIRDS AND THE BEES

bee's knees *n* An excellent person or thing (*1923+*)

beeswax *n* Business; concern : *If they did, that's their own beeswax* (*1940s+*)

beetle *n* **1** A girl; young woman : *We could find plenty of nice beetles to rub ourselves against* (*1920s+*) **2** A racehorse; ROACH : *some beetle whose neck will feel the caress of a floral horseshoe* (*1930s+ Horse racing*) **3** Trademark of a model of Volkswagen car, with a squat body curving down at front and rear (*mid-1940s+*)

beeveedees *n* BVDS

be good *interj* A parting salutation • Later expanded with "if you can't be good, be careful, and if you can't be careful, don't name it after me" (*1908+*)

behind *n* The buttocks; rump; ASS : *her broad, plain face, absence of waistline, and enormously broad behind* (*1830+*)

behind bars *adv* In jail or prison : *put him behind bars*

behind the curve *adj phr* Lagging; not abreast of current things (*1990s+*)

behind the eight ball *adv phr* In a losing or endangered position : *He was sick and broke, right behind the eight ball* [*1930s+*; fr the position of a pool player behind the black eight ball, which he must not hit]

Behind you! *interj* Look out! Someone's coming from behind! : *The waitress bellowed "Behind you!"*

beige *adj* Boring; insipid; HO-HUM (*1980s+ High-school students*)

be in someone's **face** *v phr* To confront and bother someone • The expression may come from the aggressive confrontations of basketball players : *He was totally in her face/ I was in his face about raking the leaves* (*1980s+*)

be in on the act *v phr* To be involved in an activity, esp an exciting one : *Now ABC's gotten into the act* (*1947+*)

be in the swim *v phr* To be fashionable, up-to-date, etc : *Don't use stale slang if you're in the swim* (*1869+*)

be in the weeds *v phr* To be in difficulty; be struggling : *The corporation that issues your hubby's paycheck is in the weeds* [*1980s+*; probably fr the plight of a golfer who has sent the ball into the rough]

be in the zone *v phr* To play effortlessly and without concentrated thought (*mid-1980s+ Sports*)

belch *n* **1** A complaint; BEEF (*1900+*) **2** A beer, esp of poor quality *v* **1** : *All she did was belch*

about how bad he treats her **2** To inform; SQUEAL : *I feel good that I didn't belch on my friend* (*1900+ Underworld*)

belcher *n* A beer drinker [fr the belching made by such a drinker]

belfry *See* HAVE BATS IN one's BELFRY

believe *See* YOU BETTER BELIEVE something

believer *See* MAKE A BELIEVER OUT OF someone

Believe you me! *interj* This is something you cannot dispute : *Believe you me, he is going to be mad*

bell *See* DUMBBELL, HELL'S BELLS, RING A BELL, RING someone's BELL, SAVED BY THE BELL, WITH BELLS ON

bellcow *n* A pitcher who can both start and win a game : *the one with the time and the talent to be that "bellcow" remains Al* (*1980s+ Baseball*)

bellied *See* YELLOW-BELLIED

bells *See* HELL'S BELLS, WITH BELLS ON

bells and whistles *modifier* : *If you are a bells and whistles guy, you will probably find these cars to be of more value n phr* **1** Nonessential elements, esp when impressive and decorative; frills : *the latest "bells and whistles," as high-tech frills are called/ you strip away the technological bells and whistles* **2** Accessories and accoutrements, esp of the flashier sort; refinements; adornments; finishing touches : *Maserati, with all the bells and whistles* (*1970s+*)

bells go off *sentence* Alarming recognitions and associations emerge : *What started to slow me down, though, was the little bells going off at the sight of a young black guy* (*1950s+*)

belly *n* BELLY LAUGH (*1920s+*) *See* BEER BELLY, JELLY-BELLY, POTBELLY, POTBELLY STOVE, YELLOW-BELLY

bellyache *n* A complaint; BEEF, BELCH *v* To complain, esp to do so habitually; BITCH : *You may exit the theater bellyaching about the show's unsubtleties* (*1880s+*)

belly button *n phr* The navel (*1870s+*)

belly flop *n phr* A dive in which one strikes the water stomach first; belly-whopper (*1930s+*)

bellyful *n* The limit of what one can stand; an overplus; surfeit : *I've had a bellyful of your bellyaching* (*1830s+*)

belly laugh *n phr* An especially loud, vigorous, and appreciative laugh; BELLY, boffola [*1920+*; coined by the writer Jack Conway of *Variety*]

belly stove *See* POTBELLY STOVE

belly up or **belly-up** *adj phr* Dead or ruined; bankrupt : *The whole project's belly-up v phr* To die; be down and out; collapse; GO BELLY UP : *were the schools to belly up tomorrow* (*1870s+ Cowboys*)

belly up to *v phr* To push or come up close to, esp to a bar for a drink : *the men bellied up to the bar* (*1900s+ Cowboys*)

below the belt *adj phr* Nasty; malicious; DIRTY : *That remark was below the belt/ his below-the-belt tricks* **adv phr** Not according to decent and usual practice; unconscionably irregular : *to hit below the belt/ aim below the belt* [1890+; fr boxing, where blows to the lower part of the body are forbidden] *See* HIT SOMEONE BELOW THE BELT

belt *n* **1** A blow; stroke; WHACK : *She gave it a good belt* (*1900+*) **2** A thrill; transport of pleasure; KICK : *You'll get a belt out of this one* (*1930s+*) **3** A marijuana cigarette; JOINT (*1950s+ Narcotics*) **4** A drink; swig; swallow : *He handed me the bottle and I took a belt at it* (*1920s+*) *v* **1** To hit; strike; SOCK : *Ed belts him in the kisser/ He belted the ball a mile* (*1830s+*) **2** (also **belt down**) To drink, esp vigorously and often : *I seen him come in this joint lots of times and belt them down until he's cross-eyed* (*1800s+*) *See* BORSCHT BELT, TIGHTEN ONE'S BELT

belt around *v phr* To travel or move fast : *As for Godfrey's belting around in Air Force planes* (*1890s+*)

belt out *v phr* To sing in a loud and vigorous style (*1950s+*)

Beltway *modifier* Connected with the federal government or the huge complex it occupies [*1980s+*; fr the *Beltway*, the peripheral Washington, DC, highway that is supposed to help one avoid the city's traffic] *See* INSIDE THE BELTWAY

Beltway bandit *n phr* One of the horde of businesses, consultants, lobbyists, etc who cluster about the federal government (*1980+*)

be my guest *sentence* Do as you please • Often an ironic acquiescence to something ill advised : *You want to tell the cop he's wrong? Be my guest* (*1950s+*)

bench *v* **1** To take someone out of active play in a sporting event : *coach benched him after one foul* **2** To remove someone from an activity : *Don't bench the staff for that decision*

bench jockey *n* A person who mainly sits on the sidelines and offers advice : *The bench jockeys were annoying*

benchwarmer *n phr* A person not among the most active and important members of an enterprise; esp a substitute athlete who seldom plays (*1880s+ Theater*)

bend *n* BENDER (*1870s+*) *v* To slur a note : *They alter pitch and they call it "bending"* (*1940s+ Jazz musicians*) *See* AROUND THE BEND

bend someone's ear *v phr* To talk to someone insistently and at length : *He was bending my ear about his new car* (*1940s+*)

bender *n* **1** A spree, esp a drinking spree; BAT, BINGE : *That three-day bender left Jim hurting all over/ a carrot-juice bender* (*1840s+*) **2** A stolen car [Underworld 1940s+; first sense fr *hell-bender*, "alligator," of obscure origin, which came to mean "anything spectacular and superior" and was applied to a great spree in the mid-19th century] *See* ELBOW-BENDER, FENDER-BENDER, MIND-BLOWER

bending *See* ELBOW-BENDING, MIND-BLOWING

bend (or lean) over backwards *v phr* To make every effort; strive mightily; GO OUT OF ONE'S WAY : *I bent over backwards trying to be fair* (first form *1940s+*, second form *1920s+*)

bends, the *n phr* Caisson disease, a painful result of rapid decompression after a deep dive (*1900+*)

bend the (or one's) elbow (Variations: **crook** or **tip** may replace **bend**) *v phr* **1** To drink frequently and heavily, esp whiskey : *They cautioned him that maybe he was bending the elbow a little too often* **2** To have a drink : *We'll tip the elbow over at my place* (*1825+*)

bend the law *v phr* To break the law a little; to cheat : *bent the law, but did not break it*

bend the rules *v phr* To alter the rules slightly; to interpret loosely : *Let's bend the rules a bit and have another dessert* (*1970s+*)

Benjamin or **Benji** *n* A hundred-dollar bill [fr Benjamin Franklin's image on the bill]

bennies or **benies** *n* Employer benefits such as health care, insurance, etc; FRINGES, PERKS : *I like the pay, but the bennies stink* (*1970s+*)

benny or **bennie** *modifier* : *The kid was a benny addict n* Any amphetamine pill, esp Benzedrine® (*1950s+*)

bent *adj* **1** Intoxicated, either from alcohol or narcotics (*1830s+*) **2** Having very little money : *I'm not quite broke, but quite bent* (*1940s+*) **3** Eccentric; odd; CRACKED, wacky (*1940s+*) **4** Homosexual (*1930+*) **5** Sexually aberrant; KINKY : *Charley got bent bad over women. He was kinky when it came to ladies* (*1930+*) **6** Dishonest; shady; CROOKED : *look a little bent, look like you were up for a little whoremongering and black-marketing and smuggling* (*1900s+*) **7** Stolen, said esp of a car (*1900s+ Underworld*) **8** Angry; upset; BENT OUT OF SHAPE (*1970s+ Air Force*)

bent out of shape *adj phr* **1** Intoxicated; drunk; BENT, STONED **2** Extremely upset; very angry : *He is so far bent out of shape by the press reaction/ Why are you bent out of shape?* (*1960s+ Air Force and college students*)

benz *n* **1** Benzedrine (*Drugs*) **2** A Mercedes-Benz automobile

be on it *v phr* To be prepared to act; to act on something promptly : *I'm on it, boss*

be on the lookout *v phr* To look for or establish surveillance on something or someone : *He's on the look out for babes*

Beotch *See* BITCH

be (or get) real *interj* An exhortation to be sane and sensible : *John, are you going fishing this weekend? Be real, Smitty, I have to study for a test (1980s+ College students)*

berries, the *n phr* **1** The best; an excellent person or thing; the MOST **2** Wine [1915+; fr early 1900s college slang *berry*, "something easy and pleasant, a good thing"]

berth *n* A job, appointment, situation, etc : *Dissatisfied with his prewar truck-driving berth (late 1700s+ Nautical)*

beside oneself *adj phr* Undergoing a surge or transport of emotion, esp of anger; half-crazy : *She was beside herself when she found out he was cheating/ He was beside himself with despair (late 1400s+)*

best *See* someone's LEVEL BEST

best bet *n* The most advantageous course of action : *Your best bet is to make all decisions yourself (1941+)*

best bib and tucker *n phr* One's best clothes; GLAD RAGS (*mid-1700s+*)

best bud *n* One's best friend : *Paul's my best bud*

bestest *adj* The very best : *Jim thinks the bestest thing to do with his time is take photographs*

best girl *n* One's best girlfriend or lover; sweetheart : *Bring your best girl (1880s+)*

best shot *See* GIVE something one's BEST SHOT

best (or greatest) thing since sliced bread, the *n phr* A person or thing that is superlative; a paragon; WINNER : *I thought she was the best thing since sliced bread (1960s+)*

bet one's **boots** *v phr* You can be absolutely certain : *bet your boots I'm comin'*

bet one's **bottom dollar** *v phr* To be absolutely sure of something; be totally convinced; BET THE FARM : *I'll bet my bottom dollar she'll be back (1860s+ Western)*

betcha *v phr* Bet you : *I'll betcha I can jump higher (1922+)*

bet one's **life** *v phr* BET one's BOTTOM DOLLAR (1840s+)

be there *v phr* To have the experience; learn firsthand : *You have to be there to know what I mean/ I can tell you, because I've been there myself (1880s+)*

be there or be square *sentence* One should attend an event or one will be considered an outsider : *The party? Be there or be square!*

be there with bells on *sentence* An expression of happiness about being someplace; I am eager and happy to be here : *I will be there with bells on*

better *See* GO something or someone ONE BETTER, YOU BETTER BELIEVE something

better half *n phr* One's wife; occasionally, one's husband [late 1500s+; either because the beloved is more than *half* of one or is the superior part, the soul]

Better luck next time *sentence* Maybe you will have better luck on the next try : *Missed the cutoff? Better luck next time*

bet the farm (or the ranch) *v phr* (Variations: **franchise** or **house** or **left nut** or **rent** or **shop** may replace **farm** or **ranch**) Bet everything one has; GO FOR BROKE, BET one's BOTTOM DOLLAR : *I wouldn't have bet the farm, but I'd sure bet the back forty/ I wouldn't bet the ranch that he'll be reappointed/ You can bet the rent the Jacksons will go where the big money is/ Horowitz says he'll bet his house that Ginsburg won't vote to overturn* Roe v Wade/ *nothing less than betting the franchise on this project (1980s+)*

betty *n* **1** A pretty girl, esp one regarded as sexually biddable; beddy : *Betty ... A beautiful woman* **2** An eccentric person; FREAK [1980s+ Students; perhaps fr *Betty*, a character in the TV show *The Flintstones*]

between a (or the) rock and a (or the) hard place *adv phr* In a dilemma; baffled : *So a writer is caught between the rock and the hard place/ informants, caught between the rock of prison and the hard place of the snitch (1940s+)*

bet your boots *v phr* (Variations: **ass** or **sweet ass** or **bibby** or **bippy** or **bottom dollar** or **buns** or **left nut** or **life** or **shirt** or **whiskers** may replace **boots**) To be absolutely assured; count on it : *You can bet your boots I'll be there/ You bet your sweet ass it was easier at the museum/ I'll bet my left nut that's what was happening (entry form 1800s+, variants fr then until mid-1900s+)*

bfd or **BFD** (pronounced as separate letters) *n* Something or someone of importance ● Usually said sarcastically or dismissively [fr *big fucking deal*]

B-girl *n* A promiscuous girl or woman, esp one who works in a bar as a sort of hostess to stimulate the sale of drinks; BAR-GIRL (1930s+)

bhang *n* Marijuana; a marijuana cigarette : *old bhang in his car*

bi *adj* Bisexual; AC-DC *n* : *I think maybe Vi is a bi (1960s+)*

biatch *See* BITCH

bib *See* BEST BIB AND TUCKER

bibby *See* BIPPY

bible or **Bible** *See* SWEAR ON A STACK OF BIBLES

◁**bicho**▷ (BEE choh) *n* The penis : *this little girl, she's leading you around by your bicho* [fr Spanish, literally "bug, beast," and more]

biddy *n* **1** A woman, esp an old shrewish woman ● Nearly always with "old" : *Charley* *had met an old biddy named Zoe Winthrop (late 1700s+)* **2** chick *(1780s+)* [diminutive of the name *Bridget*]

biff *n* **1** A blow with the fist; SOCK • *Biff* as the sound of a blow is attested in 1847 *(1890+)* **2** A stupid young woman *(1980s+ College students)* *v* **1** : *He wouldn't quit, so she biffed him (1890+)* **2** To fail; FLUNK *(1980s+ College students)*

big *adj* **1** Important; powerful : *the big names in this business/ the big guy (late 1500s+)* **2** Popular; successful : *If I do say so, we were very big/ The book's big in Chicago (1910+)* *adv* Successfully; outstandingly well : *The wing-dancing and funny acts catch on big (1886+)* *See* BIG WITH someone, GO OVER BIG, MAKE IT BIG, TAKE IT HARD, TALK BIG

Big *adj* Good; decent; admirable • Used as an epithet for an admired person : *Hey, what's up, Big Charlie? See* MISTER BIG

big ape or **baboon** *n phr* A large, dangerous man • Nearly always used affectionately of a man by a woman *(1940s+)*

Big Apple, the, or **the Apple** *n phr* **1** New York City • Popularized in the 1970s as a nickname : *New York is the Big Apple/ young musicians storming into the Apple (1909+)* **2** A jitterbug dance of the mid-1930s [apparently fr jazz musicians' term **apple** for a city, esp a city in the North; the dance may be so called from a Harlem club of the same name]

◁**bigass**▷ *adj* **1** Pretentiously large : *Abraham opened the door of his bigass Cadillac* **2** Pretentious; self-important : *his goddam big-ass face* [1940s+ fr black and WWII armed forces; in these and other senses *-ass* and *-assed* are used virtually as intensifiers; they may be suffixed to nearly any adjective]

◁**bigass bird**▷ *See* TAKE OFF LIKE A BIGASS BIRD

big band *modifier* : *the big-band sound/ big-band era* *n phr* A large band of dance or swing musicians, esp like the Benny Goodman or Tommy Dorsey bands of the 1930s *(1920s+)*

big bang *modifier* : *the big-bang theory/ big-bang cosmology* *n phr* The primordial explosion by which the universe was hypothetically created [1950+; The term was coined, or at least popularized, by the British astronomer Fred Hoyle in a 1950 book]

Big Blue *n phr* IBM, International Business Machines Corporation [1980s+; fr the color of the company's logo]

big board *n* The New York Stock Exchange : *down 100 points on the big board* [fr the large display *board* that reports on stocks traded on the exchange]

big boy *n phr* **1** You there; man; MAC • A term of address variously used with the intention to challenge, flatter, attract, etc : *Want a little fun, big boy? (1910+)* **2** An important man;

BIGGIE, BIG SHOT : *He tried to shake down one of the big boys (1920s+)* **3** An adult male; grown-up man • Most often used in rebuke : *Cut that out—you're a big boy now*

Big Brother or **big brother** *n phr* **1** The faceless and ruthless power of the totalitarian or bureaucratic state personified *(1949+)* **2** The tracking radar used by ground controllers *(1970s+ Airline)* [*Big brother*, "protector," is attested fr at least the 1860s; first sense fr its use by George Orwell in his novel *Nineteen Eighty-Four*; second sense quite benign]

big brown eyes *n phr* A woman's breasts; HEADLIGHTS

big bucks *n phr* A large amount of money; great sums of money; MEGABUCKS : *That car would cost you big bucks today (1970+)*

big butter-and-egg man *See* BUTTER-AND-EGG MAN

big buzz *n phr* Loudest current rumor : *The big buzz around Broadway is the announcement (1970s+)*

Big C *n phr* **1** Cancer *(late 1960s+)* **2** Cocaine *(late 1950s+ Narcotics)*

big cheese *modifier* : *without the big-cheese attitude* *n phr* **1** big bug, BIG SHOT *(1900s+)See* the CHEESE **2** A stupid or rude man; lout *(1920s+)*

big D *n phr* LSD *(1970s+)*

Big D *n phr* **1** Dallas, Texas *(1930s+)* **2** Detroit, Michigan *(1960s+)*

Big Daddy or **big daddy** *n phr* **1** You there; man; BIG BOY, MAC • Term of address used to any man, usu with a view to flattering him *(1940s+)* **2** DADDY *(1920s+ Jazz musicians)* **3** DADDY-O *(1940s+ Jazz musicians)*

Big Dance, the *n phr* The NCAA basketball tournament : *The prize will be an automatic bid to the Big Dance (1990s+)*

big deal *modifier* : *a big-deal salary/ a big-deal Boston wiseass dick; n phr* **1** Anything very important; consequential event or circumstance • Often used ironically to deflate someone or something, esp in the retort "Big deal" after someone has made an earnest reference : *Getting good grades is a big deal around here/ So you just bought an Audi. Big deal* **2** An important person; BIG SHOT : *Thinks he's a big deal 'cause he's got that fucking paper backing him up* [1940s+ Students and WWII armed forces; probably fr the Yiddish sarcastic dismissal *a groyser kunst*, "some big art," as translated and used, for example, by the comedian Arnold Stang] *See* MAKE A BIG PRODUCTION, NO BIG DEAL

Big Dick *n phr* The point or roll of ten *(1940s+ Crapshooting)*

Big Ditch, the, *n phr* Variously the Erie Canal *(1823+)*, Atlantic Ocean *(1909+)*, or Panama Canal *(1915+)*

big do *n phr* An important or popular person : *He was the big do in Green Bay* [1980s+; perhaps a shortening of *big doolie*]

big dog *n phr* An important and dominating person : *This is going to be the year of the Big Dog!* (*1840s+*)

bigdome *n* An important person, esp a manager or business executive; BIG SHOT : *if the NBA bigdomes are concerned about their image and popular appeal* (*1980s+*)

big doolie *n phr* An important person, esp a winning athlete; BIG SHOT : *I got a gold today, so I'm a big doolie* [1980s+; perhaps related to the earlier term *dooly*, "dynamite"]

Big Drink, the *n phr* Variously the Mississippi River (*1840s+*) or the Atlantic Ocean (*1880s+*)

big drink of water *n* A very tall person : *Kyle is a big drink of water See* LONG DRINK OF WATER

Big Easy, the *n phr* New Orleans (*1970s+*)

big enchilada *n phr* The chief; the head person; BOSS : *The Big Enchilada is tied up with the Chief Honcho at the moment, but the Little Enchilada can see you now* (*1970s+*)

big eyes *n* Desire; lust (*1950+ Jazz musicians*)

big fat *adj phr* Embarrassingly obvious; blatant and humiliating : *I couldn't keep my big fat mouth shut/ His big fat trademark heart greets you in this show* (*1970s+*)

big fish (or **frog** or **tuna**) *n phr* An important person; BIG SHOT : *landed herself a big fish—an old guy with money and power/ the sports authoritarian and local big tuna* (*1830s+*)

big fish (or **frog**) **in a little** (or **small**) **pond** *n phr* An important person in a relatively unimportant place [1970s+; *big toad in the puddle* is attested fr 1877]

big foot *modifier* : *George Will used his Big Foot status to get himself invited to sessions that a mere sportswriter wouldn't have been allowed near n phr* 1 A senior editor, important editorialist or columnist, etc : *an editor or pundit, a "big foot"* (*1980s+ Newspaper office*) 2 BIG SHOT : *unlike the national policy big foot she is* (*1990s+*) *v* : *DeeDee Myers was relegated to the sidelines, a victim of David Gergen's Bigfooting in the White House* [fr *Bigfoot*, one of the designations of Sasquatch, a large hairy humanoid creature thought by some to inhabit the forests of the Pacific Northwest, and probably applied to senior newspaper persons because of metaphorical size and menace]

bigger (or **other**) **fish to fry** *n phr* Other and more pressing matters to attend to; more important things in prospect : *Anyway, we've got bigger fish to fry/ Tell him to relax, we've got bigger fish to fry*

biggie *n* 1 A prominent or stellar person; BIG SHOT : *Sullivan continues putting the bee on other Government biggies* (*1930+*) 2 Something important and successful; BIG DEAL : *a tubular biggie, not only in LA and NY, but in Chicago, Detroit, and Atlanta* (*1940s+*) 3 Anything large and important : *what if a real biggie, like Brazil, went to the wall/ The next earthquake might be the biggie* (*1940s+*) *See* NO BIGGIE

biggity or **biggidy** *adj* Haughty; conceited; UPPITY *adv* : *Don't talk so biggity* (*1880+ chiefly black*)

big gun *n phr* BIG SHOT (*1830+*)

big guns *See* HEAVY ARTILLERY

big guy *n phr* Man; fellow • Used in direct address, usu with a flattering or genial purpose : *So, big guy, how's it going?/ How's it look up there, big guy?* (*1980+*)

big H *n phr* Heroin (*1950s+ Narcotics*)

big hair *n phr* A hairdo styled to add much volume and held in place with spray : *big hair is all the rage* (*1988+*)

big hand, a *n phr* Enthusiastic applause : *Let's give the little lady a big hand, folks* (*1880s+*)

bighead *n* A self-important, conceited person (*1840s+*)

big head, a *n phr* 1 Conceit : *The promotion gave him a big head* (*1850s+*) 2 The discomfort consequent upon drinking too much liquor; HANGOVER : *The rum gave me a big head next morning* (*1890+*)

bigheaded *adj* Conceited (*1940s+*)

big heat *n phr* An ostentatiously important person : *I am into so many big things, such a big heat, that I must deal as I wheel* (*1980s+*) [perhaps a synonym for *hot shot*]

big help *n* An unhelpful person or thing • usu sarcastic : *Your going to the gym for two hours was a big help while I was preparing dinner*

big house, the, or the **Big House** *n phr* A state or federal penitentiary; the big cage • The term meant "workhouse" in mid-1800s London : *to go to the big house for the rest of his life* (*1915+ Underworld*)

big idea, the *See* WHAT'S THE BIG IDEA

big jab *n* A lethal injection in carrying out a death sentence : *the governor put off the big jab*

big juice *n* 1 The person with all the power 2 A major criminal

big kahuna or **kahoona** *n phr* An authoritative person; the chief; BIG ENCHILADA, HONCHO : *Take the word "interim" out of Al Fisher's job description and insert "big kahuna"* [1950s+; fr Hawaiian *kahuna*, "shaman, medicine man, priest"; the term was apparently disseminated by surfers]

big-league *adj* Serious; important; professional : *No more fooling around, now it's big-league stuff* (*1940s+*)

big-leaguer *n* BIG-TIMER (*1910+*)

big leagues, the *n phr* 1 In baseball, the major leagues (*1890s+*) 2 The higher, more serious and arduous reaches of a profession, business, government, sport, etc; the BIG TIME, HARDBALL (*1940s+*)

big lie, the *modifier* : *the big-lie technique/ a big-lie approach n phr* A major political untruth, usu of a demagogic sort, uttered frequently by leaders as a means of duping and controlling the constituency [1940s+; fr a notion of Adolf Hitler in *Mein Kampf* (1924), that a *big lie* is often easier to foist on the masses than a little one]

Big Mac attack *n phr* A sudden, overpowering desire for fast food, like a Big Mac sandwich : *Hop in the car! I'm having a Big Mac attack*

big man *n phr* A male school or campus leader : *the prep school "big man"* (*1920s+ Students*)

big man on campus *n phr* 1 A male college student leader; BMOC (*1930s+ College students*) 2 Any preeminent man : *Griffey is the Mariners' big man on campus* (*1990s+*)

big money *See* HEAVY MONEY

bigmouth *n* 1 A person who talks constantly and loudly 2 A person who freely announces personal opinions and judgments; KNOW-IT-ALL, SMART-ASS 3 A person who can't keep a secret (*1880s+*) *See* HAVE A BIG MOUTH

big name *modifier* : *a big-name star/ They get a big-name fee n phr* 1 A celebrated person, personality, or entity, esp a star entertainer : *Hollywood figures only the big names are bankable* 2 A prominent reputation; fame : *The group has a big name in the Boston area* (*1920s+*)

big noise *n phr* An important person; most influential person : *Who's the big noise around here?* (*1900s+ British*)

big O, the *n phr* An orgasm (*1960s+*)

big of someone *modifier* Magnanimous or nice of someone : *It was big of you to pick me up when it started raining* • sometimes sarcastic

big on *modifier* Enthusiastic for : *big on yoga* (*1867+*)

big one *n phr* 1 A thousand dollars, esp as a bet : *The highjackers are handed 50 cents a gallon, which is 15 big ones and OK for a couple hours' work/ The next time you want me to do the Today show, it's going to cost you ten big ones* (*1930s+ Gambling*) 2 A serious heart attack : *not the same since the big one*

big picture, the *n phr* The large strategic situation as distinct from little details; inclusive of the surrounding circumstances (*1970s+*)

Big Pond, the *n phr* The Atlantic Ocean (*1830s+*)

big potatoes *n phr* Someone or something important or impressive : *Commencement is still big potatoes around here* [1940s+; a deliberate antonym of *small potatoes*]

big production *See* MAKE A BIG PRODUCTION

big rag, the *n phr* the BIG TOP (*1930s+ Circus*)

bigs, the *n phr* The major leagues in baseball or other areas; the BIG TIME : *When Backman was in the bigs, he wasn't your regular Mr. Sunshine* (*1960s+*)

big score, the *n phr* Huge financial success; spectacular profits : *Jobs' entrepreneurial flair and his instinct for the big score* (*1940s+*)

big shot or **bigshot** *modifier* • Often used sarcastically : *a big-shot chest surgeon/ big-shot notions n phr* or *n* A very important person; influential person; leader; BIG CHEESE, BIG-GIE • Thought to have been taken over from the idiom of Prohibition-age gangsters : *eight big shots of various farmers', manufacturers', or veterans' organizations/ "Hey, bigshot," his father would bellow on the telephone* (*1920s+*)

big sleep *n* Death [1938; popularized by the name of the novel *The Big Sleep* (1938) by Raymond Chandler, and probably coined by Chandler himself]

big (or **big-time**) **spender** *n phr* A person who is generous and extravagant, esp for lavish entertainment; HIGH ROLLER (*1920s+ Nightclubs*)·

big stiff *n phr* A large, rough man, esp one who is somewhat stupid as well • Sometimes used as a term of affection by a woman of a man (*1890s+*)

big stink *n* 1 A commotion or fuss; an argument : *her big stink about cleaning up his room* 2 A major issue or scandal : *Don't make a big stink about minor issues* (*1800+*)

big talk *n phr* Boastful and extravagant talk; esp promises or claims beyond one's capacity : *His promises were just big talk v* : *Don't big-talk a big-talker, man* (*mid-1800s+*)

big-tent *adj* Welcoming all sorts; hospitable : *NOW itself is a big-tent organization, abidingly tolerant of all attitudes* (*1990s+*)

big (or **high**) **ticket** *adj phr* Expensive; high-priced : *very low for the promotion of a big-ticket item/ More and more complete-text services are becoming available, especially in high-ticket fields like law n phr* The sale of an expensive item : *He wrote up a couple of big tickets yesterday* (*1970s+ Salespersons*)

big time *adj* Important; notable : *My book was big-time* (*1910+*) *adv* Very much; totally : *Where does it say that a congressman has the right to be on the take big time?/ It sticks big-time to any smooth surface* (*1970s+ Army*) [ultimately fr the outdated theater sense]

big time, the *modifier* : *a big-time outfit/ big-time crime n phr* The upper reaches of a profession, business, government, sport, etc; the BIG LEAGUES (*1920+*) [fr theater use of about 1910 designating certain important vaudeville circuits or houses]

big-time operator *n phr* A person conspicuously active in affairs where tradeoffs,

special favors, private understandings, etc,
are crucial; machinator; BTO, macher,
WHEELER-DEALER (*1940s+*)

big-timer *n* BIG-LEAGUER (*1930+*)

big top, the *n phr* The main tent of a circus;
also, the circus and circus life in general :
hypnotized by life under the big top (*1890s+
Circus*)

bi-guy *n* A bisexual male (*1973+*)

big wheel *modifier* : *a big-wheel attitude/ Look at
the big-wheel label on those jeans* n *phr* An
important person; BIG SHOT : *Up to that junc-
ture I was boss man of the family and big wheel*
[*1940s+*; probably connected with Chicago
underworld use *wheels,* "gang chief, big
shot," attested in 1932]

bigwig *n* A very important person, often self-
important : *bigwigs all over the restaurant*
(*1731+*)

big with someone *adj phr* Popular with; preferred by; relished by : *That's big with her* [In
this sense *big* goes back to about 1910]

big Zs *n* Lots of sleep; restful sleep : *I need the big
Zs during this project*

biker chic *n phr* The dressing style of motorcyclists: black leather garments and boots,
menacing helmets, etc : *the ghosts of all the
cattle that had died in the name of biker chic*
(*1990s+*)

bill *n* **1** A single dollar : *Can I borrow a couple of
bills until tomorrow?* (*1910+*) **2** A hundred
dollars : *I laid out four bills for that shearling*
(*1920s+*) **3** A hundred yards of gain in
football : *Coach Jackson told me I needed two
bills to win* (*1990s+ Football*) *See* PHONY AS A
THREE-DOLLAR BILL

bill and coo *v phr* To kiss and cuddle like
lovebirds : *bill and coo in the corner*

billy or **billy-club** *n* A club or truncheon, now
esp one carried by the police • Associated
with the police fr the 1850s, but a reference
of the 1880s still describes only what would
now be called a blackjack, definitely a
criminal's weapon [*1840s+*; said to be a
burglar's pet or secret name for his crowbar,
along with *Jemmy* or *Jimmy*; he also used it
as a weapon]

◁**bimbette**▷ *n* A frivolous or stupid young
woman; a man's plaything : *She was itching
to play something more demanding than bimb-
ettes and stand-by wives/ He could have any
bimbette in the state of California* [*1980s+*; fr
bimbo plus French feminine suffix *-ette*]

bimbo *n* **1** A man, esp a mean and menacing
one; BABY, BOZO : *The bimbos once helped pluck
a bank/ one of them bimbos which hurls a mean
hammer* (*1920+*) **2** An insignificant person;
NEBBISH : *Nobody listened to the poor bimbo*
(*1920+*) ◁**3**▷ A woman, esp a young
woman of hedonistic aspect : *What kind of a*

*bimbo did he think I am?/ a bimbo with legs that
go all the way up* (*mid-1920s+*) ◁**4**▷ A
prostitute; HOOKER : *Some escort services are
just fronts for prostitution that men call up and
the service just sends out some bimbo in blue
jeans from Brooklyn* (*1920s+*) [fr Italian,
"baby, bambino"; see *babe*]

Bimmer *n* A BMW car : *Bum out a Bimmer
driver. Unleash a Chevette* (*1980s+*)

bin, the *n phr* LOONY BIN (*1930s+*)

bind *n* A very tight and awkward situation;
cleft stick; BOX, JAM : *This is a nasty sort of bind*
(*mid-1800s+*) *See* IN A BIND

binders *n* The brakes of a car (*1940s+ British*)

bing *interj* An exclamation in reaction to
something sudden; BINGO (*1900s+*) *n* **1** A
packet of narcotics; bindle (*1920s+*) **2** A
prison cell used for solitary confinement; the
HOLE (*1950s+ Prison*)

binge *n* A spree, esp a drunken spree; BAT,
BENDER : *with the studios on an economy binge/
one last Häagen-Dazs binge* (*mid-1800s+*) *v* To
carouse; consume inordinately (*1900s+*)
[perhaps fr Lincolnshire dialect *binge,* "to
soak"]

binger (BING ər) *n* A home run in baseball
(*1980s+*)

bingle *n* **1** (also **bingo**) A base hit in baseball,
esp a single (*1902+*) *n* **2** A collision, esp an
automobile accident (*Australian*)

bingo *interj* An exclamation in reaction to
something sudden and unexpected, or expressing sudden success : *Have your contracts
and debts declared void and, bingo, you're back
in business* [echoic]

binocs *n* Binoculars : *Get the binocs to look at the
gopher* (*1943+*)

bio or **biog** *n* A biography, esp a brief one in a
yearbook, theater program, etc : *By now
Jenny had read my bio in the program* (first
form *1950s+*, second *1940s+*)

bioflick or **biopic** *n* A movie or television show
based on some person's life story : *stars in a
bioflick on Charlie Parker/ a big-budget Hollywood biopic* (*1980s+*)

bionic *adj* **1** Having electromechanical body
parts **2** Having extraordinary strength,
powers, or capabilities; superhuman : *a bionic appetite* [*1900s*; fr *bio-* and *electronic*]

biotch *n* **1** A woman one dislikes or disapproves of **2** An affectionate term for a girl or
woman : *Olivia? She's my biotch* **3** A man
who acts like a bitch, esp a wimpy man *See*
BITCH

bippy or **bibby** *n* The buttocks; ASS (*1960s+*)
See BET YOUR BOOTS

bird *modifier* ◁**1**▷ : *a gaggle of the guys in a
Third Avenue bird bar* (late *1800s+*) **2** : *a bird
colonel* *n* **1** A person of either sex, usu a man
and often elderly : *I'm a literary bird myself/*

She was a tall old bird with a chin like a rabbit
(mid-1800s+) **2** Somebody or something
excellent; BEAUT, lulu *(mid-1800s+)* **3** A
young woman; chick • Much commoner in
British usage; regarded by some women as
offensive *(1900+ College students)* **4** An odd
or unusual person; an eccentric; FLAKE,
WEIRDO : *He was a funny bird in many ways*
(mid-1800s+) ◁5▷ A male homosexual;
GAY *(late 1800s+)* **6** The eagle as an insignia
of a colonel's rank *(Armed forces fr WWI)* **7**
Any aircraft, esp a helicopter *(1918+)* **8** A
rocket or guided missile *(1950s+ Astro-*
nautics) **9** A communications satellite : *A*
VTR operator in Vancouver is editing a local
piece for The National. *"Gotta make the bird,"*
the guy says confidently/ an agreement to put
Satellite News Channel up on its bird (1970s+
Aerospace) [homosexual senses may be based
on or be revived by Yiddish *faygele*, "homosexual," literally "bird"] *See* EARLY BIRD, FOR
THE BIRDS, GOONEY BIRD, JAILBIRD, LOVEBIRDS,
OFF one's NUT, TAKE OFF LIKE A BIGASS BIRD,
WHIRLYBIRD, YARDBIRD

bird, the *n phr* **1** A rude flatulatory noise made
with the tongue and lips to express disapproval, derision, or contempt; BRONX CHEER,
RASPBERRY : *Give him the bird, the raspberry*
(1860s+ British) **2** the FINGER *(1960s+)* [first
sense fr the mid-1800s expression *give the*
big bird, "hiss someone like a goose"]

birdbrain *n* A person of meager intelligence;
idiot : *whatever bird-brain is rendering one of*
the ditties of the day (1940s+)

birdbrained *adj* Stupid : *Britney is unquestion-*
ably birdbrained (1940s+)

bird dog *n phr* **1** A person, like a detective,
talent scout, etc, whose job is to find something or someone *(1930+)* **2** A chaperon at
a dance or a third person on a date, appointed to be vigilant *(1930s+ Students)* **3** A
tactical officer, enforcing order and discipline *(1930s+ Service academy)* **4** A fighter
or interceptor aircraft **5** An aircraft that
spotted and marked targets *(WWII Army Air*
Forces) **6** The automatic direction-finding
instrument of an aircraft *(1970s+ Airline)* **7**
A radar detector : *The cop is sitting there with*
a bird dog (1970s+ Citizens band) *v* **1** To act
as a bird dog : *Leo Browne was doing some*
"bird-dogging" for the Yankees (1930+) **2** To
seduce or go out with another girl's boyfriend : *Sorry to bird-dog you, but the guy asked*
me to the spring concert (1990s+ Teenagers)

birdfarm *n* An aircraft carrier : *The days are*
gone when a carrier was called a flat-top. The
craft is now a "birdfarm" (Vietnam War Navy)

birdies or **bird legs** *n* Thin, bony legs *(1950s+)*
See HEAR THE BIRDIES SING

birds *See* FOR THE BIRDS, LOVEBIRDS

birds and the bees, the *n phr* The basic facts
about sex and reproduction, esp as explained to children

birdseed *n* **1** A small amount of money : *That's*
just birdseed **2** Nonsense

◁**birdshit**▷ *n* CHICKEN SHIT

birds of a feather *n phr* People who share an
interest or talent : *The teacher said birds of a*
feather flock together (1545+)

◁**birdturd**▷ *n* A despicable person; PRICK, SHIT
: *Suppose those birdturds come back here today*
(1950s+)

bird watcher *n* A male who enjoys watching
females

birdy or **birdie** *adj* Strange, possibly crazy : *acts*
birdy during her period

birthday suit *n phr* What one is wearing when
completely nude; the state of nakedness :
Naked as a jaybird, with nothing on over his
birthday suit (1730s+)

biscuit *n* **1** The buttocks; ASS, BUNS *(1930s+*
Black) **2** A small person; PEANUT *(1980s+*
Students) **3** The human head : *there's nuthin'*
but air in that biscuit See GROUND BISCUIT

bish *n* Mistake : *Oops. Big bish (1937+)*

bison *v* To vomit [likely a play on *yak*]

bissel (BISS əl) *n* A bit; a little : *I'd hold onto your*
God's little acre a bissel longer [fr Yiddish]

bistro (BEE stroh) *n* A restaurant or cafe
[1940s+; fr French]

bit *adj* Disappointed and resentful • Perhaps
the same semantics as mid-1800s *bit*,
"cheated" *(1970s+ Teenagers)* *n* **1** A prison
sentence : *Ferrati, whose "bit" was three to*
seven years (1860+ Underworld) **2** (also **bit**
part) A small part in a play or other show
(1900s+ Theater) **3** A display of pretended
feeling or an outright imitation; ACT, SHTICK :
So he does his hurt-puppy-dog bit/ You should
see my Jimmy Cagney bit (fr theater) **4** A
person's particular set of attitudes, reactions, behavior patterns, etc; style; lifestyle;
THING : *Zen never was my real bit (1950s+*
Beat & cool talk) See SIX-BIT, TWO-BIT

bitch *n* ◁1▷ A woman one dislikes or disapproves of, esp a malicious, devious, or
heartless woman • The equivalent of the
masculine *bastard* as a general term of op-
probrium : *a cold-hearted bitch (1400+)* ◁2▷
A girl : *Some boys commonly use the word*
"bitch" as a synonym for "girl" (1990s+
Black teenagers) ◁3▷ A waspish or insolent
male homosexual *(1930s+ Homosexuals)* **4**
The queen of any suit in playing cards
(1900+) **5** : *What's your bitch today?*
(1910+) **6** Anything arduous or very disagreeable : *That wind's a bitch (1814+)* **7**
(also **biatch, beotch**) A person who performs
tasks for another and is usually treated in a
degrading manner : *I'd like you to be my bitch*

today **8** Buddy; cohort *v* **1** (also **bitch and moan**) To complain; gripe; BEEF. BELLYACHE : *College students always bitch about the food (1930+)* **2** To cheat; CHISEL : *You never tried to bitch me out of anything (1920s+)* **3** (also **bitch up**) To ruin; mess up *(1820s+) See* IT'S A BITCH, SON OF A BITCH

bitchin' or **bitchen** or **bitching** *adj* Good; excellent; superior : *A bitchen new single from Southern California has been riding the airwaves to the max this summer/ Because of your bitchin' body, I'm going to put you on hold for a couple of days (1950s+ Teenagers) adv* Very; extremely : *That was a bitching good party*

◁**bitch in heat**▷ *n phr* A sexually predatory woman; promiscuous woman

bitch kitty *n phr* ◁1▷ An especially disliked or disagreeable woman *(1930+)* **2** An especially unpleasant or difficult task : *Taking the rusty muffler off the car was a bitch kitty (1930+)* **3** Anything especially pleasant or admirable; HUMDINGER : *a real bitch kitty of a performance (1940s+) See* IT'S A BITCH

bitch of a, a, or one **bitch of a** *adj phr* Very remarkable, awful, admirable, distressing, etc; a HELL OF A, SOME KIND OF : *Getting the thing together was a bitch of a job/ She's wearing one sweet bitch of a dress! (1960s+)*

bitch out *v* To complain at or denigrate : *He didn't call and she bitched him out*

bitch session *n phr* **1** A meeting where complaints and grievances are voiced, esp by labor-union representatives; GRIPE SESSION **2** BULL SESSION *(1960s+)*

bitch slammer *n phr* A women's prison : *life in the bitch slammer for Martha*

bitchy *adj* ◁1▷ Having the traits of a bitch; mean; nasty; vindictive *(1930s+)* **2** Goodlooking; chic; classy *(1930s+)* **3** Sexually provocative : *two bitchy strip queens (1920s+)*

bite *n* **1** One's share of, or the amount of, a sum owed or demanded : *We owe ten thousand, so what's my bite? (1950s+)* **2** A short excerpt or film-clip shown on television news *(1980s+)* *v* **1** To accept a deception as truth : *She said she was rich, and he bit* **2** To borrow money from; PUT THE BITE ON : *He bit me for six bills and left town/ You think I come here to bite you for money (1920s+ Australian)* **3** To anger; annoy; vex : *She wouldn't tell me what was biting her (1900s+)* **4** (also **bite on**) To appropriate; steal; take over : *to bite a popular expression (1980s+)* **5** SUCK *(1970s+ Teenagers)*

bite, the *n* Expense; charge; cost; DAMAGE : *It's a good place, but the bite is fierce (1950s+) See* PUT THE BITE ON someone

bite someone's ass *v phr* To anger; annoy : *How the hell should I know what's biting his ass? (1950s+)*

bite someone's head off *v phr* To react angrily; JUMP DOWN someone's THROAT ● **Bite someone's nose off** is attested fr 1599, and **eat someone's head off** in 1703 : *Don't mention the survey or she'll bite your head off (1850s+)*

bite me *interj* (also **bite it, bite moose, bite this**) FUCK YOU, GO TO HELL *(1940s+)* [these are all invitations to perform fellatio on the speaker, hence to be humiliated]

◁**bite my ass**▷ *interj* KISS MY ASS *(1970s+)*

bite off more than one **can chew** *sentence* To undertake more than one can do; overreach oneself *(1870s+)*

bite on someone *v phr* To copy someone else, esp to dress the same way : *Her sister was always biting on her*

biter *n* **1** Someone who copies another **2** A thief : *biters made off with his pencils* **3** Teeth ● Used in the plural

bite the big one *v phr* **1** To be a total failure *(1970s+)* **2** (also **bite the big wazoo**) To perform fellatio; SUCK *(1970s+)*

bite the bullet *v phr* To accept the cost of a course of action; do something painful but necessary : *Will he bite the bullet and become the leader that Philadelphia's black community wants and needs?/ The only thing John can do is bite the bullet* [1700s+ Military; fr the early surgical practice of having the patient bite hard on a bullet to divert the mind from pain and prevent screaming]

bite the dust *v phr* **1** To die or be killed *(mid-1700s+)* **2** To fail; be destroyed : *The ledgers showed too much red ink, and the company bit the dust (1940s+)*

bite one's **tongue** *v phr* To restrain one's speech, often with difficulty : *Hillary bit her tongue when asked that (1500s+)*

bite your tongue *sentence* Retract or be ashamed of what you just said

bit much, a *modifier* More than necessary or in good taste : *That outfit's a bit much, don't you think?*

◁**bit** (or **piece**) **of fluff**▷ *n phr* A girl or young woman; CHIT *(1840s+)*

bit part *See* BIT

bitsy *adj* Very small : *a bitsy bikini*

bit thick *modifier* Overly dramatic : *she laid it on a bit thick (1900+)*

bitty *See* LITTLE BITTY

biz *n* Business *(1860s+) See* SHOW BIZ, THAT'S SHOW BUSINESS

bizarro *adj* Bizarre : *along comes a bizarro piece of work like Trudy/ But subsequent experts on Bizarro World cinema rejected that view* [1970s+; fr a character *Bizarro* in the "Superman" comic strips]

BJ *n* A blow job; act of fellatio : *offered him a BJ*

BK *n* A Burger King fast-food restaurant

blab *n* : *That's stupid, pure blab (1400+)* *v* **1** (also **blab off**) To talk on and on, without necessarily making sense *(mid-1500s+)* **2** (also **blab off**) To say more than one ought; esp to incriminate oneself or others; SING, SQUEAL : *The gym lady blabbed to Todd/ anyone who might have something to blab to them would not be under the influence of the target's lawyer (mid-1500s+)*

blabbermouth *n* A person who talks too much, esp one who reveals personal or secret matters indiscreetly; BIGMOUTH • *Blabmouth* is found in the mid-1920s : *The blabber-mouths are likely to have the whole wretched truth beat out of them (mid-1930s+)*

black *adj* **1** Secret : *The plans for the Stealth bomber were kept in the military's black budget (1960s+)* **2** Of coffee, without cream or milk *See* IN THE BLACK

black and blue *modifier* Beat up, physically or emotionally : *black and blue from all the book editing*

black and tan *adj phr* Occupied or patronized by both blacks and whites; interracial; SALT AND PEPPER : *My place was black and tan, for colored and white alike* [1920s+; perhaps fr the same phrase used to describe an 1860s faction of Southern Republicans who proposed proportional representation for black and white voters]

black and white *n phr* **1** A capsule of an am-phetamine and a sedative, or of two am-phetamines *(1970s+ Narcotics)* **2** A police car : *Hanger was patrolling Interstate 35 in his black-and-white (1960s+)*

blackball or **blacklist** *v* To punish someone by denial of work, boycotting of products, etc • Both terms come fr the 1700s and meant "to ostracize"; the modern specialized sense appears to have developed in the labor troubles of the 1890s : *Some members of the Twilight Zone movie crew say they are being blackballed*

black book *See* LITTLE BLACK BOOK

black box *n phr* Secrecy; classified material; intelligence interests : *I suspected the project might involve secret military operations. "I knew there was black box involved with it"/ A highly confidential annex, placed in a black box, contains selected "raw material"* [1970s+; fr the use by British intelligence agencies of a *black box* for highly secret material for the prime minister and the defense and foreign secretaries]

black-collar worker *n* A person who wears black to the exclusion of other colors : *Greek ladies are black-collar workers*

black diamonds *See* DIAMONDS

black eye *n phr* **1** An eye surrounded with darkened areas of contusion; MOUSE, SHINER *(1600s+)* **2** A bad reputation; an adverse and damaging public image : *That story gave me a black eye (1880s+)*

black hat *modifier* : *the black-hat rustler in the horse opera* *n phr* **1** A villain; HEAVY : *The only way I can do that is to make you the black hat/ This time, perhaps, there are black hats on both sides* **2** The badge or symbol of a villain : *Companies have this black hat on when they go to court* *v* : *They do not try to penetrate security systems or conduct clandestine tests... "There is no black-hatting"* [1970s+; fr the Holly-wood tradition that villains in western movies always wore *black hats*]

black hole *n phr* A place where things mys-teriously disappear • An extension of the 1960s astrophysics term for a region of such extreme gravitational attraction that not even light can escape; in some minds also perhaps evoking the *Black Hole of Calcutta,* a prison cell in which some 179 Europeans were kept in 1756, and where most died : *Bureaucracy is the great black hole of both modern capitalism and modern socialism/ Banks have found a new black hole for their customers' money: leveraged buyouts (1990s+)*

blacklist *n* A list of banned or undesirable people : *the blacklist for the event* *v* To put someone's name on a list of the banned or undesirable : *blacklisted during college See* BLACKBALL

black money (or **cash**) *n phr* **1** Money obtained illegally, esp by politicians and or-ganized-crime operations, that must be "laundered" before it can be used : *Money that derives from an illegal transaction is con-sidered "dirty" or "black" cash* **2** Income not reported for tax purposes; SKIM *(1970s+)*

black-on-black *adj* Committed by black people against other blacks : *Damage is now being done by crack, AIDS, and black-on-black vio-lence (1990s+)*

black operator *n phr* A secret agent : *At the Central Intelligence Agency, he was a "black operator" who never quite made it (1980s+)*

blackout *modifier* A period during which dis-count or favorable prices on airlines are ar-bitrarily canceled : *flight from LA to NYC for free (depending on availability, blackout dates and routings) (1990s+)*

black out *v phr* **1** To faint; lose consciousness : *He slugged me with something and I blacked out (1930s+ fr Aviation)* **2** To lose one's memory of something : *He totally blacked out that evening (1930s+)* **3** To exclude an area from television coverage, esp of a sports event : *The whole region was blacked out for the final game (1980s+)*

black tar *n phr* Distilled and concentrated heroin; tootsie roll. SHRIEK *(mid-1980s+)*

blade *n* **1** A knife considered as a weapon; switchblade • This sense dates back to the early 1300s *(1940s+ esp underworld)* **2** A surgeon *(1970s+ Hospital)* **3** A dashing young man **4** A homosexual male *v* To skate on in-line skates : *Concerned that Mrs Onassis' son was blading on the day before her funeral (1980+)* [verb sense a shortening of *Rollerblade*®]

blah (also **blah-blah** or **blah-blah-blah**) *adj* **1** (also **bla**) Unstimulating; bland; featureless; dull : *makes one ponder the value of crawling out of bed on such a blah day (1919+)* **2** Tired; mildly depressed; enervated : *fever, chills, sore throat make for an allover "blah" feeling interj* An expression of disagreement, contempt, etc; BULLSHIT *(1920s+) n* Idle and meaningless talk; falsehoods and vanities; BALONEY, BUNK : *a lot of romantic blah (1918+)* [echoic; but first sense said to be fr French *blasé,* "indifferent, bored"]

blah-blah *n phr* Incessant talking : *Her mother-in-law is blah-blah, blah-blah-blah*

blahs, the *n phr* A condition of dullness, fatigue, malaise, etc : *The radicals are suffering from a case of the blahs (late 1960s+)*

blamed *adj* DARN *(mid-1800s+)*

blame game *n phr* The reciprocal process of assigning blame; ritual exchange of accusations : *Charles was the clear loser in the royal blame game (1990s+)*

blame shifting *n phr* A tactic to always push fault on another person : *their whole family practices blame shifting*

blank *n* A weakened or diluted narcotic, or a nonnarcotic substance sold as a narcotic; FLEA POWDER *(1970s+ Narcotics) v* **1** To hold an opponent scoreless; SCHNEIDER, SHUT OUT, SKUNK : *The hapless Tigers were blanked twice last week (1970s+ Sports)* **2** To kill; RUB OUT, WHACK : *the woman Loftus was with the night he was blanked (1980s+ Underworld)* [noun sense probably fr *blank cartridge,* "a cartridge without a bullet"] See DRAW A BLANK, SHOOT BLANKS

blank check See GIVE someone A BLANK CHECK

blanket *n* **1** A pancake; hotcake *(1950s+)* **2** A cigarette paper *(1950s+)* **3** An overcoat • A shortening of *blanket overcoat,* which is attested in the early 1820s *(1940s+)* See BEACH BLANKET BINGO, SECURITY BLANKET, WET BLANKET

blankety-blank *adj* or *n* or *v* A generalized euphemism substituted for a taboo or vulgar term; BLEEP, BLEEPING : *You blankety-blank idiot!/ Stick it up your blankety-blank (1880s+)*

blap *n* Stroke; bit : *little blaps of revelation and no affect v* To strike; SOCK : *continually blapped about the head and shoulders with pig bladders wielded by clowns* [1960s+; echoic]

blast (or **blast it**) *interj* An exclamation of dismay, irritation, frustration, etc; an imprecation • *(1630s+) n* **1** A blow; SOCK : *a blast in the kisser (1950s+)* **2** In baseball, a long or strong hit, esp a home run *(1950s+)* **3** : *He figures the opposition's blast won't hurt him (1940s+)* **4** A single dose or portion of a narcotic or other stimulant; BELT, FIX : *Maybe it's a little early in the day for that first blast (1950s+ Narcotics)* **5** A thrill; a transport of pleasure; CHARGE, KICK : *Meeting her was a blast (1960s+)* **6** A noisy and jolly party or other especially exciting occasion; BALL *(1950s+)* **7** Anything good or admirable; GASSER *(1970s+) v* **1** To hit : *She blasted him in the gut (1950s+)* **2** To shoot : *They blasted him with a sawed-off shotgun (1920s+)* **3** : *So the Babe blasts it right out of there (1950s+)* **4** To attack, esp with strong verbal condemnation : *He blasted the Secretary for saying that (1940s+)* **5** To defeat utterly; trounce; CLOBBER *(1960s+)* **6** (also **blast off**) To leave; BOOK, PEEL OUT, SPLIT : *He got in the Porsche and blasted out of there (1930s+)* **7** To take narcotics, esp to smoke marijuana; use : *start blasting opium from a water pipe (1930s+ Narcotics)* See BEER BLAST, FULL BLAST

blasted *adj* and *adv* **1** DARN *(late 1680s+)* **2** Intoxicated by drugs or alcohol; STONED *(1940s+)*

blast from the past *n phr* GOLDEN OLDIE *(1960+)*

blastissimo *adj* and *adv* Very, very loud; fortississimo : *You ought not to sing the berceuse blastissimo* [Musicians 1970s+; modeled on *fortissimo*]

blast off *v phr* To ignite rockets and rise from the launchpad : *The shuttle blasted off cleanly (1950s+ Aerospace)*

blather *n* Noisy nonsense; BULLSHIT *(1780s+)*

blaxploitation *modifier* : *Most of the blaxploitation films have been shoddy ripoffs n* The commercial exploitation of putative black experience, esp in films with blacks in sensational heroic roles of police officers, criminals, gamblers, etc [1970s+; blend of *black* and *exploitation*]

blaze *v* **1** To speed; rush; BARREL : *She blazed around in it like Chuck Yeager, but it scared me half to death (1980s+)* **2** To leave; BOOK, SPLIT *(1980s+ Teenagers)* **3** To set alight, esp a marijuana cigarette See LET'S BOOGIE

blaze away *v phr* To shoot at, either literally or figuratively : *The cops blazed away at the villains/ The candidates blazed away on television and radio (1770s+)*

blazes See BLUE BLAZES

blazes, as or **as hell** or ◁**as shit**▷ *adv phr* To a very great degree; TO THE MAX : *the life now is hard as blazes/ cold as hell/ tough as shit (first form 1830s+)*

blazing *adj* Seductive in dress and action;
FRONTIN', HOT *(1990s+ Black teenagers)*
bleached blonde *See* CHEMICAL BLONDE
blech (BLEKH or BLECH) *interj* An exclamation of disgust, revulsion, etc : *The House
Democratic Caucus launched its response to
Reaganomics: "BLECH!"* [1960s+; perhaps fr
the use of the term to lampoon *Breck*®
shampoo in a joke advertisement in *Mad*
magazine]
bleed *v* To take someone's money by overcharging or extortion : *His creditors bled him
to death (1680s+)*
bleeder *n* **1** A lucky or weak base hit; BLOOPER,
TEXAS LEAGUER *(1930s+ Baseball)* **2** A hemo-
philiac *(1800+)*
bleed for someone *v* To feel sympathy for :
bleed for him, but that's all I can do
bleeding heart *modifier* : *a bleeding-heart wimpy
liberal* *n phr* A person regarded as unduly
softhearted, esp towards idlers who do not
merit sympathy • Very commonly used by
the politically conservative to condemn the
politically liberal [1950s+; fr religious pictures showing the *bleeding heart* of Jesus]
bleed someone **white** or **dry** *v phr* To take all
of someone's money, esp by extortion; exact
everything : *It looks like they were bled white
and dumped*
bleep or **bleeping** or **blipping** *adj* or *n* or *v* A
generalized euphemism substituted for a
taboo or vulgar term; BLANKETY-BLANK : *your
bleeping black ass/ They're a bunch of arrogant
bleeps who think their stuff doesn't stink/ The
movie ain't no blipping good* [1970s+; fr the
practice of erasing objectionable material on
a tape or in a soundtrack with a high-pitched sound called echoically a *bleep*]
blimey *interj* An expression of surprise or excitement : *Blimey! What a ride!* [1889; contraction of *(God) blind me*]
blimp *n* An obese person [1940s+; fr the WWI
term for a nonrigid dirigible, based on *limp*]
blimp out *v* Eat too much : *Let's blimp out on
Dairy Queen*
blind *adj* **1** Very drunk; BLIND DRUNK, SNOCKERED,
ZONKED *(1630s+)* **2** Uncircumcised *(1920s+
Homosexuals) adv* Completely; COLD • Most
common in the expression *rob* someone *blind*
: *Goddam car was eating me blind (1900s+ esp
students) See* STEAL someone BLIND
blind date *n phr* **1** An arranged appointment
for a show, dance, etc, where one's partner
is a previously unknown person, usu the
friend of a friend **2** One's partner on such an
occasion *(1920s+ esp students)*
blind drunk or **blinded** *adj phr* or *adj* Very
drunk *(1840+)*
blind-side (also **blind-pop**) *v* **1** To tackle or
block someone from an unseen quarter :

*have to worry about gettin' blind-popped from a
corner blitz* **2** To be burdened or attacked
unexpectedly : *Businessmen began to be blindsided by enormous legal bills/ The state will be
coming back sometime in the future to blind-side
us (1960s+ Football)*
bling-bling *n* Jewelry, often gaudy or ostentatious : *keep trying to find some bling-bling for
my right hand* [1990s+; fr the sound it
makes]
blink *v* To blink one's eyes in a face-to-face
confrontation, a sign of weakness; BACK
DOWN : *NBC Entertainment President thinks
ABC has blinked (mid-1980s+) See* ON THE
BLINK
blinkers *n* The eyes *(1816+)*
blinking *modifier* Fucking : *I hate the whole
blinking lot of them* • Euphemistic substitute
for a strong expletive *(1914+)*
blip *adj* **1** Excellent; very good *(1930s+ Jive
talk)* **2** HIP *(1950s+ Cool talk)* *n* **1** A lumi-
nous signal on a radar screen : *Birds can
cause blips on radar screens (1940s+)* **2** A
rapid increase and decrease; quick peaking :
*The bond bulls argue that commodities' rally is
a blip/ despite temporary blips up and down
(1980s+)* *v* **1** To encroach upon, as one
aircraft's image on a radar screen might
enter the territory of another aircraft : *Car-
tridge-makers blip into Atari's airspace, attracted by the enormous profit potential
(1980s+)* **2** To censor a taped word or passage by erasing it electronically from the
tape and substituting a "bleep" : *Occasionally
Mr Carson's lines are "blipped" (1960s+)*
[most senses fr earlier *blip*, "a sharp blow or
twitch"]
blipping *See* BLEEP
blissed or **bliss out** *v phr* To become ecstatic;
go into a mystic daze, esp under the influence of a guru : *Misty was blissed and became
Dusty's instant lifelong fan/ Don't get high,
don't space out, don't get blissed out (1970s+)*
blissed-out *adj phr* In a state of exaltation or
complete contentment : *blissed-out young pil-
grims/ lives a blissed-out life with Sue (1970s+)*
2 Intoxicated : *more than blissed-out*
blissout *n* A state of exaltation or ecstasy;
mystic daze *(1970s+)*
blithering *adj* Senseless or incoherent : *blithering idiot (1889+)*
blitz[1] *v* To absent oneself from a class or examination; CUT, SHINE *(Students around
1900+)*
blitz[2] *v* To polish one's brass buttons, etc;
prepare for inspection [WWII armed forces;
fr *Blitz Cloth*, trademark for a brand of metal-
polishing cloth]
blitz[3] *n* **1** Any heavy onslaught or attack : *His
best strategy was a blitz of TV spots just before*

the election (1940s+) **2** An electronic-mail (e-mail) message *(1990s+)* **3** A chess game that must be played within ten minutes *(1990s+)* **v 1** To defeat without being scored upon; BLANK, SHUT OUT : *They blitzed the Mariners 12–zip (1970s+)* **2** To rush the quarterback in force, hoping to prevent him from completing a pass *(1960s+ Football)* **3** : *We blitzed her with questions (1940s+)* [fr German *Blitzkrieg,* "lightning war," an overwhelmingly heavy and rapid attack, using tanks and other armor, bombers, etc]

blitzed (also **blitzed out**) *adj* **1** Drunk : *Where are they going to find room in overcrowded jails for a blitzed driver?/ We were pretty blitzed out by the time Lee walked in (1960s+ College students)* **2** Completely exhausted; WIPED OUT *(1970s+)* [probably fr *blitz³,* perhaps influenced by *bliss out*]

blivit *n* Anything superfluous or annoying • Examples like the one following, though differing in the number of pounds, were ordinarily given as an explanation of the word, and the explanation was the fun : *Gerber's confession was what Keisman called a "blivit," four pounds of shit in a two-pound bag (WWII armed forces)*

blizzy *n* A marijuana cigarette

bloated *adj* Drunk *(1920s+)*

blob *n* **1** A mistake *(1900+ Students)* **2** A mass of viscous matter; an amorphous portion; GOB *(1700s+)* **3** A useless person; an oaf or wimp : *she is such a blob after work/ blobs into video games* **4** A very overweight person : *Get that blob off my couch* **v** : *He blobbed the second question*

block *adj* Stupid *(1980s+ Students)* **n** The head *(1630s+)* *See* GAPER'S BLOCK, KNOCK someone's BLOCK OFF, NEW KID ON THE BLOCK

blockbuster *n* A great success; a lavish and popular film, show, etc : *A gangster movie can be a box-office blockbuster* [1950s+; fr the large high-explosive aerial bombs of World War II called *blockbusters*]

blockhead *n* A stupid person; KLUTZ : *No man but a blockhead ever wrote except for money* [mid-1500s+; that is, a *head* no more intelligent than the *block* on which hats are made]

blogging *n* The creation of an online diary; a personal chronological log of thoughts published on a Web page : *blogging takes up much of his time (1998+)*

bloke¹ *n* A man; fellow; GUY • Chiefly British use : *Look at the bloke ridin'* [mid-1800s+; perhaps fr Celtic *ploc,* "large stubborn person"]

bloke² *n* Cocaine [narcotics 1970s+; probably echoic *blow*]

blonde and sweet *n phr* Coffee with sugar and cream *(WWII Navy)*

blond(e) moment *n phr* A lapse in one's train of thought; an instance of acting dumb or scatterbrained : *I was having a blond moment* [fr the stereotype that blondes have less-than-average intelligence]

blood *n* **1** A fashionable and popular man : *crew cut like the college blood (1900s+ College students)* **2** A fellow black; BLOOD BROTHER : *Us cats, well, we was all bloods (Black) See* MAKE one's BLOOD BOIL, SMELL BLOOD, TOO RICH FOR someone's BLOOD

blood and guts *n phr* Great vigor, violence, or fierceness; acrimony • Can be adjective, which is hyphenated : *their arguments are blood and guts*

blood brother *n phr* A fellow black; BLOOD *(1960+ Black)*

blood on the floor *n phr* The emotional residue of an intense struggle : *Women in the upper ranks of big companies are making it, but there's blood on the floor/ I don't know if there's blood on the floor after Clinton's NAFTA victory, but Democrats will reunite (1990s+)*

bloody (or **blue**) **murder** *adv phr* As if announcing general slaughter and universal destruction : *screaming blue murder on the arms of their seats (1850s+) n phr* A shattering defeat; total destruction : *After the second quarter it was bloody murder (1970+) See* YELL BLOODY MURDER

bloody well *modifier* Certainly; definitely : *You know bloody well that I hate her (1921+)*

blooey *See* GO BLOOEY

blooming *adj* and *adv* DARN • Chiefly British use [1880s+; fr the notion of full-blown or *-bloomed*]

bloop *n* An unwanted sound in a recording *(1930+) v* **1** To hit a ball relatively weakly and slowly : *He blooped a lob over her head (1940s+ Baseball)* **2** To launch and land a long, curving blow : *Turner blooped a bolo to the heart (1950s+)*

blooper *n* **1** A blow with the fist, esp a long, looping punch : *So I could hang a blooper on your kisser* **2** A high, looping pitch, throw, or hit : *I poked an easy blooper over third (Baseball)* **3** A blunder; BONER, BOO-BOO : *He may have felt he pulled a blooper*

blot someone out *v* To kill someone : *They blot someone out every 10 minutes on that show*

blotter *n* **1** The daily record of arrests at a police station *(1880s+ Police)* **2** (also **blotter acid**) A sheet of absorbent paper to which liquid LSD has been applied and then allowed to dry *(1970s+ Narcotics)*

blotto *adj* Drunk : *The drivers who are blotto (1900s+)*

bloviate *v* To talk loudly and bombastically; BLOW OFF one's MOUTH, TALK BIG • This appears to be a revival of old frontier tall-talk coinage

: *Just more bloviating by the Senator about cutting the budget/ Limbaugh chortles, crows, bloviates and denounces* [mid-1800s+; fr *blow* made into a fancy word by adding the suffix]

blow *n* **1** To do or perform something, esp to do it well : *He blows great conversation (1950s+ Beat & cool talk)* **2** Cocaine : *OK, he gets busted for blow eight times/ Hell, half the people doing blow are reacting to the cut (1960s+ Narcotics)* *v* **1** To play a musical instrument, esp in jazz style and not necessarily a wind instrument : *There will be three kids blowing guitar, banjo, and washboard/ This music is the culmination of all my writing and blowing (1900s+ Jazz musicians)* ◁2▷ To do fellatio or cunnilingus; SUCK OFF *(1930s+)* ◁3▷ To be disgusting, nasty, worthless, etc; BITE, SUCK : *This blows and you do too (1970s+)* **4** To treat someone to something; buy something expensive or unusual for someone : *I blew myself to a new pair of shoes (1870s+)* **5** (also **blow** something **in**) To spend money, esp foolishly and all at once : *The state blew my money buying votes for Roosevelt/ And blow it in on smokes (1890s+)* **6** To take a narcotic, esp but not necessarily by inhalation : *Jimi blew every kind of dope invented/ I don't know how you can blow dust and eat (1920+)* **7** To smoke marijuana; BLOW SMOKE : *He enjoys sex; he does not blow grass (1960s+ Narcotics)* **8** To leave; depart; SPLIT : *I'm blowing, I got a job in Detroit (1902+)* **9** To lose or ruin something by mistake, inattention, incompetence, etc; BLOW IT : *I blew the best chance I ever had (1920+)* **10** To forget or botch one's part in a show *(1920s+ Theater)* **11** BLOW OFF **12** To inform against someone; SING *(1840s+)* **13** To expose or publicize something secret, esp something scandalous : *Treat me right or I'll blow it about the love nest (late 1500s+)* **14** To lose one's temper; BLOW one's TOP *(1900s+)* **15** (also **blow off**) To brag; TOOT one's OWN HORN *(1400+)* **16** To sing, esp to sing well *(1980s+ College students)* See BLOW someone AWAY, BLOW one's COOL, BLOW someone's or something's COVER, BLOW someone's MIND, BLOW OFF one's MOUTH, BLOW THE LID OFF, BLOW THE WHISTLE, BLOW UP, BLOW UP A STORM, BLOW something WIDE OPEN, LET OFF STEAM, LOW BLOW, ONE-TWO

Blow *See* JOE BLOW

blow a gasket *v phr* (Variations: **fuse** or **gut** may replace **gasket**) To lose one's temper, esp to the point of insanity; BLOW one's TOP : *The higher-ups blew a gasket when they heard/ He wants more than she will give and he blows a gasket/ If Barbara sees a subpoena notice, she'll blow a gut (1940s+)*

blow away *v phr* To depart; BLOW, TAKE OFF *(1950s+)*

blow someone away *v phr* **1** To kill; assassinate; get rid of; OFF : *and boom, Jack Blumenfeld gets blown away (1900s+)* **2** To defeat utterly; trounce; CLOBBER : *And they blew away some of the best long-distance runners in the world* **3** To overcome, often with admiration; FRACTURE : *I read the book and it blew me away/ The cow connection just blew us away*

blow someone's brains out *v phr* To kill someone with a gun : *don't like movies where they blow someone's brains out*

blow by or **past** *v phr* To pitch a ball so hard and fast that the batter cannot hit it : *He blew it right by the slugger (1950s+ Baseball)*

blow by blow *adj* : *a blow-by-blow account* *adv phr* In a complete and detailed way : *I'll tell you what happened blow by blow (1930s+)*

blow chunks *v phr* (Variations: **chow** or **cookies** or **grits** or **groceries** or **lunch** may replace **chunks**, and **lose** can replace **blow**) To vomit; BARF, TOSS one's COOKIES *(1980s+ College students)*

blow cold *v* To show disinterest : *blows cold to his new ideas*

blow one's cool *v phr* To lose one's composure; become flustered, excited, or angry : *I always blow my cool when they honk at me (1960s+ Counterculture)*

blow one's cork *See* BLOW one's TOP

blow someone's or something's cover *v phr* **1** To ruin or nullify one's disguise or assumed role; reveal one's true identity : *The undercover cop had to blow his cover by pulling his gun when he thought they might have spotted him/ She called out my name, which blew my cover* **2** To reveal something, esp inadvertently or mischievously : *I'm not blowing the movie's cover story by giving you this information (1970s+ Espionage & police)*

blow someone's doors off *v phr* To utterly defeat or surpass someone : *She blows the doors off the other lexicographers*

blower *n* A supercharger for a car or airplane engine; huffer *(1920+)* See MIND-BLOWER

blowhard *n* **1** A braggart; self-aggrandizer : *His reach often does exceed his grasp, in a town of blowhards* **2** An insistent and aggressive talker *(1820s+)*

blow hot and cold *v phr* To be indecisive; dither *(1570s+)*

blow in *v phr* **1** To arrive and enter, esp from a distance : *Look who just blew in from Sri Lanka (1890s+)* **2** To spend recklessly; squander : *He blew his whole month's pay in on that one pair of shoes (1880s+)*

blow something in *See* BLOW

blowing *See* MIND-BLOWING

blow it *v phr* To fail; make a botch; ruin one's chances : *We are winning. If we don't blow it/ I think I blew it. I talked too much and said too little* (1920+)

blow it off *v phr* To fail to deal with or attend to something; neglect something deliberately : *He felt sort of blah, so he decided to blow it off and skip his morning classes* (1970s+ College students)

blow it out *interj* (Variations: **your ass** or **your asshole** or **your B-bag** or **your barracks bag** or **your ear** or **your tailpipe** may be added) A generalized exclamation of contempt, anger, incredulity, etc • Most often uttered in challenge or rebuke (WWII armed forces)

◁**blow job**▷ *n phr* An act of fellatio or of cunnilingus : *whether a blow job from a married woman is the same as committing adultery* [origin unknown; perhaps fr the use of the mouth]

blow one's **lines** *v phr* To perform badly, esp by misspeaking : *Before the week was out he had blown his lines as President, and perhaps blown the Democratic Party out of office* (1970s+ Theater)

blow someone's **mind** *v phr* To evoke deep feelings of awe, admiration, strangeness, etc; stir one profoundly : *The simplicity of the thing blew my mind* (Narcotics & 1960s+ counterculture)

blown *adj* Having a supercharger : *a blown engine* (1950s+ Hot rodders)

blown away *adj* Overwhelmed; extremely impressed : *We were blown away by her beauty*

blown-out *adj* In a state of narcotic intoxication, trance, or exhilaration; HIGH, STONED (1960s+ Narcotics)

blowoff *n* **1** A climax; a final provocation : *She said I was late, and that was the blowoff* (1900s+) **2** A quarrel : *She and Hobart have had a big blow-off* (1900s+) **3** Something very easy; PIECE OF CAKE (1970s+ Teenagers)

blow off *v phr* To avoid or shirk; not attend or attend to; ignore : *I'm not going to tell you to blow off any standing-room-only events/ It was just something he was going through, so we blew it off* (1960s+)

blow someone **off** *v phr* To rebuff; slight; treat dismissively : *Before you blow them off with a snotty comment, examine yourself/ Mike blows off Sharon Stone* (1990s+)

blow off one's **mouth** or **blow** one's **mouth off** *v phr* (Variations: **trap** or **yap** may replace **mouth**) SHOOT OFF one's MOUTH (late 1800s+)

blow off steam *See* LET OFF STEAM

blowout *n* **1** A noisy, festive occasion; SHINDIG, WINGDING (1820s+) **2** An explosive rupture of a car tire (1900s+) **3** A massive defeat; LAUGHER (1980s+)

blow someone **out** *v phr* To kill or destroy; BLOW someone AWAY : *The Redskins got blown out* (1860s+)

blow someone **out of the water** *v phr* **1** To defeat utterly; SHOOT someone DOWN IN FLAMES : *Are you afraid of being blown out of the water?/ Bradlee "blew him (Tavoulareas) out of the water"* (1960s+) **2** To astonish utterly; KNOCK one's SOCKS OFF : *These kids just blow you out of the water with the work they've done* (1990s+)

blow one's **own horn** *See* TOOT one's OWN HORN

blow smoke *v phr* **1** To boast; brag; exaggerate : *cops sitting around drinking, blowing smoke, and kidding* (1940s+) **2** (also **blow smoke up** someone's **ass** or **blow heat**) To mislead; confuse; deceive : *Anybody who tells you different's just blowing smoke up your ass* (1940s+) **3** To flatter; SWEET-TALK : *Do you mean it, or are you just blowing smoke?* (1940s+) **4** To smoke marijuana or hashish : *Everybody blew smoke there. You could buy hash* (1930s+) [fr both the presumed effects of smoking opium and the confusing and concealing effect of making a smokescreen]

blow someone's **socks off** *See* KNOCK someone's SOCKS OFF

blow the joint *n phr* To leave the place; get out, esp in a hurry : *blow the joint after running out of money*

blow the lid off *v phr* To expose a scandal, esp political or governmental corruption (1920s+)

blow the whistle *v phr* **1** To inform; SING : *She hadn't been Dutch Schultz's wife for four years not to know the penalty for blowing the whistle/ How come you're blowing the whistle?* (1940s+ Underworld) **2** To expose or begin to resist wrongdoing : *The detective who blew the whistle was also transferred* (1950s+) [fr the *whistle* once used by police officers to signal "Stop!"; influenced by the signal of a sports official that an infraction, foul, etc, has been committed]

blow someone **to** something *v phr* To treat someone to something : *Let me blow you to dinner* (late 1800s+)

blow one's **top** (Variations: **cork** or **lid** or **topper** or **stack** or **wig** may replace **top**) *v* **1** To go insane; become violently mad **2** To become wildly excited or enthusiastic : *Here's an idea'll make you blow your cork* **3** To become violently excited by narcotics; FLIP, FREAK OUT **4** To become violently and suddenly angry; have a tantrum : *a "quiet, mild-mannered man" who "blew his lid"* [entry form 1920s+; perhaps fr the violence of an oil well that *blows* as a gusher]

blow town *v phr* To get out of town, esp in a hurry : *after the robbery, blow town*

blowup *n* **1** A fit of anger (*1800s+*) **2** A quarrel; violent rift between persons (*1800s+*) **3** A photographic or other enlargement : *He already has a blowup of your proverb on a wall of his breakfast room* (*1930s+*)

blow up *v phr* **1** To enlarge a photograph (*1930s+*) **2** BLOW one's TOP **3** BLOW one's COOL **4** To forget or garble one's lines on stage; BALLOON : *Barrymore "blew up" in his lines* (*1900s+ Theater*)

blow something **up** *v phr* To assign too much importance to; exaggerate; MAKE A FEDERAL CASE OUT OF something. PUMP UP : *He'll blow it up into a world-class scandal* (*1970s+*)

blow up a storm *v phr* **1** To play, esp jazz trumpet, cornet, clarinet, etc, with great skill and verve : *He was blowing up a storm* (*1930s+ Jazz musicians*) **2** PISS UP A STORM

blow something **wide open** *v phr* To expose a scandal, esp political or governmental corruption; BLOW THE LID OFF : *That'll be the perfect time to blow this thing wide open* (*1970s+*)

blubber *n* Fat; AVOIRDUPOIS (*1700s+*) *v* To weep; snivel (*1300s+*)

◁**blubber butt**▷ *n phr* A very fat person, esp one with big buttocks; BUFFALO BUTT, FAT-ASS : *We can't have blubber butts like her on the payroll* (*1950s+*)

blue *adj* **1** Drunk : *When you were blue you got the howling horrors* (*1800s+*) **2** Lewd; rude; suggestive; DIRTY • The term covers the range from obscene to slightly risqué : *Blue humor has long been a staple of black audiences* (*1840+*) **3** Melancholy; depressed; woeful : *I feel a little blue and blah this morning* (*1500s+*) *n* ◀**1**▶ A very dark-skinned black person (*1920s+*) **2** A police officer : *By the time the first blues got there, there's like maybe ten people milling about* (*1860s+*) **3** An IBM™ computer (*1980+ Computer*) **4** A blue drug or pill, esp an amphetamine or Valium™

blue around the gills *See* GREEN AROUND THE GILLS

◁**blue-ball**▷ *n* A sexually frustrated male : *he and a fellow blue-ball did things to each other that they wanted the girls to do to them* (*1970s+*)

◁**blue balls**▷ *n phr* **1** A turgid and painful condition of the testicles due to sexual excitement and frustration : *Sex will relieve testicular congestion, or blue balls* (*1900s+*) **2** Any of various venereal diseases, esp gonorrhea or lymphogranuloma inguinale (*1930s+*)

blue blazes *adv phr* Like hell : *lying blue blazes n phr* Hell : *What in blue blazes are you up to?* [*1800s+; fr the sulfurous blue blazes of hell, an extreme environment*]

bluebook *n* A college examination : *I'm cramming for a bluebook in Econ* [*College students*

1890s+; fr the color of the examination booklet]

blue-chip *adj* Of the best sort; first-rate : *a blue-chip stock/ a blue-chip school* (*1920s+*) [fr the color of the highest denomination of gambling chip]

blue chipper *n phr* A person or thing of the highest quality, ability, etc, esp an athlete : *But the crop does not contain many blue chippers/ He did not necessarily appear to major colleges as a blue-chipper* (*1970s+*)

blue-collar *modifier* Working-class : *a blue-collar neighborhood/ blue-collar concerns* [*1940s+; fr the color of the traditional work-shirt*]

blue-collar ballet *n phr* Professional wrestling (*1990s+*)

blued *See* SCREWED, BLUED, AND TATTOOED

blue darter *n phr* A low, hard-hit line drive : *A hard line drive is a blue darter, frozen rope, or an ungodly shot* (*1940s+ Baseball*)

blue devils *n* **1** Low spirits; depression : *blue devils after giving birth* **2** Delirium tremens

blue-eyed *adj* Innocent : *all blue-eyed about it*

blue-eyed boy *See* FAIR-HAIRED BOY

blue flags *n phr* LSD (*1970s+ Narcotics*)

blue flick *See* BLUE MOVIE

blue flu *n phr* A mythical disease epidemic during a police job action when numbers of officers telephone to say that they are ill; SICK-OUT (*1960s+*)

blue funk *n phr* **1** A profoundly timorous or nervous state **2** A profoundly depressed state (*1860s+ British*)

bluegrass *modifier* : *the bluegrass sound/ bluegrass mandolin by Bob Applebaum n* Music based on the songs and dances of the Southern Appalachians and played usu at a fast tempo by a string group [fr the nickname of Kentucky, the *Bluegrass* State]

blue-hair *n* An old woman; WRINKLY : *One old blue-hair even struggled up the steps with her walker* [*1980s+; fr the blue hair tint of those who use a blue haircolor rinse on gray or white hair*]

blue hell *n phr* An extremely nasty and trying situation; unshirted hell • *Blue* here is almost an intensifier, although it carries the infernal suggestions of *blue blazes* : *It was more than tough, it was blue hell* (*1970s+*)

blue ice *n phr* Wastewater discharged from aircraft in flight, which freezes on the way to the ground [Airlines *1990s+*; fr the *blue* toilet disinfectant used]

blue in the face *See* TILL ONE IS BLUE IN THE FACE

blue-light special *n phr* A bargain; a good buy; STEAL : *Paramount may look like a blue-light special in five years* [*1980s+; fr the marking by a blue light of a particular bargain or discount in Kmart stores*]

blue meanie or **meany** *n phr* **1** A very nasty person; BASTARD : *It's not that all landlords are blue meanies* **2** Depression; melancholy; BLUE FUNK, the BLUES [1960s+; fr cartoon characters in the 1968 film *The Yellow Submarine* of the English rock group the Beatles]

blue movie (or **flick**) *n phr* A pornographic movie; erotic film; SKIN FLICK (*1960s+*)

blue murder *See* BLOODY MURDER

bluenose *n* A prude; prig; self-appointed moral arbiter : *The moral bluenoses were sniffing around* (*1920s+*)

blue note *n phr* A flatted note of the sort common in blues music (*1890s+ Musicians*)

blues, the *n phr* **1** A state of melancholy; depression (*1830s+*) **2** A usu slow style of singing, guitar-playing, and jazz originally reflecting in its melancholy and resignation the special plight of black people and the general vicissitudes of life and love; esp songs having in each stanza a repeated opening statement and single closing statement (*1912+*) **3** The police (*mid-1800s+*) [first sense ultimately fr late 1700s term *the blue devils,* "a fit of melancholy"]

blue screen of death *n phr* A fatal-error message that occurs in Windows operating systems, a blue screen that interrupts the computer's normal boot-up, indicating a fatal error in the operating system (*1991+*)

blue-sky *adj* Having no sound factual or value basis; recklessly imaginative : *a budget figure, as it turned out, and a blue-sky one at that* [1900+ Finance; perhaps fr the purveyor's fanciful description being as appealing and unclouded as the wide *blue sky*]

blue sky *n phr* **1** Speculation; guesswork : *That may sound great, but it's just blue sky* (*1980s+*) **2** Heroin : *ex-psychiatric case from Bellevue with a minor in blue sky and toot* (*1980s+ Narcotics*) *v phr* To hold a brainstorming session with no limit on the strangeness of the ideas proposed (*1980s+*)

blue state *n* Any US state that tends to vote for candidates of the Democratic party in a general election : *the blue state conservatives* (*2000+*)

blue streak, a *adv phr* (also **like a blue streak**) In a very rapid or excessive manner; extravagantly : *she talked a blue streak/ he split out like a blue streak n phr* An extreme amount, speed, etc : *He yelled a blue streak/ We ran a blue streak* [1890s+; fr the *blue streak* of a lightning bolt]

◁**blue veiner**▷ *n phr* A very stiff penile erection : *Even the Dragon Lady couldn't have given you a blue veiner* (*1970s+*)

bluff *n* : *His courage was all bluff* • A noun sense fr 1849 is "an excuse" (*1870s+*) *v* To use confident pretense as a means of winning or succeeding • The 1674 definition is "to blindfold or hoodwink"; the game of poker was originally known as *bluff* (*1670s+*) [perhaps related to, though not derived fr, a late 1700s *bluff,* "a blindfold or blinker for a horse"] *See* CALL SOMEONE'S BLUFF

blurb *n* A statement in praise of something or somebody; esp an encomious passage from a book or theater review, used as advertising [1910+; said to have been coined by Gelett Burgess (1866–1951), US humorist and illustrator; also attributed to Brander Matthews (1852–1929), US scholar and critic]

BM (pronounced as separate letters) *n* A bowel movement • Mainly a euphemism used with children

BMO (pronounced as separate letters) *n* An Arab woman [1990s+ Gulf War Army; fr *black moving object,* describing the shrouded appearance of such women]

BMOC (pronounced as separate letters) *n phr* A college-student leader or idol [1930s+; fr *big man on campus*]

B movie *n phr* A usu low-budget movie intended for the broad middle ground of taste and meant to be primarily entertaining and narrative rather than serious, artistic, etc [1930s+; fr their being the second movie in a double feature]

BMX (pronounced as separate letters) *n* Cross-country bicycle racing [1980s+; fr *bicycle moto-cross,* fr *moto-cross,* "cross-country motorcycle racing over a laid-out course," fr French *moto,* "motorcycle," and English *cross,* "cross-country"]

BO[1] (pronounced as separate letters) *n* Body odor, esp from underarm perspiration • Popularized by extensive use in ads for Lifebuoy® soap (*1930s+*)

BO[2] *adj* Theatrical appeal : *The show is really big BO n* Box office, the gauge of how well a show is doing by its receipts (*1930s+ Show business*)

board *n* **1** A ticket to a show or game; pasteboard (*1950s+ Show business*) **2** A rebound, the catching of a ball that bounces off the backboard or the basket : *We did a heck of a job on Shaq. He had 10 boards* (*1990s+ Basketball*) *v* : *If we rebound, we've got a chance. If we don't board, we can hang it up See* ACROSS THE BOARD

boat *n* **1** A car : *The little boat (automobile, in the argot of '22)* (*1915+*) **2** A big car : *Why don't you park that boat there, hop inside with me* (*1920+*) **3** A big shoe; gunboats : *leaving his boats out in the hall See* GRAVY TRAIN, MAN IN THE BOAT, MISS THE BOAT, ON THE GRAVY TRAIN, RIDE THE GRAVY TRAIN, ROCK THE BOAT

boat anchor *n* An old or useless computer; also, anything clunky and useless : *replace the boat anchors on the third floor*

boat people *n phr* Political refugees who escape by small boat (*mid-1970s+*)

bob *See* BOOB JOB, NOSE JOB

Bob *modifier* : *Bob car/ Bob clothes n* A Bedouin or Iraqi (*1990s+ Gulf War Army*)

bob and weave *v phr* To behave evasively; ROLL WITH THE PUNCHES : *For months Ross bobbed and weaved with Time's negotiators* (*1920s+ Prizefighting*)

bobber *See* DEELY BOPPER

Bobbittry *n* Militant feminism so extreme as to seem to approve sexual mutilation of the male [1990s+; fr John Wayne *Bobbitt*, whose wife was convicted of cutting off his penis]

bobble *n* : *The President's denial was a bad bobble* *v* To blunder; esp in baseball, to mishandle or drop the ball (*1900+*)

Bob's your uncle *interj* A response in conversation expressing compliance, meaning it's all right or there you are : *turn right at the light then left at the stop sign and Bob's your uncle* (*1937+*)

bobtail *n* **1** A dishonorable discharge • So called because the phrase "service honorable and faithful" was deleted from the discharge form (*1870s+ Army*) **2** A truck tractor without a semitrailer (*1940s+ Truckers*) *v* : *Returning with just the tractor (bobtailing) represented a loss* [noun sense 2 considers the semitrailer the *tail* of the rig]

bod *n* **1** A person (*1930s+ British*) **2** The body; physique : *Pamela Anderson (Brigitte Bardot hair, pouty lips, sex-doll bod)/ There are women who don't know any other way to relate except with their bods* (*1960s+*) *See* WARM BODY

bodacious (boh DAY shəs) *adj* Extreme; excellent, admirable : *That's one bodacious pair of ta-tas on that blonde* [chiefly Southern 1840s+; fr early 19th-century *bodyaciously*, "bodily, totally"]

bodacious ta-tas *n phr* Prominent attractive breasts [1980s+ College students; *tatas* is a pronunciation of "taters, potatoes," and a euphemism for "tits"; the phrase was used in the 1982 movie *An Officer and a Gentleman*]

bodega (boh DAY gə) *n* **1** A liquor store **2** A grocery store, esp in Puerto Rican areas of New York City [Mexican Spanish 1850s+; fr Spanish, "shop"]

bodice-ripper or **bodice-buster** *n* A romantic-erotic novel, esp one with a historical plot; HEAVY BREATHER : *the offensive term bodice-ripper/ literary set that swoons over such bodice-busters as "Love's Sweet Agony"* (*1980s+*)

body *See* KNOW WHERE THE BODIES ARE BURIED, WARM BODY

body and soul *n phr* One's boyfriend or girl-friend [1930s+; probably fr the title of a 1930s song, "Body and Soul"]

body count *n* **1** The total number of casualties after a conflict : *daily body count increased as the war went on* **2** The total number of people affected in a shakeup or bad situation : *body count after the layoffs* **3** The total number of people present : *body count at the meeting*

body packer or **internal** *n phr* : *These "internals" or "body packers" swallow heroin encased in condoms or other packaging, disgorging their contraband to drug dealers, if they are not killed by leaking packages first* (*1990s+ Narcotics*)

body-shake *See* SKIN-SEARCH

boff *n* **1** A blow with the fist or open hand (*1920s+*) **2** A sex act; coupling : *a quick bathroom boff* (*1950s+*) **3** A laugh, esp one following a comedian's joke; boffola (*1940s+ Show business*) **4** A joke or witty remark (*1940s+ Show business*) **5** A show that pleases the audience; SOCKEROO (*1940s+ Show business*) *v* **1** : *LaGuardia bade his cops to muss them up and boff them around on sight* **2** To do the sex act : *professors boffing coeds in their offices/ I was trying for the world boffing championship* (*1930s+*) **3** To vomit; BARF (*1950s+*) [first and second senses echoic; show-business senses probably a shortening of *boffo*] *See* THROW A FUCK INTO someone

boffer *n* A man who does the sex act; COCKSMAN : *The All-American boffer* (*1930s+*)

boffo *adj* **1** : *Hey, that's a very boffo line/ The zany Brewsters still get laughs, boffo laughs* **2** : *"Crimson Tide" rolls in as the first boffo box office/ Red-blooded boffo entertainment for both sexes* **3** Highly favorable; laudatory *n* **1** A dollar or dollar bill : *That's worth a million boffos* (*1920s+*) **2** A year, esp a one-year prison sentence; boppo (*1920s+ Underworld*) **3** A laugh, esp a loud laugh in response to a comedian; BOFF, boffola (*1940s+ Show business*) **4** A joke or a witty remark; BOFF (*1940s+ Show business*) **5** A successful entertainment; BOFF, HIT : *her string of box-office boffos* (*1940s+ Show business*) [fr a 19th-century carnival term based on the idea of a good *box office*]

bogart or **Bogart** or **bogard** *v* **1** To behave truculently; get something by intimidation : *The little old lady bogarted her way into the grocery line/ some hotshot from Brooklyn trying to Bogart a game from the regulars* **2** (also **bogart a joint**) To take more than one's share, esp of a marijuana cigarette; HOG [1960s+ Black; fr the tough roles played in films by Humphrey *Bogart*]

bog down *v phr* To become helpless and immobile, as if mired in a bog : *On the one hand* *a threat had been neutralized, but we were bogging down again (1920s+)*

bogey or **bogie** or **bogy** *n* **1** A police officer *(1930s+ Underworld)* **2** An enemy aircraft, esp an attacking fighter plane *(WWII Army Air Forces fr British RAF)* **3** A golf score of one stroke over par on a given hole *(late 1800s+ British)* [all senses fr *bogy* or *bogey*, "evil spirit, hobgoblin," the *boogy* or *boogyman* invoked to frighten children; the golf sense originated in 1890 when Dr Thomas Browne, a naval surgeon, compared his opponent, the "ground score," to the "Bogey Man" of a popular song, at any rate, so it is said]

bogsatt *n* An informal and congenial method of making decisions [1980s+ Pentagon and government; acronym fr "a bunch of guys sitting around a table talking"]

bogue *adj* **1** In need of narcotics; suffering from deprivation : *I'm bogue. I'm trying to kick (1960s+ Narcotics)* **2** False; fake; BOGUS, PHONY *(1950s+)* [origin unknown]

bogus *adj* **1** False; fake; counterfeit; PHONY *(1830s+)* **2** Ignorant; not up-to-date; unattractive; LAME, SQUARE : *"Bogus" is a different shading of "lame" (1980s+ Teenagers)* **3** Not to be trusted; useless, false, wrong, silly, incredible, etc *(1980s+ Computers)* [origin unknown; certainly connected with *bogus*, attested as name of a counterfeiting machine in 1827, whence a connection has been made with *bogy*]

boheme *n* A female style of comportment of loose funky clothing, comfortable shoes, and no makeup • Takeoff of *bohemian*

◄**bohunk**► *n* **1** An immigrant from central or eastern Europe, usu a Czech, Slovak, Hungarian, or Pole; HUNKY *(1900+)* **2** A stupid, clumsy person; lout *(1920+) (Loggers)* See BEAUHUNK

boil down *v phr* To reduce to the essential elements : *It all boils down to who gets there faster (1880+)*

boiled *adj* **1** Drunk *(1890s+)* **2** Angry See HARD-BOILED, HARD-BOILED EGG

boiler See POTBOILER

boiler room *modifier* : *The county is home to hundreds of "boiler room" telephone operations/ what law enforcement officials call a "boiler room" operation* **n** *phr* **1** A site of illegal operations, often the telephone sale of stocks, real estate, etc, by charlatans *(1930s+)* **2** A shady and provocative gathering-place; a hotbed : *the tendency of their young people to congregate in places that are boiler rooms for drugs and violence (1980s+)*

boil someone in oil *v phr* To punish or rebuke severely

boil over *v phr* To lose one's temper : *make a manager boil over (1879+)*

boil the ocean *v phr* To waste one's time on an impossible task : *You can't get him to change. It's like boiling the ocean*

boing *interj* (also **boing-boing**) An exclamation of appreciative delight and intentness at the sight of an attractive woman • An uttered equivalent of a wolf whistle : *dropped what they were doing and their eyes went "Boing, boing" (WWII armed forces)* **v** (also **boink**) To do the sex act with or to; BOFF, BONK : *Previously it was more important whether I was boinging Paula Abdul/ chicks he claims he's boinked (1980s+)* [fr the sound a plucked spring makes, suggesting tenseness and quivering response, with a hint perhaps of penile erection; verb sense related to *bang* and *bonk*]

boinkable *adj* Able, willing, and desirable for copulation : *a room full of boinkable ladies*

boinker *n* An encounter or engagement that ends in a sex act *(1980s+)*

bokoo or **boku** *n* Many • A play on French *beaucoup* : *boku people in line*

bollixed (or **bolaxed** or **bolexed**) **up** *adj phr* In a thoroughly confused and futile condition; BALLED UP, FUCKED UP : *You're getting your cues all bollixed up* [1930s+; fr *bollocks* or *ballocks*, "testicles," ultimately fr old English *bealluc*, "testicle"]

bollocks (also **ballocks**) *n* **1** Rubbish; nonsense **2** The testicles

bolo badge *n phr* A Purple Heart, esp one awarded posthumously after an injudicious maneuver [1990s+ Gulf War Army; fr the notion that one was killed because he was a poor shot]

boloney See BALONEY

bolt *v* To leave; BOOK, SPLIT *(1970s+ Students)*

bolt-on *adj* Of a woman's breasts, surgically augmented : *them's look bolt-on to me* **n** An additional part

bolts See NUTS AND BOLTS

bomb *n* **1** A conspicuous and total failure; BLAST, FLOP *(1950s+ Show business)* **2** A car, esp a hot rod *(1950s+ Hot rodders)* **3** (also **bomber**) An especially big marijuana cigarette *(1950s+ Narcotics)* **4** Heroin *(1950s+ Narcotics)* **5** Something very good : *teenagers come home from a movie and say it was a "bomb," yet insist on seeing it again and again (1990s+ Teenagers)* **v** **1** : *The show bombed everywhere on the road/ I took the test, and bombed (1960s+ Show business)* **2** To do very well at or on : *I really bombed the math test, aced it (1960s+ Students)* **3** To go very fast; plunge : *found the discarded relics ideal for bombing down the dirt slopes of Mt Tam (1960s+)* **4** To paint graffiti on; TAG : *His favorite stylin'-and-bombin' wall, tagged with the rebellious urban scrawl of graffiti artists*

(1980s+) [in the sense of failure, perhaps fr the outdated expression *make a baum of it,* "fail"]

bomb, the *n phr* **1** A very long forward pass intended to score a quick touchdown *(1960s+ Football)* **2** Something wonderful, outstanding, etc *(1990s+ Teenagers)*

bombed *adj* Drunk *(1950s+)*

bombed out *adj phr* Very much intoxicated by narcotics; very dozy or exhilarated; SPACED-OUT, STONED *(1960s+ Narcotics)*

bomber *n* A crude cocktail : *The kids had been chugging "bombers"—a mixture of liquors, wine and beer (1980s+)*

bombiosity or **bombosity** *n* The buttocks; ASS, DUFF [1930s+; fr *bombous,* "rounded, belly-shaped," fr the shape of a *bomb*]

bomb out *v phr* To fail; BOMB : *Stephanie Moody "bombed out" last year: failed to complete her opening lifts (1970s+)*

bombshell *n* **1** A startling, striking event; a stunning piece of news or something that makes one gape : *Her entrance astride the crocodile was a bombshell (1920s+)* **2** A sexually stimulating woman • Often in the expression "blonde bombshell" *(1940s+)*

bond *See* JUNK BOND

bone[1] *n* **1** Money; cash *(1970s+ Teenagers)* **2** A dollar, esp a silver dollar *(1860s+)* ◁3▷ The erect penis *(mid-1800s+)* *v* ◁1▷ (also **bone away**) To do the sex act; SCREW : *Shit! he thought. He coulda been boning by now (1980s+ Students) See* HAVE A BONE ON, JAW-BONE, TAIL BONE

bone[2] *n* A diligent student *v* (also **bone up**) To study, esp to study intensely for an examination [College students 1880s+; fr the student's use of *bohns,* "translations, ponies," named after *Bohn's* Classical Library]

bone factory *n* **1** A hospital : *taken to the bone factory* **2** A cemetery

bonehead *modifier* : *I should have been in bone-head English* **n** A stupid person : *four sons, all bone-heads* [1900s+; fr the notion of the head being all *bone,* no brain] *See* PULL A BONER

boneheaded *adj* Stupid *(1900s+)*

bonehead play or **move** *n phr* An error, esp one caused by bad judgment : *Merkel's throw was the most renowned bonehead play in history (1910+ chiefly sports)*

◁**bone-on**▷ *n* An erect penis : *Sometimes he could still get a pretty respectable bone-on (1940s+)*

bone out *v phr* To lose one's nerve; quit; CHICKEN OUT *(1990s+ Teenagers)*

boner *n* **1** A blunder; error; BLOOPER, HOWLER *(1910+ Baseball)* **2** A diligent student; BONE *(1900+ College students)* ◁3▷ An erect penis; BONE-ON, HARD-ON : *The time you coveted your neighbor's wife, you had a big boner! He*

walks around with a boner all the time *(1950s+) See* PULL A BONER

bones *n* **1** Dice • Chaucer referred to dice as "bitched *bones*" about 1390 *(1880s+)* **2** Two sticks or bones held between the fingers and used to make a clacking rhythm • Best known fr their use in post–Civil War minstrel shows, where they were wielded by a character named Mr *Bones* (late 1500s+) **3** Dollars; money *(1900s+) See* MAKE NO BONES ABOUT, SAWBONES

bone-shaker *n* Any badly sprung, springless, or violently jerking vehicle, esp a very early form of bicycle *(1860s+)*

bone up *See* BONE[2]

boneyard *n* A cemetery : *lie on a blanket out on the boneyard (1860s+)*

bong *n* A water pipe for smoking narcotics • Said to have been introduced by returning Vietnam veterans : *the array of glass and plastic water pipes or bongs (1960s+ Narcotics)* *v* **1** To smoke marijuana using a water pipe *(1960s+ Teenagers)* **2** To drink beer from a keg through a hose *(1980s+ Teenagers)*

bonged-out *adj* Intoxicated by a narcotic, esp one smoked through a bong : *You feel like a bonged-out Cubist painting (1970s+)*

bongo or **bongoed** *adj* Drunk *(1940s+)*

bonk *n* **1** A blow; BASH, SOCK *(1930s+)* **2** A single sex act; BANG, FUCK, PIECE *(1980s+ British)* *v* **1** To hit; strike; BANG, BIFF *(1930s+)* **2** Do the sex act with or to; BOFF, SCREW : *And I asked him if he was still sneaking around bonkin' that secretary/ What's this I hear about you bragging to friends that you bonked Kate Moss? (1970s+ British)*

bonkers *adj* Crazy; insane; NUTS : *Folks are going slightly bonkers these days over anything that glitters/ suffering stress-related ailments like eczema or colitis, or just plain going bonkers* [1950s+ British; probably fr *bonk,* "to hit on the head," plus the British slang suffix *-ers*]

bonnet *See* BEE IN one's BONNET

Bonus! *interj* An exclamation of strong approval, pleasure, etc: Super! You win a prize!

bonzo *adj* Crazy; NUTS : *almost drove me bonzo* **n** : *This guy is a real bonzo* [1970s+; origin unknown; perhaps influenced by *bonkers* and *gonzo;* perhaps related to a British puppy named *Bonzo,* originated in 1922]

boo[1] *adj* Excellent; remarkable : *Something that used to be known as the cat's whiskers is now called "deadly boo" (1950s+)* *n* Marijuana or another narcotic : *I got over there and she lays this dynamite boo on me, I mean super shit (1930s+ Jazz musicians)* [noun sense said to be fr black English *jabooby,* "marijuana, so called because it induces a state of fear or anxiety,", of unknown origin; but possibly fr *Budda,* "marijuana"] *See* TICKETY-BOO

boo² *interj* 1 An exclamation of disapproval, the equivalent of a hiss (*1890s+*) 2 A supposedly frightening exclamation, such as a ghost might give : *She jumped out of the closet and hollered "Boo!"* (*1940s+*) *v* : *Next time at bat he was roundly booed*

boob¹ *n* 1 A stupid person; DIM-WIT : *There are still boobs, alack, who'd like the old-time gin-mill back* (*1908+*) 2 A person who is too innocent and trusting; SUCKER : *The poor boob fell for his line and gave him the money* (*1920s+*)

◁**boob²**▷ *n* A woman's breast; BUB, knocker [*1940s+*; probably fr *boobie²*]

boob³ *n* A blunder; error; BOO-BOO *v* : *If I boob, I expect you to protect me* (*1930s+*)

◁**boobage**▷ *n* A woman's breasts; breasts in general

boobie¹ or **bubbie** See BUBBY

◁**boobie²** or **booby** or **bubbie**▷ (BOO bee) *n* A woman's breast [late 1600s+; perhaps ultimately fr Latin *puppa*, literally "little girl," which in child language became "breast"; whence Old French *pope, popel*, "breast," German dialect *Bubbi*, and so on]

◁**boob job** (or **bob**)▷ *n phr* A surgical breast enlargement : *saying that Julie had had a boob job* (*1980s+*)

boo-boo¹ *n* An error or misstep, esp one with embarrassing consequences; faux pas : *The original boo-boo that started all this public confusion* [*1950s+*; perhaps fr *boob³*; perhaps fr Yiddish *bulba*, "potato," fr Polish, which came to mean "malapropism, faux pas"]

boo-boo² *n* A minor flesh wound or blemish [*1900+*; perhaps fr *boo-hoo*, a child's crying over a minor hurt]

boob tube, the *n phr* Television or a television set; the TUBE (*mid-1960s+*)

booby hatch *n phr* 1 An insane asylum; mental hospital : *King Bolden cut hair in the booby-hatch* (*1890s+*) 2 (also **booby hutch**) A police station (*1950s+ Underworld*) [first sense perhaps connected with *Colney Hatch*, a village near London where an insane asylum was opened in 1851; the name became generic for a mental hospital]

booby trap *n phr* 1 A hidden explosive charge designed to be set off by some ordinary act, such as starting a vehicle or driving down a street, used originally in wartime to harass invaders • The British schoolboy's booby trap was a pitcher of water poised atop a door so that whoever opened the door would be doused 2 A seemingly harmless appearance that conceals vexations arranged for an unsuspecting opponent : *Don't debate him, it's a booby trap* *v* : *They booby-trapped his car and six people died* (*WWII Army; mid-1800s+ British*)

boodle *n* 1 An entire lot; a large number or amount; CABOODLE (*1830s+*) 2 Counterfeit money (*1850s+ Underworld*) 3 Bribe money or other money obtained by graft and corruption : *A few trees are planted. What happens to most of the boodle?* (*1880s+*) 4 Money in general (*1890+*) 5 Sweets; treats; delicacies (*Prison & students 1900+*) *v* To hug, kiss, etc; NECK (*1940s+ Students*) [fr Dutch *boedel*, "estate, lot"]

boog *v* To dance : *to go booging* (*1930s+ fr boogie-woogie*)

boogaloo or **bugaloo** (BOO a loo, BOOG-) *modifier* 1 : *That's really voodoo music, man, boogaloo music* 2 : *Go out and have a bugaloo good time* *n* A shuffling, shoulder-swinging dance : *feet doing a fast boogaloo in the grass* *v* 1 : *They boogalooed down the street* 2 To carry on jocularly; play; tease; FOOL AROUND [*1960s+*; apparently a rhyming form based on *boog*, like *boogerboo*]

booger or **boogie** *n* A piece of nasal mucus [*1890s+*; an extension of *bugger*, "nasal mucus"] See BUGGER

boogie or **boogey** (BOO gee, BOO-) *modifier* ◁1▷ : *a boogie hairstyle/ boogie music* *n* 1 (also **boogie-woogie**) Syphilis, esp advanced syphilis (*1900s+ Black*) ◀2▶ A black person (*1920s+*) 3 BOOGIE-WOOGIE (*1940s+*) ◁4▷ The vulva; CUNT (*1960s+*) 5 An enemy aircraft, esp a fighter plane; BOGEY (*WWII Army Air Forces*) 6 A piece of solid mucus from the nose; BOOGER *v* 1 To move, shake, and wriggle the body in time to rock-and-roll music; do a sort of boogaloo : *Amanda boogies and bangs a tambourine while her 39 sisters sit on steps and force shattered smiles* (*1940s+*) 2 To move; go; leave; LIGHT OUT : *Let's boogie, Mama—Right behind you, Big Daddy/ F16D, a jet that can really boogie/ He was here on June 16, then boogied before we got on the record* (*1970s+*) 3 To carry on jocularly; play; tease; FOOL AROUND : *back from a long weekend and ready to boogie* (*1930s+*) 4 To do the sex act : *a lot of heavy boogieing going on at Iowa State* (*1960s+*) ◁5▷ To do anal intercourse; BUGGER : *Would Ronnie be averse to being boogied by Kiss during his acceptance speech* (*1970s+*) See LET'S BOOGIE

boogie board *n phr* 1 A skateboard 2 A kind of surfboard (*1970s+*)

boogie box See GHETTO BOX

boogie down to somewhere *v phr* To go somewhere in a bit of a hurry : *boogie down to the store for some ice cream*

boogieman (also **bogeyman**) *n* An imaginary scary person or monster, an evil spirit; also, any false threat : *left the light on so the boogieman won't come*

boogie-woogie (BOO gee WOO gee, BOO-, WOO-) *modifier* : *Jimmy Yancey created the boogie woogie blues n* **1** Syphilis, esp advanced syphilis *(1900s+ Black)* **2** A fast jazz piano style with a heavy rolling bass played eight beats to the measure, often used as a song accompaniment *(1920s+ Jazz musicians) v* To enjoy oneself thoroughly *(1930s+ Black)* [origin uncertain]

book *n* **1** BOOKIE *(1860s+ Gambling)* **2** A bookie's function and place of business : *Joey keeps a book (1860s+ Gambling)* **3** The daily logbook of a police station *(1840s+ Police) v* **1** make book **2** To charge someone with a crime or misdemeanor at a police station : *They took the bum in and booked him for vagrancy (1840s+ Police)* **3** To engage or reserve in advance : *They booked eight readings in three days for the visiting poet/ Book me a table for six (1820s+)* **4** HIT THE BOOKS **5** To run or depart, esp rapidly : *And the couple booked off into the sunset for their honeymoon (1980s+ Students) See* BY THE BOOK, CRACK A BOOK, HIT THE BOOKS, LITTLE BLACK BOOK, ONE FOR THE BOOK, POUND THE BOOKS, READ someone LIKE A BOOK, STROKE BOOK, TAKE A PAGE FROM someone's BOOK, THROW THE BOOK AT someone, WRITE THE BOOK

book, the *n phr* **1** A life sentence to prison *(1920s+ Underworld)* **2** Instructions or conventional wisdom about someone's performance; form : *The "book" on this player was to leave him alone, treat him politely, and pick him up if you happened to block him (1950s+)* [first sense fr throw the book at someone; second sense fr the accumulated knowledge about horses and jockeys that gamblers study] *See* THROW THE BOOK AT someone

bookend *n* **1** : *two black bodyguards, macho bookends n* **2** (also **bookend ad**) A television commercial having two parts, separated by other unrelated commercials : *Bookends are intriguing to people because they set up a scenario v* To precede and follow; bracket : *all this is somehow bookended by the secret, shadow manuscripts of his mother and his wife/ eight big star duets, bookended by solo performances (1980s+)*

bookie *n* A person who accepts and handles bets on horse races; bookmaker *(1880s+ Gambling)*

book it *v phr* **1** To depart quickly; BOOK *(1970s+ Students)* **2** To be confident of something; count on something; Make Book on something : *I'll be back. Book it*

bookmark *v* To make a note of something, mentally or in writing ● Fr the bookmarking of Web pages

book-smarts *n* Learning; erudition : *They not only have the "book-smarts" that it*

takes, but the acting and drama ability *(1990s+)*

boola-boola *n* Noisy partisan support for one's college teams : *too much panty-raiding, fraternities, and boola-boola and all of that* [1960s+; fr a Yale University song]

boom *adj* Wonderful; fashionable; outstanding; GREAT *(1990s+ Canadian students) n* Marijuana *(1950s+ Narcotics) v* **1** To flourish; show vigor : *Business is booming! (1860s+)* **2** To promote aggressively : *There he goes booming that brand of soap (1890s+)* **3** (also **boom along**) To sail fast, under full canvas *(1600s+ Nautical) See* FALL DOWN AND GO BOOM, LOWER THE BOOM

◁**boom-boom**▷ *n* Sexual activity; copulation; ASS : *dragging girls into the woods "for a little boom-boom" (1960s+ Armed forces)*

boom box *n phr* (also **boom**) A loud stereo cassette player : *Violators risk confiscation of their boom boxes (1980s+) See* GHETTO BOX

boomer *n* **1** A migratory worker *(1890s+ Hoboes)* **2** A railroad or construction worker, logger, etc, who continually shifts from one place of work to another *(1890s+ Hoboes)* **3** A womanizer; ladies' man *(1930s+)* **4** An enthusiastic advocate of land development : *What consumes the attention of most Idahoans is the battle between the boomers (developers) and the greenies (environmentalists) (1880s+)* **5** A member of the post-WWII baby boom; BABY BOOMER : *Two quirky tales of adolescence, rooted in boomer history and sanitized for the boomer market (1980s+)*

boomerang *v* To return to the parental nest : *There's a 40 percent chance you'll "boomerang" back to live with your parents at least once (1980s+)*

boomerang baby (or **kid**) *n phr* A child who returns to the parental home even after college and other mature training; a reoccupant of the empty nest *(1980s+)*

booming or **boomin'** *adj* **1** Excellent; wonderful; BOOM, FLY, RAD **2** Playing loud bass tones on a stereo *(1980s+ Teenagers)*

boomlet *n* A minor upsurge; a small access of vigor : *sustains the boomlet in comedy-dramas about Irish village life (1880+)*

boomshakalaka *interj* An impudent exclamation similar to *in your face*

boondock *modifier* Suitable for rough outdoor use : *Marines use boondock clothes and boondock shoes for hikes and maneuvers (WWII Navy and Marine Corps)*

boondocks, the, or **the boonies** *n* Remote places; rural regions : *The people out there in the boonies may not know you're past it* [Marine Corps 1900+; fr Tagalog *bundok*, "mountain"]

boondoggle *n* : *The public's got the idea that this is a boondoggle, a Rube Goldberg* **v** To spend public funds outlandishly or on futile activity [mid-1930s+; origin uncertain; verb said to be fr the iron-smelting industry, meaning "make unprofitable attempts to retrieve good iron from slag"; noun found by 1940s meaning "an ornamental thong made by Boy Scouts" and suggesting mere make-work]

boonie rat *n phr* A combat soldier, esp an infantry private; DOGFACE, GRUNT *(Vietnam War armed services)*

booshwa or **booshwah** *See* BUSHWAH

boost *n* : *I'll give you a good boost* **v** **1** To steal, esp by shoplifting : *Someone had boosted my tape recorder out of the room/ slept on park benches and boosted from the A&P (1908+)* **2** To praise highly : *to boost one's home town (1900+)* **3** To do the sex act with or to; BONK, SCREW *(1980s+ Students)*

booster *n* **1** A shoplifter; pilferer : *Got a booster for you. The chunky girl in blue at the lace counter/ He knew they couldn't be boosters or creepers (1908+)* **2** A huckster's or auctioneer's assistant who pretends to buy in order to stimulate others; SHILL *(1905+ Carnival)* **3** A person who praises extravagantly; FAN *(1890+)*

boot *n* **1** : *Give him a boot in the ass (1940s+)* **2** : *Dark atoned for his boot by making a good play on Kiner's slow roller* **3** A thrill; surge of pleasure; BANG, KICK : *I get a boot from boats (1930+)* **4** A recruit *(1900+ Navy & Marine Corps)* ◄**5**► A black person *(1950s+ Black)* **6** (also **Denver boot**) A metal locking device put on the wheels of a scofflaw's car to prevent driving *(late 1960s+)* **v** **1** To kick, esp to give a hard kick : *Let's boot a football around (1870s+)* **2** To discharge; eject; FIRE, SACK *(1880s+)* **3** (also **boot away**) To lose or waste by incompetence, inattention, etc; botch; bungle; BLOW : *I booted three good chances (1950s+)* **4** To commit an error, esp in handling a ground ball *(1900s+ Baseball)* **5** (also **backtrack**) To inject a narcotic gradually by pulling back and reinjecting blood again and again to increase the drug's effect : *The technique, known as "booting," is believed to prolong the drug's initial effect (1960s+ Narcotics)* **6** BOOT UP *(1980+ Computer) See* TO BOOT

boot, the *n phr* Dismissal, discharge *(1880s+)*

boot camp *n phr* **1** A basic training center *(WWI Navy & Marine Corps)* **2** A penal camp, resembling a military boot camp in rigor, used as a substitute for imprisonment : *The penal system is moving toward separate drug-treatment facilities, boot camps for young offenders (1980s+)* **3** Any very strict training facility : *militant pro-life boot camp (1990s+)*

booted *adj* Intoxicated by narcotics; HIGH, STONED *(1900s+ Narcotics)*

bootleg *modifier* : *a bottle of bootleg hooch* **n** Whiskey illegally made or sold *(1880s+)* **v** **1** To make or sell illegal whiskey and other illegally repackaged products such as music recordings, movies, etc *(1906+)* **2** To carry the ball deceptively by holding it against the leg, esp after pretending to hand it off to another player *(1950s+ Football)* [fr the idea of concealment in the upper part of one's boots]

bootlegger or **booter** or **bootie** *n* A person who bootlegs : *5,000 booters on Manhattan Island alone/ That new bootie carries a powerful line of hooch (1880s+)*

bootlick *v* To serve and flatter a superior; curry favor; APPLE-POLISH, BROWN-NOSE : *Boss kisser-uppers will always be with us, boot-licking their way through the workplace (1840s+)*

boot someone out *v phr* To kick or throw someone out : *They booted me out of the soup kitchen*

boot party *n phr* Savagely kicking an offender as a form of punishment *(1990s+ Street gang)*

boots *n* A bootblack, esp in a hotel *(1840s+) See* BET YOUR BOOTS, JESUS BOOTS

boot strapper *n phr* A person who succeeds by his own efforts; self-made person : *black "boot strappers," teachers, city workers, professionals who have to struggle to make it* [1960s+; fr the expression *lift oneself by one's own bootstraps*]

boot up or **boot** *v phr* or *v* To start up or input a computer's operating system : *The typical first step in working with a computer, then, is to load the DOS programs; this is called "booting up"/ He showed me how to log in and boot the operating system* [1970s+ Computers; fr earlier *bootstrap*, because after a simple action like pressing one key, the computer loads the operating system itself, as if it were raising itself by its own bootstraps]

◄**booty** or **boody**► *modifier* : *It's about snappin' all the booty rap* **n** **1** The female body as a sex object : *You can listen to it, but you can shake your booty to it too* **2** The vulva **3** The sex act; sex; ASS : *The heroines are giving up some booty (1920s+ Black)*

◄**booty call**► *n* **1** Sexual arousal or desire to seek a sex partner : *We're in the party! Booty call!* **2** A telephone call to seek a sex partner : *high-school booty calls where they ignore you the next day*

booyah *interj* **1** An impudent exclamation similar to *in your face* : *They screamed "booyah" at the other team* **2** An excited exclamation of extreme pleasure, approval, etc : *He said "booyah!" when I told him I made tacos for dinner*

booze *n* Any alcoholic drink, esp whiskey and other spirits (*1880s+*) *v* To drink alcoholic beverages, esp to drink whiskey heavily (*1760s+*) [fr Middle English and dialect *bowse* (pronounced like *booze*), "drink, carouse," reinforced by the name of a 19th-century Philadelphia distiller, E G Booze] *See* HIT THE BOTTLE

booze artist *n* A drunk person; drunkard

boozed or **boozed up** *adj* or *adj phr* Drunk • Included as *bowz'd* in Benjamin Franklin's 1722 list of 225 words meaning "drunk" (*first form 1850+, second 1880s+*)

boozehound or **booze-fighter** *n* A person who habitually drinks a great deal of whiskey; LUSH : *Among American governors, the booze-fighters are plainly the best (first form 1940s+, second 1900s+)*

booze it (up) *v phr* To drink a great deal of liquor : *boozed it up every night after work*

boozer *n* A heavy drinker; ALKY, LUSH (*1819+*)

booze-up *n* A drinking spree; BINGE : *the morning booze-up which was still fouling his blood (1890s+ British)*

booze up *v phr* To drink a great deal of liquor (*1940s+*)

boozy *adj* Drunk • Found in the 225 terms meaning "drunk" that Benjamin Franklin published in 1722 (*1720+*)

bop *modifier* : *a bop musician* **n** 1 : *a bop on the beezer* (*1930s+*) 2 A fight among gangs; RUMBLE (*1950s+ Street gang*) 3 The sex act; SCREW (*1970s+*) 4 (also **bebop**) A style of modern jazz characterized by complex harmonies, sudden changes in register, the use of fast and nearly unintelligible lyrics, etc : *Bop is "cool" jazz (1940s+ Jazz musicians)* *v* 1 To strike, esp with the fist : *Nina reached out and bopped her on the head/ I kept my temper in check, since bopping police chiefs wasn't good PR (1930s+)* 2 To defeat : *The home team got bopped again (1980s+)* 3 : *You gotta go on bopping and hanging around street corners all your life?* 4 : *You told Esteva the cop was bopping his wife* 5 To walk or go, esp in a slow and relaxed mood : *They bopped over to the bar (1950s+ Students)* [echoic] *See* DIDDLYBOP, TEENYBOPPER, THROW A FUCK INTO someone

bop off *v phr* To depart; BOOK, SPLIT (*1950s+ Students*)

bopper *n* 1 A street-gang fighter (*1960s+*) 2 A bop musician (*1940s+*) 3 A baseball power hitter; SLUGGER : *Now I've got a big bopper at the plate (1970s+)* 4 TEENYBOPPER (*1960s+*) *See* DEELY BOPPER

bopping *modifier* : *The "bopping" cabbies were expelled* **n** Tampering with taxicab meters to register illegally high charges : *The United Cab Association here has expelled about 40 cab drivers in the last two years for "bopping" (1970s+ Philadelphia cabdrivers)*

boppy *adj* Bouncy; zesty; JAZZY : *an MTV-like newscast—everything is boppy, the pace is snappy and the graphics flashy (1980s+)*

border *See* SOUTH OF THE BORDER

bored out of one's **skull** *adj phr* BORED TO DEATH : *Stratford High School, where he was bored out of his skull for four years (1960s+)*

bored stiff *adj phr* BORED TO DEATH (*1920s+*)

bored to death *adj phr* Extremely bored (*1880+*)

bore the pants off someone *v phr* To thoroughly bore or weary : *would bore the pants off me (1937+)*

bork or **Bork** *n* : *close ranks to coordinate a huge preemptive bork* *v* To mount an intense campaign against a political appointee; BUSHWHACK : *"We're going to Bork him,"* proclaimed a feminist advocate [late 1980s+; fr the experience of Judge Robert Bork, whose 1987 nomination to the Supreme Court was rejected by strong concerted opposition]

born loser *See* LOSER

born to *adj phr* Seemingly destined and compelled to perform something indicated : *My born-to-shop bride is disappointed that all the shops are closed on Sunday/ This guy was born to run/ Weeb was born to coach (1980s+)*

borscht belt *n phr* 1 The region in and near the Catskill Mountains north of New York City where many predominantly Jewish resort hotels are found (*1930s+*) 2 Any neighborhood peopled by Russians or Russian emigrants : *Just south of the Fairfax borscht belt and across the street from the Farmer's Market (1990s+)* [fr Russian *borshch*, "beet soup" (in its Yiddish spelling), a focus of the cuisine]

borscht circuit *n phr* The resort hotels of the Catskills borscht belt, regarded as a circuit for entertainers, lecturers, etc (*1930s+*)

bosh *n* Nonsense; poppycock; BULLSHIT [1830s+; apparently fr Turkish, "empty," popularized by an 1834 British novel]

bosom buddy *modifier* : *IBM has entered a series of bosom-buddy pacts with Novell, Lotus and Borland* **n** *phr* A very close friend; best friend; MAIN MAN (*1920s+*)

boss *adj* Excellent; wonderful; the MOST • This old use seems to have been revived independently by 1950s jazz musicians and teenagers : *Aw, this is boss!/ Japan has leaped into the implements-for-bosser-living gap (1880s+)* **n** 1 The chief; the person in charge (*late 1500s+*) 2 The head of a political machine (*1860s+*) *v* : *That little guy bosses the whole operation (1850s+)* [fr Dutch *baas*, "master"] *See* STRAW BOSS

boss someone **around** *v phr* To direct or control someone in an offensively authoritarian way : *I don't mind being told, but I hate being bossed around* (1850s+)

bossy[1] *adj* Domineering; autocratic : *She's very bossy, a take-charge gal* (1880s+)

bossy[2] *n* **1** A cow **2** Beef (1930s+ *Lunch counter*) [fr Latin *bos*, "cow"]

bothered *See* HOT AND BOTHERED

both hands *n phr* A ten-year prison sentence (1930s+ *Underworld*)

both sides of the desk *n phr* The faculty and students of a school or university : *and both sides of the desk challenged the established canon* (1990s+)

both sides of the street *See* WORK BOTH SIDES OF THE STREET

both ways *See* HAVE IT BOTH WAYS, SWING BOTH WAYS, WORK BOTH WAYS

bottle, the *n phr* **1** Liquor; BOOZE : *In life he battled wives, producers, bankruptcy, and the bottle* (1600s+) **2** Male prostitution (1960s+) [sense 2 perhaps fr cockney rhyming slang *bottle and glass*, "ass"] *See* HIT THE BOTTLE

bottom *n* The buttocks; ASS (1790s+)

Bottom *See* FOGGY BOTTOM

bottom dollar *See* BET one's BOTTOM DOLLAR, BET YOUR BOOTS

bottom dropped out, the *sentence* The market collapsed; disaster struck : *And then the bottom dropped out of the market* (1935+)

bottom feeder *n phr* **1** A despicable, predatory person who exploits and fancies the squalid; SCUMSUCKER, SLEAZEBAG : *Jesse Helms, David Duke, and other political bottom feeders* **2** (also **bottom fisher** or **bottom troller**) A person or company that deliberately exploits those in difficulty and profits by their poverty or misfortune : *which has made the bottom trollers start to take notice* [1990s+; fr the presumed disgusting habits of fish and other marine forms that *feed* on the *bottom*, hence eat slime, excrement, etc; the fact that *bottom* means "ass" may not be entirely irrelevant]

bottom-feeding *modifier* Showing the instincts and practice of a bottom feeder : *bottom-feeding biographies have existed as long as people have been able to write* (1990s+)

bottom fishing *n phr* The activity of investing in securities when it is believed the market has reached bottom following a major decline; searching for investment bargains

bottomless *adj* **1** Wearing nothing; nude : *a bottomless waitress* **2** A bar, club, restaurant, etc, featuring unclad females [1960s+; by comparison with *topless*, which means nude above the waist]

bottomless pit *n* **1** A voracious and insatiable person : *Mr P is a bottomless pit* **2** An infinite resource of something **3** Something that drains all one's resources or causes infinite trouble

bottom line, the *modifier* : *a bottom-line matter* *n phr* **1** The bookkeeping figure showing profit or loss **2** The result of any computation or estimate, esp one showing total costs : *I'll go half if the bottom line's OK* **3** Any final decision or judgment : *Let me tell you the bottom line* **4** A fundamental or crucial point of fact; the essence; the NITTY-GRITTY : *The bottom line is I am paid to win games, not for goodwill* [1960s+; perhaps fr Yiddish *untershte shure*, "bottom line," as used in the financial-commercial community]

bottom man on the totem pole *See* LOW MAN ON THE TOTEM POLE

bottom of the barrel *See* SCRAPE THE BOTTOM OF THE BARREL

bottom out *v phr* To get as low or bad as possible; reach nadir : *If [Watergate] ever bottoms out, we might be all right* (1970s+)

◁**bottoms up**▷ *adv phr* DOG FASHION (1950s+)

Bottoms up *sentence* Drink up! Cheers!

bounce *n* **1** Energy; vitality; PISS AND VINEGAR, PIZZAZZ ● Perhaps fr a 1930s term for a lively jazz tempo : *more bounce to the ounce* (1940s+) **2** A prison sentence : *You're going down as an accessory to assault and battery, a serious bounce* (1950s+ *Underworld*) **3** (also **bump**) A sudden and sometime brief increase in rating, popularity, value, etc : *The Republicans got a three-point bounce out of their convention* (1980+) *v* **1** To expel; throw out : *When he started swearing, they bounced him* (1870s+) **2** To discharge or dismiss; FIRE (1880s+) **3** To be rejected for lack of funds in the bank : *His checks never bounce* (1920s+) **4** To intimidate; bully; ROUST ● Esp police use : *And I'll want to bounce this Nadine kid, see what she has to say* (1600s+)

bounce, the *n phr* **1** Forcible ejection, esp by a person hired to remove unwanted customers; the BUM'S RUSH **2** A dismissal, polite or otherwise; KISS-OFF : *After a brief dialogue with my boss I got the bounce* (1870s+)

bounce something around *v phr* To think about and discuss an idea, project, etc : *Let's bounce it around a little before we decide* (1970s+)

bounce back *v phr* To recover; return to action : *She had a bad case of flu, but bounced back in two days* (1950s+)

bounce for or **spring for** *v phr* To pay for; treat; PICK UP THE TAB : *somewhere that doesn't bounce for bluecoats* (1930s+)

bounce something off someone *v phr* To try out an idea or scheme by seeing how someone reacts; seek a quick evaluation : *He likes working with people, bouncing off people and having them bounce off him* (1970s+)

bounce off the walls *v phr* Be in a nervous and confused condition; be hyper *(1970s+ Army and medical)*

◁**bounce-on**▷ *n* A sex act; a copulation; FUCK, SCREW : *I want a bounce-on (1990s+)*

bouncer *n* **1** A person employed to eject unwanted customers from a saloon, restaurant, dance hall, etc *(1880s+)* **2** A check that is returned for lack of funds; RUBBER CHECK *(1920s+)* **3** A forged check *(1920s+ Underworld)*

◁**bouncy-bouncy**▷ *n* The sex act *(1950s+)*

bowl *See* GOLDFISH BOWL, RUST BOWL

bow out *v phr* To depart, voluntarily and often gracefully : *We wanted her to take the role, but she bowed out (1940s+)*

bowser *n* A person with a doglike or ugly face : *white bowsers on the b-ball court*

bow tie *n phr* BRUSHBACK : *"Dykstra needs a bow tie." Nolan pitched the next day, and, sure enough, Lenny got his present (1990s+ Baseball)*

box *adj* (also **boxed**) Dead *(1970s+ Medical) n* **1** A coffin *(1600s+)* **2** A safe; vault; bank vault *(1900s+ Underworld)* ◁**3**▷ The vulva; vagina : *Her box ain't no rose blossom (1600s+)* ◁**4**▷ The male genitals, esp as displayed by tight pants; BASKET *(1960s+ Homosexuals)* **5** Any stringed instrument, esp a guitar *(1930s+ jazz musicians)* **6** An accordion; groan box *(1950s+)* **7** A phonograph *(1920s+)* **8** Portable stereo radio; GHETTO BOX : *Hey, man, don't mess with my box/ They were allowed to keep their boxes because their age exempted them from normal court procedures (1970s+)* **9** A very tight and awkward situation; cleft stick; BIND : *Those guidelines put me in a hell of a box v* **1** To die : *Oh, she boxed last night (1970s+ Medical)* **2** To kill : *Samalson planned to go back Monday morning, but he got boxed (1970s+) See* FIRST CRACK OUT OF THE BOX, GO HOME FEET FIRST, IDIOT BOX, IN A BIND, IN THE BOX, NUTHOUSE, OUT OF THE BOX, SOAPBOX, SQUAWK BOX, STUFF THE BALLOT BOX

boxcars *n* **1** A throw of two sixes *(1900s+ Crapshooting)* **2** Very large shoes *(1940s+)*

box someone's ears *v phr* To punch someone's ears; also, to tell someone off : *a good mind to box your ears (1600+)*

boxed *adj* Drunk *(1940s+)*

boxed in *modifier* With few or no alternatives; in a corner : *I'm boxed in on the timeframe for this project*

box someone in *v phr* To put someone in a tight and awkward situation; incapacitate someone *(1940s+)*

◁**box lunch**▷ *n phr* Cunnilingus *(1950s+)*

box man *n phr* **1** (also **box-worker**) A criminal specializing in opening safes; PETE MAN *(1900+ Underworld)* **2** A professional blackjack or twenty-one dealer *(1950s+ Gambling)* **3** A cashier or croupier at a gambling table : *the box men, who are the cashiers of the tables (1950s+ Gambling)*

box on the table *v phr* Die on a medical operating or examining table

boy *interj* (also **boy howdy, boy o boy, boys**) An exclamation of amazement, shock, happiness, intensification, etc; JEEZ, MAN, WOW : *Boy, that was a close one!/ Boy o boy, isn't this great? (1890s+) n* ◀**1**▶ A black man : *Don't call me "boy"; I'm as old as you are if not older (1850+)* ◁**2**▷ Any male, regardless of age, working as a porter, elevator operator, etc • With the implication that it is not the job for a man. *Boy* has been used as a term of contempt since about 1300 **3** A male who takes the subservient role in a homosexual relationship; peg boy *(1970s+ Homosexuals)* **4** Heroin : *But now he had the boy; he could lie around (1920s+ Narcotics) See* BIG BOY, FAIR-HAIRED BOY, FLY-BOY, GOOD OLD BOY, OLD BOY NETWORK, ONE OF THE BOYS, PADDY, POOR BOY, PRETTY BOY, THAT'S MY BOY, TOMBOY

boyo *n* A fellow; man; friend • Often used in address [1970+; fr Anglo-Irish]

boys, the *n phr* **1** Any group of men, esp a group of drinking companions, poker players, etc : *an evening out with the boys* **2** A group of criminals or other disreputable types *(1880s+) See* ONE OF THE BOYS

boys in the backroom, the *n phr* Any group of men, esp politicians and their aides, who are privy to and control the inner workings of an enterprise or place : *the salad boys in the back room, oiling up the cabbage (1880s+)*

boys uptown, the *n phr* **1** The political bosses of a city, and their staffs; CITY HALL *(1880s+)* **2** Any group of influential and unnamed criminals : *The tricksters were "the boys uptown," not yet identified (1880s+)*

boy-toy or **boytoy** *modifier : the times Madonna has whupped her boy-toy dancers on stage n* **1** A young woman used like the plaything of a man : *when she plays boy-toy to all your crush objects (1980s+)* **2** A young man used like the plaything of a woman or man : *Paul Newman's 69 now and thinks being the boy toy of yet another generation of women is "undignified"/ a has-been silent screen legend and her young screenwriter boytoy (1980s+)*

bozo *n* A fellow; a man, esp a muscular type with a meager brain : *This bozo right here next to me [Rep. Thomas P. O'Neill incognito] could probably be a better Congressman than those guys in Congress* [1910+; origin unknown; perhaps fr Spanish *bozal*, used in the slave trade and after to designate someone who speaks Spanish badly, hence a stupid person]

bozo filter *n phr* A desirable but nonexistent device that would automatically exclude fools and louts from computer networks; also, any way of avoiding annoying people, e-mail, etc : *Do you know where I could get a good bozo filter?/ thank goodness for the bozo filter otherwise known as Caller ID (1990s+ Computer)*

◁**bra-burner**▷ (BRAH bər nər) *n* A very militant feminist : *The media decided henceforth to label feminists as "braburners"* [1910+; fr the putative symbolic burning of brassieres as a protest against the restriction of women's freedom]

brace *n* A very stiff and exaggerated standing at military attention *(1930s+ Armed forces and service academies)* *v* **1** To stop or approach a person and beg for money : *This panhandler came up to me and braced me* (1890+) **2** To confront someone with an accusation : *this would be a good chance to brace Bubba's wife without her husband being present* (1950s+) **3** : *The sergeant ordered her to brace*

bracelet *n* A radio transmitter in a band fitting on the ankle and emitting signals so that the whereabouts of the wearer may be monitored : *drug dealer was released on the condition that he wear an ankle bracelet* (1990s+)

bracelets *n* A pair of handcuffs • Old-fashioned fetters were so called in the 1600s *(1840s+ Underworld)*

bracket creep *n phr* The raising of wage earners into higher income-tax brackets, esp because of wage raises triggered by inflation : *Tax payments will mount next year from "bracket creep," the tendency of inflation to push people into higher tax brackets* (1970s+)

bragging rights *n phr* The privilege of boasting about one's accomplishments; the warrant of superiority : *the burning question of the bragging rights to the world's hottest chilies/ A town of 2,000 or more had a number of teams vying for local bragging rights (1980s+ Sports)*

braid *See* GOLD BRAID

brain *n* An intelligent person; intellectual; good scholar : *The publicity of being a brain did not further her movie career as a glamour girl* (1914+) *v* To injure with a hard blow to the head • Attested fr 1382 in the full sense, "kill by knocking out the brain" : *The left hook really brained him See* BIRDBRAIN, BUBBLE BRAIN, HAVE something ON THE BRAIN, LAMEBRAIN, NOT HAVE BRAIN ONE, PICK someone's BRAIN, SCATTERBRAIN

brain bucket *n phr* **1** A steel helmet *(1950s+ Armed services)* **2** HARD HAT

brain-burned or **-fried** *adj* **1** Mentally impaired from drug-taking **2** Unable to efficiently function mentally because of tiredness : *after a day of this, brain-fried*

brainchild *n* Someone's great idea; a product of creative thinking and word : *my brainchild, a bestseller*

braindead *adj* Stupid; dumb [1980s+ students; The more technical term designating biological death as cessation of brain activity dates fr the 1970s]

brain dish *n phr* A helmet worn for motorcycling, bicycling, in-line skating, etc : *Do I really have to wear this brain dish? (1990s+)*

brain drain *n phr* The loss of useful educated persons, esp professionals, because they can find better conditions elsewhere : *Stalled Economy Speeds Puerto Rico's Brain Drain (1960s+ British)*

brain dump *n phr* To talk, explain, expatiate : *Go hang around a mouse potato and see if you can get him to geek out and do a brain dump* [1990s+ Computer; based on *screen dump*, a computer command to print everything appearing on the monitor screen]

brained *See* AIRHEADED, BIRDBRAINED, DICKBRAINED, LAMEBRAINED, NUMB-BRAINED

brain-fade *n* Stuporous boredom; tedium : *She and her colleagues fight brain-fade by sizing up customers* (1980s+) *v* To become confused; lose coherence : *I just brain-faded; I got a little confused* (1990s+)

brainiac *modifier* : *since you've been quoting every brainiac dumb-dumb to make your points* *n* **1** An intelligent person; BRAIN : *Hugo is such a brainiac he got 100% on the algebra test* **2** An intellectual; DOUBLE-DOME, EGGHEAD [1980s+; fr a smart and nasty character in the Superman comics]

brain one *n phr* The most elementary intelligence; a minimum of sagacity : *Our leader doesn't exhibit brain one* (1970s+) *See* NOT HAVE BRAIN ONE

brain-picker *n* A person who exploits the creative notions of others : *nothing but scorn for brain-pickers and imitators* (1880s+)

brains *n* **1** Intelligence; mind; SAVVY, SMARTS *(mid-1700s+)* **2** The person who does the thinking and planning; guiding mind : *Father Paul Lucano, the real brains of the organization* (1920+) *See* BEAT one's BRAINS OUT, FUCK someone's BRAINS OUT, HAVE SHIT FOR BRAINS, SHIT-FOR-BRAINS

brains out, one's *adv phr* To one's utmost; extremely much; spectacularly; one's HEAD OFF : *So I played his brains out in spring training/ Xing his brains out*

brainstorm *n* A sudden idea, esp one that is apt and useful; a happy insight • *Brainstorm* was a medical term for "mental explosion" by the 1890s (1920s+) *v* To examine and work on a problem by having a group sit around and utter spontaneously whatever relevant thoughts they have : *We'll brainstorm the drop in enrollment* (*1920s+*)

brain surgeon *See* YOU DON'T HAVE TO BE A BRAIN SURGEON

brain surgery *n phr* Anything very difficult and technical : *This game isn't brain surgery, but it teaches them to vent without hurting someone/ If a guy doesn't know he's being tailed, well, tailing is not brain surgery* (*1990s+*)

brain-tap *n* An instance of brain-picking [1990s+; probably based on the operation called *spinal tap*, in which spinal fluid is drawn off for medical analysis]

brain-teaser *n* (also **brain-twister** and **brain-scratcher**) A puzzle; a hard or tricky question : *here is today's social brain-scratcher* (*1920s+*)

brainwash *n* : *Your line is persuasive, virtually a brainwash* *v* **1** To cause profound attitudinal changes, usu in a prisoner, by psychological conditioning, supplemented by drugs and physical abuse **2** To change or influence someone's opinions or attitude by methods less stringent than those used on prisoners : *They were brainwashed into joining that crazy cult* [1950s+; fr Chinese *hsi nao*, "wash brain," which came into US use during and after the Korean War, apparently because of its use by North Koreans and their Chinese allies as custodians of US prisoners of war]

brain wave *n phr* A sudden useful idea; BRAINSTORM : *Lou had a brain wave. He offered the boy a C note to let him drive* (*1890s+*)

brainy *adj* Intelligent; sagacious (*1840s+*)

brand spanking new *modifier* Completely new : *a brand spanking new Mini*

brand X *n phr* **1** The infantry insignia, crossed rifles (*1970s+ Army*) **2** Marijuana (*1970s+ Narcotics*) [fr the phrase used in television advertising for unnamed and allegedly inferior products]

brannigan or **branigan** *n* **1** A spree : *a prolonged crossword puzzle brannigan* **2** A brawl or fracas; DONNYBROOK : *Republicans and Democrats alike are guilty of this brannigan* (*1940+*) [1903+; fr the Irish surname, for unclear reasons]

brass *n* **1** Impudence; effrontery; CHUTZPA • Fr the late 1500s *brass* had the same meaning in the phrase *face of brass*, that is, "brazen-faced" (*1700s+*) **2** Money • Common in British usage (*late 1500s+*) **3** High officials or managers in general; the BRASS : *There's lots of vice presidents here but they're not really brass* (*1899+*)

brass, the *n phr* The upper ranks of the military or other uniformed services : *Many a GI hated the brass and the enemy* [Armed forces fr

WWII; probably a shortening of *brass hat*] *See* the TOP BRASS

◁**brass balls**▷ *n phr* Courage; audacity; GUTS : *But I had the brass balls to hold out for a piece of the action* (*1960s+*)

brassed off *adj phr* Ready to quit; sated; bored; FED UP (*WWII Royal Air Force*)

brass hat *n phr* **1** A high-ranking officer in the military or other uniformed services (*1890s+ British*) **2** Any high-ranking official; manager; chief; BOSS (*1930s+*)

brass monkey *n* Very cold weather [1857+; orig referring to a brass figure of a monkey; not, as widely believed, a nautical term relating to cannonballs]

brass tacks *See* DOWN TO BRASS TACKS

brat *n* A child, esp an obnoxious or troublesome one [1505+; origin unknown]

-brat *combining word* Designating a child raised in a stated environment : *Army brat/ opera brat/ Navy brat/ faculty brat/ Air Force brat/ Masako led a normal life—normal, that is, for a diplomatic brat with an ambitious father* (*1940s+*)

brat pack *n phr* A group of young metropolitan males deemed worthy of media attention : *Richard Price was a one-man Bronx-boy Brat Pack* [1980s+; modeled on *rat pack*]

brawl *n* A noisy, riotous party [1920s+; fr *brawl*, "a noisy fight," of obscure origin; perhaps related to Dutch *brallen*, "brag," and Low German *brallen*, "shout, roar"; perhaps fr French *branle*, "an energetic circle dance"]

Brazilian (also **Brazilian wax** or **bikini wax**) *n* A technique in which all or most of the pubic hair is removed with a hot-wax treatment : *Brazilians on "Sex and the City"*

bread *n* Money; DOUGH [1940s+, but esp cool talk & 1960s+ counterculture; probably fr *dough*; perhaps related to earlier *gingerbread,* "money"] *See* the BEST THING SINCE SLICED BREAD, SMALL POTATOES

bread and butter *modifier* : *a routine, bread-and-butter type of case* *n phr* The simple necessities of life; basic needs (*mid-1735+*)

breadbasket *n* The stomach; abdomen; KISHKES, labonza (*1750s+*)

bready *See* WHITE BREADY

break *n* **1** An escape or attempt to escape (*1830s+*) **2** A brief period of rest or relaxation : *Take a five-minute break* (*1860s+*) **3** A stroke of luck, good or bad • Probably fr the *break* in billiards, when balls arrange themselves in either a good or bad way : *I got a break and made it on time/ Football's a game of breaks to some extent* (*1911+*) **4** A stroke of mercy or favor : *Give me one break and I'll never flunk again* **5** An improvised passage; solo; LICK (*1930s+ Jazz musicians*) *v* **1** : *Let's* *break while I think about it all* **2** To interrupt or abandon some regular practice : *to break training/ break an old routine* (1400+) **3** To happen; occur; fall out : *If things break right I'll be OK* (1914+) **4** To tame a wild horse; subdue someone's spirit (late 1400s+) **5** To bankrupt a company or person (1612+) **6** To demote; reduce in rank; BUST : *They broke him back to buck private* (late 1600s+) **7** To separate, esp from a clinch : *The boxers broke and came at each other again* (1890s+) **8** (also **breakdance** or **boogie**) To do a kind of dancing that evolved in the inner-city ghettos and is characterized esp by intricate writhings and shows of balance and strength close to the floor • *Break down* was used by 1819 to describe very energetic black dancing : *You can go running. You can swim. Or you can break* (1980s+ Black teenagers) **9** (also **service break**) To win a game from an opponent who is serving (1950s+ Tennis) *See* EVEN BREAK, TAKE A BREAK

break a leg *sentence* Best wishes; good luck; I hope you do very well [fr theater; perhaps fr German *Hals und Bein brechen,* "break your neck and leg," a similar good-luck formula; the same grim warding-off spell is expressed in Italian *in bocca al lupo,* "good luck!"]

◁**break** one's **ass**▷ (or ◁**balls**▷ or **buns** or **butt** or **cork** or **hump** or **nut** or ◁**sweet ass**▷) *See* BUST one's ASS

break (or **pop**) **a sweat** *v phr* To perspire from exercise or exertion; exert oneself : *Students were not the only ones breaking a sweat Sunday/ They want to feel great and look great and not pop a sweat* (1970s+ Prizefight)

breakaway *adj* Unconventional; rebellious : *a breakaway rock group/ breakaway mind-set* (1930s+) *modifier* Made to break or collapse easily : *bashed with a breakaway chair* (1950s+ Theater)

break bad *v phr* To become hostile and menacing : *I don't want to make eye contact with this sucker because he may break bad on me* (1970s+ Black)

break someone's **balls** *v phr* **1** To give someone a hard time, esp nagging or overwhelming them : *She takes every opportunity to break his balls* **2** To overwork or be overworked : *breaking my balls to finish this in seven weeks*

break someone's **brains** *v phr* Injure someone severely : *any more of that shit and I'm gonna break your brains* (1990s+)

break (or **bust**) someone's **chops** or **balls** *v phr* **1** To verbally assault someone; harass : *I love it here. I can work hung over and nobody busts my chops/ Well, she turned absolutely livid, and ever since she's been busting my chops* **2** BUST one's ASS (1970s+)

breakdance *See* BREAK

break something **down** *v phr* To explain something; present something in detail : *Break it down for me, Baby* (1960s+ Black)

breaker *n* A person who dances with intricate writhings and shows of balance and strength close to the floor, esp and originally to rhythmic, staccato songs spoken rather than sung, in a style indigenous to the urban ghetto : *the night he and other breakers showed up, ready to boogie* (1980s+ Black teenagers) *See* BACK-BREAKER, JAWBREAKER

breakfast *See* FROM HELL TO BREAKFAST, MEXICAN BREAKFAST, SHOOT one's COOKIES

breakfast of champions *n phr* An alcoholic drink taken upon waking : *bad sign that he has the breakfast of champions*[fr the advertising phrase for the breakfast cereal Wheaties]

break someone or something **in** *v phr* To put through an initial period of easy use or training before requiring full function (1840s+)

break it up *v phr* To stop fighting, quarreling, chatting, etc : *all right, cats, break it up* • Usu a stern command (1930s+)

break out *v phr* **1** To escape from prison or some other confining situation **2** To show symptoms of disease or discomfort : *He broke out in a purple rash* (1530s+) **3** To bring out; produce for use • Originally fr nautical use where it referred to the freeing of cargo prior to unloading : *When I came he broke out the Scotch* (1890s+) **4** To be the case; be apparent : *We need donations; that's how it breaks out here* (1990s+)

◁**break out into assholes**▷ *v phr* To become very frightened [1970s+; an allusion to the loose bowels associated with fear]

breaks, the *n phr* **1** Good luck; special favors : *If I get the breaks I'll prevail* **2** Bad luck : *Them's the breaks* (1911+)

break the back *v phr* **1** To do the hardest part, or most, of a job (1890+) **2** To make ineffective; cripple : *The UN's mission is to break the back of the warlords in Somalia* (1970s+)

break the bank *v phr* To use all or most of the available money or resources to do something : *the website redesign break the bank*

break the ice *v phr* To dissipate the sense of strain among people who do not know each other : *I broke the ice by saying she looked like Charlemagne's mother* (late 1500s+)

break the points *v phr* To score enough points to cover the point-spread (1970s+ Sports & gambling)

breakup *n* A separation or dissolution (mid-1700s+)

break up *v phr* **1** To separate or to cause separation or dissolution of a close relationship : *to break up a marriage/ After ten years they* *broke up* (*mid-1700s+*) **2** To laugh or cause to laugh uncontrollably; FRACTURE. SLAY • The synonymous phrase *break all up* is attested in the 1890s : *His doctor shtick broke them up* (*1920s+*)

break wind *v phr* To flatulate; FART (*mid-1600s+*)

◁**breastworks**▷ *n* The female breasts; BAZOOM (*1860s+*)

breathe easy *v phr* To be relieved of concern; relax (*1950s+*)

breather *n* A person who makes harassing telephone calls and merely breathes, rather than talking, into the mouthpiece (*1970s+*) *See* HEAVY BREATHER, MOUTH-BREATHER

breathing *adj* Alive, at least : *They'll take any warm body that's breathing* (*1970s+*) *See* MOUTH-BREATHING

breeder *n* A heterosexual person; STRAIGHT : *the scornful term "breeders," used by some urban gays about heterosexual couples with children* (*1980s+ Homosexuals*)

breeze *n* **1** An easy task; anything easy; CINCH. CAKEWALK (*1920s+ Baseball*) **2** : *They had a breeze today at Ossining* *v* **1** To go or move rapidly and easily : *to breeze through work/ I breezed out* (*1907+*) **2** To escape from prison (*1940s+ Prison*)

breeze, the *See* BAT THE BREEZE

breezy *adj* Very easygoing and jovial; cheery : *a breezy "Good morning"* (*1870+*)

brew (*or* **brewhaha** *or* **brewski**), a *n phr* **1** A glass, bottle, or can of beer; a beer• *Brewhaha has its own variants: brewha, haha, and ha : She treated me to a brew* **2** Coffee or tea : *Dunkin' Donuts is my kind of brew* [first form 1940s+, third 1980s+; second form 1970s+ fr French *brouhaha*, "fuss, ado"]

brew-out *n* A beer party; BEER BUST (*1970s+ College students*)

brewster *n* **1** A beer drinker **2** A beer; brewski

brick *n* **1** A decent, generous, reliable person (*1830s+ British students*) **2** A kilogram (2.2 pounds) of tightly compacted marijuana (*1970s+ Narcotics*) **3** A very inaccurate basketball shot (*1980s+ Students*) [first sense said to be a clever student version of Aristotle's phrase *tetragonos aner*, "four-sided man, foursquare man," used in the *Nichomachean Ethics* to describe a person of public merit whose praise might appear on a square monument or tribute] *See* HIT someone LIKE A TON OF BRICKS, HIT THE BRICKS, SHIT A BRICK, THREE BRICKS SHY OF A LOAD

brickhouse *n* A very busty woman [1980s+ Students; because she is *built like a brick shithouse*]

bricklayer *n* An inaccurate basketball shooter : *His drawback is that he's a bricklayer from the free throw line* (*1990s+ Sports*)

bricks, the *n phr* The streets and sidewalks of a city : *I had to get out on the bricks and hustle* (*1940s+*) *See* HIT THE BRICKS

bricks and mortar *n phr* Buildings and construction, esp as an item of expenditure and administrative emphasis for an institution (*1850s+*)

◁**brick shithouse**▷ *See* BUILT LIKE A BRICK SHITHOUSE

Brickyard, the *n phr* The motor speedway at Indianapolis, Indiana, site of the annual 500-mile race [1970s+; fr the *brick* construction of the track]

bridesmaid syndrome *n phr* Misfortune of being very close, but never the winner : *Suffering from bridesmaid syndrome, which had left her the loser in 6 of the 8 finals she reached last year* (*1990s+*)

brig *n* **1** The detention cell of a ship **2** A naval prison (*1850s+ Nautical*) **3** Any military jail or prison (*1890s+*)

bright *n* Day; the daytime (*1930s+ Black*)

bright-eyed and bushy-tailed *adj phr* Eager and energetic; in splendid fettle (*1950s+ Air Force*) *See* STREET-SMART

brights *n* The bright or upper-beam headlights of a car : *into the brights of an oncoming car* (*1970s+*)

brill *adj* Brilliant : *John Turturro is brill as the gawky Jew who takes a dive* (*1981+*)

brilliant *interj* Excellent : *Go outside for lunch? Brilliant!*

◀**Brillo** *or* **Brillo-pad**▶ *n* A black person : *a black woman admitted that white teenagers called her "Brillo-pad" while she was standing at a bus stop* [1980s+; fr *Brillo*®, a brand of scouring pad with tight wiry fibers resembling tight curly hair]

brim *n* A hat : *nice brim, Indiana Jones*

bringdown *modifier* **1** : *a bringdown scene* **2** : *that bringdown face* *n* **1** A cutting rebuke or comment; a deflation : *Polite applause is a bit of a bringdown* **2** A disappointing or depressing performance **3** A morose person : *A "bringdown" is a depressing character* [1950s+ beat & cool talk fr 1940s+ jazz musicians]

bring someone down *v phr* To depress; dispirit; sadden : *I'm afraid your jolly word brings me down* (*1960s+ Students fr beat & cool talk*)

bring down the house *v phr* To score a resounding theatrical success : *Old Man Dillinger strode onto the stage and brought down the house/ first heard on a Broadway stage in 1930, when she brought down the house singing "I Got Rhythm"* (*1840s+ Theater*)

bring home the bacon (*groceries* may replace *bacon*) *v phr* **1** To achieve a tangible goal or task : *Their new tailback brought home the* *bacon* **2** To earn enough to support oneself and one's family (*1908+*)

bring it *v phr* **1** To throw a baseball fast (*1980s+ Baseball*) **2** To play very well; do the job : *He's a heck of a football player. He can bring it* (*1900s+*)

bring money *sentence* What we are talking about is quite expensive : *They have plans for two more hotels. Bring money. Breakfast for two, without champagne, can run to $50 or $60* (*1970s+*)

bring someone on *v phr* To arouse sexually

bring something to a screeching halt *v phr* To end or cease something immediately : *If I were you, I'd bring that association to a screeching halt* (*1970s+*)

bring something up *v phr* **1** To introduce into the conversation; mention : *better not bring up that new idea* **2** To vomit or cough up : *Heimlich brought up his lunch*

bring (or get or keep) someone up to speed *v phr* To give necessary information; FILL someone IN, PUT someone IN THE PICTURE : *Well, look, I appreciate your keeping me up to speed/ Johnson's teammates have gone out of their way to help him get up to speed* [fr the need to increase gradually the speed of a machine or phonograph turntable, video recorder, etc, to the proper rate]

briny, the *n phr* The ocean; the sea (*1850s+*)

Brit *adj* British : *the Brit rock scene n : two Brits and a Yank* (1900+ British)

bro' or **bro** *n* **1** Brother (*mid-1600s+*) **2** A black person : *the slick-speaking bro who scores points off the ofay* (*1960s+ Black*) **3** A man; GUY : *the pack of twenty-seven bros jamming along the freeway/ Hawk murmured, "Right on, bro," and drank some champagne* (*1970s+*)

◁**broad**▷ *n* **1** A woman • Used almost entirely by men and considered offensive by many women : *Sorry lady, no broads allowed in here/ So here was this suburban broad* **2** A promiscuous woman; prostitute [1910+; probably from the notion "broad in the beam"]

broad-assed or **broad-beamed** *adj* Wide in the buttocks (*1916+*)

broad-gauge *adj* Very versatile and competent : *We're looking for a few broad-gauge people for an exciting project* (*1970s+*)

broad strokes, the *n phr* General details; basic facts : *I don't want any details. I understand your hesitation. Just the broad strokes* (*1980s+*)

broke *adj* Entirely out of money; destitute (*1660s+*) *See* ALL HELL BROKE LOOSE, DEAD BROKE, FLAT BROKE, GO BROKE, GO FOR BROKE

broken-bat bleeder *n phr* A weak blow on which the hitter breaks his bat, and that trickles out for a hit : *It's appropriate that we*

should lose that game on a frickin' broken-bat bleeder up the middle (*1990s+ Baseball*)

broken-nose crowd, the *n phr* The organized-crime syndicates; mob • Compare *bentnose* : *There is a big-time problem here that wouldn't be one if the broken-nose crowd still ran the gambling houses* (*1990s+*)

broken record *n phr* Something or someone repetitive, tedious, and importunate : *He kept asking for a raise, like a broken record*

broke to the curb *adj phr* Ugly; ill-favored; BUCKLED, crushed, PISS-UGLY (*1990s+ Teenagers*)

brolly *n* An umbrella • Thoroughly British, with some US use (*1870s+ British schools*)

bromide *n* **1** An old, stale joke or scrap of wisdom : *a rolling illustration of the bromide that beggars can't be choosers* **2** A boring, tedious person : *Clutterbuck, with his wilted wit, was a total bromide* [1900s+; fr the use of *bromide* as a sedative]

bronc or **bronk** *n* **1** BRONCO **2** A catamite; PUNK (*Hoboes*)

bronco *n* A young male not accustomed to nor complaisant in homosexual relations (*1970s+ Homosexuals*) [fr Spanish *bronco*, "coarse, rough"]

bronco buster *n phr* **1** (Variations: **peeler** or **snapper** or **twister** may replace **buster**) A cowboy who tames broncos to riding; also, a rodeo performer who rides unruly horses in competition (*1880s+ Cowboys*) **2** CHICKEN-HAWK (*1970s+ Homosexuals*)

Bronx cheer *n phr* **1** A loud, rude, flatulating noise made with the tongue and lips; the BIRD, RASPBERRY : *The Duchess was startled but serene when the crowd greeted her with a fortissimo Bronx cheer* **2** Any outright and precise expression of derision : *That book will get Bronx cheers from every critic* (*1920s+*)

Brooklyn side *n phr* The left side of the bowling alley as one faces the pins [1940s+ Bowling; fr the location of *Brooklyn* as one looks south along the East River]

brother *interj* An exclamation of surprise, amusement, vehemence, etc; BOY, JEEZ, MAN : *"The lady was prepared to take it if it did." "Brother!"* (*1920s+*) *n* **1** A man; fellow; GUY • Used in addressing strangers : *I don't know you, brother, but you said a mouthful* (*1910+*) **2** A black person; BLOOD • Common and significant fr 1960s : *All you brothers here, and you white people too, got to take care of business* (1920+ Black) **3** A fellow professional; colleague : *I'd like to ask Brother Donaldson something, if I may* (*mid-1300s+*) *See* SOUL BROTHER

Brother *See* BIG BROTHER

brouhaha (BREW hah hah) *n* A noisy clamor; fuss; FLAP [1950s+; fr French; possibly ultimately fr Hebrew *baruch haba* "blessed are those who come (in the name of the Lord)," Psalm 118, although the line of derivation is complex and tenuous]

brow *See* HIGHBROW, LOWBROW, MIDDLEBROW

browbeat *v* To intimidate; STRONG-ARM (*1830s+*)

browbeater *n* One who intimidates : *alternately a party-throwing cheerleader and a sadistic browbeater*

brown *adj* Opposed to environmental preservation and restoration ● The opposite of *green* : *The chairman of the Council of Economic Advisers is judged brown, rather than green, on the issue of timetables for climate control* (*1990s+*) *v* ◁1▷ also **brown-hole** To do anal intercourse; BUGGER, BUNGHOLE (*1930s+*)

brown-bag or **brown-bag it** *v* To take one's lunch to the office, or one's liquor to a club or restaurant, in a paper bag : *for brown-bagging booze at places that allow this practice/ brown-bagging it for lunch* (*1960s+*)

brown bagger *n* **1** A person who brown-bags (*1960s+*) **2** A very ugly person; DOUBLE-BAGGER (*1970s+*) [second sense fr the notion that such a person should wear a bag over the head to hide the face]

browned off *adj phr* **1** Restless from waiting or wasting time; bored; BRASSED OFF (*British armed forces since WWI*) **2** Angry; PISSED OFF : *He got browned off at the way they treated the kids* (*1930s+*)

brown eyes *See* BIG BROWN EYES

Brownie points *n phr* A fancied unit of credit and approval : *I'll get Brownie points for helping him/ a place where you get big shiny brownie points, cash, sex, and adulation* [1960s+; fr merit points awarded to *Brownies* toward promotion to Junior Girl Scouts]

brown-nose *n* also **brown-noser** : *He got there by being a pious and effective brown-nose v* To flatter and pamper in order to gain approval and advantage; curry favor; APPLE-POLISH : *He's just like any other person who's in a position to screw you. You gotta brown nose* [1930s+ Military academy students; fr the color of feces presumably acquired when one has one's nose at the flatteree's anus]

brown out or **brownout** *n* A period when electricity is dimmed or fading; a partial blackout : *a brownout if some power supply is retained v* For electricity, to fade or dim

bruiser *n* A big, strong man, esp a pugilist (*mid-1700s+*)

brush *n* **1** A mustache (*1820s+*) **2** A fight; squabble; disagreement : *have had drug or alcohol problems, and have experienced a "brush with the law"* (*1840s+*)

brush, the *n phr* **1** The backwoods; jungle; the BOONDOCKS (*1770s+*) **2** A snub; quick dis-

missal; BRUSH-OFF (*1930s+*) *See* GIVE someone THE BRUSH

brushback *modifier* Pitched very close to the batter, as if to hit him : *knocked me over like a good brushback pitch n* BEANBALL, DUSTER : *Throw another brushback and you're out of the game* (*1950s+ Baseball*)

brush someone back *v phr* To pitch close to a batter in order to force him or her away from home plate and upset the batting poise (*1950s+ Baseball*)

brush-off *n* the BRUSH (*1930s+*)

brush someone off *v phr* To snub or dismiss someone pointedly; GIVE someone THE BRUSH (*1930s+*)

brush up *v phr* **1** To clean; make neat and clean (*1600+*) **2** (also **brush up on**) To improve, review, or perfect one's mastery : *Brush up your Shakespeare. Start quoting him now* (*1830s+*)

brutal *adj* Excellent; great (*1960s+ Students*)

BS or **bs** (pronounced as separate letters) *n* BULLSHIT (*1900+*) *v* To deceive or attempt to deceive with flattery, lies, etc : *Don't BS a BSer*

b school *n* Business school, esp for an MBA : *applied to b school at Yale*

BSer *n* BULLSHIT ARTIST : *He's not a big BSer* (*1900+*)

B-side *n* The second or other side of a phonograph record, of an issue, etc; FLIP SIDE (*1960s+*)

BTO or **bto** (pronounced as separate letters) *n* BIG-TIME OPERATOR (*1940s+*)

BTW (pronounced as separate letters) *adv* By the way (*1990s+ Computer network*)

bub[1] *n* BOOB, TIT (*1960+*)

bub[2] *n* A man; fellow; brother; GUY ● Used in direct address, with a slightly insulting intent : *Okay, bub, get the hell outta my way* [1830s+; fr *bubba* fr *brother*]

bubba *n* **1** Brother ● Not uncommon as a nickname : *Here comes big Bubba Jones* (*1860s+ Southern*) **2** also often **Bubba** A person of simple Southern rural culture; CRACKER, GOOD OLD BOY ● Occurrence increased enormously during the early years of the Clinton administration : *People watching "Jeopardy!" aren't just bubbas out there/ He doesn't have your typical "Bubba" approach to state government* (*1980s+*) [imitation of baby talk]

Bubbafest *n* A celebration of Southern rural culture : *Greer, SC, is holding a Bubbafest, complete with country music, sports, wading pools full of grits, a Moon Pie toss, and the crowning of the royal Bubba and Bubbette*

Bubbette *n* A woman Bubba (*1990s+*)

bubble brain *n phr* A stupid and vapid person; AIRHEAD : *Did I want to establish that, bubble* *brain though I seemed to him, there were sound reasons?* (1960s+)

bubble-brained *adj* Stupid; vapid : *Suzanne Somers' bubble-brained Chrissy* (1960s+)

bubble-butt *n* The bulbous stern found on many 1990s cars : *Chryslers and Tauruses and Toyotas all have "bubble-butts"* (1990s+)

bubble economy *n phr* An economy that overexpands and must burst : *the bubble economy of the '80s* (1990s+)

bubblegum music or **bubblegum** *modifier* : *The rap itself is sheer bubble-gum monotony/ The new album is less bubblegum, something kids and adults can relate to n phr* Rock-and-roll music that appeals to young teenagers : *young adult audience dissatisfied with "bubblegum music"/ so fundamental that one might refer to it as "heavy bubble gum"* (1960s+)

bubblehead *n* A stupid person, esp one who is frivolous and flighty; AIRHEAD, BUBBLE BRAIN : *Linda was, a polite word for dumb cunt, a bubblehead* (1950s+)

bubbles, the *adj phr* All fun; all beer and skittles : *Think life is the bubbles when you're Batman?* (1990s+)

bubble the pot *v phr* To try something out; learn by experiment : *You have to bubble the pot, stand back and see what floats to the top* (1990s+)

bubbly *n* Champagne; sparkling wine (1920+)

bubby (also **boobie, bubbe, bubbie, bubeleh**) (BU bee) *n* Darling; BABY, SWEETIE, TOOTS • A term of affection with general application : *Bubby, it's Hollywood. A little mistake* [1940s+; fr Yiddish *bubele,* an endearing epithet, fr Hebrew *buba,* "doll," which is much like Latin *pupa,* "doll"]

bubkes or **bobkes** or **bupkes** (BŎŎB kəs, BŎŎP-) *adv* Absurdly little : *That it sold bubkes may say just as much for his laziness and his hubris n* Something trivial; nothing; BEANS : *We've gone from bubkes to big deals in a year/ They've waved bye-bye to the likes of Julius Irving and gotten bubkes in return/ paying bupkes for rent* [1940s+; fr Yiddish, "goat dung," fr Russian, "beans"]

<**bubs**> (BŎŎBZ) *n* A woman's breasts; BOOB[2] (1900s+)

buck *n* **1** A dollar (1850s+) **2** A hundred dollars, esp as a bet (1960s+ Gambling) **3** BUCK PRIVATE **4** A Roman Catholic priest (1920s+ Hoboes) **5** A young male Indian; Native American brave (1800+) **6** A young black man (1830s+) **7** Any young man, esp a strong and spirited one; BUCKO (mid-1700s+) *v* **1** To resist; defy; go up against • Often in the negative : *You can't buck the system/ Life is a combination hard to buck, A proposition difficult to beat* (1850s+) **2** To work for personal advancement; aspire eagerly; covet :

I'm bucking for that dealership (1880s+) **3** To pass along a letter, memorandum, problem, etc, usu without taking action; PASS THE BUCK : *Let's buck this one to the Committee on Hot Potatoes* (WWII armed forces) [all senses ultimately fr *buck,* "male animal, usually horned"; the semantics are complex: for example, the first sense is said to be fr the fact that a *buck* deer's skin was more valuable than a female's skin; the other senses have most to do with male behavior of a butting and strutting sort] *See* BANG FOR THE BUCK, BIG BUCKS, the BUCK STOPS HERE, FAST BUCK, PASS THE BUCK, SAWBUCK

buckage *n* Money : *he's trying to get buckage off me*

bucket *n* **1** A car, esp a big, old car (1930s+) **2** A ship, esp an old and slow ship; RUST BUCKET (1840s+ Merchant marine & Navy) **3** A destroyer; CAN, TIN CAN (Navy by WWII) **4** The buttocks; rump : *Knocked him on his bucket* (1930s+) **5** The basketball net (1920s+ Basketball) **6** A basketball goal : *He'll make ten buckets a game* (1920s+ Basketball) **7** The rearmost part of the batter's box • The source expression was "have his foot in the water-*bucket*" : *had his foot way back in the bucket/ Emily steps into the bucket when going for a pitch* (1913+ Baseball) **8** Jail : *These days, the Gray Bar Motel is a synonym for "the bucket,"* which means jail (1990s+ Los Angeles police) *v* To speed; BARREL : *The kids were bucketing along* (1860s+) *See* BRAIN BUCKET, someone CAN'T CARRY A TUNE IN A BUCKET, FOR CRYING OUT LOUD, GO TO HELL IN A HANDBASKET, KICK THE BUCKET, LARD-BUCKET, RUST BUCKET, SLEAZE-BUCKET, SLIMEBAG

bucket of blood *n phr* A nasty saloon, filthy restaurant, etc : *It was about what he figured: a real bucket of blood. White tiled walls slick with grease* (1915+)

bucket shop *modifier* : *A sleazy bucket-shop operation n phr* A place where very dubious stocks, commodities, real estate, etc, are sold, often by telephone solicitation [1880+; origin uncertain; *bucket,* "cheat, swindle," is attested in 1812 and may be the source; another account has illicit traders sending down by elevator for "another *bucketful*" of dupes]

buckle *v* To hit; CLOBBER (1990s+ Teenagers)

buckled *adj* Ugly; crushed. PISS-UGLY (1990s+ Teenagers)

buckle down *v phr* To set seriously to work; put slothful ease behind one (1860s+)

buckle your seat belts *v phr* To get ready for trouble; take precautions; BATTEN DOWN THE HATCHES [1970s+; fr the pilot's order to passengers as an airplane approaches danger]

buck naked *n phr* Entirely nude; BARE-ASS : *My God, Sal, them women is buck naked in them magazines* (*1920s+*)

bucko *modifier* : *The bucko skipper was a nasty sadist* *n* **1** Fellow; friend; comrade; buddy; guy **2** A mean and dangerous man : *The mate aboard the Pride of Hoboken was a notorious bucko* (*1800s+ Merchant marine*)

buckpasser *n* Someone who rarely or never takes responsibility : *a whole family of buckpassers*

buck private *n phr* An Army private; soldier of the lowest rank [*1870s+* Army; origin unknown]

bucks *See* BIG BUCKS, IN THE BUCKS, LIKE A MILLION BUCKS

buck sergeant *n phr* An Army sergeant, wearing three stripes [Army fr WWI; origin unknown]

buck stops here, the *sentence* This is the place where responsibility must be accepted; a decision must be made here • Attributed usually to President Harry S Truman [*1940s+*; The *buck* is the same as in *pass the buck*]

buck up *v phr* To cheer up; brace : *Immigrant life lets people down as soon as it bucks them up* (*1850s+ British schools*)

bud¹ *n* **1** Friend; fellow; GUY • Used only in direct address, often with hostile intent : *Okay, bud, that'll do* (*1850s+*) **2** A very close friend; BUDDY, PAL : *Just be glad I'm your bud/ She hid out with various buds and in runaway shelters* (*1930s+*) [fr *buddy,* a childish pronunciation of *brother*]

bud² *n* Marijuana : *There was no pain yet, just numbness, kind of like smoking bud* [*1980s+* Teenagers; fr *Budda, Buddha sticks,* earlier terms for marijuana]

buddy *n* **1** BUD¹ **2** A man's closest male friend; PAL • During WWI this term took on a particularly strong sentimental value **3** A male's partner in work or sport *v* BUDDY UP [*1850+*; fr earlier *butty,* "partner, chum," said to be fr Romany; probably influenced by a childish pronunciation of *brother*] *See* ACE BOON COON, ASSHOLE BUDDY, GOOD BUDDY

buddy-buddy *adj* : *Some are buddy-buddy with the players/ He is not buddy-buddy, although he insisted that the photographer take their pictures together* *n* **1** A close friend; BUDDY (*1940s+*) **2** A person who is too friendly; an importunate acquaintance (*1960s+*) *v* : *Look at that guy buddy-buddying Joe*

buddyroo *n* BUDDY, PAL : *You should've seen the way they said hello. Old buddyroos* (*1940s+*)

buddy seat *n phr* A passenger portion on a motorcycle seat (*1950s+*) *See* IN THE DRIVER'S SEAT

buddy up *v phr* To share living quarters and conditions with; form a close association or two-person team : *These guys are alike; OK if they buddy up?/ Swimmers, buddy up* (*1930+*)

buddy up to someone *v phr* To become close and comradely with; ingratiate oneself with : *He's hanging out with Watson now and buddying up to him/ Lawrence smarmily buddies up to these women* (*1950s+*)

budget *adj* Low-quality or cheap : *No thanks on the budget toilet paper*

budget squeeze or **crunch** *n* A situation where there is not enough money for a project or plan : *college boys in a budget crunch*

buff¹ *n* A devotee or enthusiast; hobbyist; FAN, NUT : *I like to think I'm a people buff* [originally *fire buff,* because New York City volunteer firefighters about 1820 wore *buff*-colored, light brownish yellow coats; transferred to persons who like to watch fires, then to enthusiasts in general]

buff² *adj* Naked [*1604+*; probably fr the pale yellowish color of the leather called *buff,* likened to skin] *See* IN THE BUFF

buff³ *adj* (also **buffed, buffed out**) Well-built; muscular; HUNKY : *Looking mighty buff, by the way* (*1980s+ Teenagers*) *v* (also **buff out**) To do body-building; put on muscle; become brawnier : *Fudgie wondered if Tweezer had buffed out in San Quentin* (*1980s+ Teenagers*) *v phr* (also **buff up**) To be ingratiating and attentive, so as to keep on good terms : *Gotta go. Gotta buff* (*1990s+ Hollywood*) [probably fr *buff,* "polish, make attractive," a process originally done with a leather *buff stick*; the *adj* sense may be derived fr *buffalo,* as an image of strength]

buff⁴ or **buff up** *v* or *v phr* To make a patient's chart look good, esp in preparing him or her for discharge [*1970s+* Medical; fr *buff,* "to polish"]

buffalo *n* ◁1▷ A heavy or fat woman; COW (*1950s+*) ◁2▷ A black person • This sense reflects that black troopers were called *buffalo soldiers* by Native Americans (*1870s+*) *v* **1** To confuse someone purposely, esp in order to cheat or dupe (*1870+*) **2** To intimidate; cow; BULLDOZE (*1890+*)

buffalo butt *n phr* A person with large buttocks; FAT-ASS : *I mean "buffalo butt" could be a term of, uh, endearment* (*1970s+ Students*)

buffalo chips *modifier* Like the feces of a buffalo; COWFLOP : *give you that stretch valise buffalo chips thing* (*1840+*)

buffaloed *adj* Baffled; puzzled : *I didn't think Pierre would be buffaloed by it* (*1870+*)

buff the helmet *v phr* To fondle one's penis; masturbate (*1990s+ Black*)

◁**bufu**▷ (BOO foo) *n* A male homosexual; sodomite; BUGGER [1980s+ Students; fr *buttfucker*]

bug[1] *n* **1** Any insect whatever • Now US only *(1642+ British)* **2** Any upper-respiratory or flulike complaint, esp one that is somewhat prevalent : *There's a bug going around (1960s+)* **3** Any fault or defect in a machine, plans, system, etc : *You've got to get the bugs out of the program before trying to run it on the computer (1870s+)* **4** Any small, cheap item sold by a vendor or huckster *(1800s+ Circus & carnival)* **5** A joker or a wild card *(1940s+ Poker)* **6** A girl : *Boys prowl for "bugs" (1960s+ Teenagers)* **7** A semiautomatic or automatic radiotelegraph key used for fast sending *(1920s+ Radio operators)* **8** Any small symbol or label, such as a copyright or trademark symbol *(1950s+ Print shop)* **9** An asterisk printed beside the weight a horse is to carry, showing that a five-pound decrease has been granted because the jockey is an apprentice *(1940s+ Horse racing)* **10** An apprentice jockey who has ridden his or her maiden race during the current year or has not yet won his or her fortieth race *(1940s+ Horse racing)* **11** A horse that has never won a race; MAIDEN *(1940s+ Horse racing)* **12** A hot rod *(1950s+ Hot rodders)* **13** A small foreign car, esp the Volkswagen Beetle® *(1919+)* **14** A small two-person lunar excursion vehicle *(1960s+ Astronautics)* **15** An enthusiast; devotee; hobbyist; FAN, NUT : *Momma's a football bug (1841+)* **16** A compelling idea or interest : *His bug is surf-casting (1900+)* **17** An insane person; NUT : *Only a bug is strong enough for that (1880s+)* **18** An irrational, touchy mood; bad mood *(1930s+ Prison)* **19** A psychiatrist *(1950s+ Prison)* **20** A confidential message or signal; confidential information *(1925+ Underworld)* **21** A burglar alarm *(1920s+ Underworld)* **22** Small hidden listening devices for surveillance : *The team planted bugs in about six flowerpots (1940s+)* **23** Any bacterium, microbe, virus, etc : *Syph is caused by a bug (1919+)* [the sense "irritate, pester" may be a shortening of black English *humbug*, attested in such uses as "Him wife de humbug him too much"; *humbug* itself, attested in English fr the mid–18th century, is apparently found in and may derive fr Pacific Pidgin English and West African Pidgin English] *v* **1** To do a psychiatric evaluation; pronounce one insane *(1950s+ Prison)* **2** To irritate or anger someone; pester or harry someone : *I suspected something was bugging her (1940s+ Jazz musicians)* **3** To equip with a burglar alarm : *They've got that safe bugged eight ways* **4** To prepare a room or other place for electronic surveillance by installing hidden microphones; equip for electronic eavesdropping : *to bug a room/ bug the Secretary's telephone (1920+)* *See* FIREBUG, HAVE A BUG UP one's ASS, JITTERBUG, LITTERBUG, PUT A BUG IN someone's EAR, SHUTTERBUG

bug[2] (also **bug out**) *v* To protrude; bulge : *Her eyes bugged out when she saw the bill* [1870s+ Dialect; fr humorous or dialectal pronunciation of *bulge*]

-bug *combining word* A devotee or energetic practitioner of what is indicated : *firebug/ money-bug/ hockey bug* [1920s+; fr humorous or dialectal pronunciation of *bulge*]

bugaboo *n* Something that frightens or defeats one; bugbear; hobgoblin; bogy [1820s+; probably fr *Bugibu*, a demon cited in the Old French poem *Aliscans*, of 1141]

bugaloo *See* BOOGALOO

bugeyed *adj* **1** Having protruding eyeballs; exophthalmic; POPEYED **2** Startled; astonished : *gets very bugeyed about details of a failed real estate development* [fr humorous or dialectal pronunciation of *bulge*]

bug-fucker *n* A man with a tiny penis *(1970s+)*

bugged *adj* Fitted with a concealed microphone or otherwise equipped for electronic surveillance : *do-it-yourself sex manuals, bugged phones (1919+)*

bugger[1] (BUH gər, BOO-, BOO-) *n* **1** A despicable man; ASSHOLE, JERK *(1719+)* **2** Fellow; man; child; thing • Used affectionately : *What have you been up to, you old bugger?/ Ain't he a cute little bugger? (1850s+)* **3** An object, esp something admired, wondered at, or scorned; FUCKER, SUCKER : *The little buggers would outlast anything humans threw at them and dance on our graves (1940s+)* ◁**4**▷ A male with a taste for anal intercourse; sodomite *(1550s+)* **5** An arduous, painful, or difficult thing; BITCH *(1930s+)* *v* ◁**1**▷ To do anal intercourse or sodomy; sodomize; BUNGHOLE : *The proprietor wins the right to bugger him/ who immediately announced that the Reverend Mr. Alger had been "buggering" him (1590s+)* **2** (also **booger up, bugger up**) To spoil; ruin; confuse; abuse; impair; BOLLIX UP : *Between them they buggered up the mimeo machine/ The practice of how you bugger these numbers of US-Soviet armaments (1880s+ Cowboys)*

bugger[2] *or* **booger** *or* **boogie** (BUH gər, BOO-, BOO-) *n* A piece of solid mucus from the nose

bugger-all *adj* Absolutely nothing : *investments left him with bugger-all (1918+)*

buggered *adj* Damned; confounded; FUCKED : *I'm buggered if I can see anything busted on that truck (1850s+)*

bugger off *v phr* To leave; depart; FUCK OFF • Often a contemptuous command; rare in US, although adopted by the Air Force in the Korean War : *Pay no attention to my piteous Don'ts, but bugger off quickly (1920s+ British)*

bugging or **buggin'** *n* Irrational behavior; overreacting : *buggin'* ... *Irritated, perturbed* ... *Flipping out (1990s+ Teenagers)*

bugging out *n phr* Male sexual response to attractive females; protrusion of the trousers *(1990s+ Black teenagers)*

buggy[1] *n* **1** A caboose *(1890s+ Railroad)* **2** A car, esp an old and rickety one; HEAP, JALOPY : *I wouldn't exactly call my Maserati a buggy (1925+) See* HORSE-AND-BUGGY

buggy[2] *adj* Crazy; bughouse. NUTS *(1900+)*

bugjuice *n* **1** Liquor, esp inferior whiskey; ROTGUT *(1860s+)* **2** A synthetic and highly colored soft drink *(1950s+)* [fr resemblance to the *juice* secreted by grasshoppers]

bug money *n phr* Money bet on a policy operation : *a person that takes illegal bug (numbers) money (1990s+)*

bug off *v phr* To leave; depart • Often an irritated command : *I'm done with you, so bug off* [1950s+; perhaps fr *bugger off*; perhaps fr early 19th-century US **bulge** "to rush, dash"]

bugout *modifier* : *a bugout plan n* **1** A person who usually withdraws and evades; a slacker **2** A military retreat *(Korean War Army)*

bug out[1] *v phr* To bulge; protrude : *His eyes bugged out like a frog's* [1880s+; fr *bulge*]

bug out[2] *v phr* **1** To retreat; turn one's back and run *(fr Korean War Army)* **2** To leave rapidly, esp to drive away in a hurry *(1950s+ Teenagers & hot rodders)* **3** To behave crazily; FREAK OUT *(1980s+ Students)*

build *n* **1** One's physique, esp one's figure or shape; BOD : *a husky build/ sexy build (1850s+)* **2** A show whose earnings continue to increase : *The revue was a build once word-of-mouth took hold (1950s+ Theater)* **3** : *It's been a long build, but we can make our move now v* To prepare someone for swindling, extortion, etc; SET someone UP *(1920s+ Underworld)* [first noun sense perhaps influenced by earlier *build*, "the look and shape of tailored clothing"]

build a collar *v phr* To gather evidence for an arrest *(1950s+ Police)*

build a fire under someone *v phr* To encourage and incite someone forcibly : *Let's get those people moving if we have to build a fire under them (1950s+)*

buildup *n* **1** Publicity and other provisions for introducing a new product, entertainer, etc : *the buildup for a concert (1920s+)* **2** The careful preparation of a potential customer or victim *(1940s+)*

built *adj* Physically well-developed, esp in a sexually attractive way; HUNKY, STACKED : *She wasn't especially smart, but she was built* ◁**built like a brick shithouse** (or **chickenhouse**)▷ *adj phr* Very solidly and well constructed; BUILT, HUNKY • Said usually of a woman with a sturdy and attractive body, esp with large breasts *(1940s+)*

bulb *n* DIM BULB *(1960s+)*

bulge *n* **1** An advantage; a lead : *running up a 20-0 bulge/ the Californians fashioned a two-run bulge of their own (1840s+)* **2** A usu fatty surplus on the waist, buttocks, etc; SPARE TIRE *(1940s+) See* BATTLE OF THE BULGE

bull *modifier* : *a bull market n* **1** A peace officer of any kind, esp a uniformed police officer • London police constables were called *bull-dogs* by 1710 *(1850s+)* **2** An elephant, of either sex *(1920s+ Circus)* **3** An ace • Short for *bullet (1940s+ Poker)* **4** Bull Durham℗, a very popular brand of tobacco for rolling cigarettes *(1930s+)* **5** A locomotive *(1880s+ Railroad)* **6** The chief; head man; BOSS, bull of the woods *(1940s+ Loggers & cowboys)* **7** A dealer who favors higher prices and quicker selling *(1700s+ Stock market)* **8** BULLSHIT *(1900+) v* : *We were sitting around bulling/ He was bulling about his enormous talent See* ALL THAT KIND OF CRAP, BULL SESSION, BULLWORK, COCK-AND-BULL STORY, FULL OF SHIT, SHOOT THE BULL, THROW THE BULL

bulldog *modifier* : *the bulldog edition n* **1** The earliest daily edition of a newspaper *(1920s+ Newspaper office)* **2** A snub-nosed revolver *(1880s+ Police & underworld) v* **1** To advertise horse-race winners falsely; DYNAMITE *(1950s+ Gambling)* **2** To attack like a bulldog, esp to wrestle a steer to the ground by the horns *(1800s+ & esp cowboys)*

bulldoze *v* To intimidate; overcome by force • Early use of the term is connected with Southern politics of the Reconstruction period and describes the intimidation of black men who wished to vote : *to bulldoze employees* [1870s+; fr *bulldose*, "to beat, flog with a strip of leather," perhaps fr the notion of the *dose* of force needed to cow a *bull*]

bulldozer *n* **1** A person who bulldozes *(1870s+)* **2** A revolver *(1880s+)*

bulldyke *n* A lesbian, esp an aggressive one; DYKE *(1920s+ Black)*

bullet *n* **1** An ace *(1807+ Card games)* **2** Money; dollars *(1900+ Underworld)* **3** A rivet *(WWII aircraft workers)* **4** Anything thrown or hit so as to travel very fast, esp a baseball : *He's throwing bullets out there (1940s+)* **5** A record rising very fast on the popularity charts *(1970s+ Recording*

industry) **6** A one-year prison sentence;
BOFFO *(1990s+ Police)* **v** : *currently bulleting
up the charts See* BITE THE BULLET

bull fiddle *n phr* The double bass; bass fiddle
(1870s+)

bullheaded *adj* Obstinate *(1818+)*

bullhockey *n* BULLSHIT • Perhaps earlier, since
hockey, hawky, "shit," is attested as a dialect
verb in 1902 *(1960s+)*

bullish *adj* **1** Favoring and exhibiting high
prices and relatively quick turnover : *a
bullish market/ bullish advice (1880s+ Stock
market)* **2** Showing a positive and hopeful
attitude; encouraging • Often used with
"on" or "about" : *She tends to be bullish about
our prospects/ He's quite bullish on the new
restaurant*

bullpen *n* **1** A cell or secure area where prisoners are kept temporarily; TANK : *We're in
the bullpen waiting to go to court (1880s+)* **2** A
military stockade; military prison *(1900+)* **3**
A usu enclosed area where pitchers practice
and warm up : *The bullpen's getting active now
(1915+ Baseball)* **4** The relief pitching staff
of a baseball team : *They've got starters but no
bullpen (Baseball)* **5** A bunkhouse *(1930+
Loggers)* **6** A living room, lounge, etc, where
a girl's escorts and suitors are appraised
by friends and family *(1940s+ Students)*
[baseball sense perhaps fr a boys' game
called *bullpen,* attested fr 1857, in which
opponents lined up in a rectangle and threw
balls at each other; similarly, the pitchers in
the bullpen are vulnerable to being hit by
thrown and hit balls]

bullrag *n* Bovine excrement; BULLSHIT, COWFLOP
: *didn't mean bullrag in a pasture to him
(1970s+)* **v** also **bullyrag** To intimidate;
domineer over; tease *(first form 1880s+;
second form 1820s+)* [earlier forms included
balrag, ballarag, ballyrag, of obscure origin]

bull session *n phr* A discussion, esp one among
good companions passing time idly but investigating important topics [1920+ College
students; perhaps influenced by *bull,* "discuss, visit another student to pass the time,"
attested as college slang by 1850]

bull's-eye *interj* An exclamation of admiration
over a perfect answer, guess, solution, etc;
BINGO *See* HIT THE NAIL ON THE HEAD

◁**bullshit**▷ *interj* An exclamation of disbelief,
derision, and contempt in retort to some proposition *n* Nonsense; pretentious talk; bold
and deceitful absurdities; BALONEY : *I'm afraid
your theory is chiefly bullshit (1915+)* **v** : *He
tried to bullshit his way out of it (1942+)*

◁**bullshit artist**▷ *n phr* A person who habitually and effectively exaggerates, cajoles, se-
duces verbally, etc : *She's seen as a talented
maverick. "She's not a bullshit artist" (1940s+)*

bullshitter *n* Someone who bullshits *(1930s+)*

bullshooter *n* A person given to exaggeration,
boasting, or pompous inanity [fr *shoot the
bull,* and a euphemism for *bullshitter*]

bullwork *n* Tedious work requiring little
thought or skill; DONKEYWORK, GRUNT WORK,
SCUT : *sees computers taking over only the bullwork of secretaries (1970s+)*

bully *adj* Excellent; good *(1840s+)* *interj* :
Bully for you! (1780s+) *n* A track worker;
gandy dancer *(1900+ Railroad)* [first two
senses fr *bully,* "a beloved person, darling,"
of obscure origin, attested fr 1538. *Bully,*
"worthy, admirable," used of persons, is
attested in 1681]

bully pulpit *modifier* Using high office or fame
as a splendid standpoint for one's teaching
or preaching : *At the least, they hoped that his
"bully pulpit" approach would help rally public
support/ Theodore Roosevelt, rejoicing in the
president's bully pulpit, drowned out every
other voice in the United States/ Madonna has
used her bully pulpit to preach scantily clad
homilies on bigotry, abortion, civic duty, power,
death, and safe sex* [late 1980s+; Said to have
been originated by Theodore Roosevelt, and
more recently popularized by Ross Perot]

bullyrag *v* To harass or bully : *bullyrag the
substitute teacher*

bum[1] *adj* **1** Inferior; defective; LOUSY : *That's a
real bum notion you have there (1850s+)* **2** : *I
told a bum story first/ He just didn't want me to
think he had a car with a bum clutch (1859+)*
n **1** A person who seldom works, seldom
stays in one place, and survives by begging
and petty theft; vagrant; DRIFTER, hobo
(1860s+) **2** A promiscuous woman, esp a
cheap prostitute : *picking up bums in public
dance halls (1930+)* **3** Any male who is disliked by the speaker, esp for lack of energy,
direction, or talent • Often used of inept or
despised athletes : *The bum strikes out three
times in a row (1920+)* **4** A person who lives
or tries to live by his or her sports talent and
charm, usu without being genuinely professional : *Developed by volleyball bums who
hated the regimentation of the indoor game
(1950s+)* **5** An inferior animal, breed, racehorse, etc *(1930+)* **6** Anything inferior or
ineffectual : *Money is a bum, a no-good bum
(1950s+)* *v* **1** To live as a tramp, drifter, etc :
*It wasn't easy bumming that winter/ He bum-
med for a couple of years, then got a job
(1860s+)* **2** To beg or borrow; cadge : *A
schooner can be grafted if you're fierce at
bumming (1850s+)* **3** (also **bum** one's **way,
bum a ride**) To hitchhike : *They bummed all
the way to Alaska (1920s+)* **4** To deceive;
victimize : *Anyone who's seen this halfbaked
ode to mixed marital relations realizes that the*

star has been bummed into a bit role (1960s+)
5 To improve something, esp by exploiting
its full potential or rearranging its parts : I
bummed the whole program to show up all
possible mistakes (Computer) 6 (also bum out)
To become depressed, discouraged, or irritated : You don't want to pull off the information superhighway because you're already
dialed into an on-line service. Don't bum
(1960s+) [probably fr German Bummler,
"loafer"] See BEACH BUM, CRUMB-BUN, SKID ROW
BUM, STUMBLEBUM

bum² n The buttocks or anus; ASS • More
common in British usage : after getting a shot
of something in her bum [late 1300s+; fr
Middle English "anus"]

bum about v phr To be depressed about
something or someone : bummed about not
being picked for first chair

bum around v phr To go about idly; loaf : I just
bummed around last summer (1940s+)

bumblebee See KNEE-HIGH TO A GRASSHOPPER

bum check n A bad or forged bank check : no
bum check for the rent

bumf n Paper; paperwork; toilet paper •
Chiefly British : Most of the bumf he handles
himself [1880+ British schoolboys; fr bum
fodder]

◁**bum fodder**▷ n phr Toilet paper or other
material of the same use • Later, for obvious
reasons, this became a term for a newspaper
or magazine (1650s+)

◀**bumfuck**▶ v ASSFUCK (1860s+)

bummage n Despair; depression : the bummage
in breaking up just before the prom

bummed or **bummed out** adj or adj phr In a
bad mood; dejected; depressed : I'm heavily
bummed if I've realigned anybody's karma/
belonging to the most bummed-out generation
[1960s+; fr narcotics and teenager senses of
bummer]

bummer interj An exclamation of dismay : Ms.
Riner is too docile, too scared, too unsexy for the
role, and—bummer!—there seems to be a real
possibility that she's innocent **modifier** : Zonk
is rushed to the Woodstock bummer tent n 1
BUM¹ : an old bummer named Rumson (1855+)
2 An unpleasant or depressing experience
with a narcotic, esp with LSD; BAD TRIP
(1960s+ Narcotics) 3 Any bad experience or
occasion; bad situation or place : May 17—
Trip was a bummer. Instead of being off by
ourselves, we met another couple (1960s+
Counterculture) [first noun sense probably fr
German Bummler, "loafer"]

bumming adj Depressed; despairing : bumming
and need to talk

bum something off someone v phr To borrow
or beg someone for something : bum a twenty
until Friday

bum someone out v phr To depress; discourage; irritate : At a fraternity the things you
observe totally bum you out/ It bums the fuck
out of me sometimes (1960s+)

bump n 1 A job promotion : I see old Pipkin has
got the bump to full professor (1930s+) 2 In
dancing, a thrust of the pelvis : She unreeled
about fifty bumps in dazzling staccato 3 A
drink; SLUG : They go out and have a bump of
whiskey (1980s+) 4 A party (1980s+ Teenagers) v 1 To discharge; dismiss; FIRE : They
bumped him for insubordination (1915+) 2 To
take away one person's status in order to
accommodate someone of greater importance or seniority : A person is bumped by
someone with a larger number of retention
points (1860+ Railroad) 3 To cancel a reserved seat on an airline, bus, etc, because
the vehicle has been oversold : To be bumped
means to be put off a flight because too many
seats have been sold (1940s+) 4 To displace a
sports opponent by defeat : The Indians
bumped the Tigers out of third place (1950s+)
5 To kill; BUMP OFF (1910+) 6 To make
pregnant; KNOCK someone UP : She had to
blame someone for bumping her (1930s+) 7 To
do the sex act with or to (1980s+ Students)
8 To promote : He got bumped to assistant
manager (1930s+) 9 To raise a bet (1930s+
Poker) 10 In dancing, esp in striptease, to
thrust the pelvis forward and up • Nearly
always in combination with grind (1940s+
Show business) See LIKE A BUMP ON A LOG

bump, the n phr Murder; assassination;
BUMPOFF (1920+)

bump along v phr To progress haltingly : The
interest rate has been bumping along (1960s+)

bump and grind n phr The wearing tedium of
life and work; RAT RACE : the ordinary bump
and grind we call civilization/ Let us get you
through the bump and grind tomorrow
(1990s+) v phr 1 To thrust out and rotate
the pelvis in dancing, esp the striptease; an
imitation of the sex act : She bumped and
ground faster as the bass drum upped its tempo
(1940s+) 2 To play roughly; stress the
physical game rather than strategy : We
have to bump and grind. That's how the puck
went in for us (1980s+ Hockey)

bump belly v phr To oppose; confront; GO UP
AGAINST : And while bumping belly with Bob
Dole may prove tough (1990s+)

bumpdrafting n In a race, pushing the car
ahead in order to increase speed : Bumpdrafting, as the name implies, involves actually
pushing the car in front (1990s+ Car racing)

bumper music n phr Music played before a
radio show, esp a talk show [1990s+ Radio;
probably by analogy with the bumper of
a car]

bumper sticker *n* A vehicle following too closely behind another : *where are the police when this bumper sticker's around*

bumper-thumper *n* A minor car accident; BANGERS AND MASH, FENDER-BENDER (*1990s+*)

bump fuzz *v phr* To do the sex act; BOFF, SCREW : *Little did he know, all I wanted was to bump fuzz* (*1990s+*)

bumping *adj* Excellent; wonderful; COOL, RAD : *The product has kickin' taste and bumpin' packaging. (That means it tastes good and looks good)* (*1980s+ Students*)

bump into someone *v phr* To meet someone unexpectedly : *Guess who I bumped into downtown* (*1880s+*)

bumpoff *n* A killing; murder; assassination; HIT (*1920s+ Underworld*)

bump someone **off** *v phr* To kill, esp to murder; WHACK (*1908+ Underworld*)

bump on a log *See* LIKE A BUMP ON A LOG

bumps *See* GOOSE BUMPS

bump something **up** *v phr* To increase : *bumped up the price of gas* (*1940+*)

bump zone *n phr* A five-yard space downfield from the line of scrimmage, within which a wide receiver can be bumped once, and beyond which he may not be bumped at all : *The '94 rules strictly enforcing the bump zone* (*1990s+ Football*)

bum rap *n phr* 1 An erroneous conviction or sentence (*1920s+ Underworld*) 2 Any unjustified condemnation : *Reagan said, "Nancy's taken a bit of a bum rap on that buying White House china"* (*1980s+*) *v* 1 : *he had been bum-rapped* 2 : *the Philadelphia Navy Yard has been bum-rapped*

bum-rush *v* To eject someone, esp from a restaurant or other public place : *Your posse bumrushed Tatum*

bum's rush, the *n phr* 1 The ejection of a person by force, esp from a public place : *Dey gimme de bum's rush/ You want us to give 'em the bum's rush?* 2 Any discourteous or summary dismissal : *Those not in sympathy with the strike got the bum's rush/ with Stanfill telling the press that she had given her husband "the bum's rush"* (*1920s+*)

bum steer *n phr* Erroneous guidance or advice (*1924+*)

bum trip *See* BAD TRIP

bun *n* 1 A state of drunkenness; alcoholic exhilaration : *A bun is a light jag* (*1900+*) 2 The buttocks; BUM • Originally "the tail of a hare, scut"; first seen applied to persons in Scottish poetry (*1530s+*) 3 A single buttock; CHEEK : *a boil on my left bun* (*1970s+*) *See* CHEESE BUN, CRUMB-BUN, HAVE A BUN IN THE OVEN, HAVE A BUN ON

bun-buster *n* A very hard task or job; BALL-BUSTER : *This job is a bun-buster* (*1970s+*)

bunch *n* 1 A group of people (*1600s+*) 2 A particular group or set, family, etc : *I like my bunch, but yours is elitist* (*1902+*) 3 mob (*1950s+*) 4 Money, esp a large sum; BUNDLE : *He must have paid a bunch for that mink*

bunch, a *adv phr* Very much; a lot; HEAPS : *Your CIC'll be a bunch happier this way* (*1980s+*)

bunco or **bunko** *modifier* : *a bunco scheme/ the police bunco squad* (*1872+*) *n* (also **bunco game**) A swindle; CON GAME, SCAM (*1872+*) *v* To swindle; defraud; FLIMFLAM : *He was buncoed out of his seat in the House* (*1875+*) [said to be fr *Banco*, the name given in the 1850s by a crooked US gambler to the older game "Eight-Dice Cloth"; *Banco* was probably based on Spanish *banca*, a card game similar to monte]

bunco (or bunko) artist *n phr* A professional swindler; CON MAN : *Sleep, like a bunco artist, rubbed it in/ The other fellow is, in most instances, a bunko artist* (*1901+*)

buncombe *See* BUNK

bunco-steerer *n phr* An accomplice in a confidence game, esp one who makes the first contact with the victim; SHILL : *became entangled with a bunco-steerer* (*1975+*)

bundle *n* 1 A large amount of money • Originally the loot from a robbery : *Can the Pentagon Save a Bundle?/ He's dropped a bundle that way* (*1905+*) 2 An attractive woman • This term has improved: In the early 1800s it designated a camp follower, then a fat woman : *I saw Charley yesterday with this cute bundle* (*1930+*) 3 Twenty-five $5 packets of a narcotic, esp marijuana or cocaine (*1960s+ Narcotics*) *v* To gather up small political contributions into a large and influential amount : *His preferred strategy is a controversial practice known as bundling, which means rounding up contributions from friends/ The PAC bundles all the checks for presentation to the individual campaigns* (*1980s+*) *See* DROP A BUNDLE

bundle of joy or **bundle from heaven** *n* A baby : *Brad and Angelina's bundle of joy*

bundle of nerves *n phr* A very nervous person : *He was a bundle of nerves before the speech*

◁**bung fodder**▷ *n phr* Toilet paper; BUM FODDER

◁**bunghole**▷ *n* The anus (*1600s+*) *v* To do anal intercourse; BUGGER (*1940s+*)

bung up *v* or *v phr* To dent; damage; bruise; BANG : *He bunged up the left fender pretty good/ My knee is all bunged up* [*1830s+*; Used in the 1500s to mean "close the eyes or mouth with a blow, as the *bung* of a barrel is closed"]

bun in the oven *n phr* Pregnancy : *no more buns in the oven for me* (*1950+*)

bunk *n* Nonsense; pretentious talk; BALONEY, BULLSHIT (*1900+*) *v* To cheat; defraud; BUNCO : *couldn't possibly have done a better job of bunking the American people (1870s+)* [fr the explanation by a 1800s politician that his extraordinary statements were meant only for his constituents in *Bunc*ombe County, North Carolina]

bunker mentality *n phr* A sense of impending doom, stimulating the innermost defenses [1980s+; probably recalling the last days and delusions of Hitler in his Berlin *bunker*]

bunkie *n* A roommate or bunkmate; a close friend : *OK, bunkies, let's raise our right hands and make a solemn pledge (Students fr WWII armed forces)*

bunko *See* BUNCO

bunkum or **buncombe** *n* BUNK (*1840s+*)

bunned *adj* Drunk (*1908+*)

bunny *n* **1** Welsh rabbit (*1900s+ Students*) **2** A habitually puzzled or victimized person : *She is always criticizing some poor bunny (1920s+)* **3** Any young woman, esp a pert and attractive one (*1600s+*) **4** A young woman who associates with the men in some exciting, daring, or otherwise glamorous activity, sometimes as a participant; GROUPIE : *to eliminate any chance that newsroom chauvinists could tag her as an electronic bunny (1960s+)* <5▷ A prostitute who serves his or her own sex (*1950s+ Homosexuals*) **6** A layup shot (*1970s+ Basketball*) *See* BEACH BUNNY, CUDDLE-BUNNY, DUMB BUNNY, DUST KITTY, JUNGLE-BUNNY, PLAY SNUGGLE-BUNNIES, QUICK LIKE A BUNNY, SEX KITTEN, SKI BUNNY

bunny (or **rabbit**) **food** *n phr* Lettuce, salad, green vegetables, etc [1936+; *Bunny grub* is attested in British schoolboy use by 1890]

◄**bunny fuck**► *n phr* A very quick sex act; QUICKIE *v* **1** : *They pulled beside the road and bunny-fucked* **2** To stall; waste time; FUCK THE DOG : *Quit bunny-fucking and let's move (1960s+)*

bunny hill *n phr* The beginners' slope at a ski resort : *The people on the bunny hill are having just as much fun as those on the moguls (1980s+)*

bunny hop *n* Putting a bicycle in the air so both wheels are off the ground, esp in mountain biking *v* To put a bicycle's wheels in the air or jump over an obstacle without dismounting

buns *n* The buttocks, esp male buttocks : *I'll grab Ron's or Alan's buns sometimes and they're firm and hard* [1960s+; *Bun*, "buttocks," is found in the 1500s, based on an early sense, "the tail of a hare"; this later use is probably not related, being rather based on the full, round shape of an eating bun;

note that *biscuit* and *crumpet* exemplify this baked-goods analogy in other milieux]

buns off, one's *adv phr* Very energetically; with maximum effort; TO THE MAX : *You'll be playing your buns off with your left hand (1970s+)* *See* one's ASS OFF, BUST one's ASS, WORK one's ASS OFF

bun-struggle *n* A formal tea (*1890+*)

buppie *n* A black yuppie : *two proto-buppies slide instantly into Coney Island life (1980s+)*

'burb *modifier* : *They star as burbs newcomers n* A suburb : *The 'burbs, my pet name for LA-Boston-Frisco/ If he chooses to bolt to the 'burbs that's his business (1970s+)*

burg *n* A city; town; village • Usu expresses contempt : *stuck two days in this ghastly burg (1840s+ Theater)*

-burger *combining word* A sandwich made with cooked portions of what is indicated : *beefburger/ cheeseburger/ snakeburger* [1930s+; The definition does not apply to *hamburger*, the source of the term. The suffix was probably first used by the comic-strip artist E C Segar, who coined *goonburger* in the mid-1930s]

burger-flip *v* **1** To work at a fast-food restaurant **2** To work for low and insufficient wages : *the average worker has a family, which a burger-flipping job won't feed (1990s+)*

burger-flipper *n* A person who burger-flips : *pay him wages that could be topped by a burger-flipper at McDonald's (1990s+)*

burgle *v* To break into a place to rob; burglarize (*1870+*)

buried *adj* **1** Serving a life sentence or other long prison sentence **2** Languishing in solitary confinement; incommunicado (*1930s+ Underworld & prison*)

burly *adj* Very difficult; tricky; dangerous : *Check out his burly disaster slide (1990s+ Snowboarders & skateboarders)*

burn *interj* An exclamation of delight at a successful insult (*1980s+ Students*) *n* **1** Becoming angry: *He didn't blow up, just did a slow burn (1930s+)* **2** Cheat or swindle : *It was a burn, but it didn't start out to be* **3** : *I didn't mean it as a burn (mid-1890s+)* *v* **1** To cook or heat food : *Let's burn a couple of hot dogs (1950s+)* **2** To put or be put to death in the electric chair; FRY (*1925+*) **3** To kill; assassinate (*1930s+*) **4** To become angry; BURN UP : *I burned but went on singing (1930s+)* **5** To anger; infuriate; PISS someone OFF : *You must have done something to burn him (1935+)* **6** To cheat; swindle; victimize; rob; RIP OFF : *If you go along with that guy you'll get burned (late 1600s+)* **7** To assault or fight a rival gang or gang member (*1950s+ Street gang*) **8** To harass a person relentlessly; hound : *I'll burn you right off the* *force (1950s+)* **9** To insult; PUT DOWN • This seems to be a spontaneous verb form that coincides with the much older noun : *I burned this chick. "Whereja get those jeans, like Sears or something?"/ The Administration only turned to her after it felt burned by two "Eastern elitists" (1970s+ Teenagers & students)* **10** To infect or become infected with a venereal disease *(1500s+)* **11** To pass; spend; waste; KILL : *I'll start a conversation just to burn time/ if it burns tomorrow afternoon* **12** To move very rapidly; speed; BARREL :' *He wasn't just running, he was burning (1880s+)* **13** To perform, esp to improvise, superbly; excel; be hot : *The cat was getting down and burning (1950s+ Jazz musicians)* **14** To borrow; beg *(1970s+)* **15** To throw something, esp a baseball, very fast : *He burned the fastball right down the middle (1940s+)* **16** To outdo; outshine in competition : *Tony has burned the guy/ the way Dex burned Eddie on that last number* **17** To make a xerographic copy : *Will you burn me ten copies of this? (1980s+ Army)* **18** To expose as an informer : *Do you really want to spend valuable man-hours trying to find out who burned him? (1950s+ Police) See* BURNOUT, DO A SLOW BURN

burn someone's **ass (or butt)** *v phr* To anger someone; irritate someone extremely : *It burns a girl's ass when she's not supposed to go around with anybody else/ Still, it burns my ass to be so close and miss it/ That arrogance burns my butt for sure (1950s+)*

burned or **burnt** *adj* Very angry : *Everyone is sitting there really pissed, really burned/ My dad would be burned if he knew we bought it at a Chevron (1930s+)*

burned (or burnt) out *adj phr* **1** Tired; exhausted; POOPED *(1940s+)* **2** At the end of one's vigor and productivity; PLAYED OUT : *The coach said he quit because he was burned out/ an old burned-out teacher (1883+)* **3** Depressed and exhausted after the effects of a narcotic have worn off *(1960s+ Narcotics)*

burned-out (or burnt-out) case *n phr* A person who is exhausted and ineffectual; BURNOUT : *once a superior foreign correspondent but by then a burnt-out case* [1960s+; fr the title of a 1961 Graham Greene novel about a leper whose case was arrested and cured only after loss of fingers and toes]

burn one in (or over) *v phr* In baseball, to throw a fastball *(1940s+)*

burnout *n* **1** Total and incapacitating exhaustion; inability to go on • The term apparently originated among psychotherapists, describing their own overstressed condition : *Many report lawyer burnout after two or three years in practice/ high rate of teacher burnout*

(1970s+) **2** Boredom; apathy; satiation • The currency of this and the previous sense is due to the various narcotics users' meanings of burn out : *I feared polka burnout, but it never happened. I became a polkaholic (1970s+)* **3** (also **burn**) A user or abuser of drugs, liquor, etc : *There are two groups in my school, the jocks and burn-outs. The burn-outs smoke and take pills and drink/ except for the long hairs (or "burns," short for "burnouts") who hang out on the steps and smoke (1970s+ Teenagers)* **4** A very high-speed hot-rod race *(1950s+ Hot rodders)* **5** An informal match where players try to throw a baseball so hard that it cannot be caught without undue pain **6** The point where a rocket or missile has exhausted its fuel *(1950s+ Astronautics)*

burn rubber *v phr* To leave; depart, esp very precipitately : *When I got back to the flat, you had burned rubber out the back* [1970s+; fr the scorching of tires in the fast acceleration of a car]

burn up *v phr* **1** To perform very well; do superbly well : *His club is burning up the league this season (1940s+)* **2** To go very fast on • *Burn in the same sense dates from the 1870s : to burn up the base paths/ burn up the road (1940s+)* **3** To become angry *(1940s+)*

burn someone **up** *v phr* **1** (also **burn** someone **off**) To anger someone : *His egocentricity burns me up (1930s+)* **2** To put someone to death in the electric chair *(1920s+)* **3** To cheat; swindle; victimize *(1930s+ Circus)*

burp *n* A belch, esp a gentle one *v* **1** : *She burped thrice and smiled* **2** To cause a baby to belch, esp by holding it over the shoulder and patting its back *(1930s+)*

burp gun *n phr* **1** A German Schmeisser machine pistol with a very high rate of fire **2** Any submachine gun; TOMMY GUN *(WWII Army)*

burr under the saddle (or up one's rear end) *n phr* A constant annoyance; obsessive nuisance : *General Noriega has been a burr under the saddle of this Administration/ Sasha Schneider has always been a burr under the saddle of musical complacency/ For some reason, though, he had a burr up his rear end (1990s+)*

bursting at the seams *adj* Too full; almost beyond capacity : *school is bursting at the seams (1960+)*

bury *v* **1** To sentence someone to a very long prison term or to solitary confinement *(1900+ Underworld)* **2** To defeat decisively; CLOBBER *(1940s+ Sports)*

bury the hatchet *v phr* To make peace; cease hostilities : *He and Chambrun hadn't buried the hatchet after all* [1750s+; fr an American

Indian custom of burying such a weapon as a sort of peace treaty]

bus *n* **1** A car : *Whose old bus is in the drive?* (*1919+*) **2** An aircraft (*1916+*) **3** An ambulance : *Roger one-oh-four, do we need a bus?* (*1980s+ Police*) *v* To clear dirty dishes and tableware from the tables in a restaurant or cafeteria (*1913+*) [the restaurant sense probably fr the four-wheeled cart often used to carry dishes] *See* JITNEY, MISS THE BUS

bush *adj* **1** Rural; provincial; BUSH LEAGUE • The sense has gradually developed from "the wilderness" to "the country as distinct from the city"; coincidentally it has taken on the same value judgment: The city is superior, the country is inferior : *a bush town* (*1650s+*) **2** Mediocre; second-rate; amateur : *seemed pretty bush for pros* (*1650s+*) *modifier* <1▷ : *Bush shot. You could see the pubic hair, but not the sex parts* *n* **1** A beard; whiskers (*1640s+*) <2▷ The pubic hair, esp of a female; BEAVER (*1745+*) *v* To fatigue; exhaust; sap; POOP : *The climb bushed him/ Our dialogues always bush me* (*1870+*) *See* BEAT AROUND THE BUSH, BEAT THE BUSHES

bush *or* **bushes,** the *n phr* The back country; the BOONIES : *When I was working 12-hour tricks as a newspaper cub in the bushes* (*1670+*)

bushboy *n* A young, new, and naive prisoner : *That damn bushboy beats his gums too much* (*1980s+*)

bushed *adj* Tired out; exhausted; BEAT, FRAZZLED, POOPED [*1870+* Loggers; perhaps fr mid-19th-century meaning "lost in the woods"]

bush league *adj phr* Mediocre; second- or third-rate; BUSH, SMALL-TIME : *a bush-league hoodlum/ Your ideas are invariably bush league* *n phr* **1** A baseball minor league of professional or semiprofessional players (*1908+*) **2** Any subordinate, apprentice, or amateur enterprise : *The road companies are sometimes bush leagues for aspirants to Broadway* (*1908+*)

bush leaguer *or* **busher** *n or n phr* **1** A baseball player in a minor league • A 1907 example of *bush leaguer* applies to basketball rather than baseball players (*1910+*) **2** Any mediocre or second-rate performer; amateur : *He's a busher at the piano* (*1920s+*)

bush leagues, the *n phr* The mediocre and inferior reaches of business, entertainment, sports, etc; the SMALL TIME : *For years he made a perilous living as a singer in the bush leagues* (*1908+*)

bushwah (BŌŌSH wah, BOOSH-) *n* (Variations: **booshwah** or **bushwa** or **booshwa**) Nonsense; pretentious talk; bold and deceitful absurdities; BALONEY, BULLSHIT : *But the President's own managers concede this is so much bushwah* [*1906+*; seemingly a euphemism for *bullshit* fr a cowboy corruption of French *bois-de-vache*, "dried cow dung"; in some users possibly influenced by French *bourgeois* taken pejoratively]

bushwhack *v* **1** To assault, esp from ambush : *Two guys jumped out and bushwhacked him* **2** To attack violently : *After that speech the President felt bushwhacked* [*1860s+*; fr the action of cutting the bush in order to get through the forest or along an overgrown stream]

bushy-tailed *See* BRIGHT-EYED AND BUSHY-TAILED

business *n* Excrement, esp that of a house pet (*1645+*) *See* IN BUSINESS, KNOW one's ONIONS, MONKEY BUSINESS, THAT'S SHOW BUSINESS

business as usual *n phr* Persistence in the ordinary course of events despite difficulties, morality, and other hindrances : *the team that is supposed to drag America from the path of business as usual/ The riot is over, and it's back to business as usual/ If you bribe a public employee it's corruption; if he works in a private company it's business as usual* (*1885+*)

business end, the *n phr* The dangerous or operative part of something, esp the muzzle of a gun (*1878+*)

busk *v* To perform music in subway stations or other public places, taking the contributions of listeners • Very common in Great Britain, but spreading to the US (*1840s+*)

bust *adj* Out of funds; destitute; BROKE (*1840s+*) **1** A police raid : *One whiff of marijuana and we get a bust* (*1930s+*) **2** An arrest; COLLAR : *Beating a Bust: Two Views* (*1918+*) **3** : *That one bust decked me* **4** A failure; fiasco : *My try for her sweet favors was a total bust* (*1840s+*) **5** A person who fails; LOSER, nonstarter : *At baseball I was a risible bust* (*1920s+*) **6** A spree; drinking bout : *took his paycheck and went on a bust* (*1840+*) *v* **1** To break : *I busted my nose* (*1806+*) **2** To disperse or chase a rival street gang (*1950s+ Street gang*) **3** To reduce in rank; demote : *He got busted from buck sergeant to buck private* (*late 1800s+ Army*) **4** To tame a wild horse for riding : *Two rides will usually bust a bronco so that the average cow-puncher can use him* (*1890s+ Cowboys*) **5** To break open a safe, vault, etc; also, burglarize a place (*1890s+ Underworld*) **6** : *I've been busted, bring bail* **7** To catch someone in an illegal or immoral act (*1950s+ Teenagers*) **8** To hit someone : *She busted me in the kishkes* (*1808+*) **9** To fail an examination or course; FLUNK • The standard form *burst* is found in the 1850s : *I miserably busted the econ final* (*1900+ College students*) *See* BEER BUST, GO BROKE

busta *n* **1** An unemployed person who is dependent on others : *He might become a busta and live with his mother* **2** Someone who aspires to be someone else; WANNABE ; also, a kid trying to act tough : *rappers trying to be bustas*

bust a gut (or **hamstring** or **nut**) *v phr* BUST one's ASS (*first form* 1912+)

bust a move *v phr* To leave, depart

bust ass *v phr* To thrash; punish by beating; CLOBBER, KICK ASS : *A little belly, sure. But I can still bust ass* (1980s+)

◁**bust** one's **ass**▷ *v phr* (Variations: **break** may replace **bust**; ◁**balls**▷ or **buns** or **butt** or **chops** or **conk** or **hump** or **nuts** or **stones** or ◁**sweet ass**▷ or **tail** may replace **ass**) To work or perform to one's utmost; exert oneself mightily : *Yeah but, what if he busts his ass, goes to a lot of trouble/ If They Break Their Asses They Might Get into College Program/ I'm finished busting my hump on that kind of work/ I busted my butt to get those business people to sponsor me/ We're really busting our buns/ Here I was, busting my tail to develop young players* (*first form* 1940s+)

◁**bust balls**▷ *v phr* To discipline harshly; punish : *They gonna be bustin' balls, man* (1950s+)

bust one's buttons *v phr* To be ostentatiously proud and happy : *Dolores Rogan of Bay View is busting her buttons these days*

bust someone's chops *See* BREAK someone's CHOPS

busted or **bust** *adj* **1** Penniless; BROKE (1860s+) **2** Arrested or caught by an authority : *I'm so busted* **3** Intoxicated

buster[1] *combining word* Someone or something that destroys, thwarts, or otherwise defeats what or who is indicated • Revived by an early 1980s film comedy called *Ghostbusters* creating forms like *blockbuster/ chartbuster/ gangbuster/ gridlock buster/ fuzz buster/ troll buster/ virus buster* (1930s+) *n* **1** A splendid person, esp a robust one; BEAUT, CORKER : *He was a buster nigh as big as his Mammy* (1840s+) **2** (also **Buster**) Man; fellow; GUY, BROTHER • Used in direct address with a somewhat hostile tone : *Down the hall to the back room, buster* (1860s+) *See* BALLBUSTER, BRONCO BUSTER, BUN-BUSTER, CLOUD-BUSTER, SKULL-BUSTER

buster[2] *n* A weak or treacherous gang member; MARK : *Bogard accused Compton of being a "buster," meaning he was weak and unwilling to defend the gang's interests/ No fucking way. I ain't no buster!* [1990s+ Street gang; probably fr *gangbuster*]

bust hump *v phr* To work extremely hard; BUST one's ASS : *Nobody's ever accused you of being unwilling to bust hump* (1970s+)

busting out *adj phr* Doing well; looking good (1980s+ *Black teenagers*)

bustlebutt *n* A very busy, energetic person; EAGER BEAVER (1980s+)

bust on *v* To attack someone or something : *The gang's gonna bust on you*

bust-out *n* The climax of a swindle, when the victim hands over the money (1950s+ *Police*)

bust out *v phr* **1** To be dismissed from a school for academic failure (1920+) **2** To lose all one's money gambling, esp at craps; TAP OUT (1960s+) **3** BREAK OUT (1930+)

bust someone out *v phr* To win all of someone's money in a crap game, esp by cheating (1960s+)

bust-up *n* An argument, esp violent : *bust-up over unionizing* (1900+)

bust up *v phr* **1** To end a marriage, friendship, or other association (1920s+) **2** To beat or batter someone : *want me to bust you up*

bust someone wide open *v phr* To beat someone severely

busty *adj* Having large breasts; bosomy; CHESTY : *But she looked like the others, busty, too slender, bony hips* (1940s+)

busy bee *n phr* The powdered form of phencyclidine, a tranquilizer used in veterinary medicine, which as a narcotic is either sniffed or smoked in a tightly rolled cigarette; ANGEL DUST : *angel dust, also known as busy bee* [1970s+ Narcotics; fr the fact that a low dosage produces a *buzz*]

but *adv* Really; definitely : *He noticed it and began making cracks but loud* [1930s+; perhaps fr a Yiddish speech pattern]

butch *adj* : *short round blonde of butch self-sufficiency n* **1** A rough, strong man; TOUGH • Often used as a nickname (1902+) **2** An aggressive lesbian; BULLDYKE, DYKE : *Even if she has turned butch on me and twisted the family name on you* (1940s+ *Homosexuals*) [fr *butcher*]

butcher *n* **1** A surgeon, esp an incompetent one (*mid-1800s+*) **2** A brutal and sanguinary ruler : *They called Bokassa a worse butcher than Amin* (1529+) **3** : *As a carpenter I'm a butcher v* To do crudely and clumsily what should be done with finesse : *I butcher their language/ I try to paint but butcher the canvas* (1640s+)

but good *adv phr* Very well; extremely; really : *They hate us but good/ Your brother fucked you but good* [1930s+; perhaps fr a Yiddish speech pattern]

butt *adj* Bad; undesirable (1990s+ *Students*) *adv* Very; extremely; STONE : *That furniture is butt ugly* (1980s+ *Students*) *n* **1** The buttocks; rump; ASS • This sense is attested as western US in 1860. Oddly enough, *butt* looks like a diminutive of *buttock*, but to judge by the suffix, the opposite must be the case. : *So drunk he couldn't find his butt with both hands* (*1450+*) **2** The remainder of a smoked cigarette or cigar (*1930s+*) **3** A cigarette : *a pack of butts* (*1900+*) **4** The final year of a prison sentence or a term of military enlistment (*1915+ Armed forces & prison*) **5** Something or someone disliked • Somewhat derogatory : *woman is a real butt See* DUSTY BUTT, GET OFF one's ASS, GOOFY-BUTT, GRIPE one's ASS, NO SKIN OFF MY ASS, SCUTTLE-BUTT

butter *n* Flattery; cajolery; SOFT SOAP (*1823+*) *v* (also **butter up**) To flatter shamelessly and fulsomely (*1700+*) *See* LIKE SHIT THROUGH A TIN HORN

butter-and-egg man *n phr* **1** A wealthy business executive or farmer from the provinces : *The visiting Butter and Egg Men had their Whoopee in New York* **2** A person who finances a theatrical production; ANGEL (*1920s+*)

butterball *n* Any plump person : *Short and plump. A real butterball/ But butterball? That's on a par with pleasingly plump* [1940s+; The simile "as fat as a *butterball*" occurs from the mid-1800s]

butterfingered *adj* Clumsy, as if there was butter on someone's fingers (*1615+*)

butterfingers *n* A clumsy, unhandy person, esp one who regularly drops things [1850s+ Cricket; Adopted by baseball players in the 1880s]

butterflies *n* Dull spasms in one's stomach, caused by anxiety and nervousness; flutters : *I sure got butterflies thinking about it* (*1908+*)

butterfly *See* PUSSY BUTTERFLY

butterfly ball (or **pitch**) *n phr* A slow and erratic pitch; KNUCKLEBALL : *All this exertion took the butter off his butterfly ball* (*1940s+ Baseball*)

butterfly kiss *n phr* A caress made by winking an eye so that the lashes brush one's partner : *She worked her eyelashes and made butterfly kisses on my cheeks* (*1871+*)

◄**buttfuck**► *v* and *n* ASSFUCK, BUMFUCK : *to sue us for his two-thirds contingency fee and all the troopers he can butt-fuck*

◄**buttfuck buddy**► *See* ASSHOLE BUDDY

◁**butthead**▷ *n* A stupid person; oaf; BONEHEAD, DUMDUM, spazz : *Howdy is a depressingly stupid butthead* [1980s+ Students; probably fr *butthead*, "ass-headed," influenced by the 1960s student term *butterhead*, "stupid person"]

butt heads *v phr* To vie strongly; contend : *NBC's new* John Laroquette Show *butted heads with ABC's* Roseanne

◁**butthole**▷ *n* The anus; ASSHOLE : *Did those buttholes score again?* (*1950s+*)

butt in *v phr* To intrude oneself; proffer unwanted counsel; barge in : *The Wagner Act forbade any employer to butt in on such matters/ "Greenspan, don't butt in," said Gold* (*1900+*)

buttinsky *n* (Variations: **butterinsky** or **buttinski** or **butt-in**) A person who rudely intrudes himself, esp one who does so habitually [1902+; fr *butt in* plus the Slavic or Yiddish suffix **-sky**, *added for humorous effect*]

butt-kicker *n* A very effective person • Compare *asskicker* : *He's a real butt-kicker in soccer* (*1980s+ Students*)

buttload *n* A large quantity; a lot of; SHITLOAD (*1980s+ Students*)

butt naked *adj* Totally nude : *butt naked running through the boys' locker room*

button *n* **1** The chin; point of the chin : *I got clipped square on the button* (*1920+*) ◁**2**▷ The clitoris; CLIT (*1870s+*) **3** A small quantity of a narcotic : *There exists some traffic, however, in "buttons," or small amounts* (*1960s+ Narcotics*) **4** The rounded top of the peyote plant (*1960s+ Narcotics*) **5** A police officer's badge; potsy, tin (*1920s+*) **6** (also **buttons**) A police officer • *Blue and buttons* was used of the police (*1900+*) *n phr* **7** (also **button man** or **button player** or **button soldier**) A low-ranking member of the Mafia; SOLDIER (*1960s+ Underworld*) *See* BELLY BUTTON, HIT THE PANIC BUTTON, ON THE BUTTON

buttondown or **buttoned-down** *adj* Conventional; of unmistakable respectability; conservative; SQUARE : *The button-down, dispassionate, country club racism of the nouveau riche/ One of the most squeaky-clean and buttoned-down of US corporations is a partner* [1960s+; fr the wearing of *buttondown* collars by business executives and other conservatives]

button down *v phr* **1** To classify; PEG, PIGEONHOLE : *I buttoned him down from the start as a probable bore* **2** To make precise; discard all but one alternative : *First we decide to buy, then we button down the price* **3** To prepare for action; get ready : *He was all buttoned down and ready to go* [1950s+; third sense fr a military term for closing all ports and hatches for action]

buttoned-up *adj* Neat; trim; prim : *Betty Crocker's very serious, buttoned-up, orderly* (*1970s+*)

buttonhole *v* To get someone's attention as if by taking hold by a buttonhole : *listening to and buttonholing other researchers* [1880+; *Button* in the same sense is attested from the early 1860s]

buttonhook *n* A maneuver in which a pass receiver runs downfield and then suddenly spins and runs back toward the line of scrimmage [1970s+ Football; fr the resemblance of the path to a *hook* used for pulling *buttons* through the buttonholes of a pair of shoes]

button (up) one's **lip** *v phr* To stop talking; not tell what one knows : *I wish Jim Quello would button his lip* (*1847+*)

buttons *See* HAVE ALL one's BUTTONS

button up *v phr* **1** To keep quiet; BUTTON one's LIP, CLAM UP : *If you don't button up they'll shut you up* (*1850s+*) **2** To finish something, esp tidily and handsomely : *We buttoned it up in a couple days* (*1940s+*) **3** To lock up, close up, or make secure : *I told John Sanderson to button up the generator* (*1940s+*)

butt out *v phr* **1** To stop intruding; reverse one's butting in • Usu an exasperated command, based on opposition to *butt in* : *Four other guys told me I should butt out* (*1930s+*) **2** To depart, esp abruptly; BUG OUT : *I butted right out of there when it went off* (*1940s+*)

butt pack *n phr* FANNY PACK

buttplug *n* A despised person; ASSHOLE, JERK (*1980s+*)

butt ugly *adj phr* Very ugly; repulsive : *That furniture is butt ugly/ the "I feel butt-ugly" days* (*1980s+ Students*)

buy *v* **1** To believe; accept as true : *These guys bought the myth and now it's costing them dearly/ I buy it. What you told me is between us* **2** To agree to; acquiesce in : *If that's the plan, I'll buy it* (*1920s+*) **3** To do; effectuate : *She pointed her gun at me. I said, "What are you trying to buy with that?"* (*1940s+*) **4** To hire; engage : *He bought him a lawyer and filed suit* (*1650s+*) **5** (also **buy off**) To induce by money; bribe : *He tried to buy a couple of jury members* (*1650s+*)

buy-and-bust operation *n phr* A police operation in which an undercover officer buys narcotics and then arrests the seller : *The case began with a routine buy-and-bust operation* (*1980s+*)

buy a pig in a poke *v phr* To accept or agree to something without careful examination; risk the unknown : *It is unfair for anyone running for president "to ask people to buy a pig in the poke"* [*1562+*; fr dialect *poke,* "bag, sack"] *See* CAN'T BUY

buy-in *n* Acceptance; acquiescence : *Not everyone adheres to the strategy. They hedge. There's a lack of buy-in* (*1990s+*)

buy into *v phr* To accept; acquiesce in • Thought of and perhaps coined as the opposite of *sell out,* which has a more contemptuous suggestion of betrayal : *lots of guilt and I bought into that/ I bought into the whole materialistic trip/ the degree with which you bought into the pop culture of the Fifties*

buy the big one *v phr* To die : *Aunt June bought the big one*

buy the farm (or **the ranch**) *v phr* To be killed; die : *the cat that bought the farm when Harvey hit him on his bike/ Luna crash confirmed. They bought the ranch* [*1950s+* Armed forces; fr earlier Air Force term *buy a farm,* "to crash"; probably from the expressed desire of wartime pilots to stop flying, buy a farm, and live peacefully]

buy time *v phr* To be dilatory or evasive in order to gain time; temporize; STALL (*1960s+*)

buzz *n* **1** A telephone call : *I think I'll give the Guided Child a buzz* (*1910+*) **2** Subject of talk; gossip; rumor : *What's the buzz, cuz?* (*1605+*) **3** A feeling or surge of pleasure, esp a pleasant sense of intoxication; HIGH : *After two Scotches he got a nice buzz* (*1935+*) **4** A police squad car (*1950s+ Teenagers*) *v* **1** To call someone on the telephone; RING : *Why not buzz Eddy for the brawl?* (*1910+*) **2** To talk; converse : *The crowd was buzzing about some pretty raunchy divorces* (*1832+*) **3** To flatter; court (*1900+*) **4** To inform someone in confidence, esp by whispering : *You'll buzz me later* (*1950s+*) **5** To announce one's arrival or summon someone by or as if by sounding a buzzer : *Buzz when you want me* (*1950s+*) **6** To beg (*1920s+ Hoboes*) **7** To pilfer; rob; HOLD UP (*1812+ Underworld*) **8** To question or investigate someone (*1930s+ Police & underworld*) **9** To fly an aircraft alarmingly close to something, esp to the ground • A sense "to flutter or hover about, over, etc," is attested from 1650 (*WWII air forces*) **10** To roister drunkenly at : *They were all buzzing the bar* (*WWII armed forces*) **11** Kill; WASTE : *They buzz the kid and her baby?* (*1990s+ Street gang*)

buzz along *See* BUZZ OFF

buzz cut or **buzzed hair** *modifier* : *Some have buzz-cut spiked haircuts/ Fitness guru Susan Powter, she of the platinum buzz-cut hair n phr* A cutting off of all or most of the hair; a total or near-total dehairing : *A woman cadet could conceivably get a buzz cut/ Nowicki received a buzz cut from his swimmers* (*1990s+*)

buzzed *adj* Intoxicated, esp mildly so; TIDDLY : *Getting a little buzzed on a second Bloody Mary* (*1950s+*)

buzzin' *adj* Drunk (*1980s+ Teenagers*) *See* COUSIN

buzz in *v phr* To arrive : *Old JK buzzed in from Syracuse* (*1930s+*)

buzz someone *in* *v phr* To unlock an outer door for someone by actuating an electric unlatching device (*1970s+*)

buzz off (or **along**) *v phr* To depart; TODDLE OFF • First form often a command (*1914+*)

buzzword or **buzzphrase** *n* A modish technical or arcane term used to make one appear sophisticated : *The rhetoric has sputtered with buzzwords like "anticolonialist" and "progressive"*/ *I avoid buzzphrases like "this point in time"*/ *Buzzword of the Month Dept* [1946+; coined in the mid-1940s by students at the Harvard Business School and meaning "a word used to describe the key to any course or situation" in their specialized and amusingly stilted vocabulary; hence *buzz* may be a shortening and repronouncing of *business*]

buzzworthy *adj* Worthy of attention and gossip : *Is your website buzzworthy*

buzzy *adj* Drunk (*1700s+*)

BVDs (bee vee deez) *n* Underwear, esp long underwear; BEEVEEDEES : *I opened the door and caught her in her BVDs* [1920s+; fr the 1870s trademark of a brand of long underwear, the initials of the manufacturers Bradley, Voorhees, and Day]

by *prep* **1** With; as far as concerns : *Five skins is jake by me* **2** At; to; at the place of : *I'll buy you a drink by Antek* [1920s+; fr direct transcription of Yiddish prepositional use into English] *See* GET AWAY WITH something, GET BY

by a long shot (or **a jugful**), **not** *See* NOT BY A LONG SHOT

by a nose *adv phr* By a narrow margin; barely : *win by a nose* (*1908+*)

by-a-whisker *adj* Very nearly tied; very close : *the House of Representatives' by-a-whisker vote* (*1970s+*)

by cracky *interj* By Christ • A euphemistic form : *By cracky, he hit the jackpot!* (*1800s+*)

bye *See* TAKE A BYE

by ear *adv phr* : *He sort of made his judgments by ear* [fr the playing of music without the use of graphic notation, a term used since at least the 1840s] *See* PLAY IT BY EAR

bye-bye *n* Good-bye : *bye-bye for now* (*1867+*)

by George *interj* A mild exclamation of surprise, approval, determination, emphasis, etc : *By George, I'll do it/ I think she's got it, by George* [1731+; A euphemism for *by God*]

-by God- *infix* Used for emphasis : *I was born in West-by God-Virginia*

by guess and by God *adv phr* By approximation and instinct; not by precise or infallible means : *She didn't know exactly how to make a quiche, so had to do it by guess and by God* (*1940s+*)

BYOB (pronounced as separate letters) *modifier* : *a BYOB party* **v** *phr* Bring your own bottle, or your own booze (*1950s+*)

◁**by the balls**▷ *See* HAVE someone BY THE BALLS

by the bell *See* SAVED BY THE BELL

by the book *adv phr* According to correct procedures; as one should under regulations, law, contract, etc : *He said there would be no more corner cutting, we'd do everything strictly by the book* (*1840s+*)

by the numbers *adv phr* In a prescribed way; mechanically : *He even makes love by the numbers* [WWI armed forces; fr the military training device of analyzing a complex action by breaking it into a numbered series of simpler actions, performed as the *numbers* are called out]

by the seat of one's **pants** *adv phr* By instincts and feelings, without the benefit of formal training or procedures; BY GUESS AND BY GOD, BY EAR : *pushing his luck, living on the edge, playing brilliantly by the seat of his pants* (*1930s+ Aviators*) *See* FLY BY THE SEAT OF one's PANTS

by the short hairs *See* HAVE someone BY THE SHORT HAIRS

by the truckful *adj phr* (Variations: **boxcar** or **carload** may replace **truckful**) In great quantity; numerous; up the kazoo (*1960s+*)

C

C *n* Cocaine *See* BIG C, C-NOTE

cabbage *n* Money; LETTUCE : *The salad boys in the back room, oiling up the cabbage. And it's big cabbage, too* (1900+) *See* FOLDING MONEY

cabbagehead *n* A stupid person : *what cabbagehead left the light on?*

cabinet *See* KITCHEN CABINET

cabin fever *n phr* Restlessness, impatience, and other signs of having been restrained too long (1918+)

caboodle *n* A totality; discrete unit; BOODLE : *Keep the whole caboodle* [1840+; perhaps fr boodle] *See* KIT AND CABOODLE

ca-ca or **caca** or **kaka** cack (KAH kah) *n* **1** Excrement; SHIT : *Overweight is kaka* (1870s+) **2** Heroin; HORSE, SHIT (1950s+ Narcotics) [origin uncertain; perhaps fr late 1800s *cack*, "to defecate"; perhaps fr dialect *cacky*, "excrement," attested by 1899; perhaps fr Latin *cacare*, "to defecate," used as a euphemism in the presence of children; perhaps fr Modern Greek; ultimately fr the Indo-European root *kakka* or *kaka*, designating defecation]

cack *v* **1** To defecate **2** To laugh uncontrollably

cackleberry *n* A hen's egg used for food

cactus juice *n* Tequila : *drank cactus juice in Cancun*

Cad or **Caddy** or **Caddie** *n* A Cadillac car : *And we'll rent a black Caddy* (1920s+)

caddy *n* A Cadillac automobile : *Park that Caddy over there*

cadge (CAJ, CAYJ) *v* To borrow; beg; BUM, MOOCH (1800s+)

Cadillac *modifier* : *It's Cadillac all the way. It's a Cadillac operation* *n* **1** An ounce of heroin (1950s+ Narcotics) **2** The best of its kind; standard of excellence; paragon : *Republicans call New York the Cadillac of welfare states/ Revos are the Cadillac of sunglasses*

cafeteria *modifier* Allowing a range of choice; smorgasbord : *cafeteria insurance plans* (1980s+)

cafeteria Catholic *n phr* A Roman Catholic who observes church prescriptions and prohibitions at his or her own discretion : *You know, cafeteria Catholics who want to pick and choose what they want to believe of Catholic teaching* (1980s+)

cage *modifier* : *a big cage star/ the cage standing* *n* **1** A prison (1630s+) **2** A car or van : *The cage behind me bleated its horn* (1970s+ Motorcyclists) **3** A basketball basket or net (1920s+ Sports) **4** Basketball (1920s+ Sports) *v* **1** : *The punk concealed a genuine terror of being caged* **2** CADGE *See* RATTLE SOMEONE'S CAGE, RATTLE CAGES

cager *n* A basketball player : *The eight-foot cager sped down the court like a maddened giraffe* (1930s+ Sports)

cage rattler *n phr* A person not content with the humdrum or conventional : *The governor wants "cage rattlers"; thinkers, dreamers, and gadflies* (1970s+)

cahoots *See* IN CAHOOTS

Cain *See* RAISE CAIN

caj or **cas** or **cazh** (CAZH, CAYZH) *adj* Casual; acceptable (1980s+ Teenagers)

cake *n* ◁1▷ The female genitals (1940s+ Black) **2** A sexually attractive woman; FOX (1940s+ Black) **3** (also **cake-eater**) A ladies' man; DUDE : *his brown hat, fixed square-shaped the way the cakes were wearing them* (1920s+) **4** PIECE OF CAKE (1910+) *See* BABYCAKES, CUT CAKE, FRUITCAKE, ICE THE CAKE, NUTBALL, PIECE OF CAKE, TAKE THE CAKE

cake job *n phr* An easy job; sinecure : *Meter maids have a cake job* (1990s+)

cakewalk *n* Something very easy; BREEZE, CINCH, PIECE OF CAKE : *Casey on his way to a cakewalk with the Senate Intelligence Committee/ Our players thought this season was going to be a cakewalk* [1890s+; fr the name of a 19th-century dance contest, influenced by *piece of cake*]

calf love *n phr* PUPPY LOVE (1890s+)

calico *See* PIECE OF CALICO

California stop *n phr* (also **Michigan stop**) An instance of rolling slowly past a stop sign, rather than stopping (1960s+)

Californicate *v* **1** To overdevelop the land : *bumper sticker : Don't Californicate Montana* **2** To seduce and infect with the moral and social standards of Southern California : *McKellen was, in the tradition of expatriate Englishmen, Californicated into a greater sense of individual freedom* (1990s+)

Californication *n* An instance of Californicating : *Gogarty said that his task was to prevent the Californication of Ireland* (1990s+)

call *n* A decision : *It was my call* [1980s+; fr the playing decisions of managers, quarterbacks, etc, and the officiating decisions of umpires, referees, etc] *See* CATTLE CALL, CLOSE SHAVE

call someone's bluff *v phr* To force someone to justify or validate a pretense; require the truth : *When she called his bluff, he had to admit he was lying* (1870s+)

call-down *n* A reprimand; rebuke (1890s+)

71

call someone **down** *v phr* To reprimand; rebuke (*1890s+*)

call girl *n phr* A prostitute, esp one who may be engaged by telephone (*1900+*)

call hogs *v phr* To snore very loudly : *after vacation, calling hogs all night*

call in one's **chits** (or **markers**) *v phr* To collect what is owed to one, esp tit-for-tat political or other favors : *I have no chits to call in from politicians/ You're calling in your chits, Ivar/ For the Titian show, Michel Laclotte, soon to retire as director of the Louvre, has called in all his markers at once* [1980s+; fr *chit*, "notation of something owed, IOU," attested fr the 1770s; the source is Hindi *chitti*; a *marker* is also a notation of debt, esp in gambling]

call it *v phr* **1** To declare something over or done, such as to declare a medical patient dead : *surgeon called it at 1700 hours* **2** To end a current task or end one's workday : *I've written enough definitions. I'm going to call it*

call it a day (or **quits**) *v phr* To stop or terminate something; declare one has had enough : *The Iraqi leadership has hunkered down; time to call it a day/ Any sensible assassin would have called it quits* [first form 1840s+, second 1940s+; *Call quits* is attested from the 1890s]

call it like one **sees it** *v phr* To be honest and unbiased; be deaf to influence (*1980s+*)

call off the dogs *v phr* To relent; ease one's demands • A metaphor from hunting, where a trapped quarry is beset by *dogs* : *Holmgren basically called off the dogs in the third quarter* (*1930s+*)

call of nature or **nature's call** *n phr* The need to use the toilet, esp when urgent : *Where'd he go so quickly? To answer the call of nature, naturally* (*1761+*)

call someone **on the carpet** *v phr* To reprimand or summon for a reprimand; CHEW someone OUT [1890s+; probably fr early 19th-century British *walk the carpet*, having the same sense and based upon a servant's being called into the parlor to be reprimanded]

call someone **out** *v phr* To challenge someone to a fight, esp a duel : *wanted to call him out*

call shotgun *v phr* To claim the front passenger seat : *the tall guy called shotgun*

call the shots *v phr* To be in charge : *Who's calling the shots around here?* (*1960s+*)

◁**camel toe**▷ *n* Unsightly crotch cleavage when a woman is wearing tight or see-through clothing : *yogis were showing some camel toe*

camera loves someone, the *sentence* The person named is very photogenic or telegenic : *The camera loved her dark good looks*

cammies or **camies** *n* A camouflage suit or uniform : *They said théy would kill just to peel off their ripe desert cammies/ There were kids whose cammies (camouflage suits) were still on fire* (*1970s+*)

cammo *n* Camouflage : *The Cammo Dudes are here* (*1980s+*)

camp *adj* **1** : *a camp bar/ the camp scene* **2** : *a camp advertisement/ camp clothing n* **1** A male homosexual (*1940s+ Homosexuals*) **2** Effeminate behavior, such as mincing gait, fluttering gestures, or pronounced lisp (*1920s+ Homosexuals*) **3** Something, esp in art, decoration, theater, etc, so naively stylized, artificial, affected, old-fashioned, and inadequate to good modern taste as to be highly amusing and inviting to parody : *television's inexhaustible supply of crash courses in camp* (*1960s+*) *v* **1** (also **camp it up**) : *Malcolm was camping perilously in the blue-collar bar* **2** (also **camp it up**) To behave in a humorously affected, exaggerated way, esp imitating the acting and oratorical styles of the 1800s : *She started camping, vamping me like Theda Bara* (*1960s+*) [origin uncertain; perhaps, as noted in 1909, referring to a sense "actions and gestures of exaggerated emphasis," it is fr French *se camper*, "put oneself in a bold, provocative posture," attested fr the mid-1600s; the more modern senses were revived, introduced, and popularized in Susan Sontag's essay "Notes on Camp," published in 1964] *See* BOOT CAMP, HIGH CAMP, LOW CAMP

camp it up *v phr* **1** To behave dramatically or affectedly; overact : *can't help camping it up* **2** To behave effeminately, to attract homosexuals

campy *adj* **1** Effeminate; overtly homosexual (*1940s+ Homosexuals*) **2** Displaying naive, affected, and old-fashioned style : *a campy evocation of WWI patriotism* (*1960s+*)

can *n* **1** A toilet; JOHN • Said to be a shortening of *piss-can* (*1900+*) **2** The buttocks; rump; ASS : *And that's when I asked her about her fat can* (*1910+*) **3** A jail or prison; cell (*1910+*) **4** A destroyer; TIN CAN (*1930s+ Navy*) **5** A hot rod (*1950s+ Hot rodders*) **6** An ounce of marijuana or other narcotic (*1930s+ Narcotics*) **7** A canvasback duck : *I know there are a lot of hunters here this weekend to try for cans* (*1990s+*) *v* **1** To discharge an employee; FIRE : *He is not the first commentator to be canned by an editor* (*1905+*) **2** To stop; cease, esp stop objectionable behavior • Usu a stern command : *Let's can the noise* (*1906+*) **3** : *They* *caught him and canned him for two weeks* **4** To score by throwing a basket : *Shaq canned another 20-footer (1980s+ Basketball)* See ASH CAN, GET A CAN ON, IN THE CAN, SHITCAN, TIE A CAN ON someone, TIN CAN

canary *n* **1** A girl or woman; chick *(1880s+)* **2** A woman singer, esp of popular music *(1919+)* **3** An informer; STOOL PIGEON • Because a *canary* sings *(1920s+ Underworld)* *v* : *She used to canary with Stan Kenton* See MOUNTAIN CANARY

can be See EASY AS PIE

cancer stick *n phr* A cigarette : *You'll find some cancer sticks hidden* [1950s+; The origin of the term coincides with the first national awareness of the relationship between cigarette smoking and lung *cancer*]

candied *adj* Addicted to cocaine • Fr *nose candy* : *Moss is candied*

candlelight *n* Dusk or dawn

can do *modifier* : *The CIA was a can-do outfit/ So far it's been mostly a can-do spring for the 24-year-old righthander* *sentence* I can do it; I'm the one you want • The noun phrase *can do*, "good and willing worker," is attested from the 1830s : *We asked them to design a whole new bridge in a week, and they said "Can do"* *(1900s+)* See NO CAN DO

candy *n* **1** Cocaine or hashish *(narcotics 1900+)* **2** A sugar cube soaked with LSD; LSD *(1960s+ Narcotics)* **3** Any barbiturate drug; drugs in general *(1960s+ Narcotics)* **4** Something easily done; BREEZE, CINCH, PIECE OF CAKE *(1940s+)* See NOSE CANDY

candy ass *n phr* A timid person; weakling; WIMP *(1960s+)*

candy-assed or **candyass** *adj* Timid; feeble; cowardly; wimpy : *not that candy-assed dreck played by legions of Spandexed clones/ Some candyass Barry Manilow type might be at ease in this setting (1950s+)*

candy man *n phr* A narcotics supplier; CONNECTION, PUSHER *(1960s+ Narcotics)*

candy store *n phr* **1** A place where wide-eyed dreams are or may be fulfilled : *The US market is the candy store for one and all* **2** Personal territory or property; TURF : *It's Aidid's candy store (1990s+)*

candy striper *n phr* A young woman who is a volunteer nurse's aide in a hospital [1960s+; fr the *stripes* on her uniform, resembling those on peppermint *candy*]

can live with that, I *sentence* That's acceptable; I'll buy that : *You want 10 percent? I can live with that (1980s+)*

canned *adj* **1** (also **canned up**) Drunk : *They was already pretty canned/ They got canned up a little more (1910+)* **2** Recorded; played from a phonograph record or magnetic tape

: *canned music (1900+)* **3** Not fresh for the occasion; kept for easy and general use : *The candidate uttered one or two canned one-liners, to small effect (1890s+)* **4** Filmed; completed • That is, put into one of the large flat circular tin *cans* used for holding movie film : *That scene is already canned (1950s+ Movie studios)*

cannibal *n* SIXTY-NINE *(1970s+)*

cannon *n* A pistol; firearm; PIECE : *He holstered his own cannon (1900+ Underworld)* See LOOSE CANNON

cannonball *n* **1** A fast express or freight train *(1915+ Hoboes)* **2** A message sent from one prisoner to another, or from a prisoner to friends outside *(1920+ Prison)*

cannon fodder *n phr* **1** Common soldiers, esp young and relatively untrained infantry soldiers; bullet bait **2** Any relatively low-ranking employee, associate, etc : *But I'm still cannon fodder when the crunch comes (1930s+)*

◁**canoe inspection**▷ *n phr* Examination of the vulva and vagina for evidence of venereal disease • The female equivalent of the *short-arm inspection (1960s+)*

can (or tall can) of corn *n phr* A high, easy fly ball *(1930s+ Baseball)*

can (or bag) of worms *n phr* A complex and troublesome matter; a Pandora's box : *Leave it alone, don't kick the crawly old can of worms/ the current bag of worms (1950s+)* See OPEN UP A CAN OF WORMS

canoodle or **kanoodle** *v* **1** To hug, caress, etc; make love **2** To coax, esp by lavishing affection [1850s+; origin uncertain; said to be Oxford University slang, "paddle a canoe," which might lead to amorous behavior and blandishment, as little as this seems likely in an unstable watercraft]

can really pick 'em, one, or one sure knows how to pick 'em *sentence* One is very selective, accurate, and successful in choices • Nearly always used ironically : *Is this turkey your idea of a good show? You can really pick 'em (1960s+)*

cans *n* ◁**1**▷ A woman's breasts; TITS : *that chanteuse with the huge cans (1950s+)* **2** Earphones worn over the ears *(1920s+)* [second sense perhaps fr the toy telephones made by punching a hole in the bottom of a tin *can* and connecting it to another such can by a string. When drawn taut, the string would carry the vibrations of a voice from one can and reproduce it in the other] See KNOCK someone FOR A LOOP

can-shaker *n* A fundraiser • Fr the passing of a coin can, as at movie theaters

can't buy *v phr* To have no possibility of; be totally denied : *From then on, I couldn't buy a* *good review/ You couldn't find a job. You couldn't buy a job (1960s+)*

can't fight city hall, you *See* YOU CAN'T FIGHT CITY HALL

can't fight (or punch) one's way out of a paper bag *v phr* To be a very weak or ineffective puncher; put up a poor showing *(1940s+ Prizefight)*

can't find his **ass with both hands**, he *sentence* (Variations : **butt** may replace **ass**; **hold** may replace **find**; **in his back pocket** may be added) He is very stupid indeed; he is hopelessly drunk : *So drunk he couldn't find his butt with both hands/ I'm a no-good scumbag who couldn't find his ass with both hands in his back pocket (1940s+)*

can't get over something *v phr* To be surprised and unable to recover from shock : *I can't get over how much weight she lost (1899+)*

can't get there from here, you *See* YOU CAN'T GET THERE FROM HERE

can't hit the side of a barn (or a barn door), someone *sentence* Someone is unable to throw accurately enough to hit anything at all *(1930s+)*

can't win for losing, someone *sentence* Someone seems entirely unable to make any sort of success; someone is persistently and distressingly bested : *We busted our humps, but we just couldn't win for losing (1970s+)*

Canuck *modifier* : *Canuck booze/ my Canuck pal* ● Regarded as offensive by some, but apparently becoming more acceptable *n* A Canadian, esp a French-Canadian *(1840s+)*

canvas, the *n phr* A boxing ring; the squared circle *(1910+)*

can you read lips *See* READ MY LIPS

cap[1] *n* **1** Captain **2** Mister; sir ● Used in direct address to a man one wishes to flatter *(1840s+)*

cap[2] *n* A capsule of narcotics : *I didn't have the money to buy a cap with (1920s+ Narcotics)* *v* **1** To buy narcotics; COP : *I capped me some more pot (1950s+ Narcotics)* **2** To open or use a capsule of narcotics; BUST A CAP *(1950s+ Narcotics)*

cap[3] *v* **1** To best or outdo, esp with a funnier joke, stranger story, etc; TOP : *She told a lie that capped mine (1940s+)* **2** To shoot; kill by shooting ● Compare *bust a cap* : *I should just cap you right now/ I think I'm going to cap myself today (1960s+)* **3** CAP ON someone *(1980s+ Teenagers)* [all in one way or another fr *cap*, "head covering"] *See* GIMME CAP

◁**cap**[4]▷ *n* Fellatio; HEAD : *Give Jerry some cap (1960s+)*

capeesh or **coppish** or **capiche** or **capish** (kə PEESH) *affirmation* I understand : *Ten tonight? Capeesh.* *question* Do you understand?

: *All right, class, that's all there is to it. Capeesh?/ I owe it all to you. Strip Dealers School, capiche?/ Sam fixed me with a pair of very cold eyes. "Capish?" he said* [1940s+; fr Italian *capisci*, "Do you understand?"]

caper *n* **1** A drunken spree; a carouse; BINGE *(1870s+)* **2** A prank; stunt *(1840s+)* **3** A crime, esp a robbery *(1920s+ Underworld)*

capital *n* Money; cash : *short of capital after the errands*

capo (KA poh, KAH-) *n* The head of a local unit of the Mafia; Mafia captain : *identified as Mafia capo by whatever's current crime commission* [fr Italian, "head, chief"]

capo di tutti capi (KAH poh dee TOOT ee KAH pee) *n phr* The chief of all chiefs; head of all the heads, HONCHO, MISTER BIG, TOP DOG : *The dissidents convened an extraordinary meeting of every capo di tutti baseball capi/ Salvatore (Toto) Riina, the capo di tutti capi of the Sicilian mob (1970s+)*

cap on someone *v phr* **1** To outdo someone; CAP, TOP **2** To insult someone; DIS, PUT someone DOWN *(1980s+)*

capper *n* **1** A huckster's or professional gambler's helper, who attracts clients; SHILL *(1750s+)* **2** The climax or end of something *(1940s+)* **3** A story, joke, etc, that outdoes another one *(1940s+)*

car *n* A group of prisoners from the same city or other place; locational clique : *All these kids were in the Sacramento car (1980s+ Prison) See* FUNNY CAR

carb *n* Carbohydrate; food mainly consisting of carbohydrates : *can't live without carbs*

car bra *n phr* A protective covering for the front of a car, often made of black plastic *(1980s+)*

carcass *n* A human body; one's body, esp if heavy : *set his carcass on the couch*

card *n* **1** A remarkable person, esp an eccentric or amusing one *(1830s+)* **2** A portion of a narcotic; DECK *(1920s+ Narcotics)* **3** A schedule; program of events : *six fights on the card (1930s+ Sports) v* To require someone to show identification, esp at a bar or liquor store : *So far my only success was not getting carded at the Wheaton Liquor Store (1970s+) See* GET one's CARD PUNCHED, IN THE CARDS, STACK THE DECK, WILD CARD

card-carrying *adj* Authentic; genuine and long-standing : *These women tend not to be card-carrying feminists/ a service for all us card-carrying optimists* [1960s+; fr the carrying of a membership *card* in an organization; first used of Communists during the 1950s period of political inquisition]

carded or **proofed** *adj* Checked to determine if one is of legal age for a purchase or participation : *carded at the liquor store/ got carded even though she is 50*

cardsharp (or **card shark**) *n phr* A very clever cardplayer, esp an unscrupulous poker or bridge player • Shortening of earlier *card sharper* (*1880s+*)

care and feeding *n phr* Solicitous care and nurturing, like that given an infant : *Sununu devoted himself to the care and feeding of a five-member Executive Council* (*1960s+*)

carebear *n* A cuddly, nice person : *carebears won't get into fights* [*1981+*; after American Greetings character]

care package *n phr* Gifts, money, etc, given to a relative or friend : *They try to help their son with occasional care packages* [*1980s+*; fr *CARE package*, a parcel of food, clothing, etc, sent to needy persons overseas through the Cooperative for American Relief Everywhere, in the aftermath of World War II]

carhop *n* A waitress or waiter who serves food to patrons in parked cars at a drive-in restaurant; curbie *v* : *She carhopped at Beef Babylon* [*1930s+*; formed on the model of *bellhop*]

carjacking *n* The armed and violent stealing of a car from its driver; GANKING : *At 15 he was arrested for carjacking and assault* [*1990s+*; fr *car* plus hi*jacking*]

carny or **carney** or **carnie** *modifier* : *carny talk/ a carney family* *n* 1 A carnival 2 A carnival worker or member of such a worker's family : *outdoor show people, the "carnies," who travel from town to town with carnivals* 3 The occupational idiom or jargon of carnival people : *I thought you talked carney by now* (*1930s+*)

carpet *See* CALL someone ON THE CARPET, ON THE CARPET, RED CARPET, ROLL OUT THE RED CARPET

carpetbag *v* To try to make a good impression (*1930s+* Students)

carpet-bomb *v* To mount a highly destructive and intense opposition; CLOBBER : *The Bush campaign carpet-bombed Dukakis from Labor Day onward* [*1980s+*; fr a 1950s term for total area bombing, laying as it were a *carpet* of *bombs*]

carpet-rat *See* RUG RAT

carrot-top *n* A redhead (*1880s+*)

carry *v* 1 To have narcotics on one's person (*1920s+* Narcotics) 2 To be armed (*1950s+* Underworld) [fr the 1920s phrase *carry iron*, "to be armed"]

carry a load *v phr* To be drunk (*1890s+*)

carry a lot of weight *v phr* To be important; have authority : *My opinions don't carry a lot of weight* (*1690s+*)

carry a tune in a bucket *See* someone CAN'T CARRY A TUNE IN A BUCKET

carrying *adj* 1 Armed, esp with a pistol : *He carrying, Mr Esteva* (*1950s+*) 2 Having narcotics on one's person (*1920s+* Narcotics) *See* CARD-CARRYING

carry the ball *v phr* To assume the active leading role : *While the boss is away, you must carry the ball* (*1940s+* Football)

carry the something chromosome *v phr* To have the characteristics indicated : *My husband, who knows I carry the restaurant chromosome, suggested that I get up on the steel catwalk that ran along one long wall to make a toast* [*1990s+*; fr the X and Y *chromosomes* that determine sexual and hence other characteristics]

carry the load (or **the ball**) *v phr* To do or be responsible for the major part of a job : *His wife carried the load in that family* (*1950s+*)

carry the torch *v phr* To love in a suffering way, esp because the desired one does not reciprocate : *She was carrying the torch for W C Fields* [*1927+*; origin unknown; said to have been coined by a Broadway nightclub singer named Tommy Lyman, when he said, "My famous torch song, 'Come to me, my melancholy baby'"; Venus, of course, carried a torch regularly]

carry someone's water *v phr* To do the menial jobs; be an underling, esp in politics : *I have carried the water for the Democratic Party for years/ The White House doesn't have to call. They have other people carrying their water for them* (*1980s+*)

car-surfing *n* Riding on the outside of a car : *He and a 12-year-old girl tried a round of "car-surfing"* (*1990s+*)

cart *v* To transport; move; take : *I carted him over to the drug store/ Jesse James could have waltzed in there and carted off all the patio furniture* (*1880s+*)

cartload *n* A large amount; lots; HEAPS, SHIT-LOAD : *Government documents tend (especially when there are cartloads of them) to induce a certain myopia* (*1570s+*)

carve *v* To give one a thrill; SEND : *He carves me. Does he carve you?* (*1930s+* Jive talk)

carved in stone, not *See* NOT CARVED IN STONE

◁**casabas**▷ *n* A woman's breasts [*1970s+*; fr *casaba*, a kind of melon, fr *Kassaba*, a Turkish town that exported them]

Casanova or **casanova** *n* A ladies' man and seducer; LOVER-BOY : *Do ravish me, you wicked casanova you* [*1880s+*; fr the name of Giacomo Girolamo *Casanova*, 1725–98, a writer and legendary debaucher]

case *n* 1 An odd, eccentric person; CARD, CHARACTER (*1833+*) 2 : *Lefty gave the bank a case* *v* (also **case out**) To inspect, scrutinize, esp with a view to robbery or burglary • *Keep the cases* in the sense "keep close watch" is attested fr 1856, with reference to faro : *I've cased this one and it's ripe* (*1914+* Underworld) *See* COUCH CASE, GET OFF someone's CASE, GET ON someone's CASE, HAVE A CASE OF

THE DUMB-ASS, HAVE A CASE ON someone, HEAD-CASE, MAKE A FEDERAL CASE OUT OF something, NUTBALL, OFF someone's CASE, ON someone's CASE, WORST-CASE SCENARIO

case the joint *v phr* To look at how to break into a place, mainly to find something to steal; also, to check out a location : *I thought the real estate agent brought people who were casing the joint/ cased the joint for possible future parties*

cash *See* COLD CASH

cash cow *n phr* A source of money, esp a generous one : *But all this leaves The New Republic Inc without a cash cow/ For a fairly blatant cash cow, Pisces Iscariot delivers some fine milk (1970s+)*

cashed *adj* **1** Expired or depleted : *my supply is cashed* **2** Burnt out; tired : *cashed and going home*

cash flow *n* Available money; cash : *what's your cash flow tonight*

cash-for-trash *modifier* Sordid, and told only for payment : *The White House is not going to comment on any cash-for-trash stories (1990s+)*

cash in one's chips *v phr* **1** (also **cash it in**) To die; KICK THE BUCKET *(1870s+)* **2** To withdraw from some arrangement, esp a business deal *(1890s+)* [fr the redeeming of gambling chips for money, signifying the end of the game]

cash in on something *v phr* To get profit or advantage from something, esp from something unexpected *(1920s+)*

cast *n* Interpretation; opinion; SPIN, TAKE • In the sense of a personal turn or inclination of mind, *cast* is attested by 1711 : *He has his own cast on this (1990s+)*

cast a kitten *See* HAVE KITTENS

cast in concrete, not *See* NOT CARVED IN STONE

casting couch *n phr* The fancied sofa in a theatrical or film decision-maker's office upon which he appraises the talent of young women seeking roles : *only slightly detoured by a refusal to join Darryl F Zanuck on the casting couch (1920s+)*

cast-iron balls *See* HAVE BRASS BALLS

cat[1] *n* **1** A hobo or a migrant worker *(1890s+ Hoboes)* **2** A prostitute *(1535+)* ◁3▷ The vulva; PUSSY *(1730s+)* **4** A woman who, often subtly, attacks and denigrates other women; a spiteful and malicious woman : *Dorothy Parker was a super cat (1760s+)* **5** A man who dresses flashily and ostentatiously pursues worldly pleasure; DUDE, HEPCAT, SPORT : *I was a sharp cat/ The cool chick down on Calumet has got herself a brand new cat (1950s+ Black & teenagers)* **6** A jazz musician : *It was all right to the early cats (1920s+ Jazz musicians)* **7** HIPSTER *(1960s+)* **8** Any

man; fellow; GUY : *Who's that cat sitting next to the Pope? (1940s+)* **9** A sailboat with one fore-and-aft sail; a catboat : *He sails a little cat (1880s+)* **10** Metcathenone, an addictive synthetic narcotic similar to but more powerful than cocaine : *For a few hundred dollars, dealers can produce thousands of dollars' worth of cat (1990s+)* *v* **1** (also **cat around**) To spend time with women for amatory purposes; chase and stalk women; TOMCAT *(1725+)* **2** To move stealthily : *began to cat toward the door (1960s+ Black)* **3** To loaf and idle; spend one's time on street corners admiring young women *(1920s+)* [black sense, "dude," may be influenced by a Wolof term] *See* ALLEY CAT, FAT CAT, FRAIDY CAT, HELLCAT, HEPCAT, HIP CAT, LET THE CAT OUT OF THE BAG

cat[2] or **Cat** *n* A bulldozer or Caterpillar tractor [1940s+; fr *Caterpillar,* trademark for a kind of continuous-track tractor]

cat[3] *n* A catamaran boat *(1960s+)*

catbird seat *n phr* An enviable position; a controlling position : *The owners are in the catbird seat (1930s+) See* SIT IN THE CATBIRD SEAT

catch *n* **1** A highly desirable acquisition or engagement : *Getting Von Karajan for our benefit would be a catch (1740s+)* **2** A hidden cost, qualification, defect, etc; something to make one think twice : *It looks like all gravy, but there's a catch to it (1855+) v* **1** To see, hear, or attend a particular entertainment : *I caught Mickey Rooney on TV (1906+)* **2** CATCH ON *(1880s+)* **3** To do desk duty, answering the telephone and receiving complaints : *Thompson was catching in the squad room at Manhattan South (1950s+ Police)* **4** To be penetrated in an anal sex act *(1970s+ Homosexual) See* SHOESTRING CATCH

catch someone **somewhere, doing** something, etc *sentence* You will never discover this person in the situation or activity named • A vigorous denial with nearly interjectional force : *Catch Eddie allowing himself to be dated like that!/ Catch me in a tux! (1830+)*

catch-as-catch-can *modifier* Precarious; requiring keen readiness : *We lived a catch-as-catch-can life those first few years (1880s+)*

catch one's death *v phr* To get very cold, esp due to not dressing properly : *come in or you'll catch your death*

catch fire *v phr* To become markedly successful; CATCH ON : *It was a good idea, but it never really caught fire (1980s+)*

catch someone **flat-footed** (or **on their heels**) *v phr* To surprise someone; catch someone unprepared : *When the market crashed they were caught flat-footed/ Milwaukee was caught on its heels as Doran added his second goal* [1940s+; fr baseball, referring esp to a base runner who is caught off-base and thrown out]

catch flies *v phr* **1** To distract the audience's attention from another performer by making unnecessary gestures and motions *(1940s+ Theater)* **2** To gape and yawn, esp from boredom *(1940s+)*

catch hell (Variations : **holy hell** or **merry hell** may replace **hell**) *v phr* **1** To be severely rebuked or punished **2** To be severely damaged or injured : *The dock caught holy hell in that last approach (1920s+)*

catch it *v phr* To be very severely rebuked or punished : *Uh-oh! This time we'll catch it!* *(1835+)* See GET IT IN THE NECK

catch on *v phr* **1** To see and understand, esp with insightful suddenness; grasp; DIG, GET : *As long as they don't catch on, we can cheat them forever (1880s+)* **2** To be accepted and approved; succeed with the public : *The wing-dancing and funny acts catch on big (1880s+)*

catch some rays *v phr* To sunbathe : *The prince seized the opportunity to leave his chilly isle behind and catch some rays (1980s+)*

catch some z's *v phr* To get some sleep • Fr *z* as the sound of snoring : *catch some z's on the train*

catch the wave *v phr* To seize an opportunity; take advantage of present trends : *Television is the central fact of political life : deal with it or die—catch the wave* [1990s+; fr surfing, with a possible echo of Hamlet : "There is a tide in the affairs of men/ Which, taken at the flood, leads on to fortune"]

catch–22 or **Catch–22** *modifier* : *puts me in a Catch–22 fix* **n** A condition or requirement very hard to fulfill, esp one which flatly contradicts others : *It was a classic catch–22. The problem was that it was a top-secret project they weren't supposed to know about* [1960s+; fr the title of a 1961 satirical novel by Joseph Heller]

catch-up See PLAY CATCH-UP

catch someone with someone's hand in the till (or the cookie jar) See WITH one's HAND IN THE TILL

catch someone with their pants down *v phr* To find someone in the wrong with no possibility of evasion; catch someone in flagrante delicto : *Every time someone catches us with our pants down, catches us in an outright lie, up pops Ron to admit it/ The insensitive, bumbling male senators caught with their political pants down suggested a watershed in American politics (1920s+)*

catchy *adj* Seizing attention or admiration; attractive : *You need a really catchy logo (1830s+)*

Catch you later *sentence* I will see you or talk to you later : *catch you later, alligator*

catch you on the flip side *sentence* I will see you or talk to you later or tomorrow

catch Zs See COP ZS

cat fight *n phr* A particularly noisy and vicious struggle or squabble : *to judge from the cat fight that erupted among members of the advisory council (1970s+)*

Catholic See IS THE POPE POLISH

catholic bagel *n* A nontraditional bagel, esp flavored : *ok, black pepper and cheese catholic bagels*

cathouse *n* **1** A cheap lodging house; FLOP-HOUSE *(1915+ Hoboes)* **2** A brothel : *New Orleans was proud and ashamed of its cathouses (1890s+)* [second sense fr earlier *cat*, "prostitute, vulva"]

catnap *n* A short doze while sitting up : *The Senator was enjoying a cat-nap at the time* [1850s+; Attested in form *cat's nap* by 1823]

cats and dogs *n phr* Low-priced stocks, such as those returning no dividends at all *(1870s+ Stock market)* See RAIN CATS AND DOGS

cat's meow, the *n phr* (Variations : **ass** or **balls** or **eyebrows** or **nuts** or **pajamas** or **whiskers** may replace **meow**; the phrase may be shortened to **the cat's**) Something or someone that is superlative : *The cat's pajamas!—anything that is very good/ that you are on top of things and that you are, therefore, the cat's ass* [1920+; the entry form and *pajamas* form are said to have been coined by the cartoonist and sports writer Tad Dorgan, who died in 1929]

catsuit *n* A tight-fitting garment covering the entire body : *Michelle is wearing a skintight black catsuit and short high-heeled boots* [1990s+; Perhaps suggested by the seeming-epidermal garb of a character named *Catwoman*, played by Julie Newmar in the 1970s televison show *Batman*, and by characters in the show *Cats*]

cattle call *modifier* : *Nonprofessionals may vie for spaces in "cattle-call" auditions* **n phr** An audition announcement, esp for a number of extras; also the crowd resulting from such an announcement : *Mr Allen is having what is known in show business as a cattle call/ I can't speak for the other agencies, but we've just about done away with the cattle call (1950s+ Show business)*

cattle show *n phr* A convention or other occasion where political candidates display their notions, charisma, etc : *raise money for themselves by holding "cattle shows" (1970s+)*

catty *adj* Inclined to discredit others; malicious; spitefully gossipy : *Karla and Susan were being catty about Dusty* [late 1800s+; but *cat*, "spiteful woman," is attested from the 1760s]

catty-cat *See* CAT[1]

caught dead, be *See* NOT BE CAUGHT DEAD

caught in a rundown *adj phr* In an embarrassing and untenable plight : *The imperilled Cuomo seemed to be constantly in motion. Sometimes he moved so desperately that he seemed to be caught in a rundown—a reminder that he had briefly been a center fielder with a Pittsburgh Pirates farm team (1970s+ fr baseball)*

caught looking *adj phr* Called out on strikes from not swinging *(1970s+ Baseball)*

cauliflower ear *n phr* A boxer's or wrestler's ear deformed by injuries and accumulated scar tissue *(1900s+)*

cavalry *n* Last-minute rescue forces; a deus ex machina : *Powell likened the Somalia operation to "the cavalry coming to the rescue"/ not the time for a President who avoided the draft to call up the cavalry/ Democrats hear hoofbeats—the cavalry's arrival, in the nick of time* [1980s+; fr the numerous cases in cowboy movies when the US Cavalry would arrive to rescue various beleaguered persons]

cave *n* A room; PAD *(1930s+)* *v* (also **cave in**) To surrender; give way; CHICKEN OUT : *The Russians will cave when they find we are in earnest/ OK, so I caved in on the white suger, the TV, the war toys (entry form 1850s+, variant 1830+)*

cazh *adj* Casual : *don't dress up; it is cazh*

ceiling *n* An upper limit : *The Gov put a two-billion-dollar ceiling on office expenses* [1930s+; probably fr *ceiling*, "the highest an airplane can go," which is attested from 1917] *See* HIT THE CEILING

cel *n* A celluloid sheet made for an animated cartoon, now prized by collectors : *Cartoon lovers have been buying drawings and celluloids, or "cels" (1990s+)*

celeb (sə LEB) *n* A celebrity : *each a certified celeb from the realms of cafe, style, or theatrical society/ surrounded by giggling celebs (1913+)*

cellar, the *n phr* The lowest standing in a sports league, esp in a baseball league : *struggling not to finish in the cellar (1900s+)*

cellar-dwellers *n* The team in last place in a sports league *(1970s+)*

cement *See* IN CEMENT

cementhead *n* **1** A stupid person; dolt; BOOB, dufus, spazz *(1980s+)* **2** A player known more for his combative than athletic skills; GOON : *That cementhead gave him a lumber facial, but the ref didn't call it (1990s+ Hockey)*

cement overcoat (or **kimono**) *n phr* A casing of cement containing a corpse for disposal in deep water *(1940s+)*

cent *See* a RED CENT

center *See* DEAD CENTER, FRONT AND CENTER

centerfold *n* A sexually desirable person : *a woman with a centerfold's chest going for her* [1960s+; fr the photographs of such persons decorating the *centerfolds* of erotic magazines]

center stage *n phr* The place of maximum visibility; forefront : *When women's issues were brought to center stage, the Democrats caved (1990s+ fr theater)*

central *n* The most important site of what is indicated : *Israel claims U.S. is Terror Central/ quickly turned the Odessa into Mob Central/ This is a small town, but if it's cocaine central then it's a pretty tough town (1990s+)*

Central Casting *n phr* The putative office whence ideal and stereotypical persons, products, recipes, etc, come : *He is a white, male, married Protestant, middle to upper class, with children and dogs. He comes straight out of Central Casting/ This is salsa from Central Casting* [1980s+; fr the Hollywood office that provides actors for film producers]

cents *See* PUT one's TWO CENTS IN

century *n* A hundred dollars : *For two centuries a week I had me a bodyguard (1850s+)*

certifiable *adj* So deranged as to be officially certified insane : *her comments suggest she's certifiable (1939+)*

chain *See* BALL-AND-CHAIN, DAISY CHAIN, PULL someone's CHAIN

chain gang *n phr* The football officials who carry and set the chain that marks off the ten yards needed for a first down *(1980s+)*

chain-smoke *v* To smoke cigarette after cigarette, lighting the next one from the current one *(1900s+)*

chair, the *n* **1** The electric chair; the HOT SEAT **2** Death by legal electrocution : *They convicted him, and he got the chair (1895+)*

chair-warmer *n* An untalented and dispensable person; WARM BODY *(1909+)*

chalk *n* A horse favored to win [1950s+ Horse racing; References to winning by *a long chalk*, an allusion to scoring points by a chalk mark, date from the 1830s]

chalk-eater or **chalk-player** *n* A person who bets only on the horse favored to win *(1950s+ Horse racing)*

chalk-talk *n* A lecture, lesson, etc, accompanied by sketches : *The coach gave us a chalk-talk about the blitz (1880s+)*

chalk something up *v phr* To record credit or debit, as if by a chalk mark : *She won easily, and we must chalk it up to her careful preparation (late-1500s+)*

champ at the bit *v phr* To be eager or enthusiastic : *champing at the bit to run the race (mid-1600s+)*

chance *See* OUTSIDE CHANCE, a SNOWBALL'S CHANCE IN HELL

change *n* Money : *a sizable chunk of change (1880s+) See* LOOSE CHANGE, PIECE OF CHANGE, SMALL POTATOES

change, and *n phr* A small additional amount : *The book value of the Thunderbird was $3,900 and change/ At an hour and change before midnight there was still a line of people waiting to get into the Opera Cafe/ An average sentence is 27 words and change (1980s+)*

change hats *v phr* To change one's affiliations, role, etc : *changed hats and supported Maggie Thatcher (1990s+)*

change the channel *v phr* To shift the topic of conversation *(1950s+ Teenagers)*

change-up *n* **1** A slow pitch delivered after a motion that might precede a fast pitch; a change of pace *(1950s+ Baseball)* **2** Any change, esp a pronounced one : *McDowell exhibits a first-rate change-up/ Four costume changes served as a change-up in the manic pace (1970s+)* *v* : *Holy cow! He changed him up for a strike! (1950s+ Baseball)*

channel *n* A vein, usu in the crook of the elbow or the instep, favored for the injection of narcotics; MAIN LINE *(1950s+ Narcotics)* *v* **1** To lower the body of a car by opening channels around parts of the frame : *Johnny Slash, the punk in wraparound shades, lusts for a chopped and channeled '49 Merc (1950s+ Hot rodders)* **2** To be a medium of communication for a unbodied spirit : *Just some guy she channels for. Don't worry, the viewers love him (1980s+)*

channel surf *v phr* To shift rapidly from one television channel to another : *people who channel surf, using a remote control* [1990s+; *Channel-hop,* in the same sense, is attested from 1971, but did not thrive]

channel surfer *n phr* A person who channel surfs; GRAZER, TRAWLER *(1990s+)*

chap or **chappie** *n* A man; fellow; GUY, JOE • Pre-dominantly British use : *Which of you chaps is ready?/ This may amuse the chappies* [1700s+; fr a shortening of *chapman,* "peddler; peddler's customer," hence analogous with *customer* in the same sense]

chapped *adj* Angry; PISSED OFF *(1960s+)*

chaps *See* CHOPS

chapter *n* **1** A division of a sports contest, esp an inning of baseball; canto **2** An episode, period, or passage : *Please don't remind me of that revoltingly squalid chapter in my life (1940s+)*

chapter and verse *adv phr* : *He knew it chapter and verse* *n phr* **1** An exact detailed account : *I can give you chapter and verse about that night* **2** The guiding documents or principles; rules : *I know the chapter and verse of the university's policy (1700s+)*

character *n* **1** A person who behaves oddly and often amusingly; an eccentric : *My uncle's quite a character (1770s+)* **2** A person; JOKER : *You know a character name of Robert Ready? (1920s+)*

charge *n* **1** An injection of a narcotic *(1920s+ Narcotics)* **2** (also **large charge**) An acute thrill of pleasure; BLAST, KICK, RUSH : *What kind of ol' creep'd get a charge out of this stuff? (1930s+ Jazz musicians)* **3** Marijuana *(1950s+ Narcotics)* *v* To rob *(1930s+ Underworld) See* GET A BANG OUT OF someone or something

charged up *adj phr* **1** Intoxicated by a narcotic; HIGH *(1920s+ Narcotics)* **2** In a state of excited preparedness and heightened keenness; PUMPED UP : *They lost, the coach declared, because they were not charged up*

charity stripe (or **line**) *n phr* The free-throw line : *The Hawks knew the game would be decided at the charity stripe (1930s+ Basketball)*

charity toss *n phr* A free throw *(1940s+ Basketball)*

Charley *n* CHARLEY HORSE

charley (or **Charley**) **horse** *n phr* A stiff and painful inflammation of a muscle, esp of the large thigh muscle *(1887+)*

Charlie *n* The Vietcong or a Vietcong soldier [Vietnam War armed forces; fr Victor *Charlie,* military voice alphabet designation for VC]

chart *n* **1** Figures and other material showing past performance, esp of a race horse; form, TRACK RECORD *(1940s+ Horse racing)* **2** A musical arrangement or score *(1950s+ Cool musicians)*

charts, the *n phr* The listings that show the popularity of a song, a record, etc : *Stevie's latest single is way, way up on the charts (1960s+) See* OFF THE CHARTS

chase *v* To take a usually milder drink after a drink of liquor : *Let's chase this with a little Perrier (1906+) See* PAPER CHASE

chase one's own tail *v phr* To go on frantic and futile pursuits : *It's been fun watching the press chase its own tail on the persistent rumors of his extramarital escapades (1960s+)*

chaser *n* **1** A drink, often water, taken immediately after a drink of liquor *(1897+)* **2** A man in amatory pursuit of women; SKIRT-CHASER : *Mark always was a lady-killer, a chaser (1894+)* **3** An employee assigned to hurry others in their work *(1920s+ Truckers)* **4** An exit march; music played as the audience is leaving; recessional *(1930s+ Show business)* **5** A guard *(1960s+ Prison) See* AMBULANCE CHASER, FLY-CHASER, WOMAN-CHASER

chassis *n* The human physique, esp the body of a well-built woman; BUILD *(1920s+) See* CLASSY CHASSIS

chat *n* The capability of exchanging personal messages on a computer network : *As you* *play, you can exchange typed messages—that's a feature called "chat" in computer lingo—with other players (1980+ Computer)*

chat up *v phr* To charm and seduce with talk : *You hear Elvis laughing, chatting up the crowd/ while Dartmouth seniors, a little tight, chatted up Smithies* (1960s+)

chauvinist pig *See* MALE CHAUVINIST PIG

chaw-head *n* A person who chews tobacco or something else habitually : *I used to watch baseball; then I witnessed one too many newsclips of brawling, drunken chaw-heads* (1990s+)

cheap *adj* **1** Stingy; overly frugal; CHINTZY : *Cheap old bastard won't give you the time of day* (1827+) **2** Reputedly easy of sexual conquest; roundheeled : *a cheap tramp with a heart of gold* (1950s+) *See* DIRT CHEAP, ON THE CHEAP

cheap date (or **drunk**) *n phr* A person who needs very few drinks to become intoxicated : *All it took was one small sherry; she's such a cheap date* (1940s+)

cheapie or **cheapo** *modifier* : *cheapie ripoffs of The Godfather/ Our Tenth Annual Cheapo Guide n* Any cheaply made or cheaply sold item : *No ticket in town is a cheapie these days/ retreads, ethnic shoes, and Woolworth cheapos/ Wood made this fairly ordinary cheapie a mere year after* Glenn or Glenda *(first form 1898+, second 1950s+) See* EL CHEAPO

cheap is cheap *sentence* You get what you pay for : *In culture as in commerce, cheap is cheap*

◁**cheapshit**▷ *adj* Inexpensive and inferior : *ten million pair of cheapshit jeans without any labels on them* (1970s+)

cheap shot *modifier* : *some dirtymouth comedian who made cheap-shot race jokes n phr* (also **shot**) A malicious insult or action; something crude, underhanded, and damaging : *Well, the race for governor isn't a festival of cheap shots/ Keenan shouted, "Didn't you just take what is known as a cheap shot?" v phr* : *He'd say "Hey, don't cheap shot my son"/ If a person's going to cheapshot me, it just shows how low he is* (1960s+ Sports)

cheap-shot artist or **cheap-shotter** *n* A person who takes cheap shots : *Immigrant bashing is a handy charge for cheap-shotters and fearmongers (first form 1960s+, second 1970s+)*

cheapskate *n* A nasty stingy person; TIGHTWAD : *and cheapskate Goodman's not going for a renewal* (1896+)

cheat *v* To be sexually unfaithful; GET A LITTLE ON THE SIDE (1930s+)

cheaters *n* **1** Spectacles • Attributed to the cartoonist and sports writer Tad Dorgan, who died in 1929 (1920+) **2** Marked playing cards (1940s+)

cheat sheet *n phr* **1** A paper used to replace or reinforce one's memory; CRIB : *his notes and*

data on enemy hitters, which he consults in preparing game notes—a cheat sheet/ During cooking demonstrations, a paper cheat sheet sits nearby on the counter (1950s+ Students) **2** swindle sheet

check *interj* An expression of understanding, approval, etc : *I'll say check to that!/ It's time to leave? Check!* (1922+) *n* A small quantity of a drug (1950s+ Narcotics) *v* **1** (also **check that**) To cancel; introduce a correction : *He made eight yards; check that, six yards* (1950s+ Sports broadcasting) **2** To look at; pay attention to; CHECK OUT : *Check the guy at the end of the counter* (late 1700s+) *See* GIVE someone A BLANK CHECK, PICK UP THE TAB, RAIN CHECK, RUBBER CHECK, TAKE A RAIN CHECK

checkers *See* PLAY CHECKERS

check in *v phr* **1** To die; CHECK OUT (1912+) **2** To indicate one's arrival at a hotel, motel, etc (1918+)

check it *v phr* To leave; BUG OFF, SPLIT • Usu an irritated command (1990s+ Teenagers)

check minus *n* A mark indicating that one completed an effort, but it was wanting : *He got a check minus on his math homework*

check out *modifier* **1** : *a check-out counter/ check-out person* **2** : *When's check-out time tomorrow? n* : *express check-out/ slow sloppy check-out v phr* **1** To look closely at, esp for evaluation; scrutinize; GIVE someone or something THE ONCE-OVER : *For this style of music, if you prefer twang to snarl, check it out live at the Rodeo Bar* (1960s+) **2** To prove valid; be accurate : *Your story checks out* (1940s+) **3** To examine and approve one's competence : *I'm checked out on that machine* (1940s+) **4** To add up purchases and collect money at a supermarket or similar store : *I'll check you out over here* (1960s+) **5** To pay for one's purchases at a supermarket or similar store : *It took me an hour to check out of that place* (1960s+) **6** To pay one's bill and leave a hotel or motel : *When did Almendorfer check out of this fleabag?* (1920s+) **7** To leave; depart; BOOGIE, BOOK, SPLIT : *Let's check out of this joint and find a livelier one* (1920s+) **8** To die : *She checked out before they reached the hospital* (1920s+)

check that *v phr* Ignore that last remark; never mind : *Salt and pepper. Check that*

check your six *v phr* Look behind you [Fr the aviation term "your six o'clock," referring to the relative location of an aircraft with 12 o'clock being directly in front of the airplane]

cheddar or **chedda** *n* Cash; ready money : *out of chedda*

cheeba or **chiba** or **chiba chiba** *n* Marijuana (1970s+ Narcotics)

cheek *n* **1** Impudence; audacity; BRASS, CHUTZPA : *She had the infernal cheek to stick out her* *tongue at me (1840+)* **2** A buttock; BUN : *I took the injection in the left cheek (1600+)* [first sense apparently related to *jaw*, suggesting insolent speech]

cheeky *adj* Impudent; impertinent; rude *(1850s+)*

cheer *See* BRONX CHEER

cheerio or **cheery-bye** *interj* Good-bye • Used as a conscious amusing Briticism : *Cheerio, pip-pip, and all that! (1910+)*

cheers *interj* A salute or toast on taking a drink : *Cheers and bottoms up, one and all! (1919+ British)*

cheese *n* **1** Nonsense; lies; exaggerations; BALONEY : *What a line of cheese (1950s+)* **2** A fastball *(1980s+ Baseball)* **3** Vomit : *There was cheese all over the floor in the subway station* **4** Something out of date, often something so appallingly out of date that it has a certain chic appeal; CAMP, CORN : *That brown dress you're wearing is total cheese/ Lime-green shag carpeting is Cheese. Wide-bodied neckties are Cheese (1980s+ Students)* **5** Money; CHEDDAR *v* **1** CHEESE IT **2** (also **cut the cheese**) To flatulate; FART *(1970s+)* **3** To vomit; BARF *(1970s+)* **4** To make someone look outlandish; make cheesy : *A lot of actresses want to preserve the integrity of their characters, but I said "Cheese me up! Go ahead" (1990s+) See* BIG CHEESE, HARD CHEESE

cheese, the *n phr* A superior person or thing : *She's the real cheese* [1818+; perhaps fr Anglo-Indian slang *chiz* fr Hindi fr Persian, "the thing"]

cheeseball *modifier* Stupid; inferior; CHEESY : *One theater near city hall played the kind of cheeseball samurai movies that never quite made it to the more respectable Japanese theaters* • Sometimes as noun *(1980s+)*

cheesecake *modifier* : *unless one perceives in cheesecake photographs illicit and limitless pleasures n* **1** Photographs and photography of women in clothing and poses that emphasize their sexuality : *a magazine full of cheesecake (1930s+)* **2** A woman's legs, breasts, hips, etc : *standing on the corner scoping out the cheesecake (1940s+)* [apparently fr the appreciative comments of one or another New York City newspaper photographer at the ocean-liner docks who posed women so that their legs were featured, and pronounced the pictures to be "better than *cheesecake*"]

cheesed off *adj phr* Bored; disgusted : *if superbored, you're "cheesed off" (WWII Air Forces fr British Armed forces)*

cheese eater (or **bun**) *n phr* (also **cheese eater, cheesy rider**) An informer or other despicable person; RAT *(1940s+)*

cheesehead *n* **1** A stupid person : *You let this cheesehead insult me? (1920+)* **2** A native or

resident of Wisconsin : *He knows how much one of these jets costs the average Wisconsin taxpayer. Why should he upset us cheeseheads needlessly? (1980s+)*

cheese it *interj* An exclamation of alarm and warning uttered when properly constituted authorities are approaching : *Cheese it, Muggsy, the cops! v phr* To leave; depart; SCRAM *(1811+ Underworld)*

cheese whiz (also **cheez whiz**) *modifier* Out of date; CHEESY : *Her shoes were total cheez whiz* ◁*n phr*▷ An unattractive girl; DOG, TWO-BAGGER [1980s+ Students; fr the trademark name of a kind of soft cheese spread]

cheesing *adj* Smiling • Fr saying "cheese" : *cheesing for the camera*

cheesy *adj* **1** Lacking in taste; vulgarly unesthetic : *an altogether hideous room, expensive but cheesy/ The acting was so cheesy. It was like porn acting (1950s+)* **2** Of inferior workmanship; shoddy : *This is accomplished through some really cheesy special effects (1896+)* **3** Shabby; ugly : *"I thought that was kind of cheesy,"* Harding said *(1896+)* **4** Not real or genuine; false; fake. PHONY *(1970s+)* **5** (also **cheese dog**) Out of date, often so appallingly so that it has a certain chic appeal; CAMPY, CORNY : *The runway stuff? Cheese dog./ I included the big hair to cause a little friction. They both almost unanimously referred to it as "cheesy"/ And the Cheesy Award goes to Tony Bennett (1980s+ Students)*

chemical blonde *n phr* (also **bleached blonde, peroxide blonde, bottle blonde**) A blonde whose hair is given its colors by a bleach or another compound : *That's why both the chemical blonde and the pony-tailed pugilist made my stomach perform a nauseous little flip (1990s+)*

chemistry *n* Feelings between persons; attractions and repulsions, but mainly attractions : *Miss McElderry feels the unusual chemistry between her and Mr Pfeiffer has been beneficial/ He also struck up what one aide calls "instant chemistry" with US Secretary of State George Shultz*

cherries *n* The flashing lights atop a police car or other emergency vehicle; gumball, PARTY HAT *(1980s+)*

cherry *adj* ◁1▷ Virgin; sexually uninitiated : *She confessed she was cherry* **2** In an unproved or maiden state of any sort : *He hasn't published anything yet; still cherry modifier* In mint condition; pristine : *Mint is what I'm saying. Cherry/ including cherry restorations of Belairs and Fairlanes from the Fifties (1950s+ Hot rodders) n* ◁1▷ A virgin, of either sex *(1935+)* ◁2▷ Virginity : *Does he still have his cherry? (1928+)* ◁3▷ The hymen **4** An inexperienced soldier sent to the front lines

as a replacement : *A Cherry who survived long
enough earned the right to harass the next
rookie (Army)* [sexual senses fr the fancied
resemblance between the hymen and a
cherry] *See* COP A CHERRY, HAVE one's CHERRY,
POP someone's CHERRY

cherry-pick *v* To select the best and most
profitable elements; PICK AND CHOOSE : *When a
bank fails, a healthy competitor often buys it
and cherry-picks the safest and most profitable
loans/ Small insurance companies survive by
cherry-picking their clients (1990s+)*

cherry-picker *n* ◁1▷ A man who especially
prizes the sex act with young girls *(1950s+)*
2 A switch operator *(1940s+ Railroad)* **3** An
articulated crane with a bucketlike platform
: *a guy in a cherry-picker fixing the phone lines
(1940s+)*

cherry-picking *n* The selection of only what is
most helpful to one's case : *The Justice Department report on the Waco raid was cherry-
picking (1990s+)*

cherry pie *n phr* **1** Something easily done or
gotten; PIECE OF CAKE **2** Money easily obtained
(Circus) (1950s+)

chest *See* PLAY CLOSE TO THE CHEST

chestnut *n* A trite old story, joke, song, etc
[1816+; probably fr a play, *The Broken Sword*,
in which one character tells a story 27 times,
naming a *chestnut* tree, then abruptly changes
it to a cork tree, whereupon another character recalls the repetition of *chestnut*, and the
first says, "Well, a chestnut be it then"]

chesty *adj* **1** Having large breasts; bosomy :
*watching two chesty girls in tube tops
(1950s+)* **2** Prone to boast about one's virility, boldness, etc : *When you have money in
the bank it will be time enough to get chesty
(1899+)*

chev *See* SHIV

chevy *See* CHIVVY

Chevy or **Chev** (SHEH vee, SHEHV) *n* A
Chevrolet car *(1930+)*

chew *n* : *He had big chew in his cheek (1920s+)*
v **1** To chew tobacco *(1930s+)* **2** To eat
(1890+) **3** (also **chew over**) To talk; converse; discuss; JAW : *We got together to chew
about the election/ Drop up and chew it over
(1890s+)*

◁**chew** someone's **ass** (or **ass out**)▷ *v phr*
CHEW someone OUT *(WWII armed forces)*

chew someone's **ear off** *v phr* To talk overlong
and tediously to someone : *I just wanted the
time, not to get my ear chewed off (1919+)*

chewed up *adj phr* **1** Badly damaged or worn :
The transmission's all chewed up (1930s+) **2**
chewed *(1940s+ Black)*

chew gum at the same time *See* NOT HAVE
BRAINS ENOUGH TO WALK AND CHEW GUM AT THE
SAME TIME

chew light bulbs *v phr* To do something extremely painful and nasty : *Would you rather
chew light bulbs than go shopping for jeans?*
(1990s+)

chew nails *v phr* To be very angry; be livid :
*We'd better get out before he starts chewing
nails (1970s+)*

chew someone **out** (or **up**) *v phr* To reprimand severely; rebuke harshly; EAT someone
OUT, REAM : *He got chewed out for it more than
once by the platoon sergeant (WWII armed
forces)*

chew the fat (or **the rag**) *v phr* To converse,
esp in a relaxed and reminiscent way • In
earlier senses the terms meant "to complain;
wrangle" : *You want a press conference, or do
you want to chew the fat? (1900s+)*

chew someone **up and spit them out** *v phr*
To demolish someone; treat someone very
harshly *(1920+)*

chew up the scenery *v phr* To overact; HAM :
*Beery and Lionel Barrymore chew up all the
scenery that isn't nailed down/ Neeson doesn't
chew up the scenery when he works* [1930s+
Show business; originally fr a 1930 theater
review by Dorothy Parker : "More glutton
than artist, he commences to *chew up the
scenery*"; in an 1881 glossary a loud actor is
said to "eat scenes," which may or may not
be related]

chewy *adj* **1** Substantial and desirable; rich :
*Hepburn may have a less chewy part than has
Fonda/ "chewy wordplay" on Elvis Costello's
new LP* **2** Needing thought and discussion;
challenging; tricky : *The hegemony of CNN
raises lots of chewy questions (1920s+)*

Chi(town) *n* Chicago : *love visiting Chitown See*
CHI

chib *See* SHIV

chiba *See* CHEEBA

Chicago overcoat *n phr* A coffin : *A Chicago
overcoat is what blasting would get you
(1920s+)*

chichi (SHEE SHEE, CHEE CHEE) *adj* : *Fifth and
57th is no longer so chi-chi n* Something frilly,
fancy, precious, and overdecorated : *Another
bit of chichi that has come to our notice lately is
Eleanor Roosevelt's letterhead/ So much chichi.
The pretty glass people* [1940+; fr French fr
chic]

chicken *adj* **1** : *He seems like a chicken guy* **2**
CHICKEN-SHIT *modifier* : *had I written extensively about the mechanics of chicken sex n* **1**
chick *(1711+)* **2** An adolescent boy regarded as a sexual object for an adult
homosexual; catamite; PUNK *(1940s+
Homosexuals)* **3** A coward; an overly timid
person; SISSY : *Don't be a chicken; dive right in
(1707+)* **4** A trial of valor in which two
persons drive cars at each other down the

middle of a road, the first to swerve aside being designated "chicken" *(1950s+ Hot rodders)* **5** The eagle worn as insignia of rank by an Army colonel *(1920s+ Army)* **6** CHICKEN SHIT *(1940s+)* **7** The victim of a robbery or swindle; MARK, SUCKER *(1950s+ Underworld)* [homosexual senses perhaps fr late 19th-century sailor term for a boy who takes a sailor's fancy and whom he calls his *chicken*] *See* RUBBER CHICKEN

chicken feed (or money) *n phr* A small amount of money; PEANUTS, SMALL POTATOES : *Two million? That's chicken feed in this milieu* *(1830s+)*

chickenhawk *n* **1** An adult homosexual who relishes young boys as sex partners : *a "chickenhawk," a man who likes sex with "chickens," that is, boys in their middle teens (1960s+ Homosexuals)* **2** A child molester; SHORT EYE *(1980s+ Police)*

chickenhead *n* **1** A stupid person *(1950s+)* **2** A petty criminal; PUNK *(police 1990s+)* *n* or *n phr* **3** A crack-addicted woman who prostitutes herself for narcotics : *someone who would trade her body for crack, in street lingo, a chicken head*

chickenheart *n* A coward

chickenhearted *adj* **1** Cowardly; SISSIFIED : *Here's a potbellied, chickenhearted slob* **2** Squeamish; overly fastidious *(1680s+)*

chicken-livered *adj* Cowardly; CHICKENHEARTED *(1870s+)*

chicken out *v phr* To cancel or withdraw from an action because of fear; HAVE COLD FEET : *You'll think of something to chicken out/ But I chickened out. I felt sorry for him* *(1960s+)*

chickens come home to roost *sentence* (Variations : other things may replace **chickens**) Consequences, although delayed, will happen : *The chickens are coming home to roost on Reagan economics/ However the Gulf affair is resolved, it represents large chickens of the 1980s coming home to roost/ Higher interest rates are coming home to roost* *(1810+)*

chicken scratch *n* Illegible handwriting resembling the marks left by chicken feet on the ground : *can't read his chicken scratch on the grocery list*

◁**chickenshit**▷ *modifier* **1** Contemptible; trivial; petty *(1930s+)* **2** : *a chicken-shit requirement/ chicken-shit new task force (WWI armed forces, but esp WWII)* **3** Cowardly; CHICKEN *(1940s+)* *n* **1** The rules, restrictions, rigors, and meanness of a minor and pretentious tyrant, or of a bureaucracy : *The new regulations are so many parcels of chicken shit (WWI armed forces, but esp WWII)* **2** An excessive display of authority; a hectoring insistence *(WWI armed forces, but esp WWII)* **3** A coward *(1940s+)*

chicken tracks *See* HEN TRACKS

chickie *interj* An exclamation of alarm and warning, uttered when properly constituted authorities are approaching; CHEESE IT, jiggers *(1940s+ New York City teenagers)* *n* A young girl; chick : *But I do not really envy the guys my age who are making out with the young chickies* *(1920+)*

chicklet or **chiclet** *n* A young girl; chick : *Teenies and chicklets came into fashion* [1920+; a normal diminutive form, reinforced by *Chiclet*, trademark of a brand of chewing gum sold as small sugared bits]

chick movie (or flick) *n phr* A motion picture that appeals to women but not to men : *"Chick movie" is simply a shorthand term to describe the genre of films that do not feature car chases, explosions, sports, or battle scenes/ starring alongside Meryl Streep in the ultimate "chick flick"* *(1990s+)*

chief or **(head) cook and bottle washer** *n phr* The person in charge; HONCHO *(1830s+)*

child *See* FLOWER CHILD

child's play *n* Something easy to do : *writing a novel isn't child's play* *(1380s+)*

chill *adj* (also **chilled**) Excellent; wonderful; COOL, FRESH, RAD : *A "chill" outfit for a girl is tight Sergio Valente or Tale Lord jeans/ The top accolades (in 1986) include cool, chill or chilly, although froody and hondo also get high marks (1980s+ Teenagers)* *n* A glass or can of beer *(1960s+ Students)* *v* **1** To render someone unconscious; KNOCK someone OUT : *She chilled him with a kick on the chin (1930s+ Boxing)* **2** To kill; murder : *Remember the night Stein got chilled out front? (1930s+)* **3** To quench enthusiasm and amiability abruptly; snub : *He chilled me with a glance (1920s+)* **4** CHILL OUT : *As my daughter often tells me, I need to learn how to "chill" (1970s+ Students)* **5** To stay or become calm; relax; COOL IT, KICK BACK • Often a command or exhortation *(1980s+ Students)* *See* PUT THE CHILL ON someone

chiller or **chiller-diller** *n* A film, play, etc, intended to evoke delicious shudders of fear; horror show or story *(1950s+)*

chillin' *adj* **1** Excellent; the best; COOL, RAD : *But, Ma, this is "the style"! This is chillin'* **2** Relaxing; being quiet and carefree : *She told the magazine she was chillin', just having fun (1980s+ Teenagers)*

chill out *v phr* To relax; calm oneself; COOL OUT, KICK BACK : *He offers her a lit joint. "Chill out," he says/ She has become synonymous with bingeing celebrities who need to chill out (1980s+ Teenagers)*

chill pill *n phr* A tranquilizer : *They seem to have taken a chill pill musically, but the lyrics are as biting as ever* *(1990s+)*

chilly or **chili** *adj* Wonderful; excellent; COOL, NEAT : *You're chilly. You're okay, Sarge* (*1980s+ Teenagers*)

chilly mo *n phr* An aloof and unengaged person; COLD FISH [1980s+ Black; fr *mo*, "motherfucker"]

chime in *v phr* **1** To interrupt and intrude one's counsel; BUTT IN, KIBITZ **2** To offer comment : *Chime in whenever you want* (*1840s+*)

chin *n* A talk; a chat (*1890s+*) *v* **1** To talk; converse : *happily chinning in the corner* (*1870s+*) **2** To talk to : *The cop was chinning a nurse* (*1880s+*) *See* TAKE IT ON THE CHIN, WAG one's CHIN

china chin *See* GLASS JAW

◀**Chinaman's chance, a**▶ *n phr* No chance at all • Nearly always in the negative : *He hasn't got a Chinaman's chance of landing that job* [1910+; said to be fr the unfortunate situation of Chinese prospectors in the 1840s California gold rush, who were forced to work exhausted or unpromising claims, although no contemporary examples of use remain]

◀**Chinese fire drill**▶ *n phr* Something incredibly confused and confusing : *an eight-page letter with a Chinese fire drill of your life/ did their Chinese fire drill of calling the fix-it man* [perhaps fr the WWII Marine Corps expression "fucked up like *Chinese fire call*"]

chinfest *n* A session of talk and gossip; BULL SESSION, GABFEST (*1940s+*)

◀**Chink** or **chink**▶ *adj* : *Chink food/ a chink chick n* A Chinese person (*1900+*)

chin music *n phr* **1** Talk, esp inconsequential chatter; CHITCHAT : *chin music calculated to allay her trepidation* (*1830s+*) **2** Various kinds of raucous shouting at a baseball game, from the crowd, from the players to each other, from the players or manager to the umpires, etc (*1880s+ Baseball*) **3** A pitched ball that passes close to the batter's face; BEANBALL : *You ever face major league pitching, Berkowitz? You ever face chin music?* (*1980s+ Baseball*)

chintzy[1] *adj* Parsimonious; stingy; CHEAP, chinchy • The spelling imitates that of *chintzy*[2]; a dialect spelling *chinsy* is attested from 1940 : *Ask them to validate both tickets, she'd think I was chintzy* [1950s+; probably fr *chinchy*]

chintzy[2] *adj* **1** Cheap and ill-made, but showy : *the window filled with chintzy plastic couches* **2** Lacking chic and style; unfashionable : *White shoes with a dark dress is considered very definitely "chintzy"* [1850s+; fr Hindi fr *chintz*, a printed cotton fabric regarded as cheap, gaudy, and unstylish]

chin-wag *n* A conversation, esp a long and intimate chat : *You haven't had a good chin-wag with your sister-in-law since she got the joystick for her Apple* (*1870s+*)

chip *n* A flat piece of dung (*1848+*) *v* **1** To hit a short, usu high shot onto the green (*1920s+ Golf*) **2** To use a drug or drugs clandestinely while abstaining from using the drug for which one is being treated or is undergoing psychotherapy : *The men and women of the group also look at the man who is chipping. There is some palpable dismay* (*1960s+ Narcotics*) *See* BARGAINING CHIP, BLUE-CHIP, HAVE A CHIP ON one's SHOULDER

chip in *v phr* **1** To contribute, esp a share of some expense : *We each chipped in twenty bucks and got him a new suit* (*1861+*) **2** To interject a comment; contribute to a colloquy : *She chipped in some honeyed reminiscences* (*1970+*) [fr the adding of poker *chips* to the pot]

chip off the old block, a *n phr* A child that resembles one or both parents, esp a boy that resembles his father [1920s+; The form *chip of the old block* is attested fr the 1620s]

chipper[1] *n* An occasional, nonaddicted user of narcotics; JOY-POPPER : *Amy, who is only a "chipper," wanted to meet somebody* [1960s+ Narcotics; fr *chip*, "small quantity, bit"]

chipper[2] *adj* Energetic and jaunty; lively; PERKY [1830s+; fr British dialect *kipper*]

chippy or **chippie** *n* **1** A woman presumed to be of easy virtue; woman who frequents bars, public dance halls, etc : *the same as in Storyville except that the chippies were cheaper* (*1880s+*) **2** A simple buttoned dress : *A chippie is a dress that women wore, knee length and very easy to disrobe* (*1900s+*) *v* **1** To be sexually unfaithful to one's wife; CHEAT, GET A LITTLE ON THE SIDE (*1930+*) **2** To take narcotics, esp cocaine, only occasionally; CHIP (*1920s+ Narcotics*) [origin unknown; senses relating to women possibly from the chirping sound of a sparrow, squirrel, or other small creature, suggesting the gay frivolity of such women]

chips *n* Money (*1850s+*) *See* CASH IN one's CHIPS, IN THE CHIPS

chips are down (or on the table), the *sentence* The time of final decision and hard confrontation has come; resolution is at hand • Usu with *when* : *When the chips are down he goes to pieces/ For a change, when the chips were on the table, came up with some good stuff* [1940s+; fr the final bets of a poker hand]

chip shot *modifier* : *I liked my chances of kicking a chip-shot field goal n phr* **1** A shot, usu a high shot made onto the green (*1909+ Golf*) **2** An easy field goal or field-goal opportunity (*1970s+ Football*) [perhaps fr hitting under the ball as if to chop a *chip* from it]

chirp v 1 To sing : *She chirps with the orchestra*
(*1930+*) 2 To inform; SING, SQUEAL (*1830s+
Underworld*)
chisel v 1 To cheat or defraud, esp in a petty
way; deal unfairly; SCAM : *Every time I buy a
car part, he chisels a buck or two* (*1808+*) 2 To
get without necessarily intending to repay
or return; BUM, MOOCH : *Can I chisel a cigarette
from you, pal?* (*1920s+*)
chiseler n A person who defrauds : *chiseler who
we called an accountant* (*1918+*)
chisel in v phr To intrude oneself; MUSCLE IN
(*1920s+ Underworld*)
chit¹ n An impudent and spirited young
woman : *a saucy chit* [1640s+; origin un-
certain]
chit² n A bill for food or drink, which one
signs or initials instead of paying immediately [1920s+; In the sense "note," *chit*
is attested from the 1780s; shortening
of Anglo-Indian *chitty*, "letter, note," fr
Hindi]
chitchat n Talk, esp relaxed and idle conversation; CHIN MUSIC : *The members were enjoying a bit of chitchat when the gavel sounded*
(*1710+*)
chiv or chive See SHIV
chivvy or chivey or chevy (CHIH vee, CHEH
vee) v To harry and annoy; badger; BUG,
HASSLE [1821+; perhaps fr *Chevy Chase*, site
of a skirmish between the English and the
Scots, which came to mean "a running
pursuit" in Yorkshire dialect; *chivy* came to
mean "pursue"]
chiz v To relax : *chiz for a while*
◁choad or chode▷ n 1 The penis or an
imaginary penis : *choad veins are pulsing love
songs* 2 A fool; jerk : *feel like a total choad* 3
The perineum or anus : *stationary bicycle seat
irritating the chode*
◁chocha▷ (CHOH chah) n The vulva
[1960s+; fr Spanish, literally "woodcock"]
chockablock adj Crammed; crowded full : *The
plays and stories are chockablock with figures*
[1840s+ Nautical; fr a nautical rhyming
phrase used to mean that the two *blocks* of a
block and tackle are touching after the device has been tightened to its limit]
chock-full adj Absolutely full; crammed;
CHOCKABLOCK [perhaps 1400+, certainly
1751+; origin uncertain; perhaps "full to
the point of choking"]
chocoholic n A person somewhat addicted to
chocolate • Patterned on *alcoholic*
chocolate n Opium; BIG O (*1950s+*)
choice modifier Very nice; sweet : *had a choice
time at the event*
choke v To become ineffective because of tension or anxiety; CHOKE UP : *I studied all night
for my test and I totally choked* (*1980s+*)

choke a horse v phr To be very large : *That
bankroll would choke a horse* (*1900+*) See
ENOUGH TO CHOKE A HORSE
choked out adj phr Intoxicated by narcotics;
HIGH, STONED (*1990s+ Narcotics*)
choke point n phr A place where activity,
passage, etc, cannot continue; bottleneck :
*The choke point is in the few blocks between our
homes and the telephone company's switch/
Processing plants, with antiquated equipment
and unable to deal with large shipments, are
another choke point* (*1960s+*)
choker n 1 Anything worn about the neck,
such as a collar or necktie (*1840s+*) 2 A
short necklace (*1920s+*) 3 A person who
becomes ineffective because of tension or
anxiety : *Still, Jansen can't forget the sting of
being called a "choker"* (*1980s+*) See HERRING
CHOKER
◁choke the chicken or gopher▷ v phr To
masturbate (*1970s+*)
choke up v phr 1 To become tense and ineffective under pressure; CHOKE, swallow
the apple, take the pipe : *He choked up, lost his
concentration, and got clobbered in the third*
(*1940s+ Sports*) 2 To hold the bat high on
the handle, in effect shortening the bat
(*1940s+ Baseball*) 3 To cause one to be
speechless with pleasure : *Your new book
doesn't exactly choke me up* (*1960s+*) 4 To
become speechless with grief (*1960s+*)
cholo adj Very virile; MACHO (*1970s+*) n A
fellow gang member : *A cholo (street-
wise young Latino male)* (*1980s+ Prison*)
[fr Spanish, literally "mestizo, half-breed,"
used contemptuously of a lower-class Mexi-
can]
chomp v To chew [1840s+; By 1640s in form
champ]
chomp (or champ) at the bit v phr To be eager
for action; be impatient : *He'd been chomping
at the bit real hard the last three weeks*
(*1640s+*)
◁chooch▷ n The vulva; CHOCHA : *Ah, yuh
mudduh's chooch* (*1920s+*)
choo-choo See PULL A TRAIN
chop block n phr A dangerous and illegal
block made at the knees : *I can tolerate
the holding, the chop blocks I can't tolerate*
(*1990s+ Football*)
chop-chop adv Quickly; at once • Used as a
command or exhortation as well as a modifier : *They cut out chop-chop* [1830s+; fr
Pidgin English, "fast," fr Chinese]
chopped adj 1 Of a car, having the chassis
lowered or the fenders removed or both
(*1950s+ Hot rodders*) 2 Of a motorcycle,
having the front brake and fender removed,
the wheel fork extended forward, and the
handlebars raised (*1950s+ Motorcyclists*)

chopped liver *n phr* An insignificant person or thing; nothing • Often in the negative : *We have spent $25 million to adapt. And that isn't chopped liver/ It ain't chopped liver/ I'm not chopped liver. I feel too good to retire/ What the hell is the faculty lounge? Chopped liver?* (*1930s+*) *See* THAT AIN'T HAY

chopper *n* **1** A submachine gun, esp a Thompson; TOMMY GUN (*1920s+*) **2** A gangster who uses a submachine gun : *Johnny Head had met the "chopper"* (*1920s+*) **3** A helicopter : *the traffic reporter from the chopper* (*1950s+*) **4** A chopped car or motorcycle (*1950s+ Hot rodders & motorcyclists*)

choppers or **chompers** *n* Teeth, esp false teeth (*1930s+*)

chops *n* **1** (also **chaps**) The jaws; the mouth; the cheeks beside the mouth; jowls : *old turkey with pendulous chops/ Open your chops and sing* (*1500+*) **2** Musical technique or ability : *With electronically amplified music you lose your chops, your right hand, you lose your dexterity* (*1960s+ Jazz musicians*) **3** Talent or skill in general : *We'll see what kind of chops they got/ First of all, you got the chops for it, bod-wise* [senses related to skill fr notion of a jazz musician's lips, *chops*, the essential for technique in "blowing" the instrument] *See* AX, BREAK someone's CHOPS, BUST one's ASS, LICK one's CHOPS

chop shop *modifier* : *mixed up with chop shop operators in the Midwest n phr* A place where stolen cars are dismantled to be sold as parts • A slang dictionary of 1883 defines *chopped up* as "Stolen goods divided into small lots and hidden in different places" : *in Detroit, where Axel and his fellow cops are about to raid a chop shop/ I started off takin' 'em to a chop shop for $100*

chop one's teeth *v phr* bat one's gums

chow *n* Food; meals; fare : *How's the chow at Maxim's these days?* (*1856+*) *v* : *OK gang, let's chow* (*1900+*) [perhaps fr Pidgin English *chow-chow*, "a mixture (of foods)," but also a dog of China that is eaten by the poor]

chowderhead *n* A stupid person (*1830s+*)

chow down *v phr* To eat; have a meal : *They should bundle up, chow down, and stay home* (*WWII Navy*)

chow hall *n phr* A room where meals are served, esp a military mess hall (*1940s+ Army*)

chow hound *n phr* A person keenly and actively interested in eating; glutton (*1920s+ Army*)

christen *v* To use for the first time : *let's christen the new bed* (*1990+*)

chrome-dome *modifier* : *Reggie Rivers doesn't have a fancy name for his chrome-dome hairdo n* EGGHEAD : *just to catch up on what the liberal chrome-domes are thinking/ The Carter Center has its share of chrome-domes, eggheads, incompetents and hangers-on* (*1960s+*)

chrome pony *n phr* A motorcycle; BAD BOY, IRON, sled (*1990s+*)

chub(by) *n* A penile erection : *a chubby in your pants*

chubbette *n* A chubby woman, esp a small one : *The poor thing was petrified that Graig would find out what a chubbette she'd become/ a chubbette with "railroad tracks" across her teeth* (*1970s+*)

chubbo *n* An obese person (*1980s+ Students*)

chuck *n* **1** Food; a meal; CHOW, EATS : *She invited us in for some chuck* (*1850+ British*) **2** A white male • Often a term of address used by blacks *v* **1** To throw, esp to throw or pitch a ball : *chuck a mean slider* (*1590s+*) **2** To discard; throw away : *Is it possible she has chucked her aloofness* (*1850+*) **3** To vomit; UPCHUCK : *He looked like he was going to chuck his breakfast* (*1940s+*)

chuck-a-lug *See* CHUG-A-LUG

chuck something down *v phr* To eat something very quickly : *chucked down the Whopper*

chuckers or **chucks** *n* Voracious hunger; enormous appetite : *smelling the burgers, got the chuckers*

chuck it in *v phr* To give up or quit : *chucked it in a long time ago*

chuck you, Farley *interj* (Variation : **and your whole famn damily** may be added) May you and yours be reviled, abused, humiliated, rejected, etc; FUCK YOU, UP YOURS • This amusing variant of the damning formula goes beyond the brevity of an interjection but retains the force [*1970s+*; based on earlier *fuck you, Charley* and the euphemism *whole famn damily*]

chug[1] *v* To drink very quickly and in volume, as alcohol : *chugged six milks at lunch*

chug[2] *v* To move along, esp slowly and laboriously : *The USS Saratoga came chugging up the Delaware* [*1900+*; echoic of an engine, esp a steam engine, operating]

chug-a-lug or **chug** or **chuck-a-lug** *v* To drink the whole of what is in a glass or bottle without pausing : *I tried to chug-a-lug a quart bottle of Schaefer/ He chugged a liter of vodka and dropped dead* [*1940s+*; echoic of the sound of repeated swallowing; perhaps related to Scots dialect *chug*, "a short tug or pull"]

chug out *v phr* GRIND OUT : *cheerfully sifted through hard copy of the bug-checked code he'd been chugging out* (*1990s+*)

chum[1] *n* **1** A very close friend; BUDDY, PAL (*1680s+ Students*) **2** Man; fellow; GUY • Used in direct address esp to strangers, usu with mildly hostile overtones : *Keep guessing, chum* (1940s+) *v* (also **chum around**) : *He chums with Georgie Ogle* (1880s+) [origin uncertain, but earlier uses strongly suggest *chamber*-mate or *chamber*-fellow as the etymon]

chum[2] *n* : *Augie, start dumping the chum over v* To throw ground-up bait into the water to attract fish : *to chum for blues* [1850s+; origin unknown]

chummy *adj* Very friendly; BUDDY-BUDDY, PALSY-WALSY (1880s+) *n* CHUM[1] (1840s+)

chump *modifier* : *The honest, hardworking immigrant was a chump game n* A stupid person, esp a dupe; SUCKER : *I look like a chump these days* (1877+) *v* : *You were chumped, Donna Rice and Marla Trump* (1920s+) [origin unknown; perhaps an alteration of *chunk* referring to blockheadedness] *See* OFF one's CHUMP

chump change *n phr* 1 A small or relatively small and meager amount of money; a pittance : *A hundred dollars a day to the town is chump change/ Latinos rejecting $4.50 an hour as chump change* (1950s+ Black) 2 Carnival tokens customers can redeem for cash (Carnival)

chumphead *n* A stupid person : *What are you, a chumphead*

chunder *n* A substance vomited *v* To vomit [probably rhyming slang *Chunder Loo spew*, from the name of an Australian cartoon character]

◄**chungo bunny**► *n phr* A black person : *looked like he hadda be the biggest chungo bunny inna world* [1970s+; fr *jungle bunny*]

chunk *v* To throw; CHUCK (1830s+)

chunk up *v phr* To gain weight; become chunky (1990s+)

chunky *modifier* Chubby; fat : *lookin' a little chunky in that dress*

church key *n phr* A bottle or can opener (1950s+)

churn *v* To artificially increase the level of activity in a law firm, insurance company, or other enterprise in order to increase commissions, feign busyness, etc : *Policyholders have launched class-action suits alleging churning* (1940s+)

churn out *v phr* To produce written matter very rapidly and mechanically; CRANK OUT : *The sci/ fi fantasy cartoons being churned out in Japan these days* (1912+)

chute *n* A parachute (1920+) *See* POOP CHUTE

chutzpa (HŌŌTS pǝ, KHŌŌTS-) *n* (Variations : **chuzpa** or **hutzpa** or **hutzpah**) Extreme and offensive brashness; arrogant presumption; hubris : *Chutzpa is that quality enshrined in a man who, having killed his mother and father, throws himself on the mercy of the court because he is an orphan/ The hutzpah of using Studio 54 was much commented on* (1892+)

ciao (CHOW) *interj* A salutation either on meeting or parting [1920s+; fr Italian, fr *schiavo*, "I am your slave"]

cig *n* A cigarette (1880s+)

ciggy or **ciggie** *n* A cigarette : *a ciggy outside*

cinch *n* 1 A certainty; something sure to happen; SURE THING : *It's a cinch they'll win* (1880s+ Cowboys) 2 Something easily done; BREEZE, PIECE OF CAKE : *Going up is a bother, coming down's a cinch* (1890+) *v* To make something certain; CLINCH, NAIL something DOWN : *We cinched it with a last-second field goal* (1883+) [fr Spanish *cincha*, "saddle girth," which, when tight, fosters certainty] *See* HAVE something CINCHED, LEAD-PIPE CINCH

cinched *See* HAVE something CINCHED

circ *n* A circumcision (1990s+)

◄**circle jerk**► *n phr* 1 A sex party of mutual masturbation (esp teenagers) 2 Any futile occasion, meeting, session, etc (1940s+)

circle the drain *v phr* To be dying; go down the drain : *And how do some cops describe the condition of a traffic victim who is near death? Circling the drain* (1980s+ Medical and police)

circle the wagons *v phr* To take up a defensive posture or position : *"It's time to circle the wagons and suck it up," veteran guard Mark Bortz said/ You might say Polaroid Corp circled the wagons to repel a $3.2 billion assault* [1980s+; fr the action taken in a cowboy movie when a *wagon* train is threatened by hostile Indians]

circuit *See* BORSCHT CIRCUIT

circuit clout (or **blow** or **wallop**) *n phr* A home run (1908+ Baseball)

circuit slugger *n phr* A talented home-run hitter : *Gil Hodges became the greatest circuit slugger ever to wear Dodger flannels* (1940s+ Baseball)

circular file *n phr* A wastebasket (1940s+)

circus *n* 1 Any bright and uproarious occasion : *You should have been there—it was a circus* (1885+) 2 A sex show, often featuring bestial couplings (1870s+)

circus catch *n phr* A spectacularly good and difficult catch [1880s+ Baseball; fr the seemingly superhuman feats of *circus* performers]

circus play *n phr* A spectacularly good play (1880s+ Baseball)

citizen *n* A person of a more conservative, established, and prosaic caste than oneself; SQUARE (1960s+ Black & counterculture)

Citizen *See* JOHN Q CITIZEN

cits *n* CIVVIES (1829+)

city *combining word* 1 The place or milieu of what is indicated : *hamburger city* 2 A prevalence or instance of the thing indicated :

trouble city/ dumb city/ fat city [1930s+ Jazz musicians; coined on the model of the *-sville* suffix] *See* FAT CITY, FUN CITY, TAP CITY

city hall *n phr* The political powers and their haunts; those who control purse strings and patronage : *see how city hall reacts* (*1890s+*) *See* YOU CAN'T FIGHT CITY HALL

city slicker *n phr* A shrewd and modish urban person, esp as distinct from the honest and gullible provincial : *A small-town beauty shop, where city slickers can really let their hair down* (*1920s+*)

civvies *n* Civilian dress; mufti (*1880s+*)

clam *n* 1 A silent, secretive person, esp one who can be trusted with a confidence (*1860s+*) 2 A dollar : *That'll be eight clams for the oil* (*1930s+*) 3 A wrong or sour note; CLINKER (*1940s+ Jazz musicians*) 4 The vulva; BEARDED CLAM • The term is probably older than indicated. An English dialect dictionary of 1857 hints as much with two senses of *clam* : "a slut"; "to snatch, to shut" (*1916+*) *v* CLAM UP • The term must be earlier than the date given, although no examples can be provided. Middle English *clum,* "be quiet! shut up," of obscure origin, may not be related to *clam* (*1916+*) *See* BEARDED CLAM, HAPPY AS A CLAM

clambake *n* 1 Any gathering, meeting, convention, party, etc, esp a happy and noisy one (*1940s+*) 2 JAM SESSION (*1930s+ Jazz musicians*)

◁**clam bumper**▷ *n phr* A lesbian (*1990s+*)

clamp down *v phr* To increase the severity of measures against persons who break rules and laws; punish rather than tolerate : *The whole country's clamping down now on drunk drivers* (*1940s+*)

clamps, the *See* PUT THE CLAMPS ON

clam up *v phr* To stay or become silent; stand mute; BUTTON UP : *When I ask for details he just clams up* (*1916+*)

clanger *n* A big mistake : *made a clanger on that project* (*1948+*)

◁**clap, the**▷ *n* Gonorrhea : *If a guy said 'I ride bareback,' I'd tell him he needs a raincoat. Instead of gonorrhea, I'd talk about the clap* [*1587+*; fr early French *clapoir,* "bubo, swelling"]

◁**clapped-up**▷ *adj* Infected with gonorrhea : *In reality she's a gotch-eyed, clapped-up hooker* (*1960s+*)

claptrap *n* Nonsense; mendacious cant; BULLSHIT [*1819+*; fr early 1700s theatrical use, literally "a trap to get a *clap*," a device, verbal or otherwise, for milking applause]

claret *n* Blood [*1604+* Prizefight; fr the red color of *claret wine*]

class *modifier* : *a real class joint n* High quality; admirable style; cachet : *quiet dignity under fire, real class* (*1870s+*) *See* WORLD-CLASS

class act, a *n phr* A person or thing of admirable style, quality, competence, etc : *48 HRS clicks anyway. It's a class act/ Monaco was, as Arthur Lewis said, a class act* (*1970s+*)

classy chassis *n phr* A good figure; trim body : *sassy lassie with a classy chassis* (*1950s+*)

clay pigeon *n phr* 1 A person who is easily duped; EASY MARK (*1920s+*) 2 An aircraft catapulted from a ship (*1940s+ Navy*) 3 Something easily done; CINCH (*1950s+*)

clean *adj* 1 Not carrying anything forbidden, esp a firearm : *Cops gave him a body-shake and he came out clean* (*1926+*) 2 Innocent; unincriminated (*1300+*) 3 Not producing radioactive contamination : *a clean bomb* (*1950s+*) 4 Lacking money; BROKE, CLEANED OUT (*late 1900s+*) 5 Not lewd or obscene; morally unexceptionable : *a couple of clean jokes/ a clean old man* (*1867+*) 6 Trim; neat; elegant : *Mies' clean lines and crisp angles* (*1400+*) 7 Free of drug addiction (*1950s+ Narcotics*) 8 Well-dressed; clad in the latest style : *Danny, he was really clean. He had new clothes* (*1960s+ Black*) *adv* : *I was crazy about Lester. He played so clean and beautiful See* COME CLEAN, KEEP one's NOSE CLEAN, SQUEAKY-CLEAN

Clean *See* MISTER CLEAN

clean as a whistle (or **a hound's tooth**) *adj phr* Perfectly clean (*first form 1828+, second 1940s+*)

clean someone's clock *v phr* 1 To attack and punish someone : *Carlson suddenly really wanted to clean Ron Connelly's clock* 2 To defeat; trounce; CLOBBER : *The DA had his clock cleaned for him/ "She just cleaned my clock," Mrs King said* [*1960s+*; perhaps fr the notion of *clock* as "face"; perhaps fr the earlier underworld and railroad term *clean the clock,* "stop, esp suddenly"]

cleaned out *adj phr* Lacking money, esp having lost it gambling or speculating; BROKE, TAPPED OUT : *Georgie was cleaned out after the third race* (*1812+*)

cleaners, the *See* GO TO THE CLEANERS, TAKE someone TO THE CLEANERS

cleaning *See* HOUSE-CLEANING

clean someone out *v phr* 1 To win all of someone's money at gambling, esp in a crap game (*1812+*) 2 To require or use up all of someone's money : *Buying the condo just about cleaned them out* (*1860s+*)

clean sweep *n* A broad change that has a sweeping effect : *made a clean sweep of his life*

cleanup *modifier* 1 : *another cleanup campaign* 2 Batting fourth in the lineup : *He did better as the cleanup hitter* (*1910+ Baseball*) *n* An intensive effort or campaign against crime, filth, etc, of the sort periodically undertaken by the authorities : *The Mayor vowed another* *definitive cleanup of the Times Square area* (*1920s+*) [baseball sense fr the sanguine notion that the first three hitters will reach base and the bases will be emptied, *cleaned up*, by the fourth hitter]

clean up *v phr* To make a large profit; get an impressive return for one's money; MAKE A KILLING : *The West today knows many a ghost town where men of too much enterprise cleaned up and cleared out* (*1830s+*)

clean up one's **act** (or ◁shit▷) *v phr* To correct one's behavior; act properly and decently; STRAIGHTEN UP AND FLY RIGHT : *I told the kid to clean up his act or leave* (*1960s+*)

clean up on someone *v phr* To defeat someone decisively; trounce; thrash; CLEAN someone's CLOCK : *We really cleaned up on them in the second half* (*1860s+*)

cleanup spot (or **slot**), the *n phr* The fourth position in the batting order : *The manager didn't have a very reliable hitter for the cleanup spot* [1910+ Baseball; fr the fact that the batter in this position may, or ought to, get a hit and *clean* the runners off the bases by driving them in to score]

clean (or **wipe**) **up the floor with** someone *v phr* To defeat someone decisively; CLEAN UP ON someone : *If he said that to me I'd clean up the floor with the bastard* (*1890s+*)

clear *v* To earn a certain amount of money after taxes : *cleared 100 Gs*

clear someone *v* To show or declare someone free of suspicion : *He looked guilty, but the investigation cleared him* (*1940s+*) *See* READ someone LOUD AND CLEAR

clear as mud *adj phr* Entirely unclear; lacking lucidity : *I think I get it, though your explanation is as clear as mud* (*1880s+*)

clear off *v phr* To go away : *let's clear off after graduation* (*1816+*)

clear out *v phr* To depart; HIT THE ROAD : *obliged every colored man to "clear out" of the streets* (*1839+*)

clear sailing *n phr* Easy and unimpeded progress; easy going : *After a rough couple of months it was clear sailing* (*1850s+*)

clear up *v phr* To stop using narcotics; get help in withdrawing from drug addiction (*1960s+ Narcotics*)

Cleveland *n* A thousand dollars; a thousand-dollar bill : *The British publicist offered me an exclusive with King Freddy for a Cleveland—$1,000—but I passed* [1990s+; fr the presidential portrait on the banknote]

click *n* **1** An insight, esp a sudden one; flash of comprehension : *She gifts us with this click : Most men want their wives to have a jobette/ and finally to a click when it began adding up* **2** A clique (*1920s+*) **3** (also **klick, klik**) A kilometer : *a hundred and sixty clicks north of*

Saigon (*1960s+ Armed forces*) *v* (or **click with**) **1** To succeed; please an audience or constituency : *If I can click with wholesalers I should be ready to open up in about 3 weeks* (*1910+ Theater*) **2** To evoke or precede a flash of insight : *Something clicked. I thought, This is what I want to do for the rest of my life* (*1930s+*) **3** To fit together precisely; go well together : *Those two really click, like a well-oiled machine* (*1920s+*)

clicker *n* The remote-control device of a piece of electronics (*1980s+*)

cliffhanger *n* A very suspenseful story, film, game, situation, etc : *The election was a cliffhanger, right through the recount* [1937+; fr the fact that the actress Pearl White actually ended some episodes of her early serial movies *hanging* from the Palisades above the Hudson River]

climb someone *v phr* To reprimand severely; chew out. REAM ● *Climb over someone's frame* has the same sense in college slang of the 1890s : *The old man really climbed me for that stupid trick* (*WWI Army*)

climber *n* an ambitious person : *not your average social climber* (*1833+*)

climb on the bandwagon *See* GET ON THE BANDWAGON

climb (or **go up**) **the wall** *v phr* To become frantic, esp from frustration or anxiety; GO OUT OF one's SKULL : *By the time the cops came I was about to climb the wall* (*1970s+*)

clinch *n* **1** A close contact of two boxers, where they hold each other's arms to stifle blows (*1870s+ Prizefight*) **2** An embrace; passionate hug (*1899+*) *v* **1** : *Two palookas clinched through six rounds* **2** To determine conclusively; finish definitively and positively; NAIL something DOWN : *They claim new evidence that'll clinch their case* (*1716+*) [fr the bending over, clinching, of the point of a nail to ensure it does not pull out; ultimately fr *clench*]

clincher *n* The deciding or conclusive element; BOTTOM LINE : *One smudged fingerprint was the clincher* (*1830s+*)

clink *n* A black person; BROTHER (*Black*)

clink, the *n phr* A jail or prison; the SLAMMER [1770s+; fr the old prison on *Clink* Street in the Southwark district of London]

clinker *n* **1** A biscuit (*1900+*) **2** the CLINK (*1920s+*) **3** A squeak or unintended reed sound made on the clarinet, saxophone, or oboe (*1930s+ Musicians*) **4** An obvious wrong or sour note : *One of the louder sopranos hit an excruciating clinker* (*1930s+ Musicians*) **5** An error; BONER (*1934+*) **6** Anything inferior in workmanship, esp a play, movie, or other show; LEMON, TURKEY (*1940s+*) **7** An incompetent person; a failure; DUD, LOSER : *There have been some ultra-conservative judges, but there has been an absence of real clinkers* (1940s+) **8** Something damaging, esp when unseen or unforeseen; a hidden flaw : *There was a clinker in the works apart from his writing, a sort of catch* (1960s+) [fr *clinker,* "unburnable cinder"]

clip *n* **1** : *You hit him a good clip* (1850s+) ◀**2**▶ CLIPPED DICK (1940s+) **3** Pace; rate : *She took off at a real good clip* (1860s+) **4** Each one; each occasion; POP : *two treatments at $100 a clip/ Every clip cost him half a day's pay* (1801+) **5** A clipping from a newspaper, magazine, etc : *Thanks for sending the clips about the kid's wedding* (1920s+) **6** A portion of a movie or television tape : *television clips from the period of the accident* (1960s+) **7** A cut-apart or dismantled section of a car : *Salvage yards will pay $5,000 for the front end, back clip, engine, radio, doors, and bumpers* (1970s+) *v* **1** To hit; strike sharply and neatly : *He clipped and decked the local goon* **2** To steal; SWIPE : *Where'd you clip the new car?* (1930s+) **3** To cheat someone, esp by overcharging : *That joint'll clip you every time* (1920s+) **4** To arrest (1940s+) **5** To kill, esp by shooting : *You think he clipped three people, including a seventeen-year-old kid* (1920s+ *Underworld*) **6** (also **clip it**) To move rapidly; run; BARREL, carry the mail (1830s+) **7** To cut a car into sections, usu in an illegal operation (1970s+) [senses denoting fraud and theft are probably fr the practice of *clipping* bits of metal off coins and passing them at face value] *See* PUT THE CLIP ON someone, ROACH CLIP

clip-artist *n* A professional swindler or thief : *A gentle clip-artist, Abadaba robbed bookmakers as well as bettors* (1940s+ *Underworld*)

clip joint *n phr* **1** A gambling establishment where the customer is regularly cheated **2** Any business establishment that regularly overcharges, or where one is likely to be cheated : *One man's gourmet noshery is another man's clip joint* (1920s+)

clipped *adj* **1** Arrested : *clipped for petty larceny* **2** Cheated : *clipped leaving the party* **3** Circumcised : *full front showed he was clipped*

◀**clipped dick**▶ *n phr* A Jewish male (1940s+)

clipper *n* A pickpocket : *accused her of being a clipper, or pickpocket* (1970s+ *Police*)

clipping *n* **1** Illegal blocking from behind (1930s+ *Football*) **2** The repairing of a car by joining together two undamaged halves after either the front or rear end has been damaged : *Front and rear clips are attached to the remains of vehicles that have been seriously damaged, but clipping is dangerous* (1970s+)

clip someone's wings *v phr* To reduce someone's privileges as a punishment : *after the accident, they clipped his wings*

◀**clit**▶ *n* The clitoris; BUTTON (1960s+)

◀**clit-licker**▶ *n* A person who does cunnilingus; MUFF-DIVER (1970s+)

clobber *v* **1** To hit or attack very hard; BASH • Appears to have been popularized by WWII RAF **2** To defeat decisively; trounce; MURDER, WIPE OUT : *Rommel got clobbered at El Alamein* [1940s+; origin unknown; perhaps fr Scots *clabber,* "spatter, cover with mud"]

clobbered *adj* Drunk : *those who are, to use a word presently popular with the younger drinking set, clobbered* (1950s+)

clock *v* **1** To hit; SOCK : *who clocked me when I wasn't looking/ She clocked him with the portable telephone* (1920s+ *Australian*) **2** To time, esp with a stopwatch : *They clocked her at 6:05:03.65* (1880s+) **3** To achieve a specified time : *I clocked a two-minute lap yesterday* (1892+) **4** To get; amass : *Malcolm Forbes is clockin' megadollars* (1980s+ *Teenagers*) **5** To watch; keep one's eye on : *He is always clockin' girls* (1980s+ *Teenagers*) **6** To waste one's time; detain one : *Why're you clockin' me? I got people to see* (1980s+ *Teenagers*) [first sense probably related to *clock,* "face"] *See* CLEAN someone's CLOCK

clock in (or **out**) *v phr* To come or go at a certain recorded time, esp to or from a job where a time clock is used; PUNCH IN (or OUT) (1920s+)

clock (or **meter**) **is ticking** (or **running**), **the** *sentence* or *v phr* A decreasing amount of time is available; the end draws near : *Baker and Aziz were preparing to hold last-minute talks, and the clock was ticking toward war/ But the clock is ticking down for the 49-year-old ex-lineman/ One of the banks has suffered twenty million dollars in unrecoverable loans and the meter is still running* [1990s+; fr sports, astronautics, bomb disposal, and other contexts where a *clock* measures the time remaining]

clock-watcher *n phr* A person who vouchsafes more attention to the time of quitting than to work : *a hard worker, no clockwatcher* (1890+)

clod *n* A stupid person [1605+; fr *clodpate* or *clodpole,* "clodhead"]

clodhopper *n* **1** A farmer; rustic; SHIT-KICKER • Originally a plowman (1690+) **2** An old vehicle, suitable for only short passages; CLUNKER, JALOPY (1940s+)

clodhoppers *n* Strong, heavy shoes, esp workshoes; BOONDOCKERS, SHIT-KICKERS (1830s+)

clone *n* An imitation, esp a person who imitates or emulates another; a mindless copy : *Not a clone in sight. No one has the same color* *hair* [1970s+; fr clone, "the asexually produced offspring of an organism," ultimately fr Greek *klon*, "twig, branch"]

close *adj* **1** Parsimonious; stingy (*1600s+*) **2** Very good; extraordinary : *Oh, man, this is crazy close!* (*1960s+ Students*)

◁**close as stink on shit,**▷ as *modifier* Very close; intimate

close but no cigar *adv phr* Very nearly correct; not quite the thing : *One package, that was acceptable. Too many amounted to her idea of close-but-no-cigar/ If you answered George Lucas' Star Wars you're close, but no cigar* [1970s+; fr carnival feats where one gets a *cigar* as a prize]

close-fisted *adj* Unwilling to give; niggardly; stingy; CLOSE (*1608+*)

closer (KLOH zer) *n* A relief pitcher who usu comes in for the ninth inning : *You can't expect your closer to go out and save 60 games* (*1980s+ Baseball*)

close shave (or **call**) *n phr* A very narrow avoidance or evasion of some danger; SQUEAKER (*1834+*)

closet *modifier* Secret; unsuspected • Although this sense is much earlier, it has recently been revived by the homosexual use : *Puddin' calls me his closet redneck/ fellow who was known around the White House as a "closet liberal"* (*1600s+*)

closet, the *n phr* The condition of concealment in which a homosexual or other nonconforming person lives : *If you're out of the closet, you're out of the armed service* (*1960s+*) *See* COME OUT OF THE CLOSET

close to the chest (or **vest**) *adj phr* : *Janet Reno is very close to the vest about her personal feelings* (*1950s+*) *See* PLAY CLOSE TO THE CHEST

closet queen (or **queer**) *n phr* A secret male homosexual (*1960s+*)

close-up *modifier* Made or done from very near : *a close-up view/ close-up study n* **1** A photograph or movie or television sequence shot close to the subject (*1913+*) **2** A biography : *It is becoming commonplace for a literary critic to describe a biography as a "close-up"* (*1930s+*)

clothes *See* SUNDAY CLOTHES

clotheshorse *n* A fashionably dressed person; a person who wears clothes becomingly and perhaps does nothing else (*1850+*)

clothesline *n* A very flat, fast line drive; FROZEN ROPE, ROPE (*1930s+ Baseball*) *v* To block or tackle by holding out one's arm in the path of a running player : *He clotheslined him* (*1960s+ Football*)

cloud *See* ON CLOUD NINE

cloud-buster *n* A very, very high fly ball (*1950s+ Baseball*)

cloud nine (or **seven**) *n phr* A state of total euphoria : *Capriati's coach knew he had to "get*

her off Cloud 9" [1950s+; fr the notion of *clouds* as heavenly locations] *See* ON CLOUD NINE

clout *n* **1** A heavy blow : *She gave him a clout on the snoot* (*1400+*) **2** Force; power; impact; PUNCH : *This wimpish paragraph lacks clout* (*1950s+*) **3** Influence or power, esp of a political sort : *He has lots of friends in high places, but no clout* (*1950s+*) *v* **1** To hit; strike; BASH : *My old man would have clouted the hell out of me* (*1890s+*) **2** To hit the ball, esp to hit it hard (*1910+ Baseball*) **3** To steal, esp to shoplift or steal a car (*1940s+*)

clover *See* IN CLOVER, LIKE PIGS IN CLOVER

clown *n* A person for whom the speaker feels mild contempt, esp one whose behavior merits derision : *Get this clown off my back and let me help you* (*1920s+*) *v* (also **clown around**) To behave frivolously; persist in inappropriate levity (*1940s+*)

club *See* MILE-HIGH CLUB, WELCOME TO THE CLUB

clubbing *n* Participation in a party scene, individually or as part of a group, esp in an urban setting; going out to nightclubs : *tired of reading about Paris Hilton and Lindsey Lohan's clubbing*

Club Fed *n phr* A minimum-security federal prison : *Set on 42 campus-like acres, Club Fed had neither walls nor armed guards* [1980s+; after *Club Med*, trademark name of a chain of holiday resorts]

clubhouse *modifier* Having to do with routine and sometimes shady urban partisan politics : *Dinkins, 62, is a classic clubhouse politician* (*1960s+*)

clubhouse lawyer *n phr* A baseball player who is a prominent self-appointed authority on the game and its regulations, and who generously instructs his associates (*1940s+ Baseball*)

cluck or **cluckhead** or **kluck** *n* **1** A stupid person; idiot : *The champion cluck of all time/ If I defend myself you two clucks are going to need a lot more backup* (*1920s+*) ◀**2**▶ A very dark black person (*1950s+ Black*) *See* DUMB CLUCK

clue *v* or *v phr* (also **clue in**) To inform someone of pertinent facts; PUT someone IN THE PICTURE : *I'll clue ya/ Neil Sheehan and I were terribly clued-in. We had a lock on that story* (*1940s+*) *See* GET A CLUE, HAVE A CLUE, NOT HAVE A CLUE

clued out *adj phr* Unaware; ignorant : *I like Elvissa, but she can be so clued out* (*1990s+*)

clueless *adj* Ignorant; hopelessly unaware : *We'll have to endure loads of clueless reporters raving on/ You're probably just a clueless newbie* [1980s+ Students & 1930s+ Royal Air Force; perhaps a revival, perhaps a new coinage] *See* TOTALLY CLUELESS

cluelessness *n* Total stupidity or ignorance : *cluelessness in that department*

cluelessly *adv* In a clueless way : *the Bumbling Around Cluelessly Phase* (1990s+)

clunk *n* **1** : *He hit me a good clunk* **2** A stupid person; dupe; CLUCK : *scheming maids who have been working on the poor clunks all spring* (1940s+) **3** An old and worn-out machine, esp a car; CLUNKER : *Look at that fuckin' broad in the clunk next to us/ He hauled a junk car on the ice and took bets. This contest was called "Dunk the Clunk"* (1940s+) *v* **1** (also **clonk**) To hit; strike; CLOCK : *She clunked him in the teeth* (1940s+) **2** To move awkwardly and slowly : *The plot just clunks forward, for two hours and 10 minutes* (1970s+) [probably all based on *clunk*, "make a dull sound," found by 1796]

clunker *n* **1** Anything inferior; LEMON, TURKEY : *His last clunker was* Lolly Madonna (1940s+) **2** An old, worn-out machine, esp a car; CLUNK, JALOPY : *let in someone in an old clunker with a broken muffler and a fuming exhaust* (1950s+) **3** A clumsy person, esp an unskillful athlete; DUFFER, HACKER : *Tell one of those clunkers what a great stroke he has* (1940s+)

clunkhead *n* A stupid person : *Some clunkhead sent me three live quail* (1950s+)

clunkily *adv* Ungracefully; stolidly : *Her clunkily earnest lyrics are very big on concepts like the Necessity of Being Your Own Person* (1970s+)

clunky or **clunkish** *adj* Blockish and ungraceful; stolidly unsophisticated : *a pair of clunky Sonora biker boots/ a clunkish magazine called Pick-Up Times/ The ads are so clunky and quaint that they transport one back to a seemingly more innocent consumer past* (1970s+)

clutch *modifier* done or accomplished in a critical situation : *a clutch hitter/ clutch play n* **1** An embrace; CLINCH (1950s+) **2** A group; bunch : *a clutch of drunken sailors* (1908+) **3** A customer who does not tip, or tips too little; STIFF (1950s+ *Restaurant*) *v* (also **clutch up**) To panic; be seized with anxiety : *If that's what's got you clutched up, don't worry about it* (1950s+)

clutch, the *n phr* A moment when heroic performance under pressure is needed : *You could always depend on Gladys when the clutch came* (1920s+)

clutched *adj* Nervous; tense; UPTIGHT (1950s+)

clutchy *adj* **1** Likely to become nervous or anxious **2** Difficult; dangerous; HAIRY (1960s+)

clutz *See* KLUTZ

C-note *n* A hundred-dollar bill; FRANKLIN : *staring at that C-note* (1920s+)

coal *See* HAUL someone OVER THE COALS

coast *n* Effortless result; smooth ride : *The flip side gave us a coast v* **1** To go along without effort : *I coasted through the two exams* (1880s+) **2** To be exhilarated by a narcotic, by music, etc; be euphoric : *That first fix had sent him coasting one whole week* (1940s+)

coast is clear, the *sentence* Danger is past; resistance no longer impends : *I'll be back here as soon as the bomb squad says the coast is clear* (1630s+)

coat *See* PINE OVERCOAT

coattail *modifier* Based on another person's achievement or quality; derivative : *But the Sephardim are not likely to remain contented with coattail power for long v* To keep the same musical tempo : *You're still keeping the same time. We called it coattailing* (1950s+ *Musicians*) *See* ON someone's COATTAILS

cobble together *v phr* To make or construct, esp by assemblage : *They still reject computers for production, preferring to cobble together layouts by hand* (1830s+)

cock *n* ◁1▷ The penis; PRICK : *The youth's cock was by now rock hard* (1618+) **2** A friend; PAL • Chiefly British : *How goes it, old cock?* (1830s+) [origin uncertain; perhaps based on *cock*, "spigot"] *See* DROP YOUR COCKS AND GRAB YOUR SOCKS, POPPYCOCK

cockamamie or **cockamamey** or **cockamamy** (kahk ə MAY mee) *adj* Crazy; confused : *The picture ends with a cockamamie implication that love will conquer all/ this cockamamie little tort* [1920s+ New York City children; fr New York City dialect, perhaps fr British; somehow connected with *decalcomania*; perhaps because decalcomanias as given in candy boxes and chewing-gum packets were used by children for antic self-decoration]

cock-and-bull story *n phr* An improbable account, often an alibi; a mendacious farrago : *He gives me this cock-and-bull story about six flat tires* [1620+; origin uncertain; the French term "cock and donkey" is analogous]

cock a snook *v phr* To show derision and contempt by thumbing one's nose : *The "world's Greatest Rock and Roll Band" took the occasion to cock a snook at their chief competitors* [1791+; origin unknown; the spread hand resembles a rooster's head, and the dialect verb *snook* means "to seek by smelling," but the semantics are not otherwise useful]

cocked *adj* Drunk (1730s+) *See* HALF COCKED

cocker *See* ALTER KOCKER, OLD COCKER

cockeye *n* A left-handed pitcher; SOUTHPAW (1940s+ *Baseball*)

cockeyed *adj* **1** Crosseyed; walleyed; strabismic (1820+) **2** Crazy; weird; all wrong; SCREWY : *Anybody who thinks I'm kidding is cockeyed/ In* *this cockeyed caravan called the 90s* (*1930s+*) **3** Drunk : *He is in a doghouse at home on account of coming home cockeyed on his wedding anniversary* (*1722+*) **4** Unconscious : *Izzy knocks him cockeyed* (*1920s+*) **5** Genuine; absolute; FUCKING : *You're a cockeyed wonder, you know that?* (*1920s+*) *adv* Askew; crooked; slonchways : *He put his hat on cockeyed and got a polite chuckle* (*1910s+*)

◁**cock is on the block,** one's▷ *sentence* One is in grave and imminent peril : *He'll cop a plea if you tell him his cock is on the block for the murder* (*1970s+*)

◁**cocksman** or **cock hound**▷ *n* An ardent womanizer and copulator; STUD, swordsman : *In those days Harry was a big cocksman/ Valdez was a cock hound, no question* (*first form 1916+, second 1940s+*)

cocksmanship *n* The practice of being a cocksman : *In "Mambo Mouth," cocksmanship is portrayed as the only surviving romance in lives bereft of other dreams* (*1990s+*)

◀**cocksucker**▶ *n* **1** A person who does fellatio, esp a male homosexual (*1890s+*) **2** A man held by the speaker in extreme contempt; BASTARD, PRICK : *Oh, Sid, you fucking cocksucker. You nailed me again* (*1920s+*)

◀**cocksucking**▶ *adj* **1** Despicable; contemptible : *So I told the cocksucking little pimp to get lost* **2** Wretched; DAMNED • A very general intensive use, often for euphony : *Don't give me no cocksucking grief/ Here, take your cocksucking money* *adv* : *Don't talk so cocksucking silly* (*1910+*)

cocktail *n* **1** A cigarette of marijuana and tobacco, with marijuana put into the end of an ordinary cigarette **2** A cigarette of more than a single narcotic (*1960s+ Narcotics*) *See* MOLOTOV COCKTAIL

cock-tease *v* To permit sexual familiarities but deny the sex act : *They were chivying a string of suitors and behaving like overage sorority sisters. They cock-teased* (*1950s+*)

◁**cock-teaser** or **prick-teaser** or **prick-tease**▷ *n* A woman or a male homosexual who arouses a man sexually by granting certain favors, then denies him the sex act (*entry form 1891+, variants 1960s+*)

coconut *n* **1** The head (*1834+*) **2** One dollar : *the whole hundred thousand coconuts* (*1920s+*) **3** A Hispanic person who truckles to or imitates the values of the non-Hispanic majority; tio taco : *Maldonado ridicules him for selling out, for being a coconut, brown on the outside, white on the inside* (*1970s+*)

cocoon *n* One's cozy home : *Each morning he leaves his domestic cocoon in Rancho Palos Verdes* *v* To stay at home, and, often, to be inactive : *The couch potatoes are going to be cocooning in their families' personal oases* (*1980s+*)

code brown *n* A fecal accident : *code brown in the children's ward*

code yellow *n* A urinary accident : *code yellow in the baby's bed*

codger *n* An old man, esp an eccentric one • Usu with *old* : *Look at those happy codgers on the shuffleboard court* [*1756+*; probably fr *cadger*, "moocher, wheedling beggar"]

coffee *See* CUP OF COFFEE

coffee and *n phr* A cup of coffee with an accompaniment, as a doughnut or pastry : *let's stop for coffee and*

coffin corner *n phr* Any corner of the football field [*1940s+ Football*; because any player running the ball upfield from a corner is dangerously trapped]

coffin nail (or **tack**) *n phr* A cigarette; BUTT (*1880s+*)

cog in the machine *n* Someone with a necessary but insignificant role in a large organization or group : *cogs in the bureaucratic machine* (*1934+*)

coin *n* Money; BREAD, LOOT (*1870s+*)

cojones (coh HOH neez) *n* Courage; audacity; BALLS : *requiring cojones the size of the award-winning cabbages at the state fair/ You've got stainless steel cojones, Dave* [*1932+*; fr Spanish "testicles"]

coke *modifier* : *coke peddlers/ coke sniffer* *n* Cocaine (*1908+*)

Coke-bottle (or **Coke-bottle-bottom**) **glasses** *n phr* Very thick eyeglass lenses : *He had thinning hair, Coke-bottle glasses, a big nose/ Every maladjusted sociopath with Coke-bottle-bottom glasses has no trouble finding this stuff* [*1970s+*; fr their resemblance to the thickness of the bottom of a soft-drink bottle]

coked or **coked-up** or **coked-out** *adj* Intoxicated with cocaine; HIGH : *the new generation of "coked" gunmen/ the pair of strippers, a coked-out Pakistani princess and a coked-up Fire Island queen/ Marvella, you coked-out cunt* (*1920s+ Narcotics*)

cokehead *n* A cocaine addict (*1920s+ Narcotics*)

cold *adj* **1** Unconscious; OUT : *The snowball knocked him cold* (*1896+*) **2** Undergoing a spell of bad luck : *I got out of that game because I was cold and Pop was hot* **3** Without rehearsal, practice, or warmup : *When the star got sick, this woman had to take over the part cold* (*1890s+*) **4** Insulting; cruel : *That's really cold, Duffy* (*1980s+*) *adv* **1** Perfectly; in every detail; BLIND : *She knew the subject cold* (*1890s+*) **2** With no possibility of evasion; definitively; DEAD TO RIGHTS : *After that slip they had him cold* (*1908+*) *See* BLOW HOT AND COLD, HOT AND COLD

cold as (or **colder than**) **hell** *adj phr* (Variations : **a witch's tit** may replace **hell**) Very cold : *In Chicago, that December 1955, it was cold as a well-digger's ass in the Klondike/ It's cold as a witch's tit outside* [charity 1835+, witch's tit 1932+, welldigger's ass 1940s+]

cold-blooded *adj* Absolutely first-rate; the very best; ZERO COOL (*1960s+ Black teenagers*)

cold-call *n* : *Canvassing is the equivalent of cold calls in the sales field* *v* To make a sales call without an appointment : *It's difficult to cold-call a corporation and ask them to give you five figures up front* (*1970s+*)

cold cash *n phr* Unmistakably valid money, as distinct from checks, promises, etc; hard cash : *The place wants payment in cold cash, nothing less* [1884+; fr the notion that definite and inalterable things, like gold and silver coins, are *cold* and *hard*]

coldcock *n* The act of knocking someone unconscious quickly before the victim can resist *v* To knock someone unconscious; KNOCK someone OUT : *He told me to step aside and I wouldn't, so he cold cocked me/ He was going to die, cold-cocked and kicked senseless by a couple of redneck ranchers* [1918+; origin uncertain; perhaps fr the hammering of *caulking* into a boat's or ship's seams; perhaps related to Canadian loggers' *put the caulks to* someone, "stamp in someone's face with spiked boots"]

cold day in hell, a *n phr* An impossible time; never : *It'll be a cold day in hell when you catch me smoking dope* (*1940s+*)

cold deck *n phr* A dishonest deck of playing cards, usu stacked or marked (*1856+*) *v phr* To take advantage of someone; dishonestly assure one's own winning; RIG, STACK THE DECK (*1884+*)

◁**cold enough to freeze the balls (or nuts) off a brass monkey**▷ *adj phr* Very cold indeed [1928+; A politer version citing the *tail of a brass monkey* is attested in 1928]

cold feet *See* HAVE COLD FEET

cold fish *modifier* : *Jackson offered a cold-fish handshake to Antrim after the game* *n phr* A person who lacks emotional warmth, compassion, sociability, etc; iceberg (*1920s+*)

cold meat *n phr* A cadaver; corpse; DEAD MEAT (*1819+*)

cold-meat party *n phr* A wake or funeral : *You were at that cold-meat party; I spotted you coming out of the cemetery* (*1908+*)

cold one, a *n phr* A bottle or glass of beer; BREW, BREWSKI : *when someone from far away stops in for a cold one* (*1990s+*)

cold pricklies *n phr* Unpleasant and unwelcome comments; adverse criticism : *The cast needed strokes, but they got cold pricklies* [1970s+; the opposite of *warm fuzzies*]

cold shoulder *n phr* A deliberate snub; display of chilly contempt (*1816+*) *v* : *I cold-shouldered him and he looked puzzled* (*1845+*)

cold shower *modifier* : *hard-line, cold-war, cold-shower Republican Protestants* *n phr* A remedy for illusions; an imposer of reality; a dampener of spirits : *turning a cold shower on the grimy, corrosive residue of 73 years of communism* [1990s+; Attested in 1866 in the form *a douche of cold water*; it should also be recalled that *cold baths* and *showers* have been a traditional prescription for calming the rampant male]

cold snap *n phr* A short spell of cold weather (*1776+*)

cold sober *adj phr* Completely sober (*1930s+*) *See* STONE COLD SOBER

cold storage *See* IN COLD STORAGE

cold turkey *adj* Requiring abrupt and complete deprivation : *They tried the cold-turkey cure* (*1921+*) *adv phr* **1** Without warning, rehearsal, overture, etc; COLD : *simply walk in cold turkey and talk things over* (*1940s+*) **2** : *He kicked his habit cold turkey* *modifier* Basic; unadorned; HARD-CORE : *Stalin didn't like certain cold-turkey facts Kennan reported* (*1920s+*) *n phr* **1** The plain truth; the straight skinny (*1928+*) **2** Total and abrupt deprivation of narcotics, as distinct from gradual withdrawal (*1921+*) *v phr* **1** : *I'll cold-turkey right now : the butler did it* (*1920s+*) **2** To stop auction bidding and sell at a previously set price (*1940s+ Auctioneers*) *See* TALK TURKEY

collar *n* An arrest • The earliest form is *put the collar on* : *The bull makes a collar on me/ The best collar in recent years* (*1865+*) *v* **1** To seize or take, later esp to arrest : *He collared the muggers in the next block* (*1830s+*) **2** To comprehend; grasp; DIG : *I don't collar your meaning, Sam* (*1940s+ Teenagers*) *See* HOT UNDER THE COLLAR, WHITE-COLLAR

College *See* JOE COLLEGE

college try *See* THE OLD COLLEGE TRY

collywobbles, the *n phr* A stomachache (*1823+*)

color *n* Interesting background, esp details about players, etc, as used in sports coverage • A scholar in the mid-1920s wrote of *color stuff* as the enlivening human interest and spicy, inventive language used by sports writers to avoid mere facts : *doing color, spoke of a shot put up by one of the players by calling it "a Perot hook" : in, out, and in/ I told him I need some color for a magazine piece I'm doing* (*1938+ Media*) *See* OFF COLOR

Colorado koolaid *n* Coors® beer : *Colorado koolaid is always advertised on television* [1970s+; fr *Kool-Aid*®, a soft-drink powder; the beer is brewed in *Colorado*]

color me something *sentence* I am what is indicated : *Color me gone/ Color me ready*

[1980s+; fr a child's book in which *colors* are added to outline drawings]

colors *n* Dress and insignia that identify members of motorcycle clubs and other gangs : *Many bars had signs on their doors listing their dress codes or other rules. The phrase "no colors" was almost always part of such a list/ I've never seen anything that resembled colors or signs or whatever (1960s+ Motorcyclists)* See WITH FLYING COLORS

combo *n* **1** A musical group or band : *a combo like Led Zeppelin (1920s+ Musicians)* **2** The combination of a safe, lock, vault, etc *(1920s+)* **3** Any combination : *gin and tomato juice combo/ boy-girl combo (1920s+)* **4** A bisexual : *We had deep concerns that Andy was becoming a combo (1980s+ Students)*

◁**come**▷ *n* (also **cum**) Semen, or any fluid secreted at orgasm *(1920s+)* *v* To have an orgasm; ejaculate semen *(1650+)* See HOW COME, WHAT GOES AROUND COMES AROUND

come a cropper *v phr* **1** To take a sudden violent fall **2** To fail; suffer a setback [1870s+; origin uncertain; perhaps fr a British dialect word *crop*, "neck"]

come across *v phr* **1** To give something, esp to do so somewhat reluctantly : *When will you come across with the rent? (1908+)* **2** To accede to the sex act; bestow oneself sexually : *She came across without more fuss (1930s+)* **3** To seem to be; give the impression • Often with *as* or *like* : *Walter doesn't come across as a crusader, or muckraker/ This guy always comes across very hostile (1930s+)*

come again *v phr* To repeat something; RUN something BY AGAIN • Nearly always a request, or an expression of disbelief at what one has heard : *Come again? Did I hear what I hope I didn't? (1884+)*

come apart at the seams *v phr* To lose coherence; disintegrate : *It was rather a long kiss. Silas felt himself coming apart at the seams/ I would choose not to give the Republicans any advice, rather just stand back and watch them coming apart at the seams*

come at someone like six headlights (or like a Mack Truck) *v phr* To confront someone honestly and forcibly : *I'd rather sit in a room with a guy that comes at you like six headlights, like a Mack Truck (1980s+)*

comeback *n* **1** A quick and witty retort; a withering riposte : *Dorothy Parker was famous for devastating comebacks (1889+)* **2** A regaining of success, fame, health, etc : *He's trying another comeback at 38 (1908+)* **3** A customer who returns merchandise; also, the returning itself *(1950s+ Salespersons)* **4** A response to a call : *Thanks for your comeback, Dead Duck (1970s+ Citizens band)*

come back *v phr* To regain success, renown, health, etc; make a comeback : *It's hard to come back after a fiasco like that (1910+)*

come back and bite one *v phr* (Variations : **in the ass** or **in the fanny** may be added) To reappear as punishment or retribution; boomerang; backfire : *It has come back to bite him/ They don't want any of their used boxes to come back and bite them in the fanny (1990s+)*

come back for more *v phr* To return repeatedly, either bravely or foolishly, to a bad situation; not know when one is beaten : *Pathetically, no matter how treacherously venomous they were, she came back for more (1950s+)*

come clean *v phr* To tell the truth, esp the whole truth; make a plenary confession *(1919+)*

comedown *n* **1** A reduction of one's status; loss of prestige : *Riding the bus was a comedown for her (1840+)* **2** The ending of a drug experience : *I cooled it with Quaalude. The comedown wasn't too bad (1950s+ Narcotics)* **3** LETDOWN *(1950s+)*

come down *v phr* **1** To experience the ending of a drug intoxication : *as if he had just come down off methedrine (1950s+ Narcotics)* **2** To become firmly established : *when a chick's habit came down on her (1960s+ Narcotics)* **3** To happen : *Sir Morgan's cove, where the Great Event was coming down/ Something weird had to be coming down (1960s+ Black)*

come down hard on someone *v phr* To criticize or punish severely : *came down hard on him for getting home at 3 a.m.*

come down on someone **(or something)** *v phr* To criticize severely; savage : *If I did that, the press would come down on me very hard (1881+)*

come down on someone **like a ton of bricks** *v phr* To punish or suppress severely; CLAMP DOWN : *When he heard about it he came down on them like a ton of bricks* [1920s+; The earlier version *like a thousand of bricks* is found by 1836]

come down the pike *v phr* To appear; come on the scene : *every dumbass little news story that comes down the pike (1950s+)*

come hell or high water *adv phr* No matter what happens; in any event : *I'll find out come hell or high water (1916+ fr cowboys)*

come-in *n* **1** The line of people waiting to buy tickets **2** The time between the opening of the main tent and the beginning of the entry procession *(Circus)*

come in for *v phr* To receive; be given something : *He came in for a lot of grief after that decision (1665+)*

come in from the cold *v phr* **1** To retire from espionage service : *coming in from the cold and* *staying free might be out of reach* (*1960s+*) **2** To return to comfort, acclaim, etc, after a period of relative obscurity : *An Osmond comes in from the cold* (*1980s+*) [popularized by the John le Carré 1963 novel *The Spy Who Came In from the Cold*]

come-lately *See* JOHNNY-COME-LATELY

come off *v phr* **1** To succeed : *To everybody's astonishment, the scheme came off* (*1590s+*) ◁2▷ To have an orgasm; ejaculate semen; COME (*1650+*) **3** To happen; GO DOWN (*1855+*) **4** To seem to be; give the impression; COME ACROSS • Often with *as* : *Geronimo comes off as ersatz tragedy/ She comes off softer than you would think* (*1990s+*)

come off something *v phr* To stop doing or saying something immediately : *Come off that crap. Keep your jaw shut/ Give me a break and come off it* (*1880s+*)

come off it *sentence* I don't believe it : *come off it, Charlie* (*1912+*)

come off one's **perch** *v phr* To stop behaving in a superior or haughty manner; GET OFF one's HIGH HORSE (*1890s+*)

come-on *modifier* : *football bowls baited with $100,000 or so of come-on money* **n** Anything designed to attract or seduce; an enticement : *I gave her a big grin, but she knew it was a come-on* (*1902+*)

come on *interj* An exclamation of disbelief, disapproval, request, etc : *Come on, Arnold, don't give me that shit* (*1603+*) *v phr* To show as; present oneself as; act; COME ACROSS : *Your friend comes on real dumb* (*1950+*)

come on like gangbusters *v phr* To begin or proceed in a vigorous fashion : *I come on like the Gang Busters and go off like The March of Time* [*1942+*; fr the radio program *Gangbusters* of 1937–1942, which was introduced by a noisy miscellany of sirens, shots, screeches, music, etc]

come on strong *v phr* **1** To gain steadily and rapidly in a race (*1940s+ Horse racing*) **2** To be vehement and positive : *He always comes on a little too strong about taxes* (*1970s+*)

come on to someone *v phr* To make a sexual advance; PROPOSITION, PUT A MOVE ON : *The way I came on to you the other night; I thought you'd be miffed* (*1980s+*)

come out *v phr* **1** To declare oneself; take a position • The original action was that of declaring a religious conversion : *Did she come out for the Equal Rights Amendment?* (*1840s+*) **2** To end; eventuate : *How'd that whole deal come out?* (*1896+*) **3** To acknowledge one's homosexuality; COME OUT OF THE CLOSET : *Their eldest son had "come out"* (*1970s+ Homosexuals*)

come out ahead (or **on top**) *v phr* To win : *Who came out ahead in the poll?* (*1930s+*)

come out in the wash *v phr* To be dealt with as a natural consequence : *you'll see that it will come out in the wash*

come out of a bag *v phr* To act contrary to expectation (*1990s+ Black*)

come out of the chute *v phr* To begin; inaugurate something : *If we had come out of the chute conservatively, we would have been projecting a sense of doubt* [*1980s+*; fr the rodeo, where bucking horses, rampaging bulls, etc, *come out of a chute at the edge of the arena*]

come out of the closet *v phr* **1** To acknowledge one's homosexuality; COME OUT : *He came out of the closet last year and his parents damn near died* (*1960s+ Homosexuals*) **2** To reveal or acknowledge some personal conviction, political position, etc : *In 1978 Timmy came out of the closet and showed a genuine interest in the club/ James Robinson, a fiery, red-faced orator with a Bible clenched in his upraised hand, thundered that it was "time for God's people to come out of the closet and the churches and change America"*

come out of the woodwork *See* CRAWL OUT OF THE WOODWORK

come out swinging (or **smoking**) *v phr* To be eager and aggressive; COME ON STRONG : *Labor chief comes out swinging/ the fighter came out smoking, trying to dazzle the audience with a flurry of quips* (*1990s+*)

come over someone *v phr* To convince or influence, esp by force or fraud : *Then I realized he was just trying to come over me, not inform me* (*1609+*)

◁**come-queen**▷ *v* A person who prefers and practices fellatio : *a nutty come-queen named Linda Lovelace* (*1970s+*)

comer *n* A person doing very well and promising to do better in a certain field : *She's a comer, a potential champ* (*1880s+*)

come running *v phr* Join one in a hurry; appear immediately : *Once you've asked her these questions, let her make up her own mind, and be there if she comes running* (*1596+*)

comes around *See* WHAT GOES AROUND COMES AROUND

come through *v phr* **1** To succeed as expected and desired : *Jim Thorpe always came through to win* (*1899+*) **2** To cope successfully with perils and troubles; weather adversity : *All seems bleak, but we'll come through unscathed* (*1899+*) **3** COME ACROSS (*1907+*)

come (or **bring**) **to a screeching halt** *v phr* To be finished or finish abruptly and immediately : *when the 1994 season came to a screeching halt/ I've got to bring this to a screeching halt* (*1970s+*)

come unglued (or **unstuck** or **unwrapped**) *v phr* To go out of control; deteriorate to chaos; disintegrate; COME APART AT THE

SEAMS : *Mr Foster succeeded in keeping the proceedings from coming unglued/ Dole's constant anxiety that it could all come unstuck has set the dynamics of his campaign/ Everybody knew she was bound to come unwrapped* (1910+)

come up for air *v phr* To pause, take a break : *been at this since 8 and need to come up for air*

comeuppance or **come-uppings** *n* A deserved chastening, esp some event that checks a wrongdoer; just desserts (1958+)

come up roses *v phr* To turn out well; succeed : *Will Dodgers' crop come up roses?* (1960s+)

come up short *v phr* To be deficient; not add up to what it ought : *Shelton slugged 15 aces, but the rest of his game came up short* (1980s+)

come up smelling like a rose (or **with the five-dollar gold piece**) *v phr* To have extraordinarily good luck; emerge from peril with profit [1950s+; fr the traditional image of the happy person who "falls in the shitpile and *comes up smelling like a rose*"]

come up to the wire *v phr* To approach the finish; come near the end : *The crucial project is coming up to the wire and we're a bit nervous* [1970s+; fr the *wire* that marks the finish line of a race]

come up with the goods *v phr* To succeed in providing what is required : *you'll come up with the goods or be fired* (1879+)

come within an ace *v phr* To come very near to doing something, winning something, etc : *She came within an ace of getting the world title* [1704+; probably a version of the 13th-century term *within ambs ace*, "very close to," *ambs ace* being the lowest point in dice, two ones or snake-eyes, fr Old French fr Latin *ambas as*, "both ace"]

come with the territory (or **turf**) *See* GO WITH THE TERRITORY (or TURF)

comfort station *n* A restroom; public toilet : *Pull over. I need the comfort station*

comfy *adj* Comfortable and comforting; pleasant and easy : *Just reeling off their names is ever so comfy* (1829+)

comics, the *See* the FUNNIES

coming from *See* WHERE someone IS COMING FROM

coming out of one's **ass** (or **ears**) *adj phr* In surfeit; in overplenteous supply; up the kazoo : *I got plenty of problems, problems coming out of my ass/ We had weekly updates* : *We had statistics coming out of our ears* (1960s+) *See* STEAM WAS COMING OUT OF someone's EARS

commando *n* A person who behaves roughly and overeagerly, esp in lovemaking [Students fr WWII Army; fr the *Commandos*, elite British shock troops of WWII] *See* BEDPAN COMMANDO

Commie or **Commy** *adj* : *Commy plot/ Commie rhetoric n* A Communist (1930s+)

commish *n* A commissioner, esp a police commissioner : *create a high school that would focus on criminal justice studies, a kind of High School for the Commishes of tomorrow* (1908+)

comp *n* **1** A complimentary ticket; annie oakley (1885+) **2** A nonpaying guest at a hotel, restaurant, casino, club, etc (1930s+) **3** Something given free to a privileged guest or customer : *The first was the comps he got in the casino for dropping his $2,000* (1960s+) **4** Compensation, esp worker's compensation or unemployment compensation : *I've got three more weeks of comp coming* (1970s+) *v* : *The hotel will comp you for just about anything you want/ Now, because I'm a high roller, everything is comped. I don't pay for anything*

Company, the *n phr* The US Central Intelligence Agency (1960s+)

company man *n phr* One who is, esp from the point of view of union members, devoted to the interests of the employer (1920+ *Labor union*)

comped *modifier* Given free; free of charge; complimentary : *including the bill for the comped room at the Oaks and Pines* (1960s+)

compleat *See* REET

compusex or **cybersex** *n* Sexual talk, innuendo, proposals, titillations, etc, on a computer network : *But more often than not, it's a stop for compusex, that information-age version of phone sex* [1990s+; fr *computer* plus *sex*]

con[1] *n* A convict or former convict; prison inmate : *You're a "con," you've no rights* (1893+)

con[2] *n* **1** SCAM : *It's a clever con and you're a greedy rat* **2** A dishonest sort of persuasion; PUT-ON : *a slick young man with a line of deferential con* (1900s+) *v* **1** To swindle; work a confidence game : *We conned the old fart out of three big ones* (1896+) **2** : *He conned her into thinking he'd marry her*

con artist *See* CON MAN

concern *See* a GOING CONCERN

conehead *n* **1** An intellectual; POINTY HEAD : *These coneheads are retards* **2** A stupid person (1970s+)

confab (KAHN fab) *n* A talk; discussion (1701+) *v* : *Let's confab a bit about that idea* (1740+) [fr *confabulation*]

confetti *See* IRISH CONFETTI

con game (or **job**) *n phr* A confidence game; swindle; SCAM (1880s+)

congrats *interj* Congratulations : *You're in? Congrats* (1884+)

conk[1] *n* The head • *Conk* designated the nose earlier, by 1812 (1860s+) *v* **1** To hit on the nose or head : *I got conked by the bat* (1925+)

2 To defeat utterly; CLOBBER (1950s+) [probably fr *conch*] *See* BUST one's ASS

conk² *v* To die; cease to operate; CONK OUT : *A year after that, a spinster aunt conked (WWI Royal Flying Corps)*

conk off *v phr* **1** To go to sleep; sleep : *You been conking off for eight hours (1940s+)* **2** To stop work; rest when one should work; GOOF OFF (1950s+)

conk out *v phr* **1** To stop running or operating : *if this plane conked out (WWI Royal Flying Corps)* **2** To lose energy and spirits suddenly; become abruptly exhausted (1920s+) **3** To go to sleep; CONK OFF (1940s+) **4** To die : *So she's conked out, eh?/ John Le Mesurier wishes it to be known that he conked out on Nov 15. He sadly misses family and friends (1920s+)* [probably echoic]

con man (or **artist**) *n phr* **1** A confidence man (1889+) **2** One adept at persuasion, esp at dishonest or self-serving persuasion (1900s+)

connect *v* **1** To hit someone very hard : *He connected with a rude one to the jaw (1930s+)* **2** To buy narcotics or other contraband (1960s+ Narcotics) **3** To get along with; establish rapport with; CLICK : *She's never been able to connect with her tenant (1940s+)*

connection *n* A seller of narcotics; a person who can get drugs; PUSHER (1925s+ Narcotics)

connect the dots *modifier* From one fixed point to another : *rarely venture out of their own connect-the-dots puzzle : from home to work, on to local haunts, and home again* *v phr* **1** To draw a conclusion from disparate facts : *He calls this connecting the dots because it links bits of information to form a big picture* **2** To do something very simple : *He couldn't even figure out how to connect the dots* [1980s+; fr a child's puzzle, where a picture emerges when one *connects* a number of dispersed *dots* on the paper]

conniption fit or **conniption** *n phr* A violent tantrum; hysterics; catfit, DUCK FIT : *Please don't throw a conniption fit over the news* [first form 1833+, second 1848+; origin unknown; the later term *catnip fit* is a stab at folk etymology]

contract *n* **1** An arrangement to have someone murdered by a professional killer : *The word is there's a contract out for Taffy Taylor (1930s+)* **2** Any illegal or unethical arrangement : *contract, any favor one policeman says he'll do for another (1950s+ Police) See* SWEETHEART CONTRACT

contraption *n* A contrivance or device; piece of machinery : *What's this ugly contraption in the corner? (1820s+)*

conversate *v* To socialize and chat; to converse with another • Back formation from con-

versation : *We conversated about the weekend plan*

cooch *modifier* : *an old-time circus cooch show* *n* **1** Any sexually suggestive or imitative dance, esp a striptease dance; HOOTCHIE-COOTCHIE (1920s+) ◁2▷ The female crotch; vulva (1950s+)

coo-coo *See* CUCKOO

cook *v* **1** To be put to death in the electric chair; FRY (1930s+) **2** To happen; occur : *Is anything cooking on the new tax rule? (1940s+ Jive talk)* **3** To do very well; excel : *if the performers begin cooking together and most of the director's intuitions and skills pay off (1930+ Jazz musicians)* **4** To falsify; tamper with : *The British government cooked press stories shamelessly in order to deceive the Argentine enemy/ She cooked the statistics (1636+)* **5** To dissolve heroin in water over a flame before injecting it (1960s+ Narcotics)

cookbook *modifier* Routine; mechanical; unimaginative : *All he did was adopt the cookbook solution (1970s+)* *n* **1** A chemistry laboratory manual (1950s+ Students) **2** Any guide, manual, protocol, etc : *We use a* • *cookbook of procedures (1970s+)*

cooked *adj* **1** Ruined; hopelessly beaten; FINISHED : *After the fourth fumble they were cooked (1850+)* **2** Altered; falsifed; doctored : *His miracle rise turned out to be based more on cooked books than shampooed rugs (1860+)*

cooked-up *adj* Specially contrived; expedient and dishonest : *It's insane why we give ourselves cooked up reasons for not moving the issue (1940s+)*

cooker *See* PRESSURE COOKER

cook someone's goose *v phr* To ruin or destroy someone; FINISH • Very often in the passive form, "our goose is cooked" : *I know I've basically cooked my own goose here* [1845+; origin uncertain; one legend has it that a Swedish king Erik was mocked, as he approached a town, by a goose hanging over the wall, the goose being a symbol of folly and stupidity. The king thereupon burned the town and cooked the goose]

cookie or **cookey** *n* **1** (also **cookee**) A cook or cook's helper (1840s+) **2** A person who prepares opium for smoking; opium addict (1950s+ Narcotics) **3** An attractive young woman (1920+) **4** A person; GAL, GUY • Most often modified by *smart* or *tough* : *"What do you really want?" Smart cookie (1930+)* ◁5▷ (also **cookies**) The female genitals; vulva (1950s+ Black) **6** A base hit : *knowing I was going to get at least one cookie every game (1970s+ Baseball)* **7** A short line of text added to one's computer upon accessing a Web site, to identify the user *See* GRIPE one's

ASS, THAT'S THE WAY THE BALL BOUNCES, TOUGH COOKIE

cookie-cutter or **cooky-cutter** *modifier* (also **cookie-cut**) Identical and unoriginal; standardized; stereotyped : *Each store is a cookie-cutter copy, laid out according to plans devised at the corporate headquarters/ I'd never want to read that kind of cookie-cut magazine n* 1 A police officer's badge; potsy, tin *(1920s+ Circus)* 2 A weak and unenterprising person; cookie-pusher. WIMP *(1950s+)* An inadequate weapon, esp a knife *(1950s+)*

cookie jar *See* WITH one's HAND IN THE TILL

cookies *See* COOKIE, SHOOT one's COOKIES

cook the books *v phr* To tamper with and falsify records, esp financial accounts : *The managers had cooked the books to the tune of $34 million/ He's been cooking the books for so many of those companies (1940s+)*

cook up *v phr* To devise; fabricate; HOKE UP : *We'll cook up a story to explain your swollen lip (1750+)*

cook with gas (or **on the front** or **top burner**) *v phr* To perform very commendably; GROOVE : *I am cooking with gas on this project (1930s+ jive talk)*

cool *adj* 1 In control of one's feelings; stoic : *Learn to be cool under fire (by early 1700s)* 2 Aloof and uninvolved; disengaged, as an expression of alienation; BEAT, HIP : *He's cool, don't give a shit for nothing (1940s+)* 3 : *cool jazz/ a real cool passage* 4 Excellent; good : *a cool shirt/ cool sermon (1940s+)* 5 Pleasant; desirable; COPACETIC : *You enjoying it? Is everything cool? (1950s+)* 6 Not less than a certain amount : *cleared a cool million n* 1 : *He lost his cool and bolted like a rabbit (1960s+)* 2 : *My guru drifted me to a total spiritual cool* 3 Jazz marked by soft tones, improvisation based on advanced chord extensions, and revision of certain classical jazz idioms *(1940s+ Cool musicians) v* 1 To postpone; await developments in : *Let's cool this whole business for a week or so (1950s+)* 2 To kill : *Who knew what he wanted to make it look like when he cooled her (1920+) See* BLOW one's COOL, LOSE one's COOL, PLAY IT COOL, ZERO COOL

cool as a cucumber *adj phr* Very calm, and often haughty or callous *(1730s+)*

cool beans or **bananas** *modifier* Excellent; wonderful; COOL, FRESH, RAD : *Cool Beans "superlative, a highly desirable situation" (1980s+ Students)*

cool cat *n* A stylish and admirable person

cool down *v phr* To calm down : *cool down before he gets here*

cooled-out *adj* Relaxed; passionless : *a cooled-out sign linked to the mass media (1970s+)*

cooler, the *n* 1 A jail; the SLAMMER 2 A cell or cellblock for solitary confinement *(Prison) (1880s+)*

cool guy *n phr* A conventional, tedious, or pretentious person who thinks he is up-to-date, aware, interesting, etc *(1990s+ Teenagers)*

cool hand *modifier* : *these four cool-hand lunatics n phr* A person not easily disconcerted • Sir Thomas Overbury (d. 1613) wrote that a *cool hand* is "one who accounts bashfulness the wickedest thing in the world, and therefore studies impudence" *(1600s+)*

cool one's heels *v phr* To wait, esp to be kept waiting : *I cooled my heels for two hours before the great one would see me (1608+)*

cool it *v phr* 1 To relax; stop being excited or angry 2 To slow one's pace; stop being strenuous 3 To stop what one is doing, esp what is annoying the speaker • In all senses often an exhortation or irritated command *(1950s+ Beat & cool talk)*

cool million *n phr* A whole big million dollars [1890s+; *Cool* as applied to a large sum of money is attested by 1728; with currency inflation the use has progressed from hundred to thousand to million to (very likely) billion, on the way to *cool trillion*]

cool off *v phr* 1 To become calmer and less explosive; moderate : *When he cooled off I spoke sweet reason (1860s+)* 2 To kill; COOL : *Somebody cools off Mr Justin Veezee*

cool-out *n* A device or strategy intended to relax someone, esp to calm justified apprehensions : *cooperating in an Uncle Tom cool-out this late in the game/ This begins what he calls the "cool out." This prepares the man to accept defeat philosophically (1940s+)*

cool out *v phr* 1 To walk a horse after a race to calm and moderate it gradually *(1910+ Horse racing)* 2 To do the sex act *(1970s+ Beat & black)* 3 To relax; become calm; COOL IT : *He was cooling out now, not sprinting, just sitting straight up on the seat, riding without hands at a lazy relaxed rhythm (1980s+)*

cool someone out *v phr* 1 To mollify and appease someone; calm someone's apprehensions or anger : *White Americans found a new level in which to cool the blacks out/ He is the one who has to cool people out and pay off State officials (1940s+)* 2 To relax; calm someone *(1900s+)* 3 To kill someone; COOL, OFF • The date is based on an 1833 text by Davy Crockett *(1830s+)*

coolster *n* A stylish and admirable person; DUDE, STUD : *If you see said coolsters in the cafeteria, ask if it's OK to sit with them (1990s+ Teenagers)*

coolth *n* Coolness • Based on *warmth*

coon *n* **1** A black person (*1862+*) **2** (also **coon's ass**) A carnival worker who is too aggressive and mistreats the customers (*1990+ Carnival*) *See* ACE BOON COON

coon's age, a *n phr* A very long time : *I haven't seen her in a coon's age* (*1843+*)

coop *n* **1** A jail or prison (*1785+*) **2** A place, esp a patrol car, where police officers sleep while on duty : *all the cops will be in the coop* (*1960s+ Police*) *v* : *There were the cats, the milkmen, and the cops cooping in a police car at the corner* [police senses based on earlier *coop*, "any shelter used by the police to avoid the elements"; fr *chicken coop*] *See* FLY THE COOP, IN THE COOP, RAIN CATS AND DOGS

co-op or **coop** (KOH ahp) *modifier* : *co-op prices/ coop apartment complex n* A cooperative apartment house, store, etc (*1870s+*) *v* To convert an apartment or building from a rental to a cooperative unit : *The old Sussex Arms got co-oped last year* (*1950s+*)

coot *n* A stupid or silly person, usu an aged one : *a harmless old coot* (*1760s+*) *See* CRAZY AS A LOON

cootchie *See* HOOTCHIE-COOTCHIE

cootie or **cooty** *n* A body louse [WWI Army fr British; origin uncertain; perhaps fr Malay *kutu*, "dog tick"; one study suggests London cockney slang as the source]

cop *n* **1** A police officer (*1850s+*) **2** A theft **3** An arrest *v* **1** To arrest (*1850s+*) **2** To steal : *He copped six PCs from the shop* (*1900+*) **3** To win; be awarded : *to cop second place* (*1914+*) **4** To comprehend; grasp : *I don't quite cop your sense, pal* (*1940s+*) **5** To buy or get narcotics : *The pusher has appeared, and they will make their round-about way to him to "cop"* (*1960s+ Narcotics*) [origin uncertain; perhaps ultimately fr Latin *capere* "seize," by way of French; police officer sense a shortening of *copper*; second sense "seize, catch" attested by 1704] *See* GOOD COP BAD COP

copacetic or **copasetic** (KOH pə SET ik) *adj* As it should be; quite satisfactory; COOL, OK [*1919+* fr black; origin unknown; perhaps fr Louisiana Creole French *coupe-sétique* in the same sense, semantically related to *cope*, attested fr about 1880; perhaps fr Hebrew *kol ba seder*, "all in order," which may have been acquired by black customers of a Jewish merchant]

◁**cop a** (or someone's) **cherry**▷ *v phr* To deprive someone of virginity; deflower someone (*1930s+*)

cop a feel *v phr* To feel or caress someone's body, esp the sex organs, usu in a sly or seemingly inadvertent way : *I thought he wanted to help me into the car, but I think he just wanted to cop a feel* (*1930s+*)

cop an attitude *See* HAVE AN ATTITUDE

cop a plea *v phr* To plead guilty to a lesser charge than one might otherwise be tried for; escape a worse punishment by accepting a lesser one (*1920s+ Police & underworld*)

cop a tude *See* HAVE AN ATTITUDE

cop-heat *n* Police activity : *When there's cop-heat here, the prostitutes go there* [1970s+; *Heat* in this sense is attested from 1931]

cop (or **buy**) **it** *v phr* To die, esp to be killed in battle or otherwise; BUY THE FARM : *He had a feeling he wouldn't cop it that day/ The guy who buys it does it off camera* (*WWI British forces*)

cop-killer *n* A bullet capable of penetrating bulletproof vests : *the apple-green bullets they call cop-killers* (*1980s+*)

cop onto *v phr* To come to understand or become aware of : *cop onto that idea*

cop-out *n* An evasion; an excuse for inaction : *Arguing about standards is a "cop-out"* (*1960s+ Counterculture*)

cop out *v phr* **1** To be arrested (*1940s+ Underworld*) **2** To confess; plead guilty; COP A PLEA : *I copped out* (*1940s+*) **3** To avoid trouble and responsibility; evade an issue or problem; disengage oneself : *When his friends really needed help he copped out* (*1960s+ Counterculture*)

copped *adj* Arrested : *copped for stealing a baseball card*

copper[1] *n* **1** A police officer (*1846+*) **2** An informer; STOOL PIGEON (*1897+ Underworld*) **3** Time taken off a prison sentence for good behavior or because one has informed on colleagues (*1908+ Underworld*)

copper[2] *v* To bet against a card, roll of the dice, person, etc [*1864+ Gambling*; fr the use of a special metal chip, often a *copper* cent, by a gambler to indicate a bet with the bank in faro]

cop shop *n phr* A police station (*1940s+ Australian*)

cop to something *v phr* To confess to; plead guilty to : *He cops to bimbo massages, but insists he didn't go "coital"/ This gave students an opportunity to cop to secretly held feelings* [1990s+; a shortening of *cop out*]

copy *n* A subject for an article in a newspaper, magazine, etc : *She knew that Miss Gould was good "copy"* (*1880s+*) *v* To send a copy of a message to someone other than the immediate addressee : *Copy Tina and tell her the mag is fast turning to compost* (*1980s+*)

copycat *modifier* : *a copycat inventor/ copycat crime n* **1** An imitator; mimic • May be forty or fifty years older (*1890s+*) **2** A copycat crime or criminal : *Could be a copycat. Guy wants to do his wife in, covers it up by making it look like Red Rose/ I knew enough to bet the farm that this was no coincidence or copycat*

(1960s+) **v** : *Sally traps her there, and copy-cats the first murder, gore and all (1930s+)*

copycat crime *n phr* A crime committed in imitation of another crime, esp one that is sensational and highly publicized : *Copy-Cat Crimes of the Heart*

cop Zs (or some Zs) *v phr* (Variations : **bag** or **catch** or **cut** or **get** or **pile up** or **stack** may replace **cop**) To take a nap; sleep; SNOOZE : *got to peck a little, and cop me some Z's/ sits around all day cutting Zs (1950s+ Black)*

core *See* HARD-CORE, SOFT-CORE

core dump *v phr* **1** To empty out the central memory of a computer **2** To explain oneself fully; say one's piece, esp in the mode of complaint : *One of the semiconductor makers here went to see her manager the other day. Later she told a friend that she had "core dumped" on the boss (1980s+ Computers)*

Corine *n* Cocaine *(1970s+ Narcotics)*

cork *See* BLOW one's TOP, POP one's CORK

corked *adj* Drunk *(1896+)*

corker *n* A person or thing that is remarkable, wonderful, superior, etc; HUMDINGER, piss-cutter : *What a corker, this guy* [1882+; fr earlier sense "something that definitively settles a matter," perhaps fr *caulk*]

cork out *v phr* To behave very strangely; FREAK OUT : *"Hey, he/ she's corking out." (acting really weird) (1990s+)*

corn *n* **1** Corn whiskey; MOONSHINE *(1820+)* **2** Music, poetry, sentiment, etc, that is maudlin and naively affirmative of old-fashioned values; banal and emotionally overwrought material; SCHMALTZ *(1930+ Jazz musicians)* [second sense probably from the notion of *cornfed* as indicating rural simplicity and naivete]

cornball *adj* : *Where did you get those cornball notions?* *n* A person who admires or produces markedly sentimental material and utters relatively simpleminded moral convictions : *Eisenhower on no account can be called a cornball (1940s+)*

corndog *n* An eccentric and socially inept person; DWEEB, GEEK *(1980s+ Students)*

corned *adj* Drunk *(1785+)*

corner *See* COFFIN CORNER, HOT CORNER

cornfed *adj* **1** Plump and sturdy; rural or as if rural : *a corn-fed beauty (1787+)* **2** Naive and sentimental; CORNY *(1920s+)*

◀**cornhole** ▶ *n* The anus; also, a poke in the anus : *itch in the cornhole* *v* To do anal intercourse; BUGGER, BUNGHOLE : *The Germans would get castrated when they cornholed him/ Bartley had corn-holed the Irish maid in full view of wife and child (1930s+)*

corny *adj* Overly sentimental; banal; devoted to or expressing old-fashioned moral convictions; CORNBALL [1930+ Jazz musicians;

the writer Mari Sandoz (1896–1966) suggested as possible origin the corn-seed catalogs sent to Midwestern farmers before and after 1900, which were larded with tired old jokes; the jokes were called *corn jokes* and *corny*]

corral (kə RAL) *v* To find; gather : *to corral votes* [1850s+; fr Spanish]

cosmic *adj* Powerfully wonderful; excellent : *pay-per-view is cosmic*

cottage cheese thighs *n phr* Fat thighs; THUNDER THIGHS : *In Los Angeles, cottage cheese thighs are nothing to snicker about (1990s+)*

cottage industry *n phr* **1** Productive work done at home using computers or computer terminals **2** A local, esp a rural, concern or enthusiasm : *great supporter of the contras, an occupation that appears to have been an Arkansas cottage industry* [1920s+; based on the name given to the system of having piecework done at home, rather than in factories, at the beginning of the Industrial Revolution]

cotton *See* IN TALL COTTON

cotton mouth *n phr* Dryness of the mouth caused by a hangover, use of marijuana or drugs, fear, etc *(1970+)*

cotton-picking or **cotton-pickin'** *adj* Despicable; wretched; DAMNED : *They're out of their cotton-picking minds/ I don't think it's anybody's cotton-pickin' business what you're doing* [1950s+; fr the inferior status of the field hand or poor farmer in southern US society]

cotton to *v phr* Approve of; like; appreciate; fancy : *"That's a thing I didn't cotton to anyhow," said Miss Fuschia Leach, who had found her talent did not lie that way* [1605+; perhaps fr Welsh *cytuno*, "agree, consent"]

couch *See* CASTING COUCH

couch case *n phr* An emotionally disturbed person [1960s+; fr the psychoanalyst's stereotypical use of the *couch* for a reclining patient]

couch doctor *n phr* A psychoanalyst; SHRINK *(1950s+)*

couch it *v phr* To be banished to another place for sleeping by a bedmate or roommate : *He was snoring so badly, I told him to couch it*

couch potato or **sofa spud** *n phr* A habitual lounger, esp a person who spends much time watching television : *They're not couch potatoes. They're mobile, they go out/ the period that Anglophile couch potatoes find most fascinating (entry form 1970s+, variant 1990s+)*

couch surfing *n* Sleeping on the couch or extra bed of an acquaintance when traveling or when between permanent lodging places, esp to save money : *I'm interviewing in Chicago, so I'm couch surfing it at my sister's/*

She threw him out, so he is couch surfing at Shane's

cough up *v phr* **1** To pay or give something, esp with some reluctance : *Coughing it up : Dunleavy was not happy that the Bucks committed 26 turnovers* (1894+) **2** To tell or relate, esp under interrogation • Modern use, which may not truly represent a continuity with the medieval occurrence, begins in the 1890s (1393+)

coulda-been *modifier* Suggesting, often lamenting, what might have been : *other coulda-been sad-sack tales* (1990s+)

could be *sentence* It is possible • Often a reply to a speculative question : *Is he still alive? Could be/ Could be they don't like us out there* (1930s+) *See* EASY AS PIE

could eat a horse *v phr* To be extremely hungry (1936+)

could murder *v phr* To want to cause harm : *could murder him for ordering that* (1935+)

could not (or couldn't) care less *v phr* One simply does not care; one is sublimely indifferent • In a curious development, the original British negative form has been changed to affirmative by many US speakers, without change of meaning; such contradiction is more common in slang than in standard speech : *I couldn't care less if you like me or not/ I could care less if you like me or not*

could use *v phr* To want or need something : *could use a Valium* (1956+)

count *See* DOWN FOR THE COUNT, NO-COUNT

counted, be *See* STAND UP AND BE COUNTED

counter *See* BEAN-COUNTER

count for spit, not *See* NOT COUNT FOR SPIT

country club *modifier* Characteristic of the wealthy : *Tax cheating is a country-club crime, like insider trading* [1890s+; The date is based on the earliest potential use, that is, on the first occurrence of such primarily golfing clubs of generally exclusive membership]

country cousin *n phr* A distant though related person or thing : *This was country cousin to a myth that floated around St. Louis earlier, about a major utility that ordered six thousand body bags with its name imprinted on them* [1770+; The date refers to the sense "an unsophisticated rustic relative"]

country-fried *adj* Rural; unsophisticated; countrified; shit-kickin' : *Atwater, a Southerner, a country-fried Sammy Glick who learns the error of his ways* (1990s+)

country mile, a *modifier* : *Dennis Conner's country-mile victory in the first America's Cup race n phr* A very long distance : *She made it home first by a country mile* (1940s+) *See* BEAT someone or something BY A COUNTRY MILE

county mounty *n phr* A police officer. esp one patrolling the highway; a sheriff, deputy sheriff, state police officer, etc [Citizens band; second element fr *Mounty* or *Mountie*, "member of the Royal Canadian Mounted Police"]

coupe *See* DEUCE

couple something **short of**, a *modifier* Stupid; mentally deficient • A very flexible and productive formula for gently expressing an adverse judgment : *The manager is a couple cans short of a six-pack/ He's a couple bricks short of a load/ She's a couple sandwiches short of a picnic/ They were all a couple dogies short of a corral* (1980s+)

courage *See* DUTCH COURAGE

courier *n* A small-time drug dealer or drug runner : *the courier does not get much money*

course *See* CRIB COURSE, GUT COURSE, PAR FOR THE COURSE, SNAP COURSE

court *See* the BALL IS IN someone's COURT, FULL COURT PRESS, HOME-COURT ADVANTAGE, KANGAROO COURT

court-in *n* A rigorous initiation ceremony into a girls' gang : *At her court-in, a girl is christened with the nickname by which she will be known* (1990s+ Street gang)

court-out *n* Severe physical punishment for a gang member deemed disloyal : *She can face a "court-out," in which there is no time limit to the beating* (1990s+ Street gang)

cousin *n* **1** Friend; person • An amiable form of address : *How you doin', cousin?* (1430+) **2** A dupe; MARK, PIGEON (1552+ Underworld) *See* KISSING COUSIN, COUSIN

cover *n* **1** A popular song recorded by artists other than those who made it famous : *third album, like the first two, contains many covers of recent chart-busters* (1970s+) **2** An identity, usu an elaborate falsification, assumed by a secret agent for concealment : *To improve his cover he "resigned" from the agency* (1940s+ Espionage) *v* **1** To report on regularly; monitor the news at : *Who's covering the White House now?* (1893+ Newspaper) **2** (also **cover up**) To protect someone with one's testimony : *I'll cover for you if you're caught* (1940s+) **3** To substitute for someone; replace someone temporarily and protectively : *Bini was the designated cover for Placido Domingo in* La Gioconda (1960s+) **4** To attend to, esp temporarily : *Will you cover the switchboard while I'm at the dentist?* (1970+) **5** To travel : *I covered two miles in one minute* (1818+) **6** To include; account for : *That about covers what happened* (1793+) **7** To aim at with a firearm : *Freeze, I got you covered* (1687+) **8** : *They did best covering Springsteen and Stones hits See* BLOW someone's COVER

cover all bases v phr To guard against or supervise all contingencies : *The baking is done on the premises, and Ms Scherber covers all the bases (1940s+ Baseball)*

◁cover one's ass▷ (or tail) (also CYA) *modifier* : *writing long cover-your-ass memos* v phr To provide or arrange for exculpation; devise excuses and alibis : *Some call it "risk management," others "covering your ass"/ The FBI may have to let you be destroyed to cover its own ass/ CYA, you know, that old French expression that means making sure that when historians write about it all it won't be seen as happening on your shift*

cover story n phr 1 The biography and plausible account devised for a secret agent for concealment; COVER *(1940s+ Espionage)* 2 An alibi; a false narrative explanation : *We agree on the cover story, that you haven't seen me for three weeks (1940s+)*

cover-up n Anything designed to conceal or obfuscate the truth by replacement : *Sending the Navy south instead of north was an obvious cover-up (1935+)*

/ cow n 1 Milk *(1900+)* 2 A woman : *The silly cow believed everything she heard (1696+)* ◁3▷ A young woman *(1930s+ Underworld)* See CASH COW, SEA COW

cowabunga *interj* A surfer's exclamation of delight and commitment at the beginning of a ride, often used as a generalized cry of delight : *It was the real Andy Griffith, too : cowabunga (1950s+ Surfers)* n Energetic popular plaudits : *make their most open bid yet for commercial cowabunga (1980s+)* [apparently coined by Eddie Kean, writer of the television *Howdy Doody Show*, as a distress call for one of the characters]

cowboy n 1 A reckless driver or pilot : *City Subway Mishaps Attributed To Speeding "Cowboy" Motormen/ a pilot with a history of recklessness and a reputation as a "cowboy" (1920s+)* 2 The king of a suit of playing cards *(1940s+ Gambling)* 3 A violent gun-brandishing criminal : *apparently the same cowboy, a young punk with a Fu Manchu mustache, waving a nickel-plated pistol (1920s+ Underworld)* v To murder recklessly and openly : *even if we had to cowboy them (which) means that we were to kill them any place we found them even if it was in the middle of Broadway (1920s+ Underworld)* See DRUGSTORE COWBOY

cow chip n phr COWPAT, MEADOW MUFFIN : *Blue chips into cow chips. Investor loses money (1840+)*

cow college (or tech) n phr A college rurally located and of humble distinction, esp an agricultural college : *Every instructor in every cow college is trying to get to be an assistant professor (1900+ College students)*

cowpat or cow pie n or n phr A disk of cattle dung; MEADOW MUFFIN : *the meadow muffin, better known as the cow pie (1940s+)*

cowpats *interj* An exclamation of scorn, disbelief, vexation, etc; BULLSHIT : *Cowpats! He's just trying to make my life miserable (1990s+)*

cowplop or cowflop or cowflap n 1 Cattle dung : *He is dumb as cowflop and hopeless at foot shufflin' and finger snappin', but he tries hard* 2 Nonsense; pretentious talk; BULLSHIT : *I don't believe that cowflap/ Urban Cowplop (1900+)*

cowpuncher or cowpoke n A cowboy [first form 1870s+, second 1880s+; fr the use of metal-tipped prods to drive cattle into railroad cars]

coyote n A person who smuggles illegal immigrants across the Mexican-US border : *the "coyotes," the smugglers who bribe or otherwise contrive to get their charges past border authorities (1920s+)*

coyote ugly *adj phr* Extremely ugly or nasty; PISS-UGLY, ugly as catshit : *I had a coyote ugly date (1980s+ Students)*

cozy up v phr To become very friendly; court : *I find myself, too, on about the fifth trip to the hardware store, cozying up to the proprietor (1930s+)*

crab n 1 : *He's an awful crab, never gives her a moment's peace* 2 A resident of Annapolis, Maryland *(1920s+)* v 1 To complain, esp to do so regularly; nag; BITCH : *Crab, crab, crab, that was all she ever did/ So us crabbing about our zero-life factors isn't up for debate, really (1812+)* 2 To spoil; ruin : *He's trying to crab the deal (1890s+)*

crabs n An infestation of crab lice in the pubic area : *Her friends slobbered, ripped off girls' dresses at parties, had crabs (1840+)*

crack n 1 A try; attempt; SHOT : *It looks impossible, but I'll take a crack at it (1836+)* 2 A brief, funny, pungent, and often malicious remark; WISECRACK : *One more crack like that and I'm going to sock you (1725+)* ◀3▶ The vulva; CUNT *(unknown date, but very old)* ◁4▷ The deep crease between the buttocks *(unknown date, but very old)* 5 (also crack cocaine) Cocaine freebase, a very pure crystalline cocaine intended for smoking rather than inhalation; coke : *Crack's low price and quick payoff make it especially alluring to teenagers (1985+ Narcotics)* v 1 To open a safe or vault by force *(1830s+)* 2 To go uninvited to a party; CRASH *(1950s+)* 3 To gain admittance to some desired category or milieu : *He finally cracked the best-seller list (1950s+)* 4 To solve; reveal the secret of :

They never cracked the case (1930s+) **5** (also **crack up**) To suffer an emotional or mental collapse; go into hysteria, depression, etc : *After six months of that it's a wonder she didn't crack (1880s+)* **6** To break down and give information, or to confess, after intense interrogation : *Buggsy cracked and spilled everything (1850+)* **7** To speak; talk; make remarks : *Listen, Ben, quit cracking dumb (1315+)* [all senses are ultimately echoic; narcotics sense fr the sound of breaking crystals or the cracking sound the crystals make when smoked] *See* FALL BETWEEN THE CRACKS, GIVE something A SHOT, HAVE A CRACK AT something, WISECRACK

crack a book (or the books) *v phr* To study • Nearly always in the negative : *He tried to pass the course without cracking a book/ The exam's coming up and I better crack some books (1920s+ Students)*

◀**crack a fart**▶ *v phr* To flatulate; express gas anally; LAY A FART : *What's that smell? Did someone crack a fart? (1980s+ Students)*

crack a smile *v phr* To smile; start to smile : *I even wiggled my ears, but she wouldn't crack a smile (1840+)*

crackbrained *adj* Crazy; eccentric; wild; CRACKPOT *(1634+)*

crackdown *n* A particular instance or severity of punishment, law enforcement, etc : *The Mayor again vowed a crackdown on the porn shops (1930s+)*

crack down *v phr* To enforce the law or rules more vigorously; CLAMP DOWN : *Cops will crack down on drunk drivers (1930s+)*

cracked *adj* Crazy; eccentric : *You're cracked if you think I'll stay now (1692+) See* GET one's NUTS

cracked up or **cracked up to be** *modifier* Said; praised • Most often in the negative : *This beer ain't all it's cracked up to be* [1836+; fr 1300s sense of *crack*, "boast, brag"]

◀**cracker**▶ *n* A Southern rustic or poor white; more particularly, a Georgian; REDNECK [1766+; The dated sense refers to "a lawless set of rascals on the frontiers of Virginia, Maryland, the Carolinas, and Georgia" who were great *crackers*, "boasters"; these would be nearly the original frontier "tall talkers" of the Davy Crockett ilk] *See* JAWBREAKER, SAFECRACKER

cracker-barrel *adj* **1** Unsophisticated; basic : *a cracker-barrel philosophy* **2** Intimate; gossipy : *a cracker-barrel discussion of family* [1877+; fr the archetypical image of rural discussants sitting on or around the *cracker barrel* in the general store]

crackerjack or **crackajack** *modifier* : *He estimates that a crackerjack examiner working* under optimum conditions would find 10 to 15 percent of his cases to be inconclusive/ I'm a crackerjack story teller *n* A person or thing that is remarkable, wonderful, superior, etc : *Signorelli is a crackerjack* [late 1880s+; origin uncertain; perhaps a fanciful extension of *cracker* in the mid-19th-century British sense "something approaching perfection," which is also reflected in terms like *crack shot, crack troops*, etc, and based on an echoic expression of speed; hence also *cracking;* the term is reinforced in the US by late 19th-century trademark *Cracker Jack* for a popcorn and peanut confection]

crackers *adj* Crazy; CRACKED • Chiefly British use : *Also he was plain crackers* [1928+; formed with the British suffix *-ers*, like *bonkers, preggers,* etc]

crackhead *n* A user of cocaine freebase *(1980s+ Narcotics)*

crackheaded *adj* Crazy; CRACKED, CRACKERS, NUTS *(1796+)*

crackhouse or **crackshack** *n* A place where crack cocaine is sold or smoked *(1985+)*

cracking *adj* Excellent; first-rate : *a cracking meal adv* Very : *a cracking good meal* **n** : *Ragging, bagging, snapping, and cracking, these are all word games teens use as a way of competing with one another (1990s+ Teenagers)* *(1830+) See* GET CRACKING

crack one's **jaw** *v phr* To brag *(1930s+ Black)*

crack of dawn *n phr* First light; the start of sunrise *(1923+)*

crack off *v phr* To make nasty or boastful remarks *(1970s+)*

crack on someone *v phr* To insult someone; DIS, DUMP ON, TRASH *(1990s+ Black)*

crackpot *adj* : *my colleague's crackpot notions n* A crazy idiot; an addled fool; eccentric : *He's a crackpot about flying saucers (1883+)*

cracks *See* FALL BETWEEN THE CRACKS

crack the whip *v phr* To command peremptorily and fiercely; intimidate : *He has made great industrial corporations jump when he cracks the whip* [1940s+; fr the use of a whip to control animals, esp in the circus]

crackup *n* **1** A collision, crash, etc : *a bad car crackup/ airline crackup (1926+)* **2** A mental or emotional breakdown : *Have you read Fitzgerald's The Crackup? (1930s+)* **3** A very funny person or thing : *His Cagney sketch is a crackup (1960s+)*

crack up *v phr* **1** To collide; crash : *The trucks cracked up head-on (1920s+)* **2** (also **crack**) To suffer an emotional or mental breakdown; go into hysteria, depression, etc : *Jimmy felt that he was cracking up (1930s+)* **3** To have a fit of uncontrollable laughter : *He cracked up over everything Homer said (1940s+)*

crack someone **up** *v phr* To make someone laugh uncontrollably : *neighbor that cracks me up*

cradle *See* ROB THE CRADLE

cradle-robber or **cradle-snatcher** *n* **1** A person who prefers relatively younger sex or courtship partners **2** A recruiter or sports scout who solicits very young persons (*1926+*) *See* ROB THE CRADLE

cram *modifier* : *a cram session/ cram book n* A very diligent student; GRIND (*1900s+*) *v* To study intensively for an upcoming examination (*1803+ British students*)

cram it *See* STICK IT

cramp someone's **style** *v phr* To be a hindrance or distraction : *Your blank stare cramps my style* [*1917+*; Charles Lamb had written "*cramps the flow of the style*" as early as 1819]

crank *modifier* **1** Bogus; false : *crank letters/ crank phone calls* **2** Pertaining to methamphetamine : *It's connected to a crank factory, and the case goes to New Jersey, so the FBI is all over it n* **1** An eccentric person, esp one who is irrationally fixated; NUT, FREAK : *That crank wants a yogurt shampoo/ All kinds of cranks took credit for the murder* (*1881+*) **2** A crabby person **3** Methamphetamine, a stimulant; SPEED : *Ain't no calories in crank* (*1960s+ Narcotics*) [perhaps fr the *crank* of a barrel organ, by which one can play the same tune over and over again; applied by Donn Piatt to the publisher Horace Greeley]

cranked *adj* **1** Excited and eager; keen for action; CHARGED UP, CRANKED UP, PUMPED UP : *I was cranked. I was geared* **2** Angry; PISSED OFF : *He opened up the casket and, man, was he cranked about that!* (*1980s+*)

cranked up *adj phr* **1** CRANKED (*1950s+*) **2** Intoxicated by narcotics such as cocaine, esp by methamphetamine : *Was he cranked up when he did it?* (*mid-1980s+*)

cranking *adj* Excellent; wonderful; first-rate; COOL, RAD, TITS : *That party last night was so cranking* (*1980s+ Students*)

crank on someone *v phr* To vent one's anger on; HASSLE : *She must have needed someone to crank on, and I was elected* (*1980s+*)

crank something **out** *v phr* To produce or make something, esp with mechanical precision and regularity : *with the kind of junk the studios are cranking out* (*1950s+*)

crank someone or something **up** *v phr* **1** To get someone or something started; initiate action : *The people around Reagan talk about "We'll crank him up on this"/ Let's crank up the dog project tomorrow* (*1960s+*) **2** To make excited, eager, keenly ready for action, etc : *You better crank the quarterback up if you want this team to score* (*1950s+*)

cranky *adj* Very irritable; touchy : *The baby was cranky all day* (*1821+*)

crap *interj* An exclamation of disbelief, disgust, disappointment, rejection, etc; FUCK, SHIT : *Oh, crap, I broke it again* (*1930s+*) *n* **1** Feces; excrement; SHIT : *The bad news is, I look like crap* (*1898+*) **2** Nonsense; pretentious talk; bold and deceitful absurdities; BULLSHIT : *I'm not interested in stories about the past or any crap of that kind* (*1898+*) **3** Offensive and contemptuous treatment; overt disrespect : *But I don't take crap from anybody* (*1910+*) **4** Anything of shoddy quality; pretentious and meretricious trash : *Her new show is pious crap* (*1920s+*) *v* **1** To defecate; SHIT : *Where's the bathroom? I have to crap* (*1846+*) **2** To lie, exaggerate; try to deceive : *You're crapping me* (*1930+*) [by extension fr Middle English *crap*, "chaff, siftings of grain, residue"] *See* ALL THAT KIND OF CRAP, FULL OF SHIT, SHOOT THE BULL

crap around *v phr* To waste time foolishly; lack seriousness; FUCK AROUND, MESS AROUND : *Quit crapping around and get to work* (*1930s+*)

crape-hanger *n* A habitually morose person; pessimist; KILLJOY, PARTY-POOPER, WET BLANKET [*1920+*; fr the earlier funereal practice of hanging swaths of *crape* as a sign of mourning]

craphouse *n* Outhouse; privy

crap list *See* SHIT LIST

crapoid *adj* Disgusting; nasty; wretched; CRAPPY : *Clover said they were crapoid for thinking that* [*1970s+*; fr *crap* plus the suffix -oid, which became increasingly popular from the 1960s]

crapola *modifier* : *the latest trends in crapola entertainment n* Lies and exaggeration; BULLSHIT : *odious even by the usual standards of feminist crapola/ grinding out the old heartfelt crapola* (*1950s+*) [fr *crap* plus suffix -ola]

crap out *v phr* **1** To lose; fail (*1930s+*) **2** COP OUT (*1950s+*) **3** To succumb to exhaustion; CRASH, SACK OUT : *Then come back up here and crap out in that polo-field-size bed* (*1940s+*) [fr the failure of a crapshooter to make the winning point, and to roll 2, 3, or 7 instead]

crapped (out) *adj* Finished; dead : *dogs crapped out from barking*

crapper *n* **1** A toilet : *We'd just like to know if the governor of the state is aware of that damned thing in the crapper* (*1920s+*) **2** A person who regularly lies and exaggerates; a boaster and self-advertiser : *I call your great guru a mean little crapper* (*1940s+*) **3** Something disgusting, nasty, or shoddy : *Oh, Mondays are a crapper* (*1970s+*) [fr *crap*]

crappy *adj* **1** Of inferior quality; shoddy : *the crappiest shoes I ever had* **2** Very unpleasant; nasty : *Don't you feel crappy? (1846+)*

crapshoot *n* A risky gamble; something very chancy : *But who knows? It's such a crap shoot that nobody can really call it/ Such reforms would subject students to a crapshoot (1970s+)*

crash *n* **1** The empty feeling, depression, etc, felt when a euphoric intoxication ends; LET-DOWN : *The "crash" from coke is grim (1960s+ Narcotics)* **2** A collapse of a securities market *v* **1** To break into a building; enter by force : *Hoover's men crashed Doc's apartment (1920s+)* **2** To rob a place, esp by breaking in; CRACK *(1920s+)* **3** To gain admittance to some desired category or milieu : *In LA she tried to crash TV (1922+)* **4** (also **crash the gate**) To go to a party or other event uninvited or without tickets *(1922+)* **5** To sleep or live at a place for a day or so, usu without invitation : *I heard about this place and hoped I could crash here for a day or two (1960s+ Counterculture)* **6** To go to sleep *(1960s+ Counterculture)* **7** To lose consciousness from narcotics or alcohol *(1960s+ Students)* **8** To fail suddenly : *The spacecraft's No 1 computer "crashed" or shut down/ computers that can alert a mainframe owner to an impending computer "crash" (1970s+ Com-puter)* **9** To lose a significant portion of value in a short time, as with securities

crash and burn *v phr* **1** (also **crash in flames**) To fail entirely; BLOW IT : *You'd think his presidency had already crashed in flames v* **2** To collapse from exhaustion; POOP OUT : *I was just about to crash and burn (1970s+)*

crash-and-dash *See* SMASH-AND-GRAD

crash cart *n phr* A hospital cart with drugs, defibrillator, etc, summoned in cases of cardiac arrest : *Get the crash cart. We've got a code blue in 516A* [1970s+ Med-ical; probably based on *crash wagon*, an airport ambulance or emergency vehicle, so called from the 1930s]

crashed *adj* Drunk *(1970s+)*

crasher *n* A person who attends a party or event uninvited : *ruined by crashers*

crash pad *n phr* A place to sleep or live for a day or so, esp for young people traveling about more or less aimlessly and with little money : *discouraging intinerant filmmakers, homeless poets, and hangers-on of all kinds from using the room as a crash pad (1960s+ Counterculture)*

crash program (or **project**) *n phr* An intense and extraordinary effort to a specific end : *Getting the refugees housed needed a crash program* [1940s+; fr the urgency of a submarine's *crash-dive* ordered in extreme danger; *crash-dive* dates from about 1918]

crash with someone *v phr* ◁1▷ To do the sex act with someone; sleep with someone; BOFF, BONK, BOP : *You crashed with my sister (1990s+)* **2** To sleep at someone else's home : *crashed with my sister for a while*

crate *n* **1** A car, bus, airplane, etc, esp an old rickety one • Seems to have been used for airplanes before cars; this may be because early airplanes were literally wooden and cloth crates : *A "crate" is a "junker" with one surge left (1920+)* **2** A jail *(1920s+ Hoboes) v* To arrest and jail : *We crate Major and they'll go. But they won't leave him there (1990s+)*

◁**crater-face** or **pizza face** or **zit-face**▷ *n* A person with an ugly face, esp due to acne : *crater-faces along the wall*

crawl *n* **1** A dance; HOP *(1920s+)* **2** Text that scrolls up the television screen, esp explaining what happened to the characters of a "based on fact" docudrama : *And a crawl going up the screen saying she's pleaded no contest/ The use of crawl to finish a quasi-historical story (1960s+) v* ◁1▷ To do the sex act with; mount • Actually used by the 1890s to mean "mount and manage a horse" : *I finally crawled Mary Jane Cummings last night (1940s+)* **2** To reprimand severely; CHEW OUT : *"To crawl" meant what Second World War troops meant by "chew out" (WWI Army) See* PUB CRAWL

crawl (or **come**) **out of the woodwork** *v phr* To appear, materialize, interfere, etc, as or like something very loathsome : *A lot of them are weirdos who just crawled out of the woodwork/ Any time there's a juicy scandal a lot of creeps come out of the woodwork* [1960s+; fr the notion that worms, spiders, maggoty creatures, rats, etc, dwell in hidden places]

crawl with *adj phr* To be well provided with : *The place was suddenly crawling with cops (1576+)*

crazy *adj* Excellent; splendid; COOL : *If you like a guy or gal, they're cool. If they are real fat, real crazy, naturally they're real cool (1940s+ Jazz musicians) n* An insane or eccentric person; LOONY : *We're going to prevent the right-wing crazies from bombing and destroying (1867+) See* LIKE CRAZY, STIR CRAZY

-crazy *combining word* Inordinately devoted to or manic over what is indicated : *boy-crazy/ kill-crazy/ speed-crazy*

crazy about (or **over** or **for**) *adj phr* Very enthusiastic about; infatuated with; NUTS ABOUT : *I'm crazy about Ronnie (1904+)*

crazy as a loon (or **a coot** or **a bedbug**) *adj phr* Insane; NUTTY : *If you think that, you're crazy as a loon* [first form 1845+, third 1832+; fr the *loon's* or *coot's* cry, like an insane laugh, and the *bedbug's* frantic rushing about when exposed]

crazy bone *n* A point on the elbow where the ulnar nerve passes near the surface, resulting in a sharp tingling sensation when the nerve is knocked

crazy like a fox *adj phr* Very bright and canny (1908+)

crazy quilt *n phr* Something confused and patternless; a hodgepodge • Originally a bed quilt made of odd bits and pieces of cloth : *The Crazy Quilt of American Politics/ More bizarre turns in the last decade, relations among Iran, Iraq, and the US form a crazy quilt* (1880s+)

creak *v* To show signs of wear; be near collapse : *indications that their marriages are creaking* (1930s+)

cream *n* A white person; PADDY : *He was a "cream" in a car full of home boys and bloods from the black projects* (1980s+ Black) *v* **1** To cheat or deprive someone of something, esp by silky glibness : *I got creamed out of the hotel spot in Ohio/ a smoothie who wolfed on a friend and creamed his lady* (1920s+) **2** To do very well against; overcome; CLOBBER : *You didn't stop by just to tell me how you creamed the Irish* (1929+) ◁3▷ To be sexually aroused, esp so as to secrete sexual fluids, either semen or lubricants • *Cream* has meant "semen" since at least the middle 1800s : *He thinks we're gettin' all agitated over here creamin' in our drawers/ It made me cream in my panties, isn't that fun?* (1940s+)

CREAM *n* Money [1990s+ Black teenagers; fr *cash rules everything around me*]

creamed *modifier* Utterly defeated; outscored by a great amount : *creamed UConn in the Big East tournament*

◁**cream one's jeans (or silkies)**▷ *v phr* To become sexually excited; exude sexual fluids : *any idea how them ladies cream their silkies watching a muscular and handsome guy* (1940s+) See CREAM

cream puff *n phr* **1** A weakling; SISSY, WIMP : *Opponents might get the idea Lemon is a cream puff* (1930s+) **2** Something for sale, esp a used car in splendid condition and a tremendous bargain : *before you believe, much less see, any of the "creampuffs" in the classifieds* (1940s+ Salespersons)

creased *adj* Exhausted : *totally creased from this work*

creative accounting *n phr* Fraudulent or dubious bookkeeping; falsification of financial records in imaginative ways : *secret takeover deals, creative accounting just this side of Internal Revenue Service rules/ through some very creative accounting the corporations were both depriving governments of all sorts of taxes* (1970s+)

cred *n* Credibility : *you've got no cred with me*

creek *See* UP SHIT CREEK

creep or **creepo** *n* A disgusting and obnoxious person; CRUD, JERK, NERD • An isolated 1886 use seems to refer specifically to a cringing sycophant rather than a generally repulsive person : *The man is nothing but a creep/ poets loyal to Blake and Whitman, the "holy creeps"/ How to spend our money on making some creepo more creative in the growing world of weirdness* [first form 1930s+ students, second 1950s+; origin uncertain; perhaps fr one who makes one's flesh *creep*; perhaps generalized fr one who cringes and curries favor]

-creep *combining word* A gradual increase in the thing named : *My cost-of-living allowance put me into bracket-creep on my income tax/ In Somalia we saw mission-creep* (1980s+)

creeper *n* **1** The lowest gear on a truck (1930s+ Truckers) **2** A performer who moves closer and closer to the microphone (1940s+ Radio studio) **3** A sneak thief : *He knew they couldn't be boosters or creepers, not flashing their bread the way these two were doing* (1930s+ Underworld)

creepers *n* SNEAKERS (1900+ Underworld)

creepette *n* A female creep : *Surrounded by creeps and creepettes* (1990s+)

creeping crud *n phr* Any disease, esp an unnamed and prevalent flulike disorder or an unexplained and nasty rash [WWII armed forces; a reduplicating expansion of *crud*]

creep someone out *v phr* To frighten and disgust someone : *flirt alert : My teacher's creeping me out* (1990s+)

creeps, the *n phr* **1** Sensations of fear and loathing, such that one's flesh seems to formicate; revulsion; THE WILLIES : *The willies or the creeps. Call it what you like* (1864+) **2** Delirium tremens : *He was not in with the creeps but with a broken leg* (1940s+)

creepy *adj* **1** Frightening; scary; HAIRY : *a creepy show about necrophiles* (1831+) **2** Loathsome; disgusting : *a creepy little chap with an enormous bow tie* (1880s+)

creepy-crawly *adj* Loathsome; repellent; CREEPY : *The trio plunges into the creepy-crawly high life of Acapulco* (1880s+) A nasty creature, esp the caterpillar, snake, or centipede sort : *the lair, maybe, of creepy-crawlies or a ghost* (1920s+)

cremains *n* The remains of a cremated body (1990s+)

cretinoid *modifier* : *El Presidente, and others too cretinoid to mention* *n* A cretin; idiot; SPASTIC [1970s+ College students; In the standard sense "resembling a cretin" attested from 1874]

cretinous *adj* Wrong; inoperative; wretchedly designed; bletcherous (1980s+ Computer)

crib *n* **1** A translation or a set of answers used to cheat on an examination *(1827+ Students)* **2** A place where thieves and hoodlums congregate; cheap saloon : *a sleazy crib on Second Ave (1857+ Underworld)* **3** A nightclub; DIVE : *I am singing for coffee and cakes at a crib on Cottage Grove Avenue (1930s+ Teenagers)* *v* **1** : *He cribbed on the econ exam and got caught (1778+)* **2** To steal *(1748+)*

crib course *n phr* An easy college course; GUT COURSE : *Even at Stanford or Johns Hopkins the student in desperate need of a crib course can be sure to find one* [1970s+ College students; fr student senses of *crib*]

Crikey *n* or *interj* Christ : *Crikey but it was a rum go (1838+ British)*

crime *See* COPYCAT CRIME

crime, a *n phr* A misfortune; a shame : *It would be a crime if they elected that guy (1895+ College students)*

Criminy or **Crimus** (KRI mə nee, KRĬ məs) *n* or *interj* Christ • A euphemistic form : *Criminy, I've been hoodwinked/ Crimus but it's cold (1700+)*

crimp *n* A restriction; obstacle : *He kept putting crimps into my plan* *v* : *I'll crimp him good with this nasty new rule (1896+)*

crip *n* **1** A cripple; GIMP : *"Phony crips" as the fraudulent cripples call each other (1918+ Hoboes & underworld)* **2** (also **crip course**) An easy course; CRIB COURSE, GUT COURSE, SNAP *(1920s+ College students)*

Cripes or **Cripus** *n* or *interj* Christ • A euphemistic form : *Cripes, what a rotten deal (1910+)*

Crisco *n* An obese person; fatty [1930s+; fr *Crisco*, trademark for a kind of shortening sold in cans, hence "fat in the can"]

crispy *adj* Suffering the morning-after effects of alcohol; HUNG OVER *(1980s+ Students)*

crispy critter *n phr* A person, car, etc, that has been very severely burned : *Some of the soldiers wandering the graveyard joked a bit. "Crispy critters," said one, looking at the incinerated* *n phr* A person out of it from taking drugs or smoking marijuana : *no crispy-critters at the breakfast table, please* [1960s+ Army; fr *Crispy Critters*, trademark of a breakfast cereal resembling little toasted animals]

critter *n* An animal or person; cuss. CUSTOMER : *That dog is a nasty critter/ Jane's a friendly old critter* [1815+; fr *creature*]

croak *n* A mixture of crack cocaine and cocaine : *A new wave of narcotics with names such as "croak" and "parachute" is hitting the nation's streets (1980s+ Narcotics)* *v* **1** To die : *I had the horse trained, then he up and croaked on me (1812+)* **2** To kill; murder : *He croaked a screw at Dannemora (1848+)*

croaker *n* A physician : *Don't say "croaker," say "doctor" (1859+)*

crock *n* **1** A disliked person, esp an old person : *a lot of old crocks with baggy eyes (1876+)* **2** A hypochondriac and whining patient *(1950s+ Medical)* **3** A bargelike cargo ship made of cement *(WWII Navy)* **4** CROCK OF SHIT : *Spook the sponsors. What a crock/ Bonny Loo giggles, "That's a crock" (1918+)* **5** Something, esp a program, that functions, but in an ugly or awkward manner *(1980s+ Computer)* *v* **1** To hit; CLOBBER, CLOCK : *I crocked the orderly with a bedspring (1918+)* **2** To ruin; wreck; kill; QUEER : *Calling the pitch lies, as you might imagine, crocked the job (1918+)*

crocked *adj* Drunk *(1927+)*

crockery *n* **1** The teeth *(1900s+)* **2** A pitcher's arm that becomes lame and ineffective; glass arm *(1950s+ Baseball)*

◁**crock of shit**▷ *n phr* Nonsense; lies and exaggerations; mendacious cant; BULLSHIT : *characterized reports of TJ Club activity in Weinstein's campaign as a "crock of shit"/ Asked about Burns's contention, he replied, "That's a crock of shit" (1940s+)*

cromulent *adj* Appearing legitimate but actually being spurious : *These citations are indeed cromulent* [a word used by the schoolteacher, Miss Hoover, in an episode of *The Simpsons*, in which she defended one made-up word by making up another]

cronk *adj* Drunk [1850+; fr German *krank*, "ill"]

crook *n* A habitual or professional criminal; a consistently dishonest person : *The chief said, "I'm not a crook" (1870s+)* *v* To steal : *He crooked my socks (1940s+)*

crooked (KROŎ kəd) *adj* Dishonest; fraudulent; criminal [1870s+; Attested from 1225 in the larger sense "immoral, perverse, not orthodox"]

crooked arm *n phr* A left-handed pitcher; SOUTHPAW *(1940s+ Baseball)*

crook the elbow *See* BEND THE ELBOW

croon *v* **1** To sing in a relaxed and mellow style : *Rudy Vallee crooned his way to immortality* **2** To sing [1460+; fr Scots dialect; related to Dutch *kreunen*, "groan, whimper"]

cropper *See* COME A CROPPER

cross someone *v* **1** To act contrary to someone's wishes; attempt to thwart someone; contradict : *You must not cross me on this (1589+)* **2** DOUBLE CROSS *(1823+)* [both senses fr the distinction between "straight, square," and *cross*; *cross* meant "illegal practices" by 1812] *See* NAIL someone TO THE CROSS

cross-dresser *n* A transvestite : *I'm constantly getting calls from cross-dressers who think I could use their talents* (*1960s+*)

crossed wires or **lines** *n* A misunderstanding : *crossing of the political wires* (*1930+*)

cross-eyed *See* LOOK AT someone CROSS-EYED

cross my heart or **cross my heart and hope to die** *sentence* I am telling the truth; I swear this is the truth : *I love you, baby. Cross my heart* (*1908+*)

crossover *modifier* **1** : *a series of absurd moments straight outta crossover hell* **2** Bridging some gap of medium, "lifestyle," etc : *They created a lesbian comedy that is likely to be a crossover hit* (*1990s+*) *n* A shift from one musical style to another or a deliberate mixture of disparate styles (*1970s+ Musicians*)

cross someone's **palm** *See* GREASE someone's PALM

cross the aisle *v phr* To change one's affiliations, loyalties, politics, etc : *GM asked me to cross the aisle* [1980s+; fr the *aisle* that separates Republicans and Democrats in both houses of Congress]

cross someone **up** *v phr* To confuse or deceive someone : *He had to cross the blockers up* (*1940s+*)

crotchcutter *n* A woman's bathing suit with leg openings that reach above the hips and even the waist : *"Crotchcutters," the Village Voice called the suits* (*1990s+*)

crotch job *n phr* A book, television show, etc, of vulgar sensationalism : *The latter is a Fox crotch job "Roseanne : An Unauthorized Biography"* (*1990s+*)

crotch worker *n phr* A shoplifter who conceals loot under her dress (*1970s+ Police*)

crowd *n* **1** A group, faction, clique, etc : *The Hip Sing and On Leong crowds* (*1840+*) **2** An audience : *To watch Dick Enberg work the crowd* (*1863+*) *See* GO ALONG WITH THE CROWD

crowd someone *v* To press or importune someone; encroach on someone's territory or safety : *Don't crowd me now, just let me handle it* (*1839+*)

crowd someone **out** *v phr* To push or force someone by pressure as of a crowd : *I think he's trying to crowd me out of the board membership* (*1652+*)

crowd-surf *v* To be passed along overhead by the people at a "moshing" session : *The mosh pit started going full speed, complete with crowd-surfing* (*1990s+*)

crow-hop *n* A little forward jump made by an outfielder to increase the distance of a long throw : *Mike Knight shouted to him to use a crow-hop* (*1980s+ Baseball*)

crown *v* To hit someone, esp on the head; BEAN, CONK : *If she finds out she'll crown me* (*1746+*)

crown jewels *n* The male genitals : *stay away from the crown jewels*

crucial *adj* Excellent : *crucial new music video* (*1987+*)

crud or **crut** *modifier* : *It's in your ballpark, since you love the crud detail n* **1** Any venereal disease (*1920s+ Army*) **2** (also the **crud**) Any disease, esp one featuring a rash or obvious skin eruption; any unnamed disease : *I probably picked up the crud that's going around* (*1930s+ College students*) **3** A dirty and slovenly person; DIRTBALL : *I used to be a smelly crud* (*1930s+*) **4** Anything loathsome or markedly inferior : *His new show's a piece of crud* (*1930s+*) [fr Middle English, "coagulated milk or other substance, curd," of unknown origin] *See* CREEPING CRUD

cruddy *adj* **1** Nasty; loathsome; repellent : *a bar band playing cover tunes in a cruddy dive* **2** Somewhat ill and indisposed; under par; BLAH : *I'm not exactly sick, I just feel cruddy* (*1940s+*)

cruise *v* **1** To drive slowly and watchfully in the streets, walk about vigilantly in bars and parties, etc, looking for a sex partner • Streetwalkers were called *cruisers* by about 1900 : *He started cruising the singles bars* (*1903+*) **2** To make a sexual approach : *I dated girls but at the same time was still cruising guys! But what happens if, after cruising chicks you find yourself with a more cerebral companion?* (*1940s+*) **3** To be smoothly going about one's business : *He was still "cruising nice and mellow" from an acid trip two nights before* (*1960s+*) *See* LET'S BOOGIE

cruise control, on *adj* or *adv phr* Behaving or seeming to behave smoothly without conscious effort; on automatic : *In the 8th inning Clemens is on cruise control. Pitching with a 4-0 lead makes him all the more effective* [1980s+; fr *Cruise Control*, a trademark device for setting the speed of a car so that it does not vary and one does not need to touch the controls]

cruise patrol *n phr* A strolling about, usu looking for girls [1980s+; possibly influenced by *cruise control*]

cruising for a bruising *v phr* Looking for trouble; courting violence, esp while riding about in a car [1951+ Teenagers; perhaps fr or influenced by black English *cruising*, "strolling, parading," attested by 1942]

crumb or **crum** *n* **1** A louse or bedbug (*1863+*) **2** A blanket roll or pack; bindle (*1910+ Hoboes*) **3** A dirty, slovenly person; CRUD, DIRTBALL (*1918+*) **4** A loathsome, contemptible person; CREEP (*1918+*) [fr the resemblance of a louse to a *crumb*]

crumb-bun or **crumbbum** or **crum-bun** or **crumbum** *n* A contemptible person; BUM,

CRUMB : *Unlike the other critic crumb-buns, he has a soul* [based on earlier *crumb-bum*, "lice-ridden bum"]

crumbs *n* A very little, esp of money; a pittance; CHUMP CHANGE, coffee and cakes, PEANUTS : *Hell no. I won't work for crumbs—I want bread* (1856+, *but current* 1950s+)

crumb (or **crum**) **up** *v phr* 1 To spoil; confuse; LOUSE UP, MESS UP : *He tried too hard and crumbed up the whole thing* 2 To clean clothing thoroughly, esp to delouse *(WWI Army)*

crummy or **crumby** *adj* 1 Infested with body lice; lousy (1850s+) 2 Loathsome; disgusting; LOUSY : *I'd be dead of the dirty monotony around this crummy neighborhood* (1850s+) 3 Of inferior quality; shoddy; CHEAP : *This crumby razor doesn't work/ Where'd you get that crummy camera?* (1850s+)

crunch *modifier* : PARKS : *It's Crunch Time in the Havens n* 1 A crisis; a desperate climax; SQUEEZE : *Then came the political conventions that summer, and more crunches/ A "crunch" is characterized by a skyrocketing of interest rates and a choking off of the availability of credit/ The "crunch" between press and Government is inevitable in American affairs* (1930s+) 2 A kind of exercise for the stomach, in which one pulls the head off the floor while lying on one's back : *Actress Julianne Phillips keeps her stomach flat by doing 6,000 "crunches" a week* (1990s+) *v* 1 To process, usu in a wearisome way (1980s+ Computer) 2 To study intensely; PULL AN ALL-NIGHTER (1980s+ Students)

cruncher *See* NUMBER CRUNCHER

crunching *See* NUMBER-CRUNCHING, NUT-CRUNCHING

crunch numbers *v phr* To do arithmetic or mathematics; calculate : *But if the general reader is up to crunching some numbers, Sportsbiz could be a pleasing ticket to understanding the money in sports* (1980s+ Computer)

crunchy (also **crunchy granola**, **granola**) *adj* Having a healthy diet and way of living; natural; earthy : *She's a crunchy granola girl/ drew directly on their college days at Connecticut's slightly crunchy (as in granola) Wesleyan University* (1980s+ Students) *n* A person who is disagreeably intent on environmental matters, personal bodily simplicity, walking in the forest, etc • The term altered to pejorative as the student ethos altered and "political correctness" became repellent : *crunchy granola : a person who is emotionally or temperamentally still living in the 1960s/ Hippie parents, you know. Rill crunchy* (1990s+ Students) [fr the 1876 trademark of a "cooked, granulated wheat"; *crunchy*, candylike modern versions of the

cereal were much prized by some elements of the 1960s counterculture]

crunk or **krunk** *modifier* 1 Out of control; crazy and excited : *crunk during Spring Weekend* 2 Drunk 3 Hip and cool : *crunk CD*

crush *n* 1 A passing infatuation : *That's a crush, Manny is love* (1895+) 2 A thick crowd; heavily crowded place (1806+) *v* To humiliate someone; reduce someone to helpless dismay : *Her snub crushed me* (1610+) *See* HAVE A CRUSH ON someone

crusty *adj* Gruff; surly; ill-tempered; feisty : *Crusty George Meany. The downturned lips, the jowls, the half-closed lids, all were dour* (1834+)

crut *See* CRUD

crybaby *modifier* : *The Georgetown basketball team has continued its crybaby act n* A person given to weeping or lamenting at the least adversity, esp from self-pity (1852+)

cry in one's **beer** *v phr* To indulge in a session of lamentation or weeping; feel keenly sorry for oneself : *You can't make something like this make you cry in your beer* (1940s+)

crying *See* FOR CRYING OUT LOUD

crying jag *n phr* A fit of uncontrollable weeping, often accompanying drunkenness : *Florence got regular crying jags, and the men sought to cheer and comfort her* (1904+)

crying shame, a *n phr* A great misfortune; a very distressing thing; DIRTY SHAME : *That's a crying shame. I'll have to go see him* (1881+)

crystal or **crystal meth** *n* Narcotics in powdered form, esp amphetamines; SPEED (1960s+ Narcotics)

crystalhead *n* 1 A person addicted to amphetamines; SPEEDFREAK (1960s+ Narcotics) 2 A follower of New Age beliefs; a New Ager (1980s+) [second sense because such persons prize crystals for various putative powers]

cry uncle *v phr* To admit defeat and give up : *don't cry uncle after one round* (1918+)

C-section *n* A Caesarean section : *I took three weeks off for a C-section/ Although doctors have long advised against repeated C-sections, the high rate has continued* (1980s+)

C-sex *n* Computer sex; sexual talk, provocation, etc, on a computer network (1990s+)

C-Span-head *n* A devotee of the cable-television channel *C-Span*, a channel showing political events, conferences, and discussions (1990s+)

◁**ct** or **CT**▷ *n* COCK-TEASER

CTD *adj* Nearly dead [1980s+ Medical; fr *circling the drain*, that is, about to go down]

cub[1] *modifier* : *a cub reporter/ cub professor n* 1 A novice reporter (1890s+ Newspaper office) 2 Any novice or apprentice (1840+) [fr *cub*, "the young of certain animals"]

cub[2] or **cubby** *n* A room or dwelling; PAD : *Let's go to my cub* [first form 1546+, second 1860s+; origin uncertain; related to Low German of the same meaning; the 1500s form refers to an animal's stall or shed; these senses are preserved more often in black English than in standard English]

cube *n* **1** (also **cubesville**) A very conformistic and conventional person; SQUARE (1950s+) **2** A portion of LSD, hashish, or morphine : *He wanted a couple cubes, two cubes I had* (1950s+ Narcotics)

cubes, the *n phr* Dice; a pair of dice : *He chose to stake his hopes on one throw of the cubes* [The use is very, very old : the word *cube* derives from the Greek word meaning "a die for gambling"]

cuckoo or **coo-coo** *adj* Crazy; very eccentric; NUTTY : *Where do you get these cuckoo ideas?* (1918+) *n* A crazy or eccentric person (1581+) [perhaps because of the bird's monotonous, silly-sounding call]

cuddle-bunny *n* An attractive young woman, esp one who is generous with sexual favors (1940s+ Teenagers)

cuddle (or **cozy**) **up to** someone *v phr* To become friendly or cozy with someone : *Now we have the Senator cuddling up to his former opposition* (mid-1700s+)

cueball *n* A man or boy with a bald, shaven, or close-clipped head (WWII armed forces & students)

cuff *v* **1** To borrow money from someone, usu in an urgent way **2** To charge something, esp on an expense account : *No man feels he is getting ahead until he can cuff a few tabs on the firm* **3** To put handcuffs on someone : *Cuff him and book him, Flanagan* (1693+) [1920s+; first two senses fr the notion of keeping track of debts by notations on the *cuff* of one's shirt] See OFF THE CUFF, ON THE CUFF, PUT THE CUFF ON someone

◁**cuff one's meat**▷ *v phr* To masturbate : *He'd still be cuffing his meat in Spain* (1970s+)

culture vulture *n phr* An enthusiastic devotee of the arts and of intellectual pursuits, esp a pretentious one : *Culture vultures to the contrary, there is more integrity to the guy* (1940+)

◁**cum**▷ *See* COME

cume (KYUM) *n* The cumulative academic average of a student : *He didn't care about flunking, and she would say "And what about your cume?"* (1960s+ College students)

◀**cunt**▶ *n* **1** The vulva (1325+) **2** Sexual favors and indulgence; ASS, FUCKING : *But some of their daughters were giving away more cunt than Dixie was selling* (1670s+) **3** A woman : *Why didn't he spin off this stupid cunt* (1920s+) **4** A fellow male one dislikes, esp a homosexual : *And this one is from Max, the cunt* (1920s+)

◀**cuntface** or **cunthead**▶ *n* A despicable person; BASTARD : *you cunthead, you wretched fart* (first form 1940s+, second 1960s+)

◀**cunt-hair**▶ *n* A very small amount or distance; minute amount; SMIDGEN, TAD : *knows when it's off center, even when it's only a cunt hair off* (1920s+)

cupcake *modifier* Weak; soft; WIMPISH : *On cupcake opponents : It doesn't matter who you play. When you cross those black lines you should come out and play hard* (1990s+) *n* **1** An eccentric person; NUTBALL : *regarding puppeteers as kind of weird cupcakes who play with dolls/ the publishing cupcake who nailed you on the couch and then fired you* (1970s+) **2** An attractive young woman; chick : *Flossie was a saucy blonde cupcake then/ In her don't-think-I'm-just-another-cupcake suit, Geraldine A. Ferraro gave a pep talk* (1930s+)

cup of coffee *n phr* A very short visit or tenure with a team or in a major league : *After his years with the Tigers, the outfielder had a cup of coffee with the Yankees in 1950 and the Giants in 1952/ I just wanted a cup of coffee, I just wanted my foot in the door* (1900s+ Baseball)

cup (or **dish**) **of tea**, one's *n phr* One's special taste, predilection, etc; THING : *Harlem is his forte and his dish of tea* (1920s+ British)

cuppa *n* a cup of : *cuppa joe* (1934+)

curbstone *v* To pretend to sell a car for a private person while actually selling it for a dealer (1990s+ Car dealers)

curdle *v* To offend; disgust : *"It curdles me" = "I loathe it"* (1940s+)

cure *See* TAKE THE CURE

curl someone's **hair** (or **toes**) *v phr* To shock or appall ● A somewhat earlier sense is "to injure; batter" : *The prices here will curl your hair* [1940s+; fr a supposed reaction to intense fear]

curlies *See* HAVE someone BY THE SHORT HAIRS

currency *See* SOFT MONEY

curse, the *n phr* A woman's menstrual period; menstruation : *Is it any wonder that menstruation is commonly called "the curse"* (1920s+, and probably earlier)

curtain *See* BAMBOO CURTAIN

curtains *n* Death; disaster; the bitter end : *It looked like curtains for Ezra then and there* [late 1800s+; fr the final *curtain* of a show; or perhaps fr the crape *curtains* formerly hung by undertakers at the dead person's door]

curvaceous *adj* Having a generously formed female body; BUILT LIKE A BRICK SHITHOUSE, STACKED (1935+)

curve ball *n phr* Something tricky and unexpected; a sly maneuver : *Barring another last-minute curve ball from Lorenzo, Ueberroth is* *expected to win the battle for Eastern Airlines (1940s+)*

cush (KŌŌSH) *n* Money; cash : *They've put up their good cush to send me on tour* [late 1900s+; probably fr *cash*]

cushion *n* 1 One of the bases in baseball; BAG *(1940s+)* 2 Anything, esp money, kept as a safeguard against hard times : *He kept one bank account just as a cushion (1950s+) See* the KEYSTONE, WHOOPEE CUSHION

cushy (KŌŌSH ee) *adj* 1 Easy; easeful; supplying comfort and pleasure : *I landed a cushy post, a soft sinecure at the foundation* 2 Fancy; luxurious; HIGHFALUTIN, POSH : *I may not know a lot of cushy words* [1915+ British; perhaps fr Hindi *khush*, "pleasure," or Romany *kushto*, "good," or perhaps fr a shortening of *cushiony*]

customer *n* A person; COOKIE • The word has a tinge of disapproval : *a tough customer/ She's a shrewd customer* [1580s+; perhaps an expansion of *cuss*]

cut *adj* 1 : *cut whiskey/ heavily cut cocaine* 2 : *a brutally cut film/ a cut version* 3 Muscular : *cut abs* 4 Circumcised : *not cut and neither is he n* 1 : *Anybody with more than four cuts flunks* 2 A share or portion, esp of criminal or gambling profits *(1900s+)* 3 : *How much of a cut did you make?* 4 : *Welles had surrendered the right of final cut in his contract* 5 : *What a nasty cut she gave me* 6 : *That wasn't a snub, it was a cut* 7 : *I made the cut!* 8 A turn; time; CRACK, SHOT : *Have a cut at it yourself (1940s+)* 9 Swing at a baseball : *What a thunderous cut that was!* 10 A phonograph record or side, or a separate band on a record : *Osmond will perform cuts from "Donny Osmond" (1930s+)* 11 An opinion or interpretation; viewpoint; SLANT, TAKE : *I got a different cut from an American general (1990s+) v* 1 To absent oneself from without permission or legitimate excuse : *She cut choir practice twice/ to cut class (1794+ British university)* 2 : *They cut the million eight ways* 3 To dilute something, esp whiskey or narcotics : *They cut the pure stuff before they sell it on the street (1920s+)* 4 To shorten a movie, book, manuscript, etc *(1865+)* 5 To edit a film or other script *(1913+)* 6 To recur to a scene shown before • The dated form is *cut back* : *Cut back to Jazz at Lincoln Center (1913+ Movies)* 7 To injure someone with an insult or sarcasm : *That crack really cut me (1582+)* 8 To ignore someone pointedly, esp an acquaintance : *Next time I saw him I cut him (1634+)* 9 To remove someone from a team, cast, group, etc • The date reflects cowboy use for removing some cattle from a herd : *I'll be happy if Coach doesn't cut me (1880s+)* 10 (also **cut**

it, cut it out) To stop doing something; desist • Usu an irritated command : *Cut the crap, Martinez (1859+)* 11 To leave; depart : *Let's cut. We ain't no more than just time, providing we step lively (1612+)* 12 To speed; BARREL : *and "cut" about the streets like Tom Thumb's coach (1855+)* 13 To swing at the ball *(1940s+ Baseball)* 14 To outdo someone; best; surpass : *Lydia Lunch, who I feel cuts Yoko on every possible level (1880s+)* 15 To do something well; SHINE *(Black 1940s+ fr jazz musicians)* 16 To make a phonograph record, CD, or tape recording; record : *He cut a couple of demos yesterday (1937+)*

cut, the *See* MAKE THE CUT

cut a (kut AY) *See* CUT ASS

cut above *modifier* Of a superior status : *thinks she's a cut above the other neighbors (1800s+)*

cut someone a break *v phr* To give someone special favor : *He petitioned Judge Michael Wallace to cut me a break (1970s+)*

cut (or crack) a deal *v phr* To make or conclude an arrangement; transact an agreement : *Doesn't it make more sense to cut a deal with the Soviets?/ The city has done its entrepreneurial turn by cutting a deal with the Republicans in which it must approve all souvenirs (1970s+)*

◁**cut a fart**▷ *See* LAY A FART

cut a figure *v phr* To be important; be imposing; make an impression : *I cut quite a figure in this town, but nowhere else (1759+)*

cut and dried (or dry) *adj phr* Regular, predictable, and uninteresting; pro forma *(1710+)*

cut-and-paste *modifier* Crude; improvised; haphazard; SLAPDASH : *a slapdash, cut-and-paste feel*

cut and run *v phr* To leave; depart, esp hastily : *If you hear a whistle, cut and run at once* [1704+; fr the *cutting* of the anchor cable in the swift departure of a ship]

◁**cut someone a new asshole**▷ *v phr* To rebuke someone harshly; reprimand severely; REAM *(1970s+)*

◁**cut ass (or a)**▷ *v phr* To leave; depart; HAUL ASS, SHAG ASS *(1950s+)*

cutback *n* A reduction or decrease : *no cutback in prices (1940s+)*

cut back *v phr* To reduce; decrease : *They'll cut back the interest rate (1940s+)*

cut bait *v phr* To cease some activity; stop; discontinue : *Westway Trial : Lawyers Cut Bait (1970s+) See* FISH OR CUT BAIT

cut corners *v phr* To be lazy and take a shortcut; to find an easier and usually cheaper way of doing something : *Don't cut corners or you will not get another contract*

cut someone or something **down to size** *v phr* To counter and neutralize; deflate : *A few words from the judge cut him down to size* (*1930s+*)

cute *adj* 1 Shrewd; sly; tricky (*1730s+*) 2 Disrespectfully frivolous; SMART-ASS : *Don't be cute with me, you slimy pimp* (*1950s+*)

cute as a bug's ear (or as a button) *adj phr* Very attractive; pretty; DISHY (*first form 1920s+, second 1940s+*)

cutes, the *n phr* 1 Arch and simpering behavior; kittenish ways : *Lina began flapping her dress to give herself air. Then she got the cutes and asked if that was allowed/ Some of the musical background, like the narration, also suffers from the cutes* 2 The tendency or habit of constant joking; tasteless frivolity : *born with an incurable case of the cutes* (*1940s+*)

cutesey or cutesie *adj* Designedly attractive in a pert way; overtly charming : *and the children cutesy freaks/ Dutch doors, partly ivy-covered, and mostly cutesy n : The author oversimplifies everything and gets carried away with his own cutesies* (*1970s+*)

cutesy-poo or cutesy-pie *adj* Designedly arch and simpering to a nauseating degree : *saying anything narsty about so cutesy-poo an endeavor/ McWilliams writes in a cloying cutesy-pie style*

cutie or cutey or cuty *n* 1 A person or thing that is charming, attractive, clever, etc : *I'm no beauty, but am counted a cutie* (*1917+*) 2 A person who is shrewd, deceptive, and wily : *Watching a cutey spar with an ordinary dull fighter* (*1920s+*)

cutie-pie *n* A very attractive person, esp a doll-like woman : *my new cutie pies* (*1940s+*)

cut-in *n* The right to share something : *We've each got a cut-in on the profits* (*1931+*)

cut in *v phr* 1 To intrude into a conversation or discussion; barge in (*1819+*) 2 To take someone's partner away while dancing (*1896+*)

cut someone **in** *v phr* To award someone a share, esp of winnings, loot, etc : *They cut me in for 25 percent of the take* (*1930s+*)

cut it *v phr* To achieve or finish something; succeed; HACK IT : *They've been warned that a string group won't cut it with jazz fans/ But I think that you probably could cut it* (*1960+ Jazz musicians*)

cut it up *v phr* To analyze and discuss something; take a close look : *Come on, guys, cut it up* (*1950s+*)

cut something **loose** *v phr* To give something up; free oneself from something : *I want to save some bread so I can cut the hustling thing loose altogether* (*1970s+ Black*)

cut one's **losses** *v phr* To make the best compromise in a losing situation; salvage or extricate at least something : *You'd better sell right now and cut your losses*

cut someone **off** *v phr* To drive abruptly in front of someone in traffic : *He says she cut him off at the toll booth, so he shot her* (*1970s+*)

cut oneself **off at the knees** *v phr* To disable oneself; SHOOT oneself IN THE FOOT : *I don't want to cut myself off at the knees by giving figures* (*1970s+*)

cut someone **off at the knees** *v phr* To deflate or reduce someone, esp surprisingly; TAKE someone DOWN A PEG : *the nebbish with a disarming wit that could cut you off at the knees* (*1970s+*)

cut-offs *n* Pants, usu blue jeans, cut off above the knees and left to unravel (*1970s+*)

cut (or turn) **off** someone's **water** *v phr* To subdue someone; deal decisively and damagingly with someone : *I just smiled sweetly and turned off his water* (*1950s+*)

cut of one's **jib**, the *n phr* One's general character and appearance (*1790s+ fr nautical*)

cut-out *n* A person, business, etc, used to conceal the identity or purpose of a secret operation; COVER : *The firm operated as a cut-out, or front, for the FBI's purchase/ He can serve as your cut-out* (*1960s+ Espionage*)

cut out *v phr* 1 To leave; depart, esp hastily : *So you think you're cutting out? You're not leaving until I leave with you* (*1797+*) 2 To stop doing something; desist : *If you cut out the booze maybe it'll work* (*1900+*)

cut one's **own throat** *v phr* To ruin oneself; to cause harm to oneself; SHOOT oneself IN THE FOOT : *If you try to get him that way you'll cut your own throat* (*1583+*)

cuts *n* Well-defined muscles, esp of the upper body : *cuts on that guy*

cut someone **some slack** *v phr* To stop pressuring or importuning someone; let someone be; GIVE someone A BREAK : *Clinton should lie low for a while, and the rest of us should cut him some slack/ I probably cut him more slack than I have with other guys* (*1980s+*)

cutter *See* COOKIE-CUTTER, DAISY-CUTTER, RUG-CUTTER

cut the cheese *See* CHEESE

cut the mustard *v phr* To succeed; be qualified; CUT IT • Very often in the negative : *Those groups have special vested interests. And that's not gonna cut the mustard* [*1907+; probably fr cut, "achieve," and the mustard in the earlier slang sense of "the genuine thing, best thing," perhaps based on the fact that mustard is hot, keen, and sharp, all of which mean "excellent"*]

cut the (or a) **rug** *v phr* To dance, esp in jitterbug style (*1930s+ Swing talk*)

cutthroat *adj* Very harsh and barbarous : *a cutthroat game/ cutthroat competition* (1567+)

cutthroat defense *n phr* A courtroom defense in which two counsels work against each other : *The two defense counsels were working in opposition to each other—a cutthroat defense, as it is known* (1990s+)

cut throats *v phr* To lower corporate costs by reducing the number of employees; downsize : *new philosophy : cutting throats is the best way of cutting costs* (1990s+)

cut to the chase *v phr* (also **go straight to dessert**) To go to the essential matter; focus on what is most important : *It grows late, and we must cut to the chase, but further attention to the Blue Jays here is not out of place/ Want to write irresistible love letters? As you write, cut to the chase, broach the erotic. Share astonishingly intimate secrets/ Let's go straight to dessert, Marco* (1990s+)

cut two ways *See* WORK BOTH WAYS

cut-up *adj* Upset; hurt; distressed : *She was pretty cut up about not getting a paper* (1844+) *n* **1** A prankster; practical joker; antic rogue : *Uncle is a cut-up, owner of all kinds of gimmicks* (1880s+) **2** An energetic and entertaining person : *He was a great cut-up. He could dance a bit, sing better than average, and had a sense of comedy* (1880s+)

cut up *v phr* **1** To behave frivolously; be rowdyish; HORSE AROUND (1837+) **2** To divide profits, loot, etc (1930s+ Underworld) **3** To speak ill of; analyze maliciously; insult : *Or they can collectively "cut up" the girls they see around* (1759+)

cuty *See* CUTIE

cut Zs *See* COP ZS

cuz *n* Cousin

CYA *See* COVER one's ASS

cyber- *combining word* Having to do with computers and computer operations : *cybergroup, cybermuffin, cyberphobe, cybersex* [late 1980s+; fr Greek *kyber*, "rudder"; used by the mathematician Norbert Wiener in 1948 about his work on automatic control]

cyberporn or **compu-smut** *n* Pornography on computer networks : *Last week it approved a ban on cyberporn* (1990s+)

cyberpunk *n* **1** A kind of science fiction, mode of discourse, set of attitudes, etc, that combines scientific interests, esp computers, with the punk ethos : *The book was pieced togather from cybernetics and punk. Within this odd pairing lurks the essence of cyberpunk/ Cyberpunk caters to the wish-fulfillment requirements of male teenagers* (mid-1980s+) **2** A person who admires computers, esp one who uses them recreationally (late 1980s+)

cyberspace *n* The putative or apparent "space," be it mental, electronic, or "virtual," in which computer phenomena, operations, and experiences take place; in particular, the universe of computer networks [mid-1980s+; seemingly coined by the science-fiction writer William Gibson and used in his 1986 book *Count Zero*]

cyberthief *n* A computer hacker who breaks the laws against entry into private databases, telephone networks, etc : *A Most-Wanted Cyberthief Is Caught in His Own Web* (1990s+)

cycle, the *See* HIT FOR THE CYCLE

czar *n* A person appointed or elected to have great authority over a certain sport or other area; the commissioner of a sport or government department : *baseball czar/ czar of boxing/ drug czar* [1890s+; fr the title of the Russian emperors; used as the nickname of T B Reed (d. 1902), authoritarian Speaker of the House of Representatives]

D

D *n* A dollar *See* BIG D

DA (pronounced as separate letters) *n* **1** District Attorney (*1920s+*) **2** A ducktail haircut (*1951+*)

daaa *See* TAH-DAH

dab *See* SMACK

dab hand *n phr* An expert; a skilled person; an adept : *He is reportedly a dab hand at setting lofty prices* [*1828+* British; fr late 1600s *dab*, "an expert," of unknown origin]

dad *n* **1** An old man • Used as a disrespectful term of address toward older men. The similar term *pop* is not similarly disrespectful : *Okay, dad, outta the way and you won't get hurt* (*1950s+*) **2** God • Used euphemistically as an element in various old-fashioned mild oaths like *dad-blamed* (*1670s+*) *See* HO-DAD

dad-blamed or **dad-blasted** *adj* (also **dag-blamed** or **dag-blasted**) Wretched; accursed; DARN : *Git outta my dad-blamed way* (*1840s+*)

dad (or **dag**) **burn** *interj* An exclamation of surprise, irritation, frustration, etc • A euphemism for *goddamn* : *Well, dad burn it, come on* (*1829+*)

daddy *n* **1** A male lover, esp one who keeps a younger mistress; SUGAR DADDY (*1920s+* Black) **2** The most respected man in a field; cynosure; dean : *Gary Cooper, the daddy of all cowboys* (*1901+*) *See* DISNEYLAND DADDY, HO-DAD

Daddy-o or **daddy-o** *n* **1** Man; old guy; GUY • Used in addressing men, sometimes older men, respectfully and amiably **2** An older male patron, esp of a young woman; SUGAR DADDY : *like a young beauty swept out of a small Nebraska town by some Hollywood Daddy-O* (*1940s+* Bop talk)

daddy track *n phr* An arrangement of work, working hours, etc, made by men who wish to spend more than the ordinary time with their children : *the Daddy Track, about devoted dads voluntarily choosing to temper their career ambitions* (*1990s+*)

daffy *adj* Crazy; NUTS : *He tries to convince her that she is not daffy* [*1884+*; fr British dialect *daff*, "fool, simpleton"; *daffish* is attested fr the 15th century] *See* STIR-CRAZY

dag-blamed or **dag-blasted** *See* DAD-BLAMED

dag burn *See* DAD BURN

dagged *adj* Drunk

dagger *See* BULLDYKE

daggone *See* DOGGONE

dagnab *See* DOGGONE

◄**dago** or **Dago**► *adj* Italian *n* **1** An Italian or person of Italian descent • First used chiefly of Hispanics; noted as "chiefly Italians" by 1900 : *Hey, Fiorello, you're a dago* **2** The Italian language **3** A person of Hispanic birth or descent [*1823+*; fr *Diego*, "James," used in the 17th century to mean "Spaniard"]

dah *See* TAH-DAH

daily dozen *n* A set of calisthenic exercises done daily; also, a set of routine duties or tasks

daily grind *n* The routine of everyday life : *ready for the daily grind*

daisies *See* PUSH UP DAISIES

daisies, the *n phr* The outfield (*1940s+* Baseball)

daisy chain *n phr* Sexual acts shared or partly shared by more than two people at the same time in the same place; group sex (*1941+*) *v phr* To connect; link; chain : *Up to 8 EXP–16's may be daisy-chained together for a total of 128 differential inputs* (*1990s+*)

daisy-cutter *n* **1** (also **daisy-clipper**) A grounder or very low line drive (*1866+* Baseball) **2** A very low tennis shot (*1897+* Tennis) **3** A horse that trots with its hooves near the ground (*1791+*) **4** An antipersonnel bomb or mine that ejects shrapnel close to the ground (*WWII Army*)

dally *See* DILLY-DALLY

damage, the *n phr* The price; cost; esp a bill at a restaurant or bar (*1755+*)

damaged *adj* Drunk (*1851+*)

◄**damaged** (or **used**) **goods**► *n phr* A woman who is not a virgin : *Once they find out I have kids, they think of me as used goods* (*1910+*)

◄**dame**► *n* A woman; BROAD, DOLL (*1900+*)

damn *adj* (also **damned**) Cursed; accursed; wretched : *What do I do with this damned thing?* *adv* : *You seem damn stupid all of a sudden interj* (also **damn it**) An exclamation of disappointment, irritation, frustration, etc : *Damn, it's gone!* *v* To execrate; condemn; curse : *Damn this dictionary!* (*1770s+*) *See* HOT DAMN

damn, a *n phr* Nothing; very little; A FUCK, A RAT'S ASS, A SHIT : *Oh, we don't give a damn for the whole state of Michigan; we're from O-hi-o* (*1760+*) *See* NOT GIVE A DAMN

damned *See* I'LL BE DAMNED

damned if you do and damned if you don't *adj phr* Condemned, whatever decision one makes : *Investigating is delicate : Companies feel they're damned if they do, damned if they don't* (*1970s+*)

damned (or **damn**) **sight** *modifier* Very much : *a damn sight saner than other people* (*1928+*)

115

damn right *adj* and *adv phr* (also **damn skippy**, **damn straight, damn tootin'**) Certain; certainly; sure as shit : *Damn right I was mad, who wouldn't be?/ You're damn skippy. Let's go for the best record in the league/ Damn straight we used cowboy logic, if that's what you want to call it* (entry form 1940s+, probably much earlier) *See* YOU'RE DAMN TOOTIN'

damn well *modifier* Certainly; definitely : *you know damn well I have to work* (1941+)

damper *n* **1** A person or thing that depresses, takes the edge off joy, chills one's enthusiasm, etc : *The news was a damper on our hopes* (1748+) **2** A cash register or till; cash drawer (1848+) **3** A bank or money depository; treasury : *dropping bonds into the damper which are then sold to the public See* PUT A DAMPER ON

damp rag *n phr* A disappointment; a blighted hope : *That was a little bit of a damp rag* (1940s+)

damp squib *n* Something anticlimactic; something that fails to come to a conclusion; a fiasco : *his attempt at painting the house is something of a damp squib* (1845+)

Dan *See* DAPPER DAN

dance *n* A fight between rival gangs; RUMBLE : *The kids have plenty of time for pushing a dance* (1940s+ Street gang) *See* GET THE LAST DANCE, GO INTO one's DANCE, SONG AND DANCE, TAP DANCE

dance around *v phr* To improvise, tergiversate, etc, in order to avoid a question or issue; TAP DANCE : *Larson dances around the real issue of gun control/ There's always an owner willing to cave in or dance around* (1970s+)

dance card *n phr* A putative list of priorities, engagements, etc : *Kissinger's dance card that week included a party for Margaret Thatcher/ Suddenly, the Iraqi leader had maneuvered himself to the top of Mr. Clinton's dance card* (1980s+)

dander *See* GET one's DANDER UP

dandy *adj* : *a dandy idea adv* : *He does it dandy/ We get on just dandy n* A person or thing that is remarkable, wonderful, superior, etc • Attested from 1784 in the form *the dandy* : *You should get one, it's a dandy* (1880s+, very popular 1900+) *See* HOTSIE-TOTSIE, JIM-DANDY

dang *adj* (also **danged**) Wretched; nasty; accursed *adv* Absolutely; extremely : *You looked dang silly/ "Purchase what the customer intends to buy?" "Dang right" interj* (also **dang it**) An exclamation of disappointment, irritation, frustration, etc : *Dang, we missed the Welk show* [1840+; a euphemism for *damn*, which is regarded by some as taboo]

dang, a *See* NOT GIVE A DAMN

danged *adj* Wretched; accursed; DAMN : *It can tell you almost anything, but the danged thing*

doesn't speak in English (1870s+) *See* I'LL BE DAMNED

dapper (or **fancy**) **Dan** *n phr* An ostentatiously well-groomed man, usu one not inured to hard work : *the fancy Dans, dressed fit to kill* (1940s+)

dark *adj* Closed; not in operation : *Monday is a "dark" day at Heinz Hall* (1916+ Theater) *See* IN THE DARK

dark horse *modifier* : *a dark-horse candidate/ dark-horse odds n phr* A person or team, esp in sports or politics, that seems very unlikely to win but might nevertheless do so (1842+ fr horse racing)

◀**dark meat**▶ *n phr* **1** A black person, esp a woman, regarded solely as a sex partner **2** A black person's body and genitals [1920s+; fr the distinction between the *white meat* and *dark meat* of a roasted fowl, attested from the 1850s]

darn or **dern** or **durn** *adj* (also **darned** or **darnfool** or **derned** or **durned**) Wretched; nasty; silly : *sentimental songs, darnfool ditties, revival hymns adv* : *She was darn excited interj* (also **darn it** or **dern it** or **durn it**) An exclamation of disappointment, irritation, frustration, etc : *Darn, I've dropped my glockenspiel!* [1780s+; euphemism for *damn*, which is regarded by some as taboo; probably based on earlier *darnation*, "damnation," attested by 1798]

-darn- *infix* Used for emphasis : *absodarnlutely* (1918+)

darned *See* I'LL BE DAMNED

darning needles *See* RAIN CATS AND DOGS

darn tootin' *See* YOU'RE DAMN TOOTIN'

darter *See* BLUE DARTER

dash it or **dash it all** *v phr* DAMN, DARN • Chiefly British use : *Dash it, old fellow, we're dished!* (1800+)

date someone up *v phr* To schedule a social engagement or rendezvous with someone

dawg *n* **1** A dog • A colloquial or dialectal pronunciation : *That dawg won't hunt* (1898+) **2** A close male friend : *you dawg*

dawn patrol *n phr* **1** The act of getting up very early in the morning, to get a head start on the day **2** Golfers or surfers who head out early to beat others to the course or waves [fr early days of military aviation, when flights were undertaken at dawn to reconnoiter enemy positions]

day *See* HAVE A FIELD DAY, MAKE MY DAY, NOT GIVE someone THE TIME OF DAY, RED-LETTER DAY

day-glo *adj* Blatantly gaudy; cheaply flashy : *smoldering pageant turns totally day-glo/ plenty of sequins and day-glo fur/ day-glo glamor* [1950s+; fr the trademark of a brand of paint that makes things glow under a black light and produces lurid, psychedelic color effects]

day late and a dollar (or **dime**) **short,** a *adj phr* Inadequate; overdue and lacking; too little too late : *Yankee traders will be a day late and a dollar short : Visa cards are already welcome in Saigon/ Clinton's attempt to explain Whitewater is several days late and a dollar short/ "Dante Jones is a day late and a dime short,"* Butkus *said when the linebacker failed to cover Sterling Sharpe* (1990s+)

daylight *n* A clear and open space between two things, horses, players, boats, etc : *Daylight began to open between the two leaders/ He went into the line, but couldn't find any daylight* (1820+) *v* To work at a second job during the day : *who is daylighting in an ad agency as a producer of commercials* (1970s+) [verb sense based on *moonlight*] *See* PUT DAYLIGHT BETWEEN

daylight robbery *n phr* An exorbitant price : *cost of that salad was daylight robbery*

day one *n phr* The first day; the very beginning of something : *You weren't happy doing this from day one*

dazed *adj* **1** Confused : *dazed and confused really is redundant* **2** Intoxicated

dazzle *See* RAZZLE-DAZZLE

dazzle someone with footwork *v phr* To impress someone with facile virtuosity : *Hailey's 10th novel is a literary example of an old boxing adage : If you don't have the power, dazzle them with footwork* (1980s+)

dead *adj* **1** Very tired; BEAT, POOPED (1813+) **2** Not operating; not startable : *Damn battery's dead* (1902+) **3** Ruined; destroyed; FINISHED, KAPUT : *As far as another chance goes, I'm dead/ The ERA's dead again* (1400+) **4** Dull; tedious and uninteresting : *another dead sermon* (1000+) **5** Lacking brilliance and overtones; flat; dull : *The trumpets sounded dead* (1530+) **6** Absolute; assured : *It's a dead certainty he'll run again* (1589+) *adv* Extremely; very much : *I'm dead broke/ dead set against it* (1589+) *n* A letter or package that can neither be delivered nor returned • *Dead letter* in this sense is attested from 1703 (1950s+ *Post office*) [the sense "absolute, assured, certain" probably developed fr expressions like Middle English *ded oppressed,* "completely overcome," 16th-century *dead drunk,* and others suggesting the inertness of death; when inertness suggested fixedness, unchangingness, certainty, etc, the term took on these present senses] *See* DROP DEAD, KNOCK someone DEAD, NOT BE CAUGHT DEAD, STONE DEAD, STOP someone or something DEAD IN someone's or something's TRACKS

dead air *n phr* A sudden and undesirable silence (1950s+ *Broadcasting*)

dead as a dodo (or **doornail**) *adj phr* Absolutely lifeless; entirely hopeless : *The Philadelphia Bulletin is dead, dead as a doornail (first form 1904+, second 1350+)*

◁**deadass**▷ *adj* : *There are so many deadass people out there, boring each other to death adv* Completely; totally : *You're deadass wrong when you say I got nothing to go on n* A stupid, boring person; an absolute dullard : *Get some action going among these deadasses in the loony bin* (1950s+) *See* GET OFF one's ASS

deadbeat *n* A person who habitually begs or gets money from others, does not pay his or her debts, etc; MOOCHER, schnorrer : *a chance to demand immediate payment if the clerk looks like a deadbeat v* To sponge, loaf, etc : *Living off interest is not exactly deadbeating* [1863+; fr *dead,* "complete, completely" and *beat,* "sponger"]

deadbeat dad (or **daddy**) *n phr* A man who is delinquent in paying child support awards : *The champion deadbeat dad of all owes over $500,000* (1990s+)

dead broke *adj phr* Totally without money; destitute (1842+)

dead-cat bounce *n phr* A tiny rise or recovery after a decline : *Economists are arguing fiercely over whether it is a solid long-term recovery or just a dead-cat bounce* [Stock market 1990s+; fr a Wall Street saying that even a *dead cat* will bounce a little if you drop it from a high building]

dead center *n phr* A point at which nothing is happening : *Let's try to get this negotiation off dead center* (1920s+)

dead drunk *adj phr* Very drunk; stinko (1602+)

dead duck (or **pigeon**) *n phr* A person or thing that is ruined; a GONER, gone goose : *Just one more little push and she was a dead duck/ Unless somebody would start this mob to the sugar bowl, I was a dead pigeon* (1844+)

dead-fish *modifier* Limp; lifeless; unresponsive : *This yacht gives no sensory return. It's like getting a dead-fish handshake* (1980s+)

dead giveaway *n phr* An unmistakable and definitive clue : *His blushing was a dead giveaway* (1882+)

deadhead *modifier* : *a deadhead cab/ deadhead freight train n* **1** A nonpaying spectator at a game, show, etc; FREELOADER (1841+) **2** A nonpaying passenger (1869+ *Railroad*) **3** A train, bus, tractor truck, etc, carrying no passengers or freight, usu returning from a paying trip (1911+) **4** A stupid person; an incompetent; KLUTZ (1950s+) **5** An extremely boring person (1940s+) *v* : *I'll deadhead your hack back to the garage*

Deadhead *n* A devotee of the rock-and-roll group the Grateful Dead : *Tipper Gore,*

Deadhead and wife of Vice President Al Gore (*1970s+*)

dead heat *n phr* A tied race, contest, etc : *The election ended in a dead heat* [1796+ Horse racing; fr *dead,* "absolute, total, thorough," related to the finality of death, and *heat,* "a single course of a race," related either to a single firing or heating of a mass of metal, or to the heating of the body in running, or to both]

dead horse See BEAT A DEAD HORSE, FLOG A DEAD HORSE

dead in the water *adj phr* Unable to move; stalled; defunct : *Right now, the economy is dead in the water, with 10.8 percent unemployment/ Once I saw you, you were dead in the water* [fr the image of a disabled ship, unable to proceed]

dead issue *n phr* A question or topic that really does not matter any more : *his drinking's a dead issue*

dead letter *n phr* A matter no longer of concern or currency; a bygone issue (*1663+*)

deadly *adj* **1** Boring; extremely tedious; dull as death itself : *I came prepared for a long and deadly meeting* (*1300+*) **2** Excellent; admirable; COOL (*1940s+ Swing talk*) *adv* Extremely : *She is deadly serious about it* (*1300+*)

dead man's hand *n phr* A hand containing a pair of aces and a pair of eights [late 1800s+ Poker; fr the tradition that Wild Bill Hickock held such a hand when Jack McCall shot him in 1876]

dead meat *n phr* A corpse : *We don't believe in geography, teacher. Say one more word and you're dead meat/ But tell that to Toddy and you're dead meat* (*1860s+*)

dead-on *adj* Exactly right; dead nut : *One reason for the dead-on quality is the way the experiences of the Buchmans parallel the lives of its creators* (*1889+ Marksmen*)

dead on arrival or **DOA** *adj phr* Invalid and rejected : *The President's budget was dead on arrival even before it got to Congress* (*1980s+*)

deadpan *adj* : *my wife's New York ironies or her deadpan humor/ This is known as the deadpan system of prevarication* *n* **1** An expressionless face; POKER FACE **2** A person with an expressionless face : *Buster Keaton and Fred Allen were classic deadpans* *v* : *With kids packing his audiences, he deadpanned "I promise to lower the voting age to 6"* (*1930s+*)

dead pigeon See DEAD DUCK

dead president *n phr* Any US banknote [1950s+; fr the fact that banknotes show portraits of US presidents]

dead ringer *n phr* An exact duplicate, esp a person who is the double of another : *He was such a dead ringer for my ex-boss* [1891+; fr

dead, "precise, exact," and *ring in,* "substitute, esp fraudulently," an early 19th-century slang term for gambling]

dead soldier (or **marine**) *n phr* **1** An empty or emptied bottle, esp a liquor bottle • *Dead man* in the same sense is attested from 1738 (*1913+*) **2** Food or plates of food only partially eaten : *on the way to the kitchen with the dead soldiers, or leftovers* (*1920+*)

deadsville *adj* Dull; boring : *the young people who always felt that cruises were deadsville* (*1970s+*)

dead (or **bang**) **to rights** *adv phr* With no possibility of escape or evasion; in flagrante delicto; red-handed : *was caught "dead to rights" and now languishes in the city Bastille* (*1859+*)

dead to the world *adj phr* **1** Fast asleep (*1899+*) **2** Drunk, esp stuporous from drink (*1926+*)

deadwood *n* **1** Unproductive persons; lazy and useless staff **2** Anything useless, esp something useless that must be kept [1887+; fr the fact that *dead* or *rotten* wood does not produce much heat when burned]

deal *n* **1** A usu secret arrangement between politicians, rulers, business executives, etc : *He made a deal with the Republicans to suppress the charges* (*1860s+*) **2** Situation; thing in hand or at issue; affair : *Hey, what's the deal here? My car's gone/ The deal is that I'm tired of this sorry farce* (*1940+ Students*) *v* **1** To make arrangements, tradeoffs, sales, etc; WHEEL AND DEAL : *Sophie did all the dealing there* (*1500s+*) **2** To sell narcotics; be a peddler (*1920s+ Narcotics*) **3** To pitch a baseball • In the game of hurling, *deal,* "throw the ball," is attested by 1602 : *The big lefthander deals a smoker* (*1970s+ Baseball*) See BIG DEAL, GOOD DEAL, MAKE A BIG PRODUCTION, NO BIG DEAL, NOT MAKE DEALS, RAW DEAL, SWEETHEART DEAL

deal someone a poor deck *v phr* To treat someone cruelly and unjustly : *Take a thirty-year-old nurse who's bitter and thinks she's been dealt a poor deck* (*1970s+*)

dealer *n* **1** A person who makes a living from gambling, whether or not an actual dealer-out of cards • *Dealer,* "player who distributes the cards," is attested from 1600 : *A bookmaker, who is known as a dealer in refined usage* (*1950s+ Gambling*) **2** A person involved actively and aggressively in a range of negotiations, trades, purchases, etc; WHEELER-DEALER (*1950s+*) **3** A person who sells narcotics; peddler; CONNECTION, PUSHER : *The "dealer" (not "pusher") is the man who sells all this* (*1920s+ Narcotics*)

deal someone in *v phr* To make someone a participant; let someone share : *He heard we were going and said deal him in* (*1940s+*)

dealing *See* DOUBLE-DEALING

deal with *v phr* **1** To handle or cope with someone or something that is a problem : *Deal with it* **2** To kill someone : *Tony dealt with him*

deano *n* A month [Underworld; perhaps fr *deaner, deemer,* etc, because a month is about as much of a year as a dime is of a dollar]

Dear John *modifier* : *Dear-John letter n phr* A letter or other means of informing a fiancé, spouse, boyfriend, etc, that one is breaking off the relationship *(fr WWII armed forces)*

death *See* the KISS OF DEATH, LOOK LIKE DEATH WARMED OVER, SUDDEN DEATH

death warmed over *See* LOOK LIKE DEATH WARMED OVER

◁**de-ball**▷ *See* DE-NUT

debunk *n* To clear away lies, exaggerations, vanities, etc : *The author neither glorifies nor debunks* [1923+; coined by W W Woodward in a book published in 1923]

decaf *n* Decaffeinated coffee; UNLEADED COFFEE *(1980s+)*

decaffeinated *adj* Inauthentic; enfeebled • Decaffeinization of coffee dates from the 1920s : *Dress like Hemingway, but confine yourself to drinking Lite* : *This decaffeinated style is horrible (1990s+)*

Decatur *See* EIGHTER FROM DECATUR

decent *adj* Good, often very good : *makes a decent living*

deck *n* **1** The roof of a railroad car *(1853+)* **2** A package of narcotics; portion of a drug, esp three grains of heroin; BAG : *a deck of nose candy for sale (1922+ Narcotics)* **3** A package of cigarettes *(1940s+)* **4** A skateboard *(1990s+ Skateboarders)* *v* To knock someone down, esp with the fist; FLOOR : *Remember that guy I decked in the restaurant? (1940s+) See* COLD DECK, DEAL someone A POOR DECK, HIT THE DECK, ON DECK

decker *See* JOKER

decks awash *adj phr* Drunk *(1940s+)*

decompress *v* To be relieved of stress; regain equilibrium; relax; LAY BACK, unwind : *He'll be whisked away to some undisclosed place where he can decompress* [1970+; fr the gradual lowering of atmospheric pressure as one returns from a deep underwater dive]

deely bopper or **deely bobber** or **beely bopper** *n phr* A small hat equipped with bobbing wire antennas like those of an insect or some extraterrestrial creature : *a decor of remaindered Deely Bobbers and airsick bags (1975+)*

deep *adj* **1** Copious, esp well supplied with good athletes : *They may not be very deep on the bench, but they're smart/ Fudgie's set was deep, and fifty people showed up (1980s+)* **2** Intense; profound : *deep reading of philosophy books See* KNEE DEEP

deep doo-doo (or **foo-foo**) *n phr* Serious trouble; DEEP SHIT : *Deep Doo-Doo or Shallow?/ You're in a bigger paradigm, and if you break that you're in deep foo-foo (1980s+)*

deep end *See* GO OFF THE DEEP END, JUMP OFF THE DEEP END

deep freeze *See* IN COLD STORAGE

deepie or **depthie** *n* A three-dimensional movie : *The deepies released so far have been gimmick pictures (1950s+)*

deep pocket *modifier* : *No matter what fathers (deep-pocket lads) and schoolteachers (wardens) may think of current slang, to teenagers it is real George all the way n phr* Wealth; available riches and financial security : *He felt more comfortable with the deepest pocket available/ a deep pocket, that of an insurance company (1951+)*

deep pockets *n phr* Sources of much money; rich persons : *Why should she waste time with a turd-kicker like him when there are so many other applicants with deep pockets/ greater news-gathering assets than CNN and deeper pockets to offset losses*

◁**deep shit**▷ (or **trouble**) *n phr* Very serious trouble : *If they do that there'll be deep shit/ He was in deep shit with Big Lou (1972+)*

deep six *n phr* A grave *(1920s+ Underworld) v phr* To discard; jettison; throw overboard : *One White House disposal crew even unblushingly planned to deep six a file in the Potomac/ If any publication is deep-sixed, it will almost certainly be "The Car Book" (1940s+ Nautical)* [probably fr the combined notions of a grave as *six* feet *deep* and a fathom as six feet in *depth*] *See* GIVE something THE DEEP SIX

deep-think *modifier* : *do some deep-think social criticism n* Profound intellectuality • Used ironically : *a good example of university deep-think* [1963+; probably based on *goodthink, crimethink,* and other terms coined by George Orwell in *Nineteen Eighty-Four*]

deep throat *n phr* An important source of secret information : *The real "deep throat" of the rumors was someone believed to be peripherally connected with Sony or Columbia* [1974+; fr the name of a popular 1973 pornographic film, where the reference was to fellatio, applied to the prime source of secret information in the Watergate affair, where the reference was to copiousness of speech]

deep water *See* IN DEEP WATER

def or **deaf** *adj* Excellent; wonderful; COOL, RAD : *She is really def/ He's got a def girlfriend* [1983+ Black; origin uncertain; perhaps fr black English (Jamaican) pronunciation of *death,* where the semantics would resemble those of *killer, murder,* etc; certainly interpreted by many as a shortening of *definite*]

defense *See* NICKEL DEFENSE

defi or **defy** *n* Defiance; notice of act of defiance ● Use has not been continuous since the first attestation in 1580 : *on a signboard, a defi to the On Leongs* [late 1880s+; apparently fr French *défi*]

defuse *v* To ease or eliminate the danger of something menacing ● Extension of the 1940s use "to remove the fuse from an unexploded bomb" : *We might not stop it, but we might defuse it* (1950s+)

degree *See* THIRD DEGREE

déja vu all over again (DAY ZHAH VOO) *n phr* The repetition of an old story; a recurrence : *Listening to Bob Dole carp about the Democrats is déja vu all over again* [1970s+; fr the French name for paramnesia or proamnesia, said to have been used by the baseball player and manager Yogi Berra in this reduplicated form; Mr Berra is a favorite putative source of such solecisms]

deke or **deke out** *v* To trick, esp by decoying; FAKE someone OUT : *My friend, you deked me. You're not supposed to do that/ deked out all the troopers* [1950s+ Canadian hockey; fr *decoy*]

delay *See* GAPER'S BLOCK

Delhi belly *n phr* Diarrhea (1944+)

delish (dee LISH) *adj* Delicious

deliver or **deliver the goods** *v* or *v phr* To perform successfully, esp after promising; COME THROUGH : *It's a very tough assignment, but he thinks he can deliver/ He talks big, but can he deliver the goods?* (1909+)

Dem or **Demo** *adj* : *the Dem boss/ Demo congressmen n* A Democrat (*first form 1840+, second 1793+*)

demo (DEH moh) *modifier* : *Let's try the demo disk n* **1** A record or tape made to demonstrate the abilities of musicians, the quality of a song, etc : *Mark's got a good demo to pitch the new song with* (1950s+) **2** A computer disk or tape cassette made to demonstrate the abilities of a particular program : *I tried out their software demo before I bought their package* (1980s+) **3** A demonstration of protest or other conviction, esp by a large crowd with banners, etc : *a no-nukes demo* (1936+)

demolition derby *n phr* A scene or event of utter destruction and confusion : *Spectacular demolition derbies taking place in Russia, China, Cuba and Eastern Europe* [1950s+; fr a chaotic entertainment where drivers crash their old cars into each other until only one, the winner, is still running]

Denmark *See* GO TO DENMARK

den mother *n phr* The head and sometimes provider or supporter of a group of male homosexuals, often an older man : *They had a sort of den mother. A middle-aged writer type who had given up the straight life* [1970s+ Homosexuals; sardonic adoption of the term

fr *den mother*, the adult leader of a group of Cub Scouts]

◁**de-nut** or **de-ball**▷ *v* To castrate (1940s+)

Denver boot *See* BOOT

derail *v* To throw off the proper course; wreck : *He managed to derail the proposal just before Christmas* [1950s+; The source term, "To leave or cause a car or engine to leave the railroad tracks," was adopted fr French by 1850]

Derbyville *n* Louisville, Kentucky (1950s+)

dern *See* DARN

derned *See* DARN

designated something *n phr* A person formally appointed to a certain function ● The date indicates the first use in American League baseball of the *designated hitter* : '*Let us be your Designated Driver' campaign, to keep drunk drivers off the road/ Dornan, the Bush campaign's designated viper/ Dinkins was being treated this spring as a designated loser/ his minority whip and designated spitball thrower, Rep David Bonior of Michigan* (1973+)

designer *modifier* Of high quality; bearing a famous label : *Ah, designer ennui* (1960s+) *n* A counterfeiter (1940s+ Underworld)

designer drug *n phr* A synthesized narcotic, often of much higher potency than those produced from plants : *These new "designer drugs" or "super narcotics" are triply dangerous/ Out here urine testing has spawned the "designer" drug game* (1980s+)

desk jockey *n phr* An office worker : *Let some desk jockey in the home office envy you* (1950s+)

desperado *n* A person who gambles or borrows more than he can pay, and is certain to default, or who gambles with money he cannot afford to lose ● Such money is called *desperate* or *scared* [1950s+ Gambling; fr earlier *desperado*, "outlaw, fugitive," literally "desperate man," fr Spanish]

detox (DEE tahx) *v* To free someone of a narcotics addiction; detoxify : *I jumped in and out of opium habits but eventually de-toxed for good/ We can detox a heroin addict in three weeks* (Narcotics)

deuce *n* **1** A two of playing cards (1680+) **2** Two dollars ● Formerly, and still in Canada, a two-dollar bill (1920+) **3** A two-year prison sentence : *did a deuce together at Joliet* (1950s+ Prison) **4** A quitter; coward; petty thief (1940s+ Street gang) **5** (also **deuce coupe**) A powerful or handsome specially prepared two-door car, esp a 1932 Ford (1940s+ Hot rodders) **6** A table for two in a restaurant : *deuce in the corner* [hot-rod sense probably fr the *two* or *deuce* of 1932]

deuce, the *n phr* **1** the HELL (1776+) **2** Forty-second Street in New York City, mecca for many teenage runaways; forty-deuce : *in the peep shows and urinals and bars of the Deuce (1970s+ Teenagers)*

deuces wild *n phr* A team's situation with two men out, two strikes on the batter, and two men on base [1980s+ Baseball; fr the dealer's call in poker that all *deuces* may be valued as any other card]

devil, the *See* the HELL

devil-may-care *adj* Reckless; cavalier : *a devil-may-care insouciance (1790s+)*

devil of a time, a or **the** *n phr* A very difficult or annoying situation : *devil of a time untying those shoelaces (mid-1700s+)*

dew *n* Marijuana *(1960s+ Narcotics) See* MOUNTAIN DEW

dexie or **dexy** *n* A tablet of Dexedrine, trademark of a brand of amphetamine : *You can take dexies, but you can get hooked on them (1950s+ Students)*

dexter *n* A despised person who is a zealous student, computer user, etc; chiphead. PROPELLER HEAD : *A dexter, that's your basic nerd, dork, or pud (1980s+ Teenagers)*

dialed in *adj* Concentrating; focused; zoned in : *It's hard to believe how fully she's dialed in (1990s+)*

dial something out *v phr* To put firmly out of one's mind; ignore designedly : *All I had to do was concentrate on driving. I had a real excuse to dial it all out (1980s+)*

diamond in the rough *n phr* A person of exceptional qualities or potential but lacking refinement or polish; a wonderful and surprising specimen : *looked like a nerd, but rather was a diamond in the rough*

diamond lane *n phr* A highway lane designated for "high-occupancy" cars, esp for carpool cars : *The code in most states is that a carpooling vehicle can use the usually much faster diamond lane* [1990s+; because the lane is designated by *diamond*-shaped signs on the pavement]

diamonds *n* **1** (also **black diamonds**) Coal : *throwing diamonds in the firebox (1849+)* **2** The testicles; FAMILY JEWELS [the second sense reflects the idea "precious stones"]

diarrhea of the mouth *See* VERBAL DIARRHEA

dib *n* **1** A share, esp a share of money : *I ought to collect the kid's dib, too (1829+)* **2** A dollar : *fifty sweet dibs (1930s+)* [probably fr *divvy*]

dibs *n* **1** Money : *How did you make your dibs? (1807+)* **2** (also **dibs on**) A claim; a preemptive declaration : *It's mine, I said dibs first/ Dibs on the front seat* [perhaps fr *dibstones*, a children's game played with small bones or other counters]

dice *v* To jockey for position in a race : *I had no really sharp feeling about dicing with Parnelli*

[1950s+ Car racing; fr the notion of taking risks] *See* LOAD THE DICE, NO DICE

dicey *adj* Risky; perilous : *African investment is dicey/ Updike indulged in many dicey curlicues/ the dicey art of writing a farce (1940s+ British)*

dick[1] or **deek** *n* **1** A detective **2** Any police officer; BULL [1908+; fr a shortening and altering of *detective*]

◁**dick**[2]▷ *n* **1** The penis : *Now why don't you pull the weight down with your dick (1880s+ British armed forces)* **2** A despised person; PRICK : *You dick! (1960s+)* **3** Nothing; SQUAT, ZILCH, zippo : *So far we got dick/ Look, I didn't have any money, the Feds wouldn't do dick, nobody was helping out (1960s+)* *v* **1** To do the sex act with; SCREW : *If he went and dicked your twelve-year-old sister he wouldn't tell you all about it/ He was dicking everything that wiggled (1940s+)* **2** (also **dick around**) To potter or meddle; play; mess. SCREW AROUND : *That's federal merchandise you're dicking with, right, marshal?/ still in the kitchen, dicking around with the sushi (1940s+)* [perhaps fr the nickname *Dick*, an instance of the widespread use of affectionate names for the genitals; perhaps fr earlier British *derrick*, "penis"; perhaps fr a dialect survival of Middle English *dighten*, "do the sex act with," in a locution like "he dight her," which would be pronounced "he dicked her"] *See* CLIPPED DICK, DONKEY DICK, LIMP-DICK, STEP ON IT

Dick *See* BIG DICK, EVERY TOM, DICK, AND HARRY

◁**dick-brained**▷ *adj* Stupid; crazy; NUTTY : *coke-snorting super freaks, dick-brained Bob Marley tribute, and jive ooh-la-la (1980s+)*

dickens *n* The devil; a devilish person : *felt like the dickens/ let the dickens out on Halloween*

◁**dickhead**▷ *n* A despised person; BASTARD, PRICK : *Why would I possibly want to check out a dickhead like you?/ Drum the dickhead right out of the Republican party (1960s+)*

Dickless Tracy *n* A female police officer [1963+; punningly from *dick* "penis" and the name of Dick Tracy, US comic-strip detective introduced in 1931 by Chester Gould]

◁**dicklicker** or **dickey-licker**▷ *n* A person who does fellatio, most often a male homosexual; COCKSUCKER *(1940s+)*

◁**dickoid**▷ *n* A despised person; DICK[2], PRICK : *Dickoids like Martin who snap like wolverines on speed when they can't have a windown seat (1990s+)*

dick someone over (or **around**) *v phr* To victimize and maltreat someone, sexually or otherwise; fuck someone over *(1980s+ Students)*

dicty or **dickty** or **dictee** *adj* **1** Stylish; wealthy; classy : *"Dicty" is high-class* **2** Haughty;

snobbish; imperious : *These dickty jigs around here tries to smile n* A snob; aristocrat : *I don't want to be a dicty* [1926+ Black; origin unknown]

◁**dickwad** or **dickweed**▷ *n* A despised person; ASSHOLE, JERK, PRICK : *All right, you dickweeds, we gotta talk* (*1980s+*)

diddle *v* **1** (also **diddle around**) To waste time; idle; loaf (*1825+*) **2** To cheat; swindle; victimize; SCAM (*1806+*) **3** To alter illicitly or illegally; COOK, DOCTOR : *But I thought Tommy must have diddled the phone records* (*1980s+*) ◁**4**▷ To do the sex act with or to; SCREW : *Diddle your sister? Circle jerk?* (*1879+*) ◁**5**▷ (also **diddle oneself**) To masturbate (*1950+*) ◁**6**▷ To insert a finger into a woman's vulva; FINGERFUCK (*1960+*) **7** To correct or adjust a program in various small ways; tweak : *I diddled the text editor to ring the bell before it deletes all your files* (*1980s+ computer*) [cheating sense said to be fr Jeremy Diddler, a character in the 1803 novel *Raising the Wind*, by James Kenney]

diddle something out of someone *v phr* To get something from someone by deceptive means : *diddled twenty out of her for errands*

diddler *n* A child molester; short eyes (*1980s+ Prison*)

diddle with *v phr* **1** To handle casually, idly, or nervously; play with : *Stop diddling with the silverware* **2** (also **diddle around with**) To interfere with; have to do with; FOOL AROUND WITH : *Don't diddle with that button, it controls the power for the whole building* (*1940s+*)

diddly or **diddley** (Variations : **doo** or **eye** or **damn** or **poo** or **poop** or **shit** or **squat** or **squirt** or **whoop** may be added) *adj* Trivial; insignificant : *Tennis was a diddly sport back then/ If you had a choice between IBM or a diddly-squirt upstart n* Nothing at all; very little; ZILCH : *Rock critics don't mean diddley/ I don't know a diddly damn about theater/ And Hannibal, he didn't do diddly-squat/ They take this very seriously. It isn't just "diddley-eye" to them* (*1960s+*) *See* NOT GIVE A DAMN, NOT KNOW BEANS

diddlybop *n* : *They had a nice diddlybop at Gino's after work v* **1** To waste time; idle **2** To do something pleasant and exciting (*1960s+ Students*)

diddy bag *See* DITTY BAG

didie *n* A baby's diaper (*1902+*)

did you ever? *sentence* An exclamation of surprise or astonishment, contracted from "did you ever see such a thing?" (*1840+*)

die *n* To desire very strongly : *She was dying to become Miss Pancake* (*1591+*) *v* **1** To laugh uncontrollably : *When he puts a lampshade on his head you could die* (*1596+*) **2** To be left on

base at the end of an inning (*1908+ Baseball*) *See* CROSS MY HEART

died and gone to heaven *v phr* In paradisiacal euphoria; HAPPY AS A CLAM : *Looking around bug-eyed like she'd died and gone to heaven* (*1890+*)

die for something *v phr* To have a very strong desire for something : *I'm dying for a drink/ Kids die for Sugar Glops* (*1709+*)

die on someone *v phr* To die or cease to function, to the disadvantage of the speaker : *Damn motor died on me halfway up* (*1907+*)

die on one's **feet** *v phr* To become absolutely exhausted; carry on although one can hardly move (*1940s+*)

◁**diesel dyke**▷ *n phr* An aggressive, masculine lesbian; BULLDYKE : *The women regarded themselves either as butches (alternatively diesel dykes and truck drivers) or femmes/ a man fighting with a diesel-dyke over a girl they both wanted*

die standing up *v phr* To fail in a show or performance; BOMB (*1920s+ Show business*)

die with one's **boots on** *v phr* To die while still active and vital (*1873+*)

diff or **dif** *n* Difference : *What's the diff?* (*mid-1800s+*)

difference *See* the SAME DIFFERENCE

difference, the *n phr* A clear advantage; something that gives an advantage, esp a gun (*1903+*)

different animal (or **breed of cat**) *n phr* A different thing or person; SOMETHING ELSE AGAIN : *This is a different animal/ In the pros you're dealing with a different breed of cat than when you're in the college scene* (*1970s+*)

different strokes for different folks *n phr* A comment on the inevitable and tolerable variety of people and their ways : *Different strokes for different folks, I remarked/ Different strokes for different folks, he chirped mentally* (*1970s+ Black*)

dig *n* **1** A derogatory, irritating, or contemptuous comment : *It wasn't quite an insult, more a dig* (*1840+*) **2** An archaeological excavation (*1896+*) *v* **1** To interrogate or inquire vigorously : *She won't tell you, no matter how hard you dig* (*1940s+*) **2** To understand; comprehend : *Nobody ain't pimping on me. You dig me?* (*1930s+ Black*) **3** To like; admire; prefer : *Do you dig gazpacho and macho?* (*1930s+ Black*) **4** DIG UP **5** To hear or see in performance; CATCH : *dug a heavy sermon at Smoky Mary's last week* (*1930s+ Black*) [the cool senses, originally black, are probably related to the early 19th-century sense, "study hard, strive to understand"] *See* TAKE A DIG AT someone

dig at *v phr* To derogate; harass verbally; PUT DOWN : *Why are you always digging at me about my mustache?* (*mid-1800s+*)

digerati *n* Persons who use and enjoy computers; computer-literate people; CHIPHEADS : *Unix computers connect to the Well, a convivial gathering spot for San Francisco's digerati/ Wired offers in-depth reporting, fiction and profiles of the digerati* [1990s+; fr digital plus literati]

digger *n* **1** An Australian or New Zealander *(WWI Australian and New Zealand)* **2** GOLD-DIGGER : *She was just a plain digger* (1920+) **3** A pickpocket (1930s+) **4** A person who buys tickets to be sold at prices higher than is legally permitted; SCALPER : *They use diggers, dozens of guys who stand in lines and buy the maximum* (1970s+)

diggety or **diggity** *See* HOT DIGGETY

dig in *v phr* To begin to eat : *It's on the table, so dig in* (1912+)

dig oneself into a hole *v phr* To weaken or undermine one's own position, esp by a dogged defense; SHOOT oneself IN THE FOOT : *Every time the fool opens his mouth he digs himself deeper into a hole* (1970s+)

digits *n* A telephone number : *Did you get her digits*

dig out *v phr* To leave; depart; CUT OUT, SPLIT : *Supposing we dig out* (1855+)

digs or **diggings** *n* Lodgings; quarters : *Your digs, or mine?* (1890s+)

dig someone or something the most *v phr* To like or prefer; have the closest affinity : *Adam and I dig each other the most* (1950s+)

dig up *v phr* To find or discover, esp after effort : *She dug up a shirt and we went out/ What sort of evidence have they dug up?* (1860+)

dike *See* DYKE

dikey *See* DYKEY

dildo or **dildoe** *n* **1** An artificial substitute for an erect penis (1593+) **2** (also **dill** by 1950s) A stupid and despicable person; JERK, PRICK : *Yeah, I know that dildo. What's your problem with him?* (1638+) [fr Italian *diletto*, in the particular sense "a women's delight"]

diller *See* CHILLER-DILLER, KILLER, THRILLER-DILLER

dillhole *n* A person lacking intelligence; DUMBASS ; also, a person lacking soul and thereby having no compassion or people skills : *Get away from me you dillhole!/ Her old boss was a true dillhole* [fr TV series *Beavis and Butthead* as a euphemism for *dickhole*]

dilly or **dill** *n* A person or thing that is remarkable, wonderful, superior, etc; BEAUT, lulu : *The last one is a dilly if you don't have an appointment* (1935+)

dilly-dally *v* To idle; dither in an aimless or pointless fashion : *Folks who dilly-dally with dessert* (1741+)

dim *adj* Stupid; uncomprehending : *Anybody who pays to watch these teams has to be considered just a bit dim* (1892+)

dimbo *n* A stupid person; DIM BULB : *That dimbo probably couldn't find her way home from her own backyard* [1980s+ Students; perhaps a blend of *dim* and *bimbo*]

dim bulb *n phr* A stupid person; DIMWIT : *a peculiar combination of dim bulb and bump-on-a-log/ Heroes meant to be swankily sexy tend to come off as tight-lipped dim bulbs* (1920s+)

dime *n* **1** A ten-year prison sentence (1960s+ Underworld) **2** A thousand dollars, esp as a bet (1960s+ Gambling) *v* (also **drop a dime**) To inform on someone; SING, SQUEAL : *Frankie would have been okay if somebody hadn't dimed on him* (1960s+ Underworld & prison) [verb sense from the *dime* dropped into the pay telephone for the call to the police] *See* NICKEL AND DIME, ON someone's DIME, STOP ON A DIME, a THIN DIME, TURN ON A DIME

dime a dozen, a *adj* Very common; very cheap; in surplus : *Copycats are a dime a dozen* (1920s+)

dime bag or **dime** *n phr* or *n* Ten dollars' worth of a narcotic (1960s+ Narcotics)

dim view *See* TAKE A DIM VIEW OF someone or something

dimwit *n* A stupid person; BOOB : *She's the worst dim-wit on campus* (1917+)

din-din *n* Dinner : *kisses, candlelight, din-din, liqueurs* (1900+)

dine (or lunch) out on *v phr* To receive hospitality on the basis of one's particular knowledge or experience : *She dined out all year on that little adventure in the mountains/ Hitchens visited wartime Sarajevo once, two years ago. Ever since, he has been lunching out on the emotional and political insight he supposedly garnered* (1923+)

dinero (dee NAIR oh) *n* Money : *That's gonna set you back mucho dinero* [1856+; fr Spanish]

ding *modifier* Homeless : *in the ding camp at San Jose n* **1** A blow; a buffet : *We get a ding a day from the Chinese* (1825+) **2** : *She got six yeahs and five dings* **3** A letter rejecting one's application for a job or interview : *most disappointed in the dings that come on postcards* (1930+ College students) **4** A dent : *Not a nick. Not a ding. Nary a scratch* (1960s+) *v* **1** To go on the road as a hobo; BUM : *When you go bumming, you go dinging* (1950s+ Hoboes) **2** To beg; BUM, PANHANDLE (1950s+ Hoboes) **3** To vote against a candidate for membership; blackball • An 1812 sense was "to drop someone's acquaintance totally" (1930+ College students) **4** To administer a reprimand or an adverse appraisal : *If we dinged people, very seldom did they get jobs* (1970+ Army) *See* RING-A-DING-DING, RING-DANG-DO, RING-DING

ding-a-ling[1] *adj* : *to maintain the dingaling Holly Goheavily manner of life/ It's the ding-a-ling capital of the universe* (*1930s+*) *n* An eccentric person; NUT, SCREWBALL : *The impression left by all this is that Wolman and Kuharich must be a couple of ding-a-lings/ great for teenyboppers and cute little ding-a-lings* (*1930s+*) [fr the notion that such a person hears bells ringing in the head]

ding-a-ling[2] *n* The penis; COCK, DOODLE [1980s+; probably fr *dingus*]

dingbat *n* 1 An unspecified or unspecifiable object; something one does not know the name of or does not wish to name; DINGUS, GADGET : *I don't think any wire and glass dingbat is going to "oontz" out cheek-to-cheek dancing* (*1905+*) 2 A stupid person, esp a vague and inane simpleton; DIMWIT : All in the Family *was reexported to the BBC complete with "Polack pinko meatheads," "dingbats," and "spades"* (*1915+*) 3 Any of various typographic symbols used as decorations, separators, emphasizers, trademark and union-done indicators, etc (*1930s+ Print shop*) [first sense fr German or Dutch *dinges*, "thing"; second sense fr Australian *have the dingbats*, *be dingbats*, "be crazy"]

ding-dong *adj* Vigorous and spirited; KNOCK-DOWN-DRAG-OUT • Used adverbially, "with a will," by 1672 : *A ding-dong battle is in prospect* (*1870+*) *n* 1 An eccentric person; DING-A-LING[1], NUT (*1920s+*) ◁2▷ The penis; DONG : *couldn't find his own ding-dong if you told him to look between his legs/ Forget his ding-dong. Think of it as a technically superior game* (*1940s+*)

dinger *modifier* : *He was in an 11-game dinger drought n* 1 HUMDINGER : *That was a dinger, chaplain* (*1809+*) 2 A home run : *five hacks, five dingers/ The Brewers go into the afternoon with one dinger in more than two weeks* (*1970s+ Baseball*) [fr an early (by 1500) sense of *ding*, "to surpass, excel"]

dinghead *n* A stupid person : *Shut it, dinghead*

dingleberry *n* A despised person; JERK, NERD • Revived by 1980s students : *Tell that dingleberry I'm not here* [1920s+; originally one of several similar derogatory terms ending in *-berry*, for example, *huckleberry*, attested by 1835; in later use probably influenced by *dingleberry*, "a fragment of feces clinging near the anus"]

dingo *n* A hobo; tramp : *One dingo got a dollar* [1920s+ Hoboes; related to the hobo sense of *ding* and probably ultimately to the 17th-century British slang *ding-boy*, "rogue, sharper"]

ding-swizzled *See* I'LL BE DAMNED

dingus *n* 1 Any unspecified or unspecifiable object; something one does not know the

name of or does not wish to name; GADGET, GIZMO : *What's that dingus in the corner?* (*1876+*) ◁2▷ The penis (*1940s+*) [fr Dutch *dinges*, of the same meaning, essentially "thing"]

dingy *adj* Goofy; loony : *a dingy move*

dink[1] *n* 1 A tiny cap worn by freshmen; BEANIE • *Dinky cap* is attested from 1893 (*1920+ College students*) ◁2▷ The penis (*1880s+*) 3 A despised person; DORK, JERK, PRICK : *Nor, he insists, does he believe that any witless dink could learn to play like Ringo Starr within a week* (*1960s+*) 4 Very little; nothing; DICK[2], ZILCH : *He knows dink about weapons* (*1950s+*) *v* To make small exasperating movements, tennis shots, etc • First example may reflect 1920s *dinky*, "a trolley car having a short route" : *after finding that the campaign was dinking along like a Toonerville trolley/ They're not letting the combination dink them into submission anymore/ He dinked the kid to death with left-handed backspin junk* (*1939+ Tennis*) [fr *dinky*]

◁**dink**[2]▷ *n* A Vietnamese; GOOK, slope [Vietnam War armed forces; related to Australian *Dink*, "a Chinese," perhaps fr *dinge* or fr *Chink*]

dink[3] *n* A yacht's tender; dinghy [1900+; probably fr *dinghy*]

dink[4] *n* One of a childless couple, both of whom are employed : *a friend referred to two young professionals as "a couple of dinks"* [1986+; acronym fr *double income no kids*]

dink[5] *See* RINKY-DINK

dinkum *adj* FAIR DINKUM

dinky *adj* 1 Small; undersized • The earliest sense meant "small, neat, trim," and is related to later college use *dink*, "a dude" : *a dinky foreign car/ dinky little town* 2 Inadequate; substandard : *What a dinky joint!* (*1788+*)

dinner *See* SHOOT one's COOKIES

dip[1] *adj* DIPPY (*1917+*) *n* 1 A stupid person; simpleton; DIPSHIT : *That goddamned dip's worse than the Cowboys* (*1920s+*) 2 An eccentric person; NUT : *My grandmother was a woefully crazy lady, a bit of a dip* (*1920s+*) 3 A slovenly, untidy person; DIRTBAG (*1960s+ Teenagers*)

dip[2] *See* DOUBLE-DIP, I'LL BE DAMNED, SKINNY-DIP

diphead *n* A stupid person; DIP[1], DIPSHIT : *That means "the Democrats are dipheads," Phil* (*1973+ Students*)

dipped or ◁**dipped in shit**▷ *See* I'LL BE DAMNED

dippy *adj* Crazy; foolish; whimsically silly; KOOKY : *so strange and dippy as to have come from the brain of Tolkien/ Depardieu at his dippiest* [1900+; origin unknown; perhaps fr *dip*, "head," in the expression *off one's dip*, "crazy"; perhaps fr *dipsomaniac*; perhaps fr Romany *divio*, "mad, madman"]

◁**dipshit**▷ or **dipstick** *modifier* : *The dipshit broads took their lives in their own hands/ Listen, you toadying dipshit scumbag* n A stupid, obnoxious person; JERK : *You dipshit dog/ The other guy is the dipshit/ We're broke, dipstick* [1960s+; dipshit is an emphatic form of *dip*[1]; dipstick may be a euphemism or may reflect putative *dipstick*, "penis"]

dipso n A drunkard; dipsomaniac; LUSH : *Madeline Kahn is his dipso wife, Gilda Radner his ditsy daughter/ But dipsos don't count years; you take it day by day* (1880+)

dipsy *adj* 1 Drunken; bibulous; alcoholic; DIPSO : *Beryl Reid's appearance as a dipsy researcher* 2 Foolish; silly; DITZY : *Kelly, her dipsy counterpart at NBC* n DIPSY-DOODLE (1950s+)

dipsy-do n A curve ball that dips sharply; a downcurve : *[Babe Ruth] had good stuff, a good fast ball, a fine curve, a dipsy-do that made you think a little* (1940s+ Baseball)

dipsy-doodle n 1 Fraud; deception; chicanery : *I opened the front door, leaving the key in the lock. I wasn't going to work any dipsy-doodle in this place/ This dipsy-doodle allowed the Democratic candidate to preach a different sermon in every church* 2 A deceiver; swindler; CON MAN : *He's a marriage counselor, this dipsy-doodle* 3 DIPSY-DO (Sports) 4 A fight with predetermined outcome; a fixed fight (Prizefight) 5 A dance featuring dipping motions v 1 : *That smooth chap might just have dipsy-doodled us* 2 To weave among players on the ice : *Kurri dipsy-doodled down center ice to the net* (Hockey) [1940s+; most senses seem to have evolved fr the baseball *dipsy-do*, the semantic common thread being deception]

dipwad n A despised person; JERK (1970s+ students)

◁**dip** one's **wick**▷ v phr To insert one's penis; do the sex act; SCREW : *You dipped your wick just like the rest of them* (late 1800s+)

dirt n 1 Obscenity; pornography : *All you see in the movies these days is dirt* (late 1500s+) 2 Gossip; intimate or scandalous intelligence; SCOOP : *What's the dirt about your neighbors?* (1920s+) 3 A despicable person; scum; filth : *He's dirt, no better* (1300+) See DISH THE DIRT, DO someone DIRT, EAT DIRT, HIT THE DIRT, PAY DIRT, TAKE SHIT

◁**dirtbag** or **dirtball**▷ n 1 A garbage collector (WWII armed forces) 2 A despicable person; filthy lout; CRUD, SCUMBAG : *Those people in the store must have thought I was some kind of dirt bag/ Why don't you throw this dirtbag in jail, deputy?/ He ended up being chased down the hall by a dirtball with a knife* (1970s+) 3 A dirty, smelly patient brought into the emergency room off the street (1990s+ Medical)

dirt bike n scrambler (1960s+ Motorcyclists)

dirt cheap *adj phr* Very cheap : *dirt-cheap prices adv phr* : *buy it dirt cheap* (1830s+)

dirt me *sentence* Lower me to the ground (1990s+ Rock climbers)

dirt track n phr The anus; a-hole, GAZOOL, WAZOO : *Is your dirt track hanging hemorrhoids?* [1960s+; a pun on the early 1900s phrase for a racetrack with a dirt surface; hobo slang *dirt road* was semantically similar]

dirty *adj* 1 Corrupt; dishonest; shady • Often used of corrupt police officers : *If I was dirty, I would take what that Cadillac cost/ Maybe he's not dirty on Nijinsky, but he's dirty on something* (1670+) 2 Lewd; obscene; BLUE, RAUNCHY : *This dictionary dotes on dirty words/ Eschew dirty thoughts* (1599+) 3 Sexually insinuating in sound and intonation; CATHOUSE, BARRELHOUSE : *dirty blues* (1920s+ Jazz musicians) 4 Personally malicious or snide; nasty : *a dirty crack* (1920s+) 5 Addicted to narcotics (1960s+ Narcotics) 6 Having narcotics in one's possession : *Cops did a bodyshake and he was real dirty* (1960s+ Narcotics) 7 Well supplied with money; FILTHY RICH : *Paddy was dirty with fifteen thousand or so* (1919+) 8 Leaving much radioactive contamination or waste : *dirty bombs* (1950s+) adv 1 : *They fight dirty/ play dirty* 2 : *He talks dirty See* DOWN AND DIRTY, QUICK-AND-DIRTY

dirty crack n phr A rude remark : *a dirty crack about his balding*

dirty deal n phr An unfair result : *dirty deal from the professor*

dirty dog n A nasty, sneaky person : *You're the dirty dog that snuffed my brother*

dirty laundry (or **linen** or **wash**) n phr Personal or family matters; intimate details : *I won't hang out our dirty linen in front of this bunch* (1860s+) See WASH one's DIRTY LINEN

dirty little secret n phr 1 Something shameful that must be concealed; an embarrassing fact : *Power has been a dirty little secret among modern economists* 2 Anything held secret personally or communally because it is patently shameful; a skeleton in the closet : *Everybody will know the dirty little secret of American journalism/ Class Act : America's Last Dirty Little Secret* [phrase propagated by D H Lawrence, esp in his long essay "Pornography and Obscenity"]

dirty mind n phr A head full of sexual, malicious, and other reprehensible thoughts, fantasies, and implications (1930s+)

dirty-minded *adj* Inclined toward sexual, odious, or dubious notions (1930s+)

dirty old man n phr 1 A lecherous man, esp an elderly one; OLD GOAT (1930s+) 2 A male homosexual whose partner is much younger than himself : *Christopher is 20 years younger than Leo. He asks Leo to be his dirty old man* (*1960s+ Homosexuals*)

dirty pool *n phr* Unethical and dubious practice; DIRTY TRICKS : *triggered ugly accusations of dirty pool* (*1956+*)

dirty (or **low-down dirty**) **shame,** a *n phr* A person or thing that is much to be lamented; a pity; a disgrace : *He did? Ain't that a dirty shame?/ Man, you're a low-down dirty shame, you're nasty*

dirty tricks *modifier* : *the Senate Watergate Committee's chief "dirty tricks" investigator n phr* Dishonest or underhanded practices, esp in politics; malicious tactics : *make into federal crimes many "dirty tricks" in presidential and congressional elections/ Mr Clarke called the indictment "one of the greatest political dirty tricks of all times"*

dirty work *n phr* Dishonest, unethical, underhanded, or criminal acts; SKULLDUGGERY

dis *v* (also **diss; on** may be added) To show disrespect; insult by slighting; CAP ON someone : *The boys on the bus were dissing that girl/ Yet "dissin'," showing real or apparent disrespect, is cited as the motive in an amazing number of murders/ I'm tired of John dissin' on her all the time* (*1980s+ Black teenagers*)

disc jockey *n phr* (Variations : **deejay** or **Dee-Jay** or **DJ** or **dj**) A radio performer who plays and comments on phonograph records; also, the person who plays records at a discotheque : *the thunder-voiced DJ* (*1941+*)

disco *modifier* : *show up for a disco party and fashion show n* **1** A discotheque, a kind of nightclub where patrons dance to recorded music, sometimes with synchronized psychedelic and strobe lighting : *There's not much jazzing around at the disco* (*1964+*) **2** (also **disco music**) A musical style based on black soul music and marked by a strong rhythmic bass guitar (*1970s+*) *v* : *We discoed the night away*

discombobulate or **discomboberate** *v* **1** To disturb; upset; BUG **2** To perplex; puzzle : *The fancy words discombobulated me* (*1830s+*)

discombobulated *adj* Disturbed; upset; weird : *In this discombobulated society, it is far easier to get a piano shipped out to sea and lowered into the water beside the drowning man* (*1830s+*)

discombobulation *n* The condition of being discombobulated : *the Skinner course responsible for their emotional discombobulation* (*1830s+*)

disconnect *n* A disagreement; an unbridgeable disparity (as from a failure of understanding) : *Disconnect. It means a breakdown in communication* (*1990s+*)

disease *See* FOOT-IN-MOUTH DISEASE

dish *n* **1** A particularly attractive woman : *This was going to be my favorite dish/ I love this book and I think its 80-year-old author is a dish* (*1920s+*) **2** A person or thing that one especially likes; what exactly meets one's taste; one's CUP OF TEA : *Now, there is a book that is just my dish* (*1900+*) **3** The home plate of the baseball diamond (*1907+ Baseball*) *v* **1** Gossip; an item of gossip; to disparage; denigrate; DIS : *The President-elect played on the beach while his snobby neighbors dished/ We have no reason to do an anti-CBS film. There's no dishin' going on here* (*1940s+*) **2** To cheat; thwart : *I'm afraid that blackguard has dished us again* (*1798+*) **3** To gossip; have an intimate chat; DISH THE DIRT : *She sat and dished with the girls/ Now I feel free to dish about First Hair* (*1920s+*) **4** (also **dish out**) To give; purvey : *He took everything we gave and dished it right back* (*1641+*) **5** To pass the ball : *A goateed Magic in butt-tight shorts twists, whirls and dishes through his career as maestro of five NBA championships* (*1970s+ Basketball*)

dish it out *v phr* To administer punishment, injury, or abuse : *Jenny, you can dish it out, but you can't take it* (*1930+*)

dish of tea, one's *See* one's CUP OF TEA

dish out (or **up**) *v phr* **1** To distribute; issue : *The brand of drool they dished out/ What line are they dishing up today?* **2** To inflict; give : *They dished her out a horrid trouncing* (*1652+*)

dishrag *See* LIMP DISHRAG

dish the dirt *modifier* : *The first lady told her dish-the-dirt guests she called them together "to announce my candidacy" v phr* To enjoy a cozy chat about personalities : *So, dish the dirt. What was Hillary like in high school?* (*1920s+*)

dishwater *n* Weak and scarcely drinkable soup, coffee, etc (*1719+*) *See* DULL AS DISH-WATER

dishy *adj* Very attractive • Chiefly British use; the dated sense is "excellent, first rate; sharp, snaky, trim and slim, smooth" : *exactly what it is to be a dishy girl bored stiff/ We certainly don't live in one of the dishier neighborhoods/ With a new job at a ritzy club and the attentions of two dishy men* (*1940s+*)

Disneyland daddy *n phr* A divorced or separated father who sees his children rarely; zoo daddy (*mid-1980s+*)

dispose of *v phr* To kill someone : *disposed of the informer*

ditch *v* **1** To dispose of; get rid of; CHUCK : *We'll ditch this Greek and blow* (*1900+*) **2** To land an aircraft on the water in an emergency (*1940s+*) **3** To play truant; fail to go to school or to a class (*1920s+*)

Ditch *See* the BIG DITCH
dittohead *n* A person who totally agrees with a proffered system of belief, esp with the uncomplex notions of the talk-show host Rush Limbaugh : *They are happy to be known as dittoheads, from the shorthand that callers use to signify 100% agreement/ Dittoheads : people who are in perfect agreement on an issue, an idea, or a belief system* (*1990s+*)
ditty (or **diddy**) **bag** *n phr* A small bag for one's personal belongings, usu exclusive of clothing [1850s+ Nautical; origin uncertain; perhaps short for *commodity,* fr the earlier British naval term *commodity box,* which became *ditty box*]
ditz *n* A silly and inane person; a frivolous ninny : *a brainy ditz involved with a vulnerable hunk/ little more than a likable, spoiled ditz who allows herself to ruled by chemicals* (*middle-1970s+*)
ditzo *n* A person who is out of touch with reality; LUNCHBOX (*1980s+ Students*)
ditzy or **ditsy** *adj* Vapid and frivolous; silly; AIRHEADED : *Charles Ruggles's ditsy bimbo/ Is there something in the air that makes Washington wives ditsy?* [mid-1970s+; perhaps a blending of *dizzy* and *dotty*]
diva *n* A male transvestite; esp, a homosexual cross-dresser; DRAG QUEEN : *Salt-N-Pepa's divas are checking out designer creations* [1990s+; fr Italian, "goddess, lady love," used by the 1880s to designate a distinguished woman singer]
dive *n* 1 A vulgar and disreputable haunt, such as a cheap bar, nightclub, lodging house, or dancehall; CRIB : *the girl who danced in a dive in New Orleans* (*1871+*) 2 SPEAKEASY (*1920s+*) 3 A knockdown or knockout, esp a false prearranged knockout : *A dive is a phantom knockout* (*1940s+ Prizefight*) *v* : *They fixed it so that he'd dive in the fourth* [origin of first sense uncertain; perhaps fr the notion that one could *dive* into a disreputable cellar haunt (called a *diving bell* in an 1883 glossary) and lose oneself among lowlifes and criminals; perhaps a shortening of *divan,* "a smoking and gaming room," a usage popular in London in the mid- and late 19th century; the places were so called because they were furnished with *divans,* "lounges," the name ultimately fr Turkish] *See* NOSE DIVE, TAKE A DIVE
diver *See* MUFF-DIVER
divvy *n* 1 A share of profits or spoils 2 A dividend *v* (also **divvy out** or **divvy up**) To divide; apportion; piece up : *The governor and the Paris crook divvy the swag/ We would pass our hats and divvy up* (*1872+*)
dizzy *adj* Silly; foolish; inane; DITZY • Found as a noun meaning "foolish man" by 1825;

now mostly used of women, and esp, since the 1870s, of blondes : *some dizzy broad* (*1501+*)
DK *v* To claim that one does not know someone or something : *plunges the younger Sheen into trouble on a D-K (in which the buyer reneges by insisting that he "doesn't know"* (*1980s+*)
DMZ *n* An area now peaceful but recently and perhaps soon again the scene of violence : *They had long since passed Ninety-sixth Street, the infamous DMZ/ Traversing Brooklyn's DMZ to go to a steak house* [1980s+; fr the region between North and South Korea designated the *Demilitarized Zone* when the Korean War ended]
do *n* 1 A party or other gathering; affair; SHINDIG : *a few of the other main do's/ The Tweed do was held early last December* (*1824+*) 2 (also **doo**) A haircut or styling : *Your hair, your doo/ Yuppie bikers favor short fashion-boy dos or neat ponytails* (*1960s+ Black*) 3 Excrement; feces : *I stepped in doggy-do* • A children's term, perhaps first used in *dog-do* or *doggy-do* (*1920s+*) 4 Something one should do or must do • Always in the phrase *dos and don'ts* : *Being friendly is a do, but being possessive is a don't v* 1 To cheat; swindle : *He is hated by all the beggars above him, and they do him every chance they get* (*1641+*) 2 To eat or drink; partake of • The dated sense has to do mainly with drinks; the revived sense is usually in the phrase *do lunch* : *That was where I'd be "doing lunch" with Mark Bradley/ The expressions "doing lunch" and "fun" lead the 11th annual list of "banished words"* (*1853+*) 3 To use or take narcotics : *Hell, half the people doing blow are reacting to the cut/ I'd wonder why and do another line. But I never looked at it as if I were some big drug addict* (*1960s+ Narcotics*) 4 To serve a prison sentence : *He did six years up at San Quentin* (*1860s+*) 5 To visit; make the rounds of : *Shall we do Provence this summer?* (*1888+*) 6 To kill; do to death; SCRAG OFF, RUB OUT : *The guy she's having cocktails with is the one who done her?/ I'm the guy doing these colored girls* (*1350+*) 7 To do the sex with or to; BOFF, FUCK : *Heidi Does Hollywood* (*1913+*) *See* DO someone DIRT, DO-GOODER, DO IT ALL, DO one's NUMBER, DOODAD, DO someone OUT OF, DO one's STUFF, DO TIME, DO UP, DO something UP BROWN, WHOOP-DE-DO
DOA (pronounced as separate letters) *adj* Dead on arrival *n* : *Don't risk being a DOA by driving drunk*
do a deal (or **make a deal**) *v phr* To complete a negotiation or mutual arrangement; DEAL : *He had not thought about what kind of deal he wanted to do* (*1913+*)

do (or **take**) **a fade** *v phr* To sneak away or leave quietly : *do a fade from the wedding reception*

do a job on someone *v phr* **1** To injure; treat roughly : *Those motherf..in' scorpions really do a job on you* **2** DO A NUMBER ON **3** To destroy : *The pup did a job on the rug* (*1960s+*)

Doakes *See* JOE BLOW

do (or **run**) **a number on** *v phr* **1** To take advantage of, esp by deception; mistreat; SCREW : *You people ran a number on us. Whenever we brought it up, you walked away/ get even with Leonard for doing that number on her* **2** To affect adversely, esp as to morale and self-esteem : *He really did a number on her when he told her the boss didn't like her report* **3** To beat; trounce; CLOBBER : *He tells me to work this guy over, do a number on him/ Duke Does Number on Michigan* (*1970s+*)

do a slow burn *v phr* To become very angry gradually : *And I do a real slow burn* [1930s+; identified with the film actor Edgar Kennedy]

do a snow job on *v phr* To deceive or utterly confuse someone : *they did a snow job on the college applicants*

do away with *v phr* To kill : *did away with his heiress wife*

do bad things *v phr* To commit crimes of violence • An arch, childish way of euphemizing and emphasizing such atrocities : *You may have noticed there are some nuts out there who do bad things to people who deliver abortions* (*1990s+*)

do one's **business** *v phr* To defecate or urinate; ease oneself : *It's about time I let Roscoe out to do his business* (*1645+*)

dock *v* To reduce one's pay for some infraction : *I'm docking you six bucks for being sassy* [1822+; fr *dock*, "to cut off part of the tail," fr a Middle English word meaning "docked tail"]

doctor *n* A person who drugs racehorses to improve their performance (*1940s+ Horse racing*) *v* **1** To alter or tamper with something dishonestly; COOK : *We doctored the receipts/ He doctored the booze* (*1774+*) **2** To repair; mend : *Somebody's got to doctor this furnace* (*1828+*) *See* COUCH DOCTOR, PLAY-DOCTOR, SPIN DOCTOR

Dr Feelgood *n phr* **1** A physician who prescribes amphetamines, vitamins, hormones, etc, to induce euphoria : *No Dr Feelgood was in the White House administering amphetamines* **2** Any person who soothes and pleases by hedonic ministrations : *the Dr Feelgood of American politics* [1940s+ Black; fr the title of a 1960s song popularized by Aretha Franklin]

docu-schlock *See* INFOTAINMENT

do-dad *See* DOODAD

do one's **damndest** *v phr* To do one's best; exert oneself : *He swore he'd do his damndest to find her* (*1918+*)

dodge *n* A person's way of making a living, esp if illegal or dubious • Often ironically and deprecatingly used of one's own perfectly ordinary line of work : *We used to run gin, but when prohibition ended we had to give up that dodge/ One of the better practitioners of the dictionary dodge* (*1842+*)

dodger *See* ROGER

dodgy *adj* Dishonest and corrupt : *dodgy accountant* (*1860s+*)

do someone **dirt** *v phr* To cause someone trouble or embarrassment, esp by malice and slander; serve someone ill : *Don't repeat that unless you want to do him dirt* (*1893+*)

dodo *n* **1** A stupid, inept person; TURKEY (*1880s+*) **2** A boring person; FOGY : *I'm a respectable old dodo* (*1880s+*) **3** A student pilot who has not yet made a solo flight (*1940s+ Army Air Corps*) [fr the extinct *dodo* bird, rather sluggish and flightless; oddly enough, the word is fr the Portuguese name *doudo*, "simpleton, fool," given to the bird] *See* DEAD AS A DODO

◁**does a bear shit in the woods**▷ *sentence* That was a stupid question; isn't the answer very obvious? (*1970s+*)

do for someone *v phr* To harm or ruin someone; destroy someone (*1740+*)

do-funny *See* DOODAD

dog *n* **1** An unappealing or inferior person or thing; DUD, LOSER : *The new show's a total dog* (*1930s+*) ◁**2**▷ An unattractive woman : *And she was a dog* (*1930s+*) **3** An attractive woman; FOX (*1960s+ Jazz musicians*) **4** A man; fellow; GUY : *dirty dog/ handsome dog* (*1596+*) **5** An untrustworthy man; seducer (*1950s+ Black*) **6** A sexually aggressive man : *before the dogs on the ward showed their hand* (*1950s+ Black*) **7** A foot : *His left dog pained* (*1900s+*) **8** HOT DOG (*1900+*) **9** A teenager : *girls refer to boys as "dogs," and both refer to sex as a function* (*1990s+ Black teenagers*) *v* **1** (also **dog around**, **dog on**) To pester; taunt; BUG, HASSLE : *You were fully doggin' him about his hair/ My roommate was dogging on me for using up her shampoo/ In the verbal dueling of the speeded-up poetry, he doesn't bite rhymes and he doesn't get dogged or dissed* (*1970s+ Army*) **2** To perform well; defeat an adversary : *I dogged him at racquetball, though* (*1980s+ Students*) *See* BARKING DOGS, BIRD DOG, CATS AND DOGS, DOG IT, DOG TAGS, DOG UP, FUCK THE DOG, the HAIR OF THE DOG, HOT DIGGETY, HOT DOG, HOUND DOG, IT SHOULDN'T HAPPEN TO A DOG, PUP TENT, PUT ON THE RITZ, RAIN CATS AND DOGS, RED DOG, SEE A MAN ABOUT A DOG, TOP DOG

dog, the *n phr* Syphilis : *He was so far gone with the dog (1940s+ Black)*

dog and pony act (or **show**) *n phr* An elaborately prepared or staged presentation, event, etc, intended to sway or convince : *Bring them in here and do a dog and pony act* [1970s+; by the 1920s *dog and pony show* was a derisive name for a small circus] *See* GO INTO one's DANCE

◁**dog-ass** or **dog-assed**▷ *adj* Wretched; inferior; pitiable : *that dog-assed motel*

dog-doo or **dog-do** *n* Feces of the canine : *containers for picking up dog-doo*

dog-ear *v* To fold back the corner of a page to mark one's place in a book : *Those of us who still dog-ear and reread her books say "Who cares?"* [1886+; Found as *dog's-ear* by 1659]

dog-eared *adj* **1** Worn, creased, and rumpled; shabby; unkempt **2** Old; outworn; hackneyed : *Even a clean reading of a dog-eared tune is deepened* [1894+; fr the look of a book whose pages have been repeatedly folded at the corners; found in this sense by 1824]

dog-eat-dog *modifier* Ruthlessly competitive and often cruel : *dog-eat-dog world of New York City (1850s+)*

dogface *modifier* : *a dogface, paddlefoot private n* A soldier, esp an infantry private : *Few wanted to be dogfaces (1930s+ Army)*

◁**dog fashion** (or **style**)▷ *adv phr* With one partner in a sex act entering the other from the rear; BOTTOMS UP (*late 1800s+*)

dogfight *n* **1** An aerial combat among fighter planes (*WWI air forces*) **2** Any confused and riotous brawl; DONNYBROOK (*1880+*)

◀**dogfuck**▶ *v* To do a sex act with one partner entering the other from the rear : *including how to 69 and dogfuck (1960s+)*

dogger *See* HOT DOGGER

doggie *n* DOGFACE (*1930s+*)

doggo *adj* In hiding; quiet and unobtrusive; low-profile : *Hamilton, lying doggo since killing the Chicago detective/ Even doggo prospects like anthropologists and landscape architects, we learn, are still in demand (1893+ British) See* LIE DOGGO

doggone or **daggone** or **dagnab** *adj* (also **doggoned** or **daggoned** or **dagnabbed**) Wretched; nasty; silly : *This doggone thing's busted (1860+) adv* : *They left here doggone fast (1871+) interj* (also **doggone it** or **daggone it** or **dagnab it**) An exclamation of disappointment, irritation, frustration, etc; DANG, DARN : *Doggone it, leave me be! (1851+)* [probably a euphemism for *God damn*]

doggy bag *n phr* A paper or plastic bag or box given a restaurant customer to take home leftovers (*1964+*)

doghouse *n* **1** Any small structure resembling in some way a dog's individual kennel : *The boat has a doghouse over the main cabin* **2** The bass viol : *When the bull-fiddler plucks the strings he is slapping the doghouse (1920s+ Jazz musicians) See* IN THE DOGHOUSE

dog it *v phr* **1** PUT ON THE RITZ **2** To avoid or evade work; refuse to exert oneself; COAST : *He had his troubles all year long, dogging it on us and complaining all the time/ The impression comes through clearly that I was dogging it (1905+)* **3** To leave hastily; flee **4** To live as a parasite; SPONGE : *He was dogging it, mooching his room and board* **5** To behave wantonly or promiscuously (*1980s+ Students*) **6** *v phr* To make a half-hearted attempt; to fail to do one's best : *lost enthusiasm and dogged it through the rest of the project*

dogmeat *n* Something or somebody inferior or worthless; CRAP, SHIT : *Your car is a piece of dogmeat/ Columbus was dogmeat after he discovered America* [1890s+; The dated form is *dog's meat*]

do-good *adj* Overtly benign and altruistic : *This "do-good" laundry list draws sneers*

do-gooder *n* A person whose selfless work may be more pretentiously than actually altruistic; an ostentatiously right-minded citizen : *a professional do-gooder (1927+)*

dog someone out *v phr* To chide someone; criticize adversely : *Johnson is not afraid to be critical, and had heard things like "Hey, you dog me out" (1990s+)*

dogs *n* The feet [1919+; said to be short for *dog's meat*, "feet" in rhyming slang; also attributed to the writer and cartoonist Tad Dorgan] *See* BARKING DOGS, CATS AND DOGS, GO TO THE DOGS, RAIN CATS AND DOGS

dog's age *n phr* An extremely long time : *haven't seen you in a dog's age (1836+)*

dog's breakfast (or **dinner**) *n phr* A wretched mixture; an unpalatable combination; mess : *that dog's breakfast of fact and fancy docudrama/ The plot is a dog's breakfast of half-baked ideas (first form 1934+, second 1960s+)*

◁**dogshit**▷ *n* Despicable matter; pretentious trash; CRAP, DOGMEAT, SHIT : *None of this fancy-pants bullshit, poodle-top haircuts and flashy clothes. None of that dogshit (1960s+)*

dog's life, a *n phr* A wretched existence; a miserable life (*1607+*)

dog style *See* DOG FASHION

dog tags *n phr* Identification tags, esp metal tags worn around the neck by members of the armed forces : *Vets, if you still have your dog tags* [WWI armed forces; each soldier had two : one to be taken from his body if he died, the other to be left with it]

dog tent *See* PUP TENT

dog-tired *adj* Very tired; exhausted; BEAT, POOPED, WASTED [1809+; as tired as a *dog* after a hunt; Bayard Taylor called it "a German phrase" in an 1876 letter]

d'oh *interj* An exclamation of frustration or self-reprimanding realization : *I was just about to leave without my keys. D'oh* [fr the catch phrase of the character Homer Simpson on the TV series *The Simpsons*]

do-hickey or **do-hinky** *See* DOODAD, DOOHICKEY

do one's homework *v phr* To be ready and informed, esp for a meeting, interview, report, etc : *Shana Alexander has done her homework well* (*1930s+*)

do someone in *v phr* **1** To kill someone : *She did in the old woman, too* **2** To ruin someone; destroy : *why you let your brother do you in the way he did* (*1905+*)

doing *See* NOTHING DOING, TAKE SOME DOING

doings *n* **1** Happenings : *doings at the student union* **2** Nonspecific items, things one may have temporarily forgotten the name for : *the doings on the kitchen table*

do it *v phr* To do the sex act; FUCK • An arch euphemism very popular for a time in a series of bumper stickers : *Divers do it deeper/ Professors do it fifty minutes at a time/ let alone comprehend that sexual intercourse is more than two bodies "doing it"* (*1913+*)

do it all *v phr* **1** To serve a life term in prison (*1940s+ Underworld*) **2** To be versatile; be variously skilled : *Take that shortstop. He'll do it all for you* (*1960s+*)

do it the hard way *v phr* To do something in the most difficult and painful manner : *"He did it the hard way," said Johnny Croll* [*1920s+*; fr *the hard way* in craps, making the points of 4, 6, 8, or 10 with throws of a pair of 2s, 3s, 4s, or 5s]

do it up or **do it up brown** *v phr* To do something decisively and well : *Some of us really did it up in grand style* (*1880+*)

do-jigger *See* DOODAD

doke or **dokey** or **dokie** *See* OKEY-DOKE

dokle *See* OKEY-DOKE

doll *n* **1** (also **dolly**) A conventionally pretty and shapely young woman, esp a curly, blue-eyed blonde, whose function is to elevate the status of a male and to inspire general lust; BABE, BABY DOLL, BIMBO : *If a blonde girl doesn't talk we call her a doll/ the subservient dolly without a thought in her head* (*1860+*) **2** Any woman, esp an attractive one; BABE, chick • Considered offensive by many women (*1778+*) **3** A notably decent, pleasant, generous person; LIVING DOLL : *Isn't he a doll?* (*1950s+*) **4** An attractive boy or young man (*1940s+*) **5** (also **dolly**) An amphetamine or barbiturate drug in pill or capsule form (*1960s+ Narcotics*) *See* LIVING DOLL

Doll *See* BARBIE DOLL

dollar *See* BET one's BOTTOM DOLLAR, PHONY AS A THREE-DOLLAR BILL, TOP DOLLAR

dollars to doughnuts *adv phr* Very probably; almost certainly : *Dollars to doughnuts, there are more people this morning day-dreaming about old lovers than are reading this newspaper* [*1904+*; *dollars to buttons* is found in 1884, and *dollars to a doughnut* in 1890; the most common phrase is *It is dollars to doughnuts that*]

dollface *n* A person with regularly pretty features of a feminine sort (*1940s+*)

doll up (or **out**) *v phr* To dress fancily and in one's best clothes; GUSSY UP : *This year the girls are dolling up in calico patchworks* (*1906+*)

dolly *See* DOLL

do lunch *See* DO

-dom *suffix used to form nouns* The range, establishment, scope, or realm of what is indicated : *fandom/ moviedom/ klutzdom*

dome *n* The head : *But when the messenger's got a gat pointed at your dome, what are you gonna do?* (*1880s+*)

done and done *modifier* Unquestionably completed, finalized : *My to-do list is done and done*

done by (or **with**) **mirrors** *modifier* Illusory; done deceptively : *government processes done by mirrors*

done deal *n phr* Something unlikely to be altered; a fait accompli : *If Ben shook your hand, it was a done deal/ President Bush's enormous popularity may appear to make his re-election a done deal* (*1980s+*)

done for *adj phr* Ruined; doomed; FINISHED, KAPUT, SOL : *Once this gets out, we're done for* (*1842+*)

done in *adj phr* **1** (also **done up**) Very tired; POOPED : *I was done up* **2** Killed **3** Ruined; wrecked : *My plans are done in but good* (*1917+*)

done over *adj* Completely defeated : *done over by the opposing baseball team*

done to a turn *adj* **1** Cooked until well-done : *burgers done to a turn* **2** Defeated : *opponent done to a turn*

◁**dong**▷ *n* The penis [*1891+*; origin unknown; possibly fr *ding-dong* fr *dingus*, a euphemism for the unnamable thing; perhaps echoic to suggest striking; compare *wang*] *See* FLONG one's DONG, PULL one's PUD

Don Juan *n* A man who has great sexual success with a large number of women [*1848+*; fr the name of a legendary dissolute Spanish nobleman, popularized in Britain by Byron's poem *Don Juan*]

◁**donkey dick**▷ *n phr* **1** Salami and other cold-cut sausages; horse cock (*WWII armed forces*) **2** A very durable penile erection, due to an effect of heroin use : *a reward known in smack circles as "donkey dick" (1960s+ Narcotics)*

donkey's years (or **ears**) *n phr* A very long time • Chiefly British use : *I got interested in his apprenticeship donkey's years ago* [1917+; a punning allusion to the long *ears* of a *donkey*]

donkeywork *n* Tedious work needing little skill or wit; SCUT : *He uses computers to do what the "whiz kids" call their "donkey work"* (1920+)

donna *See* PRIMA DONNA

donnybrook *n* A riotous scene, esp a general and energetic brawl; BRANNIGAN : *A donnybrook began when police arrested the operators* [1852+; fr the reputation of a fair held annually at the Dublin suburb of *Donnybrook*]

do someone **nothing** *v phr* To leave one unaffected, unmoved, unpleased, etc : *This book does me nothing* [1950s+; probably a play on the Yiddish phrase *tu mir eppes*, "do me something"]

don't *n* Something one should not or must not do; NO-NO : *The do's and don'ts of sailing a leaky barge*

Don't ask *sentence* The answer is not something you want to hear : *did I eat it? Don't ask*

don't get no respect, someone or something *sentence* The subject is not treated with proper regard : *Although Luisa Miller has edged into the semi-standard repertory, it still doesn't get much respect/ We Republicans are not getting any respect from the White House/ Among superpower currencies, the Soviet ruble gets no respect* [1970s+; fr the tag line of the comedian Rodney Dangerfield]

◁**don't get your balls in an uproar**▷ *sentence* Don't get so excited; be calm; COOL IT : *Don't get your balls in an uproar. This isn't the first crime commission and it won't be the last* (1930s+)

◁**don't get your testicles in a twist**▷ *sentence* COOL IT : *I'm coming, Mr McAllister! Don't get your testicles in a twist!* [1990s+; perhaps influenced by British *Don't get your knickers in a twist*, which is attested from 1971]

don't give it a second thought *sentence* Don't worry unduly about what you said or did; FORGET IT : *You didn't mean to, I know. Don't give it a second thought* (1960s+)

don't give up (or **quit**) **your day job** *sentence* What you are planning or doing may not pan out; you may be making a mistake : *If you consider yourself to the left of, say, Michael Kinsley, then don't give up your day job* (1990s+)

don't go there *sentence* Don't bring that up; don't broach that topic : *Don't go there : in-*creasingly popular catch phrase among teenagers (1990s+ Teenagers)*

don't have a baby (or **cow**) *sentence* Calm down; relax; COOL IT : *Don't have a cow; I'm only five minutes late* (1980s+ Teenagers)

don't hold your breath *sentence* Don't count on a certain event or outcome; be patient and skeptical : *Will Clinton's vague and toothless form of workfare dissolve the welfare-based underclass? Don't hold your breath* (1960s+)

don't knock it *sentence* Don't be critical of it; appreciate its value : *Don't knock it. Nobody who lived in the past would want to live in the past/ Don't knock it. Good bucks there*

don't make a federal case out of it! *sentence* Don't make a fuss about something that is not that important : *Don't make a federal case out of my leaving crumbs on the counter*

don't make me laugh! *sentence* That is so ridiculous that I cannot believe you are saying it : *Watch basketball? Don't make me laugh*

don't pop the champagne corks yet *sentence* (also **don't uncork the champagne yet**) Don't celebrate a victory prematurely; don't count your chickens before they're hatched : *It didn't happen, but don't pop the champagne corks yet/ the S&L industry posted earnings of $1.97 billion, the first gain in five years. But don't uncork the champagne yet* [1990s+; fr the custom of pouring champagne over the victors in a sports contest]

◁**don't shit a shitter**▷ *sentence* Don't try to hoodwink an expert hoodwinker : *"Don't shit a shitter," said Dubie/ You can play it any way you like. But don't try to shit a shitter, okay?* (1970s+)

Don't sweat it! *sentence* Take it easy. Relax and don't worry : *I got your back. Don't sweat it*

don't take any wooden nickels *sentence* Take care of yourself; good-bye, and watch yourself • Used as an amiable parting salutation (1915+)

◁**don't try to shit a shitter** (or **bullshit a bullshitter**)▷ *sentence* Never try to deceive a deceiver : *We get there you can play it any way you like. But don't try and shit a shitter, okay?*

do one's **number** *v phr* To behave in an expected way; play a role; GO INTO one's ACT : *He was doing his number about how you have to alienate no one* [1920s+; fr *number*, "theatrical act or routine, shtick," which is attested by 1885]

doo *See* HOOPER DOOPER

doobie or **dubee** or **duby** *n* **1** A marijuana cigarette; JOINT : *I smoke a doobie at lunch/ and rolled myself an ample doobie* (1960s+ Narcotics) **2** A database (1980s+ Computer)

[first sense, origin unknown; second sense probably fr *database*, influenced by first sense]

doodad *n* **1** (Variations : **do-dad** or **do-funny** or **doofunny** or **do-hickey** or **doohickey** or **dohinky** or **doohinky** or **do-jigger** or **doojigger** or **doowhangam** or **do-whistle** or **doowhistle** or **do-willie** or **doowillie**) Any unspecified or unspecifiable thing; something one does not know the name of or does not wish to name; GADGET, THINGAMAJIG : *We may have turned into what looks like a nation of doohickeys/ Imagination and art aren't worth those little doowhangams you put under a sofa leg* **2** Something useless or merely ornamental : *There was not one photograph, not a doodad, not a toy, not a cup, of my own* (*1905+*)

doodle *n* **1** Wretched material; SHIT : *How can he write such doodle?* ◁2▷ The penis • A child's term (*1780s+*) *v* **1** To cheat; swindle; DIDDLE (*1823+*) **2** To make drawings and patterns while sitting at a meeting, talking on the telephone, etc : *From your doodling, the shrink sees what's in your noodle* (*1935+*) **3** To defecate • Also *doo-doo* : *dog doodled in the yard* [second sense apparently coined by Robert Riskin, screenwriter for the movie *Mr Deeds Goes to Town*; third sense perhaps fr *doo*, childish word for "shit"] *See* DIPSY-DOODLE, WHANGDOODLE, WHOOP-DE-DO

doodle-brained *adj* Stupid; silly : *singing a doodle-brained folk song about "travelin'"* [*1970s+*; fr *doodle*, "fool, simpleton," attested by 1628, whence *Yankee Doodle*]

doodlebug *n* **1** A self-propelled railroad car; a one-car train (*1940s+ Railroad*) **2** A small reconnaissance car (*WWII armed forces*) **3** A military tank, esp a light tank (*WWII armed forces*) **4** A German jet-propelled robot bomb, the V-1 (*WWII British armed forces*) **5** A divining rod or other device used for locating underground water, gas, etc (*1924+*) [all senses connected with *doodlebug*, "the larva of the tiger-beetle or various other insects"]

◁**doodle-shit**▷ *n* (Variations : **doodily-shit** or **doodley-shit** or **doodly-squat** or **doodly**) Nothing; very little; SQUAT, ZILCH : *I don't care doodily-shit about Jews and Nazis/ A whole lot of doodley-shit* (*entry form 1960s+, -squat 1930s+*)

doodling *n* Idle playing; FOOLING AROUND, NOODLING : *When Sinatra entered the wings, the doodling ceased* (*1970s+*)

doo-doo *n* Excrement; DO, SHIT : *I think doo-doo is coming out of your ears* (*1940s+*)

doo-doo head *n phr* A stupid person; an idiot; SHIT-FOR-BRAINS, SHITHEAD : *Let's face it, we're doo-doo heads for playing* (*1970s+*)

doofer or **dufer** *n* A cigarette or partial one found and saved for later [as it will "do for" later]

doofunny *See* DOODAD

doofus (also **doof** or **doofis** or **dufus**) *modifier* : *Many another dufus play among friends* **n** A fool; idiot; AIRHEAD, BIRDBRAIN, BOOB : *He'll do his best to make you feel like a doofus/ But this is the doofus you have to deal with, so hush up/ I have to be in front of this self-important doofis with his portable phone/ I felt like such a dufus/ when some big, loud, popcorn-chuggin' doof and his date sit in front of me* [*1960s+*; probably related to *doo-doo* and *goofus*]

doohickey *n* (Variations : **do-hickey** or **dohinky** or **doohinky**) Any unspecified or unspecifiable thing; something one does not know the name of or does not wish to name; GADGET, THINGAMAJIG (*1914+*) *See* DOODAD

doohinky *See* DOODAD, DOOHICKEY

doojigger *See* DOODAD

do something on top of one's **head** *v phr* To accomplish something easily : *You can do that shit on top of your head*

doop *See* WHOOP-DE-DO

dooper *See* HOOPER DOOPER, SUPER-DUPER

door *See* someone CAN'T HIT THE SIDE OF A BARN, KATIE BAR THE DOOR, REVOLVING-DOOR, SHOW someone THE DOOR

doormat *modifier* : *Cornell University's doormat status on the gridiron* **n** A person who is regularly and predictably exploited by others; constant victim : *the soulful Earth Mother doormat of the kind played by Shirley MacLaine in the fifties/ the wife a rape victim, slave, doormat* *See* TREAT someone LIKE A DOORMAT

do someone **out of** *v phr* To deprive by cheating, fraud, stealing, etc : *They did the poor jerk out of his pay* (*1825+*)

do-over *n phr* A chance to do something over; a second chance : *a do-over on the quiz*

do someone **over** *v phr* To hit repeatedly; assault by hitting : *done over by the cops* (*1860s+*)

doowhangam or **doowhistle** or **doowillie** *See* DOODAD

doo-wop or **do-whop** *modifier* : *from the do-whop music and lovingly customized cars/ lead singer of her Sixties doo-wop outfit, Patti Labelle and the Bluebelles* **n** A style of street jazz-singing, esp by black ensembles (*1950s+ Black musicians*) [echoic fr a common rhythm phrase of the songs]

doozie or **doozy** or **doosie** *n* A person or thing that is remarkable, wonderful, superior, etc; BEAUT, HUMDINGER : *a little 30-page doozey called "Making Chicken Soup"/ Want a swell Naval Air Station? I got two doozies up for grabs* [*1916+*; origin uncertain; perhaps fr a humorous repronunciation of *daisy*; certainly reinforced by *dusy, duesie,* and other short-enings of *Duesenberg,* the name of a very expensive and desirable car of the 1920s and '30s]

dope *modifier* **1** : *a dope fiend/ dope stash* **2** Wonderful; excellent; COOL, RAD, SUPER : *It's a dope day, dude!/ Redman was one of the people Andre said was dope/ have, in the parlance of the street, become "dope" and "phat,"* i.e. cool, greatest *(1980s+ Teenagers)* **n 1** Any nar-cotic drug, legal or illegal ● First applied to opium, by 1889 : *They searched him for dope/ The doctors kept him full of dope (1895+)* **2** Coca-Cola℠ : *Jim Bob sat down and ordered a large dope (1915+)* **3** Any liquid, esp a vis-cous one, used for a special purpose : *mas-saged his lamps with fragrant drug store dope (1872+)* **4** DOPER *(1909+)* **5** A stupid person; idiot; TURKEY : *Only a dope would refuse that chance (1851+ British dialect)* **6** Information; data; the LOWDOWN : *Get me all the dope you can on her colleagues/ What's the latest dope about Ruth? (1901+)* **7** A prediction, esp about a race or a game, based on analysis of past performance; form : *The dope says Dream Diddle in a romp (1901+)* **v 1** : *The nurse doped him so that he could sleep (1889+)* **2** To use narcotics : *I like to dope (1909+)* **3** To give drugs, vitamins, etc, to horses or athletes to improve their competitive prowess : *He couldn't run that fast if he wasn't doped (1875+)* **4** : *I dope it like this, Ali all the way (1920s+)* [fr Dutch *doop,* "sauce for dip-ping," with elaborate semantic shifts] *See* HIT THE DOPE

doper *modifier* : *with all these doper cops loose/ seemed merely a statement of doper hipness* **n** A narcotics addict or user : *alerting dopers of every stripe that where the penalties had been stiff, they would now be feudal/ I think to my-self, some dopers're having a disagreement (1889+ Narcotics)*

dope sheet *n phr* Printed information or in-structions, esp about the past performance of racehorses; form *(1903+)*

dope up *v phr* **1** To inject or take a dose of a narcotic : *doped up now* **2** To purchase drugs

dopey or **dopy** *adj* **1** Stuporous, esp from narcotic intoxication : *I was dopy after they gave me the shot* **2** Stupid; idiotic : *Most movies are written for women in their 20s and 30s, and these are sort of dopey parts* [1896+; fr *dope*; the word has also meant "a thief's or beggar's woman" since at least the 1850s, and this may in some minds have influenced the modern senses]

◁**dork**▷ **n 1** The penis : *the glorious acrobatics she can perform while dangling from the end of*

my dork (1964+) **2** A despicable person; JERK, PRICK : *a frightened, virtuous dork (1970s+ Students)* **v** To do the sex act with or to; ruin or confound as if by violating sexually; FUCK, SCREW : *I said to myself, "I dorked him," but the ball just kept floating like it was floating on air (1970s+)*

dorky *adj* Stupid; DOPEY, dumb : *a dorky kid with Dumbo ears/ Casually include them in chitchat about how dorky the principal's speech was (1970s+ Students)*

dory *See* HUNKY-DORY

dose *v* To infect with a venereal disease, esp gonorrhea : *What's going to happen is that you'll get dosed (1914+)*

dose, a *n phr* A case of venereal disease, esp of gonorrhea : *Don't Give a Dose to the One You Love Most (1914+) See* LIKE SHIT THROUGH A TIN HORN

do-se-do or **do-si-do** (DOH see DOH) **n 1** A dull fight, with more dancing than punching : *The guys who are supposed to do the fighting go in there and put on the old do-se-do (1930s+ Prizefight)* **2** A regular alternation; predict-able shift : *Fashion always does a do-si-do be-tween artifice and the natural (1960s+)* [fr the square-dance figure, fr French *dos-à-dos,* "back to back," in which dancers pass each other back-to-back and return to their places]

dose of salts *See* LIKE SHIT THROUGH A TIN HORN

do something standing on one's **head** *v phr* To do something easily [1896+; the dated form is *do it on one's head*]

do one's **stuff** *v phr* To perform one's role, esp something one does very well : *Get in there and do your stuff (1920s+)*

dot, the *See* ON THE DOT

do tell *interj* An exclamation of surprise, in-credulity, etc : *You shot the dog? Do tell! (1840+)*

do the math *v phr* or *sentence* Figure it out yourself; also, carry out a simple arithmetic calculation : *To live where you want, do the math*

do the nasty *v phr* To do the sex act; BOFF, BONE, DO THE BONE DANCE, SCREW *(1980s+ Students)*

do the trick *v phr* To do exactly what is needed for the desired result : *this makeup ought to do the trick*

do the wild thing *v phr* To do the sex act; BOFF, BONE, SCREW : *Elliot Gould first did the wild thing with Barbra Streisand in the early 1960s/ It was a bad thing to do the wild thing without a blessing from the Almighty (1980s+ Students)*

do one's (or one's **own**) **thing** *v phr* To follow one's special inclinations, esp despite disap-proval; to act independently or alone : *Doing* *your own thing may be all right in prescribed doses* (*1840+*)

do time *v phr* To serve a prison sentence (*1860+*)

do tricks *See* GO DOWN AND DO TRICKS

dot the i's and cross the t's *v phr* To work meticulously, esp to make something clear and accurate : *Extraneous to my investigation, but I like to dot the i's and cross the t's* (*1885+*)

double-bagger *n* A very ugly person; TWO-BAGGER [*1970s+* Teenagers; fr the fact that one needs two *bags* to obscure the ugliness, one to go over the subject's head and one over one's own head]

double-barreled slingshot *n* A bra

double cross *n phr* A betrayal or cheating of one's own colleagues; an act of treachery, often in an illicit transaction : *The two suspected dealers were planning a double-cross v : I would never double-cross a pal* [*1834+*; fr the reneging on an agreement to lose, a *cross*, by actually winning] *See* GIVE someone THE DOUBLE CROSS

double dare or **double dog dare** *v phr* To challenge provocatively : *The movie double-dared its audience to find sympathy in its dour or manic characters/ I double dog dare ya to find out which three!* [*1940s+*; fr a boys' response to "I dare you!," "I *double dare* you!"; *double dog dare* is still higher defiance]

double-dealing *modifier* : *a double-dealing little crum n* Deceitful or treacherous behavior (*1529+*)

double-dip *n* The practice of holding a second job that has retirement benefits while receiving a pension from former employment *v* **1** To dip a food item into a sauce or dip, take a bite, and then dip it in the sauce again : *You can double-dip at home, but not at a party* **2** To get money from two sources, often in a way that is not legal or by simultaneously drawing a government pension and holding a job [*1970s+*; fr an ice-cream cone with two *dips*, scoops, of ice cream]

double-dipper *n* **1** A person who double-dips : *Federal pensioners are "double-dippers" who also collect Social Security checks* (*1970s+*) **2** A person who dips an appetizer into a dip or sauce after already biting the appetizer, which is unsanitary : *She's double-dipping the Mexican layer app*

double-dome *modifier* : *None of your double-dome pomp, please n* An intellectual; scholar; EGGHEAD : *Princeton, NJ, where the double domes congregate v : legitimate double-doming I suppose, but totally without fact* (*1930s+*)

double Dutch *n phr* Language that cannot be understood, esp overly technical jargon : *Plain English will do; cut the double Dutch*

[*1864+*; *Dutch,* "German," being unintelligible, *double Dutch* is twice as opaque]

doubleheader *n* Two contests, esp baseball games, played at one meeting [*1890s+* Sports; fr earlier railroad use for a train drawn by two engines]

double-minus *See* X-DOUBLE-MINUS

double-quick *adj* Twice the usual speed; very quickly [*1822+*; orig military, from the notion of marching at twice the speed of quick time]

double-R *n* A Rolls-Royce car : *I crossed back to the Union 76, paid my ransom for Full Service, and got back in the double-R* (*1990s+*)

double sawbuck (or **saw**) *n phr* Twenty dollars; a $20 bill : *so many sheets of dollars, ten-spots and double saws* (*1850+*)

double six *n phr* A year, two six-month periods

double-take *n* A sudden second look or a laugh or gesture over something one has at first ignored or accepted; a belated reaction : *She suddenly caught the reference and did a double-take v : I double-took a little bit when she ordered a cigar* (*1940s+*)

double talk *n phr* **1** A sort of gibberish or patter that seems plausible but is nonsense, done for amusement : *Danny Kaye excelled at double talk* **2** Deceptive and insincere speech : *Don't be put off by his double talk* (*1938+*)

double-team *v* To attack or defend against someone, esp a formidable athlete, with twice the usual forces : *He was gaining every play till they double-teamed him* [*1860+*; originally fr *doubling* the *team* of horses used for a purpose]

double-time *v* DOUBLE-CROSS, TWO-TIME

double-trouble *modifier* : *a double-trouble day n* **1** Serious difficulty; DEEP TROUBLE ● This was the name of a black shuffle dance as early as 1807, showing the potential of the rhyme **2** A source or cause of great difficulty or menace; BAD NEWS : *Watch that clown, he's double trouble* (*1940s+*)

double turkey *n phr* Six strikes bowled one after another (*1940s+ Bowling*)

double whammy *n phr* A two-part or two-pronged difficulty; a dual disadvantage : *the double-whammy of steep home prices and steeper interest rates* (*1940s+*) *See* WHAMMY

◁**douche bag**▷ *n phr* A despicable and loathsome person; SCUMBAG : *dirty, filthy douchebag/ Either this guy is a bigger douche bag than I even remember or something is way out of line* [*1950s+* Students; recorded in the 1940s meaning "a military misfit"]

dough *n* **1** Money; BREAD : *And to get the dough we'll put our watch and chain in hock* (*1851+*) **2** DOUGHBOY *See* HEAVY MONEY

doughboy *n* An infantry soldier; GRUNT, paddlefoot [*1867+*; origin unknown; perhaps fr a resemblance between the buttons of the infantry uniform and *doughboys*, "suet dumplings boiled in seawater," a term fr the British merchant marine]

dough-head *n* A stupid person; idiot; KLUTZ (*1838+*)

doughnut *n* 1 A truck tire (*1930s+ Truckers*) 2 The driving of a car in tight circles, esp by hoodlums who have stolen the car : *Perform doughnuts, in which they lock the brakes, step on the gas, and send the car spinning in circles/ spotted about 7:20 doing doughnuts in the parking lot of Taco Bell* (*1980s+*) *See* TAKE A FLYING FUCK

do up *v phr* 1 To pummel and trounce; CLOBBER (*1846+*) 2 To take narcotics : *We'll do up some hash* (*1960s+ Narcotics*)

do something up brown *v phr* To do something very thoroughly : *He didn't just finish it, he did it up brown* [*1840+*; fr the *brown* color of something well baked]

dove (DUHV) *n* 1 Dear one; honey; love : *There at once, my dove* (*1596+*) 2 A person who advocates peace and nonviolence; an irenic soul (*1962+*)

dovetail *v* To say something linked and sequential : *Let me dovetail on what you just said* (*1970s+ Army*)

dovey *n* LOVEY-DOVEY (*1796+*)

dovish *adj* Tending to advocate peace over war; irenic : *more and more room for dovish interpretations* (*1960s+*)

do what comes naturally *v phr* To do the simple obvious thing; respond unthinkingly : *As might have been expected, the Joint Chiefs of Staff did what came naturally* [*1940s+*; Popularized by the song "Doing What Comes Naturally," which celebrates wholesome instinctive behavior]

do-whistle or **do-willie** *See* DOODAD

do whop *See* DOO-WOP

down *adj* 1 Depressed; melancholy; BLUE : *He's real down about losing that chance* (*1645+*) 2 Depressing; pessimistic; dampening; DOWNBEAT : *I don't see the point of making such a "down" picture* (*1950s+*) 3 Not functioning; ON THE BLINK : *The power plant has been down for two months/ The computer's down again today* (*1970s+*) 4 Coolly cognizant; at ease in one's own skin; COOL : *To show how "down" you are to youthful consumers/ Of course if you are "with it," you "be down"* (*1970s+*) 5 Excellent; good; profoundly satisfying (*1950+ Jazz musicians*) 6 (also **down-ass**) Having special affinity; linked; in league • The term was strongly revived in the 1990s by black teenagers and street gangs : *It wasn't her turf, but she wasn't down special with one gang/ You're down with the heavy metal crowd now/ I am probably one of* the few *down-ass females on his team/ You're down hard for the 'hood* (*1930s+ Jazz musicians*) 7 Finished; completed : *one down and 30 to go* *n* DOWNER (*1960s+ Narcotics*) *v* 1 To eat or drink : *I downed an enormous pizza* (*1860+*) 2 To criticize; complain of; PUT someone or something DOWN : *My friends downed me for listening to country music* (*1960s+*) [cool and teenager senses perhaps fr jazz musicians' terms like *low down* and *down and dirty* used to praise gutbucket and other jazz when especially well played] *See* GET DOWN, GO DOWN ON someone, LOOK DOWN ON someone, the LOWDOWN, LOW-DOWN, MELTDOWN, PUT-DOWN, PUT someone DOWN FOR something, UP-AND-DOWN

down (or up) someone's alley *adv phr* Of the sort one prefers or is best at; TAILOR-MADE : *That job's right down his alley* (*entry form 1941+, variant 1931+*)

down and dirty *adj phr* Nasty; low; vicious and deceptive • Also uttered in seven-card stud poker as the last cards are dealt face down : *Mississippi: A Down and Dirty Campaign/ This is down-and-dirty time. Just witness Rizzo's angry characterization of Goode* (*1950s+*)

down and out *adj phr* Penniless and hopeless; destitute : *When you're down and out, remember what did it* [*1889+*; fr the condition of a fighter who is knocked down unconscious]

down-and-outer *n* A complete failure; derelict; BUM (*1909+*)

down a peg *See* TAKE someone DOWN A PEG

downbeat *adj* Depressing; pessimistic : *a triumph of upbeat pictures over the downbeat* [*1950s+*; fr the *downbeat* of an orchestra leader's hand or baton, taken as the direction of dejection]

downer *n* 1 A depressant drug, esp a barbiturate; sedative; DOWN (*1950s+ Narcotics*) 2 A depressing experience; BAD TRIP, BUMMER, DRAG : *The opening scene's a downer* (*1960s+ Narcotics*)

down for the count *adj phr* Utterly defeated; ruined; DOWN AND OUT [*1922+*; fr the *count* of ten made over a *downed* boxer]

downhill *adj* 1 Simple and easy : *nearly done and all downhill from here* (*1719+*) 2 : *a downhill prospect* *adv* To a worse condition; to the bad : *all trends ineluctably downhill* (*1795+*) *n* The final half of a prison sentence or a military enlistment (*1930+ Prison*) *See* GO DOWNHILL

down home *adj phr* Simple; homey : *a down-home meal of roast chicken, potatoes, and peas* *adv phr* 1 In the southern US; in Dixie 2 In a Southern regional or ethnic manner : *funkier than blues and playing about as down home as* *you can get* **modifier** : *He was getting away from all that old down-home stuff* **n phr** : *old buddy from down home* (*1848+*)

down in flames *See* GO DOWN IN FLAMES

down in the dumps *adj phr* Depressed; melancholy; BLUE, DOWN [1785+; in text of 1529, *in a dump* means "melancholy, dejected"; modern use probably influenced by US *dump*, "rubbish heap," etymologically unrelated, which is attested from 1865]

down low, the *n* The information or explanation needed or wanted; the LOWDOWN : *the down low on the opposing team*

down one's nose *See* LOOK DOWN one's NOSE

down on someone or something *adj phr* Angry with or critical of : *Everybody's down on Mary since she reported Sue to the boss* (*1843+*)

down on one's **uppers** *modifier* Having no money [1895+; fr the notion of destitute people who have worn out the soles of their shoes, leaving only the uppers]

downplay *v* To deemphasize; minimize; SOFT-PEDAL : *They're downplaying the role of bias in all this* (*1968+*)

downside *n* The depressing or deflating aspect of something; the bad news : *the more ability and ambition you need to survive the "downside" of this evolutionary process/ It sounds a little too perfect. What's the downside?/ Developments of the past decades have surely had their down side* (*1980s+*)

downsize *v* To reduce the size of a company by eliminating employees, in order to increase profits (*1980s+*)

down the drain *adv phr* To a futile end; to waste : *All his best efforts seemed to go down the drain* (*1930+*) *See* POUR MONEY DOWN THE DRAIN

down the hatch *interj* A toast, followed by the swallowing of a whole drink (*1931+*)

down the pike *See* COME DOWN THE PIKE

down the river *See* SELL someone DOWN THE RIVER

down the road *adv phr* Later; in the future : *It might save us a little now, but it'll cost us down the road* (*1960s+*)

down the tube (or **tubes** or **chute**) *See* GO DOWN THE TUBE

down someone's throat *See* JUMP DOWN someone's THROAT

downtime *n* **1** Time during which a machine, factory, etc, is not operating (*1950s+*) **2** Time away from work; leisure time : *He spends most of his downtime with Toby, his wife/ He has more downtime than he did four years ago*

down to brass tacks *adv phr* Dealing with the essentials; concerned with the practical realities : *highbrow sermons that don't come*

down to brass tacks [1897+; apparently fr the *brass tacks* that were used to measure cloth on the counter of a dry-goods store, hence represented precision]

down to the wire *adv phr* Near the finish; at or to the last possible moment : *The project is getting down to the wire and things are getting frantic* [1901+ Horse racing; fr the imaginary line marking the end of a horse race; horses were said to pass "under the *wire*"] *See* GO TO THE WIRE

downtown *n* Heroin; HORSE, SHIT (*1980s+ Narcotics*)

down trip *See* BAD TRIP

Down Under *adv phr* In Australia and/or New Zealand; in the Antipodes *n phr* : *They're from Down Under* (*1890s+*)

down with someone or something *adj* **1** Comfortable; on good terms or friendly : *down with the boys in the hood/ down with Kyle* **2** Sick or ill with : *down with a cold*

down with it *adj phr* Coolly cognizant; absolutely in touch; WITH IT (*1930s+ Jazz musicians*)

down yonder *adv phr* DOWN HOME (*1840s+*)

do you eat (or **kiss your momma**) **with that mouth?** *sentence* How dare you speak so rudely and filthily! • Said to someone who uses dirty language all the time

do you want an engraved invitation *question* Must you be especially asked and pleaded with? you are being too standoffish and scrupulous (*1970s+*)

dozen *See* a DIME A DOZEN

dozer *n* **1** A powerful blow, esp with the fist; BELT, BIFF (*1950s+*) **2** DOOZIE (*1950s+*) **3** A bulldozer (*1940s+*) [except for sense 3, the sources do not clarify pronunciation; senses 1 and 2 may be pronounced *DOOzer*, which would make them different in origin from sense 3]

DQ *n* A Dairy Queen ice-cream restaurant : *DQ run for Dilly Bars*

drag *modifier* **1** : *a drag queen/ drag party* **2** : *Take the quiz and unearth your drag quotient n* **1** Influence; weight; CLOUT, PULL : *We had a big drag with the waiter* (*1896+*) **2** A street : *from some bo on the drag I managed to learn* (*1851+*) **3** An inhalation of smoke; puff; TOKE : *The ponies took last drags at their cigarettes and slumped into place* (*1914+*) **4** A cigarette; BUTT : *a drag smoking on your lip* (*1940s+*) **5** (also **drag party**) A party or gathering, usu of homosexuals, where everyone wears clothing of the other sex; a clustering of transvestites (*1920s+ Homosexuals*) **6** Clothing worn by someone of the sex for which the clothing was not intended; transvestite costume, esp women's clothing worn by a man : *We shall come in drag, which* *means wearing women's costumes/ Mother walked in, a little Prussian officer in drag (1870+ Homosexuals)* **7** drag race **8** A roll of money, purse, etc, used to lure the victim in a confidence game *(Police)* **9** A situation, occupation, event, etc, that is tedious and trying; DOWNER : *Life can be such a drag one minute and a solid sender the next/ Keeping things at the cleaners was sometimes a last-minute drag (1940s+ Jazz musicians)* **10** A dull, boring person : *Don't ask John to the party; he's such a drag (1940s+)* **v 1** : *dragging on cigars and feeling grown up (1919+)* **2** To race down a straightaway *(1950s+ Hot rodders)* **3** To move an image, a file designation, etc, or expand a designated menu on the computer screen by using the mouse : *I copied the whole file onto a floppy disk, dragged the original file into the electronic trash can (1980s+ Computer) See* MAIN DRAG

◁**drag ass** or **tail**▷ *n* : *We had twenty-five good guys on the club, no more drag-asses, no more prima donnas* **v phr 1** To depart, esp in a hurry; HAUL ASS **2** To be morose, sluggish, and whiny : *Quit drag-assing and get to work (1920s+)*

drag one's feet *v phr* To shirk; make less than a good effort, perhaps in the spirit of sabotage : *She spent a lot of time dragging her feet/ I'm not dragging my feet. I'm just scared* [fr loggers; fr the action of an unenergetic member of a two-person sawing team, who would *drag his feet* or "ride the saw" rather than contribute the proper effort]

dragged out *adj phr* Exhausted; BEAT : *I feel awful dragged out today (1831+)*

dragger *See* KNUCKLE-DRAGGER

dragging *See* one's ASS IS DRAGGING

draggy *adj* Slow; monotonous; sluggish : *a draggy movie (1922+)*

drag in *v phr* To arrive : *Where'd you drag in from? (1940s+)*

drag someone kicking and screaming *v phr* To force someone to recognize or adapt to change; educate a rigid reactionary : *we dragged him kicking and screaming out of the '60s*

Dragon Lady *n phr* A powerful, intimidating woman [1940s+; fr a character in the popular comic strip "Terry and the Pirates," which originated in the 1930s]

drag-out *See* KNOCK-DOWN DRAG-OUT

drag out *v phr* **1** To extend something tediously; make something last too long : *He dragged out the story excruciatingly (1842+)* **2** To extract; elicit : *She couldn't drag the truth out of him (1940s+)*

drag queen *n phr* **1** A male homosexual who enjoys dressing like a woman : *a rabidly right-wing congressman, a demented Southern*

drag queen, a pushy leather dyke **2** A male homosexual who affects pronounced feminine behavior; QUEEN *(1941+ Homosexuals)*

dragsville *adj* Very dull; tedious; DRAGGY, DULLSVILLE : *My much touted party proved dragsville (1960s+)*

drag one's tail (or ◁**ass**▷) *v phr* To work sluggishly; loaf; DRAG ASS, drag-tail : *Two hours off with pay, why the hell are they draggin' their tails? (1930s+)*

drain *See* BRAIN DRAIN, DOWN THE TUBE, POUR MONEY DOWN THE DRAIN

dratted *adj* Cursed; awful : *that dratted girl (1845+)*

draw *n* **1** A puff on a pipe, cigarette, etc; DRAG, TOKE *(1876+)* **2** (also **drawing card**) Something that attracts : *A skin flick is always a good draw (1881+) See* GET A BEAD ON someone or something, the LUCK OF THE DRAW, QUICK ON THE DRAW, SLOW ON THE DRAW

draw a blank *v phr* **1** To fail completely in recall : *I'm trying to remember, but keep drawing a blank (1940s+)* **2** To get nothing; have a negative result; fail : *I drew a blank when I solicited him (1825+)*

draw a picture (or **diagram**) *v phr* To explain something in very simple terms; make things transparently clear : *I just don't like him. Do I have to draw you a picture? (1960s+)*

drawer *See* TOP-DRAWER

dreadlock or **dredlock** *modifier* : *a British skinhead playing the dreadlock music of Jamaica* **n** (also **dread**) A mat or clump of long ungroomed hair as worn by Rastafarians, reggae musicians, etc : *grown his hair in long dredlocks, Rasta style/ Her dark-brown dreads are very thick and practically matted to her head* [1960+; fr the *dread* presumably aroused by the wearers]

dream *See* PIPE DREAM, WET DREAM

dreamboat *n* **1** Any very desirable vehicle : *A dreamboat for hot-rodders is a chromed roadster* **2** A very attractive person : *will star opposite James Mason, who she says is a "dreamboat" (1940s+)*

dream up *v phr* To invent; confect in the mind : *Julian has to start dreaming up a story/ conceptions of living dreamed up by such groups as the Mormons (1940s+)*

dreamy *adj* Very desirable; beautiful : *What a dreamy house you've got! (1920s+)*

dreck or **drek** *modifier* : *no point in my keeping every drek album/ an opponent of the ticky-tacky world of dreck-tech architecture* **n** Wretched trash; GARBAGE, JUNK, SHIT : *the ugliness, dreck and horror of New York City/ They may bring with them a pile of overfinished drek/ the sad glitter of desert drek* [1920s+; fr Yiddish, "feces"]

dredge up *v phr* To find or discover by effort and persistence : *Let's dredge up more dirt on the candidate* (1950s+)

dress *See* GRANNY DRESS

dress down *v phr* **1** To reprimand; rebuke; chew out (1715+) **2** To dress less formally or arrestingly than one might : *Casual Fridays raise new fashion issues. How much should you dress down?* (1960+)

dress-down Friday or **casual Friday** *n phr* The last day of the workweek, when one can dress informally : *He cites the business community's adoption of dress-down Friday as an example/ It's Friday, jeans day, pal* (1990s+)

dressed to the teeth (or to kill or to the nines) *adj phr* Extremely well and fancily dressed or decorated; DOLLED UP : *She's dressed to the teeth in magenta silks* **modifier** : *our dressed-to-the-teeth test car* *v phr* : *when she wrote articles about textured stockings and dressed to the nines* [first form 1970s+, second 1940s+, third 1859+; *to the teeth* implies "completely, from the bottom up"; *to the nines* is probably based on *nine* as a nearly perfect number just under ten, or on *nine* as a mystical or sacred number in numerology, the product of three times three] *See* the WHOLE NINE YARDS

dress something up *v phr* To alter something, usu with an aim to misleading : *It's an ugly story, no matter how you try to dress it up* (1691+)

dribs and drabs *n phr* In skimpy bits; piecemeal : *Details about Whitewater are coming out in dribs and drabs* [1850s+; *drib* is probably a shortening of *dribble*; *drab* earlier meant "a small debt"]

dried *See* CUT AND DRIED

drift *n* **1** A controlled sidewards skid : *puts his Maserati or Ferrari into a corner with a four-wheel drift* (1950s+ Car racing) **2** Meaning; intent : *Get my drift, chum?* (1526+) *v* (also **drift out, drift away**) To leave; depart : *Beat it. Drift* (1960s+ Underworld & prison) *See* GET THE DRIFT

drifter *n* A derelict; BUM (1908+)

drift off track *v phr* To deviate from proper conduct : *I sometimes drift off track a bit, but I really try to do what is right* (1970s+)

drifty *adj* Stupidly inattentive; silly; SPACED-OUT : *It makes Dede and me both look a little drifty* (1970s+)

drill *n* The way of doing something; the plan of action : *Pain in the ass, but that's the drill* (1940+) *v* **1** To speed with force, esp through obstacles : *skimmed by his head and drilled through the closed window* (1674+) **2** To shoot; kill by shooting : *Go drill the mutt. He's strictly stool* (1808+) **3** To hit a hard, straight grounder or line drive : *Lockman*

drilled a single past Hodges (1940s+ Baseball) *See* SACK DUTY

drink *See* I'LL DRINK TO THAT

Drink *See* the BIG DRINK

drink, the *n phr* A body of water; the water : *She tripped and fell into the drink* (1832+)

drinkage *n* Drinking in general; the amount drunk : *outlaw drinkage on campus/ drinkage for the evening*

drink like a fish *v phr* To drink too much; overindulge in alcohol; BOOZE, HIT THE BOTTLE (1747+)

drink one's lunch *v phr* To drink too much, esp during the working day : *I had to counsel Ames on the extent to which he was drinking his lunch* (1960s+)

drink of water *See* LONG DRINK OF WATER

drink someone under the table *v phr* To drink much more than another person or persons : *She drunk the boys under the table* (1921+)

drip *n* **1** A tedious, unimaginative, conventional person; SQUARE, WIMP • The term was apparently used a decade earlier in British schoolboy slang : *the biggest drip at Miss Basehoar's, a school ostensibly abounding with fair-sized drips/ such drips; they're just sort of dull* (1930s+ Teenagers) **2** Useless and idle talk; gossip (1930+ Hoboes)

drippy *adj* **1** Tedious; unimaginative; conventional; wimpy **2** Sentimental; lachrymose; CORNY (1940s+ Teenagers)

drive *n* **1** Dynamism; insistent power : *a song with drive* (1908+) **2** A thrill or transport of pleasure and energy; KICK, RUSH (1927+ Narcotics) *v* To play music, esp jazz, with strong forward impetus and rhythms (1930s+ Jazz musicians)

drive someone bonkers (or nuts) *v phr* To drive someone crazy : *music's driving me bonkers*

drive-by *modifier* Performed casually and callously while or as if while merely driving past : *Chicago woman convicted of the drive-by shooting of a teenage boy/ Broder and Woodward correctly chide the political press for practicing quick, drive-by journalism rather than trying to elevate the level of discussion/ a drive-by debate* (1990s+)

drive-in *modifier* : *drive-in bank/ drive-in church/ drive-in movie* *n* A place where one eats, watches movies, worships, etc, while sitting in one's parked car (1930+)

-driven *combining word* Controlled or caused by what is indicated : *ego-driven, profit-driven, tax-driven, publicity-driven*

driver's seat *See* IN THE DRIVER'S SEAT

drive the big bus *v phr* Vomit into the toilet, esp from drunkenness; BARF [1970s+ Students; fr the resemblance of a toilet seat to a steering wheel]

drive-thru childbirth (or **delivery**) *n phr* The practice of allowing only one day of hospitalization for a childbirth : *new laws designed to stop so-called drive-thru childbirth/ Drive-through delivery: Shortened hospital stay after childbirth* [mid-1990s+; fr restaurants, banks, etc, which provide quick service to customers in cars]

drive someone **up the wall** *v phr* To cause someone to become irrational or hysterical; madden : *It drives most women right up the wall/ Leave him alone and let him work. Quit driving him up the wall*

driving at *See* WHAT one IS DRIVING AT

driving while black or **DWB** *v phr* A putative motor-vehicle offense committed by blacks : *Most middle-class citizens don't know about the de facto driving violation known as DWB, driving while black (1990s+)*

drizzle or **drizzle-puss** *n* DRIP *(1930s+)*

droid *modifier* : *tends to get people in the droid positions and pay little* *n* An inferior, mechanical sort of person; robot; a semihuman drone; CLONE : *for all its ecumenical menagerie of creatures and droids* [1970s+ Teenagers; fr *android*, "humanlike," esp as used by science-fiction writers]

drone *n* **1** A boring person; DRIP, WIMP *(1930s+ Students)* **2** A small unmanned aircraft used as a target for gunnery practice *(1940s+)*

drool *n* **1** : *It gives me sharp and shooting pains, to listen to such drool* **2** DRIP *(1930s+)* *v* To talk foolishly or stupidly; utter inanities *(1900s+)*

drool for (or **over**) *v phr* To show keen appreciation; show desire : *He's still drooling for Marilyn Monroe (1940s+)*

drooly *adj* **1** Very attractive; YUMMY : *Rain can turn the sharpest dressed drooly dreamboat into a drizzly drip from the knees down (1940s+ Teenagers)* **2** Stupid; driveling : *ought to shut their fat, drooly mouths and stick their opinions in their wax-infested ears (1940s+)* *n* A popular and attractive boy : *Who's the chief drooly at Cooley? (1940s+ Teenagers)*

droop or **droopy-drawers** *n* A somewhat dull and stupid person : *He's such a droop, he can't even discuss the weather intelligently (1930s+ Teenagers)*

drop *n* **1** (also **drop joint**) A seemingly honest place used as a cover for illegal matters, esp as a depot for stolen goods; FENCE *(1930s+ Underworld)* **2** mail drop *(1950s+)* **3** A drink or drinks : *I could see by his careful walking he'd taken a drop (1775+)* **4** A homeless slum boy : *accepting anywhere from 25 cents to $1 a week for taking in drops, rustles, fetches (1950s+ Black)* **5** A paying passenger *(1950s+ Cabdrivers)* **6** The base fee on a taxi meter registered when the cabdriver acti-

vates the meter *(1950s+ Cabdrivers)* *v* **1** To be arrested; be caught with loot; FALL *(1900+ Underworld)* **2** To knock someone down; DECK *(1812+)* **3** To kill someone, esp by shooting; BUMP, OFF, WHACK *(1726+)* **4** To lose, esp money : *He dropped a bundle in the market yesterday (1676+)* **5** To collapse, esp with fatigue : *I'll drop if I don't sit down (1400+)* **6** To stop seeing or associating with someone : *She dropped her boyfriend (1605+)* **7** To take any narcotic, esp in pill or capsule form : *We want a society where you can smoke grass and drop acid (1960s+ Narcotics) See* GET THE DROP ON someone, KNOCKOUT DROPS

drop a bundle *v phr* To lose a large amount of money, esp by gambling : *He's dropped a bundle that way (1900+)*

drop a (or **the**) **dime** *v phr* **1** To inform; give information, esp to the police; DIME, RAT • New York City teenagers have equated *dime* with an amount of information and also speak of dropping a quarter, more information, and dropping a dollar, the maximum of information : *Chaney questioned the man who had dropped the dime on Madison/ And then he dropped the dime (made the phone call) and turned Vinnie in (1960s+)* **2** To point out the faults and failures of another; criticize *(1970s+ Army)* [fr the *dime* put into a pay telephone in that era]

drop-by *n* A quick visit by a celebrity, political figure, etc : *Also, his people are trying to limit this thing to a drop-by (1990s+)*

drop one's **cookies** *See* SHOOT one's COOKIES

drop dead *adj phr* **1** Unusually striking; sensational : *A drop-dead mansion in Beverly Hills, complete with his-and-hers whirlpools/ the soulful voice and the drop-dead campiness (1970s+)* **2** Absolutely final : *Schedule the announcement for December 23rd, one day before the drop-dead date, and close to the holidays (1980s+) interj* Go to hell; GET LOST • Nearly always an exclamation of curt refusal or sharp disapproval : *At that rude suggestion she told him to drop dead (1930s+)*

drop-dead gorgeous *adj phr* Extremely attractive : *drop-dead gorgeous models*

drop-in *n* **1** A place of temporary and sometimes dubious resort : *drop-ins for youths wishing marijuana revels (1950s+)* **2** A person who attends classes and other college events without being registered : *NBC did some research on college drop-ins (1960s+ Students)* **3** A new car engine as a replacement : *If you have a current model-year car, you can get a "drop-in." That's a brand new engine (1990s+)* [sense 2 is the opposite of a *dropout*]

drop someone **in** someone's **tracks** *v phr* To knock down or kill someone suddenly and sharply : *One kick dropped him in his tracks* (*1820s+*)

drop it *v phr* To discontinue or cut off a certain topic • Often an irritated command : *I'm not interested, so let's drop it* (*1844+*)

drop joint *See* DROP

drop someone or something like a hot potato *v phr* To discontinue or get rid of very quickly : *When she frowned I dropped the topic like a hot potato* (*1846+*)

drop like flies *v phr* To fall down in great numbers : *All over the hot theater people were dropping like flies* [*1940s+*; *like flies* meant "in great numbers" by 1595]

dropout *n* A person who withdraws; voluntary self-excluder, esp from school or college (*1920s+*)

drop out *v phr* To remove oneself from the conventional competitive world of politics, business, education, etc : *rush back from every excursion into Big Power and drop out with town meetings and backyard picnics* (*1960s+*)

drops *See* KNOCKOUT DROPS

drop one's teeth *v phr* To be very astonished; be gapingly shocked : *I do drop my teeth at the notion that Shakespeare is busted and needs to be fixed* (*1980s+*)

drop the ball *v phr* To fail, esp to fail in one's entrusted job or duty; FLUB THE DUB : *I think the State Department dropped the ball on Iraq* (*1980s+*)

drop the other shoe *v phr* (occasionally **let the other shoe drop**) To conclude or round out something in suspense : *The city dropped the other shoe/ Get with Martinez and drop the other shoe* (*1980s+*)

◁**drop your cocks and grab your socks**▷ *sentence* Get out of bed immediately • A jovial instruction issued by a noncommissioned officer or barracks orderly to troops quite early in the morning (*WWII armed forces*)

drowned rat *See* LOOK LIKE A DROWNED RAT

drown one's sorrows (or **troubles**) *v phr* To alleviate or obscure the chagrins of one's life, esp by getting drunk (*1674+*)

drubbing *n* Beating or total defeat : *drubbing by the rival team* (*1760s+*)

druggie or **druggy** *n* A narcotics user or addict; DOPER (*1960s+ Narcotics*)

drughead *n* A heavy user of narcotics or other drugs; hophead : *every front-page report of violence by some freaked-out drughead* (*1960s+ Narcotics*)

drugola *n* Money paid by narcotics dealers for protection, esp to the police [*1960s+ Narcotics*; based on *-ola* terms like *payola*, *plugola*, and *gayola*]

drugstore cowboy *n phr* 1 A young man who frequents public places trying to impress and

entice women; a Romeo of the street corners : *bell-bottom trousers so much in vogue with the drugstore cowboys* (*middle-1920s+*) 2 An extra in a western film (*Hollywood*) [attributed to the cartoonist and humorist Tad Dorgan, who died in 1929]

drum *See* BEAT THE DRUM

drum-beater *n* A person, esp a press agent, who insistently lauds someone or something : *I'm something of a drum-beater for my Alma Mater* [*1940s+*; *beat the drum*, "to make loud advertisement or protest," is attested by 1611]

drummer *n* A traveling salesperson [*1827+*; fr the practice of going about with a *drum* to gain attention for recruiting and other purposes; for example, the sale of fish was announced by *drumming* in the London streets]

drum up *v phr* To stimulate; promote : *Go drum up a little enthusiasm for this turkey* (*1849+*)

drunk *adj* Intoxicated by alcohol; PLASTERED, SCHNOCKERED, SHIT-FACED (*1340+*) *n* 1 A drinking bout; spree; BENDER, BINGE (*1779+*) 2 A case or occasion of intoxication : *Took him an hour to get a good drunk* (*1849+*) 3 A drunken person, esp a habitual alcoholic; drunkard, LUSH (*1852+*) [in all senses *drunk* verges on being standard English] *See* CHEAP DATE, PUNCH-DRUNK

drunk as a skunk *adj phr* Very drunk; SCHNOCKERED : *They bring beer and cigarettes, are drunk as skunks* (*1940s+*)

drunk tank *n phr* A police detention cell for intoxicated persons : *A police reporter had to pick him out of the collection in the drunk tank* (*1940s+*)

druthers *n* Wishes; desires; preferred alternatives : *We know your druthers, The Marketplace* [*1895+*; fr a dialect pronunciation of *rather* or *had rather*; used by Bret Harte in the form *drathers* in 1875] *See* HAVE one's DRUTHERS

dry *adj* 1 Not permitting the sale of alcoholic drink : *North Carolina has dry counties* (*1887+*) 2 Thirsty (*1406+*) *n* A person who favors the prohibition of alcoholic drink (*1888+*)

dry as a bone *adj phr* Very dry : *Drink, please, I'm dry as a bone* (*1649+*)

◀**dry fuck** (or **hump**)▶ *n phr* To approximate the sex act without penetration or divestiture, and typically without orgasm : *what he would call the dry humps* *v* : *Did attack-crazy kamikazes crash into dry-humping kids on the Hell's Kitchen shore?* (*1930s+*)

dry-gulch *v* 1 To murder, esp by pushing over a cliff (*1930+ Western*) 2 To knock senseless; BUSHWHACK, CLOBBER : *Then one of them got into the car and dry-gulched me* (*1940s+*) [origin uncertain; perhaps fr the practice of killing the animals of another rancher by stampeding them over a cliff into a *gulch;* perhaps fr attacking sheepherders out of a *gulch* and killing their animals]

dry out *v phr* **1** To refrain from alcohol, esp in a medical facility as a part of treatment for alcohol abuse : *He dried out a couple of weeks up in the Valley* **2** To be treated for narcotics abuse; be detoxified (1967+)

dry run *n phr* A tryout, practice version, or rehearsal of something planned : *One more dry run, then tomorrow we do it* (1940s+) *v* : *so the medical staff could "dry run" their equipment*

dry up *v phr* To stop talking; SHUT UP • Usu an irritated command : *Finally I just told him to dry up* (1852+)

DT *n* A detective; DICK.tec : *"You DT?" "No." "So what you care who piped Devona?"* (1920s+)

DTs *n* Delirium tremens; the CLANKS : *When Bix got the DT's Whiteman treated Bix to a drunk cure* (1858+)

duals *n* A pair of wheels and tires mounted as a unit on a truck or semitrailer axle (1970s+ *Truckers*)

ducat or **ducket** or **duket** (DUH kət) *n* **1** A ticket or pass to a show, game, race, etc (1874+) **2** Money; dollars : *keep him in ducats for the rest of his life* (1775+) [fr the name of an originally Venetian gold coin; adoption probably influenced by its prominence in *The Merchant of Venice*]

duck *n* **1** A man; fellow; GUY : *That duck isn't a critic* (1846+) **2** (also **ducks**) Dear one; precious; pet; DUCKY : *and his wife, a darling duck of a homebody* (1590+) **3** DUCK-EGG (1868+) **4** A hospital bedpan (1917+) **5** An amphibious vehicle, esp a WWII troop carrier designated DUKW 1942, whence the nickname (*WWII armed forces*) *v* **1** To move, weave, squat, etc, so as to avoid a blow (1530+) **2** (also **duck out**) To evade or escape : *He ducked over the wall/ They always felt she was trying to duck work* (1896+) *See* DEAD DUCK, FUCK A DUCK, HAVE one's DUCKS IN A ROW, KNEE-HIGH TO A GRASSHOPPER, LAME DUCK, SITTING DUCK

duck-egg *n* A score or grade of zero; GOOSE-EGG, ZIP (1868+)

ducks *n* Dear one; precious • Chiefly British use : *Try this one, ducks* (1930s+) *n* A person, especially one thought of as peculiar : *hand me the pliers, ducks See* HAVE one's DUCKS IN A ROW

duck soup *n phr* Anything easily done; CINCH, PIECE OF CAKE : *It would be duck soup for him to have led Willis into a trap/ Only duck soup for a guy like you* (1908+)

ducktail *n* A haircut tapered in back so that it resembles a duck's tail; DA, DUCK'S ASS (1950s+ *Teenagers*)

duck-walk *v* To move forward while squatting on one's haunches : *Maybe that reporter should duck-walk up Olympia ski hill* (1930s+)

ducky or **duckie** *adj* **1** Excellent, splendid; delightful • Often used ironically : *Everything was just ducky until Lally went into that dame's house/ Oh, me? I'm just ducky* (1897+) **2** Cute; too cute; CORNY : *Pastel phials tied with ducky satin bows* (1897+) *n* Dear one; precious; dearie, DUCKS : *Are you quite ready, duckie?* (1819+)

dud *modifier* : *a dud bomb n* **1** A failure : *The show's a dud/ He was a bit of a dud* (1908+) **2** A shell or bomb that fails to explode (*WWI armed forces*)

duddy *See* FUDDY-DUDDY

dude *n* **1** A dapper man, esp one who is ostentatiously dressed; dandy • In earliest use, to quote an 1891 source, a *dude* was "not a dandy; there is nothing gallant or dashing about him. He is soberness itself; he is as respectable as an undertaker. Yet your real dude is irresistibly comic" (1883+) **2** A guest at a Western or Western-style ranch (1883+) **3** A man; fellow; cat, GUY : *I'm sittin' in the bus stop, just me an' these other three dudes* (1918+) [origin unknown; perhaps an invented word]

dudette *n* A cool young woman, counterpart of *dude* : *party filled with dudettes*

dude up *v phr* To don fancy clothes or one's best clothes; DOLL UP (1899+)

Dudley *See* YOUR UNCLE DUDLEY

Dudley Do-Right *n phr* A person of exceptional virtue; social and moral paragon; MR CLEAN : *Bush's carefully managed image as a square-shouldered Dudley Do-Right/ a '90s breed of Dudley Do-Right is back in the saddle* [1980s+; fr a character in a television cartoon series, *Dudley Do-Right of the Mounties*]

duds *n* Clothing; THREADS : *To see them washed and put in and out of their duds was perhaps the greatest pleasure of her life* [1300+; origin unknown; perhaps fr one or another English or Celtic words meaning "cloth, rag"]

dues *See* PAY one's DUES

duff *n* The buttocks; rump; ASS : *A bunch of lazy guys sitting around on our duffs* [1830s+; origin uncertain; perhaps black slang for *fud*, "buttocks," attested by 1785; perhaps fr *duff*, "a (sailors') pudding boiled in a bag," which bag may have suggested a human fundament in shape; in this sense *duff* is a Northern pronunciation of *dough*]

duffer *n* **1** An elderly man; GEEZER, jasper • Used rather affectionately : *He's a sweet old duffer, isn't he?* **2** A mediocre or downright poor performer, esp at golf; HACKER [1840s+; perhaps fr Scots *duffar,* "dolt"]

duh or **duhh** *interj* A sound imitating that of a weak-minded person collecting his thoughts•The gesture of flapping one's lower lip with one's fingers while uttering a droning sound is used to the same effect : *Bill Cosby doesn't really serve Jell-O chocolate pudding at dinner parties? Duh/ white male artists continue to dominate (duhhh) the blue-chip market (1940s+)* ___

du jour (DOO ZHOO or JOO) *adj phr* Of today; of the day; current : *Thought du jour/ Kennedy would quiz aides about the crisis du jour/ Where would the management gurus du jour find grist for their latest bestsellers?* [1990s+; fr French, "of the day," used to identify the day's specialties in restaurants]

duke *n* **1** A hand, esp when regarded as a weapon *(1874+)* **2** The winning decision in a boxing match, signaled by the referee's holding up the victor's hand : *Even if I lose the duke I get forty percent (1930s+ Prize-fight)* *v* **1** To hand something to someone : *Duke the kid a five or ten (1940s+)* **2** To fight with the fists *(1940s+)* **3** To try to collect money from a parent for something given to a child *(1940s+ Circus)* **4** To short-change someone by palming a coin owed him *(1940s+ Circus)* **5** To shake hands; PRESS THE FLESH *(1965+)* **6** To do the sex act with or to; BOFF, SCREW : *She might even have duked one of the Hobart Street Fros sometime (1990s+ Street gang)* [perhaps fr Romany *dook*, "the hand as read in palmistry, one's fate"] *See* DUKES

duke it out *v phr* : *More than 90 percent of the fugitives don't want to duke it out (1960s+)*

dukes *n* The fists or hands : *I imagine you can handle your dukes, Jim* [1859+; said to be Cockney rhyming slang fr *Duke of Yorks*, "forks, hands"]

dukes-up *adj* Combative; feisty : *Her salty language and dukes-up style endeared her (1970s+)*

dull as dishwater *adj phr* Very tedious and unexciting; boring : *The sermon today was dull as dishwater, Your Eminence* [1940s+; the original form, and current British form, is *dull as ditchwater*, attested by the 1840s]

dull roar *n* A relatively quiet situation; a calmer situation : *checkers game kept to a dull roar*

dullsville *adj* Very dull; tedious; DRAGSVILLE : *a dullsville wimp (1960+) See* -SVILLE

dull tool *n phr* An ineffective person; dead one. LOSER *(1700+)*

◁**dumb-ass**▷ *adj* Stupid; inane; tedious : *Our private life has to take a backseat to every dumbass little news story* *n* : *to understand how a dumb-ass like Newton can have a following (1950s+) See* HAVE A CASE OF THE DUMB-ASS

dumbbell *n* A stupid person; idiot : *She's an awful dumb-bell* [1918+; fr *dumbbell*, a kind of weightlifter's barbell, attested from the 1880s]

◁**dumb blonde**▷ *n phr* A pretty but rather stupid blonde young woman; BIMBO, DUMB BUNNY, dumb dora : *Robelot's not just another dumb blonde out there; she's very aggressive (1950s+)*

dumb bunny *n phr* A naive and unwary person; silly little fool : *My dear, you are the preshest old dumb-bunny (1917+)*

dumb cluck *n phr* A stupid person; clumsy bungler; CLUCK, KLUTZ : *all those dumb clucks snickering at you (1929+)*

dumb down *v phr* To make simpler and easier, esp to alter a textbook to make it more elementary•Apparently first used of movies : *There has been a real "dumbing down" of the texts/ what some educators have called the "dumbing down" of textbooks/ There are jobs that will be dumbed down* [1940s+; attributed to *Los Angeles Times* reporter William Trombley]

dumbhead or ◁**dumbfuck**▷ *n* A stupid person : *This dumbhead has just gone nuts/ the dumbfuck who thought that up* [1887+; perhaps fr German *Dummkopf*]

dumbo (DUM boh) *n* **1** A stupid person : *an ace dumbo friend named Cleo (1950s+)* **2** A blunder; stupid mistake; BLOOPER : *if you think you've seen dumbos pulled on the highways (1970s+)*

dumb ox *n phr* A stupid, sluggish person, esp a hulking one [1847+; oddly enough, this was the nickname given by his schoolfellow to Thomas Aquinas, not for stupidity but for stolid silence]

◁**dumbshit**▷ *n* Stupid; CRETINOID, dufus : *Yeah, right. Dumbshit, two-term Reagan (1960s+)*

dumb something up *v phr* To make something simpler and easier; leach out all but the most puerile substance; DUMB DOWN : *They handed him the script and told him to dumb it up still more (1960s+)*

dum-dum or **dumdum** or **dumb-dumb** *adj* : *The only man safe enough to see is this dumdum cop* *n* A stupid or foolish person *(1940s+)*

dummy *modifier* : *a dummy machine gun/ dummy windows* *n* **1** A stupid person; idiot; CLUCK *(1796+)* ◁**2**▷ A deaf-mute or a mute *(1874+)* **3** Bread *(1890s+ Hoboes)* **4** A train carrying railroad employees *(1890s+ Railroad)* **5** A weakened or diluted narcotic; also, a nonnarcotic substance sold as a narcotic; BLANK *(1960s+ Narcotics)* **6** A pasted-up page, a blank book, or other preliminary representation of material to be published *(1858+ Newspaper office & publishing)* **7** A model or representation; mock-up *(1845+)*

v : *The designer dummied the new book* See BEAT one's MEAT

dump *n* **1** Any place so shabby or ugly as to be comparable to a depository for trash and garbage; a repulsive venue : *What a dump my hometown is now!* (*1899+*) **2** Any building or place : *Nice little dump you got here/ fanciest dump in town* (*1930s+*) **3** A prison (*1904+ Underworld*) **4** A race, game, etc, that is intentionally lost, usu for gambling advantage; FIX : *When he took a dive in the first I knew we had a dump on our hands* (*1940s+ Gambling*) **5** A defecation; a SHIT : *To start the morning with a satisfactory dump is a good omen* (*1940s+*) **6** A fund-raising event that allows many contributions to be given at once; SCOOP : *The chief has a breakfast dump at the Century Plaza, then a stump speech at 2 p.m.* (*1990s+ Politics*) *v* **1** To sell goods, stock, etc, in order to manipulate or depress a market (*1868+*) **2** : *Players accepting bribes to "dump" games* **3** To bunt a baseball : *De-honey dumped one toward third* (*1920+ Baseball*) **4** To kill (*1930s+ Underworld*) **5** To rid oneself of someone or something; DEEP-SIX : *He dumped the whole cabinet* (*1848+*) **6** To admit someone to a hospital without proper cause ● Often done as a way of avoiding responsibility for a patient (*1980s+ Medical*) **7** To assign vulnerable novices and officers with disciplinary infractions to drug-ridden precincts (*1990s+ Police*) **8** To speak openly and volubly : *I shake my head and proceed to start dumping about my mom* (*1990s+*) [origin uncertain; perhaps related to a Scandinavian term meaning "to fall suddenly," the connection being the tipping out of a load from a cart] *See* CORE DUMP, TAKE A DUMP

◁**dump a load**▷ *v phr* To defecate; CRAP (*1940s+*)

dumped on *modifier* Maligned or somehow abused; also, criticized severely ● From dump meaning "defecate" : *dumped on by her sister*

dumper *n* **1** An erratic and extravagant gambler : *Professional gamblers describe the Colonel as a dumper* (*1950s+ Gambling*) **2** A container for trash; Dumpster℠ : *It was determined that disco would be in the dumper* (*1970s+*) *See* IN THE DUMPER

dumping *n* Harsh criticism; severe derogation : *A coupon is provided on page 47 for your dumping* (*1950s+*)

dumping ground *n phr* A place to which unwanted persons and things are relegated : *Because of such appointments the Department came to be seen as "a dumping ground"* (*1885+*)

dump job *n phr* A derogatory attack; HATCHET JOB : *They did a dump job on her* (*1990s+*)

dump on (or **all over**) (also **do a dump on**) *v phr* To criticize harshly, often unfairly; complain and carp at; PUT DOWN : *If he does something right, I'm not going to dump on him/ Don't dump on the teachers we have/ an acknowledgement of the fact that he had dumped on us all year* [1940s+; perhaps fr *dump*, "defecation"]

Dumpster diving or **urban mining** *n phr* Searching through trash for something of value : *Low-end thefts range from so-called Dumpster diving, searching the garbage for discarded carbons, to old-fashioned card theft/ On Dumpster Diving: Eighner offered a sophisticated essay on the theme of surviving on refuse* [late 1980s+; fr the trademark of a type of refuse receiver]

dunk *n* **1** : *Leroy had a quick dunk in the creek* **2** A basketball field goal scored by putting the ball into the hoop from just beside or above it : *Almost all of the baskets were dunks/ basketball courts where the dunks have been so fierce lately* (*1937+ Basketball*) *v* **1** To dip something into a liquid, esp to dip food into a drink : *Scientific temperature readings cannot be taken just by dunking a thermometer on a string* (*1919+*) **2** To go into the water : *Be right back, just want to dunk* (*1940s+*) **3** : *He jumped up and dunked another one* [fr Pennsylvania German *dunken*, "dip"] *See* SLAM DUNK

dunkie butt *n phr* A large fundament : *What is a dunkie butt? It's a big butt that's shapely* (*1990s+ Rappers*)

dunk on someone *v phr* To attack someone : *He talked about my mother, talked about my shoes, my shorts, so I dunked on him* [1990s+; probably fr the notion of a violent basketball *dunk* or *slam dunk*]

dunno *v* Don't know ● Casual pronunciation of *don't know* : *dunno where he is* (*1840s+*)

dupe *n* A duplicate copy of a film or text (*1902+*)

duper *See* SUPER-DUPER

durn or **durned** *See* DARN

durn, a *See* NOT GIVE A DAMN

dust *n* Narcotics in powder form (*1960s+ Narcotics*) *v* **1** To leave quickly; flee; fly : *Dillinger used a Ford when dusting from a job* (*1850+*) **2** To hit; swat : *dusted one of the lieutenants with an old shoe for trying to talk them back to work* (*1612+*) **3** (also, earlier, **dust off**) To kill : *Watch me dust this bitch/ Don't suppose you just want to dust Esteva and go home* (*1970s+*) **4** To spray insecticide from a low-flying aircraft (*1930s+*) *See* ANGEL DUST, EAT someone's DUST, HEAVEN DUST

dust, the *See* BITE THE DUST

duster *n* **1** A pitch purposely thrown at or close to the batter to intimidate him or force him back from the plate; BRUSHBACK *(1920s+ Baseball)* 2 The buttocks See KNUCKLE-DUSTERS

dust kitty (or bunny) *n phr* One of the tufts of dust that accumulate under beds, tables, etc; ghost turds *(1980s+)*

dust someone off *v phr* To pitch a ball at or close to the batter; BRUSHBACK *(1920s+ Baseball)*

dust something off *v phr* (also **dust the cobwebs off**) To use or reuse something old; reclaim something : *Why don't we dust off a few of the good ideas our parents had?/ Hey, let's dust the cobwebs off the Declaration of Independence and take it seriously (1940s+)*

dustup *n* A quarrel or fight; altercation; SCRAP : *a big dustup in the office of a vice-president (1897+)*

Dusty *n* 1 A common nickname for a person named Rhodes, Rhoades, Rodes, etc 2 A nickname for a short person, a "dusty butt" *(1940s+)*

dusty butt *n phr* A person of short stature; SHORTY *(1940s+)*

Dutch courage *n phr* False or fleeting bravery resulting from liquor : *A man in liquor is full of Dutch courage* [1820s+; like many other pejorative uses of *Dutch*, this comes from the 17th century, when the English and the Hollanders were chronically at war. In some uses, though, *Dutch* means "German" rather than "Netherlandish," and the cases are not easily sorted]

Dutch rub *n phr* The trick or torment of holding someone's head and rubbing very hard and painfully at a small area of scalp with the fist; NOOGIE, barbershop quartet *(1910+)*

Dutch treat *adv* : *We'll eat Dutch treat tonight* n *phr* A meal, show, etc, where each person pays his or her own way *(1887+)* See GO DUTCH

Dutch twins *n phr* Two people having the same birthday *(1980s+)*

Dutch uncle *n phr* A severely censorious person, usu a man : *A "Dutch uncle" whose every word is reproof (1838+)*

duty See SACK DUTY

dweeb or dweebo *modifier* : *biggest dweeb award of all* n A despised person; CREEP, NERD *(1980s+ Teenagers)*

dweeby *adj* Revolting; silly; NERDLY : *Wear a visor (or something less dweeby) (1980s+ Teenagers)*

◁**dyke or dike▷** *modifier* : *That woman lives with her dyke daughter and her dyke daughter-in-law* n A lesbian, esp one who takes an aggressive role; BULLDYKE [1930s+; origin uncertain and much debated; perhaps fr a shortening of *morphodyke*, dialectal and substandard pronunciation of "hermaphrodite," perhaps influenced by *dick*, "penis"; a source of 1896 lists *dyke*, "the vulva"]

◁**dykey or dikey▷** *adj* Resembling or having the nature of an aggressive lesbian : *doing calisthenics with the dikey-looking brunette (1960s+)*

dynamic duo *n* A powerful pair of people or things : *dynamic duo of SpongeBob and Squidward* [fr the Batman television program]

dynamite *adj* (also **dyno-mite**) Excellent; superior; SUPER : *"Dynamite. I knew we'd get along/ DYN-O-MITE! The Blammo 12-gauge has a precision-cast hollow-core slug with stabilization tail fins for accuracy at long range* n 1 Heroin or cocaine of high quality : *a connection who deals in good-quality stuff, "dynamite" (1920s+ Narcotics)* 2 Marijuana, esp a marijuana cigarette *(1950s+ Narcotics)* 3 Something very disturbing or dangerous; a sensation : *Don't talk about it, it's dynamite (1930s+)*

dynamite charge *n phr* (also **Allen charge, deadlock charge**) A very strong charge given by a judge to a jury, seeking to ensure a verdict : *might have been better off had the jury been instructed with a dynamite charge* [1990s+ Lawyers; fr a punning use of *charge*]

dynamo *n* An energetic, hardworking, forceful person *(1890s+)*

E

each *See* PER EACH

eager beaver *modifier* : *her eager-beaver sincerity/ eager-beaver gung-ho spirit n phr* An energetic and willing worker; ambitious striver (*1940s+*)

eagle *n* A US one-dollar bill [fr the eagle pictured on the back] *See* LEGAL EAGLE

eagle-eye *n* **1** A person noted for keen vision or one who keeps a close watch : *It took a real eagle-eye to catch that* **2** A locomotive engineer (*Railroad*) **3** A detective, esp one assigned to watch for shoplifters or pickpockets

eagle-eyed *adj* **1** Having very keen vision **2** Keeping a close watch (*1601+*)

ear *v* To listen; hear : *Rosen Tapes To Be Eared By The Judge* (*1583+*) *See* ALL EARS, BEND someone's EAR, BLOW IT OUT, CAULIFLOWER EAR, CHEW someone's EAR OFF, HAVE something COMING OUT OF one's EARS, IN A PIG'S ASS, PIN someone's EARS BACK, PLAY IT BY EAR, PUT A BUG IN someone's EAR, STAND AROUND WITH one's FINGER UP one's ASS, STEAM WAS COMING OUT OF someone's EARS, STICK IT, TALK someone's EAR OFF

ear candy *n phr* ELEVATOR MUSIC (*1980s+*)

eared *See* DOG-EARED

earful, an *n phr* A large or impressive quantity of talk, esp of a rambling or gossipy sort (*1917+*)

ear-grabber *n* Something that catches one's attention; HOOK : *It's one of those short items that are perfect ear-grabbers for radio and TV* (*1990s+*)

early bird *modifier* : *an early-bird session/ early-bird radio program n phr* **1** A person who habitually gets up early in the morning; one who greets the dawn • Based on the proverb "The early bird catches the worm," attested fr the 1670s **2** A person who arrives early at a gathering, the office, etc **3** The first train, bus, airplane, etc, of the day (*1883+*)

earn one's **wings** *v phr* To prove oneself competent and reliable in one's work [*1940s+*; fr the *wing*-shaped badge awarded to graduating air cadets]

ears *n* Small boxed announcements at the upper right and left hand of a newspaper page : *space in the small boxes known as "ears" on the tops of front pages* (*1940s+*)

earth muffin or **granola** *n phr* A person who is not stylish; for example, a woman who does not wear cosmetics • Shows a mocking attitude toward "natural-looking" people and environmentalists (*1980s+ Students*)

Earth to someone *interj* Hello? Are you listening? • As if someone was on a spacecraft or is *spacy* : *Earth to Kyle, come in*

ear worm *n* A song or part of a song that is stuck in one's mind : *Billy Joel songs tend to become ear worms*

ease on (or **out** or **on out**) *v phr* To depart; MOSEY ALONG : *easing on down the road to the Land of Oz* (*1920s+*)

ease someone **out** *v phr* To dismiss or remove someone from a post or place gradually and gently (*1940s+*)

ease up *v phr* **1** To become less stringent or punishing : *Let's ease up on them; they've got no fight left* (*1915+*) **2** To become less tense, exertive, etc; GO EASY, LIGHTEN UP, relax, TAKE IT EASY : *Come on, ease up now, it's all over* (*1945+*)

easy *See* BREATHE EASY, GO EASY, OVER EASY, SPEAKEASY, TAKE IT EASY, TAKE THINGS EASY

easy as pie *adj phr* and *adv phr* (Variations: **can be** or **could be** or **falling off a log** or **hell** or **rolling off a log** or **taking candy from a baby** may replace **pie**) Very easy or easily : *He did it easy as pie/ The thing's easy as can be* (*entry form 1921+, log 1840+*)

easy eight *n phr* An easy job; sinecure : *Smith doesn't relish the work; he tells himself the job's an easy eight, but wastes his nights drinking away the haunting images of the day* (*1990s+*)

easy lay *n phr* A person easy to convince and control; PUSHOVER : *Don't expect Stone to direct: Oliver's been around the block and won't be seduced by money. He's not an easy lay* (*1934+*)

easy make *n phr* **1** (also **easy lay**) A woman easily persuaded to engage in the sex act **2** EASY MARK

easy mark *n phr* A person easily victimized or cheated; PATSY, SUCKER : *He was an "easy mark"* (*1896+*)

easy meat *modifier* : *their easy-meat score in the aerial spraying issue n phr* **1** Something done or acquired very easily (*1920s+*) **2** A person easily duped; MARK, PATSY, SUCKER (*1986+*) [fr the earlier sense that something or someone is vulnerable, easily hunted and caught, etc, esp in the sexual sense, where *meat* means "sexual victim, conquest, object, etc"]

easy money *n phr* Money easily gotten or earned : *easy money for helping in the garden*

easy on the eye *modifier* Good-looking, pleasant to look at : *cheerleaders easy on the eyes* (*1938+*)

easy street *See* ON EASY STREET

eat *v* **1** To preoccupy or upset; engross; fret : *She asked what was eating me when I frowned so* (*1893+*) **2** To be forced to swallow or recant something : *He mouths off a lot, and lately has had to eat many of his grand pronouncements* (1382+) **3** To be unable to pass the ball along : *They blitzed and the quarterback had to eat the ball* (1970s+ *Sports*) **4** To accept and enjoy; EAT UP, SWALLOW : *You really eat this shit, don't you?* (1919+) ◁5▷ (also **eat up**) To do fellatio or cunnilingus; GO DOWN ON someone : *So Little Red Riding Hood said to the wolf "Eat me"* (1916+)

eat crow *v phr* To admit that one was wrong; recant and atone [1872+; said to have originated during an armistice of the War of 1812, when an American soldier shot a crow while hunting across the Niagara River from his post; he was forced by guile to take a bite of it; he in return forced the English landowner to consume a portion]

eat dirt *v phr* To accept rebuke or harassment meekly; swallow one's pride; EAT SHIT : *I ate dirt and apologized to that bastard* (1857+)

eat someone's **dust** *v phr* To be behind someone in a race or chase : *After two laps they ate Coghlan's dust* (1940s+)

eater *See* CHALK-EATER, CHEESE BUN, FIRE-EATER, FROG, MOTHERFUCKER, PETER-EATER

eatery *n* A restaurant (1900+)

eatery/drinkery *n* A bar that serves food : *He opened an eatery/drinkery called the Chelsea Street Pub* (1980s+)

eat one's **hat** *See* EAT one's WORDS

eat high on (or **off**) **the hog** *v phr* To live very well; thrive; prosper; shit in high cotton : *You will eat high on the hog, as a member of the ruling mob/ The institute will eat high off the hog* (1940s+)

eating *See* FROG, MOTHERFUCKING

eat like a horse *v phr* To eat ravenously : *used to eat like a horse*

Eat my shorts! *sentence* Leave me alone; drop dead : *I hate you. Eat my shorts*

eat out *v phr* To have a meal away from home, esp at a restaurant (1933+)

eat someone **out** *v phr* **1** To reprimand someone severely; rebuke harshly; CHEW someone OUT : *Out came Joe McCarthy from the Boston dugout all set to eat me out* (1940s+) ◁2▷ To do cunnilingus or analingus (1960s+)

◁**eat pussy**▷ *v phr* To perform cunnilingus (1930s+)

eats *n* Food; provender : *A soft bed and good eats were paradise enow*

◁**eat shit**▷ *v phr* **1** EAT DIRT **2** To be accursed, humiliated, etc • Usu a loud oral insult; in WWII, Japanese troops attempted to arouse US troops to a reckless frenzy by shouting "Babe Ruth eats shit!" : *You eat shit, you son of a bitch! See* TAKE SHIT

eat the carpet *v phr* To be obsequious; truckle : *"Eat the carpet" is what endangered nominees*

do at confirmation hearings to make amends: *They crawl* (1990s+)

eat up *v phr* **1** To use entirely; deprive of completely; GOBBLE UP : *The rent ate up half my pay* (1535+) **2** To accept and enjoy; have delectation for; EAT : *When a man receives wolf whistles, he eats it up* (1909+)

eat one's **words** (or **hat**) *v phr* To be forced either to retract or to suffer for what one has said : *They showed him proof and he had to eat his words/ I'll eat my hat if I'm wrong* (*Words* 1891+, hat 1836+)

eat your heart out *sentence* Look at me and be envious; suffer vexation over my situation • A rather nasty taunt : *Eat your heart out, Aaron Lebedeff!* [1581+; current use influenced by Yiddish *es dir oys s'harts,* "eat out your heart"]

ech (EK) *See* YUCK

eco- *combining word* Having to do with ecology : *eco-activist/ ecofreak/ eco-terrorist/ eco-warrior* (1960+)

ecofreak or **econut** *n* An environmentalist and conservationist; duck squeezer, eagle freak : *Eco-freaks will love the clean-burning engine* (1972+)

econobox *n* A cheap car without frills : *The sleek and brightly painted Paseo's body wraps a core that is strictly econobox* (1990s+)

ecstasy or **X** *n* A variety of amphetamine narcotic : *Ecstasy, by emergency order of the Drug Enforcement Administration, illegal* (1980s+ *Narcotics*)

Ed *See* OP-ED PAGE

edge *n* **1** An advantage : *soaking up that famous New York "edge"* (1896+) **2** An irritated or sarcastic tone; sharp timbre : *She answered with a slight edge to her voice* (1908+) *See* HAVE AN EDGE ON, HAVE AN EDGE ON someone

edge, the *n phr* Perilous territory; a risky situation : *Living closer to the edge somehow makes you more than just a pampered Hollywood pretty boy* (1980s+)

Edge City or **technoburb** *n phr* A sprawling suburb lacking a downtown core but well provided with malls and other consumer amenities and serving as a place of high-tech employment : *This is the most obvious truth of family life in Edge City: The old idea of neighborhood is dead/ They're called edge cities, or technoburbs, suburbs a dozen or twenty miles outside old downtown cores that have burgeoned into centers for high-tech employment* [1990s+; the term was originated and propagated by Joel Garreau in his 1992 book *Edge City: Life on the New Frontier*]

edged *adj* **1** Drunk : *When he was nicely edged he was a pretty good sort of guy* (1894+) **2** Very angry; PISSED OFF (1980s+ *Teenagers*)

edge someone **out** *v phr* To defeat by a close margin; barely surpass : *We edged them out by just three votes* (*1940s+*)

edgy *adj* 1 (also **on edge**) Tense and irritable; nervous; UPTIGHT : *I saw he was getting a bit edgy, so I agreed to include him* (*1837+*) 2 Daringly advanced; on the cutting edge : *Spurred by the sudden obsession with youth culture, these editors are producing a series of visually edgy, culturally progressive new glossies* (*1990s+*)

educated guess *n phr* A guess made with some basis of fact and knowledge : *Economists offer some educated guesses on why the adjustment in unemployment is so skewed* (*1954+*)

-ee *suffix used to form nouns* The object of what is indicated : *baby-sittee/ kickee/ muggee*

◁**eff**▷ *v* or *n* FUCK • This curt euphemism is also the base for equivalents of *fucked, fucking,* and *fucker* : *eff off back to effing Russia/ She effed around until she was forced to work again/ this is the stupidest effing stunt you've ever pulled* (*1920s+*)

◁**effing** or **F-ing**▷ *adj* Fucking • Euphemistic : *Get that effing cat out of my office*

egg *n* 1 A person : *Evelyn's a good egg* (*1853+*) 2 Anything roughly egg-shaped, such as the head, a baseball, an aerial bomb, etc : *bopped him on the egg/ reared back and chucked the old egg* (*1589+*) [first sense altered fr the mid-19th-century term *bad egg,* "bad or rotten person"] *See* BAD EGG, DUCK-EGG, FRIED EGG, GOOSE EGG, HARD-BOILED EGG, HAVE EGG ON one's FACE, LAY AN EGG, NEST EGG, SUCK EGGS, WALK ON EGGS

eggbeater *n* 1 An aircraft propeller (*WWII Army Air Force*) 2 A helicopter • Now almost entirely superseded by *chopper* : *The "eggbeater" took off for Inchon with its burden* (*1937+*) 3 An outboard motor; KICKER : *wouldn't be caught dead with an eggbeater on their boat* (*1940s+*)

egger *See* HAM-AND-EGGER

eggery *See* HAM-AND-EGGERY

egghead *n* 1 A bald man (*1950s+*) 2 An intellectual; thinker; DOUBLE DOME • Revived in the 1950s to designate the followers of Adlai Stevenson : *An egghead is "one who calls Marilyn Monroe Mrs Arthur Miller"* (*1907+*) [second sense presumably fr the putative high, domed, *egg*-shaped *heads* of such persons; the term was used in a letter of Carl Sandburg about 1918]

egg in someone's **beer** *n phr* The height of luxury or pleasure; everything one could desire • Often part of an impatient question addressed to someone who asks for more than is merited or available : *So it's got no air-conditioning. You want egg in your beer?/ I don't call two weeks' vacation exactly egg in my beer* (*1940s+*)

ego trip *n phr* Something done primarily to build one's self-esteem or display one's splendid qualities : *The pie-thrower said the guru was on an ego trip/ This isn't any ego trip, taking a job in this administration* **v** : *I was showing off, ego-tripping* [*1960s+*; based on *trip,* "psychedelic narcotic experience"]

eh *interj* 1 An expression indicating that one is listening to what another is saying 2 An indication of slight surprise; hey! 3 An indication that one is puzzled about something said (*Canadian*)

eightball *n* ◀1▶ A black person (*1919+*) 2 A chronically unfortunate and ineffective person; LOSER, SAD SACK (*1940s+*) 3 SQUARE (*1950s+ Jive talk*) [because the pool ball numbered eight is black and is unlucky if it blocks one's cue ball] *See* BEHIND THE EIGHT BALL

eighteen-wheeler *n phr* A semitrailer truck; cab and trailer : *The driver of the eighteen-wheeler to my left was wearing the uniform of the West Virginia Highway Patrol* (*1970s+ Citizens band*)

eighter (or **Ada**) **from Decatur** *n phr* The card, roll, or craps point of eight (*1940s+ Crapshooting & poker*)

eight-hundred-pound gorilla *See* SIX-HUNDRED-POUND GORILLA

eighty-six *n* 1 A cook's term for "none" or "nix" when asked for something not available (*1930s+ Lunch counter*) 2 A person who is not to be served more liquor : *known as an "eighty-six," which means: "Don't serve him"* (*1930s+ Bartenders*) **v** 1 : *We had to eighty-six the French dip* 2 (also **eight-six**) To eject or interdict someone : *I'll have you eighty-sixed out of this bar/ I been eighty-sixed out of better situations* (*1959+*) 3 To reject; refuse; eschew : *Kids, eighty-six those video games* (*1980s+*) 4 To kill; destroy; annihilate : *There'd been serious pragmatic reasons for not eighty-sixing the man then and there* (*1970s+*) [probably fr the rhyme with "nix"]

el bonzo *adj phr* Crazy; hectic; frenetic; BONZO : *At dinner time, this restaurant goes el bonzo* (*1990s+*)

elbow *n* A police officer or detective *v* To associate with someone as a friend; RUB ELBOWS *See* BEND THE ELBOW, NOT KNOW one's ASS FROM one's ELBOW, RUB ELBOWS

elbow-bender *n* A convivial person; drinker

elbow-bending *n* Drinking liquor : *the gentlemanly art of refined elbow-bending*

elbow grease *n phr* Muscular exertion; physical effort (*1710+*)

elbow someone **out** *v phr* To eliminate or replace someone by aggressive pressure : *She looked pretty secure, but he elbowed her out of the vice presidency*

elbow room *n phr* Barely enough space for the occupant; a minimum of space : *This office is so crowded I couldn't find elbow room for anyone else/ Don't crowd so, give me elbow room* [1700s+; propagated in the US because it was a nickname for General John Burgoyne, who boasted in the 1770s that he would find *elbow room* in this country]

el cheapo *modifier* : *Beware of plaid shirts, el cheapo haircuts and candidates who talk r-e-a-l slow* **n** *phr* A cheap product; a piece of shoddy merchandise : *They bought the El Cheapos and found they didn't work* [1960s+; probably first applied like El Ropo, to cheap cigars, since many cigars have Spanish names; see *el -o*, mock-Spanish combining form]

elephant *See* SEE PINK ELEPHANTS, WHITE ELEPHANT

elephant linebacker (or **position**) *n phr* A linebacker or defensive end who specializes in rushing the quarterback on pass plays : *Now comes "elephant position"/ Paup started the first nine games at elephant, or rush, outside linebacker* (1990s+ Football)

elevate *v* To rob : *go out and "elevate" a bank* [1920s+; probably a play on *heist*]

elevated *adj* Drunk (late-1600s+)

elevator doesn't go to the top floor, one's *sentence* One is not very bright : *Those people, doesn't sound like their elevators go to the top floor/ But they should come down now. If they don't, their elevator doesn't go to the top* (1980s+)

elevator music *n phr* Bland, pretty music, of the sort played over speakers in elevators; EAR CANDY, muzak (1970s+)

elevenses *n* Light refreshments : *coffee and some sandwiches . . . "Elevenses," he said*

el foldo *n phr* Academic failure, either general or in a course (1940s+ College students) *See* PULL AN EL FOLDO

eliminated *adj* Killed : *eliminated in prison*

el -o *combining form* An amusing variation of whatever is infixed : *travel el cheapo/ flatchested el birdos in long dresses/ You still seeing El Sleazo these days?/ universal emptiness, el zilcho/ Our President did his famous el foldo/ If it is calm, it is el snoro* [1940s+; fr a common pattern in Spanish]

else *See* OR ELSE

embalmed *adj* Drunk

emcee *See* MC

emoticon *n* Symbols made from punctuation marks, used to denote emotion : :-) *n smile* ;-) ; *n smile with a wink;* 8-) *n smile from a person who wears glasses;* :-(*n frown* (1990s+ Computer)

empty-nester *n* A person whose children have grown up and moved away from home :

when my older boys were grown and I'm an empty-nester/ We are getting a lot of empty-nesters moving into a Leisure World development/ elderly "empty nesters" who sell their suburban homes and come to the city (1980s+)

empty suit *n phr* A person of some seeming distinction who is actually a product of publicity : *Steven Brill calls him an "empty suit" whose main talent is getting his name in the papers* (1980s+)

enchilada *See* BIG ENCHILADA, the WHOLE ENCHILADA

end *n* **1** A share; CUT : *Eddie would be entitled to half an end/ I muscle in for an end of the beer racket* (1903+) **2** Particular concern or portion; sector : *Selling's his end of it* (1909+) *See* GO OFF THE DEEP END, HIND END, JUMP OFF THE DEEP END, the LIVING END, REAR END, SHORT END OF THE STICK

end, the *n phr* The best; the greatest; the LIVING END : *Mr Secretary General, you're the end!* (1950s+ Beat & cool talk)

end of the line (or **road**) *n phr* The very end : *end of the line for his big plans* (1940s+)

end run *n phr* An attempt to avoid or evade higher authority by acting outside authorized channels : *McLarty gave Shalala a dressing down about doing end runs around the White House* **v** : *Special interests have found new ways to end-run our system/ the label chiefs would no longer be allowed to end-run Morgado* (1950s+ fr football)

Energizer bunny, the *n phr* Someone or something that never runs out of energy : *Nixon, like the Energizer bunny, just goes on and on and on* [1990s+; fr television ads for Energizer® batteries, which show a mechanical rabbit carrying on endlessly]

enforcer *n* A person, esp a gangster, hockey player, or other athlete assigned to intimidate and punish opponents; POLICEMAN (1930s+)

English *n* A spin imparted to a billiard ball, tennis ball, etc, to make it curve [1860s+; fr French *anglé*, "angled," similar to *Anglais*, "English"]

engraved invitation, an *See* DO YOU WANT AN ENGRAVED INVITATION

enjoy *interj* An exhortation to be happy, to enjoy oneself : *Go. Read. Enjoy. It couldn't hurt/ The trooper grinned. "Enjoy," he said, and walked on toward the cruiser* [1980s+; fr a Yiddish speech pattern, recorded but not approved by Leo Rosten]

enough is enough *interj* An exhortation to be done, to desist : *More than a few descendants of immigrants are saying enough is enough* (1546+)

enough to choke a horse *adv phr* To a very great degree; in a very large quantity : *His ego is big enough to choke a horse* (1940s+)

enviro *modifier* : *Attending an enviro benefit because he cared about the rain forest* n An environmentalist : *Even Beltway enviros not promised jobs expected something* (*1990s+*)

equalizer n A pistol or other firearm; the DIFFERENCE (*1900+*)

erase v To kill; RUB OUT (*1940s+*)

-erino *suffix used to form nouns* (also **-arino** or **-orino**) A humorous version or a remarkable specimen of what is indicated : *peacherino/ bitcherino* [1900+; probably fr the Italian diminutive suffix *-ino* combined with the agentive suffix *-er*]

-eroo *suffix used to form nouns* (also **-aroo** or **-roo** or **-oo**) Emphatic, humorous, or affectionate form of what is indicated : *babyroo/ floperoo/ jivaroo/ screameroo/ sockeroo* (*1930s+*)

-ers *suffix used to form adjectives and nouns* In the condition humorously indicated • *These are all British imports, coming ultimately from public school slang* : *bonkers/ champers/ preggers/ starkers* (*1860s+*)

-ery *suffix used to form nouns* **1** Place or establishment where the indicated thing is used, done, sold, etc : *boozery/ eatery/ minkery* (*1920s+*) **2** The collectivity or an instance of what is indicated : *claptrappery/ jerkery*

-ess *suffix used to form nouns* A woman member of the indicated group or calling • *A standard suffix now used most often in slang partly because the standard use is regarded as, and sometimes meant to be, offensive* : *loaferess/ muggess/ veepess* (*1400s+*)

-eteria *See* -ATERIA

even break n *phr* A fair and equal chance; honest treatment; a FAIR SHAKE : *The Bible, I think it is, says never to give a sucker an even break* (*1911+*)

evened out *adj phr* Restored to balance and health; rational : *"I was really emotionally fucked up." "Are you evened out now?"* (*1970s+*)

even-stephen or **even-steven** *adj* Fair; even; equitable : *Give me the hundred and fifty and we'll call it even-steven* **adv** : *And we'll do likewise for San Francisco and Odessa, or any places we want, always even-stephen* (*1866+*)

even the score v *phr* GET EVEN (*1940s+*)

ever *adv* Really; truly; certainly • *Used postpositively for emphasis* : *Boy, has it ever!/ Clinton's generation has already had its chance to make its tastes the country's tastes. Has it ever! Did we win? Did we ever!*

evergreen *modifier* : *desperately searching the shelf of "evergreen" pieces, hoping to find some picture story that we could tie in with what was happening* n **1** (also **think piece, thumbsucker**) A story that is not news, but penetrating analysis, etc : *Such articles, the desperate resort of editorial writers everywhere, are known as evergreens and think pieces* (*1980s+ Print & broadcast journalism*) **2** A perennial favorite, esp a song; GOLDEN OLDIE (*1940s+*) [journalism senses so called because such material is perdurably useful]

evergreen contract n *phr* A contract always written with a time extension : *It was an "evergreen" contract on which he'd always have two years to go automatically* (*1980s+ Sports*)

ever-loving *adj* Devoted; faithful : *And this is my ever-loving bride* **intensifier** : *Say that again and I'll bust your ever-loving ass* (*1930s+*)

everybody and his uncle (or **brother**, etc.) n *phr* Absolutely everyone : *Everybody and his uncle came to the party/ Parvin received advice from everybody and his brother/ "Will enough people see that?" "Everybody and his dog will see that,"* Smith says [1940s+; in earlier versions going back to the 1860s, *his cousin* or *their mothers-in-law* could replace *uncle*]

everything but the kitchen sink *adj phr* : *Sunday dinner—salads with an everything-but-the-kitchen-sink touch* n *phr* Everything imaginable • *First used in such phrases as* "They hit us with everything but the kitchen sink" (*WWII armed forces*)

everything's coming up roses *sentence* Everything is going marvelously well (*1980s+*)

every Tom, Dick, and Harry n *phr* Every and any man, esp a very ordinary one; ordinary joe : *letting every Tom, Dick, and Harry in on the election* (*1734+*)

every which way *adv phr* In all ways; in all directions : *Mrs Bush now has it every which way: she's the American queen mother and the master politician* (*1824+*)

evil *adj* **1** Excellent; splendid; MEAN, WICKED : *Geoffrey beats an evil set of skins* (*1950s+*) **2** Biting and sarcastic; catty; BITCHY (*1970s+ Homosexuals*)

evil twin n An illegal or nasty counterpart or duplicate of something : *Spock's evil twin*

ex or **x** n A former wife or husband, girlfriend or boyfriend, etc : *He introduced his ex rather casually, considering they were together 27 years* (*1929+*)

exam *modifier* : *exam results/ exam book* n An examination (*1848+*)

excess baggage n *phr* A person or thing regarded as unnecessary and likely to impede : *He thought his wife and kids were excess baggage* (*1909+ Theater*)

ex-con n A former convict (*1906+*)

excuse n A version or example of : *He's a rotten excuse for a lawyer* (*1940s+*)

excuse (or **pardon**) **me all to hell** *sentence* I apologize; I am sorry • *Most often said ironically, when one thinks an accusation has been undeserved or too strong*

exec *modifier* : *exec perks/ exec burnout n* **1** An executive officer *(1920s+ Navy)* **2** A business executive : *They'd never heard of female execs/ I find parking space for senior execs* *(1896+)*

expedition *See* GO FISHING

extra cheese *n* All the trimmings, all the perks : *going out with him for the extra cheese*

extracurricular *adj* Irregular; irresponsible : *not an affair, but an extracurricular fling* [fr the college sense "outside the academic curriculum"]

extra mile, the *See* GO THE EXTRA MILE

-ey *See* -IE

eye *n* A private detective; PRIVATE EYE : *an eye named Johnny O'John* *(1930+)* *See* BIG BROWN EYES, BLACK EYE, CATS' EYES, EAGLE-EYE, FOUR-EYES, GIVE someone THE EYE, GIVE someone THE FISH-EYE, GIVE someone THE GLAD EYE, GOO-GOO EYES, HAVE EYES FOR, IN A PIG'S ASS, KEEP AN EYE ON, MAKE GOO-GOO EYES, MUD IN YOUR EYE, NOT BAT AN EYE, PRIVATE EYE, PULL THE WOOL OVER someone's EYES, the RED-EYE, ROUND-EYE, SHUT-EYE, SNAKE EYES, STONED TO THE EYES

eyeball *v* To look at; look over; SCOPE ON • An isolated instance is attested in 1901 : *He would eyeball the idol-breaker/ You locate trophies before they eyeball you* *(1940s+ Black)* *See* GIVE someone THE FISH-EYE, UP TO one's EYEBALLS

eyeball to eyeball *adj phr* : *our eyeball-to-eyeball chat* *adv phr* Face-to-face; in confrontation : *We're eyeball to eyeball and I think the other fellow just blinked* *(1950s+)*

eye candy *n* Something or someone very pleasant to look at : *eye candy on campus*

eyed *See* COCKEYED, PIE-EYED, WALL-EYED

◁**eye-fuck**▷ *v* To stare intently, esp at a sex object : *That's what he believed the trio was doing, eye-fucking Callaway and Nguyen* *(1916+)*

eyeful *n* **1** A good look; close scrutiny; GANDER : *Get an eyeful of that place over there* *(1914+)* **2** A very good-looking woman; DISH *(1922+)*

eyegrabber *n* Something or someone that strongly attracts attention; GRABBER, HOOK : *Daily News front pages have been eye-grabbers on the newsstands for 70 years* *(1980s+)*

eye-grabbing *adj* Strongly attractive; magnetic : *Geena's so statuesque, she's so eye-grabbing on the screen* *(1980s+)*

eye in the sky *n phr* **1** In casinos, a security guard or video camera watching games from concealment above *(1960s+ Gambling)* **2** A reporter, police officer, etc, who watches traffic from above, usu in a helicopter *(1970s+)* **3** A coach, coordinator, etc, who watches a game from the press box and calls plays and suggestions to the coaches on the ground : *Teams have the "eye in the sky" to get an edge on defense* *(1980s+ Baseball)*

eye-opener *n* **1** A drink of liquor taken upon awaking : *He fumbled for the jug and slurped an eye-opener* *(1818+)* **2** An addict's first injection of the day *(1960+ Narcotics)* **3** Anything that informs or enlightens one : *Listening to that story was a real eye-opener* *(1863+)*

eyepopper *n* Something that makes one's eyes bulge in astonishment; EYEGRABBER : *The president added a further eyepopper* *(1940s+)*

eyes only *adj phr* Very personal and confidential [1960s+; fr the government security phrase "for your *eyes only*"]

F

fab *adj* or *interj* Excellent; wonderful; fabulous : *a man who would think it a fab idea to rent a silver limo (1950s+ Teenagers)*

face *n* **1** A celebrity, esp a show-business notable *(1960s+ Show business)* **2** A person : *bad face, a surly, mean, no-good cat (1950s+ Cool talk)* **3** A white person; FAY[1] : *Don't see why we need some high-priced face down here telling us how to live (1940s+ Black)* *v* To insult; embarrass; humiliate; BURN • This sense probably originated in basketball, where aggressive players put their hands in front of other players' faces : *face, which means to embarrass (1980s+ Students)* See BAG YOUR FACE, DOLLFACE, FEED one's FACE, GET OUT OF someone's FACE, GO UPSIDE one's FACE, HAVE A RED FACE, HAVE EGG ON one's FACE, JUST ANOTHER PRETTY FACE, LAUGH ON THE OTHER SIDE OF one's FACE, LET'S FACE IT, PALE-FACE, POKER FACE, RED FACE, SHE CAN SIT ON MY FACE ANYTIME, SHIT-FACED, SHOOT OFF one's MOUTH, a SLAP IN THE FACE, STRAIGHT FACE, SUCK FACE, TILL one IS BLUE IN THE FACE, WHAT'S-HIS-NAME

faced *adj* SHIT-FACED *(1960s+)* See POKER-FACED, RED-FACED

face someone down *v phr* To disconcert in a direct confrontation : *I am being faced down by a ten- or twelve-year-old boy (1530+)*

face fungus *n phr* A beard; whiskers : *Which do you fancy, the blue-eyed chap in the tux or the loser with the face fungus? (1972+)*

face-off *n* Confrontation, esp one before action : *continuing face-off and stalemate* [1896+; the date reflects use in hockey and lacrosse, where play begins with players scrabbling for the puck or ball]

face the music *v phr* To endure whatever punishment or rigors one has incurred; take what one has coming [1850+; origin uncertain; perhaps fr the necessity of forcing a cavalry horse to face steadily the regimental band; perhaps fr the plight of a performer on stage]

face time *n phr* Time spent face-to-face or in close proximity, esp with persons useful to one's career : *Getting 'face time,' as insinuating your way into a photograph with the President is known/ He recently spent some "face time" chatting with his new pig (1990s+)*

face up *v phr* To confront boldly; acknowledge : *It's time you faced up to how wrong you've been (1920+)*

fack *sentence* That's a fact : *She'll die a Turnipseed. Fack* *v* To tell the truth; utter facts : *Negroes know that facking means speaking facts*

[1940s+ Black; fr the normal pronunciation of *fact* in black English]

facockta *adj* Accursed; wretched; CRAPPY, SHITTY : *Robbed. Upstairs in your facockta parking lot* [1990s+; fr Yiddish, literally "shitty"]

factoid *n* A presumed fact of dubious validity; a popular assumption or belief : *Of the eight factoids pertaining to the present Administration/ a paragraph, part human interest, part factoid* [1970s+; fr *fact* plus *-oid*] See -OID

factor See FUDGE FACTOR

factory *combining word* Place where what is indicated is done, pursued, used, etc • A jocular appropriation of the term : *brain factory/ freak factory/ nut factory (1920s+)* *n* The apparatus used for injecting narcotics; works *(1940s+ Narcotics)* See BONE FACTORY, NUTHOUSE

facts See HARD FACTS

facts of life *n* An explanation of human reproduction, esp for a child : *facts of life explained in a sixth-grade film*

faddle See FIDDLE-FADDLE

fade *n* **1** A white person *(1970s+ Black)* **2** A black person who prefers white friends, sex partners, attitudes, etc; OREO *(1970s+ Black)* **3** A hairstyle with a thick upright flat top that tapers toward the ears : *Will has a fresh fade (1980s+ Black teenagers)* *v* **1** To leave; depart : *He faded to Chicago (1848+)* **2** To take one's bet; cover one's offered bet : *When I saw I was faded, I rolled the dice (1890+ Crapshooting)* **3** To lose or cause to lose power and effectiveness : *And I would try to fade the heat off me (1450+)*

fadeaway *n* A pitch that moves away from the batter so that he would have to reach out for it [1908+ Baseball; identified esp with the pitcher Christy Mathewson]

fade away (or **out**) *v phr* To depart, esp gradually *(1820+)*

fag *modifier* ◁1▷ : *frenetic hot-rhythm dancing, the cheap fag jokes/ like a fag party* *n* **1** A cigarette; BUTT, COFFIN NAIL : *He passed them swell fags around (1888+)* ◁2▷ A male homosexual; FAGGOT, QUEER : *Fags are certain to arouse the loathing of all decent fiction addicts/ sicker by a long shot than any fag, drag, thang, or simple gay man or woman (1923+)* *v* (also **fag out**) To fatigue; exhaust • The sense "to study hard, go without sleep," is attested in Cambridge University slang by 1803 : *This sort of work fags me quickly (1930+)* [origin unknown; the "homosexual" sense may be connected with the British term *fag*, "the boy

151

servant, and inferentially the catamite, of a public-school upperclassman"; perhaps influenced by Yiddish *faygele*, "homosexual," literally "bird, little bird"]

◁**fag bag**▷ *n phr* A woman married to a homosexual *(1960s+ Homosexuals)*

fag end *n phr* The useless, dreary, or extreme end of something : *The fag ends of my days are irretrievably grungy* [1622+; origin uncertain; one early sense of *fag* was "end, dragging end," and in the earliest dated example *fag end* means "ass end"; later use influenced by *fag*, "cigarette, cigarette butt," found by 1888]

fagged out *adj phr* Exhausted; BEAT, POOPED *(1833+)*

◁**faggot**▷ *n* A male homosexual : *Hot faggot queens bump up against chilly Jewish matrons/ an amazing job of controlling the faggots* [1914+; origin unknown; perhaps fr *fag*; perhaps fr *faggot*, "woman," found by 1591]

◁**faggotry** or **faggery**▷ *n* Male homosexuality : *Faggotry was at the very least a terrible embarrassment/ I have a feeling he was arrested sometime in his life. For faggery if nothing else (1970s+)*

◁**faggoty** or **faggy**▷ *adj* Homosexual, esp in an overt way • Used only of males : *who lives with his faggoty American friend (first form 1928+, second 1950s+)*

◁**fag hag** or **faggot's moll**▷ *n phr* A heterosexual woman who seeks or prefers the company of homosexual men : *Zeffirelli seems to have created a sort of limp-wrist commune, with Clare as the fag hag/ Michael once referred to her as "the fag hag of the bourgeoisie" (1969+)*

fagocite *n* An effeminate boy or man; SISSY [1930s+ New York City boys; modeled, surprisingly, on *phagocyte*, "a cell that ingests and destroys foreign particles," altered by *fag*]

fag tag *n phr* (also **fairy loop**, **fruit loop**) A cloth loop sewn into the middle pleat of the upper back of a shirt [1970s+; *fruit loop* variant fr a breakfast cereal called *Froot Loops*®]

fair dinkum *adj phr* Honest; fair and just • Still chiefly Australian use *(1894+ Australian)*

fair enough *interj* Agreed : *Want to stop now? Fair enough (1925+)*

fair-haired (or **blue-eyed** or **white-haired**) **boy** *n phr* 1 A favored or favorite man or boy : *the latest "fairhaired boy" of the musical world/ the white-haired boy of the happy family* 2 A man destined for and being groomed for principal leadership or other reward; COMER : *A job had to be found for Patten, the blue-eyed boy of British politics (first form 1918+, second 1924+, third 1923+)*

fair shake, a *n phr* Equal treatment; the same chance as others; EVEN BREAK : *He complains he didn't get a fair shake* [1830+; fr an honest shake of the dice]

fair-weather *adj* Insincere and temporary : *fair-weather fans*

◁**fairy**▷ *n* A male homosexual, esp an effeminate one; FAG, QUEER : *Too bad you weren't a fairy (1895+)*

fairy godfather *n phr* A potential sponsor, advertiser, or financial backer, esp in show business *(1930s+)*

◁**fairy godmother**▷ *n phr* A male homosexual's homosexual initiator and tutor *(1970s+ Homosexuals)*

◁**fairy lady**▷ *n phr* A lesbian who takes a passive role in sex : *Then there was the fairy lady who said "Argyle it to me!" (1950+)*

fairy tale or **bedtime story** *n* Simplistic explanation, often condescending : *don't want to hear your little bedtime story*

fake it *v phr* 1 To make a pretense of knowledge, skill, etc; bluff; cheek it 2 (also **fake**) To improvise more or less compatible chords or notes as one plays or sings something one really has not learned *(1915+ Jazz musicians)*

fake someone out *v phr* To bluff or deceive someone; mislead : *Bailey had faked out Keuper into using a preempt (1940s+ Sports)*

falderal or **folderol** *n* Wasted effort; also, mere nonsense : *the falderal involved in PTA*

fall *n* : *This your first fall, ain't it?/ Another fall meant a life sentence (1893+)* *v* 1 To be arrested; be imprisoned; DROP : *When you have bad luck and you fall, New York is the best place/ the best thief in the city till he fell (1879+ Underworld)* 2 To become enamored; become a lover : *Once Abelard saw her he fell (1906+)* See PRATFALL, the ROOF FALLS IN, TAKE A FALL, TAKE THE RAP

fall all over oneself *v phr* To be eager or confusedly effusive; to try overly hard : *He fell all over himself trying to apologize/ Administration analysts "fell over themselves" whenever he or his staff sought information (1895+)·*

fall apart *v phr* To lose one's usual poise and confidence; lose control; LOSE one's COOL : *Even the seasoned troupers fall apart (1945+)*

fall apart at the seams *v phr* To be or become spoiled or ruined : *marriage falling apart at the seams (1965+)*

fall (or slip) between (or through) the cracks *v phr* To be ignored, overlooked, mismanaged, or forgotten, esp because of ambiguity in definition or understanding : *The entire problem simply fell between the cracks/ a conviction that otherwise might have fallen through the cracks (1970s+)*

fall down and go boom *v phr* 1 To take a tumble; fall heavily 2 To fail, esp utterly and obviously *(1930s+)*

fall down on the job *v phr* To fail at one's responsibilities; shirk an obligation (*1898+*)

fall for *v phr* **1** To become enamored with; become a lover of : *He's constantly falling for long-legged brunettes* **2** To be deceived or duped by; acquiesce to : *Americans would continue to "fall for" this* (*1903+*)

fall guy *n phr* **1** An easy victim; EASY MARK, SUCKER **2** A person who willingly or not takes the blame and punishment for another's misdoings; PATSY : *He said he would not be the president's fall guy* (*1906+*)

falling-down drunk *adj phr* Too drunk to stand up; very drunk : *O'Hara was fired from most of the jobs he held; he was a falling-down, no-holds-barred, contentious drunk/ some rather large, falling-down drunk individuals* (*1980s+*)

falling off a log *See* EASY AS PIE

falling-out *n* A disagreement : *falling-out over the basketball coach*

fall off the wagon *v phr* To begin drinking liquor again after a period of abstinence; also, to breach abstinence or moderation in anything : *But like most of us, she falls off the wagon from time to time, and heads for a stadium hot dog* (*1905+*)

fall on one's **ass** *v phr* **1** (also **fall flat on** one's **ass**) To fail, esp ignominiously and spectacularly : *They want to see you fall on your ass/ Pratt and Murphy fell on their ass* (*1940s+*) **2** To deteriorate beneath operational limits • Said of the weather conditions at an airport (*1970s+ Airline*)

fall on one's **face** *v phr* (also **fall flat on** one's **face**) To make an embarrassing mistake, failed attempt, catastrophic decline, etc; FALL ON one's ASS : *Trying to be stately, I fell flat on my face/ If the dollar was stumbling, the Japanese stock market was falling on its face* (*1970s+*)

fall on one's **sword** *v phr* To commit suicide, esp after a defeat and for the good of the general cause : *Cells that become irreparably damaged are expected to fall on their swords for the greater good of the organism* [*1990s+*; fr the ancient Roman mode of self-immolation, reflected in Horatio's noble sentiment "I am more an antique Roman than a Dane"]

fallout *n* **1** An accompanying or resultant effect of something; an aftermath : *Talking to oneself is a fallout of watching too many primaries on TV* **2** Incidental products, esp when copious and of little value : *reports, memoranda, and other printed fallout from the executive suite* [*1950s+*; fr the radioactive dust and other debris of a nuclear explosion]

fall out *v phr* **1** To go to sleep or into a stuporous condition from narcotic intoxication : *Only those who are uptight fall out/ If you resist falling out and pass the barrier, the curve is up to a mellow stupor* (*1950s+ Narcotics*) **2** To become helpless with laughter or emotion; CRACK UP : *I tried double tempo and everybody fell out laughing/ sizing up audiences and delivering the goods that would make them fall out, whether in church or not* (*1950s+*)

fall through *v phr* To fail; miscarry; FIZZLE : *Our plans for the building fell through* (*1879+*)

fall up *v phr* (Variations: **by** or **down** or **out** may replace **up**) To come for a visit; arrive : *The bash is in the basement, Dad. Fall up anytime* (*1930s+ Black*)

faloosie *See* FLOOZY

falsie or **falsy** *n* **1** Anything false or artificial; a prosthesis : *Its tail, a falsy, fell off* **2** A brassiere padded to give the appearance of large breasts; also, padding worn in other places to increase the generosity of a woman's body (*1940s+*)

family jewels *n phr* The testicles; NUTS : *A kick in the family jewels will often dampen a man's ardor* (*1920s+*)

famous last words *n phr* Something said that proves singularly wrong or inappropriate • An ironic reference to the final deathbed utterances of famous people : *"I certainly hope this won't be made public," North said. Famous last words* (*1940s+*)

fanboy or **fangirl** *n* **1** A person obsessed with an element of video or electronic culture, such as a game, sci-fi movie, comic or animé, music, etc; a person obsessed with a single subject or hobby **2** A person obsessed with an actor or a fictional character (*1919+*)

fancy-Dan *adj* Pretentious; HIGHFALUTIN : *It's fancy-Dan nomenclature* (*1930s+*)

fancy (or **fast**) **footwork** *n phr* Very adroit evasion; clever dodging and maneuver : *It will take fancy footwork to explain this one/ The American Medical Association tried a little fast footwork before Congress last week* (*1900+ Sports*)

fancy pants *modifier* : *one of your fancy-pants diplomats* *n phr* **1** A dressed-up or overdressed person **2** An effete man; SISSY (*1940s+*)

fancy-schmancy *adj* Very elegant or ornate, esp pretentiously so; HIGHFALUTIN : *mostly fancy-schmancy Roman numbers like IIs and IIIs* [*1970s+*; fr the humorous and derisive Yiddish rhyming of a first word with a second one beginning *shm-*, as in "Oedipus-shmoedipus, just so he loves his mother"]

fandangle[1] *n* An ornamental object; gewgaw (*1835+*)

fandangle[2] *n* A confused profusion; generous lively miscellany : *cranes, firebirds, foxes, flamingos, a fauna fandangle hard to believe* [mid-

1800s+; fr eastern US dialect *fandango*, "a boisterous assembly," fr the Spanish dance]

fandom *n* Devotees and aficionados collectively : *All fandom welcomes the new summer football* (*1903+*)

faniggle *See* FINAGLE

fanner *n* **1** A person who locates wallets for a pickpocket to steal (*1847+ Underworld*) **2** A person who manipulates coin-return levers on pay telephones, hoping to dislodge coins : *little old lady of about 80 who was dubbed Mary the Fanner* (*1970s+*)

Fannie Mae *n phr* A publicly traded security backed by the Federal National Mortgage Association (FNMA), established in 1938 (*1948+*)

fanny *n* The buttocks; rump; ASS : *I can hardly sit down, my fanny is so sore* [1920+; fr earlier British *fanny*, "vulva," perhaps fr John Cleland's 18th-century heroine *Fanny* Hill]

fanny pack *n phr* (also **butt pack**) A small crescent-shaped cloth bag worn about the waist on a belt [mid-1980s+; a 1971 use is found in *Outdoor Life*, before use of the fanny pack became general]

fantabulous *adj* Wonderful; fantastic and fabulous : *fantabulous job at designing the set* (*1958+*)

fan the breeze *v phr* BAT THE BREEZE (*1950s+*)

fantods, the *n phr* Fidgety nervousness; uneasy restlessness; the WILLIES : *You just got the fantods, that's all* [1880s+; fr British dialect, "indisposition, restlessness," perhaps fr *fanteague*, "commotion, excitement," or fr *fantasy*]

fanzine (FAN zeen) *modifier* : *The fanzine set is not scared off by raunchy lyrics* *n* A fan magazine : *wants to start his own fanzine* (*1940s+*)

FAQ (pronounced as separate letters) *n* A set of frequently asked questions, often with their answers : *The best thing to do first is to read the FAQ, the list of frequently asked questions* (*1990s+ Computer*)

far gone *modifier* In an extreme state, such as drunk : *too far gone to help her/ fans are far gone*

Farley *See* FARLEY

farm[1] *v* To be killed in action; die in the armed services; BUY THE FARM : *Just about the whole company farmed that day* [1970s+ Army; fr *buy the farm*] *See* BET THE FARM, FAT FARM, FUNNY FARM, NUTHOUSE

farm[2] *n* A minor-league club used as a training ground by a major-league club : *Columbus is a Yankee farm* (*1898+ Baseball*)

farmisht (far MISHT) *adj* Confused; mixed up; ambivalent and/or ambiguous : *I'm afraid she's a little farmisht* [1970s+; fr Yiddish]

far out *adj* **1** Very unconventional; unorthodox and strange; WEIRD : *Drake liked "Suzie Q." Which to us was really far out/ a curious combination of far-out medicine, pampering, and very shrewd doctoring* **2** Excellent; splendid; COOL : *The next thing I heard from her was "Far out!"* (*1950s+*)

◁**fart**▷ *n* **1** A man; fellow; person; GUY : *What's that stupid fart up to?* (*1930s+*) **2** The least thing; nothing; DIDDLY, ZILCH : *It isn't worth a fart* (*1460+*) *v* To expel gas through the anus; relieve flatulence by the most immediate expedient; TOOT (*1250+*) *See* LAY A FART, OLD FART

◁**fart around** or **about**▷ *v phr* **1** HORSE AROUND **2** GOOF AROUND [1930s+; perhaps fr Yiddish *arumfartzen*, "fart around"]

◁**fart off**▷ *v phr* To waste time or goof off : *a great spring day to fart off*

fascinoma *n* An interesting, difficult, or unusual disease or condition [1970s+ Medical; fr *fascina*ting plus *-oma*, the suffix used to form the names of tumors]

fashion plate or **fashionista** *n phr* A well-dressed person, esp a stylish one : *The present-day racketeer is a veritable fashion plate* (*1920s+*)

fashion roadkill *n phr* **1** A person who tries to dress fashionably, but looks ridiculous : *young entertainers who look like fashion roadkill* **2** An outfit worn because one thinks it is fashionable, but rather is ridiculous

fast *adj* Morally lax; libertine : *on Long Island with the fast younger married set* (*1859+*)

fast (or **quick**) **buck** *modifier* : *Fast-buck speculators were getting rich on inflated FHA appraisals/ Fast-buck artists, dreamers, and even some well-heeled companies* *n phr* Money gotten quickly, esp without too fine a concern for ethics or the future : *tryin' to hustle me for a fast buck* (*1940s+*)

fasten one's **seat belt** *sentence* Prepare for difficulties; get ready for a rough time : *Fasten Your Seat Belts for the Fare War* [1940s+; fr the preflight instructions of airliners]

fast food *modifier* : *a fast-food chain* *n phr* Food like hamburgers, fried chicken, etc, cooked and served very rapidly and uniformly, usu by large catering corporations (*1951+*)

fast footwork *See* FANCY FOOTWORK

fast-forward *adj* Very much up-to-date; socially and intellectually dynamic; proactive; ahead of the curve : *hip, fast-forward people* [1980s+; fr the control on a tape player that advances the tape very rapidly]

fast lane (or **track**) *modifier* : *its glittery fast-lane image/ New York's fast-track, high-yield high culture* *n phr* A pace and quality of life emphasizing quick success against strong competition, along with the trappings of wealth and style : *amazing woman, lives on a fast lane/ Jean Piaget started academic life on a fast track/ certainly influenced the 1960s expression "life in the fast lane"* [1960s+; fr the left-hand or *fast lane* of a superhighway, which slower drivers enter at their risk, and a horse-racing *track* in good, dry condition]

fast one *n phr* A trick or deception; clever subterfuge; DIPSY DOODLE : *That was sure a fast one, you wearing the false mustache See* PULL A FAST ONE [1924+; probably fr *fast shuffle*]

fast on one's **feet** *v phr* Ready and resourceful; skillful in debate and repartee : *He is a man who knows how to ask questions and answer them. He showed himself to be fast on his feet* (1970s+ fr prizefight)

fast talk *n phr* Talk meant to deceive or confuse: glib and plausible nonsense : *Ignore the fast talk and don't sign a thing* (1950s+)

fast talker *n phr* A person who engages in fast talk : *Loose Manhattan from its moorings and let it float out to sea. Good-bye dirt, noise, crack dealers, street peddlers, fast talkers* (1950s+)

fast track, a *n phr* A very rapid and urgent information requirement : *This is on a fast track and we hope to have more information by next week* (1990s+)

fat *adj* **1** Marked by fruitfulness : *fat profits/ fat prospects* **2** Wealthy; in funds, esp temporarily so; FLUSH : *Hit him up now, he's pretty fat* (1700+) **3** (also **phat**) Attractive; up to date; COOL, DOPE, RAD • *Fat* is recorded by 1932 as meaning "hot" in US dialect, and this may underlie the teenage use : *If they are real fat, real crazy, naturally they're real cool/ Timberland boots have, in the parlance of the street, become "dope" and "phat," i.e. cool, greatest* (1951+ *Teenagers*) **4** (also **phat**) Sexy; having a shapely body • Some think this, when spelled *phat*, is an acronym for *pretty hips and thighs* : *The three boys thought that Carolyn looked fat as she walked down the street* (1980s+ *Students*) **5** Slow and easy to hit : *Williams then leaped on a fat pitch to knock the baseball 400 feet* (1940s+ *Baseball*) *n* **1** The best and most rewarding part; CREAM : *He just took the fat; screw the long term* (1570+) **2** A fat person; fatty : *I met the other 18 women or fellow fats* (1970s+) *See* BIG FAT, CHEW THE FAT

fat-ass *adj* : *Get your fat-ass self out of here n* **1** A fat person **2** A person with large buttocks; BUFFALO BUTT (1916+)

fat cat *modifier* : *the fat-cat cases, where big money is involved/ whether fat-cat contributors or New Hampshire coffee-klatschers n phr* Any privileged and well-treated person, esp a wealthy benefactor; tycoon : *A millionaire fat-cat who, when the revolution comes, will*

probably be allowed to keep at least one of his chauffeurs/ the late arrival even of such famous "fat cats"/ had jousted with Nelson Rockefeller at a formal dinner for fat cats v : *"fat-catting" ... a term applied to higher leaders who try to pad themselves with special privileges and comforts* (1928+)

fat chance *n phr* No chance at all : *entry without prior permission fell into the category of fat chance* (1906+)

fat city *n phr* **1** An ideal situation; splendid state of affairs • In earlier use *fat city* meant "vulva" : *You're in fat city while other poor slobs sweat on assembly lines/ Johnny came marching home from college and announced he was in "fat city"* (1960s+) **2** Poor physical condition, esp because of being overweight : *Its principal characters wind up in "fat city"* (argot for "out of condition") (1970s+)

fat, dumb, and happy *adj phr* Blissfully and rather bovinely contented (1970s+)

fat farm *n phr* A resort or treatment center where people go to lose weight : *It'll be adventures of me, and takes place at a fat farm/ I went to a California fat farm a couple years ago* (1960s+)

fathead *n* A stupid person; blubberhead (1842+)

fatheaded *adj* Stupid : *some fatheaded motorist* (1748+)

fat lady sings *See* the OPERA'S NEVER OVER TILL THE FAT LADY SINGS

fat-mouth *v* **1** To blab and chatter; CHEW THE FAT **2** To cajole verbally; BULLSHIT, SWEET-TALK : *I ain't asking you to fatmouth me, just as I am not interested in getting into any argument* (1970s+)

fat mouth *n phr* One who talks incessantly; MOTOR-MOUTH : *With very little prodding Jimmy began the conversation because he was feeling like a fat mouth* [1942+; probably fr the locution *I had to open my big fat mouth*]

Fats *n* (Variations: **Fat** or **Fatty** or **Fatso** or **Fat stuff**) A nickname for a fat person (1940s+)

fatso *adj* Fat, in any sense : *a fatso deal in six figures* (1940s+)

fatter *See* HAM-FATTER

faux *adj* False; fake, PHONY : *A British conglomerate told Ms Tabb to shelve her plans to sell the faux burger/ The facade drops, revealing them as the faux funsters they really are/ She had a faux art clock that ran on a battery* [1980s+; fr French]

fave or **fave rave** *modifier* : *My absolute fave-rave model was printed boldly n* or *n phr* A favorite song or musical number, film, person, etc : *That group scats Mozart, Vivaldi, Bach, and other fave raves/ includes many of the quintet's faves* (first form 1938+, second 1967+)

◀**fay**[1]▶ *n* A white person; HONKY, PECKERWOOD [1920s+ Black; fr *ofay*]

fay[2] *adj* Homosexual; GAY [1950s+ Homosexuals; fr earlier *fay*, "fairy"]

faze *v* To surprise and create discomposure : *those grades don't faze her* (1830+)

featherbed *v* **1** To work languidly and sluggishly; seek easy tasks **2** To create or retain unnecessary jobs; do essentially fictitious jobs : *featherbedding clauses in labor agreements* (1920s+)

feather (or line) one's nest *v phr* To be primarily concerned with one's own gain; take care of oneself (1590+)

feathers *See* HORSEFEATHERS

Fed *n* Any federal government worker or agent, esp in law enforcement or taxation : *right up to the day the Feds dragged him into court* (1912+)

Fed, the *n phr* The Federal Reserve System, Board, or Bank : *Now the Fed has apparently decided to let the market carry interest rates upward/ The Fed was reluctant to raise its discount rate* (1960s+)

federal case *See* MAKE A FEDERAL CASE OUT OF something

fed up *adj phr* Disgusted; tired; surfeited; BRASSED OFF : *A number of people suddenly became fed up with a slang phrase like "fed up"* [1900+; the related form *fed up to the eyelids* is found by 1882]

feeb *n* A feeble-minded person; idiot : *Then why are you treating me like a feeb?* (1914+)

feed *n* **1** A meal : *Stop by for a feed, anytime* (1830+) **2** Money (1900+) **3** Contributions of opinion, advice, etc; input : *They put their feed into the project* (1990s+) *v* To board; take one's meals; eat (1895+) *See* CHICKEN FEED

feedbag, the *n phr* A meal; food : *I'm ready for the feedbag* [1920s+; fr the *bag* of *feed*, or nosebag, hung on the head of a horse]

feed one's face *v phr* To eat (1930s+)

feeding frenzy *n phr* A scene of frantic competition, unexampled greed, etc : *First the feeding frenzy begins. We did the story for two days, then the media angle on the story, and then the legal angle* [1980s+; fr the phrase used to describe the behavior of sharks who smell blood, find meat, etc]

feed the bears *v phr* To receive a traffic ticket and pay the fine (1975+)

feed the kitty *v phr* To contribute to a fund, esp to put what one owes into the pot of a card game (1940s+ Poker)

◀**feel or feel up**▶ *v* or *v phr* To touch, caress, or handle the buttocks, breasts, legs, crotch, etc; COP A FEEL (1930+)

◀**feel, a**▶ *n phr* A caress or touch, esp of the buttocks, breasts, or crotch : *The eager amorist entreated a quick feel* (1932+) *See* COP A FEEL

feel a draft *v phr* To feel unwelcome, snubbed, etc; esp to sense racial prejudice against oneself (1940s+ Black)

Feelgood or feelgood *modifier* : *a general "relax, feelgood" vibe/ The President is running a feel-good campaign* *n* **1** DR FEELGOOD **2** A condition of contentment or euphoria : *a purveyor of religious feelgood* (1940s+)

feel good *v phr* To be slightly and pleasantly drunk : *Old Charley was feeling good that night* (1930s+)

feelie *See* TOUCHIE-FEELIE

feel no pain *v phr* To be drunk : *three men who were feeling no pain/ The anticipated audience should be feeling no pain* (1940s+)

feel one's oats *v phr* To be active and high-spirited; act brashly and confidently : *The manufacturer was just feeling his oats, having accomplished his happy intention* [1831+; fr the vigor of a just-fed horse]

feel out *v phr* To inquire or investigate tentatively : *Let's feel out the possibilities first* (1920s+)

feel the pinch *v phr* To feel the effects of not having enough money : *need a job fast, feeling the pinch* (1861+)

feep *n* The electronic bell- or whistle-like sound made by computer terminals *v* : *The machine feeped inexplicably but insistently* (1980s+ Computer)

feet *See* DRAG one's FEET, GET one's FEET WET, GO HOME FEET FIRST, HAVE COLD FEET, HOLD someone's FEET TO THE FIRE

fella *n* Fellow; guy : *fella, wipe your shoes*

fellow *See* REGULAR FELLOW

fellow traveler *n phr* A person who sympathizes with a cause or doctrine, without openly identifying himself with it : *These people are not hipsters, they are fellow travelers* [1930s+; said to have been coined by Leon Trotsky in Russian as *sputnik* and translated into English as "fellow traveler"]

◀**fem or femme**▶ *modifier* **1** : *looks more like a post deb than a femme comic/ whereas women with big heads of fat hair always look femme* **2** : *Butch-femme role players are sad relics of the uptight past* *n* **1** A woman : *He has aired the fem that got him the job* (1900+ Students) **2** A lesbian who takes a passive, feminine role in sex (1970s+ Homosexuals) **3** An effeminate homosexual male : *active or passive, manly ("stud") or womanly ("fem")* (1970s+ Homosexuals) [fr French, "woman"]

fence *n* A person or place that deals in stolen goods : *but even big fences like Alphonso can get stuck/ The loot had disappeared and been handled by a fence* (1700+) *v* : *The clown that stole the Mona Lisa found it hard to fence* (1610+) [all senses are shortenings of *defence*; in the case of criminal act, the notion is probably that of a secure place and trusty person, well defended] *See* GO FOR THE FENCES, ON THE FENCE

fender-bender *n* A minor car accident; trivial collision : *I've only had one fender-bender since I got it* (*1960s+*)

fer instance *See* FOR INSTANCE

ferret (out) *v* To search inquisitively; find by searching : *ferret out the whole story* [1570+; fr the notion of the *ferret* as a restless and assiduous searcher]

fer sure (or shure or shurr) *See* FOR SURE

fess (or 'fess) up *v phr* To confess; admit the truth : *Then why doesn't the judge come clean and fess up?/ He finally fessed up to something that I've known a long time* (*1840+*)

-fest *combining form* A celebration or extensive exercise and indulgence of what is indicated : *slugfest/ gabfest/ fuckfest/ jazzfest/ schmoozefest/ splatterfest* [1880s+; fr German, "festival"] *See* BULL SESSION

fetching *adj* Attractive : *a fetching appearance* (*1902+*)

fetch-me-down *See* HAND-ME-DOWN

few, a *See* HANG A FEW ON, WIN A FEW LOSE A FEW

few quarts low, a *adj phr* Stupid; mentally deficient; NOT WRAPPED TOO TIGHT, OUT TO LUNCH (*1980s+*)

few tacos short of a combination plate, a *adj phr* Stupid; mentally deficient; NOT WRAPPED TOO TIGHT, OUT TO LUNCH : *clearly a few tacos short of a combination plate in the intelligence area* (*1990s+*)

fickle finger of fate, the *n phr* The dire and unpredictable aspect of destiny : *It wasn't anything she specially deserved, just the fickle finger of fate at work* [1940s+; regarding *finger* as both a pointer and a violator of the body]

fiddle *n* : *His new boat is a tax fiddle* (*1874+*) *v* 1 (also **fiddle around** or <**fiddle fart around** or **fiddle-fart**▷) To waste time; GOOF AROUND, FART AROUND : *and the school board fiddled* (*entry form* 1663+) 2 To cheat; defraud (*1604+*) *See* BULL FIDDLE, PLAY SECOND FIDDLE, SECOND FIDDLE

fiddled *adj phr* Illegally altered; COOKED : *how a Park Avenue corporation based on fiddled data might have no more financial stature than an Orchard Street pushcart* (*1604+*)

fiddle factor *n phr* A cheating maneuver; tricky move : *The Navigation Foundation's study "has more fiddle factors than the New York Philharmonic"* (*1980s+*)

fiddle-faddle *interj* An exclamation of irritation, disapproval, dismissal, etc (*1671+*) *n* Nonsense; foolishness; BULLSHIT : *such homemade fiddle-faddle* (*1577+*)

fiddlesticks *n* Nonsense; foolishness; BULLSHIT : *When I explained, she only said, "Fiddlesticks!"* [1857+; the singular form is found by 1600]

field *v* To handle; receive and answer; cope with : *The secretary fielded the questions rather lamely* (*1902+*) *See* OUT IN LEFT FIELD, PLAY THE FIELD

field day *See* HAVE A FIELD DAY

fiend *combining word* A devotee or user of what is indicated : *camera fiend/ dope-fiend/ sex fiend* (*1865+*) *v* To use a choke hold on a robbery victim : *They'd take out a bodega, or fiend a few housewives* (*1980+ Underworld*)

fierce *adj* Nasty; unpleasant; awful : *Gee, it was fierce of me* (*1903+*) *See* SOMETHING FIERCE

FIFO *n* First In, First Out; the first items are on the top of the stack to be done (*Computers*)

fifth wheel *n phr* A superfluous person or thing : *I feel as though I'm a fifth wheel* [1902+; the date reflects the full form *fifth wheel of the coach*]

fifty-fifty *adv* Equally or fairly shared : *split the pizza fifty-fifty* (*1913+*)

fifty-seven varieties *n phr* A very great number; a large assortment : *She's sampled just about all 57 varieties of excess and illumination available in Western civilization* [1896+; fr the trademark designation of products made by the H J Heinz Company]

fig *n* The amount of money won or lost by a gambler [1990s+ Gambling; fr *figure*]

fight *n* A party; STRUGGLE : *the cocktail fights attended by the old man* (*1891+*) *See* CAT FIGHT, DOGFIGHT, YOU CAN'T FIGHT CITY HALL

fighter *See* BOOZEHOUND, NIGHT PEOPLE

fightin' words *n phr* Provocative speech; words inviting combat • Often said in a broad cowboy style : *I can go along with a little ribbing, but them is fightin' words, son* (*1917+*)

fight one's way out of a paper bag, can't *See* CAN'T FIGHT ONE'S WAY OUT OF A PAPER BAG

figure *v* 1 To make sense; be plausible and reasonable : *It figures he'd be next in line* (*1950s+*) 2 To be expected; be very likely : *The pup figured to be in the room when Einstein discussed the bomb with the president* (*1930s+*) *See* BALLPARK FIGURE, GO FIGURE

filch *v* To steal or grab something from someone : *filched the remote control*

file *n* 1 A pickpocket (*1754+ Underworld*) 2 A wastebasket • Often humorously called *file 17, the circular file,* etc (*1940s+*) [first sense perhaps fr the tool; perhaps related to French *filou,* "pickpocket"] *See* CIRCULAR FILE

file 17 (or 13) *n phr* A wastebasket; CIRCULAR FILE (*WWII armed forces*)

fill (or stuff) one's face *v phr* To eat a lot of food quickly : *stuffing his face at BK*

fill-in *n* 1 A summary account; information meant to supply what one does not know : *A friend gives me a fill-in on how Costello is running the country* (*1945+*) 2 A substitute, esp a substitute worker : *Get a fill-in, I gotta split* (*1920s+*)

fill in *v phr* To substitute; replace temporarily : *I'll fill in for you* (*1940s+*)

fill someone in *v phr* To complete someone's knowledge; brief someone; PUT someone IN THE PICTURE : *Fill me in so I know what's up here* (*1945+*)

fill the bill *v phr* To suffice; meet the requirement : *I'd like the job, if you think I fill the bills* (*1861+*)

filly *n* A girl; young woman [1616+; fr French *fille*, "girl"]

film *See* SNUFF FILM

filthy *adj* 1 Wealthy; rich; LOADED : *He's filthy with dough* (*1930s+*) 2 Obscene; salacious; BLUE, DIRTY : *filthy movies/ filthy minds* (*1535+*) 3 Excellent; desirable; COOL, RAD (*1990s+ Teenagers*)

filthy lucre *n phr* Money [1526+; fr the Pauline epistle to Titus]

filthy rich *adj phr* Very rich; LOADED

fin[1] *n* 1 The hand : *Reach out your fin and grab it* 2 The arm and hand (*1840+*)

fin[2] *n* A five-dollar bill; five dollars : *I gave my pal a fin/ It was the fin seen round the world. Where Reagan got the five bucks is a mystery* [1920s+ Underworld; fr Yiddish *finif*, "five"]

finagle (fə NAY gəl) (also **faniggle** or **fenagle** or **finigal** or **finagel** or **phenagle**) *v* 1 To manage or arrange, esp by dubious means; contrive : *Well, she's always trying to finagle me out of it/ He finagled the driver into doing it for him* 2 To acquire, esp by trickery : *She finagled a couple of choice seats* [1920s+; origin unknown; perhaps related to British dialect *finegue*, "to evade," or *fainague*, "to renege"]

find *n* A remarkable discovery, esp of something unexpected (*1872+*) *See* IF YOU CAN'T FIND 'EM

fine *adj* Attractive; DISHY, HUNKY : *if a guy or girl is cute, they're a "hottie" or "fine"* [1990s+ Teenagers; a revival of 1940s bop and cool use, from black, "pleasing, wonderful, exciting, cool"]

fine how-de-do (or **how-do-you-do**), **a** *n phr* A situation; usually deplorable set of circumstances : *which is a fine how-de-do in a country that prides itself on progress* [1835+; the dated instance is *pretty how do you do*]

fine kettle of fish *n phr* A nasty predicament; lamentable situation (*1800+*)

fine print, the *See* the SMALL PRINT

finest, the *n phr* The police force • Often in city name plus *finest* phrases like *San Francisco's finest, Madison's finest* (*1890s+*)

fine-tune *v* To make delicate and careful adjustments; tweak : *knowledge and techniques to fine-tune the economy* (*1960s+*)

finger *n* 1 A police informer; STOOL PIGEON (*1930s+ Underworld*) 2 A person who tells thieves about potential loot (*1920s+ Underworld*) 3 About a half-inch of liquor in a glass : *Maybe I'd better have another finger of the hooch* (*1856+*) *v* 1 To locate and point out someone : *You're the guy that fingered Manny Tinnen/ artificially heightening the tale's drama (by fingering the sponsor)* (*1920s+ Underworld*) 2 To tell thieves about the location, value, etc, of potential loot : *I fingered the robberies* (*1920s+ Underworld*) ◁3▷ To insert a finger into the vulva; FINGERFUCK : *With one hand Larry was fingering me* (*1970s+*) *See* BUTTERFINGERS, FIVE FINGERS, GIVE FIVE FINGERS TO, GIVE someone THE FINGER, NOT LAY A GLOVE ON someone, PLAY STINKY-PINKY, PUT one's FINGER ON something, PUT THE FINGER ON someone, STAND AROUND WITH one's FINGER UP one's ASS

finger, the *n phr* 1 The act of identifying or pointing out potential loot, a hired killer's victim, a wanted criminal, etc (*1920s+ Underworld*) 2 A lewd insulting gesture made by holding up the middle finger with the others folded down, and meaning "fuck you" or "up yours"; the BIRD, ONE-FINGER SALUTE (*1950s+*) *See* GIVE someone THE FINGER, PUT THE FINGER ON someone

fingered *See* LIGHT-FINGERED, STICKY-FINGERED

◀**fingerfuck**▶ *v* To insert a finger into the vulva; FRIG, PLAY STINKY-PINKY : *She wants you to fingerfuck her shikse cunt till she faints* (*1970s+*)

finger-pointing *n* The assessing of blame, guilt, etc : *Criticism of the President's foreign policy has produced a spate of finger-pointing within the Administration* (*1990s+*)

fingers *See* BUTTERFINGERS, FIVE FINGERS, GIVE FIVE FINGERS TO

fingers in the till *n phr* Stealing money from one's place of work or money for which one is responsible : *caught with his fingers in the till* (*1974+*)

finger up one's **ass** *See* STAND AROUND WITH one's FINGER UP one's ASS

finger wave *n* Giving someone the *finger* : *she gave him the finger wave when he turned away*

finigal *See* FINAGLE

finish *v* To put a disastrous end to something or to someone's prospects; COOK someone's GOOSE : *She finished him off with a passing shot* (*1755+*)

finished *adj* Ruined; no longer able to function or compete; DEAD, KAPUT : *After two tries he was finished/ She couldn't act any longer and was finished at thirty*

finish last *See* NICE GUYS FINISH LAST

finito *modifier* Ended, finished : *After that, finito*

fink *n* **1** A strikebreaker; SCAB (*1890s+*) **2** A labor spy; a worker who is primarily loyal to the employer : *unpopular with the other waiters, who thought him a fink* (*1902+*) **3** A police officer, detective, guard, or other law-enforcement agent : *This Sherlock Holmes, this fink's on the old yocky-dock* (*1925+*) **4** An informer; STOOL PIGEON : *Now he's looking for the fink who turned him in/ The glossary runs to such pejorative nouns as fink, stoolie, rat, canary, squealer* (*1920s+ Underworld*) **5** Any contemptible person; vile wretch; RAT FINK, SHITHEEL : *All men are brothers, and if you don't give, you're a kind of fink* (*1894+*) *v* : *Dutch knew I worked for his friend and I wouldn't fink* (*1920s+*) [origin unknown; perhaps fr *Pink*, "a Pinkerton agent engaged in strikebreaking," or fr German *Fink*, "finch," a university students' term for a student who did not join in dueling and drinking societies; first sense said to have been used during the Homestead Strike of 1892; fifth noun sense was unaccountably revived in the early 1960s]

fink out *v phr* **1** To withdraw from or refuse support to a project, movement, etc, esp in a seemingly cowardly and self-serving way; BACK OUT : *he will "fink out," as Kauffman believed he had done so far* (*1960s+ Counterculture*) **2** To become untrustworthy and a potential informer (*1960s+*) **3** To fail utterly (*1970s+*)

Finn *See* MICKEY FINN

finnagel *See* FINAGLE

fire *v* **1** To discharge someone from a job; dismiss, usu with prejudice; CAN, SACK (*1887+*) **2** To throw something with great force : *The big left-hander fired a fastball down the middle* (*1910+*) **3** To ask or utter with bluntness and vehemence : *The panel fired questions at me and I soon wilted* (*1850s+*) *See* BALL OF FIRE, HOLD SOMEONE'S FEET TO THE FIRE, ON THE FIRE, PULL SOMETHING OUT OF THE FIRE, SURE-FIRE

fire away *v phr* **1** To begin; go ahead ● Usu an invitation : *"Maybe this is something you can help me with" "Fire away"* **2** To attack verbally : *As soon as I walked into the room he began to fire away at me* (*1775+*)

fireball *n* BALL OF FIRE

fire blanks *See* SHOOT BLANKS

fire-breathing *adj* Fierce; menacing; dragon-like : *ABC now planned to swap Ellen with Wednesday's fire-breathing Grace Under Fire* (*1591+*)

firebug *n* An arsonist; pyromaniac [1872+; fr *fire* plus *bug*, "maniac"]

fired up *adj phr* **1** Drunk (*1850+*) **2** Angry (*1824+*) **3** (also **all fired up**) Full of enthusiasm, energy, and resolve : *If he gets fired up he's unbeatable* (*1970s+*)

fire-eater *n* **1** A quarrelsome and energetic person (*1804+*) **2** A firefighter; smoke-eater (*1920s+*)

fire in the belly *n phr* Zealous ambition; energy; high spirits : *You want someone with fire in the belly/ It's hard to get fire in the belly over health insurance when it's stuffed with pate* [1951+; probably fr the French phrase *avoir quelque chose dans le ventre*, "to have something in the gut"]

fireman *n* A relief pitcher, esp an effective one : *a four-run blast against fireman Joe in the eighth inning* (*1940s+ Baseball*)

fire on *v phr* To strike; hit : *looking at this one dude Huey had fired on* (*1960s+ Black*)

fire on all cylinders *v phr* To operate or proceed at maximum speed and efficiency : *Europe's economy will fire on all cylinders/ a world firing on all cylinders, where the US, Japan, and Europe are all growing simultaneously* (*1990s+*)

firestorm *n* An intense and often destructive spate of action or reaction : *The report has already generated a firestorm of criticism/ A lawyer from Time-Warner expected a firestorm of protest from the shareholders after the vote* [fr the catastrophic and unquenchable *fires* caused by aerial bombing of cities in World War II]

fire someone up *v phr* To fill someone with energy and enthusiasm; excite someone : *She fired them up with promises of huge winnings* (*1970s+*)

firewater *n* Liquor; BOOZE [1826+; the term is attributed to North American Indians]

fireworks *n* **1** Excitement; furor; noisy fuss; HOOPLA : *speeches that would produce the "fireworks" supporters have demanded* (*1883+*) **2** Anger; quarrels; rancorous rhetoric (*1880s+*) **3** Shooting; gunfire or cannon fire : *The riot ended when the National Guard showed up and the fireworks began* (*1860s+*)

first base *n phr* In early sexual play, holding hands : *"In sixth grade," she said, "first base is holding hands, and second base is kissing on the mouth"* (*1980s+ Schoolchildren*) *See* GET TO FIRST BASE

first crack out of the box *adv phr* Immediately; before anything else : *Get him back home and, first crack out of the box, he's run away again* (*1940s+*)

first off *adv phr* First in order; to begin with : *I said that first off I wanted an apology* (*1880s+*)

first-rate *adj* Excellent; of best quality (*1697+*) *adv* : *That'll do first-rate* [fr the rating of warships in the 1600s]

first sacker *n phr* A first baseman (*1911+ Baseball*)

fish *n* **1** A new inmate : *As a "fish" at Charlestown, I was physically miserable* (*1870s+*

Prison) **2** A nonmember of a street gang; a person regarded as inimical and distasteful by a street gang *(1950s+ Street gang)* **3** A weak or stupid person, esp one easily victimized; PATSY, SUCKER : *Why should he be the fish for the big guys?/ The superteams get stronger. They can pad their schedules with the occasional fish (1753+)* **4** A person, esp a criminal, thought of as being caught like a fish : *The cops catch a lot of very interesting fish (1885+)* **5** A heterosexual woman *(1970s+ Homosexuals)* **6** A prostitute; HOOKER • *Fish* meant "vulva" by the 1890s and retained the meaning, at least in black English, until at least the 1930s *(1930s+)* **7** A dollar : *The job paid only fifty fish (1920+)* **8** tin fish • *Fish torpedo* is found by 1876 *(1928+)* *v* **1** To seek information, esp by a legal or quasi-legal process having a very general aim; GO FISHING *(1563+)* **2** To ask for something, usu a compliment, esp in an indirect and apparently modest way *(1803+) See* BIG FISH, BIGGER FISH TO FRY, COLD FISH, FINE KETTLE OF FISH, GO FISHING, KETTLE OF FISH, LIKE SHOOTING FISH IN A BARREL, QUEER FISH

fish-eye, the *See* GIVE SOMEONE THE FISH-EYE

fish-eyed *adj* Cold, staring, and inhuman • The dated form is *fishy-eyed* : *have to persuade a fish-eyed insurance claims adjustor (1836+)*

fishhooks *n* The fingers *(1846+)*

fishing *See* GO FISHING

fishing expedition *n phr* An attempt, on the part of the police, a prosecutor, etc, to discover evidence where it may or may not be; a sort of inquisition : *She had nothing special in mind to ask Joan Tesell; it was just a fishing expedition (1961+) See* GO FISHING

fish-kiss *n* A kiss made with puckered lips : *not a real kiss, but a fish-kiss v* To kiss someone with puckered lips

fish or cut bait *sentence* Do one thing or another, but stop dithering; take action; SHIT OR GET OFF THE POT • Usu a firm or irritated demand : *The union leader warned that the city had until Feb 1 to "fish or cut bait" (1876+)*

fish story (or tale) *n phr* A series of lies or exaggerations; a false or improbable explanation : *His whole alibi is a fish story* [1819+; fr the tendency of an angler to exaggerate the size of the catch]

fish to fry *See* BIGGER FISH TO FRY

fishy *adj* Very probably false or dishonest; very dubious : *The whole proposition is decidedly fishy* [1840+; probably fr the unpleasant odor of spoiled *fish*]

fisted *See* HAM-HANDED

◀**fist-fucking**▶ *n* (also **fisting**) **1** Anal intercourse, usu homosexual, in which the hand is inserted into the partner's anus *(1970s+)* **2** Male masturbation *(1890s+)*

fistful *n* **1** A handful, usu a large amount : *I've got a fistful of overdue bills (1611+)* **2** A large amount of money : *The digital stereo set me back a fistful (1950s+)* **3** A five-year prison sentence *(1940s+ Underworld)*

fit as a fiddle *adj phr* In very good condition; in fine fettle *(1616+)*

fit to be tied *adj phr* Very angry; STEAMED *(1894+)*

five *n* The hand; the five fingers *(1950s+ Jive talk) See* GIVE SOMEONE FIVE, HANG FIVE, NINE-TO-FIVE, SLIP (or GIVE) ME FIVE, TAKE FIVE

five-finger discount *n phr* Shoplifting *(1960s+ Teenagers)*

five fingers *n phr* **1** A five-year prison sentence **2** A thief *(1940s+ Underworld) See* GIVE FIVE FINGERS TO

five it *v phr* To refuse to answer on grounds of the Fifth Amendment : *How many questions would they be able to get in before DeMeo began to "five it" (1970s+)*

Five-O *n* A police officer; the police : *Why you think you and the flap can shut the Deuce down? Five-oh can't do it* [1980s+ Teenagers; fr the television police-adventure series *Hawaii Five-O*]

five o'clock shadow *n* A growth of stubble that becomes visible in the late afternoon on the face of a man who has shaved earlier in the day *(1937+)*

five-pound bag *See* BLIVIT

fiver *n* **1** A five-dollar bill; five dollars : *For a fiver, cash, you could ride (1843+)* **2** A five-year prison sentence; FIVE FINGERS *(1940s+ Prison) See* NINE-TO-FIVER

five-second rule (also called the **three-second rule**, **10-second rule**, **15-second rule**) *n phr* The belief that if one picks up a dropped food item very quickly, it is safe to eat : *five-second rule in the cafeteria*

five-spot *n* **1** A five-dollar bill *(1890s+)* **2** A five-year prison sentence *(1900+ Underworld)*

fix *n* **1** A fight, game, etc, of which the winner has been fraudulently predetermined : *The World Series that year was a blatant fix (1890s+)* **2** (also **fix-up**) A dose of a narcotic, esp an injection of heroin; BLAST : *a fix to calm her jittery nerves (1930s+ Narcotics)* **3** Anything needed to appease a habitual need or craving • One of the common transfers of narcotics terms, like *junkie* : *He had to have his daily fix of flattery (1970s+)* **4** A difficult situation; a nasty position or dilemma : *I'm afraid her lying has gotten her into quite a fix (1809+)* **5** A clear idea; an accurate notion • The dated use refers to the determination of a point or line in navigation : *I can't get a fix on this guy's intentions (1902+)* *v* **1** To prearrange the outcome of a prizefight, race, game, etc (*1790+*) **2** To arrange exoneration from a charge, esp by bribery; have a charge quashed : *He had a pal could fix tickets for five bucks* (*1872+*) **3** To castrate an animal, esp a cat (*1940s+*) **4** To punish; injure; FIX someone's WAGON : *Make him wash the dishes, that'll fix him* (*1800+*) *See* QUICK FIX

fix, the *n phr* **1** Arrangements, esp illicit payments, assuring the prearranged outcome of a prizefight, game, race, etc : *It's in the bag. The fix is on/ If he doesn't get the Nobel, the fix is in* (*1940s+*) **2** Arrangements assuring exoneration from a police charge : *The super hisself couldn't put the fix in any faster* (*1920s+*)

fixed *adj* **1** Having the outcome prearranged : *the World Series is fixed* **2** Neutered : *fixed cats* **3** Intoxicated or drugged

fixer *n* A person who arranges shady and illegal affairs : *He's a fixer you have to see if you want to open a gambling hall* (*1889+*)

fixings *n* Things, esp food, normally accompanying some central or focal object : *turkey and all the fixings* (*1842+*)

Fixit *See* MISTER FIXIT

fix-up *n* A date arranged by a third party : *not sure if a fix-up is any better than a blind date*

fix someone up *v phr* To provide or arrange what is needed : *We can fix you up with a nice new car/ If you want a date I can fix you up with Gert* (*1861+*)

fix someone's wagon *v phr* To punish; injure; ruin; CLEAN someone's CLOCK (*1940s+*)

FIZBO *n* A person who attempts to sell property without a real-estate broker, or the arrangement for doing so : *Another is their dislike for brokers who offer their services at a discount to FIZBOS, which stands for For Sale By Owner* (*1980s+*)

fizzle *n* : *Our monster bash was a fizzle* *v* To fail; lose effect; FLOP, PETER OUT : *I bail out of all my commitments and things fizzle* [*1840s+* College students; fr the lackluster sibilance of a damp firecracker]

flabbergast *v* To amaze; perplex; THROW (*1772+*)

flack[1] or **flak** *modifier* : *The flack description is also worth quoting* *n* **1** Publicity; public relations material; ballyhoo, HYPE : *Mr Mogul's latest epic was preceded by wheeling galaxies of affecting flack* (*1940s+*) **2** (also **flacker**) A publicity person or press agent : *something that would cause your basic, self-respecting flack to want to slit his throat/ "He's shown steady improvement," said a medical flack* *v* : *his publishers, who flack it into a best seller/ He's not flakking for ulterior motives* [origin unknown; said to be fr the name of Gene *Flack*, a moving-picture publicity agent, and first

used in the show-business paper *Variety*; probably influenced by *flak*]

flack[2] or **flack out** *v* or *v phr* **1** To fall asleep; lose consciousness **2** To be tired or depressed **3** To die (*1950s+ Cool & beat talk*)

flag *n* **1** The pennant awarded annually to a league championship team (*1883+ Baseball*) **2** An assumed name; alias (*1930s+ Underworld*) *v* **1** (also **flag down**) To hail a vehicle, person, etc; signal a stop : *He was barreling along till she flagged him down* (*1850s+*) **2** To arrest; BUST : *They flagged my reefer man yesterday* (*1940s+ Underworld*) **3** To designate as someone who will not be served more liquor; EIGHTY-SIX : *Babris asked Pilone whether the men were "the local troublemakers" and then demanded that they be "flagged," the bartender testified* (*1980s+*)

flagged *adj* Forbidden further drinks because already drunk (*1980s+*)

flag it *v phr* To fail an examination or a course; FLUNK (*1950s+ College students*)

flagpole *See* RUN something UP THE FLAGPOLE

flagship *modifier* : *and not one damn word in the nation's flagship papers* *n* The most imposing constituent; premier specimen : *This car's the flagship of the line* (*1955+*)

flak *n* **1** An antiaircraft gun or guns; antiaircraft fire (*WWII armed forces*) **2** (also **flack**) Severe criticism; angry blame : *This order provoked little political flack/ Joe took considerable flak from white co-workers* (*1960s+*) **3** Trouble; fuss; dissension; STATIC : *Let's not have a lot of flak about this* (*1960s+*) [fr German *Fliegerabwehrkanonen*, "antiaircraft gun"]

flake *adj* : *Don't act so flake* (*1960s+ Baseball*) *n* **1** An eccentric person, esp a colorful individualist; BIRD : *what is known in the trade as a flake, a kook, or a clubhouse lawyer/ Users and flakes clung to her* (*1950s+ Baseball*) **2** The quality of flamboyant individualism : *The Yankees have acquired an amount of "flake"* (*1960s+ Baseball*) **3** A stupid, erratic person; RETARD (*1960s+ Teenagers*) **4** Cocaine (*1920s+ Narcotics*) **5** An arrest made in order to meet a quota; accommodation collar (*1970s+ Police*) *v* **1** To arrest someone on false or invented charges; FRAME (*1970s+ Police*) **2** To plant evidence on a suspect : *I have a throwaway gun. We're going to flake him* (*1970s+ Police*) **3** To cancel an appointment without notice; STAND someone UP : *It is already seven o'clock; I guess he flaked* (*1980s+ Students*) [all except police senses ultimately fr an attested phrase *snow flakes*, "cocaine"]

flaked-out *adj* Asleep; unconscious (*1950s+ Beat & cool talk*)

flake off *v phr* To leave; depart • Often an irritated command : *Want to brush off such* *friends? Suggest that they flake off* [1960s+ Teenagers; probably a euphemism for *fuck off*]

flake-out *n* A total failure; FLOP (*1970s+*)

flake out *v phr* **1** FLACK OUT **2** FLAKE OFF **3** To fail [1970s+; origin uncertain; *flax out* in the third sense is found in New England dialect by 1891 and is probably related]

flaky or **flakey** *adj* **1** Colorfully eccentric; buoyantly individualistic (*1960s+ Baseball*) **2** Insane; SCREWY, wacky : *a flaky old professor, a snake expert* (*1960s+*) **3** Disoriented; barely conscious; dizzy : *He played the last 23 minutes of the game in a condition that was described as "flaky" and "fuzzy"* (*1960s+*) See FLAKE

flam *See* FLIMFLAM

flamdoodle *See* FLAPDOODLE

flame *n* **1** A sweetheart; beloved (*1647+*) **2** (also **flame-mail**) An angry and often obscene message on a computer network : *countless scornful messages, called "flames" on the network/ Bill sent Michael this totally wicked flame-mail from hell* (*1980s+ Computer*) *v* **1** (also **flame it up**) To flaunt or exaggerate effeminate traits; CAMP IT UP (*1970s+ Homosexuals*) **2** To rant angrily and often obscenely on a computer bulletin board or other network : *You may even get the chance to "flame" someone else* (*1980s+ Computer*) See SHOOT someone DOWN

flame-out or **flame out** *modifier* : *Gramm, flame-out Jack Kemp n* **1** The failure of a jet engine where the flame is extinguished (*1940s+*) **2** A person of fleeting fame; FLASH IN THE PAN, HAS-BEEN : *He is the Russian Hotspur, a fiery flameout who will soon become a historical footnote/ Michael Jackson was a flame-out, too* (*1990s+*) *v phr* **1** Of a jet engine, to fail by losing the flame of its fuel (*1940s+*) **2** To lose energy; falter; collapse : *The Stevens Point native flamed out in the 1500 meters* (*1990s+*)

◁**flamer** or **flaming asshole** or **flaming fruitbar**▷ *n* or *n phr* A male homosexual; QUEEN : *It doesn't have anything to do with me being a flamer* (*1970s+ Homosexuals*)

flames *See* GO DOWN IN FLAMES

flamethrower *n* A pitcher with a very fast fastball (*1970s+ Baseball*)

flame war *n phr* An extended outbreak of vituperation on a computer network : *The whole net will basically collapse through flame-wars/ They flame back, and then a flame war begins* (*1990s+ Computer*)

flaming *adj* Blatantly homosexual, esp in an effeminate way; SWISH : *in hiding the fact that Babe Ruth and Lou Gehrig were flaming homosexuals* (*1970s+ Homosexuals*) *adv* Very • Used as an intensifier, usu preceded by "so" : *I can't believe he'd be so flaming stupid* (*1895+*) *n* (also **flamage**) The use of rude, strong, obscene, etc, language on a computer bulletin board, in computer mail, etc • This sort of verbal license is said to be common and apparently to be an effect of the medium itself (*1980s+ Computer*)

flammer *See* FLIMFLAMMER

flannel-mouth *n* An exaggerated talker (*1880s+*)

flap *n* **1** Disturbance; tumult; fuss : *Law was one direction open to me with the least amount of flap* (*1916+ British*) **2** A fight between street gangs; RUMBLE (*1950s+ Street gang*) **3** A white person : *I wouldn't give a fuck what you or the flap or anybody thought 'bout it* (*1990s+ Black street gang*) *v* To become flustered; lose one's composure : *I've seen him under hostile pressure before. He doesn't flap and he doesn't become a doormat* (*1920s+*)

flapdoodle or **flamdoodle** *n* Nonsense; foolishness; BALONEY : *He then goes on to utter other flapdoodle for the nourishment of the mind* (*1833+*)

flapjack *n* A pancake (*1600+*)

flapjaw *n* **1** Talk; discourse; chat : *We caught Mannone and Moore for a moment's flapjaw before we left* **2** A loquacious person; MOTOR-MOUTH (*1950s+*)

flapjawed *adj* Talkative; notably loquacious : *to describe the flap-jawed Turner as outspoken* (*1950s+*)

flap one's lip *See* FLIP one's LIP

flapper *modifier* : *the flapper era/ flat flapper chest n* **1** The hand; FLIPPER (*1770s+*) **2** A young woman of the type fashionable in the 1920s, with pronounced worldly interests, relatively few inhibitions, a distinctive style of grooming, etc • The date refers to two senses, "a young whore" and "a young girl"; the 1920s revival seems to blend these (*1893+*) [origin uncertain; perhaps from the idea of an unfledged bird *flapping* its wings]

flash *adj* **1** Excellent; wonderful; DYNAMITE (*1970s+ Teenagers*) **2** flashy (*1600s+*) *n* **1** Thieves' argot (*1718+*) **2** A look; quick glance : *We slid into the cross street to take a flash at the alley* (*1900+*) **3** A person who excels at something, esp in a showy and perhaps superficial way; WHIZ : *He's a flash at math* (*1603+*) **4** A display of gaudy merchandise or prizes : *expensive flash that the mark couldn't win* (*1920s+ Circus*) **5** RUSH : *Harry shot up a couple of the goofballs and tried to think a bigger and better flash than he got* (*1960s+ Narcotics*) **6** Distinctive personal style and charm; charisma : *Flash is in the clothes, the cars, the walk, the talk* (*1970s+*) **7** A sudden idea, impulse, or insight : *the joy when I get the flash, figure out who did it* **8**

Something one is currently doing; BAG, THING : *His current "flash," as he calls it, tends toward gaucho suits* (*1970s+*) **9** In decent exposure : *He gave her a flash and she squawked* **10** Urination; PISS : *and said he'd pay double in case of a "flash," which is a delicate way of describing one of nature's indelicate imperatives* (*1970s+*) **11** Showiness; superficiality; GLITTER, GLITZ : *For all the flash* Carlito's Way *is pretty tame* (*1990s+*) *v* **1** To set up a display of presumed prizes • *Flash it,* "to show the bargains offered," is found by 1849 : *Flash the joint* (*1920s+ Circus*) **2** To vomit • The dated example is *flash the hash* (*1811+*) **3** To have a hallucinatory experience from a narcotic : *He flashed he was as big as a mountain* (*1960s+ Narcotics*) **4** To feel the sudden pleasurable effect of a narcotics injection : *As soon as the needle went in, she flashed* (*1960s+ Narcotics*) **5** To have a sudden idea, insight, or impulse (*1920s+*) **6** To expose one's genitals, breasts, etc • The earlier British forms were *flash it* and *flash one's meat* : *Judy thought she was gonna flash me. She started unbuttoning her blouse* (*1846+*) **7** To display suddenly and briefly : *We flash our tin and ask him if he's lost a ballpeen hammer* **8** To climb a route on the first try (*1990s+ Rock climbing*)

flashback *n* **1** A scene or passage in a novel, movie, etc, that depicts events earlier than those in the main time frame (*1916+*) **2** A hallucination or sensation originally induced by LSD or other drugs but recurring after the drug experience has ended (*1960s+ Narcotics*)

flashforward *n* A scene or passage in a novel, movie, etc, that depicts events later than those of the main time frame (*1949+*)

flash in the pan *n phr* A person or thing that does not fulfill an apparent potential : *If he's not a flash in the pan he'll be the best poet we ever had* [*1809+*; fr the igniting charge in an old gun that goes off *in the pan* or holder without igniting the main charge]

flash on *v phr* To recall; realize vividly : *I flashed on all that stuff in basic about it being better dead than captured/ She just flashed on it for once in her life, she ought to put her own needs right up front* (*1960s+*)

flash point *n phr* The place or time when something "takes fire," becomes exciting and exemplary : *We want the White House to function as a flash point for whatever's great in this country* [*1990s+*; in the technical sense, "lowest point of ignition of a fluid, compound, etc," the term is found by the 1870s]

flat *adj* **1** FLAT BROKE (*1833+*) **2** Having to do with any gambling game, esp one in which money rather than prizes may be won

(*1940s+ Carnival*) [carnival sense fr earlier meaning of *flats,* "playing cards," or fr earlier meaning "dishonest dice"] *See* GRANNY FLAT, IN NOTHING FLAT

flat as a pancake *adj phr* Very flat : *The car was squashed flat as a pancake* [*1761+*; the form *flat down as pancakes* is found by 1611]

◁**flat-ass**▷ *adv* Totally; absolutely : *Some farmers are absolutely flat-ass broke/ It's not just that. I'll flat-ass leave her* (*1960s+*)

flatbacker *n* A prostitute : *His prostitutes are well known for being unhooked flatbackers* (*1960s+*)

flat broke *adj phr* Entirely without funds; penniless (*1842+*)

flatfoot *n* A police officer or detective : *The flatfeet scratched their heads* (*1899+*)

flatfooted *adj* Unprepared; surprised • Usu in the phrase *catch someone flatfooted* : *He just stood there flatfooted and watched it roll in* (*1912+ Baseball*) *adv* Straightforwardly; without ceremony : *If they were going to turn it down, they would have just flatfooted done it* (*1828+*)

flatline *modifier* Dead : *The defendant's face was flatline* **v** To die : *State government is in a coma. We're going to flat-line at any moment* [*1980s+*; fr the *flat line* showing no waves, hence no heartbeat, on a heart-monitoring machine]

flatlined *adj* Drunk; PLASTERED, SHIT-FACED : *I've had so many reebs I'm flatlined* (*1990s+*)

flatliner *n* **1** A dead person (*1980s+*) **2** A nontipping customer; flathead (*1990s+ Restaurant*)

◁**flat on** one's **ass**▷ *adj phr* **1** Penniless and exhausted; DOWN AND OUT : *He blew his pay pack and he's flat on his ass* (*1960s+*) **2** Incompetent; feckless : *That platoon's a loser, flat on its ass* (*1970s+ Army*) *See* FALL ON one's ASS

flat-out *adj* **1** Open and direct; unambiguous; plain : *Bunuel resorts to flat-out assertions in the last scene/ This time a flat-out demand* **2** Total; unrestricted • The noun *flat-out,* "a failure," is found by 1870; the following example is an unconscious redundancy : *a husband who was a flat-out failure/ Despite its creepshow pretensions, much of it is flat-out dull*

flat out *adv phr* At full speed; ALL OUT, WIDE OPEN : *The economy is running flat out and revenues are pouring in/ Flat out, working on it myself, it will take a week* [*1932+*; perhaps fr the elongated shape of a horse going at top speed]

flats *n* **1** Horse racing in which the jockey is mounted and the horse runs rather than trotting (*1840s+ Horse racing*) **2** A pair of dishonest dice (*1591+ Gamblers*) **3** A pair of footwear with no heels or flat heels

flat-tailed *adv* Totally; completely : *They controlled the game. They just flat-tailed beat us* (*1990s+*)

flattener *n* A blow that knocks one down and unconscious; knockout punch (*1920s+ Prizefight*)

◁**flavor** or **flava**▷ *adj* : *That's a very flava lady* *n* A sexually attractive woman (*1960s+ Black*)

flavor of the month *n phr* Something ephemeral; a short-lived phenomenon : *That 23 percent could dwindle, Mr. Perot could be the political flavor of the month/ She's not seeing him any more; turned out to be another flavour of the month* (*1990s+*)

fleabag or **fleahouse** or **fleatrap** *modifier* : *She will no longer take her dates to fleabag hotels* *n* **1** A bed; mattress; bunk or hammock (*1839+*) **2** An inferior racehorse (*1950s+ Horse-racing*) **3** A cheap and wretched hotel or rooming house; FLOP, FLOPHOUSE : *my last French hotel of the war: a fleabag two rooms wide/ He has transformed the motel from the old wayside fleabag into the most popular home away from home* (late *1820s+*) **4** Any cheap, dirty, or ramshackle public place : *unveiled at an owl show in a Forty-second Street flea bag* (*1950s+*)

flea-flicker *n* A play combining a lateral pass and a forward pass : *You won't get the flea-flickers and special-teams gambles from Holmgren* (*1920s+ Football*)

flea powder *n phr* A weakened or diluted narcotic, or a nonnarcotic substance sold as a narcotic; BLANK (*1960s+ Narcotics*)

fleece *v* To cheat or swindle : *get back the money he'd fleeced me out of/ For these traders the function of the outside public speculator is to be fleeced* (*1577+*)

flesh *See* IN THE FLESH, PRESS THE FLESH

flesh flick *See* SKIN FLICK

flesh-peddler *n* **1** A pimp or prostitute • The earlier version, *flesh-monger*, is found by 1603 (*1940s+*) **2** An actor's or athlete's agent : *The old Hollywood flesh peddlers never stop talking money* (*1930s+*) **3** A person working at an employment agency; HEADHUNTER (*1960s+*)

flesh-pressing *modifier* Handshaking, meeting and flattering voters, etc, in politics : *The flesh-pressing process remains invariable, as you will glean from the weekly schedule of City Alderman Joe Pantalone* (*1920s+*)

flexitarian *n* A vegetarian who is flexible enough to occasionally eat meat or fish • Also an adjective [*1992+*; blend of *flexi*ble + ve*getarian*]

flex one's **muscles** *v phr* To give a sample of one's power, esp in a threatening way : *I'm not sure they mean harm, probably just flexing their muscles* (*1960s+*)

flextime or **flexitime** *n* Flexible working time that varies as to hours and days worked : *flextime for working mothers and fathers in business* [*1970s+*; fr the trademark of a device used to record the hours an employee works]

flick or **flicker** *n* **1** A movie : *a cheapie hard-core porno flick/ He will play a role in the flick* **2** A movie theater [*1920s+*; fr the *flickering* of early movie images] *See* SKIN FLICK

flies *See* CATCH FLIES, NO FLIES ON

flight *n* A hallucinogenic drug experience; TRIP (*1960s+ Narcotics*)

flimflam *modifier* : *a flimflam game/ flimflam man* *n* : *Don't fall for that flimflam* *v* To cheat or swindle; defraud; BAMBOOZLE, CON : *We've been flimflammed/ He talked like some hick begging to be flimflammed* (*1538+*)

flimflammer *n* A confidence man; cheater; swindler : *an expert flimflammer who worked up crime's ladder* (*1880s+*)

fling *n* **1** A period of pleasure and indulgence, often as relaxation after or before stern responsibilities : *He had a last fling before going to the monastery* (*1827+*) **2** A try; CRACK, GO, SHOT : *Will you have a fling at climbing that wall?* (*1592+*) **3** A dance; party; SHINDIG (*1940s+ Students*)

fling woo *See* PITCH WOO

flip¹ *adj* Flippant; impudent; CHEEKY : *Mr Lawrence is flip and easy/ Someone else thought he was too flip at press conferences* (*1847+*)

flip² *n* Something that causes hilarity or pleasure : *The big flip of the year is Peter Arno's book of cartoons* (*1950+*) *v* **1** To change or switch diametrically; FLIP-FLOP : *So I flipped over to the opposite opinion* (*1900s+*) **2** To respond enthusiastically; feel great excitement and pleasure : *"They flipped over it," Riveroll recalls/ I flip over this record* (*1950+*) **3** To cause one to respond with enthusiasm; give one great pleasure : *My imitation of Mr Kissinger flipped the assemblage* (*1950+*) **4** To become angry : *When he told me what he had done, I flipped* (*1940s+*) **5** To go insane; behave irrationally; FLIP OUT : *I was flipping at first but then the marvelous vibes got to me* (*1950s+ Cool talk*) **6** To become an informer; FINK OUT, SING : *Someone had tipped the police off to where they should look: a suspect who had been persuaded to flip, become a government informant, on the night of his arrest/ It was the easiest flip Stone ever made. The man rolled over like a puppy* (*1980s+ Police*) **7** To vomit : *Many jockeys have to "flip" (regurgitate) their meals to make weight* (*1980s+*) **8** To exchange one for another; trade in : *You buy one, get it out of your system, flip it for a gray Lexus or Infiniti* (*1990s+*)

flip-flop *modifier* : *flip-flop views and reluctance to confront the issues n* A complete reversal of direction; about-face • The primary meaning is "somersault" : *Commodities have been doing flip-flops on the price ladder v* : *So Kennedy's flip-flopped again* (1900+)

flip-flops *n* A type of open shoe, often made of rubber, with a V-shaped strap that goes between the big toe and the toe next to it : *in a flowered housedress and flip-flops* (1960s+)

flip one's **lid** (or **wig** or **raspberry**) *v phr* **1** To become violently angry; BLOW one's TOP : *When she told him he flipped his lid* **2** To go insane; behave irrationally : *When he started mumbling I was sure he'd flipped his wig/ flipped his lid and blew a whole list of nuclear warhead targets* **3** To show great enthusiasm and approval : *When she finished reading, the crowd flipped its raspberry* (1940s+ Jazz musicians)

flip (or **flap**) one's **lip** *v phr* To talk, esp idly or foolishly (1940s+ Students)

flip on *v phr* To turn on; activate : *was vacationing in Norway recently when he flipped on the telly* (1990s+)

flip on someone *v phr* To rob; hold up (1990s+ Street gang)

flip-out *n* **1** A spell of anger, disturbance, craziness, etc : *Harriet has a minor flip-out and flees* **2** An exciting or wondrous experience : *Her performance was a real flip-out* (1950s+ Bop & cool talk)

flip out *v phr* **1** To evoke an enthusiastic response : *I flipped out these guys with my crazy stories* **2** To display enthusiasm; crow : *My junkie brother continues to flip out about what a cool dude I am* **3** To go insane; FLIP, FREAK OUT : *And I flipped out and went crazy* (1950s+ Bop & cool talk)

flip over *v phr* To be very or overly excited about someone or something : *flipped over the new convertibles*

flip one's **pancake** *v phr* To delight one; inspire on; turn one on : *MTV's Real World does not flip my pancake either* (1990s+)

flipper *n* **1** A hand; FLAPPER : *I manfully gripped his flipper* (1832+) **2** Traders who buy initial public offerings as the market opens and sell them when vigorous trading begins : *It's been a boom year for initial public offerings, just the right environment for "flippers"* (1990s+ Stock market) **3** A person who buys real estate and then turns around and quickly tries to sell it for a profit

flip phone *n phr* A cellular telephone with a mouthpiece that folds up to decrease total size (1990s+)

flipping *adj* Accursed; wretched; DAMN, FREAKING : *Give me the flipping thing and I'll get it fixed* [1911+ British; a euphemism for *fucking*]

flip side *n phr* **1** The reverse surface of a phonograph record; B-SIDE : *a golden oldie on the flip side* **2** The other side of a question, issue, etc : *It is true that the flip side is that/ As usual, there is a flip side. Any of the films revered by men are detested by women* **3** Tomorrow : *catch you on the flip side*

flip the bird *v phr* (also **flash the bird, fly the bird, flick off, flip off**) To make a contemptuous sign with the hand, middle finger extended; GIVE someone THE FINGER : *The six ladies flipped the bird to all their earthling viewers, lifting their minis/ He's like the jerk who whips around traffic, flashing the bird as he passes/ How did it feel to you when Mr Harrington stared you down and flipped you off in that manner?* (1980s+ Students)

flip the script *v phr* To reverse a role or situation; turn a circumstance around : *But is that still true if we flip the script?* (1990s+)

flip-top *See* POP-TOP

FLK (pronounced as separate letters) *n* An abnormal, sick, or ugly child [1960s+ Medical; fr *funny-looking kid*]

float *n* A customer who leaves while one is looking for merchandise (1950s+ Salespersons) *v* **1** To loaf on the job; GOOF OFF (1930+) **2** To disseminate; send out : *Reporters have been told to float their resumes* (1970s+)

floater *n* **1** A person who habitually moves about; vagabond; DRIFTER (1958+) **2** A blunder : *made an error, slip or floater* (1913+ British universities) **3** A slow pitch that appears to float in the air (1906+ Baseball) **4** A corpse taken from the water (1852+)

floating *adj* **1** Drunk (1940s+) **2** Intoxicated with narcotics; HIGH (1950s+ Narcotics & black)

flog *v* To offer for sale; peddle, esp in the sense of public hawking : *I went to the convention to flog a new book/ Motel and bus companies flog special charter rates* [British 1919+ fr armed forces; fr British slang *flog the clock*, "move the clockhands forward in order to deceive," applied later to the illicit selling of military stores]

flog a dead horse *v phr* To expend effort ineffectually or futilely (1870s+) *See* BEAT A DEAD HORSE

◁**flog** one's **meat**▷ *See* BEAT one's MEAT

◁**flong** one's **dong**▷ *v phr* To masturbate : *If it weren't for flonging my dong, I don't know what I'd do* (1970s+)

flood pants *See* HIGH WATERS

flooey *See* GO BLOOEY

floor *v* **1** To knock down; DECK (1812+) **2** To shock, surprise, or hurt to the point of helplessness : *I was floored when some of our players accepted their offer* (1830+) **3** (also **floorboard** or **floor it**) To drive at full speed;

push the throttle pedal to the floorboard; PUT THE PEDAL TO THE METAL : *She floored the Porsche on the freeway and got caught/ You better floor it and get out of here* (1950s+) See CLEAN UP ON someone, IN ON THE GROUND FLOOR, MOP THE FLOOR WITH someone

floozy (Variations: **faloosie** or **floogy** or **floosie** or **floozie** or **flugie**) *n* 1 A self-indulgent, predatory woman, esp one of easy morals; cheap and tawdry woman : *He'd learn more about their psychology by taking a floozie to Atlantic City/ the central figure of an adult whodunit, an obviously no-good floosie* 2 A prostitute : *You been with some floozy, George* [1911+; origin uncertain; said to be an alteration of *flossy*]

flop *n* 1 A place to sleep, esp a cheap and sordid hotel or shelter; FLOPHOUSE : *I went into the flops and the shelters and was shocked/ in a three-dollar-a-week flop* 2 : *My great idea was a total flop* *v* 1 To lie down for rest or sleep; sleep; CRASH : *"Kip," "doss," "flop," "pound your ear," all mean to sleep* (1907+ Hoboes) 2 To fail completely; BOMB : *The show flopped, ran one night only* (1893+) 3 To transfer a police officer from one station to another, one assignment to another, etc : *That's funny, Abbott's giving me advice and he's about to be flopped* (1980s+ Police) See BELLY FLOP

flophouse *n* A cheap and sordid rooming house or hotel, esp one with dormitories for men; chinch pad, FLEABAG : *I'm spending my nights at the flophouse* (1923+)

flopper See BELLY-FLOPPER

flopperoo *n* A particularly spectacular failure; FLOP : *three subdivisions: flop, flopperoo, and kerplunk* (1931+)

floppola *n* A failure, esp a severe one; FLOPPEROO : *And* Fortune's *worst floppola seems apocalyptic. Who will care for the poor?* (1940s+)

flop sweat *n phr* An actor's anxiety; fear of failure : *Flop sweat is what an actor gets when he's nervous on stage/ Lights, camera, and flop-sweat* (1960s+)

flow *v* To menstruate : *am flowing, so can't do inverted poses*

flow, the See GO WITH THE FLOW

flower child *n phr* A member of the hippie movement or counterculture, who typically advocated love, peace, and nonviolence : *a caricature of a London flower child who is about as interesting as a boiled potato/ Woodstock is long over, and the bloom has gone off these flower children/ the flower people of the late 1960s, mostly middle-class kids trying to create a gaudy secular religion* (1960s+) [plural is *flower children* or *flower people*]

flower power *n phr* The influence and merits of the pacifistic, altruistic values of the 1960s hippie movement

flub *n* 1 A stupid blunderer; LUMMOX, KLUTZ : *Pick up your feet and don't be such a flub* 2 : *The flub, as generally defined, is a mistake* *v* 1 To blunder; err; commit a gaffe; GOOF : *I flubbed as soon as I opened my big mouth* 2 To ruin by blundering; spoil with mistakes : *She flubbed the introduction, but did okay afterwards* 3 To avoid work or duty; shirk; GOOF OFF (1920s+)

flubdub *n* 1 Incompetence; ineptitude : *They would remove much of the amateur flub-dub* 2 An awkward person; blunderer; GOOF-UP, KLUTZ *v* : *I flubdubbed the stage entrance* [1920s+; first sense found by 1888 in the sense "foolishness, bunk, hot air"]

flub the dub *v phr* 1 To avoid one's work or duty; shirk; GOLDBRICK : *He learned to flub the dub, but still stay pals with his associates* 2 To think, work, move, etc, sluggishly and haplessly 3 To fail by blundering; ruin one's best chances : *I think I flubbed the dub again, bidding so late* (esp WWII armed forces)

flub-up *n* 1 A blunder : *The attempt was one big flub-up* 2 A blunderer; GOOF-UP, KLUTZ : *a kooky police cadet flub-up* (1950s+)

fluff *n* ◁1▷ A girl or young woman • Found in the sense "female pubic hair, bush, beaver" by the 1890s : *A wan little fluff steals a dress so as to look sweet in the eyes of her boyfriend/ Thanks for the great interview with Cindy Crawford. It brings the word fluff to a new low* (1903+) 2 An oral error, esp one made by an actor, announcer, etc; lapsus linguae : *A hell of a fluff, talking about Montezuma's revenge to the president of Mexico* (1891+) 3 A blunder; misplay (1920s+) *v* : *Show me an actor that never fluffed a line* See BIT OF FLUFF, GIVE someone THE FLUFF

fluffhead *n* A frivolous or stupid young woman; DITZ : *To judge masculinity you need a woman, and not some little fluffhead either* (1970s+)

fluff-off *n* A sluggard; shirker; GOLDBRICK, GOOF-OFF (WWII armed forces)

fluff off *v phr* To avoid work or duty; shirk; GOOF OFF [WWII armed forces; probably a euphemism for *fuck off*]

fluff someone off *v phr* To snub or cut someone; reject someone haughtily : *He thought he was pretty good, so he fluffed us all off* (1940s+)

flugie See FLOOZY

fluke *n* A good or bad stroke of luck; an extraordinary and unpredictable event : *My winning was just a fluke/ We got onto that flight by a fluke* [1857+; origin unknown, but perhaps fr *fluke*, "flatfish," by way of an early 1800s British slang sense of *flat*, "easy dupe, victim," altered in billiards jargon to *fluke*, to characterize the seeming chicanery of a good stroke of luck]

fluky or **flukey** *adj* Uncertain, unpredictable, and often unexpected : *It would have been a very fluky shot, even if he happened to have the camera in his hand* (1867+)

flummadiddle *n* Nonsense; foolishness; BOSH (1854+)

flummox *n* A failure; disaster; FUCK-UP : *The solemn commemoration was a total flummox* (1851+) *v* To spoil; upset; confound : *Fu-Manchu tries to abduct a missionary who has flummoxed his plans in China* (1837+) [fr British dialect, "maul, bewilder"]

flummoxed *adj* Confused and turbulent; baffling or baffled : *"One never knows, do one," I said, and left him flummoxed* (1837+)

flunk *n* : *I've got three passes and two flunks v* **1** To fail; make a botch of : *I tried selling, but flunked at that* **2** To fail an examination, a course, etc; BUST : *He flunked the final but passed the course* **3** To give a student a failing grade [1823+ College; origin unknown; perhaps a blend of *fail* with *funk*, perhaps echoic of a dull collapse]

flunk out *v phr* **1** To fail; make a botch **2** To be dismissed from school for failing work : *The great man had flunked out of Wittenberg* (1838+)

flush *adj* Having plenty of money; affluent, esp temporarily; rich : *It took money, and the jazzman wasn't ever too flush* (1603+) *v* **1** To stay away from class; CUT *(1940s+ College students)* **2** FLUNK *(1960s+ College students)* **3** To reject or ignore someone socially (1960s+) *See* FOUR-FLUSH, IN A FLUSH

flusher *n* A toilet : *right in the old flusher* (1970s+) *See* FOUR-FLUSHER

flush it *interj* An exclamation of contempt and disbelief : *I started to explain, but the cop told me to flush it* (1970s+) *v phr* To fail a course, examination, etc; FLUNK *(1960s+ College students)*

fly *adj* **1** Clever; knowing; alert; shrewd (1811+) **2** Stylish; very attractive; SHARP, SUPERFLY : *driving a Cadillac that's fly/ They tell each other they're fly when they look sharp* *(1900+ Black) v* **1** To act in a strange or bizarre way : *The broad must be flying on something (1960s+ Narcotics)* **2** To feel the effects of narcotic intoxication : *About a minute after the fix he was flying (1960s+ Narcotics)* **3** To succeed; persuade; GO OVER • Often in the negative : *They're experts on what will fly and what won't/ He glanced at Keenan to see if that statement was going to fly* (1970s+) **4** To run or travel very fast [the first adjective sense, "clever, alert, etc," is of unknown origin, though it is conjectured that it may refer to the difficulty of catching a *fly* in midair, that it may be cognate with *fledge* and hence mean "accomplished, pro-

ven, seasoned," and that it is a corruption of *fla*, a shortening of *flash;* the third verb sense, "succeed, persuade, etc," is fr a cluster of jokes and phrases having to do with the Wright Brothers' and others' efforts to get something off the ground and make it *fly;* the two adjective senses involve either a survival or a revival of an early 19th-century British underworld term of unknown origin] *See* BARFLY, CATCH FLIES, FRUIT FLY, LET FLY, NO FLIES ON, ON THE FLY

fly blind *v phr* To proceed or make decisions without enough information : *Like most benefits executives, she is largely flying blind when it comes to comparing the performances of health plans (1920s+ Aviation use)*

fly-boy *n* An aircraft pilot, esp an intrepid one in the US Air Force : *The generals are no full-throttle "fly-boys" (WWII armed forces)*

flyby *n* A ceremonial or demonstrational passage overhead by an airplane or a group of airplanes : *They saluted the President with a flyby of the newest jets* (1950s+)

fly-by-night *adj* Undependable and dishonest : *fly-by-night correspondence school*

fly by the seat of one's **pants** *v phr* **1** To pilot an airplane by feel and instinct rather than by instruments : *The old-time barnstormers had to fly by the seat of their pants (1930s+ Aviators)* **2** To proceed or work by instinct and improvisation, without formal guides or instructive experience : *The teachers are not trained to recognize it. They're flying by the seat of their pants/ Every case is different, and every investigator ends up flying by the seat of his (or her) pants* (1970s+) *See* SEAT-OF-THE-PANTS

fly-chaser *n* An outfielder *(1930s+ Baseball)*

fly high *v phr* To live in an affluent fashion; live as a successful person (1906+)

flying *adj* Useless; worthless • Used to emphasize terms meaning "something of little value," all probably variations and euphemisms of a *flying fuck* (1940s+) *See* HAVE THE RAG ON

flying boxcar *n* An airplane, esp military (1918+)

flying colors *See* WITH FLYING COLORS

◁**flying frig**▷ *See* TAKE A FLYING FUCK

◀**a flying fuck**▶ *n phr* Something of very little value; a DAMN, DIDDLY, a FUCK, a SHIT : *Your take on this isn't worth a flying fuck* [1800+; the dated instance, describing a sex act done on horseback, occurs in a broadside ballad called *New Feats of Horsemanship;* the semantics are no more nor less clear than those of simple *fuck*] *See* NOT GIVE A DAMN, TAKE A FLYING FUCK

fly in the ointment *n phr* Sticky problem; major inconvenience [1833; after Ecclesiastes 10:1, "Dead flies cause the ointment of the apothecary to send forth a stinking savor"]

fly off the handle *v phr* To lose one's temper; LOSE one's COOL (*1825+*)

fly on the wall, a *n phr* An unseen observer; inconspicuous witness : *A lot of people in NATO would have given a lot to be a fly on the wall at the Warsaw Pact discussions* (*1949+*)

fly out *v phr* To hit a fly ball that is caught for an out (*1893+ Baseball*)

fly right *v phr* To be honest, dependable, etc : *He's my son. I want him to fly right* (*1940s+*)

fly the coop *v phr* To leave, esp to escape from confinement : *He had flown the coop via a fire-escape/ Our Dubie done flew the coop* (*1910+*)

fly trap *n phr* The mouth (*1795+*)

fly under the radar *v phr* KEEP A LOW PROFILE : *We do our best to fly under the radar of the media and professions so they don't know what hit them until it's too late, Reed told them* (*1990s+*)

FOAF (FOHF) *n* : *These colorful experiences always seem to happen to a FOAF (friend of a friend), hardly ever a person with a name, address, and telephone number* (*1990s+*)

fodder *See* BUNG FODDER, CANNON FODDER

foe one one *n phr* Information; facts; the 411, the SCOOP, the SKINNY [1990s+ Black; fr *411*, the telephone number called for customers' telephone listings]

fofarraw *See* FOOFOORAW

fog *v* 1 (also **fog it**) To run; speed; hurry (*1914+ Western*) 2 To throw with great force : *Ole Diz was in his prime then, fogging a fastball* (*1930s+ Baseball*) 3 To attack; shoot • Also recorded as 1920s racketeer talk : *I takes me heat an' fogs 'em* (*1920s+ Western*) [origin unknown; probably a substitution for *smoke* in all senses] *See* IN A FOG

Fogeyville *n* Old age; senility : *I mean we are talking Fogeyville here!* (*1990s+*)

fogged out *adj phr* Befuddled and deluded by narcotics : *A lot of people were fogged out and superegotistic in that drugged-out way* (*1970s+ Narcotics*)

foggiest, the *See* NOT HAVE THE FOGGIEST

Foggy Bottom *n phr* The US Department of State : *little affinity for the "career boys" of Foggy Bottom* [1950+; fr the name of a marshy region in Washington, DC, where the State Department and other federal buildings are located; also an allusion to the murkiness of some policies and pronouncements]

fogy or **fogey** *n* 1 An old person; any very conservative, outdated person; DODO : *College students today are young fogies* (*1785+*) 2 A military longevity allowance, awarded for units of service : *He got his pension and eight fogies* (*1881+ Armed forces*) [origin uncer-

tain; perhaps fr French *fougeux*, "fierce, fiery," referring to the doughty spirit of an invalid soldier, whence *fogy*, "fierce, fiery," found by the 1860s; veteran soldiers were called *foggies* in the late 1700s, perhaps because they were regarded as moss-covered with age, *fog* being Scots dialect for "moss"]

fold *v* 1 To fail or close, esp in business or show business • The usual term earlier was *fold up* : *If the club folds* (*1930s+*) 2 To collapse; surrender; give way; CAVE : *After the President jawboned him unmercifully, the Senator folded* (*1250+*) 3 To drop out of a poker game, indicated by putting all one's cards face down on the table (*1940s+ Poker*)

folding *n* Money; FOLDING MONEY : *The socialites lose a handsome wallet stuffed with a liberal supply of folding* (*1930s+*) *See* GREEN FOLDING

folding money *n phr* (Variations: **cabbage** or **green** or **lettuce** may replace **money**) Paper money; banknotes, esp in large quantities : *They leave their folding money at home/ lacks the folding green to pick up a nightclub tab* (*1920s+*)

fold out *v phr* To abdicate responsibilities; slough off; COP OUT : *He was not a guy who would just fold out* [1980s+; fr the act of *folding*, dropping out of a poker game]

folkie *n* A folk singer or folk-music devotee : *The precious youth audience was lost to the folkies and the rockers* (*1960s+*)

folks *n* 1 A band of hoodlums (*1880s+ Underworld*) 2 A gang; one's own gang : *"What does 'folks' mean now?" Grober asks. In unison: "Gangs"* (*1990s+ Street gangs*) 3 Parents • Usu used affectionately : *I want to introduce her to my folks* (*1940s+*) 4 Ordinary people; common people : JUST FOLKS (*1619+*)

follow one's nose *v phr* To go in the most obvious direction; go straight along (*1620+*)

follow something straight out the window *v phr* To go to the extreme; follow obsessively : *When she gets hold of an idea, she'll follow it straight out the window* (*1980s+*)

follow through (or **up**) *n* : *What's the logical follow-through to what he said?* *v phr* To carry on with the next useful action; finish an action completely; pursue : *Follow up these hints, and you'll find the answer* (*1940s+*)

follow something up *v phr* 1 To carry one's investigation further; pursue a lead 2 (also **follow**) To do something appropriate subsequent to something else, or better than something already done : *How will she follow up her bestseller?/ I can't follow that line* (*1940s+*)

fonk *See* FUNK

fonky *See* FUNKY

food *See* BUNNY FOOD, FAST FOOD, JUNK FOOD, SOUL FOOD, SQUIRREL-FOOD

foodaholic *n* A compulsive eater; glutton (*1980s+*) *See* -AHOLIC

food coma *n phr* A state of uncomfortableness and drowsiness caused by overeating, esp of unhealthful food : *Most of us go into a food coma after Thanksgiving dinner*

foodie *adj* : *San Francisco, foodie capital of the USA n* A person who pays unusual attention to food, cuisine, etc; devotee of healthy gourmet cooking and eating : *To be a proper foodie, it little matters where you live as long as you own a "serious" vegetable knife* [1980s+; perhaps modeled on *groupie*]

fooey *See* PHOOEY

foofooraw or **fofarraw** or **foo-foo-rah** or **foofaraw** (FOO̅ fǝ raw) *n* 1 A loud disturbance; uproar : *Ivar, what's all the foofaraw about the Ellerbee case?* 2 Gaudy clothing and accessories, esp the latter 3 Ostentation; proud show : *The refreshing thing about it is the lack of drumbeating and foo-foo-rah* [1848+ Western; origin uncertain; perhaps fr Spanish *fanfarrón*, "braggart"; perhaps fr French *frou-frous*, "frills"]

fool *n* An adept or enthusiast in what is indicated : *Lindy was a flying fool* [1920s+; perhaps because the person is devoted to the extent of *foolishness*] *See* TOMFOOL

fool around *v phr* 1 To pass one's time idly; putter about; loaf (*1875+*) 2 To joke and tease; KID AROUND : *Mark, stop fooling around and get to work* (*1875+*) 3 To adventure sexually, esp adulterously; PLAY AROUND, SLEEP AROUND : *He had never fooled around or seen a prostitute until he came to us/ As I told Lipranzer a long time ago, Carolyn did not fool around* (*1970s+*)

fool around with *v phr* To play or tamper with; coquette with; fiddle with : *I told you not to fool around with that gun; now you've shot Aunt Bessie/ Better not fool around with him, he's a karate black belt* (*1875+*)

◁**foop**▷ *v* To do homosexual sex acts [1970s+ College students; probably a backward version of British *poof*, "male homosexual, effeminate male," fr early 1900s Australian; perhaps fr the exclamation *poof* or *pooh*, regarded as effeminate]

◁**fooper**▷ *n* A homosexual (*1970s+ College students*)

foot *See* BIG FOOT, FLATFOOT, GIVE someone THE FOOT, HAVE ONE FOOT IN THE GRAVE, HEAVY-FOOT, HOTFOOT, PUT one's FOOT IN IT, PUT one's FOOT IN one's MOUTH, SHOOT oneself IN THE FOOT, TENDERFOOT

footed *See* LEAD-FOOTED, LIGHT-FOOTED

foot-in-mouth disease *n phr* The uttering of embarrassing, stupid, or indiscreet speech : *Pat Robertson, who regularly displays symptoms of foot-in-mouth disease* [1960s+; blend of the veterinary term *hoof-and-mouth disease* and the idiom *put one's foot in one's mouth*; *put one's foot in it*, "blunder foolishly," is found by 1858]

foot it *v phr* 1 To walk : *A bus is OK during non-rush-hours if you've been footing it too long* 2 To escape by running; BEAT IT : *He stopped all of a sudden and said, "Foot it, Sonny! Foot it!"* (*1831+*)

footprint *n* 1 A history of activity; record; TRACK RECORD : *Reporters were wondering about the Justice's footprint* (*1990s+*) 2 The horizontal space needed for a machine, appliance, etc : *The new computers have a very small footprint* (*1990s+*)

foot soldier *n* A lower-ranking member of a corporation, regime, etc : *Goth's role as an SS officer and faithful foot soldier of the Third Reich is preserved/ filtered through the hazy surmises of the Cleveland footsoldiers* (*1990s+*)

foot the bill *v phr* To pay the charges; PICK UP THE TAB (*1819+*)

footwork *See* FANCY FOOTWORK

fooy *See* PHOOEY

foozle *n* 1 An error; BONER (*1890s+*) 2 A conservative, out-of-date person, esp an old man; DODO, FOGY (*1855+*) *v* To blunder; spoil by bungling; botch : *I rather foozled my first attempt at acting* (*1890s+*) [Noun sense 2 is perhaps a humorous pronunciation of *fossil*]

for all it (or **one**) **is worth** *adv phr* To the utmost; with all one's might : *She's playing the wronged woman game for all she's worth/ Push that idea for all it's worth* (*1899+*)

for a loop *See* THROW someone FOR A LOOP

for a song *modifier* For very little money; cheap : *got the Beetle for a song*

for crying out loud (or **in a bucket**) *interj* An exclamation of emphasis, surprise, disbelief, impatience, etc; FOR THE LOVE OF PETE : *For crying out loud, what half-assed thing has he done now?* [1920s+; a euphemism for *for Christ's sake*]

for free *adv phr* Without charge; gratis; free gratis : *They gave him a sandwich absolutely for free* [1940s+; based on Yiddish *far gornisht*, "for nothing"]

forget about it (also **fuhgedaboudit**, **fuhgeddabaudit**) *interj* An exclamation of dismissal and scorn • The variants represent New York City pronunciations : *Omerta. The code of silence for a sacred brotherhood. Well, fuhgedaboudit. Every time you turn around lately, a member of the Mafia is testifying at a trial/ The latest on Joey Buttafuoco's comedic debut: Fuhgeddabaudit* [1940s+; said to be also a euphemism for *fuck it*]

forget it *interj* 1 An injunction to put something out of one's hopes, concern, etc, esp because it is impossible : *If you thought you* *were next in line around here, forget it/ Forget it, she never did intend to go/ I can get up there most of the time, but in winter, forget it* **2** An exclamation of pardon; a token of forgiveness; DON'T GIVE IT A SECOND THOUGHT : *Hell no, I didn't mind. Forget it* (*1900+*)

forget you *interj* **1** An invitation or command to leave; BUG OFF **2** An exclamation of rejection or refusal; NO WAY (*1970s+ Teenagers*)

for one's **health** *adv phr* Lightly or frivolously; for one's delightful good • Always used ironically and in the negative : *I didn't make this damn stupid trip for my health, you know* (*1900+*)

for (or **fer**) **instance** *n phr* An example; an instance : *I'd understand the point better if you gave me a couple of concrete for instances* [1940s+; fr a Yiddish pattern]

forkball *n* **1** A pitch thrown from a forklike finger grip that drops sharply as it comes to the plate **2** (also **forked ball**) A spitball; spitter (*1920s+ Baseball*)

for keeps *adv phr* Forever; permanently : *They put him away for keeps/ She wanted to be married for keeps* (*1884+*) *See* PLAY FOR KEEPS

◁**forking**▷ *adj* Wretched; disgusting : *I won't eat this forking stuff adv* Very; extremely : *He sounded forking mad* [1940s+; a euphemism for *fucking*]

fork over (or **up** or **out**) *v phr* To pay; give; contribute : *Fork up the cash/ I imagine he used a picture to make you fork over the dough* (*first form 1835+*)

forks *n* Fingers : *Get your forks off that* (*1848+*) *See* RAIN CATS AND DOGS

for laughs (or **kicks**) *adv phr* For simple pleasure, usu a wicked pleasure : *Girl mobsters beating up other girls simply for laughs* (*1940s+*)

for openers (or **starters**) *adv phr* As a beginning; as a first move or suggestion : *For openers, there's the approach via the Staten Island ferry/ So, try this for openers/ expensive, for starters* [1960s+; fr the *openers*, "cards of a certain value," required in draw poker for beginning the betting]

for peanuts (or **chicken feed**) *modifier* For very little money; cheap : *a new dress for peanuts*

for Pete's sake (also **pity's sake** or **the love of Mike**) *interj* An exclamation of emphasis, surprise, impatience, disbelief, dismay, etc; FOR CRYING OUT LOUD : *For Pete's sake, get moving!* [1903+; euphemisms for *for God's sake, for Christ's sake, for fuck's sake*]

for real *adj phr* Believably existent; as good or bad as seems; authentic : *But if you ask if they are for real, the answer is right there/ I often wondered if the bastard was for real adv phr* Really; truly : *I'm gonna for real do it, right*

now [1940s+; based on Yiddish *far emmes*, "for true?"]

for serious *adj phr* : *He was for serious but she wasn't adv phr* Seriously; with a sober intent : *The Yanks took the field for serious* [1950s+; perhaps based on *for real*]

◁**for shit**▷ *adv phr* At all; in the least degree; to save one's neck, worth a damn : *They can't drive for shit* (*1940s+*)

for starters *modifier* To start or begin with (*1873+*), *See* FOR OPENERS

for (or **fer**) **sure** (or **shure** or **shurr**) *adv phr* Definitely; certainly • This old phrase was briefly resurrected in the California Valley Girls talk of the 1980s : *He is for sure a nerd affirmation* Yes : *When he asked if I'd do it I said fer sure I would* (*1553+*)

for the birds *adj phr* Inferior; undesirable; of small worth; LOUSY : *I won't buy it. It's for the birds/ A single bed is for single men, it's for the birds* [WWII armed forces; a euphemistic shortening of *shit for the birds*; because some birds eat animal feces, it is the equivalent of *bullshit* or *horseshit*]

for (or **just for**) **the hell of it** *adv phr* For no definite or useful reason; for fun; casually : *He does it, apparently, just for the adrenaline hell of it* (*1934+*)

for the long ball *See* GO FOR THE LONG BALL

for (or **over**) **the long haul** *adv phr* For a long while; for a period of difficulty and strain : *The slump in sales of women's apparel is here for the long haul* [1930s+; the *long haul*, "a transcontinental run," is found in bus drivers' talk by 1938]

for the love of Pete (or **Mike**) *interj* An exclamation of emphasis, surprise, impatience, disbelief, dismay, etc; FOR CRYING OUT LOUD : *I already did it, for the love of Pete!* (*1910+*)

fortysomething *modifier* : *the fortysomething generation/ fortysomething self-indulgence n* A person between forty and fifty years old; BABY BOOMER : *The fortysomething reminisced about seeing them on the same bill with Sonny and Cher* [late 1980s+; based on *Thirtysomething*, the title of a television series]

forty (or **six**) **ways to Sunday** *adv phr* In every possible manner, direction, etc; comprehensively : *She had him beat forty ways to Sunday* [1840+; origin unknown]

forty winks *n phr* A short sleep; nap : *He caught forty winks and perked right up* (*1828+*)

FOS (pronounced as separate letters) *n* A patient whose symptoms are psychosomatic [1980s+ Medical; abbreviation of *full of shit*]

fossil *n* An old or very conservative person; ALTER KOCKER, FOGY : *If I got to kiss old fossils to hold this job I'm underpaid* (*1850s+*)

fotog *See* PHOTOG

fouled up *adj phr* **1** Spoiled by bungling; confused; hopelessly tangled; FUCKED UP : *never seen anything more fouled up than what happened yesterday at the White House* **2** Damaged; impaired : *The kids were fouled up, came from bad homes, went to bad schools* [1940s+; a euphemism for *fucked up*]

foulmouthed *adj* Obscene and profane in speech; filthy : *a foulmouthed retort* (*1596+*)

foul-up *n* **1** A confused, tangled, hopeless situation; botch : *It's supposed to be a concert series, but it's a total foul-up* **2** A person who consistently blunders; bungler; FUCK-UP : *Why put that notorious foul-up in charge?* [1940s+; a euphemism for *fuck-up*]

foul up *v phr* To ruin and confuse a project, assignments, etc; display one's ineptitude and futility; FUCK UP, SNAFU : *I fouled up my very first chance to be a reporter* [1940s+; a euphemism for *fuck up*; possibly of naval origin, since *foul* is used of ropes, lines, anchors, sea bottoms, etc, in ways not characteristic of nonnautical speech]

foundry *See* NUTHOUSE

four *See* TEN FOUR

four-bagger *n* A home run : *It was Bobby's 31st four-bagger and his fourth at Ebbets Field* (*1883+ Baseball*)

four-banger *n* A four-cylinder motor or car (*1950s+ Hot rodders*)

four bits *n phr* Half a dollar; 50 cents [1840s+; originally a *bit* was a Mexican or Spanish *real*, worth 12½ cents, or a part of a more valuable coin, such that eight would make a dollar; ultimately fr 18th-century British slang *bit*, "a small piece of money"]

four-by-four *n* A four-wheel-drive vehicle having four forward gears (*1940s+ Army & truckers*)

four-corner town *n phr* A very small town; a crossroads : *We were flabbergasted by these four-corner towns with four bars* (*1980s+*)

four-eyes *n* A person who wears eyeglasses (*1874+*)

four-flush *modifier* : *Four-flushing hustlers who really knew how to gamble* *v* **1** To live by sponging off others, or by pretense and fraud **2** To cheat; swindle; victimize [1896+; fr a poker player's attempt to bluff when he has *four* cards of one suit showing and one of another suit not showing]

four-flusher *n* A bluffer or fraud; cheat; swindler (*1904+*)

four-letter man *n phr* **1** A stupid man • From the four letters of *dumb* **2** A detestable man; a contemptible wretch; PRICK, SHIT • From the four letters of *shit* (*1920s+*)

four-letter word *n phr* Any of several short English words generally regarded as obscene or offensive (*1920s+*)

four nines *n phr* Something pure or very nearly pure : *That is four nines, or 99.99 pure gold* (*1970s+*)

four-O *adj* Perfect; splendid; A-OK [WWII Navy; fr the point system used in Navy efficiency ratings, where 4.0 is the top rating; it is also the numerical equivalent of the grade A in most colleges]

411, the *n phr* The facts; the information; FOE ONE ONE, the SCOOP, the SKINNY : *The 4–1–1 on Urban Cool* [1990s+ Black; fr *411*, the telephone number called for information on customers' telephone listings]

four on the floor *n phr* A gearshift lever emerging from the floor of a car and controlling four speeds; hence standard as distinct from automatic shift : *This little baby's got four on the floor and leather bucket seats* (*1970s+*)

four-pointer *n* **1** A grade of A for an examination or course **2** A superior student [1960s+ College students; fr the grade-point system where an A rates at four points]

four sheets to the wind *See* THREE SHEETS TO THE WIND

four-time loser *See* THREE-TIME LOSER

four-topper *n* A restaurant table for four people : *four-topper by the window*

four-wheeler *n* An automobile; CAGE (*1960s+ Truckers*)

four wide ones *n phr* A base on balls; a walk, esp an intentional pass (*1970s+ Baseball*)

fox *n* A beautiful, sexually attractive woman or, in teenage use, man (*1940s+ Teenagers & black*) *v* To deceive; mislead; outwit; OUTFOX : *He tried to fox me with that phony accent, and did* (*1631+*) [fr *foxy*]

foxhole *n* A hole in which one conceals oneself, esp one dug for that purpose by a soldier (*WWII armed forces*)

foxy *adj* Attractive; stylish; sexually desirable : *She was 22 years old, a real foxy little chick with auburn hair/ She must be one foxy lady* (*1895+ College students*)

fracture *v* **1** To elicit loud laughter from; LAY THEM IN THE AISLES : *We're a riot, hey. We play all kinds of funny stuff. We fracture the people* **2** To evoke a strong reaction : *That flips me out and fractures me, man* (*1940s+*)

fractured *adj* Drunk (*1940s+*)

frag *v* **1** To kill or wound someone, esp a detested officer of one's own unit, typically by throwing a fragmentation grenade at him **2** To kill; ICE, WASTE : *If I hadn't've done it, he would've fragged me* (*Vietnam War armed forces*)

fragged *adj* Ruined; blown-out : *countless fragged Ferrari engines, including two that disintegrated under a CD tester's heavy foot* (*1970s+ Car racing*)

fraidy (or **'fraidy**) **cat** *n phr* A timorous person, esp a boy; coward (*1910+*)

frame *n* **1** The human body; physique; build, esp that of a woman (*1600+*) **2** A heterosexual man attractive to homosexuals; hunk (*1950s+ Homosexuals*) **3** A unit of a game or other contest; stanza : *Mel Queen lined a single to right field to open that frame* (*1910+*) **4** The incrimination of an innocent person with false evidence; FRAME-UP : *just the victim of a frame* (*1914+*) *v* : *I was framed*

frame-up *n* **1** The incrimination of an innocent person with false evidence : *I'll prove to you it's a frame-up* (*1913+*) **2** A display of goods for sale (*1940s+ Pitchmen*)

frame up *v phr* To concoct; fabricate : *What lie are you going to frame up for your father* [*1899+;* perhaps fr the carpenter's term for erecting the *frame* of a new building]

frame someone up *v phr* To incriminate an innocent person with false evidence : *They couldn't get him legally, so they framed him up with a phony burglary charge* (*1900+*)

franchise, the *n phr* A superstar athlete who constitutes the drawing and earning power of a team : *He's not just the front runner, he's the franchise/ There goes the franchise* (*1980s+ Sports*)

frank *n* A frankfurter; WEENIE (*1920s+*)

Franken- *combining word* Designating what is indicated as being genetically engineered or otherwise strangely produced : *Frankenchips/ Frankenfood/ Frankentomato* [*1990s+;* shortening of *Frankenstein,* name of the scientist in Mary Shelley's novel]

Franklin *n* A hundred-dollar bill; C- NOTE : *He peels off another five Franklins* [*1990s+;* fr its portrait of Benjamin *Franklin*]

frantic *adj* **1** Excellent; wonderful; COOL **2** Conventional; bourgeois; UNCOOL : *The man who cares is now derided for being "frantic"* (*1940+ Jazz musicians*)

frat *n* **1** A college fraternity (*1895+ College students*) **2** (also **frat rat**) A fraternity member (*1895+ College students*) **3** A male student who conforms to middle-class norms of conduct and dress : *A "frat" is a youth who dresses neatly and conforms to the accepted patterns* (*1960s+ Teenagers*)

fraternize *v* To associate closely with inhabitants of an enemy country, esp to consort sexually with the women (*WWII armed forces*)

frau (FROU) *n* One's wife : *and escort your incomparable frau to a tea dance/ his reward from the frau* [*1902+;* fr German]

frazzle, to a *adv phr* Completely; totally; to a ruined condition : *After the marathon I was beat to a frazzle* [*1865+;* fr dialect *frazzle,* "frayed end of a rope"]

frazzled *adj* **1** (also **on the frazz**) Exhausted; tired in nerve and flesh; PLAYED OUT : *He was frazzled after three weeks without a break* (*1872+*) **2** Drunk (*1940s+*)

freak *n* ◁1▷ A strange or eccentric person (*1891+*) **2** An expert; specialist; very good student (*1895+ College students*) **3** A devotee or enthusiast; buff, FAN (*1908+*) ◀4▶ A male homosexual : *"Freak" is a homosexual* (*1940s+ Jazz musicians*) **5** HIPPIE (*1960s+*) **6** An attractive person (*1990s+ Teenagers*) *v* **1** To behave strangely and disorientedly as if intoxicated by a psychedelic drug; FREAK OUT : *His publisher for the last two books "sort of freaked" when they got a look at this one* (*1960s+*) **2** (also **freak off**) To do violent and deviant sex acts (*1960s+ Prostitutes*)

-freak *combining word* A devotee or enthusiast; addict; BUG, buff, NUT : *plant freak/ radio freak/ porn-freak* See ACID FREAK, ECOFREAK, JESUS FREAK, METH HEAD, SPEED-FREAK

freak-ass *adj* Strange; freakish : *Some freak-ass accident* (*1990s+*)

freaker *n* phone phreak (*1990s+*)

freaking *adj* Wretched; accursed; DAMN, FUCKING : *who's got so much freaking talent it just turns your stomach/ all the freaking way to the bank* *adv* : *The ball just freaking found its way through n* Violent and deviant sex acts : *And there were numerous reports of lewd behavior; "freaking," after all, is a slang term for adventuresome sex* (*1960s+*) [*1920s+;* a euphemism for *fucking*]

freak-out *n* **1** An instance of freaking out : *a period which one feminist writer has called one of "mass freak-outs all over the place"/ the same freakouts, the same strange clothes* **2** A person who is freaked out **3** A frightening or nightmarish drug experience; BAD TRIP, BUMMER **4** A congregation of hippies (*1960s+ Narcotics*)

freak out (or **up**) *v phr* **1** To have intense and disturbing hallucinations and other reactions from psychedelic drugs **2** To go out of touch with reality, with or without narcotics; become irrational, esp frantically so; be intoxicated; FLIP OUT : *plus the chance to freak out, speak in tongues or talk nonsense/ I saw those golden arches and I freaked out, because I'd just seen the buttes and all that great stuff* **3** To become very excited and exhilarated, as if intoxicated with narcotics **4** To abandon conventional values and attitudes; DROP OUT (*1960s+ Narcotics*)

freak someone out *v phr* To cause someone to show the irrationality, lethargy, excitement, withdrawal, etc, of a psychedelic experience : *The heavy metal sound freaked him out* (*1960s+ Narcotics*)

freak show *n* Any show or event that is in bad taste; also, a person who behaves in a ludicrous, bizarre, or dehumanizing way : *Britney, the freak show*

freak trick *n phr* A man who demands very exotic or brutal sexual activity : *the victim of a "freak trick," a customer who gets his kicks from brutally beating girls (1970s+ Prostitutes)*

freaky *adj* Having the qualities of a freak or a freak-out; FAR OUT : *I think it would be freaky to have an affair with my barber/ There is nothing bohemian, or beat, or hippie, or freaky about them. They are straights, uptight (1960s+ Narcotics)*

◁**fred**▷ *n* A despised person; GEEK, JERK : *When Mark missed an easy shot, his friends called him a fred* [1980s+ Students; fr the name of a character in the television show and movie *The Flintstones*]

Freddie Mac *n phr* The Federal Home Loan Mortgage Corporation, which buys mortgages from lenders *(1980s+)*

Freddy *n* An employee of the National Forest Service : *"Not much to hunt around here with that type of ammo except Freddies." "Freddies?" "Employees of the Forest Service, that's what the eco-terrorists call us" (1990s+)*

free *See* FOR FREE, HOME FREE

freeball *adj* Of a male, not wearing underwear

freebase or **free base it** *v* or *v phr* To use cocaine by heating it and inhaling the smoke, its most powerful essence : *The addiction problem seems to be compounded by the fact that so many cokeheads are freebasing it (1970s+ Narcotics)*

freebie or **freebee** or **freeby** *n* Anything given or enjoyed free of charge : *That meal was a freebie and it didn't cost me anything/ Holiday Inn bartenders are enjoined from giving freebies to customers, no matter how much they spend (1900+ Black)*

free fall *n phr* An extremely rapid and unhindered descent • First used of a rocket returning to earth; then mainly of a parachutist who had not yet opened the parachute : *the bank is trying to slow the free fall of the Mexican peso/ the Russian economy is in free fall (1919+)*

freeload *n* : *During the depression women free loads were rare* *v* To be fed, entertained, supported, etc, without charge; live parasitically; SPONGE : *They will successfully free load the rest of their lives/ who gives freeloading off a famous father a bad name (1940s+)*

freeloader *n* **1** A person who freeloads; MOOCHER, SPONGER : *Congressmen are great freeloaders* **2** A gathering or party with free refreshments : *Somebody was tossing a freeloader over on Park Avenue (1930s+)*

freeloading *modifier* : *my freeloading cousins/ your freeloading pals* *v* Eating, drinking, etc, without paying : *Free loading has diminished (1940s+)*

free lunch *n phr* Something had without paying for it; an uncompensated pleasure; a perquisite or gratuity • The date shows the first occurrence of the saloon-food sense mentioned in the etymology : *pushing the free lunch* [1854+; fr the former custom of giving customers free food called *free lunch* in saloons] *See* THERE'S NO FREE LUNCH

free-range *adj* Unconfined; free to roam : *The Mall of America is not just one more amalgam of frozen-yogurt stands and packs of free-range adolescents in Guess jeans* [1960s+; fr the distinction between *free-range* chickens and battery chickens, which are raised in confinement]

free ride *n phr* **1** A base on balls; a walk *(1980s+ Baseball)* **2** A card received without betting, because no one wished to start the betting on the previous round *(1940s+ Poker)* **3** Something received without paying *(1899+) See* GET A FREE RIDE

free-rider *n* A nonunion worker who benefits from the pay and advantages gained by a union *(1950s+ Labor union)*

freeside *adv* Outside the walls of a prison : *He yearns to live freeside again (1950s+ Prison)*

free skate *n phr* Something simple and easy; PICNIC, PIECE OF CAKE : *This lawsuit isn't a free skate* [1990s+; fr the skating-rink custom of occasionally allowing an unpaid period of skating]

free ticket *n phr* **1** General freedom of action, esp of forbidden action; license; carte blanche : *He thinks the uniform gives him a free ticket to be a shitheel (1940s+)* **2** (also **free ride, free transit, free transportation**) A base on balls; walk *(1917+ Baseball)*

free-wheeling *modifier* **1** : *Jonathan himself tries opium, hash, freewheeling sex, gliders* **2** : *the free-wheeling out-of-towner* *n* **1** Independence of action and initiative; blithe and unconstrained indulgence : *No free-wheeling here, you do things strictly our way* **2** Liberal spending; easy munificence : *the free-wheeling of the new rich* [fr the feature of certain 1930s cars permitting them to coast freely without being slowed by the engine]

freeworld *modifier* : *what they called free-world punks, guys who'd been queer even before they got sent up* *n* Life outside prison; unincarcerated living *(1950s+ Prison)*

freeze *n* A stopping of change, esp in various monetary matters : *a freeze on profits/ nuclear freeze (1930s+)* *v* **1** : *The government denies it wants to freeze interest rates* **2** To stay or become motionless : *The cop hollered to him to* *freeze right there/ Your best bet is to freeze and wait. You can't get away (1848+)* **3** To treat someone with deliberate hauteur; snub; cut; PUT THE FREEZE ON someone : *Next time she froze me mercilessly (1861+)* **4** To inspire terror : *His scream froze me (1607+)* **5** (also **freeze up**) To become immobile and ineffective from fear; CLANK, PANIC : *The lifeguard should have dived in for the boy, but she froze (1970s+)* See IN COLD STORAGE

freeze one's **ass** *v phr* To become cold; freeze : *Get into your winter coat, before you freeze your ass (1940s+)*

freeze frame *n phr* A stopped or suspended condition : *Secret police files provide the historian of intelligence with a freeze frame from the secret world/ The L.A. riots put the mayoral campaign into freeze frame* [1990s+; fr the stopping of a movie, videocassette, etc, on one image]

freeze-out *n* The absence of cooperation, information, etc; a blank : *this total freeze-out on details for big Ray (1883+)*

freeze someone **out** *v phr* To exclude someone; discriminate against someone : *When I wanted to get into the game they froze me out (1891+)*

freight See PAY THE FREIGHT

◁**French**▷ *n* Cunnilingus or fellatio; the FRENCH WAY *v* : *Then the perverse chap actually Frenched her! (1917+) See* PARDON MY FRENCH

French-inhale *modifier* : *He continued to smoke in this "French inhale" style n* The trick of exhaling smoke by mouth and immediately reinhaling it by nose *(1940s+)*

French kiss *n phr* A kiss in which the tongue of one person explores the oral cavity of another, and vice versa; mouth-to-mouth resuscitation. SOUL KISS *v* : *They French-kissed and perhaps more (1920s+)*

French leave *n phr* Departure without notice or permission, esp going AWOL from a military post *(1771+)*

French letter (or **safe**) *n phr* A condom; RUBBER : *He was too shy to go in and buy a French letter (1856+)*

French postcard *n phr* A pornographic photograph, such as was fancied to be sold by furtive characters pulling at one's sleeve in the streets of Paris [1920s+; found by 1849 in the form *French print*]

French tickler *n phr* A condom with added variegated surfaces, spirals, fins, etc, to increase vaginal stimulation *(1916+)*

French (or **Spanish**) **walk** *n phr* A painful and humiliating means of hurrying one by holding his seat and neck and forcing him to walk; the BUM'S RUSH *v* (also **walk Spanish**) : *Mike Spanish-walked him swiftly across the little space/ Smith was an expert at walking 'em Spanish* • **walk Spanish** is attested from the early 1800s [1940s+; said to be fr the custom of pirates, in the *Spanish* Main, of forcing prisoners to *walk* while holding them by the neck so that their toes barely touched the deck]

◁**French way, the**▷ *n phr* Cunnilingus or fellatio [fr the conviction expressed in the classic couplet: The French they are a funny race/ They fight with their feet and fuck with their face]

fresh *adj* **1** Impudent; disrespectful; saucy; CHEEKY : *Don't be fresh to your Momma or I'll belt you one (1848+)* **2** Flirtatious; sexually bold; FAST : *I'm not that kind of girl, so don't be fresh (1870s+)* **3** Aloof and uninvolved; COOL • In 1990s use increasingly modified: *funky fresh, stupid fresh, etc* : *"We hang out with him because he's fresh," said Jesse/ Word up, fool. We be fresh tonight (1980s+ Black and teenage)* [first two senses perhaps related to German *frech,* "impudent"; third sense said to have originated with a 1970s rock group called the Fantastic Romantic Five MCs, who said "We're fresh out of the pack, you gotta stand back, we got one Puerto Rican and the rest are black"]

fresh as a daisy *adj phr* Brisk; vigorous; unfatigued : *He arrived back fresh as a daisy before their fax came through (1815+)*

freshie *n* A first-year college student [1847+ College students; fr *freshman*]

fresh meat *n phr* **1** New inmates *(1930s+ Prison)* **2** A new homosexual partner *(1970s+ Homosexuals)*

fresh one *n phr* **1** A new prisoner *(1930s+ Prison)* **2** FRESH MEAT *(1970s+ Homosexuals)*

fresh out *adv phr* Without; recently not available; OUT : *We're fresh out of bananas, Missus (1830s+)*

fribble *n* A trifle; a piece of inanity : *For every zappow fribble, there were equal servings of socially redeeming food for thought (1832+)*

fricking (also **frickin'** or **frigging**) *adj* Fucking; damn • Euphemistic : *what a fricking mess you made*

Friday See GAL FRIDAY, TGIF

fridge *n* A refrigerator

fried *adj* **1** Drunk *(1926+)* **2** Electrocuted *(1930+ Underworld)* **3** Exhausted; BURNED OUT; FRAZZLED : *Apparently, Maurice White's voice is fried/ Yeah, I know that fix destroyed the file system, but I was fried when I put it in (1980s+ Teenagers)*

fried egg *n phr* **1** A showy brass military hat decoration *(1908+ West Point)* **2** The Japanese flag : *sunk about everything the Japs owned with a fried egg on its masthead (WWII armed forces)*

friendly *n* **1** In wartime, a plane, ship, soldier, civilian, etc, of one's own side : *Friendlies, sometimes used to designate townspeople who cooperate with the Americans (WWII armed forces)* **2** An exhibition game : *Even if some current 18-year-old blossoms in the so-called friendlies, exhibition games (1980s+ Sports)*

-friendly *combining word* Easy, convenient, or amenable for what is specified : *The new PCs are quite user-friendly/ Works of art like these are more viewer-friendly than post-modernist art of 10 years ago/ The Saudi desert is not exactly visitor-friendly* [1980+ Computer; based on *user-friendly*]

friend with benefits *n phr* A friend with whom you have sexual relations, without a commitment or dating arrangement : *They started out as a couple, but ended up friends with benefits*

◁**frig**▷ *v* **1** To masturbate (*1785+*) **2** To do the sex act; FUCK (*1598+*) **3** To cheat or trick someone; take advantage of someone; DIDDLE, FUCK, SHAFT (*1920s+*) [ultimately fr Latin *fricare,* "rub"] *See* TAKE A FLYING FUCK

◁**frigging**▷ or **fricking** *adj* Wretched; accursed; DAMN, FUCKING : *if we could find the frigging truck/ You're a walkin', friggin' combat zone adv : They friggin' loved it (1930+)*

fright mail *n phr* Mail designed to resemble official government documents in order to fool the receiver into opening it : *You threw out today's fright mail, scanned a magalog, then picked up some trash cash (1990s+)*

frill *n* A woman, esp a young woman; frail (*1920s+*)

fringe *n* A benefit, like insurance coverage, added to one's pay; fringe benefit (*1960+*)

Frisco *n* San Francisco, California : *Ever been to Frisco? (1854+)*

frisk *n* : *They did a quick frisk and let him go v* **1** (also **frisk down**) To search, esp for firearms or contraband, by patting or rubbing the person in places where these might be concealed : *Raise your hands high, frisk him/ without getting taken-off, frisked-down or punched-out* **2** To inspect a building, apartment, etc, for evidence or loot : *Let's go up and frisk the apartment (1781+)*

frit *n* A male homosexual; flit (*1960s+*)

fritter away *v phr* To squander and dissipate, esp little by little : *These politicians are frittering away whatever credit they still possess with the public* [1728+; fr earlier sense of *fritter,* "to break into small pieces"]

fritz *v* To make something inoperative; put out of working order : *Lightning hit some wires and fritzed the generator (1903+) See* ON THE BLINK

fritz out *v phr* To become inoperative; break down; GO DOWN (*1960+*)

frivol *v* To behave frivolously; jape and frolic : *I wish I could frivol away my summer (1866+)*

'fro or **fro** *n* A frizzy style of coiffure; AFRO : *the curly 'fro which has found particular favor among the men (1960s+)*

frobnitz *n* An unspecified or unspecifiable object; something one does not know the name of or does not wish to name; GADGET, GIZMO (*1980s+ Computer*)

frog *modifier* ◁1▷ : *frog wine/ a Frog chick (1778+) n* ◁1▷ (also **Frog** or **froggy** or **Froggy** or **frog-eater**) A Frenchman or -woman : *My dad was in France during the last war. He knows those Frogs (1778+)* ◁2▷ The French language : *He asked me in Frog (1778+)* **3** A dull and conventional person : *Anybody who still wears saddle shoes is a "frog" (1950s+ Teenagers)* [senses referring to the French fr their eating of *frog legs*] *See* BIG FISH, BIG FISH IN A LITTLE POND, KNEE-HIGH TO A GRASSHOPPER

frogman *n* A scuba diver, esp a professional or military diver (*WWII Navy*)

from Adam *See* NOT KNOW someone FROM ADAM

from hell *adj phr* Accursed; wretched; infernal : *they struck on the title "Zarda, Cow from Hell"/ a certified, notarized, top-of-the-line day from hell* [1980s+; popularized by a comedian named Richard Lewis]

from hell to breakfast *adv phr* Thoroughly and vehemently; violently : *Police clubbed the Gophers from hell to breakfast (1920s+)*

from jump street *adv phr* FROM THE GIT-GO : *He was lying from jump street (1970s+)*

from nothing *See* KNOW FROM NOTHING

from scratch *adj phr* : *his first from-scratch musical venture adv phr* **1** From the earliest stages; from the very beginning : *We had to do it all again, from scratch (1876+)* **2** Using the separate basic ingredients or parts : *I never tired of watching my grandmother make the bread "from scratch" to feed the whole family (1950s+)* [fr the mark or *scratch* indicating the starting line of a race]

from the git-go (or **get-go**) *adv phr* From the very beginning : *It was his bust from the git-go/ Right from the get-go he came out smoking. It all went down in milliseconds* [fr black; perhaps based on *from the word go,* found by 1883]

from the hip *See* SHOOT FROM THE HIP

from (or **out of** or **straight from**) **the horse's mouth** *adv phr* From the most authentic source : *I got the tip straight from the horse's mouth* [1930+; perhaps fr the fact that a *horse's* age can be determined most precisely and directly by examining its teeth]

from the shoulder *See* STRAIGHT FROM THE SHOULDER

from the top *adv phr* From the beginning : *Let's hear it again from the top* [1950s+ Musicians; perhaps fr the musical instruction *da capo*, "from the beginning," literally, "from the head"]

from the word go *adv phr* From the very beginning; ab ovo : *He was lying from the word go* (1883+)

from way back *adj phr* Genuinely; entirely; from a long time ago : *My Dad is a Yankee fan from way back* (1887+)

from where I sit *adv phr* From my point of view; according to my notion : *Contrary to what Bernstein says, it is not clear that the idiot culture is taking over. From where I sit, we call the things he is fretting about "change"* (1980s+)

front *n* **1** The appearance and impression one presents publicly; facade : *This and his stickpin, his two diamond rings, and his shirts and the gabardine suit composed his "front"/ He's a real coon type. But that's just front* (1896+) **2** (also **front man**) A respectable and impressive person who represents or publicly supports persons lacking social approval : *Inability to hire a professional bondsman and "good front" results in a quick trial/ Ian Anderson, the band's flute-playing front man* (1920s+) **3** An ordinary and unexceptionable business used as a cover for gambling, extortion, etc, esp as a way of decontaminating ill-gotten money : *The candy store was a front for his bookie business* (1920s+) *v* **1** : *If you ask them to front for you, they know you're going to do something* **2** (also **front man**) To be the leading figure of : *Terry Frank, who fronted the blues outfit Bone Deluxe since 1980* (1990s+) **3** To give something, esp narcotics, on promise of payment : *I'll front you some of this shit if you pay me by Thursday* (1960s+ Narcotics) **4** To behave in a hostile manner; confront (1990s+) **5** To lie; renege on an agreement; COP OUT (1990s+ Teenagers) *See* OUT-FRONT, UP FRONT

frontal *adj* **1** Candid; direct; open : *He's a very direct and forceful guy, a very frontal person adj* **2** Exhibiting the front view of the naked human body [1980s+; fr *up front*] *See* FULL FRONTAL

front and center *adv phr* To the position of maximum prominence : *Because of political instability and a lack of moral leadership, race has once again moved front and center in the American mind* [1940s+ fr armed forces; fr the position in *front* of a military formation where a singled-out soldier presents himself or herself]

front money *n phr* An initial and impressive amount of money; cash as an earnest : *He had agreed to help the manufacturer get the*

$1.2 million loan in return for 7 percent of the total, plus "green" or "front money"/ in the drive for $4.5 million in "front money" by Labor Day (1920s+)

front office *adj phr* : *front-office memos n phr* **1** The chief administrative offices of a company (1930s+) **2** Managers; executives : *What's the front office think?* (1930s+) **3** A police station (1900+ Underworld)

front runner *n phr* The leader in a contest, election, etc : *That left as front runners Runcie and England's second-ranking churchman* (1914+ fr racing)

front-running *adj* Leading; first in a competition : *universally considered to be the GOP's front-running candidate* (1940s+ fr racing) *n* A type of fraud in which a trader withholds a large customer order so that he can personally profit from its effect on the market : *found David E Sitzmann guilty on eight counts of "frontrunning" in the live cattle and live hog futures markets* (1980s+ Commodities market)

frosh *n* A first-year student, or such students collectively (1915+ Students)

frosted over *adj phr* Irritated; annoyed (1970s+)

frosty *adj* **1** Unperturbed; COOL : *Stay frosty. Relax* (1970s+) **2** In a reserved manner; haughty : *her frosty glance* (1833+) *n* A cold beer : *how about a nice frosty*

frottage *n* The inducement of sexual pleasure by rubbing up against another person; masturbation by rubbing against another person (as in a crowd)

frou-frou *n* Frilly dress and adornment; frivolous bedizenment : *Is that what you want in a girl, chi-chi, frou-frou, fancy clothes, permanent waves?* [1870+; fr French, imitative of the rustling of silk]

frowsy *n* A slovenly, unkempt woman : *a few frowsies in skirts* (1900+)

froyo *n* Frozen yogurt : *froyo's not the same as the real deal*

frozen limit *n phr* Behavior, an event, etc, that is more than one can tolerate (1916+)

frozen rope *n phr* A hard line drive : *A hard line drive is a blue darter, frozen rope, or an ungodly shot* (1960s+ Baseball)

frug, the *n phr* A discotheque dance derived from the twist : *The dignified dances include the Frug (the movement is in the hips, the derivation of the name is shady)* [1960s+; origin unknown; perhaps a blend of *frig* and *fuck*]

fruit *n* **1** An eccentric person; FRUITCAKE, ODD-BALL : *I'll bet we get a lot of fruits* (1910+) ◁**2**▷ A male homosexual; FAIRY (1935+) [first sense short for *fruitcake*, as in "nutty as a fruitcake"] *See* HEN-FRUIT

fruitbar *See* FLAMER

fruitbasket *n* An insane person; FRUITCAKE, NUT, WACK : *Touched the wound, rubbed the blood on his cheeks and his forehead. Total fruitcake (1990s+)*

fruitcake *modifier* **1** : *those fruitcake sandal makers in the tractor-gear factory* **2** : *his fruitcake mannerisms n* **1** An insane person; NUT : *The shrink himself is a certified fruitcake (1950s+)* **2** An eccentric person; FRUIT, ODDBALL *(1950s+)* ◁3▷ A male homosexual; FRUIT *(1960s+) See* NUTTY AS A FRUITCAKE

◁**fruit fly**▷ *n phr* FAG HAG *(1970s+ Homosexuals)*

fruit-picker *n* A basically heterosexual man who occasionally seeks out homosexual partners *(1970s+ Homosexuals)*

fruit salad *n phr* **1** Ribbons and other badges worn on the breast of a military jacket : *You can recognize the boys from Korea by the new decoration added to the war "fruit salad" (WWII armed forces)* **2** A mixture of tranquilizers, painkillers, and other drugs from the family medicine cabinet used secretly by adolescents *(1960s+ Narcotics)* ◁3▷ (Variations: **potato patch** or **rose garden** or **vegetable garden**) A group of stroke victims or otherwise totally disabled patients *(1980s+ Medical)*

fruity *adj* **1** Eccentric; odd; NUTTY, WEIRD *(1930s+ Teenagers)* ◁2●▷ Homosexual; GAY *(1930s+)*

frump *n* A dowdy woman : *that floppy-looking frump he left you for (1817+)*

frumpy *adj* Dowdy; run-down; unattractive : *The message is that soft frumpy fellows are not only lovable but sexually attractive (1845+)*

fry *v* **1** To be executed in the electric chair, or to execute someone in the electric chair : *I built up a case against Sandmark. You probably could have fried him with it, too/ Apparently everybody in Texas thinks everybody should be fried (1929+)* **2** To punish severely; KICK ASS, ROUGH UP : *I'll call the CFTC, the FBI, George Bush, and I'll beg them to fry your ass (1920+)* **3** To upset; anger; PISS OFF *(1960s+)* **4** To fail; GO DOWN *(1980s+ Computer)* **5** To remove the kinks from hair with a hot comb or curling iron *(1950s+ Black)* **6** To take LSD; DROP *(1980s+ Teenagers) See* BIGGER FISH TO FRY, SMALL FRY

FTA (pronounced as separate letters) *sentence* Fuck the Army; also, fuck them all *(1950s+ Army)*

FTL (pronounced as separate letters) *sentence* Fuck the law : *The graffiti on the walls everywhere said "FTL"; I was told that it stood for "Fuck the Law"*

F2F or **f2f** *modifier* Face-to-face; in actual personal contact rather than computer network contact : *Cyberspace reader has been involved in serious romances, which culminated in F2F experiences (1990s+ Computer)*

fu *n* Marijuana [1940s+ Narcotics; perhaps a shortening of Portuguese *fumo d'Angola*, "Angola smoke," referring to marijuana and the smoking habit brought by slaves from Angola to Brazil]

fubar *adj* Totally botched and confused; SNAFU [WWII armed forces; fr *fucked up beyond all recognition*]

fubb *adj* FUBAR, SNAFU [WWII armed forces; fr *fucked up beyond belief*]

fubis (FOO bis) *sentence* An irritated or defiant comment [1950s+ Army; fr *fuck you, buddy, I'm shipping*]

◀**fuck**▶ *interj* An exclamation of disgust, disappointment, dismay, etc : *and yelled against the moan of the wind as loud as he could, "Fuck!" (1940s+) n* **1** An instance of the sex act : *a quick fuck (1680+)* **2** A sex partner : *She said he's not a bad fuck (1874+)* **3** A despicable person; BASTARD, PRICK : *Why don't you fucks find a cure for that already?/ "Oh yes, of course," said the fuck (1920s+) v* **1** To do the sex act with or to someone *(1200s+)* **2** To cheat; swindle; maltreat; take advantage of; FUCK OVER, SCREW : *I was with them twenty years, but they fucked me anyhow (1860s+)* **3** To curse and vilify; revile extremely; DAMN • Strongest of the cursing terms that include wishing the person or thing to eternal damnation: "damn," "to hell with," and mentally subjecting the person or thing to an act of sodomy: "fuck, screw," and British "bugger" and "sod"; has the elaborate variant *fuck them all but six and save them for pallbearers* : *Fuck the money, I'm gone go on this ride/ Ah, fuck that noise (1920s+)* **4** To botch and confuse; ruin; FUCK UP : *My God, if the doctor sent out a bill, it might fuck the whole thing (1920s+)* [origin unknown; perhaps fr or related to German *ficken*, "strike, copulate with"] *See* DRY FUCK, FINGERFUCK, a FLYING FUCK, GOAT FUCK, GO FUCK oneself, MINDFUCK, NOT GIVE A DAMN, RAT FUCK, TAKE A FLYING FUCK, THROW A FUCK INTO someone

◀**fuck, a**▶ *See* NOT GIVE A DAMN

◀**fuck, the**▶ *See* the HELL

◀**fuckable**▶ *adj* **1** Ready and willing to have sexual relations : *fuckable after three beers* **2** Highly desirable as a sexual partner : *fuckable dudes at the bar*

◀**fuck a duck**▶ *interj* An exclamation of surprise and incredulity : *He did? Well, fuck a duck! (1940s+)*

◀**fuck-all**▶ *n* Nothing; ZILCH • Chiefly British : *A good extra can pull in good money to not do fuck-all (1960+)*

◀**fuck around**▶ *v phr* **1** To idle and loaf about; MESS AROUND : *Although I do fuck* *around in home studios and things like that, I think that it's of no importance* **2** To tease; fool around annoyingly; HORSE AROUND (*1929+*) *See* FUCK WITH

◀**fuck** someone's **brains out**▶ *v phr* To do the sex act busily and for a long time : *We can spend the whole night together, fuck our brains out/ two people who'd just fucked each other's brains out* (*1970s+*)

◀**fuck buddy**▶ (or **puppet**) *n phr* A partner for sex only; a nonromantic sexual partner : *fuck buddies at college*

◀**fuck bunny**▶ *n* A female who is willing and ready to copulate : *a whole sorority of fuck bunnies*

◀**fucked**▶ *adj* Confounded; victimized; BUGGERED, DAMNED : *I'll be fucked if he's not right!* (*1940s+*)

◀**fucked out**▶ *adj phr* Exhausted; PLAYED OUT, POOPED (*1940+*)

◀**fucked up**▶ *adj phr* **1** Confused; botched; ruined; BALLED UP : *Now isn't that as fucked up as a Chinese fire drill?* **2** Mentally and emotionally disturbed; neurotic : *I was so fucked up I couldn't talk sense* **3** Intoxicated, esp by narcotics : *I was so drunk and fucked up and shaken with tenderness* (*1940s+*)

◀**fucker**▶ *n* **1** A detestable person; BASTARD, PRICK : *And the fuckers are really, really twisting us up/ The fucker stole my money* **2** Any person or thing • Often used affectionately : *Look at that little fucker go!/ Jiggs doesn't like to have anything to do with boats, "I don't want no parts of them fuckers"* (*1893+*) *See* FATHER-FUCKER, MIND-FUCKER, MOTHERFUCKER

◀**fuckery** or **fuck-house**▶ *n* A house of prostitution; brothel

◀**fuckface**▶ *n* A despicable person : *Screw you, fuckface*

◀**fuckhead**▶ *n* A despicable person; JERK : *some back-country fuckhead with a stethoscope* (*1960s+*)

◀**fucking**▶ *adj* **1** Wretched; rotten; accursed; DAMN : *hectic fuckin' business* **2** Genuine; absolute; COCKEYED : *Ain't that a fucking shame?* *adv* Extremely; very : *It's fucking difficult to get a raise these days* **intensifier** : *Why don't we go downtown and fucking get it done?* (*1893+*) *See* MOTHERFUCKING, A ROYAL FUCKING

◀**-fucking-**▶ *infix* Used for emphasis • Often printed as a separate word without hyphens : *non compos fuckin' mentis/ in-fucking-credible/ "Un-fucking-believable," they say in the booth*

◀**fucking a** (or **ay**)▶ *adv phr* : *Fucking ay right I did* **affirmation** Absolutely; definitely : *Fucking a, no one's gonna shoot Keith* **interj** An exclamation of pleasure, triumph, joy, etc; GREAT : *We won? Fucking a!* [*1940s+* fr

British; fr an affirmatory phrase *your fucking arse*]

◀**fucking well**▶ *intensifier* Absolutely : *not afraid of fucking well anything* (*1920s+*)

◀**fucking well told**▶ *adv phr* Absolutely right; FUCKING A : *"You're fucking well told," he replied* (*1940s+*)

◀**fuck like a mink**▶ *v phr* To copulate readily and vigorously • Said only of women (*1930s+*)

◀**fuck-me** or **do-me**▶ *adj* Blatantly seductive : *a brand-new pair of rhinestone fuck-me shoes* (*1980s+*)

◀**fuck nut(s)**▶ *n* An idiot; a despised person : *who's the fucknuts who turned out the light*

◀**fuck-off**▶ *n* A habitual shirker; sluggard; GOOF-OFF : *I mean, everybody's a fuck-off (WWII armed forces)*

◀**fuck off**▶ *v phr* **1** FUCK AROUND (*1940s+*) **2** FUCK UP (*1940s+*) **3** To leave; depart • Often an irritated command : *Tell 'em to fuck off, I don't want anything to do with them* (*1929+*)

◀**fuck over**▶ *v phr* To victimize and maltreat, sexually or otherwise; FUCK : *so accustomed to being used and fucked over that they probably would do nothing/ let people know who might be fucking them over* (*1960s+*)

◀**fuck-stick**▶ *n* A despised person; ASSHOLE, JERK : *real pompous little fuck-stick* (*1950s+*)

◀**fuck the dog**▶ *v phr* To waste time; idle about; temporize : *We better quit fucking the dog and get cracking* (*1930s+*)

◀**fuck-up**▶ *n* **1** A bungler, esp a chronic one : *The sergeant was a confirmed fuck-up* **2** A confused situation; botch; mess : *The operation was a royal fuck-up* **3** A blunder; GOOF : *These things are my ideas. They've all got the same fuck-ups* (*1940s+*)

◀**fuck up**▶ *v phr* **1** To fail by blundering; ruin one's prospects : *They are the prime reasons that people fuck up in bands* **2** To confuse; botch; BALL UP : *I had it right, but he fucked it up* (*1940s+*)

◀**fuck** someone **up**▶ *v phr* To injure or maltreat someone; FUCK OVER : *If anybody was to mess with your sister, you had to really fuck him up/ They didn't do it, so they fucked me up* (*1960s+*)

◀**fuck up** (or **screw up**) **a two-car funeral**▶ *v phr* To mismanage completely; botch : *D'Amato says Federal banking regulators could screw up a two-car funeral* (*1990s+*)

◀**fuck** (or **fuck around**) **with**▶ *v phr* **1** To play or toy with; meddle with : *Floyd was a little crazy and just liked to fuck with people by talking a lot of nonsense/ Every harebrain east of the Mississippi River will be fucking around with this thing* **2** To defy or challenge; provoke; MESS AROUND WITH : *"They don't fuck with me," the old man said/ to see if Buck*

Rogers was real and had come down here to fuck with Texas (1940s+)

◄**fuck-witted►** *adj* Stupid; moronic; dumb : *It's a pretty fuck-witted thing to do (1990s+)*

◄**fuck you►** *interj* An exclamation of very strong defiance and contempt : *Fuck you, friend, if that's your attitude (1940s+)*

fuddy-duddy or **fuddy-dud** *adj* : *There were a few fuddy-duddy requests for documentation* n An old-fashioned, esp a meticulous, person; an outdated conservative : *To this little squab, I evidently rated as a fuddy-duddy (1900+)*

fudge *interj* A mild exclamation of surprise, disappointment, etc; DARN *(1766+)* *v* 1 To cheat or misrepresent slightly; deviate somewhat : *so I could fudge three or four inches on my height/ if you're fudging on your income tax return (1660s+)* 2 To rub someone to orgasm; FRIG *(1950s+)* [first verb sense said to be fr the name of a Royal Navy Captain Fudge, "by some called Lying Fudge"; sailors, hearing a lie told, exclaimed "You *fudge* it!"]

fudge factor *n phr* An arbitrary percentage added to a proposed contract or estimate to allow for adverse contingencies : *How many will die? Current projections are pure darts at a board, an enormous extrapolation coupled with a fudge factor (1962+)*

fugly *adj* Very ugly; BUTT-UGLY : *That ski suit Mary has on is not just ugly, it's fugly* [1980s+; fr *fucking ugly*]

fuie *See* PHOOEY

full *adj* Drunk *(1872+)*

full blast *adj* : *a full-blast campaign for mayor* *adv phr* To the limit of capacity; with no restraint; ALL-OUT *(1839+)*

full-bore *adj* Large; fully developed : *And this track here, big, a full-bore male (1936+)*

full bore *adv phr* 1 At maximum speed and power; ALL-OUT, FULL BLAST : *We're going full bore Sheriff Wells says* 2 Absolutely; totally : *And I already full-bore suspected old Ronny* [1936+; fr the condition of an unchoked carburetor in an engine, where the *full bore* of the gas line is being used; influenced by the unchoked condition of a shotgun]

full Cleveland *adj phr* Of a man, dressed in white shoes and a white suit *(1991+)*

full-court press *n phr* Very great or maximum pressure : *an inclination not to resume a full court press for the peace plan* [fr an aggressive pressing defense in basketball, using both halves of the *court*]

full fig *n phr* Full official or ceremonial attire; full dress • Chiefly British : *Arrivals from a Swissair flight: two lushly draped, satiny ladies, a squire in noisy tweeds, a bishop in full fig* [1838+; origin uncertain; perhaps fr *full figure*, used of fashion illustrations showing the full front of the wearer]

full frontal *adj phr* Total; complete; unrestricted : *a variety of forms including iambic pentameter, full frontal rhyme and ballads* [1970s+; fr the phrase *"full frontal nudity"* used to describe the ultimate grade of nakedness, as seen in art, moving pictures, television, etc]

full monty (or **monte**) *n* A completely unclothed human body [1986+; in Montague Burton, a British firm of gentlemen's outfitters, the expression applied to a full suit of clothes]

full-moon day *n phr* A day when many disturbed patrons visit *(1990s+ Librarians)*

full-mooner *n* An insane or very eccentric person; LOONY, NUT : *in San Francisco, where there are full-mooners on every street corner/ This issue goes beyond the full-mooners* [1980s+; fr the belief that some people go crazy at the time of the *full moon*]

full of beans *adj phr* 1 Vibrant with energy; peppy : *The old guy was still full of beans (1854+)* 2 (also **full of hops**) Wrong; mistaken, esp chronically so; FULL OF SHIT : *maybe Ted Williams was full of beans (1940s+)* [first sense fr the belief that a *bean*-fed horse is particularly frisky and strong; second sense fr a connection with *beans*, hops, prunes, etc, as promoting excretion]

full of hot air *adj phr* Wrong; mistaken; pompously in error : *If she says that, she's full of hot air (1940s+)*

◄**full of piss and vinegar►** *adj phr* Brimming with energy; very peppy and assertive; FULL OF BEANS : *full of the piss and vinegar her mother lacks/ full of piss and vinegar and occasionally now, a little weed (1940s+)*

full of prunes *adj phr* 1 Vibrant with energy; peppy : *The old guy was still full of prunes (1887+)* 2 Wrong; mistaken, esp chronically so; FULL OF SHIT *(1894+) See* FULL OF BEANS

◄**full of shit►** *adj phr* (Variations: **crap** or **bull** or **it** may replace **shit**) Wrong; mistaken; not to be credited : *Oh, he's so full of shit, that self-seeking schmuck/ Anyone who says it doesn't matter is full of it/ They're all fulla shit anyway, all them goddam politicians (1940s+)*

full of the devil (or **Old Nick**) *modifier* Always causing trouble or getting into mischief : *full of the devil, and not just when he's had sugar*

full ride *modifier* : *accused of receiving a full ride scholarship from Michigan* n *phr* A full college scholarship : *seven of them got full rides to Division 1 schools (1950s+)*

full steam ahead *adj phr* Eager and energetic; GUNG HO : *BJ's rehab has gone well. He's full steam ahead (1960s+)*

full-tilt-boogie *adv* At full speed; headlong; FULL BORE : *I would rather that my state run* *full-tilt-boogie into gambling proprietorship* (*1980s+*)

full up *adj phr* Completely full : *The plane was full up by then* (*1892+*)

fully *adv* Really; certainly : *That was fully the best movie I've ever seen/ He was fully flailing on the guitar. You were fully doggin' him about his hair* (*1990s+*)

fumblerooski *n* A play in which the quarterback leaves the ball between the center's legs and fakes a hand-off, whereupon a guard takes the ball and runs with it : *and make the guard-around or "fumblerooski" play illegal/ I got you on the fumble-rooski, didn't I?* (*1980s+ Football*)

fumfer or **fumper** *v* To temporize and mumble; dither; WAFFLE : *Orrin Hatch with his quotes from* The Exorcist, *Howard Metzenbaum fumfering on about leaks/ When questioned, they fumpered around* [*1980s+; fr Yiddish*]

fumtu (FUHM tōō) *adj phr* Totally confused; botched; SNAFU [*WWII armed forces; fr fucked up more than usual*]

fun and games *n phr* Pleasure; delightful diversion; amatory dalliance • Most often ironic : *We had some fun and games a few months ago/ What happens to Romanov after that is fun and games for you, Hardy* [*1920+; based on the talk and attitude used toward children by hearty people, and analogous with show and tell*]

Fun City or **fun city** *n phr* Any city, esp New York City, fancied to be a venue for pleasure, often ironically [*late 1960s+; first used as a public relations motto for the administration of New York City mayor John Lindsay, and felt to be in ironic contrast with increasing urban shabbiness, poverty, crime, etc*]

fund *See* SLUSH FUND

fun fur *n phr* Cheap synthetic fur for casual use (*1962+*)

fungo *n* **1** A ball hit to give practice to fielders, usu by tossing it up and swinging **2** (or **fungo stick**) A long, light bat used to hit practice balls to fielders *v* : *They used to fungo that ball over your head* [*1867+ Baseball; origin unknown; perhaps fr dialect fonge, "catch," fr Old English fon, "seize, catch," or fr the German cognate fangen, in the same sense; the -o ending might indicate a shouted warning, the whole meaning "Now catch!"; Paul Dickson, the baseball lexicographer, describes five theories of origin*]

fungo stick *n phr* A bat used to hit balls for fielding practice (*1860s+ Baseball*)

fungus-faced *adj* Repulsive; GROSS : *The kids call Baker a fungus-faced toadsucker* (*1980s+ Teenagers*)

funk[1] *n* Depression; moroseness; the BLUES : *This levelheaded man of logic, however, is also a creature of moods and funks/ You guys are in a funk* (*1743+*) *v* To fail through panic; be frightened to immobility • Chiefly British : *She would have won, but suddenly funked* (*1737+*) [*perhaps fr Flemish fonck, "perturbation"*] *See* BLUE FUNK, IN A FUNK

funk[2] or **fonk** *n* A style of urban black music that relies heavily on bass guitar and exhibits elements like African rhythms, the blues, early rock and roll, jazz, etc : *There is no denying the influence of Instant Funk/ the Minister of Super Heavy Funk, the legendary James Brown/ He is New Orleans "fonk"* *v* To play or move to an urban black music that features a dominant bass guitar : *I think it's all right to funk all night* [*1950s+ Musicians; fr funky*]

funkadelic *adj* Musically hard-edged and urban while also reminiscent of the effects of hallucinogenic drugs; FUNKY : *breaks into his best funkadelic solo as the mood changes* [*1980s+; fr a blend of funky and psychedelic*]

funkified *adj* Tending toward a hard-edged, urban, black 1970s style in music : *Ornette Coleman, whose current funkified direction* (*1970s+*)

funkiness *n* The excited, hard-edged, soulful, or rhythmically compelling mood associated with funk : *Cannonball's alto sax has lost its old zesty funkiness* (*1980s+*)

funky (also **fonky** or **funky-butt** or **funkyass**) *adj* **1** Repulsive; malodorous; stinking : *What a stinking, dirty, funky bitch she was/ The Baths, though, are funky enough without booze* (*1784+*) **2** In the style of the blues; earthy; simple yet compelling, with a strong beat and powerful bass guitar : *He has combined a basically funky sound with experimentation/ the funky-butt tune high wide an' lonesome* (*1954+ Black musicians*) **3** Excellent; effective; COOL : *He wanted to get down and get funky/ There's a funkyass biker after my own heart* (*late 1960s+*) **4** Old-fashioned; quaintly out-of-date; having a nostalgic appeal : *for those of you who are not familiar with its funky splendor/ my love for funky Forties clothes* (*1960s+*) **5** Pleasantly eccentric or unconventional; OFFBEAT (*1960s+*) **6** Deviant; KINKY : *That guy's a little too funky for my taste* **7** Highly emotional; lacking affective restraint : *He hints that it may have its funky moments* (*1960s+*)

funky fresh *adj phr* Superb; the very greatest; way rad : *Funky fresh describes something that is super, exceptional, superior to fresh* (*late-1980s+*)

funnies (or **comics**), **the** *n phr* Comic strips; section or page of a newspaper with comic strips (*1928+*)

funny *adj* 1 Eccentric; odd; WEIRD 2 Insane;
NUTS *adv* In a strange way : *He looked at her
real funny (1806+)*

funny, a *n* A joke; wisecrack; witty remark
(1950s+) See DOODAD

funny business *See* MONKEY BUSINESS

funny car *n phr* A dramatically modified car,
usu having a powerful engine, oversized
wheels, a raised rear suspension, etc, esp a
drag racer so modified : *The "funny" car, built
for speed (1980s+)*

funny farm (or house) *n phr* A mental hospital, rest home for alcoholics, etc; laughing
academy : *Who put me in your private funny
house?/ They must all have died in flop-houses
or on state funny-farms (1963+)*

funny ha-ha or funny peculiar *question*
Do you mean something funny that's
amusing, or something funny that's
strange? : *Gore Vidal: You can see it in the
career of Woody Allen, who was wildly funny.
Kopkind: Funny ha-ha or funny peculiar?
(1938+)*

funny money *n phr* Worthless, counterfeit, or
play money *(1938+)*

funsies *n* Fun; FUN AND GAMES : *The driver said
they must not leave the parking area. "Oh,
funsies!" said Boots (1960s+)*

funster *n* A person who has or makes fun : *The
facade drops, revealing them as the faux funsters they really are (1784+)*

◁**fur**▷ *n* The vulva; pubic hair *(1893+)*

◁**furburger**▷ *n* 1 The vulva 2 A very attractive woman; eatin' stuff *(1960s+ College
students)*

◁**fur pie**▷ *n phr* 1 The vulva 2 Cunnilingus
(1940s+)

fuse *See* BLOW A GASKET, HAVE A SHORT FUSE

fuss *See* KICK UP A FUSS

fusspot *n* A very meticulous and finicky person; fussbudget *(1921+)*

◁**futy**▷ (FOO dee) *n* The vulva *v* 1 To do the
sex act; FUCK 2 FUTZ AROUND 3 To fuss;
grumble; BITCH *(1940s+)*

◁**futz**▷ (FUTS) *n* 1 The vulva 2 A repulsive
man, esp an old one; ALTER KOCKER : *Inside of
every American is a scrawny, twanging old futz
like me v* 1 FUCK 2 (also **futz with**) To meddle
or alter wrongfully; damage; FUCK UP : *What
is clear is that this movie has been futzed with*
[1930s+; origin uncertain; perhaps fr Yiddish *arumfartzen*; mainly perceived as a euphemism for *fuck*]

futz around *v phr* 1 To loaf and idle; FUCK OFF :
Stop futzing around and get to work 2 To experiment; try tricks; play; MESS AROUND : *The
foundation folk may get to futzing around with
their computers/ You never really had time to
sort of futz around in the sets* 3 To defy or
challenge; provoke; FUCK WITH : *I am nobody
to futz around with (1932+)*

futzed up *adj phr* Confused; botched; ruined;
FUCKED UP : *I've got her all futzed up. She does
everything I tell her (1940s+)*

fuzz *n* A police officer; the police : *Cops must be
annihilated. Kill the Fascist fuzz* [1930+; origin unknown; the form *fuzey* is found at
about the same time]

fuzzbuster *n* A device that detects police radar
signals : *Rauch discovered that I had a
Fuzzbuster, designed to warn me of radar traps*
[mid-1970s+; fr a trademark name]

fuzz-face *n* A bearded or semibearded man : *get
the shaver, fuzz-face*

fuzzled *adj* Drunk *(1621+)*

◁**fuzznuts**▷ *n* A contemptible person; JERK
(1940s+)

fuzz nutted *adj phr* Inexperienced; callow; green
: *a fuzz nutted rookie* [1970s+; fr *fuzznuts*]

fuzzy *n* 1 (also **fuzzie**) A police officer; FUZZ
(1940s+) 2 A certainty, esp a horse sure to
win; SURE THING *(1950s+ Gambling)*

F-word, the *n* A euphemized version of the
taboo word "fuck" *(1980s+)*

F/X or FX *n* Visual and other special ef-
fects • Best known after the 1986 movie *F/X*
: *The FX were tops, the tone tender* [1980s+
Movies; fr *effects* pronounced as *FX*]

G

G *n* A member of a gang; GANGBANGER, GANGSTA : *In a world of so much hate, another white "G" (1990s+ Street gangs)*

gab *v* Talk, esp of a long, prattling sort [1786+; fr Scots or Northern English dialect; perhaps related to the Old French *gab*, "mockery, boasting"]

gabby *adj* Talkative; noisily garrulous; gossipy : *They have spoken of any gabby party (1719+)*

gabfest *n* A session of conversation; a loquacious occasion; CHINFEST (1897+)

gabs See GOB[1]

gack *interj* An exclamation of disgust; YUCK [1990s+; perhaps imitating vomiting]

gacky *adj* Disgusting; bletcherous, CRUDDY, SHITTY : *The milk is gacky; throw it out! (1990s+)*

gaff *n* A concealed device or operation that makes it impossible for the customer to win; GIMMICK : *People started looking for a gaff (1893+ Carnival & hawkers) v* **1** To cheat; swindle; trick, esp by shortchanging (1893+ Carnival & hawkers) **2** To use a concealed device, esp for an illusion : *The volcano was "gaffed" with steampipes (1893+ Carnival & hawkers)* **3** To reprimand; rebuke severely (1950s+ Navy) [fr *gaff*, "a hook"]

gaffer *n* **1** One's father; OLD MAN : *Studs felt that Mr O'Brien was different from his own gaffer (1659+)* **2** An old man : *Look at that gaffer trying to stand on his head (1575+)* **3** A foreman or boss, such as the manager of a circus, head glassblower, chief electrician on a movie set, etc (1841+) [fr British dialect, "grandfather, godfather"; the dated meaning of the first sense is actually "master, governor," often synonyms of "father"] See OLD COCKER

gag *n* **1** A joke; wisecrack; trick : *I'll tell you gags, I'll sing you songs (1823+)* **2** To deceive; hoax; SCAM, TAKE IN : *his skills at what is called "social engineering" by some and "gagging" by others (1777+)* [perhaps fr obsolete *geck*, "dupe," related to German *geck*, "fool"; in the late 19th century a *gag* was "a line interpolated into a play"]

gaga *adj* Crazy; silly; irrational : *When prohibition comes up, the wets go gaga/ not to mention a ga-ga French gamine in Mickey Mouse ears* [1905+; fr French, "fool"]

gage or **gauge** (GAYJ) *adj* (also **gaged**) Intoxicated with marijuana (1950s+ Narcotics) *n* **1** Cheap whiskey (1940s+) **2** Tobacco • Also "a pipeful of tobacco," since *gage* meant "pipe" (1676+) **3** Marijuana • Perhaps related to the old meaning, "pipe" : *I could not see how they were more justified in drinking than I was in blowing the gage (1950s+ Narcotics)*

gaged (GAYJD) *adj* Drunk (1940s+) See GAGE

gag me with a spoon *sentence* I am disgusted; I am about to retch (1980s+ Teenagers)

gak *v* To speak, esp to babble on; YAK : *The pet lady then gakked on about the merits of ferrets (1990s+)*

gal *n* A woman • The female equivalent of *guy* : *She's a good gal, don't you think?/ a tough old gal (1795+)*

gal (or **girl**) **Friday** *n phr* A woman assistant or secretary, esp in an office; female factotum; GOFER [1940+; fr Daniel Defoe's novel *Robinson Crusoe*, where the servant and companion was named *Friday*]

gallery See PEANUT GALLERY, ROGUE'S GALLERY, SHOOTING GALLERY

galley-west See KNOCK someone GALLEY-WEST

galoot (gə LOOT) *n* A person, esp an awkward or boorish man • Very often in the phrase *big galoot* : *large enough for the galoots to fit through and take over/ "I really love that galoot," said Harry* [1864+; fr early 1800s British, "soldier," of unknown origin; perhaps fr the Sierra Leone Creole language Krio *galut* fr Spanish *galeoto*, "galley slave"]

galumph *v* To move or cavort ungracefully; crash heavily about : *Linda Evans galumphing around the edges like a wounded rhino/ who had seen him practically every day of his life galumphing around the house naked* [1872+; coined by Lewis Carroll in *Through the Looking Glass*]

galumphing *adj* Ungraceful; heavy and cumbersome : *his dead eyes, croaky voice, and large galumphing body (1891+)*

gam *n* A leg, esp a woman's leg • Most often in the plu-ral : *regarding her superb gams with affection/ Gavilan has spindly gams, a thin neck, and a wasp waist* [1781+; perhaps fr Northern French *gambe*, "leg"]

game *n* One's occupation; business; RACKET : *He's in the computer game these days (1860s+)* See AHEAD OF THE GAME, BALL GAME, CON GAME, the NAME OF THE GAME, ON one's GAME, PLAY GAMES, SKIN GAME, a WHOLE NEW BALL GAME, a WHOLE 'NOTHER THING

game face *n phr* The determined face one adopts in a contest; a mask of hardihood : *Just keep your game face. We've come this far/ The advancing Knicks needed to wear their game faces in a hurry, and they did (1980s+)*

game over *interj* Something has ended unsuccessfully : *Our relationship? Game over* [fr the ending text of many video games]

game plan *n phr* A strategy for winning; plan for conducting some project or affair : *That type of a game plan gave us the option to point out how badly we need a responsible press (1940s+ Football)*

gamer *n* A brave and enterprising player, esp one who works with pain or against the odds : *what is known in the business as a gamer, a guy who pitches with pain, who wants the ball/ When Jean Fuggett played for the Dallas Cowboys, his teammates called him a gamer* [1980s+ Baseball & football; probably fr *game*, "brave, determined"; in the 1620s the word meant "an athlete," and the current sense is conceivably though improbably a survival]

game, set, and match *adv phr* Thoroughly; completely : *Major announced that Britain had won game, set and match, achieving everything it wanted/ Game, Anne thought, and I think probably set and match* [1990s+; fr tennis]

game time or **showtime** *n phr* Time to play or work or accomplish what needs to be done : *It's game time*

gamy *adj* Daring; racy; slightly risqué : *shown in its gamy uncut version* [1843+; based on the taste and odor of game that has slightly decayed]

gander *n* A look; close scrutiny; glance : *I'll have a gander at the prices (1887+)* v : *Want to gander at TV for a while? (1914+)* [fr the stretched, gooselike neck of someone gazing intently] *See* TAKE A GANDER

ganef or **ganof** *See* GONIFF

◁**gang bang**▷ (Variations: **shag** or **shay** may replace **bang**) *n phr* **1** An occasion when several males do the sex act serially with one woman; TRAIN **2** A group-sex orgy : *We all ended up in a big profitable gang-bang* v *phr* : *tear the place apart, leave the owner for dead, gangbang the waitress (1953+; the variant gang shag 1927+)*

gangbanger *n* A member of a street gang; BANGER : *He lives where the city's most violent gangs live, where gangbangers cover walls, houses, even trees with arcane graffiti (1960s+ Street gang)*

gangbusters *adv* : *The big investigation still going gangbusters?/ Dad is still alive and going great gangbusters* *n* Superlative; very successful : *"Breakfast Time" does that well. I think it's going to be gangbusters* [1970s+; fr the name of a radio series that lasted from 1936 to 1957] *See* LIKE GANGBUSTERS

gangland *modifier* : *a gangland-style slaying/ gangland gorillas* *n* The world of organized crime; the gangster milieu (1908+)

gangsta (GANG stuh) *modifier* Showing the rapacious, violent, and misogynistic values of street gangs : *The group was one of the first to record "gangsta" lyrics, which focus on crime and violence* [1980s+; fr *gangster*]

gangsta (or **gangster**) **rap** *n phr* A kind of "rap," speaking words to a strong rhythmic beat, marked by rapacity, violence, and misogyny : *flirtation with gangsta rap, a style known for its profanity, violence and derogatory treatment of women/ clean up violent "gangsta rap" lyrics that they said demean and threaten women/ The stars of gangster rap have become dangerous emblems for an immensely popular, primarily black musical genre (1990s+)*

gangster glide or **pimp roll** *n phr* A style of walking used by street-gang members : *Sometimes it's called "the pimp roll," sometimes it's called the "gangster glide." It's a very exaggerated walk that some street gang members affect (1990s+)*

gang up on someone or something *v phr* To combine against a single opponent : *The nonaligned nations ganged up on Sri Lanka (1925+)*

ganja or **ganga** (GAHN jə) *n* A strong type of marijuana obtained from a cultivated strain of Indian hemp : *He remembers an uncle getting "so mean on ganja, he kills his girlfriend"* [1800+ Narcotics; fr Hindi; adopted from West Indian use]

ganking *n* The armed and violent stealing of a car from its driver; CARJACKING : *Teens engaged in "ganking" spree (1990+ Teenagers)*

gapers' block or **gawkers' block** *n phr* Traffic congestion caused by drivers slowing down to inspect an accident or other matter of interest; RUBBERNECKING (1960s+)

garage *n* A kind of house music (1980s+)

garage-sale *v phr* In skiing or snowboarding, to wipe out fantastically, often with equipment flying off

garbage (GAR bəj, gar BAHZH) *modifier* : *She uses a lot of tricky garbage shots to win games and sets/ I call it a garbage movie* *n* **1** Food or meals (1940s+ Hoboes & loggers) **2** Anything inferior and worthless, esp a literary text or other artistic work; CRAP, JUNK : *You call that piece of garbage a sonnet? (1592+)*

garbage furniture *See* STREET FURNITURE

garbage time *n phr* The last few minutes of a game whose outcome has already been decided, and when players try individually for scores to increase their averages : *Baker also played the final 2:26 of garbage time (1980s+ Basketball)*

garbology *n* The study of the refuse of a modern society [1946+; coined by W Rathje]

◁**garbonzas** or **garbanzos**▷ *n* A woman's breasts; BAZONGAS, HOOTERS, TITS [1980s+; perhaps fr Spanish *garbanzo*, "chickpea"]

gardener *n* **1** An outfielder *(1902+ Baseball)* **2** A person who plants narcotics on an airplane for smuggling *(1970s+ Narcotics)*

garden-variety *adj* Of the usual kind; ordinary; RUN-OF-THE-MILL *(1928+)*

gargle *n* A drink, esp of liquor *(1864+)* *v* To drain and flush the radiator of a truck *(1930s+ Truckers)*

garmento *n* A person in the business of designing and manufacturing garments • A deprecating term for old-fashioned practitioners, and a self-deprecating term, like *the rag trade*, for the whole industry *(1980s+)*

gas *n* **1** Empty and idle talk; mendacious and exaggerated claims; BULLSHIT : *Most of what I say is pure gas, my friend (1847+)* **2** Talk of any sort, esp conversation : *Let's get together for a good gas (1852+)* **3** Denatured alcohol or some other substitute for liquor *(1940s+ Hoboes)* **4** A fastball : *He got him out on the high gas (1980s+ Baseball)* **5** GASSER : *"What a gas!" she cried on the way from the courthouse (1957+)* **6** Anabolic steroids, used to increase body bulk : *He said about 60 percent of the wrestlers he knew during the 1980s used steroids, commonly known as "juice" or "gas" (1980s+ Athletes)* *v* **1** Talked : *I haven't gassed this long for a year* **2** To impress one's hearers very favorably; overcome with admiration : *Bird gassed them/ She gassed me, she was that good (1940s+ Cool talk)* **3** To impress an audience very unfavorably; fail with : *Our show appears to have gassed both the critics and the public (1970s+)* *See* COOK WITH GAS, RUN OUT OF GAS, STEP ON IT

gas, a *n phr* Something very impressive, pleasurable, effective, etc : *Therefore it's a gas for me to be the scribe of this weekly space/ She told me she'd been functionally fulfilled dispensing data, and it'd been a gas interfacing me (1940s+ Cool talk)*

gasbag *n* An energetic and persevering talker; WINDBAG *v* To talk energetically and perseveringly : *although we have of course plenty of gasbagging about morality (1888+)*

gas-guzzler *n* A car, esp a large American model, that uses a great deal of gasoline [1970s+; *gas eater* and *gas hound* are found by the 1940s]

gasket *See* BLOW A GASKET

gassed *adj* **1** Drunk : *I begged them not to get gassed or start any fights* **2** Overcome with admiration : *After her speech the crowd was gassed (1940s+)*

gasser *n* **1** GASBAG *(1912+)* **2** Anything or anyone exceptionally amusing, effective, memorable, etc; a GAS : *Examine this gasser (1930s+ Cool talk)* **3** Anything or anyone exceptionally dull, mediocre, inept, etc; CORNBALL, BOMB : *We planned a blast, and got a*

gasser (1940s+ Cool talk) **4** GAS-GUZZLER : *She beats the gassers and the rail jobs (1960s+ Rock and roll)*

gat *n* A pistol : *poking his gat your way* [1904+ Underworld; probably fr *Gatling gun*]

gate *n* **1** The money collected from selling tickets to a sporting or other entertainment event : *the winner to take seventy-five and the loser twenty-five percent of the gate (1886+)* **2** A performing engagement; GIG *(1940s+ Jazz musicians)* **3** A musician, a musical devotee, or any man; cat *(1920s+ Jazz musicians)* *v* GIVE someone THE GATE *(1940s+)* [musicians' senses fr the simile *swing like a gate*, "play or respond to swing music well and readily," with some influence of *'gator* and *alligator*; or perhaps fr *gatemouth*, a nickname for Louis Armstrong; first musical sense said to have been coined by Louis Armstrong] *See* CRASH, GET one's TAIL IN A GATE

-gate *combining word* An exposed affair of corruption, venality, etc, of the sort indicated : *Allengate/ Billygate/ Koreagate/ Lancegate/ Irangate* [1970s+; fr the *Watergate* scandal of the early 1970s]

gate-crasher *n* A person who attends a party, entertainment, etc, without invitation or ticket; uninvited guest : *"There are bound to be gate-crashers," Mike said (1927+)*

gatoring or **gator** *n* A sort of divertissement in which the participants writhe about among one another on the floor : *Gatoring is over (1970s+)*

gauge[1] *n* A shotgun : *a shotgun is called "the gauge," explained Officer Phil Lee/ This man took a gauge (Armond pantomimes holding a gun, then bends over to dodge from it) and two people end up dead* [1970s+ Underworld & police; fr the use of *gauge* to designate the caliber of a shotgun]

gauge[2] or **gage** *n* Marijuana; GRASS, POT, WEED [1930s+ Narcotics; origin unknown; perhaps from *gaged*, "drunk"]

gawk *v* To stare; gape stupidly : *locals gathered to gawk at strange lights/ They went in and out of the garage to gawk at the body* [1785+; fr dialect *gawk, gouk*, "fool, idiot," literally "cuckoo"]

gawky *adj* Awkward; ill-coordinated *(1759+)*

gay *adj* **1** Homosexual; homoerotic : *gay men and women/ gay attitudes (1920s+ Homosexuals)* **2** Intended for or used by homosexuals : *gay bar/ gay movies (1920+ Homosexuals)* **3** Ugly; CORNY, WEIRD : *The clarinet player looked totally gay in his USC band uniform (1980s+ Students)* *n* A male homosexual or a lesbian • Widely used by heterosexuals in preference to pejorative terms : *a hideaway for live-together couples and middle-aged gays (1920s+ Homosexuals)*

[perhaps by extension fr earlier British *gay*, "leading a whore's life"]

gay-bashing *modifier* : *after his arrest in a gay-bashing case n* The harassment of homosexuals (*1980s+*)

gay boy *modifier* : *Raoul, 24, is a cute gay-boy filmmaker n phr* A young male homosexual; GAY : *Those of you who have friendships with sweet gay boys will certainly relate* (*1990s+*)

gay-cat *n* 1 A hobo, esp a novice : *Were not these other tramps mere dubs and "gay-cats"?* (*1893+ Hoboes*) 2 (also **gey-cat**) A homosexual boy; catamite (*1902+*) 3 A novice criminal who acts as lookout, decoy, etc (*1916+ Underworld*)

gaydar *n* An internal detector of gay people; a sense of whether someone is gay or not : *gaydar on high alert in Provincetown*

gayola *adj* Homosexual; GAY : *There have to be some fulfilling alternatives to the gayola fun fair n* Bribery, blackmail, and extortion paid by homosexuals and homosexual businesses, esp to police : *for blackmail and for shakedowns by real or phony cops, a practice known as "gayola"/ Homosexual bars pay "gayola" to crime syndicates and to law enforcement agencies* [1950s+; noun sense modeled on *payola*]

gazillion *n* A very large number; JILLION, ZILLION : *This is a movie adaptation of John Grisham's gazillion-copy bestseller/ some supermodel making gazillions of dollars each year* (*1990s+*)

◁**gazongas** or **guzungas**▷ *n* A woman's breasts; GARBONZAS, HOOTERS, TITS : *I don't get these women to sweat their gazongas off*

gazoo or **gazool** *See* KAZOO

gazooney or **gazoonie** *n* 1 A catamite; PUNK (*1915+*) 2 A young and callow tramp (*1920+ Hoboes*) 3 An ignorant man (*1940s+ Merchant marine*) 4 A recruit; ROOKIE (*1940s+ Baseball*) [said to be a variant of *gunsel*] *See* GUNSEL[1]

gd or **g-d** (pronounced as separate letters) *adj* God-damned : *The biggest gd engine in the West* (*1920s+*)

g'day or **gooday** or **gidday** *interj* Good day : *g'day, mate* (*1928+ Australian*)

GDI *n* A person who is not a member of a fraternity or sorority ● Stands for "goddamned independent" : *I'm a GDI!* (*1980s+ Students*)

gear *adj* Excellent; wonderful; superb : *The opposite of "gear" is "grotty"* [1950s+ British; fr WWI British Army phrase *that's the gear*, "that's right"] *See* IN HIGH GEAR, SHIFT INTO HIGH GEAR

gearbox *n* A stupid person; idiot; DIMWIT : *only gearboxes greet strangers* (*1970s+*)

geared *adj* 1 Excited; ecstatic; HIGH : *a sexy rock star, and he got the audience so geared/ So I was cranked. I was geared* 2 Homosexual (*1930s+ Prison*)

gearhead *n* A devotee of cars, car racing, etc : *translating that into monosyllables for you gearheads/ Robin Yount has always been a gearhead* (*1970s+*)

gear up *v phr* To prepare; equip oneself : *seem ready to gear up realistically for the very tough political fight ahead/ Geriatric Gearing Up* [1890+; fr *gear up*, "to put the harness on a horse," found by 1886]

gee or **g** (JEE) *n* 1 A thousand dollars; GRAND (*1928+*) 2 Money (*1940s+*) [abbreviation of *grand*]

gee (JEE) *interj* An exclamation of surprise, pleasure, sheepishness, etc; GEE WHIZ [1895+; a euphemism for *Jesus*]

geed (or **g'd**) **up**[1] (JEED) *adj phr* 1 Crippled 2 Battered and bent [Hoboes 1940s+; perhaps from *gimp*, "limp"]

geed (or **g'd**) **up**[2] (JEED) *adj phr* Intoxicated with narcotics, esp stimulants [1940s+ Narcotics; perhaps fr *geared up*]

geek *n* 1 A sideshow freak, esp one who does revolting things like biting the heads off live chickens (*1920s+ Carnival & circus*) 2 A snake charmer (*1920s+ Carnival & circus*) 3 A pervert or degenerate, esp one who will do disgusting things to slake deviant appetites; CREEP, WEIRDO (*1920s+ Carnival & circus*) 4 (also **geekoid**) A devotee; fan; FREAK, NERD : *and assorted science-fiction geeks around the world who actually call themselves cyberpunk* (*1990s+*) [origin unknown; perhaps related to British dialect *geck, geke*, "fool"; according to David Maurer, "said to have originated with a man named Wagner of Charleston, WV, whose hideous snake-eating act made him famous"] *See* GINK

geek-chic *adj* Fashionable for the socially inept : *geek-chic earth shoes*

geekdom *n* The world or domain of geeks and nerds : *the geekdom of Silicon Valley*

geek out *v phr* 1 To speak about computers in specialized technical language, esp among noninitiates : *Go hang around a mouse potato and see if you can get him to geek out and do a brain dump* 2 To do programming with obsessive intensity : *Not infrequently, Michael locks himself inside and geeks out on code* (*1990s+ Computer*)

geekspeak *n* The jargon and slang of computer users : *The lingo: Geekspeak on the information highway* (*1990s+ Computer*)

geeky or **geekazoid** *adj* Eccentric and repulsive; WEIRD, CREEPY, NERDLY : *Kia sets her up with geeky granola-type Ely/ the geeky game played at company picnics/ Maybe you have a* *geekazoid freshman brother who is the designated wedgie-victim of the entire 11th grade* (1980s+)

gee string See G-STRING

geewhillikins or **gewhillikins** *interj* An exclamation of astonishment (1850s+)

gee whiz *adj* **1** Enthusiastic; very much impressed; youthfully optimistic : *With a very gee-whiz kid, you're not talking about a very long period/ Finch's willed naiveté frequently leads to gee-whiz insights* (1980s+) **2** Very impressive, esp in a gaudy way : *a window-less conference room that felt gee-whiz, a little Big Brother, filled with television sets* (1990s+) *interj* (also **Gee whiz, gee whillikins, gee willikers**) An exclamation of approval, surprise, mild disapproval, emphasis, etc; GOSH : *But gee willikers, he does arithmetic like lightning* (main entry 1885+; others somewhat earlier) *n phr* An armed pickpocket [1950s+ Underworld; fr *gee*, "gun," and *whiz*, "pickpocket"]

geez or **geeze** (GEEZ) *v* To have or give a dose of narcotics, esp an injection : *They drop acid, go up on DMT and "geeze" (mainline meth)/ I need to geez now, Bumper. Real bad/ I geezed that scum* (1940s+ Narcotics)

geezed or **geezed up** *adj* or *adj phr* **1** Drunk **2** Intoxicated with narcotics; GEED UP[2], HIGH (1940s+)

geezer[1] *modifier* : *Van Dyke's comeback is part of a multinetwork trend toward what could be called geezer mysteries/ "Geezer rock" goes on tour n* A man, esp an old man; DUFFER, GAFFER, GUY : *It gave him all kinds of confidence just to hear the big geezer spout/ He is a tall geezer with chin whiskers* [1885+; fr earlier and possibly Cockney *giser*, "mummer, one who puts on a guise or mask," hence a quaint figure; the origin resembles that of *guy*]

geezer[2] *n* **1** A drink of liquor; SNORT (1920s+ Prison) **2** A dose or injection of a narcotic (1940s+ Narcotics)

geezer-bashing *adj* Denigrating and blaming old people : *major media have provided ample amplification for Lead or Leave's geezer-bashing message* (1990s+)

gel or **jell** *v* **1** To come to a firm and useful form; WORK : *In this highly partisan county, it just didn't gel/ If this doesn't gel, the local people will be stuck/ Frost's saga fails to jell either as compelling drama or convincing social portraiture* (1950s+) **2** (also **jell out**) To relax; CHILL OUT, KICK BACK : *After having five hours of class today I think I'll just go home and gel* (1980s+ Students) [second sense perhaps fr the notion of productively sitting still as a *gelatin* pudding does]

gender-bender *modifier* : *a two-day search for Boy George, the 25-year-old "gender-bender"*

pop star n phr A person who tends to reverse or alter traditional notions of sex roles, dress, etc (1980+)

gender-bending *modifier* : *Madonna is known for her gender-bending antics n* The reversal or alteration of sex roles, dress, etc; androgyny : *A decade or so ago, cinematic gender-bending reached unprecedented levels* (1980s+)

general See ARMCHAIR GENERAL

generic *adj* Inferior; CHEESY, GROTTY : *Larry King doesn't appear to be generic: he has a distinctive voice, and he doesn't look like anybody else* (1980s+ Students)

gent (JENT) *n* A man; fellow; GUY : *A hefty, tough-talking gent of not quite 50* (1564+)

genuine article or **real deal** *n* The real thing, not a substitute or imitation : *that ring's the genuine article/ his artwork is the real deal*

Gen-X or **twentysomethings** *n* Generation-X, the set of white middle-class people born after the baby-boom generation : *He has a bunch of the Gen-X jargon in there* [1990s+; fr the title of a 1991 book by Douglas Coupland]

george *v* To invite to sexual activity; PROPOSITION : *One of the girls georged him, just for kicks* (1950s+ Black)

George *adj* (also **george**) Excellent; great; superb : *She's real George all the way* (1951+ Teenagers) *interj* BY GEORGE (1731+) *n* **1** The automatic pilot of an aircraft (1931+ British aviators) **2** A theater usher (1950s+ Rock and roll) [aviation sense because *George* became the term for any airman in the British forces, like "Jack" for a sailor and "Tommy" for a soldier] See LET GEORGE DO IT

George Washington *n phr* A dollar; a dollar bill [1990s+; fr the portrait on the bill]

get *n* **1** Offspring; progeny • Used contemptuously, as if of an animal (1320+) **2** GATE, TAKE (1950s+ Show business) **3** The route taken by criminals in fleeing the scene of their efforts : *The get, or getaway route* (1940s+ Underworld) *v* **1** To seize mentally; grasp; understand : *Do you get me?* (1892+) **2** To take note of; pay attention to : *Get him, acting like such a big shot* (1950s+) **3** To kill or capture; take vengeance; retaliate destructively against : *He can't say that. I'll get him* (1853+)

get one's *v phr* **1** To get the punishment one deserves : *Don't worry, he'll get his before this is all over* (1910+) **2** To become rich; get one's large share of worldly goods : *She went into this business determined to get hers by the time she was thirty* (1940s+) [probably fr the notion of *getting one's deserts*]

get a bang (or **charge**) **out of** someone or something *v phr* To enjoy especially; get a thrill out of : *The younger set is not "getting a bang" out of things anymore* (1930+)

get (or **draw**) a **bead on** something or someone *v phr* To take very careful aim at something or someone; concentrate successfully; ZERO IN : *She has, however, got a bead on her five original characters* [1841+; fr the *bead*like appearance of the front sight of a rifle; the date is for the *draw* form]

get a **broom up** one's **ass** *See* HAVE A BROOM UP one's ASS

get (or **have**) a **can on** *v phr* To get drunk : *A gal used to throw herself out the window every time she got a can on* (1920s+)

get a **clue** *v phr* To understand; grasp; become aware; DIG, WISE UP • Often in the imperative : *Get a Clue Dept: AT&T has revolutionized telecommunications* (1980s+ Teenagers)

get something **across** (or **over**) *v phr* To explain successfully; PUT something ACROSS : *He decided to devote all his energy to getting his own platform across* [1894+; fr a stage term for success, *to get it across the footlights*]

get a **crush on** someone *See* HAVE A CRUSH ON someone

get one's **act** (or ◁**shit**▷) **together** *See* GET IT TOGETHER

get (or **have**) a **free ride** *v phr* 1 To enjoy something without paying; get something gratis (1927+) 2 To get the next card without betting, because no one in the game wishes to start the betting (1940s+ Poker) 3 To get a base on balls (1980s+ Baseball)

get a **handle on** someone *v phr* To begin to understand someone; have a clue as to someone's character, behavior, etc : *That's right. I can't get a handle on him* (1972+)

get a **handle on** something or someone *v phr* To find a way of coping; discover how to proceed : *Sometimes I think I haven't got a handle on things anymore/ They've just got to get a handle on this thing* (1972+)

get a **hustle on** *See* GET A MOVE ON

get a **kick out of** someone or something *v phr* To enjoy immensely; take great pleasure in : *I sure get a kick out of the way you guys kid each other along/ I get a kick out of you* (1903+)

get a **life** *interj* An exclamation of disgust and impatience • The exhortation is very much like "Get out of my face" or "Get lost" or "Stop bugging me!" : *Upon reading Donald Trump's response to the article, I have but three words for him: Get A Life! v phr* To do something significant; stop wasting time on trivia : *When someone calls the NBA office and says "What are you going to do about Calvin Murphy putting voodoo on that man?" that person needs to get a life/ "Get a life," Captain Kirk once told some Trekkies* (mid-1980s+ Teenagers and students)

get (or **have**) a **little on the side** *v phr* To be sexually unfaithful; CHEAT (1940s+)

get a **load of** *v phr* To examine; attend to; GET : *Let him get a load of the new suit of clothes* (1929+)

get **along** (or **on**) *v phr* 1 To live without any great joy nor grief; pass through life more or less adequately; cope; GET BY (1888+) 2 To be compatible; associate easily : *He didn't get along with the boss* (1856+)

get a **move on** *v phr* (Variations: **hump** or **hustle** or **wiggle** may replace **move**) To hurry; speed up : *Tell him to damn well get a wiggle on* (*entry form* 1891+; *hump* 1892+; *wiggle* 1896+)

get an **attitude** *v phr* To become hostile and resentful : *At first I got an attitude about it. I thought it had to do with race* (1960s+ Black)

get an **eyeball on** *v phr* To spot or catch sight of someone or something : *got an eyeball of her on the recording*

get an **offer** one **can't refuse** *See* MAKE AN OFFER one CAN'T REFUSE

get another **kick at the cat** *v phr* To have another chance : *an attorney could lose one trial strategy, then present a new one to "get another kick at the cat"* (1980s+)

get a **rise out of** someone *v phr* To get a response from someone, esp a warm or angry one : *His limp joke got a rise and some projectiles out of the crowd* [1886+; fr the *rising*, the appearance, of a fish or other quarry]

get a **room** *sentence* A request for a public display of affection to be taken to a private location : *Quit making out and get a room*

get **around** *v phr* To be socially active and desirable • Often with a hint of sexual promiscuity : *she was a beautiful woman and one of modern temperament. Carolyn, we know, got around* (1928+)

get **around** someone *v phr* To persuade or fool someone, often with an illicit motive : *Somehow she managed to get around the jury* (1891+)

◁get one's **ass in a sling**▷ *See* HAVE one's ASS IN A SLING

◁get one's **ass in gear**▷ *v phr* To get into action; stop loafing and wasting time; put a verb in it : *I'd best get my ass in gear and pull this case out of sewer city* (1940s+)

get **at** someone *v phr* To influence someone illicitly : *They found there was no way to get at the judge* (1865+)

get (or **have**) a **toehold** *v phr* To get or have a precarious grip on something; get or have an uncertain command : *You've got a good toehold on the job; now let's see you take over* [1940s+; fr the sort of unsure footing one has when only the *toes* are planted and the precarious seizure one has made when only the *toe* of the quarry is in one's grip]

getaway *modifier* : *our getaway car/ getaway route/ getaway vacation package n* The act of fleeing, esp from the scene of a crime : *How about a quiet getaway from this mad scene?* (1890s+) *See* MAKE one's GETAWAY

get away with something *v phr* **1** (also **get by with** something) To go uncaught and unpunished after doing something illegal or indiscreet : *I didn't get away with hassling the committee* **2** To steal or run off with something : *He came for a friendly visit and got away with my stereo* (1878+)

get away with murder *v phr* To go unpunished or unharmed after some risk or impudence : *bitter complaints that Bush was getting away with murder in the press* (1920+)

get one's or someone's **back up** *v phr* To become angry or make someone angry, esp in a way to cause one to resist : *When they said he was lying, that got his back up* (1887+)

◁**get** one's **balls in an uproar,** not▷ *See* NOT GET one's BALLS IN AN UPROAR

get one's **banana peeled** *See* HAVE one's BANANA PEELED

get (or **groove**) **behind** *v phr* **1** To have a pleasurable narcotic intoxication (1960s+ Narcotics) **2** To enjoy something : *I can't get behind this, I keep trying to tell you* (1970s+)

get behind something or someone *v phr* To support or advocate a person, cause, etc; PUSH : *If we all get behind the amendment, it'll pass* (1903+)

get one's **bell rung** *v phr* To be injured; esp to get a head injury : *Conlon got his bell rung Tuesday night when he was accidentally kicked in the head* (1960s+ Sports)

get bent *interj* An exclamation of scorn and dismissal; DROP DEAD, GET A LIFE, go fuck yourself, GO TO HELL (1980s+ Students)

get busy (or **down**) *v phr* To do the sex act; SCREW : *Let's get busy* [1980s+ Students; fr *get down to business*]

get by *v phr* **1** To do just acceptably well; neither succeed nor fail, but survive; MAKE OUT : *We were barely getting by on two salaries* (1918+) **2** To barely escape failure; scrape by (1904+) **3** To pass inspection; stand up to scrutiny : *His work didn't get by the manager* (1914+)

get someone **by the short hairs** (or **curlies** or **knickers**) *See* HAVE someone BY THE SHORT HAIRS

get by with something *See* GET AWAY WITH something

get (or **have**) one's **card punched** *v phr* To have one's credentials, merit, etc, verified : *I'm not here to get my civil-rights card punched* [1960s+; fr the periodic punching of one's union card to show that one has paid one's dues]

get one's **clock cleaned** *v phr* To be assaulted and injured; be pummeled : *You could get your clock cleaned by a Boy Scout if you started chasing him incautiously* (1960s+)

get cold feet *See* HAVE COLD FEET

get cracking (or **cutting**) *v phr* **1** To commence : *made a mental note to get cracking on Kenneth Bodin* **2** To go or work faster : *and if we don't get cracking, get serious, and get leadership* (1925+ Royal Air Force)

get crosswise with someone *v phr* To be in conflict with someone : *He had got himself crosswise with the boss* (1990s+)

get one's **dander** (or **Irish**) **up** *v phr* **1** To cause anger; infuriate; PISS someone OFF : *That law gets my dander up* **2** To become angry; BLOW one's TOP : *They got their dander up and decided to fight the case in court* [dander 1831+; Irish 1834+; origin of dander form unknown; the form *rise my dandee up* is found in a nautical context in 1839 and is probably related]

get digits *See* PULL NUMBERS

get down *modifier* : *a get down player for those who enjoy that thumping sound v phr* **1** To stake one's money or chips; bet : *All right, get down on this card* (1901+ Gambling) **2** To make an effort; get serious; attend to the task : *so I get down now and then to try to block a couple of shots/ She's gonna get down. She just plans for it* (1960s+ Black musicians) **3** To let oneself be natural and unrestrained : *to really get down and relate/ It's really egalitarian that you can come here and just get down with regular people* (1970s+ Black) **4** To enjoy oneself; have fun : *Shoot yo' cuffs, boy, jackknife yo' legs. Get down* (1970s+ Teenagers) **5** To use a narcotic, esp heroin (1950s+ Narcotics) **6** (also **get busy**) To do the sex act; BOFF, SCREW : *a chapter on sex straightforwardly called "All About Getting Down"* (1960s+) **7** To join oneself to; get in the good graces of • Used by jazz musicians in the 1930s and revived by teenagers in the 1990s : *Groups of amateur performers can "get down with God" by recording a rap song based on the Ten Commandments* (1990s+ Teenagers) [perhaps fr *get down to it* and *get down to business,* "begin to work seriously"; perhaps from an unattested *get down and dirty*] *See* DOWN

get someone **down** *v phr* To depress or annoy; miff : *That constant whine gets me down* (1930+)

get down and boogie *v phr* To enjoy oneself; HAVE A BALL, PARTY : *That said, we're ready to get down and boogie* (1980s+)

get down on someone *v phr* To show strong disapproval or lack of trust; rebuke; upbraid : *Mama used to get down on me about hanging out with Reno* (1875+) *See* GO DOWN ON someone

get down to brass tacks *See* DOWN TO BRASS TACKS

get (or **have**) **one's ducks in a row** *See* HAVE one's DUCKS IN A ROW

get even *v phr* To take revenge; EVEN THE SCORE : *His motto was "Don't get mad, get even"* (*1858+*)

get face *v phr* To gain respect; also, to raise one's status • Opposite of *lose face* : *doing her best to get face after she was acquitted*

get one's feet wet *v phr* To initiate oneself or be initiated into something; have a first and testing experience of something : *Try one or two, just to get your feet wet* [1960s+; fr the image of a person who goes into the water very carefully rather than plunging in]

get one's finger out *v phr* To get moving and quit being lazy [1940s+; fr the notion of idleness characterized by having one's finger inserted in a bodily orifice]

◀**get fucked**▶ *interj* A rude utterance of rejection, scorn, dismissal, etc : *And Robbie said, "Get fucked, Tony," and hung up* [1970s+; possibly modeled on British *get stuffed*, found by 1952]

get someone's goat (or **nanny**) *v phr* To annoy : *His bitching gets my goat sometimes* [1910+; perhaps fr depriving a racehorse of its goat mascot; perhaps fr French *prendre sa chèvre*, "take one's source of milk or nourishment"]

◁**get one's head out of one's ass**▷ (or **tuckus**) *v phr* To start paying attention; become aware and active; GET ON THE BALL : *Make the system work. Get your head out of your Hollywood ass/ Now get your head outta your tuckus!*

get hep *v phr* To become aware; become up-to-date; GET WISE, WISE UP (*1906+*)

get one's hooks into *v phr* To get possession of, esp in a predatory way; get hold of : *If they get their hooks into you, you're a goner* (*1926+*)

get one's hooks into (or **on**) *v phr* To get a firm grasp of • Often used of a woman who has pursued and caught a man : *Once I got my hooks into those books I kept them* [1926+; fr *hooks*, "hands, fingers"]

get horizontal *v phr* To do the sex act; BOFF, SCREW : *I'll remember this when it's time to get horizontal* (*1980s+*)

get hot *v phr* **1** To start getting lucky, esp in gambling **2** To become busier, with a more hectic life

◁**get in** (or **it in**)▷ *v phr* To succeed in penetrating someone sexually; GET INTO someone's DRAWERS (or PANTS) (*1888+*)

get in (or **into**) **a jam** *v phr* (also **get jammed up**) To encounter trouble; GET INTO HOT WATER : *Call me if you get into a jam/ Stay away from those guys. You're only going to get jammed up* (*1914+*)

get in bad with *v phr* To get into trouble with someone : *got in bad with the law*

get something in edgewise (or **edgeways**) *v phr* To succeed in saying or interjecting something : *You can't even get a "Yeah, I'm still alive" in edgewise* (*1824+*)

get in someone's face *v phr* To confront someone; be present and provocative : *Don't you get in my face no more. I'll kill you/ The perpetrators bumped off someone who was apparently getting in their faces* (*1970s+*)

get in someone's hair *v phr* To annoy someone; nag at someone : *But with him always being away, we don't have time to get into each other's hair* [1851+; the dated instance is *have in one's hair*]

get in on the ground floor *v phr* To be an original participant, esp in something profitable : *Sign up today if you want to get in on the ground floor* [1904+ Business & finance; *ground floor* meaning "the very basis or beginning" is found by 1864]

get in the groove *v phr* To get in tune with someone or something : *getting in the groove of this schedule*

get into *v phr* To become deeply involved with something : *getting into yoga every day*

get into someone's drawers (or **pants**) *v phr* Get into the venue of venereal delight; enjoying sex with someone; GET IN : *You wouldn't believe how easy it is to get into her drawers* (*1960s+*)

get into hot water *v phr* To encounter trouble; incite hostility to oneself : *which reportedly got van Zuylen into hot water with the designer* (*1848+*)

get into (or **in on**) **the act** *v phr* To join in; participate; esp to intrude where one is not wanted [1940s+; popularized by Jimmy Durante's lament, "Everybody wants to get into the act"]

get in wrong *adv phr* In trouble; in disfavor : *I don't get in wrong with no fuzz/ He must have done something horrible to get that much in wrong* (*1910+*)

get one's Irish up *See* GET one's DANDER UP

get it *v phr* **1** GET IT IN THE NECK (*1851+*) ◁**2**▷ To do the sex act; BOFF, SCREW (*1889+*) **3** To understand; DIG : *I read it to him twice before he got it* (*1892+*)

get (or **catch**) **it in the neck** *v phr* To be severely punished or injured : *The poor wimp got it in the neck again* [1887+; probably an allusion to hanging]

◁**get it off**▷ *v phr* **1** To have an orgasm; ejaculate semen; COME OFF **2** To do the sex act **3** To masturbate (*1960s+*)

get it on *v phr* ◁1▷ To become sexually excited; get an erection : *Or, in the words of the young, they can get it on* ◁2▷ To do the sex act; GET IT OFF : *If Eric Valdez had gotten it on with Mrs Esteva, he was a major leaguer* **3** (also **get it off**) To enjoy something greatly; have a good time; JAM : *three, five, fifteen guys in a studio just get it off/ And they overlay their daring with pure joy. They're getting it on* (*1960s+*)

get it out *v phr* To get something off one's chest, esp tell about a problem : *we helped him get it out about his ex-girlfriend*

get it together (or **all together**) *v phr* (Variations: one's **act** or one's **head** or one's **shit** or one's **stuff** may replace **it**) To arrange one's life or affairs properly; integrate and focus oneself : *Get your shit together, said Junior Jones/ why the executive departments of government don't get their act together/ Congress has to get its shit together* (*1960s+ Counterculture fr black*)

◁**get it up**▷ *v phr* To achieve and retain an erection; GET IT ON : *I couldn't get it up in the State of Israel/ He was so bashful he could not get it up* (*1950s+*)

get jiggy *v phr* To have sexual relations with someone : *After much flirting, they got jiggy last night*

get one's jollies (or **kicks** or **cookies**) *v phr* To enjoy one's keenest pleasure; indulge oneself; GET OFF • Usually with a hint of perversion : *The owner gets his jollies by walking around in a Sioux war bonnet/ This how you get your cookies?* (*1950s+*) *See* GET one's COOKIES

get one's knickers in a twist *v phr* (Variations: one's **panties in a bunch** or one's **pants in a wad** or one's **shorts in a knot** may replace **knickers in a twist**) To become very agitated and angry : *It's the right-wingery of the Ayatollah's death sentence that gets people's knickers in a twist/ This kind of crap really gets my pants in a wad* (*entry form 1971+*) *See* NOT GET one's BALLS IN AN UPROAR

get lost *interj* An exclamation of severe and abrupt rejection; DROP DEAD *v phr* To leave; depart; SCRAM • Usually an exasperated command : *If the cops or I ask her a direct question, she'll tell us to get lost* (*1940s+*)

get one's lumps *v phr* To be severely beaten, punished, rebuked, etc : *Their greatest fun is to see a cop getting his lumps* (*1935+*)

get my drift? *sentence* Do you understand me? : *in your room, get my drift*

get naked *v phr* To have a good time; really enjoy oneself; JAM, PARTY (*1980s+*)

get next to someone *v phr* To become familiar with someone, esp in view of sexual favors : *I'm telling you, you were liable to get next to that broad* (*1896+*)

get nowhere fast *v phr* To make no progress whatever; be stuck : *He was getting nowhere fast and was more depressed* (*1920s+*)

get someone's number *v phr* To understand or realize the meaning of something, esp someone's real motives, character, etc : *I think I've got her number* (*1850s+*)

◁**get one's nuts**▷ *v phr* (Variations: **cracked** or **off** may be added) To have an orgasm; ejaculate semen : *He'd get his nuts just looking at her/ When I'd gotten my nuts off about six times, we got hungry* (*1940s+ or earlier*)

get off *v phr* **1** To get relief and pleasure from a dose of narcotics : *How we s'posed to get off with no water to mix the stuff with?* (*1950s+ Narcotics*) ◁2▷ To do the sex act; have an orgasm; GET IT OFF : *It is led by trendy bisexual types, who love to get off amidst the chic accouterments of a big smack-and-coke party* (*1860s+*) **3** To play an improvised solo (*1930s+ Musicians*) **4** To avoid the consequences of; GET AWAY WITH something : *He thinks he might get off with probation* (*1835+*) *See* TELL someone WHERE TO GET OFF

get someone off *v phr* ◁1▷ To bring someone to sexual climax : *She was really eager and it didn't take long to get her off* (*1860s+*) **2** To please greatly; move and excite : *Ron sings so fast because it gets us off/ I've got to write stuff that will get people off* (*1960s+*)

◁**get off one's ass**▷ *v phr* (Variations: **butt** or **dead ass** or **duff** may replace **ass**) To stop being lazy and inert; GET CRACKING : *He wasn't able to get his class off their dead ass* (*1940s+*)

get off someone's back (or **neck**) *v phr* To leave alone; stop nagging or annoying : *All they need is for Government to get off their backs/ Get this clown off my back* [*1880+; the date is very imprecise; the notion of being a burden, on one's back, is found by 1677*]

get off someone's case *v phr* To leave alone; GET OFF someone's BACK : *I hope you will tell your mother to get off your case/ Get off my case, O.K., Dad?* (*1960s+ Black*)

get off one's high horse *v phr* To stop being haughty and superior; deal informally; COME OFF one's PERCH [*1928+; the notion of high horse, "pretentious arrogance," is found by 1716*]

get off on *v phr* To enjoy greatly; like very much : *You get the impression she got off on it, like she wanted to roll a little in the dirt/ She really got off on Eddings* [*1950s+; fr earlier get off, and less frankly sexual*] *See* TELL someone WHERE TO GET OFF

get off the block *v phr* To start, esp to start quickly : *My game plan was to get off the block first and stay out there* [*1980s+; fr the starting blocks used by runners for initial impetus*]

get off the ground *v phr* To succeed, esp to do so initially : *Those projects misfired or didn't get off the ground at all* [1940s+; fr the takeoff of a plane]

get something off the ground *v phr* To make a successful start : *As Wilbur said to Orville, "You'll never get it off the ground"* (1940s+)

get someone off the hook *v phr* To aid someone in evading or preventing punishment, responsibility, etc : *He falls for Ilona and winds up trying to get her off the hook* (1864+)

get on (or **along**) *v phr* To grow old; age (1885+) *See* GET ALONG

get on someone *v phr* To deride; harass; HASSLE, RAG : *It helps them stay cool when their boss gets on them* (1940s+)

get on someone's case *v phr* To meddle in someone's affairs; pay unwanted, annoying attention to someone; criticize; BUG, HASSLE : *There are times when I get on his case pretty hard* [1960s+ Black; fr early 1900s black expression *sit on someone's case*, "make a quasi-judicial study and judgment"]

get on one's high horse *v phr* To become dignified and formal; assume a haughty and arrogant mien : *As soon as I said a little slang to her she got on her high horse* [1856+; *ride the high horse* is found by 1716]

get on someone's nerves *v phr* To be an irritant; annoy : *This word processor's humming gets on my nerves* (1903+)

get on the ball *v phr* To pay closer attention to doing something right; improve one's performance • Often an exasperated command [1940s+; fr *keep your eye on the ball,* fr baseball or other ball sports]

get on the bandwagon *v phr* (Variations: **climb** or **hop** or **leap** or **jump** may replace **get**) To join a person, party, cause, etc, esp one that is currently popular [1899+; fr the large circus *wagon* that carried the *band*]

get on the stick (or **wood**) *v phr* To get busy; get to work; GET OFF one's ASS : *She said he'd better get on the stick or she'd dump him* (1940s+)

get on to someone or **something** *v phr* To learn the truth about; come to understand; GET WISE : *Be careful they don't get on to your little tricks* (1880+)

get out (or **out of here**) *interj* An exclamation of disbelief; GO ON : *He really said that? Get out!/ Didn't we feel just wunderbar? Get out of here* (1940s+) *See* ALL GET OUT

get out from under *v phr* To extricate oneself from troubles, esp financial troubles : *They'll never get out from under that debt* (1875+)

get out of Dodge *v phr* To depart a location : *Hurricane's coming. I'm getting out of Dodge* [fr Dodge City, Kansas, part of a cliche from old westerns about the town]

get out of someone's face *v phr* To leave alone; stop annoying; GET OFF someone's CASE : *Get out of my face, Jelly! (1942+ Black)*

get out of the gate *v phr* To start; get under way; GET OFF THE BLOCK : *I think it was important to get out of the gate quickly* [1980s+ fr horse racing; fr the starting *gate* of a horse track]

get over something *v phr* To recover or rebound from something; be restored to the previous norm; surmount : *the 1954 equivalent of "you lost, now get over it"/ My suggestion is: GET OVER IT! and conduct a decent interview* (1687+)

get something over *See* GET something ACROSS

get (or **have**) **someone over a barrel** *v phr* To have someone in a helpless position : *Okay, you got me over a barrel/ It may look like you got me over a barrel now* (1930s+)

get something over with *v phr* To finish or end something without procrastination; come to the stopping point : *It was a very tough job, but we had to get it over with* [1765+; the date refers to the phrase *over with*]

get physical *v phr* To use the body and body contact, esp roughly or amorously : *The type who might want to get physical early in a relationship, like during the first five minutes* (1970s+)

get psyched *v phr* To get excited; become enthusiastic (1950s+ Teenagers)

get (or **be**) **real** *interj* An exhortation to be sensible, to eschew illusion : *"I'll trade them for your Reuben Kincaid sleep goggles." "Get real, pal"/ Be real, Smitty, I have to study for a test/ What other city has both a large number of Quaker activists and a dreadlocked black cult whose house the city has bombed? Get real* (1970s+)

get religion *v phr* To be chastened; learn proper behavior at last; become a convert : *It appears that Mr. Reagan has got religion on the subject of environmentalism* [1884+; in the strict sense of religious conversion, found by 1772]

◁**get one's rocks** (or **one's rocks off**)▷ *v phr* **1** To have an orgasm; GET one's NUTS : *Go out, have a few drinks, and if you're lucky, maybe even get your rocks off/ people who'd never be caught dead at a 42d Street skinflick to get their rocks off and feel intellectual about it* (1930s+) **2** To enjoy very much; GET one's COOKIES : *while everyone else was getting their rocks off at the Muse concerts/ I think she gets her rocks off turning squid inside out* (1948+)

◁**get one's shit together**▷ *v phr* To organize and manage one's affairs and life properly; HAVE one's DUCKS IN A ROW (1960s+) *See* GET one's ACT TOGETHER get one's **shorts in a knot,** not *See* NOT GET one's SHORTS IN A KNOT

get **small** *v phr* To disappear; disperse and vanish; MAKE oneself SCARCE : *Those suspects got small in a hurry* (1980s+ Police)

get **smart** *v phr* To become wisely aware of one's situation, the possibilities, etc; WISE UP : *Tell him if he doesn't get smart he'll get clobbered* (1940s+)

◁get **some**▷ *v phr* To succeed in having sex or finding a sexual partner • Euphemistic : *get some once a week* (1880s+)

get **somewhere** *v phr* To attain some success : *getting somewhere with this proposal* (1923+)

◁get **stuffed**▷ *interj* FUCK YOU (1953+ British)

get **stupid** *v phr* To have fun; enjoy oneself : *We got stupid at that picnic* (1980s+ Teenagers)

get one's **tail in a gate** ◁(or **tit in a wringer**)▷ *v phr* To get into a perilous plight; be in a painful situation : *With the whole bunch against it you got your tail in a gate/ Katie Graham's gonna get her tit caught in a big fat wringer if that's published* (1940s+)

get **taken off at the knees** *v phr* To be severely injured; be destroyed : *That guy is just waiting to get taken off at the knees* (1970s+)

get **(or sink) one's teeth into** *v phr* To undertake an activity : *as soon as I sink my teeth into this proofreading*

getter *See* GO-GETTER

get one's **testicles in a twist,** not *See* NOT GET one's TESTICLES IN A TWIST

get **the ax** *v phr* (Variations: **air** or **can** or **boot** or **chop** or **heave-ho** or **old heave-ho** may replace **air**) To be dismissed, esp to be jilted : *When she found out, he got the air/ Lefebvre got the can in Seattle after building the Mariners to their first over-.500 finish* (air 1900+; ax 1883+, boot 1888+)

get **the bird** *v phr* To be greeted with catcalls, hisses, boos, etc [1922+ Vaudeville; fr the fancied attack by *big birds,* "hissing geese," when a show is radically disliked, a notion found by 1825; the form *get the big bird* is found by 1886]

get **the business** *v phr* To be treated roughly; be punished or rebuked : *When they found out his record he got the business* (1940s+)

get **the call** *v phr* To be appointed or designated : *Boyce got the call. So it's his* (1940s+)

get **the (or one's) drift** *v phr* To see the tendency of discourse, esp what one is hinting at : *And it won't show up. Get my drift?* [1927+; *drift* in this sense is found by 1549]

get **the drop on** someone *v phr* To get someone in an inferior or threatened position; seize the advantage : *I got the drop on him with that question about oil* (1869+)

get **the goods on** someone *v phr* To find or collect decisive evidence against : *"Why did you ask me to hire a private detective?" ... "To get the goods on him"* (1913+)

get **the hang of** something *v phr* To master the particular skill needed : *If I could get the hang of it, I could live as well for $2500 as in Boston for $5000* (1847+)

get **the hook** *v phr* To be dismissed, silenced, or rejected, esp suddenly : *Just when he thought he was doing so well, he got the hook* [1940s+ Show business; fr the notion that a wretched performer, esp at an amateur night, was pulled forcibly off the stage with a *hook*]

get **the hungries** *v phr* To become hungry : *I get the hungries for some breakfast* (1980s+)

get **the jump on** someone or something *v phr* To get the lead, or an advantage, esp by alert early moves : *Never let the other guy get the jump on you* (1912+)

get **the last dance** *v phr* To be the winner in the end; triumph finally : *But Dorsey got the last dance, telling jurors Mary had "died a noble death"* [1970s+; fr the awarding by the belle of the *last dance* at the ball to the favored suitor]

get **the lead out** *v phr* (Variations: **of** one's **ass** or **of** one's **pants** or **of** one's **feet** may be added) To stop loafing; GET one's ASS IN GEAR, HUSTLE • Often an irritated command : *Get the lead out and start writing* (1920s+)

get **the monkey off (or off one's back)** *v phr* To break a narcotics habit : *so hooked on morphine that there would be no getting the monkey off without another's help* (1860+ Narcotics)

get **the munchies** *See* HAVE THE MUNCHIES

get **the nod** *v phr* To be approved; be chosen : *There were a dozen other bids but McCulloch got the nod* (1940s+)

get **the picture** or **message** *v phr* **1** To understand; CAPEESH, DIG • Often a question : *After I told him about six times he got the picture/ Well, you won't ever be promoted here. Get the picture?* **2** To mentally grasp something injurious or repellent to oneself; GET WISE : *After she caught him with that whore she got the picture* (1922+)

get **the pink slip** *v phr* To be dismissed or discharged : *When they discovered the shortage of funds he got the pink slip* (1915+)

get **there from here** *See* YOU CAN'T GET THERE FROM HERE

get **the sack** *v phr* To be dismissed, with prejudice : *If they protested, they got the sack* (1825+ British)

get **the shaft** *v phr* To be ill treated; be abused, esp by cruel deception : *He thought he'd get promoted, but he got the shaft instead* [1950s+; a euphemism for sodomization]

◁get **the shitty end of the stick**▷ *v phr* (Variations: **crappy, cruddy, dirty, little,** mucky, rough, shit, shitten, short, thick, or wrong may replace shitty) To be badly and unfairly treated; have the worst of an arrangement or of luck : *Pastorini got the shit end of the stick, as usual* (*entry form 1846+, others later*)

get the show on the road *v phr* To get started; get under way : *Good. Then I can get the show on the road* (*1940s+*)

get one's ticket punched *v phr* To be sent on one's way; be rejected or even killed : *Well, I thought my ticket had been punched/ a bus-station sit-com looking not to get your ticket punched* (*1970s+*)

◁**get one's tit in the wringer**▷ (or **tail in a gate**) *v phr* To get into great difficulty : *If you print that, Katie Graham's gonna get her tit caught in a big fat wringer* [1930s+; entry form refers to the old-fashioned washing machine with a hand- or machine-operated wringer having counterrotating cylinders]

get to someone *v phr* **1** To bribe someone : *I think maybe we can get to the Governor's butler* (*1927+*) **2** To distress or anger someone; BUG, HASSLE : *It's impossible to "get to" Oliver Barrett III/ I think it is starting to get to me* (*1950s+*) **3** To affect; make an impression : *The puppy really got to me; I couldn't send him to the shelter* (*1960s+*)

get to first base *v phr* **1** To begin well; take a successful first step • Usually in the negative : *I couldn't get to first base with the committee* (*1930s+*) **2** To initiate sexual activity successfully, esp by hugging, caressing, kissing, etc • In the same baseball analogy, get to third base means touching and toying with the genitals, and get to home plate means to do the sex act, that is, "score" (*1970+ Teenagers*)

get-together *n* A meeting or session, often social; party (*1911+*)

get under someone's **skin** *v phr* To trouble or irritate; annoy; BUG : *That cackle of his soon got under my skin* (*1896+*)

get-up *n* **1** The end of a prison term (*1925+ Underworld*) **2** Dress; costume and grooming : *Why the fancy get-up today?* (*1861+*)

get someone up *v phr* To inspire and energize someone, esp for a game, examination, or other ordeal; PSYCH someone UP : *Steinbrenner thinks he can get the players up for games* [1940s+; *up* in a similar sense, "excited, vivacious," is found by 1815]

get-up-and-go *n* Energy and initiative; pep; PISS AND VINEGAR, PIZZAZZ : *My get-up-and-go has got up and went* [1940s+; in the form *get up and get* found by 1884]

get someone where one **lives** *v phr* To affect someone profoundly; clutch at the vitals : *The psychological reaction resulting was that it got this nut and this guy where they lived* (*1860+*)

get someone where the hair is short (or **by the short hairs**) *v phr* To have complete control over a person; have a painful advantage : *We've got them where the hair is short, and they can't squirm out* (*first form 1872+, second 1888+*)

get one's wings *v phr* To get into heavy drugs and become an addict

get wise *v phr* To become impudent or defiant; be saucy : *Get wise with me, punk, and you're dead* [1890s+; the sense found in *wiseass, wiseguy,* and *wiseacre*]

get wise to *v phr* To become aware of; discover : *Had you gotten wise to me, or was it an accident?* (*1896+*)

get with it *v phr* To pay active attention to what is happening or what needs doing; GET ON THE BALL : *We'll all have to get with it if we want this to turn out right* (*1940s+*)

get with the program *interj* Do what you are supposed or expected to do; follow the rules : *No matter how many times we explain it, he can't get with the program*

get Zs *See* COP ZS

gevalt (gə VAHLT) *interj* An exclamation of woe, distress, shock, etc : *He breaks open a mezuzah, nothing inside, gevalt! but a piece of paper that says "Made in Japan"* [1960s+; fr Yiddish, "powers," hence an invocation of a higher force]

gey-cat *See* GAY-CAT

GHB *See* GRIEVOUS BODILY HARM

◁**ghetto box**▷ *n phr* (Variations: **beat box** or **boogie box** or **box** or ◁**ghetto blaster**▷ or **jambox**) A large portable stereo radio and cassette player often carried and played loudly in public places : *Hey, man, don't mess with my box/ that guy in the streets with his ghetto blaster* (*1980s+*)

ghost *n* **1** A writer paid for a book or article published under someone else's name; professional anonymous author (*1920s+*) **2** The mythical paymaster of a theatrical company, who distributes pay as he walks (*1833+*) *v* : *I "ghosted" my wife's cookbook* (*1922+*) [theater sense said to be fr a line in *Hamlet*: "The *ghost* walks," implying that pay is at hand; analogous with "the eagle shits," referring to the source of pay]

GI (pronounced as separate letters) *adj* Of, in, or from the US armed forces, esp the Army; government issue : *GI shoes/ His officious ways are very GI* (*WWI armed forces*) *n* A member of the US armed forces, esp an enlisted Army soldier serving since or during World War II : *The GIs fought furiously to hold Taejon* (*Armed forces*) *v* To scrub and make trim : *They GIed the barracks every Friday night (WWII Army) See* the GIS

GIB (pronounced as separate letters) *adj* Sexually proficient [1980s+; fr *good in bed*]

gidget *n* A lithe and pert young woman [mid-1950s+; fr *girl midget*]

gift *See* GOD'S GIFT

gift of gab (or the gab) *n phr* The ability to talk interestingly, colorfully, and/or persuasively (1650+)

gig[1] *n* **1** A party for jazz musicians and devotees; JAM SESSION : *Kid Ory had some of the finest gigs, especially for the rich white folks (1915+ Jazz musicians)* **2** A playing date or engagement, esp a one-night job : *on a gig, or one night stand/ We found some musicians and I was able to finish the gig (1905+ Jazz musicians)* **3** Any job or occupation : *It's better to take some kind of main gig for their sake (1950s+)* **4** A criminal act; swindle; JOB, SCAM : *It ain't no gig, lady, and I don't really care what you think/ On my first solo gig I was bagged, beaten shitless, and dumped in jail* **5** A demerit; report of deficiency or breach of rules (1940s+ Armed forces) *v* : *their glam-rock band, Nancy Boy, which has already gigged on both coasts/ I forget whether we're gigging in Basin Street or Buenos Aires* [origin unknown; musicians' senses are extensions of earlier meanings, "spree, dance, party," found by 1777]

◁**gig**[2]▷ *n* GIGGY [1689+; origin unknown; perhaps fr Irish or Anglo-Irish, as attested by the name *sheila-na-gig* given to carved figures of women with grotesquely enlarged vulvae found in English churches; fr Irish *sile na gcioch,* "Julia of the breasts"] *See* UP YOURS

gig[3] *n* An old car [1950+; fr *gig,* "one-horse carriage"]

gigabucks *n* Very much money • Much inflated from *megabucks* : *Silicon Valley, where the winners downloaded giga-bucks (1990s+)*

◁**giggy** or **gigi**▷ *n* **1** The vulva **2** The anus (1950s+) *See* UP YOURS

GIGO or **gigo** (GĪ goh) *sentence* The output is no better than the input [1966+ Computer; fr *garbage in, garbage out*] *See* MEGOGIGO

GI Joe *n phr* A US soldier, esp an enlisted soldier of and since World War II; DOGFACE (WWII armed forces)

gills *See* GREEN AROUND THE GILLS, LIT TO THE GILLS, SOUSED, STEWED

gimcrack or **jimcrack** *n* A gaudy trifle; gew-gaw; curiosity (1632+)

gimme or **gimmie** *modifier* : *The extent to which the "gimme" spirit has banished rationality n* **1** An acquisitive tendency; greed : *With her it's always gimme, gimme, gimme (1927+)* **2** A short putt that is conceded as sunk without actually being tried (1920s+ Golf)* **3** A gift; something freely given (1970s+)* **4** A sure win; an easy victory : *Not all that long ago, this was a gimme for the National League (1980s+ Sports)* **5** A pistol : *A "gimme" is a pistol, because they're often seen in the hands of somebody saying "gimme your money" (1990s+ Police)* [fr *give me*] *See* GIVE ME A BREAK

gimme game *n phr* An easily won game; a sure victory; LAUGHER : *We don't have any gimme games in our schedule/ We thought this was going to be a gimme game (1980s+ Sports)*

gimmick *n* **1** A secret device or hidden trick that causes something to work and assures that the customer will not win; GAFF : *A new gimmick, infra-red contact lenses, which enabled a card player to read markings on the backs of cards (1926+)* **2** Any device; GADGET (1930s+)* **3** Apparatus used for preparing and injecting narcotics; works : *A small red cloth bag with his spike needle and "gimmicks" fell out (1960s+ Narcotics)* **4** A feature in a product, plan, presentation, etc, believed to increase appeal, although it is not necessarily useful or important; GRABBER, HOOK : *This promo isn't bad, but we sorely need a gimmick (1950s+)* **5** One's selfish and concealed motive; angle, PERCENTAGE : *This looks fine, Mr Mayor. What's your gimmick, anyhow? (1950s+) v : Get a fairly good item, then gimmick the hell out of it* [origin unknown; perhaps fr *gimcrack*]

gimmickery or **gimmickry** *n* The use of gimmicks : *To juxtapose this is sheer gimmickry (1950s+)*

gimmie cap (or hat) *n phr* (also **feed cap**) A peaked cap like a baseball cap, bearing the trademark or name of a manufacturer and distributed as an advertising device : *She made him stop wearing his John Deere gimmie hat in public places/ a "macho" gimmie cap emblazoned with "Cat" (for Caterpillar Tractors)* [1970s+; probably fr the request "gimme one of those!" heard when these were available free from dealers]

gimmies or **gimmes, the** *n phr* An acquisitive zeal; greed : *They got da gimmies, always take, never give/ What they all have in common is a galloping case of the gimmies (1940s+)*

gimp *n* **1** A limp (1920s+) ◁**2**▷ A lame person; CRIP : *He'd just kick a gimp in the good leg and leave him lay (1920s+)* **3** Vitality; ambition : *All he needs is a wife with some sense and some gimp (1901+) v : The old guy was gimping across the street*

gimpy *adj* Having a limp or being lame (1920s+)

◁**ginch**▷ *n* **1** A woman, esp solely as a sexual object; chick : *the fifth ginch I'd had on those eerie sand barrier islands/ cop can't afford that kind of ginch* **2** The vulva, and sexual activity; ASS, CUNT : *all the free groupie ginch south of Bakersfield/ Hagen prowls the Stampede for ginch ahoof* [esp motorcyclists; origin uncertain; perhaps related to 1950s Australian and British sense, of surfer origin, "elegance, smartness, skill"]

ginchy *adj* Excellent; admirable; elegant; SEXY : *Annie and I were the cat's pajamas and ginchy beyond belief* (1960s+)

ginger *n* Energy; pep; PIZZAZZ : *the effervescent quality that used to be called "ginger"* [1843+; fr the practice of putting ginger under a horse's tail to increase its mettle and showiness, noted by 1785]

gink (GINK) *n* **1** A man; fellow; GUY : *Does a gink in Minsk suffer less from an appendectomy?* **2** A tedious, mediocre person; JERK [1908+; origin unknown; perhaps somehow fr Turkish, "catamite, punk," found in early 1800s sources, both British and US]

gin mill *n phr* A saloon; barroom; tavern : *There still are some boobs, alas, who'd like the old-time gin-mill back/ In some gin mill where they know the bartender* [1860+; certainly influenced by *gin mill*, "cotton mill where a cotton gin is used"]

ginned or **ginned up** *adj* or *adj phr* Drunk : *Hold me up, kid; I'm ginned* (1900+)

◀**ginnee** or **ginney** or **ginee**▶ *See* GUINEA

Ginnie Mae *n phr* A government agency that buys Federal Housing Administration loans from lenders and sells shares to investors [1970+; formed from the initials GNMA, Government National Mortgage Association]

ginormous *adj* Simply huge; extremely large [1948+; blend of *giant* and *enormous*]

gin up *v phr* To enliven; make more exciting; JAZZ UP : *To gin up support for his embattled plan, the President went to Capitol Hill on Wednesday/ Numbers of voters ginned up by the revelations may throw the bums out* [1887+; probably fr earlier *ginger up*]

◀**ginzo** or **guinzo**▶ *adj* : *What ginzo broad didn't?* *n* **1** An Italian or person of Italian descent : *Gonna have at least eight hot ginzos looking for me* **2** Any apparently foreign person; HUNKY : *a Romanian or some kinda guinzo* [1931+; fr *Guinea*]

gip *See* GYP

girl *n* **1** A male homosexual (1970s+ Homosexuals) **2** Cocaine : *They call cocaine girl because it gives 'em a shot like when they take a shot* (1950s+ Narcotics) *See* BACHELOR GIRL, BAR-GIRL, BEST GIRL, B-GIRL, CALL GIRL, GAL FRI-

DAY, GO-GO GIRL, IDIOT GIRL, PLAYGIRL, SWEATER GIRL, TOMBOY, WORKING GIRL

girl Friday *See* GAL FRIDAY

girlfriend *n* A best girlfriend; also, a female lover : *come here, girlfriend/ look, girlfriend, stay away from him*

◁**girlie**▷ *adj* Featuring nude or otherwise sexually provocative women : *To some extent, "girlie" magazines are information-getting* (1950s+) *n* A girl : *this girlie and her mother* (1860+)

girlie (or **girly**) **girl** *n* A female who dresses and behaves in a traditionally feminine style : *She doesn't fit in with the girlie girls who talk about decorating*

girlie (or **girly**) **man** *n* A male who is wimpy or soft; a male who likes to participate in activities or events thought to be mainly feminine : *That girly man loves chick flicks*

girl next door, the *n phr* A sweet and ordinary young woman, in romance regarded as preferable to a talented, sophisticated, seductive woman (1961+)

girl thing *n phr* Something only understood, experienced, or done by females; something that appeals only to women : *Using a hairdryer is a girl thing*

GIs (or ◁**GI shits**▷), **the** *n phr* Diarrhea : *An all-night bout with the GIs left him weak and weary* [WWII Army; so called because soldiers often got diarrhea after eating with unclean mess gear]

gism *See* JISM

gismo *See* GIZMO

git *interj* A command to leave; BLOW, SCRAM (1864+)

git-go *See* FROM THE GIT-GO

give *interj* A command to speak, to explain, etc : *She said, "Give!," so I told all* (1956+) *See* WHAT GIVES

give (or **write**) someone **a blank check** *v phr* To give someone leave to do whatever he or she wishes; give carte blanche : *The man gave me a blank check to order whatever I needed* (1884+)

give someone **a buzz** *v phr* To call someone on the telephone : *Just give me a buzz* (1925+)

give a damn, not *See* NOT GIVE A DAMN

◀**give a fuck**, not▶ *See* NOT GIVE A DAMN

give someone **a hand** *v phr* **1** To help : *Gimme a hand with this huge crate* (1860+) **2** To applaud someone by clapping the hands : *Give the little lady a big hand, folks!* (1890+)

give someone **a hard time** *v phr* **1** To scold or rebuke; quarrel with; GIVE someone GRIEF : *He was giving her a hard time about drinking too much* **2** To make difficulties for someone, esp needless ones; GIVE someone GRIEF, HASSLE :

Jesus, everybody was giving him a hard time (*1940s+*)

give a holler *v phr* To inform, alert, or summon someone : *You need me, Mama, just give a holler* (*1940s+*)

give someone **a jump** *v phr* To do the sex act to or with; BOFF. SCREW : *went in a bedroom there with the broad, gave her a jump* (*1980s+*)

give someone or something **a miss** (**or the go-by**) *v phr* To avoid; not opt for • *The go-by variant is attested from the mid-1600s* : *Give these girls a miss/ become fed up with a slang phrase and resolve to give it the go-by in the future* [first form 1919+, second 1659+; *miss* form is fr billiards]

give someone **a pain** *v phr* (Variations: **in the neck** or **in the ass** may be added) To be distasteful, repellent, tedious, etc : *That guy gives me a royal pain in the neck/ one of those bragging polymath types who gave everybody a pain in the ass* (*entry form 1891+, neck 1921+, ass 1940s+*)

give someone **a piece** of one's **mind** *v phr* To rebuke someone severely (*1865+*)

give someone **a ring** *v phr* To call on the telephone (*1940s+*)

give something **a shot** *v phr* (Variations: **crack** or **go** or **rip** or **ripple** may replace **shot**) To have a try at; make an attempt : *He gave the exam a good shot, but flunked it/ Let's give it a rip. We've nothing to lose* (*entry form 1840+*)

give someone **a slap on the wrist** *v phr* To give a light and insufficient punishment; RAP someone's KNUCKLES : *They caught a couple more Mafiosi and I'm sure they'll give them a real good slap on the wrist* (*1914+*)

give someone **a tumble** *v phr* To show a sign of recognition or approval; acknowledge : *The newspaper guys had the Bone Crusher pegged as a plant and wouldn't give him a tumble/ Both knew me, but neither gave me a tumble* [1921+; probably fr the earlier *take a tumble to oneself,* "examine oneself closely, esp with respect to one's faults," after which *tumble* was taken to mean "scrutiny, acknowledgment"]

giveaway *modifier* : *a giveaway show/ giveaway offer* **n 1** Anything that reveals something concealed; clue; DEAD GIVEAWAY : *She talked harsh, but the smile was a giveaway* (*1882+*) **2** A gift, prize, etc, esp one given to attract business; FREEBIE (*1872+*)

give away *v phr* To expose oneself; show one's opinion, guilt, etc : *I tried to be serious, but a grin gave me away* (*1862+*)

give away the store (**or shop**) *v phr* (also **give away the keys to the store**) To concede too much; be overly generous : *His opponents*

complained that Dinkins would give away the store to his friends in labor/ to reinforce the president without giving away the shop/ the Republican Congressional leaders had given them "the keys to the store" (*1980s+*)

giveback *n* Something previously granted, esp in a labor contract, that must now be forfeited : *The new contract has no raises and several givebacks, especially in health-care benefits* (*1990s+*)

give something one's **best shot** *v phr* To try one's hardest; do the best one can; BUST one's ASS : *For three months, they had given it their best shot/ Anyway, I gave it my best shot/ The whole thing is not easy. But you must give it your best shot/ This house was built for himself by Bruant. Naturally enough, he gave it his best shot* (*1840+*)

give one's **eyeteeth** *v phr* (Variations: **left ball** or **left nut** may replace **eyeteeth**) To pay a very high price; sacrifice much; give anything : *She said she'd give her eyeteeth for the role/ I'd give my left nut to get into NET/ I'd give my left ball for a case like that* (*entry form 1905+, variants 1940s+*)

give someone **five** *v phr* (Variation: **slap** can replace **give**) To shake hands with someone or slap someone's hand in greeting, congratulation, etc; GIVE someone SOME SKIN : *Reno put out his hand for me to give him five* (*1960s+ Black*) *See* HIGH FIVE, LOW FIVE

give five fingers to *v phr* To thumb one's nose at : *Then you could give five fingers to every cop* (*1940s+*)

give good something *v phr* To be very effective at something; work well at or as something : *Zoe Baird gives good daughter/ Mozart gives good sound track* [1990s+; based on *give (good) head*]

give someone **grief** (**or heat**) *v phr* To make difficulties for someone; harass; HASSLE : *Don't let the prof give you any grief about this/ though she gave me heat about it not being "man's work"* (*1920s+*)

◁**give head**▷ *v phr* To do fellatio; BLOW, SUCK : *Not that Linda has anything against balling customers, but she just loves to give head/ She must give extra good head or something* (*1950s+*)

give someone **hell** (**or merry hell** or **holy hell**) *v phr* To rebuke or punish severely; chew out : *The skipper gave him merry hell for crud and drunkenness* (*1851+*)

give (or **read**) someone **his** (or **her**) **rights** *v phr* To inform an arrested person formally of his or her legal rights, esp by reading him or her a "Miranda card" detailing them : *The judge threw it out because they hadn't given the crook his rights* [1960s+; fr the requirement based on the Supreme Court decision in the *Miranda* case of 1966]

give someone **his (or her) walking papers** *v phr* (Variation: **running shoes** or **walking ticket** may replace **walking papers**) To dismiss or discharge; reject : *If he doesn't stop seeing other women she'll give him his walking papers/ When he objected to the new policy they gave him his running shoes* (*entry form* 1825+)

give it (or something) a rest (or a break) *v phr* 1 To stop; ease up on ● Often a firm command : *OK, give it a rest, huh, Joe?/ You won't get anything tonight. Give it a break, okay?* 2 To stop talking about something : *your damn family; give it a rest* (*first form* 1882+)

give it a second thought, don't *See* DON'T GIVE IT A SECOND THOUGHT

give it the gun *v phr* To speed up an engine abruptly; accelerate to highest speed; FLOOR, PUT THE PEDAL TO THE METAL (1917+)

give it to someone *v phr* 1 To rebuke harshly; punish : *He really gave it to me yesterday after I totaled his car* (1864+) ◁2▷ To do the sex act with or to someone : *One minute he'd be giving it to her in his cousin's Buick* (1940s+)

give it up *interj* A request for applause or praise from the party wishing such or by a third party; clap your hands for : *Let's give it up for the drummer*

give someone **leg** *v phr* To deceive someone; fool someone; PULL someone's LEG : *Last time I saw you, you're giving me a little leg about there's nothing going on* (1970s+)

give someone **lip** *v phr* To speak to someone in an impertinent and offensive way: *People get on here all day long and all they do is give me lip/ Don't be giving me lip* (1821+)

give me (or gimme) a break *sentence* (Variations: **cut** may replace **give me**) That's enough of such foolishness; please stop it; ALL RIGHT ALREADY, GIVE IT A REST, PUT A SOCK IN IT : *Gimme a break here, Mr C/ Western journalists declare in a triumphant voice that capitalism has won. Gimme a break. I can see that socialism lost/ It's a religious sect whose secrets are known only to a few. Give me a break!/ Jamie, cut me a break. I've thought about it since* (1980s+)

give me five *See* SLIP ME FIVE

give me (or gimme) some skin *sentence* Let's shake hands : *Hi there, sweetie. Gimme some skin* (1930s+ *Black*)

give out *v phr* To collapse; cease to function; fail : *His old ticker gave out/ The bus gave out halfway up the hill* (1523+) *See* PUT OUT

gives *See* WHAT GIVES

give someone **the air** *v phr* To jilt or reject : *His last girl gave him the air* (1904+)

give someone **the ax** *v phr* (Variations: **the boot** or **the chop** may replace **the ax**) To dismiss or discharge; CAN, CUT, FIRE : *The school gave six profs the ax yesterday/ The Oval Office should give him what he really deserves: the boot/ A vast trade and business complex was given the chop* (*ax form* 1883+; *boot* 1888+; *chop* 1940s+)

give someone **the bird** *v phr* 1 To greet someone with boos, hisses, catcalls, etc (1922+ *Vaudeville*) 2 (also **give** someone **the bone**) To show contempt and defiance by holding up the extended middle finger toward someone; FLIP THE BIRD : *Do you have to give everyone who cuts you off the bone?* (1980s+ *Students*)

give someone **the brush** *v phr* To snub; treat icily and curtly; KISS OFF : *I got the brush in about two seconds in that fancy dump* (1930s+)

give someone **the business** *v phr* To give someone rough treatment; punish; rebuke : *I really gave him the business when I caught him cheating on my exam* [1920s+; *to do one's business for one,* "to kill," is found by 1773]

give someone **the cold shoulder** *v phr* To snub someone socially; be chilly toward someone (1840+)

give someone **the creeps** *v phr* To cause a feeling that loathsome things are creeping on one's skin; to cause nervous apprehension : *His smile gives me the creeps* (1849+)

give something **the deep six** *v phr* To dispose definitively of; jettison; throw overboard : *They gave those files the deep six* [1940s+ Nautical; probably fr the *six* feet of a fathom, the unit for measuring *depth*]

give someone **the double cross** *v phr* To betray or cheat one's own colleagues; act treacherously : *if you feel tempted to give the old gentleman the double cross* (1834+)

give someone **the eye** *v phr* 1 To look at in an insinuating and seductive way : *I could see he was giving you the eye* 2 To signal with a look : *Get up when I give you the eye* (1940s+)

◁**give** someone **the finger (or middle finger)**▷ *v phr* 1 To treat unfairly, dishonestly, etc; SCREW, SHAFT : *Let me show you how to give that guy the finger* 2 To show contempt and defiance by holding up the extended middle finger toward someone; FLIP THE BIRD : *leers into the rear-view mirror and gives you the finger/ It's a sort of collective giving of the finger to liberalism in all its forms/ gave me the middle finger and stormed off the set* [1940s+; fr the figurative insertion of a finger punitively into the anus]

give someone **the fish-eye (or beady eye or hairy eyeball)** *v phr* To look or stare at someone in a cold, contemptuous, or menacing way : *A well-fed man in tails opened the door, gave them the fish eye/ who gave me such hairy eyeballs that I want to slink back* (*fish-eye* form 1940s+, *others* 1960s+)

give someone **the fluff** *v phr* To snub; dismiss; BRUSH OFF : *I gave him the fluff* (1940s+)

give someone **the foot** *v phr* To dismiss or eject someone (1940s+)

give someone **the gate** *v phr* To discharge, jilt, or eject someone : *After the last goof, they gave him the gate* (1918+)

give someone **the glad eye** *v phr* To look or glance at invitingly; gaze enticingly at : *A tipsy actress gives her man, Donald, the glad eye* (1903+)

give someone **the glad hand** *v phr* To greet and welcome effusively : *I gave 'em all the glad hand, but they voted for the other bum anyway* (1895+)

give someone or something **the go-by** *See* GIVE someone or something A MISS

give someone **the heave-ho** *v phr* To dismiss or reject someone; GIVE someone THE AIR : *It took Lisa two years to give her boyfriend the heave-ho* (1940s+)

give someone **the hook** *v phr* To dismiss, silence, or otherwise reject someone, esp suddenly : *The teacher gave him the hook* (1940s+ Show business) *See* GET THE HOOK

◁**give** (or **slip**) someone **the hot beef injection**▷ *v phr* To do the sex act with or to someone (1980s+ Students)

give someone **the needle** *v phr* To nag at someone; criticize regularly and smartingly; HASSLE, NEEDLE : *The only needle she knows is the one she gives grandpa for stopping off at the bar on his way home* (1940s+)

give the nod *v phr* To give approval; confer permission : *Detroit has tightened the reins on the boys in the sheet metal design department while giving the nod to the engineers* (1940s+)

give someone or something **the once-over** *v phr* To examine quickly; glance at, esp with a view to evaluation or identification; CHECK OUT : *That guy in the corner is giving us the once-over/ I gave her papers the once-over and figured she qualified* (1915+)

give someone **the pink slip** *v phr* To discharge or dismiss; CAN, FIRE (1915+)

give someone **the raspberry** *v phr* To make a noise expressing displeasure or contempt : *audience gave her the raspberry for such distasteful jokes*

give someone **the runaround** *v phr* To be deceptive and persistently evasive with someone : *Don't give me the runaround* (1924+)

give someone **the sack** *v phr* To dismiss someone; terminate employment [1825+; origin uncertain; the phrase *donner son sac*, "to give him his sack," has been current in

French since the 1600s; *sack* may be "traveling bag, bindle"]

give someone **the shaft** *v phr* To swindle, maltreat, or otherwise deal punishingly with someone; FUCK, SHAFT : *He wasn't expecting much praise, but he sure didn't think they'd give him the shaft like that* (1940s+)

give someone **the shake** (or **the shuck**) *v phr* To rid oneself of someone; get away from someone : *He gave the cops the shake a block or so away/ I've been expecting Tish to give you the shuck* (1940s+)

give someone **the shakes** (or **shivers**) *v phr* To instill fear and trembling; intimidate : *he's being paid $5.4 million by the New York Yankees to give opposing batters the shakes* [1940s+; *the shakes*, "a fit of trembling fear," is found by 1837]

give someone **the shirt off** one's **back** *v phr* To be extremely generous • Usu in a conditional statement : *Open-handed? Why he'd give you the shirt off his back if you needed it* (1771+)

give someone **the slip** *v phr* To evade or escape someone : *They had him cornered, but he gave them the slip* (1567+)

give someone **the time of day,** not *See* NOT GIVE someone THE TIME OF DAY

give someone **the works** *v phr* To mistreat or beat severely; CLOBBER, WORK someone OVER : *They took him into the adjoining room and gave him the works* (1920+) *See* the WORKS

give someone **up** *v phr* To turn someone in to the authorities; to betray : *gave him up to the cops*

give someone **what for** *v phr* To beat or punish severely; drub either physically or verbally; CLOBBER, LET someone HAVE IT : *two or three of us would pitch on him and give him "what-for"* (1873+ British)

give with something *v phr* To give; impart : *He wouldn't give with the information/ gives with the big blue eyes as if to say: "He didn't mean to"* [1940s+ Jive talk; perhaps modeled on *make with* fr Yiddish *machen mit*]

gizmo or **gismo** or **giz** *n* **1** An unspecified or unspecifiable object; something one does not know the name of or does not wish to name; DINGUS, GADGET : *"Why weren't you using the gismo?" "I was. It didn't work"/ "What's this gizmo?" I asked. "The hand brake"/ Guy tried to shove a Pepsi bottle in his wife's giz* **2** GIMMICK (*Gambling*) **3** A man; fellow; GUY : *What's this gizmo have in mind?* [WWII Navy & Marine Corps; origin unknown; it has been suggested that it is fr Moroccan Arabic *ki smuh,* learned during the invasion of North Africa in 1942]

GKW (pronounced as separate letters) *n* Something unknown or unidentifiable : *The* *water contains GKW, God knows what/ known to paleontologists as GKWs or God knows whats*

glad-hand *modifier* Effusive and warm; cordial : *He gave me that glad-hand business* **v** : *After glad-handing the local dignitaries, he heads for the fence* (*1903+*) *See* GIVE someone THE GLAD HAND

glad-hander *n* A person who evinces a warmth and heartiness that is probably insincere; one who is designedly cordial : *He is what is known as a glad-hander, meaning that he merely shakes hands and talks* (*1929+*)

glad rags *n phr* **1** One's best and fanciest clothing; party clothes : *He was piking around in his glad-rags, with the buy-bug in his ear* **2** Formal evening wear (*1902+*)

glahm *See* GLOM

glam *modifier* **1** Glamorous; exhibiting beauty, sexiness, etc : *"Glam" is a term I'm having a little trouble with. Is this short for "glamorous"?/ the super-sexy glam vixens of the '80s/ The glam plan is neat and polished* (*1940s+*) **2** Playing a kind of rock music called "glam-rock" : *They've been asked to open a show for new glam fave Suede* (*mid-1970s+*) **v** To be glamorous; glamorize oneself (*1937+*)

glamazon *modifier* Exhibiting the attractions of a robust woman; Junoesque : *We're getting back to the glamazon look of the '80s: bigger, taller, busty models* (*1980s+*)

glam it up **v** *phr* To dress and behave glamorously; GLAM : *I haven't done the black-tie bit in ages. Why don't we glam it up just for the fun of it?/ Ellen Barkin and Naomi Campbell glammed it up at New York City's fall fashion shows* (*1990s+*)

glass *n* **1** Methedrine capsules **2** Rock cocaine (*1980s+ Narcotics*)

glass ceiling *n phr* A solid but invisible barrier against women's advancement in business and other institutions : *Women could all stop wearing lipstick and blusher tomorrow, and I doubt it would help them break through the glass ceiling/ the sound of glass ceilings breaking as women empowered by the Clinton Administration rise to new positions of influence* (*1990+*)

glasses *See* GRANNY GLASSES

glass jaw or **china chin** *n phr* A boxer's chin that cannot tolerate a hard punch (*1920+ Prizefight*)

glaum *See* GLOM

glaze someone **over** **v** *phr* To make someone ecstatic; intoxicate : *Said one enthusiastic participant: "Doesn't this just glaze you over?"* (*1980s+*)

gleam (or glimmer or twinkle) in the eye, a *n phr* A potential child; a passionate impulse with portent : *At that time he wasn't even born, wasn't even a gleam in his father's eye/*

Your weight was genetically programmed when you were only a glimmer in your parents' eye/ No, I was not even a twinkle in my mother's eye (*1940s+*)

glitch *n* **1** An operating defect; malfunction; a disabling minor problem : *despite such "glitches" (a spaceman's word for irritating disturbances)/ Most had assured themselves that the trouble signal was only a "glitch"* (*1962+ Aerospace*) **2** A sudden interruption of electrical supply, program function, etc : *The term "bug" to refer to a computer glitch* (*1980s+ Computer*) [fr German *glitschen* (or Yiddish *glitshen*), "slip"]

glitter *n* A gaudy style of dress and grooming affected by some musicians, comprising dyed hair, jewels on face and body, and refulgent jumpsuits and cowboy suits (*1960s+*)

glitterati, the *n* Famous and glamorous people; outstanding celebrities : *among the glitterati/ to film the glitterati at a Derby bash* [*1940+*; based on *literati*; in the 1920s the presumed suffix *-ati* was used to form *hustlerati* and *flitterati*]

Glitter City *n phr* Las Vegas, Nevada : *the triumph of the sturdy Midwest over Glitter City* (*1980s+*)

Glitter Gulch *n phr* **1** Reno, Nevada (*1940s+*) **2** GLITTER CITY (*1950s+*)

glitter rock *n phr* Music played by rock groups that affect a spectacular style of dress (*1972+*)

glitz *n* High gaudy finish; flashy surface : *some optional Hollywood glitz/ applied Vegas and hot tub glitz to the old Jack La Lanne* **v** (also **glitz up**) : *the Pirates of Penzance newly glitzed* (*mid-1970s+*) *See* GLITZY

glitzy *adj* Blatantly scintillant; flashy; gaudy : *and a glitzy sister who has backed into degeneracy* [*1966+*; fr German or Yiddish *glitzern,* "glitter, glisten"]

◁**globes**▷ *n* A woman's breasts : *I'd even seen Elena's soft globes* (*1889+*)

glom or **glaum** or **glahm** *n* **1** A hand, regarded as a grabbing tool **2** : *Have a glom at that leg, won't you?* **v** **1** To grasp; seize : *a contingency plan of creating wider seats for their popcorn-glomming customers* **2** GLOM ON TO **3** To steal : *"Where'd you glahm 'em?" I asked/ under the pretext of glomming a diamond from the strongbox* **4** To be arrested **5** To look at; seize with the eyes; GANDER, glim : *or walk around the corner to glom old smack heads, woozy winos and degenerates/ two new collections for the fashionable to glom* [*1907+* Underworld & hoboes; fr British dialect *glaum, glam,* "hand," ultimately fr Old English *clamm,* "bond, grasp," related to *clamp*]

glom (or glaum or glahm) on to **v** *phr* To acquire; grab; seize; LATCH ON TO : *how many*

*times the authorities might have glommed onto
this man but didn't (1907+ Underworld &
hoboes)*

gloomy gus *n phr* A morose, melancholic
person; pessimist; CRAPE-HANGER [1940s+; as
the name of a comic-strip character, *Gloomy
Gus* is found by 1904]

glop *n* **1** Any viscous fluid or mixture; GOO,
GOOK, GUNK : *dimes that rolled into the glop*
(1943+) **2** Sentimentality; maudlin trash;
SCHMALTZ : *That is very dull. I hate glop v* To
smear; daub : *By glopping strings and chorales
onto Tin Pan Alley lyrics, Nashville responded
to rock's commercial success (1980s+)*

glorified *adj* Transformed into something il-
lustrious; glamorized : *The Chrysler van is
much more than a glorified golf cart (1821+)*

glory days (or **years**) *n phr* A time of great
success and acclaim; halcyon days : *Gorelick
knows the lore of the glory days/ Natori's Glory
Days/ George Romney, the man who led the
Rambler glory years at American Motors*
(1980s+)

glory hog *n phr* A person who blatantly seeks
adulation; GLORY HOUND : *Our self-abnegating
chief turned out to be a glory hog (1960s+)*

glory hole *modifier* : *A private glory-hole club
makes a lot more sense n phr* A hole between
stalls in a toilet, through which the penis
may be put for oral sex *(1940s+ Homosexuals)*

glory hound *n phr* GLORY HOG *(1940s+)*

glossy *n* **1** A magazine printed on shiny coated
paper; a high-quality magazine; SLICK : *female editors of the powerful "glossies"/ start
their own glossies in three very different cities
(1940s+)* **2** A photograph printed on shiny
paper *(1920s+)*

glove *v* To catch and hold the ball *(1887+
Baseball) See* NOT LAY A GLOVE ON someone

glow *n* Mild intoxication; tiddliness : *After a
couple of bourbons she had a nice glow*
(1940s+)

glug *n* **1** An imitation of the sound of liquid
pouring from a bottle held upside down and
vertical *(1768+)* **2** The quantity of liquor
poured as the bottle makes one dull gurgle
(1940s+)

glurp *v* SLURP : *She glurped a milkshake (1990s+)*

glutes *n* The gluteus maximus muscles; the
large muscles of the butt : *Work those glutes*

g-ma *n* Grandmother : *and cook the g-ma some
special grub (1990s+)*

G-man *n* A Federal Bureau of Investigations
agent; feeb *(late 1920s+)*

gnarly *adj* **1** Excellent; wonderful; COOL, HAIRY,
GREAT : *That girl is gnarly. She goes to every
party there is* **2** Disgusting : *So, when the halls
became a little too gnarly for Principal Charles
Lutgen/ "Gnarly" means disgusting* [1980s+

Teenagers; said to have originated among
1970s surfers, describing a dangerous wave;
this sense persisted among skateboarders
until at least 1988]

gnome *n* An anonymous expert, esp a statistician or an industrious observer of trends;
BEAN COUNTER : *The Gnomes of Baseball/ the
inhibitions of sports announcers whose minds
have been studied by small-town station managers and network gnomes* [mid-1960s+; the
term is being extended from the first use,
gnomes of Zurich, coined in 1964 and designating the faceless little men who take account of and in part determine the curiosities
of the international money market]

go *adj* **1** Functioning properly; going as planned; A-OK : *As the astronauts say, all signs are
go in the National League (1950s+ Astronauts)* **2** Appropriate; fitting ● The phrase *all
the go,* "the fashion," is found by 1893 :
*beatniks, whose heavy black turtle-neck sweat-
ers had never looked particularly go with white
tennis socks (1960s+) n* **1** A fight : *a rip-
snorting go (1890+)* **2** A try; CRACK, WHACK :
She gave it a good go, and made it (1835+) v **1**
To die *(1390+)* **2** To rule; be authoritative :
Whatever he says goes around here (1891+) **3**
To relieve oneself; go to the bathroom : *The
dog had to go. We set him in the sink (1926+)*
4 To happen; transpire; GO DOWN : *What goes
here? (1940s+)* **5** To say; utter : *You wake up
one morning and you go, "Wait a minute"
(1960s+ Teenagers)* **6** To yield; produce :
She'll go maybe 300, 400 pounds (1816+)
See FROM THE GIT-GO, FROM THE WORD GO, GIVE
something A SHOT, HAVE A CRACK AT something, HAVE something GOING FOR someone or
something, LET FLY, LET oneself GO, NO-GO, NO
GO, ON THE GO, TELL someone WHERE TO GET OFF,
THERE YOU GO, TO GO, WAY TO GO, WHAT GOES
AROUND COMES AROUND

go-ahead, the *modifier* Putting a competitor
in the lead : *The Tigers got the go-ahead run in
the eighth and held the lead to win 9 to 8
(1960s+ Baseball) n* Permission or a signal
to proceed; consent : *She pleaded her case before state officials and got the go-ahead/ His wife
Joan had given him the go-ahead to make the
race (1940s+)*

Go ahead, make my day *sentence* Go ahead
and do what you are going to do, which is
exactly what I want [popularized in film by
Clint Eastwood's "Dirty Harry" character]

goal *See* KNOCK someone FOR A LOOP

go all the way *v phr* **1** To do the utmost; make
a special effort; GO THE EXTRA MILE : *If you
decide to do it, I'll go all the way for you
(1940s+)* **2** GO THE LIMIT

go along for the ride *v phr* To do something or
join in something in a passive way : *I don't*

expect much, but I'll go along for the ride (*1940s+*)

go along with *v phr* **1** To agree with some suggestion or statement **2** To accept or comply with some proposal; acquiesce (*1940s+*)

go along with the crowd *v phr* To lack or eschew individual judgment; do what everyone else does : *What the hell, I figured I'd go along with the crowd and vote yes* (*1940s+*)

go ape (or ◁**ape-shit**▷) *v phr* **1** To behave stupidly, irrationally, and violently; go wild : *When they told him, he went ape and wrecked his room* **2** To be very enthusiastic; admire enormously : *People are going quietly ape over the girl/ Everyone we met, experienced native and green tourist alike, went ape for it* (*1950s+*)

go around the bend *v phr* To become insane; go crazy; FREAK OUT : *Jessica Lange, who goes around the bend with more style, insight, and intensity* (*1920s+*)

◁**go around the world**▷ *v phr* To kiss or lick the whole body of one's partner, esp as a prelude to fellatio or cunnilingus (*1970s+*)

go around with someone *v phr* To be someone's frequent escort or date; be linked romantically or sexually (*1950s+*)

goat *n* **1** A car, esp an old one or one with an especially powerful engine (*1950s+ Hot rodders & teenagers*) **2** A person who takes the blame for failure or wrongdoing; scapegoat; PATSY : *After the latest flop they elected me goat* (*1894+*) **3** The most junior officer in an Army unit (*1970s+ Army*) **4** A switch engine or yard engine (*1916+ Railroad*) **5** A racehorse, esp an aged or inferior beast (*1940s+ Horse racing*) **6** A lecherous man See GET someone's GOAT, OLD GOAT

go at it hammer and tongs *v phr* To do something, esp to quarrel or fight, with great energy [*1833+*; fr the tools of a blacksmith]

gob[1] *n* **1** A mass of viscous matter; BLOB : *She chucked a big gob of plaster at me* (*1382+*) **2** (also **gabs**) A quantity, esp a large quantity : *I think he's got gobs of money* (*1839+*)

gob[2] *n* The mouth • Chiefly British use [*1550+*; fr Irish]

gob[3] *n* A US Navy sailor; SWABBY [*1915+*; perhaps fr earlier British *gabby*, "coast guard; quarterdeckman," of unknown origin]

go back on *v phr* To renege; fail to keep one's word (*1859+*)

go back to (or **be at**) **square one** *v phr* To be forced to return to one's starting point, usu after a waste of effort; make a new beginning [*1960+*; probably fr the first or starting *square* of a board game; an elaborate suggestion that it refers to a British grid system for

locating places on the soccer field, for radio broadcasting of games, cannot be verified] See BACK TO SQUARE ONE, SQUARE ONE

go back to the well *v phr* To return to a reliable source : *We just kept going back to the well and he just kept making it* (*1980s+*)

go ballistic *v phr* To become very angry and irrational; BLOW UP, HIT THE CEILING : *Either way, some constituents will go ballistic/ Henry George would go ballistic over the idea of reopening the capital gains tax break for real estate* [*mid-1980s+*; fr the extreme height attained by a *ballistic* missile, and the idea that upward motion is associated with anger]

go balls out *v phr* To make a supreme effort; GO FOR BROKE : *I went balls out on my term paper* [*1980s+ Students*; see **balls-out** and **balls to the wall**]

go bananas *v phr* **1** To become wildly irrational; FREAK OUT, GO APE : *speculation that maybe old Strom had gone bananas at last* **2** To be extremely enthusiastic; admire enormously : *She went bananas over the dress and bought one in every color* [*late 1960s+*; fr the spectacle of an ape greedily gobbling *bananas*]

go bare *v phr* To be uninsured (*1990s+ Insurance*)

go batshit *v phr* To become wildly irrational; blow one's stack, GO BANANAS : *Sal took a look at the page and went batshit/ The President said that Perot went batshit and has never forgiven him* (*1940s+ Army*)

gobble *v* **1** To make a catch (*1873+ Baseball*) ◁**2**▷ To do fellatio or cunnilingus; eat it (*1920s+*)

gobbledegook or **gobbledygook** *n* Pretentious and scarcely intelligible language, esp of the sort attributed to bureaucrats, sociologists, etc [coined in 1944 by Representative Maury Maverick of Texas]

◁**gobbler**▷ *n* A person who does fellatio or cunnilingus (*1920s+*)

gobble up *v* EAT UP (*1601+*)

go belly up *v phr* To die; collapse; cease to operate; BELLY UP : *two major credit-card firms had gone belly up* (*1870s+*)

go blooey *v phr* (Variations: **flooey** or **kablooey** or **kerflooey** or **kerflooie** or **kerfooey** may replace **blooey**) To end abruptly in failure or disaster; break down; collapse; go down the tube : *Will I make it without the air conditioner in the car going kablooey/ Then, of course, the whole thing all goes flooey* [*1920+*; echoic imitation of an explosion]

go boom See FALL DOWN AND GO BOOM

go broke (or **bust**) *v phr* To become penniless; become insolvent; GO BELLY UP, TAKE A BATH : *His newest escapade into the fashionable world of trade and manufacturing had again gone bust* (*1895+*)

gobs *See* GOB

gobsmacked *adj* Extremely surprised : *gobsmacked at the nomination* [1980s+; fr *gob*, "mouth," and *smacked*, "hit, struck," the theatrical gesture of clapping a hand over the mouth as a gesture of extreme surprise]

gob-stick *n* A clarinet [1936+; a *stick* to put in the *gob*, "mouth"]

go bust *See* GO BROKE

go-by, the *See* GIVE someone or something A MISS

go coast-to-coast *v phr* To take the ball alone from one end of the court to the other, and usu score : *He went coast-to-coast for the lay-in (1990s+ Basketball)*

go commando (or **freeball(ing))** *v phr* As a male, to go without underwear : *sure feels funny to go commando*

go critical *v phr* To become unstable and dangerous : *He felt that the Salvadoran situation was about to go critical* [1955+; fr nuclear physics, "to approach chain reaction"]

God *See* BY GUESS AND BY GOD, OLDER THAN GOD

god-awful *adj* Wretched; miserable; inferior : *cases that would never have come up but for this god-awful legislation* **adv** Extremely : *Ain't it god-awful cold in here? (1878+)*

God-damn or **God-damned** *adj* Accursed; wretched; nasty; FUCKING • Often used for euphony and rhythm of emphasis : *Take your God-damn foot off my God-damn toes* [1851+; much older than the date given; as an oath, found by 1640]

goddess *See* SEX GODDESS

godfather *n* The chief; highest authority; BOSS : *He was Life's first publisher, the godfather of the radio and film* March of Time *series* [1970s+; fr the Mafia term, "head of a Mafia family," voguish after a book and a movie] *See* FAIRY GODFATHER

godmother *See* FAIRY GODMOTHER

go down[1] *v phr* To become inoperative; stop functioning *(1980s+ Computer) See* WHAT'S GOING DOWN

go down[2] *v phr* To happen; GO : *He wanted this scam to go down as rigged/ You can't define it in terms of what kind of rap is going down (1940s+ Black)*

go down[3] *v phr* To be convicted and punished; FALL : *I want somebody to go down for killing the kid and her baby/ You going down on this thing? (1906+)*

◁**go down and do tricks**▷ *v phr* GO DOWN ON someone

go downhill *v phr* To deteriorate; worsen; GO TO POT : *It looks like his health is going downhill fast (1922+)*

go down in flames *v phr* To be utterly ruined; be wrecked : *The ballet has gone down in flames after two years/ He became Washington bureau chief of ABC News and promptly went down in flames* [1940s+; fr the fate of WWI combat pilots, who wore no parachutes]

◁**go down on** someone▷ *v phr* To do fellatio or cunnilingus; eat it, SUCK : *Only she won't go down on me. Isn't that odd?/ When I try to go down on my girlfriend, she routinely blocks my head with her thighs (1916+)*

go down swinging *v phr* To refuse surrender; show fight; nail one's colors to the mast : *The President promised he would go down swinging on that issue* [1930s+; fr baseball, "to strike out, but swing at the third strike"]

go down the line *v phr* To do whatever is necessary; GO ALL THE WAY : *Will unions go down the line for Clinton on the health bills? (1940s+)*

go down the rabbit hole *v phr* To use narcotics [1990s+ students; fr *Alice in Wonderland*, where Alice follows the White Rabbit down the rabbit hole to a land of fantasy]

go down the tube (or **tubes** or **chute** or **drain**) *v phr* To go to wrack and ruin; be lost or destroyed : *Bache was in danger of going down the chute with the price of silver/ speaks of a whole generation going down the tube/ and all of that is going right down the drain/ Should the Government sanction the act of simply sending taxpayers' dollars straight down the gurgler?/ Our foreign policy would not be down the toilet (entry form 1963+, chute 1940s+, drain 1925+, toilet 1980s, tubes 1970s)*

God's gift *n phr* A very special blessing; premier offering • Nearly always ironical : *Wall Street tells MBA's they are God's gift to investment banking/ He is becoming God's gift to columnists (1938+)*

God Squad *n phr* 1 A campus religious organization *(1969+ Students)* 2 A federal government committee that may set aside parts of the Endangered Species Act : *It was the first exemption ever granted by the committee, known as the "God Squad" because its rulings can doom a species (1990s+)*

go Dutch (or **Dutch treat**) *v phr* To pay one's own way at a dinner, show, etc : *Nobody had much money, so we all went Dutch (1914+)*

go easy *v phr* 1 To restrain oneself; control one's anger : *Go easy, fellow, he was just jiving* 2 To be lenient with; spare : *Why do the judges go so easy with these perverts? (1885+)*

goes around *See* WHAT GOES AROUND COMES AROUND

go eyeball to eyeball *v phr* To confront and contend with one another; GO HEAD TO HEAD : *He went eyeball to eyeball with a Soviet delegation (1960+)*

gofer or **go-for** or **gopher** *n* An employee who is expected to serve and cater to others; a low-ranking subordinate : *running the robo* *machine and acting as a receptionist, secretary, and general go-for/ attractive go-fers for executive editor Frank Waldrop* [1967+; *gofor,* an underworld term for "dupe, sucker," is found by the 1920s and is probably semantically related]

gofer (or **gopher**) **ball** *n phr* A pitch likely to be hit for a home run [1932+ Baseball; said to have been coined by the pitcher Vernon Louis "Lefty" Gomez; when hit, the pitch will *go for* a home run]

go figure *v phr* To try to understand, esp something contradictory or astonishing : *Evidence that drug abuse and street crime derive principally from absence of strong fathers. Go figure/ Who knows. Go figure people* [fr Yiddish *gey vays,* "go know"]

go fishing (or **on a fishing expedition**) *v phr* To undertake a search for facts, esp by a legal or quasi-legal process like a grand-jury investigation (*1960+*)

go flatline *v phr* To die : *In the ambulance he went flatline* (*1980s+*) *See* FLATLINE

go fly a kite *sentence* Cease annoying me; GO TO HELL, GET LOST : *I asked for more, and he told me to go fly a kite* (*1940s+*)

go for *v phr* **1** To be in favor of; admire; be attracted to : *I really go for her* (*1835+*) **2** To attack : *Three of the villains went for me* (*1838+*) *See* HAVE something GOING FOR someone or something

go for all the marbles *v phr* GO FOR BROKE : *He goes for all the marbles* (*1970s+*)

go for broke *v phr* To make a maximum effort; stake everything on a big try • This was the battle cry of the 442d Regimental Combat Team, made up of Japanese-Americans, in World War II [1940s+ Hawaiian English; fr a gambler's last desperate or hopeful wager]

go for it *v phr* To make a try for something, esp a valiant and risky one • Often an encouraging imperative : *Will we play it safe, or go for it?/ Go for it! You've almost got it knocked!* (*1871+*)

go for the fences *v phr* To try to make long base hits, esp home runs; SLUG (*1970s+ Baseball*)

go for the gold *v phr* To strive for the highest reward; GO FOR BROKE : *Everything else looks real. They were going for the gold/ Any time Hollywood goes for the gold there are bound to be contestants that finish dead last* [1980s+; fr the *gold medal* awarded to the first-place finisher in Olympic competitions]

go for the jugular *v phr* To compete in dead earnest; give or take no quarter : *They were a tough team that always went for the jugular* [1980s+; fr the *jugular vein* in the neck, severance of which is usually fatal; the image is of a wolf or other attacking animal]

go for the long ball *v phr* To take a large risk for a large gain; GO FOR BROKE : *entering the fall campaign, might decide to go for the long ball* [fr football 1970s+; fr a *long* pass, the "bomb," thrown in a football game]

◀**go fuck** (or **impale**) oneself▶ *sentence* May you be accursed, confounded, humiliated, rejected, etc; GO TO HELL : *Oh, go fuck yourself, Stern/ Ah, go impale yourselves, the bunch of you v phr : If people were only interested in it 'cause she balled Paul McCartney "then they could go fuck themselves"* (*1960s+*)

go full bore *v phr* To go at the utmost speed : *We're going full bore, Sheriff Wells says* (*mid-1930s+*) *See* FULL BORE

go full term *v phr* To reach completion or fruition : *Although today's test did not go full term, we were impressed with the professional manner with which the launch team responded* [1990s+; fr the obstetrical designation *full term,* "full development of the fetus at birth"]

go gangbusters *See* GANGBUSTERS

go-getter *n* A vigorous and effective person; WINNER : *sometimes enviously referred to as a go-getter, a hot shot, a ball of fire* (*1921+*)

go-go *adj* **1** Having to do with discotheques, their music, style of dancing, etc (*1960s+*) **2** Stylish; modish; TRENDY : *She may be getting on in years, but she certainly is a go-go dresser* **3** Showing vitality and drive, esp in business and commerce; urgent and energetic : *Religion is a really go-go growth industry these days/ Japan's go-go entrepreneurs can turn their operations into the new Goliaths n* **1** A bar or club with go-go girls : *It surely won't keep minors out of go-gos* (mid-1980s+) **2** The penis : *Mrs Bobbitt cut off her husband's go-go* (*1990s+*)

go-go girl (or **dancer**) *n phr* A scantily clad or partly naked young woman employed to do solo gyrational dancing in a discotheque or club on a small stage or platform, in a cage, etc (*1967+*)

go gold *v phr* To sell enough copies to become a gold record : *A rerelease of his album recently went gold* (*1990s+*)

go great guns *v phr* To do extremely well; succeed remarkably : *He's going great guns as a wine-taster* [1913+; fr the early 1800s nautical expression *blow great guns*]

go gunning for someone *See* GUN FOR someone

go halvsies (or **halvies** or **halfies**) *v phr* To award an equal share; divide in two equal parts : *I may go halvsies/ If he stonewalled them or went halvesies with the truth* [1940s+; *go halves* is found by 1848]

go haywire *v phr* **1** To become inoperative; break down unexpectedly; GO BLOOEY : *This radio's gone haywire* **2** To go crazy; become confused and disoriented : *Remember that I tried to talk you out of it, and don't go haywire* [1929+; fr the ramshackle condition of something that must be hastily repaired with *haywire*]

go head to head *v phr* To confront and contend with one another; GO EYEBALL TO EYEBALL : *Lawyers Susan Sarandon and Tommy Lee Jones go head to head over the fate of an eleven-year-old boy* (1960s+)

go (or **run**) **hog-wild** *v phr* To be wildly excited and unrestrained : *I'm going to take a round-house wallop at the first thing I see and run hog-wild on the bases/ A person easily excited goes "hog-wild and crazy"* (1904+)

go Hollywood *v phr* To affect arrogance, gaudy dress, and other presumed traits of motion-picture success : *It is at this point that the Hollywood ingenue goes Hollywood* (1929+)

go home feet first (or **in a box**) *v phr* To die : *Make one wrong move and you go home feet first* (1940s+)

goifa *See* GREEFA

going *See* HAVE something GOING FOR someone or something

going concern, a *n phr* A project, business, operation, etc, that is successfully launched and functioning smoothly : *Just an idea last year, now it's a going concern* (1881+)

going down *See* WHAT'S GOING DOWN

going out of style *See* LIKE IT'S GOING OUT OF STYLE

going-over, a *n phr* **1** A beating; trouncing : *The goons gave him a brutal going over* (1940s+) **2** An examination; scrutiny : *Give these records a going-over, please* (1919+) [related to the first sense, "a scolding, a dressing-down" is found by 1872]

goings-on *n* Happenings, events : *keeps her up on the group's goings-on*

go into one's **act** *v phr* DO one's NUMBER (1940s+)

go into one's **dance** *v phr* (Variations: **dog and pony show** or **song and dance** may replace **dance**) To begin a prepared line of pleading, explanation, selling, seduction, etc : *He went into his dance, but she wasn't convinced* (1980s+)

go into orbit *v phr* To reach very extreme and apparently uncontrolled heights : *those whose stocks can absorb, say, $50 million or more without going into orbit* (1960s+)

go into the dumper *v phr* To fail utterly; be discarded : *Gone to Carnival had gone straight into the dumper* [1990s+; *dumper* is probably a shortening of *Dumpster*, trademark for a refuse bin]

go into the tank *v phr* To lose a fight, game, etc, deliberately; THROW : *Some night you*

went *inna tank?* [1940s+ Prizefight; fr the resemblance between a fighter hitting the canvas and a person *taking a dive into a tank*]

go it alone *v phr* To do something arduous or tricky by oneself : *She tried going it alone but found it scary* [1842+; fr the game of euchre, where one may play against combined opponents]

go jump in the lake *sentence* May you be accursed, confounded, humiliated, etc; DROP DEAD, GO FUCK oneself : *Go jump in the lake (or perhaps something a little stronger), Wauwatosa Ald Joseph Ptaszek essentially told several people/ 'So far,' Rothschild said, 'Nader hasn't told us to jump in the lake.'* (1912+)

go kerplunk *v phr* To fail; FLOP, GO BLOOEY : *If they go kerplunk, someone will have to scrape up the pieces* (1940s+)

gold *n* A high grade of marijuana (1960s+ Narcotics) *See* ACAPULCO GOLD

gold braid *n phr* Naval officers, esp high-ranking ones : *It is evident that the gold braid doesn't think enough of the order* (1940s+)

goldbrick *n* (also **goldbricker**) A shirker; a person who avoids work or duty; GOOF-OFF (WWI armed forces) *v* **1** : *She made him promise to quit goldbricking* **2** To swindle; cheat; CON (1902+) [fr the convention of the confidence trickster who sells spurious *gold bricks*]

gold-digger *n* A woman who uses her charms and favors to get money, presents, etc, from wealthy men : *Lorelei Lee, the crazy-like-a-fox gold-digger* (1920+)

golden *adj* Supremely fortunate; excellent : *I'm golden*

golden-ager *n* An elderly person : *golden-agers playing bingo*

golden boy *n phr* A favored and especially gifted boy or man; FAIR-HAIRED BOY : *Casey regarded Inman as a brittle golden boy, worried about his image* [1937+; popularized by the title of Clifford Odets's 1937 play about a boxer]

golden handcuffs *n phr* Arrangements, options, perquisites, etc, that induce one to stay in one's job : *These ties that bind have become known in industry as golden handcuffs* (1976+)

golden oldie or **oldie but goodie** *n phr* An old record, song, person, etc, still regarded as good, esp one that has revived or sustained popularity : *a golden oldie like "Honeysuckle Rose"/ All the golden oldies are replayed and the untied threads neatly resolved/ Oldies but Goodies Could Put Success in Senior Tours: There's a golden patch of oldies who can still play great tennis/ oldies but goodies such as "Down by the Riverside"* [mid-1960s+; probably influenced by association with the *gold* phonograph record struck for a recording that has sold a million copies and more]

golden parachute (or **handshake**) *n phr* Very high sums, benefits, etc, offered for taking early retirement : *"Golden parachutes" or severance packages are all becoming more common/ A parting golden handshake with GM included a valuable Cadillac franchise (first form 1980s+, second 1960+)*

◁**golden shower**▷ *n phr* Urination on someone who sexually enjoys such a wetting : *what girls do through the bladder, which is otherwise known as the "golden shower"/ Golden showers? Not me (1940s+ Homosexuals & prostitutes)*

goldfinger *n* A type of synthetic heroin *(1960s+ Narcotics)*

goldfish bowl *n phr* A place or situation where one is exposed; a venue without privacy : *Celebrities must live in a goldfish bowl (1935+)*

goldilocks *n* **1** Any pretty blonde woman • Often used ironically : *Well, thought Jimmy, it won't be because of you, goldilocks (1598+)* **2** A burglar who breaks into a house, eats, and otherwise makes himself at home, but takes nothing of value *(1990s+)* [second sense fr the folk tale *Goldilocks and the Three Bears*]

gold mine, a *n phr* A fortunate or unexpected source of great wealth : *I didn't think much of the book, but the royalties have been a gold mine* [1882+; a somewhat ambiguous use in 1664 probably refers to an actual *gold mine*]

gold piece *See* COME UP SMELLING LIKE A ROSE

golf widow *n phr* A woman often left alone while her mate plays golf *(1908+)*

golly *interj* A mild exclamation of surprise, dismay, pleasure, etc; GOSH : *Golly, Mom, did you really win it? [1775+;* a euphemism for God]

gomer *n* **1** A patient needing extensive care; a vegetative comatose patient : *We got a real gomer in from ICU yesterday/ He says the guy's a total gomer now (1960s+ Medical)* **2** A first-year Air Force Academy cadet, esp a clumsy trainee *(1950s+)* [origin uncertain; medical sense said to be an acronym of "get out of my emergency room"]

gon or **gond** *See* GUN²

go native *v phr* To take on the behavior and standards of the place one has moved to or is visiting, esp when this means a loss of rigor, respectability, etc : *On Bleecker Street he went native and donned a black sweatshirt and sneakers (1901+)*

gone *adj* **1** Intoxicated, esp with narcotics *(1940s+ Jazz musicians)* **2** In a trancelike condition; meditative : *gurgling forth a flow of words, a "gone" expression on his face*

(1940s+ Cool talk) **3** Excellent; wonderful; COOL : *a real gone chick (1940s+ Cool talk)*

gone on (or **over**) *adj phr* In love with; enamored of : *I was so gone over her (1885+)*

goner, a *n* Someone or something that is doomed; someone dead or about to die; DEAD DUCK : *pray, or you're a goner/ for Rome will be a goner (1850+)*

gong *n* **1** (also **gonger**) An opium pipe *(1914+ Narcotics)* **2** A military decoration; medal or ribbon *(British WWII use)* [both senses probably fr *gong*, "saucer-shaped metal bell," of Malayan origin; the sense "opium pipe" may be related to the general association of *gongs* with Chinese matters, and the military sense to the notion that a decoration is something like the ceremonial sounding of a *gong*]

gonged *adj* **1** Intoxicated with narcotics; HIGH, STONED : *She's sitting in the front row gonged to the gills with acid (1900s+ Narcotics)* **2** Dismissed; FIRED, SACKED : *Just ask Pat Sheridan, who was gonged by WISN last fall (1980s+)* [second sense fr television *Gong Show*, where performers were dismissed by the sound of a *gong*]

gongoozler *n* A person who stares idly or protractedly at something *(1900s+)*

goniff (GAH nəf) *n* (Variations: **gonef** or **gonif** or **gonof** or **gonoph** or **ganef** or **ganof** or **guniff**) A thief; a person who is in effect a thief, like an unethical salesperson : *And who is this arch-goniff?/ a gonof like Glick/ all the other gonophs, consultants who peddle bullshit, builders who build badly (1845+)* *v* : *Are you trying to goniff me, pal?* [fr Yiddish, "thief," fr Hebrew *gannabh*, "thief"]

gonk *See* CONK

gonna *v phr* Going to • Casually pronounced form : *I'm gonna veg out tonight (1913+)*

go no-go *adj phr* Pertaining to the last critical moment at which a project, plans, etc, can still be canceled; relating to the point of no return : *It's go no-go. Either we do it or we kill it (1960s+ Astronauts)*

go nowhere *v phr* To be unsuccessful or frustrated in an attempt : *her proposal went nowhere*

go nowhere fast *v phr* To proceed very slowly; be stalled : *The proposal is officially still pending but going nowhere fast (1940s+)*

gonsil or **gonzel** *See* GUNSEL

go nuclear *v phr* GO BALLISTIC : *Susan and poor, meek little Emmett Couch went nuclear (1990s+)*

gonzo (GAHN zoh) *adj* Insane; wild; bizarre; confused; CUCKOO, BANANAS, NUTSO : *established Hunter Thompson as the father of gonzo journalism, a flamboyant if controversial style/ the gonzo idea of a cross-country street race* *n* :

The Gonzo and the Geeks/ These double-gaited gonzos are perpetrating a plague of best-selling takeoffs [1971+; fr Italian, "credulous, simple, too good"]

goo *n* **1** Any sticky and viscous substance; GLOP, GUNK : *fell in the goo rounding third/ a layer of goo on the skin* (1903+) **2** Sentimentality; maudlin rubbish; GLOP, SCHMALTZ (1922+) **3** Fulsome flattery; overly affectionate greetings : *They ladle out the old goo* [perhaps sound symbolism, influenced by *glue;* perhaps fr *burgoo,* "oatmeal porridge"]

goob or **goob-a-tron** *n* A tedious, contemptible person; DORK, NERD : *Nerds can be "goobs" or "tools"/ A Goob-a-tron's Guide to Rad Speak* [1980s+ Students & teenagers; fr *goober*]

goober *n* **1** A minor skin lesion; ZIT : *whiteheads, blackheads, goopheads, goobers, pips* **2** A stupid and bizarre person; GEEK, WEIRDO [1970s+ Teenagers; fr *goober,* "peanut," fr Kongo *nguba,* "kidney, peanut"; first sense probably because the first syllable describes the *goo* that exudes from or is squeezed from the lesion]

good *See* BE GOOD, DO-GOOD, DO-GOODER, FEEL GOOD, HAVE IT GOOD, MAKE GOOD, NO-GOOD

good and mad *modifier* Thoroughly angry : *good and mad at you*

good buddy *n phr* **1** The person one is cordially addressing (1970s+ Citizens band) **2** One's homosexual lover (1970s+ Homosexuals) **3** A male homosexual : *It turns out that the most famous term in the CB vocabulary has become slang for "homosexual"* (1980s+ Citizens band)

good-bye *See* KISS something GOOD-BYE

Good call! *interj* That was a good decision : *Chinese takeout? Good call!*

good cop bad cop or **nice cop tough cop** *modifier* Marked by alternations between friendliness and hostility, easiness and rigor, etc : *Successful management requires a variation of the "good cop, bad cop" routine/ In short, a "nice cop" Rousseau and a "tough cop" Rousseau/ I think that she's the good cop and he's the bad one, and I think it's quite deliberate* [fr the interrogation technique by which one police officer pretends to sympathize with the suspect and to protect him from a pitiless and menacing fellow officer]

good deal *interj* An exclamation of agreement, pleasure, congratulation, etc : *You made it? Good deal!* *n phr* A pleasant and favorable situation, life, job, etc : *He had a good deal there at the bank, but blew it* (WWII armed forces)

good egg *n phr* A decent and kindly person; a reliable and admirable citizen : *Henry Fonda frequently was cast as the good egg* [1903+; modeled on *bad egg,* found by 1855]

gooder *See* DO-GOODER

good-for-nothing *adj* : *You good-for-nothing bastard, you* (1711+) *n* A worthless person; scoundrel; BUM (1751+)

good golly Miss Molly *interj* An exclamation of emphasis, surprise, indignation, etc; goodness gracious : *Good golly, Miss Molly! Lascivious lyrics were not, after all, introduced to the lower orders from above* [1950s+; fr the title of a 1950s song by Little Richard (Richard Penniman)]

good hair day *n phr* A day when things go right; good day : *She said she was having a good hair day as she arranged the seating for the photos during the interview* (1990s+) *See* BAD HAIR DAY

goodie or **goody** *modifier* : *Then I got out my goodie bag n* **1** GOODY-GOODY **2** A special treat; something nice to eat : *a huge basket of goodies* (1940s+) **3** Something nice; a pleasant feature; something very desirable : *headlight with a middle beam, the goodie you've been waiting for/ The local population took to the goodies of Western culture with avidity* (1940s+) **4** (also **good guy**) Someone on the side of virtue and decency, in contrast with a villain : *It's much easier to make a girl a baddie than a goodie* (1930s+ Motion pictures) *See* GOLDEN OLDIE

good-looker *n* Someone or something that is handsome and attractive, esp a woman; LOOKER : *Is she a good looker?* (1893+)

good night *interj* An exclamation of surprise, irritation, emphasis, etc : *Good night! Must you chew that gum so loud?* [1880s+; a euphemism for *good God*]

good old (or **ole**) **boy** *modifier* : *Kevin Baker and Fred Ward have good-ol'-boy chemistry n phr* A white Southerner who exemplifies the masculine ideals of the region; BUBBA : *The helpful truck driver was a good old boy from around Nashville* (1970s+)

good one *n phr* A lie • Euphemistic : *You passed? Good one*

goods *n* Narcotics of any sort (Narcotics) *See* GREEN GOODS, PIECE OF CALICO, STRAIGHT GOODS

goods, the *n phr* **1** Something or someone of excellent quality; just what is wanted : *She's the real goods* (1904+) **2** The evidence needed to arrest and convict a criminal : *We've got the goods on him* (1908+) **3** Stolen property; contraband : *They caught him with the goods in his pocket* (1900s+) *See* DELIVER THE GOODS, GET THE GOODS ON someone

◁**good shit**▷ *interj* GOOD DEAL *n phr* Anything favorable or pleasant; something one approves of : *This place is real good shit, ain't it?* (1950s+)

good sport *n phr* A person who plays fair, accepts both victory and defeat, and stays amiable : *I just want to be a good sport and get along with people* (1917+)

good time *n phr* Time deducted from a prison term for good behavior : *a period of solitary confinement and a loss of "good time"* (1870+ Prison)

good-time Charlie *n phr* A man devoted to partying and pleasure; bon vivant (1927+)

good to go *interj* A rallying cry; battle cry; GUNG HO : *the similar "good to go" that came out of the Gulf* (Persian Gulf War Army)

good word *See* WHAT'S THE GOOD WORD

goody-goody *modifier* : *what might have been a goody-goody role* (1871+) *n* A prim and ostentatiously virtuous person : *I'm not a mammy boy nor a goody-goody* (1873+)

goody gumdrops *interj* An unenthusiastic exclamation of semiapproval : *watching more TV, goody gumdrops*

goody two-shoes *modifier* : *in spite of its Goody Two-Shoes ecological image n phr* An obviously innocent and virtuous young woman; GOODY-GOODY ● Most often used mockingly or contemptuously (1766+) [fr the name of the heroine of a 1760s children's story, probably by Oliver Goldsmith, about a little girl who exulted publicly at the acquisition of a second shoe]

gooey *adj* Consisting of, covered with, or resembling goo : *These passages seem affected and a bit gooey/ the story of Teresa Stratas, without gooey heaviness* (1906+)

goof *n* 1 A stupid person; BOOB, KLUTZ, SAP : *two goofs can't agree on how many orgasms they should have/ High school girls now talk of the "goofs we go with"* (1916+) 2 An insane person; mental case : *He couldn't have acted more like a goof* (1940s+) 3 One's cellmate (1930s+ Prison) 4 A blunder; bad mistake; BOO-BOO : *They covered their goof quite well* (1950s+ Jive talk) *v* 1 : *You goofed again; it's a one-way street* (1941+) 2 To pass one's time idly and pleasantly; GOOF OFF : *In Sarajevo, members of a student volunteer brigade goofed and joked as they worked* (1932+) 3 GOOF AROUND (1940s+) 4 To fool; KID : *Don't goof your grandpa* (1940s+) [fr British dialect *goof, goff,* "fool"]

goof around *v phr* 1 To pass one's time idly and pleasantly; potter about; FART AROUND 2 To joke and play when one should be serious; FUCK AROUND, HORSE AROUND : *The monarch ordered the field marshal to quit goofing around and win the goddamn war* (1940s+)

goofball *n* 1 A stupid and clumsy person; GOOF : *roles that earned him the affectionate labeling as a "goof ball"* (1959+) 2 An eccentric person; ODDBALL, WEIRDO (1959+) 3 A pill or capsule of Nembutal® (1940s+ Narcotics) 4 A barbiturate, tranquilizer, etc, used as a narcotic

: *took over three hundred goof balls* (1940s+ Narcotics) 5 A portion or dose of a narcotic; BALL, gb : *A goof ball is a narcotics preparation which is burned on a spoon and inhaled* (1930s+ Narcotics) 6 Marijuana (1930s+ Narcotics)

goof-butt *See* GOOFY-BUTT

goofed *adj* Intoxicated with a narcotic, esp marijuana; HIGH, STONED (1950s+ Narcotics)

goofer or **goopher** *n* 1 A fool; GOOF : *Don't be a critical goopher or you can't go* (1925+) 2 An intrepid fighter pilot (WWII Army Air Forces)

◁**go off**▷ *v phr* To have an orgasm; COME OFF (1928+)

go off half-cocked *v phr* To make a premature response, esp an angry one : *Let's not go off half cocked/ But before I went off half-cocked, I had to check the alibis* [1833+; fr the accidental firing of a gun at *half cock*]

go off on someone *v phr* To lose one's temper; attack someone : *Now think about this before you go off on me* (1980s+ Students)

go off the deep end *v phr* To go into a violent rage; BLOW one's TOP [1921+; perhaps fr the notion of jumping into a pool at the *deep end,* hence being in *deep* water, in trouble] *See* JUMP OFF THE DEEP END

go off the rails *v phr* To behave abnormally; lose stability : *Most of what she said was okay, but she went off the rails with that last remark* (1848+)

goofiness *n* The acts, ways, ideas, etc, of those who are goofy : *an unparalleled tolerance for goofiness* (1920s+)

goof-off *n* 1 A person who regularly or chronically avoids work; FUCK-OFF : *getting kicked out of seminary as a goof-off* 2 A period of relaxation; respite : *A little goof-off will do you good* (WWII armed forces)

goof off *v phr* To pass one's time idly and pleasantly; potter about; shirk work; GOOF AROUND : *My goofing off in the final period had knocked down a possible A average/ Are you trying to tell me my son is goofing off?* (WWII armed forces)

goof on someone *v phr* To play a joke on someone; fool someone (1970s+ Teenagers)

goof-proof *v* To ensure against mistakes; forestall errors : *her own formulas for goof-proofing a party* (1970s+)

goof-up *n* A blunder, esp a serious one; FUCK-UP, SNAFU (1960s+)

goof up *v phr* 1 To spoil; disable; QUEER : *He goofed up the whole deal by talking too soon* 2 To blunder; GOOF : *that can look at a child when he goofs up and reflect, "I understand and I love you"* (1960+)

goofus *n* 1 THINGAMAJIG (1940s+) 2 A small calliope (1915+ Circus) 3 A saxophone-shaped, breath-operated reed instrument with a keyboard covering two octaves, intended as an easy aid to the musically uneducated • The name may have been given by the jazz saxophonist Adrian Rollini, who led a group called *The Goofus Five,* featuring the instrument; it was originally known as the Couesnophone after the French manufacturer Couesnon et Compagnie *(mid-1920s+)* **4** A stupid person; DIMWIT, DOPE, spazz : *The networks always remind me of slow-witted goofuses squatting out there in the L A glare (1918+)* **5** A rural person; naive spectator; EASY MARK *(1920+ Circus & carnival)* **6** Tasteless and meretricious material or entertainment designed for the unsophisticated *(1950s+ Show business)*

goofy *adj* Silly; foolish; crazy; dotty • Nearly always has an affectionate and amused connotation : *a goofy grin/ a goofy awkward kid/ And he looked, well, goofy (1921+)*

goofy about *adj phr* CRAZY ABOUT *(1921+)*

goofy-butt or **goof-butt** *n* A marijuana cigarette; JOINT *(1950s+ Narcotics)*

googly *adj* Protruding; exophthalmic : *her great big googly eyes* [1901+; origin uncertain; perhaps fr *goggle,* which meant "stare at admiringly or amorously"; perhaps fr mid-1800s *google,* "the Adam's apple," where the eyes are thought of as similarly protruding; perhaps influenced by *goo* in the sense of "sentimental, amorous"; popularized by the hero of a comic strip]

goo-goo or **gu-gu** *adj* Infantile; cooing : *talking goo-goo talk to her, like you would to a baby (1863+)*

goo-goo eyes *n phr* Eyes expressing enticement, desire, seduction, etc [1897+; probably fr *googly,* with which it is synonymous in early uses] *See* MAKE GOO-GOO EYES

gook[1] or **guck** *n* Dirt; grime; sediment; GLOP, GOO, GUNK : *Glim gets the gook off/ Joan has white guck all over her face (1940s+)*

◀**gook**[2]▶ *modifier* : *Give it to the gook hospitals n* An Asian or Polynesian; slope • Originally a Filipino insurrectionary, then a Nicaraguan, then any Pacific Islander during WWII, the term embraced Koreans after 1950, Vietnamese and any Asian fr 1960s; sometimes used of any colored person : *take it on the chin better than an American or a Zulu or a gook/ the way he felt about Vietnam and the gooks/ It was there that I first heard of dinks, slopes, and gooks* [1900s+ Army; fr *gugu,* a term of Filipino origin, perhaps fr Vicol *gugurang,* "familiar spirit, personal demon," adopted by US armed forces during the Filipino Insurrection of 1899 as a contemptuous term for Filipinos, and spread among US troops to other places of occupa-

tion, invasion, etc; probably revived after 1950 by the Korean term *kuk,* which is a suffix of nationality, as in *Chungkuk,* "China," etc]

◁**gooky**▷ *adj* Sticky; viscid; greasy : *Greaseless. Nongooky (1940s+)*

goombah (also **goombar** or **gumba** or **gumbah**) *n* **1** A friend; companion; trusted associate; patron; PAL : *They called him Joey Gallo's rabbi or his goombah/ trying to make these old goombars understand/ We want all our gumbahs to come over and get rich* **2** An organized-crime figure; Mafioso : *I'm gonna kill any greasy Guinea goombah that tries to stop me/ This big dumb gumba can send you home with your nuts in a paper bag* [fr dialect pronunciation of Italian *compare,* "companion, godfather"]

goon *modifier* : *goon squad/ his goon tactics n* **1** A strong, rough, intimidating man, esp a paid ruffian : *Fondled, pinched, handled by a big red-haired goon who was our jailer* **2** Any unattractive or unliked person; JERK, PILL : *He had the face of a pure goon* **3** The police [mid-1930s+; origin uncertain; perhaps entirely fr the name of Alice the Goon, a large hairy creature who appeared in E C Segar's comic strip "Thimble Theatre" in 1936, but who had a very gentle disposition; perhaps connected with Frederick Lewis Allen's term for "a person with a heavy touch," that is, a literary or stylistic touch, found by 1921; perhaps fr *gooney*]

go on *interj* A mild exclamation of disbelief, esp when one is praised : *Oh, go on, I'm not that good (1940s+)*

goon boy *n phr* A despised person; GEEK, JERK, NERD *(1950s+ Students)*

go something or **someone one better** *v phr* To surpass or outbid; raise the standard : *That wasn't a bad offer, but I'll go you one better* [1845+ Gamblers; fr the raising of bets in poker]

gooned or **gooned out** *v phr* Intoxicated; HIGH, STONED : *Getting gooned on Nyquil (1960s+)*

gooney *n* A stupid person; simpleton; fool [1895+; fr earlier *goney, gonus,* "simpleton," found by 1580, and of obscure origin]

gooney bird *n phr* The DC-3 airplane : *Pilots everywhere refer to it with great affection as the "Gooney Bird" after the albatross* [WWII aviators; fr the slow but sure flight of the *gooney bird,* "black-footed albatross," the bird so called by seamen because of its foolish look and awkward behavior when on the ground]

goonk *See* GUNK

goon squad *n phr* A group of ruffians • Used of the opposition by both sides in labor disputes : *A few weeks later, another "goon squad," as* *they have been rightly labeled/ What some doctors deride as investigative "goon squads"* (mid-1930s+)

go on the hook for something *v phr* To go into debt : *So you'll go on the hook for one of those eighty-dollar sports-car coats* (1950s+)

go on track *v phr* To patrol an area seeking prostitution customers; HOOK : *Then I'd go on track till 4 AM, sleep two more hours, and start over* (1970s+ Prostitutes)

goop or **goup** *n* **1** A nasty viscid substance; GLOP, GOO : *Suck up the goop and then spill it over* **2** Stupidly sentimental material; sugary rubbish : *who can't transcend the Positive Mental Attitude goop she is forced to utter* [1940s+; probably fr *goo*]

goopher *See* GOOFER

goopy *adj* **1** Viscid; nastily sticky : *You certainly tend to get goopy fancy food these days* **2** Stupidly sentimental; maudlin; GOOEY : *There's no way to talk about that without sounding goopy/ Please, not another goopy eulogy to the past* (1940s+)

goose *n* **1** A rough prod in the anal region : *He threatened a goose, and I cringed* **2** A strong verbal prodding : *The whole bunch needed a good goose* *v* **1** To prod someone roughly and rudely in the anal region, usu as a coarse and amiable joke : *As she was bending over her lab table, a playful lab assistant goosed her* (1881+) **2** To exhort strongly and irritably; goad harshly : *and goosed the media into hyping them/ Every once in a while goose it with defense spending* (1930s+) **3** To run an engine at full speed or with spurts of high speed; GUN : *Vroom-vroom-vroom, he goosed the engine to full-throated life* (1940s+) [fr the presumed prodding action of an angry *goose*; influenced by an earlier sense, "to do the sex act to; screw," where the instrument is a tailor's goose, a smoothing iron with a curved handle, found by 1690] *See* COOK someone's GOOSE, LOOSE AS A GOOSE

goose bumps (or **pimple**) *n phr* A roughness of the skin or the production of small pimples on the skin as the result of fear, cold, or excitement; gooseflesh (*first form* 1930s+, *second* 1914+)

goose egg *n phr* Zero; nothing; a score of zero; ZILCH : *My contribution appears to have been a great big goose egg* (1866+ Baseball)

goose something **up** *v phr* To make something more exciting, intense, impressive, etc; JAZZ something UP : *If we tried to goose it up too much, it wouldn't help anybody* (1970s+)

goosy or **goosey** *adj* Touchy; jumpy; sensitive : *I feel a little goosy about the whole thing/ Hennessey was goosey anyway, and he jumped* (1906+) *See* LOOSE AS A GOOSE

go out *v phr* **1** To die (1888+) **2** (also **go out like a light**) To lose consciousness; PASS OUT : *Last thing I heard before I went out was the siren/ Something swished and I went out like a light* (1930s+)

go out of one's **skull** *v phr* **1** To become very tense; get nervous : *You can go out of your skull while they're doing that* **2** To become very excited; be overcome with emotion; GO APE : *They went out of their skulls when she grabbed the mike to sing* **3** To be overcome with tedium; fret with boredom : *The silence made him go right out of his skull* (1960s+)

go out of one's **way** *v phr* To make a special effort; try very hard; BEND OVER BACKWARDS : *I went out of my way to be nice to the guy* (1876+)

go out on a limb *v phr* To put oneself in a vulnerable position; take a risk : *OK, I'll go out on a limb and vouch for you* (1897+)

go over *v phr* To succeed; be accepted : *This demonstration will never go over with the hard hats* [1910+; *go* in this sense is found by 1742]

go over big *v phr* To succeed very well; be received with great approval : *Her proposal went over big with the biggies* [1920s+; the form *go big* is found by 1903]

go overboard *v phr* **1** To be smitten with love or helpless admiration : *He went overboard for her right away* **2** To commit oneself excessively or perilously; overdo : *Take a couple, but don't go overboard* **3** JUMP OFF THE DEEP END (1931+)

go over like a lead balloon *v phr* To fail miserably; FLOP : *The whole thing went over like a lead balloon* (1940s+)

go over the hill *v phr* To go absent without leave from a military unit (1920s+ Armed forces)

go over with a bang *v phr* To succeed splendidly; be enthusiastically approved : *My idea for a new bulletin board went over with a bang* (1928+)

go pfft (or **phut** or **phffft** or **poof**) *v phr* To end or fail; dissolve; break up; FIZZLE : *Their romance went pfft after that/ This year, two ballyhooed mergers have gone phffft/ New opportunities are emerging even as old ones go poof* [1930s+, second form by 1880s; used by gossip columnists; fr the British echoic phrase *go phut*, "come to grief, fizzle out," found by 1888, and imitative of the sound of a dull impact]

gopher[1] *n* **1** A young thief or hoodlum : *tough West Side gophers who wouldn't hesitate to use a gun* (1893+) **2** A safecracker (1901+ Underworld) **3** A safe or vault (1970s+ Underworld); (1870s+) **4** GOFER

gopher[2] *v* To hit a GOFER BALL in baseball : *only about the fifth or sixth that Orosco had gophered home the eventual gamer*

gopher ball *See* GOFER BALL

go pittypat *v phr* (also **pit-a-pat** or **pitterpat**) To beat strongly and excitedly; pump with joy and anticipation : *My veteran heart went pittypat* (1601+)

go places *v phr* To do very well in one's work; have a successful career; make good (1930s+)

go postal *v phr* To succumb to tension and fatigue; LOSE IT, STRESS OUT [1990s+ Computer; a grim reference to "the unfortunate number of postal employees in recent years who have snapped or gone on shooting rampages"—*Macon Telegraph*]

go public *v phr* To reveal oneself; acknowledge openly; COME OUT OF THE CLOSET : *how she adjusted to going public as a single-breasted woman/ Rumor is that the FBI is about to go public with another suspect* [fr the financial idiom *go public*, "offer stock for sale in the stock market after it had previously been held in a family or otherwise privately"]

gorilla *n* 1 (also **gorill**) A ruffian; GOON : *Strong-arm men, gorillas, and tough gangsters/ Those gorills do not care anything about law* (1904+) 2 A hired killer; HIT MAN (1920s+) 3 Anything very powerful and unstoppable; anything very forceful and intimidating : *It is very simple to create the appearance of a "gorilla," a product with a lot of momentum* (1980s+) *v* 1 To steal or rob with threat and violence : *if you let somebody gorilla you out of some money* (1960s+) 2 To beat someone up; savage someone; CLOBBER : *If that doesn't work, we'll gorilla a little bit/ You ain't gonna gorilla anybody* (1960s+) *See* SIX-HUNDRED-POUND GORILLA

gork *n* 1 A stuporous or imbecilic patient; a patient who has lost brain function : *The gork in that room has the "O" sign, did you notice?/ By any definition, a gork. Lived a few minutes* (1980s+ Medical) ◁2▷ A despised person; DORK, GEEK, JERK : *Hubert is such a gork. His glasses are always falling off his nose, and he wears plaids with stripes* (1980s+ Students) *v* To sedate a patient heavily (1980s+ Medical) [said to be fr *God only really knows*, referring to a patient with a mysterious ailment]

gorked or **gorked out** *adj* or *adj phr* Stuporous; semiconscious; heavily sedated; SPACED-OUT (1980s+ Medical)

gork out *v phr* To become stuporous or comatose (1980s+ Medical)

gorm *v* To eat voraciously [1850+ Students; fr *gormandize*]

gormless *adj* Stupid; slow-witted; dumb [1746+ British; fr British dialect *gaumless*, "half-silly," lacking *gaum*, "understanding"; the dated sense is in the form *gaumless*; the entry spelling is found by 1883]

go-round *n* A turn; a repetition : *That was nice. Let's have another go-round* (1960s+)

go round and round *v phr* To quarrel; squabble; fight : *They went round and round on the same issues for hours* [1970s+; *go-round*, "a fight," is found by 1891]

gorp[1] *v* To eat greedily; GOBBLE, GORM [1940s+; probably fr British *gawp up*, "to devour"]

gorp[2] *n* A food mixture of dried fruit, nuts, and seeds, consumed esp by hikers, alpinists, etc [1980s+; said to be fr *good old raisins and peanuts* and probably related to *gorp*[1]]

go screw *sentence* or *v phr* GO FUCK oneself : *Until that time, all those more experienced guys could go screw*

gosh *interj* A mild exclamation of pleasure, disbelief, surprise, etc : *Gosh but I'm tickled, Reverend* [1757+; a euphemism for *God*]

gosh-awful *adj* Wretched; miserable; DARNED : *Isn't that picture gosh-awful? adv* Extremely : *Wasn't it gosh-awful dark in there?* (1900+)

◁**go shit in your hat**▷ *See* SHIT IN YOUR HAT

go sit on a tack *sentence* Cease annoying me; GO FLY A KITE, GO TO HELL (1900+)

go slumming *See* SLUM

go soak yourself (or **your head**) *sentence* Cease annoying me; GO TO HELL : *When I asked for a date she told me to go soak my head* (1884+)

go sour *v phr* To become unsatisfying; fail; disappoint : *After a couple of years of fame it all went sour* (1935+)

go south (also **head south**, **take a turn south**) *v phr* 1 To disappear; fail by or as if by vanishing : *He played unbelievably, then all of a sudden he just went south/ North Goes South/ Royals' offense heads south when Cone takes turn on mound* (1940s+) 2 To abscond with money, loot, etc : *She went south with a couple of silk pieces/ I hope he doesn't go South with the winnings* (1925+) 3 To cheat, esp to cheat at cards : *go south* 1: *Palm cards or chips* 2: *Quit a game while winning, pretending to have suffered losses* (1950+ Underworld) 4 To lessen; diminish : *concern about injury went south/ His salary request needs to take a turn south/ The price immediately heads south in a highly competitive market* (1980s+) [probably fr the notion of disappearing *south of the border*, to Texas or to the Mexican border, to escape legal pursuit and responsibility; probably reinforced by the widespread Native American belief that the soul after death journeys to the south, attested in American

Colonial writing fr the mid-1700s; *GTT,* "Gone to Texas, absconded," is found by 1839]

gospel (truth) *n* The absolute truth : *His book's the gospel*

go steady *v phr* To have a constant and only boyfriend or girlfriend : *Going steady means taking out one girl until a better one comes along (1905+)*

go straight *v phr* To renounce a life of crime; reform; slipper *(1919+ Underworld)*

go straight to dessert See CUT TO THE CHASE

got See NO GOT

gotcha *interj* Got you; caught you : *a gotcha campaign n* **1** A wound or injury, usu minor like a slight razor slice incurred while shaving : *Remember the gotchas you got from that worn old wrench?* **2** A capture; a catch; an arrest : *"This is a gotcha," Johnson allegedly told Jaffee* **3** Gleeful and persistent faultfinding and personal recrimination, esp a particular fault loudly found : *The Admissions office at Georgetown revealed that blacks on average had lower test scores. "Gotcha!" was the attitude among critics/ a gigantic game of "gotcha," leading the Senate into what he described as "uncharted waters" (1980s+)* [fr got you]

got it made *v phr* To have all the trappings for success; to be in an advantageous position : *with all those degrees, she has it made (1955+)*

go the distance *v phr* To finish an arduous effort; persist to the end : *Don't start this if you can't go the distance (1940s+ fr horse racing)*

go the extra mile *v phr* To make an extra effort; do more than usual : *It is time to communicate that. It is time to go that extra mile/ But for women, you have to go the extra mile to prove your credibility (1980s+)*

go the limit (or all the way) *v phr* To do the sex act, as distinct from heavy petting, foreplay, etc : *all-American girl must not "go the limit"* [1925+; entry form fr poker, "to bet the maximum allowed"]

go the whole hog or **go whole hog** *v phr* To do the utmost; not slacken; pursue to the limit; GO THE WHOLE NINE YARDS : *He decided to go the whole hog and buy a real big boat* [1828+; fr the notion of buying an entire animal and not a butchered part of it; *go the whole animal* is found as a variant by 1890]

go the whole nine yards *v phr* To do the utmost; GO THE LIMIT, GO THE WHOLE HOG : *I went the whole nine yards (1960s+) See* the WHOLE NINE YARDS

go through *v phr* **1** To search and rob a place *(1860+)* **2** To use up, esp eat or spend in a short amount of time

go through changes *v phr* **1** To work very hard; strive; HUSTLE **2** To pass through various emotional difficulties; be unstable and unsure : *Since last July 31, he has "gone through every change, from suicidal to who gives a shit" (1952+ Black)*

go through the cellar *v phr* To plummet; fall disastrously; GO SOUTH : *The ratings went through the cellar (1980s+)*

go (or be) through the mill *v phr* To have practical experience of something; be thoroughly seasoned : *I think you can rely on her; she's been through the mill (1859+)*

go through the motions *v phr* To imitate some action rather than perform it; simulate a feeling, stance, etc : *Are you really remorseful, or just going through the motions? (1816+)*

go through the roof *v phr* To become very upset and angry; GO BALLISTIC, HIT THE CEILING : *All I said was "Cool it," and she hit the roof (1950s+)*

go Titanic *v phr* To sink or fail : *project went Titanic* [from the sinking of the famous ship *Titanic*]

go to bat *v phr* To be tried for a crime *(1940s+ Underworld)*

go to bat against *v phr* Oppose; contend against : *None of her victims would go to bat against her (1940s+)*

go to bat for *v phr* To support or defend; help : *to judge by how he'd gone to bat for him*

go to bed *v phr* To be in final form ready for the press : *I can predict before the paper goes to bed (1930s+ Newspaper office)*

go to bed with someone *v phr* To do the sex act with someone; SLEEP WITH someone *(1940s+)*

go to blazes *sentence* GO TO HELL *(1853+)*

go to Denmark *v phr* To have a sex-change operation; become a transsexual [1960s+; fr the fact that such operations were originally done primarily in Denmark]

go toe to toe *v phr* To fight, esp to fight hard; SLUG IT OUT : *They are going toe-to-toe with Cosmo, Glamour/ Men in the courtroom can go toe to toe and then go off patting each other on the back (1940s+)*

go-to guy *n phr* **1** A player to whom the ball is thrown for a fairly sure score : *He was our go-to guy down low. And you knew if he got fouled he'd make his free throws/ He's once again the go-to guy on the best team in the conference (1990s+ Basketball)* **2** (also **go-to office**) The best person or place to go for information, action, etc : *Professor Wilson is the main go-to guy on race and poverty for the institutions that shape agendas/ His became the go-to office for getting things done (1990s+)*

◁**go to hell**▷ *sentence* May you be accursed, confounded, humiliated, etc; DROP DEAD, GO FUCK oneself : *He wanted me to lie, but I told him to go to hell (1836+) v phr* To deteriorate; be ruined : *The whole town's gone to hell, with that new mayor/ Old Joe's gone to hell a bit lately* (*1930s+*)

go to hell in a handbasket (or a bucket) *v phr* To deteriorate badly and rapidly; GO DOWN-HILL : *White people can go to hell in a hand-basket. They can go to Burger King and not have their way* (*1980s+*)

go to pot *v phr* To deteriorate; worsen; GO DOWNHILL, GO TO HELL : *A group of men who had literally and figuratively let themselves go to pot get back into good physical condition/ A middle-aged man going to pot gets more than muscle tone from heavy exercise* [*1831+*; fr the con-dition of an animal no longer useful for breeding, egg-laying, etc, that will now be cooked in the *pot*]

go (or be taken) to the cleaners *v phr* To lose all one's money, esp gambling at craps; TAKE A BATH (*1907+*)

go to the dogs *v phr* GO TO HELL, GO TO POT [*1864+*; fr the notion that something unfit for human food would be given to the lowly *dogs*]

go to the glass *v phr* To shoot for a basket [*1990s+* Basketball; fr the *glass* backboard of the basket]

go to the mat *v phr* To fight; contend mightily : *They soon stopped sparring and went to the mat* [*1908+*; fr the *mat* used as a wrestling site]

go to the wall *v phr* **1** To be ruined and des-titute; collapse : *if a real biggie, like Brazil, say, went to the wall* (*1589+*) **2** To do sacrifice oneself; give way to another's interest; GO ALL THE WAY : *We've gone to the wall for you* (*1858+*) [first sense fr the plight of someone being executed by being shot, against a *wall*]

go to (or down to) the wire *v phr* To be in very close competition until the very end; be NIP AND TUCK : *The 1928 pennant race between the As and the Yanks went to the wire* (*1901+*)

go to town *v phr* **1** To do very well; succeed; perform impressively **2** To throw off re-straint; let go (*1933+*)

got up on (or out of) the wrong side of the bed *v phr* To be peevish, perverse, etc; be in a nasty mood : *He just about bit my head off, must have got up on the wrong side of the bed* (*1930s+*)

got what it takes *v phr* To have the right tools or aspects for success : *that singer's got what it takes*

gouge *v* To cheat; FLIM-FLAM, SCAM : *Looks re-spectable, but this place regularly gouges the customer* (*1875+*)

go under *v phr* To fail; sink; esp to lose con-sciousness (*1880+*)

go underground *v phr* To go into hiding; to operate in secret : *the school newspaper went underground/ the persecuted go underground*

goup *See* GOOP

go up against *v phr* To confront; face; chal-lenge : *So that's the kind of piffle actors have to go up against* (*1940s+*)

go up in smoke or **flames** *v phr* To be ruined; be destroyed : *He just saw his beautiful scam go up in smoke* (*1933+*)

go (or hit) upside one's **face (or head)** *v phr* **1** To beat and pummel, esp around the head **2** To defeat utterly; trounce; CLOBBER (*1960s+ Black*)

go up the wall *See* CLIMB THE WALL

gourd *n* The head; skull (*1844+*) *See* OUT OF one's HEAD

go west *v phr* To be spoiled or ruined; also, to die : *valuable evidence gone west* (*1910+*)

go whole hog *See* GO THE WHOLE HOG

go with *v phr* To date exclusively or go steady : *he's gone with her for four years* (*1890s+*)

go with the flow *v phr* To consign oneself to the order and pace of things; be passive : *They pondered a while and decided to go with the flow and they all went back to sleep/ Really, I'm just trying to go with the flow* [*1960s+* Counterculture; probably a reference to Taoism]

go (or come) with the territory (or turf) *v phr* To be an integral part of some occupation or status, esp a part that is not especially de-lightful : *At EPA It Goes With the Territory/ Tierney's answer was that such speculation "goes with the territory"/ Such embarrass-ments come with the turf, however* [*1960s+*; fr the conditions implicit in a sales represen-tative's covering of a certain *territory*, pop-ularized by use in the Requiem section of Arthur Miller's 1949 play *Death of a Sales-man*]

grab *n* An arrest; BUST, PINCH : *We will get credit for the grab, and we will also profit/ The only thing worse than no grab is a bad grab* (*1753+* Police) *v* To seize the admiration or attention of; impress : *How does that grab you?/ to reflect on a whole lot of things that had been grabbing me* (*1966+*)

grab a handful of air *v phr* To apply the brakes of a truck or bus quickly [*1930s+* Truckers; fr the fact that such vehicles have *hand*-operated *air* brakes]

◁**grab-ass** or **grab-arse**▷ *n* Sexual touching and clutching : *less anxious, less suspicious about my merry games of grabarse* (*1940s+*) *See* PLAY GRAB-ASS

grab-bag *n* A miscellaneous mixture; random collection : *the grab-bag of memories in my muddled head* [*1855+*; dated sense refers to a carnival game in which one may reach in-side a bag of small prizes after paying a fee]

grabber *n* Anything that seizes and rivets the attention; something that commands immediate admiration; HOOK : *Dance within the regular format is a solid grabber/ He's found a real grabber* (1966+) *See* MOTHERFUCKER

grabby *adj* **1** Greedy; acquisitive; selfish : *Share that, don't be grabby* (1910+) **2** Seizing; arresting; riveting : *spent hours working on a goddamn grabby lead* (1960s+)

grabs *See* UP FOR GRABS

grab shot *n phr* A photograph taken in great haste, without time for proper focusing, exposure-setting, etc; a photograph of opportunity (1980s+)

grab your socks *See* DROP YOUR COCKS AND GRAB YOUR SOCKS

grad *modifier* : *a grad student/ grad reunion* *n* A graduate : *college grad* (1871+ Students)

grade, the *See* MAKE THE GRADE

grade-grubber *n* A very hardworking student who is also popular with teachers

graft *n* **1** One's occupation; GAME, RACKET (1853+ British) **2** The acquisition of money by dishonest means, esp by bribery for political favors : *the usual charges of graft at City Hall* (1865+) [origin unknown; an 1883 source connects the two senses: *Graft. To work. Grafting.* Helping another to steal]

grain *n* Marijuana; GRASS, POT : *You been smoking too much grain. You head is juiced* (1980s+ Narcotics)

gramps *n* Grandfather; any old man : *Need any help, gramps?* [1940s+; *gramp* is found by 1898]

gran *n* Grandmother : *gran made cookies*

grand *n* A thousand dollars; GEE : *A banker would scarcely call one thousand dollars "one grand"* [1920+ Underworld & sports; said to have originated with Peaches Van Camp, a criminal who flashed such *grand* notes for ostentation]

grand bounce, the *n phr* the BOUNCE

Grand Central Station *n phr* Any place that is overcrowded and busy; MOB SCENE : *My office was like Grand Central Station this morning*

granddaddy of all something *n phr* The most venerable, most impressive, largest, etc, of what is named; dean; MOTHER OF ALL something : *The Newport is the granddaddy of all jazz festivals* (1956+)

grandfather *v* To give someone a special status or privilege because of service before the time a new or definitive arrangement is made : *Some farmers just got grandfathered in, that's true* [1900+; fr the *grandfather clause* often written into new arrangements in order to be fair to older incumbents or practitioners; the date indicates the earliest instance of *grandfather clause*]

grandma *n* **1** The lowest and slowest gear of a truck; CREEPER (1940s+ Truckers) **2** Any old woman : *Can I carry your groceries, grandma?*

(1940s+) [the second sense's date must be much earlier]

grand slam *modifier* : *grand-slam home run* *n phr* **1** The winning of all the goals, games, prizes, etc, available; total comprehensive victory : *Nobody won the tennis grand slam last year* (1814+) **2** GRAND SLAMMER (1940+ Baseball) [fr a bridge term for winning all the tricks in one hand]

grand slammer *n phr* A home run hit when all the bases are occupied, and scoring four runs (1940+ Baseball)

grandstand *modifier* : *a grandstand catch* *v* To play or perform in a brilliant and spectacular way, esp in order to get the approval of an audience; HOT DOG, SHOW OFF : *Coach told him to stop grandstanding and take care of business* (1895+ Students)

grandstander *n* A person who habitually grandstands; HOT DOG, SHOW-OFF (1895+ Students)

grandstand play *n phr* **1** A play made with special brilliance and brio, esp in order to impress the spectators **2** Any action, speech, tactic, etc, designed to appeal to spectators; a tour de force : *The President's pronouncement's just a grandstand play* (1888+ Baseball)

granny dress *n phr* A floor-length dress, usu with long sleeves and a high neckline (1960s+)

granny (or **grampa**) **dumping** *n phr* The abandonment of helpless and destitute old people by families that cannot care for them : *Some overwhelmed families turn to granny dumping, abandoning their relatives at hospital emergency rooms/ John Kingery, 82, victim of Alzheimer's, found abandoned in his wheelchair at a dog track, drew national attention to the phenomenon of grandpa dumping* (1991+)

granny flat *n phr* A small cottage or apartment where elderly people may live near but not actually with their children's family; mother-in-law apartment (1965+)

granny glasses *n phr* Eyeglasses with small, circular steel or gold frames (1960s+)

granny tax *n phr* A state tax on nursing-home beds : *Groups who represent the elderly consider Thompson's proposal a "granny tax"* (1990s+)

granola *modifier* : *geeky granola-type Ely/ Fort Collins isn't really into hard music. There's a granola scene here* *n* A person who is objectionably or prissily devoted to the 1960s values of environmental awareness, multi-ethnic tolerance, healthy "natural" diet, usu vegetarian, precious antiquated tastes, etc; EARTH MUFFIN : *Stephanie turned into a granola when she started college. She won't even eat at McDonald's/ Elizabeth was far too granola for Jason, what with her herb garden and Celtic record collection* [late 1980s+ Students; fr a multigrain WK Kellogg breakfast cereal devised around 1886]

grape *n* Wine or champagne (*1636+*)

grapefruit league *n phr* The association of major-league teams as they play each other in preseason training [*1937+* Baseball; fr the fact that most spring training camps are held in citrus-growing regions]

grapevine *adj* Coming from an unofficial source of rumor or news : *a grapevine item/ grapevine gossip* (*1863+*)

grapevine, the *n* The source and route of rumors and unofficial news : *I heard it through the grapevine (Civil War)*

grass *n* **1** The straight hair typical of Caucasians (*1950s+* Black) **2** (also **grass weed**) Marijuana; POT : *smoking a little grass and passing on venereal disease/ Scoring grass here is easier than buying a loaf of bread* (*1930s+* Narcotics) *See* one's ASS IS GRASS

grass-cutter or **grass-clipper** *n* A very hard-hit ground ball (*1868+* Baseball)

grass widow *n phr* A woman who is alone because of divorce, separation, rejection, etc [*1839+*; because her husband is still above the *grass* rather than under it]

grave *See* HAVE ONE FOOT IN THE GRAVE

gravel *See* HIT THE DIRT

graveyard shift *n phr* A working shift that begins at midnight or 2 AM (*1907+*)

graveyard watch *n phr* A period of guard or watch duty from midnight to 4 AM or 8 AM (*1927+* Railroad & Navy)

gravity check *n phr* A fall from a surfboard, snowboard, etc

gravy *n* Money or other valuables beyond what one actually earns or needs; a bonus or excess : *Once we make back our expenses, everything else is gravy* (*1910+*)

gravy train (or **boat**), **the** *n phr* A chance, job, business, etc, that gives a very ample return for little or no work; an obvious sinecure; the LIFE OF RILEY : *His job's a permanent gravy train/ Thus, railroad workers referred to a short haul that paid well as a "gravy train"* (fr railroad *1927+*) *See* ON THE GRAVY TRAIN, RIDE THE GRAVY TRAIN

gray market *n phr* The sale of reputable products, esp cameras and electronic equipment, by persons who have not bought them from the manufacturers' authorized distributors and hence offer lower prices because the products do not qualify for the makers' guarantees : *There is a growing "gray" market for Levi's* (*1960s+*)

gray matter *n phr* Intelligence; BRAINS, SMARTS (*1899+*)

graze *v* To eat small amounts often : *"I don't eat meals," she said. "I graze all day long"/ Cindy Crawford grazing at the salad bar* (*1980s+*)

grazer *n* **1** A person who grazes rather than eats meals **2** A person who shifts rapidly from one television station to another; CHANNEL SURFER : *Comedy will come in quick bursts, aimed at TV grazers who flip around the dial with their remotes* (*1980s+*)

greafa or **greapha** *See* GREEFA

grease *n* **1** Money (*1800s+*) **2** Bribe or protection money; money given for corrupt purposes : *They get so much grease it takes them half a block just to change direction* (*1823+*) **3** Butter (*WWII Army*) **4** Food (*Persian Gulf War Army*) **5** A gun : *You handled the grease real good, but not good enough, you didn't kill them v* To shoot, esp to kill by shooting : *He has a gun and might try to grease you (WWII armed forces)* [the verb *to grease*, "to bribe," is found by 1557; last two senses fr *greasegun*, a WWII submachine gun] *See* ELBOW GREASE, GREASE someone's PALM

greaseball *n* ◀**1**▶ A dark-skinned, dark-haired person of Mediterranean or Latin American origin; DAGO, GREASER : *taking knives away from greaseballs in zoot suits/ This time the greaseball smacked her. They were taking turns smacking her* (*1915+*) **2** A dirty tramp (*1920s+* Hoboes) **3** A cook or kitchen worker (*WWII Navy*) **4** A hamburger stand or concession (*1940s+* Circus) **5** An actor who uses too much makeup or greasepaint (*1920s+* Theater)

greased lightning *n phr* Something or someone extraordinarily fast; a BLUE STREAK : *He got out of there like greased lightning* (*1848+*)

grease joint *n phr* **1** The cookhouse and eating tent (*1920s+* Circus & carnival) **2** A hamburger stand (*1914+*)

grease monkey *n phr* **1** A worker who lubricates machines, esp automobiles : *Good grease monkeys all, they could think better with a grease rack to lean against* **2** A stoker, oiler, or wiper on a ship (*Merchant marine*) **3** Any mechanic, esp an automotive mechanic (*1920s+*)

grease (or **cross** or **oil**) **someone's palm** *v phr* To pay someone for a corrupt purpose; bribe; buy favors : *If you grease the commissioner's palm, you can get anything fixed/ Officials whose palms have been crossed* (*1581+*)

greaser *n* ◀**1**▶ GREASEBALL • Used esp in referring to a Mexican or an Italian (*1849+*) **2** A hoodlum, petty thief, etc; PUNK : *Stradazzi. Looks like a greaser, too* (*1950s+* Teenagers) **3** A very smooth landing (*1980+* Aviators) [second sense fr the *grease* used for their typical combed-back hairstyle]

grease the wheels *v phr* To make things go smoothly; facilitate (*1809+*)

grease trough (or **pit**) *n phr* A lunch counter or lunchroom : *Imagine yourself in the grease* *trough again/ a shadowy grease pit midway between (1940s+)*

greasy *adj* **1** Repellent in an unctuous and cunning way; OILY *(1529+)* **2** Muddy and slippery : *to negotiate a "greasy" mile before an approving audience (1950s+ Horse racing)*

greasy spoon *n phr* A small, cheap restaurant, lunchroom, or diner : *The Marx brothers ate in coffee pots and greasy spoons/ your above-average greasy spoon in Boston's Back Bay (1925+)*

great *adj* Excellent; wonderful : *Hey, that's really great (1848+)* *n* A famous person, esp an athlete or entertainer : *Weiss, a former football "great" (1400+)*

great divide *n phr* A divorce

greatest, the *n phr* A person or thing of superlative quality; the MOST *(1950s+ Bop & cool talk)*

greatest thing since sliced bread, the *See* the BEST THING SINCE SLICED BREAD

great guns *See* GO GREAT GUNS

Great something or somebody in the Sky *n phr* Heaven; God; the ultimate authority : *Senator Levin will be in the Great Committee Room in the Sky before Congress revisits the lobbyist mess/ We'll leave this play to that Great Critic in the Sky (1970s+)*

great shakes *See* NO GREAT SHAKES

great unwashed, the *n phr* The common people, hoi polloi : *in the auditorium with the great unwashed*

greedygut or **greedyguts** *n* A glutton; CHOW HOUND, PIG : *One has no problem with Clifford Irving, a mere greedyguts (1546+)*

greefa *n* (Variations: **goifa** or **greafa** or **greapha** or **greefo** or **greeta** or **grefa** or **griefo** or **griffa** or **grifo**) Marijuana or a marijuana cigarette [1930s+ Narcotics; fr Mexican Spanish *griffa,* "weed"]

Greek *n* **1** A Greek-letter fraternity member *(1900+ College students)* **2** A professional gambler, esp a cardsharp *(1528+ Gambling) See* ALL GREEK TO

◁**Greek way (or style), the**▷ *n phr* Anal intercourse, esp heterosexual : *Another request is for Greek style. That is, anal sex*

green *adj* Advocating environmental protection; pro-ecological ● The opposite of *brown (1970s+)* *n* Money, esp ready cash; FOLDING MONEY : *plus "green" or "front money" to pay off others (1920s+ Underworld & sports) See* LONG GREEN, MEAN GREEN

green apples *See* SURE AS GOD MADE LITTLE GREEN APPLES

green (or blue) around the gills *adj phr* Sicklooking; pale and miserable; nauseated : *He was looking green around the gills, so I told him to lie down* [1930s+; the date should prob-

ably be earlier; *gills,* "face," is found by 1626]

◁**green-ass**▷ *adj* New and inexperienced; callow; green : *I spent thirty-four months havin' green-ass corporals chew me up (1940s+)*

greenback *n* A dollar bill [1870+; said to have been coined by Salmon P Chase, who died in 1873]

green fingers *n phr* Exceptional skill at growing plants *(1934+)*

green folding *n phr* FOLDING MONEY *(1950s+)*

green goods *n phr* Counterfeit paper money *(1887+)*

greenhorn *n* An inexperienced person; newcomer; neophyte; ROOKIE *(1753+)*

greenie *n* **1** GREENHORN *(1830s+)* **2** A heart-shaped green stimulant pill of dextroamphetamine : *Do you take something, like greenies?/ Greenies are pep pills and a lot of baseball players couldn't function without them (1960s+ Narcotics)* **3** A traffic ticket *(1990s+ Los Angeles police)*

green-light *v* To approve; sanction : *Who in the world thought that Levinson's screenplay should be greenlighted? (1968+)*

green light, the *n phr* Permission, esp a superior's approval to proceed; the GO-AHEAD : *When she got the green light, she invited the couple to see her in Washington/ have also been given the green light to advertise special plates (1937+)*

greenmail *n* The buying, at a premium price, of the stock holdings of someone who is threatening to take over a company, in order to induce the person to cease the attempt : *The most cited recent case of greenmail occurred this spring and summer as Walt Disney Productions fought to escape a takeover/ But Wall Street analysts agreed that CBS was unlikely to consider such action, since it amounts to "greenmail"* [1983+; modeled on *blackmail*]

green money *n phr* Paper money; ready cash; FOLDING MONEY : *shooting for green money (1940s+)*

green one *n phr* A dollar bill; dollar; BUCK, CLAM : *Alphamassage, only 15,000 green ones at Hammacher Schlemmer, plus 125 for shipping and handling (1980s+)*

green stuff, the *n phr* Money; ready cash; paper money; FOLDING MONEY, LONG GREEN : *He really poured the green stuff to the bookies (1880s+)*

green thumb, a *n phr* **1** A special talent for gardening **2** The ability to make projects succeed like flourishing plants : *possessor of a green thumb when it comes to making musicals blossom (1940s+)*

greenwash or **greenwashing** *n* The practice of promoting environmentally friendly programs to deflect attention from an organization's environmentally unfriendly or less savory activities : *using greenwashing techniques to sell themselves* [*green*, "environmentally friendly," and (*white*)*wash*, "conceal flaws"]

greeta or **grefa** *See* GREEFA

gremlin *n* **1** An imaginary imp who caused malfunction in machines, problems in projects, confusion in arrangements, etc • The Royal Naval Air Service apparently used the term in WWI *(WWII Army Air Forces fr British)* **2** (also **grem, gremmie**) A person, esp a girl, who frequents surfing beaches without surfing; BEACH BUNNY : *gremlins, usually girls, those hangers-on who may never get wet (1960s+ Surfers)* [origin unknown; probably modeled on *goblin*, with the first syllable perhaps fr Irish *gruaimin*, "irascible little creature"]

grid or **gridiron** *modifier* : *the grid squad/ gridiron victories n* A football field

G-ride *n* Car theft; grand theft auto *(1990s+ Los Angeles police)*

gridlock *n* A blockage; paralysis : *Until the emotional and psychological gridlock over the Federal deficit is broken* [1980+; fr the traffic term designating a total blockage of traffic caused by cars stopping in intersections behind other stopped cars and blocking traffic on the intersecting street]

grief *n* Complaints; faultfinding; reprimand : *I don't want no grief from the fourteenth floor (1929+) See* GIVE SOMEONE GRIEF

griefo or **grifo** or **griffa** *See* GREEFA

grievous bodily harm or **GHB** *n phr* An illegal steroid substance, gamma hydroxybutyric acid; SCOOP : *GHB crossed over onto the club circuit, where users refer to it as Grievous Bodily Harm (1990s+)*

grift *n* **1** Money gotten dishonestly and by one's wits, esp by swindling **2** Any dishonest way of getting money by cunning, esp the deceptions of confidence tricksters, hawkers, etc *v* : *He grifted a couple years then got a regular job (1914+ Carnival & circus)*

grifter *n* **1** A gambler *(Circus)* **2** A confidence trickster, hawker, minor criminal, etc **3** A hobo; vagabond; DRIFTER *(1915+ Carnival & circus)*

grin and bear it *v phr* To exercise forbearance and fortitude; TOUGH IT OUT *(1864+)*

grinch *n* A person who spoils a happy occasion, esp Christmas; spoilsport; SCROOGE : *The grinch at City Hall/ Mecham of Arizona is drawing fire as a new kind of grinch* [1980s+; fr a character in Dr Seuss's 1957 book *How the Grinch Stole Christmas*]

grind *n* **1** : *to wow the audience with her bumps and grinds (1940s+)* **2** : *No one except a few*

notorious *grinds studied that night (1864+ Students)* **3** : *They heard the hawker go into his grind* **4** A hawker or barker *(1925+ Circus)* **5** Any obnoxious or annoying person; JERK, A PAIN IN THE ASS, PILL : *The prof's a tedious old grind (1890+)* **6** Any very difficult and trying task, esp one that lasts a long time and is slowly and painfully done : *Writing dictionaries is indeed a grind (1852+) v* **1** To rotate one's pelvis in the sex act or in imitation of the sex act • Nearly always in combination with *bump* : *the strippers bumping and grinding away (1940s+)* **2** To study diligently : *Five days to grind and two days to be social, the way it was at Yale (1864+ Students)* **3** To attract and address a crowd at a show or concession; spiel *(1925+ Circus) See* BUMP AND GRIND, IF YOU CAN'T FIND 'EM

grindcore *n* A variety of hard-rock music : *This veteran quintet may be the purest and most primal grindcore band (1990s+)*

grinder *n* **1** A barker or hawker *(1925+ Circus & carnival)* **2** A stripteaser; STRIPPER *(1950s+)* **3** A car, esp an old and ramshackle one : *bought a brand new Chev to take the place of her old grinder (1940s+)* **4** HERO SANDWICH *(1950s+)* **5** A parade ground; drill field *(1940s+ Marine Corps)*

grind-house or **grind movie** *n* or *n phr* A theater that runs continuously without intermissions, holidays, etc : *Four years ago, it would have been restricted to a few downtown grind-houses/ He dragged me to the Times Square grind-house to which it had been relegated* [1930s+ Theater; probably fr *grind show*, perhaps influenced by the burlesque and sexual connotations of *grind*]

grind something out *v phr* To produce or make something, esp with uninspired precision or long and painful effort : *They sat down and ground the script out in two days/ They just grind them out ten a day (1940s+)*

◁**gringo**▷ *n* English people or Anglo-Americans : *gringo, used contemptuously by Spanish-Americans (1849+)*

grip *n* **1** A stagehand or stage carpenter : *crowded with assistant directors, character actors, movie stars, grips and electricians (1888+ Theater & movie studio)* **2** A traveling bag; valise : *Gonna pack my grip and make my getaway (1879+)* [second sense a shortening of *gripsack*]

gripe *n* **1** : *I want to clear my desk of various matters, mostly gripes (1934+)* **2** griper *(1930s+) v* **1** To complain, esp habitually and trivially; groan; BITCH, KVETCH, PISS : *He got good and sore and griped (1932+)* **2** To annoy or disgust; afflict; distress : *What's griping him is that he can't do anything for the* *kids* (*1559+*) [ultimately fr *griping of the gut,* "colic, bellyache, stomach cramp"]

◁**gripe** one's **ass**▷ *v phr* (Variations: **balls** or **butt** or **cookies** or **left nut** or **middle kidney** or **soul**, or some other organ or possession at the whim of the speaker, may replace **ass**) To disgust or annoy someone extremely : *His sycophancy gripes my ass* (*1940s+*)

gripe session *n phr* A conversation or discussion consisting primarily of complaints (*1940s+*)

grit *n* **1** Courage; fortitude and stamina (*1825+*) **2** The roadpath beside a railroad track (*1950s+ Railroad*) **3** (also **grits**) Food (*1930s+ Black*) ◁**4**▷ A Southerner : *He's a hotshot down here among the grits. A good Yankee guard would eat him alive* (*1960s+*) **5** (also **Grit**) A white person : *It's a God's wonder some Grit didn't kill us* (*1960s+ Black*) *v* To eat (*1930s+ Black*) [food senses at least partially fr *hominy grits*, although *grit* was British military slang for "food" in the 1930s; Southern dialect sense probably ironically fr Civil War use of the expression *true Yankee grit* by Northern soldiers and writers] *See* HIT THE DIRT

gritch *v* To complain : *gritching about the dog next door*

gritty *See* the NITTY-GRITTY

grody or **groady** or **groaty** or **groddy** *See* GROTTY

groceries *n* A meal or meals : *I got hooked for the groceries* (*1940s+*) *See* BRING HOME THE BACON

grog *n* Liquor (*1770+*) [fr British naval *grog,* "rum and water," so called because it was introduced in the mid-18th century as a sailor's ration by "Old *Grog,*" Admiral Sir Edward Vernon, who habitually wore a *grogram* coat]

grogged *adj* **1** Drunk **2** Sleepy; GROGGY

groggy *adj* Sleepy; dazed; semiconscious : *Conlon was so groggy that he wanted to know why Nelson was not coaching the Warriors* (*1832+*)

grok (GRAHK) *v* **1** To communicate sympathetically : *all rapping and grokking over the sound it made/ All the Romans grokked like Greeks* (*1961+ Counterculture & students*) **2** (also **grok on**) To get into exquisite sympathy with : *She met him at an acid-rock ball and she grokked him/ The Handbook of Highway Engineering, they totally grokked on it* (*1961+ Counterculture & students*) **3** To understand : *You've come to grok that Cronenberg's narrative is merely the pretense for his imagery* (*1980s+ Computer*) [coined by Robert A Heinlein as a Martian word in the 1961 science-fiction novel *Stranger in a Strange Land*]

grollo *n* GROWLER

grommet *n* A young surfer • Apparently a borrowing from Australia, where it is also spelled *grummit* : *an ersatz club scene for junior high-schoolers, grommets, kiddies* (*1986+*)

gronk *n* Any nasty substance, like a collection in one's belly button or between one's toes : *use a Q-Tip on that gronk*

gronk out *v phr* To cease functioning; GO DOWN : *The terminal gronked out about ten minutes ago* (*1980s+ Computer*)

grooby *adj* Excellent; GROOVY : *You, too, can get on the grooby side* (*1943+ Teenagers*)

groove *n* Any habitually preferred activity; what excites and gratifies one; BAG, KICK (*1958+*) *v* **1** To enjoy intensely; take gratification, esp rather passively and subjectively; GO WITH THE FLOW : *To groove means to yield yourself to the flow of activity around you/ I just like to get out there and groove a little* (*1960s+*) **2** To like and approve; DIG : *They see the spade cats going with ofay chicks and they don't groove it* (*1960s+*) **3** To perform very well; be effective : *really grooving on that funny trumpet* (*1935+*) [fr the sense that a musician is in a definite and exciting track, has hit a perfect stride, when playing well, esp a solo; perhaps influenced by the *grooves* of a phonograph record] *See* IN THE GROOVE

groove on something or someone *v phr* To enjoy intensely; GROOVE : *I can really groove on the Beatles/ She walks for blocks grooving on Reality* (*1960s+*)

groovy *adj* **1** Playing and enjoying music well and with concentration; HEP, IN THE GROOVE (*1930s+ Jive talk*) **2** Excellent; wonderful; FAR OUT : *"Hey, groovy," said Sally* (*1944+ Teenagers*) **3** Obsolete; out-of-date : *a way of describing, with heavy sarcasm, maroon polyester suits: "Groovy!"* (*1980s+ Teenagers*)

grope *v* To touch, feel, caress, fondle, etc, with seeming or actual sexual intent (*1250+*)

gross *adj* Disgusting; rebarbative; GROTTY : *at this moment (how gross!) blowing kisses into the phone* (*1958+ Teenagers*)

grossed out *adj phr* Disgusted; revulsed (*1960s+ Teenagers*)

gross-out *modifier* : *The Animal House gross-out movies are all about groups/ gross-out scenes of the Dalmatian mounting the smaller dog* **n** Something particularly disgusting; repellent trash : *He attempts the ultimate gross-out: "self-expression" of the kind found in Greenwich Village* (*1960s+ Teenagers*)

gross someone **out** *v phr* To disgust or offend, esp with crude and obscene language and behavior : *They're grossing me out, too, you know/ Being a mother really grosses me out* (*1968+ Teenagers*)

grotty (GROH dee, -tee) *adj* (Variations: **grody**
or **groaty** or **groddy** or **groady; to the max**
may be added) Disgusting; nasty; repellent;
bizarre; GRUNGY, SCUZZY : *The magazines had*
covers with those grotty weirdos on them **n** : *the*
introspective hedonism and political individual-
ism of the second group, called groddies [mid-
1960s+ Teenagers; fr *grotesque*; popularized
by the Beatles in the 1960s; perhaps fr
Merseyside dialect]

ground *See* BEAT TO THE GROUND, NOT KNOW one's
ASS FROM one's ELBOW, NOT KNOW someone or
something FROM A HOLE IN THE GROUND, RUN
something INTO THE GROUND, STAMPING GROUND

ground someone *v phr* To deny privileges to
someone, esp to keep someone confined at
home as a punishment : *If my father got a*
pair of bell-bottoms, I think I'd ground him
[1940s+; fr the practice of not permitting a
pilot to fly, as a punishment, the word found
by 1931]

ground biscuit *n phr* alley apple (*1920s+*)

grounder *n* **1** A cigarette butt (*1930+ Hoboes*)
2 A batted baseball that rolls along the
ground (*1861+ Baseball*) **3** A homicide case
that be easily and quickly solved : *decided to*
hand Kennedy the 23rd Street jumper, which he
thought was a grounder (1980s+ Police)

ground floor *See* IN ON THE GROUND FLOOR

ground-pounder *n* A military infantry soldier

ground rations *n phr* The sex act [1950s+
Black; probably fr the sexual sense of *grind*
plus the frequent association of the sex act
with eating]

group *See* IN GROUP

groupie *modifier* : *The "groupie" syndrome,*
personified by adulatory novices of science
flocking around the luminaries **n** **1** A young
woman who seeks to share the glamour of
famous persons, esp rock musicians, by offering help and sexual favors; BUNNY : *No*
fool, no groupie, no teeny-bopper, she takes rock
music, rightly, seriously **2** An ardent devotee
and votary; FAN : *like many of Hollywood's*
young trendies, a political groupie/ the Ameri-
can literary groupies (1960s+ Rock and roll)

grouse *v* To complain; BITCH : *No grousing, no*
foot-dragging, both signs of a solid pro (1887+
British armed forces)

growl *v* To complain; mutter angrily (*1707+*)

growler *n* **1** (also **grollo**) A container used to
carry beer home from a bar : *A can brought in*
filled with beer at a barroom is called a growler
(*1888+, now obsolete*) **2** A public-address
loudspeaker or system; bitch box, SQUAWK
BOX (*WWII Navy*) **3** A small iceberg (*1912+*)
4 A police squad car; prowl car : *They got*
back into the growler and took off (1980s+
Police)

grrrl *modifier* Aggressively feminist, as expressed in music, fashion, ideas, etc : *leader*
of the hard-core feminist riot grrrl movement/
media overkill about the Riot Grrrl fashion
trend [1990s+; a blend of the angry animal-
like utterance *grr!* with *girl*] *See* RIOT GRRRL

grrrldom *n* The realm and principles of an
aggressive feminism : *the humorless man-*
hating axis of riot-grrrldom (1990s+)

grub *n* Food : *goods one can exchange at the*
kitchen door for grub/ nonchalantly gobble up
mounds of this grub (1659+) v : Come over and
grub with us (Black)

grubbies or **grubs** or **grubbers** *n* Older, worn-
out clothes, esp worn for hanging out or
doing dirty work : *Wear grubbies for the ar-*
chaeology dig

grubbin' *n* Good food (*1990s+ Teenagers*)

grubby *adj* Not clean; dirty : *grubby kid*

grub-pile *n* A meal (*1863+ Cowboys*)

grub-slinger *n* A cook (*1912+ Cowboys*)

grubstake *n* The money needed for a new
venture, new start, etc : *Nobody knows how*
much he gave away in grubstakes (1863+)

grudge fight (or **match**) *n phr* A sports contest
in which personal animosity figures : *Their*
every match is a grudge match (1930s+)

gruesome twosome *n phr* A couple going
steady (*1940s+ Teenagers*)

grunge or **grunch** (GRUHNJ, GRUHNCH) *adj*
1 Boring (*1960s+ Teenagers*) **2** GRUNGY
(*1960s+ Teenagers*) *n* **1** A dull, tedious person; NERD, PILL **2** Slovenliness; sloppiness
(*1960s+ Teenagers*) **3** Something nasty :
Those globs of guitar grunge get me off every
time (1960s+ Teenagers) **4** A style of dress
featuring mismatched and rumpled garments, mostly suggesting lumberjacks, appearing to have been bought at thrift shops
and donned at random, and favored by
grunge rock musicians : *"Stuff We Hate"*
grunge as high fashion/ Garth's wardrobe is
mostly grunge (1990s+) **5** A kind of rock
music originally associated with Seattle, WA
: *Nirvana and Pearl Jam are two of the best*
grunge bands (1990s+)

grungy (GRUHN jee) *adj* Shabby; squalid;
dirty; GROTTY, SCUZZY : *I put down in my*
grungy little notebook that Max Frisch was a
wise man/ the peerless, fearless, slightly grungy
Grodin to investigate [1960s+ Teenagers;
origin unknown; perhaps sound symbolism
resembling *gross, mangy, mung, stingy,* etc]

grunt *n* **1** A line repairer's helper who works
on the ground and does not climb poles
(*1900+ Line repairers*) **2** A locomotive engineer; hogger (*1940s+ Railroad*) **3** An infantry soldier : *I was drafted and served twelve*
months as a grunt in Vietnam/ Now there's a

willingness to tell the story of the poor grunt who got his tail shot off (Vietnam War armed forces) **4** Any low-ranking person, neophyte, etc : *The attitude among the reporter grunts was pretty much "them against us" (late 1960s+)* **5** A bill for food or drink : *I just hope Toots didn't bring along any of the grunts I must have left in that oasis (1940s+)* **6** A diligent student; GRIND : *A grunt is a student who gives a shit about nothing except his sheepskin (1980s+)*

grunt work (or **labor**) *n phr* Hard and/or tedious toil; BULLWORK, scut work : *The machine will do the grunt work, filing, typing lists, comparing, sorting/ Congress returned to Washington and settled down for a month of grunt work/ Whereas Agassi's every second of court time is grunt labor (1977+)*

G-string or **gee string** *n phr* or *n* A breechcloth, or brief covering for the genitals, worn esp by striptease dancers : *Thus the G-string became an integral part of a stripper's apparatus* [1878+; origin unknown; the dated use refers to Plains Indian use of a loincloth; the stripper sense is found in the 1930s]

guardhouse lawyer *n phr* latrine lawyer *(1888+ Army)*

Gucci Gulch *n phr* A fashionable shopping street or mall in Washington, Los Angeles, etc : *I'm gonna have to kill some time at Gucci Gulch/ Yes, Wisconsin's red and white army shopped the gold and jewels of Gucci Gulch* [1990s+; fr the posh and pricey Florentine retail house of *Gucci*]

guck *n* Any thick, gooey substance : *guck on the windowsill*

guesstimate *n* An approximation based on calculation and guesswork *v* : *Let's guesstimate a yield of four percent (1934+)*

guess what or **who** or **why** *v* To feign a conjecture when the truth is blatantly obvious; you'll never guess, SURPRISE SURPRISE : *The only one bold enough to call the proposal a smoke screen disguising congressional complicity was Colorado Republican Armstrong. Guess what? He's retiring this year/ Kissinger's scheme outlined a framework between the two superpowers to be arranged by a secret envoy (guess who?)/ The stoppages were unpopular; the Western press—guess why?—is no longer keen on Polish strikes (1930s+) See* BY GUESS AND BY GOD

guest shot *n phr* A guest appearance on a television show : *I get a big guest shot for big bucks on his next special (1980s+)*

guff *n* **1** Nonsense; pretentious talk; bold and deceitful absurdities; BULLSHIT : *his ability to listen to all the guff, through all the tedium (1888+)* **2** Complaints, abuse : *Don't take any guff from him v* To lie; exaggerate; BULLSHIT : *Quit your guffing and tell it right* [perhaps fr Scots *gaff*, "loud, rude, merry talk"; *gaff* in the first sense, now obsolete, is found by 1825]

Guido or **guido** *n* A gaudy macho type : *Guido: a greasy, pimpy, open-shirted, hairy-chested, gold-chain-danglin' sleazoid/ It's not my fault I look like a Guido* [1980s+ Teenagers; the name of a character in the 1983 movie *Risky Business*]

guilties, the *n phr* Feelings or pangs of guilt : *Sometimes we get the guilties on this account (1980s+)*

◄**Guinea►** (GIHN ee) (also **ghinney** or **ginee** or **ginnee** or **ginney** or **guin** or **guinea** or **guinie;** any of the variants may begin with a capital letter) *adj* : *a tough Ginney bootlegger n* **1** An Italian or person of Italian descent *(1896+)* **2** A native of a Pacific island, including Japan *(WWII armed forces)* [perhaps fr contemptuous association with the outdated term *Guinea Negro*, "black slave from the Guinea coast"]

guinea pig *n* Person or thing used in an experiment, sometimes without agreement : *the guinea pigs for her cooking*

◄**guinzo►** *See* GINZO

gulch *See* DRY-GULCH

gum *v* **1** To talk; chatter : *The he-gossips at the Press Club have been gumming about another romance (1940s+)* **2** GUM UP *(1901+) See* BUBBLEGUM MUSIC

gumbah *See* GOOMBAH

gum-beater *n* A persistent talker, esp a pompous braggart; BLOWHARD *(1930s+ Black)*

gum-beating *n* **1** A conversation; chat; RAP **2** Vain and exaggerated talk; BALONEY, BULLSHIT *(1930s+ Black)*

gumby *n* **1** A dull, tedious person, esp one out of touch with current fashions; NERD, PILL : *You can become a gumby by wearing the wrong plaid stretch pants (1970s+ Canadian teenagers)* **2** A slanted box haircut : *Murph has a gumby (1980s+ Teenagers)* [first sense fr a repulsive character, Mr *Gumby*, in the television series *Monty Python's Flying Circus*; second sense fr a person-shaped toy rubber (gum) figure named *Gumby*, seen in television shows and also portrayed by the comedian Eddie Murphy on the television series *Saturday Night Live*]

gummy *adj* **1** Inferior; tedious; unpleasant : *He found himself in a very gummy situation, with both of them berating him (1922+)* **2** Sentimental; maudlin; CORNY : *a gummy, gooey tearjerker of a film (1940+)* [like *icky* and *sticky*, fr the unpleasant feel of glue or slime]

gump *n* **1** A fool; dolt; KNUCKLEHEAD *(1825+)* **2** A chicken, esp a stolen one *(1899+ Hoboes)* **3** A male homosexual *(1950s+ Prison)* [fr British dialect, "fool"]

gumption *n* Initiative; enterprise; courage; SPUNK *(1831+)*

gumshoe *n* (Variations: **gum boot** or **gumfoot** or **gumheel** or **gumshoe man**) A police officer, esp a detective or plainclothes officer : *It made him a good gumshoe* *v* **1** (also **gumheel**) To work as a police officer or detective : *Still gumheeling?* **2** To walk a police beat : *Police now ride prowl cars instead of gumshoeing around the block* **3** To walk quietly and stealthily [1906+; fr *gumshoe*, "rubber-soled shoe"]

gum up or **gum up the works** *v phr* To ruin; spoil; throw into confusion; BOLLIX UP, FUCK UP [1890+; fr dialect *gaum*, "handle improperly, damage," found by 1656, influenced by the stickiness and clogging capacity of *gum*]

gun[1] *n* **1** An armed criminal : *They hired a gun to blast the competition (1859+)* **2** An important person; BIG GUN : *He's quite a gun around there now (1830+)* **3** The throttle of a car, airplane, etc : *Get your stupid foot off the gun (1900s+)* **4** A hypodermic needle *(1930s+ Narcotics)* **5** A long, heavy surfboard *(1960s+ Surfers)* **6** Throwing arm, esp a strong and accurate one *(1929+ Baseball)* *v* **1** To shoot someone : *Canales had no motive to gun Lou (1898+)* **2** To speed up an engine or vehicle, esp abruptly; GOOSE : *He gunned the Rolls into the parking spot (1940s+) See* BIG GUN, BURP GUN, GIVE IT THE GUN, JUMP THE GUN, SCATTERGUN, SIX-SHOOTER, SMOKING GUN, SON OF A BITCH, TOMMY GUN, ZIP GUN

gun[2] *n* (also **gon**) A professional thief, esp a pickpocket [1858+; fr Yiddish *gonif*]

gunboats (also **battleships**) *n* **1** A pair of shoes or galoshes, esp of large size : *He brought some of the 14EE gunboats with him from the States* **2** A pair of large feet *(1886+)*

gun someone down *v phr* To shoot so as to fell or kill : *They gunned him down in a barber chair (1898+)*

gun (or **go gunning**) **for** someone *v phr* **1** To seek out or pursue with harmful intent; aim to punish : *He gunned for her after she slapped him with a lawsuit (1888+)* **2** To pursue actively : *She's gunning for a new image (1940s+)*

gunge *n* An irritation of the groin region; crotch rot

gung ho *adj phr* Very zealous; totally committed; enthusiastic : *They were gung ho about the opportunity, their talk charged with an eagerness/ reminiscent of the gung-ho shot*

making that brought him so many grass-stained knees at Wimbledon [WWII Marine Corps; fr the name of a Chinese industrial cooperative organization, *kung ho,* "work together," adopted as *Gung ho!* to be the battle cry of a Marine Corps raiders group in World War II]

guniff *See* GONIFF

gunk or **goonk** *n* **1** Any sticky, viscous liquid, esp hair tonic, cosmetics, lubricants, or cleaning fluids; GLOP, GOOK[1] **2** Dirt; slime; oily grime; muck : *The anchor was clotted in noisome gunk* [1932+; fr a trademark, *Gunk,* for a degreasing compound, and part of a cluster of nearly synonymous terms beginning with *g*]

gun moll *n phr* A female criminal or a criminal's consort [1908+; fr *gonif* rather than fr the firearm; *Moll* is a diminutive of *Mary* and has been identified with notorious women since the early 1600s]

gunner *n* **1** A flashy performer; GRANDSTANDER, HOT DOG : *the reputation of a gunner and a hot dog, playground terms for players who showboat (1960s+ Basketball)* **2** A student who aggressively courts attention in class ● In earlier use, *gunner* meant a sexually aggressive student : *"Gunners" are people who raise their hands in class repeatedly just to impress (Students 1990s+)*

guns *See* HEAVY ARTILLERY

gunsel[1] (also **gonsil** or **gonzel** or **guncel** or **guntzel** or **gunzl**) *n* **1** A sexually vulnerable boy or young man; catamite; PUNK *(1914+ Underworld)* **2** A male homosexual *(1931+)* [fr Yiddish *gantzel,* "gosling"]

gunsel[2] *n* (Variations: see **gunsel**[1]) An armed criminal; HOODLUM : *The reformed gunzl took a quick gander/ The gunsels killed each other off* [1950s+; fr a blend of *gonif, gunsel*[1], *gunman,* etc]

gun-shy *adj* Apprehensive; reluctant; fearful : *He's still gun-shy about putting things on paper (1884+)*

gunslinger *n* **1** An armed criminal : *The gunslinger will spend his life behind bars/ He thought of himself as a lone gunslinger, like John Wayne (1920s+)* **2** An inmate who habitually exposes himself to female guards : *the sexually aggressive inmates, known as "gunslingers" in prison lingo (1990s+ Prison)*

guppie *n* A homosexual yuppie (young urban professional) [1984+; *gay* and *yuppie* blend]

guru *n* **1** A leader, expert, or authority in some field, esp a charismatic or spiritual figure who attracts a devoted following : *turning for guidance to such gurus as Paul Goodman and Herbert Marcuse/ That genial guru of the right, Barry Goldwater (1960s+)* **2** A psychiatrist; SHRINK *(1960s+)* **3** A person who aids and supports someone having a psychedelic drug experience *(1960s+ Narcotics & counterculture)* **4** A computer expert : *when you were with gurus (read: seasoned computer veterans) (1990s+ Computer)* [fr Sanskrit, "venerable"]

Gus *See* GLOOMY GUS

gussy up *v phr* **1** To dress in one's best clothes; adorn oneself; DOLL UP **2** To clean or make neat : *The freak had the little apartment all gussied up* **3** To decorate or elaborate on a plain design **4** To refurbish, renovate; polish : *They're gussying up the same old tiredness* **5** To decorate; make fancy : *It resembled a gussied-up Studebaker* [late 1940s+; origin unknown; perhaps fr *gusset,* a triangular insert that might be used to prettify a dress; perhaps fr someone or some place named *Augusta*]

gusto *n* Beer : *get some gusto*

gut *adj* **1** Basic; essential; most immediate : *the gut issues in the forthcoming election (1964+)* **2** Deep and not essentially rational; visceral; intuitive : *this deep, gut feeling that they want to be part of things/ He has to convince me on a gut level that I can do things my mind resists/ Whether the messenger is a top Government official or an ordinary Russian with a gut instinct (1968+)* **3** Easy : *a "gut" humanities course where the professor is said to put on a good show (1916+ Students)* **n 1** The stomach; abdomen; paunch; BAY WINDOW, POTBELLY *(1000+)* **2** GUT COURSE : *considered a gut by at least 50 percent of the students (1916+ Students)* **v** To remove all unessentials *(1950s+ Hot rodders)* *See* BUST A GUT, POTBELLY, ROTGUT, SPILL one's GUTS, TUB OF GUTS

gut course *n phr* (also **gut**) An easy course in college [1916+ College students; perhaps fr earlier sense *gut,* "a feast," hence a course that one can "eat up"]

gut it out *v phr* To be strong and resistant; be sturdily stoic; persist; TOUGH IT OUT : *Cook claimed that he was innocent of any wrongdoing and until last week insisted that he would "gut it out" (1970s+)*

gutless *adj* Cowardly; feeble; CHICKEN *(1915+)*

gutless wonder *n* A totally insipid and spineless person : *gutless wonders never knowing which way is up*

gut reaction *n phr* An immediate and instinctive response; an intuition; HUNCH : *if the public-opinion polls and gut reaction count for anything (1968+)*

guts *n* **1** The insides of a person, machine, etc; viscera; INNARDS : *He removed the cover and exposed the guts (1580+)* **2** The most essential material or part; essence : *The guts of the matter is that they are not here (1950s+)* **3** Courage; nerve; BALLS : *the guy who had guts enough to croak "Tough Tony" (1893+) See*

HATE someone's GUTS, SPILL one's GUTS, TUB OF GUTS

gutsy *adj* **1** Brave : *a gutsy lady* **2** Energetic and tough; ZINGY : *a gutsy car (1930s+)*

gutter *n* A dive in which one lands flat on the water; belly-whopper *(1950s+) See* HAVE one's MIND IN THE GUTTER

gutter, the *n phr* A wretched and lowly venue; the PITS : *Without jobs they'll never get out of the gutter (1846+)*

gutter language *n phr* Profanity and obscenity; scabrous speech : *This dictionary has a selection of gutter language* [1890+; *gutter,* "appropriate to the gutter or sewer," is found by 1849]

guttersnipe or **gutterpup** *n* A vulgar person; a vile wretch [1869+; in the sense "a curbside stock broker" found by 1856]

gut-thumper *n* An exciting and suspenseful occasion; CLIFFHANGER : *It wasn't a cakewalk, but it wasn't exactly a gut-thumper either (1980s+)*

gutty *adj* **1** Forceful and assertive : *a good gutty rock number (1939+)* **2** GUTSY *(1950s+)* **3** Capable of high speed; having a powerful engine *(1950s+ Hot rodders)*

gut-wrenching *adj* Emotionally shattering; extremely disturbing : *graphic, gut-wrenching description of gang violence/ Thursday's gut-wrenching roll-call victories represented a down payment on Clinton's campaign promises to get the country moving again (1990s+)*

gut-wrenchingly *adv* In a gut-wrenching way; shattering : *Many of Breyten's poems included gut-wrenchingly vivid evocations of his actual situation (1990s+)*

guy *n* **1** A person of either sex, esp a man; fellow • Used of and to women in address, and then almost invariably in the plural, but seldom in reference or in the singular *(1876+)* **2** A woman's fiancé, husband, lover, etc : *Just remember he's my guy (1940s+)* **3** A thing referred to, esp something one does not know the name of; BABY, GADGET, SUCKER : *I'll have this guy, this guy, and this guy (1980+)* **v** To mock; ridicule *(1869+)* [ultimately fr the name and reputation of *Guy* Fawkes, and esp of his ugly effigies burnt in England on November 5 to commemorate the foiling of the Gunpowder Plot, his plot to blow up the Houses of Parliament] *See* FALL GUY, ONE OF THE BOYS, REGULAR FELLOW, SMART GUY, TOUGH GUY, WISE GUY

guy thing *n* Something only understood, experienced, or done by males; something that appeals only to men : *reading on the toilet is a guy thing*

guzzle *n* goozle *v* **1** To drink, esp rapidly : *He guzzled a Coke (1500s+)* **2** To drink liquor, esp to excess : *He guzzled a lot when he got worried* [fr French *gosier,* "throat," or perhaps like that French word, echoically based on the sound of swallowing]

guzzler *n* A heavy drinker of alcohol : *guzzlers at the VFW*

◁**gweebo**▷ *n* A tedious and contemptible person; DORK, NERD *(1980s+ College students)*

gym rat *n phr* An athlete; a person who frequents gymnasiums : *a thin, fortunate group of very highly paid gym rats (1970s+)*

gyp or **gip** or **jip** *modifier* : *a gyp joint/ gyp terms n* **1** (also **gyp artist** or **gypster**) A swindler; cheater; CROOK : *denunciations of punks, tinhorns, and gyps (1889+)* **2** : *the victim of any such gyp (1914+)* **3** A cabdriver who does not start the meter, hence can pocket the fare *(1930+ Cabdrivers) v* To cheat; swindle; CON : *We got gypped out of it all in two days* [fr *gypsy*]

gyp joint *n phr* Any business place that overcharges, cheats, etc; CLIP JOINT : *Cops tried to shut down the midtown gyp joint (1935+)*

gypsy *n* **1** GYPSY CAB *(1940s+)* **2** A truck driven by its owner rather than a union driver *(1942+ Truckers) v* To make a risky bet or call : *You will find players consistently gypsying, flat-calling with kings up or less (1940s+ Gambling); (1950s+)*

gypsy cab *n phr* A taxicab operating without a taxi license or medallion, or with only a livery license that does not entitle it to pick up passengers on the street : *the advent of the latest taxi competitor: the gypsy cab (1970s+)*

gyve *See* JIVE

H

H *n* Heroin *(Narcotics) See* BIG H

hab *n* A French-speaking resident of Quebec [1980s+ Canadian; fr French *habitant*, "a French settler or a descendant of one"]

habit *n* Drug addiction : *I had a great big habit (1897+ Narcotics)*

ha-cha-cha *See* HOTCHA

hack[1] *n* **1** A taxicab *(1704+)* **2** A bus *(1950s+ Bus drivers)* *v* To drive a taxi or bus : *I worked in an office for years. Then I took to "hacking" (1931+)* [ultimately fr *hackney*, "horse," fr *Hackney*, a village incorporated into London, fr Old English "Haca's island" or "hook island"; presumably the horses were associated with the place]

hack[2] *n* **1** A persistent, often nervous, cough : *oughta see someone about that hack (1885+)* **2** A try; attempt; WHACK : *Let George take a hack at it (1836+)* **3** A mediocre performer or worker; tiresome drudge : *They are not the hacks that Eric's scholarship would make them (1700+)* **4** (also **hack writer**) A professional, usu freelance, writer who works to order • This sense belongs to *hack* reflecting the notion that such a writer was for hire like a horse, but its own derivatives blend with those of the meaning "try, stroke, etc" *(1810+)* **5** A computer program, esp a good one : *A well-crafted program, a good hack, is elegant (1980s+ Computer)* **6** A guard : *The guards, the hacks, as they called them/ The hacks didn't worry about the old convicts too much (1940s+ Prison)* **7** A white person; HONKY, OFAY *(1940s+ Black & prison)* *v* **1** : *If you quit smoking maybe you won't hack like that* **2** To cope with, esp successfully; manage; HANDLE • Most often in the negative : *"I can't hack this," Sandy remarked/ I couldn't hack the lines, so I used Mother Nature's privy (1940s+)* **3** (also **hack at**) To attempt; do persistently but mediocrely : *Do I play tennis? Well, I hack at it (1940s+)* **4** : *They hacked for some of our most respected leaders (1813+)* **5** To work with a computer or computer program, esp to do so cleverly, persistently, and enthusiastically • This term has many specialized senses in computer slang *(1980s+)* **6** To annoy; anger; BURN : *That attitude really hacks me (1892+)* [nearly all senses ultimately fr *hack*, "cut, chop"; black and prison senses fr identification of prison guards with white persons in the pattern identical with that of *the man*; prison guards perhaps so called because they sometimes beat prisoners]

hack (into) *v* To gain unauthorized access to a computer system : *hack into my site (1985+)*

hack around *v phr* To do nothing in particular; idle; loaf; BEAT AROUND : *He says he's been hacking around in some bar/ So I quit Butter, hacked around for a while (1960s+)*

hacker[1] *n* A persistent but generally unskillful performer or athlete; DUFFER *(1950s+)*

hacker[2] *n* **1** A skillful but not necessarily elegant computer programmer • This term has many senses in computer slang; the core notion is simply "someone who enjoys messing with computers, cleverly or not" : *When a hacker programs, he creates worlds/ As a hacker, McLachlan is a member of an intense, reclusive subculture of the computer age (1976+ Computer)* **2** A person who with evil, inquisitive, or self-aggrandizing intent intrudes into computer networks and files : *He said computer intruders, commonly referred to as hackers, who take over a router can do whatever they want (1980+ Computer)* [said to be fr *hack*[2], computer jargon for a clever and subtle correction of a flow in a computer program]

hackery *n* Routine mediocrity; esp the dull performance and tone of an average political professional : *the gray, self-serving hackery of previous City Councils (1970s+)*

hackie *n* (also **hacker** or **hacky**) A taxicab driver : *He enriched another hacker by an even $5,000/ He actually found a hackie named Louis Schweitzer (1937+)*

hack it *v phr* To cope successfully; CUT IT, HANDLE • Often in the negative : *John Fist can't hack it anymore (1940s+)*

hack on someone *v phr* To ridicule someone; PUT someone DOWN *(1990s+ Students)*

had (or taken or took), be *v phr* **1** To become a partner in the sex act *(1594+)* **2** To be duped or cheated; be victimized : *You practically need a finance degree to know that you are being had (1805+)*

had it *See* ONE HAS HAD IT

ha-ha *adj* : *even made a ha-ha pass at him/ ha-ha candles made to look like penises n* A joke; something funny; stroke of wit : *That's a ha-ha all right* [1940s+; *ha-ha* represented the sound of laughter by 1000] *See* the MERRY HA-HA

Hail Mary *modifier* Done in pious hope and desperation : *Staubach hurls a Hail, Mary pass into the end zone/ "We did what could be described as the Hail Mary play," Gen.*

Schwarzkopf says/ You know a Hail Mary moment when you see one: It happened at the Redskins-Cardinals game [1980s+ Football; fr the liturgical prayer *Hail, Mary, full of grace,* etc]

haimish or **heimish** (HAY mish) *adj* Friendly and informal; unpretentious; cozy : *No one in his right mind would ever call Generals de Gaulle or MacArthur haimish* [1960s+; fr Yiddish, with root of *haim,* "home"]

hair *n* Complexity : *a system with a lot of hair (1980s+ Computer) See* CURL someone's HAIR, FAIR-HAIRED BOY, GET IN one's HAIR, HAVE A BUG UP one's ASS, HAVE someone BY THE SHORT HAIRS, IN someone's HAIR, LET one's HAIR DOWN, LONGHAIR, NOT HAVE A HAIR ON one's ASS

hairball or **furball** *n* **1** A noisy, destructive drunk : *Jon was being a hairball last night. He got heated and thrashed the whole upstairs (1980s+ Students)* **2** A repulsive person; scumball, SLEAZEBAG : *makes a nice change from the hairballs featured in most crime novels (mid-1980s+)*

haired *See* LONGHAIR, FAIR-HAIRED BOY

hairnet *See* WIN THE PORCELAIN HAIRNET

hair of the dog (or **of the dog that bit** one), the *modifier* : *Does the hair-of-the-dog procedure eventually desensitize key cells in the immune system to the offending allergen? n phr* A drink of liquor taken as a remedy for a hangover; in general, the use of a harmful agent against itself [1546+; fr the belief that the bite of a *dog* could be healed by applying its *hair* to the wound]

◁**hair on** one's **ass**▷ *See* NOT HAVE A HAIR ON one's ASS

◁**hair pie**▷ *n phr* **1** Cunnilingus; BOX LUNCH **2** The female genitalia; the vulva; PUSSY [1930s+; a pun on *hare pie*]

hair wrap *n phr* A hair braid interwoven with colored thread : *doing hair wraps, those vaguely Rastafarian braids woven with Technicolor threads (1990s+)*

hairy *adj* **1** Old; hoary : *a hairy tale (1940s+)* **2** Difficult; rough; TOUGH : *We had a hairy time getting it all organized (1848+)* **3** Frighteningly dangerous; hair-raising; scary : *Campus guards would comb the dorm "It was hairy"/ the hairy strip of 42d Street (1940s+ Teenagers)* [last sense probably fr the *hairy* monsters of horror films, but the sense of "difficult" was used at 19th-century Oxford, and that of "dangerous" in the British armed forces of the 1930s]

hairy eyeball *See* GIVE someone THE FISH-EYE

half *See* BETTER HALF, a LAUGH

◁**half-and-half**▷ *n* Fellatio plus copulation *(1960s+ Prostitutes)*

half a shake *n phr* A moment; a trice : *I'll be there in half a shake* [1930s+; fr the expres-

sion *two shakes of a lamb's tail,* "a very short time"]

◁**half-assed** or **half-ass**▷ *adj* Ineffectual; incompetent; half-hearted; HALF-BAKED : *You first ran into censorship problems with the words "half-assed games"/ So far it's been a half-ass investigation* [1932+; perhaps fr a humorous mispronunciation of *haphazard*]

half a yard *n phr* Fifty dollars : *A "yard" and "half a yard" meaning one hundred dollars and fifty dollars respectively (1940s+)*

half-bagged *adj* Drunk : *They keep half-bagged all day and bore their new friends silly with stories (1950s+)*

half-baked *adj* Foolish; ill-conceived; not completely thought out; HALF-ASSED *(1621+)*

half cocked *adj* : *a half-cocked start adv* Prematurely; unprepared : *not going into this half-cocked (1940s+) See* GO OFF HALF COCKED

half crocked *adj phr* Drunk; half-drunk : *laying around on a settee, sort of half crocked/ I came out at twelve, one o'clock, half-crocked, really snockered (1920s+)*

halfies or **halvies** or **halvsies** *n* One half of what is indicated, esp as an equal share : *She found it, but I claimed halvsies because I did most of the work (1960s+) See* GO HALFIES

half in the bag *adj phr* Drunk; half-drunk : *He was half in the bag. He always is at Christmas/ Billy Small was half in the bag even that early (1920s+)*

half of it *n phr* The most significant or important part of something • Usu in negative contexts : *her attitude is not the half of it (1932+)*

half-pint *modifier* : *half-pint showman n* **1** A short person : *the little half-pint that she was* **2** A boy *(mid-1920s+)*

half seas over *adj phr* Drunk [1736+; fr the notion that one is like a ship low in the water and burdened so that relatively low waves, *half seas, sweep over its deck*]

half-shot *adj* Drunk; half-drunk : *when they were half shot with beer (1837+)*

half-step *v* **1** To act tough but then back down when challenged **2** To do something halfway, insufficiently, or incompetently

half-stewed *adj* (Variations: **screwed** or **slewed** or **snapped** or **sprung** may replace **stewed**) Drunk; half-drunk *(1737+)*

half-wit *n* A foolish person : *half-wits in the phys ed class (1755+)*

hall *See* CHOW HALL

halvsies *modifier* Split equally between two; GO DUTCH : *let's go halvsies on dinner See* GO HALVSIES

ham[1] *modifier* : *a ham radio operator/ ham network n* An amateur radio operator [1928+; fr *amateur*]

ham² *modifier* : *ham actor/ ham performance n*
1 An actor who overacts, dramatizes himself, emotes too broadly, etc : *had been roasted by the critics as a ham/ Variety never referred to actors as "hams"* (1882+) **2** A person who uses overtheatrical and overly expressive airs and actions : *Miss Moment was no doubt the biggest ham of a teacher* (1940s+) *v* **1** (also **ham it up**) : *The famous star was hamming all the way* (1933+) **2** (also **ham it up**) : *The prof strode into the lecture hall hamming and mugging* (1940s+) [fr *ham-fatter*]
ham-and-egger *n* **1** An average, predictable person or thing; ordinary joe : *The new People Wieners album is a ham and egger* (1920s+) **2** An average or mediocre prizefighter (1920s+ Prizefight)
hambone *modifier* : *The night's most ebullient winner was Finkel, who plays the hambone attorney n* A person who fancies himself an actor; histrionic self-advertiser; HAM : *Every hambone from the deep sticks was constrained to make a speech for the benefit of the cameras* (1893+)
hamburger *n* **1** A scarred and unvictorious prizefighter **2** A hobo or mendicant **3** An inferior racing dog (1940s+) *See* MAKE HAMBURGER OUT OF someone or something
ham-fatter *n* HAM, HAMBONE [1882+; fr a minstrel song of 1887, "The Hamfat Man," having to do with a second-rate actor, and the use of *ham fat* as greasepaint to remove makeup]
hamfist *n* A large fist, big as a ham : *His huge hamfist had landed me a vicious blow* (1920s+)
ham-handed or **ham-fisted** *adj* Crude and clumsy; lacking in finesse : *his hamfisted approach to a delicate matter (first form 1918+, second 1928+)*
ham-handedness *n* Crudeness; clumsiness; lack of polish : *In selecting the rottenest apples, one seeks the pretension and the exploitation rather than mere ham-handedness* (1928+)
hammer *n* **1** A sexually desirable woman; FOX ● Regarded by some women as offensive (1960s+ Black) **2** The accelerator of a truck (1960+ Truckers) ◁3▷ The penis : *How's your hammer hangin', Tiger?* (1960s+) *v* **1** To denigrate severely; DUMP ON : *You can be playing outside the pearly gates and you're still going to get hammered* (1900+) **2** To beat down the price of a stock : *Beverly's stock was being hammered by the company's persistent losses* (1846+ Stock market)
hammer and tongs *adv phr* Very violently; with full force : *We went at each other hammer and tongs* [1708+; reflecting use of both the blacksmith's main tools]
hammer away at someone or something *v phr* To persist in a line of questioning or declaration; attempt to persuade or break down by force : *The prosecutor kept hammering away at the alibi/ He hammered away at my credibility* (1887+)
hammer down *adv phr* Going full speed; with throttle to the floor; WIDE OPEN : *a herd of L A rednecks, all of 'em pie-eyed and hammer down* (1960+ Truckers)
hammered *adj* Drunk : *I don't get hammered anymore* (1950s+)
hammerhead *n* A stupid person : *The best way out is for one of the three to be a hammerhead* (1930s+)
hammer lane *n phr* The fast lane of a superhighway : *The passing lane can be "centerfield," "the hammer lane," or "the showoff lane"* [1980s+ Truckers; fr the trucker sense hammer, "accelerator"]
hammer-man *n* An authoritative person; strongman [1950s+ Black; perhaps an echo of *John Henry*]
hams *n* Legs or hips; the hamstring muscles : *worked her hams at the gym*
hamster-wheel brain *n* An instance or condition where one's mind goes over and over an issue or problem without reaching a solution : *I'm mostly worrying about work, with my hamster-wheel brain running*
ham up *v phr* To make histrionic; overexpress; HAM : *The baseball umpire was hamming up his signals for the benefit of the television audience* (1929+)
hand *v* To give, esp something not desired; bestow forcefully, fraudulently, etc : *The Red Sox handed the Yankees a 12 to 3 shellacking/ What kind of con job was he trying to hand you?* (1919+) *See* BOTH HANDS, COOL HAND, DEAD MAN'S HAND, GIVE someone THE GLAD HAND, GLAD-HAND, HAVE one's HANDS FULL, NOT LAY A GLOVE ON someone, TIP one's MITT, WITH one's HAND IN THE TILL, WITH ONE HAND TIED BEHIND one's BACK
hand, a *n* **1** A round of applause : *Well she got a big hand* (1838+) **2** Help; aid (1960+) *See* GIVE someone A HAND
hand someone **a lemon** *v phr* To take advantage of; cheat; GYP : *if they hand me a lemon* (1860s+)
handbasket *See* GO TO HELL IN A HANDBASKET
handcuffs *See* GOLDEN HANDCUFFS
handed *See* HAM-HANDED, LEFT-HANDED, RIGHT-HANDED
hander *See* GLAD-HANDER
handful *n* **1** A five-year prison sentence or term (1930+ Underworld) **2** A great deal to manage; burdensome task : *That kid of yours is a handful* (1887+) *See* GRAB A HANDFUL OF AIR
hand someone **his head** *v phr* To destroy; figuratively to decapitate someone and hand him his own head; CLOBBER : *Do what they*

want, or they'll hand you your head/ when the press is handing Francis Coppola his head (*1970s+*)

hand-holding *n* Support; reassurance; encouragement : *Congress wants some hand-holding from Clinton on Somalia* (*1908+*)

hand-in-glove *adv* In close cooperation or relationship; going together naturally : *those two ambitions work hand-in-glove*

hand it to someone *v phr* To compliment; praise someone for a success • Often said with overtones of reluctance : *I got to hand it to you* (*1906+*)

◁**hand job**▷ *n phr* An act of masturbation, usu done for one person by another : *rolled over on top of me and started giving me a real good hand job/ If you were unlucky, all you got was a hand job* (*1940s+*)

handle *n* **1** A person's name, nickname, or alias : *He is known by that handle ever since to all his pals/ Many people use handles for themselves instead of their real names* (*1870+*) **2** The gross receipts or the profit of a sporting event, a gambling game, an illegal operation, etc : *A total handle of between 4 and 10 billion a year in the handbooks, the numbers, and the slots* (*1920s+*) **3** The amount of money bet on a specific race or game, or in a particular day or week, etc : *The handle at Belmont dropped today on account of the blizzard* (*1920s+ Gambling*) **4** A way of approaching or grasping something; an initial and relevant insight : *Women, I don't seem to have a handle on them/ So we may have less handle on him than we did before* (*1972+*) *v* To cope with; manage; HACK : *He can handle Tom's temper tantrums very well/ My wife left me and I don't know how to handle it* (*1970s+*) *See* FLY OFF THE HANDLE, GET A HANDLE ON something, PANHANDLE

handler *n* A person who seconds, supports, advises, etc, a principal : *Bush and his political handlers believe, as Reagan did, that the way to the people's heart is paved with unshucked corn* [*1950+* Prizefighting; the term was used of those who handled gamecocks, dogs, etc, by *1825*] *See* PANHANDLER

handles *See* LOVE HANDLES

hand-me-down or **fetch-me-down** *modifier* : *a pair of hand-me-down pants/ fetch-me-down ski boots n* Something, esp clothing, used by one person and then passed to another, esp to a younger sibling : *I wore mostly my brother's hand-me-downs* (*1874+*)

handout *n* **1** Food, money, or other donations received or given • Nearly always with the implication that the giver is overgenerous or self-interested, and the recipient undeserving : *Damn hippies lived on food stamps and other bleeding heart handouts* (*1882+ Hoboes*)

2 A leaflet or flyer passed out on the streets **3** An official press release or communiqué : *The newspaperman's slightly derogatory slang term for the news release is "handout"* (*1941+*)

hand over fist *adv phr* Very energetically, persistently, and rapidly : *It was a treat to see them go at it hand over fist* (*1833+*) *See* MAKE MONEY HAND OVER FIST

hands *See* BOTH HANDS, HAVE one's HANDS FULL, SIT ON one's HANDS

hands are tied, one's *sentence* One is unable to act : *I'd like to help, but my hands are tied* (*1940s+*)

hands down *adv phr* Very easily; without effort • Most often in the phrase *win hands down* : *She entered the race unheralded, and won it hands down/ We just loafed along, but beat them hands down* [*1867+* fr horse racing; fr the gesture of a jockey who drops his hands and lets the reins go loose in an easy victory]

hands-off *adj* Noninterfering; passive : *the president's hands-off policy* (*1902+*)

handsome *See* HIGH, WIDE, AND HANDSOME

hands on *adj* Practical and active rather than theoretical : *what we labeled a hands-on mayor/ No Hands-On Achiever Need Apply adv phr* Manually, by direct control rather than automatic control : *The ship was then flown hands on modifier* : *hands-on landing of the aircraft* (*1960s+*)

hand up *v phr* To testify against; betray; RAT ON : *He said he'd do life before he'd hand up his associates/ This, like the problem of cops refusing to hand up other cops* [*1893+*; the dated instance is from British schoolboy slang]

hand-waving *n* A signal that one does not want to give a full explanation; also, an argument that is not fully supported or fully convincing : *They asked him about progress, but he just offered some hand-waving. / She tried to explain why she forgot, but the hand-waving said it all*

hand-wringing *n* An ostentatious show of grief, remorse, etc : *hand-wringing on the part of the press* (*1603+*)

handyman's special *n phr* Something, esp a house, in dire need of major repair; a wreck : *"Hudson River Castle for Sale: Handyman's Special with View"* (*1970s+*)

hang *v* **1** To spend time; frequent; GOOF OFF, HANG OUT : *Who runs the coffeepot where they hang?/ If a person is goofing off, he's hanging* (*1951+ Teenagers*) **2** To endure a situation; survive; handle pressure : *No one ever chants I am somebody. If you weren't, you couldn't hang/ This is so stressful. I can't hang* (*1980s+ Students*) *See* HAVE IT ALL HANGING OUT, LET IT ALL HANG OUT

hang a few on *v phr* To have several drinks of liquor : *He had only hung a few on and was, for him, slightly sober* (1950s+)

hang a left (or a right) *v phr* To turn left or right, to round a corner : *Bellsey hung a left on 53rd Street* [1960s+ Teenagers; perhaps fr surfers' phrases *hang five, hang ten*]

hang around *v phr* **1** To idle about; loiter; HACK AROUND **2** To stay where one is; remain : *I decided to hang around and see what went down* (1847+)

◁**hang-down**▷ *n* The penis; PRICK : *like the horse's hang-down that I am, get myself shit-faced* (1970s+)

hanged *See* I'LL BE DAMNED

hanger *See* CLIFFHANGER, CRAPE-HANGER

hang five *v phr* To ride forward on the surfboard so that the toes of one foot are over the edge (1960s+ Surfers)

hang in (or in there) *v phr* To endure in some difficult action or position; persist tenaciously; HANG TOUGH : *He didn't pack it up, of course, he hung in there and saw the story through/ Rosemary Woods is hanging in* (1969+)

hanging *See* HOW THEY HANGING

hang it up *v phr* To retire; cease working, competing, etc : *since Joe Namath and Sonny Jurgenson hung it up/ After a serious injury they wanted me to hang it up* (1874+)

hang (or stay) loose *v phr* To be relaxed and nonchalant; be uninvolved; COOL IT ● Often heard as a genial exhortation : *I needed to hang loose, breathe free, get lost, take a trip/ You're healthier and happier when you hang loose/ Stay loose, man* (1950s+ Hot rodders)

hang of something, the *See* GET THE HANG OF something

hang on *v phr* To endure; persist; HANG IN

hang something on someone *v phr* To place the blame on : *Don't hang that mistake on me*

hang (or tie or pin) one on *v phr* **1** To get very drunk; go on a drinking spree (1900+) **2** To hit someone hard; CLOBBER : *Will you hang one on my jaw?* (1908+)

hangout *n* **1** A place for loitering, loafing, and passing time, esp with congenial companions : *a grad student hangout on Mirandola Lane/ a gay hangout* (1893+) **2** One's home; DIGS (1920s+)

hang out *v phr* To pass time; loaf pleasantly about; loiter; HANG : *Just us five hangin' out/ The best hours of my youth were spent loitering in front of Simon's Candy Store doing nothing, just hanging out* (1844+) *See* HAVE IT ALL HANGING OUT, LET IT ALL HANG OUT

hang out the wash *v phr* To hit a hard line drive [1930s+ Baseball; because the ball's path resembles a taut clothesline]

hang someone out to dry *v phr* **1** To punish someone severely, esp as a scapegoat : *The*

company silently took the fall; Storms was hung out to dry/ J R Rider says he was "hung out to dry" by Nevada–Las Vegas officials **2** To defeat utterly; CLOBBER : *hang Sox out to dry* **3** To catch a base-runner in a rundown; pick off a base runner : *I was hacking because I didn't want to leave Listach out to dry* (1980s+ Baseball) (1980s+)

hangover *n* The headache, morbid sensitivity, nausea, etc, felt upon awakening some hours after drinking too much liquor (1912+)

hang ten *v phr* To ride forward on a surfboard so that the toes of both feet are over the edge (1960s+ Surfers)

hang time *n phr* The time that a punted ball stays in the air : *He's got lots of great stats, hang time* (1980s+ Football)

hang tough *v phr* To endure in a difficult plight; show plucky and stoic persistence; HANG ON, TOUGH IT OUT : *You've got a friend at Chase Manhattan, if you've still got a traveler's check to cash. Otherwise, hang tough/ Mr Shannon glorifies Kennedy for his ability to "hang tough"* (1960s+)

hang-up *n* **1** A mental block; a psychological disturbance, fixation, or problem : *ribald anecdotes concerning his hang-up on strong women* **2** Anything encumbering, frustrating, distressing, etc; an impediment : *You couldn't carry around an amplifier and electric guitar and expect to survive, it was just too much of a hang-up/ The only hang-up we can see right now is that business of paying the doctors* (1959+)

hang up *v phr* To become fixated : *Why did you get hung up on Proust, anyhow?* (1960s+)

hang someone or something up *v phr* To stall or immobilize; frustrate; paralyze : *The four would not be able to hang the entire jury up/ or some other means of transcending the realities that hang one up* (mid-1800s+)

hang something up *v phr* To abandon one's efforts; CALL IT QUITS : *Police have hung it up* (1854+)

hang up (or out) one's shingle *v phr* To commence professional practice; open a law office, doctor's office, etc : *He's passed his bar exam now, so he can hang up his shingle* (1871+)

hang with *v phr* To seek and prefer the company of; consort with : *Sondra didn't hang with nobody but doctors* (1950s+)

hankie or **hanky** *n* A handkerchief (1895+)

hankty *See* HINCTY

hanky-panky *n* Anything dishonest, deceptive, or unethical; esp, in recent use, sexual infidelity; MONKEY BUSINESS : *She seems just to be along for some hanky-panky with her pal, General Von Griem/ can be an assurance against* *clandestine wrongdoing and political hanky-panky (1841+)*

happening *adj* **1** Up-to-date and desirable; chic; COOL, HIP, WITH IT : *That dress is definitely happening; you look great/ This music is happening* **2** Lively; vibrant : *It's a way happening town n* An event : *the concert was a happening (1980s+ Students)*

happenings *n* Narcotics; JUNK *(1950s+ Narcotics)*

happy *adj* Drunk, esp slightly so; TIDDLY *(1893+)*

-happy *combining word* Somewhat insane over or excessively wrought upon by what is indicated : *bomb-happy/ car-happy/ power-happy/ trigger-happy* [1930s+; probably modeled on *slap-happy*]

happy as a clam *adj phr* Very happy; euphoric : *She's happy as a clam with contractor Roe Messner/ on a posing dais in front of a full-length mirror, happy as a clam* [1636+; fr earlier locution *happy as a clam at high tide*, that is, when it cannot be dug]

happy as a pig in slop *adj phr* Very happy; euphoric : *happy as a pig in slop just to be playing in the National Football League* [1970s+; a euphemism for *happy as a pig in shit*, found by 1896]

happy camper *n phr* A contented person; someone well pleased : *Quayle called the people of American Samoa "happy campers"* [1980s+; said to have originated among California movie and show-business people; the reference is probably to child clients of summer camps]

happy face *n phr* A stylized circular smiling face, drawn or pasted up as a talisman : *I don't want to put one of those Chuck Tanner happy faces on this season (1960s+)*

happy hour *n phr* **1** The hour or so of relaxation with drinks after work; cocktail hour **2** A specified period of time, usu in early evening, in some restaurants and bars when drinks are sold at lower prices or when free food is provided *(1980s+)*

happy-juice *n* Liquor : *The increased taxes on happy-juice have cut the revenues from liquor sales (1950s+)*

happy pill *n phr* A tranquilizer pill *(1956+)*

happy talk *modifier* : *as for the happy-talk format that sandwiches cheerful repartee between the fire and robbery reports n phr* Informal chat and chaffing among news broadcasters during the program, as an element of entertainment : *Later, happy talk evolved, to break the tension created by the action, that is the violence, shown on TV news* [1980s+ Television studio; fr the title of a song in the 1949 Rodgers and Hammerstein musical *South Pacific*]

haps, the *n phr* Events; happenings; attractions : *Free Haps/ E-mail our trend hotline with the haps in your town (1990s+)*

hard *adj* **1** Demonstrable; verifiable; not dependent on subjective judgment, emotion, etc : *A comprehensive set of hard figures emerged for the first time (1960s+)* **2** TOUGH *(1818+)* **3** Excellent; good; COOL *(1930s+ Jive talk) n* ◁**1**▷ HARD-ON *(1893+) See* TAKE IT HARD

hard (or tough) act to follow *n phr* Something or someone difficult to rival or beat : *Dr Nick's going to be a hard act to follow* [1975+; from the notion of a performer coming next on a variety bill]

hard as nails *adj phr* Extremely durable and grim; TOUGH *(1850s+)*

◁**hard-ass** or **hard-assed**▷ *adj* : *Some are hard-ass disciplinarians/ even your most hard-assed rightwingers had some showboat in them n* A severe and often pugnacious person; : *I've gotten the reputation as being a hard-ass (1940s+)*

hard at it *adj phr* Doing the sex act; SCREWING : *Was you and she not hard at it before I came into the room? (1749+)*

hardball *modifier* : *fields hardball questions in a practice TV interview/ despite his hardball attitude toward sponsors of offensive TV shows n* Serious and consequential activity, work, etc; perilous and responsible doings : *It's hardball now, it's not games anymore/ It's going to be hard ball. We're talking about physicians losing income v* PLAY HARDBALL *(1973+)*

hard-boiled *adj* Severe and uncompromising; strict and pugnacious; TOUGH : *The rather hard-boiled painting that hangs in Father's office* [1886+; fr *hard-boiled egg*]

hard-boiled egg *n phr* A severe and pugnacious person; TOUGH GUY : *Our basic idea of a hero is really a "hard-boiled egg"* [1880s+; because "it can't be beat"]

hard (or heavy) breathing *n phr* Passionate lovemaking *(1970s+)*

hard case *n phr* A rough and dangerous person; TOUGH GUY : *Most of the hardcases knew their rights better than the cops (1836+)*

hard cheese *n phr* **1** An unfortunate outcome or situation • Still chiefly British; often an interjection : *This is hard cheese indeed (1876+)* **2** A fastball; SMOKE *(1980s+ Baseball)*

hard coin *n phr* Large amounts of money; MEGABUCKS : *There's some hard coin being made by the music magnates (1970s+)*

hard copy *n phr* A printed copy of a computer document; printout : *Millie, can you give me a hard copy of that? (1964+)*

hard-core *adj* Essential and uncompromising; unmitigated : *a hard-core Republican/ hard-*

core pornography (1951+) *n* Pornography that openly depicts complete sex acts : *He sort of likes dirty stuff, but not real hard core* (1970s+)

hard drug *n phr* A narcotic, like heroin or morphine, that is powerfully addictive and injurious : *The American problem is heroin, as "hard" a drug as there is* [1960s+ Narcotics; probably modeled on *hard liquor*]

hard facts *n phr* Information that is dependable and verifiable (1887+)

hard hat *modifier* : *Caution, this is a hard-hat zone n phr* **1** A derby hat : *The boys with the hard hats always ask a lot of questions about murders* (1935+) **2** (also **brain bucket**) The steel or plastic helmet worn by various sorts of workers, esp construction workers : *From here on we wear hard hats/ They lay aloft at 1930 with their "brain buckets" (hard hats) and bags of tools* (1953+) **3** A worker who wears a hard hat : *The hard hats sat around and whistled at the passing girls* (1960s+) **4** A very conservative right-winger; a reactionary : *He knows he can count on the hard hats to support him* (1970s+) **5** A regular Viet Cong soldier, who wears a military helmet, as distinct from a guerrilla or reservist : *Some 50,000 are "hard-hats" (full-time fighters) (Vietnam War armed forces)* [the political sense fr the vocal and sometimes violent opposition of many construction workers to the US peace movement during the Vietnam War, reinforced by terms like *hard line* and *hard core*]

hardhead *n* An obstinate or stupid person (1519+)

hard-headed *adj* **1** Obstinate; stubborn; PIG-HEADED (1583+) **2** Realistic; practical; unevasive; HARD-NOSED (1779+)

hard line *adj* : *the President's hard-line views on abortion n phr* A policy or attitude based on severity and lack of compromise : *Take a hard line with them or they'll murder you* (1960s+)

hard liquor *n phr* Whiskey, rum, gin, brandy, etc., as distinct from wine and beer; spirits; strong waters (1879+)

hard look, a *n phr* **1** An intense and unblinking scrutiny; strict examination : *Take a hard look at what's going on upstairs/ We'll have a hard look at the income and expenses* (1960s+) **2** A menacing or hostile stare : *She gave me a real hard look when I blurted her name* (1888+)

hard-luck story *n phr* A tale calculated to gain sympathy and help : *He gives me the same old hard-luck story every time* (1900+)

hard news *n phr* Information that is definite and verifiable, free of conjecture (1938+)

hard-nosed *adj* **1** Stubborn; obstinate (mid-1920s+) **2** Severe and practical; harshly realistic; HARD-HEADED, TOUGH : *They'll take a hard-nosed look, then report* (1940s+)

hard nut *n* A difficult or uncompromising person : *was a hard nut, that's for sure* (1888+)

◁**hard-on**▷ *n* **1** An erection of the penis : *It was another one of those subway things. Like having a hard-on at random* (1893+) **2** A severe and intolerant person, esp a martinet leader or superior : *Stone is turning into a world-class hard-on* (1980s+) See HAVE A HARD-ON FOR someone or something

hard-rock *adj* Severe; dour and pugnacious; TOUGH : *the old hard-rock guy who would line up all the cocaine users and shoot them* [1923+; probably fr the difficulty of *hard-rock* mining as distinct fr other kinds; influenced by *rock-hard*]

hard rock *n phr* A form of rock-and-roll music with a simple, driving beat, usu played on heavily amplified guitars (1960s+ Rock and roll)

hard (or tough) row to hoe, a *n phr* A difficult task; a period of trouble and travail; HARD TIMES : *If he focused on Rwanda, where would he get the interest and support? It's going to be a hard row to hoe* (1835+)

hard science *n phr* A science such as chemistry or physics where the data and conclusions are supportable by objective criteria (1960s+)

hard sell *n phr* An act or policy of selling aggressively, forcibly, loudly, etc : *Joe is a master at hard sell* (1950s+)

hard-shell *adj* Strict; conservative; HARD-CORE : *her hard-shell manner, her hipped-up weariness*

hard stuff *n* **1** Whiskey and other strong liquors; spirits; HARD LIQUOR : *The troubles the hard stuff inflicts on men with no defense against it* (1891+) *n phr* **2** HARD DRUG (1960s+ Narcotics) **3** Money, esp loot or other illicit gain (1910+ Underworld)

hard swallow *n phr* Something hard to accept : *Clinton's change of policy is a hard swallow for Ghali* (1990s+)

hard time *n phr* Time actually spent in prison by a sentenced criminal : *Hard men are serving hard time 10 miles down the road* (1930s+ Underworld) See GIVE someone A HARD TIME

hard times *n phr* A period of economic depression, poverty, etc (1705+)

hardtop *n* **1** A car with a metal roof, esp one resembling a convertible or with a convertible counterpart (1940s+) **2** A paved area or road : *Park over there on the hardtop* (1950s+)

hard up *adj phr* **1** Poor; penniless : *It was no disgrace to be hard up in those times* (1821+) **2** Sexually frustrated; needing sexual gratification; HORNY : *He declared he was so hard up* *he'd fuck mud (1940s+)* [apparently fr a nautical expression meaning the helm is *hard up,* that is, held all the way to windward while beating and so pinched as tight as possible]

hard up for something *adj phr* Lacking; deficient in : *We're hard up for booze around here (1840+)*

hardware *n* 1 Weapons and other war matériel : *military "hardware," tanks, planes, guns, rockets, weapons (1865+)* 2 Military insignia or medals worn on a uniform *(WWII armed forces)* 3 Badges and other identification jewelry *(1930s+)* 4 HARD DRUG, HARD LIQUOR

hard way, the *n phr* 1 The repetition of an even number that came up on the first roll, made by rolling two even dice that add up to it *(1950s+ Crapshooting)* 2 The most difficult and strenuous way of doing anything : *Wideman is building a picture of the world the hard way—person by person, life by life (1931+)*

hard-wired *adj* Determined by innate brain functions; not a matter of choice : *These individuals seem hard-wired only to show up at work, do their task and leave with a paycheck/ We're hard-wired to be social creatures* [1970s+; fr the definiteness of an actual wired connection in a computer, as distinct from something depending on a program]

hardwood, the *n* A basketball court *(1940s+ Basketball)*

harness *n* The dress and equipment of special categories of persons, such as telephone line repairers, police officers, train conductors, motorcyclists, etc : *Wise detectives, who dread going back into "harness" or uniform (1841+) See* IN HARNESS

harrumph *v* To speak disparagingly or indignantly : *Louise Trubek harrumphed that title insurance is regarded as a "consumer rip-off"/ She harrumphed and slammed her door closed (1940s+)*

Harry *See* EVERY TOM, DICK, AND HARRY

harsh *v* To nag and complain; NUDGE *(1990s+ Teenagers)*

Hart, Schaffner and Marx *n phr* Three jacks [1960s+ Poker; fr the name of a men's clothing manufacturer]

has-been *n* 1 A person who was once famous, successful, courted, etc, but is no longer so : *Some has-beens make spectacular comebacks (1786+)* 2 BACK NUMBER

hash *adj* Excellent; wonderful; COOL *(1960s+ Cool talk) n* Hashish *(1950s+ Narcotics) v* 1 To discuss, esp at length; HASH OVER : *They had hashed and rehashed for many a frugal conversational meal (1920+)* 2 HASH UP *(1663+) See* MAKE HAMBURGER OUT OF someone or something, SLING HASH

has had it, one *sentence* 1 (Variations: **up to here** or **up to one's ass** or **up to one's eyebrows** or some other anatomical feature may be added) One is exhausted, disgusted, unwilling to put up with any more : *All at once I've had it up to here with psychiatry* 2 One has been given a last chance and has failed : *That's the ball game, buddy, you've had it* [WWII armed forces; fr shortening of WWII British Royal Air Force slang: He's *had his time,* "He's been killed"]

hasher *n* 1 A waiter or waitress : *going to give them jobs as hashers* 2 A cook or kitchen worker *(1916+)*

hashery *n* A restaurant or lunch counter, esp a small or cheap place : *We'll inhale a few hamburgers at some fashionable hashery (1870+)*

hash head *n phr* A frequent user of hashish or marijuana *(1950s+ Narcotics)*

hash-house or **hash joint** *n* A restaurant or lunch counter, esp a cheap one; HASHERY : *the sort of language that one would expect to hear from a hobo in a Bowery hash-house (1875+)*

hash mark (or **stripe**) *n phr* 1 A service stripe, worn on the sleeve of a military uniform to mark each four-year period of service : *the voice of a subaltern of God, hashmarks running down his arm for a thousand miles (1909+ Armed forces)* 2 An inbounds line marker used to help fix the point where the ball is put in play, and spaced one yard from the next mark *(1960s+ Football)* [military sense apparently fr the number of years one has had free food from the Army]

hash over (or **out**) *v phr* 1 To discuss, esp repeatedly and lengthily : *We kept hashing over the same tired old topics/ She thought we should hash it out right now* 2 To rehash, review : *Asked him in to hash over a point or two* [1931+; fr the notion of chopping something fine]

hash session *n phr* GABFEST *(1940s+)*

hash-slinger *n* 1 A waiter or waitress, usu in a cheap restaurant or lunch counter : *Hash-slingers are plentiful, but well-trained waitresses are scarce (1868+)* 2 A cook or kitchen worker *(1868+)*

hash up *v phr* To ruin; spoil; FUCK UP, MESS UP *(1940s+)*

hassle or **hassel** *n* 1 A disagreement; quarrel; fight : *A hassel between two actors touched off the riot/ The hassle over putting fluoride in drinking water* 2 A difficult or tedious task or concern : *Getting those tickets was a real hassle v* 1 : *They were hassling about who would pay the bill* 2 (also **hass**) To harass; treat rudely and roughly : *I went to an assistant DA and told him I wanted to discuss being hassled by the* *police/ What you going to do if you find the hobo that hassed him?* **3** To get narcotics with difficulty : *He finally hassled one bag (1950s+ Narcotics)* [1920s+, but mainly 1940s+; origin unknown; probably fr *hatchel*, "to harass," found by 1800, a *hatchel* being an instrument for beating flax, and related to *heckle*; perhaps fr *hazel*, with a variant *hassle*, the switch used for beatings; *hazel oil* meant "a beating" by 1678]

hassle-free *adj* Without difficulties and worries : *The bliss of hassle-free existence depends first and foremost on other people who can dispense with all the pesky minutiae of daily life. In other words, you need staff (1980s+)*

hat *n* A condom *(1990s+ Teenagers) See* BRASS HAT, GIMMIE HAT, HARD HAT, HIGH-HAT, OLD HAT, PARTY HAT, PASS THE HAT, SHIT IN YOUR HAT, TALK THROUGH one's HAT, THROW one's HAT IN THE RING, UNDER one's HAT, WEAR TWO HATS, WHITE HAT, WOOL HAT

hatch *n* The mouth and throat : *DeCasseres would hurl the first legal drink down his hatch (1931+) See* BOOBY HATCH, DOWN THE HATCH, NUTHOUSE

hatchet job *n phr* **1** A malicious attack; a diatribe or indictment meant to destroy : *By hatchet job is meant here a calculated attempt to demolish the author* **2** A discharge or dismissal; AX *(1940s+)*

hatchet man *n phr* **1** (also **hatchet**) A professional killer; HIT MAN *(1880+)* **2** A person whose task and predilection is to destroy an opponent, often by illegitimate means *(1944+)*

hate someone's **guts** *v phr* To have an extreme hatred for someone; absolutely execrate someone : *I dislike him, but I don't hate his damn guts (1918+)*

hate-jock *n* A radio talk-show host who encourages bigotry : *a protest against the racism of white hate-jock Bob Grant (1990s+)*

hat in hand *adv phr* Obsequiously; tamely; pleadingly : *The President stands there, hat in hand, begging the Congress for their votes*

hat trick *n phr* **1** The scoring of three goals in a single game by the same player in hockey or soccer *(1877+ British sports)* **2** The feat of hitting a single, double, triple, and home run in one game *(1980s+ Baseball)* [fr cricket, "the bowling down of three wickets with successive balls," probably compared with the magician's trick of pulling a rabbit out of a hat; also said to be a feat that entitled the player to the proceeds of a collection, that is, a passing of the *hat*, or to a new *hat*]

hatty *See* HIGH-HAT

haul *n* **1** Profits or return, esp illicit ones; loot : *The show yielded a huge haul* **2** The proceeds from any activity : *a haul for the canned goods*

collection [1776+; fr the contents of a fish net that is *hauled*] *See* FOR THE LONG HAUL, GET one's ASHES HAULED, LONG HAUL, OVER THE LONG HAUL

◁**haul ass**▷ *v phr* **1** (also **haul a**) To leave; depart; BUG OUT, CLEAR OUT, DRAG ASS : *If you're smart you'll haul ass out of here before you get in big trouble/ Time to haul a, man! (WWI Navy)* **2** To act quickly, esp in response to a command : *being ready to haul ass when the ball was hit* **3** To drive or travel very fast : *They were really hauling ass when they hit that curve (1950s+ Hot rodders)*

haul someone **in** *v phr* To arrest someone; RUN someone IN : *The police decided to haul them all in (1940s+)*

haul it *v phr* To run away; flee; escape [1940s+ Black; fr *haul ass*]

haul off *v phr* To launch an attack, diatribe, etc : *The parson hauled off and told that bunch of jerks they were a bunch of jerks* [1870+; probably fr the action of drawing away to make more room for launching the fist, and *haul* suggests a nautical origin]

haul off on someone *v phr* To hit or beat someone; launch a blow at someone : *counting fifty before they hauled off on a Red (1930s+)*

haul (or **rake**) someone **over the coals** *v phr* **1** To rebuke someone harshly; castigate; chew out **2** To put someone through an ordeal [1719+; fr the old ordeal by fire]

hausfrau (HOUS frou) *n* A woman whose primary interests are keeping house, raising children, etc • Often used in mild contempt, and to suggest a lack of chic [1918+; fr German, "housewife"]

have *v* ◁1▷ To do the sex act with; possess sexually : *I had Mary Jane in her own bathtub ten times (1594+)* **2** To cheat; deceive; DIDDLE : *I'm afraid it's a scam, they have had us (1805+)* **3** To gain an advantage over : *I have you there, old man! (1596+) See* be HAD

have a bag (or **half a bag**) **on** *v phr* To be drunk : *He had half a bag on and looked it (1940s+)*

have a ball *v phr* To enjoy oneself particularly well and uninhibitedly : *After the dean left we had us a ball (1940s+)*

have a bellyful *v phr* To get more than one wants; be unpleasantly surfeited : *I've had a bellyful of your bitching (1886+)*

have a big head *v phr* **1** To think of oneself as superior **2** To have a hangover

have a big mouth *v phr* To be inclined to say embarrassingly too much, esp about others' personal affairs : *Marcel Proust sure had a big mouth/ When he heard that, my pal told me I had a big mouth* [1960s+; popularized by the comedian Jackie Gleason, who often said it of himself]

◁**have a bone on**▷ *v phr* To have an erect penis [1920s+; fr a hubristic anatomical misstatement]

have a bone to pick with someone *v phr* To have a matter to complain about or go into with someone (*1565+*)

◁**have a broom up** one's **ass**▷ *v phr* (Variations: **get** may replace **have**; **stick** may replace **broom**; **in** one's **tail** may replace **up** one's **ass**; **butt** may replace **ass**) To work diligently and eagerly; be an overachiever [1930s+; fr the willing or harried worker in a joke, whose hands are full, but who would sweep the floor if one placed a *broom* in the worker's nether cavity]

◁**have a bug (or hair) up** one's **ass (or up** one's **nose)**▷ *v phr* To be very irascible and touchy : *These people with little bugs up their ass, they come here to cause trouble/ Obviously the chief had a bug up his ass, and this was not the time to start an argument/ Cheatham had a hair up his ass, was the consensus/ He had some bug up his butt and insisted I come down last night* (*1940s+*)

have a bun in the oven *v phr* To be pregnant : *The outspoken Miss Bow, who had a bun in the oven, replied* (*1940s+*)

have a bun on *v phr* To be drunk (*1900+*)

have a can on *See* GET A CAN ON

◁**have a case of the dumb-ass**▷ *v phr* To do something stupid; err idiotically (*1970s+ Army*)

have a case on someone *v phr* To be infatuated with or in love [1852+; *case* was specialized to mean "a case of being in love" by the mid-19th century]

have a chip on one's **shoulder**▷ *v phr* To be very touchy and belligerent; be easily provoked (*1855+*)

have a clue *v phr* To know; be aware or apprised of • Often in the negative : *Do you have a clue about what's going on here? (WWII British armed forces) See* NOT HAVE A CLUE

have a cow *See* HAVE KITTENS

have (or take) a crack at something *v phr* (Variations: **go** or **rip** or **ripple** or **shot** or **whack** may replace **crack**) To make an attempt at something; have a try : *He said he wasn't sure he could, but he'd have a crack at it* (*1836+*)

have a crush on someone *v phr* To be infatuated or enchanted with someone, esp to be secretly in love with someone older and more worldly than oneself (*1913+*)

have a field day *v phr* To indulge oneself freely and successfully; have it entirely one's way; go all out : *When the news gets out, the press will have a field day/ I'm afraid the bunnies have*

had a field day with the hyacinths [1827+; fr mid-1700s field day, "a military review"]

have a finger in the pie *v phr* To participate in an intrusive way; meddle : *I'm afraid the Commissioner has a finger in this pie* (*1659+*)

have a free ride *See* GET A FREE RIDE

have a full (or much on one's**) plate** *v phr* To be very busy; be preoccupied and overburdened : *I know you have a full plate and can't give any one case the coverage it needs/ I have so much on my plate and so little time* (*1924+*)

have a go *v phr* To make an attempt; have a try; HAVE A CRACK AT something : *Thought I'd have another go at friend Gary* (*1835+*)

◁**have a hair on** one's **ass, not**▷ *See* NOT HAVE A HAIR ON one's ASS

have a hair up one's **ass** *See* HAVE A BUG UP one's ASS

◁**have a hard-on for** someone or something▷ *v phr* To have antipathy for; hate : *He knows I'm a federal cop, so he's got to figure I got a hard on for Panthers/ couple heavy-duty Cubans worked for the CIA when the CIA had a hard-on for Castro* (*1970s+*)

have a heart *interj* A pleading exclamation : *Have a heart, baby, I only did it once!* (*1916+*)

have a hole in one's **head (or wig)** *v phr* To be very stupid; be insane; HAVE ROCKS IN one's HEAD (*1940s+*)

have a leg up on someone or something *v phr* To have a good start on some project, process, in some competition, etc; be well on the way to a goal : *She just started, and they already have a leg up on it* (*1940s+*)

have a little on the side *See* GET A LITTLE ON THE SIDE

have all one's **buttons (or marbles)** *v phr* To be normal or mentally sound; be sane; be shrewd and aware • Most often in the negative : *When I'm sure I no longer have all my buttons I'll quit this line of work/ The old guy doesn't seem to have all his marbles, the way he mumbles to himself* [1860+; *buttons* probably refers to the neatness and completeness of a normal mind compared with the uncertainty and slovenliness of clothes lacking buttons] *See* LOSE one's MARBLES

have all one's **ducks in a row** *See* HAVE one's DUCKS IN A ROW

have all the moves *v phr* To be very skillful; be expert, esp and originally in a sport or game (*1970s+*)

have a load on *v phr* To be drunk; FEEL NO PAIN (*1598+*)

have a lock on something *v phr* To be assured of some result; be certain of success : *Catholics constantly yearn for moral conviction, and Mr Powell's got a lock on that* [1970s+; fr *lock*, "a wrestling hold"]

have a mind like a sieve *v phr* To be very forgetful (*1893+*)

have a monkey on one's **back** *v phr* To be addicted to narcotics [1930s+ Narcotics; perhaps related to the same phrase, meaning "to be angry," found by 1860]

have (or cop) an attitude (or a tude) *v phr* **1** To dislike and complain about one's plight; BITCH, KVETCH : *If you'd put up as many bonds for nothing as I have, you'd have a fucking attitude too/ "Go ahead, cop an attitude," she says and pulls away from him/ If you're going to cop a tude because I was a few minutes late, then I'll just go home* **2** To be arrogant or haughty (*1980s+ Black*)

have an (or the) edge on someone *v phr* To have an advantage; enjoy a superior or winning position : *The slim and handsome will always have the edge on the rest of us* (*1896+*)

have a (or one's) nerve *v phr* To be impudently aggressive : *You sure have your nerve, telling him off that way* (*1890+*)

Have a nice day *sentence* A saying said upon parting, often by someone who is not an acquaintance : *store employees trained to say "Have a nice day"*

have another think (or thing) coming *v phr* To be wary of a fixed opinion; be skeptical of one's certainty : *For lo! I have another think a-coming* (*1901+*)

have ants in one's **pants** *v phr* To be nervous or anxious; to be fidgety : *he has ants in his pants waiting for the audition See* ANTS OR ANTS IN ONE'S PANTS

have any, not *See* NOT HAVE ANY

have a party *v phr* To do the sex act; SCREW (*mid-1930s+*)

◁**have a pot (or without a pot) to piss in,** not▷ *See* NOT HAVE A POT TO PISS IN

have a prayer *v phr* To have a chance; be able • Very often used in the negative : *The Eagles don't have a prayer, and neither will Murray* (*1941+*)

have a problem with something *v phr* To find hard to accept; be unable to agree immediately : *I said we'll split it. You got a problem with that?* (*1970s+*)

have a red face *v phr* To be embarrassed; have a guilty and sheepish mien; HAVE EGG ON one's FACE : *The Chief had a red face when he was found in possession of stolen property* (*1937+*)

have a screw loose *v phr* To be crazy; be eccentric : *that his brains, in her opinion, were twisted, or that he had a screw loose/ Sometimes I think she must have a screw loose* (*1810+*)

have one's **ashes hauled** *See* GET one's ASHES HAULED

◁**have a shit fit**▷ *v phr* To become very upset or furious; SHIT A BRICK, shit green : *Some people are going to have a shit fit when they read it* (*1970s+*)

have a short fuse *v phr* To have a quick temper; be irascible; SHOOT FROM THE HIP (*1960s+*)

have a soft spot for *v phr* To regard favorably; like; enjoy; approve of (*1902+*)

◁**have** someone's **ass**▷ *v phr* To punish someone; retaliate severely : *If you utter one word, I'll have your ass* (*1940s+*)

have one's **ass handed to** one *v phr* To be decisively defeated : *If he runs again he'll have his ass handed to him* (*1990s+*)

have one's **ass (or tail) in a crack** *v phr* To be in a bad situation; be in trouble (*1980s+*)

◁**have** one's **ass in a sling**▷ *v phr* (Variations: **get** or **put** may replace **have**; the locution may be one's **ass is,** **was,** etc, **in a sling**) To be in serious trouble : *Allen has taken an introspective, but not innocent, bystander, and put his ass in a sling* [1930s+; the similar *have one's eye in a sling* is found by 1909]

have one's **ass to the wind** *v phr* To be vulnerable, as if naked : *They're telling Harold he's wearing a beautiful suit, and he's got his ass to the wind* (*1980s+*)

have a thing about *v phr* To be especially concerned with, in love, hate, or fascination; be strongly emotional about : *She really has a thing about pyramids* (*1936+*)

have a tiger by the tail *v phr* To be in a nasty situation, esp innocently or unexpectedly, that will get much worse before it gets better (*1972+*)

have oneself a time *v phr* To enjoy oneself hugely : *Everybody had himself a time* (*1882+*)

have a toehold *See* GET A TOEHOLD

have a turkey on one's **back** *v phr* To be drunk (*1980s+*)

◁**have (or get)** one's **banana peeled**▷ *v phr* To do the sex act; copulate (*1889+*)

have bats in one's **belfry** *v phr* To be crazy; be eccentric (*1901+*)

have brain one, not *See* NOT HAVE BRAIN ONE

◁**have brass (or cast-iron) balls**▷ *v phr* To have audacity; be foolhardy : *Which one of you worthless nits had the brass balls enough to cough when I was talking* (*1970s+*)

◁**have** someone **by the balls**▷ *v phr* To have someone in a very perilous and painful position; have a firm grip on someone; HAVE someone BY THE SHORT HAIRS : *I didn't want to do it, but they had me by the balls* (*1940s+*)

◁**have (or get)** someone **by the short hairs (or curlies or knickers)**▷ *v phr* To have someone in a painful and helpless situation;

have absolute control over; HAVE someone BY THE BALLS : *When life gets you by the short hairs, it doesn't let go/ Someone nasty and ruthless has him by the short hairs/ You're in no position to make deals. We got you by the curlies/ We've got him by the knickers and he's hurting* [1891+; fr the *short hairs* growing on the scrotum]

have someone or something **by the tail** *v phr* 1 HAVE someone BY THE BALLS (*1940s+*) 2 To have control of : *I know all young people are sure they can have it by the tail* (*1796+*)

have one's **card punched** *See* GET one's CARD PUNCHED

◁**have** one's **cherry**▷ *v phr* 1 To be a virgin (*1889+*) 2 To be unproved or untried in the sense indicated : *He's never been bankrupt; still got his cherry* (*1970s+*)

have something **cinched** *v phr* (Variations: **iced** or **knocked** or **made** or **taped** or **wired** may replace **cinched**) To be entirely sure of a favorable outcome; be sure of success, well-being, etc : *Then you see the helicopter and you know you've got it knocked/ A veteran bank shot artist who has the back boards at West 4th Street wired, does anything he pleases/ I thought I had it iced* [entry form 1900+, most others 1950s+; *have something cinched* is fr cowboy usage, referring to a tightly and securely *cinched* saddle; the variants *have something made, taped,* and *wired* fr poker terms, also fr cowboy use]

have one's **claws out** *v phr* To be intent on committing injury; be in a damaging or fighting mood : *Maggie Siggins certainly had her claws out when she wrote about Bill* (*1940s+*)

have (or **get**) **cold feet** *v phr* To be timorous or afraid; have second thoughts : *Ella was coming too, but she had cold feet* (*1893+*)

have someone **coming and going** *v phr* To have someone in an inescapable situation : *What could I do? They had me coming and going* (*1903+*)

have something **coming out of** one's **ears** *v phr* To have something in great abundance : *He's got talent coming out of his ears* (*1940s+*)

have dibs on *v phr* To have a claim or option on : *No, sorry. This guy has dibs on me* (*1930s+*)

◀**have** one's **dick in** one's **zipper**▶ *v phr* To be in a difficult and embarrassing plight : *And Buster's got his dick in his zipper now* (*1980s+*)

have something **down pat** (or **cold**) *v phr* To know something or be able to do something perfectly; be perfect master of something : *I had my story down pat, so I almost believed it myself* (*first form 1896+, second 1915+*)

have one's **druthers** *v phr* To have one's preference; have it one's way : *if George Bush*

had his druthers/ But personally, if I had my druthers, I would like nothing better than to run off to the country with some guy (*1895+*) *See* DRUTHERS

have (or **get**) one's **ducks in a row** *v phr* (Variations: **have** [or **get**] one's **ducks all in a row** or **have** [or **get**] **all** one's **ducks in a row**) To be fully prepared; to be organized; DO one's HOMEWORK : *You have five years to get all your ducks in a row/ Want to get all your ducks in a row? Get ChemPlus* [1970s+ Army; perhaps fr a mother duck's marshaling of her ducklings in a neat flotilla behind her; perhaps fr some game]

have one's **ears on** *v phr* To have one's receiver turned on (*1970s+ Citizens band*)

have egg on one's **face** *v phr* To be caught in an embarrassing or guilty plight; be rueful and embarrassed : *Steve Brill, the editor, should have egg on his face this week/ He left President Reagan with egg on his face* (*1950s+*)

have eyes for *v phr* To desire; wish for; have a lech for someone or something : *But the chick who has eyes for some cat would be uncool if she told him so directly/ Then suddenly she finds out he's got eyes for another woman* (*1810+*)

have (or **eat**) someone **for lunch** *v phr* To defeat and destroy someone; CLOBBER, eat someone's lunch : *Then Ronald Reagan had Walter Mondale for lunch* (*1980s+*)

have game *v phr* To have high skills; also, to bring spirit and heart into an activity : *his dunking showed he still has game*

have something **going** (or **working**) **for** someone or something *v phr* To enjoy a certain advantage; have particular assets : *You've got more going for you with NTS home training/ The best thing this mall has going for it is it's just a test* (*1960s+*)

have something **going with** someone *v phr* To be amorously tied to someone (*1970s+*)

have one's **hands full** *v phr* To be occupied up to one's limit, esp in an emergency : *When the water main burst, the utility workers had their hands full* (*1546+*)

have (or **need**) one's **head examined** *v phr* To be crazy or seriously consider that one is crazy : *you should have your head examined for making that decision* (*1949+*)

have one's **head handed to** one *v phr* To be severely punished : *The emir said nothing at all, and sped off to his palace. This is just the sort of thing that has gotten other rulers their heads handed to them* (*1980s+*)

have one's **head pulled** *v phr* (Variation: **out of** one's **ass** may be added) To be intelligent and sensible; be aware (*1970+ Army*)

have one's **head screwed on right** *v phr* To be sane and sensible : *No matter what he sounds* *like, he really has his head screwed on right* (1821+)

◁**have** one's **head up** one's **ass**▷ *v phr* To behave stupidly and blindly; be chronically wrong : *Why you gommy, stupid shit. Your head is up your ass/ He's one of the few bosses in this job who doesn't have his head up his ass* (1970s+)

have someone **in the palm of** one's **hand** *v phr* To have control of someone; have someone at one's command : *We had her in the palm of our hands* (1940s+)

have it *v phr* To be talented; be competent and effectual : *He tries hard, but he just doesn't have it* [1940s+; probably a shortening of *have it on the ball*] *See* LET someone HAVE IT

have it all *v phr* To enjoy everything life might offer : *These days women are telling her they can't have it all. You've spent so long getting where you are—how does a baby fit in?* (1970s+)

have it all hanging out *v phr* To be concealing nothing; be entirely candid and undefensive; LET IT ALL HANG OUT : *As the current saying goes, NCR has it all hanging out* (1960s+)

have it all over someone or something *v phr* To be superior; surpass or outstrip : *In advanced technology, the North has it all over the South* (1922+)

have (or get) it all together *v phr* To have one's life, feelings, energies, etc, satisfactorily arranged; be free of emotional and behavioral dysfunctions : *Dr Jung says we'll all be OK when we have it all together* (1960s+)

have it bad *v phr* To be very much in love; be powerfully infatuated : *They would say that mouse has got it for Joey but bad/ He warbled the old song, "I got it bad and that ain't good"* (1872+)

have it both ways *v phr* To hold or esp to profit from two contrary positions; WORK BOTH SIDES OF THE STREET • Usu in the negative : *Make up your mind which one you'll support, because you can't have it both ways* (1914+)

have it going on *v phr* To be attractive; be chic and up-to-date : *So you think you've got it going on, huh?* (1990s+)

have it good *v phr* To enjoy prosperity, health, regular meals, and pleasures, etc : *I had it real good up there, till they canned me/ We never had it so good!* (1940s+)

have it in for someone *v phr* To be angry with; feel vindictive toward; bear a grudge : *Hatfield had it in for McCoy* (1849+)

have it made *See* HAVE something CINCHED

◁**have it off**▷ *v phr* To do the sex act; copulate • Still chiefly British : *who has had it off with both of them* [1930s+ British; fr earlier use, "to achieve a crime or shady transaction,"

pull something off," probably transferred to sexual activity on analogy with *cheating* and *hanky panky*, and by psychological suggestions related to *pull off* and *come off*]

have kittens or **cast a kitten** *v phr* (Variations: **a cat** or **a cow** or **pups** may replace **kittens**) To manifest strong and sudden feeling; have a fit of laughter, fear, anger, etc : *He got so mad I thought he was going to have kittens/ In addition to shy clients and those who don't want their parents to have a cow* (1900+)

have lead in one's **pants** (or ◁**in** one's **ass**▷) *v phr* To be very sluggish and lazy; move or work slowly; be unresponsive : *Frank's got lead in his ass, go jazz him up* (1950s+)

◁**have lead in** one's **pencil**▷ *v phr* **1** To be sexually potent; have an erect penis **2** To be keenly needful of sexual gratification (1916+)

have lockjaw *v phr* To be silent or reticent : *PUSH is not an organization that has lockjaw when it comes to issues* (1980+)

have loose lips *v phr* To be unable to keep a secret or keep quiet (1940s+)

have something made *See* HAVE something CINCHED

have one's mind in the gutter *v phr* To be preoccupied with or devoted to crudeness and smut (1940s+)

have one's moments *v phr* To have intermittent success : *she has her moments singing in the shower* (1925+)

have money to burn *v phr* To be wealthy; have more money than one needs : *Last year he was a bum, but he hit the lottery and has money to burn* (1896+)

have no bones about *See* MAKE NO BONES ABOUT

have-not *modifier* : *the have-not nations of the Third World* *n* A poor person, region, etc (1919+)

have nothing on *v phr* To be surpassed by : *I have nothing on her in the experience department* (1906+)

have someone's **number** *v phr* To know the exact truth about someone, though it be disguised; know someone completely : *She knew what I meant, and she knew I had her number/ They'd all had Dixon's number for years* (1853+)

have one foot in the grave *v phr* To be nearly dead; be doomed (1621+)

have one in the hopper *v phr* To be pregnant; have a pregnant wife : *I've only been married a short time, but we've got one in the hopper* (1970s+)

have something on the ball *v phr* To be talented; HAVE IT [1912+; fr the skill of a baseball pitcher, who puts speed, motion, etc *on the ball*]

have something **on the brain** *v phr* To be obsessed with : *She's got folk-dancing on the brain* (1862+)

have someone **over a barrel** *v phr* To have someone at a disadvantage or in an awkward position [1938+; apparently in allusion to the state of someone placed over a barrel to clear the lungs of water after being rescued from drowning]

have one's **plate full** *See* HAVE one's HANDS FULL

have pups *See* HAVE KITTENS

have rocks in one's **(or the) head** *v phr* To be wrong, stupid, crazy, etc : *Kid, you got rocks in your head* (1940s+) *See* ROCKS IN one's HEAD

haves, the *n* The people who have money, wealth, etc : *the haves just keep on getting more*

◁**have shit for brains**▷ *v phr* To be very stupid (1940s+)

have something on someone *v phr* To know incriminating information about someone : *now I have something on her* (1919+)

have the drop on *v phr* To get an advantage over someone; put someone in a disadvantageous situation [1867+; fr an earlier more specific sense, beat someone to the draw with one's firearm]

have the edge on someone *See* HAVE AN EDGE ON someone

have the foggiest notion or **idea,** not *See* NOT HAVE THE FOGGIEST NOTION

have the goods *v phr* To be talented; be effective; HAVE IT, HAVE WHAT IT TAKES : *She had the goods to hold on to a tried and true audience* (1980+)

have the goods on someone *v phr* To have incriminating evidence : *They can't convict him because they don't have the goods on him* (1913+)

◁**have the hots for** someone▷ *v phr* To desire someone sexually : *The stocky instructress was glaring at them. "Think she's got the hots for you"/ I know Grodin has the hots for you* (1940s+)

have the inside track *v phr* To have a strong advantage, esp one based on some fortuitous circumstance : *All the candidates look OK, but Hester has the inside track because she's single* [1857+; fr the advantage that a racer has by being nearest the *inside* of the *track* and having therefore the shortest distance to run]

have the jump (or jump on) *v phr* To enjoy a lead or advantage; be ahead of : *Who has the jump in this election?* (1912+)

have them in the aisles *See* LAY THEM IN THE AISLES

have (or get) the munchies *v phr* To be hungry, esp for sweets and starches after using marijuana : *I just smoked the smoke and got the munchies and I got real fat* (1960s+ Narcotics & counterculture)

◁**have the rag on**▷ *v phr* To menstruate; fall off the roof (1940s+)

◁**have the world by the balls**▷ *v phr* (Variations: **by the tail** or **on a string** may replace **by the balls**) To be in a very profitable and dominant situation; HAVE something CINCHED, shit in high cotton : *Dunning had the world by the balls/ With a good agent, you've got the world by the balls* (1970s+)

have one's **ticket punched** *v phr* To be a legitimate member of something; be fully warranted in experience, qualification, etc; PAY one's DUES : *These women have had their "tickets punched" in the corporate world* (1970s+)

◀**have** one's **tits in a wringer**▶ *v phr* To be in trouble; be distressed : *Even as she watched her tits being pulled into the wringer* [1940s+; referring to the old-fashioned *wringer* for wet laundry]

have something to burn *v phr* To have something in great abundance; HAVE something COMING OUT OF one's EARS : *This guy has chutzpah to burn* (1896+)

have two left feet *v phr* Be clumsy : *you've got two left feet* (1915+)

have what it takes *v phr* To have the right abilities, personality, etc, for success : *Do you have what it takes? Let me enhance your gifts!* (1934+)

have one's **work cut out** *v phr* To have something difficult to do : *telling him the news, she has her work cut out for her* (1862+)

hawk[1] *v* To clear one's throat; cough up and spit : *let out of their cells to wash, hawk, stretch* (1583+)

hawk[2] *n* **1** A person who advocates a strong and bellicose policy or action : *Some were doves on Vietnam and hawks on Iran* (1960s+) **2** A person who attracts and procures young men and boys for homosexuals, esp older men : *The police believe he was acting the role of a "hawk," finding "chickens" (young boys) for older men* (1970s+ Homosexuals)

hawk[3] *n* A imitation Indian haircut affected by punk rockers; MOHAWK : *egg or soap it into the hawk* (1980s+)

hawking *n* To drive slowly and watchfully in the streets, walk about vigilantly in bars and parties, etc, looking for a sex partner; CRUISE : *If you're out searching for a date, you're "cruising," "hawking," or "macking"* [1990s+ Teenagers; perhaps related to *hawk*[2], "a pimp for homosexuals"]

hawkish *adj* Having the attitude of one who advocates strong action on national policy : *These people are as hawkish as Lyndon Johnson* (1965+)

hawkishness *n* The quality of being an advocate of a bellicose policy; belligerence : *A few of the Republicans objected to Nixon's hawkishness* (*1967+*)

hay *n* Marijuana; HERB [Narcotics;1940s+] *See* HIT THE HAY, THAT AIN'T HAY

hay, the *n* Bed : *He is in his hotel room in the hay* (*1912+*) *See* HIT THE HAY

haybag *n* A woman (*1851+*)

haymaker *n* **1** A very strong blow with the fist : *smashes the kid with a wild haymaker* **2** Any powerful stroke or felling blow : *Having her arrested would be a haymaker to your father* **3** Any supreme or definitive effort, performance, etc; WINNER : *Her blues number was a haymaker* [*1912+*; probably fr the wide swinging stroke of a scythe in cutting hay]

hayseed *adj* Rural; provincial : *The bad actors perform worse plays in hayseed theaters* *n* (also **hayseeder**) A farmer; country person : *There's still a lot of hayseed in Senator Chance* (*1888+*)

haywire *adj* **1** Functioning erratically; out of order; ON THE BLINK : *This meter's haywire* **2** Makeshift; precariously operative : *What sort of haywire gadget are you using for a pump?* **3** Crazy; confused; COCKEYED : *He never looked inside an almanac, and was sure that anyone who did was haywire* (*1905+ Loggers*) *See* GO HAYWIRE

haze *See* IN A FOG

HAZMAT *n* Hazardous material : *The ambulance crew checked the site for hazmats* (*1990s+*)

head *n* **1** A headache, esp as a component of a hangover; a BIG HEAD : *You won't believe the head I had next morning* (*1893+*) **2** The foam on a glass of beer (*1893+*) **3** A person : *at twenty-five cents a head, no reserved seats/ One head that used to claim to sell stockings called* (*1551+*) ◄**4**► Fellatio or cunnilingus; BLOW JOB, HAIR PIE : *Some quiff is going to give you head* **5** A narcotics user, esp an addict : *My trip is to reach as many heads in this country as I can, and turn them around* (*1911+ Narcotics*) **6** The feeling of euphoria produced by a narcotic; HIGH, RUSH : *I take two Tuinals and get a nice head/ much of the head, or psychic lift, that users experience* (*1960s+ Narcotics*) **7** A toilet or restroom : *in the head, back in a sec* *See* ACID FREAK, AIRHEAD, BANANAHEAD, BEANHEAD, BIGHEAD, a BIG HEAD, BITE someone's HEAD OFF, BLOCKHEAD, BONEHEAD, BUBBLEHEAD, CHEESEHEAD, CHICKENHEAD, CHOWDERHEAD, CLUNKHEAD, COKEHEAD, DEADHEAD, DOO-DOO HEAD, DUMBHEAD, FATHEAD, GET one's HEAD OUT OF one's ASS, GIVE HEAD, GO SOAK YOURSELF, HARDHEAD, HASH HEAD, HAVE A HOLE IN one's HEAD, HAVE one's HEAD PULLED, HAVE ROCKS IN one's HEAD, one's HEAD IS UP one's ASS, HEAD SHOP,

HEAD-SHRINKER, HIT THE NAIL ON THE HEAD, HOTHEAD, IN OVER one's HEAD, JARHEAD, KNUCKLEHEAD, LUNKHEAD, MEATHEAD, METAL HEAD, METH HEAD, MUSCLEHEAD, MUTTON-HEAD, NEED someone or something LIKE A HOLE IN THE HEAD, OFF one's NUT, OFF THE TOP OF one's HEAD, OUT OF one's HEAD, OVER one's HEAD, PIGHEAD, PILLHEAD, PINHEAD, POINTHEAD, POINTY-HEAD, POTATO-HEAD, POTHEAD, PUDDINGHEAD, PUMPKINHEAD, ROCKS IN one's HEAD, SAPHEAD, SHITHEAD, SOFT IN THE HEAD, STAND ON one's HEAD, TALKING HEAD, USE one's HEAD, WEEDHEAD, WHERE someone's HEAD IS AT, WOODENHEAD, WOODHEAD, YELL one's HEAD OFF

-head *combining word* Addicted to or using the narcotic specified : *acidhead/ pothead* (*1911+ Narcotics*)

head, the *n phr* The toilet; CAN [*1748+* Nautical; fr the location of the crew's toilet in the bow or *head* of a ship]

headache *n* Any trouble, annoyance, vexation, etc : *another headache for pro coaches* (*1934+*)

headbanger *n* A devotee of heavy metal rock music, a style dating from the mid-1960s : *Hip headbangers, it seems, want nothing more than to see Bon Jovi fall off the face of the earth/ The show's naked emotionality feels as false and forced as an arena full of headbangers holding their lighters aloft during a power ballad* [*1970s+*; fr the frenetic reactions of such persons to the music, including actual banging of the head]

headcase *n* An insane or very eccentric person; NUT : *dedication to a cause that marked them as fanatics of a sort, the wealthy headcases, and professional haters* (*1970s+*)

head cook and bottle washer *See* CHIEF COOK AND BOTTLE WASHER

-headed *combining word* Having a head, esp a mind, of the specified defective sort (*1386+*) *See* AIRHEADED, BIGHEADED, BONEHEADED, BULLHEADED, FATHEADED, MEATHEADED, PIGHEADED, WOOLLY-HEADED

header *n* **1** A head-first dive, fall, or plunge (*1849+*) **2** A pass, shot at the goal, etc, made by batting the ball with one's head (*1906+ Soccer*) *See* DOUBLEHEADER

head for *v phr* To start out for or toward; HIT FOR : *I headed for the door/ He's headed for a disappointment* [*1835+*; fr the pointing of a ship's bow or *head* toward a destination]

head game *n phr* A process of manipulation, something like brainwashing; MIND-FUCK : *I was playing head games/ Coach Riley is a headgamer who uses players as pieces in a board game* (*1990s+*)

headhunt *v* To act as a headhunter

headhunter *n* A person or agency that seeks out and recruits employees, esp business executives and highly paid professionals, as candidates for usu high-paying or prestigious jobs : *Headhunters head for Washington as a capital place to find executives (mid-1960s+)*

◁**head is up** one's ass▷ *sentence* One is behaving stupidly and blindly : *were even saying that, skill-wise, the FBI's head was up its ass (1970s+)*

◁**head job**▷ *n phr* Fellatio or cunnilingus; oral sex : *receiving a listless headjob from an aging black prostitute (1960s+)*

head kit *n phr* The set of implements used for taking narcotics; drug apparatus; works : *Head kits are constantly being found (1960s+ Narcotics)*

headless chicken *n* A panic-stricken person who is behaving illogically : *running around like a headless chicken at holiday time* [1993+; alluding to a chicken's behavior after its head is cut off]

headlights *n* 1 The eyes *(1920s+ Prizefight)* ◁2▷ A woman's breasts *(1940s+)*

headliner *n* The main or chief performer; main attraction : *She was the headliner last week at the Seven Seas (1896+ Show business)*

head off, one's *adv phr* To one's utmost; extremely much; spectacularly; one's ASS OFF, one's BRAINS OUT : *one time when Joey was vomiting his head off (1920+)*

head someone or something off at the pass *v phr* To forestall or prevent by anticipation : *A single mother has to establish control fast, before the coercive cycle builds. You have to head it off at the pass* [1930s+; fr the stock situation in western movies, where typically the leader of a force pursuing thieves or rustlers through rough ground declares, "We'll head them off at the pass"]

head of steam *n phr* Full speed and impetus : *Stephanopoulos acknowledges a steady series of peaks and valleys: "You get up a head of steam and then—oops! What's coming around the corner?"* [1835+; the date refers to the actual boiler pressure of a machine]

headrush *n* The feeling of euphoria produced by a narcotic; HEAD, RUSH : *There are so many people packed into one place it almost gives you a headrush (1960s+ Narcotics)*

head shop *n phr* A shop selling various accessories of the drug culture and hippie culture, such as water pipes, holders for marijuana cigarettes, psychedelic posters, incense, etc *(1960s+ Counterculture)*

headshrinker or **headpeeper** *n* Any psychotherapist, psychiatrist, psychoanalyst, etc; SHRINK : *with a good deal more understanding than any clergyman or headshrinker/ You lousy smug headpeeper (1950+ Medical)*

head south *See* GO SOUTH

heads-up *adj* Clever; alert; shrewd : *They're playing real heads-up football (1940s+)* **modifier** : *Daschle was on Mitchell's heads-up list for good reason* *n* A warning; a meeting where warning is given : *blamed Young for not giving regents a "heads up" about the controversy/ Altman called a brief heads-up designed to tell the White House what procedures the RFC would follow (1990s+)*

heads up *interj* A warning of some impending danger or need to be alert : *Heads up, for heaven's sake (1940s+)*

heads will roll *sentence* People will be dismissed, punished, ruined, etc : *If eventually the authorities catch up with you, no heads will roll/ I promise you: if this package is not delivered on time, heads will roll* [1930+; the source is a quotation from Adolf Hitler]

head trip *modifier* : *The Head-Trip Dodge, verbalizing without involvement, the educated filibuster* *n phr* 1 A mental exploration; an adventure of thought, esp of a new sort; a delectable fantasy : *Private head trips seemed to be adjuncts or companions of social movements* 2 HEAD GAME, MIND-FUCK : *Considering the estrangements and head trips your family has put you through, it's a wonder you can still smile* *v phr* : *Man seeks companion for head-tripping, studying together, Scrabble, etc*

head up *v phr* 1 To be the chief of; supervise; direct : *Stan Baker will head up our new Verbal Economy Division (1930s+)* 2 To confront or attack someone : *Fudgie wouldn't want to head up with him/ You niggers burn those ribs, I'm a head you up (1990s+ Black)*

heap *n* 1 A car, esp an old ramshackle one; JALOPY : *I keep hoping somebody will steal this heap* 2 Any old vehicle [1924+; a motorcyclists' shortening of *scrap heap*] *See* JUNK HEAP

heap, a *adj phr* Very much : *Thanks a heap, old buddy (1930+)*

heaps *adv* Very much : *She loved him heaps, but kept mum* *n* Very many; a flock, OODLES : *I've got heaps of scratch (1547+)*

heart *n* A tablet of an amphetamine, esp Dexedrine® *(1960s+ Narcotics) See* BLEEDING HEART, CROSS MY HEART, HAVE A HEART, PURPLE HEART

hearted *See* CHICKENHEARTED

hear the birdies sing *v phr* To be knocked unconscious; be unconscious *(1940s+)*

hear the wheels going around *v phr* To be aware of another's thought process; notice cerebration : *Kennedy could hear the wheels going around (1970s+)*

hear things *v phr* To have delusions of hearing; hear voices : *she's hearing things again* [1991, but certainly must be earlier]

hearts and flowers *n phr* **1** Sentimentality; maudlin appeals, etc : *I believed all the hearts and flowers you gave me about being in love with your husband (1920s+)* **2** A knockout *(1940s+ Prizefight)* [fr the name of a mournful and sentimental song of about 1908]

heartthrob *n* One's deeply beloved : *Who's your heart-throb this week? (1920s+)*

heat *n* **1** Pursuit, prosecution, and other sorts of involvement with the law : *types of cash mark which do not involve federal heat (1928+ Underworld)* **2** (also **heater**) A good fastball *(1980s+ Baseball)* **3** Any sort of trouble, pressure, or recrimination, esp the angry complaining of irritated persons; FLAK, STATIC : *We better expect heat when this report gets out (late 1920s+)* **4** (also **heater**) A firearm, usu a pistol : *I was packing about as much heat as you find in an icicle without a gun (late 1920s+)* **5** A round in boxing, inning in baseball, etc • *Heat*, "a horse race," is found by 1663 *(1940s+ Sports) See* BITCH IN HEAT, DEAD HEAT, GIVE someone HEAT, PACK HEAT

heat, the *n phr* The police; a police officer : *Try operating an American city without the heat, the fuzz, the man/ until the heat pulls up in one of those super paddy wagons (1937+) See* IF YOU CAN'T STAND THE HEAT STAY OUT OF THE KITCHEN, PUT THE HEAT ON someone, TAKE HEAT, TAKE THE HEAT OFF

heat is on, the *sentence* Extreme pressure and pursuit are afoot, esp by the police against criminals : *The heat is on dope. That's a big bust if they get hold of you (1934+)*

heave *n* A shelter : *Heave. Any shelter used by a policeman to avoid the elements (1950s+ Police)* *v* To vomit; BARF *(1868+)*

heave-ho, the, or the old *n phr* Forcible ejection; summary and emphatic dismissal; the BOUNCE : *If you make any noise, you get the heave-ho/ And he gave me the old heave-ho* [*heave and ho*, the sailors' cry when hauling, is attested from the 1500s] *See* GET THE AIR, GIVE someone THE AIR

heaven *See* HOG HEAVEN, STINK TO HIGH HEAVEN, TO HELL

heavy *adj* **1** Serious; intense • The ancient sense was revived during the 1920s : *heavy petting/ heavy correcting (1971+)* **2** Excellent; wonderful; COOL : *These guys were not simply cool. They were heavy, totally hip, and totally trustworthy (1960s+ Counterculture)* **3** Important; consequential; prominent : *The heaviest art form on the planet is certainly films/ You said we were meeting this heavy actress/ He must have been blowing some heavy politics (1842+) n* **1** A thug; hoodlum; GOON *(1920s+)* **2** The villain in a play, movie, situation, action, etc; BADDIE, dirty heavy : *It*

mattered not at all that his employers were the heavies of the piece (1880+ Theater) **3** An important person; BIG SHOT, HEAVYWEIGHT : *will continue to stitch up the local heavies (1940s+)* **4** A big wave : *good set of heavies (1970s+ Surfers)*

heavy artillery or **big guns** *n phr* The most impressive and persuasive arguments, evidence, persons, etc, available : *The Republicans are rolling out their heaviest artillery for this debate/ Against these big critics' big guns I offered the author some shelter (first form 1809+)*

heavy breather *n phr* BODICE-RIPPER *(1970s+)*

heavy breathing *n phr* Pompous opinionating; punditry : *Give us the tabloids, and even transcripts in the serious newspapers, but spare us the prime-time writhing and op-ed heavy breathing (1990s+) See* HARD BREATHING

heavy click time *n phr* The moment when television viewers most likely change the channel : *They ponder "pod positioning" and "heavy click time" (the moments when most viewers reach for their remote controls) (1990s+ Television)*

heavy date *n phr* **1** A very important rendezvous, esp with someone of the other sex for sex : *A heavy date with a light lady* **2** One's partner on a heavy date **3** Any important, urgent engagement : *a heavy poker date for this afternoon (1923+)*

heavy-duty *adj* Very active; highly productive : *The sting identified 46 "heavy-duty taggers"* [1940s+; fr the term for a particularly strong and durable machine, found by 1914]

heavy-foot *n* A habitually fast driver; speeder *(1940s+ Police)*

heavy (or long-ball) hitter *n phr* A person of achievement; an expert; MAJOR LEAGUER : *There was no one-upmanship dealing with a heavy hitter like Cifelli/ Hitler was a heavy-hitter if there ever was one/ I knew immediately that Annette Bening was a long-ball hitter, emotionally, intellectually and artistically* [1980s+; fr a baseball term, "player who hits the ball hard," found by 1883; *long-ball* variant found in baseball by 1950s]

heavy (or heavily) into *adj phr* Much engaged in; prominent in : *his family very heavy into potato chips/ Us niggers be very heavy into stockings over our faces doing houses and Seven Elevens (1970s+)*

heavy lifter *n phr* The one who does the heavy lifting : *The NRA is the heavy lifter (1990s+)*

heavy lifting *n phr* The hardest work : *Baker reckons that he has done most of the heavy lifting, whereas it is his friend who got first prize/ It's going to be some really heavy lifting (1990s+)*

heavy metal *modifier* : As the prototypical *heavy metal band, Led Zeppelin has created its fair share* **n** *phr* A style of simple music characterized by extreme loudness, distortion, and pounding drums and played through great banks of amplifiers and speakers : *With all the sudden interest in heavy metal, Deep Purple has decided to give it a go once again/ a degree of internal intricacy that belies popular conceptions of heavy metal (1960s+ Rock and roll)*

heavy money *n phr* (Variations: **big** or **important** or **real** may replace **heavy**; **dough** or **jack** or **sugar** may replace **money**) A large amount of money; impressive sums; MEGA-BUCKS : *Why did she walk out on a movie career which was paying her heavy money?/ I've been busy cleaning up some heavy dough/ So nobody's about to pay big money for the site fee of a Tyson versus Ribalta (1924+)*

heavy petting (**or necking**) *n phr* Very passionate kissing, fondling, etc, stopping short of the sex act proper *(1940s+)*

heavy scene *n* A serious or difficult state of affairs, often emotional : *heavy scene after the funeral*

heavyweight *n* An important person; BIGGIE : *He's some sort of heavyweight in the rag trade (1890+)*

heck *interj* HELL *(1887+)*

heck, the *See* the HELL

hedge *n* Something that offsets expected losses : *People were buying gold as a hedge against inflation* **v** (also **hedge off**) To transfer part of one's bets to another bookmaker as a means of reducing possible losses if too many of one's clients were to win : *Big banks use derivatives to hedge their bets on which way the markets are going (1672+)*

H-E-double toothpicks *n phr* HELL : *I caught H-E-double toothpicks for saying I liked the perfume-scented inserts in magazines (1940s+)*

heebie-jeebies, the (Variations: **the heebies** or **the jeebies** or **the leaping heebies**) *n phr* **1** A very uneasy and jumpy feeling; nagging frets; the WILLIES : *Mr Perot worked off his heebie-jeebies by trashing Mr Bush's chance for re-election/ His several disquisitions on the jeebies/ I always get the heebies there* **2** Delirium tremens [1923+; said to have been coined by a cartoonist named Billy De Beck]

heel *n* **1** A sneak thief; petty criminal; PUNK *(1914+ Underworld)* **2** A petty hawker; SHILL *(1930+ Carnival)* **3** A contemptible man; blackguard; BASTARD, PRICK, SHITHEEL : *His friend turned out to be a heel, and ran off with his wife and money (1925+)* **4** : *They made a clean heel from Leavenworth* **v 1** To escape from prison *(1950s+ Underworld)* **2** To get a gun for oneself or another person *(1873+)*

[last sense fr *heel*, "arm a fighting cock with a gaff or spur," found by 1755] *See* COOL one's HEELS, SHITHEEL

hefty *adj* **1** : *a hefty matron over at the corner table* **2** Large; considerable : *not only romance, but a hefty dose of fantasy these days* **n** A stout or obese person : *While other hefties count their calories, he counts the dollars (1871+)*

heh *interj* A half laugh offered as a nonnegative response or to express surprise : *He said he'd call, heh*

◁**heifer**▷ *n* A young woman, esp an attractive one; FILLY *(1853+)*

heimish *See* HAIMISH

heinie *n* The buttocks; ASS, BUTT, KEISTER : *I think it was her heinie. That high, insolent ass* [1930s+; probably fr *hind end*]

heinous *adj* Bad; CRAPPY, GROSS, LAME *(1980s+ Students)*

Heinz 57 variety *n phr* **1** A mutt; a dog of no discernible lineage; a mongrel : *Chloe's her dog,"a Heinz 57 variety," says Ivey (1896+)* **2** Any mixture of variable or undetermined parts : *a Heinz 57 buffet See* FIFTY-SEVEN VARIETIES

heist *n* A robbery or holdup : *Led Zeppelin was the victim of the heist (1930+ Underworld)* **v 1** To steal; stick up; rob *(1931+ Underworld)* **2** To highjack *(1920+ Underworld)* [fr an early and dialectal pronunciation of *hoist*; in an 1883 source *hoist* is defined as "to rob houses by climbing in a window," because one thief climbs or hoists himself up over another] *See* SHORT HEIST

heister *n* A shoplifter or robber *(1927+)*

hell *interj* **1** An exclamation of disgust, regret, emphasis, etc : *Oh hell, they're back/ Hell, darling, I didn't mean it (1678+)* **2** An exclamation of strong denial, disbelief, defiance, etc; IN A PIG'S ASS, MY EYE : *"Retreat hell!" said the general (1893+) n* **1** Strong rebuke or punishment; MERRY HELL : *Your old man'll give you hell/ I caught hell from the tax people (1851+)* **2** A bad experience : *Dinner with my in-laws is usually pure hell (1374+)* **v 1** hell around *(1897+)* **2** To speed; BARREL : *An ambulance, helling out the state road (1929+) See* ALL HELL BROKE LOOSE, BLAZES, BLUE HELL, CATCH HELL, COME HELL OR HIGH WATER, EASY AS PIE, EXCUSE ME ALL TO HELL, FOR THE HELL OF IT, FROM HELL TO BREAKFAST, GIVE someone HELL, GO TO HELL IN A HANDBASKET, HOT AS HELL, LIKE A BAT OUT OF HELL, LIKE HELL, PLAY HELL WITH something, RAISE HELL, a SNOWBALL'S CHANCE IN HELL, TAKE OFF LIKE A BIGASS BIRD, TO HELL

hell, the *adv phr* **1** (also ◀the fuck▶) Completely and immediately • A hostile intensifier : *The hell're we doing sitting here?/ Anybody who hasn't learned this yet had better grow the fuck up/ Kid, shut the fuck up* **2**

(Variations: **deuce** or **devil** or **◀fuck▶** or **heck** may replace **hell**; in **God's name** or in **hell** may replace **the hell**) In fact; really ● Mainly used for rhythmic fullness in a hostile question : *What the hell do you mean by that?/ What the deuce are you about, you blackguard?/ Tell me what the devil you have in mind/ How the fuck would he meet the taxes and pay so many salaries?* [1911+; probably derived from expressions of incredulity like "in the world," which altered to "in hell"]

hellacious *adj* Excellent; wonderful; GREAT : *It was a hellacious picnic (1930s+ College students)*

hell-bent *adj* Strongly determined; recklessly eager : *They are hell-bent to cut taxes again before election (1835+)*

hellcat *n* A volatile and dangerous woman *(1605+)*

heller *n* An energetic and aggressive person, esp one who is mischievous and menacing : *He was quite a heller when young (1895+ Students)*

hell-for-leather or **hell-bent-for-leather** *adv* Rapidly and energetically; ALL-OUT, FLAT OUT : *Frank and Pat had gone hell-for-leather over this territory* [1889+; origin unknown; perhaps related to British dialect phrases *go hell for ladder, hell falladerly, hell faleero,* and remaining mysterious even if so, although the *leather* would then be a very probable case of folk etymology with a vague sense of the *leather* involved in riding tack]

hellhole *n* Any unpleasant or morally degenerate place; DUMP : *I was so glad to get out of this hellhole/ Emerson is a hellhole (1866+)*

hellish *adj* 1 Very; extremely : *hellish expensive* 2 Unpleasant; deplorable : *hellish noise coming from the vacuum*

hell of a, a or **helluva** or **one hell of a** *adj phr* Very remarkable, awful, admirable, distressing, etc; a BITCH OF A, SOME KIND OF : *They could have done a helluva lot better than cold cereal (first form 1776+)*

hell of a note, a *n phr* Something amazing, disgusting, surprising, etc : *She drank it, ain't that a hell of a note?/ What a hell of a note this is, a lousy flat tire (1940s+)*

hell of a (or **no**) **way to run a railroad,** a *n phr* An incompetent, overcomplex, or disastrous way of doing something; a flawed and botched methodology : *When she saw how our department was organized she told us it was a hell of a way to run a railroad, and she suggested some improvements (1940s+)*

hell of it, the *n phr* The worst part of something; what makes something very nasty : *The hell of it is that I tried all week to renew my license before they caught me (1940s+)* See FOR THE HELL OF IT

hell on wheels *n phr* A very impressive, nasty, violent, etc, event, person, etc : *This house is going to be hell on wheels in six months/ And considering what hell on wheels she'd been during our divorce* [1843+; origin uncertain; said to be fr mid-1800s characterization of the gambling places and houses of prostitution loaded on flatcars for railroad workers in the West, but the first instances predate this; perhaps fr earlier *on wheels,* "smooth, rapid, impressive"]

hell or high water See COME HELL OR HIGH WATER

hell-raiser *n* 1 A person likely to cause trouble and disturbance, esp by an active and defiant spirit : *This town needs a few hell-raisers to liven it up* 2 A person who leads a life of low pleasures; profligate; libertine; HELLER : *He was barred from the Muskie train after lending his press pass to a drunken hell-raiser (1914+)*

hell's bells *interj* An exclamation of impatience, anger, emphasis, etc : *Hell's bells, Maude, I did that two whole years ago (1912+)*

hell to pay *n phr* A very large fuss with dangerous implications; violent repercussions : *Hell to pay, in other words, for anyone who was unyielding (1901+)*

helmet *n* The foreskin of the penis or the end of the penis (glans penis) ● Fr its shape : *clipped helmet*

he-man *modifier* : *a regular he-man cop n* A very masculine man; HUNK, MACHO *(1859+)*

hem and haw *v phr* To hesitate; tergiversate; temporize : *Stop hemming and hawing and do something (1580+)*

hemp *n* Marijuana; Indian hemp *(1940s+ Narcotics)*

hen *modifier* By, of, and for women : *hen party/ hen talk n* 1 A woman, esp a fussy or gossipy woman ● This and other senses regarded as offensive by some women : *That old hen made him sick* 2 A young woman; chick *(1626+)*

hen party *n phr* A party for women only : *Men have stag parties; girls have hen parties (1887+)*

henpecked *adj* Dominated by women, esp by one's wife; PUSSY-WHIPPED *(1690+)*

hen tracks *n phr* (Variations: **chicken** may replace **hen; scratches** or **scratchings** may replace **tracks**) Illegible handwriting; scrawl *(1907+)*

hep *adj* Aware; up-to-date; HIP, WITH IT ● Taken up by jazz musicians to the extent of being identified with them : *By running with the older boys I soon began to get hep/ But I'm hep, man; for example, I had my vasectomy already* [1908+ Underworld; origin unknown; a 1914 source says it is based on the name of "a fabulous detective who operated in Cincinnati"]

hepcat *n* A man who appreciates the right sort of music, leads a life of fashionable pleasure, etc; cat, DUDE : *a big-timer, a young sport, a hep cat, in other words, a man-about-town* [1920s+ Jive talk; fr *hep cat*; a possible supplementary origin fr Wolof *hipicat*, "man who is aware," has been suggested]

hepster *n* A hep person; HEPCAT *(1930s+ Jive talk)*

hep to *adj phr* Aware of; cognizant of : *How little we've been personally hep to what's actually going on (1908+ Underworld) See* HEP

hep to the jive *adj* Aware; informed; initiated; WITH IT : *I commenced getting hep to the jive (1915+ Jazz musicians)*

herb[1] *n* A tedious, contemptible person; DORK, GEEK, NERD : *think you're a couple of reality-impaired herbs (1990s+ Students)*

herb[2] or **herbs** *n* Marijuana; POT : *So you get fines to pay and you've lost your herbs (1960s+ Narcotics)*

herd *See* RIDE HERD ON someone

here *See* UP TO HERE

here goes *interj* Let's begin : *Ready to jump. Here goes (1829+)*

here's mud in your eye *See* MUD IN YOUR EYE

Here's the deal *interj* Here is the plan or the way it is : *You want in? Here's the deal*

Herkimer Jerkimer *n phr* Any rustic, fool, or eccentric [1940s+; based on a *jerk from Herkimer*, that is, from a distant provincial place]

herky-jerky *adj* Jerky; spasmodic; not smooth : *bellow and quiver with those herky-jerky spasms/ herky-jerky instability of Shepard's plays/ producing a herky-jerky style of governing* (mid-1950s+)

hero sandwich or **hero** or **Hero** *n phr* or *n* A sandwich made with a loaf of bread cut lengthwise and filled with a variety of cheeses, sausages, vegetables, etc; GRINDER, HOAGIE, POOR BOY, SUBMARINE, TORPEDO (1955+)

◁**herring choker**▷ *n* 1 A Scandinavian (1940s+) 2 A New Brunswick native or ship (1899+) *n phr* 3 A Nova Scotian person or ship; bluenose : *No price for lobster, cause of the Herring-Chokers (1899+)*

hess *See* MELL OF A HESS

hetero *adj* Heterosexual (1933+)

hex *n* A jinx or curse; the indian sign, whammy : *I lose every time, must be a hex on me* [1909+; ultimately fr German *Hexe*, "witch"]

hey *interj* An exclamation used to underscore mildly what is said : *Pennzoil has been arguing that, hey, they are reasonable people/ I tried explaining that, hey, basically a goose is just a big duck/ Hey, I'm only human* [1980s+; the use is attenuated from the ancient call for attention found by 1225]

hey Rube *n phr* The traditional warning and rallying cry of circus and carnival people, used esp when they are attacked by righteously indignant citizens [1935+ Carnival; fr *hay-rube*, "hayseed, rube, rustic," found by 1908]

hi or **hiya** *interj* A salutation upon meeting : *The staccato cry of "Hi!," which we judged to be the almost universal greeting* [first form 1862+, second 1940+; probably based on *hi*, "hey," exclamation used to call attention, found by 1475]

hiccup *n* A brief interruption; spasmodic stoppage : *The violence in Moscow is another hiccup in Russia's drive for democracy (1980s+)*

hick *modifier* : *wasn't bad looking in a hick way/ that hick chief of police* **n** A rural person; a simple, countrified man or woman; apple-knocker, RUBE : *The automobile largely nullified the outward distinctions between hick and city slicker* [1565+; fr a nickname of Richard, thought of as a country name, as Reuben is the base of "rube"]

hickey or **hickie** *n* 1 Any unspecified or unspecifiable object; something one does not know the name of or does not wish to name; DOODAD, DOOHICKEY, GADGET : *We have little hickeys beside our seats (1909+)* 2 A blackhead, pimple, or other minor skin lesion; ZIT (1915+) 3 A mark on the skin made by biting or sucking during a sex act : *line of hickeys, or love bites/ Violet came home from the mall with a leather bustier and a hickey (1956+)*

hick town *n phr* A small or rural town : *any hick town in Kansas (1920+)*

hickville or **hicksville** *adj* 1 DULLSVILLE 2 CORNY (1940s+)

hideaway *n* 1 A private retreat; personal refuge; HIDEOUT (1930+) 2 A small, remote place, esp a small nightclub, restaurant, etc : *The vaudeville performer on the two-a-day has played to punks in the hideaways (1929+)*

hide or hair *n phr* (also **hide nor hair**) No sign or part of the person mentioned : *No one has seen hide or hair of him since (1830+)*

hideout *n* 1 An inmate who hides with the intention of escaping at night (1915+ Prison) 2 A place of relative obscurity and safety; HIDEAWAY : *The gang had a hideout in a ruined warehouse near Hoboken (1885+)*

hide out *v phr* To hide, esp from the police or other pursuers (1884+)

hide the weenie *See* PLAY HIDE THE WEENIE

hidey hole *modifier* : *conceal themselves in one of the hidey hole apartments of their proliferating step-parents* **n phr** A place to hide; HIDEAWAY (1817+)

higgledy-piggledy *adj* Confused; chaotic; messy : *I was walking in dark corridors that* *were all higgledy-piggledy* [1598+; origin uncertain; perhaps fr the disorderly herding configuration of *pigs*]

high *adj* **1** Drunk, esp slightly so : *high, slightly alcoholic, above the earth* (1627+) **2** Intoxicated by narcotics, esp in an easy and lighthearted condition induced by drugs; GEEZED : *An actor has less license to get high during working hours than does a musician/ the smoker uses them in big puffs getting high* (1932+ Narcotics) **3** : *The congregation was all high on gospel enthusiasm* (1960s+) *n* **1** : *He took a few tokes and got a pretty good high* (1960s+ Narcotics) **2** A nonintoxicated feeling of exhilaration or euphoria; LIFT : *Weddings are a high* (1960s+) *See* MILE-HIGH CLUB

high and dry *modifier* Abandoned; being in a helpless condition : *thought he was helping out, but left me high and dry* [as a beached vessel]

high as a kite *adj phr* Intoxicated or exhilarated to an important degree (1939+)

highball *n* **1** A signal denoting a clear track or clearance to start or accelerate (1897+ Railroad) **2** A train running on schedule, or an express train (Railroad) **3** An iced, mixed alcoholic drink taken in a high glass : *He quaffed a couple of rye highballs and left* (1898+) **4** A military salute (WWI Army) *v* To speed; rush : *A train was thirty yards away, highballing down the track/ One New York distributor highballed 30 trucks through the Holland Tunnel* (1925+ Railroad) [fr the former use of a railroad trackside signal using a two-foot globe, raised or lowered, to instruct the engineer; the military sense fr the use of a railroad conductor's raised hand or fist as a signal to the engineer to start, the term transferred from the mechanical signal; the drinking sense is probably fr a *ball*, "drink of whiskey" in a *high* glass]

highbrow *adj* **1** (also **highbrowed**) Idealistic; snobbish : *all them high-brow sermons* (1891+) **2** Impractical; unrealistic : *another silly highbrow scheme n* An intellectual; person of notable education and culture; DOUBLE DOME, EGGHEAD : *One does not need to be a "highbrow" to read this book* (1902+) [said to have been coined by the humorist Will Irwin as a back formation fr *high-browed*]

high camp *n phr* Artwork, theater performance, items of decoration, etc, that are so outrageously old-fashioned, so blatantly injurious to good contemporary taste, as to assume a sort of special value by their very egregiousness : *His way of lisping Shirley Temple lyrics is high camp* (1954+) *See* CAMP

higher-up *n* One of the persons in charge; a member of the upper echelon; BIG SHOT • Most often in the plural : *A conference with the*

Higher-ups and Tammany Hall/ She always fought with the movie higher-ups (1916+)

highfalutin or **highfalutin'** or **hifalutin** *adj* Overblown and pretentious; bombastic; stilted : *take one with ideas less "highfalutin'"/ stilted, overstrained, and as the Americans would say, hifalutin* [1848+; origin unknown; originally a gerund, seemingly based on a verb *high falute*, suggesting a humorous alteration of *flute*; perhaps fr a blend of *highflown* with some other element; perhaps fr Dutch *verlooten*, "stilted"]

high five *n phr* A way of greeting or congratulating by slapping raised palms together • Chiefly used by and adopted from athletes, who themselves adopted the style from black colleagues : *handshaking, even a few high-fives from the younger alums v phr* GIVE someone FIVE : *Roberts is not the kind to engage in trash-talking or high-fiving*

high flyer *n phr* A very adventuresome and impressive person (1690+)

high gear *See* IN HIGH GEAR, SHIFT INTO HIGH GEAR

high-hat *adj* (also **high-hatty**) : *his high-hat posturings/ high-hatty pretentions* (1925+) *n* **1** (also **high-hatter**) A person who behaves arrogantly and snobbishly; a putatively important person : *a lot of lowbrows pretending to be intellectual high-hats* (1925+) **2** A set of two cymbals, the upper of which is crashed on the lower by operating a foot pedal; SOCK (1932+ Jazz musicians) *v* : *How come you're high-hatting me, old buddy?* (1925+)

high heaven *See* STINK TO HIGH HEAVEN, TO HELL

high horse *See* GET OFF one's HIGH HORSE, GET ON one's HIGH HORSE

highjack *See* HIJACK

high-jinks *See* HI-JINKS

high-maintenance *adj* Requiring much care and effort to maintain : *high-maintenance hair/ high-maintenance girlfriend*

high muckety-muck *n phr* (Variations: **muck-a-muck** or **mucky-muck** may replace **muckety-muck**) A very important person, esp a pompous one; BIG SHOT, HIGHER-UP : *I'm gonna meet a couple of the high muckety-mucks at the university tomorrow* [1856+ Western; fr Chinook jargon *hiu muck-amuck*, "plenty to eat," transferred to the important individual who has plenty to eat]

high-octane *adj* Forceful; energetic; HIGH-POWERED, PUNCHY : *A pompous classical overture gives way to a jittery, high-octane beat and frayed guitar riffs* [1980s+; fr the *octane* rating of motor fuels, from about 1930]

high old time, a *n phr* A very pleasant occasion; a BALL : *They had them a high old time on that trip* (1834+)

high on someone or something *adj phr* **1** Very favorable toward; enthusiastic about :

I'm not as high on Wallace Stevens as I once was (1942+) **2** Intoxicated by; exhilarated with : *He says he's high on Jesus/ She gets high on wine and pot (1932+)*

high on the hog *See* EAT HIGH ON THE HOG

high-powered *adj* Forceful; energetic; HIGH-OCTANE, PUNCHY : *George is a real high-powered salesman* [1930s+; used of cars by 1903]

high puller *n phr* Frequent and inveterate players at slot machines : *the "high pullers" at the dollar machines* [1980s+ Gambling; modeled on *high roller*]

high-rent *adj phr* Chic and expensive; classy. high-class : *with some kind of high-rent bitch from a women's magazine (1970s+)*

high-res or **hi-res** *adj* High-resolution; of satisfyingly high quality : *a high-res monitor*

high rider *n phr* A car or truck that has been fitted with very large tires : *A high rider is a normal sized car, camper, or pickup that is mounted on oversized, "monster" tires (1980s+)*

high roller *n phr* **1** A person who gambles for high stakes : *for the high rollers in the mysterious world of wheat and corn futures (1902+ Gambling)* **2** BIG-TIME SPENDER *(1881+)* [gambling sense probably influenced by the idea of *rolling* the dice in craps]

high sign, the *n phr* A signal to an associate, esp one given inconspicuously by gesture : *waiting by prearrangement in the dark blue Lincoln Town Car, and George gave him the high sign (1903+)*

hightail or **hightail it** *v* or *v phr* **1** To leave quickly; LIGHT OUT : *She took one look and hightailed for home* **2** To speed; rush; HIGHBALL : *We better hightail it if we want to make the first show (1925+ Cowboys)*

high ticket *See* BIG TICKET

high-up *n* An important person; BIG SHOT. HIGHER-UP • Most often plural : *Rico got in touch with some of the high-ups (1868+)*

high water *See* COME HELL OR HIGH WATER

high waters *n phr* (also **high water pants** or **high waders** or **flood pants**) Trousers that are shorter than current fashion dictates, esp that end above the ankles : *Look at his high waters!* [fr the notion that the trousers have been chosen or rolled up for walking through *high water*]

highway robbery *n phr* An unconscionable price asked by a merchant : *Highway robbery is no name for it/ 100 bucks? That's highway robbery! (1886+)*

high, wide, and handsome *adj phr* : *a high-wide-and-handsome win adv phr* Easily, triumphally, and masterfully; WITH FLYING COLORS *(1907+)*

high-wire act *n phr* A perilous policy, procedure, etc : *Nixon remained skeptical of Kis-*

singer's high-wire act in Vietnam [1970s+; fr *high wire,* an 1880s term for the funambulist's high tightrope]

hijack or **highjack** *v* **1** To rob, esp to rob a vehicle of its load : *Hijack the truck (1923+)* **2** To commandeer a public vehicle, esp an airliner, for some extortionary or political purpose : *Two more planes were hijacked to Cuba last week (1960s+)* **3** To appropriate unjustifiably; annex; steal : *The 40th anniversary of D-day was hijacked by Reagan's PR men/ When Petersen, the director, is stuck, he just hijacks an idea or two from Hitchcock to get him to the next point in the picture/ How was the Bharatiya Janata Party able to hijack Hinduism? (1980s+)* [origin uncertain; said to be fr the command *High, Jack,* telling a robbery victim to raise his hands; an early 1900s hobo sense, "traveling hold-up man," is attested, which suggests that the source may be railroad and hobo slang; said to have originated in the California wheat fields and among the Wobblies; the name of the 1875 skit *High Jack the Heeler* is interesting but probably coincidental] *See* BALL THE JACK

hi-jinks or **high-jinks** *n* Boisterous fun; uninhibited jollification; pranks and capers : *the dashing hi-jinks of the Katzenjammer Kids/ The out-of-towner cuts the hi-jinks here* [1861+; fr the name of a dice game played for drinks, found from 1690]

hike *n* : *The government got a big tax hike v* **1** To raise; increase; boost : *They won't hike our wages this year (1867+)* **2** hike a check [fr mid-1800s term *hike up,* "go or raise up," related to *hoick* of the same meaning, both probably fr the basic dialectal sense "go, go about"] *See* TAKE A HIKE

hill *n* The pitcher's mound *(1908+ Baseball) See* GO OVER THE HILL, OVER THE HILL

Hill *See* SAM HILL

Hill, the *n phr* **1** Capitol Hill in Washington, DC : *They're all over the Hill, and can frighten members* **2** The US Congress : *Republicans or Democrats on the Hill (1970s+)*

hillbilly *adj* **1** : *hillbilly music/ hillbilly crafts* **2** Countrified; unsophisticated; HICK : *This ain't no hillbilly joint. We got some class here n* **1** A southern Appalachian hill dweller • Regarded as offensive by some *(1900+)* **2** A country bumpkin

hill of beans, a *See* NOT GIVE A DAMN

himbo *n* A male bimbo; a male who uses his good lucks but is superficial and unintelligent [1988+; a blend of *him* and *bimbo*]

hincty (Variations: **hinkty** or **hinktyass** or **hankty**) *adj* **1** Snobbish; aloof; STUCK-UP : *hinkty motherfucker/ like you do a hankty heifer in the bed and make her like it* **2** Pom-

pous; overbearing **3** HINKY ◀*n*▶ A white
person; OFAY [1924+ Black; origin unknown]
hind end *n phr* The buttocks; ASS, HEINIE
(1915+)
hinders or **hind legs** *n* or *n phr* The legs • Often
in phrases connoting resistance or defiance :
*He stood up on his short little hinders and got
himself a lawyer/ The Packer defense rose on its
hind legs again* (1940s+)
hindsight *See* TWENTY-TWENTY HINDSIGHT
◁**hind tit**▷ *See* SUCK HIND TIT
hinge *n* A look or glance; GANDER (1930s+)
hinky *adj* Suspicious; curious : *Something hinky
is going down/ driver of the pimpmobile looks
hinky* [1970s+; origin unknown] *See* DOO-
DAD
hip *adj* **1** HEP (1904+ Black) **2** Being and/or
emulating a hipster, hippy, beatnik, etc;
COOL, FAR OUT : *"I'm hip"means Cool/ to be hip
is to be "disaffiliated"* (1951+) *v* To make
aware; inform : *educating the masses of
America, hipping black people to the need to
work together* (1932+) [fr hep] *See* SHOOT
FROM THE HIP
hip cat or **hipcat** *n phr* or *n* **1** HEPCAT **2** HIPSTER
(1944+ Beat & cool talk)
hip chick *n phr* An alert and up-to-date young
woman, esp in matters of popular culture,
music, etc; flychick (1944+ Beat & cool talk)
hip-hop or **Hip Hop** *adj* or *adj phr* Of or pertaining to contemporary black urban youth
culture *n* or *n phr* **1** rap song **2** BREAK
DANCING **3** The activities that are emblematic
of contemporary black urban youth culture :
*What is "hip-hop"? That phrase includes such
activities as break dancing, rap music, and
graffiti art/ Most of them are young Hispanics,
more connected to Hip Hop than High culture*
[1980s+; echoic, said to have originated
with a New York disc jockey called Holly-
wood]
hip-huggers *n* Pants having a low waistline,
usu below the navel (mid-1960s+)
hipped on *adj phr* Enthusiastic about; obsessed
with : *I ain't hipped on her, sort of hypnotized
by her, anymore/ I'm hipped on Freud and
all that* [1920+; ultimately fr hip or the hip,
"hypochondria," hence obsession]
hipper-dipper *adj* Excellent; superb; SUPER-
DUPER : *a hipper-dipper display n* A prizefight
where the result is prearranged; tank fight :
*the last fight being a "hipper-dipper" (Prize-
fighting)* [1930s+; the boxing sense perhaps
related to *dipper*, "small swimming pool," in
which one goes up to the hips; modeled on
take a dive and *tank*]
hippie or **hippy** *modifier* : *Saigon has acquired
an elaborate hippie culture n* One of a group of
usu young persons who reject the values of
conventional society and withdraw into

drifting, communes, etc, espouse peace and
universal love, typically wear long hair and
beards, and use marijuana or psychedelic
drugs; BEAT, BEATNIK [1960s+ Counterculture; fr *hip*]
hippie-dippy *adj* Hippie; of the 1960s hippie
culture : *None of that hippie-dippy, war-
protesting, free-loving, drug-chugging stuff for
him* [fr HIPPIE + *dippy*, "weird, crazy"]
hippiedom or **hipdom** *n* **1** Hippies collectively
2 The hippie movement, world, culture, etc
(1960s+ Counterculture)
hippity-clippity *adj* Rapidly; at once : *I ran
hippity-clippity down the siding* (1980s+)
hip-pocket bookie *n phr* A betting agent who
has only a few large bettors as clients
(1960s+ Gambling)
hippy *adj* Having wide and prominent hips
(1919+) *See* HIPPIE
hipster *n* **1** HEPCAT, HEPSTER, HIP CAT **2** BEATNIK,
HIPPIE (1941+)
hip to *adj phr* Aware of; knowledgeable and
informed of : *Why don't you get hip to yourself?/ They were hip to me too and just waiting
for the right moment* (1920s+)
hired gun *modifier* : *elaborated on his "hired
gun" reference in an interview n phr* **1** A
professional killer; HIT MAN (1958+) **2** An
employee or agent, esp in some aggressive
capacity : *We're not just "hired guns" out to
raise a few bucks for the place/ Keith is not
going anywhere as a hired gun for one year*
(1970s+)
hissing match *n phr* A disagreeable confrontation; spat : *refused to get into a hissing match
with former union director Marvin Miller*
[1990s+; probably a euphemism for *pissing
contest*]
hissy fit *n phr* A noisy fit of anger; catfit, CON-
NIPTION FIT, DUCKFIT : *the vile, know-nothing
hissy fit loose in our land/ and write that memo
before the boss has a hissy fit that registers on
the Richter scale* [1990s+; *hissy* in the same
sense is found by the 1940s as a South-
western usage]
history *adj* Finished; done with; hist : *It's been
history, I'd say, four months* (1980s+ Students)
hit *modifier* : *a hit musical/ a hit song n* **1**
Anything very successful and popular, esp a
show, book, etc : *He wrote two Broadway hits*
(1815+) **2** A stroke of good fortune at
gambling, on the stock market, etc; LUCKY
BREAK : *a big hit on the commodities exchange*
(1666+) **3** A premeditated murder or organized-crime execution, esp one contracted
for with a professional killer : *"He can order a
hit," a police officer says/ There is no set price
for a hit* (1970+ Underworld) **4** A stroke of
severe criticism; attack; assault : *the club*

hired the firm to counter the hits it was taking
in the media/ Zavala took a double hit because
her husband also refused to cross the picket line
(1668+) **5** A dose, inhalation, etc, of narcotics; FIX • Hit the pipe, "smoke opium," is
found by 1886 : The current price of cocaine
was about $10 a "hit"/ He held a long hit in his
mouth, then expelled it slowly (1951+ Narcotics) **6** A drink; swallow; SNORT : a tall glass
of thick, slightly green fluid, and said, "Take a
big hit off this, Felix" (1950s+) **7** A pleasurable sensation; RUSH : People jockeyed for position around the foyer to get a little hit of
darshan (1960s+ Narcotics) **8** A cigarette
into which heroin has been introduced : GIs
sit smoking the mixed tobacco-and-heroin cigarettes called "hits" (1960s+ Narcotics) **9** A
dilution or "cutting" of a narcotic : You give
it a full hit, you already double your price
(1970s+ Narcotics) **10** Each separate occasion; each time; POP, SHOT : You should be on a
tour, where you can get 2,000 people a hit
(1980s+) **11** An unwanted, unwarranted,
hospital admission : The ambulance people
asked which hospital would take the hit
(1980s+ Medical) **12** A match between a
search item and an item in a database : That
year, Popcorn racked up 58 Nexis hits
(1990s+ Computer) **13** An interpretation;
idea; TAKE : My hit on this is he heard about
Brian (1990s+) **v 1** : I think this show will hit
2 : She hit real big at the track last week **3** RUB
OUT, WHACK : The mob figure got hit last night in
his car (1955+) **4** To reach; visit; attain : His
new book hit the best-seller list/ The market hit
a new high today (1888+) **5** To pass an examination, esp with a good grade; ACE : I
really hit the eco final (1950s+ Students) **6** To
cause a strong reaction; have a strong impact : The injection hit the heart like a runaway
locomotive (1891+) See BANJO HIT, MAKE A HIT,
PINCH HIT, SMASH

hit someone *v phr* **1** (also **hit someone up**) To
solicit money, a favor, etc : I'll hit Joe for ten
bucks/ She hit him up for a big raise (1882+) **2**
To have a strong impact on; distress; overwhelm : Kennedy's death hit me pretty hard
(1891+) **3** To present; reveal : I wanna hit
you with a very profitable idea (1960s+) **4**
To deal another card (1940s+ Cardplaying)
5 To serve another drink : He signaled
the bartender. "Hit us again" (1940s+) **6** To
administer a narcotic, esp by injection
(1940s+ Narcotics)

hit a brick wall *v phr* To encounter an insu-
perable obstacle : Negotiations seem to have
hit a brick wall this week [1960s+; brick wall
in this sense is found by 1886]

hit someone below the belt *v phr* To hurt
or exploit unfairly, esp with words : call-

ing her white trash was really hitting below the
belt

hit by a Mack truck *adj phr* Astonished;
stunned; bowled over : What's up? You look
like you been hit by a Mack truck [1940s+;
Mack is a trademark make of truck]

hitch *n* **1** A problem or difficulty; delaying defect; CATCH, GLITCH : Everything went off
without a hitch (1748+) **2** A period of enlistment : 42 percent have "reupped" for another hitch (1835+ Armed forces) **3** A ride,
esp one gotten by hitchhiking; LIFT (1923+)
v **1** HITCHHIKE (1940s+) **2** To marry; be
married (1844+)

hitch a ride (or **a lift**) *v phr* To get a free ride,
esp by hitchhiking (1940s+)

hitched *adj* Married (1857+)

hitchhike *v* To get free rides by standing beside
a road and signaling drivers; HITCH, THUMB
(1923+)

hitfest *n* A baseball game with many hits and
runs; SLUGFEST : pathetic parodies of the old
hitfests (1950s+)

hit for (or **out for**) *v phr* To start for or toward;
HEAD FOR : One time we hit for K C (1905+)

hit for the cycle *v phr* To hit personally a
single, a double, a triple, and a home run all
in one game (1960s+ Baseball)

hit it *v phr* To begin playing music; attack
(1930s+ Jazz musicians)

hit it a lick *v phr* To hit something very hard
(1940s+)

hit it big *v phr* To succeed splendidly : Pitchers
who hit it big as soon as they escaped from the
Trappers' pocket-sized park (1940s+)

hit it off *v phr* **1** To like one another : The pair
hit it off right from the start **2** To work well
together **3** To succeed with others : He hit it
off with the whole class (1780+)

hit someone like a ton of bricks *v phr* To have
a great sudden impact on, esp by surprise :
Then the answer hit me like a ton of bricks
[1920s+; based on the mid-1800s term fall
upon someone like a thousand bricks]

hit list *n phr* A putative or actual list of persons
who are to be removed from office, pun-
ished, murdered, etc : EPA officials maintained a "hit list" of employees (1976+)

hit man *n phr* An assassin, esp a professional
killer; HIRED GUN, MECHANIC : Like every professional hit man I've ever known, I've always
used a gun/ A State Police detective, posing as a
hired killer "flown in as a hit man" (1970+)

Hit me *interj* **1** Please deal me another card **2**
Please serve me another drink **3** Give me a
high five

hit on someone *v phr* **1** To ask for a favor;
solicit; pester; HIT someone : Everyone's been
hitting on her lately to help save something or
other (1970s+) **2** To make advances to;

PROPOSITION : *What if muscle-bound jocks hit on her all day long?/ I fired my last studio manager for hitting on one of the girls/ It's amazing that a man of my own age would be hitting on me (1980s+ Students)*

hit on all six (or **on six**) *v phr* To do very well; operate smoothly and effectively : *He's sure hittin' on all six* [1916+; fr the smooth operation of a *six-cylinder* engine]

hit pay dirt *v phr* To find what one is looking for or needs; garner profit; STRIKE OIL : *I didn't hit pay dirt until near the bottom of the second box (1850s+)*

hit (or **slap**) **skins** *v phr* To do the sex act; SCREW : *She'd be like, "Did you ever hit skins?" (1990s+ Black teenagers)*

hit squad *n phr* A group of assassins, severe critics, "hatchet men," etc : *André Breton commanded and organized literary hit squads, practicing intimidation in the name of Surrealist dogma (1976+)*

hitter *n* HIT MAN (1970+) *See* NO-HITTER, SWITCH-HITTER

hit the books *v phr* To study, esp in an intensive way (1920s+ Students)

hit the bottle (or **the booze** or **the sauce**) *v phr* To drink liquor, esp rapidly and to excess; BOOZE : *If he keeps hitting the bottle they'll have to dry him out (1889+)*

hit the bricks *v phr* **1** To go out and start walking on a street or sidewalk **2** To be released from prison : *He'll hit the bricks tomorrow, having been paroled (Prison)* **3** To go out on strike : *Teachers won't be as quick to hit the bricks* **4** To live in the streets because one is homeless *(Hoboes)* (1931+)

hit the bullseye *v phr* HIT THE NAIL ON THE HEAD (1940s+)

hit the ceiling (or **roof**) *v phr* To become violently angry; BLOW UP : *according to one source, hit the ceiling with rage (1914+)*

hit the deck *v phr* **1** To be knocked down (1940s+) **2** To get down on the ground quickly; duck down flat : *When I heard that airplane shoot, I hit the deck (1940s+)* **3** To get out of bed; rouse oneself *(WWI armed forces)*

hit the dirt (or **gravel**) *v phr* **1** To slide into a base *(Baseball)* **2** (also **hit the grit**) To jump off a train, esp a moving one *(Hoboes)* **3** To get down and take cover, esp from gunfire

hit the dope *v phr* To use narcotics [1920s+; *hit the pipe*, "smoke opium," is found by 1886]

hit the fan *v phr* To cause or experience extensive trouble and chaos : *A month later it all hit the fan/ Meanwhile the mailings had hit the fan See* THE SHIT HITS THE FAN

hit the ground running *v phr* To make a quick and eager start; not waste time : *Boot camp legislation hits the ground running/ The new*

Administration should hit the ground running (1950s+ Marine Corps)

hit the hay (or **the sack**) *v phr* To go to bed; CRASH, FLOP, SACK OUT *(first form 1912+, second 1943+)*

hit the jackpot *v phr* To win or succeed spectacularly; get the most available : *I hit the jackpot with this new job (1944+)*

hit the nail on the head *v phr* To be exactly right; say precisely the most accurate thing : *His few quiet remarks hit the nail on the head (1574+)*

hit (or **push**) **the panic button** *v phr* To give way to alarm and terror; declare a general emergency : *He hit the panic button when he saw the month's figures/ a move characterized by many as pushing the panic button (1950s+ Air Force)*

hit the road *interj* An irritated request that one leave : *Hit the road, Jack, and don't you come back no more v phr* To leave; get on one's way : *We better hit the road, it's a long way home (1873+)*

hit the roof *v phr* To become very angry : *hit the roof over finding beer in his car (1925+)*

hit the sauce *See* HIT THE BOTTLE

hit the sheets *v phr* **1** To go to bed : *After the long day, I watched TV and hit the sheets* **2** To have sexual relations with someone : *hit the sheets after the fraternity party*

hit the skids *v phr* **1** To fail; GO BELLY UP : *But if HBJ hit the skids, could the building ensure the integrity of retirees' pensions?* **2** To show a precipitous decline; fall disastrously : *Home sales are down and sales of large cars have hit the skids/ Eventually they had hit the skids* [1918+; *skids* are various planks or rollers used to move heavy objects]

hit the spot *v phr* To be very satisfying, esp to some appetitive need : *That cup of coffee really hit the spot (1940s+)*

hit the trail *v phr* To depart, leave : *hit the trail before it gets dark*

hit the wall *v phr* To come to one's limit of energy and capability, esp in a marathon or other arduous race : *I hit a wall of shock and pain/ Sampras Slams Into the Wall/ if he wears down and "hits the wall" as Avent did last season (mid-1980s+ Sports)*

hit up *v phr* To inject a narcotic; SHOOT UP [1940s+ Narcotics; an earlier related sense, "to drink to excess," found by 1900]

hit someone up *v phr* To request something, esp a loan; importune : *I'm sure your only salvation is to hit up your rents (1917+)*

hit upside one's **face** (or **head**) *See* GO UPSIDE one's FACE

hit someone where one **lives** or **hit** someone **where it hurts** *v phr* To deliver a very painful blow, insult, insinuation, etc; have a strong impact : *The Third Movement hits me right where I live (1860+)*

hit someone **with** something *v phr* To present an idea, plan, etc, esp with great enthusiasm and spontaneity : *I hit them with my idea to go to Camden*

hive *v* To understand *(1935+ West Point)*

hivey *adj* Sharp-witted; perceptive *(1935+ West Point)*

hiya *See* HI

hizzoner *n* The mayor : *Hizzoner, looking game but a tad uncertain*

◄**HMFIC**► (pronounced as separate letters) *n* Commanding officer; officer in charge : *HMFIC can be rendered politely as "head military person in charge"* [Persian Gulf War Army; fr *head motherfucker in charge*]

ho[1] or **hoe** *n* A prostitute or other disreputable woman : *like many of her sisters of the streets (she calls them "hos")/ The bar was a hangout for players and hos* [1960s+; fr Southern or black pronunciation of *whore*]

ho[2] *See* the HEAVE-HO, RIGHT-O

hoagie *n* HERO SANDWICH *(1967+)*

hobnob with someone *v phr* To be on friendly terms with someone [1866+; fr earlier *hob and nob*, "to drink familiarly together," suggesting two men calling each other by nicknames]

hock *n* The state of pawn : *I've got to get my typewriter out of hock v* To pawn : *I hocked my diamond ring (1878+)* [apparently fr Dutch *hok*, "prison"; the earliest US use was *in hock*, "in prison"; perhaps also fr the underworld phrase *in hock*, "caught," fr the notion that one is taken "by the heels," or *hocks*] *See* IN HOCK

hockable *adj* Pawnable : *The "ice" was always hockable (1878+)*

◄**hockey** or **hocky**► *n* **1** Feces; excrement; SHIT : *Great big blooping hunks of dog hockey/ But it's a lot of horse hockey, on both sides* **2** Empty and pretentious nonsense; BULLSHIT : *any of that hocky about being a white man* **3** Semen; CUM [1923+; origin unknown; perhaps fr a variant pronunciation of the *hokum, hokey, hocus-pocus* cluster, suggested by some spellings, and hence originally "falsehood, pretentious exaggeration, etc," whence "bullshit," whence "shit";]

hocktooey *interj* An imitation of hawking and spitting, taken as a sign of machismo : *masculine in a cigar-smoking, crotch-grabbing, hocktooey! way (1990s+)*

hocus *v* To falsify or misrepresent; also, to adulterate : *hocus the presentation/ hocus the punch*

hocus-pocus *n* Sleight-of-hand; trickery; MONKEY BUSINESS [1694+; originally a term for a juggler, and probably derived fr a juggler's

spoken formula imitating the Church Latin phrase *hoc est corpus*, "this is the body"]

◄**hod**► *n* A black passenger; scuttle [1920s+ Cabdrivers; probably because a *hod* is a container for coal]

ho-dad (also **hodad** or **ho dad** or **ho-daddy**) *n* **1** A person who claims knowledge and authority he or she does not possess; BLOWHARD, WISE GUY : *"ho-daddy" (intruding wise guy)* **2** A nonparticipant who seeks the company of athletes and performers; hanger-on : *The true surfer is scornful of the "ho-daddies"* **3** An obnoxious and contemptible person; JERK, PHONY, WIMP [1960s+ Surfers; origin unknown; perhaps fr a surfer's cry *Ho, dad!*]

hoe *See* a HARD ROW TO HOE

hoedown *n* **1** (also **hoe-dig**) A country square dance *(1807+)* **2** A lively and noisy argument *(1950s+)* **3** A riotous fight; brawl : *Mr Clinton has put more energy into such old-politics hoedowns (1950s+)* **4** A fight between gangs; RUMBLE : *Anything can start a hoedown (1950s+ Street gangs)*

hog *n* **1** A locomotive, originally a heavy freight engine *(1915+ Railroad & hoboes)* **2** hogger *(1915+ Railroad & hoboes)* **3** A Harley-Davidson® motorcycle : *Harley, perhaps best known for its big-engine "hogs"/ a hundred Hell's Angels on their Hogs (1960s+ Motorcyclists)* **4** A large car, esp a Cadillac® : *"I got a Hog, a Cadillac" (1950s+ Black)* **5** (also **the hog**) PCP or a similar addictive drug : *climbed on stage and threw thousands of caps of "the hog" into the crowd (1960s+ Narcotics)* **6** A sexually appealing male; adonis, HUNK *(1980s+ Students)* *v* To take or eat everything available for oneself; claim and seize all : *appeared simultaneously with ET and suffered as the little fungiform geek hogged the box office/ Mara had deliberately hogged the spotlight (1884+)* [railroad and hobo senses fr the fact that large locomotives consumed a great deal of coal] *See* EAT HIGH ON THE HOG, ON THE HOG, WHOLE HOG

hog (or **pig**) **heaven** (or **paradise**) *n phr* A place of total bliss, esp for the gluttonous; FAT CITY : *For the sports junkie, this is Mecca. For the gambler, it is hog heaven/ It doesn't put Wisconsin in pig heaven/ Jesse Helms must be in pig paradise (1940s+)*

hogs *n* Dollars, esp only a few dollars *(1940s+)*

◄**hog's-breath**► *n* A despicable person; disgusting wretch; CRUD, GEEK, SCUMSUCKER : *The unshaven hog's-breath of a transient thief stands out like a green-glowing extraterrestrial (1990s+)*

hogster *n* An owner, admirer, etc, of Harley-Davidson® motorcycles, which are called "hogs" : *The unlikely collection of hogsters arrived in Milwaukee last month* (1980s+)

hogwash or **hogslop** *n* Empty and pretentious talk; nonsense; BALONEY, BULLSHIT : *It's hogwash. There's no such thing/ Bradley is too soft, too fragile. Hogslop* [first form 1882+, second 1990s+; fr the house waste fed to hogs; the date of *hogslop* is probably earlier; *hogslosh* in the same sense is found by the 1940s]

hog-wild *See* GO HOG-WILD

ho-hum *adj* Unexciting; mediocre; dull : *hohum sex and the dregs of countless six-packs/ After a ho-hum second quarter, stocks have perked up* (1960s+) *interj* An expression of boredom (1924+) *n* Boring matter; dull tripe (1960s+) *v* To be bored with; be indifferent to : *On the other hand, we shouldn't ho-hum the situation* (1960s+)

hoist *n* : *Crooks speak of a job of hold-up as a "hoist"* *v* 1 To rob; steal; HEIST : *The stall distracts the sales force while the hoister hoists* (1708+ *Underworld*) 2 To drink some beer or liquor : *Let's stop at Harry's and hoist a few* (1940s+)

hoisted *adj* Stolen : *among the hoisted articles recently* (1708+ *Underworld*)

hoister *n* A shoplifter (1847+)

hoity-toity *adj* Snobbishly exclusive; haughty; uppish; SNOOTY : *in the hoity-toitiest of Fifth Avenue shops/ Will he go all hoity-toity on us?* (1668+) *interj* (also **highty-tighty**) : *Highty tighty! What a debil of a rage* (1695+) [fr earlier *highty-tighty*, "peremptory, quarrelsome," perhaps related to the notion of being *high* in the sense of "superior"]

hoke *n* HOKUM (1921+) *v* (also **hoke up**) To make fun of; treat insincerely; overplay : *But don't hoke it too hard, Beatrice/ It's all right to hoke the incident, but not the theme/ Halaby hoked up a special ceremony* (1935+)

hoked-up *adj* False; dishonestly confected; PHONY : *hoked-up or fictionalized biographies/ a zest for hoked-up violence* (1940s+)

hokey *adj* False and meretricious; very dubious; PHONY : *hokey confections that public taste ought to repudiate/ The radio is jammed with hokey copies of US and European rock and roll songs* (1927+)

hokey-dokey *See* OKEY-DOKE

hokey-pokey or **hoky-poky** *adj* : *It might sound weird or hokey pokey, but it works* **modifier** : *candy bars on the hokey-pokey counter* *n* 1 Cheap ice cream and sweets made primarily to attract children (1884+) 2 False and meretricious material; deception; HOKUM : *too much of "Hollywood hokey-pokey"* (1840s+) [fr an earlier sense of *hokey-pokey*, "cheat, swindle," ultimately fr *hocus-pocus*; the ice cream is said to have

been named in Italian, *O, che poco*, a child's cry at the paucity of the portion]

hokey-pokey, the *n phr* A simple, informal sort of circle dance : *People across the globe will join hands, form huge human circles. The hokey-pokey* (1960s+)

hokum *n* 1 Pretentious nonsense; inane trash; BUNK : *more hokum from the Department of State* 2 A trick, gag, routine, etc, sure to please a gullible public : *There is some hokum in "King Penguin" (Theater)* 3 HOKEY-POKEY [1917+; origin unknown; perhaps a blend of *hocus-pocus* and *bunkum*]

hold *v* 1 To have narcotics for sale 2 To have narcotics in one's possession (1930s+ *Narcotics*) *See* ON HOLD

◀**hold someone by the nuts**▶ *v phr* HAVE someone BY THE BALLS : *Would you rather have the cops holding you by the nuts?* (1940s+)

hold someone's coat *v phr* To stand back and let others fight : *A lot of people are willing to hold our coats and let those 200,000 soldiers in the Persian Gulf go to war* (1940s+)

holder *See* ROACH CLIP

hold everything *sentence* Stop what you are doing; let's stop right now : *Hold everything, here's new evidence!* (1924+)

hold someone's feet to the fire *v phr* To subject someone to strong and painful persuasion; use maximum pressure : *helping hold the President's feet to the fire* (1980s+)

hold one's horses *v phr* To be patient; stop importuning; HOLD one's WATER • Often an irritated command : *Wait a second, Bradley, hold your horses* (1844+)

holding *adj* 1 Wealthy : *Respect for people who are "holding"* (1940s+) 2 Possessing narcotics (1930s+ *Narcotics*)

holding pattern *See* IN A HOLDING PATTERN

hold one's liquor *v phr* To be able to drink a quantity of alcohol and have one's wits about them : *can hold her liquor at home, but not in public*

hold onto your hat *v phr* To get ready for trouble; take precautions; BUCKLE YOUR SEAT BELTS : *Hold onto your hats for the craziest ride through the truth that's ever been done on television* (1970s+) *See* HAT

holdout *n* 1 A person, esp a professional athlete, who refuses to sign a contract until the salary is raised (1911+) 2 A person who refuses to agree to something : *coerce reluctant hold-outs into "kicking in"* (1940s+) 3 A playing card sneakily kept from the deck by the dealer (1894+ *Gambling*)

hold out or **hold out on** *v phr* 1 To refuse to do something until one gets certain conditions; to refuse to give information : *The union held out for a 10 percent raise/ he's holding out on me about the girlfriend* (1907+) 2 To endure;

persist : *This tire won't hold out another mile* (*1593+*)

holds *See* NO HOLDS BARRED

hold the fort *v phr* To remain at a location and handle matters : *Can you hold the fort while I go downtown for a walk*

hold the phone *v phr* To wait a minute; delay; HOLD EVERYTHING ● Often a request for respite and thinking space : *body jerked back in a kind of W C Fields double take. "Hold the phone," I said* (*1930s+*)

holdup *modifier* : *the full-fledged hold-up business n* 1 A robbery, esp the armed robbery of a person, bank, store, etc; STICKUP : *Give us no nonsense. This is a holdup* (*1851+*) 2 The demanding of exorbitant prices, wages, etc : *That was no sale, it was a holdup* 3 A delay; stoppage; cause of delay : *a brief holdup in our magnificent progress/ What's the holdup?* (*1843+*)

hold up *v phr* 1 To rob, esp at gunpoint : *They were holding an old man up at the corner* (*1851+*) 2 To extort or demand higher prices, wages, etc : *That shop held me up!* 3 To delay; cause a delay or stoppage : *The strike held up our flight for six days* (*1843+*) 4 To point to; single out : *Is this the one you held up as such a great example?* (*1602+*)

hold one's water *v phr* To be patient; stop importuning; HOLD one's HORSES ● Often an irritated command : *I know that, fuckface. Just hold your water/ Hold your water, Mr McAllister!*

hole *n* 1 Any nasty or unpleasant place; DUMP, JOINT : *The restaurant turned out to be a loathsome little hole* (*1616+*) ◁2▷ The vulva or anus (*1340+*) *See* ACE IN THE HOLE, BROWN, BUNGHOLE, CORNHOLE, IN A HOLE, IN THE HOLE, the NINETEENTH HOLE, NOT KNOW one's ASS FROM one's ELBOW, RATHOLE

hole, the *n* 1 Solitary confinement or a cell used for it; BING : *I was slapped with the organizing label and put in the "hole"/ I was thrown in the hole for it* (*1535+ Prison*) 2 A subway (*1950s+ Underworld*) *See* ACE IN THE HOLE, IN THE HOLE

hole card *n phr* A card dealt face down in stud poker (*1908+ Poker*)

hole in the doughnut, the *n phr* What is lacking; an obstacle of omission : *The hole in the doughnut in helping the homeless is substance-abuse treatment* (*1990s+*)

hole in the ground *See* NOT KNOW one's ASS FROM one's ELBOW

hole in the (or one's) head, a *See* HAVE A HOLE IN one's HEAD, NEED someone or something LIKE A HOLE IN THE HEAD

hole in the wall *n phr* A small and usu unpretentious dwelling, shop, etc : *Nothing fancy, just a hole in the wall on Park Lane* (*1822+*)

hole out *v phr* To finish a hole by putting the ball in the cup (*1867+ Golf*)

hole up (or **in**) *v phr* 1 To hide; take refuge; HIDE OUT : *Long Island, where he might hole up for a day or two* 2 To stay for a time; lodge; CRASH : *thinking about holing up for the night* (*1875+*)

-holic *See* -AHOLIC

holiday *n* 1 A small area missed while painting 2 A forgotten or neglected task (*1935+ Navy*)

holier-than-thou *modifier* Condescending; thinking one is superior to others : *holier-than-thou attitude gains him no friends*

holler *n* (also **holler-song**) A Southern black folk song with spoken or shouted words, a precursor of the blues song : *You find hollers in many of Leadbelly's recordings and songs* (*1930s+*) *v* 1 To shout (*1699+*) 2 To inform; SING, SQUEAL : *You think he wouldn't holler if they turned the heat on him?* (*1940s+*) 3 To complain; BITCH : *What's he hollering about now?* (*1904+*)

hollow *See* BEAT ALL HOLLOW

holy cow *interj* (Variations: **cats** or **gee** or **mackerel** or **moley** or **Moses** or **schmuts shit** or **smoke** or **sox** may replace **cow**) An exclamation of surprise, wonder, dismay, admiration, etc; Wow! : *All he could manage to say upon seeing the nude blonde was "holy cow!"/ Holy shit, the police/ And I think holy shit, this could be a Hitler/ Holy schmuts, that would be the pride and glory* [entry form 1940s+, cats 1900+, gee 1895+, mackerel 1903+, Moses 1900+, schmutz 1990s+, shit 1940s+, smoke 1889+, sox 1909+; euphemisms for *holy Christ*; *moley* is from comic-book character Captain Marvel]

holy hell *n phr* Vehement rebuke; severe punishment; HELL, MERRY HELL : *I caught holy hell when the thing broke* (*1940s+*) *See* CATCH HELL, GIVE someone HELL

Holy Joe *modifier* : *these Holy Joe voices n phr* 1 A clergyman; chaplain : *needs twelve Holy Joes to get him past them Pearly Gates* (*1874+*) 2 A sanctimonious, pietistic person : *In the east they're all holy Joes and teach in Sunday schools* (*1889+*)

holy terror *n phr* A troublesome, energetic, and aggressive person : *He's a holy terror around the house* (*1887+*)

hombre (HAHM bray, AHM bray) *n* 1 A Hispanic person 2 A man; fellow; GUY : *a real cool hombre* [1846+; fr Spanish, "man"] *See* WISE GUY

home *See* BRING HOME THE BACON, HOME BOY, MONEY FROM HOME, NOBODY HOME, NOTHING TO WRITE HOME ABOUT

home boy or **homeboy** or **home girl** or **homegirl** *n phr* or *n* 1 A person from one's hometown *(1940s+ Black)* **2** A simpleton; naive bumpkin : *Youse just a home boy, Jelly. Don't try to follow me (1940s+ Black)* **3** (also **home**) A close friend, or someone accepted like a friend • Used also by Chicanos in Los Angeles, some of whom apparently dispute the black origin : *Home boy, them brothers is taking care of business!/ He stormed outside with two homeboys: one called "Gino," and Kevin Baca, 17, whom he'd met a month before (1970s+ Black)* **4** A black male; BRO, BLOOD, HOME SLICE : *black faces, fucking home boys with skin the color of bunker oil and the threat coming off them in waves (1980s+)* **5** An easygoing, unpretentious person *(1970s+ College students)*

homebuddy *n* HOME BOY : *Don't want what you can't have, or what your homebuddy has (1980s+ Black)*

home-court advantage *n phr* The psychological and other favorable elements that come from being in familiar surroundings, with a sympathetic audience, etc : *Yojimbo is less than sympathetic here (it's clear who has the home-court advantage) (1970s+ Sports)*

home free *adj phr* Successfully arrived or concluded; at or assured of one's goal; out of trouble : *I hear things been a little tight. Well, you home free now/ I think you're home free. If you'll forgive me for saying this*

home in on someone or something *v phr* To approach purposefully; go straight toward : *I saw these two guys homing in on her at the bar* [1950s+; fr the movement of an airplane, ship, missile, etc, that follows a radio beam or other signal to approach a destination or target; *home* is found by 1920; perhaps reinforced by the behavior of a *homing* pigeon]

home plate *n phr* The landing field, aircraft carrier, etc, where an aircraft is based [1950s+ Air Force; fr the baseball sense, regarded as a goal and safe haven] *See* GET TO FIRST BASE

homer *n* **1** A home run; CIRCUIT BLOW *(1891+ Baseball)* **2** An official who favors the home team : *A lot of refs get reputations as "homers", which means they give all the tough calls to the home team (1980s+ Sports)* *v* : *Kaline homered in the sixth*

homeskillet *n* A good friend; HOME BOY : *a "homeskillet," a good friend (1990s+ Students)*

homeslice or **home slice** *n* or *n phr* **1** A good friend; one's best friend; BUDDY, HOME BOY : *That's my homeslice out on the court (1980s+ Teenagers)* **2** A black person; BROTHER, BLOOD : *And "home slice" is a black person (1990s+ Black)*

homework *See* DO one's HOMEWORK

homie *modifier* : *and "homie love," the camaraderie among members of his gang* *n* **1** (also **homey**) A close friend or a fellow townsperson; BUDDY, HOME BOY : *is expecting more than her homies to support her/ Then get yourself a job, homie (1970s+ Black)* **2** A male homosexual; FAGGOT, QUEER *(1940s+)*

◁**homo**▷ *modifier* : *homo slang/ a homo bar* *n* A homosexual man or woman : *I knew nothing about "homos" at that time (1929+)*

hon (HUHN) *n* Sweetheart; honey • Used in direct address : *What's that, hon? (1906+)*

honcho (HAHN choh) *n* The person in charge; chief; BIG ENCHILADA, BOSS : *better known as the honcho of Scientific Anglers, Inc (1947+)* *v* : *honcho a staff* [fr Japanese *hancho,* "squad leader"; *han,* "small group," and *cho,* "leader"]

hondo *adj* Excellent; desirable; CHILL, COOL, way rad : *froody and hondo also get high marks at some schools/ If a guy is better than cool "he's really hondo"* [1980s+ Students; fr Spanish, "deep"]

honest-to-God *adj* Genuine; real; NO-SHIT : *What is certain is the damage of an honest-to-God fight to the finish involving the debt ceiling (1916+)*

honey *n* **1** One's sweetheart, beloved, spouse, etc *(1880+)* **2** Any pleasant, decent person; PUSSY-CAT, SWEETIE *(1880+)* **3** A person or thing that is remarkable, wonderful, superior, etc; DILLY, HUMDINGER : *Ain't this a honey of a show? (1888+)*

honeycakes *See* BABYCAKES

honeymoon or **honeymoon period** (or **stage**) *n* An early stage in a project or activity before there are problems and disagreements : *honeymoon is over when the new employee has his bearings*

◁**honeypot**▷ *n* The vulva or vagina *(1719+)*

honk *v* **1** To sound the horn of a car *(1895+)* **2** To make a sexual, esp a homosexual, advance by handling or pressing a man's genitals : *He's making a move to honk you, just grab his hand (1960s+)* **3** To vomit; BARF, HURL *(1990s+)*

honked or **honked off** *adj* Angry; PISSED OFF : *I'm going to have people really honked at me no matter what I do/ a honked-off Torcivia wrote to Wineke (1980s+) See* HONK OFF

honker *n* The nose; SCHNOZZ : *and she has a honker as big as yours (1940s+)*

honking *adj* Large; HUMONGOUS : *We have a honking textbook in my management class (1980s+ Students)*

honk off *v phr* To anger; PISS OFF : *He honked off some natives, who thought the Veep was being more than a tad condescending/ While that's honking off some bird lovers* [1980s+; origin unknown; perhaps fr the annoyance shown by *honking* the horn of a car]

◀**honky** or **honkie**▶ *modifier* : *No talkin' or we'll bust your honky heads* **n** A white person; gray, OFAY *(1967+ Black)* [fr *hunky*[1], as often normally pronounced in black English]

honky-tonk *modifier* **1** Gambling and drinking: *wisely emphasizes Brown's down-and-dirty honkytonkin' side* **2** Prostitution: *the honky-tonk district* **n 1** A cheap, usu disreputable saloon and gambling place; JOINT : *rode to my honky-tonk on a bus* **2** A cheap, small-town theater : *playin' the sticks, the honky-tonks* **3** A brothel **v** : *his honky-tonking ended, naturally, at Filly's, the urban cowboy saloon* [1894+; origin unknown]

hoo-boy *interj* An exclamation of surprise, consternation, amazement, etc : *Hoo-boy! The cheapest way to have your family tree traced* [1950+; perhaps a blend of *hoo ha* with *oh boy*; popularized by Walt Kelly's comic strip "Pogo"]

hooch[1] **n** Liquor; strong drink; BOOZE : *and the bottles of hooch, and the free food on the job/ or guzzles hooch that he hides inside a big toy duck* [1897+; fr the liquor made by the *Hoochinoo* Indians of Alaska]

hooch[2] or **hootch** **n 1** A Korean house, room, shack, etc : *giggle timidly and plead: "Come on to my hooch"* **2** A Vietnamese village hut **3** An American barracks, esp a Quonset-style barracks in Vietnam [Korean & Vietnam War armed forces; fr Japanese *uchi*, "house"]

hooch[3] *See* the HOOTCHIE-COOTCHIE

hood[1] (HOOD, HŌŌD) *modifier* : *has been in the hood hierarchy for decades* **n** HOODLUM : *those St Louis hoods/ the procession of hoods on the witness stand* (1930+)

hood[2] or **'hood** **n** Neighborhood • First associated with black Los Angeles neighborhoods : *Who know the defendant from the 'hood. It's part of the job* (mid-1980s+)

hoodge **v** To take someone's nipple between thumb and forefinger and squeeze it painfully; RAT (1980s+)

hoodie **n** A hooded sweatshirt or top : *hoodies in every color and style*

hoodlum **n** A petty criminal; a street tough [1868+; origin unknown, although many suggestions have been made; the term appears to have originated in San Francisco]

hoodoo **n** A person or thing that brings bad luck; JINX : *A mascot and a hoodoo, meaning one who brings ill fortune, are terms invented in the theater* [1882+; said to be an alteration of *voodoo*]

hooey **n** Nonsense; foolishness; BALONEY : *lip-smacking imps of mawk and hooey write with us what they will/ a dangerous mix of electio-*

neering hooey and religious clap-trap [1889+; origin unknown]

hoof **n** A foot : *Take your goddam hoof the hell off my fender* (1598+) **v 1** To walk; HOOF IT : *I better hoof over to the garage* (1888+) **2** To dance : *She's hoofing in that show about cats* (1921+)

hoofer **n** A dancer, esp a professional dancer in nightclubs, musical plays, etc : *The hoofers and the chorines of a cabaret* (1921+)

hoof-in-mouth disease **n** *phr* A tendency to speech before thought; the habit of opening one's "big fat mouth" : *Among the most notable practitioners of hoof-in-mouth disease in the past year* [1960s+; fr *put one's foot in it* with a pun on the *hoof-and-mouth disease* of farm animals, so designated by 1887]

hoof it **v** *phr* **1** To walk : *Get off the bus and hoof it home* (1728+) **2** To dance : *then hoofed it a bit herself with old friend Gene Kelly* (mid-1920s+)

hoo-ha[1] *interj* An exclamation of astonishment, admiration, envy, scorn, deflation, etc : *Does she gossip? Hoo-ha* [1930s+; fr Yiddish]

hoo-ha[2] **n 1** Disturbance; brouhaha; uproar : *What was I supposed to do in the middle of such a hoo-ha?/ In case you're wondering what all the hoo-ha is about* **2** A noisy celebration; a raucous fete : *But Northampton, Mass, held a week-long hoo-ha for its favorite son* [1931+; perhaps influenced by *hoo-ha*[1]; first attested in early 1900s British armed forces as "an argument; an artillery demonstration," and probably echoic-symbolic of a loud fuss, like *hoopla, to-do, brouhaha, foofooraw*, and *hooley*]

hook **n 1** An anchor *(1940s+ Nautical)* **2** A curveball *(1910+ Baseball)* **3** A hypodermic needle or bent pin used for injecting a narcotic *(1950s+ Narcotics)* **4** A narcotic, esp heroin *(1950s+ Narcotics)* **5** A prostitute; HOOKER : *Janie Ruth looked at the hook* (1915+) **6** Something that strongly attracts, esp something catchy in the lyrics or music of a song : *The musicians push a good hook, a high, ragged guitar line/ You just won't tell me much at a time about life. It's your hook/ There are no hooks, either, like the mechanical bull or dancing* (1930+) **7** A patron; a helpful connection : *Why have I been in a radio car for over twenty years? Because I don't have a hook* *(1980s+ Police)* **8** A grade of C *(1960s+ Students)* **v 1** To steal, esp to shoplift : *Hooking merchandise from department stores requires no training* (1615+) **2** To get; find : *Where can we hook a good meal around here?* (1940s+) **3** To arrest; stop and ticket : *My cab driver got hooked for speeding* (1920s+) **4** To entice successfully; procure more or less against one's will : *They hooked me for the* *main speech* (*1764+*) **5** To cheat; deceive ● Most often in the passive voice : *He got hooked into paying the whole bill* (*1940s+*) **6** To work as a prostitute; whore : *They stress the fact that they strip and don't hook/ Carl supplemented their income by hooking from the notorious bus bench* (*1959+*) **7** To drink, esp quickly at a gulp : *You pour a half-glass of Dewar's, hook it down and fan out the flames with a bottle of beer* (*1880s+*) *See* BUTTON-HOOK

hook, the *n phr* A violent football tackle in which the head of the ball-carrier is caught and held in the crook of the tackler's arm (*1970s+ Football*) *See* GET someone OFF THE HOOK, GET THE HOOK, GIVE someone THE HOOK, GO ON THE HOOK FOR someone or something, LET someone OFF THE HOOK, OFF THE HOOK, ON THE HOOK, RING OFF THE HOOK

hooked *adj* **1** Addicted to a narcotic : *Once a week wasn't being hooked/ I was the pusher who got you hooked* (*1925+ Narcotics*) **2** Captivated as if drug-addicted : *a shock to discover my wife was hooked on needlepoint/ Once you buy his preposterous premise and get to know his pleasantly insane characters, you're hooked* (*1960s+*) **3** Married; HITCHED (*1889+*)

hooker *modifier* : *hooker district* *n* **1** A prostitute : *drunken sportswriters, hard-eyed hookers, wandering geeks and hustlers/ The thirtyish ex-hooker was answering questions* (*1845+*) **2** A person who recruits, enlists, snares, etc : *Hooker, a person who induces union members to act as spies* (*1850s+*) **3** A drink of liquor; SNORT : *It took a stiff hooker of whiskey to thaw her* (*1887+*) [first noun sense apparently fr the notion that such women are "*hookers* of men"]

hook (or rook) someone into something *v phr* To obligate or involve someone by force or trickery : *They hooked me into paying for everybody's lunch/ She got rooked into a very boring cocktail party* (*1940s+*)

hook, line, and sinker *modifier* Totally; completely : *she's got you hook, line, and sinker*

hooks *n* The hands (*1846+*) *See* FISHHOOKS, GET one's HOOKS INTO, LUNCH-HOOKS, MEATHOOKS

◁**hookup**▷ *n* A sex act; SCREW, PIECE OF ASS (*1990s+*)

hook up *v phr* **1** To do the sex act; DO THE WILD THING, SCREW : *We didn't do nothing wrong, 'cause it's not illegal to hook up* (*1990s+*) **2** To meet and become associated, or cause somebody to meet and become associated, with somebody else

hook someone up *v phr* To arrest someone; COLLAR, PINCH [1990s+ Police; probably fr the act of handcuffing someone]

hooky *adj* Captivating; very attractive; catchy : *It's also more insinuatingly hooky than Led Zep ever was/ After the first few merely hooky tracks* (*1930s+*) *v* PLAY HOOKY (*1950s+*)

hooligan *n* **1** ruffian; street tough; GOON, HOODLUM : *Beat me up with your hooligans* (*1898+*) **2** GUN **3** The Wild West tent of a circus or show (*1940s+ Circus*) [origin unknown; perhaps fr a rowdy Irish family named *Hooligan* of Southwark, London, England; perhaps fr Irish *Uillegán*, a nickname for William, with confusion by Americans over vocative "Oh, Willie," spread to all Irishmen; circus sense perhaps related to Western *hoolian* or *hooley-ann* or *hoolihan*, "throw a steer by leaping on its horns, bulldog"; all senses perhaps related to Irish *hooley*, "noisy party, carousal"]

hoop *modifier* Having to do with basketball : *a hoop team/ hoop scores* (*1940s+ Basketball*) *n* **1** A finger ring : *the old hoop on that finger* (*1859+ fr underworld*); **2** The basketball net or basket; BUCKET (*1930s Basketball*) **3** A basketball goal; BUCKET : *He made six hoops last night* (*1940s+ Basketball*) *v* To vomit; BARF, OOPS : *One of the guys from Emergency Services hooped into his boots over it* (*1980s+*)

hoop-a-doop or **hoop-de-doop** or **hoopty-do** *See* WHOOP-DE-DO

hoopla or **whoopla** *n* **1** A joyous and boisterous clamor; HOO-HA : *Is this hoopla for my birthday?* **2** A noisy fuss; a commotion : *His arrival started a big hoopla* **3** Advertising or promotion; ballyhoo, FLACK : *I say this is a lot of unnecessary hoopla* [1877+; perhaps fr *hoop-la!*, the stagecoach driver's exhortation to his horses]

hoop-man or **hoopster** *n* A basketball player (*1940s+ Basketball*)

hoops *n* The game of basketball : *meet to play hoops at the Y* *See* JUMP THROUGH HOOPS

hoopty-doo *See* WHOOP-DE-DO

hoosegow (HOOS gou) *n* A jail [1911+; fr Mexican Spanish *juzgao*, "*tribunal, court*"]

Hoosier *n* A native or resident of Indiana (*1826+*)

hoot, a *n* **1** Something or somebody very funny and pleasant : *Life is a hoot/ Wouldn't it be a hoot to wake up one morning and find yourself in Gracie Mansion?* (*1915+ Students*) **2** A person; COOT *See* NOT GIVE A DAMN

hoot and a holler, a *n phr* A short distance : *The gas station's just a hoot and a holler that way* (*1940s+*)

hootch *See* HOOCH

◁**hootchee** or **hotchee**▷ *n* The penis (*Korean War armed forces*)

hootchie-cootchie (or **hootchy-kootchy** or **hooch**), the *n* **1** An erotic dance in which the woman rotates her hips, etc **2** A woman who dances the hootchie-cootchie [1890+; origin unknown; "The Hootchy-Kootchy" was the name of a song associated with the dancer Little Egypt at the Chicago World's Fair of 1893, but the term is found several years earlier in the context of the minstrel show]

hootenanny (HOOT ən annee) *n* **1** Any unspecified or unspecifiable object; something one does not know the name of or does not wish to name; GADGET, GIZMO : *He took a little hootenanny off the shelf and blew into it* (1925+) **2** A folk-music entertainment, esp one where the audience participates (1940s+) [one of many fanciful coinages for something unspecified; probably related to *hooter*, "anything trifling," found fr the mid-1800s, and to *hewgag*, "an indeterminate, unknown mythical creature," similarly found; the syllable *hoo-*, which is prominent in such coinages, probably represents the interrogative pronoun *who*; the folk-music sense is based on this, in spite of a fanciful explanation by the singer Woody Guthrie, involving a loud singer called *Hootin' Annie*]

hooter *n* A marijuana cigarette (1960s+ Students)

◁**hooters**▷ *n* A woman's breasts : *Hooters (a synonym, I learn, for knockers) is a nice little play* (1980s+)

hoot it up *v phr* To laugh; cackle : *Goodman and Francie were hooting it up* [1980s+; *hoot*, "to laugh," is found by 1925]

hooty *adj* Excellent; delightful; amusing : *Wasn't that a hooty rendition?* (1980s+)

hoover *v* **1** To eat or drink up, esp greedily : *instead of the moussaka and lamb that everyone else was hoovering* ◁**2**▷ To do fellatio or cunnilingus with or to; EAT : *Will you hoover me immediately, before I pay any attention to you* **3** To elicit information from : *a chance to hoover your brains* [1980s+; fr the *Hoover*® vacuum cleaner]

hop *n* **1** A dance or dancing party : *We went to a hop* (1731+) **2** A hotel desk porter; BELLHOP : *The hop was tall and thin* (1940s+) **3** A trip; stage of a journey; airplane flight : *a long hop to Singapore* (1909+) **4** A beer : *a hop with those quesadillas* *v* **1** : *They hopped over to Brussels* **2** To board : *to hop a plane* (1909+) See CARHOP, TABLE-HOP

hope to die See CROSS MY HEART

hopjoint *n* An opium den (1887+)

hop on the bandwagon See GET ON THE BANDWAGON

hopped up *adj phr* **1** Intoxicated by narcotics; GEEZED, gowed up : *The newer generation of "coked" or "hopped up" gunmen* (1924+ Narcotics) **2** Excited; highly stimulated : *What are you so hopped up about?* (1923+) **3**

Made very exciting; deliberately intensified; JAZZED UP : *those hopped-up novels in which passion is named but not felt* (1940s+) **4** SOUPED UP (1942+)

hopper *n* A ground ball that hops along (1940s+ Baseball)

hopper, the *n phr* The imagined place where proposed ideas, actions, etc, are placed; the place where proposed bills are filed for legislative consideration; PIPELINE : *Can't look at it now, put it in the hopper* [1950s+; fr the *hopper* device that feeds mills, etc, so called fr its shaking]

hopping mad *adj phr* Very angry; livid; STEAMED (1840+)

hops *n* Beer (1930+) See FULL OF BEANS

hopscotch *v* To leap about; make long and diverse transits : *The show hopscotches from Toronto and Boston to Lake Tahoe and Las Vegas* [1970s+; fr the children's game]

hopup (HAHP up) *modifier* Used to increase the power and speed of a car engine : *a pretty good selection of hopup and speed equipment* (1950s+ Hot rodders)

hop up *v phr* **1** To administer narcotics : *He hopped himself up on heroin* (1940s+ Narcotics) **2** To drug a horse for speed; DOPE : *to hop up or slow down their horses* (1940s+ Horse racing) **3** To increase the speed and power of a car; SOUP UP : *How to Hop Up Chevrolet and GMC Engines* (1940s+)

horizontal bop, the *n phr* (Variations: **mambo** or **rhumba** may replace **bop**) The sex act; copulation : *while he did the horizontal bop with this girl/ Clark, you can do the horizontal rhumba with the entire Metnet cheerleading squad if you want* [1980s+; *horizontal refreshment* in the same sense is found by 1893]

horn *n* **1** Any wind instrument (1940s+ Jazz musicians) **2** The trumpet (1900+ Jazz musicians) ◁**3**▷ A penile erection; HARD-ON : *I could have beat up five guys with the horn I had on* (1785+) **4** The telephone : *I get straight on the horn to Eckert* (1940s+) See LIKE SHIT THROUGH A TIN HORN, TOOT one's OWN HORN

horn, the *n phr* The telephone : *Regional representatives got on the horn with the Louisville headquarters* (1940s+)

horner *n* A person who has a tender, runny nose from inhaling cocaine (1960s+ Narcotics)

horn in *v phr* To intrude; thrust oneself in; BUTT IN : *Some wallie tried to horn in on our gang* (1912+)

horniness *n* Sexual craving; lust and lustfulness; HOT ROCKS : *the lure of High Art to mask the visceral odors of simple human horniness* (1960s+)

hornswoggle *v* To cheat; swindle; dupe; CON (1829+)

◁**horny**▷ *adj* Sexually excited and desirous; keenly amorous; lustful; HOT • Of recent years applied to women as well as men, despite being derived fr *horn,* "erect penis" : *his horny teen-age daughter/ At first it eased my head and made me less horny/ a few scenes between a horny housewife and a guy in a Lone Ranger mask* (1889+)

horrors, the *n phr* Delirium tremens; the SHAKES (1860+)

horse *n* 1 Heroin; SHIT : *They shoot horse in the john at the local high school/ After about 1952, nobody called it horse any more* (1940s+ Narcotics) 2 A hard-drug addict (1940s+ Narcotics) 3 A prison guard paid by inmates to smuggle letters and other contraband in and out • See *mule,* "a person paid to carry smuggled drugs" (1960s+ Prison) 4 A truck or a tractor (1940s+ Truckers) 5 An honest, hardworking police officer : *We know who the horses are around here, every cop in the department knows* (1960s+ Police) *v* 1 To play and idle; FOOL AROUND, HORSE AROUND : *He wasn't just horsing now/ The Badgers lapse into their old ways, horsing up shots* (1927+) ◁2▷ To do the sex act with or to; SCREW : *there ain't goin' to be any immoral horsin' goin' on* 3 To fool; ridicule; trick (1901+) [the sense "heroin" may have derived fr *shit,* "heroin," by way of *horseshit,* although the derivation might well have gone in the other direction; or perhaps the sense is based on the sobriquet of a Damon Runyon character *Harry the Horse* by way of the partial rhyme of *Harry* with *heroin;* second verb sense used of stallions and mares by 1420] *See* DARK HORSE, DEAD HORSE, ENOUGH TO CHOKE A HORSE, FROM THE HORSE'S MOUTH, GET ON one's HIGH HORSE, ONE-HORSE, ONE-HORSE TOWN, WARHORSE

horse-and-buggy *adj* Old-fashioned : *a horse-and-buggy leisureliness* (1927+)

horse apple *n phr* 1 A ball of horse feces 2 Pretentious trash; HORSESHIT : *all that particular pile of horseapples boiled down to* (1940s+)

horse around *v phr* To joke and caper pleasurably; indulge in horseplay; FOOL AROUND : *He was horsing around and he got caught* (1927+)

horsefeathers *interj* An exclamation of disbelief, rejection, contempt, etc : *Mail comes urging that something be done to "rescue children from guns, daggers, and soldier worship." Horsefeathers!* *n* Nonsense; BALONEY, BUNK, HORSESHIT : *Don't give me that horsefeathers about your saintly momma* (1928+)

horsehide *n* A baseball (1895+ Baseball)

horselaugh, the *n phr* A loud, nasty, and dismissive laugh at someone; the MERRY HA-HA : *When I asked for more time I just got the horselaugh* (1738+)

horse opera (or **opry**) *n phr* 1 A cowboy movie; western; oater (1927+) 2 A circus show featuring horses (1857+ Circus)

horseplay *n* Rough and boisterous playing; coarse physical merriment (1589+)

horse race *n* A serious contest; a hard-fought competition : *Suddenly what looked like a shoo-in turned into a real horse-race* (1970s+)

horses *n* A pair of dishonest dice, esp of mismatched dice that can produce only specific combinations : *Karnov explained the use of "horses"* (1940s+ Gambling) *See* HOLD one's HORSES

◁**horse's ass** (or **derriere**)▷ *n phr* A contemptible person; a persistent and obnoxious fool; JERK : *I just regard the critic privately as being the biggest horse's ass in the western world/ If, however, he wanted to present himself in Texas as a real horse's ass, none of us would dispute him/ We just hope history will prove we were visionaries and not horses' derrieres*

horse sense *n phr* Good sense and shrewdness : *horse sense needed before taking on something like that* (1832+)

◁**horseshit**▷ *interj* An exclamation of disbelief, disapproval, and contempt : *Horseshit! I'll never believe that modifier* (also **horse-bleep**) : *Superstar! What a horseshit idiot!/ and the overall horsebleep pitching n* 1 Nonsense; pretentious talk; bold and deceitful absurdities; BALONEY, BULLSHIT : *You give me all that horseshit about the conditions here* 2 Something of very poor quality; DRECK, GARBAGE : *I'm not a cheerleader; if we're horseshit, I'll say so* 3 Trivialities; nonessentials; CHICKENSHIT : *Don't bother me with that niminy-piminy horseshit v* : *He was horseshitting about what a great sailor he is* (1940s+)

◁**horseshit and gunsmoke**▷ *n phr* Excitement and confusion; chaos [1970s+ Army; fr an evocation of a cavalry skirmish or a cowboys-and-Indians battle]

horse's mouth *See* FROM THE HORSE'S MOUTH

horse-trading *n* Negotiating reciprocal concessions and benefits, esp of a political sort : *Vintage Washington politics as usual was not good enough anymore, that horse-trading, your bill for mine, was part of the old-time religion* (1940s+)

hose *n* 1 A sexually promiscuous woman (1980s+ Students) ◁2▷ The penis *v* ◁1▷ To do the sex act with or to; BONK, JAZZ, SCREW : *Do you still want to hose her some more tonight?* (1940s+) 2 To cheat; deceive; dupe; SCREW, SHAFT : *He's not going out of his way to hose Nico/ I got news for you. You got hosed* (1940s+) 3 To turn down; reject; snub : *They're afraid of getting hosed* (1960s+ Students) [origin uncertain; perhaps fr a rare but found *hose,* "penis," whereupon the

hosed

term would be analogous to *diddle, fuck, screw, shaft,* etc]

hosed *adj* Being in a bad spot or unfortunate situation; screwed : *hosed on the shipping cost*

◀**hose job**▶ *n phr* BLOW JOB : *Looks like the hooker was doing a hose job on one of the truckers (1980s+)*

◁**hoser**▷ *n* **1** A contemptible and obnoxious person, esp a man; DORK, JERK : *Reagan is a hoser (1980s+ Students)* **2** (also **hosehead**) A Canadian, esp a simple and durable northern type • Originated by comedians Dave Thomas and Rick Moranis for the television skits called "The Great White North," where it was used by the mentally challenged Mackenzie brothers : *unavailable to us hosers, but can be bought down south/ unlike their hoser cousins (1980s+ Canadian)* **3** A very sexually active male; COCKSMAN, swordsman : *Bill has slept with three girls this week. What a hoser! (1980s+ Students)*

hosing *n* Abuse, esp a beating with a hose *(1931+ Prison) See* TAKE A HOSING

hostess with the mostest, the *n phr* The most successful, lavish, and well-connected party-giving woman [1950s+; fr a popular song fr the 1950s show *Call Me Madam,* "The Hostess with the Mostest on the Ball"]

hot *adj* **1** Capable of high speed; moving very fast : *Hot crate, a fast plane (1868+)* **2** Selling very rapidly and readily, hence very much in demand : *paralleled the rise of the "hot" ticket/ Xaviera Hollander is the hottest thing in the business promoting her own work (1960s+)* **3** Performing extremely well; certain to win : *When you're hot you're hot/ The big fork-baller is real hot today, folks (1895+)* **4** Angry; furious; PISSED OFF : *Don't get so hot about it, it was just a goof (1225+)* **5** Lively; vital; vibrant : *This is a hot town/ A "hot" magazine is one that's sizzling and bubbling with activity (1911+)* **6** Sexually excited; afire with passion; lustful; HORNY : *Hot faggot queens bump up against chilly Jewish matrons/ the hottest little devil I ever met (1500+)* **7** Pornographic; salacious; DIRTY : *a real hot movie (1892+)* **8** Eager; ANTSY : *Why so hot to get started? (1971+)* **9** Exciting, rapid, strongly rhythmical, eliciting a visceral response : *The old jazz was mostly hot, then it was cool, and now even cool cats blow hot licks now and then (1920+ Jazz musicians)* **10** Stolen, esp recently stolen; contraband : *Stolen bonds are "hot paper" (1925+ Underworld)* **11** Wanted by the police : *Where would a hot can of corn like Dillinger hide out (1931+ Underworld)* **12** Dangerous; menacing; potentially disastrous : *Things were getting too hot/ It's so hot out there, man, I'm thinking about getting into another game*

(1618+) **13** Extremely infectious; having lethal potential : *The garbage bags held seven dead monkeys, and they were hot as hell. Presumably lethal (1990s+ Medical)* **14** New, esp both brand-new and interesting : *a hot tip/ the hot news from upstairs (1908+)* **15** Having electrical potential; live; switched on : *Is this mike hot?/ Can I touch this wire, or is it hot? (1925+)* **16** Radioactive *(1942+)* **17** Excellent and very good-looking : *Hot means cool and extremely good-looking (1980s+ Teenagers)* [stolen-goods sense may derive fr *hot,* "too well known," found by 1883] *See* BLOW HOT AND COLD, NOT SO HOT, RED HOT

hot air *n phr* **1** Nonsense; pretentious talk; bold and deceitful absurdities; BALONEY, BULLSHIT : *The Jefferson family tree will never be blown down by any hot air from me* **2** Pomposity and vanity; bombast : *The old fraud talks a lot of hot air (1900+) See* FULL OF HOT AIR

hot and bothered *adj phr* Angry; fiercely indignant; PISSED OFF, STEAMED UP : *Now don't get all hot and bothered just because he didn't call (1921+)*

hot and cold *n phr* A mixture of heroin and cocaine; h and c, SPEEDBALL *(1960s+ Narcotics) See* BLOW HOT AND COLD

hot as blazes (or **hell**) *adj phr* Very hot indeed *(first form 1849+, second 1912+)*

hot bed or **hotbed** *n phr* or *n* **1** A bed used both day and night, by shifts of sleepers *(1945+)* **2** A place that produces or is prominently rich in specified things : *College these days is a hotbed of sobriety (1768+)*

hot button *modifier* : *his subtle tilts to the center on hot-button issues such as abortion and gun control n phr* An inflammatory topic or area; a tender public nerve : *The Horton spot hit a "hot button"/ more low-income housing, a political hot button in town* [1980s+; perhaps fr the earlier *hot button,* "the clitoris"; perhaps fr the button or key of a news teletype that sounded a bell to announce "hot" news]

hotcha *adj* Sexually attractive and energetic : *He run Sternwood's hotcha daughter, the young one, off to Yuma interj* (also **hotcha-cha** or **ha-cha-cha**) An expression of pleasure, approval, relish, etc [1933+; a derivation fr Yiddish *hotsa,* "hop!" has been suggested, based on the joyous repetition of the word as one bounces an infant on one's knees; perhaps fr *hot;* according to Gelett Burgess, *hotcha-cha* was coined by the comedian Jimmy Durante, with whom one identifies the utterance]

hot corner *n phr* **1** Any very dangerous and crucial place : *The North African front is a "hot corner" (1854+)* **2** Third base, esp as a fielding position *(1889+ Baseball)* [baseball sense reflects the time when most sluggers were right-handed hitters]

hot damn *interj* An exclamation of pleasure, gratification, etc; HOT DOG, HOT SHIT (*1936+*)

hot diggety (or **diggity**) *interj* (Variations: **dog** or **doggety** or **damn** may be added; **ziggety** or **ziggity** may replace **diggety**) HOT DOG (*1924+*)

hot dog *interj* An exclamation of delight, gratification, relish, etc; HOT DAMN, HOT SHIT : *Did you have a good time? "Hot dog!"* (*1906+*) *modifier* 1 : *a hot-dog stand/ embattled hot-dog vendor* 2 : *I don't appreciate that hot-dog garbage in my ball park n phr* 1 A frankfurter or a frankfurter sandwich (*1900+*) 2 HOT SHOT (*1900+*) *n* 3 : *Walter is one of the good guys, not a hot dog* (*1966+*) *v phr* 1 To perform in a brilliant, spectacular way, esp in order to seize the admiration of an audience; GRANDSTAND, play to the grandstand, SHOW OFF : *a little careless against Bob Cousy's Royals, hot-dogging their passes and loosening their defenses* (*1960s+*) 2 To surf spectacularly : *Surfers may "hot dog," do acrobatics* (*1960s+ Surfers*) 3 To do hot-dog skiing (*1970s+ Skiers*)

hot dogger *n phr* GRANDSTANDER, HOT SHOT (*1960s+*)

hot-dog skiing *n phr* Free-style skiing that features somersaults, midair turns, balletlike figures, and other feats rather than speed : *A whole new style of baroque skiing has developed. Known as "free-style," "exhibition," or "hot-dog" skiing* (*1970s+ Skiers*)

hotfoot *adv* At once; immediately : *I'll walk hotfoot to the doctor's office* (*1835+*) *v* 1 (also **hotfoot it**) To go fast; hurry : *The boys would hotfoot back when they heard the mess call/ Tell him to hotfoot it to the sheriff's office* (*1838+*) 2 give someone a hotfoot

hot for *adj phr* 1 Very desirous of; lusting for; wishing to possess : *She seemed hot for you/ a young outfielder everyone in the Mets' organization was hot for* 2 Very eager over; enthusiastic about : *He's real hot for the new promotion policy* (*1667+*)

hothead *n* 1 An irascible person; one quick to anger; 2 A fanatical, emotional person; fiery militant (*1660+*)

hot iron *n phr* HOT ROD (*1950s+ Hot rodders*)

hot item *n* 1 An item that sells very well : *reading glasses are a hot item* 2 A fairly new and serious romantic couple : *they became a hot item after the prom See* HOT NUMBER

hot knife through butter *See* LIKE SHIT THROUGH A TIN HORN

hot line or **hotline** *n phr* or *n* An emergency telephone line or number : *Clearly, hot lines are no cure for the complex, overall problem of drug abuse/ a community "hot line" to head off* gang wars [mid-1950s+; popularized by the telephone line between the White House and the Kremlin]

hot number (or **item**) *n phr* 1 A very sexy man or woman; HOT PANTS 2 Something that is selling rapidly and well (*Salespersons*) (*1930s+*)

hot on *adj* Very fond of; enthusiastic for : *hot on renting movies from Blockbuster* (*1865+*)

hot pants *n phr* 1 Strong sexual desire; lust; carnal craving : *His hot pants will get him in trouble* (*1927+*) 2 A very passionate, lustful, and potentially promiscuous person : *Catherine the Great was apparently an imperial hot pants* (*1966+*) 3 Very brief women's shorts (*1960s+*)

hot patootie *n phr* A sexually attractive and sexy woman : *He calls the object of his affection a "hot patootie"* [*1928+*; fr *hot potato,* with a play on *potato* as used, like *tomato,* to mean "a person"]

hot poo *n phr* or *interj* 1 HOT SHIT *n phr* 2 (also **hot poop**) Recent and authoritative information; the latest word (*1950s+*)

hot potato *n phr* Something embarrassing and troublesome; a tricky and sticky matter : *Everyone can see how the boss looks when he handles a hot potato* (*1846+*) *See* DROP someone or something LIKE A HOT POTATO

hot property *n phr* Someone or something very valuable and marketable, esp an athlete, desirable executive, entertainer, etc : *Timmons and Co, knowing a hot property when it signs one up* (*1958+*)

hot rock *n phr* HOT SHOT

◁**hot rocks** (or **nuts**)▷ *n phr* Male sexual craving; powerful lust; HORNINESS

hot rod *modifier* : *hot-rod manual/ hot-rod club n phr* 1 A car specially modified and fitted with a powerful or rebuilt engine so as to be much faster than one of the same stock design; a-bomb. CAN. ROD : *Special Racing Cars and Hot Rods, a technical book explains the principles of supercharging, carburetion, suspension, shock absorbers. A complete speed manual* (*1945+ Hot rodders*) 2 (also **hot rodder**) A driver or devotee of hot rods : *Right away he thinks he's a hot rod* (*1949+ Hot rodders*)

hots, the *n phr* 1 Strong liking; predilection : *I'd never got the deep undying hots for that rah rah collitch boy/ If a girl calls and asks me out, she's got the hots for me* 2 Lust; HOT PANTS : *A bare-chested photograph of this guy can give 2,300 women the hots* (*1947+*) *See* HAVE THE HOTS FOR someone

hot seat, the *n phr* 1 The electric chair : *He draws the hot-seat for taking that rat* (*1925+*) 2 A place where one is under uncomfortable scrutiny and pressure, esp the witness stand

: *Deane was succeeded in the hot seat by a very small pot from the State Department/ always on the cutting edge, always in the hot seat* (1942+) *See* ON THE HOT SEAT

hot sheet *modifier* Catering to quick assignations; permitting short-term occupancy : *The "Strip Tease" murder includes a brief, touching appearance of the forlorn manager of a hotsheet place called the Flightpath Motel/ Investigating shady insurance claims lands Jack in the usual hot-sheet motels in North Dallas* [1980s+; modeled on *hot bed*]

◁**hot shit**▷ *modifier* : *Thought he was a hot shit basketball player/ to get the hot-shit, thick-book education he could well afford* n *phr* or *interj* **1** HOT DOG *n phr* **2** Someone or something very remarkable and attractive, irresistible, etc; HOT STUFF : *He thinks he's real hot shit* **3** An aggressive, self-assured person; BIG SHOT : *something sensitive and probing like all the rest of these hot shits* (1940s+)

hot shot *modifier* **1** : *In just a year I'm claiming to be a hot-shot Columbia man myself/ a young, hot-shot second lieutenant* **2** : *a hot-shot freight* n *phr* **1** An especially gifted and effective person; a notably successful person; BALL OF FIRE, WINNER • Often used ironically : *What has been written about executives has usually dealt with the hot shots/ You're not pushing around some crummy client to show him what a hot-shot you are* (1933+) **2** A fast train or express train (1930+ *Railroad*) **3** A news bulletin; a news flash : *When that hot-shot came in about Monahan's death* (1940s+) **4** A narcotics injection that is fatal because of an impurity or poison : *You got a hot shot! You're dead* (1950s+ *Narcotics*)

hot spot *n phr* **1** TIGHT SPOT (1932+) **2** A dangerous place, esp a combat zone : *Sarajevo is a hot spot again* (1941+) **3** A popular nightclub, esp one with sexy entertainment : *became 52d Street's hot spot* (1931+)

hot stove league *n phr* The off-season entity of devotees, arguments, etc, that keeps baseball serious and topical from October to April [1912+; as applied to horse racing, the term is found by the 1870s]

hot stuff *n phr* **1** A person of exceptional merit, talents, attractions, etc; HOT SHOT • Almost always used ironically : *I guess they think they are hot stuff/ Don't you think I'm hot stuff* (1889+) **2** Material, entertainment, etc, that is very exciting, esp salacious : *Those magazines are real hot stuff* (1904+) **3** Stolen goods; contraband (1924+ *Underworld*) **4** News or information that is very important, fresh, sensational, forbidden, etc : *I peeked in your briefcase, and that's hot stuff!* (1931+) **5** Food, drinks, etc, that are very hot : *Hot stuff coming through* (1940s+)

hotsy-totsy or **hotsie-totsie** *adj* Satisfactory; fine; COPACETIC : *All's hotsie-totsie here, thank you so much* (1926+)

hot ticket *modifier* : *Willenson is a hot ticket item in the media these days* n *phr* A very popular show; HIT : *Mr. Martins's staging of Sleeping Beauty was such a critical success at its premiere that it became an instant hot ticket* (1960s+)

hottie *n* An attractive person; beddy, DISH : *if a guy or girl is cute, they're a "hottie" or "fine"* (1990s+ *Teenagers*)

hot to trot *adj phr* Afire with craving, esp for sexual activity; lustful : *to ask her bluntly if she was hot to trot/ Somebody was hot to trot for a Japanese sedan/ who claims her hot-to-trot boss gave her a chase around the office* (1950s+ *Black*)

hot under the collar *adj phr* Very angry : *The Puerto Ricans who get hot under the collar and curse aloud if anyone should question their being Puerto Rican* (1895+)

hot up *v phr* **1** To become more exciting and dangerous; heat up : *Then things really hot up and January falls in love with an aging macho novelist* (1936+) **2** To make something hot or hotter : *I'll just hot up some soup for lunch* (1903+)

hot war *n phr* A war with combat and killing; shooting war • An isolated use in 1768 means "a vigorous war," lacking the modern contrast with *cold war* (1947+)

hot water *n phr* Difficulty; trouble; embarrassment : *got herself into hot water by marrying a Siamese prince* (1875+) *See* IN HOT WATER

hot-wire *v* **1** To start a car, truck, etc, by electrically bypassing the ignition lock : *He could hot-wire any car in about 20 seconds* (1961+) **2** To activate illegally; tamper with : *let the affected corporations hot-wire the regulatory process* (1970s+) [fr the notion of attaching an electrically *hot* wire to the starter-motor relay]

Hot ziggety! *interj* Wow! : *A babysitter for junior? Hot ziggety See* HOT DIGGETY

hound *v* To harass, pester, or annoy someone; BURN : *I hounded him. Oh fuck, what a loser I was* (1605+) *See* BOOZEHOUND, CHOW HOUND

-hound *combining word* A person devoted to or addicted to what is indicated : *autograph hound/ boozehound/ newshound/ nicotine hound/ thrill-hound*

hound dog *n phr* A contemptible man, esp a woman-chaser [1940s+; a Southernism popularized by an Elvis Presley song lyric: "Ain't nothin' but a hound dog"]

house *n* **1** A brothel; CATHOUSE, WHOREHOUSE • Earlier occurrences, from 1726 on, have modifiers: *of ill repute, of ill fame, of as-*

signation, of accommodation, etc : *A House is not a Home* (1865+) **2** The audience at a theater (1921+) **3** A kind of dance music derived from soul, rock, and jazz, with a strong percussive beat, originally a black Chicago style • Comes in many varieties: deep house, garage, tribal, progressive, etc : *to introduce Southern California to "house," the technologically sophisticated dance music that has taken the country by storm/ For years, dance-club regulars have been expecting the boom-chucka-boom beat of house music to conquer pop* (mid-1980s+) [third sense fr *the Warehouse,* a Chicago club] *See* BARRELHOUSE, the BIG HOUSE, BRING DOWN THE HOUSE, CATHOUSE, CRACK HOUSE, FLEABAG, FLOPHOUSE, FUNNY FARM, GRIND-HOUSE, HASH-HOUSE, NOTCHHOUSE, NUTHOUSE, ON THE HOUSE, POWERHOUSE, ROUGHHOUSE, ROUNDHOUSE, STROKE HOUSE, WHEELHOUSE, WHOREHOUSE

house ape *n phr* A small child; an infant; curtain climber. RUG RAT (1980s+)

housebroken *adj* To be generally observant of the amenities; tame [1932+; fr the condition of a pet who will soil the house with excreta]

house-cleaning *n* A reorganization of a business or government department, esp with dismissal of incompetent or dishonest employees; SHAKE-UP : *Honest cops, instead of welcoming a house-cleaning, resent it* (1928+)

house-sit *v* To live in and care for a house free of charge or for a fee while the owner is away [1970s+; modeled on *baby-sit*]

how *See* AND HOW, KNOW-HOW

how about (or **what do you know about**) **that** *interj* An exclamation of surprise, pleasure, admiration, etc : *We've only got a year to go. How about that!/ I should worry. What d'yuh know about that?* [first form 1939+, second 1920s+; first form popularized by the baseball anouncer Mel Allen]

how something can you get *sentence* It is impossible to be or behave to a more extreme degree; this is the utmost : *"How tacky can you get?" Maddie said disgustedly/ He did? How stupid can you get?* (1951+)

how come *sentence* What is that? what is the reason? : *"Change of plans. We move today" "How come?"* (1848+)

how do you like (or **how about**) **them apples** *interj* An exclamation of pleasure and triumph, usu inviting admiration for something one has done or acquired : *How do you like them apples, huh, Ma?!/ How about them apples, Goodman?* (1940s+)

howdy *interj* An exclamation upon greeting : *Howdy, pardner, what's up?* [1843+; fr *how do you do*]

how it shakes out *adv phr* The consequences; the fate of an idea, experiment, endeavor, etc

: *This may or may not fly; we'll just wait and see how it shakes out* (1990s+)

howl, a *n* **1** Something amusing; a funny event; a HOOT (1934+) **2** BEEF, STINK : *I do not want any friends to make a howl through the press* (1886+)

howler *n* A very funny mistake, esp in something written or spoken rather solemnly; also, a serious and obvious mistake : *His misuse of "Rappaport" for "rapport" was the season's howler* (1844+)

howling *adj* Conspicuously successful : *The Peoples' theatre is doing a howling biz* (1887+)

how's about *prep phr* What do you feel or think about : *How's about a drink?* (1925+)

how's tricks *sentence* How are you? how are things going for you? (1904+)

how're they (or **how they** or **how's it**) **hanging?** *sentence* How are you? • A genial greeting, usu from one man to another; an inquiry as to the condition of the genitals : *Dude, how's it hangin'* (1940s+)

HUA (pronounced as separate letters) *adv phr* Stupidly; blindly; inattentively : *You're driving pretty HUA today* [1980s+; fr *head up ass*]

hubba-hubba *adv* Quickly; immediately; ON THE DOUBLE *interj* An exclamation of delight, relish, etc, esp at the sight of a woman [WWII armed forces; origin unknown; perhaps a version of a Chinese greeting *how-puhow,* apparently adopted by US airmen from Chinese pilot trainees; perhaps originally a bit of gibberish used to imitate the clamor of conversation, esp when soldiers get the command "Parade rest," after which one can talk, as distinct from the command "At ease," after which one must remain silent and contribute to no *hubbub*]

hubby *n* Husband (1798+)

huck *v* To throw; CHUCK : *We'd each huck a dart standing on one foot, gulping a beer* (1990s+)

huckleberry *n* **1** A man; fellow; GUY : *Well, I'm your huckleberry, Mr Haney* (1883+) **2** A sweet, agreeable person, hence sometimes a dupe • A very mild and affectionate insult (1895+ Students)

huckster *n* An advertising person or publicity agent : *so the television hucksters can peddle their shaving cream* [1945+; popularized by the 1946 novel about advertising, *The Hucksters,* by Frederick Wakeman]

huddle *n* A conference; closed and intense discussion : *He went into a huddle with his aides* *v* : *We'll have to huddle on that one* [1929+; fr the *huddle,* esp of the offensive team, before most plays in football]

huffy *adj* Angry; petulant; irritable; IN A HUFF : *I didn't mean to get huffy* (1848+)

huggy-huggy *adj* (also **kissy-huggy** or **kissy-kissy**) Very affectionate; BUDDY-BUDDY,

PALSY-WALSY : *We are all very huggy-huggy with each other/ This is not gonna be a kissy-huggy book/ The kissy-kissy socials had all but disappeared* (*1980s+*)

hug the porcelain god(dess) (or **throne**) *v phr* To vomit in the toilet : *Memorial Day weekend hugging the porcelain god*

hulking *adj* Large : *hulking muscles bulging* (*1700+*)

hum (or **hmmm**) **babe** *interj* An utterance of various meanings, often of encouragement : *Piece of cake, can of corn, hum babe* [*1980s+* Baseball; perhaps fr exhortations to the pitcher to throw a devastating *hummer*]

humdinger *n* A person or thing that is remarkable, wonderful, superior, etc; BEAUT, LOLLAPALOOZA : *Arnold Moss gave us a humdinger of a talk* (*1905+*)

hummer *n* **1** A person or thing that is remarkable, wonderful, etc; HUMDINGER : *This is Mason's first book, and it's a hummer* (*1907+*) **2** A fastball (*1940s+* Baseball)

humongous (hoo MAWN gəs) *adj* Very large; gigantic : *a humongous chain* [*1960s+* Students; perhaps a sort of echoic-symbolic blend of *huge* with *monstrous*]

hump *n* A contemptible constable; an incompetent • Apparently sometimes used jovially to mean simply "cop" : *I don't believe that hump! I'm trying to develop a case, and he acts like I'm a hysterical old maid looking for rapists under the bed* (*1990+* Police) *v* **1** (also **hump it**, **hump along**) To move or go, esp with difficulty; slog : *lack the nerve to hump it through to the end/ put on that pack and hump for miles through the boonies* <2▷ To do the sex act with or to; FUCK : *from the brave pilots who hump the nubile hostesses to the dialect-spouting steerage passenger* (*1785+*) **3** To exert oneself mightily; work hard • To work as if carrying something on one's back, or *hump* : *and humped the big tractor trailer right off 128 and down ramp/ The groundskeepers have been humping to prepare the stadium for the big game* (*1835+*) *See* BUST ONE'S ASS, BUST HUMP, DRY FUCK, GET A MOVE ON, OVER THE HILL

hump oneself *v phr* To hurry : *You better hump yourself over to the police station and explain* (*1883+*)

hump day *n* The middle of the workweek, usu Wednesday, seen as the hill to get over in moving toward the weekend and time off (*1965+*)

<1▷**humpery**▷ *n* The sex act; coupling; FUCKING : *refused to change the X rating on Fritz the Cat on the ground that it depicted "anthropomorphic humpery"* (*1970s+*)

humpin' *adj* Attractive; good-looking; DISHY (*1990s+* Black)

<1▷**humpy**▷ *adj* Sexually arousing; lubricious; sexy : *flashy, precise, and humpy as in a Czardas* (*1970s+*)

humvee or **hummer** *n* A small military vehicle : *She and others were traveling in a humvee when one of the Jeeplike vehicles rolled over a mine/ Some 20,000 Humvees were used in the Persian Gulf War* [*1990s+*; fr *high mobility multipurpose wheeled vehicle*]

hunch *modifier* : *This was too good a hunch play to let drop n* An intuitive premonition; a shrewd idea or notion : *I gotta hunch she won't come back v* : *As I hunch it, the answer is triple* [*1904+*; said to be fr a gamblers' belief that touching a *hunchback's* hump would bring good luck]

hung *adj* **1** HUNG OVER (*1958+*) **2** In love (*1955+* Rock and roll) <3▷ Having impressive male genitals; HUNG LIKE A BULL, WELL-HUNG (*1641+*)

<1▷**hung like a bull** (or **a horse**)▷ *adj phr* Possessing large genitals; HUNG, WELL-HUNG (*1960s+*)

hung over *adj phr* Suffering the ill effects of a hangover : *looking as hung over as you can get* (*1940s+*)

hungries, the *See* GET THE HUNGRIES

hungry *adj* Very ambitious; extremely eager to succeed : *He won't make it because he's not hungry enough*

hung up *adj phr* **1** Limited by conventional beliefs and attitudes; SQUARE, UNCOOL : *Either you're way out, pops, or you're hung up* (*1940s+* Jazz musicians) **2** Agitated or immobilized by emotional disturbance; stalled : *She suddenly got all hung up around Christmas* (fr beat & cool talk) **3** Delayed; detained : *He got hung up with a phone call as he was leaving* (*1712+*)

hung up on *adj phr* Obsessed with; stalled or frustrated by; suffering a hangup over : *I'm hung up on fried rice* (*1957+* Beat & cool talk)

hunk *n* **1** A man or woman considered primarily as a sex partner; PIECE, PIECE OF ASS : *He came back to the hot little hunk he used to run around with* (*1940s+*) **2** A very attractive man, esp a muscular and sexually appealing one; STUD MUFFIN : *Wherever she goes she always manages to pick up a hunk* (*1945+*)

hunker down *v phr* **1** (also **hunker**) To squat on one's haunches : *He heads for the inevitable mariachi square, hunkers down in the dark, wet and shivering/ Fiona had just hunkered down, abandoned all caution/ Jon was hunkered in the dark, silently chain-smoking* (*1720+*) **2** To get into the mood and posture for hard work : *Now that summer's gone we must hunker down and get that report finished* (*1970s+*) **3** To take a sturdy defensive attitude; become hard to move : *As the public responds, the*

*defense lawyers hunker down/ "We'll just have
to hunker down," said Jody Powell (1970s+)*
[fr southern US fr northern British dialect
hunker, "haunch"]

hunk of change *See* PIECE OF CHANGE

hunkorama or **hunkster** *n* A very attractive
man, esp a muscular and sexually appealing
one; HUNK, STUD MUFFIN : *all 6 feet 2 inches of
blond hunkorama/ Holy Hunksters! It's Batman forever! (first form mid-1980s+, second
1990s+)*

◄**hunky**[1]► (also **hunkie** or **Hunky** or **Hunkie**
or **Hunk** or **hunks**) *modifier* : *hunky talk/
dumb hunkie brain* **n 1** A foreigner, esp a
Hungarian, Slavic, or Baltic laborer; BOHUNK,
GINZO (1910+) **2** HONKY : *99 white workers
got killed in a coal-mine disaster, man! Do you
know what I mean? So I can't call everybody no
Hunkie (1960s+ Black)* [fr *bohunk*]

hunky[2] *adj* Attractive, esp sexually desirable;
MACHO : *hunky, bearded actor-troubadour/ the
hunky blond who cranks the ferry* [1978+; the
related sense, "thick-set, solidly built," is
found by 1911]

hunky-dory *adj* Satisfactory; fine; COPACETIC :
*That may be hunky-dory with the jumping and
jiving youngsters* [1866+; origin uncertain;
hunky was a generalized term of approval by
1861; as to *dory*, according to one proposal
of 1876 it was brought back by sailors from
Yokohama, Japan, where *Honcho dori* is a
street where they found their diversions; the
term was popularized by a Christy Minstrels
song of about 1870]

hunter *See* HEADHUNTER

hunt up *v phr* To search for diligently; search
out : *Let's see if we can hunt up a place to get
this fixed (1791+)*

hurl *v* **1** To pitch : *after hurling five frames in
three games (1908+ Baseball)* **2** To vomit :
*Somebody hurled, which was so gross it made
somebody else hurl (1992+)*

hurler *n* A pitcher (1908+ Baseball)

hurrah's nest, a *n phr* Confusion; chaos; SNAFU
(1829+)

hurry up and wait *v phr* To be rushed only to
then have to wait : *another hurry up and wait
situation before the kids' soccer game*

hurt *adj* Ugly; ill-favored; PISS-UGLY : *I never saw
anyone as hurt as her boyfriend (1980s+
Teenagers)*

hurting *adj* In great need; in distress : *Guys, the
last thing we want is to seem to be hurting
for money (Armed forces & students fr black
1940s+)*

husband *n* **1** A pimp : *She has a pimp she calls
her "husband" (1960s+ Prostitutes)* **2** The
dominant, masculine member of a homosexual couple, male or female (1960s+
Homosexuals)

hush-hush *adj* Very secret; classified : *a hush-
hush border meeting* **n** : *Why all the hush-hush
about Walden? (1916+)*

hush money *n phr* Money paid to ensure silence : *You can't give "hush money" to someone who's already talked (1709+)*

hustle *n* **1** : *Put a little hustle in it now* **2** : *I guess
one man's "hustle" is another man's "promo-
tion" (1963+)* **3** A swindle: *You know I can't
pay out five bills for a wash if I wasn't planning
a hustle* **v 1** To hurry : *We better hustle, the
thing leaves in five minutes (1844+)* **2** To
behave, play, perform, etc, very energetically and aggressively : *The reason they're
losing is they don't hustle (1888+)* **3** To beg :
You'll hustle for an overcoat (1891+) **4** To
work as a prostitute; HOOK : *whores that
hustle all night long (1930+)* **5** To cheat;
swindle; victimize; CON : *It took a hell of a
caddy to hustle a pro and a greenskeeper/ Lar-
abee, he decided, was trying to hustle him
(1887+)* **6** To steal : *We must hustle us a car
(1915+)* [criminal senses may be related to
early 19th-century *hustle*, "do the sex act,
fuck"] *See* GET A HUSTLE ON, GET A MOVE ON, ON
THE HUSTLE

hustler *n* **1** A thief or a dealer in stolen goods :
*and sells to hustlers like Tommy at about one-
third its retail value (1825+)* **2** A confidence
trickster or swindler, esp one who pretends
ignorance of a game where he or she is in
fact an expert and sure to win; CON MAN,
SHARK (1914+) **3** A prostitute; HOOKER : *I
ain't nothing but a hustler (1924+)* **4** An energetic, aggressive performer or worker : *An
active and successful businessman achieves the
honorable distinction of a "hustler" or a "rustler" (1882+)*

hutzpa or **hutzpah** *See* CHUTZPA

◄**Hymie**► *n* A Jewish male • Apparently
chiefly black use : *A little curly-haired Hymie
pleading his case* [1980s+; fr the Jewish given
name *Hyman*]

hype[1] *n* **1** A hypodermic needle; hype-stick
(1913+ Narcotics) **2** An injection of narcotics (1925+ Narcotics) **3** An addict who
injects narcotics : *and heroin substitutes don't
work with a stone hype (1924+ Narcotics)* **4** A
seller of narcotics; CONNECTION : *any hype that
wants to get you hooked* [fr *hypodermic* referring to a needle or an injection]

hype[2] *n* : *without any advance PR hype* **v 1** :
*exercises no stock options, hypes no quick
secondary stock offering/ unless Margaret's
hyping the gate for a rematch (1937+)* **2**
To trick; deceive; originally, to shortchange
(1914+) **3** HYPE UP (1938+) [origin unknown; perhaps related to *hyper*, "hustle," of
obscure origin, found from the mid-1800s;
recent advertising and public relations

senses probably influenced by *hype¹* as suggesting supernormal energy, excitement, etc, and by *hyper²* and *hyperbole*; verb sense 3 supported by a 1914 glossary: *"Hyper, current among money-changers. A flimflammer"*] *See* MEDIA HYPE

hype, a *n phr* 1 A high-pressure advocacy or urging; a publicity or public relations invention : *The nostalgia for the Fifties is not entirely a media hype/ This is gonna sound like a hype (mid-1960s+)* 2 A person or thing promoted by hype *(mid-1960s+)* 3 A swindle; CON, SCAM *(1962+)*

hyped-up *adj* 1 False; fake; HOKED-UP, PHONY : *no hyped-up glamour/ the woman's archly hyped-up language (1940s+)* 2 Excited; overstimulated; HYPER : *I leave early, hyped-up, impressed, nauseated/ The game gets him "hyped up," and "releases energy" in the same way that football does (1938+)*

hyper¹ or **hype artist** *n* or *n phr* A publicist; promoter; advertiser; FLACK [1960+; fr *hype²*]

hyper² *adj* 1 Overexcited; manic; overwrought; HYPED-UP : *She tells how the grownups gave her Nembutal when she was eight years old, because "I was hyper"/ It's this flaky hyper hour/ She's a hyper-person, accustomed to constant activity (1942+)* 2 Exceeding most; very superior; : *with harem cushions, a hyper-hi-fi set, ha-ha candles (1970s+)* [fr Greek *hyper,* "super," and in the first sense probably fr medical terms like *hyperactive, hyperkinetic, hyperthyroid,* etc; in some sources this term is associated with *hipped* and *hippish,* fr *hypochondriac,* "melancholic," first found in the early 18th century] *See* THROW A FIT

hype up *v phr* 1 To fake; manufacture; invent; HOKE : *They had to hype up a convincing story* 2 To promote or advertise by blatant, obnoxious means 3 To give something a false impact, appeal, energy, etc : *other chemicals to hype up the produce and fool the buyer (1940s+)*

hypo *n* 1 A hypodermic needle 2 A hypodermic injection 3 A drug addict who injects narcotics; HYPE¹ *(1940s+ Narcotics)* *v* To stimulate or strengthen; BEEF UP : *a wilted record player hypoed by a pooped-out public address system (1960s+)* [1904+; fr *hypodermic,* referring to a needle or an injection]

I

I bet or **I'll bet** *interj* I doubt it : *You're ready to go? I'll bet* (1857+)

ice *adj* Excellent; fine; COOL (1960s+ Cool talk) *n* **1** Di-amonds; a diamond : *a two-carat hunk of ice* (1906+) **2** Gems and jewelry in general : *Gonna wear your ice?* (1906+) **3** Extra payment given for a desirable theater ticket : *a slight fee, say $100 worth of tickets for $120. The $20 is the "ice"* (1927+) **4** Protection money; bribery; PAYOFF : *syndicate that paid out $1,000,000 in ice to the police* (1948+) **5** Methamphetamine crystals (1980s+ Narcotics) *v* **1** To make something certain; CINCH, SEW something UP : *They iced the game in the ninth with two more runs* (1930s+) **2** (also **ice someone out**) To ignore someone; snub; cut; COLD SHOULDER : *how women were "iced" by peers during corridor conversations/ I've had doors closed and I've been iced out* (1836+) **3** To defeat utterly; trounce; CLOBBER : *Nebraska iced Kentucky 55 to 16* (1960s+ Sports) **4** To kill; OFF •Probably a shortening of *put on ice* : *Ice a pig. Off a pig. That means kill a cop* (1960s+ Underworld) See BREAK THE ICE, ON ICE

icebox *n* **1** A solitary confinement cell; the HOLE : *When a prisoner is sent to the "icebox"* (1920s+ Prison) **2** A prison (1920s+ Prison) **3** The imagined place where persons and things are held in reserve; ON THE BACK BURNER : *I got a left-hander in the icebox* (1940s+) **4** A very cold place : *This building's an icebox* (1940s+)

ice cream (or **snow**) **cone** *n phr* A ball that is caught but can be seen protruding from the glove or mitt; a barely caught ball (1980s+ Baseball)

iced See HAVE something CINCHED

ice maiden (or **queen**) *n phr* A very cool and composed woman; a chilly woman; iceberg : *Margaret Thatcher, the Ice Maiden, branded the conservative Gorsuch "the Ice Queen"/ Ms Stone plays Sally, a powerful woman, another ice queen whose roiling emotions remain contained* [1970s+; perhaps modeled on the title of Hans Christian Andersen's tale *The Snow Queen*]

iceman *n* **1** A jewel thief (1940s+) **2** A very calm person, performer, etc : *An iceman is a gambler who never loses his head* (1940s+) **3** A professional killer; HIRED GUN, HIT MAN : *Maybe I hadn't seen the iceman with Bobb/ Go play iceman* (1970s+ Underworld)

ice princess *modifier* *Blond, beautiful, smart, impeccably dressed, ice-princess cool and very direct* *n phr* A chilly, reserved woman; ice-

berg, ICE MAIDEN : *the travails of growing up with a politician for a father and an ice princess for a mother* (1970s+)

ice (or **put the icing on**) **the cake** *v phr* To put a victory beyond question; ensure a favorable result : *He iced the cake with a knockdown in the seventh* (1940s+)

icing on the cake *n phr* An enhancement; a bonus : *going out to dinner and a movie is icing on the cake*

ick *interj* An exclamation of disgust; GROSS, YECCH, YUCK (1948+)

icky (Variations: **ickie** or **icky-poo** or **icky-sticky** or **ickey-wickey**) *adj* **1** Overly sentimental; maudlin; SCHMALTZY : *That music pleased my icky, lachrymose sensibility/ The prose gets a mite too icky-poo for comfort* (1939+ Jive talk) **2** Unpleasant; revolting; nasty; GROSS, GRUNGY : *Those cool comedies and quizzes became dumb, boring, icky, weird/ refuse to get involved in anything outside their own little ickey-wickey bailiwicks/ The acting is icky* (1960s+) *n* A conventional, tedious person; SQUARE : *She turned out to be an icky* (1935+) [fr baby talk, "sticky, nasty"; although perhaps fr Yiddish *elken* or *iklen*, "to nauseate, revolt"]

icy *adj* Excellent; good; COOL : *The old Valley Girl terms "rad" and "icy" still describe the very cool* (1980s+ Teenagers)

idea See WHAT'S THE BIG IDEA

idiot box *n phr* A television set; television; the BOOB TUBE (1959+)

idiot light *n phr* A usu red light on a car's dashboard that glows to announce some sort of fact, such as the discharge of a battery, overheating, etc : *replaced by too-late-to-react idiot lights* (1968+)

-ie (also **-ey** or **-y** or **-sie** or **-sey** or **-sy**) *suffix used to form adjectives* Having the quality indicated : *comfy/ creepy/ swanky* *suffix used to form nouns* **1** Diminutive, affectionate, or familiar versions of what is indicated : *auntie/ cubby/ thingy/ tootsie/ folksy* **2** Coming from the place or background indicated : *Arky/ Okie/ Yalie* **3** A person of the sort indicated : *weirdie/ hippy/ sharpy*

iffy *adj* **1** Uncertain; doubtful; improbable : *His chances were a bit iffy/ Would the DA take the case, knowing the chances of a conviction would be iffy?* **2** DICEY (1937+)

-ific or **-iffic** *suffix used to form adjectives* Extremely marked by what is indicated : *horrific/ beautific* [fr *terrific*]

if I had a nickel (or **dime**) **for every time something happens** *adv clause* A somewhat

265

rueful complaint about the frequency of the named event : *If I had a nickel for every time I'm called homophobic, I could buy New York* (1970s+)

if it ain't broke, don't fix it *sentence* If it is functioning, don't meddle; leave well enough alone : *The economy ain't broke, so don't fix it* (1970s+)

if looks could kill *adv clause* The extreme fanciful gauge of a disapproving look : *If looks could kill, she would have been guilty of my murder* (1922+)

If the shoe fits, wear it *sentence* If the statement applies to you, admit it or do something about it

if you can't stand the heat, stay out of the kitchen *sentence* Do not undertake a hard job if you lack the stamina and thick skin to endure sharp criticism [1940s+; a favorite saying of President Harry S Truman, referring to the presidency]

I kid you not *sentence* I am perfectly serious; I am not misleading nor joking with you : *There were daily departures of a yacht called, I kid you not, the* Alter Ego/ *It's rough out there, I kid you not* [1950s+; popularized by the television comedian Jack Paar]

ill *adj* 1 Arrested or detained on suspicion; jailed (1960s+ *Underworld*) 2 Very good; excellent; COOL : *Ill: very good or bad* (1980s+ *Black teenagers*) 3 Very bad : *Ill: very good or bad* (1980s+ *Black teenagers*)

I'll be damned *sentence* (Variations: **danged** or **darned** or **ding swizzled** or **dipped** or ◄**dipped in shit**► or ◄**fucked**► or **jiggered** or **jigswiggered** or **hanged** or **hornswoggled** or **a monkey's uncle** or **switched** may replace **damned**; **damned** may also be omitted) May I be maltreated, confounded, accursed, etc; an exclamation of surprise or determination : *I'll be damned, we made it!/ I will be dipped in shit/ I'll be a monkey's uncle if you put that over on me!/ Well I'll be, he made it!* [entry form 1920s+, *ding swizzled* 1940s+, *dipped* 1940s+, *jiggered* 1837+; *dipped* forms fr 1600s British *be dipped* or *dipped in wing*, "get into trouble; be defeated"]

I'll drink to that *sentence* I agree; you are quite right; I approve (1960s+)

I'll eat my hat *sentence* I am absolutely convinced that a given statement is true, a named event will occur, etc : *I'll eat my hat if he doesn't come back tomorrow* (1837+)

I love it *sentence* Believe it or not : *They want to search us on the way out. I love it* (1990s+)

I may be stupid, but I'm not dumb *sentence* : *From a distance, Brett looked as if he would run right over McClelland, but the umpire stands 6 foot 6, weighs 250 pounds, has protective equipment on and is holding a bat in his hand.*

As Brett said, "I'm stupid, but I'm not dumb" (1990s+)

IMHO *adv phr* In my humble opinion : *The roast quail with polenta was dynamite, IMHO* (1990s+ *Computer network*)

I'm outta or **outa here** *sentence* I am leaving now : *If it gets into blamin' me or stuff like that, I'm outta here/ "So what are you going to do?" "I'm outa here"* (1984+)

I'm sideways *sentence* I'M OUTA HERE (1990s+ *Teenagers*)

I'm there *sentence* I am ready and willing to go someplace; your invitation is accepted : *Cubs game? I'm there*

in *adj* 1 In fashion at the moment; now preferred : *Violence is in, sentiment is out* (1960+) 2 Accepted; acceptable; belonging to a select group; IN LIKE FLYNN : *one of the in people/ Bullock made it to the "in" crowd a few years later* (1960+) *n* 1 An advantage, esp through an acquaintance; entree : *Get me an in with the skipper of that precinct* (1920s+ *Underworld*) 2 A person who holds office or other power or position : *Will the Democrats ever be the ins again?* (1768+) *See* GET IN, HAVE IT IN FOR someone

-in *combining word* A communal occasion where one does what is indicated : *be-in/ lie-in/ love-in/ pray-in* (1960s+)

in a bad way *adj phr* In great difficulty; badly damaged or injured : *I'm afraid our poor friend is in a very bad way after the wreck* (1809+)

in a big way *adv phr* Very much; extremely : *The soldiers went for pin-ups in a big way* (1903+)

in a bind (or **box**) *adj phr* In a very tight and awkward situation; stalled by a dilemma; IN A BOX : *I'm in a bind, damned if I do and damned if I don't* [1940s+ *Loggers*; fr the situation of a logger whose saw is caught and held tight by the weight of a tree or branch]

in a box *adv phr* In an awkward situation; IN A BIND : *No, and don't put me in a box* [1913+; the related and perhaps original sense "short of money" is found by 1891] *See* GO HOME FEET FIRST

in a bucket *See* FOR CRYING OUT LOUD

in a fix *adv phr* In difficulty; in a tight spot : *under a cloud, up a tree, quisby, done up, sold up, in a fix* (1837+)

in a fog (or **haze**) *adj phr* In a dazed, disoriented, confused state; inattentive : *He was so tired he was walking around in a haze* (1888+)

in a funk *adj phr* Depressed; melancholy : *Steve's been in a funk since he lost his dog* *adv phr* In a depressed, nervous, or frightened state : *Jackson left San Francisco in a funk, he looked tired and sounded like a morose, defeated candidate* (1743+ *British*)

in a holding pattern *adv phr* In abeyance; not in an active status; ON THE BACK BURNER [1950s+; fr the aviation term, found by 1948, for airplanes that are flying a prescribed circling route while awaiting clearance to land]

in a hole *adj phr* In grave and probably insurmountable difficulties; UP SHIT CREEK : *The death of my brother leaves me in a deep legal-financial hole* (1762+)

in a huff *adj phr* Angry; petulant; grumpy [1694+; fr a *huff* or gust of anger]

in a jam *adj phr* In trouble, esp serious trouble : *If you're in a jam, he'll fight for you* (1914+)

in a jif(fy) *See* JIFFY

in a lather (or lava) *adj phr* Angry; upset; IN A SWEAT : *this business of your being in a lather about it/ The editors say they are not in a lava over the coincidence* [1828+; fr the resemblance between an agitated sweat, esp the frothy sweat of horses, and frothy washing lather thought of as the result of vigorous agitation; found by 1660 in the form *lavour*]

◁**in-and-out** or **in-out**▷ *n* The sex act; copulation; FUCKING : *The pages of romances offered less in-and-out than a downtown parking garage/ Her refreshing answers about the old in-and-out bluntly demystified any last glitches/ the endlessly hypnotic spectacle of the old in-out* [first form 1620+; fr the 1600s idiom *play at in-and-out*, "do the sex act, copulate"]

in an uproar *See* NOT GET one's BALLS IN AN UPROAR

in a pickle *adj phr* In a disagreeable situation; in a sad predicament : *Today I find myself in a pickle, bind, and jam* (1585+)

◁**in a pig's eye**▷ (or **ass** or **asshole** or **ear**) *adv phr* Not at all; never; LIKE HELL • Used for vehement denial : *In a pig's ass, I did/ Yeah, we'll get it back. In a pig's eye/ In a pig's asshole!*

in a pinch *adv phr* **1** If necessary; if need be : *In a pinch we could make that do* **2** IN A JAM (1903+)

in a poke *See* BUY A PIG IN A POKE

in a row *See* HAVE one's DUCKS IN A ROW

in a spot *modifier* In a difficult position or situation (1929+)

in a state *adj phr* **1** Agitated; upset; tense : *She got home and found her husband in a state* (1837+) **2** Untidy; disheveled; chaotic : *I'm afraid my room's in a state* (1879+)

in a stew *adj phr* **1** Chaotic and muddled; in disarray : *The whole place is in a stew about the new appointment* **2** Angry and irritable; upset; IN A SWEAT : *Well don't get in such a stew about it* (1809+)

in a sweat *adj phr* Upset; irritated; tense; scared : *Don't get in a sweat, I'll return it at once* (1753+)

in a tailspin *adj phr* Dangerously out of control : *I knew he'd be upset, but he's gone into a tail spin over this* [1928+; fr the downward spinning of an airplane, for which the term is found by 1917]

in a tizzy *adj phr* Very much upset; distractingly disturbed; in a state : *I have been in a tizzy since reading his accusations* [1935+; origin unknown]

in at (or for) the kill *adv phr* Participating in the finish of something, esp when it is very satisfying and vindictive : *Tell me when the thing'll be signed, I want to be in at the kill* [1814+; fr a fox-hunting term]

in a walk *See* WIN IN A WALK

in a zone *adj phr* Daydreaming, esp from narcotics; SPACED-OUT [1970s+; said to be fr *ozone*, implying very high up in the sky or toward outer space]

in bad *adj phr* In difficulty; embroiled : *When did you get in bad with the cops?* (1911+)

in bed with someone (or **in bed together**) *adj phr* In close association with; on good terms with : *Lefcourt, who was in bed with the mob, as you know* (1970s+)

in one's book *adv phr* In my opinion; as I believe : *"Is he a competent investigator?" "In my book?"* (1964+)

in business *adj phr* In operation; under way : *One more day or so of prep and we're in business/ The space shuttle is finally in business* (1950s+)

in cahoots *adj phr* In partnership; acting in a common purpose : *Louise Peccoralo and her husband claim they were not in cahoots with William Perone of Arizona* [1829+; origin uncertain; perhaps fr French *cahute*, "cabin"]

in clover *adv phr* In a position of ease and affluence; HAPPY AS A CLAM (1710+)

include one **out** *v phr* To exclude one : *Counties began asking the DNR to include them out* [1937+; said to have been uttered by the movie mogul Samuel Goldwyn upon resigning from the Hays organization that monitored Hollywood films for moral content]

in cold blood *modifier* Without feeling; also, with cruelness : *shot down the idea in cold blood*

in cold storage (or **the deep freeze**) *adv phr* Held in abeyance; reserved to be dealt with later; ON HOLD, ON THE BACK BURNER : *The plan's in cold storage for now/ Well, let's just keep that one in the deep freeze for a few months* (1940s+)

in concrete or **cement** *adj phr* Firmly set; fixed and determined : *The most recent thing I heard is 45 days to two months, but nothing's in concrete/ The President seems to be in cement* (1960s+)

indeedy *adv* Indeed; certainly : *No, indeedy* (*1856+*)

in deep ◁**doo-doo** (or **shit**)▷ *n phr* Very serious trouble : *He was in deep shit with Big Lou/ Boy, is your ass in deep shit* (*1970s+*)

in deep water *adv phr* In a difficult situation, esp where one is not fitted to cope; out of one's depth (*1861+*)

Indians *See* TOO MANY CHIEFS AND NOT ENOUGH INDIANS

indie *adj* Playing indie rock : *Really they're just five soft-spoken indie prepsters who happen to rule nice-kid noise pop* (*1990s+*) *modifier* : *one indie pic company n* An independent, esp an independent movie producer (*1928+ Movie studio*)

indie rock *modifier* : *its purposeful indie-rock slag at commerciality/ Stars of the indie-rock scene dig into formidable pop catalogue n phr* A kind of rock music of no particular style but of the small-company, college radio, etc, milieu (*1990s+*) [fr *indie*, "independent," for the relatively small companies and labels involved]

indigo *n* A kind of marijuana (*1990s+ Narcotics*)

industrial *adj* **1** Very masculine; manly; MACHO, STUDLY : *If you can get a date with Bambi, you'll be so industrial, dude!* (*1980s+ Students*) **2** INDUSTRIAL-STRENGTH : *an industrial dose of Thorazine* (*1980s+*) *modifier* : *and the harsh industrial pop of Nine Inch Nails n* A variety of rock music : *industrial music is "the sounds our culture makes as it comes unglued"* (*1990s+*)

industrial-strength *adj* Powerful, sturdy, weighty, etc, as if fit for use in industry; heavy-duty : *drinking a cup of industrial-strength coffee out of a pig-shaped mug/ industrial-strength smog/ ripe for heavy, industrial-strength investigation* [*1980s+*; the descriptive and advertising term is found by about 1920]

in Dutch *adj phr* In disfavor; in trouble : *You have to promise, Pop, not to get me in Dutch with Mrs Skoglund* [*1912+*; origin uncertain; perhaps fr bookmaking; *Dutch book,* "a bad risk with a bookmaker," is found by 1915]

Indy or **Indy 500,** the *n phr* The annual Indianapolis 500 car race (*1960s+*)

in one's ear *See* STAND AROUND WITH one's FINGER UP one's ASS, STICK IT

in one's face *adj phr* Irritating; pestering : *he's in my face about more new ideas*

in fine feather *modifier* In good form or well-dressed; also, in excellent spirits or condition : *in fine feather today*

in flames *See* GO DOWN IN FLAMES

info *n* Information; POOP : *I can slip you the info* (*1906+*)

infobahn *n* The Information Superhighway, a projected system of linked computer networks; i-way : *Walt is already ahead of everyone on the Infobahn* [*1990s+*; fr *info* plus *bahn,* fr German *Autobahn,* "multilane automobile highway"]

infomercial *n* A television program that tells or teaches something and is also advertising a product : *has been doing infomercials, a Taco Bell ad/ Infomercials got their initial boost in 1984, when the FCC freed local stations from limits on the amount of commercial time they could air* [*1983+*; fr *information* plus *commercial*]

in for it *adj phr* Committed willy-nilly; about to suffer trouble, attack, etc : *When they saw the black clouds they knew they were in for it/ If they nab us with the pope's ring, we'll really be in for it* (*1698+*)

infotainment *n* Televisions programs that teach while entertaining : *"infotainment," an information-entertainment program* [*1983+*; fr *information + entertainment*]

in front *See* UP FRONT

in God's name *See* the HELL

in-group *n phr* An exclusive group or clique, esp of influential persons (*1907+*)

in someone's hair *adj phr* Constantly annoying; nagging at : *You'll have one of these professors in your hair* (*1851+*)

inhale *v* To eat or drink, esp rapidly : *I inhaled my lunch because I didn't have much time to eat* (*1924+*) *See* FRENCH-INHALE

in harness *adj phr* Working; actively employed rather than resting, retired, on holiday, etc : *He didn't know how to relax after all those years in harness* (*1875+*)

in heat *See* BITCH IN HEAT

in heck *See* the HECK

in hell *See* the HELL

in high (or **tall**) **cotton** *adj phr* Happy; pleased; fortunate; FAT, dumb, AND HAPPY : *We're in high cotton tonight to have with us Mr Big/ would greet them from this office, this desk, this chair, high and dry in tall cotton* [*1920s+* Southern; fr the double fact that the crop is well developed and is easier to pick because the picker need not stoop over]

in high gear *adj phr* In the most active, rapid, impressive phase; at full tempo : *The advertising campaign is in high gear* (*1940s+*) *See* SHIFT INTO HIGH GEAR

in hock *adj phr* **1** Accepted for pawn; in a pawnshop **2** In debt; mortgaged : *We're deeply in hock to the bank* (*1883+*) *See* HOCK[1]

in hot water *adv phr* **1** In trouble, esp with the law, one's superiors, etc : *I'm in hot water with the cops again* **2** In difficulties, esp in serious trouble; IN THE SOUP : *I got you in some hot water with the boss* (*1765+*)

ink *n* **1** Coffee *(1940s+ Hoboes)* **2** Cheap, often red, wine : *a cheap local "ink" (1930s+ Black)* ◄**3**► A black person *(1940s+)* **4** Press notices; print publicity : *New York Day's got lots more ink than Paul will get for his memoir/ NBC thought it might as well hang onto the one show that was getting good ink (1980s+)* **5** Tattoos in general; the amount of tattooing on someone's body : *the ink on those college basketball players* **v** To write; sign, esp a contract : *He also inked the plays/ has inked to helm two more pictures (1940+) See* RED INK

ink-slinger *n* **1** A writer; author; newspaper reporter or writer **2** A clerk; office worker *(1900s+ Lumberjacks, cowboys & hoboes) (1877+)*

in like *adv* To like someone romantically, be fond of • A take on *in love* : *in like with the boy in study hall/ The teenagers are completely in like with each other*

in like Flynn *adj phr* Accepted; acceptable; belonging to a select group; IN : *"Are you in or out right now?" "I'm in like Flynn. Didn't you notice the picture on my desk?"* [1940s+, perhaps fr US Army Air Corps; origin uncertain; perhaps merely a rhyming phrase; perhaps associated with the sexual and other exploits of the actor Errol *Flynn*]

in line *adj phr* **1** Within appropriate bounds; acceptable; IN THE BALLPARK : *Yes, those prices are about in line* **2** Behaving properly; out of trouble : *Can't you keep your kids in line? (1920s+)*

in line for *adv phr* In position to get; about to get : *Hey, you're in line for a big bonus (1940s+)*

in living color *adj phr* Displayed with complete accuracy and lifelike tones : *The rules and rituals of life inside IBM are all here, and in living color: the army of lawyers, tangle of procedures and endless slide presentations (1990s+)*

in luck *adj phr* Lucky [1857+; the opposite of earlier *out of luck*]

in mothballs *adj phr* In reserve; ON ICE *(late 1940s+)*

innards *n* **1** The viscera; GUTS, INSIDES, KISHKES : *got a feeling in my innards it won't work (1825+)* **2** The inner parts or workings; INSIDES : *Let's look at the innards of this gizmo and see what's going on (1921+)*

innie *modifier* : *a tidy innie belly button/ I suspect that the Cardinal arts editor has an outie belly button, and I have an innie belly button* **n** A concave navel *(1980s+)* [probably a children's term]

in nothing (or no time) flat *adv phr* Very quickly : *When I heard the signal, I got over there in nothing flat (1940s+)*

-ino *See* -ERINO

in on (the act) *adv* Involved in what is going on : *I'm in on the deal/ in on the act with James*

in one piece *See* ALL IN ONE PIECE

in on the ground floor *adv phr* Engaged early and profitably in a project, investment, etc : *You better act now if you want to be in on the ground floor (1872+)*

in orbit *adj phr* Having a free and exhilarating experience; HIGH, WAY OUT : *One slurp of gin and he's in orbit (1960s+ Teenagers)*

in over (or above) one's head *adv phr* In a situation one cannot cope with; helplessly committed and likely to lose : *He tried to stop, but he was in over his head (1622+)*

in one's pants *See* ANTS

in play *adv* Actively going on; being played or executed : *the ball's in play so stay off the sideline/ stock deals in play*

in someone's pocket or **hip pocket** *adv phr* Under someone's absolute control : *Don't worry, I have him in my pocket/ He's in the hip pocket of the networks (1940s+)*

in rare form *adv* At one's best : *She's in rare form after working 10 hours*

inside *adv* In prison *(1888+ Prison) See* ON THE INSIDE

inside dope *n phr* The privileged information; inside story : *want the inside dope on the apartment*

inside job *n phr* A robbery, stroke of espionage, etc, done by someone or with the aid of someone within the target organization : *The cops think the hotel murder is an inside job (1908+)*

insider *n* A person who has special knowledge, authority, etc, because he is within or part of some privileged group : *The insiders are saying that the President will veto it (1850+)*

insides *n* INNARDS

inside skinny *n phr* by 1972 The confidential and little-known truth : *This guy gave us the inside skinny on Prozac See* SKINNY

inside the Beltway *adv phr* In US government and other Washington circles : *You don't know this yet, but it's an old story inside the Beltway (1980s+)*

inside track, the *See* HAVE THE INSIDE TRACK

in one's sleep *adv phr* Very easily : *There's a lot of prose so negligent that Mr. Leithauser could have written it in his sleep (1953+)*

insource *v* To assign a task or job internally rather than farm it to an outside vendor

in spades *adv phr* To the utmost; in the highest degree : *What Aleksandr Solzhenitsyn did for the Gulag he has now done in spades for the Soviet Union as a whole/ I detest them right back, in spades (1929+)*

instant replay *n phr* Immediate repetition and additional judgment : *If anyone mistakes the new regimen for freedom, the full trappings of*

martial law remain available for instant replay
[1970s+; fr the re-viewing of a sports play
on television, sometimes in order to confirm
or change an official's call]

in stitches *adv* Laughing very hard (*1935+*)

in sync (or **synch**) *adv phr* In order; in harmony; synchronized; without jar or clash : *to
bring the author back into sync with his existentialist colleagues/ perfectly in sync with
Thicke's outrageous style* [1940s+; fr *in synchronism*, used in radio, television, etc, to
express exact matching and timing between
audio and video]

inta *See* INTO

intense *adj* Excellent; COOL (*1970s+ Teenagers*)

internal *See* BODY PACKER

in the air *See* a BEAR IN THE AIR

in the altogether *adj phr* Naked (*1894+*)

in the bag *adj phr* **1** Certain; sure; ON ICE : *It's in
the bag. The fix is in* (*1926+*) **2** Ruined; destroyed; FINISHED, KAPUT, OUT OF THE BOX : *If an
actor is hurt or killed doing a stunt the whole
film is in the bag* (*1970s+*) [fr game shot and
stuffed *into the game bag*; second sense fr the
use of the heavy plastic body bag for the
handling of military and other casualties]
See HALF IN THE BAG

in the ballpark *adj phr* Within general appropriate limits; not exorbitant, outrageous,
etc : *react to an analyst's estimate by telling
him whether it is too high, too low, or "in the
ballpark"* (*1968+*)

in the barrel *adj phr* Without money; BROKE : *A
red hot pimp like you ain't got no business being
in the barrel* [1940s+ Black; fr the archetypal
image of a destitute man who wears a *barrel*
for clothing]

in the belly of the beast *adv phr* In an extremely difficult plight; beleaguered : *Esa-
Pekka Salonen is in the belly of the beast. The
brilliant young Finnish conductor has begun his
third season as music director of the Los Angeles
Philharmonic* [1990s+; perhaps an allusion
to the plight of Jonah, swallowed by a great
fish]

in the black *adj phr* Profitable; solvent; not in
debt : *We toyed with bankruptcy for a while,
but now we're in the black* [1928+; fr the color
of ink traditionally used by bookkeepers to
record assets, profits, etc]

in the boat *See* MAN IN THE BOAT

in the bubble *adj* In winning form; playing very well; IN THE ZONE, ON A ROLL [mid-
1980s+ Sports; said to have been the reply
of basketball player Julius Erving when he
was asked what a winning streak felt like]

in the bucks *adj phr* Having money, esp a lot
of it; in funds; FLUSH, LOADED : *right after
Christmas and we're not in the bucks* (*1920s+*)

in the buff *adj phr* Naked; BARE-ASS, BUCK NAKED,
IN THE ALTOGETHER : *There we stood, in the buff
and abysmally embarrassed* [1960s+; *in buff*,
"in the bare skin," is found by 1602]

in the can *adj phr* Successfully finished; ready
for release, consumption, etc [1940s+
Movie studio; fr the large, flat, circular tin
can into which finished movie film is put]

in the cards *adj phr* Very probable; likely to or
about to happen : *Another tax cut is in the
cards* (*1936+*)

in the catbird seat *See* SIT IN THE CATBIRD SEAT

in the chips *adj phr* Having money; affluent;
FLUSH, LOADED [1938+; *chips*, "money," is
found by 1859]

in the clear *adj phr* Apparently not involved;
not suspected of wrongdoing; CLEAN : *After
thorough investigation they declared him in the
clear* (*1901+*)

in the clutch *adv phr* At the moment when
heroic performance under pressure is needed : *He's a good one to have around in the clutch*
[1920s+; probably a baseball term originally]

in the coop *adj phr* Sleeping on the job; off
duty for unauthorized rest : *The cruise car for
that street was supposed to be in the coop*
(*1960s+ Police*)

in the cross-hairs *adv phr* Fixed as a target;
aimed at : *Detroit's Big Three found themselves
again in the media cross hairs* [1884+; the
date shows the earliest use of the term for a
telescope or telescopic sight indicator]

in the cut *adj phr* Relaxed; calm; COOL, LAID
BACK [1990s+ Street talk; perhaps fr the
confidence of one who *makes the cut*; perhaps
a version of *in the* (or *a*) *groove*]

in the dark *adj phr* **1** Uninformed; ignorant;
uncognizant : *We'll keep 'em in the dark about
this until the time is right* **2** Mystified; puzzled
: *You maybe told me, but I'm still sort of in the
dark* (*1901+*)

in the (or **a**) **doghouse** *adj phr* In a position or
status of obloquy; out of favor, esp temporarily : *The press secretary is in the doghouse
for cussing out a reporter/ He was in a doghouse
at home on account of coming home cockeyed on
his wedding anniversary* (*1932+*)

in the driver's (or **buddy**) **seat** *adj phr* In the
position of authority; in control : *With that
kind of vote, we're in the driver's seat/ You
don't make it very easy, do you? Always in the
driver's seat*

in the dumper *adj phr* **1** Bankrupt; ruined;
insolvent; in the tub **2** Lost; irretrievably
forfeited or taken away : *Fifteen years plus,
and his pension, in the dumper* (*1970s+*)

in the face *See* a SLAP IN THE FACE, TILL one IS BLUE
IN THE FACE

in the family way (also **in that way, in a way**) *modifier* Pregnant • Euphemistic : *had got them in the family way* (1740s+)

in the flesh *adj phr* : *an in-the-flesh presentation* *adv phr* In person; in propria persona : *The great movie star appeared there in the flesh* [1865+; an allusion to the corporeal resurrection of Jesus]

in the foot *See* SHOOT oneself IN THE FOOT

in the groove *adj phr* **1** Making good sense; saying what needs saying : *Right! You're in the groove now* **2** In good form; working smoothly and well : *The professor of Classics was, as she would have put it, "in canaliculo," in the groove* **3** Playing well and excitingly; HEP (Jive musicians) (1930s+ Jive talk)

in the gutter *See* HAVE one's MIND IN THE GUTTER

in the hay *adv phr* In bed, either sleeping or cavorting : *Joe's in the hay, zonked out/ a toss in the hay with her boss* [1940s+; probably fr hit the hay, found by 1912]

in the hole *adv phr* **1** Dealt face down, in stud poker : *What's he got in the hole?* (1915+ Poker) **2** In debt : *He is in the hole to the tune of $9,000* (1890+) *See* ACE IN THE HOLE

in the hopper *See* IN THE PIPELINE

in the hot seat *See* ON THE HOT SEAT

in the know *adj phr* Well informed, esp having current, advance, or confidential information : *Those in the know tell me to sell* (1902+)

in the life *adj phr* Occupied or engaged in some specialized and usu socially despised way of living, such as the homosexual subculture or prostitution : *By the time strippers are "in the life" they have developed an exploitative attitude to men and people in general* (1970s+)

in the long run *adv phr* After a long period of time, trial, endurance, etc : *It looks grim now, but in the long run you'll see it'll get better* [1768+; the form *at the long run* is found by 1627]

in the loop *adv phr* **1** In a select company, esp in the communicating circle of the powerful : *no force in the administration, observes simply, "He's not in the loop"/ Sometimes they are not even "in the loop" to get important information* **2** Being circulated and processed; IN THE PIPELINE : *It's in the loop now, and who knows when I'll get it back* [1980s+; probably an alteration of the military idiom *in the net*, of the same meaning, fr the use of radio *nets* or communications nexuses that include or exclude certain headquarters]

in the money *adj phr* Having money, esp in large amounts; IN THE BUCKS, FLUSH : *I'm in the money at last* (1902+) *adv phr* Providing winnings to bettors : *None of his horses finished in the money today at the track* (1928+ Gambling & horse racing)

in the mud *See* STICK IN THE MUD

in the paint *adv phr* The area of a basketball court extending from the basket to the three-point line, hence the site of most action : *"In the Paint" refers to being in the center of the action of a basketball game/ who can crash the boards, feed and run the break, wheel and deal in the paint, and shoot from the three-point range* [1990s+ Basketball; fr the fact that it is often painted a different color from the rest of the floor]

in the picture *adj phr* Probable; distinctly conceivable : *It just isn't in the picture that they'll get married/ I'd like to travel, but it doesn't seem like it's in the picture for a year or so* (1923+) *adv phr* In a position to understand what is happening; in an informed position : *OK, now that you're one of us, I want you in the picture* (1900+) *See* PUT someone IN THE PICTURE

in the pink *adj phr* In good health; ruddy and in fine fettle (1914+)

in the pipeline *adj phr* (also **in the hopper** or **in the works**) Being prepared, processed, or worked on; ON THE FIRE : *almost 10 times that amount in infrastructure projects were in the pipeline/ We got a little gizmo in the works that'll give them a duck-fit* (1955+) *adv phr* Riding inside the curled-over front of a wave (1963+ Surfers)

in the raw *adj phr* **1** Naked; IN THE BUFF : *Leonotra always liked sleeping "in the raw," as she called it* **2** Without amenity or polish; relatively crude and primitive : *Up there they lived life in the raw/ His work is sculpture in the raw* (1930s+)

in there *adv phr* **1** IN THERE PITCHING **2** Pitched across home plate for a strike (Baseball) (1940s+) *See* HANG IN

in the red *adj phr* In debt; losing money; insolvent : *The huge corporation has been in the red for eight years* [1926+; fr the color of ink traditionally used by bookkeepers to record debts, losses, etc]

in there pitching *adv phr* (also **in there** or **right there** or **right in there**) Making a great effort; coping energetically and successfully; ON TOP OF : *I'm on the go night and day, and I'm in there pitching/ When they needed a strong guide, he was in there* (1940s+)

in the ring *See* THROW one's HAT IN THE RING

in the sack *adv phr* Doing the sex act; making love : *Like Kirkland's book, Tharp's even includes a discussion of what Baryshnikov is like in the sack* (1960s+)

in the saddle *adv phr* **1** In a controlling position; in charge : *I see old Wilcox is in the saddle again* (1738+) **2** On duty; working; IN HARNESS : *on duty since six that morning. Close* *to eighteen hours in the saddle (1940s+)* **3** Doing the sex act; in flagrante : *Maybe Caroline caught old Bailey in the saddle up there (1940s+)*

in the same boat *adv phr* Equally sharing a situation, plight, etc : *City, country, slum, farm, we're all in the same boat (1550+)*

in the soup (or **<the shit>**) *adv phr* In trouble; in peril; IN DEEP DOO-DOO : *He'd better clear this one fast or he's in the soup/ Maybe that's why I'm in this soup to begin with/ Jeeves cocks an eyebrow, and Bertie knows he's in the soup (first form 1888+, second mid-1800s+)*

in the spotlight *adj phr* Singled out for close attention; prominent : *He was a public figure, but hated being in the spotlight (1904+)*

in the tank *adv phr* Woefully ineffectual; inept; LAME : *The Rockies are in the tank; they have lost twelve games in a row* [1990s+; a 1930s sports sense was "losing games or fights intentionally"] *See* GO INTO THE TANK, TANK

in the toilet *adj phr* In very dire straits; standing a clear last : *Thirty-one years ago, when the Mets were really in the toilet, sportswriters rallied New Yorkers by touting the Mets' incompetence as symbolic of underdog struggle (1980s+)*

in the tooth *See* LONG IN THE TOOTH

in the trenches *adv phr* In the workplace; in contact with the people or problems in a situation; unprotected by distance or illusion : *I needed to be back in the trenches where I could really relate to a community/ More retrospective accounts are elegant and noble. Watson told it like it was in the trenches (1970s+)*

in the water *See* DEAD IN THE WATER

in the wind *See* TWIST SLOWLY IN THE WIND

in the woods *See* DOES A BEAR SHIT IN THE WOODS

in the works *See* IN THE PIPELINE

in the wrong *adj phr* Mistaken; wrong; erring : *He's usually in the wrong when he discusses music* **adv phr** In an unfavorable light or position : *This guy is always putting me in the wrong (1400+)*

in the zone *adj phr* (also **zoned**) Playing easily and spontaneously : *Just that one time, I was in the zone/ She is zoned in the second set (1980s+ Tennis)*

into or **inta** (IN tōō, IN tōō, IN tə) *prep* Currently interested in; now practicing or absorbed in : *a former Ivy Leaguer named Crimpcut who is into Buddha/ Cool it, woman, I'm inta my thang/ if you're into Chinese cuisine (1960s+)*

into oneself *adj phr* Absorbed; introspective : *If a bear appears when you are into yourself (1990s+)*

into someone for *adj phr* In debt to; owing, esp money : *The guy's into me for five grand! (1970s+)*

into the ground *See* RUN something INTO THE GROUND

in tow *adv* Carried along; joining : *with a huge bag in tow/ baby in tow (1896+)*

in transition *adj phr* Unemployed; AT LIBERTY : *in transition: A many-headed euphemism read: unemployed (1990s+)*

intro *n* An introduction or prelude of any sort : *"Listen to that intro," she says. "How awful"/ the kind of intro which is important* **v** : *Who'll intro the archbishop? (1923+)*

in two (or **three**) **shakes of a lamb's tail** *modifier* Very quickly or fast; in a minute (1816+)

invent the wheel *v phr* To labor unnecessarily through the obvious and elementary stages of something : *Hey, cut to the chase! You don't have to invent the wheel*

invitation *See* DO YOU WANT AN ENGRAVED INVITATION

invite (IN vīt) *n* An invitation : *You can't go in there without an invite (1615+)*

in-your-face *adj* Confrontational; hostile; impudent; SASSY : *We're just playing in-your-face football, and we feel we can stand up to anybody/ verbal mud-wallowing that proudly wears its in-your-face machismo smut/ takes its title from "Seasons in the Sun," which is as in-your-face as it gets (1980s+)*

I only (or **just**) **work here** *sentence* I can't answer your question; I don't know what is going on, even though I probably should (1950s+)

IOU (pronounced as separate letters) *n* A promise to pay; written acknowledgment of a debt : *had won $800,000, in cash, not IOUs (1618+)*

<Irish confetti> *n phr* Bricks, stones, blocks thrown in an altercation (1935+)

iron *n* **1** A motorcycle; motorcycles collectively; bike, SCOOT : *competing on old British and American iron (1920s+ Motorcyclists)* **2** A car : *On this big piece of German iron there's a bumper sticker (1935+)* **3** A firearm, esp a pistol; SHOOTING IRON (1775+) **4** The weights used in weightlifting (1972+) *See* HAVE BRASS BALLS, HOT IRON, PUMP IRON, SHOOTING IRON

iron-fisted *adj* Having a fist or grip strong as iron : *The company appears to have iron-fisted control of the market (1828+)*

iron out *v phr* **1** To kill, esp with a gun, an "iron" : *You weren't at home when he was ironed out* **2** To arrange satisfactorily; straighten out; WORK OUT : *Ironing out the kinks this way made them aware of just how weak their endgame was (1920s+)*

ish kabibble (ISH kə BIB əl) *interj* An exclamation of indifference, nonchalance, etc : *"Ishkabibble," or "I should worry"/ It was a pretty abrupt transition from la belle époque into the Space Age, but ish kabibble* [1921+; origin unknown; perhaps an alteration of Yiddish *nit* or *nisht gefidlt;* apparently introduced and perhaps coined by the comedienne Fanny Brice]

issue *n* A problem • Colloquial : *We have an issue with irregular newspaper delivery*

Is the Pope Polish (or Italian or Catholic) *sentence* That was a stupid question; isn't the answer very obvious? DOES A BEAR SHIT IN THE WOODS [1970s+; first variant used since the accession of John Paul II]

it *modifier* : *Clara Bow, the original it girl n* **1** Sex appeal, esp female : *a girl with lots of it* (1904+) **2** The sex act; copulation; SCREWING • Used in numberless unmistakable but quasi-euphemistic contexts like *do it, go at it, want it, have it off, make it,* etc (1611+) *See* IT GIRL

it ain't over till it's over *sentence* Don't give up hope; the decision is not yet made : *It ain't over 'til it's over. So reason America's steelmakers, who began a broad campaign last week to reverse recent tariff rulings* [1970s+; fr a heartening observation by the New York Yankees catcher and manager Yogi Berra]

itch *See* SCRATCH

itchy *adj* Eager; restless; ANTSY (1940s+)

itchy feet *n phr* The desire to travel : *been six months, getting itchy feet* (1943+)

it couldn't happen to a nicer guy *sentence* What punishment or damage was received was richly deserved • The sentiment is quite ironic : *Joe got canned? It couldn't happen to a nicer guy!* (1940s+)

item *See* HOT NUMBER

item, an *n phr* An unmarried but sexually linked couple; a NUMBER : *Book Says Ava and Adlai Were An Item/ Carolyn and Larren used to be an item a long time ago* [1970+; probably a shortening of "an *item* in the gossip columns"]

it girl *n phr* A young woman with sex appeal (1920s+)

-itis *suffix used to form nouns* An excessive and probably unhealthy involvement with or prevalence of what is indicated : *committeeitis/ symbolitis* (1903+)

it is dollars to doughnuts *See* DOLLARS TO DOUGHNUTS

it rules *sentence* It is wonderful, impressive, awesome (1980s+ Teenagers)

it's a bitch (or bitch kitty) *sentence* The thing referred to is very impressive, very difficult, very complicated, very sad, or in some other way extraordinary : *She shook his knee playfully. "It's a bitch, isn't it?"/ The last couple of laps are a real bitch kitty* (1814+)

it's all good *sentence* Everything is fine; there is nothing to worry about : *the meaning of "It's all good" is straightforward. It means "no worries"*

◁**it's one's ass**▷ *sentence* One is doomed, or in great difficulty; one's ASS IS GRASS • Usu a conditional statement : *But I lend you my iron and it's my ass/ You write anything about me in an article again and it'll be your ass/ We have to find this outlaw an hour after daybreak or it's our asses!* (1940s+ Army)

it's at *See* KNOW WHERE IT'S AT

it's been real or **it's been** *sentence* It has been nice to meet you; it has been a nice time or party, etc • Often used ironically (1950s+)

it shouldn't happen to a dog *sentence* What has happened, often to the speaker, ought not to happen even to the lowliest of creatures; it is atrocious : *The trouble I had getting this ticket, it shouldn't happen to a dog* [1940s+; fr Yiddish speech patterns]

it's (or the opera's) never over till the fat lady sings *sentence* Things are never finished until they are finished; further possibilities of action exist here : *Like they say around here, "The opera's never over till the fat lady sings." What hotel are you staying at, little lady?* [1970s+ Baseball; originated by Dan Cook, a San Antonio broadcaster, and based on Yogi Berra's "It ain't over till it's over"]

itsy-bitsy or **itty-bitty** *adj* Tiny; esp, small and cute; LITTLE BITTY, TEENSY-WEENSY : *I can't find even an itty-bitty scrap of paper to show who these Wunderkinds are* [late 1930s+; fr baby talk]

it's you *sentence* The thing is precisely appropriate or integral to you : *Oh my sweet, that mauve cummerbund, it's you!* (1960s+)

it's your nickel *sentence* Its is your prerogative to act, speak, etc, since you are paying for it : *"Go ahead, it's your nickel," he said quaintly* [1940s+ Students; fr the former 5-cent charge for a telephone call]

it takes two to tango *sentence* This cannot happen or have happened without more than one person; cooperation or connivance is indicated : *It takes two to tango, said the mediator/ Now, it takes two to tango, but I still think it was more her fault* [1952+; the name of a 1950s song]

it up *suffix used to intensify verbs* Doing energetically, vehemently, loudly, etc, what is indicated : *camping it up/ hamming it up/ laughing it up*

it works for me *sentence* The idea or plan is fine and I like it

ivories *n* **1** The teeth : *as fine a display of ivories as we've seen in our time* (*1782+*) **2** Dice; a pair of dice (*1830+*)

ivories, the *n* Piano keys; the piano (*1918+*) *See* TICKLE THE IVORIES

ivory tower *n* A place or attitude of retreat, especially preoccupation with lofty, remote, or intellectual considerations : *Come out of that ivory tower*

ixnay *negation* No; no more; none : *Ixnay on the kabitz* [*1930+*; pig Latin for *nix*]

J

J *n* (also **jay** or **jay smoke** or **J smoke**) A marijuana cigarette; JOINT [1960s+ Narcotics; fr the *J* of *Mary Jane*, "marijuana," or the *j* of *joint*]

jabber *n* A hypodermic needle *(1915+ Narcotics)* *v* To talk incessantly; chatter on *(1499+)* *See* JIBBER-JABBER

◁**jaboney** or **jiboney** or **jibone**▷ *n* **1** A newly arrived immigrant; a naive person; GREENHORN : *Vinny, you're a real jibone, you know that?* **2** A hoodlum; thug; GORILLA : *He had a couple of his jiboneys with him* **3** A frequent television guest expert : *"Nightline" is desperate for a jaboney tonight. They tried for Kissinger (1990s+ Television)* [origin uncertain; perhaps fr Italian dialect *giappone*, literally "a Japanese," but extended to any strange- or foreign-looking person]

jabroni *n* **1** (or **jobber**) A professional wrestler who loses in order to make another wrestler look good **2** A loser

jack *n* **1** Money : *the fans which paid their jack/ I figured it would be an easy way to make some jack (1859+)* **2** Nothing; JACK SHIT, ZIP : *What did you do today? Jack (1980s+ Students)* *v* **1** To take twisting evasive action in an airplane; jank. jink *(Vietnam War Air Force)* **2** To steal; rob : *Two men who "jacked," or stole, a 1991 Plymouth Colt (1990s+ Teenagers)* [money sense probably fr the expression *hard Jackson* or *hard Jackson money*, referring to President Andrew Jackson and found by 1838; first verb sense perhaps related to mid-1800s British criminal slang *jack*, "run away, escape," or perhaps by folk etymology fr *jank*, an echoic companion of *jink*; compare *jink-jank* with *yin-yang* and *zig-zag*; stealing sense probably fr *hijack* and related to *carjacking*] *See* BALL THE JACK, HEAVY MONEY, HIJACK, PIECE OF CHANGE

Jack *n* Man; friend; fellow; MAC • Used in addressing any man, whatever his name : *Man, he's murder, Jack/ That supposed to be funny, jack?* *(1889+)*

jack around *v phr* **1** To idle about; FART AROUND, SCREW AROUND : *He and LD had been jacking around in practice and LD fell on his leg* **2** To meddle with; FOOL AROUND : *and jack around with somebody else's wife/ until the lawyers started jacking around with the structure* [1960s+ Students; origin uncertain; perhaps fr *jack off*]

jack someone around *v phr* **1** To tease; KID : *These guys are only trying to jack you around* **2** To victimize; HASSLE. JERK someone AROUND :

Don't you think I know when people are jacking me around? (1960s+ Students)

◁**jackass**▷ *n* A stupid person; idiot; dolt; fool; LUNKHEAD, SHIT-FOR-BRAINS *(1823+)*

jacked in *adj phr* Up-to-date and aware; ON TOP OF : *I'm impressed by the level of techiness: people here are fully jacked in* [1990s+; fr *jack*, "male plug used in telephone and electronic patching," hence "totally connected"]

jacked up *adj phr* **1** Stimulated; exhilarated; HIGH : *all the parents jacked up on coffee/ I was jacked up, coming in, then I faced reality* **2** Elevated, esp by artifice; JUMPED-UP : *That he is a jacked-up cowboy and minor film star is a libel* [1970s+; first sense probably fr *jagged up*, "drunk," found by 1737]

jacket *n* A criminal record; RAP SHEET [1940s+ Police; fr the cardboard folder or *jacket* used to hold the papers]

jack (or jake) it *v phr* To play half-heartedly, claiming an injury; malinger : *Piniella's charge that Henderson was "jacking it"* [1970s+ Baseball; fr earlier *jake*, "a player who loafs or stalls," apparently based on the name of Jake Stahl, who played and managed various teams between 1903 and 1913, because his surname rhymes with "stall"]

◁**jack-off** or **jagoff**▷ *n* A stupid, incompetent person; JERK : *What's that jack-off up to now?/ those two slick-haired jagoffs (1930s+)*

◁**jack off**▷ *v* To masturbate; JERK OFF • Said chiefly of males [1916+; ultimately fr *jack*, "penis"]

jack out *v phr* To pull out; seize and expose : *could jack his gun out kind of fast (1940s+)*

jackpot *n* The largest win available in a slot machine [1940s+ Gambling; fr the *progressive jack pot* in poker, which stipulates that if no player has a pair of jacks or better to open, then on the next hand, after anteing again, someone must have queens or better, and so on; thus the *pot* could become quite large; the poker use, "a very large win," is found by 1881] *See* HIT THE JACKPOT

jack-rabbit *v* To advance by leaps, like a jack-rabbit : *a stock market jack-rabbiting past the Dow Jones 5,000 (1990s+)*

jackroll *v* To rob, esp a drunken man; ROLL : *Father had recently been "jackrolled" while drunk (1915+)*

◁**jack shit**▷ *n phr* Nothing at all; DIDDLY. ZILCH : *They had it, but jack shit was what they had/ I didn't know jackshit about it/ "Ex-model" means jackshit (1970s+ Southern students)*

275

jack *n* Nothing at all, zero; nada; JACK SHIT : *You don't know jack squat about going to college these days*

jack up *v phr* 1 To inject a narcotic; SHOOT UP *(1960s+ Narcotics)* 2 To stimulate; exhilarate : *Aren't you getting jacked up? Ain't it great? (1970s+)* 3 To raise; increase : *Did they jack up the price again? (1904+)*

jack someone up *v phr* 1 To rebuke, esp to revive a sense of duty : *The sergeant had to jack the whole platoon up (1896+)* 2 To rob, esp at gunpoint *(1960s+)* 3 To thrash; trounce; CLOBBER *(1960s+)* 4 Of the police, to stop and search someone, demand identification, question harshly, etc; ROUST, TAKE ON *(1960s+ Black)*

jack with *v phr* To play or toy with; mess with : *mechanic jacked with the poor woman customer* See MESS AROUND WITH

jag *n* 1 A drinking spree; BENDER 2 A spell or spree of a specified sort : *One had a "crying jag"/ the annual Christmas gift-buying jag* [1887+; fr *jag*, "a load," found by 1597, whence "as much liquor as a man can drink," found by 1678] See CRYING JAG

Jag *n* A Jaguar automobile *(1950s+)*

jagged (JAGD) *adj* Drunk *(1737+)*

jagoff See JACK-OFF

jail *v* To live tolerably in jail; survive imprisonment : *Roy taught me how to jail (1980s+)*

jail bait *n phr* ◁1▷ A girl or boy below the legal age of sexual consent, copulation with whom would constitute statutory rape; san quentin quail 2 Any person or thing likely to tempt one to crime and imprisonment *(1934+)*

jailbird *n* A convict or ex-convict *(1618+)*

jailhouse lawyer *n phr* A prisoner who, authoritative or not, is disposed to lengthy discussion of his legal rights and those of other inmates; GUARDHOUSE LAWYER : *an avid reader of good literature and a "jailhouse lawyer" (1940s+)*

jake *adj* Excellent; very satisfactory; HUNKY-DORY : *She said the whole college seemed jake to her* **adv** : *You never can tell on a day like this, things could be goin' jake one minute, then presto, before you know it you're history* [1914+ Underworld; origin unknown]

jalopy or **jaloppy** or **jalop** *n* 1 An old and battered car or airplane; HEAP : *A jalopy is a model one step above a "junker"* 2 Any car; any vehicle; BUGGY : *Let them search every jalop on the road* [1924+; origin unknown; perhaps fr *Jalapa*, a Mexican city to which many US used cars were sent]

jam[1] *modifier* : *Jam bands do have styles* **n** 1 A predicament; BIND, TIGHT SPOT *(1914+)* 2 (also **traffic jam**) A tight crush of cars, people, etc; JAM-UP *(1917+)* 3 Small objects like rings and watches that are easy to steal *(1925+ Underworld)* 4 A party or gathering where jazz musicians play for or with one another; JAM SESSION : *Bix and the boys would blow it free and the jam was on (1930s+ Jazz musicians)* 5 A party : *Are you going to the jam tonight? (1930s+)* ◁6▷ The vulva; a woman's genitals *(1896+)* 7 Cocaine; NOSE CANDY *(1960s+ Narcotics)* **v** 1 To play jazz with great spontaneity, esp to improvise freely with other musicians and usu without an audience *(1930s+ Jazz musicians)* 2 To have a good time; party joyously; GET IT ON : *As for us, we danced, we jammed, and we wondered* 3 To make up a rap song, esp in a competitive situation *(1970s+ New York teenagers)* 4 To make trouble for; coerce or harass, esp with physical force : *than when they're jammin' me for a penny every time I walk down the street/ He knows what to say that will jam you and not jam you (1960s+)* ◁5▷ To do the sex act; copulate; SCREW : *Did what? Jammed (1970s+ Students)* 6 To auction; act as an auctioneer *(1950s+ Hawkers)* 7 To send an interfering signal on a broadcast channel one wishes to make unintelligible : *An attempt was made to jam (1914+)* 8 To run away; SKEDADDLE : *Let's jam!/ I shifted ionto high gear and jammed it up to Santa Teresa (1990s+)* 9 To pitch the ball close to the batter, so that he is forced to hit it close to the gripped end of the bat *(1960s+ Baseball)* 10 SLAM DUNK *(1990s+ Basketball)* [all senses have some relation to the basic notion of squeezing or crushing so as to make *jam*] See IN A JAM, LOGJAM, TOE JAM

jam[2] *n* A heterosexual man [1970s+ Homosexuals; said to be fr *just a man*]

jamble See JIMBLE-JAMBLE

jambox See GHETTO BOX

jammed *adj* Drunk : *He got jammed (1922+)*

jammed up *adj phr* IN A JAM : *You are jammed up (1940s+)*

jammer *n* A musician who takes part in jam sessions : *the likely jammers being the four ex-Beatles, Leon Russell, Mick Jagger, and a few other "friends" (1930s+ Jazz talk)*

jammies *n* Pajamas : *who conclude the revue clad in jammies/ into the bedroom, into his jammies, into the bed (1980s+)*

jammin' *modifier* 1 Very busy, esp with people : *coffee shop is jammin'* 2 Excellent; first-rate : *That was a jammin' set, man*

jamoke[1] or **Jamoke** (jə MOHK) *n* Coffee [1914+; perhaps a blend of *java* and *mocha*]

jamoke[2] or **jamoche** *n* A despised man; JERK : *I don't rate your chances none too good if that jamoke's going to defend you/ You really think this jamoche is gonna give you somethin'?* [origin unknown]

jam-packed *adj* Very tightly packed; very crowded : *those jam-packed suburban classes* (1925+)

jams, the *See* the JIM-JAMS

jam session *n phr* A gathering of musicians, esp jazz musicians, playing freely and for one another, but sometimes in a public performance; JAM : *Here's Dodo on the piano and Tiny on the bass. Looks like we'll have a fine jam session* (1930s+ *Jazz musicians*)

jam-up *n* A tight crush of people, cars, etc, preventing normal movement; JAM : *to forestall the possibility of another jam-up* (1940s+)

jam up *v phr* To encumber; disable by overburdening : *to file complaints was a sure way to jam up a cop* (1940s+)

jangle *See* JINGLE-JANGLE

jarhead *n* **1** A mule (1918+) **2** A US Marine; gyrene (*WWII armed forces*)

java or **Java** *n* Coffee [1907+; fr *Java*, an Indonesian island whence some coffee was exported]

jaw *n* : *ain't had a good jaw together* (1842+) *v* **1** To talk; chat; converse : *Can't stand here jawing with you all day* (1760+) **2** To exhort; lecture; strive to persuade orally; JAWBONE : *had kept sober for several months by jawing drunks, unsuccessfully* (1810+) *See* CRACK one's JAW, FLAPJAW, GLASS JAW

jawbone *n* **1** Credit or trust, esp financial : *Try as he might he got no jawbone from the bankers* (1862+) **2** : *The President launched a sustained and hot jawbone on the budget cuts* *v* **1** To borrow; obtain on credit : *He jawboned enough to set up an office* (1862+) **2** To discuss; talk over, esp extensively and profoundly : *a distinguished group of presidential biographers to jawbone about the situation* (1966+) **3** To exhort and earnestly urge in order to persuade • Used predominantly to describe high-level pressure applied on economic issues, and popularized under President Lyndon Johnson : *the Presidential promise not to "jawbone" business into not raising prices/ chiefly direct controls on all pay and prices or "jawboning" against individual wage and price rises* (1969+) **4** To fire a weapon in practice, esp for formal qualification to use it (*WWII Army*)

jawboning *n* Strong exhortation; potent oral pressure : *The technique was called "jawboning." Lyndon Johnson and Mr Nixon used it* (1960s+)

jawbreaker or **jawcracker** *n* **1** A long word or a word difficult to pronounce : *Diphenylpentoactomaggetoneplangianoliosis is something of a jawbreaker* (1835+) **2** A piece of hard candy, esp a spherical piece with bubblegum in the center (1875+)

jaw dropper *n phr* Something astonishing; an awesome event : *Wasn't that a jaw dropper! Imagine Ted being elected Dalai Lama!/ That first show was a jaw-dropper* [1990s+; fr the instinctive gaping response to such an event]

jaw-hanging *adj* Causing the jaw to gape in awe; riveting : *You have to have cutting-edge, jaw-hanging graphics* (1990s+)

jay[1] *n* **1** A rustic; simpleton; HICK, RUBE (1523+) **2** An easy victim; MARK, PATSY, SUCKER (1884+ *Underworld*) [fr the raucous bird]

jay[2] *n* Marijuana or a marijuana cigarette; J : *Let's do up a jay and truck on down to the libo* (1960s+ *Narcotics*)

jazz *modifier* : *a jazz trumpet/ jazz riffs* *n* **1** : *This place needs more jazz and pizzazz* **2** A kind of popular, often improvised, and emotive instrumental music originating among Southern black people in the late 19th century and still evolving as an American and a world style (1900s+ *Jazz musicians*) **3** Empty talk; nonsense; lies; BALONEY, BULLSHIT, JIVE : *You mean her most eloquent pledges were jazz?* (1918+) **4** Ornamentation; embellishment, esp when merely superficial : *a clean design, without a lot of jazz* (1960s+) *v* ◁1▷ To do the sex act with or to; FUCK : *I jazzed her, too/ what he's going to do to a guy he finds out's been jazzing his wife* (late 1800s+ *Black*) **2** To increase the tempo, animation, or excitement of something; JAZZ something UP : *Come on, jazz yourself, we're late* (1875+ *Black*) **3** To arrange or play in a jazz style : *They jazzed the National Anthem* **4** : *Stop your jazzing and merely adduce the data* [origin unknown; *jass* was an earlier spelling]

jazz-bo *n* **1** A flashily groomed man or woman; cat. DUDE : *her stage image as a witchy little jazz-bo with a boxer's shuffle and a baseball player's kick* (1923+) ◀2▶ A black man, esp a black soldier (1919+)

jazzed *adj* Eager and energetic; PSYCHED UP : *I'm really jazzed. I want to train for '96* (1960s+ *Teenagers*)

jazzed up *adj phr* Made faster, more exciting, interesting, active, etc; HOPPED UP, HYPED-UP : *They were riding motorcycles, the big jazzed-up ones* (1930s+)

jazz something up *v phr* **1** To make faster, more exciting or stimulating, etc : *He tried to jazz the meeting up* **2** To play in the musical style indicated (1930s+)

jazzy *adj* **1** Resembling or partaking of the musical style indicated : *He could turn a Beethoven sonata into a jazzy little number* **2** Exciting; stimulating; SEXY : *He wore bow ties and jazzy suits* (1915+)

jeebies *See* the HEEBIE-JEEBIES

Jeepers Creepers or **Jeepers** *interj* An exclamation of surprise, dismay, emphasis, etc :

Jeepers Creepers, another busted leg! [1929+; a euphemism for *Jesus Christ*]

Jeez *interj* (also **jeez** or **Jeeze** or **jeeze** or **Jees** or **jees** or **jeezy-peezy** or **Jeezy-peezy**) An exclamation of surprise, dismay, emphasis, etc; JEEPERS CREEPERS [entry form 1923+, *jeeze* 1920+, *jees* 1931+, *jeezy-peezy* 1942+; fr *Jesus*]

jelly-belly *n* A fat person (*1896+*)

jelly-roll *n* ◁1▷ The vulva; vagina (*1870s+ Black*) ◁2▷ The sex act; copulation; FUCKING (*1870s+ Black*) **3** A man obsessed with women; woman-chaser; COCKSMAN, LOVER-BOY (*1870s+ Black*) **4** A lover or mistress; SWEET PAPA, SWEET MAMA (*1870s+ Black*) **5** Large round hay bales; big round bales (*1980s+*) [sexual senses perhaps related to *jelly*, "semen," found by 1622]

jerk *modifier* : *a couple of jerk wops* *n* **1** A short branch railroad line : *a small "jerk" with only two locals a day* (*1892+*) **2** A short ride (*1920s+ Cabdrivers*) **3** A tedious and ineffectual person, esp a man; fool; ninny; ass; BOOB, TURKEY : *Jeez, what a jerk!* (*Carnival 1935+*) **4** A contemptible and obnoxious person, esp a man; ASSHOLE, BASTARD : *Dr Johnson admired Goldsmith's literary talent, although he considered him a jerk/ A jerk not only bores you, but pats you on the shoulder as he does so* (*1935+*) **5** soda jerk (*1923+*) *v* ◁1▷ JERK OFF (*1940s+*) [the derogatory term comes fr *jerk off*, "masturbate"; the form *soda jerker* is found by 1883] See CIRCLE JERK, KNEE-JERK, PULL someone's CHAIN

jerk around *v phr* To idle about; play casually; FOOL AROUND : *if kids are jerking around and enter a system as a lark with no intent to deprive* (*1980s+*)

jerk someone **around** (or **off**) *v phr* To victimize or harass : *Salespeople feel that men who want hand holding are often jerking them around/ bumming cigarettes and generally jerking him around throughout the broadcast/ I think Coyle was jerking you off* (*1980s+*)

jerk (or **yank**) someone's **chain** *v phr* To victimize or dupe; harass; JERK someone AROUND : *You came out to jerk my chain tonight/ the perception white voters got that Jackson was jerking their chains/ Are you guys yanking my chain?* [1980s+; fr the notion of a chained man, monkey, etc, being harassed]

Jerkimer See HERKIMER JERKIMER

◁**jerk-off**▷ *adj* Stupid; JERKY : *It's too much of a jerk-off idea/ preparing an answer to the jerkoff question modifier* Useful for masturbation : *an electric suction jerk-off device n* A person who jerks off, either literally or figuratively : *I'd be tickled to death to lose the jerk-offs* (*1960s+*)

◁**jerk off**▷ *v phr* **1** To masturbate; JACK OFF : *I went ahead as usual and jerked off into my sock/ KB was always trying to jerk off* (*1916+*) **2** To idle about; FUCK OFF, GOOF OFF (*1950s+*)

jerk over *v phr* **1** To victimize; treat disrespectfully; DIS : *My professor jerked me over when he refused to accept my paper two days late* (*1980s+ Students*) **2** To treat ineffectually; FUCK UP, MESS UP : *Well, you know, just generally jerking it over* (*1980s+*)

◁**jerk the gherkin**▷ *v phr* To masturbate; pound one's pud : *Your gherkin is for firkin', not for jerkin'* (*1940s+*)

jerk (or **jerkwater**) **town** *n phr* A small town; an insignificant village : *to fool around a jerk town* (*1899+*)

jerkwater *adj* Insignificant; trivial : *These seem like jerkwater sentiments* (*1897+*)

jerky *adj* Having the traits of a jerk : *any jerky Joe* (*1940s+*) See HERKY-JERKY

jerry-rigged *adj* Patched or cobbled; HOKED-UP : *these would be much better than something jerry-rigged on my Olivetti* [1980s+; a blend of *jerry-built*, "badly or flimsily built," found by 1869, with *jury-rigged*, "rigged temporarily or in an emergency," found by 1788; the origin of both of these is unknown]

Jesus boots *n phr* Men's sandals (*1960s+ Counterculture*)

Jesus Christ *interj* An exclamation of surprise, dismay, emphasis, etc; JEEPERS CREEPERS (*1592+*)

Jesus freaks (or **people**) *n phr* Members of an evangelical Christian religious movement among young people, esp ex-hippies and drug addicts : *in this light the herds of Jesus freaks/ Jesus freaks, gypsies, lunatic right-wingers, leering conventioneers* (*1960s+ Counterculture*)

Jesus H Christ or **Jesus** *interj* An exclamation of surprise, dismay, emphasis, etc; JEEPERS CREEPERS [1840s+; the intrusive *H* may reflect IHC, fr Greek IHSOUS, "Jesus Christ," found by 950 and still embroidered on vestments of the Church of England, or it may be an infix for oral emphasis]

jet *v* To leave; AIR OUT, SPLIT (*1990s+ Teenagers*)

jet set, the *n phr* The group of wealthy, chic people who move about from one costly venue to another : *a charter member of the international jet set* (*1951+*)

◀**Jew** (or **jew**) **down**▶ *v phr* To bargain and haggle in an attempt to get a lower price : *but then the guy started jewin' me down* [1848+; *jew* in the same sense is found by 1824]

jewel in one's **crown**, the *n phr* One's most precious and distinguished possession : *Once the jewel in Luce's crown, Time was seen by its* *new managers as just another rhinestone* (*1873+*)

jewels *See* FAMILY JEWELS

◄**Jewish American Prince►** *n phr* A pampered and usu wealthy young man who feels he deserves special treatment (*1970s+*)

◄**Jewish American Princess** or **JAP** or **Jap►** *n phr* A pampered and usu wealthy young woman who feels she deserves special treatment : *plenty of Jewish American Princesses in their wigs and false eyelashes/ the unofficial, secret JAP within me* (*1970s+*)

Jheri curl (or **Kurl**) *n* Staightened kinky hair : *He was a tall motherfucker with a Jheri curl, looked like a baboon* (*1990s+ Black*)

◄**jibagoo►** *See* JIGABOO

jibber-jabber *v* To talk nonsense; JABBER : *Time for Congress to quit jibber-jabbering/ We just jibber-jabbered these things all day*

jiboney *See* JABONEY

jiffy, a *modifier* : *Let's make a jiffy dessert n phr* (Variations: **jif** or **jiff** or **jiffin** or **jiffing**) A short space of time; an instant : *drop off to sleep for a jiffy/ I'll have coffee ready in a jiff* (*1793+*) [said to be fr thieves' slang *jeffey* or *jiffey*, "lightning"]

jig *n* **1** A dancing party or public dance ◄**2►** JIGABOO (*1923+*)

◄**jigaboo►** (also **jibagoo** or **jigabo** or **jig** or **zig** or **zigaboo** or **zigabo**) *modifier* : *a jig band n* A black person (*1909+*)

jigger *n* **1** An artificially made sore, usu on the arm or leg, useful in begging : *whether it will pay to use his "jigger"* (*1890s+ Hoboes*) **2** A liquor glass of one-and-a-half ounce capacity; SHOT GLASS (*1857+*) **3** THINGAMAJIG (*1874+*) *v* **1** To interfere with; QUEER : *jigger our riding on the railroad* (*1890s+ Hoboes*) **2** To tamper with or falsify; DOCTOR : *There is pressure from Casey to jigger estimates/ how the gold trading was jiggered* (*1970s+*) [*giger*, "lock," is found by 1612, apparently coined by Thomas Dekker, and is probably the source of the third noun sense] *See* DOODAD, I'LL BE DAMNED

jiggered *See* I'LL BE DAMNED

jiggery-pokery *n* Deception; trickery; SKULLDUGGERY : *or what some term jiggery-pokery/ could have prevented most of the jiggery-pokery* [*1893+*; probably fr Scottish *joukery-paukery* fr *jouk*, "trick"]

jiggins *See* JUGGINS

jiggle or **jiggly** *modifier* : *the ads for comedies in the jiggle genre/ a brand of show so dependent on buxom starts and wet T-shirts that it was called jiggle television n* **1** The bouncing and shaking of a woman's parts, esp of the breasts • Hence the whole tone and style of blatant female sexual exploitation : *help put the jiggle back in the series "Charlie's Angels"* **2** A TV program featuring the bouncing and shaking of a woman's parts : *when advertisers see wall-to-wall jigglies in prime time v : She swims, jumps rope, and practices jiggling in front of the mirror* (*1970s+*)

jiggy *adj* **1** Excellent; cool : *jiggy with that idea* **2** Excited or involved, esp sexually : *gotten jiggy with a few men interj* Excellent; sweet *n* **1** Sexual relations **2** Money; wealth (*1990+*)

jig is up, the *sentence* The criminal enterprise is discovered (*1800+*)

jig-swiggered *See* I'LL BE DAMNED

jillion *n* (also **gadzillion** or **gillion** or **kajillion** or **skillion** or **zillion** or **quadzillion**) A great many; an indefinitely large number; SCADS : *a jillion jackpots/ The beautiful people who would be at her cocktail party ("A zillion horny studs!")/ All those years we paid no official notice to those gadzillions of Chinese/ This instant, in fact, quadzillions of these particles may be streaking harmlessly through our bodies* (*1940s+*)

jimble-jamble *adj* Mixed; motley : *a jimble-jamble sort of crowd* [*1970+*; modeled on *skimble-skamble*, found by 1826]

Jim Crow *modifier* : *Jim Crow laws n phr* ◄**1►** A black man; African-American (*1828+*) **2** Segregation and discrimination against black people, and the laws and practices that accompany them : *My first experience with Jim Crow/ Jim Crow killed Bessie Smith* (*1940s+*) *v* : *I would like to say that the people who Jim Crow me have a white heart* [fr a character in a minstrel-show song by T D Rice]

jim-dandy *adj* : *Anacin is a jim-dandy remedy n* A person or thing that is remarkable, wonderful, superior, etc; BEAUT, HUMDINGER (*1844+*) [perhaps fr an early 1840s song "Dandy Jim of Caroline"]

jim-jams *n phr* the HEEBIE-JEEBIES : *Two-seaters are high therapy from life's imbalances, emotional dross and other colitis-causing jimjams* (*1880+*)

jimmies *n* Bits of candy put onto ice cream as a topping (*1960s+*)

jimmy or **jimmy hat** *n* A condom : *That's right, condom fashions, with small pockets for what kids call jimmys* (*1990s+ Teenagers*)

jingle *n* A telephone call; a ring; TINKLE : *We never hear from you, not even a jingle*

jingle-jangle *adj* In poor condition; ramshackle : *driving down to Big Sur in their funky bus or some jingle-jangle car* (*1970s+*) *n* (also **jing**) Money; coins : *I've got some jingle-jangle in my jeans/ A lot of bars have fundraisers and donate a big chunk of their jing to AIDS groups* (*1950s+*)

jinks *See* HI-JINKS

jinx *n* **1** A cause of bad luck : *Somebody around here is a jinx (1911+)* **2** A curse; assured ill fortune : *Looks like the place has a jinx on it (1911+) v : Somebody jinxed him (1917+)* [apparently fr *jynx* or *iynx*, "wryneck woodpecker," fr the use of the bird in divination]

jip *See* GYP

jism *n* ◀**1**▶ CUM *(1899+)* **2** (also **gism**) Liveliness; excitement; SPUNK; ZING *(1842+)* [origin unknown]

◀**jit**▶ *n* A black person *(1931+)*

jitney or **jit** *adj* Cheap : *a jitney dance hall (1916+) modifier : cracked down today on illegal jitney service n* **1** A nickel *(1903+)* **2** (also **jitney bus**) A small bus used as public transportation • Formerly, jitneys were cars operating for low fare in more or less unregulated competition with taxis, buses, and streetcars *(1914+)* **3** Any car, esp a small or cheap one *(1917+)* [origin unknown; perhaps fr Yiddish]

jitter *v* **1** To tremble; quiver : *A line of half-washed clothes jittered on a rusty wire (1931+)* **2** To be nervous; be agitated; fret : *I jittered around the house, unable to concentrate on anything (1932+)* [echoic-symbolic]

jitterbug *n* A devotee of swing music, esp one who dances to swing : *Jitterbugs are the extreme swing addicts v* To dance to swing music : *Do you feel like jitterbugging a little bit? (1930s+ Jive talk)*

jitterbug, the *n phr* A fast, freely improvisational, and vigorous dance done to swing music, with passages where the couple separates to do more or less spectacular solo figures *(1930s+ Jive talk)*

jitters, the *n phr* A state of nervous agitation; acute restless apprehension : *I had the jitters (1925+)*

jittery *adj* Nervous : *He felt all jittery and uptight (1931+)*

jive[1] *modifier* : *jive records/ jive dancers n* **1** Empty and pretentious talk; foolishness; BALONEY, BULLSHIT : *Sugar Mouth Sammy with the same ol' tired jive/ male chauvinist, damsel in distress, and all that jive (1929+)* **2** Trifles; trash : *I bought a lot of cheap jive at the five and ten cent store (1920+)* **3** Swing music of the 1930s and '40s, esp as played by the big bands and played fast and excitingly : *Man, what solid jive! (1938+)* **4** (also **gyve**) Marijuana or a marijuana cigarette : *So Diane smoked jive, pot, and tea (1938+) v* **1** To banter; jest; tease; KID : *She told him to quit jiving (1938+ Black)* **2** To deceive, but not seriously; mislead, esp playfully *(1928+)* **3** To play or dance to fast, exciting swing

music *(1938+)* [origin unknown; perhaps fr Wolof *jev*, "talk disparagingly"] *See* JUKING AND JIVING, SHUCK

jive[2] *v* To jibe; chime • The form **gibe** is found by 1813 : *The two answers do not jive (1940+; origin uncertain; perhaps related to chime; the form gibe is found by 1813]*

jive and juke *v phr* To have a very good time *(1970s+ College students) See* JUKING AND JIVING

◁**jive-ass**▷ *adj* **1** Deceitful; undependable : *Damn his lazy, jiveass soul/ You better find out some place else, you jiveass punk* **2** Ridiculous, stupid • Usu objectionable : *jive-ass bitch n* Pretentious and deceitful talk; BULLSHIT, JIVE : *That's like jive-ass* [1940+ Black; in the phrase *jive-ass motherfucker* said to have originated with the musician Charlie "Bird" Parker]

jive talk *n phr* A rapid, pattering way of talking, accompanied with finger-snapping and bodily jerks and using the swing and jive vocabulary, affected by teenagers during the swing and jive era of the 1930s and '40s *(1930s+ Jive talk)*

jive turkey *n phr* A stupid person : *Get those jive turkeys off my car*

◀**jizz** or **jizzum**▶ *n* Semen; CUM, JISM : *puts a little body in his jizz, pumps a baby a year into the wife (1960s+)*

J/O *modifier* Masturbation : *Since the confusing days of AIDS, one of the main attractions of group J/O scenes was precisely the ecstatic sexual energy that only a group can generate* [1980s+; abbreviation of *jack off*]

job *n* **1** (also **jobbie**) A specimen or example, either of a thing or a person : *I lost two $110 imported jobs before a locksmith told me what I was doing wrong/ She's a tough little job/ one of those big 18-wheel jobbies (1927+)* **2** (also **jobbie**) A car : *She was driving a little red job (1940s+)* **3** A crime; a criminal project; CAPER : *a big payroll job (1667+ Underworld) v* To deceive; cheat; DOUBLE CROSS, FRAME : *Crying that he had been jobbed/ got absolutely jobbed out of the Heisman (1731+) See* BAG JOB, BLOW JOB, BOOB JOB, CON GAME, HAND JOB, HATCHET JOB, INSIDE JOB, LAY DOWN ON THE JOB, LUBE, NOSE JOB, PUT-UP JOB, SHACK JOB, SNOW JOB, TORCH JOB

jobber *See* JABRONI

jobbie *v* To befoul : *any ladies out there who will jobbie their pants for the camera*

jock *n* **1** A jockey *(1670+)* **2** Disc jockey *(1970s+)* **3** The penis; the crotch : *I'll be beating the bushes with snow to my jock (1790+)* **4** An athletic supporter; jockstrap : *I asked him if he wanted some sweat clothes, or a jock (1952+)* **5** (also **jocko**) An athlete • Now used of both men and women, despite the phallic derivation : *The players themselves are a curious blend of woman and jock/ the lucrative job proper to an all-Ivy jock* (*1963+*) [the basic etymon is *jock*, "penis," fr *jack*, probably the diminutive of *John*, which fr the 14th century has been applied to males, malelike things, and male organs; the sense "athlete" is fr *jockstrap*]

jockey *n* The driver or pilot of any vehicle : *airplane jockey/ tank jockey* (*1912+*) *See* DESK JOCKEY

Joe or **joe** *adj* Informed; aware; HEP (*1940s+ Underworld*) *n* **1** Coffee (*1940s+*) **2** Man; fellow; GUY : *never seemed to share much of the problems of the ordinary joe* (*1846+*) **3** GI JOE (*WWII Army*) *v* : *Let me Joe you to that racket* (*1940s+ Underworld*) *See* HOLY JOE, SLOPPY JOE

Joe Average *n phr* The ordinary or typical citizen : *For Joe Average, the game simply doesn't exist* (*1990s+*)

Joe Beige *n phr* A bland, colorless person : *I don't find you very interesting. "Joe Beige"* (*1980s+*)

Joe Blow *n phr* (Variations: **Doakes** or **Storch** or **Zilch** may replace **Blow**) Any man; the average man; JOHN DOE : *the average black "Mr Joe Blow"* [entry form 1920s+ Jazz musicians, *Doakes* 1943+, *Storch* 1960s+, *Zilch* 1925+; fr the *blowing* of the musician, later probably thought of as referring to big talk]

Joe College *n phr* A young man whose dress and manner betoken the nonacademic aspects of college life : *a real Joe College type* (*1932+*)

Joe Lunch Bucket *modifier* : *Royko's Joe Lunchbucket persona may lie at the heart of his appeal n phr* The ordinary or typical working man : *Three years ago the Packers got Jim Thorpe in the draft, and now they get Joe Lunch Bucket* (*1990s+*)

Joe Public *n* The general public : *Joe Public first was theatrical slang* (*1942+*)

Joe Schmo (or **Schmoe**) *n phr* An undistinguished and unfortunate person [1960s+; fr *schmo*, a Yiddish or quasi-Yiddish word meaning "unfortunate person, *schlemiel*"]

Joe Six-pack *n phr* An ordinary American male; JOE, JOE AVERAGE, JOE BLOW : *Do you think that Joe Six-pack in Illinois cares?/ a sleazy bar where go-go girls perform for goggle-eyed Joe Six-packs* [fr the six-bottle or -can packets of beer these men typically consume]

john[1] *n* A toilet; CAN : *I made a brief visit to the john* [1930s+; probably an amusing euphemism for *jack* or *jakes*, 16th-century terms for toilet; some say fr Sir *John* Harington (1561–1612), who originated a form of water closet, but evidence for the attribution

is lacking; *cuzjohn*, "cousin john," in the same sense is found in 1735]

john[2] or **John** *n* **1** Any man; an average man; JOE : *We don't want no poor johns on here* (*1920s+ Black*) **2** A man regarded as an easy victim, a potential easy sale, etc : *He's pretty smart at figurin' out what a John'll pay* (*1946+*) **3** An Army recruit (*1940s+ Army*) **4** A man who keeps a girl; DADDY, SUGAR DADDY (*1950s+*) **5** (also **johnson**) A prostitute's customer : *even for girls turning their first tricks, pulling their first real John/ shot an 18-year-old hooker then plugged a john who was present* (*1911+ Prostitutes*) **6** An older homosexual male who keeps a younger one (*1950s+ Homosexuals*) **7** JOHN LAW *See* DEAR JOHN

John Doe or **Richard Roe** *n phr* Any man; the average man; JOE [1768+; originally the fictitious plaintiff and defendant in a lawsuit]

John Hancock (or **Henry**) *n phr* One's signature [1903+; fr the fact that *John Hancock* of Massachusetts was the first to sign the Declaration of Independence in 1776; *John Henry*, possibly by confusion with *Patrick Henry*, because of the prominence of *John Henry* as a folklore hero, and by near-rhyming resemblance]

John Law *n phr* A police officer; the police : *had been gathered in by John Law* (*1907+*)

Johnny or **johnny** *n* Any man; JOE, JOHN ● Chiefly British : *The big johnny came over to talk* (*1673+*) *See* STAGEDOOR JOHNNY

Johnny-come-lately *modifier* : *a Johnny-come-lately quasi-solution n* **1** A person or thing only recently arrived, esp as compared with the more seasoned : *Postwar planning was no Johnny-come-lately* (*1839+*) **2** An upstart (*1839+*)

Johnny-on-the-spot *n* A person who is ready and effective when needed : *Ed was Johnny-on-the-spot and we got it cleaned up quick* (*1896+*)

John Q Citizen (or **Public**) *n phr* Any man, esp the average or typical man; JOE AVERAGE : *John Q Citizen seems to yearn for the big cars* (*1940s+*)

johns *See* LONG JOHNS

◁**johnson** or **Johnson** or **jones**▷ *n* The penis : *beat out time with their titties and their johnsons/ I've only got one Johnson, and he winks/ Enough is enough, turn my jones loose* [1863+; origin unknown; such a use is recorded fr Canada in the mid-1800s, perhaps as a euphemism for the British euphemism *John Thomas*, "penis"] *See* JOHN[2]

John Thomas *n* The penis : *John Thomas up and raring to go* (*1879+*)

joined at the hip *adj phr* Very closely associated; inseparable; symbiotic : *Weldon writes as if she were Virginia Woolf and Roseanne*

Arnold joined at the hip/ Frequently in the past, Main Street and Wall Street have had their differences, but today as never before they are joined at the hip [1990s+; fr the condition of some Siamese twins]

joint *n* **1** Any disgusting or disreputable place; DIVE, DUMP : *That evening the joint buzzed with sedition/ a vile Kansas "joint"* (*1821+*) **2** Any place or venue, including a home : *It's a swell joint, all right* (*1905+*) **3** A marijuana cigarette; REEFER : *inhale a joint or two of cannabis/ I've had to hold joints in my hand but I never smoked even one* (*1950s+ Narcotics*) **4** The apparatus for injecting narcotics; HEAD KIT, works (*1940s+ Narcotics*) ◁5▷ The penis (*1960s+*) **6** A concession (*1940s+ Carnival*) [place senses fr early 1800s Anglo-Irish *joint*, "low resort," perhaps from its being a nearby, joined room rather than a main room] *See* BEER JOINT, CLIP JOINT, EAT HIGH ON THE HOG, GREASE JOINT, GYP JOINT, HOP-JOINT, JUKE JOINT, PULL one's PUD, PUT someone's NOSE OUT OF JOINT, SQUARE

joint, the *n phr* Jail; prison : *in the joint* (*1927+*)

joke *See* SICK JOKE

joke, a *n phr* Someone or something not to be taken seriously; a laughingstock : *So nobody's about to pay big money for the site fee of a Tyson versus Ribalta. I mean, Ribalta's a joke* (*1791+*)

joker *n* **1** (also **joker in the deck**) A hidden cost, qualification, defect, nasty result, etc; CATCH : *It all looks very sweet, but there's a joker* (*1904+*) **2** A man; fellow; GUY, CHARACTER, CLOWN • Often derogatory : *Ask that joker who the hell he thinks he is* (*1811+*) [first sense fr the *joker* card included in a new deck, which may be used as a trump or a wild card]

jollies *n* Pleasure and gratification; thrills, esp when somewhat disreputable; BANG, KICKS : *People that drive Buicks are getting some kind of jollies* (*1957+*) *See* GET one's COOKIES

jolly *v* To cajole with humor and bonhomie : *I was pretty upset, but she jollied me along/ We jollied her into coming along with us* (*1876+*)

jolt *n* **1** The initial impact of a narcotic injection; the potency of a type of drug; RUSH (*1916+ Narcotics*) **2** A narcotic injection; a dose of a drug (*1916+ Narcotics*) **3** A marijuana cigarette; JOINT (*1950s+ Narcotics*) **4** A drink of strong liquor or the potency of a type of alcohol; SNORT : *a wee jolt of Bourbon/ got a jolt from one seven-and-seven* (*1904+*) **5** A prison sentence : *to get a jolt in the stir* (*1912+ Underworld*) *v* : *We didn't want to jolt*

Jones or **jones** *n* **1** Heroin; HORSE, SHIT **2** A drug habit : *works at two jobs to keep up with the "Jones"* **3** Any intense interest or absorption : *The twenty-something elite definitely has a*

jones for Jones *v* : *She's jonesing for those diamond earrings* [1960s+ Narcotics; origin unknown; perhaps an innocent code word used by addicts and dealers] *See* JOHNSON

Joneses *See* KEEP UP WITH THE JONESES

jook *See* JUKE

Jose *See* NO WAY

josh *n* : *It was just a tasteless little josh* (*1978+*) *v* To joke; banter; KID : *continued Brian, unwilling to be joshed out of it* (*1845+*) [origin unknown; the earliest example is capitalized, suggesting a proper name; Eric Partridge gives "a country man; a rustic" as one sense, so perhaps the primary meaning is "to behave like a bumpkin" or "to fool one by seeming to be a rural simpleton"]

joy-juice *n* Liquor (*1950s+*)

joy-popper *n* **1** A newcomer among narcotics users, esp among marijuana smokers **2** A person who takes, or claims to take, only an occasional dose of narcotics : *For the "joy-poppers" had no intention of becoming addicts in the true sense* (*1930s+ Narcotics*)

joy ride *n phr* A ride or trip taken solely for pleasure, esp a fast and merry junket that is in some way forbidden : *They stole the police car and had themselves a joy ride* (*1908+*)

joy-stick *n* **1** The control lever of an airplane (*1910+*) **2** The steering wheel of a car, esp a hot rod (*1950s+ Hot rodders*) **3** The control lever for a computer or video game (*1967+*) **4** An opium pipe (*1940s+ Narcotics*) ◁5▷ (also **joy-knob**) The penis (*1920+*) [the origin of the control-lever senses is uncertain; perhaps fr the tremulous shaking of the stick, perhaps fr the joyful sensation experienced while flying]

j-school *n* A school or college of journalism : *I did not say that j-school was a worthless educational experience, only that the degree was not highly regarded by potential employers/ Truman is trying to entertain J-school questions about the future of American magazines* (*1990s+*)

J smoke *See* J

juco (JOO koh) *n* **1** A junior college; community college **2** A junior-college student or graduate : *those fugitives from a real education, those, those "jucos"* (*1939+*)

Judas Priest *interj* An exclamation of surprise, dismay, emphasis, etc [1914+; a euphemism for *Jesus Christ*]

judy *n* **1** A sexually promiscuous girl or woman (*1823+*) **2** A girl or woman (*1885+*)

jug *n* **1** A bottle of liquor : *Fetch me my jug, son* (*1886+*) **2** A relatively cheap wine, usu bought in large bottles; JUG WINE : *Far more people drink jugs these days* (*1980s+*) **3** A vault or safe (*1925+ Underworld*) **4** A bank

(1845+ Underworld) **5** A carburetor *(1960s+ Hot rodders)* **6** A good holding place : *"jug"—a nice big hold (relative to the rest of the route) (1990s+ Rock climbers)* **v** To put in jail; imprison : *I get jugged for parking in the wrong places? (1834+)* [rock-climbing sense fr *jug-handle* in the same sense, found by 1955]

jug, the *n phr* Jail; prison : *Refusal will result in a quick trip to the jug (1834+)*

jugful *See* NOT BY A LONG SHOT

juggins or **jiggins** *n* **1** A stupid person; dolt; jughead *(1882+ British schoolboys)* **2** A dupe; EASY MARK, PATSY, SUCKER *(1940s+ Underworld)*

juggle *v* To alter, esp with a view to deception and advantage : *Owners Might Juggle Lineup Before Facing Players/ They discovered that the CEO had been juggling the books (1813+)*

jughead *n* A stupid person; fool; KLUTZ *(1926+)*

◁**jugs**▷ *n* A woman's breasts; HOOTERS [1920+ Australian; abbreviation of *jugs of milk*]

jugular *adj* **1** Bent on destruction; ruthless; savage; CUTTHROAT : *inert and inept troop of Democrats unable to beat back an aroused and jugular band of Republicans* **2** Vital; crucial; life-and-death : *a jugular issue for the industry/ Barbara has a very strong respect for power and position. She will not ask the ultimate jugular question* [1960s+; based on the phrase *go for the jugular*]

jug wine *n phr* A relatively cheap domestic wine, usu bought in large bottles *(1980s+)*

juice *modifier* : *a juice dealer/ juice man* **n** **1** Liquor; BOOZE, the SAUCE : *liquor much stronger than the present-day juice/ Those people just don't hold the juice (1828+)* **2** Money, esp illegally obtained and used by gamblers, loan sharks, etc : *The juice, the C, the commission (1940s+ Underworld)* **3** The interest paid on a usurious loan; VIGORISH : *interest, known in the trade as vigorish, vig, or juice (1940s+ Underworld)* **4** Electricity; current and voltage : *Turn on the juice so we can see something (1896+)* **5** Gasoline; motor fuel : *If you have a light supply of juice you climb at about 200 mph (1909+)* **6** A fuel additive for cars, esp hot rods; POP *(1960s+ Hot rodders & car racing)* **7** Nitroglycerin; SOUP *(1925+)* **8** Influence; CLOUT, PULL : *"What's juice?" "I guess you'd call it pull. Or clout" (1935+)* **9** Methadone, often administered in fruit juice *(1960s+ Narcotics)* **10** Anabolic steroids : *About 60 per cent of the wrestlers he knew during the 1980s used steroids, commonly known as "juice" (1980s+)* **11** Authority; power : *It was the stuff of cool and ultimate victory. The Redskins have the juice, the Broncos don't/ As one of the oldest gangsters in the neighborhood, Bogard had the credibility, or "juice," to call the shots (Black 1980s+ hip-hop & street talk)* **v** To hit the ball hard and far; SLUG² : *The club starts struggling a bit, so he starts trying to juice the ball (1960s+ Baseball) See* BUG JUICE, HAPPY-JUICE, JOY-JUICE, LIMEY, MOO-JUICE

juiced or **juiced up** *adj* or *adj phr* **1** Intoxicated, either by liquor or narcotics; HIGH, STONED : *Crabs was already pretty juiced up/ You been smoking too much grain. You head is juiced up (1937+)* **2** Excited, perhaps overly so; enlivened; inspired; PUMPED UP : *When they get into (regular season) games, they get all juiced up. You try to protect them (1960s+)* *adj phr* **3** Manufactured or tampered with so as to travel longer and farther : *One thing about the ball that never changes is the occasional claim that it's "juiced up"/ When a little singles hitter like the Mets' Howard Johnson connects for a tape-measure homer, all you hear is "The ball is juiced, it's hot" (1980s+ Baseball)*

juiced up *adj phr* **1** Using anabolic steroids *(1990s+)* **2** SOUPED UP *(1940s+ Hot rodders) See* JUICED

juicer *n* An alcoholic *(1967+)*

juice up *v phr* **1** To energize; invigorate; PUMP oneself UP : *A thing like that can really juice you up/ He seems, if anything, to be juicing up the pace these days* **2** To fuel : *They juiced the car up and set out* **3** SOUP UP *(1940s+ Hot rodders)* **4** To use anabolic steroids *(1980s+)*

juicy *adj* Interesting in a sexy or scandalous way; sensational; RACY : *He spared us none of the juicy details (1883+)*

juju *n* Magical or supernatural power : *has some juju going for him*

juke¹ or **jook** *n* **1** juke house **2** JUKE JOINT **3** JUKEBOX **4** Liquor; BOOZE : *That is some juke, man. That is some bad beverage (1990s+ Black street talk)* **v** **1** To tour roadside bars, drinking and dancing : *I want you to go juking with me* **2** To have a good time; disport oneself, esp at a party *(1970s+ College students)* **3** To dance *(1970s+ College students)* **4** To do the sex act; BOFF, SCREW : *"Did you juke?" "No, we just met" (1980s+ College students)* **5** To kill; OFF, SCRAG : *A man said the lady who got juked was Alice Carmody (1980s+)* **6** To absent oneself from school; PLAY HOOKY *(1970s+ Canadian teenagers)* [1900s+; fr Gullah fr Wolof and/or Bambara, "unsavory"] *See* JIVE AND JUKE, JUKING AND JIVING

juke² *v* To swerve and reverse evasively; trick a defender or tackler; jink : *Rather than to juke a defensive back, then duck inside/ Zaffuto juked past Peters on the right side* [Sports; fr Scots *jouk*, of uncertain origin]

jukebox *n* A coin-operated record player in a restaurant, bar, etc (*1930s+*)

juke joint *n phr* A usu cheap bar, roadside tavern, etc, with a jukebox (*1935+*)

juking and jiving *modifier* : Hart despises "the jukin' and jivin' phoniness of politics" *n phr* Frivolity and evasiveness; triviality and inanity (*1970s+ College students*) *See* JIVE AND JUKE

jumbo *adj* Very large; gigantic; HUMONGOUS : *I had a jumbo portion* [1897+; fr the London Zoo's great elephant, sold in 1882 to P T Barnum; *Jumbo* is a version of the word for "elephant" in various West African languages, for example, Kongo *nzamba*]

jump *modifier* : *a jump tune/ jump music* *n* 1 SWING (*1930s+ Jive talk*) 2 A dance where the music is swing or jive; HOP (*1930s+ Jive talk*) 3 A street fight between teenage gangs; RUMBLE (*1950s+ Street gangs*) 4 The continuation of a news story on a later page : *Wednesday's Times had to concede, in the jump, that Kennedy didn't make any Cabinet appointments until December 1st* (*1920s+ Newspapers*) 5 A base runner's lead off base in a possible steal (*1960s+ Baseball*) *v* 1 To attack; assault : *We jumped him as he left the place* (*1789+*) 2 To rob, esp at gunpoint; HOLD UP (*1859+*) 3 To be furiously active; be vibrant with noise and energy : *Before long the joint was jumpin'* (*1930s+ Jive talk*) ◁4▷ To do the sex act with or to; SCREW : *She admitted she always wanted him to jump her* (*1638+*) *See* GET THE JUMP ON someone or something, HAVE THE JUMP

jump all over (or **up and down on**) someone *v phr* To rebuke and berate someone very severely; savage someone : *He jumped all over her for not telling him/ The critics loved to jump up and down on Brubeck: He only once won a* Down Beat *critics' poll* (*1950s+*)

jump at *v phr* To agree eagerly : *They all jumped at the idea of a picnic* (*1769+*)

jump bail *v phr* To default on one's bail (*1872+ Underworld*)

◁**jump** (or **jump on**) someone's **bones**▷ *v phr* 1 To make strong sexual advances; sexually assault : *All these spades is gonna jump on your bones and pull your pants off/ Have I tried to jump your bones?* 2 To do the sex act with someone : *how you wish to deal with the question of me jumping your bones* (*1960s+*)

jump down someone's **throat** *v phr* To make a violent and wrathful response : *When I hinted he might be mistaken he jumped down my throat* (*1916+*)

jumped-up *adj* Elevated above one's proper status; JACKED UP • Chiefly British : *The elite regard me as a jumped-up interloper* (*1835+*)

jumper *See* PUDDLE-JUMPER

jump someone **in** *v phr* To initiate a gang member by beating : *Gang members asked if she wanted to be "jumped in" to their gang* (*1990s+ Street gangs*)

jump (or **go**) **off the deep end** *v phr* To act precipitately; take drastic action : *He jumped off the deep end and got married again* (*1940s+*) *See* GO OFF THE DEEP END

jump on someone *v phr* JUMP ALL OVER someone : *When severe reproof is administered, the culprit is said to be jumped on* (*1868+*)

jump on the bandwagon *See* GET ON THE BANDWAGON

jump someone **out** *v phr* To eject someone from a gang, usu with beating : *So I didn't have to go through the beat-down or be jumped out (practices in which the gang members are physically beaten if they decide to leave)* (*1990s+ Street gangs*)

jump out of one's **skin** *v phr* To react vehemently from joy or fear : *If that promotion comes through, he'll jump out of his skin/ When it thundered she jumped out of her skin* (*1798+*)

jump page *n phr* A page on which stories are continued : *the mixup of several paragraphs appearing on the inside "jump page"* (*1920s+ Newspapers*)

jumps, the *n phr* the JITTERS (*1899+*)

jump salty *v phr* To become angry (*1938+*)

jump ship *v phr* To desert or abandon one's job; change jobs : *Why did CBS' Deborah Norville jump ship to replace Bill O'Reilly* (*1940s+*)

jump-start *n* The act or process of starting or setting in motion something that is stalled or sluggish : *Linden teacher gives kids jump-start on information highway* *v* To start a car by attaching cables to the battery from a car that runs; start anything that resists going : *They finally jump-start that poor dumb animal/ Mubarak Tries to Jump Start Stalled Mideast Peace Talks* (*1980s+*)

jump street *n phr* The very beginning; the GIT-GO, SQUARE ONE : *One usually starts at the beginning of the endeavor, or from Jump Street* [1980s+; *at the first jump* in the same sense is found by 1577]

jump the couch *v phr* To exhibit frenzied or aberrant behavior that makes others think one is insane [2005+; fr Tom Cruise's antics on *Oprah* TV show]

jump the gun *v phr* To act prematurely : *We planned it well, but jumped the gun and ruined it* [1940s+; *beat the pistol* is found by 1905]

jump the shark *v phr* To resort to stunt programming when a television show is past its peak [1998+; fr episode on *Happy Days* TV show in which this was the actual stunt]

◁**jump through** one's **ass**▷ *v phr* To make a very quick response to a sudden difficult demand : *Old Man says we'll have to jump through our ass to get that done by tomorrow* (*1970s+ Army*)

jump through hoops *v phr* **1** To serve, obey, or accommodate someone without question, esp in a harried, frantic way : *You had to jump through hoops to please that guy* **2** To exert oneself mightily; strain : *I had to jump through hoops to get you that job* [1917+; fr the image of a trained animal *jumping through hoops* in a show, circus, etc]

jumpy *adj* Nervous; apprehensive; JITTERY : *One of our pals is jumpy and he needs a bodyguard tonight* (*1879+*)

jungle *n* **1** A camp or regular stopping place near the railroad on the outskirts of a town : *always leaves the jungle like he found it* (*1914+ Hoboes*) **2** Any place of notable violence, lawlessness, etc : *The neighborhood's becoming a jungle* (*1906+*)

◀**jungle-bunny**▶ *n* A black person : *It's no longer open season on Jungle bunnies. That day is gone* (*1950s+*)

junk *modifier* **1** : *junk jewelry/ junk mail* **2** : *one of the most dangerous junk neighborhoods in the city n* **1** Worthless and shoddy things; useless and inept productions; trash; DRECK, SHIT : *Why do you always buy such junk?* (*1842+*) **2** Tricky serves and lobs; soft, hard-to-reach shots : *He is a master of control and of dealing "junk"/ looping junk, the players' term for soft, short shots* (*1970s+ Tennis*) **3** JUNK-BALL (*1950s+ Baseball*) **4** Narcotics; DOPE : *Canales has a noseful of junk a lot of the time/ Sherlock Holmes. All he does is play a fiddle and take junk* (*1920s+ Narcotics*) **5** Unspecified heaps and objects; stuff; crap : *Men carry more junk in their pockets than women do in their pocketbooks* [fr a British nautical term for old or weak rope or cable, found by 1485]

junk-ball *modifier* : *Eddy Lopat, another "junk ball" pitcher n* A deceptive and unorthodox pitch; JUNK (*1950s+ Baseball*)

junk bond *n phr* A bond having high yield but relatively little security, used as a payment for one company by another in a corporate merger : *Fed adopts "Junk Bond" curbs* (*mid-1970s+*)

junked up *adj phr* HOPPED UP (*1940s+ Narcotics*)

junker *n* **1** JUNKIE (*1920s+ Narcotics*) **2** A narcotics dealer; CONNECTION, juggler (*1920s+ Narcotics*) **3** A car or other machine that is worn out and ready to be discarded, or that has been discarded; something that ought to be discarded; PIECE OF SHIT : *You can't litter the countryside with the kind of crap that the junkers are/ driving a junker around and around one of the chicken coops* (*1950s+*)

junket *n* A tour undertaken by a government official at public expense and often for no public benefit : *An agricultural junket through nine European countries* (*1886+*) *v* : *junketed like contemporary tourists* [fr *junket,* "feast; merrymaking," found by 1530 and of obscure origin; the verb is found by 1821, meaning "take a pleasure trip," without the US political sense]

junk fax *n* An unsolicited and unwanted fax message

junk food *n phr* Foods like potato chips, popcorn, sugar-coated cereals, and the like, esp popular with children and having little nutritional value (*1970s+*)

junk heap *n phr* **1** A worn and ramshackle old car; HEAP, JALOPY (*1940s+*) **2** Any unsightly or chaotic place : *His room was always a mephitic junk heap* (*1906+*)

junkie or **junky** *modifier* : *Junkie logic is the ability to justify whatever needs to be done to support an addiction n* **1** A narcotics addict : *I didn't want to be a junkie/ The man I was to find was both a junkie and pusher* (*1923+ Narcotics*) **2** A devotee or addict of any sort : *Zuckerman describes himself as a "newspaper and magazine junkie"/ Growth junkies, snipes one former insider, go-go boys*

junk mail *n phr* Mail, usu third class, consisting of advertising circulars, appeals for money, etc, and sometimes addressed to "resident" (*1950s+*)

junkyard dog *n phr* A particularly vicious dog or person : *If the unions took over our plants, we would turn as mean as a junk-yard dog/ He's a junkyard dog. He's tough. He's nasty* (*1980s+*)

jury is still out, the *sentence* No decision has yet been made; the question is open : *The jury is still out on whether he's fitting in/ The jury is still out on whether the traditional union is necessary for the new workplace/ The jury may remain out on Mr. Clinton's contradictory character for a long time* (*1980s+*)

just another pretty face, not See NOT JUST ANOTHER PRETTY FACE

just around the corner *adv phr* Nearby; imminent : *Prosperity is just around the corner, the President said* (*1914+*)

just fallen off the turnip truck *adj phr* Unfledged; inexperienced; ignorant : *Detective Benjamin Calazo was not a cop who had just* *fallen off the turnip truck* [1980s+; the agricultural source suggests an earlier date]

just folks *n phr* Ordinary people; common people; hoi polloi : *The Mayor moved about in a warm-up jacket, playing just folks* (1908+)

just for the hell of it *See* FOR THE HELL OF IT

just off the boat *modifier* Just in from a foreign country; also, naive and gullible : *They don't understand; they are just off the boat*

just one of those things *n phr* Something that can hardly be predicted, justified, explained, or avoided, but is an intrinsic and sometimes a distressful part of living•The gestural equivalent is a shrug : *Their divorce was just one of those things* (1930s+)

just the ticket *adv* Just the thing needed or wanted : *cup of coffee will be just the ticket*

just what the doctor ordered *n phr* Exactly what is needed : *Account Supervisors: We're just what the doctor ordered for your career* (1914+)

just whistling Dixie *See* NOT JUST WHISTLING DIXIE

juve or **juvie** or **juvey** *adj* Juvenile; youthful : *the next monster juve act would be* (1940s+) *modifier* 1 : *Andrews became the archetypal juve lead on British television* 2 : *juvey hall/ juvey books* *n* 1 A young person; child; juvenile, esp a juvenile offender : *I'm a juve* (1940s+) 2 An actor who plays youthful roles; a juvenile lead : *No juve in this show?* (1935+) 3 A juvenile court or a reformatory : *I was desperate. You ever been in juvie?* (1940s+)

K

K *n* **1** A thousand dollars : *Four bastards no smarter'n you and me got ninety-seven K out of some little bank* (*1970s+*) **2** A kilogram, esp such a quantity of narcotics; KEY : *even occasional Ks (kilograms) of cocaine* (*1960s+ Narcotics*) **3** A strikeout (*1861+ Baseball*) [fr the Greek prefix *kilo-*, "one thousand"; baseball sense said to have been originated in a scorecard notation system either by Henry Chadwick or M J Kelly]

kabibble *See* ISH KABIBBLE

kablooey *See* GO BLOOEY

kaka *See* CA-CA

kamikaze *modifier* Violent and reckless; self-destructive : *his kamikaze style would lead to fine, suspension, or tragic injury* (*1960s+*)

kangaroo *v* To convict someone with false evidence; FRAME (*Prison*)

kangaroo court or **club** *n phr* **1** A mock court : *The toughest prisoner announced that he was president of the Kangaroo Club and would hold court* (*1853+*) **2** A small-town police court where traffic fines to transients are high and usu divided among the police (*1940s+*) [origin unknown]

kaput or **kapoot** (kah PŌOT) *adj* Inoperative; ineffective; FINISHED : *I would be "kaput" without a folding machete/ Only sixteen of us. After that, kapoot* [1914+; fr echoic-symbolic German slang]

Katie bar the door *sentence* Get ready for trouble; a desperate situation is at hand : *If you fall too far behind, it'll be Katie-bar-the-door real quick/ If they were on to him, well, that's all she wrote. Katie bar the door* (*1930s+*)

katrinka *n* An old car : *makes it clear that some of the old katrinkas are worth their weight in gold* (*1990s+*)

kayo or **kay** *n* A knockout; KO (*1923+ Prizefight*)

kazoo or **gazoo** or **gazool** *n* **1** The buttocks; anus; ASS : *an impossible, unreliable, self-destructive pain in the kazoo/ We have subcommittee staff running out the kazoo/ You know he's off balance and you'd like to stick it in his gazoo* **2** Toilet; CAN : *I tore it up and flushed it down the kazoo* [1970s+; origin unknown; perhaps fr Louisiana French *zoozoo*, "buttocks, ass"; perhaps *kazoo*, known in its standard sense fr the 1880s, suggested the anus in being tubular and emitting sounds]

kee *See* KEY²

keed *n* KID (*1920+*)

keel over *v phr* To fall down; collapse : *He was so tired he was about to keel over* [1876+; fr nautical careening of a ship so that the keel is raised]

keen *adj* Excellent; wonderful; NEAT : *I think she's a keen kid/ "Keen?" Blanche said. "I haven't heard that word in 20 years"* (*1900+ Teenagers & students*) *See* PEACHY

keep someone *v phr* To support and maintain someone for sexual purposes : *She has "an old man" who "keeps" her/ Maybe some day some guy'll even keep me* (*1560+*)

keep (or **maintain**) **a low profile** *v phr* To stay inconspicuous; try not to attract much attention : *Better keep a low profile until this blows over* [1975+; originally a military term, based on the idea of offering a small target; *low profile* is found by the 1960s]

keep an eye on someone or something *v phr* To watch; guard over : *So I paid her a visit so as I could keep an eye on the house* (*1818+*)

keep one's chin up *v phr* To maintain a positive attitude (*1938+*)

keep one's cool *v phr* To retain one's composure; stay calm; COOL IT : *We'd all better keep our cool and not provoke him* (*1950s+ Beat & cool talk*)

keeper *n* Someone or something worth keeping or trying to keep : *This husband's a keeper*

keep one's eye on the ball *v phr* To pay strict attention to what one is doing; be alert and undistracted (*1907+*)

keep one's eye peeled (or **skinned**) *v phr* To be vigilant; look carefully : *I keep my eye peeled for bargains* (*entry form 1853+, second 1833+*)

keep one's hair on *v phr* To stay unruffled; be calm; COOL IT : *I'm coming. Just keep your hair on, won't you?* (*1885+*)

keep someone honest *v phr* **1** To pose a requirement or test so that someone does not go unchallenged : *We'll ask her a few questions just to keep her honest* **2** To pitch close to a batter; throw at a batter : *Keep him honest, which means, make the batter afraid of you* (*Baseball*) (*1960s+*)

keep it down to a dull (or **loud**) **roar** *v phr* To be quiet, or quieter : *How about keeping the noise level down to a dull roar?/ Earl thrives on controversy, and we're trying so hard to go the other way or, at least, keep it to a loud roar* (*1940s+*)

keep it on the DL *v phr* To keep something secret [1990s+ Teenagers; fr *keep it down low*]

keep it real *interj* Be yourself; don't be a fake : *They all pretend to be sophisticated, but I'm keeping it real*

287

keep one's **nose clean** *v phr* To avoid doing wrong or seeming to do wrong; stay above reproach : *If you only keep your nose clean, you'll have it* [1887+; fr a traditional injunction of a mother to a child to wipe its *nose*, wash behind its ears, etc]

keep someone **on a short leash** *v phr* To keep someone under close control : *We must keep that crazy kid on a short leash* (1970s+)

keep someone **on ice** *v phr* To keep someone under one's authority : *complete control to keep Dubie on ice indefinitely* (1894+)

keep on keeping on *v phr* To persist; hold one's course; KEEP ON TRUCKING : *He would keep on keeping on and worry later about his destination* (1970s+)

keep something on the down low *v phr* To keep quiet about a matter; to not divulge information : *Please keep this idea on the down low*

keep someone **on the reservation** *v phr* To ensure and require orthodoxy, esp in politics : *White House chief of staff McLarty kept Penny, McCurdy and Stenholm completely on the reservation* [1990s+; fr the notion of confinement to an Indian *reservation*]

keep on trucking *v phr* To carry on; continue what one is doing, esp working, plugging away, etc; KEEP ON KEEPING ON (1972+)

keep one's **pecker (or rocket) in** one's **pocket** *v phr* To refrain from the sex act; practice continence : *Another professor remarked crudely, "You had better teach your husband to keep his pecker in his pocket, so you can get your research done"* (1990s+)

keep one **posted** *interj* Please keep me informed of what is going on; supply up-to-date information (1800s+)

keeps See FOR KEEPS, PLAY FOR KEEPS

keep several balls in the air (or irons in the fire) *v phr* To be involved on multiple jobs, projects, etc [1980s+; fr the image of a juggler]

keep one's **shirt (or pants) on** *v phr* 1 To stay unruffled; be calm; COOL IT : *He was beginning to holler, so I told him to keep his shirt on* 2 To be patient; wait a bit; HOLD one's HORSES : *Keep your pants on and the guy will be back* (1854+)

keep tabs on *v phr* To keep informed about; keep watch on or over : *Who's gonna keep tabs on the receipts?* [1888+; fr *tab*, "bill, account"]

keep the faith (baby) *interj* Stay encouraged and positive : *a 60s chant to keep the faith*

keep one's **trap shut** *v phr* To stay or become silent; SHUT UP : *Otherwise you do yourself a favor and keep your trap shut, you understand?* (1899+)

keep something under one's **hat** *v phr* To keep something quiet, or a secret; keep to oneself : *Payne, keep this under your hat, will you?* (1885+)

keep up with the Joneses *v phr* To strive, esp beyond one's means, to keep up socially and financially with others in the same neighborhood or in the same social circle : *Never keep up with the Joneses; drag them down to your level, it's cheaper* [1913+; fr the title of a 1913 comic strip by Arthur R Momand]

kee-rect (KEE rekt) *adj* Correct (1950s+)

kef (KEEF, KAYF) *n* (also **keef** or **kief** or **kif**) Marijuana, hashish, or opium [1878+ Narcotics; fr Arabic, "pleasure"]

kegger or **keg party** *n* A beer party; BEER BUST (1960s+ Teenagers & students)

keister (KEE stər) (also **keester** or **keyster** or **kiester** or **kister**) *n* 1 The buttocks; rump; ASS : *I've had it up to my keister with these leaks/ What a sensation; we'll knock them on their keister* (1931+) 2 A rear trousers pocket (1930s+ Pickpockets) 3 A suitcase that opens into a display of goods : *the typical "keister" of the street hawker* (1930s+ Hawkers) 4 A safe; strongbox; CRIB (1914+ Underworld) [fr British dialect *kist* or German *Kiste*, "chest, box," transferred to the buttocks perhaps by the pickpocket sense or by the notion that something may be concealed in the rectum]

ker- (KURR or KUH) *prefix* A particle that intensifies echoic terms for blows, splashings, hard efforts, etc : *kerbang/ kerblam/ kerplunk/ kerslosh/ kerwallop* (1840s+)

kerflooie or **kerflooey** See GO BLOOEY

kerfuffle *n* Disorder; confusion : *Don Imus has thrown the capital into a kerfuffle* [1813+; fr Scots dialect; often spelled *curfuffle*]

kerplunk See GO KERPLUNK

kettle of fish See FINE KETTLE OF FISH

key[1] *adj* 1 Essential; crucial : *U.S. commitment and pressure are key to what happens next/ The attendance of cute guys at this party is key* (1980s+) 2 Excellent; splendid; FRESH, KILLER, AWESOME (1980s+ Students) *n* 1 A typical Ivy League student; white shoe (1950s+ College students) 2 The area on the court legal for free throws : *Best way to choose a nominee? "Personally," said Bradley, "I favor a jump shot from the top of the key"/ knocked home a 19-footer from the top of the key* (1990s+ Basketball) *v* To vandalize a car by scratching it with a key : *Well, did you key her car?* (1980s+) See CHURCH KEY

key[2] or **kee** or **ki** *n* A kilogram (about 2.2 pounds) of a narcotic : *enough opium to produce a key (kilo) of heroin/ Anybody who can handle a key of pure coke is dealing big* [Narcotics; fr *kilo*]

key on something *v phr* To regard something as important; discover that something is "key" : *One of the things I kept keying on was this notion of a distinctly hand-oriented society* (1990s+)

keyster *See* KEISTER

keystone or **keystone sack** or **keystone cushion,** the *n phr* Second base *(1917+ Baseball)*

ki *See* KEY

kibbles and bits *n phr* Crumbs of cocaine [1990s+ Teenagers; fr *kibbles*, "products of a kind of grinding," found by 1891; the verb is found by 1790; today chiefly a form of dog-food pellets]

kibitz or **kabitz** *n* : *Ixnay on the kabitz. Get me?* *v* **1** To give intrusive and unrequested advice while watching a game, performance, etc : *He was kibitzing us all the way* **2** To banter, comment : *We were kibitzing around* [1920s+; fr Yiddish fr German *Kiebitz*, "peewit, lapwing," a noisy little bird]

kibitzer *n* A person who gives intrusive advice : *I don't mind admitting that a good kibitzer has 20-20 hindsight* (1920s+)

kibosh *v* To eliminate; terminate; kevork, KILL : *That was kiboshed promptly by the White House spokesman* (1884+)

kibosh, the *n phr* The termination; sad end; sudden doom : *This latest goof is probably the kibosh* [1834+; origin unknown and very extensively speculated upon; perhaps, e.g., fr Irish *cie bais*, "cap of death," referring to the black cap a judge would don when pronouncing a death sentence; perhaps fr Yiddish] *See* PUT THE KIBOSH ON someone or something

kick *n* **1** : *If you got any kicks, you can always quit* (1839+) **2** A pocket, esp a pants pocket : *I have a hundred thousand boo-boos in the kick* (1849+) **3** A surge or fit of pleasure; a feeling of joy and delight; BELT, CHARGE : *He was having a real kick/ I get a kick out of you* (1941+) **4** Anything that gives one a feeling of pleasure, joy, etc : *That's a kick. Ridin' a guy down Wilshire in daylight* (1941+) **5** A strong personal predilection; THING : *Arthur is on the Paris kick/ several opportunities to let her wail on a comic kick* (1940s+) **6** Power; impact; potency : *One of those stories with a kick* (1844+) **7** A shoe : *Hey, nice kicks* (1904+) **8** A spurt of speed at the end of a footrace : *Full into his kick as he passed them* (1980s+ Sports) *v* **1** To complain; protest; BITCH : *She can just kick all she wants to* (1388+) **2** To end one's drug habit; become "clean" *(1936+ Narcotics)* [pocket sense fr late 17th-century *kicks*, "breeches"] *See* GET A KICK OUT OF someone or something, ON A ROLL, SIDEKICK

kick around *v phr* **1** To idle about; drift around rootlessly; BAT AROUND : *He put in a couple years just kicking around California* **2** To acquire experience; become seasoned : *sound like a band that's kicked around for a long time*] [1940s+; the sense "walk around" is found by 1839]

kick someone **around** *v phr* To abuse; repeatedly maltreat : *Mr Nixon said the press wouldn't have him to kick around anymore* *(1912+ Students)*

kick something **around** *v phr* To discuss or think about something; consider from all angles : *It's something we've been kicking around for about 10 years* (1940s+)

kick-ass *adj* (also **kick-butt** or **kick-yer-ass**) Rough; powerful; ROUGH-ASS, TOUGH : *that kick-ass attitude/ gave up its last drop of kick-ass Gewurztraminer/ the only team without a kick-butt run blocker on their line* *n* Power; energy; virility : *He's the guy who coaxed the kick-ass back into the torque/ with the gall to label such Muzak kick-ass* (1970s+ Army)

kick ass *v phr* **1** To assert power; be rough; punish : *He once again kicked ass with the Wagner 6 to 1 triumph/ Geometry and algebra were kicking my ass/ We kicked a little ass last night* **2** To have power; have unpolished vigor : *just country that kicks ass and entertains* (1970s+ Army)

kick ass and take names *v phr* To behave very roughly and angrily; KICK ASS : *screaming, berating, threatening, kicking ass and taking names/ Paschal ain't gonna do nothing but kick ass and take names* [1970s+ Army; fr the image of a rough and punitive police officer, drill sergeant, prison guard, etc]

kickback *n* Money given to someone illegally or unethically : *Buying another poor devil's job for $50 or a kick-back from his pay/ All the cops were on the pad, getting kickbacks from the hookers* (1934+)

kick back *v phr* **1** To return or restore, esp to give back stolen property : *Stolen goods returned to the rightful owner are "kicked back"* *(1926+ Underworld)* **2** To give part of wages, fees, etc, illicitly to another in return for one's job or other advantage : *The cabbies had to kick back a lot to the dispatchers* (1934+) **3** To relax; CHILL OUT : *Use the pool, kick back. Who knows?/ That's when I started kicking back with my brothers and homeboys* (1980s+ Students fr black)

kick booty *v phr* KICK ASS (1980s+)

kicker *n* **1** A complainer; KVETCH (1876+) **2** A small motor, esp an outboard, used for a boat; EGGBEATER (1928+) **3** Anything that gives great pleasure; KICK : *The kicker was the station wagon* (1940s+) **4** A hidden cost, qualification, defect, etc; CATCH : *The kicker is that if you are subject to this requirement, your homeowner's policy will not cover the injuries/ The kicker to this one is simple* (1970s+) [fourth sense probably fr poker, "a high card kept, along with a pair, in draw poker," found by 1892]

kickers *n* Shoes, esp tennis shoes *(1950s+ College students)*

kickin' *adj* Excellent; BAD, COOL, way rad : *a creamy Italian dressing with kickin' taste and bumpin' packaging/ The game was kickin'* *(1980s+ Black teenagers)*

kick in *v phr* **1** To pay up money; make one's proper contribution; FORK OVER : *to ask you guys to kick in your share of the expenses* (1908+) **2** To begin action; take effect; begin to function : *The endorphins were beginning to kick in/ Now the morphine was kicking in/ The motel kitchen was kicking into action* (1980s+) [second sense perhaps fr earlier phrase *kick it in gear*, "shift the gears of a car"]

kicking ass *n phr* A good time; a BALL : *We went downtown and had a kicking ass* *(1980s+ College students)*

kick in the ass (or **the [seat of the] pants**), a *n phr* **1** A surprising and dampening rebuff, misfortune, etc; a slap in the face **2** A strong stimulus or impetus; a SHOT IN THE ARM : *If this campaign doesn't get a kick in the ass we're dead/ The sizzle of the 24-valve V8 Mercedes M3 assures the driver of the right kind of kick in the pants* (1940s+)

kick it *v phr* **1** To rid oneself of narcotic addiction : *I don't think anybody knew anyone who had kicked it* (1936+ Narcotics) **2** To play swing or jazz very vigorously *(Jazz talk & jive talk)* **3** To idle about with nothing much to do : *Dude canceled his party, so we'll probably end up kickin' it/ I didn't really have any friends at school, I just used to kick it by myself* *(1980s+ Black teenagers)*

kick it up a notch *v phr* To make something more exciting, intense, or interesting, as a food dish or a social gathering : *He's adding garlic to kick it up a notch/ She broke out the martini ingredients to kick it up a notch* [1990s+; fr chef Emeril Lagasse, whose other catch phrases are "BAM!" "Feel the love," and "Oh yeah, babe"]

kickoff *modifier* : *kickoff dinner/ kickoff speech n* The beginning; inauguration : *He planned the kickoff of his campaign for Texas* (1875+)

kick off *v phr* **1** To die : *after his wife kicked off* (1921+) **2** To leave; depart (1950+) **3** To begin something; inaugurate : *the chain of thought kicked off by it/ a relative newcomer who kicked off her film career with Menace II Society*

kick someone **out** *v phr* To eject, expel, or dismiss someone; BOUNCE : *She kicked Peter out of the apartment* (1711+)

kick over *See* KNOCK OVER

kicks *n* **1** Pleasure and gratification; BANG, JOLLIES : *Sock cymbal's enough to give me my kicks* (1950s+) **2** Shoes (1891+) *See* GET one's COOKIES

kick-start *n* To inaugurate; launch, esp vigorously : *Clinton's speech was a kick-start for his health plan* [1990s+; fr the starting of a motorcyle by a *kick* downward on the start pedal]

kick the bucket *v phr* To die : *Old man Mose done kicked the bucket* [1785+; origin uncertain; perhaps fr the *bucket* a suicide might kick from beneath him in hanging himself]

kick-the-cat *modifier* Angry and frustrated : *puts the IRS in a surly, kick-the-cat mood* [1990s+; fr the image of one who *kicks the cat* when the real target of anger is unknown or unreachable]

kick the tires *v phr* To make a quick and superficial inspection; do cursory checking : *simplistic agrarian vision bought by the warweary nation without kicking the tires/ has asked PC Magazine to kick the tires and slam the doors* [1970s+; fr such an examination made while appraising a car]

kick someone **to the curb** *v phr* To be no longer employed or wanted; made surplus : *It shall be rendered, as the British say, redundant. Or as my contemporaries would observe, kicked to the curb* (1990s+)

kick-up *n* **1** A dance or dancing party (1778+) **2** A commotion; disturbance; RUCKUS (1793+)

kick up a fuss (or **a row**) *v phr* To make a disturbance; complain loudly and bitterly; RAISE CAIN : *I don't want his lawyer to kick up a fuss about this/ I'm afraid the opposition will kick up a row over this* (entry form 1848+, variant 1759+)

kick someone **upstairs** *v phr* To remove someone from office by promotion to a nominally superior position : *It is conceivable but not likely that Mr Gromyko has been kicked upstairs where he'll no longer influence Soviet foreign policy* (1821+)

kicky *adj* **1** Very chic and modish : *a lot of kicky clothes, many of them imports/ so easy and smooth in their short, kicky skirts, pantyhose* **2** Exciting; ravishing; FAR OUT : *It's very kicky to be able to drive right over sand dunes/ a kicky way to spend a couple of years* (1950s+)

kid *modifier* : *his kid sister/ my kid cousin n* **1** A child : *She's a cute little kid* (1599+) **2** A young or relatively young man or woman : *the kids in college* (1884+) *v* **1** To joke; jest;

banter; JOSH : *a funny guy, always kidding* (1891+) **2** To attempt to deceive; try to fool : *Are you kidding me?* (1811+) [fr *kid*, "an infant goat"; bantering and fooling senses perhaps fr an alteration of dialect *cod*, "hoax, fool"] *See* I KID YOU NOT, NEW KID ON THE BLOCK, WHIZ KID

Kid, the *n phr* A copilot; meter-reader *(WWII Army Air Forces)*

kid around *v phr* To jest and banter; avoid seriousness; FOOL AROUND (1940s+)

kiddie or **kiddy** *n* A child [1889+; the form *kiddey* is found by 1823]

kidding *See* NO KIDDING

kiddo or **Kiddo** *n* A person, esp one younger than oneself • Used nearly always in direct address : *Look, kiddo, I don't think you quite understand/ There's a lot of loot there, kiddo* (1905+)

kidney *See* GRIPE one's ASS

kid stuff *n phr* **1** Something too easy to challenge an adult; CINCH, PIECE OF CAKE : *That swim to Catalina's kid stuff* **2** Activity not appropriate for an adult; childish concerns : *Give up the kid stuff and find a real job* (1923+)

kief or **kif** *See* KEF

kiester *See* KEISTER

◄**kike**► *adj* : *kike neighborhood n* **1** A Jew • Sometimes used by Jews of other Jews they regard with contempt; several early occurrences are found in a theatrical context (1904+) **2** A low or shady merchant or shop • The 1916 advertisement quoted here was placed by a Jewish merchant : *Go into any little kike, little hole-in-the-wall* (1916+) [origin unknown and much speculated upon; the most plausible explanation, published by J H A Lacher, a former traveling salesman, is that the established German-American Jewish salesmen ridiculed their Eastern European colleagues in the 1890s with the name *kiki* because so many of their surnames ended in "ki" or "ky," whence *kike*]

kill *n* **1** A murder : *for the Shannon kill* (1930s+) **2** An enemy airplane, ship, tank, etc, destroyed *(WWII armed forces)* *v* **1** To drink or eat up : *The lady killed a dozen oysters* (1833+) **2** To spoil or ruin : *One bad grade killed his chances for med school* (1573+) **3** To demoralize totally; make hopeless : *The third defeat killed him* (1940s+) **4** To be extremely successful with : *The Evergreen Review kills him* (1899+) **5** To make an audience helpless with laughter; FRACTURE : *My McEnroe act kills 'em* (1856+) **6** To do very easily; ACE : *I killed the geology final* (1900+ *Students*) **7** To eliminate a newspaper story or part of it (1865+) **8** To extinguish a light (1934+) **9**

To stop or turn off a motor (1886+) *See* IN AT THE KILL, KILLER

kill, to *See* DRESSED TO KILL, DRESSED TO THE TEETH

killer *adj* (also **killer-diller**) : *not only was it a killer version/ The killer idea of the century is about to be laid on you* (1970s+) *n* **1** A very attractive person : *Ain't she a killer?* (1937+) **2** (also **killer-diller**) A person or thing that is remarkable, wonderful, superior, etc; BEAUT, DOOZIE : *The song's a killer!/ The famed quartet steams out "killer-dillers"* (1930s+) **3** A marijuana cigarette; JOINT (1940s+ *Narcotics*) *See* LADY-KILLER

kill for something *v phr* To be willing to go to great extremes to get something : *I'd kill for a beer now*

killing *adj* Excellent; FRESH, GREAT, KILLER, way rad : *And good things are known as "rad, tough, booming, legit, fly, kill, killing, chilling, fresh or nasty"* [1980s+ Teenagers; the sense "fascinating, bewitching, irresistible" is found by 1619, but the current use is an independent phenomenon rather than a survival] *See* MAKE A KILLING

killjoy *n* A morose pessimist; CRAPE-HANGER, GLOOMY GUS

kill the clock *v phr* To use delaying tactics and plays at the very end of a period or game : *and ran double tight-end formations sets to kill the clock* (1960s+ *Sports*)

kill (or **shoot**) **the messenger** *modifier* : *In a shoot-the-messenger diversionary tactic, the spotlight swung away from Clarence Thomas and smack onto Totenberg v phr* To punish the bearer of bad news : *Dreyfus is right. Let's not make the mistake of killing the messenger* (1980s+)

kilter *See* OUT OF KILTER

kimono *See* PINE OVERCOAT

kin *See* KISSING COUSIN

kind (or **sort**) **of** *See* SOME KIND OF

king *n* **1** (also **kingpin**) The leader; chief : *king of the motorcycle jumpers* (entry form 1382+, variant 1867+) **2** A prison warden (1940s+ *Underworld*) **3** A yardmaster or freight conductor (1940s+ *Railroad*)

King Kong *n phr* **1** Something huge and threatening; SIX-HUNDRED-POUND GORILLA : *"It wouldn't matter if you put King Kong in the Treasury," complained Sir Teddy Taylor. "The Germans control our economy"* (1955+) **2** Cheap and strong liquor : *No six-year-old child got no business drinking that King Kong* (1960s+ *Black*) [fr the 1933 movie *King Kong*, about a gargantuan gorilla]

king-size or **king-sized** *adj* Very large; extra large : *Your nagging gives me a king-size headache/ The new king-sized rockets stopped three Red tanks* (1940s+)

kink *modifier* : *a kinko diner who tries to attract Chong's attention* **n** **1** (also **kinko**) A person with deviant or bizarre tastes, esp sexual : *I'm not some kind of kink* (1960s+) **2** A deviant practice or predilection, esp sexual : *a Nazi with a kink for prepubescent girls/ the female staffer whose kink is making love down in the morgue* **3** A style featuring deviation and oddness : *blend of leaden TV-style melodrama and deadpan modernist kink* (1990s+) **4** A defect or flaw, esp a minor one; BUG : *We'll work the kinks out of the plan before we announce it* (1868+)

kinky *adj* **1** Dishonest; illegal; CROOKED : *"kinky" gambling paraphernalia* (1927+) **2** Stolen : *a kinky car* (1927+ Underworld) **3** Eccentric; crotchety (1860+) **4** Bizarre; weird : *no offense so kinky that the Maximum Enchilada and his consigliores wouldn't commit it* (1950s+) **5** Deviant and abnormal, esp sexually : *a very kinky guy, likes being beat up* (1950s+) **6** Showing or pertaining to sexual deviation : *kinky photos/ kinky porn* [the stronger fifth sense is said to have originated among British homosexuals in the 1920s]

kipe *v* To steal : *kiped some cherries from the bar* (1960s+)

kishkes or **kishkas** *n* The entrails; innards; GUTS : *His kishkas were gripped by the iron hand of outrage and frustration* [1959+; fr Yiddish]

kiss *n* KISS-OFF (1950s+) *See* BUTTERFLY KISS, FRENCH KISS, SOUL KISS

KISS (KIS) *sentence* Keep it simple, stupid, or keep it simple and stupid (1980s+)

kiss and make up *v phr* To become reconciled; forget past animosity : *Mandela and his rival Chief Buthelezi, whose followers have been slaughtering one another by the thousands, have kissed and made up* (1940s+)

kiss and tell *modifier* Gossiping about one's friends, esp about sexual exploits : *Reagan condemned these "kiss and tell" books by former government servants/ those juicy kiss-and-tell escapades that seem so much a part of the professional athlete's life* (1695+) **n phr** : *Don't look for a kiss-and-tell from Ulichny* (1980s+) [the dated instance for the first sense is in the original verb form]

◁**kiss-ass** or **kiss-butt**▷ *modifier* (also **kissy-ass**) : *another kiss-ass review of an extremely bad album/ his tone much different, being efficient and a little kissy-ass* **n 1** A toady; sycophant; BROWN-NOSE, ASS-KISSER : *and not have people think, "Oh, what a kiss-butt"* **2** Sycophantic flattery : *using the old kiss-ass with the colonel* (1960s+)

◁**kiss ass**▷ *v phr* To flatter one's superiors; BROWN-NOSE : *He likes to be perfect and kiss ass* (1930s+)

◁**kiss someone's ass**▷ *v phr* To flatter someone; curry favor with superiors : *I didn't kiss anybody's ass and I didn't expect anybody to kiss mine* (1749+)

kisser *n* The mouth; the face : *It would be a pleasure to drop one on your kisser, I admit/ show the good side of my kisser/ Reagan had that quizzical "do I talk now?" look on his kisser* (1860+) *See* ASS-KISSER, MOTHERFUCKER

kiss something goodbye *v phr* To take leave of something, often unwillingly; bid farewell : *I figure, this is it, say your prayers and kiss your butt goodbye* (1930s+)

kissing *See* MOTHERFUCKING

kissing cousin (or **kin**) *n* **1** A relative close enough to be kissed in salutation, hence anyone with whom a person is fairly intimate : *The two species will often prove to be kissing cousins, for they'll crossbreed/ You guys talk like kissing cousins* **2** A close copy : *He had a kissing cousin of Montgomery's mustache* (1940s+)

◁**kiss my ass**▷ *sentence* An invitation to perform an obsequious and humiliating act; GO FUCK oneself, FUCK YOU • Always an insulting challenge and rejection : *"What should I say?" asked Belle. "Tell him to kiss my ass"/ I want him to kiss my ass in Macy's window and tell me it smells like roses* (1705+)

kiss of death *n phr* The reason something will end or die; something causing ruin : *Interviewing with them could be the kiss of death*

kiss-off *n* (also **California kiss-off** or **New York kiss-off**) A dismissal, esp a rude one; the BOUNCE, BRUSH-OFF, KISS : *He got up out of his chair, the standard kiss-off* **v** To die (1940s+ Black)

kiss off *v phr* **1** To dodge; evade : *had kissed off all raps* (1930s+) **2** To kill : *who kissed off Martin* (1940s+)

kiss someone or something off *v phr* **1** To dismiss rudely; BRUSH someone OFF : *The receptionist kissed me off quite cheekily* **2** To let go of, to attempt to forget; KISS something GOODBYE : *You can kiss that money off* (1930s+)

kiss someone out *v phr* To deny someone their share : *When a member of a mob is deprived of his share he is "kissed out"* (1920s+ Underworld)

kiss the canvas (or **the resin**) *v phr* To be knocked unconscious, esp in a boxing match (1919+)

kiss the dust *v phr* BITE THE DUST (1940s+)

kiss up to *v phr* To flatter obsequiously : *kisses up to the popular crowd*

kissy-face (also **kissy-huggy** or **kissy-kissy** or **kissy-poo**) *modifier* : *But she was such a kissy-face up person/ Pauley and Norville's kissy-poo exchange on Today/ For two weeks* *after that kissy-face weekend, our love connection continued/ is not gonna be a kissy-huggy book/ Many of the rich and famous, the kissy-kissy socials had all but disappeared* **n 1** Displays of affection; cuddling; blandishments : *From now on it's all PR work and kissy-kissy here and kissy-kissy there* **2** A kiss : *The symbol of welcome is a handshake, not a kissy-poo* **v** : *I've trained poodles so that they won't kissy-face everybody* (1980s+) See PLAY KISSIE

kister *See* KEISTER

kit *See* HEAD KIT

kit and caboodle (or **boodle**) **n phr** The totality; everything : *the whole kit and caboodle, go hang/ the whole kit and boodle of 'em* [1861+; fr 1700s British *kit*, "outfit of equipment," plus early 1800s *boodle*, "lot, collection," perhaps fr Dutch *boedel*, "property, effects"]

kitchen **n 1** The cab of a locomotive *(1940s+ Railroad)* **2** The stomach **3** The space over home plate where a batter finds it easiest to hit a fair ball; a batter's preferred point of delivery; WHEELHOUSE : *He'd throw it in my kitchen, so I moved up a step toward the plate* *(1970+ Baseball)* [baseball sense perhaps ultimately fr *kitchen*, "stomach," found by 1594] *See* IF YOU CAN'T STAND THE HEAT STAY OUT OF THE KITCHEN

kitchen cabinet **n phr** An unofficial set of advisers to a president or chief, made up of close friends and cronies, originally of President Andrew Jackson *(1832+)*

kite **n 1** A letter or note, esp one smuggled into prison *(1851+ Underworld)* **2** An airplane • Chiefly British *(1917+)* **v** To write a check when one does not have the funds to cover it, hoping to find them before the check is cashed : *The bill was due before payday, so I had to kite the check* *(1934+)* [*fly a kite* in the verb sense is found by 1808] *See* GO FLY A KITE, HIGH AS A KITE

kitsch or **Kitsch** (KITCH) **n** Literature or art having little esthetic merit but appealing powerfully to popular taste : *It stands unchallenged as a masterpiece of kitsch/ The closest I can come to America is through its Kitsch* [1925+; fr German, "trash, rubbish"]

kitschy **adj** Being or resembling kitsch : *Visconti's kitschy film/ Its kitschy Lupe Velez ambiance* *(1960s+)*

kitten *See* HAVE KITTENS, SEX KITTEN

kitty **n** The pot or pool of money in a gambling game, made up of contributions from the players; a contributed fund : *Each put $25,000 in the kitty* *(1891+ Gambling)* See BITCH KITTY, DUST KITTY, FEED THE KITTY, IT'S A BITCH

klepto **n** A kleptomaniac : *"Bloody klepto,"* says *Siddhartha* [1940s+; fr a Greek combining word *klepto-*, "thief"]

klick or **klik** *See* CLICK

kluck *See* CLUCK, DUMB CLUCK

klutz or **clutz** (KLUTS) **n 1** A stupid person; idiot; BLOCKHEAD : *Now, klutz that I am, I thought of Neal/ A small crowd of first-class clutzes* **2** A clumsy person; a lubberly lout : *I am the world's biggest klutz. I trip over my own feet, drop things* [1968+; fr Yiddish, "blockhead," literally "block"]

klutzy **adj 1** Stupid; idiotic : *any clever kid playing a klutzy kid* **2** Clumsy; unhandy *(1968+)*

kneecap **v 1** To shoot someone in the kneecap or legs : *There was another drive-by and one of the deacons got kneecapped* **2** To disable as if by kneecapping : *The law-and-order issue, which Republicans have used for a generation to kneecap Democrats at will, has been coopted* *(1975+)*

knee-deep **adj phr** Overwhelmed; oversupplied; very much involved; UP TO one's ASS IN something : *I never even tried to make money, and now I'm knee deep in the stuff* *(1940s+)*

knee-high to a grasshopper **adj phr** (Variations: **bumblebee** or **duck** or **frog** or **mosquito** or **spit** or **splinter** or **toad** may replace **grasshopper**) Very short or small, esp because young : *He's been smoking since he was knee-high to a grasshopper* [1851+; *knee high to a toad* is found by 1814]

knee-jerk **modifier** : *one more gesture to the knee-jerk hawks in the Congress/ Yet McDonald is no mere knee-jerk critic of the evangelicals* **n 1** A reflexlike action or response : *Being nasty to women is a knee-jerk with him* *(1958+)* **2** A person who reacts with a reflexlike response : *a seventy-year old knee-jerk best remembered for castigating the Reverend Bill Moyers for dancing the frug in the White House* *(1958+)* **v** : *We need less kneejerking on both sides in these arguments about the environment* *(1980s+)* [fr the patellar reflex, described as *knee jerk* by 1876]

knees *See* BEES KNEES, CUT oneself OFF AT THE KNEES, CUT someone OFF AT THE KNEES, GET TAKEN OFF AT THE KNEES

kneesies **n** Clandestine amorous friction of the knees : *We got back to the table and played kneesies while we talked* [1951+; modeled on *footsie*]

knee-slapper **n** Something very funny, esp a joke; boffola : *That's a knee-slapper/ If she ever told a knee-slapper, I wasn't there* *(1966+)*

knickers *See* HAVE someone BY THE SHORT HAIRS

knob **n 1** The head : *Can you get that through your ugly knob?* *(1725+)* **2** A despised person; DORK, JERK, PRICK : *Don't they know what a knob he is? (1990s+)* [*knob,* "penis," was British use in the 1800s, according to Tony Thorne]

knobber *n* A male homosexual transvestite prostitute : *It is where the knobbers, or transvestites, hang out* [1970s+; perhaps fr their wearing of false *knobs,* "female nipples or breasts"; perhaps because they give *knob jobs*]

knobby *See* NOBBY

◁**knob job**▷ *n phr* An act of fellatio; BLOW JOB *(1960s+)*

◁**knobs**▷ *n* A woman's breasts or nipples; KNOCKERS *(1970s+) See* WITH BELLS ON

knock *n* : *It wasn't a disinterested comment—it was a knock/ The knock on Fernandez is he can't field v* **1** To deprecate; criticize severely; dispraise; PUT someone or something DOWN : *by knocking Hymie Salzman (1896+)* **2** To borrow or lend; ask or beg *(1950s+ Black)* **3** To give : *C'mon, baby, knock me a kiss (1944+ Black) See* DON'T KNOCK IT, HAVE something CINCHED

knock, the *n phr* The bill for food, drinks, etc; check; the DAMAGE, TAB : *By the way, I'm picking up the knock (1970s+)*

knockabout *adj* **1** Casual; informal : *These are my knockabout clothes (1880+)* **2** Noisy; raucous; crude : *Beverly Hillbillies has knockabout humor/ in the contest of a knockabout comedy it's deeply offensive (1892+)*

knock around *v phr* To idle about; loaf; KICK AROUND *(1834+)*

knock back *v phr* To drink in one gulp : *The Colonel got his drink, and after he had knocked it back with one swift motion, he began to feel better/ there to mull their downside risks and knock back free champagne (1915+)*

knock someone's **block off** *v phr* To hit very hard; give a severe trouncing; CLOBBER : *One more word and I'll knock your block off* [1908+; *block,* "head," is found by 1635]

knock someone **cold (or cuckoo)** *v phr* To knock unconscious or semiconscious *(1896+)*

knock someone **(or knock 'em) dead** *v phr* To delight or impress someone extremely; KILL, KNOCK someone's SOCKS OFF, WOW : *I want a fantastic scenery number for my life's movie. Something that'll knock 'em dead (1917+)*

knockdown *modifier* Designed to be sold unassembled and to be easy to assemble and disassemble : *a knockdown kitchen set (1795+) n* **1** An introduction : *You want a knockdown to something (1865+)* **2** An invitation *(1940s+)* **3** Money stolen from one's employer : *considered the "knock-down" a perfectly legitimate source of profit (1860s+)*

knock down *v phr* **1** To pocket money taken from one's employer : *clerk who was knocking down on the till (1850s+)* **2** To earn : *Hommuch he knock down a week? (1929+)*

knock something **down** *v phr* To sell something at auction : *I'll knock it down to you for three bucks* [1760+; probably fr the gavel blow given by an auctioneer to signal and conclude a sale]

knock-down-drag-out *adj phr* Very violent; unrestrained; ALL-OUT : *They were having a knock-down-drag-out argument when I got there n* : *Seems the neighbors were having a knockdown-drag-out (1827+)*

knocked *adj* Arrested *(1920s+ Police) See* HAVE something CINCHED

knocked out *adj phr* **1** Drunk *(1940s+)* **2** Intoxicated with a narcotic; HIGH, STONED *(1940s+ Narcotics)* **3** Overcome with delight; extremely pleased : *and were really knocked out with it/ Everybody was knocked out to be asked (1940s+)* **4** Very tired; exhausted; POOPED *(1950s+)*

◁**knocked up**▷ *adj phr* Pregnant *(1813+)*

◁**knockers**▷ *n* A woman's breasts; HOOTERS : *Dumb broads with big knockers, that's what guys go for (1941+)*

knock someone's **eyes out** *v phr* To astonish and delight someone : *But wa-ait a minute! I'm going to knock your eyes out! (1930s+)*

knock someone or something **for a loop** (Variations: **throw** may replace knock; **goal** or **row** or **row of ash cans** or **row of milk cans** or **row of Chinese pagodas** or **row of tall red totem poles** may replace loop) *v phr* **1** To hit someone or something very hard; CLOBBER : *We knocked the villain for a row of ash cans/ You certainly knocked him for a row of tall red totem poles* **2** To unsettle severely; disrupt calm and confidence; discombobulate : *It must have thrown him for a loop, but he asked* **3** To delight extremely; thrill and amaze; KILL, KNOCK someone's SOCKS OFF : *if this climactic sequence doesn't knock you for a loop/ Wouldn't that knock the boys for a row or two/ guaranteed to knock the keenest mind for a loop* **4** To cope with very well; ACE, CREAM : *Would he hit Math 1 in the eye? He'd knock it for a loop (1920+)*

knock heads together *v phr* To exercise persuasive or punitive force; KICK ASS : *Oakley has spent much of his time in Somalia opening dialogue between different elements trying to knock heads together to get them to talk (1940s+)*

knock someone or something **into the middle of next week** *v phr* To hit extremely hard; CLOBBER *(1836+)*

knock it off or knock it *v phr* To stop doing or saying something; desist; cut it out • Often a stern command : *I told you creeps to knock it off, now I'm gonna waste you* (1902+)

knock someone's **lights out** *v phr* **1** To beat severely; BEAT THE SHIT OUT OF someone, CLOBBER **2** To impress enormously; KNOCK someone's SOCKS OFF : *I have a story that would knock your lights out* [1940s+; probably based on the expression *liver and lights*, "liver and lungs," used of animals by at least 1704; influenced by *lights*, "eyes"]

knockoff *modifier* : *extra pieceworkers to turn out knockoff blouses/ knockoff Coach bags bought in Chinatown* *n* A copy or close imitation : *Clint Eastwood's Pale Rider is a contemporary knockoff* (1966+)

knock off *v phr* **1** To stop, esp to stop working; desist (1649+) **2** To produce, esp with seeming ease and rapidity : *He knocked off a couple of portraits at $40,000 each* (1820+) **3** To delete; shorten by : *Let's knock off this last paragraph/ If you do that I'll knock off half the purchase price* (1811+) **4** To consume, esp to drink; KNOCK BACK, KNOCK DOWN : *after knocking off a glass of wine/ while I knock off two or three or four drinks* (1950s+) **5** To kill; murder; assassinate; RUB OUT : *Before long the spiders knock off Michael/ sent to a lonely spot and knocked off* (1919+) **6** To die; pass away (1704+) **7** To arrest, esp after a raid : *Local cops had free authority to knock them off* (1926+) **8** To rob; HOLD UP, KNOCK OVER : *The pair knocked off several shops, a bank, and jewelry stores* (1919+) ◁9▷ To do the sex act with, esp as a prostitute; satisfy a sex client : *if you're a street hooker and knock off twenty or thirty guys a day/ She couldn't see anybody just knocking her off one time* (1940s+) **10** To defeat; overcome : *The Tigers knocked off the Yankees today* (1950s+) **11** To attain; operate at : *The old tub was knocking off 12 knots and groaning like a cow in labor* (1940s+)

◁**knock off a piece**▷ *v phr* To do the sex act; copulate; SCREW (1940s+)

knock someone or something **off** one's **pins** *v phr* To stun; bowl over; invalidate : *Nature knocked our theories off their pins* (1880+)

knockout *modifier* : *That was a knockout plot/ a knockout wife and two daughters* *n* An especially attractive person or thing; DISH : *Saaay, you know, you're a knockout* (1906+)

knock oneself **out** *v phr* **1** To work very hard; do one's utmost : *They like "knocking themselves out" for Variety* **2** To have a splendid and exhausting time : *They knocked themselves out drinking and dancing* [1936s+; perhaps fr Yiddish *aroysshlogn zikh*]

knock someone **out** *v phr* **1** (also **knock** someone **stiff**) To make someone unconscious, esp with a blow (1896+) **2** To delight

or impress someone extremely; KILL, KNOCK someone's SOCKS OFF : *I read a lot of war books and mysteries and all, but they don't knock me out too much/ He knocked me out. He just killed me!* (1942+)

knock something **out** *v phr* To make or - produce, esp rather quickly and crudely : *I haven't got time to knock the script out myself* (1856+)

knockout drops *n phr* Chloral hydrate or another stupefacient drug, esp when put into a drink of liquor; MICKEY FINN (1876+)

knockover *n* A robbery; HEIST (1940s+ Underworld)

knock over *v phr* **1** (also **kick over**) To rob; HOLD UP, KNOCK OFF : *made regular sweeps by jet, knocking over airport motels/ We kick over the spot/ to prevent people from coming in to case the joint so they can knock it over later* (entry form 1928+, variant 1930+) **2** To raid : *knocked over a reputed bookmaking parlor* (1931+)

knocks *n* Extreme pleasure; gratification; COOKIES, JOLLIES, KICKS : *They get their knocks that way*

knock (or **blow**) someone's **socks off** *v phr* To delight extremely; thrill and amaze; KILL, SEND : *It's undressing that really knocks your socks off/ We got a sound that's gonna knock your socks off/ a "surprise special" that we think will blow your socks off* [1845+; these senses fr mid-1800s sense "defeat utterly," fr the notion of hitting someone so hard that he is lifted right out of his shoes and *socks*]

knock the habit *v phr* To stop taking drugs, esp end a drug addiction

knock them in the aisles *See* LAY THEM IN THE AISLES

knock the props from under (or **out from under**) *v phr* To make a position, argument, opinion, etc, invalid; call into serious question : *What he found out knocks the props from under her story* (1910+)

knock the spots off someone *v phr* To defeat someone decisively; CLOBBER (1950+)

knock the tar out of *v phr* To beat up; KNOCK THE SHIT OUT OF someone or something

knock (or **throw**) **together** *v phr* To make or produce something quickly : *what you said about knocking something together that we could eat/ In the few minutes available they threw together a cover story* (1874+)

knock someone **up** *v phr* ◁1▷ To make pregnant (1813+) **2** To awaken someone; arouse by knocking • Fr a British term meaning to awaken someone with a knock at the door (1663+)

know *See* IN THE KNOW

know all the angles *v phr* To understand all the aspects of something; to be extremely knowledgeable : *know all the angles of this business*

know (or **have**) **all the answers** *v phr* **1** To claim or affect special intimate knowledge : *That little creep over there always thinks he knows all the answers* **2** To have a jaded, cynical, spiritless sort of wisdom : *She don't bother anymore, knows all the answers* **3** To know a case or subject thoroughly • Most often in the negative : *Even your doctor doesn't have all the answers* (*1940s+*)

◁**know one's ass from one's elbow** (or **from a hole in the ground**), not▷ *See* NOT KNOW one's ASS FROM one's ELBOW

know a thing or two *v phr* To have practical sagacity; be worldly-wise; KNOW WHAT'S WHAT (*1792+*)

know beans, not *See* NOT KNOW BEANS

know Dorothy *See* BE A FRIEND OF DOROTHY'S

know from *v phr* To know about; be acquainted with : *I don't know from trees much* [1940s+; fr Yiddish *vos vayz ikh fun*]

know someone from Adam, not *See* NOT KNOW someone FROM ADAM

know someone or something from a hole in the ground, not *See* NOT KNOW someone or something FROM A HOLE IN THE GROUND

know (or **not know**) **from nothing** *v phr* To be ignorant; be deeply uninformed or ill-informed : *Gallo knows from nothing* [1936+; fr Yiddish *nit zu wissen fin gornisht*]

know-how *n* Skill, esp technical skill; practical competence : *Takes know-how to run that thing* (*1838+*)

know something **inside out** (or **backwards** or **backwards and forwards**) *v phr* To be very familiar with something : *know baseball inside out/ know parallel parking backwards*

know-it-all *n* A person who pretends to virtual omniscience; BIGMOUTH, SMART-ASS : *Just what we need around here, another know-it-all* (*1895+*)

know something **like the back of one's hand** *v phr* To understand something intimately : *know this school like the back of my hand*

know one's onions *v phr* (Variations: **beans** or **business** or **stuff** may replace **onions**) To be very competent and authoritative in one's work : *I'm glad the tax accountant knows his onions* (*1922+*)

◁**know shit from Shinola,** not▷ *See* NOT KNOW SHIT FROM SHINOLA

know the ropes *v phr* To be seasoned and informed; know the intricacies of a job, situation, etc; KNOW one's WAY AROUND [1874+; fr nautical; fr the myriad *ropes* of a sailing vessel]

know the score *v phr* To have essential and current information; understand what is

important : *You look like a smart lad who knows the score* (*1940s+*)

know the time of day *v phr* To be knowledgeable (*1897+*)

know one's way around *v phr* To be informed and experienced; be seasoned and reliable : *He's been at the job for two years but still doesn't know his way around* (*1940s+*)

know what one **can do with** something *v phr* (Variations: **where** one **can put** [or **shove** or **stick** or **stuff**] may replace **what** one **can do with**) To know that one's offer, request, possession, etc, is held in extreme contempt • A euphemized way of saying that one can take something and stick it up his or her ass : *I saw the contract, and he knows what he can do with it/ I told him where he can shove that great idea of his* (*1950s+*)

know what one **is talking about** *v phr* To be very knowledgeable • Often used in the negative, denoting speaking in ignorance : *popped off without knowing what he was talking about* (*1920+*)

know what's what *v phr* To have practical sagacity; KNOW WHICH WAY IS UP (*1553+*)

know when to hold them and when to fold them *v phr* To be aware of probabilities and consequences; KNOW THE SCORE : *Jackson knows instinctively how to bluff and bargain, when to hold 'em and when to fold 'em* [1980s+; fr a Kenny Rogers song, and fr poker]

know where it's at *v phr* To be up-to-date and cognizant : *the NOW generation, who, like, know what's happening and where it's at* (*1960s+ Counterculture*)

know where the bodies are buried *v phr* To have intimate and secret knowledge, esp of something criminal, scandalous, etc : *The president reckoned he had to keep that lawyer quiet, because he knew where the bodies were buried* (*1960s+*)

know which way (or **end**) **is up** *v phr* To have practical sagacity; KNOW WHAT'S WHAT : *Beneath the tunes and the glories, Mozart knew which way was up, and had a first-class comic imagination/ They was all badly scared and muddled, and didn't know which end was uppermost* (*1891+*)

knuckle *See* WHITE KNUCKLE

knuckleball or **knuckler** *modifier* : *a knuckleball artist n* A pitch thrown from the knuckles that moves slowly and erratically; BUTTERFLY BALL : *Leonard's tantalizing knucklers* (*1906+ Baseball*)

knuckle down *v phr* To work hard and seriously; stop loafing; BUCKLE DOWN [1866+; fr the act of putting one's *knuckles down* to the taw or marble preparing for a careful shot in the game of marbles, a use dating fr the mid-18th century]

knuckle-dragger *n* A rough, somewhat stupid and crude man; GORILLA, STRONG-ARM MAN : *the tendency of some covert agents, "the knuckledraggers" of the Special Operations Group, to revel in deception* [1970s+ College students; from the image of a gorilla whose *knuckles drag* on the ground when it walks]

knuckle-dusters *n* Brass knuckles (*1858+*)

knucklehead *n* A stupid person; BONEHEAD : *Movies are made by unappreciative knuckleheads* [1940s+; fr earlier *knuckle*, "bone"]

knuckler *See* KNUCKLEBALL, WHITE KNUCKLER

knuckles *See* RAP someone's KNUCKLES

knuckle sandwich *n phr* A hard blow to the mouth or face : *I feed him a knuckle sandwich/ You keep that up and you're going to get a knuckle sandwich* (*1973+*)

knuckle under *v phr* To yield; THROW IN THE SPONGE : *It's a shame she had to knuckle under to those bigots* (*1860+*)

KO (pronounced as separate letters) *modifier* : *a KO punch* *n* A knockout; KAYO (*1922+ Prizefight*) *v* : *He KOed six in a row* *See* TKO

kocker *See* ALTER KOCKER

KOed *adj* Knocked out, esp from drinking or tiredness : *KOed from the long week*

Kong or **kong** *n* KING KONG (*1960s+ Black*)

kook (KŌŌK) *modifier* : *did a kook piece with dancers* *n* **1** An eccentric person; NUT, SCREWBALL : *The bomb cannot be exploded by a single "kook"/ The early Streisand played kook* (*1950s+ Teenagers*) **2** A novice surfer (*1961+ Surfers*) [fr *cuckoo*]

kookie or **kooky** *adj* Crazy; eccentric; DIPPY, GOOFY : *make you seem a little kookie/ the kooky stunt so pleased him* (*1950s+ Teenagers*)

kootchy *See* the HOOTCHIE-COOTCHIE

kopasetic *See* COPACETIC

kosh *n* cosh

kosher *adj* Proper; as it should be; legitimate : *Everything looks kosher* [1896+; fr Yiddish fr Hebrew *kasher*, "fit, proper"]

◄**kraut** or **Kraut** or **krauthead**► *adj* : *kraut wine* *n* A German, esp a German soldier : *Oh, that kraut-head* (*WWI armed forces*) [fr *sauerkraut*, regarded as a favorite and characteristic German food]

kvetch (kə VECH) *n* : *I am another kvetch when it comes to wind chimes/ right in tune with the city medical spirit, which is basically one of kvetch* *v* To whine; complain; be consistently pessimistic : *I know you know. I'm just kvetching/ Dealing with a controversial idea of public importance, Mobil kvetched* [1960s+; fr Yiddish, literally "squeeze, press"]

L

lab *modifier* : *a lab report* *n* **1** A laboratory (*1895+*) **2** (also **Lab**) A Labrador retriever (*1960s+*)

labor *See* GRUNT WORK

lace into *v* To attack and beat; thrash; CLOBBER : *I rushed at the fellow and fairly laced into him/ Reviewers laced into the play* [*1920s+; lace* in the same sense is found by 1599]

la-di-da (also **lah-de-dah** or **la-de-da** or **lah-di-dah**) *adj* **1** Very refined and respectable : *Nobody weren't going to make her live in a lah-di-dah place like that* (*1940s+*) **2** Carefree and nonchalant : *Her emotions at the dissolution of her 25-year marriage are anything but la-de-da* (*1970s+*) *interj* A phrase used to mean the equivalent of "It doesn't matter" : *You're canceling our date? Oh well, lah-di-dah* (*1970s+*) *n* A dandyish or sissified man; superrefined and delicate person : *Some lah-de-dah with a cane* (*1883+*) *v* To treat in a nonchalant, offhand manner : *The outfielder la-di-da'd the catch* (*1970s+*) [an imitation of casual and aristocratic speech]

ladies' (or **lady's**) **man** *n phr* **1** A man who pursues and otherwise devotes himself to women to an unusual degree; LOVER-BOY **2** A man who is attractive to many women : *He's so conceited. Thinks he's a real ladies' man* (*1842+*)

ladies who lunch *n* Women who are well-off, style-conscious, and somewhat conservative in dress : *The title character, played by Mia Farrow, is a pampered Upper East Side lady who lunches/ Chic fleet—for tony ladies who lunch* [*1970+*; fr a song by Stephen Sondheim]

lady-killer *n* A man who is irresistible to women or has the reputation for being so; LADIES' MAN (*1811+*)

lady of the night (or **evening**) *n* : A prostitute (*1925+*)

lag *n* A convict : *lags who escape from the county pokey* (*1930s+ Underworld*) *v* To arrest or imprison a criminal (*1940s+ Underworld*)

laid *adj* Having had sex; copulated with : *definitely got laid*

laid out *adj* Drunk (*1929+*)

la-la (or **la la** or **lala**) **land** (also **Lotusland**) *n phr* **1** Los Angeles and Southern California in their reputed glamour and trendiness : *Suddenly the real Los Angeles intrudes itself. La-la land with its beaches and movie stars, Rolls Royces and Evian, Italian suits and car phones, coke-sniffing boy-girl bimbos, was gone/ I just wanted to show you we ain't asleep down here in Lotusland* **2** An unreal and hallucinatory place; dreamland; Never-Never Land; Lotus Land : *After the operation I was in la-la land/ This is directed at President Clinton, Mike McCurry, and anyone else in that la la land they call Washington/ Stanford is a multicultural lala land; it's not the real world* (*1980s+*)

lallygag *See* LOLLYGAG

lam *v* **1** To depart; go, esp hastily in escaping : *lammed for Cleveland* **2** To escape from prison [*1886+ Underworld*; ultimately fr British sense "beat," found by 1596, hence the same semantically as *beat it*] *See* ON THE LAM, TAKE IT ON THE LAM

lamb *n* A dear, sweet person : *Mary is such a lamb* (*1923+*)

lambaste or **lambast** (lam BAYST, lam BAST) *v* **1** To hit very hard; thrash; CLOBBER : *They lambasted the suspect mercilessly* **2** To disparage strongly; castigate : *A woman psychologist today lambasted the idea that "mom is to blame"* [*1637+*; ultimately fr British *lam* and *baste*, both "beat"]

lambie or **lambie-pie** *n* One's sweetheart; beloved : *It was a dithering meditation on a lackluster Don Juan. Are Reynolds and Edwards such unmanly lambie-pies?* (*1940s+*)

lame *adj* **1** Socially awkward; clumsy; KLUTZY : *Cindy normally tells such great jokes, but that last one was really lame* (*1942+*) **2** (also **lamed** or **lame-o**) Stupid; inept : *I automatically inherit this lame "slacker" attitude/ Don't try and sell us this lame-o "throwback to a bygone era" argument* (*1950s+ Students*) **3** : *a lame assault on boomers/ Their performances were sloppy, sometimes even lame* (*1950s+ Teenagers* fr *jazz musicians*) *n* An old-fashioned, conventional person; SQUARE : *and not worry about anybody naming me a lame/ not have been as quick to judge him as a lame* (*1950s+ Teenagers* fr *jazz musicians*)

lamebrain *n* A stupid person; DOPE, KNUCKLE-HEAD : *Not all the lamebrains on Capitol Hill frequent the House or Senate* (*1929+*)

lamebrained *adj* Stupid; KLUTZY (*1929+*)

lame duck *modifier* : *lame-duck president* *n phr* **1** A public official who has lost an election or one who is not permitted by law to seek re-election for an additional term but is serving out a term (*1863+*) **2** A speculator who has taken options on stocks he or she cannot pay for (*1751+ Stock market*) [political sense attributed to Vice President Andrew Johnson, referring to a Colonel Forney]

lame-o *adj* Stupid; inept : *That's a lame-o excuse if I ever heard one* *See* LAME

lamster *n* An escaped convict [1904+ Underworld; fr *lam*]

lane *See* FAST LANE, HAMMER LANE

lap-dance *v* To perform an erotic dance straddling a customer's lap : *To lap-dance, you undress, sit your client down, order him to stay still and fully clothed, then hover over him, making a motion that you have perfected by watching Mister Softee ice-cream dispensers* (1990s+)

lap dancer *n phr* A woman who does lap dances : *Of course, not every coming film exalts women: audiences will also see them as lap dancers, strippers, and phone-sex workers* (1990s+)

lapdog *n* A subservient person; eager sycophant : *The leading Singapore newspaper, the Straits Times, enthusiastically fills the role of government lapdog/ employee committees that labor leaders charge will be lapdogs of management* (1980s+)

lapel-grabber *n* A person who seizes and holds one's attention by grasping one's lapels, either actually or in effect : *The style is the man; Hoving of the Met has always been a lapel-grabber/ Margaret Mead is the most famous of these lapel-grabbers* (1980s+)

lap something **up** *v phr* To accept or believe eagerly; to take in something delightful : *Tell 'em you'll lower their taxes and they'll lap it up/ lapped up the praise* (1922+)

lard *See* TUB OF GUTS

◁**lard-ass** or **lard-bucket**▷ *n* A fat person; CHUBBO, TUB OF GUTS (1946+)

large *n* A thousand dollars; BIG ONE, GRAND : *with new Beverly Hills basic wheels going for fifty large* (1980s+)

lark *n* A merry time • Chiefly British (1811+) *v* : *This is no time to go larking* (1813+) [origin uncertain; perhaps fr an allusion to the bird, since *skylark* in the same sense is found somewhat earlier]

last *See* NICE GUYS FINISH LAST

last dance, the *See* GET THE LAST DANCE

last-ditch *modifier* Ultimate; final and heroic : *They pumped themselves up for a last-ditch effort* [1940s+; fr earlier *last-ditcher*, ultimately fr *die in the last ditch*, "die at the last defense line," found by 1715 and attributed to William of Orange]

last hurrah *n phr* The end for someone or something : *Last hurrah for some write-offs/ I want this book to be my last hurrah* [1956+; fr the title of Edwin O'Connor's 1956 novel about a politician's final campaign and bow]

last of the big-time spenders, the *n phr* The last lavish spender and host • Always ironical, meaning its opposite [1970s+; *big spender* is found in the New York night-life milieu in the 1920s]

last straw *n* The final insult; an act that calls for a response : *her yelling at him was the last straw*

latchkey (or **doorkey**) **child** or **kid** *n phr* A child whose parents are working and who must spend part of the day unsupervised at home : *A latchkey child, Nikki would always go home, stay inside, and do her homework/ Personally, I always wanted to be a latchkey kid, or at least have a key* (1944+)

latch on to or **latch on** *v phr* **1** To get; obtain; GLOM ON TO : *Latch on to the first seat that's empty* **2** To comprehend; grasp; DIG : *He finally latched onto the truth* **3** To attach oneself to; be dependent on : *He latched on to me as soon as I arrived* (1930s+ Black)

lately *See* JOHNNY-COME-LATELY

later *interj* A parting salutation : *I dug right away what the kick was, so I said, "Later," and he split/ Later, baby. Catch you later* (1980s+ Teenagers fr black) *See* SEE YOU LATER, ALLIGATOR

lather *v* To hit; strike : *He lathered the ball out of the park* [1797+; fr the notion that frothy washing *lather* is produced by vigorous agitation or beating] *See* IN A LATHER

lats *n* The latissimus dorsi muscles : *checking the cut of their lats in shiny windows* (1980s+)

laugh *See* BELLY LAUGH, the HORSELAUGH

laugh, a, or a **laugh and a half** *n phr* Something funny; a cause of amusement, esp of contemptuous derision : *You're gonna cook? That's a laugh*

laugh all the way to the bank *v phr* To be amused and gratified by a victory where a defeat was predicted : *The film, with horrible reviews, grossed more than $30 million. Disney laughed all the way to the bank* (1970s+)

laugher *n* A laughing matter, esp a game in which one team scores an annihilating victory : *The two games he mentioned were laughers, Oklahoma 41–7 over North Carolina/ I like to see it about 16–0. I like laughers* (1960s+ Sports)

laugh something **off** *v phr* To dismiss something with a laugh : *It's hard to laugh that insult off, isn't it?* (1715+)

laugh on (or **out of**) **the other side of** one's **face** *v phr* To lament and moan; suffer a change of mood from joy to distress; undergo a defeat : *When they get through with him he'll be laughing out of the other side of his face* (1779+)

laugh up (or **in**) one's **sleeve** *v phr* To laugh covertly : *After you had that accident she was laughing up her sleeve* (1560+)

launder *v* To transfer or convert funds so that illegal or dubious receipts are made to appear legitimate : *The account money that had been "laundered" by being siphoned from this* *country into Mexico and returned under an alias (1961+)*

laundry *n* **1** A bank or other place used for legitimizing illegal or dubious money *(1960s+)* **2** A board of faculty members that passes on flying cadets *(WWII Air Forces)* [second sense from the fact that some cadets were *washed out*, "failed," by such a board]

laundry (or **shopping**) **list** *n phr* A long bill of items to be obtained, discussed, done, or not done : *This "do-good" laundry list draws sneers/ The cadets didn't need a laundry list of prohibitions/ A shopping list is not a strategy (1958+)*

lav *n* Lavatory; bathroom : *ladies in the lav*

lava *See* IN A LATHER

lavender *adj* Homosexual : *Alberta Maged had marched with a coalition of groups including the Lavender Left and the Commie Queers/ Clinton dropped the gays like a flaming potato, suggesting they might serve in special lavender units* [1970s+; both blue and *lavender* are colors associated with homosexuality]

Law *See* JOHN LAW

law, the *n phr* Any police officer, prison guard, etc; the HEAT *(1920s+ Underworld)*

lawnmower *n* A hard-hit grounder *(1891+ Baseball)*

lawyer *See* CLUBHOUSE LAWYER, JAILHOUSE LAW-YER, SEA LAWYER

lay *n* ◁1▷ A person regarded merely as a sex partner or object : *The two girls looked like swell lays/ She's a great lay (1932+)* ◁2▷ A sex act; PIECE OF ASS : *Anyone who is looking for an easy lay (1936+)* *v* ◁1▷ : *five cadets who swore they'd all laid the girl one night (1934+)* **2** To bet : *I laid her six to one he wouldn't show up (1300+)* *See* EASY MAKE

layabout or **lie-about** *n* A lazy person; shirker *(1930s+)*

◁**lay a fart**▷ *v phr* (Variations: **cut** or **let** or **rip** may replace **lay**) To flatulate; FART : *This guy laid this terrific fart (1940s+)*

lay a glove (or **finger** or **hand**) **on** someone, not *See* NOT LAY A GLOVE ON someone

lay an egg *v phr* To fail; BOMB, FLOP : *The plan's going to lay an egg unless we give it a shot in the arm* [1929+; fr earlier British *lay a duck's egg*, "make a score of zero"]

lay a trip (or **scene**) **on** someone *v phr* To attribute something to someone; burden someone with something; accuse someone of something : *But if you try and lay a trip on somebody through psychoanalysis, it's nonsense/ Don't lay this scene on me. I did the best I could/ Vote for Walker. But don't lay any undue trips on him (1960s+ Counterculture fr black)*

lay back *v phr* To relax; take one's ease : *It is not a Southern-rock band. They don't lay back (1970s+ fr black)*

lay down on the job *v phr* To loaf; dawdle and shirk *(1918+)*

lay down the law *v phr* To cite the rules, or one's rules, sternly : *He overheard a father laying down the law to three sheepish kids (1762+)*

lay eyes on *v phr* To see : *never laid eyes on him before (1200s+)*

lay for someone *v phr* To watch for one's chance to take revenge; vigilantly stalk : *I'd lay for him in town some night (1494+)*

lay into someone *v phr* To attack someone, physically or verbally : *That's why I laid into Eckert and made him drive me down that night (1838+)*

lay it on *v phr* To exaggerate; overstate; • Often used of flattery and cajolement : *I overheard you laying it on to the boss. Shame! (1560+)*

lay it on someone *v phr* To tell; inform; CLUE : *If you know it, please lay it on me (1960+)*

lay (or **put**) **it on the line** (or **on the table**) *v phr* To speak candidly and straightforwardly; TELL IT LIKE IT IS : *They are more likely to give it to you if you lay it on the table (1940s+)*

lay it on thick *v phr* To exaggerate; overstate; hyperbolize; LAY IT ON : *"I tell them it's something their father and I always talked about" "That's laying it on a bit thick, isn't it?" (1740+)*

lay it on with a trowel *v phr* LAY IT ON THICK : *The film has too many slow spots, and its message is laid on with a trowel (1600+)*

lay low *v phr* To stay out of sight; remain inconspicuous; KEEP A LOW PROFILE, LIE DOGGO : *We're layin' low a couple days (1839+)*

layoff *n* **1** A dismissal or furlough from a job *(1919+)* **2** The part of a bookmaker's bets placed with another agent to forestall catastrophic loss *(1950s+ Gambling)* **3** An unemployed actor : *A couple of layoffs were walking out of the hotel (1950s+ Theater)*

lay off *v phr* **1** To stop troubling or harrying someone; leave someone in peace • Often an irritated command or entreaty : *So lay off or I'll split your head, baby (1908+)* **2** To dismiss or furlough an employee : *Half the staff at IBM has been laid off (1868+)* **3** To place a portion of bets or debts with other agents so as to reduce one's possible losses : *That's a lot of cash to come up with. We could lay some of it off, you know it'd be easier for us (1950s+ Gambling)*

lay someone **off** *v phr* To terminate someone's job *(1868+)*

lay something **on** someone *v phr* **1** To present; give : *And the sisters laid the revolutionary ideology right on them/ will suck his dick to oblivion if he lays some coke on them* **2** To tell or inform : *I have something heavy to lay on* *you, I'm afraid* **3** LAY A TRIP ON someone : *The media says I'm not a journalist. I never said I was. They're laying something on me I never laid on myself* [1960s+ counterculture; fr 1930s+ black]

lay one on someone *v phr* To hit hard; punch; HANG ONE ON : *She laid one on him, when he least expected it* (*1940s+*)

lay (or **put**) something **on the line** *v phr* To put deliberately at risk; put in peril as a wager or hostage : *If you try this, remember you are laying your ass on the line* (*1950s+*)

layout *n* **1** A place; house; living arrangements : *Nice little layout you got here* (*1869+*) **2** Place, equipment, apparatus, etc, for a particular purpose : *who may never have seen such a layout* (*1886+*)

lay rubber *v phr* To accelerate rapidly and speed in a car, so as to leave black tire marks on the road (*1940s+ Teenagers*)

lay them in the aisles *v phr* (Variations: **have** or **knock** or **put** may replace **lay**) To entertain, amuse, or impress an audience extravagantly; WOW (*1934+*)

lazybones *n* An indolent person; slugabed (*1593+*)

lead *n* Bullets; gunfire (*1809+*) *See* GET THE LEAD OUT, HAVE LEAD IN one's PANTS, HAVE LEAD IN one's PENCIL

lead balloon *n phr* A dismal failure; FLOP : *His run for office was a lead balloon* (*1940s+*) *See* GO OVER LIKE A LEAD BALLOON

lead someone **down the garden path** *v phr* To deceive someone; hoodwink someone : *Will anyone know who led whom down the garden path?* (*1870+*)

leaded coffee *n phr* Coffee with caffeine, as distinct from decaffeinated coffee : *Coffee? You want leaded or unleaded?* (*1980s+*)

lead-foot (LED fŏŏt) *v* To drive fast : *Starting Friday, speeders will pay an extra $20 when caught lead-footing* (*1940s+ Truckers*)

lead-footed (LED fŏŏt əd) *adj* **1** Sluggish and awkward; clumsy : *The bungling, lead-footed fellow* (*1596+*) **2** Tending to drive very fast (*1940s+ Truckers*) [the first dated form is *leaden-footed*]

lead in one's **pencil** *n phr* A penile erection (*1930+*) *See* HAVE LEAD IN ONE'S PENCIL

lead-pipe (or **lead-tight**) **cinch** *n phr* **1** A certainty; inescapable fact : *not early enough to move no tables, that's a lead-pipe cinch/ calls Coleco Vision a "lead-pipe cinch" for making a strong showing at Christmas* **2** Something very easy; CINCH, PIECE OF CAKE : *a lousy lead-tight cinch that any freshman in law school could have won* [1898+; fr the fact that a *lead pipe* can be easily bent, in case one has bet on such a feat]

lead with one's **chin** *v phr* To make oneself vulnerable : *If you tell him that right away you'll be leading with your chin* (*1940s+*)

leaf, the *n phr* Cocaine (*1960s+ Narcotics*)

league *See* BIG-LEAGUE, BUSH LEAGUE, GRAPEFRUIT LEAGUE, HOT STOVE LEAGUE, MAJOR-LEAGUE, MINOR-LEAGUE, OUT OF one's LEAGUE

leaguer *See* TEXAS LEAGUER

leagues *See* the BIG LEAGUES, the BUSH LEAGUES

leak *n* **1** The divulgence or divulger of secret information : *A famous leak was called Deep Throat* (*1873+*) ◁2▷ An act of urination; a PISS (*1930s+*) *v* **1** To give information to the press or other recipient secretly : *Then the FCC report was "leaked" to the press* (*1859+*) ◁2▷ To urinate; PISS : *He said he had to leak; his back teeth were floating* (*1930s+*) *See* TAKE A LEAK

lean and mean *adj phr* Desperately and somewhat menacingly ambitious; HUNGRY : *"Lean and mean" is the byword in publishing these days/ A fat and lazy firm must become lean and mean, or see its capital redeployed* (*1970s+*)

lean on someone *v phr* To put pressure on someone, esp with violence or the threat of it : *And he thinks he can lean on me!/ Several restaurants and clubs were being leaned on* (*1950s+*)

lean over backwards *See* BEND OVER BACKWARDS

leaping heebies, the *See* the HEEBIE-JEEBIES

leap on the bandwagon *See* GET ON THE BANDWAGON

leap tall buildings at (or **in**) **a single bound** *v phr* To do something impossible : *She is under the impression that you can leap tall buildings at a single bound* [1940s+; one of the feats of the comic-strip character Superman]

learn the ropes *v phr* To learn the elements of a task or profession; serve one's apprenticeship : *Stokovich and a mope from Justice who was at the time learning the ropes* (*1977+*)

leary *See* LEERY

least, the *n phr* The worst; the dullest, most conventional, etc (*1950s+ Beat & cool talk*)

leatherneck *n* A US Marine; gyrene [1914+ Navy; fr the *leather* collars of their early uniforms; the term is found by 1890 as British sailors' name for a soldier]

leave *See* FRENCH LEAVE

leave a calling card *v phr* To defecate in a public or inappropriate place : *after a passing horse had left its calling card on the street* (*1940s+*)

leave something or someone **be** *v phr* To leave alone (*1825+*)

leave someone **flat** (or **cold**) *v phr* To leave a person suddenly and definitively : *When he lied once too often she left him flat* (*1902+*)

leave someone **holding the bag** *v phr* 1 To cause someone to take all the losses; dupe someone to his disadvantage : *Don't you let them leave you holding the bag* (*1906+*) 2 To maneuver so that one takes individual blame for a failure or a crime [fr 1600s *give the bag to hold*, "victimize in a game of snipehunt"; the form *hold the sack* in the first sense is found by 1904]

leave someone **in the lurch** *v phr* To abandon someone in a difficult plight : *They all cleared out and left me in the lurch* (*1596+*)

lech or **letch** *n* 1 Strong desire, esp sexual; lust; the HOTS : *his lech for cam shafts and turbines/ He had a lech for his fifteen-year-old daughter* (*1796+*) 2 A lecher : *under the illusion that the lech is as enamored as she is/ who also appears as a good-natured lech* (*1943+*) *v* : *when Henry goes letching after Anne/ keep Junior from leching* (*1911+*) [fr *lecher, lechery*, ultimately fr the notion of licking]

leech *n* A human parasite (*1784+*) *v* : *insisted that MCI was not leeching off the successful campaign of its competition* (*1960s+*)

leery or **leary** *adj* Untrusting; suspicious; wary : *He was leery of toting so much money/ Cheyfitz and Farrell exchanged leery glances* [*1718+*; probably fr British dialect *lere*, "learning, knowledge"]

left *See* HANG A LEFT

Left Coast *n phr* The Pacific Coast : *That's not what they're saying out on the Left Coast*

left-field *adj* Unorthodox; unexpected; wacky : *Abril stuffs her first starring role in an American movie with the kind of willful, left-field behavior that she learned from working with Almodovar* (*1950s+*) *See* OUT IN LEFT FIELD

left-handed *adj* 1 Undesirable; unlucky (*1940s+ Merchant marine*) 2 Irregular; illicit; dubious : *left-handed honeymoons with someone else's husband* (*1612+*)

left-handed compliment *n phr* Praise that is subtle dispraise; reluctant and dubious praise : *Telling her she has the constitution of a horse is maybe a left-handed compliment* (*1881+*)

left-handed monkey wrench *n* A nonexistent tool

left nut *See* GRIPE one's ASS

lefty or **leftie** *modifier* : *a lefty hurler/ leftie tennis ace n* 1 A left-handed person, esp a left-handed pitcher or other athlete (*1886+*) 2 A person of liberal or socialist political beliefs; radical; liberal : *such urban lefties as Bella Abzug* (*1930s+*)

leg *n* 1 An infantry soldier; GRUNT (*Vietnam War Army*) 2 A woman, esp a sexually promiscuous one (*1960s+ College students fr black*) *v* (also **leg it**) To go; travel : *I was legging down the line* (*1601+*) *See* an ARM AND A LEG, BOOTLEG, GIVE someone LEG, HAVE A LEG UP ON someone or something, PEG LEG, PULL someone's LEG, SHAKE A LEG, TANGLE-FOOTED

legal eagle (or **beagle**) *n phr* A lawyer, esp a clever and aggressive one : *In 1979 Davis' legal eagles got him acquitted again/ Software turns you into a regular legal beagle*

legit (lə JIHT) *adj* 1 Legitimate; KOSHER : *She's a legit farmer/ by legit, or honest, people* (*1931+*) 2 Having to do with or being of the legitimate theater : *specialists in legit reviewing* (*1923+*) *n* The legitimate theater, or one such theater (*1897+*) *See* ON THE LEGIT

legless *adj* Drunk (*1976+*)

leg man *n phr* 1 A newspaper reporter who goes out to gather facts and may or may not write the story (*1923+ Newspaper office*) 2 Any person who works actively and outside, rather than in, an office (*1950s+*) 3 A man whose favorite part of the female body is the legs (*1940s+*)

legs *n* The ability of a show, song, public figure, etc, to be an enduring success; staying power : *whether a movie will have legs, the power to entice audiences week after week/ runaway success, bigger than disco, with stronger legs/ There is no other theory with legs* (*1970s+ Show business*) *See* BIRD LEGS, HINDERS

leg up, a *n phr* 1 Aid; a boost : *He'll do OK, but he needs a financial leg up to get started* (*1837+*) 2 An advantage : *You can go in with a leg up on other people* (*1901+*) *See* HAVE A LEG UP ON something

legwork *n phr* Peripatetic work done outside the office : *I figured Wendell must be somewhere close, and I did a little legwork* (*1891+ Newspaper office*)

lemme *v* Let me ● Casual-pronunciation spelling : *Lemme open that for you*

lemon[1] *n* 1 Anything unsatisfactory or defective, esp a car; CLINKER : *His tale brought back memories of my first lemon/ That show's a lemon* (*1909+*) ◁2▷ A light-skinned and attractive black woman; HIGH YELLOW (*1940s+ Black*) 3 A sour, disagreeable person (*1925+*) 4 (also **lemonade**) Weakened or diluted narcotics, or a nonnarcotic substance sold as a narcotic; BLANK (*1960s+ Narcotics*) *See* HAND someone A LEMON

lemon[2] *n* A Quaalude® [1960s+ Narcotics; *Lemmon* is the name of a pharmaceutical company that once manufactured the drug]

length *n* Female sexual gratification (*1968+*)

◁**les** or **lessy** or **lez** or **lezzie** or **lezzy**▷ (LEZ) *modifier* : *It was a fantastic turn-on, watching a lezzie scene n* A lesbian : *Mary is a les and John is a fairy/ I'd have figured you for a lez* (*1929+*)

◁lesbo or lesbie▷ (LEZ boh) *n* A lesbian : *where the Lesbos even come and watch the dress rehearsals/ a carefree single lesbo looking for love* (1940+)

let a fart *See* LAY A FART

letch *See* LECH

letdown *n* **1** A disappointment; COMEDOWN : *Actually meeting him was something of a letdown* (1889+) **2** The gradual descent of an airplane toward a landing (1945+)

let fly (or go) *v phr* **1** To launch vigorously into something; begin with projective energy : *She took a deep breath and let fly* (1654+) **2** To hurl; shoot; fire : *The gunman let go with both automatics* (1624+)

let George do it *sentence* Let someone else besides me take care of it [1910+; perhaps fr a learned journalist's recall of the French *laissez faire à Georges*, "let George do it," referring to Cardinal Georges d'Amboise, a church and government official under Louis XII in the late 15th and early 16th centuries]

let oneself go *v phr* To behave in an unrestrained way; be uninhibited : *Come on, Herbert, let yourself go, have another cookie* (1926+)

let one's hair down *v phr* To be very open and candid, esp about personal matters : *A lot of men that I have been with do not let their hair down/ A small-town beauty shop, where city slickers can really let their hair down*

let someone have it *v phr* **1** To hit someone, esp powerfully; CLOBBER : *Then let him have it, right on the chin* (1840+) **2** To attack verbally, esp punitively; GIVE IT TO someone : *He allows me to count on his affection. Then he lets me have it* (1891+)

let her (or 'er) rip *v phr* To let something go at full speed; take off all restraints : *He decided to buckle his seat belt and let her rip* (1879+)

let it all hang out *modifier* : *I enjoy our let-it-all-hang-out relationship* *v phr* To be entirely candid; be free and unrestrained; LET one's HAIR DOWN : *You'll feel better if you let it all hang out* (1960s+ Counterculture fr black)

let it go at that *v phr* LET IT SIT : *You'll eat half of it? OK, let it go at that* (1898+)

let it sit *v phr* To decline to object or interfere; acquiesce : *"He wasn't perfect, but he tried." I let that one sit there, unwilling to challenge her version of events/ "Let it sit, then," he said with the slightest of shrugs* (1990s+)

let someone off *v phr* To decline to pursue or prosecute someone : *The prosecutor let him off because he was a pal of the mayor* (1828+)

let (or blow) off steam *v phr* To talk loudly and angrily as a method of relieving the pressure of one's feelings; express one's anger or frustration : *He's not serious, just letting off steam/ I've blown off steam/ They're bored, just blowing off steam* (1837+)

let someone off the hook *v phr* To relieve someone of responsibility or menace : *They had already given me a lot. I wanted to let them off the hook* (1960s+)

let on *v phr* To reveal; hint : *Guys fool around, they sort of joke about it, they sort of let on, you know?* (1825+)

let out (or slip) *v phr* To reveal : *They let out that they were already married* (1870+)

let something ride *v phr* To let something go on as it is; decline to change or intervene : *Let the same order ride for now* (1921+)

let rip *v phr* To accelerate; to let something go unchecked (1843+) *See* LET HER RIP

let's blow this Popsicle stand *sentence* Let's get out of here : *This game is a blowout. Let's blow this Popsicle stand*

let's boogie *sentence* (Variations: **cruise** or **blaze** may replace **boogie**) Let us leave [1950s+ Teenagers; originally "let's dance to boogie-woogie music"]

let's face it *sentence* Let us freely admit it; let us accept the unhappy truth : *Let's face it, kids, we're all to blame some* (1911+)

let's get the (or this) show on the road *sentence* We should get started; we should become active (1957+)

letter *See* DEAD HORSE, FRENCH LETTER, POISON-PEN LETTER, RED-LETTER DAY

letter man *See* FOUR-LETTER MAN

let the cat out of the bag *v phr* To reveal a secret, usu without intending to : *Her guilty smile pretty much let the cat out of the bag* (1760+)

let the good times roll *v phr* To enjoy oneself; be joyous, gregarious, and bibulous [1900+ Jazz musicians; the phrase is still associated with New Orleans]

lettuce *n* Money, esp paper money; CABBAGE : *That's a lot of lettuce/ the man who nipped all this lettuce from the Playboy patch* (1929+) *See* FOLDING MONEY

level *adj* True : *There's never a place for guys like me. That's level* *v* To tell the truth; be honest and candid : *Don't laugh. I'm leveling/ It's on this level that they tell you that they are "leveling" with you* (1920+) *See* ON THE LEVEL

level best, someone's *n phr* The utmost one can do; one's honest greatest effort : *I'll do my level best to keep you* (1851+)

level playing field *n phr* Equality of opportunity; fair terms on all sides : *It's no level playing field if you always get to pick first* (1981+)

lez *See* LES

◁**lezzie**▷ *See* LES

liaise (lee AYZ) *v* To cooperate; get into regular contact : *told her to liaise with the FBI* [1916+; shortening of *liaison*]

lib *n* Liberation, esp as the aim of various movements : *animal lib* (*1960s+*)

libber *n* A member of one of the liberation movements, esp of the women's lib movement (*1960s+*)

libe *n* A library, esp a college library *v* To study in a library (*1915+ Students*)

liberate *v* To steal or appropriate, originally something in conquered enemy territory (*WWII Army*)

liberty *See* AT LIBERTY

license to print money, a *n phr* A very lucrative business : *The railways are not, like some predecessors, a license to print money/ In the past, owning a movie studio was like having a license to print money*

lick *n* **1** A blow; stroke : *I got in a couple good licks before he decked me* (*1678+*) **2** Censure; adverse criticism; HIT, KNOCK : *The show is no winner, but doesn't deserve the licks it's taken* (*1739+*) **3** A try; attempt; CRACK, SHOT, WHACK : *I probably won't make it, but I'll give it a good lick* (*1863+*) **4** A time at bat : *So the Yankees come up for their last licks* (*1883+ Baseball*) **5** A short figure or solo, esp when improvised; BREAK, RIFF : *a few solid licks on the sliphorn/ that I know are exactly the licks that I play* (*1920s+ Jazz musicians*) *v* **1** To beat; pummel; LAMBASTE, larrup (*1563+*) **2** To defeat; CLOBBER : *Next time we'll lick 'em for good* (*1800+*) *See* HIT IT A LICK

lick and a promise, a *n phr* A hasty job; a cursory performance [1860+; fr the notion that one does one *lick* or stroke of what is appropriate, and *promises* to do the rest]

lick into shape *v phr* WHIP INTO SHAPE

lick one's chops *v phr* To display hunger and anticipation for food or for something else desired : *We all sat licking our chops as the turkey was carved/ I licked my chops when I thought of that huge bonus* (*1655+*)

lick one's wounds *v phr* To attempt to heal one's injuries or hurt feelings

licker *See* ASS-KISSER, CLIT-LICKER, DICK-LICKER

lickety-split or **lickity-split** *adv* Very fast : *Felt he just had to get a lawyer lickity-split* [1859+; fr *lick*, "speed, a spurt of speed," found by 1809; earlier forms *lickety-cut, lickety-click, lickety liner*, and *lickety switch* are found in the 1830s and 1840s]

licorice stick *n phr* The clarinet (*1930s+ Jive talk*)

lid *n* **1** A hat (*1896+*) **2** One ounce of marijuana : *a shutdown on grass, lids were going for thirty dollars/ lifted out the back seat and found a lid of marijuana* (*1960s+ Narcotics*) *See*

BLOW THE LID OFF, FLIP one's LID, PUT A LID ON something or someone. SKID LID

lie *See* the BIG LIE, a PACK OF LIES

lie doggo *v phr* To stay in hiding; secrete oneself; LAY LOW • Chiefly British : *You better lie doggo a while till it blows over* [1893+; probably fr the silent and unobtrusive behavior of a hunting or herding *dog* when stalking]

lie like a rug (or **wet rug**) *v phr* To be very mendacious : *They say the truth is not in us, first of all. They say we lie like wet rugs* (*1940s+*)

lie low *v phr* To hide or behave so as to not attract attention; LAY LOW, LIE DOGGO : *lie low for a month* (*1880+*)

lie through one's **teeth** (or **dentures**) *v phr* To be radically untruthful; LIE LIKE A RUG : *Carl, what you already did is called lying through your dentures* (*1940s+*)

lieut (LOOT) *n* Lieutenant; looey, LOOT (*1843+*)

life *See* BET YOUR BOOTS, LOW-LIFE, NOT ON YOUR LIFE

life, a *n phr* Another chance to get a hit, score, etc, esp after a fielding error : *The Tigers got a life when the second baseman bobbled an easy one* (*1868+ Baseball*) *See* GET A LIFE

life, the, or **the Life** *n phr* **1** Prostitution, esp as a business : *a hooker from LA who knows this is her ticket out of the life/ this latter often purchased "hot" from others in the life* **2** The homosexual life, esp that of an effeminate transvestite male prostitute : *She had lived the life so long now* (*1970s+*) *See* IN THE LIFE

lifejacket *n* A condom : *take a lifejacket to the prom*

life of Riley, the *n phr* An easy, luxurious, and pleasant life; the GRAVY TRAIN : *I took the money, went to Mexico, and lived the life of Riley* [1919+; origin uncertain; perhaps fr an 1880s song about a man named O'Reilly, who became rich and sybaritic]

lifer *n* **1** A convict serving a life sentence (*1830+*) **2** A career Army officer : *"lifers" (the contemptuous GI term for career officers)* (*WWII Army*)

lift *n* **1** A surge or feeling of exhilaration; a transport of exuberance; HIGH, KICK, RUSH : *I get a lift from watching that kid* (*1861+*) **2** A ride : *I need a lift to the bus terminal downtown* (*1712+*) *v* **1** To steal : *He got caught lifting a chicken from the convenience store* (*1526+*) **2** To plagiarize : *whole pages lifted from my book* (*1892+*) *See* HITCH A RIDE

lift a finger *v phr* To help • Used in the negative to denote unwillingness to make an effort (*1833+*)

lifted *adj* Intoxicated by narcotics; HIGH, STONED (*1990s+ Narcotics*)

light *See* the GREEN LIGHT, IDIOT LIGHT, OUT LIKE A LIGHT, REDLIGHT

lighten up *v phr* To become less serious; be easy; relax • Often a more or less gentle admonition : *Schofield lightens up and improves at bat/ Aw, come on, everybody, lighten up a little. It wasn't that bad. The decade, I mean/ You have to lighten up, Chief. The men are giving it everything they have* (late 1960s+)

light-fingered *adj* **1** Inclined to steal; thievish; STICKY-FINGERED (1547+) **2** Having a light and nimble touch : *The light-fingered thoughtfulness, the ironic lyricism of the most civilized playwright of the era* (1804+)

light-footed *adj* Homosexual; effeminate (1955+)

light into *v phr* To attack; excoriate; LAY INTO : *He lit into the Administration's tax bill with some sparkling epithets* (1878+)

lightning *n* Cheap, raw whiskey; WHITE LIGHTNING (1781+) *See* GREASED LIGHTNING, WHITE LIGHTNING

lightning rod *n* Someone or something that draws the attention, esp criticism, for an issue or problem : *press secretary is the lightning rod for the President*

light on one's **feet** *adj phr* Homosexual; effeminate : *Some models are light on their feet* (1960s+)

light out *v phr* To leave, esp hastily; TAKE OFF, HIGHTAIL : *Jack, estranged from his father by his brother's death in a helicopter crash, lights out for the territories* [1870+; fr earlier nautical *light out*, "move out, or move something out," of obscure origin; perhaps "move or move something lightly, quickly, handily"]

lights *n* A police car : *There were five lights at Dunkin' Donuts* (1980s+ *Teenagers*)

lights out *n phr* **1** Bedtime : *Lights out is at 10:30* **2** The end; death; CURTAINS : *otherwise lights out for me See* PUNCH someone's LIGHTS OUT, SHOOT THE LIGHTS OUT

lightweight *adj* Inconsequential; unserious (1809+) *n* : *He seems like a lightweight to me, don't pay him any attention* (1882+)

like *adv* As if; really; you know; sort of • A generalized modifier used to lend a somewhat tentative and detached tone to the speaker, to give the speaker time to rally words and ideas : *Like I was like groovin' like, you know what I mean? (1950s+ Counterculture & bop talk) v* To pick; bet on : *I liked Felton. I took his folder and read it again* (1950s+) *See* MAKE LIKE

like a bandit *adv phr* Very successfully; thrivingly : *coming out of the battle with Bendix like a bandit* (1960s+) *See* MAKE OUT LIKE A BANDIT

like a bat out of hell *adv phr* Very rapidly; LICKETY-SPLIT : *They split like a bat out of hell* (1921+) *See* TAKE OFF LIKE A BIGASS BIRD

like a blue streak *See* a BLUE STREAK

like a bump on a log *adv phr* Idly; uselessly; inertly : *He just sits there like a bump on a log* (1863+)

like a bunny *See* QUICK LIKE A BUNNY

like a dream *modifier* Easily, smoothly : *drove like a dream* (1949+)

like a hole in the head *See* NEED someone or something LIKE A HOLE IN THE HEAD

like a million bucks *adv phr* Very good; superb : *In that blouse she looks like a million bucks* (1930s+)

like a shot *modifier* Very fast : *bumblebee went by like a shot* (1800+)

like a streak *adv phr* LIKE GREASED LIGHTNING (1839+)

like a ton of bricks *See* COME DOWN ON someone LIKE A TON OF BRICKS

like crazy *adv* With great speed or effort : *ate chocolate like crazy*

like death warmed over *adv* Looking quite pathetic, tired or ill : *after that nap, looking like death warmed over*

◄**like fuck**► *adv phr* LIKE MAD : *coding like fuck every day* (1990s+)

like gangbusters *adv phr* Very energetically and successfully : *Everyone knows I'm getting into your pants like gangbusters/ The rest of the year the economy will be going like gangbusters* (1942+) *See* COME ON LIKE GANGBUSTERS

like greased lightning *adv phr* Very rapidly; LIKE A STREAK : *The little car went by like greased lightning* (1833+)

like hell (or **blazes**) *adv phr* **1** In an extravagant way; very forcefully : *walleyes feed like crazy and "bite like hell"/ Started screaming like hell* (entry form 1855+, variant 1845+) **2** (Variations: **fun** or **shit** may replace **hell**) Never; it is impermissible; IN A PIG'S ASS : *Like hell you will!/ when the prostitute says "Like fun you are"* (entry form 1925+, fun 1909+)

like it is *See* TELL IT LIKE IT IS

like it or lump it *adv phr* Whether or not one wishes : *We have to go now, like it or lump it* (1833+)

like it's going out of style or **like there's no tomorrow** *adv phr* Extravagantly; wildly; recklessly; with abandon : *spending money like it was going out of style/ boozing like there was no tomorrow* (1970s+)

likely story (or **tale**) *n phr* A probable lie; a statement that seems incredible (1740+)

like mad (or **crazy**) *adv phr* Extravagantly; wildly; violently : *tearing around like crazy/ Then everybody laughs like mad* (entry form 1653+, variant 1924+)

like nobody's business *adv phr* Very much; extraordinarily : *He loves her like nobody's* *business/ That hurts like nobody's business* *(1938+)*

like pigs in clover (or ◁**in poo**▷) *adj phr* Very happy; euphoric : *Paramount's general counsel laughs, "This part of the job I enjoy. We're like pigs in clover"* [1800s+; probably a euphemized version of *happy as a pig in shit; pigs in clover* is a children's game first marketed in 1889]

like pulling teeth *adj phr* Very slow and arduous : *Interviewing movie stars can be like pulling teeth, but Nicole Kidman was a delightful surprise: relaxed, natural, and a lot of fun* [1970s+; *like pulling gum-teeth* in the same sense is found by 1872]

◁**like shit through a tin horn**▷ *adv phr* (Variations: **a dose of salts** or **a hot knife through butter** or **off a shovel** may replace **through a tin horn**) Very rapidly and easily; effortlessly : *He went through the defense like shit through a tin horn/ The pension bill went through like a dose of salts* (*dose of salts 1837+, tin horn 1940s+*)

like shooting fish in a barrel *adj phr* Very easy; much too easy : *Home shopping is like shooting fish in a barrel* (*1940s+*)

like something the cat dragged in *adj phr* Revolting; rebarbative; GROSS, YUCKY : *Jesus, get cleaned up. You look like something the cat dragged in/ Sometimes the glue smells like something the cat dragged in*

like that *See* ALL LIKE THAT THERE

like there was no tomorrow *adv* In excess, as if there would not be another opportunity : *drinkin' like there's no tomorrow*

like white on rice *adv* Right on top of something; as close as something can get : *The cat's on me like white on rice*

lily *n* ◁**1**▷ A homosexual; PANSY, QUEER (*1940s+*) **2** Something remarkable, superior, etc; lulu : *I told my best joke. It's never missed, it's a lily*

lily-white *adj phr* Desiring or having only Caucasian residents, workers, etc : *The thugs would never think to look for him in a lily-white suburb* (*1903+*)

limb *See* GO OUT ON A LIMB, OUT ON A LIMB

limey or **lime-juicer** *n* **1** An English person : *The "Doctor" was a lime-juicer* (*1888+*) **2** A British ship (*1919+*) [fr the ration of *lime juice* given to British sailors as an antiscorbutic; the dated use for the first sense is strictly "an English immigrant to the Antipodes"; the generalized term probably reflects the US use, "English sailor or soldier," found by 1918]

limit, the *n phr* A person, thing, etc, that exceeds or outrages what is acceptable : *I've seen some stupid things, but this is the limit/*

Ain't he awful, ain't he just the limit? (*1900+ College students*) *See* GO THE LIMIT

limo (LIHM oh) *n* A limousine : *disapproves of this vast fleet* (*789 limos*) *of luxury transportation* (*1946+*) *v* : *Check your reso before you limo to Manhattan See* STRETCH LIMO

◁**limp-dick**▷ *adj* : *I called myself every limp-dick name I could think of n* An ineffectual man; an impotent man; WIMP (*1970s+*)

limp dishrag *n phr* An ineffectual person; NEBBISH, WIMP : *Sandy is discarded as if she were, well, a limp dishrag* (*1970s+*)

limp noodle *adj* : *outdated postures, overused jokes, and limp-noodle romantic ballads n phr* Something or someone feeble, tasteless, and without distinction : *Warren Christopher has shown himself to be a limp noodle of a persuader* (*1970s+*)

limp wrist *modifier* : *a limp-wrist hangout n phr* A male homosexual : *I reminded her that Boke Kellum was a limp wrist/ Barbara Hutton could only marry herself seven or eight limp wrists* (*1950s+*)

limp-wristed *adj* Effeminate; slack and sinuous; homosexual : *His art always has this subtle, limp-wristed style to it/ the most limp-wristed "stud" in the Philadelphia metropolitan area* (*1950s+*)

line *n* **1** One's way of talking, esp when being persuasive or self-aggrandizing; SPIEL : *of what in a later generation would have been termed her "line"/ You've got some line* (*1903+*) **2** One's occupation, business, etc; RACKET : *What's my line? Herring in brine* (*1655+*) **3** A musical solo or figure, esp personal and innovative : *Coasters talk of "lines," not licks, breaks, or riffs* (*1930s+ Jazz musicians*) **4** A bookmaker's odds on a sports event : *Baseball, basketball, and hockey lines are available on the day or night of the games* (*1970s+ Gambling*) **5** A dose of cocaine, usu formed into a thin line to be nasally ingested (*1980+ Narcotics*) *v* **1** To hit the ball in a line drive (*1892+ Baseball*) **2** Take cocaine : *They lined twice last night, no wonder they're tired See* someone's ASS IS ON THE LINE, the BOTTOM LINE, HARD LINE, HOT LINE, IN LINE, IN LINE FOR, LAY IT ON THE LINE, MAIN LINE, ON LINE, ON THE LINE, OUT OF LINE, PUNCH LINE, PUT one's ASS ON THE LINE, TOE THE MARK

line, the *n phr* **1** The chorus girls of a show **2** An assembly line (*1940s+*) *See* TOE THE MARK

linen *See* DIRTY LINEN, WASH one's DIRTY LINEN

line one's nest *See* FEATHER one's NEST

line out *v phr* **1** To sing, esp in a loud strong voice; BELT OUT (*1970s+*) **2** To hit a line drive that is caught (*1890s+ Baseball*) [musical sense perhaps fr church practice of having a hymn read one line at a time, then having the congregation sing the line]

line (one's **own**) **pocket(s)** *v phr* To be greedy, esp by stealing or extortion : *lining their pockets from the donations at the theater*

liner *See* HEADLINER, ONE-LINER

line up with *v phr* To support; take sides with : *Who will you line up with on this thorny issue?* (*1940s+*)

lion's share *n phr* A major proportion or part of something; the largest portion : *He does the lion's share of the housework*

lip *n* **1** Insolent, impertinent, or presumptuous talk; SASS, SAUCE : *I don't want none of your lip* (*1821+*) **2** A lawyer; MOUTHPIECE (*1929+ Underworld*) *v* To play a musical instrument, esp in jazz; BLOW : *He couldn't lip anything proper anymore* (*1950s+ Jazz musicians*) *See* FLIP one's LIP, ZIP one's LIP

lip lock *n phr* A kiss : *the Rubbles in a passionate lip lock* (*1990s+*)

lip mover *n phr* A dull and stupid person; BLOCKHEAD : *between those countless millions of lip-movers and the minuscule audience for better novels* [*1980s+*; fr the habit of uneducated or dull people of *moving their lips* while reading to themselves]

lippy *adj* **1** Insolent; brash and arrogant : *He's smart, but much too lippy* (*1875+*) **2** Talkative (*1893+*)

lip service *n* Insincere expression of friendship, admiration, agreement, support, etc : *lip service for the volunteers*

lip-sync or **lip-synch** (LIP sink) *v* To move the lips silently in synchronism with recorded singing or speaking, to give the illusion of actual performance : *Having taped his lines before the show, he lip-synched his pronouncements/ staying home with her sister lip synching to Leon Russell records* (*late 1950s+*)

liquefied *adj* Intoxicated from alcohol; drunk (*1939+*)

liquidate *v* To kill [*1924+*; based on Russian *likvidirovat*, "liquidate, wind up"]

liquid crack *n phr* : *40-ounce bottles of malt liquor sometimes have a nickname among the young people who drink them dry in one sitting: "liquid crack"* (*1990s+*)

liquid lunch *n phr* Excessive drinking at lunch; drinking alcohol instead of eating lunch : *picked Sundays for a liquid lunch*

liquor *See* HARD LIQUOR

liquored up *adj* Drunk (*1921+*)

list *See* HIT LIST, SHIT LIST, WISH LIST

listen-in *n* An instance of eavesdropping or wiretapping : *an occasional listen-in on the line* (*1940s+*)

listen up *v phr* To listen closely; pay strict attention • Often a brusque command : *He can*

make you listen up with that violin of his (*1960s+ Armed forces fr black*)

lit[1] *n* Literature : *comp lit/ black lit* (*1850+*)

lit[2] *adj* Drunk (*1917+*)

lit-crit *modifier* : *Gallop, a celebrity in lit-crit circles, could be described as a sort of post-structural Mae West* *n* Literary criticism (*1963+*)

lite *adj* Not serious; not scholarly; watered down; popularized : *there's myth lite apres Joseph Campbell, Pinkola Estes, etc* [*1980s+*; fr the misspelling of *light* used to identify less fattening, less intoxicating, etc, products, esp beer]

litterbug *n* A person who throws trash in the streets, parks, etc [*1947+*; coined for a New York Police Department campaign against littering; modeled on *jitterbug*]

little bitty *adj phr* Very small; ITTY-BITTY : *I got four little bitty kids* (*1940+*)

little black book *n phr* The private notebook in which one is supposed to keep telephone numbers and details of potential and actual sex partners; secret record (*1940s+*)

little boys' (or **girls'**) **room** *n phr* The men's (or women's) restroom : *trip to the little boys' room*

little game, someone's *n phr* Someone's devious scheme; someone's wretched stratagem : *The crowd dropped to his little game* (*1884+*)

little green apples *See* SURE AS GOD MADE LITTLE GREEN APPLES

little green men *n phr* Aliens from outer space, said to have been seen descending from flying saucers : *Search for Extraterrestrial Intelligence, which has long been derided as a quest for "little green men"* (*1961+*)

little secret *See* DIRTY LITTLE SECRET

little shaver *n phr* A young boy (*1843+*)

◁**little shit**▷ *n phr* A nasty or insignificant person; creep : *die, you little shit*

little woman, the *n phr* One's wife • Once regarded as affectionate, this term is now patronizing and demeaning : *tooling along with the kiddies and the little woman in his costly can* (*1881+*)

lit to the gills *adj phr* Drunk (*1917+*)

lit up or **lit up like a Christmas tree** *adj phr* **1** Drunk : *I found Uncle Peter and he was also lit up* (*1902+*) **2** Intoxicated with narcotics; HIGH (*1960s+ Narcotics*)

live *adj* **1** Not recorded or taped : *live music/ a live telecast* (*1934+*) **2** Of current importance; still to be decided : *Is metrication really a live issue today?* (*1900+*)

live high on the hog *See* EAT HIGH ON THE HOG

live-in *adj* Sharing one's domicile : *Coe's former live-in girlfriend/ J Edgar's "longtime live-in* *lover"* (1955+) *n* A housekeeper or care-giver who lives in one's home : *After they had their second child, they hired a live-in* (1955+)

live it up *v phr* To live joyfully and extrava-gantly : *After retirement we decided to live it up for a while* (1951+)

live one *n phr* **1** A lively person; up-to-date person; LIVE WIRE (1920s+) **2** A likely target for a confidence scheme or fast sell : *Hey, Eddie, looks like we got us a live one here* (1920s+ Carnival)

live on the edge *v phr* To life dangerously; court disaster : *dumped about a quarter-cup of salt on top. "I like to live on the edge," she explained/ pushing his luck, living on the edge, playing brilliantly by the seat of his pants* (1990s+)

liver *See* CHOPPED LIVER, THAT AIN'T HAY

lives *See* HIT someone WHERE one LIVES

live wire *n phr* An energetic, vibrant person : *Jimmy's a live wire, all right* (1909+)

living doll *n phr* A notably decent, pleasant person : *Isn't the emcee a living doll?* (1960s+)

living end, the *n phr* A person, thing, etc, that is about as much as one can stand; the END, the LIMIT • Usu highly complimentary (1950s+ Beat & cool talk)

living large *v phr* Doing well : *responded that he is living large*

◁**living shit,** the▷ *See* SCARE THE SHIT OUT OF someone

lizard *See* LOUNGE LIZARD

load *n* **1** Enough liquor to make one drunk : *He's taking on a load again* **2** A dose of nar-cotic smoked in a water pipe *(esp teenagers)* ◁**3**▷ The semen of a single orgasm **4** An old car *(1980s+ Teenagers)* **5** An obese person; CHUBBO : *It's sort of OK to be a load, because it's what's inside that counts/ I'm not going to camp with a bunch of fat loads* (1990s+) **6** (also **load of shit**) Nonsense; lies and exag-gerations; mendacious cant; BULLSHIT, CROCK OF SHIT : *the whole thing about O J threatening to blow his head off was a load* (1990s+) *See* CARRY A LOAD, CARRY THE LOAD, FREELOAD, GET A LOAD OF, HAVE A LOAD ON, a SHITLOAD, SHOOT one's LOAD, THREE BRICKS SHY OF A LOAD

loaded *adj* **1** Drunk : *Men should act different when they get loaded/ Jerry got so loaded at the party last night that we were afraid to let him drive home* (1886+) **2** Containing whiskey or other liquor : *We sipped our loaded coffee* (1930s+) **3** Intoxicated with narcotics; HIGH, STONED : *And then you get loaded and like it* (1940s+ Narcotics) **4** Well supplied; abound-ing in; LOUSY WITH : *She's loaded with talent/ He died loaded with honors* (1709+) **5** Weal-thy; FILTHY RICH : *They're all loaded in that neighborhood* (1910+) **6** Full of information;

prepared *(1895+ Students)* **7** Carrying sig-nificance beyond the obvious or surface meaning : *That was a loaded remark* (1942+) **8** Prearranged; biased : *The interview was loaded in my favor* (1940s+)

loaded dice *n phr* Dice of which the weight distribution has been altered so that the roll is predictable (1781+)

loaded for bear *adj phr* Ready and anxious for a fight; heavily prepared for conflict, debate, etc : *I went to the board meeting loaded for bear* [fr the notion that a hunter must use par-ticularly powerful ammunition, or *load*, to kill a *bear*; the phrase meant "very drunk" by 1896]

loader *See* FREELOADER

loading *See* FREELOADING

loads of something *n phr* A great number; many; much : *The old lady has loads of charm and loads of money* (1880+)

load off someone's **mind, a** *n phr* A great mental and emotional relief; an end to fret-ting : *When I heard she was OK it was a great load off my mind* (1852+)

load the dice *v phr* To prearrange or bias some result : *a man who helped load the dice against the dissidents within the government* [1714+; the date applies to the literal sense; the metaphorical is hard to date]

load up *v phr* **1** To tamper with the ball by covertly applying spit, hair oil, Vaseline, etc *(1980s+ Baseball)* **2** To drink heavily; get drunk : *John always loads up before he goes to fraternity parties* (1980s+ Students)

loan shark *n phr* An underworld usurer; juice dealer, SHYLOCK (1905+)

lobster shift (or **trick**) *n phr* A working shift beginning about midnight [1920s+ News-paper office; perhaps fr *lobster,* "fool, dupe," found by 1896]

local yokel *n phr* **1** A town or city police officer *(1970s+ Citizens band)* **2** A resident of a small town or rural area *(1940s+)*

lock *v* To be seemingly paralyzed and helpless; CHOKE : *He locked on Letterman* (1990s+) *See* LOCKDOWN

lock, a *n phr* A certainty; SURE THING, SHOO-IN : *This guy looks like a lock now/ no longer a lock to win the NFC East* [1940s+; fr *lock,* "wrestling hold"] *See* HAVE A LOCK ON some-thing, MORTAL LOCK

-lock *combining word* A stoppage or restric-tion of or by the indicated thing : *gridlock/ job lock/ marriage lock/ timelock* [1980+; mod-eled on *gridlock*; perhaps based on wrestling holds called *locks*]

lockdown (or **lock**) *n* **1** The state of being grounded and denied privileges : *can't go to the mall; I'm on lockdown* **2** A relationship in which one is controlled or confined by the other : *wanted to go to the party, but his girl's got him in lockdown*

lock down *v phr* To confine all prisoners to their cells : *The prison was locked down and sharpshooters were aiming their guns at the barred windows (1980s+ Prison)*

lock horns *v phr* To contend with; fight : *They had locked horns with a better man/ She has also locked horns with the network (1839+)*

lockjaw *n* : *McKellen's Richard, his defects minimized and with a ruling-class lockjaw accent, is elegantly carved in ice (1980s+) See* HAVE LOCKJAW

lockup *n* A cell, esp a detention cell or holding cell; the COOLER, TANK *(1839+)*

lock someone up and throw away the key *v phr* To imprison someone for a very long time : *A lot of people feel good when you lock these criminals up and throw away the key (1940s+)*

loco[1] *adj* Crazy; NUTS : *He took one look and just went loco (1887+) n : She's acting like a loco* [fr Spanish, "insane"]

loco[2] *n* A locomotive *(1940s+ Railroad)*

log *See* BEAT one's MEAT, EASY AS PIE

logjam *n* An immovable static situation; GRIDLOCK : *He broke the logjam of negotiations with the cable companies (1890+)*

logrolling *n* The congressional practice of canny reciprocal assistance in getting votes : *Thus, when members of Congress find themselves not able to secure the passage of a measure of purely local interest, they are apt to resort to logrolling* [1823+; said to be based on a proverbial phrase, "You *roll* my *log* and I'll roll yours"]

lol *v phr* Computer network abbreviation for "laughed out loud" *(1990s+ Computer)*

lollapalooza, (lah lə pə LOO zə) (Variations: **lollapaloosa, lallapaloosa, lala-, lolla-, -pa-looser, -paloozer**) *n* A person or thing that is remarkable, excellent, wonderful, superior, etc; BEAUT, HUMDINGER : *He's got a lollapalooza of a cold (1904+)*

loll (or laze) around *v phr* To dispose or comport oneself idly; GOOF OFF, LOLLYGAG, LOUNGE AROUND : *We were lolling around at the pool when the thing fell* [1940s+; *loll*, "lean idly," is found by 1377]

lollipop *n* A pitch that is easy to hit : *will they chuckle when out-of-shape lefties lob up lollipops? (1960s+ Baseball)*

lollygag or **lallygag** (LAH lee gag) *v* **1** To idle about; GOOF OFF : *He has the summer free for play, swimming, berry picking, and general lallygagging/ when my nephew and his companion lollygagged back to my house (1862+)* **2** To kiss and caress; dally; MAKE OUT, NECK, trade spit *(1868+)*

lonesome *See* ALL BY one's LONESOME

long arm, the *n phr* A police officer; the LAW [1940s+; fr the phrase *the long arm of the law*]

long as your arm, as *See* AS LONG AS YOUR ARM

long ball *See* GO FOR THE LONG BALL

long block *v phr* : *A "long block" is a complete engine minus the oil pump and oil pan (1990s+ Car mechanics)*

long (or tall) drink of water, a *n phr* A very tall, thin person : *Bill Bradley is sure a long drink of water/ We have an expression in the Midwest: "a tall drink of water" (1940s+)*

long dry spell *n phr* A period of disappointment; sterile period : *It's been a long, dry spell for Atari game players (1970s+)*

long green (or bread) *n phr* Paper money; bills; FOLDING MONEY : *that dear old affectionately regarded long green* [1891+; perhaps influenced by earlier sense "home-grown, home-cured tobacco"]

longhair *adj* **1** (also **long-haired**) : *longhair tastes in poetry* **2** (also **longhaired**) : *sonatas and other longhair stuff n* **1** An intellectual; EGGHEAD *(1920+)* **2** Classical music ● Originally the term was used for musicians who play from written music, and for the music they play : *sometimes called Western music, sometimes European music, and sometimes just longhair (1920s+ Jazz musicians)* **3** A young man with long hair, esp a hippie : *another longhair, a member of our commune (1960s+)* [earlier senses fr the stereotype of an intellectual or esthete as being strange and wearing *long hair*]

long haul *n phr* A long and arduous period : *It looks like it'll be a long haul (1940s+) See* FOR THE LONG HAUL, OVER THE LONG HAUL

long in the tooth *adj phr* Aged; advanced in age : *The actor is a bit long in the tooth to be playing Tom Sawyer* [1852+; fr the practice of judging the age of horses by the *length* of *teeth*]

longjohn *n* A man who is copulating with a prisoner's wife; jody : *That longjohn out there is gonna die when I hit the street (1990s+ Prison)*

long johns or **long ones** *n phr* Long winter underwear : *A generation or so ago, men, women, boys and girls put on long ones in October and wore long ones until spring/ Pop, will you dig that dish out of your long johns (1940s+)*

long on *modifier* Having a large amount of something : *long on patience (1913+)*

long run, the *See* IN THE LONG RUN

long shot *modifier* : *a long-shot victory n phr* **1** A person, horse, project, etc, that seems not likely to win or succeed; DARK HORSE : *But it's a pretty long shot I'm afraid (1869+)* **2** A scene photographed from a distance; a long-range photograph (*1940s+*) *See* NOT BY A LONG SHOT

long story short *v phr* To make a longer tale into a nutshell : *long story short, school's out baby*

long suit, someone's *n phr* Someone's best gift or quality; forte; strong point : *His gift of gab is his long suit. He can call a bird off a tree* [*1895+*; fr cardplaying, "suit in which you hold originally more than three cards," found by 1876]

long time no see *sentence* I haven't seen you for a long time (*1900+*)

loo[1] *n* A toilet • Chiefly British : *everything you'd find in a powder room except the loo* [*1940+*; origin uncertain; perhaps fr *Waterloo* in proportionate analogy with *water closet*; perhaps fr the Edinburgh cry "*Gardyloo*" uttered when one threw the contents of the slopjar into the street; Mrs. Virginia Burton of Lynchburg, VA, suggests it may be a pronunciation of French *lieu*, "place," in the phrase *lieu d'aisance*, "toilet, lavatory"]

loo[2] *n* (also **Loo**) A lieutenant, esp of police : *All lieutenants were called Loo* (*1990s+*)

loogie *n* A mass of phlegm and saliva that is ejected from the mouth : *The immature kids hocked loogies*

look *See* a HARD LOOK

look-alike *n* **1** A person who closely resembles another; DEAD RINGER, double : *Barratt had an interview with his noted look-alike* (*1947+*) **2** A compatible machine : *an IBM PC look-alike* (*1980s+ Computer*)

Look alive! *interj* Get ready; act alert; get ready to move : *Look alive, the train's coming*

look at someone **cross-eyed** *v phr* To commit even a tiny fault; offend in the least way : *who would yell copper if you looked at them cross-eyed* (*1940s+*)

look daggers *v phr* To look at with anger; glare at : *I wondered why they were looking daggers at me* (*1833+*)

look down one's **nose** *v phr* To behave with hauteur; act condescendingly : *He looked down his nose at me as if I were some loathsome thing in his path* (*1921+*)

look down on someone or something *v phr* To hold in contempt; scorn : *He looks down on us as newcomers* (*1711+*)

looker *n* **1** A good-looking person of either sex, but esp a woman : *That waitress is a looker, a real dish* (*1902+*) **2** (also **lookie-loo**) A person who inspects merchandise but does not buy : *A "looker" is to the used car lot what a browser is to a bookstore/ Yard/garage/tag sales are plagued by "lookie-loos"* (*1940s+ Salespersons*) *See* GOOD-LOOKER

looking *adv* Watching the pitch without swinging the bat : *The Russian infielder struck out three times, looking* (*1970s+ Baseball*)

looking at (or **talking**), be *v phr* To have as a subject; direct the mind to; specify; contemplate : *We're looking at about 3 billion here/ John Glenn, not known for his humor, slammed Reagan's top aides. Instead of serving four more years, he said, some are looking at ten to 20/ What we're talking here is seventy-five a key/ Rita Rose. You're talking Rita Rose, right?* (late *1970s+*)

looking good *interj* An exclamation of encouragement, praise, reassurance, etc; WAY TO GO : *They hollered "Looking good!" as the leader passed* (*1970s+*)

look like a drowned rat *v phr* To have a singularly disheveled, subdued, and unsightly appearance : *When they got off the boat after a weekend they looked like drowned rats* (*1508+*)

look like death warmed over *v phr* To look miserable; look ill and exhausted; have a wretched mien : *I don't know what the news was, but Frank looks like death warmed over* (*1939+*)

look-see, a *n phr* A look; an inspection : *Let's have a look-see at our friend/ I stopped in at Jerry's for a lager and a look-see* (*1883+*)

look see *v phr* To look; have a look : *I'm dropping down to look see* (*1930s+*)

loon *See* CRAZY AS A LOON

loony or **looney** or **luny** *adj* Crazy; NUTTY : *You looney punk/ "I think, sir, he's a little luny," replied Ginger Nut, with a grin* (*1853+*) *n* (also **loon** or **loonball**) : *the inspired looney who hated killing/ would have shown up in a Mel Brooks epic had that loonball thought of it first* (*1884+*) [probably fr both *lunatic* and *crazy as a loon* (found by 1845)]

loony bin *n phr* A mental hospital; NUTHOUSE : *that fugitive from a loony-bin/ So how come I felt like a loony in a loony-bin?* (*1919+*)

loony-tune or **loony-tunes** (Variations: **looney** may replace **loony**; **toon** may replace **tune**) *modifier* : *the loony-toon acting debut of writer Stephen King/ It's been kind of a looney-tunes week n* A crazy person; NUT : *Jesus, what a loony tune/ Loony-tunes Dennis Hopper wires a city bus to blow up* (*1980s+*) [fr *Looney Tunes*®, a series of short cartoon-film comedies, a paraphrasing of *Silly Symphonies*, also short cartoon-film comedies]

loop *See* IN THE LOOP, KNOCK someone FOR A LOOP, OUT OF THE LOOP, THROW someone FOR A LOOP

looped or **looping** *adj* Drunk : *The end result is a looped group/ Was she drunk? Looping* (*1934+*)

looper *n* A fly ball hit between the infield and outfield (*1937+ Baseball*)

loopy or **loopy-loo** *adj* Crazy; silly; NUTTY : *that loopy guy whose handkerchief you cry into/*

visually complemented the singer's loopy Balkan bop/ even loopier bids for the few works in Wood's small mature oeuvre (1925+)

loose *adj* **1** Relaxed; easy; COOL : *No wonder you guys were really loose/ You are loose in the rush, misty and safe (1950s+ Cool talk)* **2** Sexually promiscuous *(1595+) See* ALL HELL BROKE LOOSE, HANG LOOSE, a SCREW LOOSE

loose as a goose *adj phr* **1** (also **loosey-goosey**) Very relaxed; perfectly easy; COOL : *loose-as-a-goose, completely relaxed on the field/ a big party place; people slept with each other, it was loosey-goosey (1950s+ Cool talk)* **2** Of a car engine, needing new bearings and other repairs *(1950s+ Hot rodders)* [probably both fr the rhyme and the perception that a *goose* has *loose* bowels; first sense may be related to an earlier "weak, flimsy," with the notion of "loosely articulated," hence relaxed to the point of languor]

loose cannon *n phr* A person who is quite likely to cause damage; a wildly irresponsible person : *Haig is a loose cannon on a pitching deck/ His detractors call him a loose cannon who makes recommendations in public before consulting (1977+)*

loose change *n phr* Money at hand and to spare; available money : *I wanted to help, but didn't have any loose change (1827+)*

loosen (or **loose**) **up** *v phr* To speak more freely; become loquacious; loosen one's tongue : *Fatigue and a drink or two loosened him up and he told us the whole story/ Debating Perot is a mistake. They will loose him up (1911+)*

loot *n* Money, esp a large amount of money : *Rich planters would come and spend some awful large amounts of loot/ There's a lot of loot there, kiddo (1930+ Jazz musicians)*

lord *See* TIGHT

lose a bundle *v phr* To lose a lot of money : *lost a bundle on that handbag*

lose one's ass *v phr* To be badly defeated; lose everything : *We would have lost our ass if we had gone in the way Colin wanted (1960s+)*

lose one's cookies *See* SHOOT one's COOKIES

lose one's cool *v phr* To become angry or flustered; lose composure; LOSE IT : *Easy, dude, don't lose your cool (1950s+ Cool talk)*

lose it *v phr* To become very distraught; lose control of oneself; suffer a kind of breakdown; CRACK UP : *told me to keep an eye on Dennis, that he looked like he was losing it/ of being totally stressed out, of "losing it"/ Thieu was really tough, but that day he lost it. His spirit was broken* [1990s+; probably fr the notion of *losing* one's grip on reality]

lose one's marbles *v phr* To become foolish, irrational, forgetful, etc, as if senile [1920s+; fr an earlier phrase *let his marbles go with the*

monkey, fr a story about a boy whose marbles were carried off by a monkey; *lose one's taw* (a choice playing marble), "go crazy," is found by 1902]

loser *n* (also **born loser**) A person or thing that fails, esp habitually; BUST, DUD, LEMON, nonstarter *(1950s+ Students) v* : *I don't want them to think I'm losered out*

lose one's shirt *v phr* To lose one's money or property; go broke : *lost his shirt on investments*

lose sleep over something *v phr* To worry overmuch about something; be very anxious about something • Often in the negative : *Murray doesn't seem to have lost a lot of sleep over working without a strong black literary tradition to rely on/ Do you lose sleep over your investments? (1942+)*

losing *See* someone CAN'T WIN FOR LOSING

losses *See* CUT one's LOSSES

lost *See* GET LOST

lost cause *n phr* A hopeless or worthless pursuit; a person or thing that can no longer hope to succeed or be changed for the better : *tried to reform her, but she is a lost cause*

lot *See* ALL OVER THE LOT

lot of weight *See* CARRY A LOT OF WEIGHT

lotsa *adj* Lots of : *needs lotsa attention (1927+)*

lots of luck or **good luck** *interj* A rueful and ironic way of wishing someone success when it is obviously impossible : *Vance played a key part in negotiating the Camp David agreements on the Middle East, but lots of luck in getting him to say so/ Looking for a lady loan shark? Good luck; mob jobs remain male turf* [the first form is sometimes uttered in a jokey Asian way: "Rots of ruck"]

Lotus Land *See* LA-LA LAND

loud *adj* Vulgar and gaudy in taste; garish : *Isn't his dress rather loud? (1849+) See* FOR CRYING OUT LOUD, READ someone LOUD AND CLEAR

loudmouth *n* A loud and constant talker, esp a braggart and self-appointed authority; WINDBAG : *Maybe poking Loud Mouth in the kisseroo would solve everything (1934+) v* : *Don't you loudmouth me!*

lounge around *v phr* LOLL AROUND : *What are you lounging around here for? Get to work! (1940s+)*

lounge lizard *n phr* LADIES' MAN [1918+; fr the notion that such a man *lounges*, frequents cocktail *lounges*, and is as colorful, indolent, and reptilian as a *lizard* in the sun]

louse *n* An obnoxious and despicable person, esp one who is devious and undependable; BASTARD, CRUMB : *We kicked the dirty louse out when he said that (1633+)*

louse up *v phr* **1** To ruin or spill; botch; BOLLIX UP : *Boy, you certainly loused that up* **2** To fail;

SCREW UP : *He'll get promoted next month if he doesn't louse up* (1938+)

lousy *adj* Bad; nasty; CRUMMY : *Crab was all she ever did. What a lousy sport/ Yuh lousy boob* (1690+) *adv* : *I did pretty lousy on that test*

lousy with *adj phr* Well provided with; swarming with : *Everybody will come home lousy with cash/ That hotel was lousy with perverts* (1843+)

love *See* CALF LOVE, FOR THE LOVE OF PETE, PUPPY LOVE

love, a *n phr* Any notably decent, pleasant, generous person; LIVING DOLL : *Be a love and bring me another drink* (1841+)

lovebirds *n* Lovers : *the two lovebirds* (1911+)

love bug *n phr* **1** An imagined insect whose bite causes one to fall in love (1937+) **2** A notably decent, pleasant, generous person; DOLL, LIVING DOLL, LOVE : *But once you know her, she's a love bug* (1975+)

love drug *n phr* A drug thought to be an aphrodisiac, such as methaqualone (1960s+ Students)

love handle *modifier* : *who come in rarely, and mostly for love-handle removal* *n phr* A bulge of fat at the side of the abdomen : *when I have strapped the metal thing to my love handles* (1960s+)

love-in *n* A gathering, esp of hippies, devoted to mutual love and understanding : *Tulsa recently had its first love-in* (1960s+ Counterculture)

lovely *n* An attractive woman : *where flabby lovelies in polka-dot bikinis lobbed beachballs around* (1940s+)

love me, love my dog *sentence* If you accept me, you must accept what belongs to me or comes with me : *Our stations are not for sale separate from the network. Our attitude is Love me, love my dog* (1546+)

◁**love-muscle**▷ *n* The penis (1930s+)

love nest *n phr* A place where two can make love, esp adulterous love (1930s+)

lover *See* MOTHERFUCKER

lover-boy *n* **1** A handsome man; matinee idol **2** A womanizer; CASANOVA, LADIES' MAN, STUD, WOMAN-CHASER (1940s+)

◁**lovesteak**▷ *n* The penis; COCK, DONG, DORK : *Playgirl always has men with big lovesteaks as their centerfolds* (1980s+ Students)

love (or like) the sound of one's own voice *v phr* To have a high opinion of one's self; enjoy self-esteem : *Clifford was a man who clearly loved the sound of his own voice* (1960s+)

love-up *n* An instance of caressing, fondling, etc (1953+)

lovey-dovey *adj* Affectionate; amorous : *My, aren't they lovey-dovey?* *n* **1** Affection; friendship : *a reign of peace, prosperity, and lovey-*

dovey **2** A wife, mistress, sweetheart, etc : *their foreign lovey-doveys* (1904+)

loving *See* EVER-LOVING, MOTHERFUCKING

low *adj* Sad; melancholy : *I was so low and depressed* (1744+) *n* A bad reaction to a narcotic; BUMMER (1960s+ Narcotics) *See* KEEP A LOW PROFILE, LAY LOW, LIE LOW

low-ball *v* To report as lower; reduce : *Had Feldstein deliberately low-balled the original numbers?/ But he apparently lowballed the amount of money he gave Medlar*

low blow *n phr* An unfair and malicious stroke; CHEAP SHOT : *"They'd be rendered mute if they couldn't use sports analogies." "Low blow, Alice"* [1940s+; fr the illegal *blow below the belt* in boxing]

lowbrow *adj* : *What are you always pulling that lowbrow stuff for?* *n* A person lacking education and refinement; an ignorant lout (1902+) [said to have been coined by the humorist Will Irwin]

low camp *n phr* Entertainment or art characterized by very broad and vulgar features : *Low camp would mean doing it with winks and leers at the audience, in jeering collusion* (1960s+)

lowdown, the *n phr* The truth; the authentic facts : *eager to get the low-down on new aircraft* (1915+)

low-down *adj* **1** Vulgar; despicable; vile : *a dirty low-down trick* (1888+) **2** Intense and insinuating, in the blues style : *a babe with a low-down voice* (1900+ Jazz musicians) *See* a DIRTY SHAME

low-down dirty shame *See* a DIRTY SHAME

lower the boom *v phr* **1** To deliver a knockout punch : *When he got his Irish up, Clancy lowered the boom* **2** To punish; exact obedience and docility : *if we lower the boom on every nonconformist in society/ My patience evaporated and I lowered the boom on them* (1940s+)

low five *n phr* A greeting or gesture of approval made by slapping hands at about waist level : *San Diego hand-slapping, high fives, low fives* (1980s+) *v phr* GIVE someone FIVE

low-key *adj* Quiet; modest; unassertive : *She is low-key but is happy to talk about things that Wayans doesn't do for himself* (1965+) *v* To treat with little emphasis; PLAY DOWN : *They were low-keying it because of the controversy* (1960+) [in adjective sense, a technical term in photography, "with tones lying in the gray scale," found by 1907]

low-life *adj* : *fancies himself in love with the raucous, lowlife Doreen* (1794+) *n* A person of reprehensible habits; BUM (1909+)

low-octane *adj* Feeble; ineffectual; low-powered : *The songs earned the obligatory pan from Rolling Stone: "low-octane operatic drivel"* (1990s+)

low profile *adj* : *a low-profile discreetness n phr*
Inconspicuousness; recessiveness; modesty :
*He thought he'd do better with a low profile
the first year or so* (*1960s+*) *See* KEEP A LOW
PROFILE

low-rent or **low-end** *adj* Cheap; second-rate;
inferior : *and from that low-rent lunch at the
Century Plaza/ Plug themselves into some low-
rent section of the brain. Some dud bit of the
brain/ I'm having trouble deciding whether he's
classically Rabelaisian or just low-end*

low rent *n phr* A sexually promiscuous
woman; PUSHOVER (*1960s+ Students*)

low-res or **lo-res** *adj* Low resolution; of lesser
or poor quality : *low-res monitor*

low ride *adj phr* Socially inferior; vulgar; TRA-
SHY : *For teenagers any mixing with the Indians
or low ride Mexicans down in the valley is
slumming* (*1950s+ Southern California*)

low rider *n phr* **1** A person who drives a car
with a radically lowered suspension **2** A car
with a lowered suspension **3** A motorcyclist,
esp one who rides a customized motorcycle
with the handlebars very high **4** A rough
young man from a black ghetto : *A group of
low riders from Watts assembled on the basketball court/ There are what the blacks call low
riders, these people who run around pushing
their weight around* [*1950s+ Southern California; extended fr the ghetto style, among
blacks and Chicanos, of the cool young man
who wished, according to Calvin Trillin, "to
lower his car to within a few inches of the
ground, make it as beautiful as he knows
how and drive it very slowly"*]

LSD *n* Lysergic acid diethylamide, a hallucinogenic drug; acid : *There is no rite of passage,
such as smoking pot or tripping with LSD*
[*1960s+ Narcotics*; found as a chemical
abbreviation by 1947 in a Swiss journal]

lube *modifier* : *lube rack n* **1** (also **lube job**) A
lubrication; grease job; a greasing : *accused
the Packers of giving their jerseys a lube job
to prevent offensive linemen from holding*
(*1950s+*) **2** (also **lubricant**) Butter (*Students*)
[last sense from the likening of *butter* and
grease]

lubricated *adj* Drunk; OILED (*1927+*)

luck *interj* A wish that one have good luck :
"Luck," I said. "You too," Conway said
(*1980s+*) *See* IN LUCK, OUT OF LUCK, POT LUCK,
SHIT OUT OF LUCK

luck into *v phr* To get something by luck :
*Alain lucked into a goldmine with an idea for a
magazine* (*1950s+*)

luck of the draw, the *n phr* The way fortune
would have it; THAT'S THE WAY THE BALL
BOUNCES (*1967+*)

luck out *v phr* **1** To be very unlucky; be
doomed (*WWII Army*) **2** To be lucky; get

something by good luck : *that he will luck out
after his search and create operation* (*1954+*)
[one of the slang expressions that can mean
opposite things]

lucky break *n phr* A stroke of good luck; HIT :
Finding the guy was sure a lucky break
(*1938+*)

lucky stiff (or **dog**) *n phr* A fortunate person :
You've done it again, you lucky stiff (first form
1914+, variant *1844+*)

lucre *See* FILTHY LUCRE

lude or **'lude** *n* Quaalude®, a depressant drug;
any methaqualone capsule or pill : *Only this
year "ludes" (Quaaludes or "downs") were the
hot sellers/ Dropping the Last 'Lude* (*1960s+
Narcotics*)

lug *n* **1** A stupid man; dull fellow; BOZO : *Those
lugs in the band would begin to kid me about
it/ a simple-minded lug like Moose Malloy*
(*1924+*) **2** A demand for money, esp bribe or
protection money : *a captain of detectives who
was collecting the lug from the gambling houses*
(*1934+*) *v* To solicit money; borrow [origins
and derivations uncertain; the first noun
sense is probably fr *lug*, "something heavy
and clumsy," attested in the 16th century
and retained in several English dialects
where it is used derogatorily of persons]

LUG *n* : *At colleges as diverse as Smith and Ohio
State, for example, episodic lesbians are numerous and open enough to have spawned an
acronym: LUG, short for Lesbian Until Graduation* (*1990s+*)

lughead *n* A stupid person : *lugheads lifting
weights*

lulu *n* A person or thing that is remarkable,
wonderful, superior, etc; Darb, HUMDINGER,
PISSER : *He said the aquarium was a lulu/
Burrows was permitted his own bower, and it
was a lulu* [*1886+*; origin unknown; earlier
looly, "beautiful girl," is attested; perhaps fr
the cowboy term *loo loo*, "a winning hand,"
explained as a hand invented by local people
in order to win a game from a stranger "for
the good of the *loo*," where *loo* means "party,
set, community"; this sense of *loo* is related
to the popular 18th-century card game of the
same name, fr *lanterloo* fr French *lanterlu*, a
nonsense phrase in the refrain of a song]

lumber *n* A bat (*1940s+ Baseball*) *v* To take
advantage of someone; make someone a
scapegoat ● Chiefly British : *He was totally
lumbered. It was a terrible travesty* (*1845+*)
[verb sense fr *lumber*, "to fill up or obstruct
with lumber," found by 1642]

lummox or **lummux** *n* A stupid, clumsy person; KLUTZ [*1841+*; fr British dialect fr *lum-
mock*, "lump"]

lump *n* **1** A packet of food : *"Lumps" are possible
at any time during the day* (*1912+ Hoboes*) **2**

A dull, stupid person; CLOD, KLUTZ : *What an unspeakable lump I was* (*1597+*)

lump it *v phr* To accept or swallow something one does not like : *It was a lousy deal, but I just had to lump it* [1791+; fr earlier sense of *lump*, "dislike, reject," probably related to the sense "strike, thrash"] *See* LUMPS, LIKE IT OR LUMP IT

lumps *n* Severe treatment; punishment; a beating : *Somebody was out to give him his lumps* [1935+; ultimately fr late 1700s *lump*, "beat, thrash"] *See* GET one's LUMPS, TAKE one's LUMPS

lumpy *adj* Badly played (*Cool talk*)

lunatic fringe *n phr* The radical and irresponsible sector of a group or party : *The party has been turned over to its lunatic fringe* [1913+; apparently coined by Theodore Roosevelt in *History as Literature*]

lunchbox or **lunchsack** *n* A confused or ignorant person; someone out of touch with reality; DITZO (*1960s+ Students*)

lunch-bucket or **lunch-pail** *modifier* 1 Working-class; blue-collar; proletarian and ordinary : *Phillips is a regular commentator on NPR, that bastion of lunch-bucket values/ The fight made Tomashek a lunch pail hero/ hard worker, good player, overlooked contributor, a lunch-pail guy* 2 Favoring the political interests of the working class : *Traditional lunch-pail liberals and progressive Democrats are beginning to question the vitality of their own programs* (*1990s+*)

lunch-hooks *n* The hands; fingers; MEATHOOKS : *get a set of predatory lunch-hooks into him* (*1896+*)

◁**lungs**▷ *n* A woman's breasts; BOOBS, KNOCKERS : *pushed a whole blouse full of lungs against my arm/ She has a great pair of lungs*

lunk *modifier* : *four books about a lunk hero Carlo Reinhart* *n* A stupid person; LUNKHEAD : *Lunks, Hunks and Arkifacts/ a character whom Tristan describes as "a big lunk"* (*1867+*)

lunkhead *n* A stupid person; BOOB, DOPE, LUNK : *a bulky, duckfooted lunkhead/ Tenors have been traditionally stereotyped as vain lunkheads* (*1852+*)

lunky *adj* Stupid : *conflict between paternal authority and lunky adolescent waywardness* (*1940s+*)

lurk *v* 1 To ride about looking for sex partners; CRUISE : *Me and the boys are going lurken' tonight to pick up some foxy broads* (*1960s+ Black*) 2 : *Lurk: To log onto a bulletin board and read the discussion without participating or making your presence known* (*1990s+ Computer*)

lurker *n* 1 A person who "lurks" : *according to David Brooks, a pro-gun control lurker/ You just sneak around and listen without revealing your presence, thus becoming what internauts pejoratively call a lurker* (*1990s+ Computer*) 2 A person who enters a computer system illegally; an uninvited computer eavesdropper : *Ian had found a lurker in the system* (*1970s+ Computer*)

lush *n* A drunkard; an alcoholic; DIPSO : *She is still plastered, the little lush/ The father was by no means a lush, but the son carried temperance to an extreme* (*1890+*) *v* : *lushing, stowing wine into our faces* [origin unknown; probably related to *lush*, "liquor, booze," which is found by 1790 and may be fr Romany or Sehlta (tinkers' jargon)]

lushed or **lushed up** *adj* or *adj phr* Drunk (*1926+*)

luv *n* A woman, said affectionately : *Please pass the potatoes, luv* (*1957+*)

M

M *n* **1** Morphine : *You've got to get M to get that tingle-tingle (1912+ Narcotics)* **2** Marijuana *(1960+ Narcotics)*

ma'am *See* WHAM-BAM THANK YOU MA'AM

ma-and-pa *See* MOM-AND-POP

mac[1] *n* Man; fellow; BUSTER, JACK • Used in direct address, often with a mildly hostile intent : *Take it easy, mac* [1928+; fr the many surnames beginning *Mac* or *Mc*]

mac[2] *v* (also **mac out, mac on**) To eat; gorge : *Let's go mac/ He really macked out last night/ mac on hamburgers and fries* [1980s+ Students; fr the *McDonald's*® chain of fast-food restaurants]

MacGuffin or **McGuffin** *n* A plot or movie device that raises a seemingly crucial question in the minds of the audience, but may well be a cunning deception : *The writers wanted a MacGuffin which would set up a series of absurd rules for us/ You still haven't told me what the McGuffin is. Why were the government and Mr D so interested* [1930s+; first used by the director Alfred Hitchcock, and perhaps suggested by *McGuffin*, "a gift that is not to be opened until Christmas," hence something tantalizing, found by 1925]

machinery *n* **1** A drug user's paraphernalia; ARTILLERY *(1940s+ Narcotics)* **2** The male genitals : *You could see the bulge of his machinery there at the crotch (1980s+)*

machisma (mah CHIZ mə) *n* The female counterpart of machismo : *Machisma, Women, and Daring (1970s+)*

machismo (mah CHIZ moh) *n* Aggressive masculinity; blatant virility : *machismo, a he-man complex/ with Chicago machismo, also universal adolescent horniness* [1960s+; fr Spanish]

macho (MAH choh) *adj* : *a typical macho Mailerism/ list of macho jobs as long as a master sergeant's sleeve of hash marks n* **1** An aggressively masculine man; HE-MAN **2** Aggressive maleness; MACHISMO : *It was not just a question of executive macho* [1970s+; fr Spanish]

macking *n* **1** Heavy petting and other sex play : *Mackin' Making Out* **2** To drive slowly and watchfully in the streets, walk about vigilantly in bars and parties, etc, looking for a sex partner; CRUISE [1990s+ Teenagers; perhaps related to *mack*, "pimp"]

mack on *v phr* **1** To make a sexual proposition : *mack on anything with breasts* **2** To make out with someone : *macking on his girlfriend*

Mack truck *n phr* Something very powerful; SIX-HUNDRED-POUND GORILLA : *Marilyn Horne, the greatest coloratura mezzo of our time, is a Mack truck of a voice with awesome flexibility* [1980s+; fr the trademark of a line of heavy trucks]

mad *adj* **1** Angry *(1400s+)* **2** Excellent; exciting; CRAZY *(1950s+ Bop & cool talk) See* LIKE MAD

-mad *combining word* Devoted to, manic over, obsessed with what is indicated : *money-mad/ computer-mad/ horse-mad*

mad about someone or something *adj phr* CRAZY ABOUT : *Aren't you just mad about her new book? (1744+)*

mad as a wet hen *adj phr* Very angry; infuriated; PISSED OFF : *When he got the letter he was mad as a wet hen (1823+)*

mad-dog *v* To stare at someone steadily and provocatively; stare someone down : *Torres thought the man had challenged or "mad-dogged" him/ He kept his stare on Hawk. It was what the gang kids called mad-dogging (1990s+ Street talk)*

made, be *v phr* be TAKEN *(1950s+)*

made for someone *adj phr* Exactly fitted to one's desires, looks, etc : *Mr and Mrs Smith were not exactly made for each other*

made man (or **guy**) *n phr* A man who has been initiated into the Mafia : *He was a mob hanger-on, but not a made man/ a made guy, one of them (1960s+)*

made of money *adj phr* Very rich; LOADED : *Well off? Why the guy's made of money (1849+)*

madhouse *n* A scene of confusion : *a madhouse at the grocery store*

Madison Avenue or **Mad Ave** *modifier* : *Madison Avenue hype n phr* The values, behavior, business, milieu, etc, of advertising and public relations *(1950s+)*

mad money *n phr* **1** Money carried by a woman with which to pay her way home if her escort becomes offensive **2** Money saved by a woman against the time when she wants to make an impulsive or therapeutic purchase *(1922+)*

Mae West *n phr* A bulky life preserver [1930s+ British aviators; fr the generous bosom of the actress]

mag *n* **1** A magazine *(1801+)* **2** A magneto *(1920+)* **3** A car wheel made of a magnesium alloy *(1960s+)* *v* To search someone with a magnetometer device : *no unscheduled stops and limited contact with people who haven't been magged (1990s+)*

maggot *n* A white person; OFAY : *Maggot: street slang for anyone white (1980s+ Black)*

magic bullet *n phr* A miraculous remedy for some social, economic, etc, ill : *We know no one chancellor has a magic bullet to turn the school system around* [1960s+; fr the name given in 1910 to salvarsan, formerly a trademark, discovered and proposed by the bacteriologist Paul Ehrlich as a cure for syphilis]

magic (or sacred) mushrooms *n* A type of mushroom (genus *Psilocybe*) that when eaten causes hallucinations, etc

magnum-force *adj* Very powerful : *one of Thomas Hearns's magnum-force punches* [fr the powerful *Magnum* revolver (a trademark since 1935)]

maiden *n* A racehorse, regardless of sex, that has never won a race; BUG *(1880+ Horse racing)*

mail *See* AIR MAIL, GREENMAIL, JUNK MAIL

main *adj* Favorite; most admired; beloved : *This is my main nigger, my number one nigger (1960s+ Black) See* MAINLINE

main cheese *n* A high-ranking or important person *(1900+)*

main drag (or stem) *n phr* The major street of a town or city • Main stem was used of a railroad line by 1832 : *We begged together on the "main drag"/ We sifted along the main stem (entry form 1851+, variant 1900+)*

mainline or **main** *v* 1 To inject narcotics into a blood vessel; SHOOT UP : *after mainlining heroin the night before (1930s+ Narcotics)* 2 To take or administer stimulants or depressants of various sorts : *because the economy was mainlining bigger and bigger fixes of inflation/ LA and the San Joaquin valley mainlined northern California water and couldn't wait for the next fix*

main line *n phr* 1 (also **Main Line**) The wealthy and fashionable elements of a place; high society and its area of residence, esp that of Philadelphia : *so young and handsome and so popular with the Main Line (1930s+)* 2 A vein in the arm, the median vein, into which narcotics may be injected *(1920s+ Narcotics)* [first sense fr the railroad between Philadelphia and the wealthy suburbs to the west]

main man *n phr* 1 One's best friend : *Lou Reed, he my main man (1960s+ Black)* 2 The most important player, person, etc : *the team's main man (1990s+)*

main queen *n phr* 1 One's steady girlfriend *(1950s+)* 2 A male homosexual who takes the passive role, esp one much sought after by other homosexuals *(Homosexuals)*

main squeeze *n phr* 1 The most important person; BIG ENCHILADA, BOSS : *Vance seems to be the main squeeze (1896+)* 2 One's sweetheart, lover, etc : *which center on his main squeeze, a girl in his Shakespeare class (1980+)*

maintain *v* To stay under control; to keep one's composure : *While he gives this silly speech, I need to maintain*

maintain a low profile *See* KEEP A LOW PROFILE

maisie *See* S AND M

major *adj* Impressive; weighty; important, SERIOUS : *The TV pictures of the smoking problem showed over-accessorized secretaries with major hair smoking in dark doorways of an office building (1990s+)*

major-league *adv* Very much; totally; BIG TIME : *We've been major-league screwed. I just found out the trains are stopped (1990s+)*

major leaguer *n phr* A person of achievement; an expert; HEAVY HITTER : *If Eric Valdez had gotten it on with Mrs Esteva, he was a major leaguer*

majorly *adv* Very; extremely : *Both are majorly distraught over the wife/mommy's death/ I remember once when I was majorly depressed (1990s+)*

make *n* 1 Positive identification : *The woman gave us a make on the guy who slugged her* ◁2▷ A person regarded merely as a sex partner; LAY : *an easy make (1918+)* *v* 1 To rob; steal; HEIST *(1700+ Underworld)* 2 To recognize or identify; make an identification : *The dealer-suspect "made" (i e, correctly identified) one of the staked-out 53 cars/ He made me the minute he saw me (1906+ Underworld & police)* 3 To understand; grasp; DIG : *I don't make you, kid. What did the boy do? (1912+)* 4 To bring fame, success, wealth, etc : *That one show made her (1460+)* ◁5▷ To do the sex act with; LAY, SCREW : *Not only is the King in love with me, but the Queen tried to make me too/ in the sense of "making" handsome men (1918+)* 6 To arrive at; HIT : *We'll never make Padanaram before dark (1624+)* 7 To defecate; DUMP, SHIT *(1950s+)* 8 To initiate one into the Mafia : *The purpose of a particular meeting had been to make us "to incorporate individuals as new members of the family" (1960s+)* 9 (also **make up**) To shuffle playing cards : *Peter made the cards and handed them to Stern to deal See* EASY MAKE, ON THE MAKE, ON THE TAKE, PUT THE MAKE ON someone, RUN A MAKE

make a believer out of someone *v phr* To convince someone, esp by forceful or harsh means : *I never worried about it much, but that one wreck made a believer out of me (1960s+)*

make a big production (or big deal) out of something *v phr* To overdo; overreact, overplan, etc; MAKE A FEDERAL CASE OUT OF something : *All she wanted was a simple wedding, but he had to make a big production out of it (1960s+)*

make a bundle *v phr* To acquire a lot of money; CLEAN UP : *John really made a bundle on the deal (1905+)*

make a federal case out of something *v phr* To overemphasize the importance of something; exaggerate or overreact; BLOW UP : *I merely bought a new car, so don't try to make a Federal case out of it* [1950s+; popularized after being spoken by a judge in the 1959 movie *Anatomy of a Murder*]

make a go of *v phr* To achieve success in : *to make a go of the list book business* (*1877+*)

make a hash of something *v phr* To make a jumble of; mangle; botch : *The newspapers made a total hash of what I had said* (*1735+*)

make a hit *v phr* To be successful; be received with approval, gratitude, etc : *She made a hit with my family* (*1829+*)

make a killing *v phr* To get a large, quick profit; win hugely : *Where did he get all that money? Made a killing on the stock market, he says* (*1888+*)

make a mess *v phr* To defecate; CRAP, SHIT : *I'm afraid the kid has made a mess in his pants* (*1903+*)

make a mess of something *v phr* To make a jumble of; mangle; botch; MAKE A HASH OF something : *He gave it his best shot, but made a mess of it* (*1862+*)

make a monkey out of someone *v phr* To make someone seem stupid or inept; make a fool of someone : *Are you trying to make a monkey out of me?* (*1900+*)

make a move on someone *See* PUT A MOVE ON someone

make (or get) an offer one **can't refuse** *v phr* To coerce or menace, esp with an ostensibly plausible offer : *"He's a businessman," the Don said blandly. "I'll make him an offer he can't refuse"/ The North Atlantic allies last week got an offer they couldn't brusquely refuse* [1960s+; popularized by Mario Puzo's 1969 novel *The Godfather* and the subsequent movie]

make a pass at someone *v phr* To make a sexual advance; PROPOSITION, PUT A MOVE ON someone : *He got high one time and made a pass at her* [1928+; fr early 1800s in the sense of "strike at, attack"]

make a pitch *v phr* To make a persuasive case; advocate strongly • Do a pitch in the same sense is found by 1876 : *The theatrical agent came in and made a pitch for her client* (*1960s+*)

make a pit stop *v phr* To urinate [1970s+; fr the *pit stop* for refueling, etc, in a car race, found by 1932]

make a play for *v phr* To attempt to get or seduce, esp by applied attractiveness : *He's making a play for that cute millionaire* (*1905+*)

make a scene (or a stink) *v phr* To exhibit anger, indignation, fiery temper, hysterics,

etc, in a public outburst : *I asked her to be quiet and not make a scene/ Why don't these pay cable services make a public stink about the Time Inc-Manhattan Cable monopoly?/ "I never made a big stink about it," says Righetti* (*entry form 1804+, variant 1812+*)

make a score *v phr* **1** To buy narcotics; SCORE : *this Jewish cat looking to make a score* (*1960s+ Narcotics*) **2** To win a bet : *But I make scores and they keep me going for a while/ ran wild in the cabaret as soon as they made a big score* (*1950+ Gambling*)

make a splash *v phr* To produce a strong and usu favorable impression; be very conspicuous : *That's the book that made such a big splash a couple of years ago* (*1820+*)

make (or have) a stab at something *v phr* To make an attempt; have a try : *I've never done this before, but I'll make a stab at it* (*1895+*)

make a thing of (or about) *v* To overexaggerate the importance of something • Usu used in the negative : *Don't make a thing about my going to Monday Night Football* (*1934+*)

make one's bed *v phr* To be the cause of one's own bad situation or misery : *make your bed and lie in it*

make one's (or the) blood boil *v phr* To make one very angry; infuriate one : *a devastating combination of logic, analysis, and case studies, makes the blood boil* (*1859+*)

make book on something *v phr* To bet on; offer odds on : *This time she really means it, and you can make book on that* (*1940s+*)

make one's day *v phr* To ensure the pleasure and distinction of one's whole day : *getting the computer fixed made her day* (*1909+*)

make deals, not *See* NOT MAKE DEALS

make for *v phr* **1** HEAD FOR (*1633+*) **2** To encourage; promote : *This will make for renewed confidence* (*1526+*)

make one's getaway *v phr* To escape; flee; fly, esp from the scene of a crime : *The thugs made their getaway in a souped-up Sherman tank* (*1893+*)

make good *v phr* To succeed; do what one set out to do in career or life (*1899+*)

make goo-goo eyes *v phr* To look at someone longingly, lovingly, seductively, etc : *make goo-goo eyes near a tropical lagoon* (*1900+*)

make hamburger (or hash or mincemeat) out of someone or something *v phr* To defeat definitively; trounce; CLOBBER : *They made hamburger out of the wilting opposition* [entry form 1980s+, *mincemeat* variant 1708+; *make meat of,* "to kill," is found by 1841]

make it *v phr* **1** To succeed; GO OVER : *The charts showed we had made it, and big* (*1925+*) **2** To survive; live : *He's so sick, I don't think he'll make it* (*1940s+*) **3** To get to a particular goal or place : *He didn't quite make it to the john* (1885+)

make it big *v phr* To succeed extraordinarily well • *Big* in this adverbial sense is found by 1886 (1960s+)

make it (or things) hot for someone *v phr* To make things unpleasant for someone : *Maybe if we make it hot for them they'll leave/ citizens of obvious substance, who might make things hot for them* (1830+)

make it snappy *v phr* To hurry; go faster; act quickly; GET THE LEAD OUT, SNAP TO IT (1915+)

make it with someone *v phr* <1▷ To do the sex act with or to someone; SCORE : *Man, don't think I didn't make it with her* 2 To succeed with someone : *Talking that way he'll never make it with the committee* (1950s+ *Cool talk*)

make kissy-face *v phr* To purse the lips and imitate a kiss; give an "air kiss" : *Rush guffaws, he blusters, he bats his eyes, he makes kissy-face* (1980s+)

make like *v phr* To pretend to be; imitate : *A cop picked it up and made like a bookie/ Brewster's gonna make like a canary* [1940s+; fr Yiddish *makh vi*]

make mincemeat out of someone or something *See* MAKE HAMBURGER OUT OF someone or something

make money hand over fist *v phr* To earn a large income; prosper hugely; coin money • *Hand over fist* is used about winning money by 1833 (1888+)

make one's move *v phr* To take a first and crucial action, esp one that will start a chain of reactions : *The cops are just waiting for the guy to make his move* [1970s+; probably fr sports, where opponents watch the person with the ball to see where he *moves*]

make my day *sentence* Go ahead and do what you appear to threaten, so that I can trounce you and have a successful day : *"Make my day" is much used in the New York subway system, where life is raw and tempers are short* [1971+; popularized by the movie star Clint Eastwood, who used the line in one of his *Dirty Harry* police thrillers]

make nice *v phr* To pet; cosset, caress : *Public officials make nice to politicians they cannot stand because they need their goodwill* [1970s+; perhaps fr Yiddish syntax]

make (or have) no bones about *v phr* 1 To be entirely candid about; to be open about; be UP-FRONT : *They make no bones about what they're going to do* (1548+) 2 To show or feel no doubt or hesitation about : *This spirited Labrador had no bones about venturing out* [origin unknown; the form *find no bones,* found by 1459, may indicate that the reference is to bones in soup or stew, which

would hinder the eating, hence hold the matter up]

make noises *v phr* 1 To express oneself; speak, esp initially and somewhat vaguely : *The Russians began to make noises about leaving* 2 To talk insincerely or uselessly : *Do they mean it, or are they making noises?* (1951+)

make no never mind *v phr* To make no difference; be insignificant : *Makes no never mind what he thinks, I'm going* (1940s+ *Black*)

make out *v phr* 1 To understand; DIG : *I couldn't quite make out what he was getting at* (1646+) 2 To succeed, esp by a slim margin; manage; GET BY : *Did you make out OK with that new machine?* (1776+) 3 To pet heavily; kiss and caress; NECK : *holding hands, slow dancing, making out to a point/ nostalgic for duck-tail haircuts, and making out in the back seat* (1940s+ *Teenagers & students*) 4 To succeed in sexual conquest (1939+)

make-out artist *n phr* 1 A man known for sexual success; COCKSMAN, STUD, swordsman : *The correct description for such a fellow is "make-out artist"* (1940s+) 2 A man who tries to charm and impress his superiors (1950s+)

make out like a bandit *v phr* To emerge very successfully; win everything : *You'd make out like a bandit/ Some of the people who came on early were making out like bandits/ "How did you make out?" "Like a thief"* [1960s+; based on Yiddish *bonditt,* "bandit; clever, resourceful fellow"]

make one's pile *v phr* To earn or win a fortune : *George made his pile investing in Microsoft* (1975+)

make (or score) points with someone *v phr* To be more highly prized with someone : *That's no way to make points with the voters these days* (1960s+)

maker *See* WAVE-MAKER, WIDOW-MAKER

make oneself **scarce** *v phr* To depart, esp hastily and under threat; BUG OUT, SKEDADDLE : *Yonder comes the law; we better make ourselves scarce* (1749+)

make something out of *v phr* To interpret as a cause for combat; regard as a challenge or insult : *So you heard what I said, huh? You want to make something out of it?* (1940s+)

make something **stick** *v phr* To cause an accusation, assertion, etc, to be believed; validate or prove something : *They accused him of rape, but they'll never make it stick* (1932+)

make the cut *v phr* To survive an elimination when a team or group is being chosen : *those mediocre actresses even made the cut* (1980s+ *fr sports*)

make the fur fly *v phr* To promote a lively conflict; stir things up : *When the Senator hears about this, he'll make the fur fly* (1834+)

make the grade *v phr* **1** To succeed : *He made the grade as a lawyer* **2** To meet certain standards : *His work just didn't make the grade* [1912+; perhaps fr a train's ability to climb up the *grade* or slope of the track]

make the rounds *v phr* To be passed from person to person; circulate : *A theory about the cause is making the rounds now* [1970s+; *go the rounds* in the same sense is found by 1669]

make the scene *v phr* **1** To arrive; appear : *I hope I can make the scene Saturday night* **2** To succeed; achieve something : *With this album they'll sure make the scene* **3** To do; experience : *I think I'll make the political scene next* (*1950s+ Beat & cool talk*)

make time *v phr* To go fast; travel at a good speed : *They really made time after they let the passengers off* (*1887+*)

make time with someone *v phr* To succeed sexually with someone, esp to make or approach a rapid conquest : *He was making time with Ezra's girl* (*1934+*)

make tracks *v phr* To depart; CLEAR OUT, MAKE oneself SCARCE : *If you know what's good for you, make tracks right now* (*1839+*)

make up for lost time *v phr* To work, play, travel, etc, very fast to compensate for a slow start (*1774+*)

make waves *v phr* To cause trouble; upset things : *What he said has made waves/ John Quinn had always been a team player who didn't make waves/ The case continues to make waves in the state* [1962+; fr the joke in which a person just arrived in hell, and hearing beautiful serene singing, finds that it is being done by inmates standing in chin-high excrement and cautiously chanting "Don't make waves"]

make whoopee *v phr* **1** To have a very good time; PARTY : *70 degrees and humidity 50 percent, which is when fleas make serious whoopee* (*1928+*) <2▷ To copulate; SCREW : *"What do you mean, done, Ethan?" "You know, made whoopee, for Christ's sake"*

make with *v phr* To use; exercise : *The poor man's Bing Crosby is still making with the throat here in Chi* [1939+; fr Yiddish *machen mit*, "swing or wave something about, brandish something"]

-making *combining word* Causing what is indicated : *nervous-making/ puke-making/ shy-making/ sick-making* (*1970s+*)

makings, the *n phr* The ingredients; what is necessary for : *He's young, but he's got the makings of a real pro* (*1613+*)

malarkey *interj* BULLSHIT *n* Lies and exaggerations; empty bombastic talk; BALONEY, BULLSHIT : *Hollywood is in the business of manufacturing malarkey as well as movies/ That's a lot of malarkey* [1929+; origin unknown]

male chauvinist pig or **porker** *modifier* : *male-chauvinist-pig-type man to the contrary notwithstanding/ the arrogant male chauve resident* *n phr* A man who believes in and proclaims the superiority of men over women; MCP : *Is it all right to call a priest a male chauvinist pig?/ And the men who ran the AVP were even worse oinking porkers* (*entry form 1972+, variant 1990s+*)

male member *See* MEMBER

mall rat or **mallie** (MAW lee) *n* or *n phr* A person, esp a teenager, who frequents shopping malls for sociability, excitement, etc : *"Mallies" always hang around the pay telephone/ A mall rat is someone who is here every day* (*first form 1980s+, second 1986+*)

mama *n* **1** A sexually attractive or sexually available woman : *"Say, baby, you sportin' tonight?" "Yeah, Mama, if I could find somebody to sport with"* (*1925+ Black*) **2** A woman who belongs to a motorcycle gang : *If a girl wants to be a mama and "pull a train," she'll be welcome at any Angel party* (*1960s+ Motorcyclists*) **3** The passive partner of a homosexual couple (*1970s+ Homosexuals*) *See* RED-HOT MAMA, SWEET MAMA

mama-and-papa *See* MOM-AND-POP

mama's boy or **mammy boy** *n phr* A soft or effeminate boy or man; a male overly attached to his mother : *the stale old mama's-boy-liberated-by-looney-lovely* (*1896+*)

man *interj* An exclamation of surprise, delight, emphasis, etc; JEEZ, WOW : *Man! I almost missed it!* (*1896+*) *n* A dollar; iron man : *You oughta grab about 300 men* (*1921+*) [in the first sense, the very similar *man alive* is found by 1839] *See* ASS MAN, BACKDOOR MAN, BOX MAN, BUTTER-AND-EGG MAN, CANDY MAN, COMPANY MAN, CON MAN, DIRTY OLD MAN, FOUR-LETTER MAN, G-MAN, HAMMER-MAN, HATCHET MAN, HE-MAN, HIT MAN, HOOP-MAN, LADIES' MAN, LEG MAN, POINT, POOR MAN'S something, ROD-MAN, SEE A MAN ABOUT A DOG, SHACK MAN, STRAIGHT MAN, SWEET MAN, TIT MAN, TRIGGER MAN, WHEEL MAN

man, the, or **the Man** *n phr* **1** Any man in authority; BOSS, HIS NIBS : *See the guy in front? That's the man* (*1918+*) **2** A police officer, detective, prison guard, etc; the HEAT : *Careful, here's the man* (*1960s+ Narcotics & underworld*) **3** A supplier of narcotics; DEALER (*1960s+ Narcotics*) **4** A white man; the white establishment : *a super nigger who spends his life trying to prove he's as good as the Man/ That's what "the man" wants you to do—to riot, so he can shoot you down* (*1963+ Black*)

man about a dog, a *See* SEE A MAN ABOUT A DOG

man-about-town *n* A sophisticated urban man and cynosure; boulevardier (*1734+*)

manage *v* To cope satisfactorily; survive; GET BY : *It's a lot to pay, but we'll manage* (*1655+*)

man bag or **purse** *n phr* A handbag carried by a male, esp a metrosexual

man boobs (or **breasts**) *n phr* Abnormally enlarged pectoral area on a male, giving the illusion of being breasts

man-eater *n* A sexually voracious woman; also, a femme fatale (*1906+*)

manhandle *v* To treat roughly; beat; banjax, CLOBBER : *They manhandled him pretty thoroughly before they let him go* (*1865+*)

manicure *v* To care for meticulously • The standard sense "care of the hands and fingernails" is found by 1889 : *Dutch farmers' constant manicuring of the land has driven out numerous native plant and animal species/ the manicured playing fields of international finance* (*1922+*)

man on (or **in**) **the street** *modifier* : *and some man-on-the-street TV commercials for post-convention use* **n phr** The average person; the ordinary person; JOE AVERAGE, JOHN Q CITIZEN (*1830+*)

man-sized or **man-size** *adj* Large; HEFTY : *Crump bet man-sized money* (*1934+*)

man upstairs, the *n phr* God : *I'm talking about the man upstairs. God himself* (*1961+*)

◁**man with a paper ass**▷ *n phr* A person whose ideas are not important; a trivial man; LIGHTWEIGHT (*1970s+ Black*)

many *See* ONE TOO MANY

map *n* **1** The face : *A funny look spread over Kenney's crimson map* (*1908+*) **2** A bank check (*1950s+ Gambling*)

map out *v phr* To plan : *Let's map out what we're gonna do tomorrow* (*1853+*)

◁**maracas**▷ *n* A woman's breasts; BOOBS : *gams and a pair of maracas that will haunt me in my dreams* (*1939+*)

marbles *See* GO FOR ALL THE MARBLES, GO FOR BROKE, HAVE ALL one's BUTTONS, LOSE one's MARBLES

marching orders *n phr* A directive to get going or carry out instructions : *marching orders for the husbands* (*1937+*)

Mari *See* MARY

marinate *v* To think about something or to wait for something to happen : *Let me marinate on that idea*

Marines *See* TELL IT TO THE MARINES

mark *n* **1** The target or victim of a swindle, esp one who is easily duped; PATSY, SUCKER : *not that he's more of a mark than other horse nuts/ his "marks," as the gullible are called by a pitchman* (*1883+*) **2** An outsider or member of the local community; home guard : *Marks aren't allowed in* (*1940s+ Carnival*) *v*

To inform; SQUEAL : *He swore he wouldn't mark if they caught him* (*1970s+ Teenagers*) *See* EASY MARK, HASH MARK, TOE THE MARK, UP TO SCRATCH

marker *n* **1** IOU : *He is willing to take Charley's marker for a million* (*1887+*) **2** A point or score : *eight markers in the first period* (*1940s+ Sports*)

market *See* GRAY MARKET, MEAT MARKET

marks the spot *See* X MARKS THE SPOT

mark time *v phr* To wait or do nothing while waiting : *marking time while she looked through clothing stores*

marquee *adj* Famous and influential; star; stellar : *Sawyer is likely to escalate demands from other marquee names/ When you play a marquee player like Shaquille O'Neal, if you block his shot, you want to let him know* **modifier** Publicity; HYPE : *That Pasolini was offered these public forums suggests that there was a certain marquee value attached to his name* [late 1980s+; fr the important names featured on a theater *marquee*]

marriage *See* SHOTGUN WEDDING

marry *v* To join; bring together : *He tries to marry the Canadian producers with the foreign buyers* (*1526+*)

marshmallow *n* A white person : *an Oreo fronting for a "marshmallow"/ Not bad for a kid whose mother was probably knocked up by a marshmallow* (*1960s+ Black*)

Mary *n* **1** A male homosexual who takes the passive, "feminine" role : *He passed two willowy-looking queers, Mary's who'd decided to settle for each other* (*1970s+ Homosexuals*) **2** (also **Mari**) Marijuana (*1960s+ Narcotics*)

Mary Ann or **Mary Jane** *n phr* Marijuana or a marijuana cigarette (*1920s+ Narcotics*)

mash *n* **1** Love or a love affair : *just another mash* (*1920s+*) **2** A lover, of either sex : *her latest big mash* (*1879+*) *v* **1** To make a sexual advance to; PROPOSITION : *I wouldn't try to mash anybody like you* (*1882+*) **2** To neck, pet, etc; MAKE OUT : *My blind date and I felt just a little uncomfortable when you guys started mashing in the backseat last night* (*1980s+ Students*) [apparently fr Romany, "allure, entice," and so used in mid-1800s vaudeville by a Gypsy troupe] *See* MISH-MASH

masher *n* A man who habitually makes sexual approaches to women; LADY-KILLER, WOLF (*1875+*)

mash note *n phr* A very flattering letter, esp one proposing or offering sex : *He gets mash notes by the ton/ showered him with embroidered pillows, mash notes, and cigars* (*1880s+*)

massage *v* **1** To beat; drub; ROUGH someone UP : *caught and massaged with rubber hoses* (*1924+*) **2** To handle, process, or manipulate data, esp computer data : *The results all depend on how you massage it* (1966+)

massage someone's **ego** *v phr* To soothe and flatter someone; STROKE : *He felt all strong and confident after she massaged his ego at lunch* (1980s+)

massage parlor *n phr* A place that provides sexual services under the guise of legitimate body massage; rap club (1970s+)

master cylinder *n* The most important part of a system, esp that can start or stop a process : *Who's the master cylinder in this operation*

mat *n* The floor; deck (1950s+ Navy) See GO TO THE MAT, ON THE MAT

match See the WHOLE SHOOTING MATCH

mate or **matey** *n* A friend of the same sex; a friend or companion : *Give me a hand, mate* (1380+)

matter See GRAY MATTER

max *adv* At the most; at the highest limit : *I do three cars a week, max* (1970s+) *v* To win; do the very best (1950s+ College students) [fr *maximum* "the highest possible grade," found by 1851] See TO THE MAX

maxed *adj* Intoxicated with a narcotic; STONED [1960s+ Narcotics; perhaps related to *max*, "gin, brandy, liquor," found from 1811]

maxed out *adj phr* Having reached a specified upper limit : *People have less money and are maxed out on their credit cards* (1990s+)

maxi *adj* : *long black pants under a maxi coat n* **1** A below midcalf or ankle-length skirt or coat **2** The ankle-length depth of hemline : *Is the new length a midi or a maxi?* [1960s+; fr *maximum*]

max out *v phr* **1** MAX To make the best score, or one's best score (1970s+ Army) **2** To do or contribute the maximum possible amount : *go to the people with the potential of, as they say in the business, "maxing out"* **3** To go to sleep (1970s+ College students) **4** To reach the highest possible point; peak : *It doesn't look to be a trend that's maxed-out* (1990s+) **5** To be used to the maximum : *There's been a great outpouring of affection. The phones have been maxed out/ teen angst is something that happens when your credit cards max out* (1990s+)

mayo *n* Mayonnaise (1930+)

mazuma (mǝ ZOO mǝ) *n* (also **mezuma** or **mazume** or **mazoomy** or **mazoo** or **mazoola** or **mazula**) Money : *You have to leave your mazuma behind* [1901+; fr Yiddish fr Hebrew; perhaps fr a Chaldean word meaning "the ready necessary"]

Mc- *prefix* Indicating various qualities associated with the McDonald's® restaurant chain and its food, such as rapidity, brevity, disposable packaging, small size, strict standardization, etc • The prefix reflects a scornful comparison with the things : *McFirm/*

McJob/ McLibrary/ McLunchroom/ McMyth/ McNews/ McPublisher/ McSchool/ McSurgery center/ McTheater/ McWine/ McWorld [1980s+]

MC or **emcee** (pronounced as separate letters) *n* A master of ceremonies (1929+) *v* : *MC'd by Bob Hope/ George Jessel emceed the event*

McCoy *adj* Genuine; legitimate; KOSHER : *like every other McCoy biz* (1930+)

McCoy, the See the REAL MCCOY

McDs or **McDucks** or **Mickey Ds** *n* McDonald's®, a fast-food restaurant [1980s+ College students; reference to Disney's *Donald Duck*]

McFly *n* A stupid or simple-minded person : *duh, McFly* [1985+; fr character in the film *Back to the Future*]

MCP or **mcp** *modifier* : *a sort of anarcho-Marxist MCP/ Somehow his senior mcp act doesn't really threaten women n* MALE CHAUVINIST PIG (1971+)

meadow muffin *n phr* A large, flat, dried piece of dung; a buffalo chip : *the meadow muffin, better known as the cow pie* (1980s+)

meal See SQUARE

meal ticket *n phr* **1** A superstar athlete who constitutes the drawing and earning power of a team, manager, etc; the FRANCHISE : *with his meal ticket, the Brown Bomber himself* (1905+ Sports) **2** Any person, skill, part of the body, instrument, etc, that provides one's sustenance : *His looks are his meal ticket* (1902+)

mean *adj* Excellent; wonderful; classy, WICKED : *This girl has already proved she can play a mean game of tennis/ And Wheelright had a great, mean ear for dialect* (1900+ Black) See LEAN AND MEAN

mean business *v phr* To be seriously in earnest : *show these guys that we mean business* (1857+)

mean gene *n phr* A postulated genetic basis for a violent personality (1990s+)

mean green *n phr* Money : *Mean green won out over neighborhood purity in the end* (1970s+ Black)

meany or **meanie** *n* A cruel, unkind person; villain; HEAVY (1927+) See BLUE MEANIE

measly *adj* Contemptibly inadequate; petty : *Should I work for a measly five bucks an hour?* (1864+)

meat *n* ⊲1▷ A person considered merely as a sex partner or object; ASS (1597+) ⊲2▷ The vulva; CUNT (1611+) ⊲3▷ The penis; PRICK (1595+) **4** A stupid person; MEATHEAD : *to see a bunch of meats play* (1970s+ Students) **5** The depth of tread on a car tire (1970s+ Car racing) **6** Solid value or meaning; substance : *The ones that contained real meat were milked capably by the cast* (1886+) See BEAT one's

MEAT, COLD MEAT, DARK MEAT, EASY MEAT, MAKE HAMBURGER OUT OF someone or something, WHITE MEAT

meat, one's *n phr* **1** An easy and favorite opponent; a chosen opponent : *He wins every time, guess I'm his meat* **2** One's preferred work, play, effort, etc : *Tennis is his meat* [1899+; probably based on the older sense of *meat,* "food, sustenance, game"]

meat, the *n phr* The essential part; core : *Now we see the meat of the problem* (1901+)

meat and potatoes *modifier* : *It's the meat-and-potatoes appeal, the old pull at the heart-strings* *n phr* The simple fundamentals; the NITTY-GRITTY (1940s+)

meatball *n* **1** A stupid, tedious person; an obnoxious or disgusting person; CREEP, JERK : *"How come?" "Because he's a meatball"* (1940+) **2** A signal flag with a black dot on a yellow field (WWII Navy) **3** The Japanese flag (WWII Navy)

meat grinder *n phr* A place or situation of extreme destruction : *An Iraqi battalion had blundered badly, sending thinly armored personnel carriers across the border into a meat grinder, where Saudi and American missiles had all but demolished the invaders* (1951+)

meathead *n* A stupid person; MEATBALL : *The copper was a big meathead/ Take your hand off that door, you meathead* (1945+)

meatheaded *adj* Stupid : *some meatheaded tart* (1949+)

meathooks *n* The hands or fists; biscuit hooks (1919+)

meat market *n phr* **1** A place where one looks for sex partners; the milieu of the singles; MEAT RACK : *men, who are now in the meat market, just like women have always been/ They go out to the meat markets, then come back and say how awful it was* (1896+) **2** Any place where people are displayed, appraised, etc, and generally treated like cattle : *the free gear, the summer job, the horrific meat market of the Nike summer camp for prime national hoop prospects* (1980s+)

meat rack *n phr* A gathering place, often public like a park bench or a shopping mall, where one seeks out sex partners; MEAT MARKET : *trailers parked near the river in Greenwich Village, the strip some people call "the meat rack"/ Crescent Beach was the local meat rack where the beautiful young women from the university drifted across the sand* (1972+ Homosexuals)

meat wagon *n phr* **1** An ambulance : *He woke up in the meatwagon/ I got a lift in the meat wagon to the hospital where I got the treatment of a fuckin' king* (1925+) **2** A hearse : *They have the meat wagon following him around* (1950s+) **3** A group or stable of second-rate fighters : *Montoya was known for running a meat wagon, a wholesale source of journeymen opponents* (1980s+ Prizefighting)

mechanic *n* **1** An expert cardplayer, esp one adept at cheating; CARDSHARP : *No "mechanics" (sharps) were tolerated* (1909+ Gambling) **2** A professional killer; HIRED GUN, HIT MAN : *Some prison mechanic will take him out on the lunch line* (1973+)

media circus *n phr* An occasion of very extravagant media coverage, esp television : *It'll be a media circus* (1990s+)

media hype *n phr* Concentrated favorable publicity for a person, corporation, candidate, etc : *Instead of dealing in the media hype, Coplon should have pursued the reasons* (1970s+)

medicine *See* TAKE one's MEDICINE

meds *n* Medications : *an angry, alienated 25-year old who swallows anti-psychotic "meds" to curb his demons* (Medical)

meemies, the *See* the SCREAMING MEEMIES

meet *n* **1** A point where trains are scheduled to meet (1940s+ Railroad) **2** A meeting, esp for some illegal purpose : *She went out to make a "meet" to buy more bogus bills/ I'll call you next Friday, same time, and set up a meet* (1879+) **3** JAM SESSION (1950s+ Bop musicians & cool musicians)

meets the road *See* WHERE THE RUBBER MEETS THE ROAD

mega *adj* Much : *I got mega homework tonight* *adv* Very : *This dude is mega gross* (1980s+ Students & teenagers)

mega- *prefix* A very large specimen, quantity, etc, of what is indicated : *megabitch/ megablitz/ mega-cost/ megafame/ megagreed/ megahopes/ megamodel/ megatravel* (1981+)

megabucks *n* (also **megageeters**) Much money, literally, "millions of dollars" • **Megabuck,** "a million dollars," was coined by nuclear scientists in 1946, but the plural form was not popularized until the 1960s and '70s : *the simple faith that moves mountains and grosses megabucks/ He was doing okay, but she's got megabucks of her own/ after two years on the road you'll be knocking down megageeters* (1946+)

megillah, the, or the **whole megillah** (mə GILL ə) *n phr* Something very long and tedious told or explained exhaustively : *I've been listening to all this here Megillah/ Let's not have the megillah/ a whole megilla (song and dance)* [1909+; fr Yiddish fr Hebrew, "scroll, volume," esp the Book of Esther read aloud in its entirety at Purim celebrations]

MEGO (MEE goh) *sentence* This is a smashingly boring affair [1980s+ chiefly news media; fr *mine eyes glaze over*]

MEGOGIGO (MEE goh GĪ goh) *sentence* This is totally tedious [1980s+ Teenagers; fr *mine eyes glaze over, garbage in garbage out*]

-meister *combining word* Very active in, adept at, or in charge of what is indicated • These words have proliferated hugely since the 1960s, apparently on the model of **schlockmeister** : *admeister/ attackmeister/ blurbmeister/ budgetmeister/ burgermeister/ coupmeister/ dealmeister/ frissonmeister/ hypemeister/ kinkmeister/ megadealmeister/ mudmeister/ mushmeister/ opinionmeister/ ordealmeister/ packmeister/ perkmeister/ processmeister/ quote-meisters/ rapmeister/ schlockmeister/ shuttlemeister/ sleazemeister/ spinmeister/ spookmeister/ symbolmeister/ talkmeister/ trashmeister/ yakmeister* [fr German, or fr Yiddish *mayster*, "master"; what was probably a Yiddish word was given, as is the custom, a German spelling] *See* SCHLOCKMEISTER

mell of a hess, a *n phr* A dire situation; SNAFU : *You better come over, Doc, there's a mell of a hess here/ Some mell of a hess you got us into* [spoonerism for *hell of a mess*]

mellow *adj* 1 Slightly drunk; TIDDLY (*1690+*) 2 Sincere and skillful • Said of a musical performance (*1935+ Jazz musicians*) 3 Relaxed; at ease; laid-back (*1950s+ Cool use*) 4 Very friendly; intimate (*1950s+ Cool use*) *n* A close friend; BUDDY (*1950s+ Cool use*) *v* MELLOW OUT (*1980s+ Students*)

mellow-back *adj* Smartly dressed (*1930s+ Black*)

mellow out *v phr* (also **mellow**) To become relaxed and easy : *wondering why the family in "The Grapes of Wrath" didn't move to LA and mellow out/ Even the testiest groups and crews can be mellowed out after spending time at Alpine* (*1970s+ Students*)

mellow yellow *n* A banana peel used as an intoxicant; also, LSD (*1967+*)

melon *n* The sum of profits, loot, etc, to be divided : *The stockholders have a meager melon to share this year* (*1906+*)

melonhead *n* A stupid person; KNUCKLEHEAD, MEATBALL : *She called Greenwood a "melonhead"* (*1980s+*)

◀**melons**▶ *n* A woman's breasts, esp large • Usu objectionable : *the melons on that girl*

meltdown *n* A disaster : *They are facing a credibility meltdown/ The Glenn campaign has achieved almost total meltdown* [1970s+; fr the nuclear power-plant disaster in which the core of radioactive material *melts down* into the earth below, the term found by 1963]

melt down *v phr* To be disastrously affected : *When you put on that kind of outfit, boys are going to melt down* (*1990s+*)

member *n* 1 A fellow black person; BROTHER, SISTER (*1958+ Black*) ◁2▷ The penis (*1356+*) [second sense a euphemism for the even more euphemistic *membrum virile*]

mend one's fences *v phr* To establish or restore good relations : *I had better get home and mend my fences* (*1880s+*)

mensch or **mensh** *n* 1 An admirable and substantial person; a decent and mature person : *wear good clothes and look like a mensch/ A generous little mensch gets French manicure gift certificates for his girlfriend* 2 A virile man • Can also be used of women : *mensch, a stand-up he-man/ Trigere, almost alone, is mensch enough to candidly dismiss the misogynous midi* [1909+; fr Yiddish, literally "person, man"]

mental *adj* Crazy; deranged; NUTTY : *And the son, William, went absolutely mental* (*1927+ British*) *n* A deranged person; NUT (*1913+ British*)

meow *See* the CAT'S MEOW

merchant *combining word* A person who esp indulges or purveys in what is indicated : *heat merchant/ speed merchant* (*1914+*)

merry ha-ha, the *n phr* A ridiculing and dismissive laugh at someone; the HORSELAUGH (*1906+*)

merry hell *n phr* A severe rebuke or punishment : *He gave us merry hell for that caper* (*1911+*) *See* CATCH HELL, GIVE someone HELL

merv *n* A student who studies hard; pencil neck, POINDEXTER (*1980s+ Students*)

mesc *n* Mescaline, a hallucinogenic drug (*1960s+ Narcotics*)

meshuga (mə SHOO gə, -SHIH-) *adj* (also **meshigga** or **meshugah** or **meshiggah** or **mishugah** or **mishoogeh**) Crazy; NUTTY : *Mishoogeh or mishugah, spelled either way, means crazy* [1892+; fr Yiddish fr Hebrew; the variant pronunciations reflect major dialects of Yiddish]

meshugana or **meshiggana** or **meshiganer** (mə SHOO gə nə, -SHIH-) *n* A crazy person; NUT [fr Yiddish fr Hebrew]

mess around *v phr* To idle about; loaf; work indolently; GOOF OFF : *Stop messing around and get to work* (*1932+*)

mess someone around (or **over**) *v phr* To victimize and exploit; maltreat; FUCK OVER : *being messed over by Goldberg all the time/ Here's a young black dude in a Cadillac, we'll just mess him around* (*1960s+ Black*)

mess around with or **mess with** *v phr* 1 To become involved with : *I don't mess with married or attached women* (*1913+*) 2 To defy or challenge; provoke; FUCK WITH : *Nobody dared to mess around with Slippers/ They go around messing with us, because we're trying to do something* (*1950s+*) 3 To play or tinker with : *I caught him messing around with the heating control* (*1940s+*)

messed up *adj phr* **1** Quite confused : *messed up over the breakup* **2** Intoxicated from drugs or alcohol : *got messed up last night*

mess up *v phr* **1** To disarrange; muddle : *Who messed up these figures?* (*1909+*) **2** To injure; damage : *The drugs and booze messed up her mind* (*1919+*) **3** To get into trouble; make a botch; FUCK UP : *If you don't mess up you get an automatic promotion* (*1915+*)

mess someone up *v phr* **1** To thrash; beat up; WORK someone OVER : *They sent a couple of goons to mess him up when he wouldn't pay* **2** To damage or injure someone : *The wreck messed him up so he can't walk* (*1940s+*)

metal *n* HEAVY METAL *v* To play loudly amplified rock and roll music : *Nobody can metal like Blue Oyster Cult* (*1973+*) *See* HEAVY METAL, PUT THE PEDAL TO THE METAL

metal head *n* A devotee of heavy-metal rock music : *The standard uniform of the metal-head is Led Zeppelin T-shirt, jeans, shoulder-length hair* (*1970s+*)

meth *n* Methedrine℠; methadone, or meth-amphetamine : *Eight hours after snorting cocaine for two days and doing crystal meth* (*1960s+ Narcotics*)

meth head (or **freak**) *n phr* A habitual user of Methedrine℠ (*1960s+ Narcotics*)

me-too or **me-tooistic** *adj* Imitative; COPYCAT : *Big companies brought out many me-too drugs and had to slim down* (*1940s+*)

metrosexual *adj* Of a male, exhibiting a strong aesthetic sense and inordinate interest in appearance and style *n* An urban male of any sexual orientation who has a strong aesthetic sense and spends a great deal of time and money on his appearance and lifestyle (*1994+*)

◀**Mex**▶ *adj* Mexican : *Ensenada is all Mex n* A Mexican (*1854+*)

◀**Mexican breakfast**▶ *n phr* A cigarette and a glass of water or cup of coffee (*1950s+*)

Mexican standoff *n phr* A stalemate; deadlock; STANDOFF • First referred to a tie baseball game (*1891+*)

mezuma *See* MAZUMA

MF or **mf** *n* A despicable person; MOTHERFUCKER : *He used to look right at them MFs/ kill some of the Uncle Tomming mfs* (*1960s+ Black*)

mick[1] *modifier* Easy : *Russian 27A is a mick course n* An easy course; GUT COURSE, pipe course : *I heard that Astro 3 is a mick* [*1980s+ Students*; fr *Mickey Mouse*]

◀**mick**[2] or **Mick**▶ *adj* **1** : *a mick politician* **2** : *my one mick friend, although he isn't Irish n* **1** An Irishman or person of Irish descent **2** A Roman Catholic [*1856+*; fr the nickname of the common Irish name *Michael*]

mickey or **Mickey** *n* **1** A potato : *We stole our first mickies together from Gordon's fruit stand/ roast mickies in the gutter fires* (*1940s+*) **2** MICKEY FINN : *Mickeys act so drastically that one may kill a drunk with a weak heart* (*1915+*) **3** A half-bottle of liquor (*1914+*) **4** (also **Mickey Mouse**) A white person; irish, OFAY : *and the Mickey, which is you, be dead a long time ago, except he says no* (*1970s+ Black*) [potato sense probably by association with the common phrase *Irish potato*] *See* SLIP someone A MICKEY

Mickey Ds *n phr* A McDonald's® fast-food restaurant (*1970s+ Teenagers*)

Mickey Finn or **mickey finn** *n phr* **1** A strong hypnotic or barbiturate dose, esp of chloral hydrate, put secretly into a drink; KNOCK-OUT DROPS : *The drug, sometimes known as "knockout drops" or Mickey Finn is a sedative/ Sometime during the nineties, technology finally brought refinement to the art, in the form of the Mickey Finn* (*1890s+*) **2** A purgative similarly administered (*1935+*) [origin unknown and richly conjectured, chiefly being fathered on various bartenders or saloon proprietors with names like *Mickey Finn*]

Mickey Mouse or **mickey mouse** *adj phr* **1** (also **micky-mouse**) Sentimental and insincere : *A "micky-mouse band" is a real corny outfit/ to the dead beat of mind-smothered Mickey Mouse music* (*1935+ Musicians*) **2** Showy; meretricious, merely cosmetic : *And I don't think Mickey Mouse changes are going to work* (*1951+*) **3** Shoddy; inferior : *The carpentry work was just Mickey Mouse* (*1960s+*) **4** Simple; elementary; easy : *A "Mickey Mouse course" means a "snap course"* (*1950s+ Students*) **5** Petty; inconsequential : *A Mickey Mouse survey of popular culture/ A lot of the Mickey Mouse stuff has been eliminated from the program/ got picked up on a Mickey Mouse thing in August by the State Patrol* (*1951+ Students*) *n phr* **1** : *It's hard to get past the mickey mouse and see what the hell they're driving at* (*1960s+*) **2** : *That book's pure mickey mouse* (*1960s+*) **3** A blunder due to confusion and stupidity; SCREW-UP : *The only big Mickey Mouse was a brief shortage of jungle boots* (*1960s+ Armed forces*) **4** (also **Mickey**) A stupid person, esp a white person or a police officer (*1970s+ Black*) *v phr* To treat someone shabbily; ill-use someone; SCREW, SHAFT : *"I think we got Mickey Moused," Williams said. "My best pitcher is washed right down the drain, and I don't like it"* (*1980s+*) [apparently this pejorative trend began after the wide distribution of cheap *Mickey Mouse* wrist watches, showing the cartoon character on the face, with his arms as the watch's hands, which were regarded as shoddy, gimmicky, etc, at that time; the diminutive rodent continues to be extremely popular with children]

middlebrow *adj* : *a middlebrow magazine/ middlebrow audience* *n* A person of average intelligence and taste (*1925+*)

middle kidney *See* GRIPE one's ASS

◁**middle (or third) leg**▷ *n phr* The penis (*1922+*)

middle name, someone's *n phr* Someone's most characteristic feature, gift, concern, etc; someone's forte or "trademark" : *The CIA's middle name is intelligence, which Webster defines as the faculty of understanding/ Baseball is my middle name* (*1920+*)

middle of nowhere, the *n phr* A very remote area; an isolated place; the BOONDOCKS : *They moved out of Manhattan way into Jersey, the middle of nowhere* (*1960+*)

middy *n* A midshipman (*1818+ Nautical*)

midnight requisition *n phr* A wrongful acquisition, esp of military property in a nonregulation manner : *One of our sergeants was quite skillful at the midnight requisition* (*WWII armed forces*)

mike *n* **1** A microphone (*1927+*) **2** A Mikado engine, a type of locomotive having eight drive wheels, produced in the 1890s for the Japanese state railroad and also used in the US (*1950s+ Railroad*) **3** A microgram; a millionth of a gram : *I feel like I've been up on 300 mikes of acid* (*1970+*) *v* To amplify with a microphone : *The club was so small they decided not to mike the show*

mile *See* GO THE EXTRA MILE, STICK OUT

mileage *n* Profit; productive potential : *Do they think there's any mileage in my idea?* (*1945+*)

mile-high club *n phr* The putative association of persons who have done the sex act more than a mile high in the sky : *They had stayed behind to renew their membership in the mile-high club by sinking into one of the leather banquettes and making passionate love* (*1970s+ Airline*)

milk *v* **1** To exploit something to the utmost : *The ones that contained real meat were milked capably by the cast* (*1921+ Show business*) **2** To get something, esp money, unfairly or fraudulently : *The agents had regularly been milking the tenants for exorbitant rents* (*1532+*) ◁**3**▷ To masturbate (*1970s+*)

milk cans *See* KNOCK someone FOR A LOOP

milk run *n phr* **1** A scheduled airline passage with many stops; : *followed by a milk run to Charleston, Jacksonville, Daytona Beach, and Tampa* (*1970s+ Airline*) **2** An easy bombing mission : *It looked like a milk run* (*WWII Air Forces*) [fr the stopping of a train at every rural station to pick up *milk* for delivery to the cities]

◁**milk the lizard**▷ *v phr* To masturbate; JACK OFF, SPANK THE MONKEY (*1990s+*)

mill[1] *n* A million dollars : *That'll cost the government a cool six mill* (*1955+*)

mill[2] *n* **1** A prizefight : *the night of the KO Kelly mill* (*1842+ Prizefighting*) **2** A military prison or guardhouse (*WWI armed forces*) **3** A car or motorcycle engine : *Has it got the magnum mill?/ They both chuckled and fired up their mills* (*1918+*) **4** A car : *A squirrel is a reckless driver of a mill (automobile)* (*1950s+ Teenagers*) **5** A locomotive (*1925+ Railroad*) **6** A typewriter (*1919+ Newspaper office*) *See* GIN MILL, GO THROUGH THE MILL, RUMOR MILL, RUN-OF-THE-MILL, THROUGH THE MILL

million bucks *See* LIKE A MILLION BUCKS

mincemeat *See* MAKE HAMBURGER OUT OF someone or something

mince words *v phr* to restrain oneself in conversation to avoid offense

mind *See* BLOW someone's MIND, DIRTY MIND, HAVE A MIND LIKE A SIEVE, a LOAD OFF someone's MIND, MAKE NO NEVER MIND, ONE-TRACK MIND

mind-blower or **mind-bender** *n* **1** A hallucinogenic drug **2** Something exciting, beautiful, shocking, etc : *That little book's a mind-bender* (*1960s+ Counterculture & narcotics*)

mind-blowing or **mind-bending** *adj* **1** Hallucinogenic; psychedelic **2** Overwhelming; exciting; staggering : *The speech was mind-blowing* (*1960s+ Counterculture & narcotics*) (*1960s+ Counterculture & narcotics*)

mind-boggling *adj* So astonishing or complex as to overwhelm the mind : *The school problem is absolutely mind-boggling* [*1964+*; *boggle,* "to be disablingly frightened, take alarm," is found by 1598; a *bogle* or *boggle* was a spook that horses were reputed to see]

minded *See* DIRTY-MINDED

◀**mind-fuck**▶ *n* : *such supposedly Caucasian specialties as stance and persona and pop mind-fuck* *v* To manipulate someone to think and act as one wishes; BRAINWASH : *He was totally mind-fucked but he seemed to know his stuff* (*1970s+*)

◀**mind-fucker**▶ *n* **1** A person who manipulates others, esp for his or her own profit : *Most gurus are magnificent and filthy-rich mind-fuckers* (*1970s+*) **2** A distressful situation; BAD SCENE (*1970s+*)

mind game *n phr* A toying with psychological influence for one's advantage : *She was moving with a fast bunch of kids who did drugs and played mind games and had group sex and I don't know what else/ It isn't a subtle mind game to make the airport seem bigger than it is* (*1990s+*) *v* PSYCH, psych out : *They try to mind-game you*

mind one's **p's and q's** *v phr* To take care of one's affairs carefully and exclusively : *What* the hell are you staring at, madam, you mind your p's and q's [1779+; fr the fact that the two similar letters are particularly hard to distinguish in type, where their ordinary shapes are reversed]

mind the store *v phr* To attend to routine business; carry on : *Who'll mind the store while Mr Clinton is overseas?* [1970s+; fr the joke about the dying man who, finding by patient inquiry that all his children are at his deathbed, inquires testily who is *minding the store*]

mine *See* RUN-OF-THE-MILL

mingy (MIN jee) *adj* Parsimonious; mean; tight-fisted [1911+; said to have been coined by the author Noel Busch; perhaps a blend of *mean* and *stingy*]

mini *adj* : *She looked out of place in her mini dress* *n* **1** A very short dress, skirt, or coat ending well above the knee **2** The fashion or style of wearing such short garments (1965+)

mini- *prefix used to form nouns* Small; miniature; short : *minibus/ minicab/ minivan/ minicam/ mininuke/ minisemester/ miniskirt* [late 1930s+; fr *miniature*]

mink *n* **1** A sexually promiscuous person; lecher; nymphomaniac : *The doctor was a regular mink* **2** A pert and attractive young woman; DISH, FOX ◁3▷ A woman's genitalia, pubic hair, etc; BEAVER (1940s+) *See* FUCK LIKE A MINK, TIGHT

minor-league *adj phr* Not of the highest quality or type; second-rate : *This author exhibits a minor-league talent/ With my 50-word vocabulary I'd be a busher in that company, having had no minor league experience* [1926+; the original baseball use is found by 1884]

mint, a *n phr* Very much money; MEGABUCKS : *The old guy must be worth a mint* [1874+; the full phrase *mint of money* is found by 1655]

minus *n* A disadvantage : *that degree is actually a minus for him* (1708+)

minuteman *n* : *Youth gangs use minors as gun runners, calling them "minutemen" because if they're caught they're out (of jail) in a minute* (1990s+ Street gang)

Mirandize *See* GIVE someone HIS RIGHTS

mish-mash (MISH mahsh) *n* (also **mish-mosh**) A confused mixture; an indiscriminate miscellany : *regarded as a hopeless mishmash/ as untidy as untangling the Starrett mishmash* [1450+; apparently originally fr German *Mischmasch*, but probably in its modern use chiefly fr Yiddish]

mishugah or **mishoogeh** *See* MESHUGA

miss, a *See* GIVE someone or something A MISS

missionary position *n phr* The sexual posture in which the male lies over the female between her spread legs : *Most of them have* never gone beyond three furtive minutes in the missionary position/ enjoying sex in that reliable missionary position [1960s+; fr the fancied distinction between this coital configuration of Christian *missionaries* and those of the peoples among whom they labored]

miss out on something *v phr* To fail to see, enjoy, etc, something; MISS THE BOAT : *I'm sorry I missed out on the ice cream* (1929+)

Miss Right *See* MISTER RIGHT

miss the boat or **bus** *v phr* To lose an opportunity; fail; BLOW IT : *Tom really missed the boat when it came to making friends/ In Bartlett's book the Byzantine Empire and Kievan Russia seem to have missed the bus* (1940s+)

missus, the, or **the missis** or **the Mrs** *n phr* One's wife; the LITTLE WOMAN : *He wanted the missus to get some sleep* (1833+)

mister *n* Man; fellow; GUY • Always used in direct address, usu to a stranger : *Hey, mister, where's the turn-off for Bogota?* (1760+)

Mister Big *n phr* The chief or most important person; BIG ENCHILADA, HONCHO : *I predict in three or four years he'll be Mister Big* (1940+)

Mister Clean *modifier* : *Ramos operated in the cutthroat Marcos administration and emerged with his Mr Clean reputation largely intact n phr* A man, esp a politician, unsullied by suspicion of corruption or bad character; DUDLEY DO-RIGHT : *a female version of a managerial Mr Clean* (1970s+) [fr the trademark name of a household detergent]

Mister Fixit *n phr* A person who can and does repair, adjudicate, resolve, etc, difficulties : *has earned a reputation as an ingenious Mr Fixit/ Peter Ueberroth, the Mr Fixit of the 1984 Olympics, was called upon to save Los Angeles even as the fires were raging*

Mister Happy *n phr* The penis; COCK, DORK : *Is Mr. Happy taking longer to snap back to attention? Sexually speaking, a man is never what he used to be* (1980+ Students)

Mister Man *n phr* The leader of a gang : *He was trying to be Mister Man* (1990s+ Street gang)

Mr Nice Guy *n* A sweet, friendly person, often male : *postman is Mr. Nice Guy*

Mister (or **Miss** or **Ms**) **Right** *n phr* The person one would and should happily marry; one's dream mate : *The Kathleen Norris heroine who didn't wait for Mr Right* (1937+)

mitt *n* **1** The hand : *snatched right out of his mitt* (1896+) **2** A boxing glove : *have the big mitts on* (1812+ Prizefighting) **3** mitt-reader (1914+ Circus & carnival) *v* **1** To clasp hands above one's head as a sign of victory and acknowledgment of applause : *sitting in his corner and mitting the crowd* (1920s+ Prizefighting) **2** To shake hands : *Mitt me, pal, I done it* (1924+) [fr *mitten*] *See* TIP one's MITT

mixed up *adj phr* 1 Confused; chaotic; messy : *His mind's all mixed up (1862+)* 2 Involved; implicated : *I think he was mixed up somehow in the failure of those banks (1912+)*

mixer *n* 1 A person who easily becomes acquainted and sociable with others; a gregarious person *(1896+)* 2 A party or other gathering intended as an occasion for people to meet and become acquainted with one another *(1920s+)*

mix it or **mix it up** *v phr* To fight; HASSLE : *Candidates for the Milwaukee School Board took off their gloves and mixed it up a little with each other/ didn't seem to want to mix it/ Richards, the traditional marketing man, mixing it up with the culture gang (1900+)*

mix-up *n* 1 Confusion; chaos; mess : *There's an awful mix-up over at the plant today (1898+)* 2 A fight, esp a free-for-all *(1841+)*

MJ *n* Marijuana [1960s+ Narcotics; fr Mary Jane, an earlier name for marijuana]

mo *n* A moment : *Give me half a mo (1896+)*

mob (or **Mob**), the *n* Organized crime; the Mafia; the syndicate : *I heard it's controlled by the mob (1927+)*

mobile *adj* Attractive; DISHY *(1990s+ Teenagers) See* PIMPMOBILE

mob scene *n phr* A very crowded place or occasion : *And the secretaries soon report that the reception room is a mob scene (1922+ fr motion pictures)*

moby *adj* Very large, complicated, and impressive : *Some MIT undergrads pulled off a moby hack at the Harvard-Yale game* [1980s+ Computer; probably fr the white whale in Herman Melville's *Moby Dick*]

mod *adj* Modern; up-to-date, esp in the styles of the 1960s : *shows off her attributes in a mod wardrobe (1960s+)*

Model-T *adj* Old-fashioned; old-timey : *a real Model-T speakeasy out of an early Warner Brothers movie* [1940s+; fr the *Model T* Ford car of the early 1900s]

Moe, Larry, and Curly *n phr* The pilot, copilot, and navigator of an airplane *(1990s+ Airline stewardesses;* from the Three Stooges comedy team)

Mohawk *n* A haircut in which the side hair is shaved off, leaving a brushlike line of hair down the middle of the scalp : *like this guy that comes into Mattie's all the time with a Mohawk/ all make a good Mohawk* [1970s+; fr its fancied resemblance to the hairstyle of *Mohawk* Indian males; the style was much affected by the punk rockers]

mojo[1] *n* 1 A charm or amulet worn against evil; hence power, luck, effectiveness, etc : *When you got the mojo, brother, when you're on the inside, the world is fantastic/ gets his mojo going for conventions and elections/ The office bears a sort of superstitious, bad-mojo stamp* 2 Power; charisma : *her mojo gets her into a lot of high places* 3 Sex appeal; also, one's sex drive : *He had his mojo going at the party* [1920s+ Black; origin unknown; probably fr an African language]

mojo[2] *n* Any narcotic, esp morphine [1935+ Narcotics; perhaps fr Spanish *mojar,* "celebrate by drinking"]

mole *n* A person who works undercover within an organization and passes information about it to others *(1974+)*

moll *n* 1 A woman *(1700s+ British)* 2 A prostitute *(1604+)* 3 A criminal's woman companion, accomplice, girlfriend, etc; GUN MOLL *(1823+)* [fr *Molly,* nickname for Mary]

Molotov cocktail *n phr* A grenade made by pouring gasoline into a bottle, adding a cloth wick, and igniting it [WWII; fr Vyacheslav *Molotov,* Soviet premier, used and satirically named by Finnish fighters against the Soviet invasion of 1940]

mom-and-pop *adj* Run by a couple or a family; small-scale : *still seem wedded to the "mom and pop store," small-business approach/ All kinds of neighborhoods have them, mom-and-pop stores, laundromats/ The constitution says nothing about a mom and pop presidency (1951+)*

momism (MAHM izm) *n* Maternal domination; matriarchalism; mother worship • Disseminated by Philip Wylie's book *Generation of Vipers (1942+)*

momma *n* Any specified object, esp a large, admirable, or effective one; MOTHER, MOTHERFUCKER : *It's time to put this momma in the oven (1970s+ Black)*

mommy track *n phr* : *Should corporations set up a two-track system for women managers, a fast track for childless women and a slower "mommy track" for women with children? (1987+)*

mom-word *n* MOTHERFUCKER : *"Hit the ground, you (obscenity)." (All right, if you must know, he was using the mom-word) (1990s+)*

momzer or **momser** (MUHM zər, MAHM-) *n* 1 A person who expects many loans and favors; MOOCHER, SPONGER 2 A contemptible person; BASTARD, SHITHEEL : *A very cool customer, this momzer* [1562+; fr Yiddish fr Hebrew, "bastard"; used in the 4th-century Latin Vulgate Bible; despite this ancient lineage, modern use is ordinary demotic Yiddish]

Monday morning quarterback *n phr* A person who is good at predicting things that have already happened and at pointing out the errors of quarterbacks and other leaders; ARMCHAIR GENERAL [1932+; fr the fact that *Monday* is the first weekday or business day after the weekend, when school and college football games are played]

mondo or **mundo** or **mongo** *adj* Very large or very much; HUMONGOUS, important : *She had a lot of things on her desk top, including a mondo-size slo-mo printer/ I've got a mongo bruise on my leg from field hockey/ You'd think it took some kind of miracle, or some mondo engineering breakthrough* *adv* Very; totally; FULLY, WAY : *Your dad is mondo cool!/ mondo fun at the beach* [1979+; fr Italian *mondo,* "world"; the *mongo* variant is probably just imitative]

money *See* BAIT MONEY, BLACK MONEY, BUG MONEY, CHICKEN FEED, FOLDING MONEY, FRONT MONEY, FUNNY MONEY, GREEN MONEY, HEAVY MONEY, IN THE MONEY, a LICENSE TO PRINT MONEY, MAD MONEY, MAKE MONEY HAND OVER FIST, ON THE MONEY, PUT one's MONEY WHERE one's MOUTH IS, RIGHT MONEY, the SMART MONEY, SOFT MONEY, THROW MONEY AT something, TIGHT MONEY

moneybags *n* 1 A rich person : *some aged moneybags* (1818+) 2 A military paymaster *(WWII Navy)*

money from home *n phr* Something very welcome and useful, esp when gratis and unexpected : *but for the TV news boys this was money from home* (1913+)

money grubber *n* A stingy person : *refuses to buy a newspaper, he's such a money grubber*

money pit *n phr* A project, possession, etc, that costs more and more money : *See that boat? I call it my Money Pit* (1990s+)

money talks *sentence* 1 Wealth is power : *In New York, boy, money really talks, I'm not kidding* (1891+) 2 (also **money talks, bullshit walks**) PUT UP OR SHUT UP, PUT one's MONEY WHERE one's MOUTH IS : *Money talks and you know what walks/ Money talks, bullshit walks* [the second sense's variant is found by 1987]

money-washing *n* The "laundering" of illicit money to make it seem legitimately earned : *Soon the Caymans became a great capital of money-washing* (1972+)

mongo *n* Something valuable found in an abandoned building, a trash bin, etc [1979+; origin unknown] *See* MONDO

monicker *n* (also **moniker** or **monniker** or **monacer** or **monica** or **monaker**) A person's name, nickname, alias, etc; HANDLE : *His "monica" was Skysail Jack/ Ricord picked up a new moniker among US narcotics agents* [1849+ British street talk; origin unknown and very broadly speculated upon; perhaps fr transference fr earlier sense, "guinea, sovereign," when used by hoboes as an identifying mark; perhaps related to the facts that early 1800s British tramps referred to themselves as "in the monkery," that monks and nuns take a new name when they take their

vows, and that *monaco* means "monk" in Italian; perhaps, as many believe, an alteration of *monogram*]

monkey *n* 1 A man; person; GUY • Mildly contemptuous : *a smart monkey* (1914+) 2 A child or young person • An affectionate use (1605+) ◄3► A Chinese or Chinese-American (1912+) 4 A person who is not a hobo, carnival worker, etc; ordinary person *(1940s+ Hoboes)* 5 A victim; MARK *(1940s+ Carnival)* 6 Narcotics addiction; a drug habit : *went from monkey to nothin' in twenty-eight days (1940s+ Narcotics)* 7 A kilogram of a narcotic : *And you call and you want 100 monkeys (1960s+ Narcotics)* *v* 1 To tinker or tamper; intrude one's action : *Look, it's running fine, don't monkey with it* (1881+) 2 monkey around or about *See* GET THE MONKEY OFF, GREASE MONKEY, HAVE A MONKEY ON one's BACK

monkey around *v phr* 1 To idle about; loaf; GOOF AROUND : *I'm just monkeying around, nothing special* (1891+) 2 To tinker or tamper; attempt to use or repair : *Please stop monkeying around with that machine* (1894+)

monkey (or funny) business *n phr* 1 Frivolous pranks; japes and jests, etc : *He was full of monkey business, the clown* 2 Dubious and dishonest stratagems; trickiness : *Show these kids that you're going to stand for no monkey business* (1883+)

monkey-monk *See* HIGH MUCKETY-MUCK

monkeyshines *n* Tricks; japes and capers; pranks (1832+)

monkey suit *n phr* 1 A fancy uniform or formal suit; tight uniform : *Neither of my two hats went well with the monkey suit* (1886+) *n* 2 A baseball uniform *(1929+ Baseball)*

monkey's uncle *See* I'LL BE DAMNED

Monkey Ward *n phr* The Montgomery Ward retail company *(1930s+)*

monniker *See* MONICKER

mono (MAH noh) *n* 1 Mononucleosis *(1960s+ Students)* 2 A monophonic recording *(1950s+)*

monster *modifier* 1 : *users of scag and monster drugs* 2 Enormous; overwhelming; HUMONGOUS : *his monster ego/ a monster rally* (1837+) 3 Very good; COOL, KILLER, RAD *(1990s+ Teenagers)* *n* 1 A narcotic that acts on the central nervous system *(1960s+ Narcotics)* 2 A bestseller, esp a recording *(1970s+)*

Montezuma's revenge *n phr* Diarrhea, esp traveler's diarrhea; AZTEC TWO-STEP, TURISTA : *It was regarded as unfortunate that the President joked about Montezuma's revenge when he introduced the president of Mexico* (1962+)

month of Sundays, a *n phr* A very long time :
*He hadn't seen the family in a month of Sun-
days (1841+)*
moo[1] *n* **1** Beefsteak : *slab of moo (1916+)* **2** Milk
(1940s+)
moo[2] *n* MOOLA *(1945+)*
mooch *n* **1** MOOCHER *(1914+)* **2** A gullible
customer; dupe; MARK *(1929+ Carnival)* **3** A
person who listens to the pitch, but does not
buy *(1940s+ Carnival)* **4** A customer who
painstakingly examines the merchandise before buying *(1940s+ Carnival)* *v* **1** To
beg; borrow; CADGE, SPONGE : *The geisha girls
are forever mooching chocolates (1857+)* **2** To
steal *(1862+)* **3** To stroll; loaf along *(1851+)*
[fr earlier *mowche,* "to pretend poverty; play
truant," found by 1460, fr Old French
muchier, "to hide, skulk"]
moocher *n* A beggar; borrower; DEADBEAT,
SPONGER : *He heard a moocher deliver the following spiel/ Minnie the moocher, she was a
low-down hootchy-cootcher (1857+)*
moo-juice *n* Milk or cream *(1941+ Lunch
counter & Army)*
moola or **moolah** *n* Money : *So put a little moola
in your portfolio and get yourself a cash cow/
He who rips off jazz makes mucho moolah*
[1920+; origin unknown]
moon *n* Cheap whiskey, esp whiskey made
by unlicensed distillers; MOONSHINE : *a couple
of pints of moon/ using it to transport moon*
(1928+) *v* **1** To behave in a pleasantly listless and dreamy way : *I was sitting there
mooning over her latest letter (1848+)* **2**
To exhibit one's bare buttocks as a defiant
or amusing gesture, usu out a window
(1960s+ Teenagers & students) [second noun
sense fr *moon,* "buttocks," found by 1756]
mooner *n* **1** A criminal or eccentric active
during the period of the full moon *(1950s+
Police)* **2** A person who "moons" *(1960s+
Teenagers & students) See* FULL-MOONER
moonlight *v* To work at a job in addition to
one's regular job : *a million guys moonlight-
ing, holding a little back (1957+)*
moonlight requisition *n* A nighttime foray to
steal something : *moonlight requisition in the
cafeteria*
moonshine *n* **1** Whiskey made by unlicensed distillers; corn whiskey; MOUNTAIN
DEW : *the moonshine distilled in the mountains*
(1877+) **2** Any cheap, inferior whiskey;
ROTGUT *(1920+)* **3** Any liquor or whiskey
(1920+) **4** Exaggerated talk; vain chatter;
BALONEY, BULLSHIT : *His story's plain moonshine (1843+)*
moony *adj* Behaving in a pleasantly listless
and dreamy way : *in a back booth at Ca-
ballero's where Carolyn and I talked and became
drunk and moony (1848+)*

moosh (MOOSH) *v* To mash; squash : *I see it's
all mooshed out of shape* [1990+; the date
should certainly be much earlier, since this
is a variant spelling of *mush,* which is found
by 1781] *See* MUSH[2]
mopped *adj* Thoroughly beaten; CLOBBERED
(1990s+ Teenagers)
mop (or **mop up**) **the floor with** someone *v
phr* To defeat thoroughly; trounce; CLOBBER
(1940s+)
mop top *modifier* : *curly-haired mop-top head-
shop owner n phr* A person with a thick head
of hair : *Those with only a receding hairline
are in no greater danger than the mop tops*
(1990s+) [mop-head in the same sense is
found by the late 1700s, so the date is
probably earlier than shown]
more fun than a barrel of monkeys *adj phr* A
very good time; a pleasant occasion *(1895+)*
more than you can shake a stick at *n phr*
Much; a lot : *He's got more money than you
can shake a stick at (1818+)*
morning glory (or **missile**) *n* A penile erection upon waking : *a morning missile wakes
him up*
morph *n* **1** Morphine *(1912+ Narcotics)* **2**
morphodite *(1940s+)* *v* To change one image into another by a computer technique :
*One of the most popular techniques in TV ads
has been to "morph" a Democratic rival into
Clinton, employing special effects to have the
candidate's face change into the President's/
One thing morphs into another before your very
eyes (1990s+)* [fr Greek *morphe,* "form"]
mortal lock *n phr* A certainty; CINCH, SURE
THING : *Brown is what bettors would call a
mortal lock to win/ a mortal lock to get on the
front page* [1950s+ Gambling; fr a wrestling
hold]
mortar *See* BRICKS AND MORTAR
mosey or **mosey along** (MOH zee) *v* or *v phr*
To move along, esp to walk slowly; saunter;
EASE ON : *A mild river that moseyed at will/ The
Wheaton cruiser moseyed on by me and turned
back toward town* [1829+; perhaps fr Spanish *vamos;* perhaps fr British dialect *mose
about,* "walk in a stupid manner"] *See* VA-
MOOSE
mosh (MAHSH) *v* To dance to heavy metal
music in a tight-packed arena called a "mosh
pit," with a certain amount of physical violence : *They don't dance. They mosh. They slam.
They skank and thrash, too/ Gearshift would
give the crowd something to mosh to* [late
1980s+ fr British; fr British dialect, "mash,
smash," found by 1848]
moshing *n* : *Pearl Jam pulled out of a concert in a
dispute with security forces over how to handle
"moshing," the rowdy, high-contact dancing
common at their shows (late 1980s+)*

mosh pit *n phr* The place where "moshing" is done : *It's unspeakably hot, often painful, certainly claustrophobic, all in all, just another night in the mosh pit/ Mosh pits are a lot like armpits; they both are sweaty, hairy, and they stink (late 1980s+)*

mosquito *See* KNEE-HIGH TO A GRASSHOPPER

moss *n* Hair; among black people, straightened or processed hair : *Moss is hair (1940s+ Black) See* RIGHTEOUS MOSS

mossback *n* A very conservative person; FOGY : *The real mossbacks will vote for the governor* [1878+; said to have been a description of a group of poor white Carolina swamp dwellers who had lived among the cypresses until the *moss* grew on their *backs*]

most, the *n phr* The best; the GREATEST : *New Jetliner The Most, Reds Say (1950s+ Beat & cool talk)*

mostest, the *n phr* the MOST [1885+; fr Southern dialect and black normal superlative of *much*] *See* the HOSTESS WITH THE MOSTEST

mothball *v* To take something out of active use and preserve it for the future, as clothing is stored with mothballs : *"It's really sad to see Buran on the ground." It was used in 1988 and then mothballed (1949+) See* IN MOTHBALLS

moth-eaten *adj* Worn out by long or rough usage or by neglect : *moth-eaten school (1550+)*

mother *modifier* : *Every mother other one of 'em cried foul n* **1** The leader, usu the elder and mentor, of younger homosexuals *(1970s+ Homosexuals)* **2** A despicable person; MOTHERFUCKER : *I looked into the wallet of one of the mothers (fr black)* **3** A fine, interesting, or remarkable event, object, or person; MOMMA : *Grab these mothers. They'll really do the job/ When a good-looking girl passes a "big man" on the street, instead of a whistle she gets an approving Motha Higby, especially if she's a cool mother (1950s+ Black)* **4** A problem or difficulty; MOTHERFUCKER [both black senses fr the very useful and general *motherfucker*]

◄**motherfucker►** (Variations: **eater** or **grabber** or **jumper** or **kisser** or **lover** or **nudger** or **rammer** or some other two-syllable agent word may replace **fucker**; **mammy** or **mama** or **momma** may replace **mother**; other alliterating or rhyming terms like **motorscooter** may replace the whole form) *modifier* : *a mammyrammer blowhard fart that has no respect n* **1** A detestable person; BASTARD, SHITHEEL : *"You motherfucker!" she screamed, "You bastard!"/ blew this motherfucker's brain out* **2** An admirable or prodigious person : *We will joyfully say, "Man, he's a motherfucker"/ You old benevolent motherjumper, I love you* **3** A fine, interesting, or remarkable

event, object, or person; MOMMA, MOTHER, SUCKER : *We had a motherjumper of a winter. Snow up the yin-yang* **4** A problem or difficulty; MOTHER *(1950s+ Black)*

◄**motherfucking►** *adj* (Variations: see *motherfucker* for base forms from which *-ing* forms may be made) Detestable; disgusting; nasty; accursed; GOD-DAMN ● Often used for rhythmic and euphonious emphasis : *went down there with his motherfucking gun, knocked down the motherfucking door/ what he describes as "three hard mothergrabbin' years" (1950s+ Black)*

mother-nudger *See* MOTHERFUCKER

mother of all something *n phr* The largest, most impressive, utterly unsurpassable example of something; GRANDDADDY OF ALL something : *The plan to fix the Hubble telescope in orbit is the mother of all repair missions/ I have the mother of all pains in the back* [1991+ Gulf War; Muslim tradition fr Ayesha, second wife of Mohammed, and the *Mother of Believers;* used by Iraqi President Saddam Hussein to describe the battle in which he would annihilate invading forces]

motor *n* An amphetamine, esp Methedrine®; SPEED : *"What's motor? Speed?" "Un huh" (1990s+ Narcotics) v* **1** To perform well and without apparent effort; CRUISE : *Agassi is motoring through the match (1970s+)* **2** To leave; BOOGIE, BOOK, SPLIT : *I have to motor if I want to be ready for the funeral (1980s+ Teenagers)*

motor-mouth *adj* : *I didn't know he was motormouth/ The gangsta rapper is wrecking the mike with motormouth rhymes n* A very talkative person; a compulsive jabberer; FLAPJAW, WINDBAG : *What else can you do with this motor-mouth but grin and bear it?/ He keeps on talking. A motor-mouth, this guy (1971+)*

Motown *n* Detroit, the Motor City : *records made in Motown*

mountain (or **Rocky Mountain**) **canary** *n phr* A donkey; burro *(1905+)*

mountain dew *n phr* Raw and inferior whiskey, esp homemade bootleg whiskey; MOONSHINE *(1839+)*

mountain (or **prairie**) **oysters** *n phr* Sheep or hog testicles used as food *(1890+) See* ROCKY MOUNTAIN OYSTER

mounty *See* COUNTY MOUNTY

mouse *n* **1** A bruise near the eye, caused by a blow; BLACK EYE, SHINER : *One of the Kid's eyes has a little mouse under it (1842+)* **2** A young woman : *a little mouse I got to know up in Michigan/ I'm pouring Dom Pérignon and black eggs into this little mouse (1655+)* **3** A term of endearment for a woman : *Just stepping out for a minute, mouse (1520+)*

mouse potato *n phr* : Mouse potato, the digital age's version of the couch potato: a person who is habitually on-line or otherwise occupied at the computer (1990s+)

mousetrap *n* A small, inferior theater or nightclub : He walked out on the stage of a mousetrap called the Blue Angel (1950s+) *v* To trick someone into a trap, esp by various feints (1950s+ Sports)

mouth *n* Impudence; backtalk; SASS : I've had about enough of your mouth (1926+) *v* : They jounced and mouthed each other See BAD-MOUTH, BIGMOUTH, BLOW OFF one's MOUTH, COTTON MOUTH, FOOT-IN-MOUTH DISEASE, FOULMOUTHED, FROM THE HORSE'S MOUTH, LOUD-MOUTH, MOTOR-MOUTH, MUSHMOUTH, POOR-MOUTH, RUN OFF AT THE MOUTH, SHOOT OFF one's MOUTH, SMARTMOUTH, WATCH one's MOUTH, ZIP one's LIP

mouth-breather *n* A stupid person; moron; idiot : Some mouth-breather in the office told me it would be OK [1970s+; fr the noisy breathing of an adenoidal idiot]

mouth-breathing *adj* Stupid; moronic : If the dumb mouth-breathing bastards in the street only understood/ a quirky Canadian sport run by morons, played by barbarians, and watched by mouth-breathing, two-fisted slobbers (1970s+)

mouthful, a *n phr* Something hard to pronounce or speak; JAWBREAKER : Diphosphopyridine nucleotide is a mouthful (1884+) See someone SAID A MOUTHFUL

mouth off *v phr* 1 To talk; make comments; chat 2 SHOOT OFF one's MOUTH (1970s+)

mouth on someone *v phr* To inform on; SQUEAL : He got busted, and he mouthed on everybody he knew (1960s+)

mouthpiece *n* 1 A lawyer; LIP : inability to hire a professional bondsman and "good front," "mouth-piece" or lawyer (1857+) 2 A spokesperson : Each tong has an official "mouthpiece" (1805+)

move *v* 1 To steal; pilfer 2 To sell merchandise; dispose of a stock : We better move these monster Teddy Bears quick 3 To be desirable to customers; sell quickly : Those pet rocks are not moving any more (1950s+) See MAKE one's MOVE, PUT A MOVE ON someone

move into high gear See SHIFT INTO HIGH GEAR

move on *v phr* To attempt to seduce someone : She moved on the single men at the bachelor party

movers and shakers *n* People who accomplish things, get things done : Movers and shakers are influential people

moves See HAVE ALL THE MOVES

move up *v phr* To buy a more expensive or more cherished thing : The smoker is exhorted to "move up" to a particular brand of cigarettes, the motorist to a new car (1970s+)

movie See BLUE MOVIE, B MOVIE, GRIND-HOUSE, SNUFF FILM

mower See LAWNMOWER

moxie *n* 1 Courage; GUTS : You're young and tough and got the moxie and can hit 2 Energy; assertive force; PIZZAZZ : We knew you had the old moxie, the old get out and get 3 Skill; competence; shrewdness : showed plenty of moxie as he scattered seven hits the rest of the way [1908+; the semantic history is not entirely clear; best known fr the advertising slogan "What this country needs is plenty of Moxie," used for a brand of soft drink registered in 1924; but other Moxie drinks preexisted this: a patent "nerve medicine" of the same name was marketed in 1876; the name may be based on a New England Indian term found in several Maine place names and perhaps in the name of a plant, moxie-berry]

Ms Right See MISTER RIGHT

mucho *adj* Very; a lot of : mucho dinero/ wanting mucho nachos

muck *n* HIGH MUCKETY-MUCK ● Always used with big, high, etc : the way some of these big mucks do

muck-a-muck See HIGH MUCKETY-MUCK

muck around *v phr* To tinker or tamper; interfere in; FUCK AROUND : I found myself mucking around my life as well as Jean's/ He believed that other Brewer coaches were mucking around too much in his area of expertise [a euphemism for fuck around]

muckety-muck See HIGH MUCKETY-MUCK

muck up *v phr* To damage; ruin; FUCK UP : And let's not muck up our public spaces before we find the answers/ Mucking up the enterprise are fatuous passages about smugglers, espionage, and computers [a euphemism for fuck up, probably influenced by mid-1800s mucks, "disarrange, discompose, make a muddle," fr British dialect muxen, "make filthy"]

mucky-muck See HIGH MUCKETY-MUCK

mud *n* 1 Defamatory assertions and accusations : Watch out, they'll throw a lot of mud at you (1786+) 2 Opium before it is readied for smoking (1922+ Narcotics) 3 Coffee (1925+ Hoboes) See someone's NAME IS MUD, STICK IN THE MUD

mudder *n* A racehorse that runs very well on a muddy track (1905+ Horse racing)

mud (or here's mud) in your eye *interj* A toast; a health : He raised his glass and said "Mud in your eye" (1927+)

mudslinging *n* The use of defamation, insinuation, etc, esp in politics; SMEAR (1884+)

mud wrestle (or wrestling) *n phr* Low and slanderous political devices; DIRTY TRICKS : The mud wrestle was mostly over how to craft a law that would fatten the ranks of new

Democratic voters at the expense of Republicans/ What we have now is mud wrestling and dirty tricks and Willie Horton [1980s+; fr a form of entertainment in which lightly clad women *wrestle* in *mud*]

muff *n* **1** : *dropped the ball, "the $75,000 muff," as it was called* **2** A wig; a toupee; RUG : *wasn't wearing his muff* (*1940s+*) ◁**3**▷ The vulva and pubic hair; BEAVER (*1699+*) *v* To fail; botch, esp by clumsiness • The older example refers to playing cricket : *This is a ripe one. Don't muff it, Billy* (*1837+*) [verb sense fr the clumsiness of someone wearing a *muff* on the hands]

◁**muff-dive**▷ *v* To do cunnilingus • Sometimes used as a plain insult : *You muff-diving, mother-fucking son of a bitch* (*1935+*)

◁**muff-diver**▷ *n* A person who does cunnilingus; CLIT-LICKER (*1935+*)

◁**muffins**▷ *n* A woman's breasts (*1950s+*)

mug or **mugg** *n* **1** The face : *showing so unperturbed a face, so impudent a "mug"* (*1708+*) **2** A photograph of the face; MUG SHOT : *a police mug, front and profile* (*1887+*) **3** A man; fellow; esp a tough, rude sort or a pugilist or hoodlum : *Those mugs on the corner seem menacing* (*1895+*) *v* **1** To photograph a person's face, esp for police records : *When crooks are photographed they are "mugged"* (*1899+*) **2** To make exaggerated faces, grimaces, etc, for humorous effect : *while Danny mugs through his program* (*1855+*) **3** To assault and injure someone in the course of a robbery : *The victims were mugged in the hallways of their homes* (*1818+*) [probably fr drinking *mugs* made to resemble grotesque human faces; the sense of violent assault comes fr mid-1800s British specialization of the term "rob by violent strangulation," probably fr *mug-hunter*, "a thief who seeks out victims who are mugs" (easy marks)]

mugger *n* **1** An actor or comedian who makes exaggerated faces, grimaces, etc, for humorous effect : *where this trivial mugger is performing* (*1892+*) **2** A thief who uses extreme physical violence : *apparently the victim of muggers/ A knife or an armlock around the throat has been the favorite technique of muggers* (*1865+*)

mug shot *n phr* A photograph of a person's face, esp the front and side views made for police records; art : *passed around a mug shot of Willie/ She had identified a "mug shot" from the books as the man who attacked her* (*1940s+*)

◁**muh-fuh** or **mo-fo**▷ *n* A despicable person; MOTHERFUCKER : *Them muh-fuhs are superbad* (*1970s+ Black*)

mule *n* **1** A stubborn person : *He's a hardheaded mule* (*1848+*) **2** Crude raw whiskey; MOONSHINE, white mule (*1926+*) **3** A person who carries, delivers, or smuggles narcotics or other contraband : *The danger to the mule is that a packet may rupture/ "Mules" carry coke in picture frames and sealed in the sides of suitcases/ American currency was spirited out of the country then, often by "mules"* (*1935+ Narcotics*) **4** A condom stuffed with narcotics, carried in the vagina or rectum (*1970s+ Narcotics*) *v* : *Sometimes they mule it in small amounts/ otherwise law-abiding countrymen into performing muling favors*

mulligan *n* **1** A stew, esp one made of any available meat and vegetables (*1904+ Hoboes*) **2** : *A mulligan is the taking of an extra shot contrary to the rules* (*1940s+ Golf*) [perhaps fr the proper name *Mulligan*]

mulligrubs, the *n* the BLUES [1619+; origin unknown]

multi-culti *modifier* Multicultural; expressing or advocating multiculturalism : *Kalman wasn't hired by Benetton because they hoped his multi-culti graphics would put the company out of business* (*1990s+*)

mum's the word *interj* Please keep quiet; don't say anything (*1704+*)

munchies *n* Snacks; food : *take the joy out of America's favorite munchies, from burgers to pasta to popcorn* • Often with *the* (*1950s+*)

munchies, the *n phr* Desire for food after smoking marijuana (*1971+*) *See* HAVE THE MUNCHIES

Munchkin *n* A low-ranking employee, staff member, etc; a menial : *Justice Department spokesman Thomas De Cair sniffed that Honegger was "a low-level Munchkin"/ Most of the munchkins, junior campaign aides, won't make it to the transition staff* [1970s+; fr the name of the dwarfish helpers in L Frank Baum's 1900 book *The Wonderful Wizard of Oz*]

munch out (or **up**) *v phr* To eat, esp to consume hungrily; PIG OUT : *You'll get together with your friends, right, and you'll be munching up or something/ She knew she shouldn't be munching out on carbos like this*

mung *n* Anything nasty; filth; GLOP : *Jones noticed the mung on Lydon's never-brushed teeth/ Fold the table down, and generations of crud and mung appear* (*1960s+ Students*) *v* **1** (also **mung up**) To spoil; botch (*1960s+ Students*) **2** To make changes, often undesirable ones, in a file (*1980s+ Computer*) **3** To destroy : *The system munged my whole day's work* (*1980s+ Computer*) [origin unknown]

mung up *v phr* To make filthy : *I munged up my shoes walking across the field* (*1970s+ Teenagers*)

mungy *adj* Messy, gloppy, often gooey or oily : *mungy leftovers*

murder *n* 1 the MOST, the GREATEST • Sometimes pronounced with equal stress on each syllable, as noted by 1943 *(1935+ Jive talk)* 2 A very difficult or severe person or thing : *Baseball is murder on families* v 1 To defeat decisively; trounce; CLOBBER : *They murdered them all season (1950s+)* 2 To make someone helpless with laughter; FRACTURE, KILL : *This one'll murder you (1970s+) See* BLOODY MURDER, GET AWAY WITH MURDER

murder one *n phr* The criminal offense of murder in the first degree : *when he did get to trial, and they were going to go for murder one (1971+)*

murphy *n* 1 A potato *(1811+)* 2 A confidence game in which the victim is left with a sealed envelope supposed to contain something valuable, but in fact filled with blank paper *(1960s+ Underworld)* 3 WEDGIE *(1980s+ Students)* v : *Mayor Smitherman was "murpheyed" by the Negro confidence man*

muscle *n* 1 A strong-arm man; GORILLA : *some gowed-up muscle (1929+)* 2 Power; influence; CLOUT : *DiBona will have a lot of muscle when it comes to Penn's Landing (1931+) See* FLEX one's MUSCLES, LOVE-MUSCLE

muscle car *n phr* A powerful car, esp one admired by teenagers : *Chrysler's hot-selling Viper muscle car is $50,000/ the Sacramento Valley is "car country," where blue-collar kids drive "muscle cars" (old Pontiacs, newish Corvettes if they're making money) and are slurred as "the Camaro crowd"/ The undercover cops had a sporty muscle car. It was mean. It was fast. It was cool (1980s+)*

musclehead *n* 1 A stupid person; KLUTZ 2 A strong-arm man; MUSCLE : *I saw three or four muscleheads gleefully beat up on a kid (1950s+)*

muscle in *v phr* To force one's way in, esp into someone's criminal operation : *attempt to muscle in on some graft out of his own domain/ afraid you're muscling in on his scam (1929+ Underworld)*

muscle man *n phr* A muscular male, esp from lifting weights *(1929+)*

muscle out *v phr* To force out : *If she persists, she'll be muscled out of the movement (1950s+)*

museum piece *n phr* Something old-fashioned : *His hat's a museum piece (1950s+)*

mush¹ *n* 1 Empty and exaggerated talk; BALONEY : *Don't hand me that mush, pal (1841+)* 2 Sentimentality; saccharinity; CORN, SCHMALTZ : *They were all weeping over the Dickensian mush (1908+)* [perhaps an alteration of *mash*, "something soft and pulpy"]

mush² or **moosh** (often M$\overline{OO}$SH) *n* The face, esp the mouth and jaws : *He pulled his mush away from the plate and sighed* [1859+; origin unknown; perhaps fr Romany, "man"]

mushmouth *n* A person who talks indistinctly and slurringly : *Say it again so I can hear it, mushmouth (1950s+)*

mushroom *n* 1 A person who is deliberately kept ignorant and misinformed 2 : *The growing contempt for accidental victims is even indicated by the name killers give them: "mushrooms" who "pop up" in the line of fire (late 1980s+)*

mushy *adj* Sentimental : *The kid got mushy with the broad/ If you expected Al Unser Sr to get all mushy-gushy and misty-eyed, you don't know Al Unser Sr (1839+)*

music *See* BUBBLEGUM MUSIC, CHIN MUSIC, ELEVATOR MUSIC, FACE THE MUSIC, SOUL

musical *modifier* Changing rapidly from one to another possessor : *At night in Port-au-Prince a massive game of musical houses is going on/ The revolving cast of Love Letters has become something of a game of musical celebrities/ Neither partner will relinquish the co-op; this is black comedy, a wickedly funny tale of musical apartments and malfunctioning appliances* [1924+; the date refers to the first occurrence of *musical chairs*, the game in which players circle a set of chairs and sit in any one available when the music stops]

musical beds *n phr* Sexual promiscuity; SLEEPING AROUND : *The soaps were conspicuous for their preoccupation with musical beds See* MUSICAL

muss or **muss up** *v* or *v phr* To disarrange; dishevel : *He mussed his hair all up* [1899+; fr *mess*]

mussy *adj* Disarranged; rumpled : *rumpled now, and mussy (1899+)*

must, a *adv* Necessarily; imperatively : *Solaris is definitely a must-have game/ I don't think the element of fantasy ruins the movie, which in my book is a must-see n phr* Something that must be seen, experienced, done, etc : *Having two cars is a must these days (1892+)*

mutant *n* A weird and disgusting person; shpos : *Marvin is a mutant; he's constantly licking his nose in public (1980s+ Student)*

mutt *n* 1 A dog, esp a hybrid; mongrel *(1906+)* 2 A stupid person; KLUTZ, MUTTONHEAD : *A mutt? Yeah, he's that all right. Not too much brains (1901+)* 3 A criminal; suspect; mope. PERP *(1980s+ Police)*

Mutt and Jeff *n phr* A mismatched pair of people [1917+; fr the names of two characters, one tall and the other short, in a popular cartoon series by H C Fisher, American cartoonist]

muttonhead or **mutton-top** *n* A stupid person (*1803+*)

muzzed *adj* Drunk; intoxicated (*1836+*)

◁**my ass**▷ *interj* An exclamation of strong denial, disbelief, defiance, etc; IN A PIG'S ASS : *"Looks like you had a pretty good hunch, Mr Light" Pretty good hunch, my ass* [1796+; a dysphemism for *my eye*]

my bad *interj* : *My bad: My fault or my mistake. A term of apology (1990s+ Teenagers)*

my boy *See* THAT'S MY BOY

my eye or **my foot** *interj* IN A PIG'S ASS, MY ASS : *She's the greatest my eye/ You'll do that my foot* [first form 1842+; in the early and obsolete meaning "nonsense," perhaps fr a Joe Miller joke in which a Latin nonsense phrase *O mihi, beate Martine* ("O, to me, blessed Martin") is pronounced as *all my eye and Betty Martin*]

my foot *interj* I do not believe that; like hell, that's true : *She's better than me? My foot*

my man *n phr* One's particular friend; BUDDY, HOMIE, PAL : *"Serve it up, my man," said Tump. Tump never even saw it (1930+ Black jazz musicians)*

mystery *n* Hash (*1885+*)

mystery meat *n phr* Meat not readily identifiable, esp as served in a student dining hall, fraternity house, etc : *Parents must follow the rules: They are forbidden to smoke or leave the building, must show up at homeroom and eat mystery meat at lunch like the rest of their classmates* [1970s+ Students; meat loaf was called *mystery loaf* by the 1940s]

N

nab *n* (also **nabs**) A police officer or detective *(1950s+ Street gang)* *v* To catch; seize; arrest; COLLAR : *The officers nabbed him around the corner (1686+)* [fr dialect *nap* as in *kidnap*, perhaps related to Swedish *nappa*, "catch," or Danish *nappe*, "pull"; probably related to *nip*; the noun sense is recorded in British criminal slang by 1813]

nabe *n* **1** A neighborhood; HOOD : *The nabe is a zzzhoney, architecturally (1937+)* **2** A neighborhood movie theater : *The current films eventually make their way to the nabes (1935+)*

nada *n* Nothing ; *it's free, zip, zero, nada*

◁**nads** or **'nads**▷ *n* The male gonads; testicles; BALLS, FAMILY JEWELS : *Apparently I was no longer rousing his 'nads/ When we found him his nads were gone* [1980s+; *nard*, "testicle," is found in 1960s student slang and is probably also a shortening of *gonad*]

naff *adj* Not very good; lacking taste or style *(1966+)*

naff (off) *interj* Get away *v phr* (also **about**) To goof off, fool around [1959+; British euphemism for *fuck off*]

nag *n* A horse, esp an old and worn-out racehorse : *to make dough on the nags* [1400+; origin unknown]

nail *n* A hypodermic needle *(1960s+ Narcotics)* *v* **1** To catch; seize; NAB : *the feared and famous Batman and Robin who'd nailed him (1766+)* ◁**2**▷ To do the sex act to someone; FUCK : *the publishing cupcake in the Florsheims who nailed you on the couch and then fired you* **3** NAIL something DOWN : *We've got it nailed See* HARD AS NAILS

nail-biter *n* Something very worrying and suspenseful : *If Lucas looked this nervous as the Spurs were blowing out the Clippers, how would he react during a nail-biter?/ The gain in compliance cases brought by the SEC has been a nail-biter for brokerage executives (1990s+)*

nail-down *n* an advertised price to lure one into the store that is attached to exactly one item *(1980s+)*

nail something **down** *v phr* To make something securely final; CINCH : *They nailed down the arrangement and had a drink (1880+)*

nailed *adj* **1** Identified correctly **2** Arrested; apprehended : *nailed for speeding*

nail in the coffin *n phr* Something that hastens defeat or death : *The Houston convention was one very big nail in Bush's re-election coffin/ Whittle's proposal is the first nail in the coffin of public education (1824+)*

nail someone or something **to the cross (or the wall)** *v phr* To punish severely and publicly; make an example of; crucify : *We are going to nail them to the cross/ We would not nail an airline to the wall if it made its best effort/ I wonder why nobody tried to nail his hide to the wall for the Irish jokes he told over the years (1990s+)*

naked *See* BUCK NAKED

naked as a jaybird *adj phr* Entirely unclothed; BARE-ASS *(1930s+)*

Nam or **'Nam** *n* Vietnam : *not like the gooks back in 'Nam who always got their goddam hands out/ I was in Nam and Nam made me like that (Vietnam War armed forces)*

name *modifier* Being well known or prestigious : *a name band/ name brand (1938+)* *n* A very important person, esp in entertainment; HEADLINER : *I saw three or four names there/ He's a name in the carpet business (1611+) See* BIG NAME, WHAT'S-HIS-NAME, YOU NAME IT

name-calling *n* The assigning of malicious designations in politics, debate, etc; character assassination; vilification : *They soon sank to simple name-calling (1853+)*

name-drop *v* To mention the names of important persons as if they were friends and associates [1955+; back formation fr *name-dropper*]

name-dropper *n* A person who ostentatiously mentions the names of important people as if they were friends and associates : *Well, she may know Barbra Streisand, or she may just be a name-dropper (1947+)*

name-dropping *n* The practice of a "name-dropper" *(1949+)*

name is mud, someone's *sentence* One is in trouble; one is doomed : *If they catch him, his name is mud* [1823+; fr earlier British dialect *mud*, "fool"]

name (or number) is on something, one's *interj* One has been singled out as being responsible or to blame for something [1925+; used with reference to a bullet, shell, etc, with the implication that one is doomed to be killed by it]

name names *v phr* To make accusations, esp against one's former associates : *A genuinely guilty collaborator in Czechoslovakia can now, it seems, easily save his or her own hide by "naming names" and implicating independent-minded dissidents (1950s+)*

name of the game, the *n phr* **1** What matters most; the essence : *In business, the name of the game is the bottom line/ Good gun dogs are the name of the game* **2** The inevitable; the way things are : *Telling lies in politics? Hell, that's just the name of the game* (1966+)

names *See* KICK ASS AND TAKE NAMES

name your poison *sentence* Say what you would like to drink : *Sally, name your poison*

nance or **nancy** or **Miss Nancy** *modifier* : *with his talk of nancy poets, his anti-intellectualism* n 1 A male homosexual who takes the passive role (1904+) 2 An effeminate man; LILY : *Where you need desperately a man of iron, you often get a nance* (1883+) [said to be fr the nickname of Miss Anna Oldfield, an actress who died in 1730 and was noted for her extreme vanity, fashionable dress, etc]

nanny *See* GET someone's GOAT

nanny tax *n phr* The legal requirement, enacted in 1951, that full-time domestic childminders be treated like other employees under the Social Security law : *The Social Security "nanny tax," made famous last year in confirmation hearings will be eased under legislation Congress passed Thursday* [1980s+; fr British *nanny*, "childrens' nurse," a nickname for *Ann*, and found by 1795]

-napping *combining word* The stealing of the indicated animal : *The judge was told of the monkeys' disappearance; the monkey-napping had its serious side* [1939+; based on *kidnapping*; the dated example is *dognapping*]

nappy *adj* Dirty; messy : *Kelly's panties are nappy. No doubt, she's been wearing them for a week* (1980s+ Students)

narc or **narco** *modifier* : *down to the narco police on the beat* n A narcotics agent or police officer; gazer : *another drug-scare hoax promulgated by the "narcs"/ the ritual of dodging the "narcos"* (1960s+ Narcotics)

nark *n* 1 A police informer; STOOL PIGEON (1860+) 2 KIBITZER, BUTTINSKY (1950s+) 3 A decoy; SHILL : *information about known gamblers, little bookmakers, and their narks* (1960s+ Gambling) *v* (also **narc**) : *He will nark on him if the first guy doesn't keep playing games/ felt the Fraynes and their youngsters had narced on them* [fr Romany *nak*, "nose"]

nash *See* NOSH

nasty *adj* Good; stylish; admirable (1834+) *n* 1 Something unpleasant, repulsive, etc : *pathos, poverty, and other real-life nasties* (1971+) 2 The sex act : *We caught them doing the nasty in his bedroom* 3 A vicious person; villain : *takes her family on a river trip, where they are taken prisoner by nasties/ a few of the nasties are scenery-chomping, world-class scum* (1930s+)

natch *adv* Naturally; certainly : *will be in riding clothes (habits of the rich, natch)/ The two men, natch, are soul buddies* **affirmation** Of course; right : *Do I like it? Natch, what else?* (1945+)

native *See* GO NATIVE

natives are restless, the *sentence* One can expect some opposition; discontent appears to be afoot : *Meanwhile, the natives are restless: Polls indicate rising feeling that the President is paying too much attention to foreign matters* [1930s+; fr a trite line in many old jungle movies as native drums throb]

natty *adj* Neat; spruce; stylish : *The fitted shirt gave him a natty appearance/ A natty convertible* (1806+)

natural-born *adj* Total; absolute; innate : *The man's a natural-born spaz/ a natural-born artist* (1930s+ Black)

nature of the beast, the *n phr* The innate characteristics of someone or something : *The shared experience is the value of network television; it's the nature of the beast* [1678+; the earliest occurrence is in a collection of English proverbs]

nature's call *See* CALL OF NATURE

naughty bits *n* The genitals [1960+; euphemism fr *Monty Python's Flying Circus* skits]

near thing *n phr* Something that barely succeeds or nearly ends in failure or disaster : *It was a near thing, but I kept my job* (British)

neat *adj* 1 Excellent; wonderful (1920s+ Teenagers) 2 Without water or another mixer; undiluted; STRAIGHT, STRAIGHT UP • Used to describe spirits : *I'll take my Scotch neat, please* (1579+)

neatnik *n* A neat or tidy person, as distinct from a "beatnik" (1959+) *See* -NIK

neato *adj* NEAT : *with nothing to his name but a variety of neat-o consumer electronics* (1968+ Teenagers)

nebbie *See* NIMBY

nebbish or **neb** *n* A person without charm, interesting qualities, talent, etc; WIMP : *"Nebbish" is simply the one in the crowd that you always forget to introduce/ Don't be a nebbish/ poor little nebs like Julian* [1941+; fr Yiddish fr Czech *neboky*]

necessary, the *See* the NEEDFUL

neck *v* To kiss, embrace, and caress; dally amorously; MAKE OUT, SMOOCH : *At least you'd want to neck me/ You "spooned," then you "petted," after that you "necked"* (1825+) *See* GET OFF someone's BACK, GIVE someone A PAIN, LEATHERNECK, NO-NECK, a PAIN IN THE ASS, REDNECK, ROUGHNECK, RUBBERNECK, STICK one's NECK OUT, TO SAVE ONE'S NECK

necking *n* The pleasures and procedures of those who engage in kissing, embracing, and caressing : *pupils resort to necking/ It was the closest we ever got to necking* (1825+) *See* HEAVY PETTING

neck of the woods *n phr* An area, neighborhood, etc : *Hey, you live right in my own neck of the woods* (1839+)

necktie party (or **social** or **sociable**) *n phr* A hanging or lynching (*1871+*)

needle *n* **1** Criticism or goad : *a really nasty needle* **2** A hypodermic injection; SHOT (*1943+*) *v* **1** To nag at someone; criticize regularly and smartingly; HASSLE : *He keeps needling the guy about his looks* (*1940+*) **2** To age or strengthen an alcoholic beverage artificially, esp by using an electric current passed through a needlelike rod (*1920s+*)

needle, the *n phr* **1** Injurious and provocative remarks; nagging criticism : *He's always ready with the needle* (*1940+*) **2** Narcotics injections; the narcotics habit : *The needle finally killed him* (*1940s+ Narcotics*) *See* GIVE someone THE NEEDLE

needle beer *n phr* Beer reinforced with alcohol or ether (*1928+*)

needle park *n phr* A public place where addicts regularly gather to deal in drugs and to take injections; SHOOTING GALLERY : *Drug addicts have turned the Platzspitz in Zurich, once elegant, into a needle park* (*1966+*)

needles *See* RAIN CATS AND DOGS

need someone or something **like a hole in the head** *v phr* To have emphatically no need whatsoever for someone or something [*1951+*; fr Yiddish *loch in kop*, "hole in head"]

neg *v* To reject; turn down : *I was negged from Princeton but accepted at Yale* (*1980s+ Teenagers*)

negative *n* A negative element in judgment; a minus : *"drove up Dukakis' negatives" in voter surveys* (*1647+*)

negatory *negation* No; NIX, NOPE : *Mrs. Shrub sternly took Shrub's arm. "Were you really going to ruin his daughter's wedding?" The Shrub said, "Negatory"* [*1950s+ Air Force*; an adjective sense, fr French *négatoire*, is found by 1580; the modern sense was popularized by the citizens band phenomenon of the 1970s]

nellie or **nelly** *adj* **1** Homosexual; effeminate; GAY, SWISH : *Well, his backstroke is a little Nellie/ what in the past would have been described as a Nelly queen* **2** Overfastidious; finicky; schoolmarmish : *"As follow" is Nellie usage and probably incorrect* (*1960s+*) *See* NERVOUS NELLIE

nemmie or **nemish** *See* NIMBY

nerd *modifier* : *Norton represents a new type of American rich person: the nerd tycoon/ a mix between journalism and nerd heaven, with its sophisticated desktop equipment and absence of paper* **n** **1** (also **nerdboy** or **nurd**) A tedious, contemptible person; DORK, DWEEB, JERK : *In Detroit, someone who once would be called a drip or a square is now, regrettably a nerd, or in a less severe case, a scurve/ What about a total*

dweeb? *Yup. Geek? Yup. Nerdboy? Yup.* (*1951+ Teenagers*) **2** An overstudious person, esp a computer devotee, usu pictured with horn-rimmed spectacles and often buck teeth : *She's definitely a word nerd ● In some uses nearly synonymous with "hacker"* (*1980s+ Students*) [probably fr the 1950 children's book *If I Ran the Zoo*, by "Dr. Seuss," where a *nerd* is one of the desired animals]

nerdacious or **nerdly** *adj* Nerdlike; NERDY : *and nerdacious mutterings full of buried Hobbit references* (*1990s+*)

nerdling *n* An inexperienced and naive computer "hacker" (*1980s+*)

nerd pack *n* A plastic shield worn to keep ink off shirt pockets (*1980s+ Teenagers*)

nerdy *adj* Characteristic of a nerd : *Above all, stay away from anything nerdy/ When the trendy become mainstream, the hip go nerdy* (*1970s+ Teenagers*)

nerts or **nertz** *See* NUTS

nerty *See* NUTTY

nervous Nellie *n phr* A timid or cautious person; a worrier : *a nervous Nellie a bit like Jeanne Dixon* [late 1930s+; perhaps fr *Nervous Nellie*, the nickname of Frank B Kellogg, secretary of state 1925–29, who negotiated the Kellogg-Briand differences]

nervy *adj* **1** Nervous; JUMPY (*1891+*) **2** Impudent; bold (*1896+*)

nest *See* FEATHER one's NEST, LOVE NEST

nest egg *n phr* Saved money, esp for use in retirement or an enterprise, emergency, etc (*1700+*)

nester *See* EMPTY-NESTER

net (or **Net**), **the** *n* The Internet : *Like many newcomers to the "net," which is what people call the global web that connects more than thirty thousand on-line networks* (*1990s+ Computers*)

net down *v phr* To be equivalent to; amount to : *Hostile takeovers net down to a power grab* (*1980s+*)

netiquette *n* The etiquette of the Internet; polite online behavior : *the "netiquette" that prevailed in its early days is breaking down/ This clash isn't even about the future of "netiquette"* (*1990s+*)

net result *n phr* The final result after everything has been added and subtracted, after everything has occurred : *net result of your efforts*

net sex or **cybersex** *n* Sexual expression and interchange on the Internet : *I think I'll head back to the house for a little cybersex and a nap* (*1990s+*)

netter *n* A tennis player : *The Jefferson High School netter took second in the Southern Lakes Conference tournament last year* (*1932+*)

never follow a dog act *sentence* Be very careful about whom you are to be immediately compared with ● Often a rueful comment after one has been outshone *(1960s+ Show business)*

never mind *v phr* Forget it. It does not matter anymore : *Need you to get me a towel. Oh, never mind See* MAKE NO NEVER MIND

new *See* WHAT ELSE IS NEW

new ball game *See* a WHOLE NEW BALL GAME

newbie (also **noob**) *n* A person new to computers and computer networks; computer neophyte : *You'd copy it because you didn't want to seem like a newbie (read: clueless computer rookie)/ Newbies sometimes get flamed just because they are new (1990s+ Computer)*

new boy *n phr* A novice; beginner : *Not a bad start for a new boy* [1970s+; fr the British term for a beginning school student, found by 1847]

new fish *n phr* : *For first-time prisoners ("new fish," in prison parlance), once bail is revoked the darkness descends quickly (1940s+ Prison)*

new kid on the block *n phr* Any newcomer or recent arrival : *The newest kid on that ostentatious block is O'Neal, who, after signing with Orlando, was snatched up by Reebok*

new look, the *n phr* A new fashion; new practice, fad, etc : *Here's the new look in computer software, folks* [1947+; fr a fashion sensation notable chiefly for the long skirts of Christian Dior dresses]

new one on someone, a *n phr* Something not heard or experienced before : *Isn't this a new one on you, Messrs. Police? (1887+)*

news *See* BAD NEWS, NOSE FOR NEWS

newshawk or **newshound** *n* A newspaper reporter *(first form 1929+, second 1936+)*

newsy *adj* Containing or offering a lot of news : *her newsy Christmas cards*

newt *n* An uninteresting person; also, a stupid person : *Be practical, you newt*

new wrinkle *n phr* A novel idea or technique; expedient; trick : *Hey, that little gismo is a new wrinkle (1899+)*

newy or **newey** or **newie** *n* Something new; a novelty : *You'll like this one, it's a newy and a goody (1940s+)*

New York kiss-off *See* KISS-OFF

New York minute *n phr* A very short time; a JIFFY : *In the computer world, nouns like modem and fax become verbs in a nanosecond, almost as short as a New York minute/ I would sign a woman in a New York minute (1990s+)*

next *See* GET NEXT TO someone

next off *adv phr* Next; at that point : *Next off, Hutch give a yell (1920s+)*

next to nothing *n phr* Almost nothing; a very little bit : *It's been very useful and cost me next to nothing (1656+)*

next week *See* KNOCK someone INTO THE MIDDLE OF NEXT WEEK

nibbled to death by ducks *adj phr* Subject to constant petty annoyances : *Writing in such an editor-dominated environment was like being nibbled to death by ducks/ is being nickeled-and-dimed, nibbled to death by ducks (1950s+)*

nibs *See* TOUGH SHIT

nice *See* MAKE NICE

nice as pie, as *adj phr* As pleasant and harmless as could be : *It didn't make any difference to her. You know? She was as nice as pie (1922+)*

nice guys finish last *sentence* It is foolish to be fair and decent; look out only for yourself [late 1940s+; attributed to the baseball manager Leo Durocher]

nice work if you can get it *sentence* That would be a very pleasant thing to do; wouldn't that be fun? ● An admiring comment made when one sees something easy, pleasant, attractive, etc, used esp with sexual overtones : *They're paid salaries totaling millions, they get the best tables in restaurants, the valets never keep them waiting for their Mercedes, they glide from one studio job to another. Nice work if you can get it* [1930s+; this was the title of a George and Ira Gershwin song of 1937]

nic-fit *v* To crave nicotine; suffer from withdrawal : *It's so incredibly bad to nic-fit, it's not even funny (1990s+)*

nick *n* NICKEL BAG *(1990s+ Narcotics) v* **1** To rob or steal : *The bank is gonna be nicked (1869+)* **2** To charge; overcharge; exact : *I think you can nick her for one fifty if you get tough (1921+)*

nickel and dime *modifier* Inconsequential; trivial; TWO-BIT : *You realize you've smashed a grape with a hammer, whacking some nickel-and-dime guy (1970+) v phr* **1** To drain in small increments; nibble away at : *The mack started nickel-and-diming him into the poorhouse/ He said the grizzly habitat was being nickeled-and-dimed out of existence (1970s+)* **2** To quibble; niggle; bring up all sorts of trivia : *is being nickeled-and-dimed, nibbled to death by ducks (1970s+)*

nickelback *n phr* The fifth backfield player in the "nickel defense" : *When peace was restored, the officiating crew ejected end Tom Briggs and nickel back Leroy Axem (1980s+ Football)*

nickel bag *n phr* A five-dollar packet of narcotics *(1960s+ Narcotics)*

nickel defense *n phr* A defensive formation in which a fifth defensive back is added to cover an almost certain pass receiver *(1980s+ Football)*

nickels and dimes *n phr* Very small amounts of money; PEANUTS : *We can get the improved roads for nickels and dimes* (1893+)

nifty *adj* Smart; stylish; NEAT, SLICK : *a great many niftier and hotter words/ a nifty way to upstage the president* (1868+) *adv* : *You did that real nifty* **n 1** : *his six blonde nifties/ Another nifty is the circularization of telephone subscribers* **2** A fifty-dollar bill [origin unknown; called by Bret Harte, in the 1868 example, "Short for *magnificat*"]

◄**nig**► *n* A black person (1932+)

◄**nigga**► (NIGG uh) *n* A black person • Not a taboo word as used by one black person to or about another, esp by rap singers : *For several years, it has become common for young blacks to greet each other as "nigga"* (1925+)

◄**nigger**► *modifier* : *a nice nigger lady n* A black person • Not a taboo word as used by one black person to or about another (1786+)

niggle *v* **1** To complain **2** To spend time on inconsequential things; trifle • With *niggling* as the adjective form : *niggle over the details* (1886+)

night *See* AMATEUR NIGHT, GOOD NIGHT, SATURDAY NIGHT SPECIAL

nightcap *n* **1** A drink taken just before going to bed or the last drink of the evening, esp an alcoholic drink : *Let's stop at Joe's for a nightcap* (1818+) **2** The second game of a doubleheader (1917+ *Baseball*)

nightie or **nighty** *n* A nightgown : *Aphrodite in her nightie, Oh my God what a sightie* (1894+)

night-night or **nightie-night** *interj* An amiable parting salutation at night (1896+)

nightowl or **nighthawk** *n* NIGHT PERSON (*first form 1846+, second 1868+*)

night people (or **fighters**) *n phr* People who work at night or prefer to be up late at night : *I happen to be "night people" and I'm always up late/ Night people, the professor and his wife used to retire about 2:30 to 3 Am* (1950s+)

night person *n phr* One of the night people : *She's a night person, never gets up before the afternoon* (1950s+)

nightspot *n phr* A nightclub; cabaret; Boite, nitery (1936+)

-nik *suffix used to form nouns* A person involved in, described by, or doing what is indicated : *beatnik/ computernik/ peacenik/ nogoodnik* [1940s+; fr Yiddish fr Russian and other Slavic languages]

nimby *n* (also **nimbie** or **nebbie** or **nemmie** or **nemish**) Nembutal® or any barbiturate (1950+ *Narcotics*)

NIMBY (also **Nimby** or **nimby**) *modifier* Exclusivist; fiercely protective : *The local perspective is a recipe for disaster: ignorance, Nimby selfishness, isolationism, tribal and ra-* cial strife *n* not in my back yard : *Institutions that no organized community wants in its backyard, prisons, sanitation works and other NIMBYs, have followed* (1980+) [fr "not in my backyard"]

nimrod *n* : *Of course, there's always the middle ground, reserved for friends who commit a blunder. For these, we have "nimrod," "klutz," and "geek"* [1980s+ Teenagers; fr the name of Nimrod, the "mighty hunter before the Lord" in Genesis]

nincompoop (also **ninny** or **ninnyhammer**) *n* A fool or stupid person (1676+)

nine *n* A nine-millimeter semiautomatic pistol : *There was a fight. I saw a man running with a nine/ People seeking guns for personal combat want reliable stopping power, revolvers or semiautomatic pistols known as "nines"* (1990s+) *v* : *Motherfucker tried to stiff me on a buy and I nined him right there*

nine-hundred-pound gorilla *See* SIX-HUNDRED-POUND GORILLA

nines, the *See* DRESSED TO THE TEETH

nineteenth hole, the *n phr* A drink or a spell of drinking after finishing a golf game (1901+ *Golf*)

nine-to-five *adj* Occupying the time period of a regular, salaried, probably dull office job : *a nine-to-five drag of a job* (1950s+) *v* To be regularly employed, esp in an office job : *even when he was nine-to-fiving* (1962+)

nine-to-fiver *n* **1** A person who is steadily employed : *As early as the 1920s they were called white-collar slaves and by the 1950s nine-to-fivers* **2** A regular job, esp a salaried office job (1959+)

nine yards *See* the WHOLE NINE YARDS

◄**ninnies**▷ *n* A woman's breasts; JUGS, HOOTERS : *Ordell saw what looked like a swimsuit bra covering her ninnies* (1990s+)

nip *n* A small quantity, a taste, of a drink : *Well, give me just a nip, then* [1796+; apparently fr *nipperkin*, "small measure of drink," found by 1694]

nip and tuck *adj phr* **1** Equally likely to win or lose; even; neck and neck : *Near the finish they're nip and tuck* **2** Of equal probability; equally likely : *It's nip and tuck whether I'll get there in time or not* [1857+; earlier versions included *rip and tuck, nip and chuck,* and *nip and tack,* making the original semantics somewhat difficult to assess; the term might be from sailing or from sewing and tailoring]

nipper *n* A small boy; lad • In British dialect, the youngest child of a family : *warning that America's nippers are turning into microchip golem* [1859+; perhaps because he *nips,* "moves quickly"]

◄**nips**▷ *n* The nipples : *Barb's nips are not big and dark* (1970s+)

nitpick *v* To quibble over trivia; NIGGLE : *so all that remains is for them to sit and lie there and nitpick over trivialities or talk about what's on TV*

nitpicking *adj* : *a highly nit-picking attitude n* The act and pleasure of one who quibbles over trivia [from the very slow and attentive work of a person or a simian picking tiny *nits*, "insect eggs," out of hair or fur]

nitro (NĪ troh) *n* **1** Nitroglycerin; SOUP *(1935+)* **2** Nitromethane, a fuel additive for cars *(1960s+ Hot rodders)*

nitty-gritty, the, or the **nitty** *adj phr* : *a lot of nitty-gritty campaigning as well n phr* **1** The most basic elements, esp when unwelcome or unpleasant; harsh realities : *from what they call the nitty gritty and the grass roots/ the awesome and awful nitty gritty of today's urban condition/ and shifting from ideology to the nitty (1960s+ Black)* **2** Practical details [fr the repellent association of *nits*, "the eggs of hair lice, young hair lice," and *grit*, "abrasive granules"]

nitwit *n* A stupid person; fool; BOOB [1922+; perhaps fr *nit*, fr German dialect, "no," found by 1909, plus *wit*]

nix *n* **1** Nothing : *wasn't taking her out here in the park for nix (1789+)* **2** A refusal; veto : *if the Petrillo nix stands (1951+)* **negation** No : *I asked her for one and she said nix (1909+)* *v* To veto; reject : *had been considering marriage but have apparently nixed the idea/ and he was afraid that might nix his CBS deal (1903+)* [fr German *nichts*, "nothing"]

nixie *n* A piece of mail that cannot be delivered because of damage, illegibility, etc *(1885+ Post office)*

nix on *v phr* To forbid • Used only as an imperative : *Nix on the hurry talk/ Nix on swiping anything (1902+)*

nix sign *n phr* : *A local cafe sells a T-shirt showing a howling coyote in a circle with a slash through it—the international nix sign (1990s+)*

no-account or **no-count** *adj* Worthless; untrustworthy; incorrigible : *I'm a lazy no-account bum (1845+) n* : *A no-count that never did a right thing in his life*

no bargain *n phr* A person or thing that is not especially desirable or good; NO PRIZE PACKAGE : *Well, he's OK, but no bargain* [1940s+; fr Yiddish *nit ka metsie*]

nobby *adj* Stylish; fashionable; smart : *Polo shirts, nobby ties/ In 1903 Larkin picked up a nobby one-cylinder Winton* [1788+; fr *nob*]

no better than one ought to be *adj phr* Sexually promiscuous; loose *(1815+)*

no big deal *n phr* Nothing important; no problem : *I kept telling him that it wasn't any big deal*

no biggie *n phr* NO BIG DEAL *(1970s+ Teenagers)*

nobody, a *n* A person lacking fame, status, importance, etc; an uninteresting person; NEBBISH *(1581+)*

nobody home *modifier* : *Forrest Gump wears an expression of nobody's-home innocuousness throughout the picture sentence* This person is crazy, stupid, or feeble-minded; OUT TO LUNCH *(1919+)*

nobody likes a smart-ass (or **wise-ass**) *sentence* What you just said is very offensive; you are too smart and acid for your own good : *Nobody likes a minority smart-ass/ "And you will notice that I am not sweating." "No one loves a smartass" (1980s+)*

no bones *See* MAKE NO BONES ABOUT

no-brain *adj* Stupid; vapid : *The show was a loser right up to its no-brain ending (1980s+)*

no-brainer *modifier* : *Alden Essex is currently the undisputed king of no-brainer novels/ Lansing, with the help of no-brainer sequels such as Wayne's World 2 and Addams Family Values, has the studio back on track n* Something very simple, requiring no intelligence : *The question of which CAD program to buy is a no-brainer; Autodesk's AutoCAD dominates the market/ Passing it seemed like a no-brainer, but it failed (mid-1980s+)*

no can do *sentence* I am unable or unwilling to do that : *On that schedule? No can do* [1923+; a phrase in pidgin English probably adopted and disseminated by seamen; popularized in the 1940s by a song having the phrase as a title]

no-count *See* NO-ACCOUNT

nod *v* To be intoxicated with narcotics to a very drowsy or stuporous state : *with slews of rich kids nodding in the Scarsdale woods* [1960s+ Narcotics; the underlying sense, "let the head fall forward when drowsy," is found by 1562]

nod, a *n phr* A stuporous state following an injection of narcotics : *He goes on a "nod," his head drooping, eyelids heavy/ Here was Pimp in a nod (1960s+ Narcotics)*

nod, the, *n phr* The affirmative decision; the signal of choosing or preference; THUMBS UP : *Bold Ruler gets the nod over Gallant Man in today's renewal of the Carter Handicap (1920+ Sports) See* GET THE NOD

noddle *See* NOODLE

no dice *adj* Worthless; CRUMMY : *a little no-dice paper called the* Rome American *negation* No; absolutely not; NO SALE, no soap, NO WAY : *A Nuevo Laredo judge said no dice/ Nice, but no dice (1931+)* [fr the call of a crapshooter that the roll just made is not valid]

nod off *v phr* To fall asleep *(1845+)*

no earthly reason *n phr* No conceivable reason : *There's no earthly reason to keep this crap*

no end of (or **to**) *n phr* An never-ending resource; something that goes on and on : *no end to her nagging*

no flies on someone or something *n phr* Nothing impeding one's energy, awareness, soundness, up-to-dateness, etc : *There's no flies on Jersey. It's got more and better bookmakers* [1888+; fr the image of an active cow, horse, etc, on which *flies* cannot settle; the similar term *no flies about* is found in Australia by 1848]

no-frills *adj* Restricted to the essentials; without frivolous ornamentation or flourishes : *Imagine a no-frills warehouse crossed with an abattoir* (1960+)

noggin *n* The head : *the psychiatrist after diagnosing his noggin* [1866+; fr *noggin*, "mug," itself used for "face"] *See* MUG

no glove no love *modifier* Forbidding sex without a condom : *Female rappers have become front-line teachers of the "no glove, no love" school* (1990s+)

no-go *adj* Not ready to proceed; inauspicious; blocked : *This looks like a no-go situation* [1960s+; probably stimulated recently by astronauts' use] *See* GO NO-GO

no go *n phr* An unlikely success; a sure failure; an impossibility : *We tried to save him, but it was no go* (1825+)

no-good or **no-gooder** *adj* : *His father was a no-good drunk n* An unreliable or deplorable person; BUM, NO-ACCOUNT, NO-GOODNIK : *A high-living no-good in a derby hat (first form 1924+, second 1950s+)* [*no-good-boy* is found by 1908]

no-goodnik *n* NO-GOOD (1924+) *See* -NIK

no great shakes *adj phr* Mediocre; not outstanding; rather ineffective; NOTHING TO WRITE HOME ABOUT : *I'm no great shakes at serve-and-volley* [1819+; origin unknown]

no-hitter *n* A game in which at least one side gets no base hits *(1948+ Baseball)*

no holds barred *adj phr* : *The commission was to produce a "no-holds-barred" study adv phr* Free and uninhibited; with no limits or reservations : *They went at it no holds barred* (1940s+) [fr the rules of a wrestling match]

no-hoper *n* A person who has no hope of success : *Stand-ins are the film industry's no-hopers, the ones who never made it* [1957+; found in Australian racing slang by 1943 as "a horse with no hope of winning"]

nohow *adv* In no way; under no circumstances : *We tried, but couldn't manage to score nohow* (1775+)

noise *n* **1** Empty talk; meaningless verbiage; bluster : *That press release is plain noise* (1940s+) **2** Heroin *(1920s+ Narcotics) See* BIG NOISE, MAKE NOISES

no joke *n phr* A serious matter (1920+)

no kidding or **no joke** *adv phr* Really; factually • Often a question asked when one hears something astonishing or doubtful [first form 1914+, second 1880+; the earlier form *no kid* is found by 1873]

no more Mister Nice Guy *n phr* No longer a decent, fair, trustworthy, amiable, etc, person : *If I get the nomination, it'll be no more Mr. Nice Guy/ No More Mr. Nice Guy. Shevardnadze declares war on Georgia's rebels* (1970s+)

noncom (NAHN kahm) *n* A noncommissioned officer (1747+)

non compos *modifier* Not in control of the mind • Short for Latin *non compos mentis* (1628+)

no-neck *modifier* : *Andrew Giuliani, the executive moppet, strolled uninvited to the lectern, as uninhibited as one of Tennessee Williams's no-neck monsters n* A stupid, bigoted person; a brute; REDNECK : *the moral and intellectual sleaziness of the media and its no-necks in residence* (1970s+) [fr the thick, *neckless* aspect of very muscular men, gorillas, etc]

nonevent *n* **1** An apparent event staged or produced for or by the media **2** Something invalid; something that in effect did not happen : *"As a practical matter" the new rules are "a nonevent"* (1962+)

no never mind *See* MAKE NO NEVER MIND

no-no, a *n phr* Something forbidden; something very inadvisable : *The company says mustaches are a no-no/ allowing members to enjoy such former no-nos as corn on the cob* (1940s+)

noodge *See* NUDGE

noodle[1] *n* The head; the mind : *Most of the fellows running television today are sick in the noodle* (1914+) *v* **1** To play idly at an instrument; improvise lazily : *I noodled a bit on it and instantly realized I could express me/ Members of an avian orchestra are already softly noodling (1937+ Musicians)* **2** (also **noodle around**) To think, esp in a free and discursive way; indulge in mental play : *as many drafts and as much noodling as I wanted to/ still noodling around with our calculators and the latest census data* (1970s+) **3** To play; toy : *noodling nervously with a glass of water* (1970s+) [origin unknown; the "play around" senses perhaps influenced by *doodle*; *noddle* in the noun sense is found by 1579] *See* OFF one's NUT

noodle[2] *n* A stupid person; fool; simpleton • Still predominantly British : *Something that noodle at Interior might reflect on* [1753+; origin unknown; perhaps fr *noodle* the food, fr German *nudel*, because of its limp and wormlike connotations]

noogie (NOO gee, NOŎ-) *n* A painful rubbing of the scalp with the knuckles; DUTCH RUB :

Tomashek was probably the first challenger in heavyweight history whose most effective tactic was a noogie (1960s+ Teenagers) See TOUGH SHIT

◁**nookie** or **nookey** or **nooky**▷ (NŎŎK ee) *n* 1 Sexual activity; the sex act; ASS, COOZ : *a young kid tryin' to get his first nookey/ if you can't give her a little nooky* 2 A woman regarded as a sex partner; ASS, CUNT [1928+; origin unknown; perhaps fr Dutch *neuken*, "to fuck"]

no one loves a smartass See NOBODY LIKES A SMARTASS

nooner *n* A sex act done at midday : *putting a tax on anyone who checks into a motel for what is crudely called a "nooner"/ so she invited this boy here for a nooner (1980s+)*

nope *negation* No [1888+; fr *no* plus an intrusive stop resulting from the closure of the lips, rather than the glottis as is normal]

no picnic *n phr* A difficult or trying experience; a hard time or task : *While the ground crew didn't exactly have to carry me onto the plane kicking and screaming, it was no picnic/ It's no picnic, teaching people to play (1888+)*

no prize package or **no prize** *n phr* A person or thing of little worth, interest, charm; NO BARGAIN : *He's well qualified on paper, but no prize package (1940s+)*

no problem or **no prob** *interj* An assurance that everything is under control, that no difficulties are at hand in spite of appearances; NO SWEAT : *You'd like a red one? No problem (1963+)*

north *adv* In the direction of increase; upward : *A few months ago the cost of a 4-megabit memory chip was $11 on the spot market. Last week, it was $20 and heading north (1864+)*

north of *adj phr* More than; above : *Credit Lyonnais will probably pay Ovitz north of $30 million/ a good guess would be somewhere north of $5 million (1990s+)*

no sale *negation* No; absolutely not; NO DICE, no soap, NO WAY : *Sorry, Still No Sale; Assad still denied that terrorism had been discussed with the White House* [1934+; fr the sign that rose into the glass indexing window of a cash register when the *No Sale* key was punched]

nose *n* A police informer; STOOL PIGEON *(1830+ Underworld)* See BY A NOSE, HARD-NOSED, HAVE A BUG UP one's ASS, KEEP one's NOSE CLEAN, LOOK DOWN one's NOSE, NO SKIN OFF MY ASS, ON THE NOSE, PAY THROUGH THE NOSE, POKE one's NOSE INTO something, POWDER one's NOSE, PUT someone's NOSE OUT OF JOINT

nose around *v phr* To show strong inquisitiveness; investigate, esp closely and slyly; pry : *Why are you nosing around in my life in the first place? (1879+)*

nosebleed *modifier* : *Sitting next to Bob Ueker up there in Nosebleed Heaven/ I passed the evening of January 1 in the nosebleed section of the Louisiana Superdome watching Alabama claim the championship/ were forced to watch the show standing behind nosebleed seats in the balcony n* Putative nasal bleeding caused by high altitudes : *$50. This is the dreaded 400 section of Madison Square Garden. Short of flying on the Concorde, a seat here offers one of the most glamorous nosebleeds available anywhere (mid-1980s+ Sports)*

nose candy *n phr* A narcotic, esp cocaine, taken by sniffing : *a deck of nose candy for sale (1930s+ Narcotics)*

nosed See HARD-NOSED

nose dive *n phr* A sudden and large decrease : *The price of gold took a nose dive (1920+) v* : *Our morale nose-dived yesterday* [fr the precipitate descent of an airplane, found by 1912]

no see See LONG TIME NO SEE

no-see-um *n* Any tiny biting insect; midge; gnat [1847+; fr a presumed Indian term]

nose for news *n phr* Special ability and eagerness for learning news : *A good reporter has, first of all, a keen nose for news (1893+)*

nose job *n phr* Plastic surgery to beautify a nose; rhinoplasty (1963+)

nose someone out *v phr* To defeat by a small margin; barely win over; win by a nose : *He nosed out the leading candidate in Iowa (1940s+)*

nose out of joint See PUT someone's NOSE OUT OF JOINT

nosh or **nash** (NAHSH) *n* : *He always liked a little nosh between meals v* To have a snack; nibble : *noshing on more fruits and veggies* [1957+; fr Yiddish]

noshery *n* A restaurant or delicatessen, esp for snacking (1963+)

no shinola *interj* No shit. No kidding : *no shinola, gas prices are high*

◁**no shit**▷ *interj* Is that right; you wouldn't "shit" me, would you; NO KIDDING : *"No-o," said Gold with extravagant amazement, "shit"/ Uh, now, you mean? No shit (1940s+) modifier* Genuine; real; HONEST-TO-GOD : *the man from Santo Domingo, a no-shit revolutionary full of zeal*

◁**no shit, Sherlock**▷ *interj* No kidding. That is obvious

no-show *adj* Designating a nonexistent worker or job, usu on the public payroll : *a no-show job Sonny got him n* Someone or something that fails to keep an appointment, use a reserved seat, etc : *Snowstorm a no-show/ The airline figures about 20 percent no-shows (1941+)*

no siree or **no siree bob** *negation* No; absolutely no : *Nope, never, no way. No siree bob* (*first form 1848+, second 1890+*)

◁**no skin off my ass**▷ *adj phr* (Variations: **butt** or **ear** or **nose** may replace **ass**) Of no concern, esp damaging concern, to me; immaterial : *And if you fall on your face, no skin off my nose* (*entry form 1920+, nose 1909+*)

no slouch *adj phr* Very able or competent; skilled • Often followed by *at* something : *She's no slouch at finding good restaurants/ When it comes to golf he is definitely no slouch* [1796+; fr British dialect *slouch*, "awkward, lazy person," found by 1515]

no spring chicken *modifier* No longer young • Often said of a woman : *She looks great, but she's no spring chicken* (*1910+*)

no strings attached *adj phr* Free of conditions, limitations, etc : *He's giving us the house with no strings attached* [1940s+; fr *string*, "a restriction," found by 1888; the similar form "no strings to something" is found by 1909]

no sweat *n phr* No problem or difficulty; an easy thing : *No sweat, though!/ It was no sweat for me* (*1950s+*)

nosy or **nosey** *adj* Inquisitive, esp overly so; prying : *Everyone on the staff must be super nosy/ We shall not be nosey* (*1882+*)

nosy parker or **nosey parker** *n phr* A nosy, overly inquisitive person • Sometimes capitalized [1907; picture postcard caption referring to a peeping Tom in Hyde Park]

not *negation* What has just been stated is emphatically not true : *Millions of animals in experimental labs die annually. Shock value? NOT!/ Hooray for Pat Buchanan, not!/ Dan Quayle has already filmed a commercial declaring Murphy Brown his favorite show ... "not"* (*1990s+*)

not a (or **snowball's**) **chance** (**in hell**) *interj* No

not a dime's worth of difference *n phr* Hardly any difference : *There's not a dime's worth of difference between the candidates on health care* (*1990s+*)

not all beer and skittles *adj phr* (also not all skittles and beer) Not entirely pleasant or easy; not a picnic, cinch, piece of cake, etc [1857+; fr *skittles*, a bowling game played in taverns and pubs; Dickens used the form *all porter and skittles* in 1837]

not all there *adj phr* **1** Stupid; feeble-minded : *The poor creature who's not quite all there* **2** Crazy; eccentric; NUTS, OUT TO LUNCH (*1864+*)

not bat an eye *v phr* To not show surprise, reluctance, etc : *"I'm leaving," she said. He didn't bat an eye* (*1904+*)

not be caught dead *v phr* To be defiantly set against; be extremely reluctantly found or

seen : *I wouldn't be caught dead in that dress* (*1940s+*)

not (or **barely**) **break a sweat** *v phr* To do something very easily; be entirely nonchalant; not turn a hair : *The touring Soviet squad barely broke a sweat in the 6–2 victory over the Badgers* (*1970s+ Prizefighting*)

not buttoned up too tightly *adj phr* Feeble-minded; eccentric; NOT ALL THERE, NOT WRAPPED TIGHT : *a nice old gentleman, but not buttoned-up too tightly, as you've noticed* (*1980s+*)

not by a long shot *adv phr* Not at all; emphatically not : *It's not my best work, not by a long shot* (*1861+*)

not carved (or **etched**) **in stone** *adj phr* (also **not cast in concrete**) Not having ultimate and permanent authority; able to be altered : *It's a good policy, but it's neither carved in stone nor set in concrete* [1970s+; fr the *carved stone* tablets of the Decalogue]

notch *v* **1** To score; achieve : *a pacy serve that's notched a few aces in its time* (*1623+*) ◁**2**▷ To do the sex act • Use attributed to volleyball players : *Guys don't fuck, they notch* (*1970s+*) [first sense fr use of the term in cricket, and influenced by the cowboy tradition of filing a *notch* in the handle of one's pistol for each man killed] See TOP-NOTCH

notch baby *n phr* A person born between 1917 and 1921, and who is said to receive less of Social Security benefits thereby (*mid-1980s+*)

not count for spit *v phr* To be very insignificant; be trivial : *An aptitude for speaking amusingly doesn't count for spit* [1980s+; *spit* is a euphemism for *shit*; *count*, "to be of importance," is found by 1857]

note *See* BLUE NOTE, C-NOTE, a HELL OF A NOTE, MASH NOTE

not enough Indians *See* TOO MANY CHIEFS AND NOT ENOUGH INDIANS

not even *interj* An exclamation of disagreement or disapproval : *You think I will give him money? Not even*

◁**not get one's balls** (or **bowels**) **in an uproar**▷ *v phr* To avoid becoming excited or upset; stay calm; COOL IT • Often an attempt to soothe someone : *Come on! Don't get your feminist balls in an uproar* (*1930s+*)

not get one's knickers in a twist *v phr* To avoid becoming tense and upset (*1971+ British*)

not get one's shorts in a knot *v phr* To avoid becoming upset or stressed : *Don't get your shorts in a knot, it's only a suggestion* (*1990s+*)

◁**not get one's testicles in a twist**▷ *v phr* To avoid becoming tense and upset; NOT GET one's KNICKERS IN A TWIST : *I'm coming,*

Mr. McAllister! Don't get your testicles in a twist! (1990s+)

not give a damn *v phr* (Variations: **dang** or **darn** or **dern** or **durn** or **diddly-damn** or **diddly-shit** or ◀**flying fuck**▶ or ◀**fuck**▶ or **hill of beans** or **hoot** or **piss** or ◁**rat's ass**▷ or **rat's behind** or **rat's rump** or **rip** or ◁**shit**▷ or **spit** or **squat** or **two hoots in hell** may replace **damn**) To be indifferent to or contemptuous of; not care one whit : *I don't give a damn what they do to me/ Nobody gave a flying fuck who their influences were/ When do celebrities give a hoot about people who interview them?/ We all busted up because George didn't give a rat's ass/ The average American child does not give a rip about O J Simpson/ Me, I don't give a shit, high road, low road, I go either way/ Anyway, who gives a fuck, actually? (entry form 1895+, fuck 1929+, hill of beans 1863+, hoot 1878+, rip 1940s+)*

not give someone the time of day *v phr* Not do the slightest favor for; not greet or speak to; have contempt for : *Like him? I wouldn't give that bastard the time of day* [1593+; the dated instance, from Shakespeare, is not in the negative]

not have a clue *v phr* To be uninformed or ignorant about something; be "clueless" : *"You know who I was?" "Haven't got a clue" (WWII British armed forces)*

not have a leg to stand on *v phr* To lack support for one's position, arguments, etc : *My lawyer told me I didn't have a leg to stand on, so I shouldn't sue the company (1594+)*

◁**not have a pot (or without a pot) to piss in**▷ *v phr* To be very poor and deprived; be penniless : *entering their middle years without a pot to piss in (1930s+)*

not have a prayer *See* HAVE A PRAYER

not have brain one *v phr* To be very stupid *(1960s+)*

not have brains enough to walk and chew gum at the same time *v phr* To be lacking the most elementary intelligence *(1960s+)*

not have the foggiest notion (or the foggiest) *v phr* To be entirely ignorant and uncertain : *I didn't have the foggiest notion what "the right thing" was (1917+ British)*

not having any *v phr* To refuse to accept; reject; ignore : *Home buyers weren't having any and more than a few developers went belly-up (1903+)*

nothing *adj* Inane; lacking charm, talent, interest, etc; worthless : *That was a real nothing experience (1950s+) See* DO someone NOTHING, KNOW FROM NOTHING

nothing, a *n phr* Someone or something that lacks all talent, charm, qualities, etc; NEBBISH : *This show's a total nothing (1950s+)*

nothing doing *n phr* A lack of activity; stasis : *Nothing doing on the job front (1827+)* **negation** No; absolutely not; NIX, NO WAY : *Buy that piece of crap? Nothing doing (1910+)*

nothing flat *See* IN NOTHING FLAT

nothing to it *interj* That is easy

nothing to sneeze at (or about) *n* Something of consequence, like an amount of money : *her raise, nothing to sneeze about*

nothing to write home about *n phr* A very ordinary or mediocre person or thing; nothing special; NO GREAT SHAKES : *His pitch was nothing to write home about (1914+)*

not in my backyard or **NIMBY** *interj* It is not ok with me that something is here where I live or exist

not in my book *adv phr* Not in my opinion; not according to my beliefs : *type of behavior is not ok in my book*

not just another pretty face *n phr* Not someone or something of no particular distinction; not a specious person or thing : *He had a time convincing them he was a genuine expert, not just another pretty face* [1970s+; fr the plight of a young woman, esp in popular fiction or film, who has intelligence, talent, etc, but fears she is being treated by males as only an ordinary sex object]

not just whistling Dixie *v phr* To be saying something important or useful : *When they warned us about this they weren't just whistling Dixie See* WHISTLE DIXIE

◁**not know one's ass from one's elbow**▷ *v phr* (Variations: **a hole in the ground** or **third base** may replace one's **elbow**) To be very ignorant; be hopelessly ill informed; be stupid; KNOW FROM NOTHING : *Well, he obviously didn't know his ass from a hole in the ground/ He doesn't know his ass from third base (1930+)*

not know beans *v phr* (Variations: **diddly** or **diddley** or **diddly-damn** or **diddly-poo** or **diddly-poop** or **diddly-shit** or **diddly-squat** or **diddly-squirt** or **diddly-whoop** or **shit** or **squat** or **zilch** or **zip** may replace **beans**) To be very ignorant; not know even the fundamentals ● In each case the positive and negative idiom have the same meaning : *You don't know beans, do you?/ may have been England's greatest mathematical puzzle inventor, but he knew beans about spiders and flies* [1833+; entry form fr an old joke question, found by 1830, "How many blue beans make five white?"]

not know enough to come in out of the rain *v phr* To be quite stupid, esp in practical matters : *Ross thought that people with talent didn't in general know enough to come in out of the rain* [1884+; the positive form is found by 1599]

not know someone **from Adam** *v phr* (also **Adam's off ox** or **from Adam's house cat**) To be entirely unacquainted with or uncognizant of : *We're bigger than 90 percent of the companies on the Big Board, but nobody knows us from Adam/ I didn't know from Adam's house cat who Nolan Ryan was* (entry form *1843+, ox 1890+, cat 1908+*)

not know from nothing *See* KNOW FROM NOTHING

not know something **if it bit** someone *v phr* To be quite ignorant and unperceptive : *Kuttner wouldn't know a strategic trade policy if it bit him on the leg* (*1990s+*)

◁**not know shit from Shinola**▷ *v phr* NOT KNOW one's ASS FROM one's ELBOW • Often euphemized : *a tightfisted banker who doesn't know what from Shinola/ In high school I didn't know shoot from Shinola* [1930+; fr *Shinola*™, a brand of shoe polish; used partly for a suggestion of brown color, mainly for alliteration]

not lay a glove (or **finger** or **hand**) **on** someone *v phr* To leave unscathed; fail to hurt : *To this point, they haven't laid a glove on him* (*1940s+ Prizefighting*)

not make deals *v phr* To refuse to operate by or tolerate clandestine or unethical arrangements : *I don't make deals, especially not with crooks* (*1960s+*)

not (**so**) **much** *interj* No : *Did you like the movie? ... Not so much*

not much to look at *adj phr* Unattractive (*1861+*)

no tomorrow *See* LIKE IT'S GOING OUT OF STYLE

not on your life *negation* No; absolutely not; NOTHING DOING, NO WAY : *Drink that? Not on your life* (*1896+*)

not play for someone *v phr* To be unappealing or unconvincing for one : *I like the idea, but it may not play for you* (*1990s+*)

not put it past someone *v phr* To believe someone capable of an indicated act, opinion, etc : *I wouldn't put it past you to believe such hogwash* (*1870+*)

not say boo *v phr* To keep silent; not respond : *He didn't say boo when I called him a thief* [1940s+; perhaps fr earlier *not say boo to a goose*, "to be afraid or too timid to speak"]

not so hot *adj phr* Not very good; mediocre; poor : *I didn't flunk, but my record isn't so hot* [1926+ Teenagers; the form *not so warm* is found by 1900]

not to be sneezed at *adj phr* Not to be underrated; of considerable value : *It's not a big salary, but still not to be sneezed at* (*1813+*)

not too shabby *adj phr* Quite good; highly acceptable : *The Angels train in Palm Springs, California, which isn't too shabby* (*1980s+*)

not touch someone or something **with a ten-foot pole** *v phr* To be loath to have anything to do with; be suspicious or apprehensive; reject : *If I were you I wouldn't touch that proposition with a ten-foot pole* [1909+; semantically akin to the proverb advising us to use a long spoon when we eat with the devil; an earlier and once more common version spoke of a *forty-foot pole*]

not to worry *sentence* There is nothing to worry about : *Not to worry, I bought plenty of food for everybody* (*1958+*)

not what it or something **is cracked up to be** *adj phr* Of low quality; inferior or unsatisfactory (*1836+*)

not worth a damn (or **a shit**) *adj phr* : *Those promises aren't worth a damn* *adv phr* Not well at all : *This guy doesn't sing worth a damn/ She doesn't like me worth a shit* (first form *1817+, second 1920s+*)

not worth a hill of beans *adj phr* Worthless; useless (*1863+*)

not worth a plugged nickel *adj phr* Valueless : *His word isn't worth a plugged nickel* [1940s+; a *plugged* coin was counterfeit or had an insertion of inferior metal]

no two ways about it *adv phr* Clearly; definitely; sure as shit : *No two ways about it, this guy is nuts* (*1818+*)

not wrapped tight *adj phr* Crazy; eccentric; NOT ALL THERE, NOT BUTTONED UP TOO TIGHTLY : *Your father was not wrapped real tight. His loaf was missing several slices/ Some MEs, who weren't wrapped too tightly to begin with* [1968+; fr the image of something *wrapped* neatly without loose ends, spillage, etc]

now *adj* Up-to-date; very much au courant; thoroughly modern : *tripping out on now words/ the Right On, Now Generation* (*1967+*)

no way or **no way, Jose** or **no way in hell** *adv phr* Never; under no circumstances : *No way will I resign. You'll have to fire me negation* No; absolutely not; NO DICE : *No good. No go. No way, Jose/ You absolutely no way in hell can use my name* (*1960s+*) *See* THERE'S NO WAY

no way to run a railroad *See* a HELL OF A WAY TO RUN A RAILROAD

now generation *n* People who want instant gratification becoming more prevalent in late 20th century and 21st century : *Baby Boomers as the first Now Generation*

nowhere or **nowheresville** *adj* Inferior; tedious; drab : *If you're not with it, you're nowhere/ rows of folding chairs, nowheresville decor* (*1940+*) *See* the MIDDLE OF NOWHERE

no-win *adj* Impossible to win; hopeless : *This tax business is a no-win situation/ Furious Volley in a No-Win Match*

nudge (NŎŎJ, NŎŎD jə) (also **noodge** or **nudjh** or **nudgy** or **nudzh**) *n* A chronic nagger, kibitzer, or complainer : *He's not a writer, he's a nudge/ not as an assassin, but as a nudge and a nerd* (1960s+) *v* : *Usually he comes up to nudgy me while I'm writing/ and oh nudjh, could he nudjh!* [fr Yiddish fr Slavic "fret, dully ache"; perhaps influenced by English *nudge*]

nudge elbows *See* RUB ELBOWS

nudging *See* MOTHERFUCKING

nudie *modifier* : *I bought a couple of nudie magazines n* **1** A movie, play, etc, in which players appear naked **2** A nude or nearly nude female performer : *some of the worried little nudies* **3** A magazine, book, etc, featuring pictures of nudes; SKIN MAGAZINE (1935+)

nudnik (NŎŎD nihk) *n* An annoying person; pest; nuisance; NUDGE : *the story of a gang of nudniks trying to defeat the establishment/ remains an unreconstructed nudnik throughout* [fr Yiddish *nudne*, "boring"] *See* -NIK

nuff said *sentence* Enough has been said; that closes the topic : *I will not go, never. Nuff said* (1841+)

nuggets *n* The testicles

nuke *n* A nuclear device or facility; nuclear weapon; nuclear power plant (1959+) *v* **1** To destroy with a nuclear weapon or weapons : *The global village has been nuked* (1969+) **2** To destroy; eliminate; KILL : *Jesus Christ, I can nuke this guy/ Nuke this whole paragraph* (1986+) **3** To cook or heat in a microwave oven (1987+)

nuke oneself *v phr* To go to a tanning salon (1980s+ Students)

nuker *n* A microwave oven : *popcorn in the nuker*

numb *adj* Stupid; unresponsive (1950s+)

numb-brained *adj* Stupid; dull-witted : *recruits from the numb-brained hanger-on* (1930+)

number *n* **1** A person, esp one considered to be clever and resourceful or attractive; ARTICLE, HOT NUMBER • Always preceded by an adjective or by the locution "quite a" : *some dizzy broad that must have been a snappy number/ bored-looking number* (1919+) **2** A piece of merchandise, esp of clothing; ARTICLE : *I found a number I liked pretty well* (1894+) **3** A theatrical act or routine, esp a song; SHTICK : *He does that number with the tablecloth* (1885+ Show business) **4** A tactic or trick; ACT : *When he's pulling one of his numbers, he knows what he's doing* (1970s+) **5** A casual homosexual partner; TRICK (Homosexuals) **6** A marijuana cigarette : *smoked a couple of numbers in the room* (1960s+ Narcotics) [merchandise sense fr the model *number* that most retail items have] *See* BACK

NUMBER, BY THE NUMBERS, DO A NUMBER ON, DO one's NUMBER, HAVE someone's NUMBER, HOT NUMBER

number, a *n phr* Something noted, esp a sexual relationship; an ITEM : *Hey, we're a number. We have a non-casual relationship now* (1980s+)

number cruncher *adj* Requiring mathematics, statistics, etc : *number-cruncher course n phr* **1** A computer or mechanical calculator (1966+) **2** (also **numbers cruncher**) One who regularly processes or works with figures, statistics, records, etc, esp with a computer : *As a veteran numbers cruncher, I find that good research often raises more questions than it answers/ promote clerks rather than bring in fancy number-crunchers from outside* (1971+)

number-crunching *n* Doing serious and difficult mathematics by computer : *played chartered accountant for a few sessions of number crunching* (1980s+ Computer)

number is up, someone's *sentence* One is dead or about to die : *I'm glad we never know when our number is up until it's up* (1899+)

Number One or **number one** *n phr* **1** One's own self, esp as competitive with others; NUMERO UNO : *Always look out for Number One, he says* (1704+) **2** Urination (1902+) *v* : *The little kid had to number one real bad*

numbers *n* A player's averages, statistics, etc; STATS : *I've always thought numbers were a hill of beans. The only numbers that matter are wins and losses (Sports) See* BY THE NUMBERS

numbers, the *n phr* An illegal gambling game in which players bet that a certain number will appear somewhere; the policy racket : *Poor people lose a lot playing the numbers* (1897+)

number two *n phr* Defecation (1902+) *v phr* : *He ran off into the woods, having to number two*

◁**numb-nuts**▷ *modifier* : *not the numbnuts chatter cornballs like Bob Hope or Yellowman peddle n* A despicable person; JERK, LIMPDICK : *You gotta get a better job, numb-nuts* (1960s+)

Numero Uno or **numero uno** *n phr* **1** One's own self, esp as the object of one's best efforts; NUMBER ONE **2** The chief; leader; BOSS, HONCHO : *a clear understanding between the brothers about who is Numero Uno* **3** The most distinguished person in a field or endeavor : *now an also-ran, but for many years Numero Uno* [1883+; fr Italian or Spanish]

nurse *v* **1** To consume one's drink slowly : *He ordered a highball and nursed it all evening* (1942+) **2** To handle or drive slowly and carefully : *I nursed it away from the curb and went out Main Street* (1980s+)

nut *n* **1** The head (*1846+*) **2** A crazy or eccentric person; maniac; FLAKE, SCREWBALL : *It is forbidden to call any character a nut; you have to call him a screwball* (*1903+*) **3** A very devoted enthusiast; BUG, FREAK : *He's a nut about double crostics* (*1934+*) **4** The investment needed for a business; capital and fixed expenses : *producing a daily income that barely met the nut/ Our nut is high, but our variable expenses are practically nothing* (*1912+*) **5** Any illegal payoff to a police officer : *what they called "the nut," payoffs to the police* (*1960s+ Underworld*) **6** A share in the graft collected by police officers (*1960s+ Underworld*) ◁7▷ A testicle; BALL : *He said it griped his left nut* (*1899+*) [insanity sense probably fr late 1800s *off* one's *nut*, that is, head; senses 4, 5, and 6 fr the custom of taking the retaining *nut* from the wheel of a circus wagon, to be returned when all bills were paid] *See* GRIPE one's ASS, OFF one's NUT, TOUGH NUT, a TOUGH NUT TO CRACK

-nut *combining word* A devotee or energetic practitioner of what is indicated; buff, FREAK : *when one football nut writes a book/ But he's not just a word nut* (*1930s+*)

nutball (Variations: **bar** or **cake** or **case** may replace **ball**) *adj* : *murdered by nutball moneybags Harry K Thaw/ Use the nutbar examples we've provided here/ not such a nutcake question n* A crazy or eccentric person; NUT : *A lot of nutballs accost you at that corner/ The Protestants in Ireland also have their share of nutcakes/ I'm not a nut case* (entry form, bar, and cake 1970s+, case 1950+)

nut-crunching *n* The sapping or destruction of masculinity; figurative castration; BALL-BUSTING : *Adrienne Barbeau, playing a government investigator whose best defense is nut-crunching* (*1970s+*)

nuthouse *n* (Variations: **box** or **college** or **factory** or **foundry** or **hatch** may replace **house**) A mental hospital; insane asylum : *He has been recalled by the nut college/ goes away to the nut house/ exceptional privacy and independence even in a nut hatch/ a general air of having been redecorated by a parolee from a nut hatch* (entry form 1920s+, box 1960s+, college 1934+, factory 1915+, foundry 1932+, hatch 1940s+)

nuts or **nerts** or **nertz** or **nurts** or **nutz** *adj* Crazy; very eccentric; bughouse, MESHUGA : *Are you nuts to turn your back on a deal that could mean life or death?/ Heir Rejected 400G, Is He Nuts?* (first form 1914+, second 1932+) *interj* An exclamation of disbelief, defiance, contempt, dismay, etc : *General McAuliffe replied "Nuts!" to the Germans at Bastogne* (*1931+*) *n* ◁1▷ The testicles; BALLS, FAMILY JEWELS : *They want to get their nuts out of the sand* (*1899+*) **2** Nonsense *See* BUST one's ASS, the CAT'S MEOW, GET one's NUTS, HOT ROCKS, NUMB-NUTS

nuts, the, or the **nerts** or the **nertz** *n phr* The very best; the GREATEST : *eulogizing anything as "the nuts"* [first form 1932+, second 1934+; probably a shortening of *the cat's nuts*] *See* the CAT'S MEOW

nuts about (or **over** or **on**) *adj phr* (Variations: **nutty** may replace **nuts**) Very enthusiastic about; devoted to; CRAZY ABOUT : *I think I'm nuts about you/ I'd be simply nutty about the quadrangles at Oxford* [1918+; fr British slang *nutty,* "piquant, fascinating," fr earlier sense "rich, tasty, desirable, like the kernel of a delicious nut," altered in slang to *nuts* and originally in the phrase *nuts upon,* found by 1785; the US form *nuts about* may be based on all this or on the notion *crazy about,* and probably on both]

nuts and bolts *modifier* : *Berger's nuts-and-bolts discussion of film-TV music n phr* The fundamentals; the practical basics : *the nuts and bolts of wildland preservation/ men who are dealing with the nuts and bolts of negotiations* (*1960+*)

nutshell *v* To condense; sum up : *If I'm forced to nutshell it, the show is about community, it's about the workplace and the town* [1883+; fr the idiom *put something in a nutshell*]

nutso or **nutsy** *adj* Crazy; NUTTY : *I have to keep up with 29 (mostly nutso) ballot initiatives/ drove each other nutsy with crashing self-confidence* (first form 1975+, second 1923+)

nutsville *adj* crazy : *This city is nutsville* (*1980s+*)

nutter *n* A crazy person; NUT, NUTBALL : *the Zodiac killer or some nutter on the loose/ Mick Jagger says there will always be the nutters* [1958+; a British coinage and still chiefly British; perhaps influenced by *Nutter,* trademark name of a butter made from nuts, found by 1906]

nuttiness *n* Craziness; insanity; GOOFINESS : *Booth's capacity for nuttiness became a legend* (*1916+*)

nutty *adj* Crazy; very eccentric; NUTS : *I was just about nutty, I was so lonely* (*1898+*) *See* SLUG-NUTTY

nutty as a fruitcake *adj phr* Crazy as can be; extremely eccentric : *"That's me," Calazo said. "Nutty as a fruitcake"* (*1935+*)

nut up *v phr* To go crazy; GO APE : *He'll just about nut up when you tell him that* (*1970s+ College students*)

nympho *n* A nymphomaniac : *no boozing broad, no nympho, no psycho, no bitch* (*1935+*)

O

-o *suffix used to form adjectives* **1** Having the indicated characteristics : *berserko/ luxo/ neato/ sicko/ wrongo* **suffix used to form nouns 2** : *foldo/ freako/ klutzo/ muso* • This fanciful formation is increasingly current [1960s+; fr a humorous imitation of Spanish or Italian words, more probably Spanish because of the similar *el -o* pattern of coinage] *See* FIVE-O, FOUR-O

oak *See* OK

obit (OH bit) *modifier* : *This is not the obit page n* An obituary, esp in a newspaper : *getting left out of the pious obits in* The Times (*1874+*)

OD (pronounced as separate letters) *n* An overdose of narcotics : *I guess he'd taken a light OD v* **1** : *met Jesus one day when I was ODing on speed in my room* **2** To overindulge in or on anything : *Viewers may have OD'd on athletics and turned to reruns* (*1960s+ Narcotics & medical*)

oddball *adj* **1** Strange; weird : *sensible drug users and the odd-ball drug users* **2** Nonconformist : *He had some pretty oddball ideas n* **1** An eccentric person; a strange one; WEIRDO : *This little guy, opinionated, emotional, sensitive, was definitely an oddball/ This weird guy, this oddball with his long neck and his funny talk* **2** A nonconformist; outsider; odd man out : *We were generally considered to be a family of hopeless oddballs* (*1940s+*)

odd bod *n* **1** An eccentric, strange person (*1955+*) **2** A person with an odd body; also, a strange body : *tough to find jeans for my odd bod*

odd couple *n phr* Two people who seem unlikely as partners, mates, etc : *The odd couple, Gen. Humberto Ortega and President Violeta Barrios de Chamorro of Nicaragua, have arrived at a working relationship* [1965+; fr the title of a 1965 Neil Simon play]

odd man out *n phr* Someone who is not included in a game, arrangement, business deal, etc : *United Artists seemed the odd man out in Transamerica's financial services game* (*1889+*)

odds and ends *n phr* A miscellany of leftovers, outsizes, scraps, unmatched bits, etc (*mid-1700s+*)

odds-on *adj* Favorable; sure to win : *This one's so successful the odds-on betting was it'd never burn down* (*1898+ Gambling*)

of (uhv) *v* Have • In verb constructions, used for humorous or dialect effect : *I must of gone crazy or something* (*1844+*)

◁**ofay**▷ *modifier* : *ofay business men and planters n* A white person; FAY. Gray : *Let the ofays have Wall Street to themselves/ a white boy, an ofay* (*1917+ Black*) [probably fr pig Latin for *foe*]

off *adj* **1** Not performing well; : *Perot had an off-night* (*1846+*) **2** Spoiled; not fresh : *the milk's a bit off* (*1896+*) **3** Eccentric; abnormal; WEIRD : *That girl is off* (*1866+*) **4** Canceled; not going to happen : *Let's call the whole thing off/ The deal's off* (*1882+*) **5** Not working; not engaged : *The cook is off today* (*1861+*) *prep* Not using; no longer addicted to : *She's off H now/ I've been off the sauce for four years* (*1930s+ Narcotics*) *v* **1** To kill or destroy; WASTE : *ordered him to mess up a couple of guys, but instead he offed them/ We'll off any pig who attacks us* (*1930+*) ◁**2**▷ To do the sex act with or to; SCREW : *When I off a nigger bitch, I close my eyes and concentrate real hard* (*1950s+ Black*)

off and running *adj phr* Started and making good headway : *by hitting one of his rare home runs, and I thought we were off and running* [1960s+ Horse racing; *they're off!* to signal the start of a race is found by 1833]

off one's ass *adv phr* Extremely; TO THE MAX : *My roommate was wasted off his ass by the time the party was over, and I had to carry him to bed* (*1980s+ Students*)

off at the knees *See* CUT ONESELF OFF AT THE KNEES

off base *adj phr* **1** By surprise; unawares : *The lawyer tried to catch him off base with some unexpected questions* (*1936+ fr baseball*) **2** Not appropriate; uncalled for : *Some of his questions were way off base* **3** Presumptuous; impudent; OUT OF LINE : *When I asked for her number she said I was off base* (*1950s+*) **4** Incorrect; inaccurate : *These stats are a mile off base* (*1947+*)

offbeat *adj* Unusual; unconventional; strange : *the off-beat death in an off-Broadway hotel/ its offbeat ad seeking 10 Renaissance-type men* [1935+; fr the interruption of a regular rhythm in music]

off one's block (or nut) *adv phr* **1** Crazy : *off your nut to go mountain biking* **2** Intoxicated by alcohol

off someone's case *See* GET OFF someone's CASE

off color *adj phr* Somewhat salacious; risqué; BLUE : *a couple of off-color jokes/ Some of his observations were a bit off color* (*1875+*)

offer *See* MAKE AN OFFER one CAN'T REFUSE

office *n* The cockpit of an airplane (*1917+ Aviators*) *See* FRONT OFFICE

off one's noodle (or gourd or onion or rocker) *adj phr* Crazy; deluded; MESHUGA, NUTS : *I've been as near off my noodle as a sane*

351

man can get/ I suppose he was off his rocker (*entry form* 1945+, *onion* 1890+, *rocker* 1897+)

off one's **plate** *adv phr* No longer a matter of one's responsibility and concern : *Congress would like to get the abortion issue off its plate* (1980s+)

off-putting *adj* Distressing; unsettling; discomfiting : *Nor do I find pubic hair ugly or off-putting/ an off-putting chip on the shoulder* (1828+)

off-road *modifier* : *This baby is an off-road, all-terrain vehicle* v To drive in deserts, mountains, forests, beaches, etc, away from roads : *People with a little too much enthusiasm for nocturnal off-roading were a problem for the Santa Monica Mountains Conservancy* (1990s+)

off the bat *See* RIGHT OFF THE BAT

off the beam *adv phr* Distant from truth or accuracy; in error : *That idea is way off the beam* [1940s+; fr the radio *beam* that guides aircraft to an airport or runway]

off the charts *adj phr* Too great to be measured; off the scale : *His popularity, high before, is now way off the charts* [1980s+; fr the published *charts* that show the best-selling musical records and albums]

off the cuff *adj* : *a good off-the-cuff talker adv phr* Extemporaneously; without rehearsal : *I don't speak well off the cuff* (1938+) [fr the notion of speaking from notes made on one's shirt *cuff*]

off the deep end *See* GO OFF THE DEEP END, JUMP OFF THE DEEP END

off the grid *adv phr* Not using or requiring utilities such as electricity, water, etc : *living off the grid in Maine* (1991+)

off the ground *adj phr* Started; in operation; OFF AND RUNNING : *We have to decide how to get the project off the ground* [1970s+; fr the putative conversation of airline pilots at takeoff: "Let's see if we can get this thing *off the ground*"]

off the hog *See* EAT HIGH ON THE HOG

off the hook *adj phr* Free of responsibility, blame, punishment, etc; CLEAR : *Shagan gets Harry off the hook/ In brief, parents are off the hook* (1954+) *See* LET someone OFF THE HOOK, RING OFF THE HOOK

off the pace *adv phr* Behind the leader or leaders : *The red car is about two laps off the pace* (1951+)

off-the-rack *adj* Mass-produced or ready-made; not tailored or specially designed : *Buying an off-the-rack reno is expensive and not very adventurous* (1963+)

off the record *adv phr* Confidential; not for publication or attribution : *The mayor would only speak off the record, and very cryptically at that* (1933+)

off-the-shelf *modifier* Readily available from retail sources; not customized : *a drastically scaled-down program that involves purchasing off-the-shelf computer software* (1936+)

off the top *adv phr* Before any deductions are made; UP FRONT : *He demanded his percentage right off the top* (1970s+)

off the top of one's **head** *adv phr* Without thought or calculation; impromptu : *I can't give you the figure off the top of my head, but it's around, say, 500* (1939+)

off the wagon (or **water wagon**) *adj phr* Drinking liquor after a period of abstinence : *Like the bartenders, they fall off the wagon* (1904+) *See* FALL OFF THE WAGON

off the wall *adj phr* **1** Unusual; outrageous; ODDBALL, OFFBEAT : *his off-the-wall sense of humor/ the totally off-the-wall absurdity of existence* (1968+) **2** Crazy; very eccentric; OFF one's NOODLE : *Mrs Morea was "very, very distraught, really incoherent, off the wall"/ They're describing him as "off the wall"* [probably fr the medical term *bounce off the walls*, referring to the behavior of a psychotic patient] *See* BOUNCE OFF THE WALLS

oh-so- *adv* Very; extremely; WAY : *Patriotism provides an oh-so-convenient way to confuse the higher ideals it announces with the narrow interests it claims to transcend/ The administration's bank regulators are moving oh-so-slowly in seizing insolvent banks*

oh yeah *interj* An exclamation of defiance or disbelief; izzatso : *I told her I'd make her a star, and she said, "Oh yeah?"* (1930+)

-oid *suffix used to form adjectives* Resembling or imitating what is indicated : *blitzoid/ cheesoid/ technoid/ zomboid suffix used to form nouns* Something resembling or imitating what is indicated : *flakoid/ fusionoid/ Grouchoid/ klutzoid* • This suffix is increasingly current, probably because of the popularity of fantasy and science fiction, esp among teenagers [fr the scientific suffix *-oid*, fr Greek *-oeides*, ultimately fr *eidos*, "image, form"; dictionaries list over 1,800 *-oid* compounds, most of which date from the 1700s and 1800s]

oiled *adj* Drunk : *Choose your companions, and get properly oiled as well* (1737+) *See* WELL OILED

oil someone's **palm** *See* GREASE someone's PALM

oily *adj* Cunning and ingratiating; sly and unctuous : *his perfect-pitch portrayal of Artie, the oily producer of* The Larry Sanders Show (1879+)

oink out *v phr* To overeat; pig out : *oinking out on Peeps*

OK (also **ok** or **okay** or **oka** or **okeh** or **okey** or **oak** or **oke**) *adj* **1** Agreeable; COPACETIC : *He made an OK decision* **2** Acceptable but not excellent; satisfactory : *The play's okay, but I still prefer the book* **3** Good; excellent : *He had worked with Sergeant Boone before and knew he was an okay guy* **adv** Right; that's understood, let's get on : *So I told you about that, okay, so the next thing was he jumped the fence* **affirmation** Yes; I agree; I accept that; I will do that **affirmation** or **question** Is that all right? is that understood? COPPISH : *I'm going now, okay?* [1839+; origin uncertain and the subject of essay after essay; Allen Walker Read is the great authority and has shown that the locution began as a bumpkin-imitating game among New York and Boston writers in the early 1800s, who used *OK* for "oll korrect"]

okey-doke *affirmation* or *question* (also **hokey-dokey** or **okie-doke** or **okey-dokey** or **okie-dokie** or **okle-dokle**) Yes, satisfactory, alright, etc; OK : *Suppose I pick you up at seven? Okie doke* (1932+ Students)

◁**Okie**▷ *n* **1** A migratory worker, esp one in the 1930s who had to leave home because of dust storms; arky **2** A native or resident of Oklahoma; SOONER (1935+)

-ola or **-olo** *suffix used to form nouns* An emphatic instance or humorous version of what is indicated : *buckola/ crapola/ schnozzola* [1940s+; probably modeled on *Pianola*® and *Victrola*®, both found by 1905; *-ola* compounds proliferated after the Charles Van Doren *payola* scandal of 1959; *-ola* compounds, numbering about 40, offer no real semantic core]

old *adj* Good; dear; well-liked : *What's old Donald up to now?* (1598+) *See* ANY OLD

old army game, the *See* the ARMY GAME

old bag or **old bat** *n phr* An old woman, esp a repulsive, gossipy old shrew [first form 1920s+, second 1940s+; both *bag* and *bat* earlier meant "prostitute"]

old biddy *n phr* An old woman, esp an unpleasant one : *Talk to the old biddy for me. She likes you* [1940s+; ultimately fr *biddy*, "chicken, hen," found by 1601]

old bird *n phr* An old man; GAFFER, GEEZER (1853+)

old boy *n phr* A graduate; alumnus : *Thousands of Princeton old boys flexed their wrists and learned to Frisbee* (1868+ British schools) *See* GOOD OLD BOY

old boy network or **old boys' system** *n phr* A reciprocally supportive, exclusive, and influential group of men, esp those who were friends at some prestigious school or college; IN-GROUP : *an "old-girl" network to rival the much-ballyhooed "old-boy" network/ It's an old boys' system. Once you have a few commissions under your belt, one architect recommends you to another* (1959+ British)

old cocker *n phr* ALTER KOCKER : *I said good morning to the two Old Cockers who ambled along every day kidding themselves they were exercising/ a lot of old cockers out there who wanted to hear a ball game* (1980s+)

old college try, the *n phr* One's utmost effort; GIVE something one's BEST SHOT : *It's not going to be the end of the world. You give it the old college try* [1927+; fr the early and innocent legends of college football]

◁**old crock**▷ *n phr* An old person, esp a man, who is broken down and physically debilitated : *That old crock still plays tennis?* [1880+; *crock* is found in several Germanic languages as "a broken-down horse"; noted in 1969 as medical slang for a neurotic complainer]

older than God (or **baseball** or **dirt**) *adj phr* Very, very old : *Robert Penn Warren is older than God/ Dick James, who remembers the Philadelphia Athletics, older than dirt*

◁**old fart**▷ *n phr* An old man; a superannuated man; ALTER KOCKER, POOP : *I feel like an old fart. My back's stiff, my knees hurt, my teeth hurt* (1968+)

old flame *n phr* An ex-sweetheart or lover : *saw my old flame at the reunion*

old fogy (or **fuddy-duddy**) *n phr* An old person, esp a man who clings to old-fashioned ways [first form 1790+, second 1899+; of fuddy-duddy, origin unknown] *See* FOGY

old geezer or **goat** *n phr* An old man, esp an unpleasant one : *Get that old geezer out of here* (1897+) *See* GEEZER

old girl *n phr* An old woman; also, a wife (1791+)

old hand *n phr* An experienced person; a seasoned veteran : *She's an old hand at these diplomatic remedies* (1785+)

old hat *adj phr* Out of style; old-fashioned : *Tubular stuff is now old hat* (1911+ British)

old heave-ho, the *See* the HEAVE-HO

oldie or **oldy** *n* An old thing or person, esp an old song, movie, or story : *Our pet oldie concerns the India rubber skin man/ as good as a W C Fields oldie* [1930s+; the late pianist Eubie Blake dated this phrase from about 1900] *See* GOLDEN OLDIE

oldie but goodie *See* GOLDEN OLDIE

old lady *n phr* **1** One's wife; a wife : *Losin' his old lady is what crazied him* (1836+) **2** A girlfriend, mistress, woman living companion, etc : *He introduced this chick as his old lady* (1950s+) **3** One's mother; a mother : *The little kid went to ask his old lady if he could come along* (1836+)

old man *n phr* **1** One's husband; a husband : *She can't bear to see her old man lose his money* (1895+) **2** A boyfriend or lover : *Her old man was a bass guitar player in a rock group*

(1950s+) **3** One's father; a father : *My old man wasn't mean* (1768+) **4** A man who supports a mistress; JOHN, SUGAR DADDY : *"Old Man," the name we used to have for a common-law husband/ She has an "old man" who "keeps" her* (1935+) **5** A pimp *(Prostitutes)* **6** Old friend (1870+) *See* DIRTY OLD MAN, SO'S YOUR OLD MAN

old man, the *n phr* The chief or boss, esp the captain of a ship, aircraft, or military unit; HONCHO (1830+)

old money *n phr* Inherited wealth, as distinct from that of the nouveaux riches : *Bush attended two fund-raisers in Highland Park, the center of what passes in Dallas for old money, rooted in real estate, cotton, and oil in the early years* (1963+)

old one-two, the *See* ONE-TWO

old pro *See* PRO

old school *modifier* From an early time, favoring traditional ways; retro or vintage : *old school fraternity hazings/ strictly old school*

oldster *n* An older person, as opposed to a youngster : *We oldsters can beat you* (1848+)

old timer *n phr* A seasoned veteran, esp a man • Often used in direct address, generally affectionately : *Although younger agents find them exciting, old-timers resist them* (1860+)

old-time religion *n phr* The tried-and-true way of doing things; hallowed wisdom : *that horse-trading, your bill for mine, was part of the old-time religion/ If Cuomo does run, he will have money, eloquence, labor unions and the power of old-time Democratic religion behind him* [1930s+; fr the hymn tune "Give me that *old-time religion*"]

old woman *n phr* OLD LADY

-olo *See* -OLA

on *adj* **1** Aware; informed; alerted : *I saw he was on, and quit talking* (1885+) **2** Not canceled; scheduled to happen : *The deal's still on/ It's on for tomorrow night* (1908+) **3** Accepted and confirmed as a partner, competitive bettor, etc : *He said he bet he could do it, and I told him he was on/ You want to go up there with us? You're on* (1812+) **4** Performing; presenting a talk, appeal, etc, as if one were on stage : *She's never relaxed, she's always on/ Better review your points, since you're on next* (1793+) **prep 1** Paid for by; with the compliments of : *This was to be on him* (1871+) **2** Taking; using; addicted to : *He had her on penicillin/ He was on acid and barbiturates at the time* (1936+ *Narcotics)*

on a cloud *adj phr* Very happy; euphoric; in a blissful transport : *Oh, world, I'm on a cloud today!* (1950s+)

on a dime *See* STOP ON A DIME, TURN ON A DIME

on a plate *adv* In an easy situation; easily acquired : *a win on a plate* (1935+)

on a roll *adj phr* **1** Having great success; enjoying a winning impetus : *The tax cut's a smash. You're on a roll, Mr President/ But Brad was on a roll now* (1976+) **2** (also **on a kick**) Doing something enthusiastically and constantly : *She was on a philosophy roll* (1970s+) [fr a crapshooting term meaning "very, very lucky; unbeatable with the dice"]

on a shingle *See* SHIT ON A SHINGLE

on a shoestring *adv* For very little money; on a tight budget : *put the party together on a shoestring*

◁**on** one's **ass**▷ (or **ear**) *adv phr* In or into a sad and helpless condition; supine; DOWN FOR THE COUNT : *He lost three jobs, and now he's on his ass/ His hat store went kerflooie, and he's on his ear now* (entry form 1950s+, variant 1940s+) *See* FALL ON one's ASS, FLAT ON one's ASS, SIT ON one's ASS

on someone's ass *adj phr* Annoying or harassing one : *The paparazzi have been on my ass all day* (1980s+)

on a tear (TAIR) *adj phr* Very angry, esp punitively so; PISSED OFF : *Ronald Reagan is on a tear over leaks* [1880s+; the dated example is in *a tear]*

on someone's back *adv phr* Persistently annoying or harassing someone; ON someone's CASE : *The cops were on my back after that* (1776+)

on board *adv phr* Serving as a member of a team, government, or other group: *The President said he was glad to have the new Secretary on board* (1980s+)

on someone's case *adv phr* Paying close and esp meddling or punitive attention to someone : *Maybe the world isn't on my case. Maybe the problem is me/ These people got on my case heavy the first day the ol' man was dead* [1970s+ *Black*; fr the black expression *sit on someone's case*, "discuss and judge someone's problems, behavior, etc," based on a judicial analogy]

once in a blue moon *adv phr* Very rarely : *Herb? I only see him once in a blue moon* (1864+)

once-over or **once-over lightly,** a *n phr* A hasty cursory performance or preparation; a LICK AND A PROMISE : *a razor for a hasty once-over* (1940s+)

once-over, the *n phr* A look or glance of inspection; scrutiny; the double-O : *The first thing we went to buy after giving all the pavilions the once-over was tomatoes* (1915+) *See* GIVE someone or something THE ONCE-OVER

on cloud nine (or **cloud seven**) *adj phr* At the very pinnacle of bliss; euphoric; ON A CLOUD : *She came back home and he's on cloud nine* (1950s+)

on someone's **coattails** *adv phr* Profiting from someone else's success, esp in a decisive election : *when all these rube politicians come riding in on Reagan's coattails* [1909+; Abraham Lincoln used *under that coattail* in the same sense in 1848, referring to the winning influence of Andrew Jackson]

on deck *adj phr* **1** : *the on-deck hitter* **2** Present and ready; on hand and prepared : *If you need anybody else, I'm on deck* (1889+) *adv phr* Waiting to be the next batter, usu in a special circle marked for the purpose (1867+ Baseball)

on someone's **dime** (or **nickel**) *adv phr* At someone's expense other than the speaker's : *On the dime of Universal/ Hicks and Sims went home, on their own nickel, to their own miseries* [fr the *dime* or *nickel* formerly needed to activate a pay telephone]

one *See* FAST ONE, FRESH ONE, HANG ONE ON, SQUARE ONE, THIN ONE

One *See* MURDER ONE, NUMBER ONE

one and only *n phr* One's beloved, fiancée, sweetheart, etc : *My one and only, what am I going to do if you turn me down when I'm so crazy over you* (1906+)

on one's ear *See* ON one's ASS

one-arm (or **one-armed**) **bandit** *n phr* A slot machine (1938+)

on easy street *adv phr* In a condition of solvency, ease, and tranquility (1901+)

one-bagger *n* A one-base hit; single *(1880s+ Baseball)*

one better *See* GO something or someone ONE BETTER

on edge *See* EDGY

one-eyed demon (or **snake**) *n phr* The penis : *Safe sex education blew it. The emphasis should be on the psychology that goes into wrestling with that one-eyed demon* [1990s+; fr regarding the meatus as an eye]

one-finger salute *n phr* A lewd insulting gesture made by holding up the middle finger with the others folded down, and meaning "fuck you" or "up yours"; the FINGER *Then he put his arm out the window and raised his hand in the one-finger salute* (1980s+)

one foot in the grave *See* HAVE ONE FOOT IN THE GRAVE

one for the book (or **books**) *n phr* Something remarkable; an amazing thing, case, etc : *That storm was really one for the book* (1922+)

one for the road *n phr* A last drink of the evening, party, carouse, etc; stirrup cup (1943+)

one hell of a *See* a HELL OF A

one-horse *adj* Insignificant; inferior : *It's a one-horse operation he's got there* (1853+)

one-horse town *n phr* A small town; JERK-WATER TOWN (1855+)

one-liner *n* A quick joke or quip; a funny observation; WISECRACK : *a new neighbor who exchanges one-liners with Lianna in the laundry room* (1964+)

one-man show (or **band**) *n phr* An enterprise, business, etc, controlled by one person : *The company had previously been run as a "one-man show"* (entry form 1921+, variant 1938+)

one-night stand *n phr* **1** A performing engagement for one evening only : *Not a bad gig, but just a one-night stand* (1880+) **2** A casual sex act; a brief sexual encounter : *He never enjoyed one-night stands* (1963+) **3** A person who has a casual sexual encounter : *emerges as less the femme fatale than a one-night stand gone wrong*

one-off *n* Something unique; something not repeated : *encouraged band member Jim Warchol to think of 5th and National as more than a one-off* (1934+)

one of the boys (or **the guys**) *n phr* An ordinary, amiable man; a man without side or lofty dignity; ordinary joe : *His Eminence was trying hard to be one of the boys* (1893+)

one of those things *See* JUST ONE OF THOSE THINGS

101, something *n phr* The introductory course in something : *You should be teaching police-amatic Bullshit 101 at John Jay/ College Slang 101/ Is Pistol-Packing 101 the 80s equivalent of Drivers' Ed?* (1980s+)

one on one *adv phr* In immediate confrontation; person to person; EYEBALL TO EYEBALL, mano a mano : *I go on the basketball court and have a 15-year-old guy beat me one on one/ John Rhodes was very effective, one-on-one* (1967+) *n phr* : *have a one-on-one with him*

one piece *See* ALL IN ONE PIECE

one red cent *See* a RED CENT

one-shot *modifier* : *He put her in a one-shot whodunit/ Maybe it was a one-shot shakedown* *n* **1** A story or article that appears once, with no sequel (1942+) **2** Any transaction, event, etc, that occurs only once; ONE-OFF : *He was doing poetry readings, one-shots* (1937+) **3** A woman who accedes to the sex act once, then refuses repetitions (1950+)

one size fits all *adj phr* Of broad or universal application : *Social Security is a one-size-fits-all program, run entirely out of Washington/ A one-size-fits-all approach in public education is unfair to youngsters with disabilities* [1990s+; fr the labels on caps, gloves, and other products that accommodate all wearer sizes]

one-stoplight town *n phr* ONE-HORSE TOWN : *No one seemed interested in how many "steppenwolfs" were playing one-stoplight towns* (1980s+)

one thin dime *See* a THIN DIME

one too many *n phr* Enough liquor to make one drunk, and possibly more : *Its driver had obviously had one too many* (1937+)

one-track mind *n phr* A mind limited to or obsessed with a single idea, theme, etc (1927+)

one-trick pony *n phr* A person having a single accomplishment : *As he proved during exquisite ballads and mid-tempo tunes, he's no one-trick pony/ For years, Twentieth Century Fund has been known to investors as a one-trick pony* (1990s+)

one-two *modifier* : *good potent one-two punches n* (also **the old one-two** or **one-two punch** or **one-two blow**) A combination of two blows with the fists, a short left jab plus a hard right cross, usu to the chin : *zipping "one-twos" to the jaw* (1811+)

one-up *adv phr* **1** In a superior position; at an advantage : *I always try to be one-up* (1919+) **2** Ahead by one : *The Pinks were one-up on the Puces, 109 to 108 v* To get the advantage over : *I wasn't trying to one-up Arthur Schwartz*

one-upmanship *n* The technique and practice of having the advantage over one's opponent, esp keeping a psychological advantage by low cunning and subtle brilliance : *a wide-open but good-humored game of political one-upmanship* [1952+; coined by the late British humorist Stephen Potter as a book title]

on one's game *adj phr* Performing very well; HOT : *When I was out in the water and on my game, nothing existed but the wave* (1920+)

on one's head *See* STAND ON one's HEAD

on one's high horse *adj phr* Behaving arrogantly and pompously [1805+; the form *ride the great horse* is found by 1716]

on hold *adv phr* In postponement or abeyance; suspended; IN COLD STORAGE : *Our plans are on hold for a while* [fr the button on a telephone marked *hold*, used to switch temporarily from the conversation]

on ice *adj phr* **1** Certain of being won or of turning out well; IN THE BAG : *The deal's on ice* (1890+) **2** (also **on tap**) In reserve; ready to play a role; IN COLD STORAGE : *If this one fails, I've got another on ice/ Who arranged Dubie to be on tap* (1894+) *adv phr* In prison, esp in solitary confinement (1931+)

onion *n* The head (1890+) *See* KNOW one's ONIONS, OFF one's NOODLE

on line *adj phr* Available; ready for use; installed : *The Navy's announced plans for a new destroyer class are on line* (1980s+)

only *See* EYES ONLY, ONE AND ONLY

only game, the *n phr* (also **the only ball game**) The only choice available : *For export industries "development bank" projects are the only game in town/ They are the only ball game*

for maintenance [a shortening of the expression *I know it's crooked, but it's the only game in town*]

only way to go *n phr* The best way to do something; the optimal choice : *Taking the free vacation is the only way to go*

on paper *adv phr* Only by abstract report or reputation; theoretically : *It works on paper, but I've never actually tried it* (1795+)

on spec *adv phr* As a venture or gamble; hoping to profit : *They said they would take the case on spec* (1832+)

on tap *See* ON ICE

on task *adv* Concentrating or focusing on what is to be done : *like them to stay on task in the classroom*

on the back burner *adv phr* Not being actively considered; in reserve; ON HOLD : *I have some good projects on the back burner right now* (1960+)

on the ball *adj phr* Skillful, alert, and effective; WITH IT : *FBI agents were very much on the ball in the Bremer snatch* [1912+; fr the advisability of keeping one's eyes *on the ball* when playing a ball game] *See* GET ON THE BALL, KEEP one's EYE ON THE BALL, SOMETHING ON THE BALL

on the bandwagon *adv phr* Agreeing with the majority; following popular opinion : *so many on the bandwagon with wearing flip-flops in the winter*

on the beam *adv phr* On the proper track or course; performing correctly : *It took a while, but he's on the beam now* [1941+; fr the radio beam used to guide aircraft]

on the bleeding edge *adv phr* Having or using advanced technology • More advanced than *cutting edge* : *the bleeding edge of electronic manuscripts*

on the blink *adj phr* (Variations: **bum** or **fritz** or **Fritz** may replace **blink**) Not functioning properly; in poor condition : *His pacemaker just went on the fritz* [entry form 1904+, fritz 1903+, bum 1896+; origin unknown; perhaps fr the notion that defective eyes or lights blink]

on the brain *See* HAVE something ON THE BRAIN

on the bubble *adv phr* In a precarious position : *That could place guard Conner Henry on the bubble* [1980s+; because the *bubble* might burst]

on the button *adj phr* Perfectly placed; absolutely correct; ON THE MONEY, ON THE NOSE, SPOT-ON : *Your estimate was right on the button adv phr* Precisely; exactly; ON THE DOT, ON THE NOSE : *The meter says 35 on the button* (1937+)

on the carpet (or **mat**) *adv phr* In the situation of being reprimanded : *Next time they caught him asleep he was on the carpet* [1899+;

probably fr *walk the carpet* or *carpet*, "reprimand, rebuke," found by 1823]

on the cheap *adj phr* : *Prices still delight the on-the-cheap set* **adv phr** cheaply : *selling just about anything on the cheap* (*1859+*)

on the cuff *adj phr* Free : *On-the-cuff drinks are delicious* **adv phr 1** On credit : *The mutt puts me on the cuff for the drinks* **2** Free of charge : *He promised me lodging on the cuff* [mid-1920s+; fr the practice of noting debts on the *cuff* of the shirt, esp on a detachable *cuff*]

on the dot *adv phr* At the exact moment; punctually : *I got there on the dot* (*1909+*)

on (or at) the double *adv phr* **1** At twice the rate of ordinary marching **2** Quickly; rapidly : *When I holler, come on the double* (*1892+*)

on the draw *See* SLOW ON THE DRAW

on the edge *See* LIVE ON THE EDGE

on the fence *adv phr* Not taking a stand or making up one's mind; straddling (*1828+*)

on the fire *adj phr* **1** Pending; in preparation; IN THE PIPELINE : *We've got a great new model on the fire for next year* **2** Being cooked; in preparation (*Lunch counter*)

on the fly (or **the gallop**) *adj phr* : *an on-the-fly decision* **adv phr** Hastily in passing; without preparation or forethought : *We had to make up our minds on the fly/ He objected to disposing of the case "on the gallop"* (entry form *1851+*, variant *1693+*)

on the fritz *See* ON THE BLINK

on the front burner *adj phr* Getting immediate attention (*1970+*)

on the go *adj phr* **1** Active; energetic; indefatigable : *I'm on the go day and night* **2** Always moving about; restlessly in motion : *I'm on the go all the time and don't see my family* (*1843+*)

on the gravy train (or **boat**) *adv phr* Enjoying an effortless and prosperous life; FLUSH : *After a couple of years on the gravy train the bottom fell out of things* (*1927+*)

on the ground floor *See* IN ON THE GROUND FLOOR

on the head *See* HIT THE NAIL ON THE HEAD

on the hog *See* EAT HIGH ON THE HOG

on the hook *adv phr* **1** In trouble; liable to blame : *You're on the hook for this mess, junior* **2** Trapped; ensnared : *She had the old fool on the hook right soon* (*1940s+*)

on (or in) the hot seat *adv phr* In an uncomfortable situation; IN A JAM : *You're on the hot seat every day in that job* (*1960s+*)

on the house *adj phr* Free of charge; free gratis : *Breakfasts, luncheons, and dinner. All "on the house"* (*1889+*)

on the hustle *adj phr* Living by constant petty frauds and crimes; watchful for dupes : *sleeping till ten in the morning, on the hustle in the streets or the poolrooms* (*1970s+*)

on the inside *adv phr* Having access to the most confidential information; near the focus of power and influence (*1932+*)

on the lam or **on the run** *adj phr* In hiding from the police; wanted as a fugitive : *So I went on the lam* [first form 1931+, second 1887+; the form *on a lam* is found by 1904] *See* TAKE IT ON THE LAM

on the legit *adj phr* or *adv phr* Lawful; legal; ON THE LEVEL : *strictly on the legit* (*1931+*)

on the level *adj phr* Honest; candid; ON THE LEGIT : *to swear that I'm on the level* (*1875+*) *adv phr* : *and would fight on the level*

on the line *adv phr* In a risky or vulnerable position; at risk, esp deliberately; UP FOR GRABS : *The whole season's on the line this inning* [1968+; origin unknown; perhaps fr a gambling game where the bet is placed *on a line*; perhaps fr the commercial slang expression *lay* (*the price* or *payment*) *on the line*, "pay, pay up"; perhaps fr the sense of *line* as separating combatants or duelists] *See* LAY IT ON THE LINE, LAY something ON THE LINE, PUT one's ASS ON THE LINE

on the make *adv phr* **1** Aspiring and ambitious, esp in a ruthless and exploitive way; careeristic; HUNGRY : *The rookies are very much on the make* (*1869+*) **2** Offering and seeking sexual pleasure and conquest; openly amorous : *whether they are on the make, and they all are* (*1929+*) *See* ON THE TAKE

on the map *adj phr* Excellent; COOL, way rad : *That movie was on the map* (*1990s+ Teenagers*)

on the mat *See* ON THE CARPET

on the mend *adv phr* Recovering health (*1802+*)

on the money *adj phr* Absolutely perfect; precisely as desired; accurate : *good hit, right on the money* (*1971+*)

on the nose *adj phr* Perfectly placed; exactly as desired; ON THE MONEY : *Your guess was right on the nose* **adv phr** Precisely; exactly; ON THE DOT : *It's six on the nose* (*1937+*)

on the one hand *interj* Something to consider is : *on the one hand, there's college*

on the outs *adj phr* Estranged; alienated : *The young couple are on the outs now* (*1887+*)

on the prowl *adj phr* Actively seeking; abroad and searching, esp for prey (*1836+*) *adv phr* Seeking sexual pleasure and conquest; ON THE MAKE (*1940+*)

on the QT *adj phr* : *Remember, what I said is on the QT* *adv phr* Secretly; quietly : *We did it on the QT* (*1884+*) [fr the first and last letters of *quiet*]

◁**on the rag**▷ *adj phr* **1** Menstruating : *Maybe I'm on the rag* (*1940s+*) **2** Irritable; in a bad mood (*1960s+ Students*) [fr *rag* used as a sanitary napkin]

on the road *adv phr* Traveling from place to place with a show, musical program, etc *(1870+ Show business)*

on the rocks *adv phr* **1** In a ruined condition; hopelessly wrecked; KAPUT : *My little enterprise is on the rocks (1889+)* **2** Poured over ice : *Scotch on the rocks'll be fine (1946+)*

on the ropes *adj phr* Defeated; bested; CLOB- BERED : *His career as a promoter is on the ropes* [1924+; fr the plight of a boxer who must lean on the *ropes* of the ring or fall down]

on the same wavelength (or **page**) *adj phr* In agreement; in harmony; TUNED IN : *Her door's open, but we are not on the same wavelength/ We do now have a long-range plan. Everybody's on the same page (1962+)*

on the sauce *adj phr* Drinking liquor, esp heavily : *on the sauce in a charming school-boy way* [1970s+; *sauce,* "liquor," is found by 1940]

on the shelf *adv phr* Not in active use or consideration; deferred; ON THE BACK BURNER : *We'll have to put some of those plans on the shelf for a while (1815+)*

on the side *adv phr* Extra; additionally : *He moonlights as a hackie on the side (1893+)*

on the skids *adj phr* On a failing or declining course; deteriorating : *After that scandal his whole career was on the skids* [1921+; ulti- mately fr the *skids,* "long pieces of timber," on which barrels, logs, and other heavy objects were rolled or slid, sometimes on a downgrade]

on the sly *adv phr* Secretly and deceptively : *sold that equipment on the sly*

on the spot *adj phr* **1** Expected to cope, explain, react, etc, at once; under sharp pressure : *She can't make it, so I guess you're on the spot (1928+)* **2** Available and ready; keen and at hand : *When I need him he's never on the spot (1884+) adv phr* Immediately; at once and at the place in question : *I was able to fix it on the spot (1687+)* [the adverbial dated form is *upon the spot*] *See* JOHNNY-ON- THE-SPOT

on the take (or the **make**) *adv phr* Amenable to bribery and graft; on the pad : *spent 30 years fighting everything from pigeons to cops on the make (1930+)*

on the throne *adv phr* On the toilet; in the bathroom

on the town *adv phr* Enjoying the pleasures of a city, esp the night life; roistering and rev- eling urbanly [1712+; the dated example is *upon the town*]

on the up and up *See* UP AND UP

on the uptake *See* SLOW ON THE DRAW

on the wagon (or **the water wagon**) *adj phr* Abstaining from liquor; teetotal, at least temporarily : *Monty didn't drink, and Clifton*

James went on the wagon [1904+; first at- tested as *on the water cart* in 1902]

on the warpath *adj phr* Truculent; looking for a fight • The original Native American sense is found by 1841 *(1880+)*

on to someone *adj phr* Aware of, esp of some- thing shady or forbidden; WISE TO : *Watch it now, I think the guard is on to you (1877+)*

on top *See* COME OUT AHEAD

on top of *adv phr* **1** Actively coping with the problem; able to guide and control the matter; JACKED IN : *It's a nasty outlook, but I think we can get on top of it* **2** Fully informed about something : *Get on top of this latest development right away (1970s+)*

on track *See* GO ON TRACK

on one's uppers *adj phr* Penniless; destitute; DOWN AND OUT [1891+; fr the notion that one has worn out the soles of one's shoes and is walking *on the uppers* only]

on someone's watch *adv phr* During some- one's tenure of responsibility; while some- one is in charge, esp of protection : *Jerusalem and the West Bank were lost to Jordan and the Arab world on his watch* [1980s+; fr the nautical setting of *watches,* the designating of officers and crew members who run the ship for a specified period]

on wheels *adj phr* To the utmost extent; of the purest sort; IN SPADES : *We agreed she was a bitch on wheels/ He thinks he's shit on wheels* [1940s+; modeled on *hell on wheels,* found by 1843] *See* SHIT ON WHEELS

ooch or **oonch** *See* SCRUNCH

oodles *n* A large amount; lots; a shithouse full, a SHITLOAD : *They have oodles of charisma* [1869+; perhaps fr *boodle, caboodle*]

ooh and ah *v phr* To express wonder, amaze- ment, etc : *the spectators oohed and aahed at the trapeze artist (1953+)*

ooky *adj* Repellent; slimy; YUCKY : *The Addams family are definitely mysterious and undoubt- edly ooky (1964+)*

oomph *n* **1** Sexual attractiveness; compelling carnality; IT **2** Energy; CLOUT, PIZZAZZ : *sub- stance, drive, authority, emotional power, and oomph* [1937+; an echoic coinage suggest- ing the gasp of someone hit hard by a blow, a transport of desire, etc]

oops *interj* An exclamation of surprise, dismay, apology, etc, esp when one has done some- thing awkward : *Mr Belve, oops, I mean Webb, is ecstatic (1933+) n* A blunder; serious mis- take; GOOF, WHOOPS : *Might have saved her life. Basic oops (1980s+) v* (also **oops up**) To vomit; BARF *(1980s+)* [echoic, fr the invol- untary lip-rounding and expulsion of breath that accompany a regrettable mistake, and from an approximation of the sound of vo- miting]

ooze *v* To move or walk slowly; glide or slide; saunter : *I'd ooze across the street and into the bar (1940s+ Black)*

Op-Ed (or **op-ed**) **page** *n phr* A newspaper page, usu appearing across from the editorial page, made up of columns and short essays [1970+; fr *opposite editorial*]

opener *See* EYE-OPENER

openers *See* FOR OPENERS

open season *n phr* The time when persons may be harmed, insulted, etc, with impunity : *If we leave, it will be open season on Americans globally* [1914+; fr the time when game may be legally hunted, the term found by 1896]

open up *v phr* **1** To speak and inform candidly; SPILL one's GUTS : *You must open up and tell us all about what happened (1921+)* **2** To cause or induce someone to speak : *the DA, who opens Leo up with the threat of a perjury charge*

open up a (or **that**) **can of worms** *v phr* To broach a very complicated and troublesome matter; set something messy in motion : *Merit pay? Let's not open up that can of worms (1962+) See* CAN OF WORMS

open one's yap *v phr* To open one's mouth, esp to speak; speak up; say something : *every time you open your yap to say something (1937+)*

opera *See* HORSE OPERA, SOAP OPERA, SPACE OPERA

opera ain't over till the fat lady sings, the *sentence* Things are never finished until they are finished; IT AIN'T OVER TILL IT'S OVER [1977+; coined by Dan Cook, a San Antonio sportscaster, and modeled on the Yogi Berra dictum entered here as a synonym]

operator *n* **1** A person who busily deals and manipulates, often self-importantly; DEALER, WHEELER-DEALER (1875+) **2** LADIES' MAN (1950s+)

opry *See* HORSE OPERA

oral diarrhea *See* VERBAL DIARRHEA

-orama *See* -RAMA

orbit *See* GO INTO ORBIT, IN ORBIT

orc or **orch** *See* ORK

order *See* APPLE-PIE ORDER

or else *prep phr* Otherwise; or this unhappy thing will follow• Used at the end of a command or warning to encourage compliance : *Get that damn thing out of here or else (1833+)*

◁Oreo▷ *n* A black person whose values, behavior, etc, are those of the white society; AFRO-SAXON : *I've been called a "zebra" and an "Oreo"* [1960s+ Black; fr the trademark of a brand of sandwich cookies that have a white cream between round chocolate biscuits]

org *n* An organization : *The Joe Breen (Hays org) influence on pix (1936+)*

-orino *See* -ERINO

-orium *See* -ATORIUM

ork or **orc** or **orch** *n* An orchestra (1936+)

orphan *n* A model of a car, boat, computer, etc, which is no longer being manufactured, and for which spare parts are hard to find (1940s+)

or what *question* Or is it not? what else can it be? : *Was that exciting, or what?/ Is this the old trickle-down the-ory or what? (1990s+)*

O sign *n phr* A sign of death: the patient's mouth is wide open (1980s+ Medical)

ossified *adj* Drunk; STONED (1901+)

other fish to fry *See* BIGGER FISH TO FRY

other half, the *n phr* One large sector of population, usu the rich as distinct from the poor or the poor as distinct from the rich• Nearly always in the expression "see how *the other half* lives" : *Young people from West Berlin now spend their weekends "over there," trying to find out how the other half lives* [1532+; the dated example is from Rabelais]

other side of one's **face** *See* LAUGH ON THE OTHER SIDE OF one's FACE

ouch *n* An injury; a hurt : *A very serious injury is a "big" ouch* [1873+; fr the pained interjection *ouch* fr German, probably Pennsylvania German, *autsch*, found by 1838]

ought to have one's **head examined,** one *sentence* One has done something very stupid or strange : *He paid full price? He ought to have his head examined (1940s+)*

out *adj* **1** Attractive; au courant; HIP, WAY OUT : *Man, that Modigliani is really out (1942+ Beat & cool talk)* **2** Not modern, popular, or in accord with current taste : *Those neckties are out this year (1966+)* **3** Openly avowing homosexuality; OUT OF THE CLOSET (1970s+ Homosexuals) **4** (also **out cold**) Unconscious or intoxicated : *The folks who use it are usually too luded out or preoccupied (1936+)* **5** Rejected; not to be considered • Said to be fr the editing or cutting room in a movie studio : *Ask him again? No, that's out (1923+)* *adv* To the point of surfeit or exhaustion : *I'm coffeed out for the time being/ I don't want them to think I'm losered out (1990s+)* *n* A way of escape; a plausible alibi or evasive course; LET OUT : *You have an out, though. You can talk (1919+)* *v* : *Some gay activists have undertaken a campaign of outing, exposing well-known people who are believed to be gay (late 1980s+) See* ALL GET OUT, FAR OUT, GET OUT, WAY OUT

outa or **outta** *adv phr* Out of• Eye dialect : *We're outta here*

out-and-out *adj* Thorough; complete : *an out-and-out idiot* [1813+; as an adverb, found by 1325]

outasight *See* OUT OF SIGHT

out cold *adv phr* Unconscious; knocked out : *out cold after drinking Yagermeister*

outed *modifier* **1** Revealed as being a homosexual; having one's sexual preference revealed : *outed by his mother* **2** (also **offed**) Killed : *outed by the mob*

outercourse *n* Noninvasive sex : *Thousands of American women have told Ann Landers, in their sex lives they would like more talking, more hugging, more outercourse (1990s+)*

outer garden *n phr* The outfield *(1907+ Baseball)*

outfit *n* **1** A company or group working together : *that outfit I used to work for* **2** A set of clothing; also, a set of items or things for a task or job : *outfit looks good on you/ the outfit you need for the dig*

outfox *v* To outwit; outsmart; FOX *(1962+)*

out from under *See* GET OUT FROM UNDER

out-front *adj* Honest; candid; unevasive; UP FRONT : *intelligent, very open, out-front people (1960s+)*

outie *modifier* : *I suspect that the Cardinal arts editor has an outie belly button, and I have an innie belly button n* A convex navel *(1980s+)* [probably a children's term]

outing *n* **1** A particular game or performance : *Eldred rebounds from his lone poor outing (1980s+ Sports)* **2** (also **outage**) The exposure of someone as homosexual *(late 1980s+)*

out in left field *adj phr* **1** Very unorthodox and wrong; weirdly unconventional; crazy *(1959+)* **2** Disoriented; confused *(1960+ Medical)*

out like a light *adj phr* Unconscious; fast asleep *(1934+)*

out loud *See* FOR CRYING OUT LOUD

out of one's ears *See* HAVE something COMING OUT OF one's EARS

out of gas *adj phr* Exhausted; BEAT, POOPED : *So I started the second game, damn near out of gas (1975+)*

out of one's head (or **skull** or **gourd**) *adj phr* **1** Insane; crazy; NUTS : *You're out of your head if you think I'll do that* **2** Dazed; delirious; OFF one's NOODLE : *He took one sniff and went right out of his gourd* (*entry form 1825+, variants 1950s+*)

out of hell *See* TAKE OFF LIKE A BIGASS BIRD

out of it *adj phr* **1** Unable to win or succeed : *The Hawks are out of it this season (1940s+)* **2** Not a part of the trend or scene; uninitiated : *Everyone was out of it in the Fifties (1960+)* **3** Unattending because of drugs, disease, etc : *We could accept him as being out of it (1963+)*

out of joint *See* PUT someone's NOSE OUT OF JOINT

out of kilter *adj phr* Not in order or repair; OUT OF WHACK [1628+; fr British dialect *kilter* or *kelter*, "condition, state, frame," of obscure origin]

out of one's league (or **ballpark**) *adj phr* **1** Not comparable or equal in talent, importance, remuneration, etc : *I'd love to have Reba McEntire, but she's completely out of our ballpark* **2** Not in one's proper province : *The matter's fortunately out of my league (1966+)*

out of left field *adv phr* Unexpectedly; suddenly and surprisingly : *When they needed a new idea, this guy appeared out of left field (1953+)*

out of line *adj phr* **1** Not in accordance with what is appropriate or expected : *You was considered out of line if your coat and pants matched* **2** Behaving improperly, esp presumptuously : *Maybe I'm out of line. I just feel I must say something (1940+)*

out of luck *adj phr* Having no chance of success; already too late for what one wants : *Those looking for New Jersey organic turkeys are out of luck See* SHIT OUT OF LUCK

out of pocket (or **the pocket**) *adj phr* Absent or otherwise unavailable : *I'm out of the pocket for a bit, but I'll get back at ya (1974+)*

out of shape *adj phr* Very upset; angry; hysterical *(1970s+) See* BENT OUT OF SHAPE

out of sight *adj phr* **1** (also **outasight**) Excellent; superior; WAY OUT *(1891+)* **2** Very high-priced; exorbitantly priced : *That hat's out of sight (1940s+)*

out of style *See* LIKE IT'S GOING OUT OF STYLE

out of sync *adj phr* Not coinciding or compatible; arrhythmic, esp in relation to something else, a context, etc : *his presence just self-consciously regular enough to be out of sync* [1961+; fr the lack of *synchronism* sometimes noted between a movie or TV image and its sound track]

out of the box *adj phr* Out of contention; ruined; FINISHED, KAPUT *(1970s+) adv phr* (also **outside the box**) In an original and creative manner : *Thinking out of the box. Creating new processes, not just tinkering with old formulas (1990s+)* [first sense fr the condition of a baseball pitcher who has been knocked out of the box and hence has probably lost the game; second fr the notion that conventional thinkers are *in a box*]

out of the closet *adj phr* **1** Openly avowing homosexuality **2** No longer secret : *The last American taboo, that of talking about indebtedness, may be out of the closet at last (1970s+) See* COME OUT OF THE CLOSET

out of the fire *See* PULL something OUT OF THE FIRE

out of the gate *adv phr* Immediately : *The booing began in the first inning, when Cal Eldred spotted the Detroit Tigers three runs right out of the gate* [1990s+; fr the start of a horse race]

out of the loop *adj phr* Not one of the inner and influential group; not in the network :

George Bush was out of the loop an ineffective second in command [late 1980s+; probably fr the military notion of radio *nets*, conceptually like *loops*, connecting various commanders]

out of the picture *adv phr* Not relevant; no longer around or needed : *with her back, his other girl friend is out of the picture/ with Erin out of the picture, I'm queen*

out of the water *See* BLOW someone OUT OF THE WATER

out of the woods *adj phr* Out of danger; safe : *This does not get us out of the woods in terms of the growth curve of prison costs* [1792+; the dated example reads *out of the wood*]

out of the woodwork *See* CRAWL OUT OF THE WOODWORK

out of this world *adj phr* Excellent; wonderful; superior; the GREATEST, WAY OUT : *She had a figure that was out of this world* (1938+)

out of one's tree *adj phr* Insane; crazy; APE : *I think she's got to be out of her tree* (1966+)

out of turn *adj phr* Behaving improperly : *You're strictly out of turn.* Get in line (1930+ Underworld) *See* TALK OUT OF TURN

out of one's way *See* GO OUT OF one's WAY

out of whack *adj phr* **1** Not operating; out of order; ON THE BLINK, OUT OF KILTER : *My car's out of whack, so I'll take yours* **2** Not in adjustment, harmonious synchronism, etc; not in proper order : *Our priorities are out of whack* **3** Strange; inexplicable; not right : *It seems out of whack to me, then, that Jakobek was the only aldermanic candidate who had a great deal of support from the young* [1885+; probably fr *whack*, "share, a just proportion," so called perhaps fr the blow that divides something or, like the auctioneer's hammer-rap, signals a fair share or deal]

out on a limb *adv phr* In a very vulnerable position; exposed; in peril : *The announcement put the Mayor out on a limb* (1841+) *See* GO OUT ON A LIMB

◁**out on** one's **ass**▷ *adj phr* (also **out on one's ear**) Discharged; rejected; superseded; FINISHED : *She's the First Lady now, and I'm out on my ass* (1940s+)

outside chance *n phr* A remote possibility; a slim likelihood : *He may have an outside chance to pass* (1909+)

outtake *n* An excerpt; an extracted passage : *Is this an outtake from the $1.98 Beauty Show?* [1977+; originally, by 1960, a rejected part of a film]

out (or up) the wazoo *adv phr* **1** UP THE ASS : *You can be full of warts, have a scarred-up body, have disadvantages out the wazoo* (1990s+) **2** In excess : *She has work up the wazoo*

out the window *adj phr* Wrecked and futile; go down the tube. KAPUT : *All our plans are out the window now, so forget it* (1939+)

out to lunch *adj phr* Insane; crazy; eccentric : *On critical issues of fact and analysis he is out to lunch* (1955+ Students)

out to pasture *See* PUT someone or something OUT TO PASTURE

over *See* the ONCE-OVER

over a barrel *adv phr* In a helpless situation : *I knew enough about him that I had him over a barrel* [1939+; perhaps fr the tying *over a barrel* of a person about to be flogged]

over-amped *adj* Unduly stimulated; too expectant; PSYCHED UP, PUMPED UP : *Couples who fall in love and marry instantaneously often find themselves "over-amped"* (1990s+) *See* AMPED

overboard *See* GO OVERBOARD

overcoat *n* A parachute (WWII Air Forces) *See* CHICAGO OVERCOAT, PINE OVERCOAT

over easy *adj phr* Of eggs, fried on both sides, lightly on one (1940s+)

over someone's eyes *See* PULL THE WOOL OVER someone's EYES

over one's head *adj phr* Too difficult for one mentally; incomprehensible : *The concept's way over my head* (1622+) *adv phr* Better than one's usual standard; in an inspired way : *The team played over its head, and by God they won* (1970s+) *See* IN OVER one's HEAD

overhung *adj* Suffering from having drunk too much alcohol (1964+)

overjolt *n* An overdose of drugs • Can also be in verb form : *overjolt of heroin*

overkill *n* An excess, esp of needed action : *Going twice would be overkill, don't you think?* [1958+; fr the use of the term in connection with the *killing* potential of nuclear arms and arsenals]

over my dead body *interj* An expression of refusal, denial, or rejection; not happening : *Over my dead body will she live with us* (1936+)

overserved *adj* Drunk, having been given too much alcohol • Euphemistic : *overserved again*

overshot *adj* Drunk (1605+)

over the coals *See* HAUL someone OVER THE COALS

over the hill *adj phr* **1** Middle-aged or past middle age : *a film for, and about, the over-the-hill gang* (1940s+) **2** No longer effective; worn out; ausgespielt (1940s+) **3** Most of the way to success or completion : *I think that you can say that we're over the hill* (1970s+) **4** Absent without leave; AWOL (1940s+ Army) [first three senses fr the notion that one is no longer going upward toward the summit, but is descending the far side of the imagined hill]

over the hump *adj phr* Most of the way to success or completion; OVER THE HILL [1925+; a 1914 source defines *hump* as "the halfway point in a prison sentence"]

over the long haul *See* FOR THE LONG HAUL

over the moon *modifier* Very happy; delighted (*1936+*)

over the top *adj phr* Beyond reason; outlandish : *Makes no sense at all. Simply hilarious and over the top/ It would be over the top! It would be redundant! It would be ridiculous* (*1968+*)

own someone *v* To dominate, rule over; to kick (someone's) ass : *chief resident owns the newbies*

ownage *n* The stuff that one owns; also, the acquisition of stuff : *mother-in-law into ownage*

own horn, one's *See* TOOT one's OWN HORN

ox *See* DUMB OX

oy *interj* An exclamation of multiple significance : *Oy may be employed to express anything from ecstasy to horror* [1892+; fr Hebrew]

oyster *See* MOUNTAIN OYSTERS, the WORLD IS one's OYSTER

oy vay *interj* (also **oy gevalt** or **oy vey iz mir**) An intensification of "oy" as an exclamation of alarm, distress, etc : *Oy Gevalt! New Yawkese An Endangered Dialect?/ Oy Vay! Bigamy on the Lower East Side/ The Six-Day War altered my mindset for good: from Oy vey iz mir to Never again!*

P

pace *See* OFF THE PACE

pack *v* To carry, esp a weapon (*1890+*) *See* NERDPACK, RAT PACK

package *n* **1** A large sum of money; BUNDLE : *That must have cost a package* (*1956+*) **2** The collective terms of a contract or agreement : *The lefthander signed for a package including 10 million in two years, three McDonald's franchises, and the state of South Dakota* (*1952+*) **3** A particular combination or set : *That rental car is part of the vacation package* (*1931+*) **4** The manner and quality of presentation, the trappings and ornamentation, etc, of something : *It isn't what you've got, it's the package that impresses people* (*1947+*) **5** Someone who has an array of good qualities, plus good looks : *She's the total package/ package that walked in my life v : He never peddled his idea because he didn't know how to package it* (*1947+*) *See* NO PRIZE PACKAGE

packer *n* A male homosexual : *There were a few packers at the party last night* [1980s+ Students; fr homosexual slang *pack fudge*, "do anal intercourse," found by the 1940s]

pack heat *v phr* To carry a gun : *They knew all along that Elvis was packin' heat/ If you pack heat, you got to know what you're doing* (*1940s+ Underworld*)

packie *n* A package liquor store (*1980s+*)

pack in (or up) *v phr* To cease; give up; retire from : *I intended to pack up playing all together/ told the FBI men he is "packing in"* (*1940s+*)

packing or packed *modifier* Armed, esp with a pistol; CARRYING : *The policeman was packed before he raided the building* (packed *1980s+ Teenagers*, packing *1990s+*)

pack it in *v phr* To stop; desist or give up what one is doing; to order to stop doing something annoying : *I decided to pack it in and move to New York/ Who can fault them for not quite yet wanting to pack it in and quietly go home* (*1940s+*)

pack of lies, a *n phr* A set or series of lies; COCK-AND-BULL STORY : *That whole eyewitness account is a damn pack of lies* (*1763+*)

pack rat *n phr* A person who cannot discard anything acquired; a compulsive keeper and storer (*1850+*)

pad *n* **1** A bed or place to sleep temporarily; CRASH PAD • Revived and popularized in 1960s : *The girl shares her pad with other hippies* (*1718+*) **2** A room, apartment, etc, where narcotics addicts and users gather to take drugs : *There were plenty of pads* (*1930s+ Narcotics*) **3** One's home; residence : *He and I used to live in the same pad for two years* (*1973+*) **4** A prostitute's working room; CRIB (*1915+ Prostitutes*) **5** An automobile license plate : *The job was wearing California pads* (*1948+*) *v* To increase the amount or length of : *He was padding his expense account* (*1913+*)

padding *n* Text added, often gratuitously and for mere bulk, to an essay, book, speech, etc (*1861+*)

paddle *See* UP SHIT CREEK

paddle one's **own canoe** *v phr* To deal with one's own problems, advancement, etc : *My Dad kicked me out and told me to paddle my own canoe* (*1828+*)

◀paddy or Paddy▶ *modifier* : *I know I can't be tight with this paddy boy n* **1** An Irish person or person of Irish extraction (*1780+*) **2** (also patty) A white person : *Even a drunken black shoeshine man could handle the likes of this paddy* (*1946+ Black*) [fr the nickname of the given name *Patrick*]

paddy wagon *n phr* A police patrol wagon or van; black maria : *The cooperative family was being escorted into the paddy wagon* [1930+; fr patrol wagon, perhaps influenced by the fact that many policemen were of Irish extraction, hence *paddies*]

page *See* OP-ED PAGE, TAKE A PAGE FROM someone's BOOK

page turner *n phr* A book that is so absorbing that one reads it without stopping, although not necessarily for serious literary or intellectual quality : *a book that unquestionably deserves the description page turner* (*1976+*)

pain *See* FEEL NO PAIN

pain, a *n phr* **1** Annoyance; irritation; HEAD-ACHE : *Marvin is a real pain* **2** PAIN IN THE ASS, a : *It's very much like the Internet equivalent of having your windows soaped. But it's still a pain to clean up after* (*1908+*) *See* GIVE someone A PAIN

◁pain in the ass, a▷ (or butt or neck or rear) *n phr* An annoying, obnoxious person or thing : *This proved a major pain in the ass as too many casual favorites fell to the wrong side* (entry form *1934+*, variant *1924+*) *See* GIVE someone A PAIN

paint, the *n* The foul zone; lane : *get the hell out of the paint* (*1990s+ Basketball*)

paint oneself **into a corner** *v phr* To put oneself into a frustrating or helpless situation : *Paul has painted himself into a corner with that unlikely explanation* (*1980s+*)

paint the town or paint the town red *v phr* To go on a wild spree; carouse : *Well, sport, let's go out and paint the town a new color* (*1884+*)

◁**pair**▷ *n* A woman's breasts • Regarded as offensive by many women (*1922+*)

pajamas *See* the CAT'S MEOW

pal *n* A friend, esp a very close male friend; boon companion; BUDDY : *has many devoted friends, but he is nobody's "pal"* (*1681+*) *v* PAL AROUND (*1899+*) [fr Romany *phral, phal,* "brother, friend," ultimately fr Sanskrit *bhratr,* "brother"]

palace *n* A grand venue for something • Always ironically used of a fairly seedy though perhaps ornate place (*1834+*)

pal around *v phr* To be "pals"; consort as "pals" : *the people he palled around with* (*1915+*)

pale (or green) around the gills *adj phr* Looking sickly or nauseous (*1959+*)

paled or **paled out** *adj* or *adj phr* Completely exhausted, esp by drugs or liquor; WASTED (*1970s+ Canadian teenagers*)

paleface *n* **1** A white homosexual (*1970s+ Black homosexuals*) **2** A circus clown (*1940s+ Circus*)

palimony *modifier* : *a much-heralded palimony suit n* Money awarded, property shared, etc, when an unmarried couple separate (*1979+*) [fr *pal* plus *alimony;* coined for or at least popularized by a lawsuit against the film star Lee Marvin]

pally or **pallie** *adj* Very friendly; affectionate and familiar; PALSY-WALSY (*1895+*) *n* PAL (*1940+*)

palm *v* To conceal a playing card against the palm in order to use it in a gambling hand : *It was five cards that he palmed, three aces and a pair of queens* (*1673+*) *See* GREASE someone's PALM

palm something off *v phr* To bestow something inferior as if it were of good quality; foist; fob off : *He palmed the leaky old place off like it was the Ritz* (*1822+*)

palm oil *n phr* Money used for bribery and graft (*1627+*; because it is used to *grease* one's *palm*]

palooka or **paluka** or **palooker** *n* **1** A mediocre or inferior boxer : *a paluka who leads with his right* (*1925+*) **2** A professional wrestler (*1940+*) **3** Any large and stupid man (*1940s+*) [origin unknown; said to have been coined by the sports writer and humorist Jack Conway]

palsy-walsy (PAL zee WAL zee) *adj* Very friendly; CHUMMY : *breezy, palsy-walsy with Baskerville, who's not a breezy type* (*1940s+*) *n* : *Hey, palsy-walsy, what's going down?*

pan *n* **1** The face; MUG : *too great for them to keep their pans shut* (*1923+*) **2** : *an out-and-out pan v* To criticize severely and adversely; derogate harshly; ROAST : *The Daily Worker panned his first novel* (*1909+*) [noun sense 2 and

verb sense fr the fact that roasting is done in a *pan*] *See* DEADPAN, FLASH IN THE PAN

panhandle *v* To beg, esp by accosting people on the street : *The boys deal drugs or panhandle, even become male prostitutes* [*1903+*; fr *panhandler*]

panhandler *n* A person who begs, esp by accosting people on the street; beggar : *This panhandler came up to me and braced me* [*1897+*; fr the stiff arm held out by the beggar]

panic *n* A very funny person; an effective comedian; a STITCH (*1924+*) *v* **1** To become frightened and confused, esp suddenly; FLIP : *He panicked and dropped the ball* (*1910+*) **2** To get a strong favorable reaction, esp to get loud laughter from an audience; FRACTURE : *Mr Todd knows how to panic the rubes* (*1920+*)

panic button *See* HIT the PANIC BUTTON

panky or **pank** *See* HANKY-PANKY

pan out *v phr* To be productive; succeed; PAY OFF : *Ryan thought about what he'd be living with if the FBI profile panned out* [*1868+*; fr the practice of *panning* gold in river sediments]

◁**pansified**▷ (PAN zi fīd) *adj* Effeminate; SISSIFIED (*1941+*)

◁**pansy**▷ *adj* : *Stage and screen voices in recent years have become so pansy n* **1** A male homosexual; QUEEN : *if someone had bluntly said that her friends were pansies* **2** A weak or effeminate male; LILY, SISSY (*1929+*)

◁**panther piss (or juice or sweat)**▷ or **panther** *n phr* or *n* Raw and inferior whiskey; ROTGUT (*1929+*)

pantry *n* The stomach; BREADBASKET : *another real fine left to the pantry* (*1950+ Prizefight*)

pants *v* **1** To pull the pants, shorts, etc, down or off, esp as a prank : *We pantsed him at the swimming pool* **2** To be dealt a crushing defeat; to exact a crushing defeat : *Our soccer team was pantsed again/ We pantsed the other teams at the spelling bee See* ANTS, CREAM one's JEANS, FANCY PANTS, FLY BY THE SEAT OF one's PANTS, GET THE LEAD OUT, HAVE LEAD IN one's PANTS, HIGH WATERS, HOT PANTS, RAGGEDY-ASS, SEAT-OF-THE-PANTS, SHIT one's PANTS, SMARTY-PANTS

pants off someone, the *adv phr* (also **someone's pants off**) To the utmost; to an extreme degree : *I'm going to sue the pants off you this time, meathead* [*1933+*; the intensifier became popular in the 1930s, mostly with menacing verbs like *beat, bore,* and *scare,* but also with *charm* and *flatter;* the semantics are not apparent, except perhaps that one feels helpless with one's pants off]

panty raid *n phr* A male invasion of a women's dormitory, the purpose being to take underwear as trophies (*1950s+ Students*)

pantywaist *n* A weak or effeminate male; PANSY : *The hurt pantywaist ran off a number of copies of his letter* [1936+; fr a child's garment with short *pants* buttoned to the *waist* of a shirt]

papa *n* A male lover; DADDY *(1785+ esp black); (1922+) See* SWEET MAN

paper *n* **1** A forged or worthless check *(1850+)* **2** A pass or free ticket; annie oakley *(Theater)* **3** A packet of narcotics; BAG *(1960s+ Narcotics)* **4** Money : *pass him paper in exchange for goods* *v* **1** To use or pass counterfeit money or worthless checks; lay paper : *papered Queens and Long Island with bum checks* (1925+) **2** To give out free tickets in order to get a large audience : *The show was not doing well, so they papered the theater (1879+ Theater)* **3** To write traffic and parking tickets : *The captain complained that the patrolmen were not papering enough (1960s+ Police) See* BAD PAPER, ON PAPER, PEDDLE one's PAPERS, WALKING PAPERS

paper bag *See* CAN'T FIGHT one's WAY OUT OF A PAPER BAG

◁**paper bag case**▷ *n phr* An ugly woman *(1980s+ Students)*

paper chase *n phr* An intense searching and collation of files, books, documents, etc, esp for the needs of bureaucratic pomp : *Manuel's history of ideas carries the reader not on a paper chase but on a fascinating voyage* [1932+ British; fr the game of hare and hounds in which the quarry would leave a trail of scraps of *paper*, the term found by 1856; popularized in the US as the title of a film and a TV series, where the *paper* was a Harvard Law School degree]

paper over *v phr* To conceal or gloss over; fail to deal with : *If the tiff were nothing but a clash of personalities it might be quickly papered over* [1955+; based on *paper over the cracks*, found by 1910 and based on a phrase of Bismarck's]

paper profits *n phr* Monetary gains recognizable by accounting but not realized in palpable money or goods *(1940s+)*

papers *See* PEDDLE one's PAPERS, WALKING PAPERS

paper tiger *n phr* A menacing person or thing that in fact lacks force; a blusterer : *doing battle with a paper tiger when he aims his wrath at the white liberal* [1952+; fr the Chinese expression *tsuh lao fu*, "paper tiger," given currency by Mao Zedong]

paper trail *n phr* Records, documents, etc, that lead to a conclusion : *Officials had expected to find a damning paper trail of incriminating evidence (mid-1980s+)*

pappy *n* Father; pap : *Harry Light? His pappy*

parade *See* RAIN ON someone's PARADE

paralyzed *adj* Very drunk *(1888+)*

parboiled *adj* Drunk *(1935+)*

pard *n* Friend; partner; PAL *(1872+)*

pardon me all to hell *See* EXCUSE ME ALL TO HELL

pardon (or excuse) my French *interj* An exclamation of apology for the use of profane or taboo language : *That Goddamned blankety-blank, pardon my French/ You will excuse my French. I am only quoting Mr Clemens (entry form 1895+, variant 1940+)*

parental unit or **unit** *n* Parent : *The parental units are away for the weekend (Teenagers)*

par for the course *n phr* What is to be expected : *He had to take a little crap from the clerk, but that's par for the course (1947+)*

park *v* **1** To put or place; locate : *Park yourself anywhere, I'll be right back (1922+)* **2** To manipulate records illegally so as to conceal true ownership of stocks : *If you're caught "parking" stock, your defense is everybody does it but I didn't know it was going on (1990s+) See* BALLPARK, BALLPARK FIGURE

park one *v phr* To hit a home run : *A cheer would go up across the street, and someone who had a transistor radio would holler, "Mantle just parked one" (1940s+ Baseball)*

parlay *v* To build or increase something from a small initial outlay or possession : *She parlayed her dimples into movie superstardom* [1942+; fr horse racing, "place a series of increasing bets," found by 1895, fr *paralee* or *parlee*, an early 1800s faro term fr Italian *parole*, "words, promises"]

parley-voo *v* To speak, esp a foreign language : *She wondered if he parley-vooed Chinese* [WWI Army; fr French *parlez-vous*, "do you speak?"]

parlor *See* MASSAGE PARLOR

part *See* BIT

party *n* **1** A person *(1460+)* **2** A bout of sex play or sexual activity *(1935+)* *v* (also **partay**) To go to or give parties; be energetically social; LIVE IT UP, MAKE WHOOPEE : *You don't party with the right people, kiss your ass goodbye (1922+) See* COLD-MEAT PARTY, HAVE A PARTY, HEN PARTY, NECKTIE PARTY, POT PARTY, STAG, TAILGATE PARTY

party animal (or **reptile**) *n phr* An enthusiastic party-goer : *Apparently Salman has turned into a major party animal (1980s+)*

party hat *n phr* **1** The array of lights on the roof of a police car or emergency vehicle; gumball *(1960s+)* **2** A condom : *In the heat of the moment he realized he didn't have a party hat (1980s+ Students)*

party hearty *n phr* PARTY ANIMAL : *He attracted a Hollywood set of Hawaiian-shirt party hearties who sunned themselves like alligators down in Key West (1990s+)*

party is over, the *sentence* The fun is finished; reality impinges *(1937+)*

party line, the *n phr* The accepted view; conventional wisdom : *The party line on Matisse* [1942+; popularized in the 1930s as "the official dogma of the Communist Party"]

party pooper or **party poop** *n phr* A morose, pessimistic person; KILLJOY, WET BLANKET : *No one can call Mr Bulganin and Mr Kruschchev party poopers/ What a party poop you are today, Sally* (1951+)

pass *n phr* A sexual advance; PROPOSITION (1928+) *v* **1** To be thought to be something one is not, esp to be thought white when one is actually black : *the oldest daughter, so fair she could pass* (1940s+) **2** To suffice or be adequate, only just barely : *It's not great pasta, but it'll pass* (1565+) **3** To decline to do something, take something, etc : *I'll pass on the French fries, but take the onions* (1869+) [in the first verb sense, *pass oneself off as* is found by 1809] *See* MAKE A PASS AT someone

pass go *v phr* To complete a difficult task or pass an important milestone in a project • Usu negative : *Execs go to jail, do not pass go in the scandal* [fr the game of Monopoly]

passion pit *n phr* **1** A drive-in movie theater : *taking his buxom daughter off to the local passion pit* (1951+ *Teenagers*) **2** A room used for seduction : *some minor-league Don Juan's passion pit* (1970s+)

passout *n* A person who has passed out, esp from drinking : *finding yourself with an 18-year-old passout on your hands* (1950s+)

pass out *v phr* **1** (also **pass out cold**) To lose consciousness; faint; go to sleep, esp from drinking too much liquor (1918+) **2** To die : *He left us a lot of jack when he passed out* (1899+)

pass the buck *v phr* To refer a problem or responsibility to someone else, esp to a higher authority; decline to take action : *We chickened out and passed the buck to the dean* [1865+; fr poker games where one would *pass the buck,* usu a pocketknife with a *buck* horn handle, on to the next person, thereby passing the deal on]

pass the hat *v phr* To ask for contributions of money; collect money from a group : *We passed the hat until we had her plane fare* (1762+)

pass something **up** *v phr* To choose not to take, attend, etc; GIVE someone or something A MISS : *I guess I'll pass up the concert tonight* (1896+)

paste *v* **1** To hit; strike very hard : *She grabbed the broom and pasted me* (1846+) **2** To defeat decisively; trounce; CLOBBER : *The Jets got pasted* (1940s+ *Sports*) [origin unknown; perhaps an alteration of earlier *baste,* "strike, trounce," of obscure origin and preserved in *lambaste*]

pasties *n* Adhesive patches worn over the nipples by nude dancers (1961+)

pasting *n* A beating; drubbing (1851+)

pasture *n* The outfield of a baseball field (1891+ *Baseball*) *See* OUTER GARDEN, PUT someone or something OUT TO PASTURE

patootie or **sweet patootie** *n* or *n phr* **1** One's girlfriend or boyfriend; sweetheart : *Tell their patooties how pretty they are* **2** A young woman : *a batch of pretty-panned patooties* [1921+; perhaps fr a play on *sweet potato* suggested by *sweetheart* and *potato* as used, like *tomato,* to mean a person]

patsy *n* **1** A victim; dupe; SUCKER : *a patsy, a quick push, a big softie/ But to retain lawyers is clear proof that you're a patsy* **2** A person who takes the blame for a crime, who is put up against a superior opponent in order to lose, etc; FALL GUY [1903+; apparently fr the name of *Patsy Bolivar,* a character in a minstrel skit of the 1880s, who was blamed for whatever went wrong]

pattern *See* IN A HOLDING PATTERN

patter of tiny feet (also **pitter-patter**) *n phr* Having young children around; also, imminent childbirth

patty *See* PADDY

pavement, the *See* POUND THE PAVEMENT

pavement princess *n phr* A prostitute who solicits business over a radio band [1976+; Citizen's band terminology]

paw *n* A hand : *You let me get my paws on the money* (1605+) *v* To touch and handle, esp in a crude sexual way (1701+) *See* SOUTHPAW

pay *See* HELL TO PAY

payback *n* Revenge; retaliation : *Payback is the idiom of East Africa, but the rule is that innocents always get hurt* (1970+)

pay dirt *n phr* Profit and success : *I'll try a fast-food franchise, where there's sure to be paydirt* [1873+; in the sense "richly yielding ore," found by 1856] *See* HIT PAY DIRT

pay one's **dues** *v phr* To serve and suffer such that one deserves what good comes to one; go through the mill : *We elderly have paid our dues* [1943+; an isolated example is found in 1878]

payoff *n* **1** Payment, esp of bribery, graft, etc : *The villains were waiting for their payoff* (1930+ *Underworld*) **2** The final outcome or bit of information, esp when it is surprising or amusing : *OK, here's the payoff, she's the Albanian consul!* (1926+)

pay off *v phr* **1** To give someone bribe money, blackmail money, or the like : *We'll have to pay them off handsomely to keep quiet* (1930+ *Underworld*) **2** To bring in profit; succeed; pay : *Getting another degree will pay off someday* (1951+)

payola *n* Graft; extortion money; bribery, esp that paid by recording companies to disc jockeys for playing their records on the radio [1938+; coined probably fr *payoff* and the ending of *Pianola*, trademark of an automatic piano-playing device, or *Victrola*, trademark of a gramophone]

pay the freight *v phr* To pay for; compensate for; bear the expense of; PICK UP THE TAB : *We may have to "pay the freight for well-meant efforts at improvement"* (*1970s+*)

pay through the nose *v phr* To pay exorbitantly; give too much in recompense (*1672+*)

pay up *v phr* To pay in full; settle one's account : *Pay up and be done with it* (*1434+*)

PC *adj phr* (also **pc**) Exhibiting political correctness *n* **1** Political correctness; conformity with a set of progressive social ideals (*1990s+*) **2** A personal computer : *Turn on your PC and type in CHKDSK* (*1978+ Computer*) **3** A pilot check flight or ride, where a pilot's continued qualification to fly is periodically tested (*1970s+ Airline*)

PCP *n* Phencyclidine, an animal tranquilizer smoked as a narcotic; ANGEL DUST (*1960s+ Narcotics*)

p'd *See* PISSED OFF

PDA *n* Public display of affection : *It's uncomfortable to be an adult and see PDA at the mall*

PDQ *adv* Pretty damn quick (*1875+*)

pea *See* SWEET PEA

pea-brain *n* An unintelligent or empty-headed person : *a pea-brain for a mom* (*1959+*)

peacenik *n* A member of a peace movement; pacifist; antiwar demonstrator (*1965+*) *See* NIK

peach *n* **1** An attractive young woman : *She really was a "peach"* (*1754+*) **2** Any remarkable, admirable, amiable, or attractive person : *You're a peach* (*1904+*) **3** Anything superior or admirable : *The hotel was a peach* (*1870+*)

peach-fuzz *modifier* Young; inexperienced : *I asked one of Clinton's peach-fuzz counselors how they could still be learning to govern after running the country for two years* (*1990s+*)

peachy or **peachy-keen** *adj* Excellent; wonderful; GREAT, NEAT : *this president's political health, which Wirthlin thinks is peachy (first form 1900+, second 1955+)*

peanut *adj* : *a peanut operation n* A small or trivial person; something insignificant (*1934+*)

peanut gallery *n phr* **1** The topmost rows of a theater (*1888+*) **2** A group or individual whose opinion is considered inconsequental

peanuts *n* A small amount of money; a trivial sum; NICKELS AND DIMES : *They got you working for peanuts* (*1934+*) *See* THAT AIN'T HAY

pearly whites or **pearlies** *n* The teeth : *shining those pearly whites at me* (*1935+*)

pea-shooter *n* **1** A firearm, esp one so called by a person who scorns its small caliber (*1950s+*) **2** A fighter pilot or plane (*WWII Army Air Force*) [fr a child's toy, a long tube through which he *shoots peas*, found by 1803]

pea soup (or **souper**) *n phr* A thick fog, esp one plaguing London (*1849+*)

pec *n* A pectoral muscle : *All the male weight lifters love her a bushel and a pec* (*1966+*)

peck *n* <1▷ PECKERWOOD (*1940s+ Black*) **2** Food (*1960s+ Teenagers*) **3** A perfunctory kiss : *She gave him a friendly peck and got back to work* (*1893+*) *v* To eat (*1960s+ Black*) *See* a PECK OF TROUBLE

◁**pecker**▷ *n* The penis (*1902+*)

◁**peckerhead**▷ *n* A despicable person; ASSHOLE, JERK : *Do you hear me, peckerhead?* (*1955+*)

◁**peckerwood**▷ *n* **1** A poor Southern white, esp a farmer; CRACKER, REDNECK **2** Any white Southern man : *Any white man from the South is a "peckerwood"* [*1929+ esp black*; fr rural black use of the red-headed *woodpecker*, with dialect inversion of the word elements, as a symbol for white persons in contrast with the blackbird as a symbol for themselves; the red head may be the semantic base, suggesting *redneck*]

peck of trouble, a *n phr* Much difficulty : *Looks like that young fellow got himself into a peck of trouble* (*1535+*)

pedal *See* PUT THE PEDAL TO THE METAL, SOFT-PEDAL

peddle one's **papers** *v phr* To go about one's business ● Often an irritated command that one leave the speaker alone : *I told him to go peddle his papers* (*1936+*)

pee *n* Urine *v* To urinate; PISS, WHIZ (*1880+*)

peed off *See* PISSED OFF

peekaboo *adj* Made of a sheer fabric or decorated with holes; SEE-THROUGH (*1895+*)

peel *v* **1** To undress; strip (*1785+*) **2** PEEL OUT (*1950s+ Hot rodders*) **3** : *Many of the young people describe stealing a vehicle as "peeling it"* (*1980s+ Street talk*)

peeler *n* A striptease dancer; STRIPPER : *grinders, peelers, and bumpers* (*1940s+*) *See* BRONCO BUSTER

peel out *v phr* (also **peel rubber** or **peel wheels**) To leave quickly; SPLIT [*1950s+ Hot rodders*; fr the notion of *peeling* off the tread of a tire]

◁**peenie**▷ *See* POUND one's PEENIE

peep *n* **1** A word; the slightest sound : *If I hear a peep out of you, you've had it* (*1903+*) **2** People ● Often plural

peeper *n* A private detective; PI, PRIVATE DICK : *And don't bother to call your house peeper* (*1940+*) *See* HEADSHRINKER

peepers *n* **1** The eyes : *If anything was wrong with my peepers the army wouldn't of took me* (*1700s+*) **2** A pair of sunglasses; SHADES : *I'd come through the employee door with one of my peepers on* (*1970s+*)

peep show *n phr* **1** A supposedly private view, as if through a hole in the wall, of some forbidden sexual activity (*1914+*) **2** leg show (*1940s+*) [found by 1851 as "an exhibition of pictures viewed through a lens in a small hole"]

peeve *n* : *You probably have a long list of peeves* (*1911+*) *v* To annoy; irritate : *That crap really peeves me* (*1908+*) [by back formation fr *peeved,* which in turn derives by back formation fr *peevish,* fr Middle English *peivish,* "perverse, wayward, capricious," perhaps fr Latin *perversus*] *See* PET PEEVE

peeved or **peeved off** *adj* or *adj phr* Annoyed; irritated; irked : *He got peeved* (*1908+*)

peewee *n* A short or small person, animal, etc : *That peewee doesn't scare me* (*1877+*)

peezy *See* JEEZ

peg *n* A throw, esp a hard one : *His peg missed and the runner scored* (*1862+ Baseball*) *v* **1** To identify; classify; pick out; BUTTON DOWN : *I could peg a joint like that from two miles away* (*1920+*) **2** To taper or bind a pair of trousers at the lower end : *Pants must be pegged to fit snugly around the ankle* (*1935+*) **3** : *He pegged it sharply to first* **4** To derogate; speak unfavorably of; BAG ON someone, put someone or something DOWN, TRASH : *It's good he wasn't at the party, because he was really pegged* (*1980s+ Students*) *See* SQUARE PEG, TAKE someone DOWN A PEG

peg leg *modifier* : *Watch me pass that peg-leg gimp* *n phr* A person who wears a wooden leg (*1872+*)

peg out *v phr* To die : *Harrison actually pegged out in 1841* [*1855+;* fr the ending of play in cribbage by *pegging*]

pegs *n* Legs; PINS : *He was wobbly on his pegs* (*1847+*)

pen *n* A prison of any sort, esp a penitentiary (*1845+*) *See* BULLPEN, PIGPEN, POISON-PEN LETTER

pencil *v* To work out details; study : *Let me pencil this idea for a while* (*1990s+*) *See* HAVE LEAD IN one's PENCIL

pencil someone or something in *v phr* To make a tentative arrangement : *Why don't I pencil in an appointment for next Thurday?* (*1940s+*)

pencil-pusher (or **-driver** or **-shover**) *n* An office worker, esp a clerk, bookkeeper, or the like; DESK JOCKEY : *The number of pencil pushers and typists has increased* (*1881+*)

penguin suit *n phr* A tuxedo; TUX : *Yes, it is possible to do serious rock 'n' roll in a penguin suit* (*1967+*)

penny ante *adj* : *I despised his penny-ante ideas* *n phr* A trivial transaction; a cheap offer, arrangement, etc (*1935+*) [fr the minimal ante required in a cheap poker game]

penny-pincher *n* A stingy person; miser; TIGHTWAD (*1934+*)

penny stock *n phr* : *That minimum would exclude penny stocks, which are cheap, risky stocks that usually have prices below $1 a share* (*1932+*)

pen-pusher *n* PENCIL-PUSHER (*1913+*)

pension off *v phr* To remove or dismiss because of old age or obsolescence : *pensioned off when he got senile* (*1848+*)

people *n* A person : *She's great people* (*1926+*) *See* the BEAUTIFUL PEOPLE, BOAT PEOPLE, JESUS FREAKS, NIGHT PEOPLE, STREET PEOPLE

people person *n phr* A sociable and compassionate person : *And the fact that he could tolerate a query about personality flaws proved he's not all that bad a "people person"* (*1990s+*)

Peoria *See* PLAY IN PEORIA

pep *modifier* : *pep talk/ pep pill* *n* Energy; vitality; PISS AND VINEGAR, PIZZAZZ (*1912+*) [fr *pepper*]

pepped out *adj phr* Exhausted; sapped : *I'm tired and pepped out* (*1920+*)

pepper *n* **1** Energy; vitality; PEP : *The old moral support is what gives we players the old pepper* (*1895+*) **2** A fast and hard session of pitch-and-catch; BURNOUT (*1920s+ Baseball*) ◄**3**► (also **pepper belly**) A Mexican or person of Mexican extraction (*1920s+*) *v* To throw a baseball very hard; BURN (*1920s+ Baseball*) *See* SALT AND PEPPER

pepper-upper *n* A thing, food, drink, person, etc, that imparts pep; stimulant : *"Say, fellows," said a uniformed pepper-upper to a bunch of GI assault troops* (*1937+*)

pep pill *n phr* Any amphetamine pill; UPPER (*1930s+ Narcotics*)

peppy *adj* Energetic; vital; ZINGY (*1918+*)

pep rally *n phr* A meeting where the participants are stimulated to some activity, harder effort, etc : *Ceausescu's pep rally becomes a revolution*

pep talk *n phr* A hortatory speech, usu given by a team coach or other leader : *I always had to give myself a pep talk before I went out to sing*

pep up *v phr* To stimulate; energize; brighten; JAZZ something UP : *Pep up your winter wardrobe* (*1925+*)

perc *See* PERK

percentage *n* Profit or advantage : *I don't see any percentage in doing it that way* (*1862+*)

percolate *v* **1** To run smoothly and well : *The little engine was percolating nicely* (*1925+*) **2** To saunter; stroll; OOZE : *Percolate on down the*

Avenue (1942+ Black) [all senses fr the coffee-making device; sense of "run well," for example, fr the steady cheery bubbling of the coffeemaker]

per each *adv phr* For each; apiece; a THROW : *Those are $8 per each, to you* [1906+; fr a humorous insertion of Latin *per* in imitation of pretentious business use]

perform *v* To do a sex act; function sexually : *She didn't love him, but liked the way he performed* (1916+)

period *interj* End of story. That is final : *Don't ask me again. Period*

perk[1] or **perc** *n* Percolated coffee (1950s+) *v* To run smoothly and well; PERCOLATE : *The project's perking now* (1925+)

perk[2] or **perc** *n* Extra money, privileges, fringe benefits, etc, pertaining to a job or assignment : *His men were delighted to be in Afghanistan, he said, mostly because of the perks* [1824+; fr *perquisite*]

perk up *v phr* 1 To stimulate; invigorate : *Gotta perk up this class* (1965+) 2 To recuperate; recover; gain energy : *He's perked up after a two-week illness* (1706+) [origin uncertain; perhaps related to *perch*, and semantically to the notion of being placed high]

perky *adj* Energetic and jaunty; lively; CHIPPER (1855+)

peroxide blonde *See* CHEMICAL BLONDE

perp *n* A criminal engaged in a specific crime : *The perp stood up, stepped back, took out a handgun and fired at least two shots* [shortened form of *perpetrator*]

perp walk (or parade) *n phr* A public display of a criminal defendant by the police : *an extended jaunt around the block, which is known as a perp parade/ The perp walk is a ritual, a vital part of New York's criminal-justice system* (1940s+)

persnickety or **pernickety** *adj* Overfastidious; finical; fussy [first form 1905+, second 1814+; fr Scots dialect]

persuader *n* A handgun; HEAT (1884+)

per usual *See* AS PER USUAL

perv or **perve** *n* A pervert; one with unconventional sexual tastes : *perv at the convenience store* (1944+)

pesky *adj* Vexatious; annoying; pesty [1775+; origin unknown]

pet *n* Darling; sweetheart; DOLL : *It's you, pet! How frightfully tickety-boo!* (1755+) *v* To kiss and caress : *torrid hugging, smooching, and petting* (1924+) *See* HEAVY PETTING

Pete *See* FOR THE LOVE OF PETE, PISTOL PETE, SNEAKY PETE

◁**peter**▷ *n* The penis [1902+; fr the association with *pee*, "urine"]

◁**peter-eater**▷ *n* A person who does fellatio, esp homosexually; COCKSUCKER (1970s+)

peter out *v phr* To become exhausted; dwindle away in strength, amount, etc : *They ran well the first mile or so, then petered out* [1858+; origin unknown; a 1908 article says it may be fr *peterboat*, a sharp double-ended vessel, hence "grow small or thin"]

pet peeve *n phr* One's particular and most cherished dislike or annoyance : *long been one of my pet peeves* (1919+)

petrified *adj* Drunk; OSSIFIED, STONED (1903+)

petting *n* Amorous caressing and kissing : *Petting is necking with territorial concessions* (1924+) *See* HEAVY PETTING

pfft *See* GO PFFT

phat or **PHAT** *adk* 1 Excellent; very good, pleasing, desirable : *everything is phat* 2 Musically, describing a full, deep, and bassy sound originating from hip-hop [fr black slang; first sense originally used to describe a woman as "sexy, attractive"] *See* FAT

phenagle *See* FINAGLE

phenom (FEE nahm) *n* A phenomenally skilled or impressive person; a performing wonder, esp in sports : *Veeck was a phenom, too* (1890+ Baseball)

Philadelphia lawyer, a *n phr* One who makes things unnecessarily complicated and obfuscates matters [1834+; fr a traditional reputation for the shrewdness of such attorneys, and the phrase *it would puzzle a Philadelphia lawyer*, found by 1788]

Philly or **Phillie** *n* Philadelphia (1891+)

phish *v* To lure unsuspecting Internet users to a fake Web site by using authentic-looking e-mail with the real organization's logo, in an attempt to steal passwords or financial or personal information or introduce a virus attack; the creation of a Web site replica for fooling unsuspecting Internet users into submitting personal or financial information or passwords (1996+)

phiz or **phizog** (FIZ, FIZ ahwg) *n* The face; MUG [1688+; fr *physiognomy*]

◁**phlegmwad** or **flemwad**▷ *n* A despised person; JERK, PRICK, ASSHOLE (1990s+) *See* -WAD

Phoebe or **little Phoebe (or fever)** *n* or *n phr* Five or the point of five (1940s+ Crapshooting)

phone *See* FLIP PHONE, HOLD THE PHONE

phone it in *modifier* Lackadaisical and half-hearted in playing (1980s+ Sports)

phone tag *n phr* A repetitive cycle of telephoning, leaving messages, missing replies, etc • Referring to the pervasive round-robin of messages left and phone calls missed : *"Having computers in our volunteers' homes has eliminated phone tag," says Power* (1990s+)

phony or **phoney** *adj* Not real or genuine; false; fake : *You phony little fake* (1900+) *n* 1 A fake thing : *That window's a phony, it don't* *open* (*1902+*) **2** A person who affects some identity, role, nature, etc; poseur : *some phony calling himself a writer* (*1902+*) *v* : *I ain't phoneying them woids* (*1942+*) [fr late 1700s British underworld slang *fawney* fr Irish *fáinne*, "ring," referring to a swindle in which the *fawney-dropper* drops a cheap ring before the victim, then is persuaded to sell it as if it were valuable; as the sequence of spellings, *phoney* and later *phony*, indicates, the US spelling is probably based on an attested folk etymology revealing the notion that one's feelings or even identity could be readily falsified on the *telephone*]

phony as a three-dollar bill *adj phr* Very false indeed; not remotely genuine (*1940s+*)

phooey *interj* (also **phoo** or **pfui** or **fooey** or **fooy** or **fuie**) An exclamation of disbelief, rejection, contempt, etc [1929+; fr Yiddish fr German; popularized by the newspaper columnist Walter Winchell]

photog or **fotog** (FOH tahg) *n* A photographer : *The Swedish fotogs were actually saving film* (*1913+*)

photo op *n phr* A brief period during which the press is allowed to photograph a dignitary or celebrity; a photographic opportunity (*1980s+*)

phreaking (FREE king) *n* The imitation of telephone touch-tone signals by whistling or by using mechanical devices so that free calls may be readily made : *and "phreaking," the art of using the telephone for fun but no profit for the company, came into being* (*1972+*)

physical *adj* Using the body, esp roughly or intimately : *Vanderbilt is a lot better than last year and more physical* (*1970+*) See GET PHYSICAL

PI *n* (pronounced as separate letters) *n* **1** A pimp (*1931+*) **2** A private detective; op (*1960+*)

piano legs *n phr* Thick calves and ankles : *Claudia Schiffer, the Bardot look-alike with a slight case of piano legs, stumps down the runway appallingly clumsy* (*1960s+*)

pic *n* A picture, and later esp a movie; FLICK : *Raft's next pic* (*1884+*)

◁**piccolo player**▷ *n phr* A person who likes and does fellatio [1950s+; fr a double reference to the *picklelike* shape of a penis and the fact that fellatio is referred to as "playing the skin *flute*"]

pick *See* NIT-PICK

pick and choose *v phr* To select very carefully (*1577+*)

pick someone's brain *v phr* **1** To question someone closely for one's own profit; exploit someone's creativity by imitation; be an intellectual parasite **2** To inquire of someone;

ask someone for information, advice, etc (*1885+*)

pick 'em *See* one CAN REALLY PICK 'EM

picker *See* BRAIN-PICKER, CHERRY-PICKER, FRUIT-PICKER

picker-upper *n* A person or thing that picks up : *A hitchhiker caught a ride. The picker-upper was soon arrested* (*1936+*)

picking *See* COTTON-PICKING

pickings *See* SLIM PICKINGS

pickle *n* **1** (also **picklement**) A parlous situation; predicament; dilemma : *I was in a sad pickle when I lost my job* (*1609+*) **2** A torpedo (*WWII Navy*) **3** A bullet : *He fired six pickles at the knob* (*1940s+*) *v phr* **1** To hit the ball very hard (*1908+ Baseball*) *v* **2** To ruin; wreck : *This will promptly pickle her college chances* (*1950s+*) [first noun sense fr 1500s British slang *in a pickle* and may refer to the situation of a mouse fallen into a pickling vat; *picklement* is a handy echo of *predicament*]

pickled *adj* Drunk; SOUSED (*1842+*)

picklepuss *n* A frowning and pessimistic person; SOURPUSS (*1940s+*)

pick-me-up *n* **1** A drink or snack that invigorates; PEPPER-UPPER, PERKER-UPPER **2** A drink of liquor taken to restore tone and morale (*1867+*)

pick off *v phr* To shoot, esp with careful aim (*1810+*)

pick someone or something to pieces *v phr* To be exquisitely critical : *We were sitting around picking the speech to pieces* (*1859+*)

pickup *adj* **1** Impromptu; unceremonious : *We'll have a pickup lunch in the kitchen* (*1859+*) **2** For one occasion; temporary; ad hoc : *a pickup band/ a pickup corps of waiters* (*1936+*) *n* **1** A person accosted and made a companion, esp in a bar, on the street, etc, for sexual purposes : *His next girlfriend was a pickup he made at Rod's* (*1926+*) **2** An arrest (*1908+*) **3** (also **pickup truck**) A small truck having a cab and cargo space with low sidewalls (*1932+*) **4** The ability of a car to accelerate rapidly, esp from a halt (*1909+*) **5** The act of getting or acquiring something : *He made the pickup at the post office* (*1938+*)

pick up *v phr* **1** To get; acquire : *He picked up a few thou hustling* (*1608+*) **2** To make things clean and neat; tidy up : *You'd better pick up in your room. It's a godawful mess* (*1874+*) **3** To answer the telephone (*1970s+*)

pick someone up *v phr* **1** To arrest someone : *The cops picked up six muggers and hauled their asses in* (*1871+*) **2** To make someone's acquaintance boldly, esp in a bar, on the street, etc, for sexual purposes : *She lets the soldiers pick her up* (*1698+*)

pick something **up** *v phr* To notice; discover; learn : *Did you pick that wink up?/ He picked up pitching in no time* (1857+)

pick up on something *v phr* **1** To notice; become aware of : *I pick up on people's pain, Alexander* (1935+) **2** To refer to and add to; bring back to notice, esp in order to query : *I want to pick up on what you just said about Philadelphia* (1970s+)

pick up the tab (or **check**) *v phr* To pay; assume the expense; PAY THE FREIGHT : *somebody to pick up the tab, which was important to her* (1945+)

picky *adj* Very niggling; CHICKENSHIT, PERSNICKETY : *For growing a beard. A lot of little picky things like that* (1917+)

picnic *n* **1** Something very easy; an easy undertaking; CINCH, PIECE OF CAKE : *That job's a picnic* (1880s+) **2** A good or enjoyable time; a BALL, BLAST : *The last week we had a picnic* (1909+) *See* NO PICNIC

picture *See* DRAW A PICTURE

picture, the *n phr* The situation; present shape of things (1922+) *See* the BIG PICTURE, GET THE PICTURE, PUT someone IN THE PICTURE

piddle *n* Urine (1901+) *v* **1** To urinate; PEE : *So you piddled on the floor. But you don't have to have your face wiped in it* (1796+) **2** To waste; idle : *You just piddle the day away* (1545+) [a euphemism for *piss*]

piddling or **piddly** or ◁**pissy-ass**▷ *adj* Meager; trivial; paltry : *It was an effort, though a piddling one/ The case was "a piddly little misdemeanor"/ Make your pissy-ass point again* (first form 1559+, second 1940s+)

pie *n* An easy task or job; GRAVY : *That's pie for him* (1889+) *See* APPLE-PIE ORDER, CUTESY-POO, CUTIE-PIE, EASY AS PIE, FUR PIE, HAIR PIE, SWEETIE-PIE

piece *n* **1** A share; portion; financial interest; a PIECE OF THE ACTION, SLICE : *a piece of the racket* (1929+) **2** A gun; pistol : *They step up to the driver's side and shove a piece in his ear* (1581+) ◁**3**▷ PIECE OF ASS (1785+) **4** An ounce of heroin or other narcotic : *He buys heroin in "pieces"* (1960s+ Narcotics) **5** A graffito on a subway car : *A train rumbles in and we all pause to view its pieces* (1970s+) **6** A tiny ponytail worn by males **7** Something worthless; PIECE OF SHIT : *that car is a piece* [second sense, US underworld use since about 1930] *See* ALL IN ONE PIECE, COME UP SMELLING LIKE A ROSE, KNOCK OFF A PIECE, MOUTHPIECE, MUSEUM PIECE, TEAR OFF A PIECE, THINK-PIECE

◁**piece of ass** (or **tail**)▷ *n phr* **1** The sex act; a completed sex act **2** A person regarded as a sex object, organ, or partner [first form 1930s+, variant 1917+; the date should

probably be earlier, in view of the 1785 occurrence of *piece* in the first sense] *See* TEAR OFF A PIECE

piece of cake *n phr* Anything very easy; anything easily or pleasantly done; BREEZE, DUCK SOUP • Originally British : *It's a piece of cake because you don't have the fear that they are going to pitch out on you* (1936+)

piece of calico (or **goods**) *n phr* A woman [first form 1880+, variant 1751+; *piece* meant "woman" as long ago as the 1400s]

piece of change *n phr* (Variations: **hunk** may replace **piece**; **jack** may replace **change**) Money, esp a large amount : *which would come to quite a piece of change* (1914+)

piece of fluff *See* BIT OF FLUFF

piece of meat *n phr* A person regarded as merely a physical body; unaccommodated man : *I'm just a piece of meat, but I know I'm a good piece of meat* (1940s+)

piece of one's **mind, a** *See* GIVE someone A PIECE OF one's MIND

◁**piece of shit** (or **junk** or **crap**)▷ *n phr* **1** Something or someone inferior or worthless : *a film he didn't want to make, and was a piece of shit* **2** A lie; hypocrisy; a PACK OF LIES : *Everything she said is a big piece of shit* (1950s+)

◁**piece of tail**▷ *See* PIECE OF ASS

piece of the action (or **pie**), **a** *n phr* A share of something, esp in profits, a business, or speculation, etc : *a piece of the "Gunsmoke" action/ Health expenditures consume an ever growing piece of the pie* [first form 1966+, variant 1970s+; fr *action*, "gamble, gambling"]

piece of work *n phr* A person remarkable either for good or ill; a prodigious person : *And pow along comes a bizarro piece of work like Trudy the dietitian* [1928+; fr Hamlet's paean "What a piece of work is a man"; the date belongs to the first occurrence of *nasty piece of work*, but it should probably be earlier; the phrase is listed among those children like in a 1900 compilation, and seems to refer to persons]

pie-eyed *adj* **1** Drunk : *the pie-eyed brothers* (1904+) **2** Astonished; wide-eyed : *Randall was pie-eyed. His mouth moved, but nothing came out of it* (1940+)

pie-faced *adj* Stupid; foolish : *a pie-faced boy from Minnesota* (1923+)

pie in the sky *modifier* : *It was a bit of a pie-in-the-sky idea n phr* The reward one will get for compliant behavior, later; hence wishful thinking or utopian fantasies [1911+; fr a Wobbly expression of contempt for those who maintained that suffering and penury on earth would be compensated by bliss and luxury in heaven; the locus classicus is a 1911 parody of the hymn "In the Sweet By and By," by the Wobbly martyr Joe Hill]

piffed or **piffled** *adj* Drunk *(first form 1900+, second 1934+)*

piffle *interj* A mild exclamation of disbelief, contradiction, rejection, etc *(1914+)* *n* Nonsense; BALONEY, BUNK : *the kind of piffle actors have to go up against (1890+)*

pifflicated *adj* Drunk *(1905+)*

◁**pig**▷ *n* **1** A police officer *(1811+ Underworld)* **2** A glutton *(1890s+)* **3** A promiscuous woman, esp one who is blowsy and unattractive : *spoke of a pig he had recently picked up (1927+)* **4** A racehorse, esp an inferior one; BEETLE : *why the hell that pig didn't win (1940s+ Horse racing)* *v* PIG OUT : *When you eat too much, you can say "I pigged" See* LIKE PIGS IN CLOVER, MALE CHAUVINIST PIG, RENT-A-PIG

pigeon *n* **1** An informer; STOOL PIGEON : *I don't like pigeons (1849+ Underworld)* **2** The victim of a swindle; dupe; MARK, SUCKER : *I'm your pigeon now and you guys are gonna rip me off (1593+)* **3** A young woman; chick *(1586+)* **4** A former alcoholic in the care of a helpful sponsor or guardian *(1980s+)* [first sense see **stool pigeon**; the second sense probably derives fr the expression *pluck a pigeon* and may be based on a notion that *pigeons* are easy to catch; the sense "young woman" is probably fr or related to *quail* and again suggests an easy victim] *See* CLAY PIGEON, DEAD DUCK

pigeonhole *v* **1** To classify; identify; BUTTON DOWN, PEG : *I pigeonhole this clown as a total bigmouth (1870+)* **2** To put away or aside *(1855+)* [fr the separate compartments of a desk or sorting system, likened to the orifices in a *pigeoncote*]

piggyback *n* The transport of loaded containers or semitrailers on railroad flatcars *(1953+)* *v* To originate or prosper with the help of something else : *Aerobic dancing piggybacked on the jogging craze (1968+)* [fr the term for carrying someone, esp a child, on one's back, derived by folk etymology fr *pick-a-back*, of unknown origin]

piggy bank *n phr* A source of funds : *Portland GE has $25 million in the company's piggy bank* [1941+; the date refers to the first notice of pig-shaped banks for children]

pighead *n* A stubborn person *(1889+)*

pigheaded *adj* Stubborn; stupidly obstinate *(1620+)*

pig-ignorant *adj* Crassly ignorant; very stupid due to ignorance : *pig-ignorant about the fact that we are grown people (1972+)*

pig in a poke *See* BUY A PIG IN A POKE

pig-out *n* A gluttonous occasion : *Thanksgiving was a total pig-out (1979+ Teenagers)*

pig out *v phr* **1** To overeat; PIG : *we ordered a pizza and totally pigged out* **2** To overindulge in anything : *It was time to pig out on rock and roll (1979+ Teenagers)*

pigpen *n* (also **pigsty**) Any filthy, littered place : *His room's a pigpen (1872+; 1820+ pigsty)*

◁**pig's ass** (or **ear** or **eye**)▷ *See* IN A PIG'S ASS

pigskin *modifier* : *the pigskin parade/ a pigskin superstar n* A football *(1894+)*

pike *See* COME DOWN THE PIKE

piker *n* **1** A mean and stingy person; miser; TIGHTWAD *(1872+)* **2** A shirker; loafer *(1889+)* [originally a vagrant, esp a gambler, who wandered along the *pike*; hence a poor sport, a cheapskate]

pile *v* To dash; run; thrust oneself : *I piled after her hell to split (1948+) See* GRUB-PILE

pile, a *n phr* A large amount of money; a fortune; BUNDLE *(1741+)*

◁**pile of shit**▷ *n phr* **1** CROCK OF SHIT **2** Something inferior or worthless; a shabby performance or product; PIECE OF SHIT : *The whole project's a pile of shit (1940s+)*

pile on *modifier* : *Contributing to the pile-on tactics, both big corporate media (including the Washington Post) and putative defenders of free expression strafed Moldea I from the start v phr* To throw oneself on a downed opponent unnecessarily : *It constitutes what is known in football as piling on, and they penalize you for it (1980s+ Football)* [pile onto, "assail," is found by 1894]

pileup *n* A wreck, esp one involving a number of cars : *6-car, end-to-end pile-up on the New Jersey Turnpike (1929+)*

pile up *v phr* To wreck; RACK UP, TOTAL : *after he piled up his car (1899+)*

pile up Zs *See* COP ZS

pill *n* **1** A boring, disagreeable person; a PAIN IN THE ASS : *Oh, don't be a pill, Valerie (1871+)* **2** A baseball or golf ball *(1906+)* **3** An opium pellet for smoking *(1887+ Narcotics)* **4** A Nembutal® capsule; NIMBY *(1950s+ Narcotics)* **5** A bomb, cannonball, bullet, etc : *He was drinking coffee when the big pill came down (1626+) See* PEP PILL

pill, the, or the **Pill** *n phr* Any oral contraceptive for women : *now that the joint and the pill are with us*

pillage *v* To eat voraciously or steal food : *pillaged the office fridge when no one was looking*

pillhead or **pill popper** *n* A person who habitually takes tranquilizers, amphetamines, barbiturates, etc, in pill or capsule form : *Papoose and me were a bunch of pillheads (1960s+ Narcotics)*

pillow talk *n phr* Intimate talk, esp that between a couple in bed *(1939+)*

pill-popping *adj* Addicted to or using narcotics in pill or capsule form : *The prostitute is now a* *suicidal, pill-popping* Newsweek *reporter n phr* The use of narcotics in pill form *(1960s+ Narcotics)*

◁**pill-pusher** or **pill-roller** or **pill-peddler**▷ *n* 1 A physician : *gynecological phenomena you pill-peddlers are always talking about* 2 A pharmacist or student of pharmacy (*first form 1857+, second 1926+, third 1927+*)

pimp *n* 1 A very cool person : *Pimp, a cool guy who's popular with girls (1990s+ Teenagers)* 2 An informer

pimping *n* Rapid questioning of a trainee by a superior [1980s+ Medical; fr initials of *put in my place*]

pimpish *adj* Stylishly dressed *(1980s+ Teenagers)*

pimpmobile *modifier* : *The pimpmobile mantle will be donned by the 1983 Cougar n* 1 A fancy car used by a prostitute's procurer and manager : *There's a red Cadillac pimpmobile parked outside* 2 Any very fancy and overlavish car *(1973+)*

pin *n* A leg *(1530+) v* 1 To classify and understand someone; PEG, PIGEONHOLE : *He was pinned as a bad doctor (1960s+)* 2 To look over; survey; DIG : *just pinning the queer scene (1960s+)* 3 To declare a serious commitment to someone by giving or taking a fraternity pin *(1935+ Students) See* HAIRPIN, KING, PIN someone DOWN, PIN something DOWN, PIN someone's EARS BACK, PIN ON, PINS

pinch *n* : *make a respectable number of pinches to stay off the transfer list (1900+) v* 1 To steal; SWIPE : *Who pinched the script? (1656+)* 2 To arrest; BUST : *The stores will invite ill will if they pinch indiscriminately (1837+) See* IN A PINCH

pinched *adj* 1 Arrested; apprehended : *pinched as he sped down the empty road* 2 Not having enough money to pay for necessities : *pinched until payday*

pincher *See* PENNY-PINCHER

pinch-hit *v* 1 To bat for a player who has been removed from the lineup, usu at a critical point in the game *(1927+ Baseball)* 2 To substitute for someone else : *Silvey has been pinch-hitting as an assistant director (1927+)*

pinch hit *n phr* A hit made by a player who bats in place of another *(1907+ Baseball)*

pinchpenny *adj* : *your pinchpenny budgets n* A miser; pinch-gut, TIGHTWAD *(1412+)*

pin someone **down** *v phr* 1 To get a definite answer, commitment, piece of information, etc, from someone : *He wouldn't say just when, I couldn't pin him down (1951+)* 2 To make someone immobile, esp to keep soldiers in place with constant or accurate fire *(1940s+)* 3 To identify or classify someone definitely; PEG, PIN : *I can't pin her down, but I've seen her before (1960s+)*

pin something **down** *v phr* To recognize, identify, or single out something definitely; make explicit : *I can't quite pin my feeling down (1951+)*

pineapple, the *n* The dole; unemployment benefits : *too many people on the pineapple* [1937; fr the brand Dole *Pineapple*]

pin someone's **ears back** *v phr* To punish someone, either by words or blows; chasten : *a flip-lipped bastard who should have had his ears pinned back long ago (1941+)*

pine (or **wooden**) **overcoat** *n phr* A coffin, esp a cheap one : *what they call in the army a pine overcoat (entry form 1896+, variant 1903+)*

ping *v* To get someone's attention with a sharp sound or other form of communication : *ping my accountant with April 15 getting close*

pinhead *n* A stupid person *(1896+)*

pink *adj* 1 Politically liberal; radical : *pink perspective on Palestine (1837+)* 2 Homosexual *(1972+ Homosexuals) n* 1 A white person; gray *(1926+ Black)* 2 A politically liberal or mildly socialist radical; parlor pink *(1927+)* 3 A legal certificate of car ownership *(1950s+ Hot rodders) See* IN THE PINK, TICKLED PINK

pink collar *adj phr* 1 Traditionally held by women of the middle class : *Mature women tended to gravitate toward pink collar jobs as secretaries, teachers, nurses, and saleswomen* 2 Working in a job traditionally held by women of the middle class : *the TV character to whom real-life blue- and pink-collar working women most relate* [1977+; modeled on *blue collar* and *white collar*]

◁**pinko**▷ *adj* : *How come those Niggers and those creepy pinko hippies call us names like "pigs"? (1957+) n* A person of liberal or mildly radical socialist political opinions; PINK : *Nixon liked to call people pinkos (1936+)*

pink slip *n phr* 1 A discharge notice; WALKING PAPERS : *All 1,300 employees got pink slips today (1915+)* 2 A legal certificate of car ownership; PINK : *I got the pink slip, daddy (1950s+ Hot rodders) v* : *They had pink-slipped Hartz one brutal afternoon (1915+) See* GET THE PINK SLIP, GIVE someone THE PINK SLIP

pinky or **pinkie** *modifier* : *pinky ring n* The little finger : *Pardon my lifted pinky (1860+)* [fr an earlier adjective sense, "small, tiny"] *See* PLAY STINKY-PINKY

pin on *v phr* To make an accusation; inculpate; HANG ON : *Police indicated they had little to pin on them*

pin one on *See* HANG ONE ON

pins *n* The legs : *knocked clean off his pins (1530+)*

pin-splitter *n* An excellent golfer; also, an accurate shot made by such a golfer, to the pin *(1926+)*

pint *See* HALF-PINT

pint-size or **pint-sized** *adj* Small, like a child or small person [1938+; fr the notion of a pint being a small amount]

pin-up *modifier* : *pin-up collections and books n* **1** A picture, usu a provocative photograph, esp of a pretty young woman **2** A young woman shown in a pin-up : *Dorothy Lamour was the Army's favorite pin-up* (1941+)

pin-up girl *See* SWEATER GIRL

pip, a, or **a pipperoo** or **a pippin** *modifier* : *a pipperoo flick n phr* A person or thing that is remarkable, wonderful, superior, etc; BEAUT, HUMDINGER : *His wildest dreams have to be pips (first form 1912+, second 1942+, third 1897+)* [fr *pippin*, a prized kind of apple; the shift was probably fr *peach* as one kind of excellent fruit to *pippin* as another]

pipe *n* **1** A signal; letter or note (1940s+ Underworld) **2** A telephone (1960s+) **3** (also **pipeline**) The tubular inner section of a breaking wave (1963+ Surfers) *v* **1** : *Bill Johnson pipes from Frisco that times are hard* **2** To speak up; say something; PIPE UP : *But I am not supposed to know that and do not pipe* (1784+) **3** To look at; see; notice : *Did you pipe her hands?* (1846+) **4** To hit someone on the head, esp with a metal pipe : *Someone was gonna pipe me (1970s+ Underworld)* **5** To shoot or kill with a gun; NINE : *So what do you care who piped Devona? (1990s+ Black street talk)* [all senses probably derived fr *pipe* as a conduit or a musical instrument; the sense "look at" is related to criminal slang "follow, keep under surveillance," of obscure origin and difficult to relate to any sense of *pipe*; *pipe-gun*, "crude gun made of a pipe," is found by 1973] *See* DOWN THE TUBE, LEAD-PIPE CINCH

pipe down *v phr* To stop talking; speak more quietly : *The others got sore at him and told him to pipe down* [1900+; fr naval jargon, probably related to the use of the boatswain's *pipe* for giving commands, or to its shrill noise]

pipe dream *n phr* An improbable and visionary hope, ideal, scheme, etc, such as an opium smoker might have : *He has some ambitious plans, mostly pipe dreams* (1896+)

pipeline *modifier* Directly communicated : *a pipeline review n* **1** A channel of communication, esp a direct and special one : *You'd think he has a pipeline to Jesus* (1921+) **2** A channel or course for routine production, processing, etc : *We'll have fewer men in what we call the "pipeline" who are moving* (1955+) *See* IN THE PIPELINE, PIPE

pipe someone off *v phr* To blacklist someone [1940s+ Nautical; fr the nautical practice of blowing the boatswain's *pipe* to welcome someone aboard or usher someone off a ship]

pipes or **set of pipes** *n* or *n phr* The voice, esp the singing voice : *to bring that great set of pipes into your very own living room*

pipe up *v phr* To speak up; raise one's voice; SING OUT : *He piped up with a couple of smart-ass cracks* [1889+; perhaps fr a play on the nautical *pipe down*; perhaps fr the playing of the *pipe* or *pipes*]

pipsqueak *n* A small and insignificant person or thing [1910+; fr *pip*, high-pitched sound, and *squeak*]

pisher *adj* Insignificant; trivial; PIDDLING : *I'm only sad that critics take it seriously. It's just a little pisher half-hour n* A young, insignificant person; SQUIRT : *Roth's rise in a few short years from Hollywood pisher to Hollywood mogul was a classic movie scenario* [1942+; fr Yiddish, "bed-wetter"]

◁**piss**[1]▷ *adj* Of wretched quality; PISS POOR : *Europe is a piss place for music* (1970s+) *n* **1** Urine (1386+) **2** A bad-tasting or poor-quality beer or liquor *v* **1** : *He had to piss* (1290+) **2** (also **piss and moan**) To complain; grumble; BITCH, KVETCH : *Angie's mother pissed and moaned about it for months* (1940s+) *See* FULL OF PISS AND VINEGAR, NOT HAVE A POT TO PISS IN, PANTHER PISS, TICKLE THE SHIT OUT OF someone

◁**piss**[2]▷ *combining word* A term placed before an adjective to intensify its meaning : *piss-awkward/ piss-elegant/ piss-poor/ piss-ugly* (1940s+)

◁**piss and vinegar**▷ *n phr* Energy; vitality; PEP, PIZZAZZ : *I was seventeen years old and 150 pounds of piss and vinegar* [1942+; full of vinegar, "interesting, entertaining," is found in college slang by 1926] *See* FULL OF PISS AND VINEGAR

◁**piss and wind**▷ *n phr* Pretentious but feeble show; gaudy display : *They strut with the piss and wind traditional among victors in political intrigues* [1922+; perhaps fr the situation of a person who can urinate and flatulate, but not achieve a substantial defecation]

◁**pissant**▷ (PIHS ant) *adj* Insignificant; paltry : *this little pissant country n* A despicable person; an insignificant wretch : *That sorry damn pissant* [1903+; extension of *pissant*, "ant," which is found by 1661]

◁**piss around**▷ *v phr* To deliberately waste time or annoy somebody and waste their time : *just pissing around and will never be ready to go*

◁**piss artist**▷ *n phr* An unpleasant or despicable person, esp one who is drunk (1975+)

◁**piss something away**▷ *v phr* To waste and dissipate something foolishly; squander :

There was a part of him that wanted to piss it away and be a loser (1930s+)

◁**pissed off**▷ *adj phr* (Variations: **pissed** or **p'd** or **peed off** or **p o'd**) Angry; profoundly annoyed; indignant : *His face got all red-colored whenever he was pissed off/ He gets a little pissed like I'm making fun of him*

◁**piss-elegant**▷ *adj* (Variations: ◁**piss-ass** or **pissy** or **pissy-ass**▷) Ostentatiously elegant; affecting great refinement; HOITY-TOITY : *a piss-elegant new wave Chinese restaurant and bar/ He was a jerk for needing to hang around with pissy queens (1972+)*

◁**pisser**▷ *n* 1 A very difficult job or task; BALL-BUSTER, BITCH : *That climb was a pisser* 2 A person or thing that is remarkable, wonderful, superior, etc; piss-cutter, PISTOL : *You're a pisser, you are* 3 A very funny person or thing : *What a pisser when he opened the wrong door by mistake* 4 A toilet : *windowless with a pisser and no benches* [1940s+; third sense fr the notion that one laughs hard enough to *piss* in one's pants]

◁**pisshead**▷ *n* A despicable person; a stupid bore; ASSHOLE : *who made such a pisshead of herself (1970s+)*

◁**piss ice water**▷ *v phr* To be very cool; exhibit sangfroid : *Patrick Stone had a reputation for pissing ice water at times like these (1980s+)*

◁**pissing contest (or match)**▷ *n phr* 1 An argument; disagreement; confrontational debate : *warned him against getting into a pissing contest with Bittman/ I'm not going to sit here and get in a pissin' match about petty problems like work shoes* 2 A contest; an unofficial competition [1970s+; perhaps fr actual vying among boys as to who can project the urinary stream farthest]

◁**piss in(to) the wind**▷ *v phr* To waste one's time and effort : *Why do you think the smart people get out of the job? Because they realize they're pissing into the wind* [1980s+; he who pisseth against the wind, wetteth his shirt is found as an Italian proverb by 1642]

◁**piss-off**▷ *n* Anger; indignation : *There's a basic, well-justified piss-off all over the country (WWII armed forces)*

◁**piss off**▷ *interj* Leave me alone; get lost : *Piss off, you jerk (1958+) v phr* To anger someone : *Don't piss off the policeman (1946+)*

◁**piss someone off**▷ *v phr* To make angry; arouse indignation *(WWII armed forces)*

◁**piss on someone or something**▷ *v phr* To dismiss or treat contemptuously; defile or violate; DAMN, FUCK, SOD ● Often used as an angry and defiant dismissal : *I said thanks for the flower. He said piss on the flowers (1720+)*

◁**piss poor**▷ *adj phr* 1 (also **pea-poor**) Of wretched quality; inferior; bad : *outgrow its*

status as one of the many piss-poor modern dance groups playing college campuses/ I thought the tight ends were pea-poor (1946+) 2 Penniless; in pauperdom : *They're all born piss-poor (1957+)*

◁**piss-ugly**▷ *adj* Very ugly; nasty and menacing : *Beer-bellied brutes peered at the world through piss-ugly eyes (1970s+)*

◁**pissy** or **pissy-ass**▷ *adj* Stupid; silly; offensive : *Oh, don't be so pissy. You know I will when I'm sure (1973+) See* PIDDLING, PISS-ELEGANT

pistol *n* 1 A person or thing that is remarkable, wonderful, superior, etc; BEAUT, pip, piss-cutter : *That Ruby Jean, she's a pistol (1984+)* ◁2▷ A woman's breast; BAZOOKA, JUG, TIT : *Whoa! Look at the pistols on that new French teacher (1990s+)* 3 Hot pastrami (1950s+ Lunch counter) [first sense probably a euphemism for *pisser*; lunch-counter sense because the eater feels as if shot in the stomach soon after eating hot pastrami]

pistol Pete *n phr* A zealous and effective lover; COCKSMAN [1940s+; fr the usual jocular analogue between *pistol* and "penis," "shooting" and having an orgasm, etc, reinforced by alliteration and the fact that *Peter* means "penis"]

pit bull *n phr* An extremely vicious and aggressive person ● *Rottweiler* is more common in British use : *Perot hired legal pit bull Roy Cohn to sandbag the Vietnam Memorial because he hated the design (1980s+)*

pitch *n* 1 A hawker's or street vendor's place of business; high pitch, low pitch (1849+) 2 The sales talk or spiel of a hawker : *He recited a part of his pitch/ other gifts to prospective brides, along with a pitch to honeymoon at Holiday Inns (1876+)* 3 A sexual approach, esp a tentative one; PASS : *I never made a pitch with Herta (1930s+) v* 1 : *Louie pitches kitchen gadgets/ He pitches household items like the Magic Towel* 2 : *I wouldn't try to pitch to that Ice Maiden* 3 To penetrate the anus in sex (1970s+ Homosexuals) *See* BUTTERFLY BALL, IN THERE PITCHING, MAKE A PITCH, THROW

pitchforks *See* RAIN CATS AND DOGS

pitch in *v phr* To set to work vigorously; help : *Let's all pitch in and get it done (1843+)*

pitching *See* IN THERE PITCHING

pitch into someone or something *v phr* To attack; assail forcibly (1829+)

pitchman *n* 1 A person who sells novelties, household items, clever toys and tricks, etc, on the streets or at a fair or carnival 2 Any advocate, promoter, persuader, spokesman, etc : *chief pitchman for Big Oil (1926+)*

pitchout *n* 1 A pitch thrown wide of the plate so that the catcher can more easily throw to one of the bases to forestall an attempted

steal *(1910+ Baseball)* **2** A lateral pass from
one back to another *(1947+ Football)*

pitch out *v phr* To make a pitchout *(1910+
Baseball)*

pitch (or fling) woo *v phr* To kiss and caress;
NECK : *And she pitches some more woo with Dr
Jan (1930s+ Teenagers)*

pits, the *n phr* **1** The most loathsome place or
situation imaginable : *This school is the pits* **2**
The armpits : *Your pits have BO (1953+)*

pit stop *n phr* A stop so that people may go to
the toilet : *Pit stop. Head run* [fr the *pit stops*
made by racing cars for service, repair, rest,
etc; possible pun on *piss stop*]

pix *modifier* : *pix credit n* **1** Movies; the movies;
the FLICKS : *You ought to be in pix* **2** Photographs, esp the artwork of a newspaper,
magazine, book, etc; graphics *(1932+)*

pixilated *adj* **1** Crazy; eccentric; confused
(1848+) **2** Drunk *(1955+)* [fr enchantment
by *pixies*; revived and popularized by the
1936 movie *Mr. Deeds Goes to Town*]

pizzazz *n* Energy; power; PEP, PISS AND VINEGAR :
What's missing is overall pizzazz and pace
[1937+; origin unknown; perhaps echoically
suggested by *piss*, *ass*, and *piss and vinegar*]

PJs or **pjs** *n* **1** Pajamas; JAMMIES, peejays : *New
arrivals like me still flapped about in pj's and
robes/ as though I were running around in my
PJs (1964+)* **2** Housing projects : *We always
lived in the PJs (1990s+ Black teenagers)*

places *See* GO PLACES

plain Jane *adj phr* Unadorned; stark; NO-FRILLS :
*"Plain Jane" is how one gun collector describes
the look* [1912+; the earliest examples read
plain Jane and no nonsense]

plain vanilla *adj phr* Unadorned; simple; basic
: *more lushly appointed variants of plain vanilla
family cars are due to arrive* [1970s+; fr vanilla ice cream, considered less fancy than
other flavors]

plain (or plain white) wrapper *n phr* An un-
marked police car *(1970s+ Citizens band)*

◁**plank**[1]▷ *v* To do the sex act with or to;
SCREW : *had witless good fun with his children while his wife was out getting planked*
[1970s+; origin unknown]

plank[2] *See* WALK THE PLANK

plunk down (Variations: **plump down** or
clunk down or **plank down** or **plank out**
or **plank**) *v phr* **1** To put down with a thud
or crash; place decisively : *an overstuffed chair
some admirer had planked down next to the
booth* **2** To pay money; put down or put up
money; offer or bet money : *planked down
a cool $8,000,000/ plunked down $65,000*
[1839+; fr the hard striking of the *plank* of a
table]

plant *n* **1** SHILL *(1925+)* **2** A cache, esp of stolen
goods *(1785+)* **3** Evidence placed so as to

incriminate *(1912+)* **4** A spy, esp a police
spy : *The new guy turned out to be a plant
(1812+)* *v* **1** To bury; hide *(1610+)* **2** To
place evidence secretly so that someone will
be incriminated : *Someone is planting evidence
(1865+)* **3** To place a blow : *He planted a left
on my poor snoot (1920+)*

plaster *n* **1** A banknote, esp a one-dollar bill : *If
you need a couple of plasters until Ed gets out,
tell me (1940s+)* **2** A person who surrepti-
tiously follows another; shadow; TAIL : *He
probably knew he had a plaster by this time
(1940s+)* **3** A subpoena or summons; arrest
warrant *(1950s+)* *v* To cover or apply generously : *They plastered the city with leaflets
(1585+)* [money sense fr *shinplaster*, an early
19th-century term for "currency of little
value or very small denomination"]

plastered *adj* Drunk *(1912+)*

plastic *adj* False and superficial; meretricious;
HOKED-UP, SLICK, PHONY : *in California, a plastic
society (1960s+ Counterculture) n* A credit
card; monetary credit afforded by the use of
credit cards *(1979+)* [second sense fr *plastic
money*, which is found by 1974]

plate *See* HAVE one's HANDS FULL, HOME PLATE, OFF
one's PLATE

platter *n* A phonograph record *(1931+)*

play *n* Publicity; media coverage : *The dangers
of the Free Trade Agreement are getting more
play (1929+)* *v* **1** To acquiesce; cooperate;
PLAY BALL : *They'd come back and get her, if
I didn't play with them (1937+)* **2** To go
very well; succeed : *The O'Connor appointment's playing. You're on a roll, Mr President
(1980s+ Show business) See* BONEHEAD PLAY,
GRANDSTAND PLAY, MAKE A PLAY FOR

play along *v phr* PLAY BALL *(1929+)*

play around *v phr* **1** To do something, esp
one's job, casually or frivolously; HORSE
AROUND : *Quit playing around and start playing hardball (1960+)* **2** To be sexually promiscuous; SLEEP AROUND : *She plays around
(1929+)*

play around with someone *v phr* **1** To flirt or
dally with; have a sexual involvement with
(1929+) **2** To treat lightly or insultingly;
challenge or provoke : *I wouldn't play around
with that gorilla if I were you (1960+)*

play at something *v phr* To pretend to do
something : *Play tennis? Well, I play at it
(1840+)*

play ball *v phr* **1** To begin; get started : *Let's
play ball now; it's time (1867+)* **2** To cooperate; collaborate; acquiesce : *I might have
played ball just a little, but I scorned to
(1903+)* **3** To deal honestly and fairly : *He
was playing ball with Artrim (1944+)* [fr
baseball; the first date refers to the first record of a baseball umpire's call *Play ball!*]

playboy *n* A man devoted to amusement; bon vivant; GOOD-TIME CHARLIE, MAN-ABOUT-TOWN (*1829+*)

play catch-up (or **catch-up ball**) *v phr* **1** To play a game determinedly and desperately when one is losing : *when college wishbone teams go to the air to play catch-up* **2** To work to recover from a disadvantage, defeat, etc : *For the last two years it's been a matter of playing catch-up ball with the budget* (*1971+*)

play checkers (or **chess**) *v phr* To move about from seat to seat in a movie theater, soliciting possible sex partners (*1972+ Homosexuals*)

play close to the chest (or **the vest**) *v phr* To be secretive and uncommunicative; keep one's counsel : *So you had to play your cards very close to your chest/ Nominees have played their cards close to the vest* [1950s+; fr the practice of a careful cardplayer]

play dirty *v phr* To use unethical, illegal, or injurious means; be deceptive and tricky; chicane : *When he started in politics he didn't mean to play dirty* [1940s+; the related form *play dirt* is found by 1908]

play doctor *n* A writer who specializes in altering and improving other writers' plays (*1940s+ Theater*)

play down *v phr* To treat with little emphasis; LOW-KEY : *They decided to play down the chief's faux pas* (*1934+*)

played out *adj phr* **1** Exhausted; worn out; ausgespielt, FRAZZLED : *I was played out, and quit at once* **2** No longer useful, viable, fashionable, etc : *I think the alienation theme is about played out* (*1862+*)

player *n* **1** A bettor : *A lot of players are avoiding OTB* (*1483+*) **2** : *some of his fellow "players" (as pimps refer to themselves)* (*1974+*) **3** An active participant : *Man, I'm a player. I gotta be watched* (*mid-1980s+*) *See* CHALK-EATER, PICCOLO PLAYER

play fast and loose *v phr* To behave in a recklessly irresponsible or deceitful manner toward someone or something; to treat someone or something quite unfairly or carelessly : *playing fast and loose with the facts*

play footsie (Variations: **footsy-footsy** or **footsy-wootsy** or **footy-footy**, or all these spelled with **ie** replacing the final **y**) *n* **1** Amorous and clandestine touching and rubbing of feet between a couple; pedal dalliance : *I played footsie with her during* Carmen **2** Any especially close relationship between persons or parties : *Truman is plenty burned up over the way Chiang Kai-shek played footy-footy with the Republicans* (*1935+*)

play someone for a fool (or **sucker**) *v phr* To take advantage of someone's gullibility, greed, etc : *Some blokes can never see when they are being played for suckers* (*1881+*)

play for keeps (or **rough**) *v phr* To be intent and serious to the point of callousness; PLAY HARDBALL : *We're out here man for man and playin' for keeps* [1861+; fr the game of marbles and other children's games where the tokens may be either returned or kept by the winner]

play games *v phr* To maneuver and manipulate cunningly; toy and gamble : *Don't play games with me, Linda* (*1970s+*)

playgirl *n* A woman devoted to amusement (*1934+*)

◁**play grab-ass**▷ *v phr* To indulge in sexual clutching and touching; to feel and fondle; GROPE • Sometimes used metaphorically : *were currently inside a doughnut shop, playing grabass with the counter girl/ His reluctance to play what he called grab-ass with Congress* (*1940s+*)

play hardball *v phr* To be intent and serious to the point of callousness; PLAY FOR KEEPS : *You want to play hardball, here we go* [1973+; fr the presumed distinction in difficulty, severity, and manliness between baseball, that is, *hardball*, and softball]

play hell (or **merry hell**) **with** something *v phr* To damage or destroy : *The rain had played hell with business/ Gloria played merry hell with the filing system* [1803+; fr *play hell and Tommy*, attested in the mid-19th century and said to be fr earlier *play Hal and Tommy*, in reference to the behavior of Henry VIII and his minister Thomas Cromwell]

◁**play hide the weenie** (or **salami** or **sausage**)▷ *v phr* To do the sex act; copulate; SCREW : *So Craig suggested that we play hide the salami* (*1980s+*)

play hooky (or **hookey**) *v phr* To stay away from work and duty, or esp from school without an excuse; be truant [1848+; probably fr *hook it*]

play in Peoria *v phr* To succeed in areas distinct from such foci of power as Washington and New York or the Northeast in general : *When you're under a deadline, it's hard to judge what will play in Peoria* [1970s+; fr the theater sense of *play*, to succeed on the stage; perhaps echoing Harold Ross's criterion that he wanted *The New Yorker* to appeal to "a little old lady in *Peoria*"]

play into someone's **hands** *v phr* To give an advantage to one's opponent : *Signing that is just playing into their hands* (*1705+*)

play it by ear *v phr* To handle a situation instinctively and extemporaneously, rather than by informed planning; improvise : *We didn't have much to go on, so we just had to play it by ear* [1961+; fr the playing of music imitatively, without training and notation; the phrase is found by 1674]

play it cool *v phr* To behave in a calm, controlled, uncommitted way; be watchful and impassive : *We asked for a price and the agent "played it cool"* (1955+)

play it (or **play**) **safe** *v phr* To choose a cautious line of behavior; avoid much risk : *Now we're ahead, let's play it safe* (1919+)

play kissie (Variations: **kissy-face** or **kissy-facey** or **kissie-kissie** or **kissy-poo** or **lickey-face** or **smacky lips** may replace **kissie**) *v phr* 1 To kiss and caress; MAKE OUT, NECK : *Salesmen got them to buy an awful lot of perfume when they weren't busy playing lickey-face/ Newlyweds play kissy-poo in a resort hotel* 2 To be friendly and flattering; PLAY UP TO someone : *We have to play kissie with him* (1970s+)

playmate *n* One's companion in the pursuit of pleasure, esp of sexual delight (1970s+)

play out *v phr* To develop; transpire; BREAK OUT, SHAKE OUT : *How do you see this playing out in your own State?* [1854+; fr the finishing of a stage *play*]

play pattycake *v phr* To cooperate cozily; PLAY FOOTSIE : *They point to the hypocrisy of local law enforcement that plays pattycake with the Mafia up on the Strip* [1976+; fr a game one plays with infants]

play rough *See* PLAY FOR KEEPS

plays *See* the WAY IT PLAYS

play second fiddle *v phr* To be in an inferior position; lack power or will to lead : *They won't play second fiddle to their spouses anymore* (1809+)

play snuggle-bunnies *v phr* To kiss and caress; cuddle amorously; PLAY KISSIE : *Mr De Varennes is playing snuggle-bunnies with Mrs Martin* (1970s+)

◁**play stinky-pinky** (or **stink-finger**)▷ *v phr* FINGERFUCK (1903+)

play the something card *v phr* To use an exploitive or inflammatory maneuver : *Milosevic saw that the best way to hold on to power was to play the nationalist card* (1886+)

play the field *v phr* To have a number of sex or love partners, rather than settling on one [1936+; fr gamblers who bet on other horses than the favorites]

play the ponies *v phr* To bet on horse races (1908+)

◁**play the skin flute**▷ *v phr* To do fellatio (1940s+)

play up *v phr* To emphasize; feature; make the most of : *Hey, don't play up your bad points* [1909+; fr the featuring of a story in a newspaper]

play up to someone *v phr* To flatter; be compliant : *If you play up to him he'll think you're brilliant* [1826+; fr the behavior of an actor who gives featuring support to another]

◁**play with** oneself▷ *v phr* To masturbate; JACK OFF : *I was going with girls and I didn't feel the urge to play with myself* (1896+)

play (or **deal** or **operate**) **with a full deck** *v phr* 1 To be sane and reasonable; have normal intelligence • Usu in the negative : *Neither of the poor things was playing with a full deck/ But she is dealing with a full deck, as it were/ He wasn't playing with a full deck of cards* 2 To be honest and straightforward; avoid deception : *He has bluffed you into thinking he was playing with a full deck* (1970s+)

play with fire *v phr* To do something risky or dangerous : *playing with fire to put too much into that new Web site*

play with someone's head *v phr* To toy with psychological influence for one's advantage; play a "mind game" : *He's playing with my head, and I don't like it* (1990+)

plea *See* COP A PLEA

plebe *n* A first-year student at Annapolis or West Point [1833+ Service academy; fr *plebeian*, "lower-class person," fr Latin]

pledge *n* A student who has agreed to join a certain college fraternity or sorority (1901+ Students) *v* : *Without a second thought MacCrimmon pledged Xi Phi*

plenty *adv* Very; very much; extraordinarily : *I was plenty cautious* (1842+)

plink *v* 1 To shoot : *I could walk up to him, plink his eyes out* (1966+) 2 To make a series of short, light, ringing sounds

plonk *n* 1 Inferior wine; cheap wine : *It's a humble plonk, but you'll like it* (British fr Australian 1930+) 2 A boring and obnoxious person; PILL (1960s+) [wine sense fr French *vin blanc*, "white wine"; second sense perhaps fr the dull sound *plonk*]

plonked *adj* Drunk (1943+)

plotzed *adj* Drunk : *even smashed as you were, friend, plotzed out of your wits* [1962+; probably fr Yiddish *plotzen*, German *platzen*, "burst, split," reflecting the same notion of violent destruction as *smashed, bombed*, etc]

◁**plow** or **plough**▷ *v* To do the sex act with or to a woman; SCREW (1606+ and probably before)

plow (or **plough**) **into** *v phr* 1 To collide with very hard; ram : *so long as they don't fry in the sun or plow into an atmosphere* (1972+) 2 To attack heartily; assault (1940s+)

pluck[1] *v* To rob or cheat; fleece : *These bimbos once helped pluck a bank* [1400+; fr the image of *plucking* a chicken]

◁**pluck**[2]▷ *v* To do the sex act with or to; SCREW [1950s+; a euphemism for *fuck*]

plug[1] *n* 1 An inferior old horse; NAG (1860+) 2 An average or inferior prizefighter (1915+) [perhaps fr Dutch *plug*, "a sorry nag," related to Swiss-German *pflag* and to Danish *plag*, "foal"]

plug[2] *adj* (also **plugged**) Worthless; PHONY : *And furthermore the author does not give a plug damn* (*1888+*) *n* A silver dollar (*1900+*) *v* **1** To shoot, esp shoot to death : *The mugger got plugged by an indignant on-looker* (*1870+*) **2** To do the sex act to; BOFF, POKE, SCREW (*1901+*) [all senses fr the notion of *plug* as hole-filler; the second sense may be influenced by the notion of inferiority in *plug*[1]] *See* PULL THE PLUG, SPARK PLUG

plug[3] *n* Positive publicity : *I certainly would appreciate him giving me a plug with the owners* (*1902+*) *v* **1** (also **plug along** or **plug away**) To work or study steadily and fairly hard; keep busy but not excitingly so : *She's plugging away, though* (*1888+*) **2** To give a flattering appraisal, esp with a view to selling something; advocate and support; cry up : *Cosmetic manufacturers plugged products to give women ersatz tan/ If you'll plug my book, I'll plug yours* (*1906+*) [fr Oxford University slang, apparently in imitation of heavy plodding steps, or perhaps the steps of an old and tired horse; sense of selling or advocating fr the fact that such commendation was originally constant and repetitive]

plug for *v phr* To support actively; cheer for; ROOT FOR : *She was plugging for the coalition candidate* (*1900+*)

plugged in (or **into**) *adj phr* **1** In direct touch with; sensitive to and aware of : *She's plugged in, in ways I don't quite understand* **2** TURNED ON [late 1960s+; fr the metaphor of a person as an electrical or electronic device]

plugged nickel *See* NOT WORTH A PLUGGED NICKEL

plugger *n* **1** A diligent but not brilliant worker or student; dependable drudge (*1900+*) **2** A hired killer; HIT MAN (*1940s+ Underworld*) **3** : *The Packers reluctantly shifted George Koonce from the inside linebacker (plugger) position* (*1990s+ Football*)

plug in (or **into**) *v phr* **1** To become a part of; participate in; gain access to : *Parents were beginning to be plugged directly into the decision-making process* **2** To discover and exploit to one's advantage; tap : *Nixon has plugged into a great national yearning* [late 1960s+; fr the notion of the electrical *plug* and socket]

plug-ugly *n* **1** A rowdy; tough; GORILLA, HOOD (*1856+*) **2** A prizefighter; PUG (*1940s+*) [origin unknown; perhaps fr rowdy fire companies in Baltimore, hence fr *fireplug*; perhaps fr New York toughs of the 1830s who wore top hats over their ears as helmets; perhaps related to *plug-muss*, "a fight," found by the early 1950s]

plum *modifier* : *who recently got the plum job of heading the county's Department of Human Resources n* Something highly prized, esp an easy job with high pay and prestige, often given for political favors : *The winners get to pick all the plums* (*1825+*) [probably influenced by Little Jack Horner's feat of reaching in his thumb and pulling out a *plum* (in fact a raisin); compare early 1800s British *plummy*, "good, desirable"]

plumb *adv* Completely; entirely; STONE : *What he said was plumb silly* [*1748+*; fr notions of exact extent and precision associated with the *plumb* bob or sailor's *plumb* line (for measuring depth of water), ultimately fr Latin *plumbum*, "lead"]

plumber *n* **1** A urologist (*1950s+ Medical*) **2** A member of a White House group under President Richard M Nixon, which exerted itself to stop various leaks of confidential information : *One of the jobs carried out by the plumbers was burglarizing the office of Dr Daniel Ellsberg's former psychiatrist* (*1972+*) *v* To botch; ruin : *I tho't I plumbered it* (*1930s+*)

plumber's (or **working man's**) **smile** *n phr* A view of the upper cleft of the gluteus maximus as a male's pants descend when he is bent over doing work : *don't want to see plumber's smiles from the town road crew*

plumbing *n* **1** A trumpet (*1930+ Jazz musicians*) **2** The digestive, excretory, and reproductive systems and organs (*1950s+*)

plummy *adj* Rich and sonorous; orotund and fruity; unctuous; SMARMY : *the rich, plummy voice of Edward Arnold* (*1881+*)

plump or **plunk** *adv* Precisely; exactly; squarely; SMACK [*1734+*; fr *plumb*]

plump for someone or something *v phr* To choose; support; advocate (*1834+*)

plunk *n* A dollar : *my five thousand plunks* (*1891+*) *v* To shoot (*1888+*) [echoic]

plush or **plushy** *adj* Luxurious; stylish; costly : *a swank, plush, exclusive cabaret club/ singer Ella Logan at the plushy Casablanca* (*1927+*) *n* : *All the plush in the world won't tidy up his vulgar soul* [fr the soft and costly fabric, fr French *pluche*]

po *See* PISSED OFF

pocket *See* DEEP POCKET, IN someone's POCKET, OUT OF POCKET

◁**pocket pool** (or **polo**)▷ *n phr* The fondling of one's own genitals with a pocketed hand (*entry form 1930s+, variant 1980s+*)

pocket rocket *n phr* A penis, esp one with an erection : *covering the pocket rocket with a towel*

po'd *See* PISSED OFF

Podunk (POH dunk) *n* The legendary small country town; east jesus; JERK TOWN [*1843+*; originally an Algonquian place name meaning "a neck or corner of land," used for several places in New England; also the name of a small tribe]

poetry slam *n phr* : *A poetry slam is a contest for poets. Anyone who spends his or her leisure hours pouring his or her soul onto paper can enter a slam* (1990s+)

poindexter *n* An overly studious person; MERV. NERD, pencil neck (1980s+ Students)

point *n* **1** The jaw (1925+ Prizefighting) **2** A hypodermic needle; SPIKE (1960s+ Narcotics) **3** (also **point man**) A forward reconnaissance man; lookout man; scout who warns his associates of danger and may get the first shock of attack : *He is the point man for organized labor* (1940s+ Armed forces & underworld) See BROWNIE POINTS

pointer *n* An item of advice or instruction : *She gave me a few pointers about how to say it* (1883+) See FOUR-POINTER

point man (or **person**) *n* A person who plays a crucial, often hazardous role in the forefront of an enterprise; a person designated to take the lead in a project or task : *point man on the new project*

point-shaving *n* The illegal practice, esp on the part of athletes, of controlling the score of a game, match, series, etc, so that professional gamblers will have to pay less to the bettors or will win for themselves (1971+ Sports & gambling)

point the finger *v phr* To accuse or vilify : *Don't be too quick to point the finger in his case* [1829+; the dated instance refers to the *finger of scorn*]

pointy-head or **pointhead** *n* **1** A stupid person; TURKEY **2** An intellectual; EGGHEAD : *The "pointy heads" are impractical as politicians* (1972+)

poison *n* **1** A situation, person, event, etc, that portends harm and evil; MURDER : *Don't try that route, it's poison* (1918+) **2** Liquor, esp cheap whiskey (1805+) See NAME YOUR POISON

poison-pen letter *n phr* A malicious anonymous letter; an obscene crank letter (1929+)

poison pill *n phr* Any financial stratagem that causes a company to be unattractive to takeover bidders : *Time Warner's poison pill effectively bars an investor from owning more than 15 percent of the company's outstanding shares* (mid-1980s+ Business & finance)

poke[1] *n* **1** A cowboy : *Each poke pays his own transportation to the Rodeo* (1928+) **2** SLOW-POKE (1940s+) ◁3▷ The sex act; PIECE OF ASS (1700+) *v* **1** To herd cattle (1940s+) **2** To hit the ball, esp to hit fairly lightly with precise aim : *He just poked it into the hole* (1880s+ Baseball) ◁3▷ To do the sex act

with or to; SCREW (1868+) See BUY A PIG IN A POKE, COWPUNCHER

poke[2] *n* **1** A wallet, pocket, or purse : *with only about $85 in my poke* (1859+) **2** Money; one's bankroll (1926+) [fr Southern dialect, "pocket, bag," fr Middle English, ultimately fr Old Norman French]

poke around *v phr* To examine or search, esp in a dilatory way : *He might know we've been poking around the computer files* [1809+; the dated instance reads *poke about*]

poke fun *v phr* To tease; jape; mock (1840+)

poke one's nose into something *v phr* To pry and meddle; examine : *and to poke your nose into all the most interesting places* (1860s+)

poker face *n phr* **1** An expressionless face; neutral mask; DEADPAN **2** A person whose face is usually expressionless (1885+)

poker-faced *adj* Without expression; showing a neutral mask; DEADPAN, STRAIGHT-FACED : *She's great at poker-faced zingers* (1923+)

pokery See JIGGERY-POKERY

pokey[1] or **poky** *n* A jail; CLINK, SLAMMER : *My thoughts centered around the prospect of the "Pokey"* [1919+; origin unknown]

pokey[2] or **poky** *adj* **1** Slow; dawdling; sluggish : *What a pokey waiter* (1856+) **2** Insignificant; paltry : *a pokey little town* (1849+) See HOKEY-POKEY

pol (PAHL) *n* A politician : *only another pol on the take* (1942+)

◀**polack**▶ (POH lahk) (also **Polack** or **pollack** or **Pollack** or **pollock** or **Pollock**) *n* A Pole or a person of Polish extraction • It is curious that this word is somewhat pejorative in English even though it is the Polish word for "Pole" (1879+)

pole See BEANPOLE, NOT TOUCH someone or something WITH A TEN-FOOT POLE

police or **police up** *v* or *v phr* To clean up a camp, barracks, parade ground, etc; make neat and orderly (1851+ Army)

policeman *n* ENFORCER : *You had to bring in somebody who was as tough, or brutal, as they were. The kind of terminology for this role in hockey was "policeman"* (1980s+)

Polish See IS THE POPE POLISH

polisher See APPLE-POLISHER

polish off *v phr* **1** To eat; consume, esp quickly and heartily : *I had polished off a platter of beans* (1873+) **2** To finish; accomplish : *He polished off the week's quota in four days* (1837+) **3** To put out of action; defeat; kill : *Polish him off by crowning him with a Coca-Cola bottle* (1829+) [fr the notion of finishing a piece of work by giving it a final *polish*]

politician *n* A person who succeeds through charm, diplomacy, mutual favors, etc • The term is mildly derogatory in suggesting a lack of true substance : *If you called him an asshole to his face you're no politician* (*1592+*)

politico (pə LI ti koh) *n* A politician, esp a spectacular or unscrupulous one : *the heavy-duty Bay State politicoes* [*1630+*; fr Spanish or Italian]

pollack or **pollock** or **Pollock** *See* POLACK

polluted *adj* Drunk (*1912+*)

Pollyanna *n* An irrepressibly cheery person; undaunted optimist : *or were we all a crowd of Pollyannas?* [*1913+*; fr the title and heroine of a novel by Eleanor Hodgman Porter, 1868–1920]

◁**pom-pom**▷ *n* The sex act; SCREWING [WWII Army; perhaps fr the echoic name *pom-pom* of various rapid-fire automatic guns, found by 1889]

pond, the *n* The ocean (*1641+*) *See* the BIG POND

pond scum *n phr* A worthless person, often mean-spirited (*College students*)

pony *n* **1** A literal translation of a foreign-language school text, used as a cheating aid (*1827+ Students*) **2** Any cheating aid used by a student (*1970s+*) **3** A small, bell-shaped liquor glass, used esp for brandy and liqueurs (*1849+*) **4** A racehorse : *Do you follow the ponies?* (*1907+*) **5** A chorus girl or burlesque dancer : *The ponies slumped into place* (*1905+*) [in all senses fr the thing being small like a *pony*; the student senses, which have or have had *horse* and *trot* as synonyms, may also suggest something that carries one, gives one a free ride]

pony act *See* DOG AND PONY ACT

pony up *v phr* To pay; FORK OVER : *He had ponied up a silver quarter* [*1824+*; fr earlier British *post the pony*, "pay," fr 16th-century *legem pone*, "money," fr the title of the Psalm for Quarter Day, March 25, the first payday of the year]

poo or **pooh** *interj* A mild exclamation of disbelief, dismay, disappointment, etc : *Oh poo, I dropped it* (*1602+*) *n* Excrement; DO, POO-POO • Along with *poop*, this is a euphemism used by and to children : *Zoo Poo garden fertilizer is made from the waste of all manner of exotic creatures* (*1950s+*) *See* CUTESY-POO, HOT POO, ICKY

-poo *combining word* Little; silly little • A nonsense word used after diminutive forms to give an arch baby-talk effect : *settled down for a well-bred nappy-poo* (*1970s+*)

pooch *n* A dog : *a card for your pooch* [*1924+*; origin obscure] *See* SCREW THE POOCH

◁**poof**▷ *n* (also **poofter** or **poove** or **pouffe**) A male homosexual; FAGGOT, QUEER [British 1850+, poofter fr Australian by 1903; origin unknown; perhaps fr *puff*, attested in mid-1800s British hobo slang as "homosexual"]

pooh-bah *n* An important person; a self-important person; BIG SHOT, HONCHO, VIP : *where presidents and pooh-bahs commune* [*1888+*; fr the character in Gilbert and Sullivan's *The Mikado* who holds many high offices, the name probably coined fr two exclamations of contempt and derision]

poohed or **poohed out** *adj* or *adj phr* POOPED (*1940s+*)

pooh-pooh or **poo-poo** *v* To dismiss lightly and contemptuously; airily deprecate; deride : *I don't poo-poo his talent, just his character* (*1827+*)

pool *See* DIRTY POOL, POCKET POOL

◀**poon tang** or **poon**▶ *n phr* or *n* A black woman regarded as a sex object or partner : *Eye that poon tang there/ just about to get a little poon/ watching all that young poon* [*1910+*; probably fr French *putain*, "prostitute," by way of New Orleans Creole]

poop[1] *n* Information; data; SCOOP : *The girl's given us the complete poop See* POOP SHEET (*1930s+ Army & students*)

poop[2] *n* **1** Excrement; POO • Along with *poo*, this is a euphemism for use to and by children (*1744+*) **2** A contemptible, trifling person; PILL • Often used ironically and affectionately, esp of an old person : *a sweet old poop who was seventy-six* (*1915+*) *v* **1** : *The dog pooped on the rug* (*1903+*) **2** To tire; fatigue; BUSH : *Being with him poops me exceedingly* (*1932+*) [probably fr a merging of 14th-century *poupen*, "to toot," with 15th-century *poop*, "the rear part of a ship," fr Latin *puppis* of the same meaning; the fatigue sense may be related to the condition of a ship that is *pooped*, "has taken a wave over the stern"]

◁**poop chute**▷ *n phr* The anus : *I fingered her pussy and poop chute* (*1970s+*)

pooped or **pooped out** *adj* or *adj phr* Exhausted; deeply fatigued; BEAT, BUSHED : *starting to get pooped out* [*1930+*; fr a British nautical term describing a ship that has been swept by a wave at the stern; perhaps related to *pooped*, "overcome, bested," found by 1551]

pooper *n* The posterior; ASS, BUTT : *What a fuckin' pooper on that little snatch* (*1970s+*) *See* PARTY-POOPER

pooper (or **poop**) **scooper** *n phr* A shovel and container set designed for cleaning one's dog's feces off the sidewalk, and, by extension, anything so used : *to buy a pooper scooper or something like it* (*1972+*)

poophead *n* A very unhappy person; also, someone who acts stupidly

poo-poo *n* Excrement; POO, POOP • A euphemism used to and by children : *He reverts to that childishness of poo-poo caca* [*1970s+*; fr *poop*]. *See* POOH-POOH

poop (or **poo**) **out** *v phr* To fail; lose energy and impetus; FIZZLE : *They would have won, but they suddenly just pooped out* (*1926+*)

poop sheet *n phr* Any set of data, instructions, official notices, etc : *Here's the poop sheet from the comptroller* [1935+ Army & students; origin unknown; perhaps fr *poop,* "excrement"; improbably but possibly an unaccounted shortening of *liripoop,* "lore, tricks of the trade," as found in the 1500s phrases *to know one's liripoop, to teach someone his liripoop,* perhaps related to *lerrie,* "something learned or spoken by rote"]

poopsie or **poopsy** or **poopsie-woopsie** *n* Sweetheart; BABE, HONEY ● Often a term of endearment : *I hear you, poopsie* (*1940s+*)

poopy or **poopie** *adj* Depressed; also, ineffectual : *She felt poopy when they left her out* (*1957+*) *n* Excrement ● Mainly a children's word : *poopy in the diaper*

◁**poor-ass**▷ *adj* Wretched; nasty; LOUSY : *a poor-ass place to live* (*1960s+*)

poor boy *n phr* A very large sandwich; dagwood, HERO SANDWICH [1921+; coined and invented by Clovis and Benjamin Martin, who opened a New Orleans restaurant in 1921]

poor deck *See* DEAL someone A POOR DECK

poor man's something or someone *n phr* A thing or person less glamorous, desirable, famous, etc, than the top grade : *the Poor Man's Palm Beach* (*1854+*)

poor-mouth *v* **1** To deny one's wealth and advantages; emphasize one's deficiencies; talk poor mouth : *Richard Nixon often poor-mouthed his chances* (*1965+*) **2** To deprecate severely; BAD-MOUTH : *I'm not going around poor-mouthing the war* (*1967+*) [*make a poor mouth,* "to whine, make the worst of things," is found as Scots dialect by 1822]

◁**poot**▷ *interj* : *I checked my watch. Poot. It was only twelve forty-five* *n* **1** Excrement; CRAP, SHIT : *Did she think I usually walked around festooned in pigeon poot?* **2** A contemptible person; PILL, POOP : *some old poots patrolling with a dog or two* **3** : *The dog laid a loud poot* *v* To flatulate; FART [1970s+ Black; probably a variant of *poop*]

poot around *v phr* To waste time; behave frivolously; CRAP AROUND : *There's been a lot of pootin' around but very little maximum effort* (*1970s+ Black*)

pop[1] or **pops** *n* **1** Father; POPPA (*1838+*) **2** An older or elderly man ● Used in informal, yet respectful, direct address : *Hey, pop, slow down a bit* (*1889+*)

pop[2] *n* **1** Flavored carbonated water; soda; soda pop (*1882+*) **2** Ice cream or flavored ice on a stick; Popsicle® (*1923+*) **3** Nitromethane or any other fuel additive for cars : *fuel additives*

called pop (*1960s+ Car racing & hot rodders*) **4** A quantity of narcotics; BAG : *Each of them had a couple of pops on 'em* (*1960s+ Narcotics*) ◁**5**▷ The sex act; sexual activity; ASS (*1950s+*) **6** POP-UP (*1895+ Baseball*) *v* **1** To take narcotics by injection; SHOOT UP (*1950s+ Narcotics*) **2** To take pills, esp barbiturates, amphetamines, etc, and esp habitually (*1960s+ Narcotics*) ◁**3**▷ To do the sex act with or to; JAZZ, SCREW : *Well, did you pop her?* (*1950s+*) **4** To hit; smack : *She popped him on the snoot* (*1386+*) **5** To shoot; kill; DRILL : *You might avoid going to the joint, or getting popped, today's term for murder, if caught* (*1762+*) **6** To catch; arrest : *But what I need is probable cause to pop a guy* (*late 1960s+*) [all senses related to *pop* as an echoic term for a sharp noise or a sharp blow; in the first sense, "ginger beer," found by 1836]

pop[3] *adj* Popular; having a very broad audience : *Tom Wolfe, the pop journalist* [1910+; found by 1862 in the senses "a popular concert," "popular music"]

pop, a *n phr* A time; each occasion; CRACK : *Steinem gets $3000 a pop for talking* (*1939+*; fr *pop,* "blow, stroke, crack," and according to Eric Partridge used by the Australians in the 1920s]

pop a wheelie *v phr* To raise the front wheel of a motorcycle or bicycle off the ground in order to ride on the rear wheel only (*1960s+ Motorcyclists & bicyclists*)

◁**pop** someone's **cherry**▷ *v phr* To terminate someone's virginity : *I would definitely pop his cherry* (*1930s+*)

◁**pop** one's **cookies** (or **rocks**)▷ *v phr* To have an orgasm; climax; COME : *Madam Gray, who couldn't ever pop her cookies enough* (*1970s+*)

pop one's **cork** *v phr* To become furious; explode angrily; BLOW one's TOP : *I didn't expect her to pop her cork either* (*1930s+*)

Pope *See* IS THE POPE POLISH

Popemobile *n* A car specially designed and built to display and protect the Pope : *I had chased his Popemobile as he toured western Sicily on a weekend pastoral jaunt* (*1979+*)

popeyed *adj* **1** Having protuberant eyes; exophthalmic; BUGEYED (*1830+*) **2** Astonished; amazed : *I just stood there popeyed* (*1906+*)

pop for *v phr* To pay for, esp as a treat to others; PICK UP THE TAB : *Go to a veterinarian or pet groomer and pop for the flea dips* (*1940s+*)

popgun *n* A pistol (*1849+*)

popoff *n* **1** A death or killing (*1880s+*) **2** A bragging, blatant, brash, and/or stupid declaration : *It was a typical senatorial popoff* (*1940s+*) **3** BIGMOUTH, LOUDMOUTH (*1940s+*)

pop off *v phr* **1** To die : *If he had popped off sooner, less trouble for all (1764+)* **2** To talk loudly and perhaps prematurely; SHOOT OFF one's MOUTH : *I'm not popping off about the pennant until we get it (1933+)* **3** To leave; depart *(1919+)*

pop someone off *v phr* To kill someone, esp by shooting : *The police never found who popped the informer off (1824+)*

poppa *n* **1** One's father *(1765+)* **2** Any older man *(1765+)* [fr *papa*, which is found by 1681]

poppet *n* A young child • Usu a term of endearment *(1849+)*

poppycock *n* Nonsense; foolishness [1865+; apparently fr Dutch *pappekak*, "soft dung"]

pop quiz or **shotgun quiz** or **pop test** *n phr* A surprise test; an unexpected examination [1940s+ College students; *pop*, "to announce or produce unexpectedly," is found by 1529]

pop the question *v phr* To propose marriage *(1826+)*

pop-top *n* **1** A small sailboat, camper, etc, whose top rises to provide headroom and sleeping room **2** (also **flip-top**) A beverage can with a preperforated opening and a ringlike lever on the top for access to the liquid *(1970+)*

pop-up *n* A high fly ball in the infield *(1908+ Baseball)*

pop up *v phr* **1** To appear suddenly : *for the universe to pop up tackily out of nowhere (1706+)* **2** To hit a high fly ball in the infield, either fair or foul *(1867+ Baseball)*

porcelain god *See* PRAY TO THE PORCELAIN GOD

pork *n* **1** Federal appropriations obtained for particular localities or interests *(1862+)* **2** The police; PIG *v* ◁1▷ To do the sex act; copulate; SCREW : *I decided to lay some groundwork for porking her brains out (1980s+)* [origin uncertain; perhaps fr *poke*]

pork barrel *adj* Involving spending large amounts of money in an area that generates consumer popularity *n* A legislative appropriation designed to ingratiate legislators with their constituents *(1909+)*

◁**porked**▷ *adj* Copulated; deflowered

◁**porker**▷ *n* An overweight person : *porkers in line at McDonald's*

pork out *v phr* To eat overheartily; overeat; PIG OUT : *We were porking out on three sweet rolls (1980s+ Students)*

pork up *v phr* To put on weight; fatten oneself : *Jeff Daniels porked up for* Dumb & Dumber *role (1990s+)*

porky *adj* Obese; porcine : *a porky, middle-aged waitress with a mustache and bad feet (1852+)*

porn or **porno** *adj* : *The very best porn film ever made/ little prospect of pay-TV turning our* homes into porno palaces *n* Pornography; a pornographic film, book, etc : *the merry world of pimps and porno/ or witness the amount of porn around/ I found out about the porno Rita'd made (first form 1970+, second 1952+)*

porny *adj* Pornographic *(1961+)*

portsider *n* **1** A left-handed person; SOUTHPAW : *We despair that portsiders will ever get their rights (1934+)* **2** A left-handed baseball pitcher *(1926+ Baseball)*

POS *n* PIECE OF SHIT : *coffeemaker's a POS*

poser *n* A person who pretends to have various desirable traits and tastes; poseur : *My son also told me that there are also people called "posers" who DRESS like "bassers" but are, in fact, secretly "preppies"* [1980s+ Teenagers; the revival of a term found by 1888]

posh *adj* Luxurious; fancy; chic; CUSHY, SWANKY : *The apartment is now rather posh* [1903+; origin uncertain; perhaps fr the mid-1800s term *posh*, "money," fr Romany *pash*, "a half," referring to a half-penny; perhaps fr mid-1800s *posh*, "a dandy," of unknown origin; perhaps fr early 1900s Cambridge University slang *push* or *poosh*, "stylish"; perhaps a mispronunciation of *polish*; improbably an acronym for *port out starboard home*, said to be the formula for choosing the side of the ship with the most comfortable cabins on the steamer route from England to India or return; perhaps none of the above]

posse *n* : *I thought posses were Jamaican. Language changes very fast here, now it just means a small gang* [1980s+ Black teenagers; probably fr the sheriff's *posse* seen so often in cowboy movies]

possession *n* The state of having illegal drugs *(1970+)*

postal *adj* : *postal—2) Whacko, flipped* *n* : *postal—1) A state of irrational, psychotic anger and disorientation (mid-1990s+ Teenagers) See* GO POSTAL

postcard *See* FRENCH POSTCARD

posted *adj* Informed; IN THE PICTURE : *If you hear anything, you might keep me posted (1850+)*

poster boy (or **girl** or **child**) *n phr* Someone given prominence in a certain cause : *The Bible-thumpers portray Col. North as the poster boy for the religious right/ Mary Matalin, for all her new visibility as a GOP poster girl, is actually a moderate/ Marky Mark became the poster child of the baby teens, smiling with sweet innocence in his Calvin Klein underwear from billboards around the country* [1980s+; fr the appealing children appearing on posters in the 1930s and following, soliciting money for various disease-fighting organizations]

pot[1] *n* **1** The total amount bet on a hand of poker or some other gambling matter; KITTY

: *The goulashes' takeout was 5 percent of the pot (1847+ Gambling)* **2** A rather obnoxious person, esp an unattractive woman; PILL : *one of the pots that sat at the table (1930+)* **3** BEER BELLY, POTBELLY *(1928+)* **4** A carburetor *(1941+)* **5** A car engine *(1950s+ Hot rodders)* **6** A locomotive *(1930+ Railroad) v* To shoot : *He potted a woodchuck (1860+)* [all senses fr cooking *pot*, as something containing a *pot*-luck mess of food, something sooty and unattractive, something fatlooking, something to be filled by hitting the hunt's prey, etc] *See* GO TO POT, NOT HAVE A POT TO PISS IN, SEXPOT, a SHITLOAD

pot² *modifier* : *a pot party n* Marijuana; GRASS, tea : *Most of the parties I had been invited to recently, pot had been passed around freely* [1930s+ Narcotics; perhaps fr Mexican Spanish *potiguaya*, "marijuana leaves"]

pot³ *n* A potentiometer *(1940s+)*

pot, the *n phr* The toilet; CRAPPER : *closed the stall door, and sat down on the pot* [1705+; fr *chamber-pot*, which is found by 1570] *See* SHIT OR GET OFF THE POT

potato *n* **1** A dollar : *You can get this wonderful coat for 497 potatoes (1931+)* **2** A baseball *(1940s+ Baseball) See* COUCH POTATO, HOT POTATO, MEAT AND POTATOES, SMALL POTATOES, SWEET POTATO

potato-head *n* A stupid person *(1832+)*

potato soup *n phr* Vodka • Generally made from potatoes

potbelly or **potgut** *n* **1** A protuberant belly; paunch; BEER BELLY, POT **2** A person with a potbelly, esp a man *(first form 1714+, second 1909+)*

potbelly (or belly) stove *n phr* An old-fashioned stove, esp a rotund one : *rickety armchairs around the big belly stove (mid-1800s+)*

potboiler *n* A book, play, etc, written just to get money, esp something done rather badly by a writer who can do very well [1864+; fr the notion that one does such work only to keep the food *pot boiling* in the domicile]

pothead *n* A user of marijuana, esp a heavy user : *a few potheads who don't move up from marijuana (1960s+ Narcotics)*

pot party *n phr* A gathering or party for the purpose of smoking marijuana in company; blast party *(1960s+ Narcotics)*

potshot *See* TAKE A POTSHOT AT someone

potted or **potted up** *adj* or *adj phr* **1** Drunk *(1922+)* **2** Intoxicated by marijuana or another narcotic : *all potted up on something (1960s+ Narcotics)*

◁**pot to piss in, a**▷ *See* NOT HAVE A POT TO PISS IN

potty *adj* Slightly crazy; eccentric; dotty, GOOFY *(1920+) modifier* : *time out for a potty break n* **1** A young child's toilet seat and chamber

pot *(1940s+)* **2** : *failure to perform potty at the proper hour* **3** Any toilet *(1940s+)*

potty-mouth *n* A person who uses foul and scatological language : *Margaret Cho describes herself as a kind of potty-mouth in her standup act (1960s+)*

potty talk *n phr* Foul and scatological language : *The use of profanity, epithets, and potty talk on TV jumped 45 percent from 1990 to 1994 (1990s+)*

pouffe *See* POOF

pound *v* ◁1▷ To do the sex act to or with; SCREW *(1970s+)* **2** To drink, esp beer : *Let's knock off and go pound some Budweiser (1980s+)*

◁**pound one's meat**▷ *See* BEAT one's MEAT

pound something out *v phr* To work hard at a keyboard : *pounds out the great American novel at night*

◁**pound one's peenie**▷ *v phr* To masturbate; BEAT one's MEAT : *Who is he mooning over as he pounds his peenie? (1970s+)*

pound the books *v phr* To study hard; HIT THE BOOKS *(1935+ Students)*

pound the pavement (Variations: **pavements** or **the sidewalks** or **the streets** may replace **the pavement**) *v phr* **1** To walk a police beat **2** To trudge about the streets, esp looking for work : *the liberal arts graduates pounding the Park Avenue pavements (1940s+)*

pour cold water on *v phr* To put an end to something or dampen the efforts of someone : *poured cold water on my vacation idea*

poured into one's **garment** *adj phr* Wearing very tight and revealing clothing : *She's in those TV commercials, poured into her jeans (1940s+)*

pour it on *v phr* **1** To make an intense effort; maximize striving : *Henry Gonzalez was pouring it on thick* **2** To exert all one's charm and persuasiveness; COME ON STRONG : *He was really pouring it on to that judge* **3** To speed; pour on the coal : *The driver was pouring it on to close the gap (1940s+)*

pour money down the drain (or **the rathole**) *v phr* To waste money utterly; spend hugely for nothing : *The Legislature is not going to pour more money down that rathole (1970s+)*

pow *interj* An imitation of a blow, collision, explosion, etc, used for sudden emphasis or to show sudden understanding : *Suddenly bells went off and I knew that was it! Pow! (1881+) n* Power; influence; CLOUT : *only be apprehended by government action, that is, by political "pow" (1960s+)* [noun sense reinforced by *power*]

powder *n* **1** : *Bonnie murdered a constable during the powder* **2** The speed of a pitch, esp very high speed; STUFF *(1932+ Baseball) v* **1** To leave; depart hastily, esp in escaping : *We* *better powder (1920+ Underworld)* **2** To hit very hard; PULVERIZE : *after he had powdered the second pitch (1940s+ Baseball)* [sense of running away probably fr similar *dust* fr the notion of raising dust as one runs; perhaps, in view of *take a powder* and *run-out powder*, the basic notion is reinforced by that of taking a medicinal *powder*, esp a laxative, so that one has to leave in a hurry, or perhaps a magical *powder* that would cause one to disappear] *See* FLEA POWDER, RUN-OUT POWDER, TAKE A POWDER

powder one's **nose** *v phr* To excuse oneself to visit the restroom • Jocular use

powderpuff *adj* **1** For or involving women; women's : *the pampered, powderpuff existence of the Ultra-feminine (1930s+)* **2** Trifling; insignificant : *Reagan offers reporters only powder-puff photo opportunities (1930s+)* *n* A cautious, agile fighter as distinct from a slugger *(1940s+ Prizefighting)* *v* : *He just powderpuffed his opponent until he tired*

powder room *n* A bathroom, esp public restroom : *to the powder room at intermission*

power *v* To hit the ball very hard : *He powered that one to the wall (1940s+ Baseball) See* FLOWER POWER

powerhouse *n* **1** A formidable team, organization, etc : *Georgia Tech, another powerhouse/ Texas Instruments, a powerhouse in electronics* **2** An energetic and effective person **3** A vigorous, muscular person, esp an athlete **4** Anything that constitutes winning force : *If you control six votes that's a powerhouse (1915+)*

power lunch *n* (Variations: **breakfast** or **feeding** may replace *lunch*) A meal calculated to increase or negotiate matters of influence; a feed where important matters are on the table : *Mr. Trump was seen at both a power breakfast and a power lunch yesterday/ If you still believe that the Four Seasons and 44 are the only places that matter for Manhattan media power feeding (mid-1980s+)*

power tool *n* An extremely hardworking student : *power tools cramming all night*

power trip *n phr* A show of personal power, esp of a blatant sort : *the classic Latin American dictator's power trip* [mid-1960s+; based on the narcotics sense of *trip*]

powwow *n* A meeting; discussion : *The directors are having a crucial pow-wow* [1625+; ultimately fr an Algonquian word for "medicine man," meaning "he dreams," extended to mean counsel and a council]

PR or **pr** (pronounced as separate letters) *modifier* : *the PR department n* Public relations *(1940s+)*

prairie dog *v phr* To pop up one's head from an office cubicle : *Dilbert depicts prairie-dogging*

prairie oysters *See* MOUNTAIN OYSTERS

pratfall *n* **1** A fall on one's rump, esp by a clown or comedian : *a perfect pratfall (1939+)* **2** A humiliating defeat; an embarrassing humiliation : *the principles and pratfalls of the rhyming racket (1950+ fr theater)*

prayer *See* HAVE A PRAYER

pray to the porcelain god *v phr* To vomit in the toilet *(1970s+ College students)*

preemie or **preemy** or **premie** *n* A premature baby : *like a human preemie, it was placed in an Isolette (1927+)*

preggers *adj* Pregnant : *Meredith gets preggers by Jos (1942+)*

prego *adj* Pregnant : *as if one-half the female population is prego n* A pregnant teenager *(1980s+)*

prelim (PREE lim) *n* **1** A professional boxing match coming before the main match in a given program *(1930s+ Prizefighting)* **2** A preliminary qualifying examination *(1891+)*

premed (PREE med) *modifier* : *a required premed course n* **1** A premedical student **2** A premedical course of study or major *(1940s+ College students)*

pre-nup *n* A premarital agreement, primarily about money and property, made by persons about to marry : *A Federal court decision may mean hundreds of thousands of pre-nups are irrelevant* [1990s+; shortening of *pre-nuptial*]

prep *adj* Preparatory; preparing a student for college or university *(1895+)* **1** A preparatory school : *She went to Georgetown Prep (1895+)* **2** PREPPY : *If you don't listen to Green Day or Nirvana, then you're a "prep" (1980s+)* **3** Preparation; preliminary steps : *The nurses did the prep for the operation (1927+ Medical) v* **1** To go to preparatory school : *Where'd you prep? (1915+ Students)* **2** To prepare; get ready : *a pitcher who has prepped earnestly for many years (1934+)* [*prep*, "student at a preparatory school," is found by 1890, and *prepster* by the 1940s]

preppy or **preppie** *adj* Typical of the manners, attitudes, folkways, etc, of preppies : *The handshake is firm and preppy n* (also **prepster**) A student or graduate of a preparatory school : *Wouldja please watch your profanity, Preppie?/ five soft-spoken indie prepsters who happen to rule nice-kid noise pop (1970s+)* [*preppy*, "silly, immature," is found by 1900]

prep school *adj* : *prep school grad n phr* A preparatory school, usu rather expensive and aristocratic *(1895+)*

prequel *n* A book, episode, etc, that precedes an existing work in time • Not very precisely differentiated from *flashback* : *what Hollywood calls a "prequel," an adventure that takes* *place at the start of his career* [1973+; based on *sequel*]

pres (PREZ) *n* (also **prez** or **prex** or **prexy** or **prexie**) A president (*1940s+, prex 1828+, prexy 1871+*)

presenteeism *n* The habit of being present; working constantly instead of taking earned or available time off • A play on the opposite *absenteeism*

press *See* FULL COURT PRESS

press roll *n phr* A snare-drum roll in which the loosely held sticks are pressed onto the drumhead and allowed to vibrate (*1934+ Musicians*)

press the flesh (or **the skin**) *adj* : *Williams conducted a press-the-flesh campaign* **v** *phr* To shake hands • Used chiefly of politicians and others who ingratiate themselves with the public (*1926+*)

pressure cooker *modifier* : *flung into the pressure-cooker existence of live TV* **n** *phr* A place or situation of great personal stress : *the pressure cooker on the Hudson* (*1958+*)

pretty *adv* Quite; more than a little : *The weather's pretty rotten* (*1565+*) *See* be SITTING PRETTY

pretty boy *modifier* : *their "pretty boy" young preacher* **n** 1 A man who is good-looking in an epicene way; an effeminate dandy (*1885+*) 2 A bouncer or professional strong man (*1931+ Circus*)

pretty face *See* NOT JUST ANOTHER PRETTY FACE

pretty kettle of fish *n phr* A new and probably unfortunate circumstance : *Here's a pretty kettle of fish; his teeth went down the drain* (*1742+*)

pretty penny, a *n phr* A lot of money : *That car cost him a pretty penny* (*1768+*)

previous *n* An earlier conviction : *Kid looks clean; no previous* (*1935+*)

prexy or **Prexy** or **prexie** or **Prexie** *See* PRES

prez or **Prez** *See* PRES

priceless *adj* Very funny or amusing : *priceless observation* (*1907+*)

pricey or **pricy** *adj* Expensive; dear • Chiefly British : *Godiva chocolates and other pricey goodies* (*1932+*)

◁**prick**▷ *n* 1 The penis; COCK (*1592+*) 2 A detestable person, esp a man; obnoxious wretch; ASSHOLE, BASTARD : *He's an antagonistic prick* (*1929+*) [Farmer and Henley's *Slang and Its Analogues* includes six and a half pages of synonyms in the 1896 volume]

pricklies *See* COLD PRICKLIES

◁**prick-teaser**▷ *See* COCK-TEASER

prima donna *n phr* A person of great and touchy self-esteem; a person who requires to be the sole focus of adulatory attention and who indulges in temperamental displays [1936+; fr Italian, literally "first lady,"

a title for superstar opera singers and the like]

prince *n* A very decent and admirable person; ACE • Often used ironically : *He told me he thinks you're a goddam prince* (*1911+*)

print *n* A fingerprint : *My prints ain't on that gun* (*1924+*) **v** : *They printed me* (*1938+*) *See* the SMALL PRINT

print money *See* a LICENSE TO PRINT MONEY

prior *n* An earlier conviction; PREVIOUS : *"Any priors on him?" "Dinged once, in Rapid City"* (*1978+*)

prissy *adj* Overfastidious; primly censorious : *He has a prissy distaste for heavy shoes* (*1895+*) *n* : *these do-gooding prissies* [origin uncertain; perhaps a blend of *prim* or *precise* with *sissy*]

private *See* BUCK PRIVATE

private dick or **private eye** *n phr* A private detective; a private investigator; PI (*entry form 1908+, variant 1938+*)

privates *n* The genitals; private parts (*1846+*)

privy *n* An outdoor toilet without plumbing; backhouse. Chic Sale (*1662+*)

prize package, no *See* NO PRIZE PACKAGE

pro[1] *modifier* : *pro ranks* **n** 1 A professional in any field, as distinct from an amateur, and mainly distinguished by superior and dependable performance : *hear his song played and sung by pros* (*1866+*) 2 A prostitute : *He treats all women like pros and all men like enemies* (*1937+*) [the last sense perhaps fr *professional* reinforced by *prostitute*, or vice versa]

pro[2] *n* A prophylactic for preventing venereal disease; condom; RUBBER (*WWII armed forces*)

pro[3] *n* 1 Probation as a judicial sentence (*1950s+*) 2 A person on probation

pro-am *adj* Admitting or including both professional and amateur performers, esp athletes; open : *a pro-am golf tournament* (*1949+*)

problem *See* HAVE A PROBLEM WITH something

production *See* MAKE A BIG PRODUCTION

production line *n phr* A high-scoring offensive line [1940s+ Hockey; based on the industrial *production line*, the term found by 1935]

prof *n* Professor (*1838+ College students*)

professional student *n phr* A person who continues to take courses and earn degrees over a number of years instead of entering a profession related to the degrees

profile *v* 1 To strut and attitudinize; SHOW OFF : *Now, right now, you're profiling. And I'm being bored* 2 To display prominently and proudly; SHOW OFF : *He was profiling his new Mercedes* [1960s+ Black; fr the notion of displaying one's handsome *profile*] *See* KEEP A LOW PROFILE, LOW PROFILE

program *v* To train; predispose by rigorous teaching, condition : *He's programmed to be* *polite to old ladies and all (1966+ fr computers) See* CRASH PROGRAM

project *See* CRASH PROGRAM

prole (PROHL) *n* A member of the lower or working class : *Chez Tom Wolfe proles, for example, wear new down coats* [1887+; fr *proletarian,* "member of the working class," ultimately fr Latin; popularized by George Orwell's 1949 novel *Nineteen Eighty-Four*]

promise *See* a LICK AND A PROMISE

promo (PROH moh) *n* **1** Advertising and promotion : *Who's handling the promo for this show?* **2** A film, tape, printed piece, etc, for promotion : *He shot some promos for his syndicated TV show* (1963+)

promote *v* **1** To get, esp by theft, hard persuasion, or begging : *We got to promote a boat to run the stuff in* (1920+ *Underworld*) **2** To accost in an acquisitive spirit; HIT : *begun promoting him for something to drink* (1934+)

promotion *See* MEXICAN PROMOTION

◁**prong**▷ *n* The penis; PRICK *v* To do the sex act to or with; SCREW : *every guy who had ever pronged her* (1969+)

◁**prong on**▷ *n phr* A penile erection; HARD-ON : *I got this huge prong on* (1970s+)

pronto *adv* Immediately; quickly; PDQ [1850+; fr Spanish]

prop[1] *n* An article used on stage or in a film; property (1841+ *Theater*)

prop[2] *n* A propeller (1914+)

propeller head *n phr* A computer expert or enthusiast; GEEK, NERD : *Interactive multimedia software? The propeller heads live for this stuff* [mid-1980s+; fr their visualization as wearing ridiculous little beanies with propellers on top]

property *See* HOT PROPERTY

proposition *n* An invitation or request for sexual favors; PASS : *He made a rude proposition and got his ears pinned back v* To request sexual favors; COME ON TO someone, MAKE A PASS AT someone : *He propositioned every woman at the party* [1924+; defined as "a proposal of marriage" in a 1908 source]

props *n* **1** The property manager at a theater or movie studio (1900+ *Theater*) **2** falsies *See* KNOCK THE PROPS FROM UNDER

prowl *v* To search by running the hands over the person; FRISK : *prowled me over carefully with his left hand* (1914+) *See* ON THE PROWL

prune *n* **1** A pedantic, stiff, and prudish person; PRISSY (1895+) **2** A dehydrated nursing-home patient (1980s+ *Medical*) *v* To accelerate faster than another car in a race (1940s+ *Hot rodders*)

prunes *See* FULL OF BEANS

p's and q's *See* MIND one's P'S AND Q'S

pseud (SOOD) *adj : That guy is really pseud, with all his big talk* (1962+) *n* Someone or

something false; a fraud; fake. PHONY (1968+) [fr *pseudo*]

pseudo *adj* False; bogus, sham : *offering pseudo interest in her*

psych *modifier* Psychiatry; psychiatric : *makes it down from the psych ward on the 15th floor* (1940s+) *n* Psychology, esp as an academic study (1895+ *College students*) *v* (also **psych out**) **1** To outsmart another person : *The bastards psyched me* (1934+ *College students*) **2** To sense or infer the motives, behavior, etc, of others; feel out a situation : *an uncanny ability to "psych out" audiences and make them love her* (1961+) **3** To unnerve someone; cause someone to lose composure, will, skill, etc : *He won't psych me as he did her* (1960s+)

psych oneself or **psych** oneself **up** *v phr* To arouse oneself emotionally, spiritually, mentally, etc, to a maximum effort; raise oneself to a state of keen readiness and capability; PUMP oneself UP : *That's almost a whole year of psyching yourself up as high as you can go/ I tried to psyche myself for this new challenge* (1972+)

psyched or **psyched up** *adj* or *adj phr* In a state of excited preparedness and heightened keenness; PUMPED UP : *They were all psyched up to carry the blue and white banner of Catawba College/ are generally so psyched that elation becomes their bottom line* (1968+) *See* GET PSYCHED

psycho *adj : a special psycho channel that I know nothing about n* A crazy person; maniac; psychopath; NUT : *no buzzing broad, no nympho, no psycho, no bitch* (1942+) [probably fr *psychotic*; the form *psychot,* "psychopath," is found by the 1940s]

psychobabble *n* Talk about self, feelings, motives, etc, esp in psychological jargon : *His characters have absorbed the attitudes of post-1960s psychobabble, and tend to say things like "Viet Nam is a reality warp"* (1976+) *v : "If you want space," she tells a psychobabbling boyfriend, "go to Utah"*

psych up *v phr* To bring to a state of keen attention; excite and incite; PUMP UP (1957+)

psywar (SĪ wawr) *modifier : an impressively orchestrated psywar operation n* Psychological warfare (1954+)

◁**pt** or **PT**▷ (pronounced as separate letters) *n* PRICK-TEASER (1960s+)

pub[1] *n* A saloon; bar; tavern : *a round of Long Island pubs* [1859+ British; fr British *public,* fr *public house*]

pub[2] *n* Publicity : *You know Dallas is going to get all that pub* (1990s+)

pub crawl *n : They went on a memorable pub crawl afterwards v* To carouse about from one saloon to another *(1910+ British)* [*gin crawl* is found by 1883, and *beer crawl* by 1902] *See* BARHOP

pubes (PYOO beez) *n* Adolescent females; TEENYBOPPERS [1960s+ Students; fr *pubescent*]

pucker *modifier* : *The U.S. ships were taking no chances: as Capt. Mathis told his crew members, one mine is enough to keep the pucker factor up n* Fear; state of fright : *Don't get into such a pucker (1741+)*

◁**pucker-assed**▷ *adj* Timid; fearful; CHICKEN [1970s+; fr *pucker*]

◁**pud**▷ (PUHD, POOD) *n* **1** The penis *(1939+)* **2** An obnoxious person; DORK, JERK : *A dexter, that's your basic nerd, dork, or pud (1980s+ Teenagers)* [fr slang sense of *pudding*] *See* PULL one's PUD

◁**pudding**▷ *n* The penis : *You can't even come off unless you pull your own pudding (1719+)*

puddinghead *n* A stupid person, esp one who is also amiable : *a natural nitwit, a puddinghead, a stand-up comedian (1851+)*

puddle-jumper *n* **1** A small or rickety vehicle : *I wouldn't ride in that puddle-jumper* **2** An aircraft that makes several stops along a cross-country route *(1932+)*

◁**pudlicker**▷ *n* A person who does fellatio; COCKSUCKER, DICKLICKER : *asking when my new column, "Pudlicker to the Celebrated," was going to start (1990s+)*

◁**pud-pulling**▷ *modifier* : *a stupid pud-pulling jerk n* Masturbation : *a frenzied bout of pud-pulling (1939+)*

puff *n* (also **puffery** or **puff job**) A specimen of extravagant praise, esp for commercial or political purposes; PLUG *(1732+, puffery 1782+)* *v* : *There is little need for us to puff this book (1858+) See* CREAM PUFF, POWDER-PUFF

puff piece *n phr* Something written in extravagant praise, esp for sales purposes; HYPE : *But as my brassy page-one editor would say, those portrayals are puff pieces (1980s+)*

puffy *adj* **1** Obese; bloated : *these strutting athletes and puffy officials (1664+)* **2** Very favorable; adulatory; drum-beating : *Even the stern People's Daily ran extraordinarily puffy coverage of Reagan (1980+)*

pug *n* A prizefighter or boxer; pugilist [1858+; fr *pugilist*]

puggled *adj* **1** Exhausted; pooped **2** Intoxicated with alcohol

pug-ugly *adj* Quite ugly; having a face resembling a dog's : *pug-ugly white boys on the teams*

puh-leez *interj* Give me a break; I do not believe or accept that : *You're my friend? Puhleez* • Said with disgust

puke *n* **1** Vomit; spew **2** Something so disgusting that it might be vomit and the cause of vomit : *Who wrote this puke? (1961+) v* To vomit *(1600+)*

puke hole *n phr* **1** A toilet **2** One's mouth : *Shut your puke hole* • Often offensive

puky or **pukey** *adj* Nasty; inferior; disgusting : *It's a pukey sort of ballad (1965+)*

pull *n* **1** Influence; special power or favor; CLOUT : *irregularities and instances of political pull (1886+)* **2** A gulp of a drink, a puff on a cigarette, etc : *I took a big pull at my drink and looked up (1575+) v* **1** To drink; take a swallow : *a 17-year-old kid pulling on a beer (1436+)* **2** (also **pull down**) To earn; receive : *I pulled an A on the quiz/ The seven magazines pull down nearly $700 million a year (1937+, variant 1917+)* **3** To do; perform; effect, esp a trick or shady act : *What are they trying to pull now? (1916+)*

pull a boner (or **a bonehead play**) *v phr* To blunder; commit an error, esp an egregious one : *I'm afraid you've pulled a boner this time; the thing sank (1913+)*

pull a fast one *v phr* To execute or attempt a deception; achieve a clever fraud or swindle; PULL something ON someone : *You're accusing me of trying to pull a fast one?* [1933+; probably fr *fast shuffle*]

pull a job *v phr* To carry out a crime, esp stealing : *pulled a bank job (Police and underworld)*

pull an all-nighter *v phr* To study all night *(1980s+ Teenagers & students)*

pull (or do) an el foldo *v phr* To lose energy; wilt; fade; FOLD : *The Saints chose that time to pull an el foldo (1962+) See* EL FOLDO

pull a one-eighty *v phr* Make a complete change of direction; make an about-face : *Of course the right quickly found itself obliged to pull a one-eighty* [because *180* degrees indicates an exactly opposite heading on an azimuth compass]

◁**pull a train** (or **the train** or **the choo-choo**)▷ *v phr* Of a woman, to do the sex act with several men serially : *taking some dame in the woods and making her pull a train (1965+ Motorcyclists)*

pull a vanishing act *v phr* To disappear; TAKE A POWDER : *That may be exactly why he's pulled a vanishing act* [1981+; fr a magician's *vanishing* or causing someone to do so; in the form *do a vanishing act* found by 1923]

pull oneself (up) by one's (own) bootstraps *v phr* To improve one's position by one's own efforts *(1936+)*

pull someone's chain (Variations: **yank** or **jerk** or **rattle** may replace **pull**; **string** may replace **chain**) *v phr* **1** To deceive; fool, victimize; PULL A FAST ONE : *too busy trying to figure out if I had been pulling his chain* **2** To upset someone, esp by teasing or harassing;

anger someone : *I did not know you can rattle his chain with marvelous results/ He was insecure and sensitive. It was easy to pull his string* [1980s+; probably fr the image of a person who upsets a captive animal by *pulling* or *jerking* at its *chain*]

pull down *v phr* To earn a certain amount of money : *pulls down 100K*

pull one's **finger out** *v phr* To get moving; to demand effort of a lazy person : *Pull your finger out and let's get cracking* (1941+)

pull one's **head out** *v phr* To pay attention to one's affairs; wake up : *You better pull your head out and get to studying or you won't graduate* [1960s+ Students; shortening and euphemizing of *pull your head out of your ass*]

pull in *v phr* To arrive : *She pulled in about noon* [1905+; fr railroad]

pull someone **in** *v phr* To arrest someone; RUN someone IN (1891+)

pull it off *v phr* To accomplish something; succeed; MAKE IT : *pull it off and keep the patients coming back for more* (1887+)

pull someone's **leg** *v phr* To deceive in fun; fool; KID : *I suspected that he was pulling my leg* [1886+; fr the act of playfully tripping someone]

pull numbers or **get digits** *v phr* To succeed in getting the telephone numbers of potential dates, escorts, etc (1990s+)

pull off *v phr* **1** To succeed in or at; achieve : *Fegley managed to pull off a hat trick for this issue* (1883+) ◁2▷ To masturbate : *At Smolka's signal, each begins to pull off* (1922+)

◁**pull** oneself **off**▷ *v phr* To masturbate; JACK OFF (1900+)

◁**pull** someone **off**▷ *v phr* To cause someone to ejaculate semen by manipulating the penis (1900+)

pull something on someone *v phr* To deceive or cheat; take advantage of; PULL A FAST ONE : *At first she thought I was trying to pull a slick scam on her* (1916+)

pull out *v phr* **1** To leave; depart : *He pulled out after 45 minutes and disappeared* (1884+) **2** To withdraw; terminate one's association : *He threatened to pull out if we didn't raise the ante* (1887+)

pull out all the stops *v phr* To do everything possible; to use everything available : *pulled out all the stops to keep her from leaving* [fr organ stops being pulled out to extend the sound]

◁**pull something out of** one's **ass**▷ *v phr* To produce something, esp information or an idea, unexpectedly (1970s+ Army)

pull something out of the fire *v phr* To salvage something; rescue : *They got hot and pulled the game out of the fire* (1893+)

◁**pull** one's **pud**▷ (PUHD, PŌŌD) *v phr* (Variations: **dong** or **joint** or **wang** or any other word for "penis" may replace **pud**) To masturbate; JACK OFF (1944+)

pull one's **punches** *v phr* To soften one's blows; be lenient and moderate : *Ouch. You don't pull your punches* (1934+ Prizefighting)

pull rank *v phr* To overwhelm with one's authority; be officiously arrogant : *Each was frightened that the other would pull rank* (1923+)

pull strings (or **wires**) *v phr* **1** To exert influence; use one's power, esp clandestinely : *If she pulls a few wires I think I might get the job* [entry form 1860s+, variant 1893+; probably fr the use of *strings* or *wires* to control marionettes; *work wire* is found by 1886] **2** To exert private or secret influence : *pull wires to get visitation* (1862+)

pull teeth *v phr* To do something in the most difficult way; do something the hard way (1970s+ Armed forces) • Fr earlier *pull teeth through the armpit*

pull the plug[1] *v phr* **1** To terminate something; end support or cooperation : *if the affiliates rise up in rebellion and pull the plug* (1940s+) **2** To terminate various mechanical and electronic efforts being used to keep life in a moribund patient (1960s+) [fr the disconnecting of an electrical *plug*]

pull the plug[2] *v phr* To dive in a submarine; submerge [1970s+ Navy; fr the withdrawing of a bathtub *plug*]

pull the rug from under (or **out from under**) *v phr* To undermine or disable; put opponents at a great and often sudden disadvantage : *They were intended to pull the rug out from under left-wing critics* (1946+)

pull the string *v phr* **1** To pitch a change-of-pace ball, a very slow ball after the motion for a fast one (1937+ Baseball) **2** To rudely reveal the truth, previously kept hidden; unveil true intentions; reveal the catch • The full form is *pull the string of the shower bath* : *They doubled their efforts, showering her with affection, then they pulled the string* (1928+) [perhaps fr the use of a *string* to fasten and release a concealing sheet on something about to be unveiled; perhaps fr *pull the lanyard*, "to fire a cannon"]

pull the wool over someone's **eyes** *v phr* To deceive; mislead : *The whole indignant act was an attempt to pull the wool over the voters' eyes* [1842+; a slightly earlier form is *spread the wool over* someone's *eyes*]

pull up one's **socks** *v phr* To correct one's behavior; look to one's performance; GET ON THE BALL : *Whittingham was terminated after having failed to pull up his socks enough during six months on probation* (1893+)

pull up stakes *v phr* To depart; decamp : *If things don't get better we'll pull up stakes* (1817+)

pull wires *See* PULL STRINGS

pulp *modifier* : *a pulp romance n* A magazine printed on rough paper and devoted to adventure, science fiction, cowboy stories, rude erotica, etc (1931+)

pulverize *v* To defeat thoroughly; punish; CLOBBER (1631+)

pummelled *adj* Intoxicated with alcohol; also, beat up

pump *n* 1 (also **pumper**) The heart; TICKER : *He had a hole through his pump* (1885+) 2 A home run; TATER : *He had three pumps yesterday. Three home runs!* (1980s+ Baseball) *v* ◁1▷ To do the sex act; FUCK, HUMP : *Duffy wondered if Jert had been pumping Tish* (1730+) 2 To question long and closely; extract information : *The cops pumped him for three days straight* (1667+) 3 To excite; AMP, HYPE, PUMP UP, TURN ON : *That stripper at the party last night really pumped me* (1980s+ Students)

pumped up *adj phr* 1 (also **pumped**) Excited and expectant; PSYCHED UP • Used often of athletes in or before competition : *The girls were really pumped up/ was returning to play in his first game in more than two years and this city was pumped* (1980s+) 2 Exaggerated; artificial; PHONY : *He showed pumped-up conviviality. Concannon didn't like it* (1904+) *adj* 3 Pregnant : *She got pumped and had to quit her job* (1960s+ Students)

pump iron *v phr* To lift weights; do bodybuilding (1980s+)

pumpkin or **pumkin** or **punkin** *n* 1 The head (1890s+) 2 One's sweetheart, beloved, spouse, etc; DOLL, HONEY, SWEETIE : *We're allies in everything, pumpkin* (1940s+)

pumpkinhead or **punkinhead** *n* A stupid person (1848+)

pump up *v phr* 1 To exaggerate; assign too much importance to; BLOW UP : *He wanted a scandal and wanted to fry Maxine Waters. They wanted to pump it up* (1970s+) 2 To persuade to keen excitement; AMP, HYPE, TURN ON : *Experts like Dr Edward Teller have steadily "pumped up" Reagan about the potential of such defensive-weapons systems* (1980s+)

pump oneself **up** *v phr* To arouse oneself emotionally, spiritually, mentally, etc, to a maximum effort; PSYCH oneself • Much used by sports commentators, esp by baseball announcers of pitchers : *The big lefthander's really pumped himself up for this crucial encounter* (1970s+)

punch *n* Power; force; impact; CLOUT : *This article has no punch* (1911+) *See* CAN'T FIGHT one's WAY OUT OF A PAPER BAG, ONE-TWO, SUCKERPUNCH, SUNDAY PUNCH

punch cows (or **cattle**) *v phr* To herd or drive cattle (1890+)

punch-drunk *adj* 1 Exhibiting brain damage from repeated blows to the head; slow in movement, slurring in speech, disoriented and shambling; PUNCHY, SLAP-HAPPY 2 Dazed from overwork, excessive stress, etc : *He was punch-drunk after the annual meeting* (1915+)

punched *See* GET one's CARD PUNCHED, HAVE one's TICKET PUNCHED

punched-up *adj* Improved; increased in energy, impressiveness, impact, etc : *no more than a punched-up form of the sentiment that the prose style of most social scientists "is Greek to me"* (1950s+)

punches *See* PULL one's PUNCHES, ROLL WITH THE PUNCHES, TELEGRAPH one's PUNCHES

punch in (or **out**) *v phr* To come or go at a certain time, esp to or from a job; CLOCK IN (or OUT) [1934+; fr the stamping of one's work card at a time clock]

punching bag *n phr* A target; butt; whipping boy; scapegoat : *Milken has come to be regarded as a handy punching bag for everything that went wrong in the 1980s* (1980s+)

punch someone's **lights out** *v phr* To beat or defeat someone severely; trounce; CLOBBER : *Sugar Ray Leonard punched Thomas Hearns's lights out* [1970s+; fr the earlier *beat out someone's liver and lights*, where *lights* reflects a Middle English word for "lungs, esp of a slaughtered animal or game animal," now certainly interpreted as "eyes" and as "electric lights"]

punch line *n phr* The last line or part of a joke, which makes it funny; KICKER, ZINGER : *I remember the jokes, but not the punch lines* (1921+)

punch out *v phr* 1 To beat, esp with the fists; BEAT UP, CLOBBER : *I punched out this guy* (1970s+) 2 To use the ejection seat for escape from a aircraft (1970s+ Air Force)

punch the clock *v phr* To do the minimum routinely required : *The public has good instincts for when people are doing significant or courageous things in space and when merely punching the clock* (1940s+)

punch up *v phr* 1 To improve; increase the energy, impressiveness, etc, of; JAZZ something UP : *I guess they hired me because their material needed punching up* (1950s+) 2 To bring a specified part of a recording tape into view, into place at the playing head, etc 3 To call up a software program (1980s+ Computers)

punchy *adj* 1 Exhibiting brain damage from repeated blows to the head; PUNCH-DRUNK : *Sailor Bob, a punchy stumble-bum* (1937+) 2 Feeling somewhat confused and battered, as if punch-drunk : *Even if she's a little punchy* *and hyper from doing a dozen interviews that day (1940s+)* **3** Having force, impact, energy, etc; potent; JAZZY, ZINGY : *The English language may someday be as colorful and punchy as it was in Elizabethan times (1926+)*

punk[1] *n* **1** A catamite; young companion of a sodomite; GUNSEL[1] *(1904+)* **2** (also **punk kid**) Any young or inexperienced person; boy; KID : *Sparky was always a fresh punk (mid-1920s+)* **3** A petty hoodlum; meager minor tough or criminal : *to emphasize just how tough a Division Street punk could be (1917+)* **4** Any inferior, insignificant person, like an ineffective fighter, jockey, pool player, waiter, porter, etc *(1917+)* **5** Any young circus animal *(1926+ Circus)* **v** ◁1▷ To sodomize; do anal sex to; BUGGER, CORNHOLE : *The guy peeled off Tate's pants and punked him (1970s+)* [ultimately fr 1500s British, "prostitute, harlot," of unknown origin]

punk[2] *adj* Inferior; poor; bad : *The idea strikes me as punk (1896+)* **modifier** : *the punk workers who sell corn removers n* **1** Bread *(1891+)* **2** A patent medicine *(1940s+)* [probably early 1700s, "rotting wood, touchwood," of unknown origin, usu taken to be fr *spunk,* of the same meaning, fr Gaelic *spong,* "tinder"]

punk[3] *adj* : *The atmosphere in North London's pubs is really punk n* (also **punker**) An adherent to a style of dress and behavior marked by seemingly threatening, dangerous, and aggressive attributes, such as safety pins worn through ear lobes, razor blades around the neck, and torn clothes : *In the beginning, punk wasn't just fashion. Punk was outrage (1976+)* [originally meant to be reminiscent of the hoodlums called punks in the 1950s, but soon an independent style]

◁**punk-ass**▷ *adj* Unpleasant, deplorable • Used to describe a person : *your punk-ass white friend (1920+)*

punked out *adj phr* Having the style of dress and behavior marked by seemingly threatening, dangerous, and aggressive attributes : *I am a punked-out loner boy-repellent (1980s+)*

punkette *n* A young woman who adopts the manners and appearance of the punk milieu : *a scruffy, androgynous punkette with close-cropped hair and dressed all in black except for a pair of electric-red socks (1980s+)*

punkin *See* PUMPKIN

punk out *v phr* **1** To quit, esp from fear; CHICKEN OUT, FOLD : *The Soho News punked out (1920+)* **2** To adopt the style of a punk rocker *(1980s+)*

punk rock *n phr* Loud and crude rock-and-roll music played by persons who purport, in their dress, vile behavior and language, re-

pellent names, and ugly appearance, to be loathsome louts : *The bad equivalent of "bubble-gum," it was called punk-rock, and it was totally utilitarian music (1976+)*

punk rocker *n phr* **1** A player of loud and crude rock-and-roll music who purports to be a loathsome lout **2** A person who adheres to a style of dress and behavior marked by seemingly threatening, dangerous, and aggressive attributes; PUNK *(1976+)*

punt[1] *v* To gamble; bet [1706+; fr French *ponte,* Spanish *punta,* "point," used for playing against the banker in faro and other games]

punt[2] *v* **1** To drop a course in order not to fail it **2** To give up; withdraw; COP OUT : *I hate to punt, but I just don't have time to finish this job* **3** To improvise or do something different when faced with few or no choices : *had to punt when he didn't get in his first-choice school* **4** To return something; throw (or kick) something back : *The high court punted the usetax issue back to Congress and cleared the way for future legislative action* **5** To stall for time; to delay; to relinquish control : *Clinton suddenly punted on health reform and shifted to welfare* [1970s+ College students; fr the kick out of danger in football, fr mid-1800s Rugby football, "kick the ball before it hits the ground," of unknown origin; perhaps echoic]

punter *n* A gambler; a bettor : *Inside the clubhouse, the punters sit enraged on their slatted benches* [1706+; fr French *punter,* "to place a bet against the bank in a card game," of uncertain origin]

punt someone or something off *v phr* To deliberately forget; ignore and evade; BAG : *He decided to punt the whole problem off (1970s+ College students)*

pup *n* **1** A young, inexperienced person; KID, PUNK *(1890+)* **2** HOT DOG *(1940s+)* **3** A small four-wheeled truck trailer *(1940s+ Truckers)* **4** (also **puppy**) A thing; BABY, SUCKER : *I guess we turn this pup around/ You can mail this puppy in or you can appear at the tribal court (1980s+)* [ultimately fr French *poupée,* "doll"] *See* GUTTERSNIPE

puppies or **pups** *n* The feet; DOGS *(1923+)*

puppy *n* **1** A wimp or softie : *You're such a puppy* **2** A thing or part of a thing : *Put that puppy down and help me*

puppy love *n phr* Love or infatuation of very young persons; CALF LOVE *(1834+)*

pup (or **dog**) **tent** *n phr* A small tent; an Army shelter tent : *The crew loaded pup tents and cooking equipment into motorcycle sidecars (1863+)*

purgatory *n* An extremely unpleasant experience; a temporary condition of suffering : *the purgatory of drug abuse (1807+)*

purple haze *n phr* LSD mixed with methedrine (1967+)

purple heart *n phr* Any barbiturate, or a mixture of a barbiturate and morphine; GOOFBALL, NIMBY [1960s+ Narcotics; fr the US decoration awarded for a combat wound]

push *n* **1** A fight between street gangs; RUMBLE (1940s+ Street gang) **2** A supervisor : *Jigger's first season as a camp push* (1930+ Loggers) **3** A radio frequency, such as is tuned by pressing a push-button (1970s+ Army) **4** An intense sustained effort : *They made a big push to get the damn thing done* (1940s+) *v* **1** (also **push across**) To kill someone : *when one of our boys gets pushed/ He might have pushed Foster across* (1940s+) **2** To approach a specified age : *You're pushing 50* (1937+) **3** To advertise; publicize; promote : *They don't have to push reference books too much* (1894+) **4** (also **push for**) To recommend; boost; GET BEHIND : *He decided to push my idea, and push for two new labs* (1888+) **5** To sell, esp in an aggressive way; hawk : *Push the specials today, okay?* (1940s+) **6** To press or importune, esp too often and too hard : *I'll probably do what you want, just stop pushing* (1578+) **7** To sell narcotics; peddle; DEAL : *Funny cigarettes ain't all that one pushes* (1930s+ Narcotics) **8** To distribute and pass counterfeit money (1940s+ Underworld)

push a button *v phr* To provoke a response; reach one's feelings; hit a "hot button" : *Don't push my button. I haven't exactly been behind him, pushing and clapping/ The issue of domestic disputes pushes buttons, summons up personal emotions* (1980s+)

push comes to shove *sentence* A touchy situation becomes actively hostile; a quarrel becomes a fight; the CHIPS ARE DOWN : *If push comes to shove, can you count on him?* (1958+)

pusher *n* **1** A narcotics peddler or distributor; CANDY MAN, CONNECTION : *queen of the Broadway narcotics pushers* (1935+ Narcotics) **2** A distributor or passer of counterfeit money; paperhanger (1940s+ Underworld) *See* PENCIL-PUSHER, PEN-PUSHER, PILL-PUSHER, WOOD-PUSHER

pushing (number) *v phr* Used to denote that someone is nearly a particular (advanced) age : *She is pushing 50* (1974+)

push one's luck *v phr* To take additional risks when things are going well : *He pushed his luck and lost the whole bundle* (1911+)

push off *v phr* **1** To leave; SHOVE OFF (1918+) **2** To kill; murder; PUSH (1940s+ Underworld)

pushover *modifier* : *He wasn't a pushover kind of cat* **n 1** A person who is easily defeated, imposed upon, convinced, etc : *an eight-round preliminary with some pushover* (1926+) **2**

punchboard, roundheel (1906+) **3** An easy job or task; CINCH, DUCK SOUP : *Two ways to do it. One was a pushover* (1906+)

◁**push-push**▷ *n* The sex act : *If they don't go where she wants, it's no push-push for him that night*

push the envelope *v phr* To expand possibilities; innovate boldly; take risks : *What we want is to create the next computing revolution. We want to push the envelope* (late 1980s+)

push the panic button *See* HIT THE PANIC BUTTON

push up daisies *v phr* To be dead; be buried (1860+)

puss[1] *n* The face : *one sock in the puss* [1890+; fr Irish *pus,* "lip, mouth"] *See* PICKLEPUSS, SOURPUSS

puss[2] *adj* Excellent; wonderful; GREAT, RAD, TITS [1990s+; fr *pussy*]

pussy *adj* Harmless and undemanding; fit for the timid : *The bumper cars are pussy* (1970s+) *n* ◁1▷ The vulva or vagina (1879+) ◁2▷ A woman as a sex object or partner; ASS, TAIL : *Where I come from we call that kind of stuff table pussy* (1879+) ◁3▷ A harmless person, either gentle or timid or both; PUSSYCAT : *Space Invaders are pussies compared to the marketing aggression of the major producers* (1859+) [fr *pussy,* "cat," found by 1726]

◁**pussy butterfly**▷ *n phr* An intrauterine contraceptive device; IUD (1980s+)

pussycat *n* **1** A harmless, gentle, or timid person : *Iacocca is no closet pussycat masquerading as a tiger* **2** A pleasant and amiable person; DOLL, HONEY (1859+)

pussyfoot or **pussyfoot around** *v* or *v phr* To be careful and hesitant; be evasive; tergiversate; BEAT AROUND THE BUSH : *Please stop pussyfooting and get to the point* [1903+; fr the nickname of W E Johnson, given because of his catlike stealth as a law-enforcement officer in the Indian Territory (Oklahoma); Johnson became a famous advocate of Prohibition, and the term briefly meant "prohibitionist"]

◁**pussy-whipped**▷ *adj* Dominated by one's wife or female lover; obsequiously uxorious; henpecked : *Francie had had it with bore-ass "pussy-whipped" men* (1956+)

◁**put**▷ *v* To proffer or do the sex act; LAY : *With men buyers, you get them put and you can sell them the Brooklyn Bridge* [1930s+; a shortening of *put out*] *See* KNOW WHAT one CAN DO WITH something, TELL someone WHAT TO DO WITH something

put a bug in someone's **ear** *v phr* To give someone a special and private piece of information, esp in the hope of favorable action (1940s+)

put a cork in it *v phr* To keep silent; SHUT UP • Often an irritated command : *A New York judge has mercifully told Woody and Mia to put a cork in it* (1990s+)

put a crimp in someone or something *v phr* To thwart or hamper; block or interfere with; STYMIE : *How can we put a crimp in this guy's plans?* [1896+; fr the notion of a severe pinching-in as an obstacle]

put something **across** (or **over**) *v phr* 1 GET something ACROSS 2 To succeed; PULL IT OFF : *Ask her, she knows how to put it across* (1917+)

put a damper on *v phr* To discourage or dishearten; also, to decrease the intensity of something : *Insects put a damper on my plans to move to Maine*

put a lid on someone or something *v phr* To suppress; quiet; quell : *Putting a Lid on The Kid* (1970s+)

put a move on someone *v phr* (Variations: **make** can replace **put**; **the move** or **the moves** can replace **a move**) To make a sexual advance to someone; PROPOSITION : *Why don't you put a move on that Tuck girl?/ tryin' to put the moves on every girl in the place* (1980s+ Students)

put (or **stick**) **a sock in it** *interj* Please keep quiet; SHUT UP : *Would you please be so kind as to force the media to put a sock in it/ And they can stick a sock in it. Or maybe a bratwurst* (1919+)

◁**put** one's **ass in a sling**▷ *See* HAVE one's ASS IN A SLING

◁**put** one's **ass on the line**▷ *v phr* To assume risk and responsibility; put oneself in peril : *I agreed with him, but I wasn't going to put my ass on the line to prove the point* (1940+)

put away *v phr* To eat or drink, esp heartily or excessively : *They were able to put away a lot of noodles, turkey hash, corn, Jell-O, bread, peanut butter, jelly, and water* (1878+)

put someone or something **away** *v phr* 1 To commit to an asylum or send to jail, an old-age home, nursing home, etc (1872+) 2 To kill someone (1588+) 3 To please someone enormously; KNOCK someone's SOCKS OFF : *It put me away. It destroyed me* (1970s+)

put daylight (or **distance**) **between** *v phr* To separate things, esp to separate oneself from someone or something disadvantageous : *The President is trying hard to put daylight between himself and the National Rifle Association* (1970s+)

put-down *n* Something disparaging, humiliating, or deflating; a reducing insult; KNOCK : *since it is such a neat put-down of the arrogant administrator* (late 1950s+)

put someone or something **down** *v phr* 1 To kill : *Criticizing Jim Brady's wife Mohan said,*

"Because of all her barking and complaining, she really needs to be put down. A humane shot at a veterinarian's would be an easy way to do it" (1560+) 2 To criticize adversely and severely; denigrate; DUMP ON, KNOCK : *Not that I mean to put down the Old Masters* (late-1950s+)

put someone or something **down for** something *v phr* To identify or classify; recognize; PEG : *When I see a guy with a pull-over sweater under a double-breasted suit, I put him down for an Englishman* (1950s+)

put one's **finger on** something *v phr* To recall or specify a desired matter with precision; define exactly : *I remember it, but can't quite put my finger on the outcome* (1889+)

put one's **foot in it** *v phr* To get into difficulties, esp by blundering : *Trying to be delicate, I put my foot right in it* (1856+)

put one's **foot in** one's **mouth** *v phr* To make an embarrassing comment; say something stupid : *part of the same hysterical syndrome that caused me to put my foot in my mouth* (1940s+)

put someone **in the picture** *v phr* To give necessary orienting data; brief; BRING someone UP TO SPEED : *Nobody put me in the picture, and I was confused for weeks* (1942+)

put in one's **two cents worth** *See* PUT one's TWO CENTS IN

put it on ice *v phr* To make victory certain; ensure success : *Back-to-back doubles put it on ice in the ninth inning* (1918+)

put it on the line *See* LAY IT ON THE LINE

put it on the street *v phr* To disclose something, esp rather publicly : *So we put it on the street that she was leaving* (1970s+)

put it over on someone *v phr* To deceive; fool : *Be careful, nobody puts it over on her* [1913+; found slightly earlier as *put it all over on*]

put it past someone *See* NOT PUT IT PAST someone

◁**put it to** someone▷ *v phr* To do the sex act with or to; SCREW (1940s+)

put one's **money where** one's **mouth is** *sentence* Support your statements, brags, opinions, etc, with something tangible; PUT UP OR SHUT UP : *I won't believe he's leaving until he puts his money where his mouth is and goes away* (1942+)

put someone's **nose out of joint** *v phr* To make someone envious or jealous (1581+)

put-on *adj* Feigned; affected : *his put-on machismo* (1621+) *n* 1 An act, remark, etc, intended to fool someone; a more or less amiable deception : *a master of the "put-on," a mildly cruel art/ They nudge us that what they're doing is just a "put-on"* (1896+) 2 (also **put-on artist**) A pretender; PHONY : *to equate an original talent like Kenneth Anger with a put-on like Andy Warhol* (1960s+)

put someone on *v phr* To fool someone, esp by pretending; tease : *The Countess who adores the poet pities him and puts him "on"* (1896+)

put on airs *v phr* **1** To affect a refinement and hauteur one is not born to : *Now that I have the Rolls Royce I'll put on airs* **2** To be snobbish and aloof (1781+)

put on an act *v phr* To behave misleadingly, esp pretentiously; shoot someone a line (1934+)

put one over on someone *v phr* To deceive someone; best someone by a trick (1912+)

put something or someone on hold *v phr* To defer an immediate decision; postpone consideration : *I'm afraid that whole matter is on hold just now* [1960s+; fr the *hold* function of a telephone, with which one can close off a conversation temporarily]

put something on the line *See* LAY something ON THE LINE

put on the ritz (or the dog) *v phr* **1** To make a display of wealth and luxury : *everything they could to put on the ritz/ put on the dog and give him the ritz like this* **2** To dress stylishly and flashily **3** PUT ON AIRS [entry form 1926+, variant 1934+; fr the name of the Swiss César Ritz and the various luxurious European hotels he built; *put on the dog* fr a late 1800s college, esp Yale, expression]

put someone on the spot *v phr* **1** To require action, a solution, etc, at once : *It had to be ready tomorrow, which put our department on the spot* **2** To embarrass; put in a difficult position : *I don't want her to put us on the spot again* (1929+)

put something on the street *v phr* To make known publicly something that others may not want known : *put it on the street that he was into illegal stuff*

put someone on to someone or something *v phr* To introduce someone; get someone access to : *that little Andronica you put me onto* (1887+)

putout *n* An out, other than a strikeout (Baseball)

put-out *adj* Angry; upset; offended : *I know you will be put out at my not writing* (1887+)

◁**put (or give) out**▷ *v phr* To proffer sexual favors, esp to do so readily; be promiscuous : *A guy gives a dame a string of beads and she puts out/ As a Yale woman I am resented because I will not "put out" for Yale men/ A guy buys a gift for his wife because he knows she won't give out if he don't*

put someone out *v phr* To impose upon; cause inconvenience (1940s+)

put someone or something out of the way *v phr* To remove an obstacle, eliminate a barrier : *put that project out of the way to concentrate on this*

put someone or something out to pasture *v phr* To retire; take out of active use, practice, etc, usu after long service : *That old machine's about shot, and we should put it out to pasture* [1930s+; fr the farm practice of letting an old horse graze at will and work no longer]

put paid to *v phr* To finish; also, to put to rest or finish off (1919+; British)

put one's pants on one leg at a time *v phr* To have traits of ordinary humanity : *Even giants put their pants on one leg at a time* (1960s+)

put one's skates on *v phr* To hurry (1895+)

put that in your pipe and smoke it *sentence* Take that : *I'm not going. Put that in your pipe and smoke it*

put the arm (or the sleeve) on someone *v phr* **1** To detain or arrest, esp by force : *It was a signal for the waiter to hustle over and put the arm on the customer who was trying to stiff him* **2** To hit; beat up : *in case a tough greengrocer tries to put the arm on you* **3** To ask for a loan; PUT THE BITE ON someone or something : *writing a letter to my friend Ted without putting the arm on him for a couple of bucks* (1930s+)

put the bite (or the bee) on someone or something *v phr* **1** To ask for money, esp for a loan : *And how do you put the bite on me* (1900s+) **2** To make a request; solicit : *Sullivan continues putting the bee on other government agencies* (1933+)

put the clamps on *v phr* To seize, esp to steal (1940s+)

put the fear of God into *v phr* To terrify (1905+)

put the finger on someone *v phr* **1** To locate and identify a victim; FINGER **2** To provide evidence leading to the arrest of a criminal; betray a criminal to the police : *He put the finger on my husband* (1926+ Underworld)

put the freeze (or chill) on someone *v phr* To reject; treat very coldly : *Women are quick to put the freeze on free loaders* (1960s+)

put the hammer down *v phr* To accelerate; go full speed : *Guerrero put the hammer down and passed Unser a few laps later* (Car racing 1960+, fr truckers)

put the heat on someone *v phr* To use coercive pressure; LEAN ON someone : *He put the heat on me to vote that way* (1936+)

put the icing on the cake *See* ICE THE CAKE

put the kibosh on someone or something *v phr* To quash or stifle; put the quietus to : *I was praying that the kid wouldn't put the "kibosh" on me* [1836+; origin unknown and richly speculated upon; many regard it as probably fr Yiddish because it sounds as if it ought to be; Padraic Colum, however, attributed it to Irish *cie bais*, "cap of death," presumably the black cap donned by a judge before pronouncing the death sentence, which is a semantically appealing suggestion; the phrase was used by Dickens in his first published book, in 1836, and put into the mouth of a London urchin]

put the make on someone *v phr* To make sexual advances; MAKE A PASS AT someone : *The codger was horny and put the make on the lady cop* (1970s+)

put them in the aisles *See* LAY THEM IN THE AISLES

put the moves on *v phr* To try to seduce someone : *put the moves on her lab partner*

put the pedal to the metal *modifier* Regulating or deregulating highway speeds : *President Clinton will sign what friends and foes alike call "the pedal to the metal bill" v phr* To accelerate; go fast; GIVE IT THE GUN : *Bolan settled back on creaky springs, and put the pedal to the metal* (1980s+)

put the screws to (or **on**) someone *v phr* To use extreme coercive pressure; harass; PUT THE HEAT ON someone : *The only reason Fidel agreed was to put the screws to Reagan* [1940s+; fr a torturer's use of *thumbscrews; put the screws on* is found by 1834]

put the squeeze on someone *v phr* To put under heavy pressure or exigency; LEAN ON someone, PUT THE HEAT ON someone : *She hired me to put the squeeze on Linda for a divorce* (1941+)

put (or **run**) someone **through the mill** *v phr* To subject to an arduous experience; be rough on someone : *She's quite eager to try again, although they really put her through the mill* (1818+) *See* GO THROUGH THE MILL, THROUGH THE MILL

put someone through the wringer *v phr* To subject to harsh treatment, esp by severe interrogation [1942+; fr the image of squeezing something out by passing it through a clothing *wringer*]

putting *See* OFF-PUTTING

put-together *adj* : *Calm, cool, and collected. Never blew his stack. Never raised his voice. A real put-together guy* (1970+)

putt-putt *n* **1** A small marine engine **2** A motorboat, esp a slow one : *A sneaker's no good.*

Got to use a putt-putt **3** Any small motor vehicle *v* : *We'll putt-putt over to the island* [1905+; fr the sound of a two-cycle engine]

put (or **add**) one's **two cents** (or **two cents worth**) **in** *v phr* To volunteer one's advice, esp when it is not solicited; KIBITZ : *If I may put my two cents in, I think we should shut up* (1930s+)

putty *n* A very malleable or biddable person or persons : *they'll be putty and do exactly what you want (as they should)* (1924+)

put someone under *v phr* To arrest someone; COLLAR, HOOK SOMEONE UP, PINCH [1990s+ Police; shortening of *put someone under arrest*]

put someone under the table *v phr* To remain sober while one's drinking companion(s) becomes drunk : *She can drink most under the table* (1921+)

put up *v phr* To contribute or pay money, esp money bet or promised (1865+)

put someone up *v phr* To provide lodging for (1800+)

put-up job *n phr* A prearranged matter; a contrived affair : *The surprise award was a put-up job* (1838+)

put up or shut up *sentence* PUT one's MONEY WHERE one's MOUTH IS (1878+)

put someone up to something *v phr* To incite or persuade someone : *I know who did it, but not who put him up to it* (1824+)

put up with someone or something *v phr* To tolerate or accept : *I'll put up with it if you think I should* (1755+)

◁**putz**▷ *n* **1** A detestable person; obnoxious wretch; PRICK, SCHMUCK : *Here comes the Moravian putz* (1964+) **2** An ineffectual person; NEBBISH : *There wasn't much that worried him. Dying like a putz in a fucked-up gag was one thing that did* (1964+) **3** The penis (1934+) [fr Yiddish, literally "ornament"]

putz around *v phr* To behave idly; putter around; FOOL AROUND, FUTZ AROUND : *Dad was putzing around in the background* [1970s+; fr *putz* and semantically related to *dick around, fuck around,* though less coarse than these to any but, probably, Jewish ears]

pyro *n* A pyromaniac, lover of fire (1977+)

pythons *n* Quite muscular upper arms : *flexing his pythons after going to the Y*

Q

QT, the *See* ON THE QT

quack *n* An incompetent and fraudulent doctor [1659+; a shortening of *quacksalver,* "a person who boasts about the virtues of his worthless remedies"; fr Dutch and found by 1579]

quackery *n* The practices of "quacks" : *and knew it was "world-class quackery"* (1709+)

quad *n* **1** Any architectural quadrangle, esp one at a college or university (1820+) **2** quod (1804+) **3** A car having four headlights (1950s+ Hot rodders) **4** An idiot; fool; SPAZ, TARD : *I feel like such a quad, falling on my face while skating with those cute boys* (1990s+ Canadian students) [said to be a shortening of *quadrilateral,* "square"]

quarterback *v* To lead or direct; control; manage : *and quarterbacking the rise of* Action News *at Channel 6* (1945+) *See* MONDAY MORNING QUARTERBACK

queen *n* **1** A woman, esp a wealthy and gracious one : *Wouldn't it be luck if some ritzy queen fell for him!* (1900+) **2** A male homosexual, esp one who ostentatiously takes a feminine role : *The queens look great strutting along the boardwalk* (1924+ Homosexuals) *v* (also **queen it**) To behave in a refined and haughty way (1611+) [homosexual sense probably a late 1800s alteration of *quean,* "harlot, prostitute," influenced by connotations of *queen,* "aged, dignified, tawdry, and overadorned"] *See* CLOSET QUEEN, DRAG QUEEN, MAIN QUEEN, SIZE QUEEN, TOE-JAM QUEEN

queer *adj* **1** Counterfeit (1740+) ◁2▷ Homosexual; CAMP, GAY • In the early 1990s *queer* was adopted as a nonpejorative designation by some homosexuals, in the spirit of "gay pride" : *Some girls said that I was queer* (1922+) *n* **1** (also **the queer**) Counterfeit money : *eagle-eyed concessionaires always on the lookout for the queer* (Underworld 1900s+); (1812+) ◁2▷ (also **queerie**) : *a lot of queeries in the State Department* (1932+) *v* To spoil; ruin; GOOF UP : *Food is what queered the party* (late 1700s+ British); (1812+)

◁**queer as a three-dollar bill**▷ *adv* Obviously homosexual • Usu considered offensive : *He is queer as a three-dollar bill*

◁**queerbait**▷ *n* **1** A person who attracts gay people; a person who acts gay but claims to be straight **2** A person held in disdain : *Hey, queerbait! What are you looking at*

queer fish *n phr* A strange or weird person; odd fellow; WACK, WEIRDO (1750+)

Que pasa? *sentence* What's happening? What's going on? : *Hey, baby. Que pasa*

quick-and-dirty *adj* Hastily done as an expedient; slipshod : *The gossip in this quick-and-dirty, self-pitying memoir* (1977+) *n* GREASY SPOON (1968+)

quick buck *See* FAST BUCK

quick fix *n phr* A hasty repair or relief job : *He called my idea a quick fix at best, but he'd do it* [1966+; fr *fix* as "repair" influenced by *fix* as "dose of narcotics"]

quickie *modifier* : *the new "quickie divorce" law n* **1** (or **quicky,** also **quick one**) A quick drink of liquor (entry form 1940+, variant 1928+) **2** Anything taken or done very hastily; something rushed : *a "quickie," one of those overnight film concoctions* (1926+) **3** The sex act done very hastily : *We may have time for a quickie* (1940s+) **4** An unauthorized strike; WILDCAT (1943+)

quick like a bunny *adv phr* Very quickly [1940s+ Students; possibly a reference to the rapid copulation of rabbits]

quick on the draw (or the trigger or the uptake) *adj phr* Quick to respond or react; touchy; sensitive (1940s+)

◁**quim**▷ *n* The vulva or vagina; CUNT [1613+; origin unknown]

quits *See* CALL IT A DAY

quit while one is ahead *v phr* To stop doing something after achieving success or at least partial success : *had won at slots, so he quit while he was ahead*

quote unquote *interj* An expression to emphasize a word or phrase, esp for irony or sarcasm : *your quote unquote friends*

R

rabbit food *See* BUNNY FOOD

rabbit punch *n* A very quick punch, esp a short blow to the neck

race *See* HORSE RACE, RAT RACE

rack *v* **1** (also **rack out**) To sleep; nap; COP ZS : *I'll rack out for awhile on the grass till I get it together* (1960s+ Teenagers) **2** To denigrate severely; TRASH : *Why rack Clinton?* (1990s+) [probably fr torture on the *rack*, a stretching machine, the verb found by 1433] *See* MEAT RACK, OFF-THE-RACK, RIM-ROCK

rack, the *n* Bed; SACK : *Jeanne is pretty good in the rack* (1940s+ Navy)

racked *adj* Hit in the testicles *adv* For certain; under control; taped : *As for the next step, I have that racked* [1960s+; probably fr the *racking* of the balls before a pool game, putting them in a precise pattern]

racked out *adj phr* Asleep; in bed (1960s+ Teenagers)

racket *n* **1** Any illegal concern or enterprise; a criminal business; DODGE, GRIFT : *G Marks and Abe Cohn have a new racket now of promenading Clinton Street dock* (1785+) **2** A party or dance, esp a noisy one • In recent usage this is most common among the police : *passing evidence around like a pretzel tray at a retirement racket* (1745+) **3** Any concession, stand, etc (1940s+ Circus & carnival) *v* To lead a busy life professionally and socially : *Monk's seesawing years, from 1935 to 1940, were spent racketing endlessly back and forth between Europe and New York, an itinerant pianist and boulevardier* (1760+) [fr early 1800s British underworld fr *racket*, "noise, confusion," etc]

racketeer *n* A person who works in an illegal racket; a member of the rackets; gangster, mobster, WISE GUY (late 1920s+)

rackets, the *n phr* Organized crime; the syndicate; the Mafia; the MOB (late 1920s+)

rack up[1] *v phr* To register or post; accumulate; achieve : *more representative of actual consumer use than 60,000 miles would have been if racked up in short order* [1960s+; probably fr the *racking up* of pool balls in a triangular frame before a game]

rack up[2] *v phr* To wreck; ruin; damage severely; TOTAL : *He got caught raping a nine-year-old Japanese girl. He got racked up* (1970s+) *See* RACK

racy *adj* Somewhat indecent; RAUNCHY : *The movie has a lot of racy dialogue* (1901+)

rad *adj* Extraordinary; wonderful; AWESOME, CHILL, GNARLY : *Want to go to this way rad party? (late 1970s+ Teenagers)* *n* A radical (1820+)

raft *n* A large number; OODLES, SLEW : *I have rafts of reasons for not doing that* [1833+; fr earlier uses of *raft* to mean a dense flight of waterfowl, a mass of logs in a river, etc]

rag *n* **1** An article of clothing : *She got into her rags* (1855+) **2** A tent (1940s+ Circus) **3** The pennant awarded to the annual winner of a league championship (1908+ Baseball) **4** A newspaper or magazine, esp one that the speaker does not like : *This so-called revolutionary organ is a horrible rag* (1734+) **5** ragtime (1897+) **6** A piece of ragtime music (1897+) *v* **1** To play in a ragtime style : *The street bands ragged a tune by taking one note and putting two or three in its place* (1897+) **2** To tease; banter disparagingly with; NEEDLE, RIDE : *Sometimes we'd rag one another in the rough manner that is safe only for friends* (1808+) *See* the BIG RAG, DAMP RAG, GLAD RAGS

◁**rag, the**▷ *n* **1** A sanitary napkin or tampon : *She told him she had the rag on, which cooled his ardor some* **2** Menstruation; the CURSE (1930s+) *See* CHEW THE FAT, HAVE THE RAG ON, ON THE RAG

rag bag *modifier* : *a rag-bag collection, but an interesting one* *n phr* Any miscellany, esp a very random and confusing one : *What he calls his philosophy is a rag-bag of trite trivialities* (1820+)

rage *n* A good party : *This is a rage, man* (Australian 1980+, Canadian 1990s+)

ragged *See* RUN SOMEONE RAGGED

◁**raggedy-ass**▷ or **raggedy-pants** *adj* Inferior; sloppy; HALF-ASSED : *some kinda raggedy-ass agreement she thinks is a legal will/ picked up from some raggedy-pants US trackside* [WWI armed forces; found as *ragged-arse* by 1896]

rag on someone or something *v phr* To disparage; strongly deprecate; TRASH : *Ivey, who was hosting the show, began ragging on him/ He overheard Mel ragging on one of his shots* (1980s+ Students)

rag out (or **up**) *v phr* To dress in one's best clothes; DOLL UP (entry form 1875+, variant 1934+)

rags *See* GLAD RAGS

rag-tag and bobtail *n phr* The rabble; hoi polloi : *Oh Lord, deliver me from the rag-tag and bobtail* [1820+; *tag-rag and bobtail* is found by 1659; *bobtail*, "cur, lout," by 1619]

ragtop or **rag-roof** *modifier* : *I sure wouldn't sleep in that rag-top car* *n* A convertible car :

It's been a while since the ragtops rolled off the assembly line/ Return of the rag roofs (1955+)

rag trade, the *n phr* The clothing and fashion industry; the garment industry; SEVENTH AVENUE : *the enormously canny middle-aged men of the rag trade (1890+)*

rah-rah *adj* Naively enthusiastic and hortatory, esp in a partisan collegiate context : *Some are rah-rah types, some are hard-ass disciplinarians (1911+) n : I just couldn't see myself spending four years of my life with rahrahs like them* [a shortening of *hurrah,* found by 1877 as used in cheers]

rail *n* **1** A thin row of powdered narcotic to be sniffed; LINE : *I snorted the rails that Hondo offered (1960s+ Narcotics)* **2** An elongated sort of competition hot rod *(1970s+ Hot rodders)*

railroad *v* **1** To convict and imprison someone very rapidly, perhaps unjustly or illegally : *The prisoner is railroaded to jail* **2** To force a resolution of something quickly, perhaps without due process : *if all cases were railroaded through that quick (1884+) See* a HELL OF A WAY TO RUN A RAILROAD

rain cats and dogs *v phr* (Variations: **chicken coops** or **darning needles** or **pitchforks** may replace **cats and dogs**) To rain very hard [entry form 1738+, *pitchforks* 1850+; origin unknown; although many improbable derivations have been proposed, from classical Greek to pagan Scandinavian; rain dogs and polecats is found by 1652]

rain check *n phr* A postponement or delay, with promise of renewal, of a sports event, dinner, party, date, receipt of a sale item at a store, etc [1884+ Baseball; fr the ticket stub that permits one to see another baseball game if the game one has a ticket for is not played on account of rain] *See* TAKE A RAIN CHECK

raincoat *n* A condom; RUBBER : *If a guy said "I ride bareback," I'd tell him he needs a raincoat. Instead of gonorrhea, I'd talk about the clap (1980s+)*

rainmaker *n* A powerful and successful representative or agent, esp for a law firm : *to a six-figure "rainmaker" generating fees for one of the most politically connected law firms in the state (1968+)*

rain on someone's **parade** *v phr* To spoil someone's day, performance, special occasion, etc *(1941+)*

raise *v* To leave; CUT OUT, SPLIT *(1990s+ Black) See* MEXICAN PROMOTION

raise a stink *v phr* RAISE CAIN : *I didn't even raise a stink when Bradley's stylist guy came over* [1970s+; *kick up a stink* is found by 1948; *stink,* "fuss, disturbance," is found by 1812]

raise Cain (or **a ruckus**) *v phr* To make a disturbance; complain loudly and bitterly; KICK UP A FUSS *(1840+)*

raise hell *v phr* **1** (Variations: **living hell** or **merry hell** or **unshirted hell** may replace **hell**) RAISE CAIN : *They raised living hell/ cold frosts raise unshirted hell with fishing (first variant 1980s+)* **2** To carouse and celebrate boisterously **3** To rebuke strongly; castigate : *He raised hell with me when he found out (1896+)*

raiser *See* HELL-RAISER

raise the roof *v phr* **1** To complain angrily and bitterly; issue a strong rebuke : *When the president sees this fuck-up, she'll raise the roof (1860+)* **2** To make a boisterous noise; carouse raucously *(1894+)*

raisin ranch *n phr* A retirement community • Referring to wrinkles : *raisin ranches all over Florida*

rake in *v phr* To acquire large sums of money : *The Yosemite Fund has so far raked in $200,000 from the sale of 15,000 plates (1583+)*

rake on someone *v phr* To denigrate and humiliate someone *(1980s+ Students)*

rake someone **over the coals** *See* HAUL someone OVER THE COALS

rally *See* PEP RALLY

ralph *v* (also **Ralph** or **ralph up** or **rolf**) To vomit; BARF : *He ralphs up the downers and the quarts of beer* [1967+ Teenagers; probably echoic]

-rama or **-arama** or **-orama** *suffix used to form nouns* A spectacular display or instance of what is indicated : *boatarama/ bunsorama/ videorama* [1824+; fr *panorama,* ultimately fr Greek *horama,* "sight"]

Rambo *modifier* Violent; loutishly aggressive : *Each day Bush ratchets up the Rambo rhetoric and closes more alleys of diplomatic escape for Saddam Hussein* [1985+; fr the main character of the movie *Rambo*]

rambunctious *adj* Boisterous; obstreperous; wild [1859+; origin unknown; *rumbunctious* is found by 1830]

ram something **down** someone's **throat** *v phr* To force someone to hear or do something : *ramming religion down our throats*

◁**ram it**▷ *v phr* STICK IT *(1950s+)*

rammer *See* MOTHERFUCKER

ranch *See* BUY THE FARM

R & R *n* Rest and relaxation or recuperation : *lots of R & R after this is over (Military)*

randy *adj* **1** Sexually aroused; HORNY : *a desperately randy brain surgeon* **2** Desirous; yearning : *randy for the smell of setting cement* [1847+; origin unknown; various dialect senses suggest a possible derivation fr "wild movement," "boisterousness," "wantonness"]

rank *adj* Inferior; contemptible *v* **1** To say or do something that reveals another's guilt : *She ranked him by busting out with that new fur so soon after the robbery (1920s+ Underworld)* **2** To harass; annoy; KID, NEEDLE : *the fine, foul art of "ranking." Light insults were his way of making friends (1934+)* [second sense used by 1960s teenagers in the preferred variant *rank out*, both as a verb phrase and a noun phrase] *See* PULL RANK

rank someone (out) *v phr* To chastise or criticize someone : *ranked Terry out for smoking*

rank on someone *v phr* To insult; disparage; PUT someone or something DOWN : *Fred ranked on Dawn after the fight was broken up (1980s+ Students)*

rap[1] *n* **1** A rebuke; blame; responsibility; KNOCK : *Who'll take the rap for this? (1777+)* **2** Arrest, indictment, or arraignment for a crime : *Gangs with influence can beat about 90 percent of their "raps" (1903+)* **3** An official complaint or reprimand : *Honest cops will often take a "rap" or complaint rather than testify against a fellow cop (1928+) See* BEAT THE RAP, TAKE THE RAP

rap[2] *n* **1** Informal talk; candid conversation and communion *(1929+)* **2** rap song *(1970s+ Black)* *v* **1** To converse; chat and exchange views, esp in a very candid way : *drugs, youth cult, ecstasy questing, rapping (1929+)* **2** To chant a rap song *(1970s+ Black)* [origin unknown; perhaps related to *repartee*, perhaps to *rapport*, perhaps to *rapid*]

rap someone's knuckles *v phr* To give a light and insufficient punishment; GIVE someone A SLAP ON THE WRIST : *Tokyo had been rapped over the knuckles* [1749+; the dated instance might indicate a more severe punishment than modern use does]

rapper[1] *n* **1** A person who charges or identifies another as a criminal *(1904+)* **2** A judge or prosecutor *(1904+)* **3** A crime for which someone not guilty has been punished : *a couple of gang murders solved, but they were just rappers (1940+)*

rapper[2] *modifier* : *rapper talk, which pulls in language from 40s hipsters, 60s hippies, and even cockney rhyming slang n* **1** A person who converses and chats, esp a member of a rap (discussion) group *(1960s+ Counterculture)* **2** The chanter of a rap song *(1970s+ Black)* **3** A devotee of rap music and its attendant styles of dressing, dancing, etc : *as rappers pick up on a little new wave style and make their moves (1970s+ Black)*

rap session *n phr* **1** A conversation; a bout of candid chat : *talk shows featuring rap sessions between hosts and listeners* **2** A meeting of a discussion group : *I was asked to lead a rap session (1970+)*

rap sheet *n phr* : *Their rap sheets listed convictions for the possession or sale of controlled substances (1960+) See* RAPPER[1]

rare back *v phr* To gather one's strength; poise oneself for action : *She rared back and let him have it* [1930s+; fr the verb *rear*, and the image of a horse *rearing* on its hind legs]

rare bird *n phr* Someone or something quite different and remarkable : *rare bird of a man who will do housework*

raring to go, be *v phr* To be very eager and keen to begin; lean forward in the saddle [1927+; fr the image of a *rearing*, mettlesome horse]

raspberries or **razzberries** (RAZ behr eez) *interj* An exclamation of disbelief, defiance, disgust, etc; NUTS *(1925+)*

rat *combining word* A frequenter and devotee of the place indicated : *arcade rat/ rink rat (1970s+) n* **1** A treacherous and disgusting person : *He's acting like a prime rat on this (1629+)* **2** An informer; STOOL PIGEON : *In most cases they were "rats" and the best tools the keepers had (1902+) v* **1** To betray; desert; turn one's coat *(1812+)* **2** : *an inmate, rankled by Angelo's attempts to woo his daughter, ratted on them (1910+)* **3** HOODGE *(1980s+) See* LOOK LIKE A DROWNED RAT, PACK RAT, RUG RAT, SHACK MAN, SMELL A RAT

◁**rat-bastard**▷ *n* A thoroughly despised or wretched person : *the rat-bastards who live here*

ratchet *v* To change by increments in one direction : *Gold had ratcheted down to 385* [1977+; fr the *ratchet* action of a winch or of a wrench, where an increasing pressure, torque, pull, etc, is registered by the clicking of a pawl on a gear wheel]

rate *v* **1** To merit; deserve : *He rates a big cheer, folks (1920+)* **2** To be highly esteemed : *What stunt did he ever pull that makes him rate? (1940s+) See* FIRST-RATE

rated *See* X-RATED

rate with someone *v phr* To be highly regarded, cherished, trusted, etc, by someone : *That sort of persuasion doesn't rate a damn with me (1928+)*

rat fink *modifier* : *the rat-fink Eastern press n phr* A treacherous and disgusting person; BASTARD, SHITHEEL : *that rat-fink Danny's kid (1963+ Teenagers)* [perhaps originally fr labor-union use, since both terms mean "scab"]

◀**rat fuck**▶ *adj phr* **1** Unacceptable to conventional moral traditions **2** FAR OUT *n phr* A despicable person; RAT FINK : *You lousy bastard rat-fuck v phr* **1** To have a good time; JAM **2** To loaf and idle about; rat around *(1950s+ College students)*

rathole *n* A wretched, messy place; a filthy hovel; DUMP : *Those days we lived in a rathole* (1812+) *v* To store up food and supplies; stockpile; STASH (1950s+) *See* POUR MONEY DOWN THE DRAIN

rations *See* GROUND RATIONS

rat on someone *v phr* To inform on someone; give evidence against someone; SQUEAL : *No power on earth can keep her from ratting on you* (1932+)

rat out *v phr* To abandon or desert; withdraw; FINK OUT : *I wouldn't feel you were ratting out* [1941+; fr the *rats* that desert a sinking ship]

rat someone **out** *v phr* To betray or inform on someone; RAT ON someone : *My little brother ratted me out, though* (1990s+)

rat pack *n phr* A teenage street gang : *juvenile gangs, sometimes called rat packs* (1951+)

rat race the *n phr* A job, situation, milieu, etc, marked by confusion and stress; futile and enervating hyperactivity; the everyday world of toil and struggle; the routine workaday : *the rat-race of ordinary social gatherings* [1939+; found by 1937 as the name of a dance]

rats *interj* An exclamation of disgust, disappointment, dismay, etc (1886+)

◁**rat's ass, a**▷ *See* NOT GIVE A DAMN

◁**rat's asshole**▷ *n phr* A despicable person; BASTARD, RAT FINK : *You rat's asshole* (1970s+)

rattle *v* **1** (also **rattle on**) To talk on and on, esp foolishly or pointlessly; babble (1594+) **2** To confuse; upset; disturb concentration : *I rattled him with veiled menaces* (1869+)

rattle someone's **cage** (or **caboose**) *v phr* **1** To criticize; needle; sting; BUG : *Reiner and friends affectionately rattle the cage of rock music and its every pretension* **2** To make a scene or disturbance; RAISE CAIN : *I'm going into his office and rattle his cage* (1980s+)

rattle cages *v phr* To cause excitement; shake things up : *"You like to rattle cages," the saleswoman observed, explaining that it was a California expression* (1980s+)

rattle someone's **chain** *See* PULL someone's CHAIN

rattled *adj* Confused and upset : *rattled by the news*

rattlesnakes *See* UP TO one's ASS IN something

rattletrap *n* A ramshackle coach or other vehicle, esp an old car (1822+)

ratty or ◁**rat-ass**▷ *adj* Shabby; slovenly; SCRUFFY, TACKY : *The skinny Berkley, with her ratty hair and sharp teeth/ the rat-ass rags he's always wearing* (1867+)

raunch *n* Vulgarity; smut; PORN : *No obscenities in Glen's Bar. Too tired for raunch/ the latest batch of 8mm raunch* (1964+) *v* To do the sex act with or to; SCREW : *just because she's raunched a few law students* (1970s+) [back formation fr *raunchy*]

raunchy *adj* **1** Sloppy; slovenly; careless : *depending on how good or how "raunchy" we were* (1939+) **2** (also **rotchy**) Inferior; cheap; CRUMMY, GRUNGY : *my raunchy old jeans* (1950+ Teenagers) **3** Vulgar; salacious; DIRTY : *In the beginning there was Playboy, then came raunchy Penthouse* (1967+) [origin uncertain; the pronunciation and the early currency among aviation cadets in Texas suggest a possible origin in Spanish *rancho,* "ranch," found by 1857, and called by 1864 "a place of evil report"; a ranch, of course, may be regarded as a place of animal filth, odors, etc]

rave *modifier* : *rave notices* *n* **1** : *The critics gave it a rave* (1926+) **2** : *Organized on the fly (sometimes by electronic mail) and often held in warehouses, raves are huge, nomadic dance parties that tend to last all night, or until the police show up/ all-night, Ecstasy-fueled parties known as raves/ Rave head dictates nonviolent fashion and dancing spasmodically to very fast "techno" music* (1990s+) *v* To commend or applaud enthusiastically : *He's raving over this new book* (1816+) [*rave* meant "party" in British slang by 1960] *See* FAVE

raver *n* A person who has a wild time, especially sexually (1959+)

rave-up *n* **1** A wild party (1940+ British) **2** Something loud and exciting : *in "Take Me Back," a lively rave-up* (1967+)

raw *adj* **1** Inexperienced; unfledged; callow : *a raw young actress* (1561+) **2** Harsh; inhospitable : *a raw reception* (1546+) **3** Nude; naked; IN THE RAW : *You can't go raw on this beach, ma'am* (1931+) **4** Vulgar; salacious; dirty; raunchy : *He offended us all with a very raw story* (1940s+)

raw deal *n phr* A case of harsh, unfair, or injurious treatment; a ROYAL FUCKING : *The Academy officers were heaping raw deal after raw deal on him* (1912+)

ray of sunshine *n phr* An infectiously happy person (1915+)

rays *n* Sunshine : *soaking up some rays* (1980s+) *See* BAG SOME RAYS

razz *v* To insult and ridicule; NEEDLE, RIDE : *Is there ever any razzing about the fact that you report to your wife?* [1920+; fr *raspberry;* found in the form *razoo* by 1890]

razz, the *n phr* Mocking insults; rude splatting sounds; the RASPBERRY : *They begin to give him the razz* (1920+)

razzle-dazzle *adj* : *its razzle-dazzle weapons and command and control systems* *modifier* : *a razzle-dazzle quarterback* *n* **1** Adroit deception; slick dodging and feinting; DIPSY-DOODLE,

RAZZMATAZZ : *suspecting some sort of razzle-dazzle* (*1898+*) **2** Excitement; gaudiness; spectacular show : *put razzle-dazzle into the grocery business* (*1889+*) **3** An exciting carnival ride (*1935+ Carnival*) [probably a reduplication of *dazzle*]

razzmatazz or **razzamatazz** *adj* Spectacular; showy; dazzling; RAZZLE-DAZZLE : *a razzmatazz New Year's Eve bash n* **1** Swift and adroit deception; slick jugglery; RAZZLE-DAZZLE : *more glitter, more razzmatazz, more false human interest* (*1894+*) **2** Anything outdated, esp old and sentimental; CORN, RICKY-TICK[1] : *"Razzmatazz" is corny jazz* (*1950s+ Jazz talk*)

reach-me-down *adj* Inferior; shoddy : *the nice and the reach-me-down manners n* HAND-ME-DOWN (*1862+*)

reaction *See* GUT REACTION

read *n* **1** A book or other printed matter : *Ultimately, it's Maas' reporter's eye for detail that makes "China White" a great read* (*1958+*) **2** Understanding; interpretation; TAKE : *What's your read on this?* (*1990s+*) *v* **1** To inspect clothing for lice (*WWI Army*) **2** To receive and interpret a radio signal; understand : *He's breaking up and I can't read him* (*1940s+ Radio operators*) **3** To understand; DIG : *I read you, baby, and I flatly agree* (*1956+*)

read 'em and weep *sentence* Here is some probably unwelcome information for you; here is the truth [1940s+ Gambling; fr the crapshooter's or poker player's injunction that his opponents look carefully at a winning roll or hand]

read from the same page *v phr* To agree; see eye to eye : *These guys, reading from the same page for the first time in years, signed the pact* (*1990s+*)

read someone his rights *See* GIVE someone HIS RIGHTS

read someone like a book *v phr* To know and understand someone thoroughly, including deep motives and likely actions : *She thinks she's pretty clever, but I read her like a book* (*1844+*)

read someone loud and clear *v phr* To understand someone very well; comprehend perfectly : *Do you read me loud and clear, mister?* (*1940s+ Radio operators*)

read my lips or **can you read lips** *sentence* I am thinking but not uttering something obscene, insulting, or otherwise not for the public ear : *Psst. Hey, parents! Read my lips v phr* You seem to be too stupid to understand what I'm saying, so look at me very attentively and try (*1980s+*)

read the riot act *v phr* To rebuke firmly; reprove severely, esp in the vein of a stern warning (*1819+*)

ready, the *n phr* Money : *Take the ready and send it along* [1688+; fr *ready* money]

ready for this? (are you) *interj* Get ready to hear something surprising

real *adv* Really; truly (*1658+*) *See* FOR REAL, IT'S BEEN REAL

◁**real bitch**▷ *n phr* A particularly nasty, difficult, or annoying person or thing : *Opening that is a real bitch*

real cheese, the *See* the CHEESE

reality check *n phr* A confirmation of fact, esp when compared with fantasy : *Proxmire's pronouncements provided a reality check on spending requests* (*1990s+*)

really pick 'em *See* one CAN REALLY PICK 'EM

real McCoy, the, or the **McCoy** *n phr* Any genuine and worthy person or thing; the genuine article : *egg bagels, a sweeter variety of the real McCoy/ You can trust her, she's the McCoy* [1922+; origin uncertain; *the real Mackay* is found by 1883; revived during Prohibition times to describe liquor]

real money *See* HEAVY MONEY

real pro *See* PRO

ream *v* **1** (also **rim**) To cheat; swindle, esp by unfair business practice; SCREW : *A new technique for reaming the customers* (*1914+*) **2** (also **ream out**) To rebuke harshly; BAWL SOMEONE OUT, CHEW SOMEONE OUT : *I've seen him just ream guys out for not getting the job done* (*WWII armed forces*) ◁**3**▷ (also **rim**) To stimulate the anus, either orally or with the penis (*1942+ Homosexuals*)

rear end *n phr* (also **rear**) The buttocks; ASS : *She's a pain in the rear end* (*1937+, variant 1796+*) *v* To hit a car from the rear : *his Grand Am was rear-ended* (*mid-1970s+*)

rear-ender or **back-ender** *n phr* An automobile accident in which the victim is hit from behind

rec *Modifier* Recreation : *worked for park and rec for years* (*1929+*)

recap (REE kap) *n* : *I gave her a quick recap of the incident v* To repeat, esp in a summary form; recapitulate; REHASH (*1940s+*)

recharge (one's **batteries**) *v phr* To replenish one's energies, resources, etc : *I came to New York to recharge my cultural batteries* (*mid-1970s+*)

recon *n* Reconnaissance : *orders for recon only* (*1966+ Military*)

record *See* BROKEN RECORD, OFF THE RECORD, TRACK RECORD

◁**red ass**▷, the *n phr* Anger; PISS-OFF (*1940s+ Southern*)

◁**red-assed**▷ *adj* Very angry; livid; PISSED OFF (*1940s+ Southern*)

red carpet *adj phr* Luxurious; plush; RITZY : *Jewelry gives you a red carpet elegance* (*1950s+*) *n phr* A sumptuous welcome : *He* *was sort of expecting the red carpet and not the fish-eye (1934+)* [fr an ancient custom, at least as old as Aeschylus's *Agamemnon*, of putting down a *red carpet* over which a welcomed dignitary would walk] *See* ROLL OUT THE RED CARPET

red cent, a (or one) *n phr* (Variation: a (or one) red) A cent; the least amount of money; a THIN DIME : *The poor man claimed he didn't have a red cent* [1839+; fr the fact that a copper *cent* is *red*]

red dog *n phr* A defensive assault in which the linebacker goes directly for the quarterback *(1966+ Football)*

red-eye, the, or the **red-eye special** *n phr* An airline flight from coast to coast, esp from west to east, that leaves one coast late at night and arrives early in the morning : *I just flew in on the red-eye* [1968+; fr the bleary sleepless look of overnight passengers]

red face *See* HAVE A RED FACE

red-faced *adj* Embarrassed; abashed; guilty-looking *(1950s+)*

redflag *v* To inject narcotics by hypodermic needle; MAINLINE, SHOOT UP : *take it home and redflag the works into your arm (1990s+ Narcotics)*

red flag *modifier* Subject of a special warning or suspicion : *His article identifies several "red flag" professions that have a higher-than-usual chance of being audited* [1976+; found as a sign of warning by 1777]

red herring *n phr* Something used to divert attention from the real issue or matter : *All this talk of deficits is just a red herring* [1884+; fr the use of a dead *red herring* to confuse or test the scent of hunting dogs, found by 1686]

red hot *adj phr* Very hot; sizzling • An intensive of all slang senses of *hot* (1758+) *n phr* A frankfurter; HOT DOG *(1892+)*

red-hot mama *n phr* 1 A type of heavy, loud, and somewhat vulgar woman singer of the 1920s *(1926+)* 2 An especially lively, amorous, and attractive woman *(1936+)*

red ink *n phr* 1 Red wine, esp of an inferior sort : *A pint of red ink still sells for two bits* *(1919+)* 2 Financial loss or losses : *a flood of red ink totaling close to $80 billion (1929+)*

red-letter day *n phr* An important day; a memorably happy or noteworthy day : *red-letter days marked on the calendar*

redlight *v* 1 To push someone off a moving train; kill by pushing off a train : *Who'd you red-light, Ferris? (Circus & carnival)* 2 To eject someone from a car

red light, the *n phr* A warning or command to stop : *We were all set, but the boss gave us the red light* [1931+; found by 1849 in the time before traffic lights]

redneck *modifier* : *This is a redneck rural county* *n* 1 ◄CRACKER► *(1893+)* 2 A bigoted and conventional person; a loutish ultraconservative : *Fred is a crude redneck, and Carol is his latest bimbo (1975+)* [perhaps fr the characteristic ruddy *neck* of an angry person, and influenced by the image of a bigoted rural Southern white person; perhaps fr the fact that pellagra, a deficiency disease associated with poor Southern whites, produces a dermatitis that turns the neck red; first noun sense found by 1830 in a more specialized derogatory use, "the Presbyterians in Fayetteville"]

redshirt *n* 1 A student whose period of athletic eligibility has been extended 2 An act of redshirting : *Indiana forward Alan Henderson is recovering from knee surgery, so a medical redshirt is a possibility v* 1 To extend a college student's period of athletic eligibility 2 Various noncollege and nonsports instances of providing an extra year of eligibility : *It is a capricious misuse of scarce resources when public schools provide redshirting, borrowing the term used in college athletics/ To get them eligibility for additional schooling: Under the redshirt plan, special education students could extend their high school program by at least one year* [1955+ Sports; fr the *red shirts* worn by such athletes in contrast with varsity players]

red state *n phr* Any US state that tends to vote for candidates of the Republican party in a general election *(2000+)*

red tape *n phr* Delay and complication; bureaucratic routine; petty officious procedure [1736+; fr the tape used for tying up legal and official documents]

red tide *n* A woman's menstrual period : *down with the red tide*

red zone *n phr* The part of the field closest to the defender's goal line : *We wouldn't be talking about a lull if we wouldn't have made the mistakes in the red zone (1990s+ Football)*

reefer[1] *n* A refrigerated railroad car, truck, ship, etc; FREEZE : *A malfunction in a refrigerated trailer, or reefer, raises the temperature* [1914+; fr *refrigerated*]

reefer[2] or **reefer weed** *n* 1 A marijuana cigarette; JOINT 2 A person who smokes marijuana; POTHEAD [1920s+ Narcotics; origin unknown; perhaps originally *rifa* fr Mexican Spanish *grifa*, "marijuana," the *g* lost because it is not aspirated or exploded in Spanish pronunciation and hence not readily heard by English speakers]

reentry *n* The act of descent from a narcotic ecstasy *(1960s+ Narcotics)*

reet or **reat** *adj* (also **reet** and **compleat**) Good; proper; excellent; right : *With her good looks,* *she was still "reet" with me/ looking extremely reet and compleat (1930s+ Jazz musicians) See* ALL REET

ref *n* A referee (1899+) *v* : *I started reffing basketball in southern Illinois in 1957* (1929+)

refi *n* Refinancing : *a year ago, many refis*

refrigerator mom *n phr* A working or absentee mother who communicates with her children by notes on the refrigerator door : *Autistic kids are not due to refrigerator moms* (1990s+)

register *v* To express with the face and body : *I jumped up and registered horror* (1901+)

regs *n* Regulations; rules : *All regs say you can't* (1940s+)

regular *adj* **1** Real; genuine : *He thinks he's a regular Casanova* (1821+) **2** : *regular coffee n* A cup of coffee with the usual moderate amount of cream and sugar • In New York City no sugar is included *(1950s+ fr lunch counter)*

regular fellow (or **guy**) *n phr* An honest, pleasant, convivial person, esp of the moral bourgeoisie : *I know I'm not a regular fellow, yet I loathe anybody else that isn't/ She's like Wallace. A real fighter. A regular guy (first form 1920+, second 1840+)*

rehab (REE hab) *modifier* : *more work-release and rehab centers n* Rehabilitation, esp of a drug addict, alcoholic, etc : *After a few weeks' rehab they sent him back home* (1948+) *v* To rehabilitate, esp a building, factory, etc : *Williams has worked for minimum wage, rehabbing houses/ had to give up a sublease because the building was rehabbed* (1970s+)

rehash *n* : *a rehash of stale political charges v* To review; discuss again; repeat; RECAP : *the things they had hashed and rehashed for many a frugal conversational meal* [1880+; called vulgar in the dated source]

reinvent the wheel *v phr* To go laboriously and unnecessarily through elementary stages in some process or enterprise; waste time on tediously obvious fundamentals (1980s+)

rejigger or **rejig** *v* To alter or readjust; tinker with : *sought to raise output this year by rejiggering its agricultural policies* [first form 1940s+, second 1960+; fr mid-1800s *jigger*, "shake or jerk rapidly," related to *jig* as a rapid movement, dance, etc, hence "rearrange or readjust by shaking," semantically similar to *shake up*]

religion *See* GET RELIGION

reloading *n* : *In one of the worst scams, called "reloading," consumers who have already lost money are bilked again by companies that offer to recover their losses* (1940s+)

◁**reltney**▷ *n* The penis : *My reltney was ready for action* [origin unknown]

rent *See* BET THE FARM, HIGH-RENT

rent-a-cop or ◁**rent-a-pig**▷ *n* A uniformed security guard; square badge : *a part-time rent-a-cop, somebody's doorman* [1970s+; coined on the model of *rent-a-car*, on which model depends also the coinage *Rent-a-Kvetch* and many others]

rent-boy *n* A male prostitute, esp young (1969+)

rent party *n phr* A party where one's friends and neighbors buy drinks, food, etc, and help one pay the rent; percolator. SHAKE (1925+ Black)

rents or **'rents** *n* Parents; PARENTAL UNIT(S) : *I'm sure your only salvation is to hit up your rents* (1960s+ Teenagers)

rep[1] *n* Reputation : *gettin' the rep a not havin' a big schnozz* (1705+)

rep[2] *n* A representative : *The sales rep from Kokomo* (1896+) *v* : *Both of whom are repped by yours truly*

rep[3] *modifier* : *a rep company n* Repertory : *She played in rep a couple years* (1925+ Theater)

rep[4] *n* A repetition : *I mused on this while I did 15 reps at 250* (1864+)

repeaters *n* Loaded dice (1950s+ Gambling)

repeat on someone *v phr* To cause eructation or belching : *I never eat chili because it always repeats on me* (1930s+)

replay *See* INSTANT REPLAY

repo[1] (REE poh) *n* A car repossessed for non-payment of installments (1970s+) *v* : *when the best times are to repo or rip off cars*

repo[2] (REE poh) *n* A type of investment : *investments known as retail repurchase agreements, or repos for short* (1963+)

repo (or **snatch**) **man** (REE poh) *n phr* A person employed to confiscate repossessed cars : *He had become unpopular as a result of his work as a repo man, work that had required him to carry a sawed-off shotgun/ Baraka gave young black artists a place to go outside of white bohemia and black academia, though some of us still landed in those two purgatories to stay ahead of the snatch man* (1970s+)

res (REHZ) *n* An Indian reservation : *He won't get off the res* (1990s+)

resin *See* KISS THE CANVAS

rest *See* GIVE IT A REST

restless *See* the NATIVES ARE RESTLESS

◁**retard**▷ (REE tard) *n* A stupid person; AIRHEAD, SPAZ : *the stereotype of the crazy retard* [1960s+; fr mentally *retarded*]

◁**retarded**▷ *modifier* Defective and annoying : *this retarded bicycle*

retread (REE tred) *n* **1** A used tire with new tread (1914+) **2** A former military person recalled or accepted for additional service *(WWII armed forces)*

retro *adj* Nostalgic; historically resurrectional : *I'm going to give them retro names like Madge or Verna or Ralph* *n* A retrospective art exhibit, movie festival, etc : *the Bleecker's current Godard retro* [1974+; fr *retrospective*]

re-up *v* **1** To re-enlist : *Are you really going to re-up and go to that chopper school?* **2** To obligate or engage oneself again : *paying him $6,000,000 to re-up with the Cubs* [1906+ Army; fr the requirement of holding up one's right hand while taking an oath]

rev or **rev up** *v* or *v phr* **1** To speed up a motor; increase the rpms (*1916+*) **2** To stir up; stimulate; enliven; JAZZ something UP : *seems to think he has to really rev his prose every now and again* (*1956+*)

revamp *v* To improve by remaking; renovate; revise : *We can't just patch it up; we need to revamp the whole proposal* [1850+; fr shoemakers, "to replace the upper front part of a shoe"]

revolving-door *modifier* Of short duration; helter-skelter; transient : *revolving-door presidents and prime ministers, that's what's happening*

revved up *adj phr* Excited; expectant; PUMPED UP : *We were really revved up that here was somebody who was going to try to run up the middle* (*1931+*)

rhoid *n* A truly annoying person; PAIN IN THE ASS

rhubarb *n* A loud quarrel or squabble; a controversy of riotous potential, esp among baseball players on the field : *beanball throwing, rhubarbs, and umpire baiting* [1938+ Baseball; origin unknown and richly speculated on; said to have been first used in a broadcast by Garry Schumacher]

rib *n* : *Carson sensed that he was the victim of a rib* *v* To tease; make fun of; KID, RAG, RIDE : *His trick is gently ribbing the audience* (*1930+*) [origin unknown; perhaps fr a symbolic nudge in the *ribs*]

ribbie or **ribby** or **rib-eye steak** *n* A run batted in; RBI : *had two other big ribbies/ Brandon had two homers and seven rib-eye steaks (RBI)* (*first forms baseball 1960s+, third 1990s+*)

rib-tickler *n* Something amusing, esp a joke (*1933+*)

rice-burner or **rice-grinder** or **rice-rocket** *n* A motorcycle of Japanese manufacture (*1980s+ Motorcyclists*)

rich *See* STRIKE IT RICH, TOO RICH FOR someone's BLOOD

Richard Roe *See* JOHN DOE

◁**rich bitch**▷ *adj phr* : *his rich-bitch mother-in-law* *n phr* A wealthy woman (*1940s+*)

rich rich *adj phr* Very rich : *They're rich, OK, but not rich rich* [1963+; found by 1725 in a poem of Edward Taylor, but the meaning is not clearly the same]

ricky-tick[1] (also **ricky-ticky** or **rinky-tink**) *adj* Old-fashioned; outworn; CORNY : *a brassy, ricky-ticky big band sound (1930+ Jazz musicians)* *n* Bouncy ragtime music of the 1920s (*1930+ Jazz musicians*)

ricky-tick[2] *adj* RINKY-DINK

ride *n* **1** A sexual encounter : *He asked her for a ride and she slapped him (1937+)* **2** An improvised passage; BREAK, RIFF *(1930+ Jazz musicians)* **3** A saddle horse *(1787+)* **4** A psychedelic narcotic experience; TRIP *(1960s+ Narcotics)* **5** A car : *This you ride, man? (1929+)* *v* **1** To tease; heckle; make fun of; NEEDLE, RIB : *I can remember riding Pete Rose to death from the bench (1912+)* ◁**2**▷ To do the sex act with or to a woman; mount; SCREW *(1250+)* **3** To hit the ball hard; POWDER : *Goslin rode it right out of the park (1929+ Baseball) See* FULL-RIDE, GO ALONG FOR THE RIDE, HITCH A RIDE, JOY RIDE, LET something RIDE, SLEIGHRIDE, TAKE someone FOR A RIDE, THUMB

◁**ride** someone's **ass**▷ *v phr* To harass someone; BUG, HASSLE : *somebody wants to bother you, man, really ride your ass* [1980s+; *ride* is found by 1583 in the stronger sense "to dominate cruelly, oppress"]

ride herd on someone or something *v phr* To keep someone or something under control; monitor and correct; manage : *Chief Suarez hasn't been riding herd on his guys (1897+)*

rider *See* BAREBACK RIDER, FREE-RIDER, LOW RIDER

ride shotgun *v phr* **1** To act as a guard, esp on a vehicle; keep a vigilant eye peeled; ensure safety : *beefing up security and changing the pattern of deliveries, although nobody will start to ride shotgun/ Several wives have gotten wise and are riding shotgun on who checks in and out (1963+)* **2** To ride in the front passenger seat of a car *(1960s+ Teenagers)* [fr the Old West practice of having an armed guard with a *shotgun riding* beside the driver on the stagecoaches]

ride the gravy train (or **gravy boat**) *v phr* To enjoy a good and effortless life; bask in prosperous ease (*1927+*)

ride the pine (or **pines**) *v phr* To sit idle on the player's bench : *who right now seems destined to ride the pine a lot behind Mark Jackson/ I'd rather ride the pines on Mars than play the outfield for these mo'fuckers (1980s+ Sports)*

rif (pronounced as separate letters or as an acronym, RIF) *n* **1** A dismissal; layoff **2** A demotion *v* **1** To notify an employee of dismissal or layoff : *when he receives his Reduction in Force letter, and he will say, "I've been riffed"* **2** To demote : *had been "rif'd" back to sergeants* [1953+; fr *reduction in force*]

riff *n* **1** An improvised passage, esp a solo; BREAK, LICK : *an initially funky bass riff (1917+ Jazz musicians)* **2** A solo passage of any sort : *He never inflates a movement, never accelerates into showy riffs of excess energy (1917+ Jazz musicians)* **3** A particular variation or version : *I have actually eaten something called a pastrami burrito dog, sort of a riff on the oki dog (1990s+)* **4** A piece of personal behavior, esp of entertainment; SHTICK : *allow the star to do character riffs that approximate the sort of things she does as monologues in her one-woman show/ She can make out the riffs and scams of the inner city like a dog picking up a scent (1980s+)* [origin unknown; perhaps echoic; perhaps fr *refrain;* perhaps fr *riffle* or *ripple* in the sense of "try, shot, crack"]

riffle[1] *n* A hard swing at the ball; RIPPLE : *gives it a really good solid riffle* [1932+ Baseball; probably fr *ripple* fr *rip*]

riffle[2] *n* : *Give that deck a good riffle* **v** To shuffle playing cards *(1894+ Cardplaying)* [probably echoic]

rig *n* **1** (also **rig-out**) Clothing; outfit : *How come you're wearing that rig?/ a waiter's or a chef's rig-out (1843+)* **2** A truck, bus, ambulance, etc *(1930s+ Bus drivers & truckers)* **v** To prearrange or tamper with a result or process; FIX : *Prizefights or horse-races have been rigged (1930s+)*

right *adj* Reliable; safe : *He assured them his partner was all right (1856+)* **affirmation** Yes; correct : *Did you say left? Right! (1588+)* **question** Am I not right? CAPEESH, OK : *He's in charge, right? (1961+) See* ALL RIGHT, ALL RIGHT ALREADY, DEAD TO RIGHTS, FLY RIGHT, HANG A RIGHT

Right *See* MISTER RIGHT

right as rain, (as) *modifier* Completely correct : *right as rain, son*

righteous *adj* Excellent; genuine; the GREATEST : *what we used to call the righteous jazz/ "Is that righteous gold?" "Righteous it ain't, but gold it is" (1900+ Jazz musicians)*

righteous moss *n phr* Hair of a Caucasian sort; nonkinky hair; GOOD HAIR : *It looked just like that righteous moss (1942+ Black)*

right-handed *adj* Heterosexual; STRAIGHT : *He was about 60 percent right-handed and he ended up as a male go-go dancer (1970s+)*

right money *n phr* the SMART MONEY : *It's the combination of likely lad and a good horse that makes "right money" dig down in its jeans (1941+)*

right-o *affirmation* (also **righto** or **right-ho** or **rightho**) Yes; correct; all right *(1896+ British)*

right off the bat *adv phr* Immediately; without delay : *I normally get four cars right off the bat [1914+; hot from the bat is found by 1888]*

right on *adj phr* Precisely right; very effective : *Michael Caine is right on as the medic (1960s+)* **interj** An exclamation of approval, encouragement, agreement, etc : *Oh mercy, baaabeh, riiight onnnn! (1925+ Black)* [interjection sense popularized as a Black Panther usage in the middle 1960s]

rights *See* DEAD TO RIGHTS, GIVE someone HIS RIGHTS

right stuff, the *n phr* by 1848 The best human ingredients, such as fortitude and resolution : *a heart that was made of the right stuff to set off to advantage his iron frame* [popularized by Tom Wolfe's 1979 book about the first astronauts]

right there *See* IN THERE PITCHING, THERE

right up one's **alley** *modifier* Perfect for someone; exactly what someone is best at : *Teaching grammar is right up her alley*

right up there *adv phr* Among the leaders, the most distinguished, etc; in contention : *Two weeks to go and the Mets are still right up there (1970+)*

righty *n* A right-handed person, esp a baseball player; northpaw *(1940s+) See* ALL RIGHTY

◁**rim**▷ *v* To lick or suck the anus *(1959+ Homosexuals) See* REAM

rinctum *n* The rectum *(1950s+ Black) See* SPIZZERINKTUM

ring *v* **1** To substitute one horse illegally for another in a race : *to attempt ringing (1812+ Horse racing)* **2** (also **ring up**) To call on the telephone; GIVE someone A RING : *I rang him the next day, but he was out (1940s+, variant 1880+) See* THROW one's HAT IN THE RING

ring a bell *v phr* To remind one of something; sound familiar : *"Nineteen seventy-six. June 25." "Ring a bell?" (1934+)*

ring-a-ding-ding or **ring-a-ding** *adj* : *Our new stack addition is a huge brick building full of metal, a ring-a-ding book box* **n** Glamour and show; spectacular impressiveness; RAZZLE-DAZZLE : *an aura of breathless showbiz ring-a-ding-ding (1970s+)*

ring someone's **bell** (or **chimes**) *v phr* To be sexually attractive to someone; TURN someone ON *(1970s+)*

ring changes *v phr* To make or try out variations, esp ingeniously : *Berle could do the same mugging bits and ring many more changes on them* [1614+; fr *change-ringing,* the elaborate esp British ringing of sets of church bells]

ring-dang-do (RING DANG DOO) *n* A complicated process, scene, affair, etc; rigmarole : *the whole ring-dang-do of moral Darwinism (1970s+)*

ring-ding *n* A stupid person; DING-A-LING : *that South American ring-ding with his sequined rodeo shirt (1970s+)*

ringer *n* **1** A person or animal substituted for another, esp a racehorse put in to run in place of an inferior beast : *"ringers," good horses masquerading as poor ones (1890+ Horse racing)* **2** A person who arranges the illegal substitution of a horse : *the master horse ringer of them all (1890+ Horse racing)* **3** A person or thing that closely resembles another; DEAD RINGER : *With the mustache and glasses, Blackmer is a ringer for Teddy (1891+)* [fr the expression *ring someone in*, "announce or herald someone"]

ring off *v phr* **1** To end a telephone conversation; hang up *(1882+)* **2** To stop talking; SHUT UP *(1895+)*

ring off the hook (or **the wall**) *v phr* To ring constantly and often : *Says the director of the hotline: "The phones have been ringing off the hook" (1970s+)*

ringtail *n* **1** A grouch *(1931+ Hoboes)* **2** An offensive person; BASTARD, JERK *(1931+ Underworld)* ◄**3**► An Italian dockworker or one of Italian extraction *(1940s+ Dockworkers)* ◄**4**► A Japanese *(WWII Navy)* [origin unknown]

rinktum *See* SPIZZERINKTUM

rinky-dink *adj* (also **ricky-tick**) Inferior; cheap; CRUMMY : *described by federal attorneys as rinky dink and a very strange document/ its deserted beaches, summer houses, and ricky-tick towns (1913+) n* **1** Cheap and gaudy merchandise; DRECK, JUNK *(1912+ Carnival)* **2** Used merchandise; secondhand articles : *Let's go see what sort of rinky-dink the Salvation Army has this week (1913+)* **3** A small, cheap nightclub, cabaret, etc; HONKY-TONK : *as she was called when she played the rinky-dinks (1912+)* **4** A deception; swindle; THE RUNAROUND : *Don't give me the rinkydink (1912+) See* RICKY-TICK

rinky-tink *See* RICKY-TICK

riot, a *n phr* A very amusing person or thing, joke, occasion, etc; a HOOT, a SCREAM *(1909+)*

riot act, the *See* READ THE RIOT ACT

riot grrrl *n phr* A militant female feminist : *Watching this magazine drool like a dirty old man over riot grrrls is very amusing. Like a riot grrrl would ever have sex with an Esquire reader (1990s+)*

rip[1] *n* A debauched and dissolute person; libertine : *the proper way to treat a rip* [1797+; perhaps a variant of *rep* fr *reprobate*]

rip[2] *n* **1** An official demerit or fine *(1939+ Police)* **2** An insult; a disparagement; KNOCK : *master of the off-field rip (1940s+)* **3** A joy; a pleasure : *What a rip it is to know there are still people who feel for the cars they put to-gether (1970s+)* **4** A try; attempt; CRACK, RIPPLE, SHOT : *I'll have a rip at that old record (1940s+)* **5** RIPOFF *(1990s+) v* **1** To strongly criticize, disparage : *William Proxmire who is usually ripped for refusing to bring home the bacon (1857+ British dialect)* **2** (also **rip-ass**) To speed; BARREL, TEAR : *cars rip-assing up and down the street (1853+)* [all, one way or another, fr *rip*, "tear"; third noun sense perhaps related to *ripping*, "excellent, first-rate," found by 1846] *See* GIVE something A SHOT, HAVE A CRACK AT something

ripe *adj* **1** Smelly or foul : *smelling a bit ripe* **2** Intoxicated by alcohol : *bit ripe after three Heinekens*

ripoff *n* **1** A theft; an act of stealing **2** A fraud; swindle; SCAM : *The whole arms-reduction policy is a big ripoff* **3** (also **ripoff artist**) A person or company that steals or swindles : *He was the biggest ripoff ever seen, even in Congress (1960s+ Black)*

rip off *v phr* **1** To steal : *Somebody ripped off my bike* **2** To swindle; defraud; GYP : *I don't know who rips us off more, business or government* [1960s+ Black; *rip*, "to steal," is found by 1200]

rip on someone *v phr* To harass and insult; RIP : *When those two get together they totally rip on Jeff (1960s+ Black)*

ripped *adj* **1** Intoxicated, either from narcotics or alcohol; HIGH : *I'm ripped to the tits as it is (1971+)* **2** Showing well-defined muscles : *So ripped you can see her liver, or think you can (1980s+ Students)*

ripper *n* One that is an excellent or admirable example of its kind : *Every episode is a ripper (1838+)*

ripple *n* A try; an attempt; CRACK, RIP, SHOT : *I'll never figure out how these pieces fit, so why don't you have a ripple?* [origin uncertain; perhaps fr *rip* in the sense of a strong action, attempt, or blow; perhaps fr 1800s *make a riffle* or *ripple*, "to succeed, make it," based on crossing or getting through dangerous rapids in a river] *See* GIVE something A SHOT, HAVE A CRACK AT something

rip-roaring or **rip-snorting** *adj* Boisterous, vigorous : *rip-roaring good time*

◄**ripshit**► *adj* Very angry; PISSED OFF, STEAMED : *Michael was ripshit (1980s+)*

ripsnorter *n* A person or thing that is remarkable, wonderful, superior; etc; BEAUT, HUMDINGER : *The villain is a real ripsnorter (1840+)*

rise, a *See* GET A RISE OUT OF someone

ritz, the *See* PUT ON THE RITZ

ritzy *adj* **1** Elegant; luxurious; classy. POSH. SWANKY : *The ritziest dance hall was the Haymarket* **2** Haughty; supercilious; STUCK-UP *(1920+)*

river See SELL someone DOWN THE RIVER, SEND UP, UP THE RIVER

roach n 1 A police officer (1932+ Prison & black) 2 A racehorse, esp an inferior one; BEETLE (1940s+ Horse racing) 3 The stub or butt of a marijuana cigarette : He lighted the toke again, a roach now that he impaled on a thin wire (1938+ Narcotics) 4 An unattractive woman (1960s+ Students) [narcotics sense perhaps fr earlier roach mane, a horse's mane clipped very short and tied; perhaps fr the insect]

roach clip (or holder) n phr Any tweezerlike device for holding a marijuana cigarette stub too short to be held in the fingers; crutch : necessitating the invention of the "roach clip," which holds roaches (1960s+ Narcotics)

road modifier Traveling; touring, itinerant : a road show (1900+ Theater) See GO THE HANG-PUT ROAD, HIT THE ROAD, LET'S GET THE SHOW ON THE ROAD, ONE FOR THE ROAD, ON THE ROAD, WHERE THE RUBBER MEETS THE ROAD

road hog n phr A driver who takes more than his or her share of the road (1891+)

roadie n (also **roadster**) A person who travels with a musical, political, theatrical, or other group to handle booking, business arrangements, equipment, etc : Microphones tossed by Chapman land in unlikely places, one on a roadie, another in the lap of the audience (1969+)

road kill n phr 1 A person or animal struck by a car and killed; ROAD PIZZA : After screeching to check for roadkill, these young motorists started howling, laughing it up (1980s+) 2 Something undesirable and unpalatable, like the meat of an animal killed in traffic : Plagiarism proclaims that some written words are valuable enough to steal. But what if the borrowed stuff is a flat, lifeless mess, the road kill of passing ideas? (1980s+) 3 : Nothing like a road kill. For our young guys who are new to the team, nothing is better than getting a road win (1990s+ Sports)

road pizza n phr 1 A dead animal smashed in traffic (1980s+) 2 (also **road rash**) Abrasions from a crash (1990s+ Cyclists)

road rash n A skin injury from rubbing up against concrete or the ground : road rash from skateboarding

road warrior n A person who travels frequently, especially on business (1980s+)

roam v To use a cellular phone outside of one's own service area : Hi honey. I'm roaming in San Francisco (1990s+)

roast n : this national love for a good "roast," this spirit of mockery v To make fun of; ridicule; insult, often in an affectionate way : had been roasted often by the critics as a ham (1710+)

roasting adj Uncomfortably hot (1768+)

robber See CRADLE-ROBBER

rob someone blind v phr To steal from someone, esp by overcharging : robbed him blind buying pre-made salad at the grocery

robocop n A robot police officer (1990s+)

rob the cradle v phr 1 To marry or date someone much younger than oneself 2 To recruit, use, or exploit young persons (1940s+)

rock n 1 A dollar; BUCK : I want to see you make twenty rocks (1840+) 2 Any precious stone, esp a diamond (1908+ Underworld) 3 A rock-and-roll devotee : teenagers called "rocks" (1950s+) 4 Rock-and-roll music : hard rock (1950s+) 5 A small cube of very pure cocaine, intended for smoking rather than inhalation : Dealers sell pellet-size "rocks" in small plastic vials (1980s+ Narcotics) 6 A cellblock : When is the wagon due back on this rock, Pops? (1970s+ Prison) 7 A basketball (1980s+ Basketball) v <1▷ To do the sex act with or to; SCREW, RIDE : My man rocks me with one steady roll (1900+) 2 To move, dance, writhe, etc, to rock-and-roll music; BOOGIE, BOP : Soon just one couple was rocking in the middle of the floor (1950s+) 3 To be resonant with and physically responsive to rock-and-roll music; JUMP : Soon the whole room was rocking (1950s+) See GLITTER ROCK, HARD ROCK, HOT ROCK, PUNK ROCK, RIMROCK

rockabilly modifier : showing up at rockabilly dances and clubs in full '50s regalia n A blend of black rhythm and blues with white hillbilly music (1956+)

rock bottom modifier At the lowest level or part, esp in price : rock-bottom prices on Easter stuff n The lowest level or part : hit rock bottom last week

rock 'em, sock 'em adj phr Violent and energetic; concussive : the rock 'em, sock 'em action that goes on inside a full-sized truck (1970s+)

rocker[1] n 1 A rock-and-roll musician, singer, radio station, etc : general manager of rhythm-and-blues rocker WOL in Washington, DC 2 A rock-and-roll song : classic country rockers, sometimes with an old-timey flavor (1950s+) See PUNK ROCKER, TEENYBOPPER

rocker[2] See OFF one's NOODLE

rocket n A complaint or rebuke; BEEF, DING • Chiefly British : You get a rocket from one of the parties (1941+)

rocket scientist See YOU DON'T HAVE TO BE A BRAIN SURGEON

rocking or rockin' adj Excellent : rockin' time on New Year's Eve

rock jock n phr A rock climber; mountain climber; Alpinist : In about a year she's gone from novice climber to total rock jock (1980+)

rock on *interj* A happy greeting or good-bye; an admonishment to carry on because everything is copacetic; also, party on : *Rock on, roadmeister*

rock out *v phr* To totally enjoy a rock-and-roll song : *rocked out to Nirvana*

rocks *n* 1 Ice cubes (*1946+*) ◁2▷ The testicles; FAMILY JEWELS, NUTS (*1948+*) [*stones* in the second sense is found by 1154] *See* GET one's ROCKS, HAVE ROCKS IN one's HEAD, HOT ROCKS, ON THE ROCKS, TOUGH SHIT

rocks in one's (or **the**) **head** *n phr* Stupidity; foolishness; mental incapacity : *dedicated to whiny losers with rocks in their heads* (*1951+*) *See* HAVE ROCKS IN one's HEAD

rock the boat *v phr* To cause trouble; create inconveniences; disrupt things : *Fritz Mondale doesn't want to rock the boat* (*1931+*)

rocky *adj* 1 Drunk 2 Weak and unsteady; groggy; WOOZY : *came back to work, looking pale and rocky* (*1895+*) 3 Difficult; trying; TOUGH : *That was a very rocky time for our family* (*1873+*)

Rocky Mountain canary *See* MOUNTAIN CANARY

Rocky Mountain oysters *n phr* A lamb's testicles used as food (*1889+*)

rod *n* 1 A pistol : *Here's a rod, blow your brains out* (*1903+ Underworld*) 2 A car, esp a specially prepared car; HOT ROD : *A restless youth buys a broken-down rod* (*1940s+ Hot rodders*) ◁3▷ The penis; SHAFT (*1902+*)

rod-man *n* A gunman; TORPEDO (*1929+ Underworld*)

Roe *See* JOHN DOE

Roger or **rodger-dodger** *affirmation* Yes; I understand; OK : *Get your asses over there, Roger* [WWII armed forces; fr the US military phonetic alphabet word designating *R* for "received," said also to have been used by the Royal Air Force by 1938]

rogues' gallery *n phr* 1 A police collection of photographs of criminals; MUG SHOTS 2 Any group or collection of unsavory persons; den of thieves : *The new building commission is a plain rogues' gallery* (*1859+*)

'roid or **roid** *n* 1 A steroid drug used for bodybuilding : *'Roids, dude. The Wheaties of the '80s* (*late 1980s+*) 2 Hemorrhoids : *cream for his roids*

'roid (or **roid**) **rage** *n phr* : *Normally easygoing, he recalls bouts of roid rage, an urge to destroy that often strikes steroid users* (*late 1980s+*)

rolf *See* RALPH

roll *n* 1 Money; funds; BANKROLL (*1846+*) 2 The sex act; a ROLL IN THE HAY (*1940s+*) *v* 1 To rob, esp a stuporous or helpless drunkard who is literally rolled over for access to pockets : *rolling a stiff/ the less perilous profession of rolling lushes* (*1873+*) 2 To displace

another worker : *Negro firemen on the good runs should be "rolled" by whites* (*1950s+ Railroad*) 3 To run or start a movie camera : *Quiet, and roll 'em* (*1939+ Movie studio*) *See* JACKROLL, JELLY-ROLL, MICHIGAN ROLL, ON A ROLL, PRESS ROLL, ROCK

rollback *n* A reduction, esp of wages or production (*1942+*)

rolled *modifier* Nabbed by law enforcement, esp for minor infractions : *They got rolled for having alcohol in the dorm room*

roller *n* 1 A prison guard (*1940s+ Prison*) 2 A police officer (*1964+ Black*) 3 A thief who robs drunks (*1915+*) [first two senses fr late 1700s British *rollers*, "horse and foot patrols of police"] *See* HIGH ROLLER, PILL-PUSHER, STEAMROLLER

rollin' *adj* On a roll; having great success : *Now she is rollin' on the project*

roll in *v phr* To arrive; SHOW UP : *What time did you finally roll in?* (*1940s+*)

rolling doughnut *See* TAKE A FLYING FUCK

rolling in money (or **it**) *modifier* Enjoying wealth (*1782+*)

rolling off a log *See* EASY AS PIE

roll in money *v phr* To be very rich (*1773+*)

roll in the hay *n phr* The sex act, esp when regarded as casual and joyous : *A roll in the hay with Seattle Slew cost $710,000* (*1940s+*)

roll out the red carpet *v phr* To give someone a very sumptuous or ceremonious welcome (*1952+*)

rollover *n* The last night of a prison sentence (*1940s+ Prison*)

roll over *v phr* 1 To reinvest bonds, certificates of deposit, or other monetary instruments upon maturity, rather than liquidating them (*1957+*) 2 To inform on one's criminal associates; SQUEAL : *It was the easiest flip Stone ever made. The man rolled over like a puppy and proceeded to hand up his associates so fast that Stone had to tell him to slow down* (*1973+ Police*)

roll over and play dead *v phr* To surrender or acquiesce, esp without resisting : *We're not about to roll over and play dead while the Republicans rubber stamp their extremist agenda* [*1940s+*; fr a trick one would teach a dog]

roll the bones *v phr* To play craps [*1929+*; *bones*, "dice," is found by 1386]

roll with the punches *v phr* To behave so as to defend oneself against damage and surprise; absorb punishment and survive : *"You roll with the punches. My experience was, I was going to lose her. But I'm thankful for what I've gotten so far"* [*1951+*; fr the evasive action of a boxer who does not avoid a *punch* but reduces its effect by moving in the direction of the blow]

romp *n* A fight, esp between street gangs; RUMBLE *(1960s+ Street gang)* *v* : *The gangs romped on Thursday*

ronchie *See* RAUNCHY

-roo *See* -EROO

roof *See* RAISE THE ROOF

roof falls (or caves) in, the *v phr* A sudden and total catastrophe occurs; one's joy and world collapses : *long before the roof fell in on Gossage/ But then the roof caved in on the Bucks (1958+)*

rook *n* : *Balcony seats for 40 bucks are a real rook* *v* To cheat; defraud; GYP : *who would rook them for two dollars (1577+)* [probably fr the thieving habits of the rook, which it shares with other corvine birds like the crow and magpie]

rookie or **rookey** or **rooky** *modifier* : *The shooting of "rookie" patrolman James A Broderick* *n* A newcomer; recruit; tyro : *the rookies and substitutes (1892+)* [probably fr shortening of *recruit;* perhaps fr the black, rook-colored coat worn by some British army recruits]

roost *n* One's home; PAD *(1940s+)*

root[1] *v* **1** To cheer; applaud; urge on : *We rooted and rooted, but our side folded* **2** To eat food like an animal; PIG OUT [1888+; origin obscure]

root[2] *n* **1** A cigarette *(1900+)* **2** A marijuana cigarette *(1960s+ Narcotics)* [perhaps fr *cheroot* or *cigaroot*]

◁**root**[3]▷ *n* The penis [1846+; fr something that is or can be planted]

rooter *n* A supporter or fan, esp of a team, fighter, school, etc *(1890+)*

root for *v phr* **1** To be a regular supporter of; be a fan of : *He rooted for the Giants (1889+)* **2** To urge hopefully : *I'm rooting for the tax bill (1922+)* [perhaps fr British dialect *route,* "roar, bellow"]

rootin'-tootin' *adj* Boisterous; noisy; vigorous : *He's a hifalutin' rootin'-tootin' son of a gun from Arizona* [1924+; probably fr *rooting,* "cheering loudly," and *tooting,* "blowing a horn"]

rooty-toot *n* Old-fashioned music; CORN, RICKY-TICK *(1936+ Musicians)*

rope *n* **1** A cigar; el ropo. HEMP *(1934+)* **2** A hard-hit line drive; CLOTHESLINE, FROZEN ROPE *(1960s+ Baseball)* *v* **1** (also **rope in**) To ensnare someone with amity and concern as a means of swindling; ROPE IN *(1848+)* **2** : *Surhoff roped an RBI double to the gap in left-center See* GOAT FUCK, KNOW THE ROPES, SUCK

ropy or **ropey** *adj* Of low quality; bad; inferior; unsatisfactory *(1942+)*

◁**rosebud**▷ *n* The anus *(1970s+ Homosexuals)*

rosy *adj* **1** Slightly drunk; TIDDLY *(1905+)* **2** Promising; favorable; COPACETIC : *Things look rosy now (1887+)*

rot *n* Nonsense; BALONEY, BULLSHIT *(1848+)* *v* To be deplorable, nasty, inept, bungled, etc; STINK, SUCK : *This idea of yours rots (1960s+ Teenagers)*

rotgut *n* Inferior liquor; PANTHER PISS : *pre-Prohibition rotgut (1597+)*

Roto-Rooter *n* **1** Any medical device that clears or cleans out obstructions in tubes : *More than 100,000 Americans had a surgical procedure known as carotid endartectomy, a kind of Roto-Rooter for cleaning out clogged arteries* **2** : *The number of computers directly connected to the Internet is updated periodically by sending a computer program crawling around like a Roto-Rooter tallying the number of connections* [1980s+; fr a trademarked plumber's device for cleaning out clogged pipe]

rotten *adj* Deplorable; nasty; inept and bungled : *This is a rotten situation altogether (1880+)*

rotten apple *n phr* A corrupt or unfit person who may corrupt others : *But a certain number of rotten apples, predisposed to brutality, make it through psychological testing that can be woefully inadequate* [1940s+; fr the saying "one rotten apple can spoil a barrel"; stated in a 1528 source as "For one rotten apple lytell and lytell putrifieth an whole heape"]

rotten egg *n* A bad or despicable person : *acts like a rotten egg sometimes*

rough *adj* **1** Lewd; salacious; DIRTY, RAUNCHY : *Some of the jokes were pretty rough (1958+)* **2** Difficult; dangerous; TOUGH : *Conditions were very rough that winter (1856+)* *n* A used car that has been in a wreck *(1950s+ Salespersons) See* PLAY FOR KEEPS

rough-and-tumble *adj* Free and uninhibited; with no limits or reservations; NO HOLDS BARRED : *It was a rough-and-tumble confrontation* [1832+; originally of a fight where the usual rules were not observed; an article of 1810 says that "in roughing and tumbling it is allowable to peel the skull, tear out the eyes, and smooth away the nose"]

rough around the edges *adj phr* Somewhat crude; unpolished : *a slightly rough-around-the-edges New York manner (1940s+)*

◁**rough-ass**▷ *adj* Harsh; crude; KICK-ASS : *She liked his rough-ass ways for a while (1940s+)*

roughhouse *adj* : *rough-house work for the political boss* *n* **1** Boisterous and rowdy behavior; more or less harmless scuffling *(1897+)* **2** Physical violence; mayhem *(1887+)* *v* **1** : *The kids roughhoused half the night (1900+)* **2** : *Gun-toting bodyguards roughhoused Swedish citizens (1902+)*

roughie *n* 1 A tough or crude person 2 A shrewd or unfair trick : *sprang a roughie on him* 3 A long shot to win *(Australian)*

rough it *v phr* To live under harsh or primitive conditions : *roughing it in the woods*

roughneck *n* 1 A thug and brawler; PLUG-UGLY, TOUGH : *The so-called roughneck is hit with everything (1836+)* 2 A worker or laborer, esp in a circus or on an oil-drilling rig *(1917+) See* RUFFNECK

rough stuff *n phr* 1 Physical violence; mayhem : *have graduated from the "rough stuff" class (1913+)* 2 Obscenity; profanity; PORN *(1950s+)*

rough trade *n phr* A sadistic or violent sex partner, often heterosexual; ruffianly partner of a homosexual : *I hope the next time he meets some rough trade from uptown (1935+ Homosexuals)*

rough someone up *v phr* 1 To hit or pummel, esp as intimidation : *He told it like a good citizen, and got roughed up for his pains* 2 To injure someone : *The wreck roughed me up some (1920+)*

roulette *See* VATICAN ROULETTE

◁**round-eye**▷ *modifier* : *a round-eye woman* *n* A Caucasian as distinct from an Asian *(Korean War armed forces)*

roundhouse *modifier* 1 : *He swung a roundhouse left* 2 : *a roundhouse pitch* *n* 1 A long, looping punch to the head *(1920+ Prizefighting)* 2 A sweeping curveball *(1910+ Baseball)*

round the bend *adj phr* 1 AROUND THE BEND *(1929+)* 2 STIR-CRAZY *(WWII prisoners of war)*

round the horn *See* AROUND THE HORN

round-tripper *n* A home run : *a round-tripper in the ninth (1950s+ Baseball)*

round up *v phr* To find and bring together, esp to a police station or lockup : *Round up the usual suspects* [1885+; found by 1847 of the collection and corralling of animals]

roust *n* Raid or harassment : *What's the roust? You gonna close this place?* *v* 1 Esp of police officers, to harass someone; CHIVVY, ROUGH UP : *always being rousted by cops* 2 To arrest : *Try rousting me and see what real resistance is like* 3 To raid : *They're rousting all the gay bars* [1970s+; fr *rouster* or *rooster,* "a deckhand or waterfront laborer," attested fr the mid-1800s, hence with connotations of roughness; related to *roustabout,* fr British dialect *rous-about,* "unwieldy," *rousing,* "rough, shaggy," and *rousy,* "filthy"; the semantic core seems to combine roughness with laziness, in the old heroic mold, and to be associated with the behavior of the *rooster,* who combines rough vigor with long periods on the perch; first verb sense found in

1904 prison slang in the sense "to jostle," and by the 1940s in the sense "to jostle so as to pick a pocket"]

roustabout *n* A general laborer, esp an oil-rig worker *(1948+)*

routine *n* 1 A passage of behavior; act; BIT, RIFF, SHTICK : *They did a Laurel and Hardy routine (1926+ Show business)* 2 An evasive or contrived response : *I look for revelation and get routine (1950s+ Cool talk)*

row *n* An elongated pile of narcotic, esp cocaine, for sniffing; LINE : *and snorted a row of coke (1960s+ Narcotics) See* a HARD ROW TO HOE, HAVE one's DUCKS IN A ROW, KNOCK someone or something FOR A LOOP, SKID ROW

royal *adj* Thorough; definitive : *gives me a royal pain in the ass (1940s+)*

◀**royal fucking,** a▶ *n phr* Very rough and unfair treatment; RAW DEAL *(1940s+)*

royal pain *n* A thoroughly annoying person or thing; PAIN IN THE ASS : *Finishing this is a royal pain*

rub *n* 1 A dancing party *(1920s+ Students)* 2 A session of hugging and kissing *(1930s+ Students)* 3 A complaint; BEEF, BITCH : *What's your rub? (1990s+)* *v* RUB OUT *(1848+)*

rubber[1] *n* ◁1▷ A condom : *"Rubbers," Cushie told him (1930s+)* 2 Automobile tires : *The thing's a wreck but has good rubber (1961+)* *v* To gaze; gape : *Don't be rubbering at McCorn (1896+) See* BURN RUBBER, LAY RUBBER

rubber[2] *n* A professional killer; HIT MAN *(1934+ Underworld)*

rubber check *n phr* A check that cannot be cashed because not enough money is on deposit [1927+; because it "bounces"]

rubber-chicken *modifier* Featuring the unappetizing usual sort of banquet food occupationally eaten by politicians, lecturers, etc : *She's on the rubber-chicken circuit (1959+)*

rubber duck *See* TAKE A FLYING FUCK

rubber meets the road *See* WHERE THE RUBBER MEETS THE ROAD

rubberneck *n* (also **rubbernecker**) A person who stares and gapes; gawking spectator : *The courtroom was full of rubbernecks/ These were rubberneckers, staring curiously at a bloody accident (1896+) v* : *They all slowed down and rubbernecked at the wreck*

rubbernecking delay *n phr* A traffic slowdown due to drivers staring at a wreck *(1980s+)*

rubbish *n* Something of inferior quality; nonsense *(1600+)*

rube or **Rube** *adj* Green; newbie : *a rube police force* *n* 1 A rustic; farmer; HAYSEED 2 An unsophisticated person, esp a newcomer; GREENHORN 3 A member of the audience or public; CITIZEN : *Mr Todd knows how to panic the rubes (Circus)* [short for *Reuben*] *See* HEY RUBE

Rube Goldberg *n phr* A much overcomplicated machine or arrangement : *The public's got the idea that this is a boondoggle, a Rube Goldberg* [1940+; fr the fancifully articulated machines drawn by the cartoonist Rube Goldberg (1883–1970); the British artist Heath Robinson (1872–1944) amused his public with similar gadgets]

rub (or **nudge**) **elbows** *v phr* To meet and consort; spend time together; mingle : *colleagues with whom we rub elbows in the course of a day's work*

rub it in *v phr* To increase the pain or embarrassment of something; exacerbate something : *always trying to rub it in* (1870+)

rub someone's nose in it *v phr* To punish or chide with undue harshness : *I screwed up that one time, and they rubbed my nose in it for years* [1940s+; fr the punishment of a puppy or kitten that has irresponsibly evacuated]

◁**rub off**▷ *v phr* To masturbate (1903+)

rubout *n* A murder; gangster-style killing : *the hombre she blamed for Paddy's rub-out* (1927+ Underworld)

rub out *v phr* To murder; kill; HIT : *whose husband you rubbed out* (1846+)

◁**rub the bacon**▷ *v phr* To do the sex act; FUCK, SCREW : *January und Trumball are rubbing the bacon* (1980s+)

rub someone the wrong way *v phr* To be distasteful or obnoxious to someone's sensibilities; regularly displease : *I don't quite know why, but that woman rubs me the wrong way* [1883+; *rub the hair the wrong way* is found by 1868]

ruckus *n* A disturbance; uproar; brawl; RUMPUS [1890+; perhaps fr *ruction* plus *rumpus*]

ruffneck *modifier* Violent; rabble-rousing; GANGSTA : *Even some rappers are having trouble drawing a line between their "ruffneck" lyrics and real life n* A devotee of rap music; B-BOY : *He is also a B-boy. That's right, a ruffneck* (1990s+ Black)

rug *n* A toupee; hairpiece; divot : *I even wear a little rug up front* (1940s+ fr theater) *See* CUT THE RUG, PULL THE RUG OUT FROM UNDER

rug-cutter *n* A person who dances to swing music : *the rug-cutter's way of saying "all right"* (1938+ Jive talk)

rug rat or **carpet rat** or **rug ape** *n phr* (Variations: **yard** may replace **rug** or **carpet**) An infant or small child; crumbcatcher : *He lived with his wife and their two rug apes* (1960s+)

rule *v* To dominate; to be the most important : *Girls rule!*

rum bag *n phr* A drunkard; LUSH : *a lot of cowardly rum bags* (1940s+)

rumble *n* **1** Information or notification given to the police : *The cops had gotten a rumble that gangsters were holed up* (1911+ Underworld) **2** A police search or raid; ROUST : *If there's a rumble, we do the time* (1940s+ Police) **3** A fight between street gangs : *Teenagers Injured in Brooklyn Rumble* (1940s+ Street gang) *v* To steal; loot : *ending a run by rumbling everything from airline glasses to grub* (1970s+ Airline)

rum-dum *adj* Stupefied by liquor; DEAD DRUNK *n* A stupid person, esp one slow-witted from habitual drunkenness : *The murmuring rum-dums were being let out to wash* (1891+)

rummy or **rummie** *n* A drunkard; LUSH : *He spotted the old rummy at the corner* (1851+)

rumor mill *n phr* The source of rumors, esp those that seem to be deliberately passed along : *There has been a rumor mill on him for years* (1973+)

rumpus *n* A disturbance; uproar; RUCKUS [1764+; origin unknown]

rumpus room *n phr* A family room used for games, parties, etc (1939+)

run *n* A route followed by a vehicle, esp regularly : *In the middle of her run, the bus driver was attacked by a gang of thugs* (1925+) *v* **1** To be in charge of; manage; supervise : *Who's running this operation, anyway?* (1864+) **2** To drive; convey; transport : *If you keep jerking me around, I'm going to run your ass down to the drunk tank* (1864+) **3** To play basketball on a pickup basis : *Enough of this crap, let's run* (1980s+ Black) **4** To go on; proceed; happen; SHAKE OUT, WORK OUT : *That's the way it'll run. They'll throw me the bone* (1374+) *See* CUT AND RUN, DRY RUN, IN THE LONG RUN, MILK RUN, TAKE A RUN AT someone

run after *v phr* To seek a sexual relationship with : *ran after him all of high school* (1526+)

run a game on *v phr* DO A NUMBER ON : *Then he had to run a game on Iris* [fr black; perhaps fr running a whole *game* of pool without yielding the cue]

run a make *v phr* To perform a checking procedure for identifying someone, that is, for "making" an identification (1970s+ Police & prison)

run-and-gun *adj* : *the Lakers' run-and-gun offense v* To play in an aggressive single-handed way, for high scoring : *as a big city ball player looking to run-and-gun* (1970s+ Basketball)

run-and-shoot *modifier* Combining running and passing, in an offense : *The Lions' run-and-shoot offense almost exclusively uses four receivers* (1980s+ Football)

run a number on *See* DO A NUMBER ON

runaround, the *n* Deceptive, evasive, and diversionary treatment, esp in response to a request : *All he gets is a polite runaround* (1915+) *See* GIVE someone THE RUNAROUND

◁**run around with** one's **finger up** one's **ass**▷ *v phr* To be frantically ineffectual : *You* *and your little band of merry men scoff up truckloads of narcotics while we run around with our fingers up our asses* (1970s+)

run something **by again** *v phr* To repeat; COME AGAIN : *Just run that name and address by me again, will you?* (1980s+)

run circles around someone or something *v phr* To be much faster or more effective than someone or something : *They follow directions and they run circles around other teams* (1940s+)

rundown *n* A summary or account : *a brief rundown of what happened* (1945+)

run someone **down** *v phr* To disparage; denigrate; BAD-MOUTH : *He's your pal, so I won't run him down* (1668+)

run something **down** *v phr* To tell or explain completely : *Maybe one day I'll run it down to you* (1964+ Black)

run hog-wild *See* GO HOG-WILD

run-in *n* A quarrel; an unpleasant confrontation : *Sorry we had the run-in* (1905+)

run someone **in** *v phr* To arrest; PULL someone IN : *Am I going to have to run you in?* (1859+)

run interference *v phr* To provide justification, protection, etc : *The average personnel department merely pushes paper, occasionally running interference for the line managers who actually make hiring decisions* [1947+; the primary football use is found by 1929]

run (or work) something **into the ground** *v phr* To overdo; carry too far : *You already warned us, so now don't run it into the ground* (1826+)

run one's **mouth** *v phr* To talk too much : *running her mouth again about nothing important* (1940+)

runner *n* **1** A messenger **2** A deliverer of illegal drugs or other contraband *See* FRONT RUNNER

running gag *n phr* A recurrent thematic pleasantry : *which are actually just a running gag that allows Martin to stammer, stumble and mug appealingly* (1980s+)

run off at the mouth *v phr* To talk too much; SHOOT OFF one's MOUTH : *I'm not about to run off at the mouth to the tabloids* (1909+)

run-of-the-mill or **run-of-the-mine** *adj* Ordinary; average; GARDEN-VARIETY (1930+)

run on all cylinders *v phr* To run well, smoothly, and efficiently

run on empty (or on fumes) *v phr* **1** To be ineffectual; fail : *As televison, "The Africans" is sometimes stunning; as scholarship it runs on empty* **2** To be nearly devoid of resources : *The school system is running on empty, too, with a $400 million deficit/ Our bank account must be running on fumes again* [1980s+; fr the needle of a fuel gauge indicating "Empty"]

run-out *n* A fleeing; desertion; escape : *has taken a run-out with the bankroll* (1928+)

run out of gas (or steam) *v phr* To lose impetus, effect, etc; fail; stall : *He ran out of gas a lot slower/ A succès d'estime is a success that's run out of steam* (1920s+)

run out on *v phr* To abandon, leave (1920+)

run over someone *v phr* To treat arrogantly, slightingly, or flippantly (1836+)

run someone **ragged** *v phr* To exhaust; wear out (1918+)

runs, the *n phr* Diarrhea; the GIS (1962+)

run scared *v phr* To show signs of panic and fear; try to escape : *Members aren't exactly running scared* (1950s+)

run short *v phr* To lack resources; exhaust one's supply : *Please send me two dollars. I run short* (1752+)

run the table *v phr* To finish a season undefeated : *When a team runs the table in a major conference and then wins one of the big bowl games, it usually finds a national title at the end* [1990s+ Football; fr the feat of sinking all the balls on the table successively in pool]

run-through *n* A rehearsal; DRY RUN : *After the first run-through, Mr Berlin casually tossed out three songs* (1923+)

run through *v phr* To rehearse : *I ran through my story once more, to polish it* (1923+)

run-up *n* A substantial increase over a relatively short period of time

run up against *v phr* To meet someone or something as an opponent or obstruction : *We were doing fine until we ran up against those real scumbags* (1821+)

run something **up the flagpole** *v phr* (Variation: **and see if anybody salutes** may be added) To test the reaction to; try out an idea, concept, etc : *Television runs these vapidities up the flagpole and we salute as though we had been programmed to do so* [1960s+; an expression attributed to the Madison Avenue advertising milieu, along with others like "Put it on a train and see if it gets off at Westport"]

run with it *v phr* To grasp and capitalize on something : *"Say nothing about this, until I can get something solid in our hands." "Please. Take it and run with it"* [1980s+; fr the notion of seizing and *running with* a football]

rush *n* **1** : *appears to want to give her a big rush* **2** A motion-picture print made immediately after the scene is shot (1924+ Movie studio) **3** An intense flood of pleasure, with quickened heart rate, felt soon after ingestion of a narcotic : *He didn't have to wait long for the rush* (1960s+ Narcotics) **4** A surge of pleasure; an ecstasy : *To Friend, it's a kind of a* *rush, the last big high/ gives her a unique rush* *(1960s+)* **v 1** To court a woman ardently : *He had "rushed" her, she said, for several months (1899+)* **2** To entertain and cultivate a student wanted as a fraternity or sorority member *(1890s+ College students)*

rushee *n* A person being rushed, esp by a college fraternity or sorority *(1916+)*

rush hour *n phr* The times when people are going to or leaving work, notable for heavy traffic *(1890+)*

rust bowl (or belt) *modifier* : *Wall Street, Chrysler, high-tech enterprises vs "rust bowl" basic industries* **n phr** The beleaguered and declining industrial areas, esp of the Middle West : *in the midwestern middle, the "rust bowl"/ Breaking the Rust Belt loose (1984+)* [modeled on the 1930s term *dust bowl* and the 1970s term *sun belt*]

rust bucket *modifier* : *the recent grounding in New York of a rust-bucket freighter* **n phr 1** An old worn vessel *(WWII Navy)* **2** An old car • Originally Australian : *Has your old rust bucket driven its last mile? (1969+)*

rustle *v* **1** (also **rustle** one's **bustle**) To bestir oneself; GET OFF one's ASS *(1882+)* **2** (also **rustle up**) To find and produce : *where I knew I could rustle up the Lompoc phone book (1844+)* [origin unknown; perhaps fr *rush* plus *hustle*]

rutabaga *n* A dollar : *We've spent 60,000 rutabagas (1940s+)*

S

sac fly *n phr* A sacrifice fly, a fly ball that permits a runner to score [1980s+ Baseball; the unshortened form is found by 1908]

sack[1] *modifier* : *sack duty* *n* **1** A bed, bunk, sleeping bag, etc; sleeping place; RACK : *Let me stay in the sack all day* (1829+) **2** Sleep; sack time : *He needed some sack* (1940s+) **3** A dress that fits loosely over the shoulders, waist, and hips and is gathered at the hemline (1957+) **4** A base; BAG, pillow : *He slid into the sack* (1891+ *Baseball*) *v* To discharge; dismiss; CAN, FIRE : *by refusing to sack his aide* (1841+) [verb sense probably fr the notion of giving a discharged person a traveling bag or *sack*, since the earliest expression was *get the sack*] *See* HIT THE HAY, the KEYSTONE, SAD SACK

sack[2] *n* **1** : *The Lions made 18 sacks in the first half* (1972+ *Football*) **2** An assault or blow : *You have to credit Dim Rome for hanging in there and taking the sack he accused Everett of being afraid to take* (1990s+) *v* To tackle the quarterback behind the line of scrimmage (1969+ *Football*) [fr *sack*, "to assault and pillage"]

sack, the *n phr* **1** Discharge from a job; dismissal; the BOOT : *He was late once too often and got the sack* (1825+) **2** Bed as the site of sexual activity : *Was this guy also a miracle worker in the sack?* (1980s+) [first sense apparently fr an old practice of giving someone a *sack* when sending him away; corresponding expressions are found in French: *donner son sac à quelqu'un*]

sack artist *n phr* **1** A chronic loafer; GOLDBRICK, GOOF-OFF (WWII armed forces) **2** A sexual virtuoso : *Goddess, riot grrrl, warrior, tattooed love child, sack artist, leader of men: The 21st Century Woman* (1990s+)

sack duty (or **drill** or **time**) *n phr* Sleeping time; sleep; loafing : *Get in some sack drill* (WWII armed forces)

sacker *See* FIRST SACKER, SECOND SACKER, THIRD SACKER

sack out (or **in** or **up** or **down**) *v phr* To go to bed; sleep; HIT THE HAY : *Well, it's time to sack out* (WWII armed forces)

sacred cow *n phr* Someone or something that may not be questioned or altered : *Everything is on the table. There are no sacred cows* [1910+; fr the venerated status of *cows* in Hinduism]

sad or **sad-ass** or **sad-assed** *adj* Inferior; botched or bungled; CRUMMY : *It's a sad dump/ What a sad-ass town* (first form 1899+, second 1971+ third 1974+)

saddled with *adv* Burdened with something or someone : *saddled with doing all the laundry*

sad sack *n phr* An awkward, unfortunate, harried, and maladjusted person; EIGHTBALL, SCHLEMAZEL : *nevertheless stuck with an inexplicable sad sack of a leading man* [Students 1920s+ & esp WWII armed forces; fr the unflattering image of a human being as primarily a container for feces]

safecracker *n* A person who blows or breaks open safes; BOX MAN, pete-man (1930s+)

said a mouthful, someone *sentence* Someone spoke accurately and cogently; someone said something very important • Often an ex- Often an expression of vehement agreement : *Daisy sure said a mouthful* (1922+)

said it *See* YOU SAID IT

sail in *v phr* To go boldly to the attack or to the rescue (1856+)

sailing *See* CLEAR SAILING

sail into *v phr* To attack; criticize severely; LAMBASTE : *He quickly sails into anyone that complains* (1856+)

salt *n* **1** A sailor, esp an old and seasoned one (1840+) **2** Heroin in powder form (1960s+ *Narcotics*)

salt and pepper *adj phr* **1** Interracial; BLACK AND TAN : *a salt and pepper neighborhood in Detroit* (1950s+) **2** Referring to hair that is turning gray (1915+) *n phr* Impure or low-grade marijuana (1960s+ *Narcotics*)

salt away *v phr* To save or store, esp money; hoard : *tapping the millions he had salted away to finance the company's renaissance* (1902+)

salt mines, the *See* BACK TO THE SALT MINES

salts *See* LIKE SHIT THROUGH A TIN HORN

salty *adj* **1** Audacious; daring; aggressive : *I relaxed, smiled. Salty little bugger* (1920+ *Navy*) **2** Terrible; nasty; unpalatable (1940s+ *Jive talk*) **3** Angry; hostile (1938+ *Black*) **4** Expensive; also, falsely bid higher

salute *See* RUN something UP THE FLAGPOLE

salvage *v* To steal; loot; LIBERATE (WWI Army)

salve *n* **1** Butter (1915+ *Hoboes*) **2** Cajolement; flattery; SOFT SOAP : *I handed him a little salve* (1864+) **3** A bribe; PALM OIL (1940s+) **4** Money, esp as a remedy or reward for something unpleasant (1940s+)

same difference, the *n phr* The same thing; something exactly equal : *So they fire him or he quits, it's the same difference* (1945+)

same here *interj* An exclamation of agreement (1895+)

same old same old *n phr* The same old thing • Said with resignation : *What's new? Same old same old*

417

same old story *n phr* An often-repeated story or occurrence : *Every time we ask him to check in, it's the same old story*

same wavelength, the *See* ON THE SAME WAVE-LENGTH

Sam Hill *n phr* Hell : *Where in Sam Hill do you think you're going?* [1839+; an echoic euphemism]

sammich *n* A sandwich, esp a savory one : *I'll make you the best sammich you ever ate* • Purposeful mispronunciation

sandbag *n* A type of life preserver *(WWII Navy)* *v* **1** To attack someone viciously, esp with a blackjack or similar bludgeon; BUSHWHACK : *I was sandbagged from behind* (1887+) **2** To intimidate; cow; BULL-DOZE : *Persuasion didn't work, so they tried to sandbag her* (1901+) **3** To check and then to raise the bet *(1940+ Gambling)* **4** To pretend weakness or ineptitude; mislead an opponent by apparent inferiority : *He charged that the Aussies were "sand bagging" (deliberately losing) to take the limelight off their disputed keel* (1970s+) **5** To drive a hot rod very fast *(1950s+ Hot rodders)*

sandbagged *adj* Temporarily evicted from one's dormitory room so that one's roommate can entertain a lover : *Bill's girlfriend came up for the weekend and Bob got sandbagged again* *(1980s+ Students)*

sandlot *modifier* : *sandlot ball n* A rough or improvised baseball field; hogan's brickyard *(1890+ Baseball)*

S and M or **S/M** or **sadie-maisie** *n phr* or *n* Sadomasochism; perverse sexual practices featuring whips, chains, etc *(1960s+)*

sandwich *See* HERO SANDWICH

sap[1] *n* A stupid person; fool, esp a gullible one : *Quit acting like a sap* [1815+; fr British dialect, short for *sapskull*, "person with a head full of soft material"; probably influenced by early 1800s British schoolboy slang, "compulsive studier, grind," which is probably fr *sap* as an ironic abbreviation of Latin *sapiens*, "wise," and is hence semantically akin to *sophomore*]

sap[2] *n* A blackjack; bludgeon : *The sap, a nice little tool about five inches long, covered with woven brown leather* (1899+) *v* : *One of the others sapped him from behind with the blackjack* (1926+) [perhaps fr Middle English *sappe*, "shovel," the shovel being for ages a popular club]

saphead *n* A stupid person; BLOCKHEAD, SAP : *one young woman who just seems to be a saphead* (1798+)

sappy *adj* **1** Stupid; foolish; GOOFY : *Lay off them sappy songs* (1670+) **2** Sentimental; mawkish; SCHMALTZY : *the Velveeta-voiced crooner of sappy tunes*

sarge *n* A sergeant (1867+)

sashay *v* To go; walk; flounce : *after a great deal of extravagantly publicized sashaying about* [1836+; fr the square-dance gait, fr French *chasser*, "chase"]

sass *n* Impudence; impertinent back talk : *if this reporter was going to give her any sass* (1835+) *v* : *He kept sassing his mama till she decked him* [fr *sauce*, "rude and impudent language or action"]

sassy *adj* Impudent; impertinent; IN-YOUR-FACE (1831+)

satch *n* **1** (also **satchelmouth**) A man with a large mouth **2** An overly talkative man; WINDBAG : *in the days when I was fearlessly denouncing old satch* (1940s+)

satchel *n* **1** The buttocks; rump; KEISTER : *a chance to rest my satchel* **2** SATCH **3** A jazz musician who plays a horn *v* To prearrange the outcome of a fight, race, etc; FIX, RIG : *It was satcheled against him* [1940s+; verb sense fr *in the bag*]

saturated *adj* Drunk : *to keep them saturated indefinitely* (1902+)

Saturday night special *n phr* **1** A cheap, small-caliber revolver quite easy to obtain : *Detroit lawmen began to refer to the weapons as "Saturday night specials"* (1968+) **2** A person, often an alcoholic, who comes to a hospital on weekends seeking a bed and board *(1970s+ Medical)* [*Saturday night pistol*, "25-caliber semi-automatic," is found by 1929]

sauce *n* **1** Impudence; impertinence; LIP, SASS (1835+) **2** A steroid drug used for body-building; 'ROID *(mid-1980s+) See* APPLESAUCE

sauce, the *n* Liquor; whiskey; BOOZE : *It made him sad and he almost began hitting the sauce* (1940+) *See* HIT THE BOTTLE, ON THE SAUCE

saucebox *n* An impudent person (1588+)

saucers *n* The eyes (1864+)

sausage *n* **1** A prizefighter, esp one with a swollen and battered face (1930s+) **2** A stupid person; MEATHEAD (1940s+) ◁3▷ A penis

sausage hound (or **dog**) *n phr* A dachshund; WIENER DOG *(1940s+)*

save someone's ass *v phr* To rescue someone : *I figure I better come down and save your ass* (1980s+)

save one's bacon *v phr* To save oneself; work one's preservation : *We'd better act right now if we want to save our bacon* (1654+)

saved by the bell *adj phr* Rescued, relieved, or preserved at the last moment : *Some Republicans argue that the threat of recession makes serious deficit cutting unwise right now. Saved by the bell!* [1950s+; fr the plight of a boxer who is being severely punished when the bell rings to end the round]

savvy or **savvey** *adj* : *a very savvy lady* *n* Comprehension; intelligence; BRAINS. SMARTS : *He's a guy with much savvy* (1785+) *v* To understand; know; grasp : *I'm the honcho here, savvy?* (1785+) [fr West Indian pidgin fr Spanish *sabe usted,* "do you know?"; modern use influenced by French *savez,* "you know"]

sawbones *n* A surgeon; a physician : *without being able to rouse a sawbones* (1830+)

sawbuck *n* A ten-dollar bill; ten dollars [1850+; fr the resemblance of the Roman numeral X to the ends of a *sawhorse*] See DOUBLE SAWBUCK

saw wood *v phr* 1 To sleep, esp very soundly 2 To snore [1940s+; fr the sound of snoring]

sax *modifier* : *a sax virtuoso* *n* A saxophone (1923+)

say See WHAT DO YOU SAY

say a mouthful *v phr* To say something true, important, etc • Usu a conversational response : *He is stupid? You said a mouthful* (1918+) See someone SAID A MOUTHFUL

say boo *v phr* To make an innocuous threat • Often in the negative : *No politician will say boo to the tobacco industry* (1932+)

say cheese *interj* Please smile for the camera

say-so *n* One's word, report, recommendation, etc : *No jury'll convict Manny on your say-so alone* (1637+)

says you or **says who** *interj* (Variations: **sez** or **sezz** may replace **says**) An exclamation of defiance, disbelief, mere pugnacity, etc; izzatso : *I'm in the wrong seat? Says who?* (1926+)

say that again See YOU CAN SAY THAT AGAIN

say uncle *v phr* To surrender; give up; KNUCKLE UNDER (1918+)

say what *interj* A request for more information; excuse me? • Sometimes with the sense of not believing what one has heard : *Marvella put her apple down. "Say whuuut?"* (1970s+ Black)

scab *n* A nonunion worker, esp one who attempts to break a strike; FINK (1777+)

scads *n* 1 A large quantity of money (1890+) 2 A large quantity of anything; BAGS, OODLES : *I have scads of studying to do* (1809+) [origin unknown; perhaps fr British dialect, "shed," and hence semantically akin to a *shithouse full*]

scag See SKAG

scairdy cat See SCAREDY CAT

scale *n* The regular rate of pay for a union worker : *paid scale for the day*

scalp *v* To sell tickets at a higher than normal or legal price (1883+)

scalper *n* 1 A person who scalps tickets (1869+) 2 A person who places bets and backs bets in such a way that he will win

whether the horse wins or loses (1960s+ Gambling)

scam *n* 1 (also **scambo**) A swindle; confidence game; fraud; CON : *It was a full scam/ Looking for a good scambo for April Fool's Day* (1963+) 2 The information; the LOW-DOWN, the SCOOP : *Here's the scam. We're holing in for the night* (1964+) *v* 1 (also **scam on**) : *You guys are scamming me* 2 To fool around and waste time : *scamming in the back room* [origin unknown; perhaps related to early 1800s British *scamp,* "cheater, swindler"]

scammer *n* A swindler or hustler

scandal sheet *n phr* A sensationalistic and vulgar newspaper, magazine, etc; cheap tabloid; RAG (1939+)

◁**scank**▷ *n* An unattractive girl (1970s+ Black teenagers)

scankie *adj* Disheveled; sloppy (1970s+ Black teenagers)

◁**scared shitless**▷ *adj phr* Very frightened; terrified : *And the producer is scared shitless of the sponsor* [1936+; based on the expression *scare the shit out of* someone]

scared stiff *adj phr* Very frightened; paralyzed by terror [1900+; fr the notion of being *scared to death*]

scaredy (or **scairdy**) **cat** *n phr* FRAIDY CAT (1933+)

◁**scare someone shitless**▷ (or **spitless** or **witless**) *v phr* To frighten very much; terrify : *It scared me shitless, but that didn't stop me from watching it again and again* (1936+)

◁**scare the shit out of** someone▷ *v phr* (Variations: **living shit** or **bejesus** or **daylights** may replace **shit**) To frighten very much; terrify : *Their strategy was to maximize the threat of bloodshed, to scare the shit out of the KGB/ It scares the living shit out of them/ These complexities would scare the bejesus out of David Cronenberg* (entry form 1930s+, others perhaps earlier)

scare up *v phr* To find and produce; RUSTLE : *was among the goodies scared up at a flea market* [1853+; fr the rising or starting of wildlife, which sense is found by 1846]

scarf *n* Food; a meal; CHOW, SCOFF (1930s+ Teenagers fr black) *v* 1 (also **scarf down** or **scarf up**) To eat or drink, esp voraciously; consume : *puffing on his morning joint, eating cereal, and scarfing up a beer/ People scarf up food after truck overturns/ scarfed down Milky Ways flambe* (1950+) ◁2▷ To do cunnilingus : *Scarf her a few times: eat her box, in other words* (1960s+)

scarf out *n phr* : *eat all I wanted in the cafeteria, really a scarf out* *v phr* To eat very heartily; overeat; PIG OUT : *I took the band there and we scarfed out* (1970s+)

scary *adj* Very good; first-rate : *And there are some pretty scary community players out there; it's not as if just anyone can come in and play (1990s+ Musicians)*

scat[1] *modifier* : *precise "scat" singing n* Pattering staccato gibberish sung to songs, esp jazz songs : *Then I'd carry on some of my scat v* : *Scatting has almost always been used by jazz singers as an interlude* [1926+ Jazz musicians; origin unknown; probably one of the nonsense syllables used]

scat[2] *v* To drive or otherwise move very fast [1950s+ Teenagers; fr early 1800s *ss cat*, a hissing address designed to drive away a cat; the earliest occurrence is in the expression *quicker than ss'cat*]

scatback *n* A very fast and agile backfield runner *(1946+ Football)*

scatterbrain *n* A silly or stupid person, esp one who cannot attend properly to a subject or get simple things done; DITZ, rattlebrain : *He's such a scatterbrain I don't look for a plausible theory from him (1790+)*

scatterbrained *adj* Silly or stupid; mentally unstable; DITZY *(1804+)*

scattergun *modifier* Broadly and imprecisely directed; crudely comprehensive; SHOTGUN : *the scattergun memo (1952+) n* 1 A shotgun *(1836+)* 2 A machine gun, submachine gun, or machine pistol; BURP GUN *(WWII Army)*

scene *n* 1 The setting or milieu of a specific activity or group; specialized venue : *the rock "scene"/ It is really quite difficult to understand their scene* 2 One's particular preference, activity, etc; BAG, THING : *I mean that's not my own scene or anything (1960s+ Counterculture) See* BAD SCENE, LAY A TRIP ON someone, MAKE A SCENE, MAKE THE SCENE, MOB SCENE, SPLIT THE SCENE

scenery *See* CHEW UP THE SCENERY

scenic route *n* The long route or way, often due to one's losing one's way : *missed the Garden State Parkway and ended up taking the scenic route*

schizo (SKITSO, SKIH zoh) *adj* 1 : *a schizo drug addict* 2 (also **schizy** or **schizzy** or **schizie**) Crazy; demented, esp in a self-contradictory way; psychotic; NUTTY : *People in democracies are a little schizzy about authority/ this same schizy little brain (1920s+ fr hospital) n* (also **schiz**) A schizophrenic : *Docs find he's a schizo (1945+, variant 1955+) [fr schizophrenic, schizophrenia]*

schiz out *v phr* To go crazy; become schizophrenic; FLIP : *She thought he'd schizzed out completely/ on the perpetual verge of schizing out (1980s+ Students)*

schlang *See* SCHLONG

schlemazel or **schlimazel** or **schlemasel** or **shlemozzle** (shlə MAH zəl) *n* An awkward,

unfortunate, maladjusted person; SAD SACK [1940s+, but probably earlier; fr Yiddish *shlimazel* fr *shlim mazel*, "rotten luck"; British slang *shemozzle, shlemozzle*, "a muddle, an unhappy plight," is found by 1889 and is probably related]

schlemiel or **schlemihl** or **shlemiel** (shlə MEEL) *n* A stupid person; fool; oaf; esp. a naive person often victimized : *Don't talk like a schlemiel, you schlemiel/ playing the lovable schlemiel to Brooklyn Jews* [1892+; fr Yiddish *shlemiel*, probably fr the name of the main character in A von Chamisso's German fable *The Wonderful History of Peter Schlemihl*, 1813]

schlep or **schlepp** or **shlep** *n* 1 : *even with the four-flight schlep to the editorial office (1964+)* 2 (also **schlepper** or **shlepper**) A stupid person; oaf; LOSER, KLUTZ, SLOB : *dead schleps playing behind him/ Poor John was a schlepper of the first order (1939+) v* 1 To carry; drag along : *schlepping the male's genetic material so his baby inherits half its genes from each parent (1922+)* 2 To move or advance with difficulty; drag : *Then I'd have to schlep around to the Quarter Note (1922+) [fr Yiddish shleppen]*

schleppy or **shleppy** *adj* Awkward; stupid; KLUTZY *(1940s+)*

schlock *adj* : *unlike all those schlock films n* (also **schlack** or **schlag** or **shlock**) Inferior merchandise; an inferior product; CRAP, JUNK : *That "Macbird" is a piece of schlock/ are bringing out schlock so they can pay for the books they care about (1915+) [fr Yiddish fr German schlag, "a blow," perhaps because the merchandise has been knocked around, or knocked down, or perhaps because, as Eric I Bromberg wrote in American Speech in 1938, "to schlach is to cut or raise a price according to a customer"; the New York Times speculated in 1922 that the underworld use schlock, "a broken lot of loot," was adopted because junk had recently come to mean "narcotics, dope"]*

schlockmeister *n* A successful maker or seller of schlock : *Low-budget, high-profit exploitation has solidified their position as Hollywood's premier schlockmeisters [1965+; fr schlock plus German Meister, "master"]*

schlocky or **shlocky** *adj* Inferior; shoddy; cheap and gaudy; JUNKIE *(1968+)*

◁**schlong**▷ *n* (also **schlang** or **shlang** or **shlong**) The penis; PRICK : *you know with his schlong hanging out there [1969+; fr Yiddish shlang, literally "snake"]*

◁**schlontz** or **shlontz**▷ *n* The penis [1970s+; perhaps a blend of Yiddish *shlong* and *shwants*]

schloomp (SHLŌŌMP) (also **schlump** or **shloomp** or **shlump**) *n* A stupid person;

KLUTZ : *For openers, he looks like a shlump* v
(also **shalump** or **schloomp around**) To loaf;
idle about; GOOF OFF : *She shalumps around the
Ritz in her loose clothes and sneakers* [1930s+;
fr Yiddish *shlump*, related to German *Schlu-
mpe*, "a slovenly woman"]

schlub *See* ZHLUB

schmaltz or **shmaltz** (SHMAWLTS) *n* Blatant
sentimentality, esp musical or theatrical
material of a cloyingly sweet and maudlin
sort; CORN : *happy combination of good theater
and good pathos known as schmaltz* [1935+
Swing musicians; fr Yiddish *shmalts*, literally
"rendered fat"]

schmaltzy or **schmalzy** or **shmaltzy** *adj* Sentimental; sweetly melancholy; CORNY, ICKY :
this schmaltzy king of schlock and roll (1935+)

schmancy *See* FANCY-SCHMANCY

schmatte (SHMAH tə) *n* (also **schmattah** or
schmatteh or **shmatte** or **shmotte**) A shabby
or unstylish garment : *She had on a tired old
schmattah* [1970+; fr Yiddish *shmatte*, literally "rag"]

schmear[1] or **shmear** or **shmeer** *n* A bribe :
*Since the rest of the tables were all unoccupied,
it would seem to call for a bit of a shmear* v 1 To
bribe; GREASE someone's PALM : *see this here
Rabbi and schmear him a thousand dollars*
(1909+) 2 To flatter and cajole someone;
SOFT SOAP (1930+) [fr Yiddish *shmeer*, literally
"grease"]

schmear[2] *n* An accusation or innuendo meant
to harm someone's reputation; a slander *v*
To treat someone very roughly; CLOBBER,
CREAM, SMEAR [1950s+; fr a humorous mispronunciation of *smear*]

schmear, the *n phr* the WHOLE SCHMEAR
[1940s+; fr Yiddish *shmeer*]

schmeck or **shmeck** *n* A taste; a bite : *How
about a little schmeck?* (1968+) 2 Heroin;
SMACK : *She's hustling right now, schmeck, tail,
abortion, the whole bit* (1930s+ Narcotics) [fr
Yiddish *shmek*, "a smell, sniff," related to
German *schmecken*]

schmegeggy or **shmegeggy** or **schmegegge**
(shmə GEG gee) *n* 1 A stupid person; oaf;
SCHLEMIEL : *the shmegeggy she lives with/ a new
story about some gringo schmegegge exchanging his dollars for a worthless mess of Batista
money* 2 Nonsense; foolishness; BALONEY
[1964+; fr Yiddish *shmegegi*, of unknown
origin, perhaps coined in American Yiddish]

schmendrick or **shmendrick** *n* A stupid person, esp an awkward and inept nonentity;
SCHLEMIEL : *a schmendrick with a noodle for a
brain* [1951+; fr Yiddish *shmendrik*, fr the
name of a character in an operetta by A
Goldfaden]

schmo (also **schmoe** or **shmo** or **shmoe**) *n* 1 A
naive and hapless person; fool; GOOF : *I've*

been standing here like a schmoe for 20 minutes
2 A person; man; GUY : *Them big-time
schmoes was stockholders* [1947+; perhaps a
euphemistic alteration of Yiddish *shmok*,
"penis"; perhaps a quasi-Yiddish coinage for
amusing effect; the term has been adopted
into American Yiddish] *See* JOE SCHMO

schmooz (SHMOOS or SHMOOZ) (also **schmoo**
or **schmooze** or **schmoos** or **schmoose** or **sch-
moozl** or **schmoozle** or **schmoosl** or **schmo-
osle** or **schmuss** or any of these spelled with
sh-) *n* : *Two buddies enjoying a quiet schmooz* v
1 To converse, esp lengthily and cozily : *stop
and chat* (*Schmoos, he calls it*)/ *lawyers
schmoozing in the halls* (1897+) 2 To seduce
with flattery; SOFT SOAP : *What he does is he
hooks up with these dumb women whom he
schmoozes and lives off* (1990s+) [fr Yiddish fr
Hebrew *schmuos*, "things heard"]

schmoozefest *n* A meeting, conference, etc,
where people chat; GABFEST : *where they're on
their way to yet another promotional schmoozefest* (1990s+)

schmoozer *n* A person who schmoozes, esp as
an aspect of personality : *He has none of the
small coin of politics. He's not a schmoozer*
(1909+)

schmuck or **shmuck** *n* A detestable person; an
obnoxious man; BASTARD, PRICK : *You must be
a real schmuck* [1892+; fr Yiddish *shmok*,
"penis," literally "ornament"]

schmucky *adj* Detestable; obnoxious : *The fact
that this kid might be schmucky hurt his
chances* (1975+)

schmutter or **shmutter** *n* A garment (1970+;
Yiddish)

schmutz or **shmutz** *n* Filth; smut [1967+; fr
Yiddish]

schneider or **schneid** *n* : *The Yanks took four
straight, a schneider/ The AFC might have
teams capable of breaking the Super Bowl
schneid* v 1 To win before one's opponent has
scored; SHUT OUT 2 To defeat decisively;
trounce; CLOBBER [fr German, literally "tailor," probably by way of Yiddish; the term
is used in various card games for a clean
sweep]

schnockered or **snockered** *adj* Drunk : *Better
quit before you get schnockered/ while all the
male guests get snockered* [1955+; origin
uncertain; perhaps fr Irish *snagaireact*, pronounced with initial *sh-*, "tippling, stam-
mering"]

schnook or **shnook** (SHNŎŎK) *n* An ineffectual person; a naive person often victimized;
PATSY • A more affectionate and compassionate way of designating a schlemiel :
Don't be such an apologetic schnook [1940s+;
fr American-Yiddish *shnook*, said to be fr
German *Schnucke*, "small sheep"; probably

related to the pet names *snooks, snookums,* etc]

schnozz *n* (also **schnoz** or **schnozzle** or **schnozzola** or any of these spelled with **sh-** or **snozzle**) The nose, esp a large one; bugle : *the rep of not havin' a big schnozz/ Five players broke their schnozzolas* [entry form 1942+, *schnozzle* 1934+, *schnozzola* and *snozzle* 1930+; fr Yiddish *shnoz* fr *shnoitsl* fr German *Schnauze,* "snout"]

schpritz *See* SHPRITZ

schtick *See* SHTICK

schtoonk (SHTOŌNK) *n* (also **schtunk** or **shtoonk** or **shtunk**) A person one detests or despises; JERK, STINKER [1968+; fr Yiddish *shtunk,* "stink, scandal"]

schtup *See* SHTUP

schvantz or **schvontz** *See* SHVANTZ

◀**schvartze**▶ (SHVAHR tsə) *n* (also **shvartzeh** or **shvartze** or **schwartze** or **schvartzer** or **shvartzer** or **schwartzer**) A black person : *irons even better than the schvartze/ A shwartze. Some wife killer who'd faked it* [1961+; fr Yiddish fr *shvartz,* "black"]

schwing *interj* An exclamation of delight, esp sexual; HUBBA-HUBBA : *As a child, he found cartoon characters (in particular Bugs Bunny) arousing. Schwing!* [1990s+; popularized by the 1992 movie *Wayne's World*]

science *See* HARD SCIENCE

sci-fi or **sciffy** *modifier* : *sci-fi fans secretly crave* *n* Science fiction (1955+)

scillion *See* SKILLION

scoff *n* Food : *Beef heart is their favorite scoff* (1846+) *v* **1** To eat or drink, esp voraciously; SCARF : *I'll take you over so you can scoff* (1846+) **2** To steal; seize; plunder; SWIPE : *Who scoffed my butts?* (1893+) [origin uncertain; perhaps fr Afrikaans *schoft,* defined in a 1600s dictionary as "eating time for labourers or workmen foure times a day"; perhaps fr British dialect *scaff*; South African use in current senses is attested in late 1700s]

scoffings *n* Food; meals : *A hard town for "scoffings"* (1892+ Hoboes)

scooch *v* To move or push in a direction by a small amount • Also as a noun : *Scooch your leg forward with your hand if you can't get there See* SCRUNCH

scoop *n* **1** : *The paper scored a major scoop with that revelation* (1874+ Newspaper office) **2** A standard hemispherical portion of ice cream, mashed potatoes, etc; dip (1950s+ Lunch counter) **3** A fund-raising event that allows many contributions to be given at once; DUMP (1990s+ Politics) **4** A designer drug, gamma hydroxybutyrate; GHB, GRIEVOUS BODILY HARM (1990s+ Narcotics) *v* **1** To publish or file a news story before another newspaper or another reporter : *I was afraid of being scooped, because I knew a lot of reporters were on the same story* (1884+ Newspaper office) **2** In singing, to attain a desired note by beginning lower and sliding up to pitch : *In the video* Forza del Destino, *Renata Tebaldi sometimes scoops and has occasional bouts of flatness* (1927+) **3** To steal; pilfer (1960s+ Students)

scoop, the *n phr* News or data, esp when anxiously awaited, heretofore secret, etc; POOP : *Oh, come on. What's the scoop?* (1940s+ Students & armed forces)

scooper *See* POOPER SCOOPER

scoop on someone *v phr* To make sexual advance; HIT ON someone : *I saw him trying to scoop on Nancy at the party* (1980s+ Students)

scoot *n* **1** A dollar : *Greg could have the sixty scoots, the guns, everything* (1970s+) **2** A motorcycle; bike, IRON (1960s+ Students) *v* **1** To move rapidly, esp in fleeing or escaping : *When they saw the cops they scooted right out of there* (1841+) **2** To slide, esp suddenly as on a slippery surface : *Let's scoot this thing into the corner* (1838+) [origin unknown; perhaps ultimately fr a Scandinavian cognate of *shoot,* by way of Scottish dialect; British naval *scout,* in the first verb sense, is found by 1758; the first noun sense may have an entirely different derivation than the two verb senses]

scope out (or **on**) *v phr* To look at; examine; CHECK OUT, DIG : *scoping on the foxy sisters/ I'd scoped him out pretty well* [1980s+ Teenagers fr black; probably fr *periscope*]

scorch *v* **1** To travel very fast; BARREL : *I proceed to scorch to make up for lost time* (1891+) **2** To throw the ball very fast and hard; BURN : *You had to love how he scorched Buddy Ryan* (1940s+ Baseball)

scorched earth *n phr* : *Scorched Earth: a self-destructive strategy in which a company seeks to discourage a takeover by making itself less attractive* [1990s+ Business; translation of Chinese *jiaotu,* describing the 1930s strategy adopted in defense against the invasion by Japan, under which retreating troops destroyed everything useful]

scorcher *n* **1** A very harsh remark, review, etc; ZINGER (1842+) **2** A very hot day (1874+) **3** A very hard-hit ball (1900+ Baseball)

score *n* **1** A success or coup : *This was the big score for him, the chance he'd been waiting for all his life* (1970s+) **2** The loot or proceeds from a robbery, swindle, gamble, etc; also, the amount of such loot; HAUL (1914+ Underworld) **3** A share of loot; CUT (1930s+ Underworld) **4** Accomplishment; payoff : *He was always looking for an easy score* (1960+) **5** The client of a prostitute : *The little hooker* *got only five scores all evening (1960s+ Prostitutes)* **6** A planned murder; HIT *(1970s+ Underworld)* **7** A buy of narcotics : *He's out looking for a score (1950s+ Narcotics)* **8** : *The Mollen Commission focused on clusters of officers who profited from scores, a code word for stealing and extorting narcotics and cash from drug dealers (1990s+ New York City police)* **9** A summary or conclusion : *Bartender, what's the score?* **v 1** To succeed, esp to please an audience, interviewer, or others who judge; RATE : *The show didn't score with the TV critics (1884+)* ◁**2**▷ To do the sex act with or to someone; MAKE IT WITH someone *(1960+)* **3** To find a client for prostitution *(1960s+ Prostitutes)* **4** To buy or get narcotics : *You go score what you need for the trip (1950s+ Narcotics)* **5** To get; acquire : *Most of them score their clothes as gifts from parents (1970s+ Students) See* EVEN THE SCORE, MAKE A SCORE

score, the *n* The main point; crux; the BOTTOM LINE : *I heard the facts, now what's the score? (1938+) See* KNOW THE SCORE

scosh *See* SKOSH

scrag[1] *v* **1** To kill; murder : *overshoot or undershoot and scrag some scared civilian (1930+)* **2** To destroy or severely damage; ruin : *The beet sugar people try to scrag the cane sugar people (1835+)* ◁**3**▷ To do the sex act with or to; SCREW, SCROG : *the middle-American hobby of scragging the random housewife at any opportunity (1970s+)* [fr earlier slang, "hang by the neck"]

◁**scrag**[2]▷ *n* An unattractive woman; DOG [1940s+ Students; probably fr *hag* reinforced by the name of the ugly *Scraggs* family in the comic strip "Li'l Abner" and possibly by earlier slang, "a raw-bones; a skinny person," found by 1542]

scraggy *adj* Gaunt and wasted; lean; bony : *snapshot of a scraggy Sindona as an apparent captive (1611+)*

scram *n* : *I got ready for a sudden scram* *v* To leave quickly; flee; BEAT IT : *Customers scrammed screaming when the trailer went on/ Scram, you kids (1928+)* [fr *scramble*]

scramble *v* : *Some girls I know "scramble," which means sell drugs, to get it (1980s+ Teenagers)*

scrambled eggs *n* **1** Gold braid, embroidery, etc, on the uniform of a senior officer, esp on the bill of a hat **2** Senior officers; BRASS, the TOP BRASS *(WWII armed forces)*

scrap *n* A fight; quarrel; DUSTUP *(1846+)* *v* : *They scrapped for days over the appointment* [origin uncertain; probably fr *scrape*]

scrape along (or **by**) *v phr* To survive; carry on; GET BY, MAKE OUT : *I'm not flourishing, but I'm scraping along, barely (1884+)*

scrape the bottom of the barrel *v phr* To use one's last and worst resources; be forced to desperate measures : *He scraped the bottom of the barrel when he proposed that topic for his paper (1942+)*

scrape (or **scratch**) **up** *v phr* To get, esp laboriously and bit by bit : *Dollar by dollar they scraped up a million/ even if you can't scratch up all of that cash now (first form 1617+, variant 1922+)*

scrappy *adj* Inclined to fight; pugnacious *(1895+)*

scratch *adj* Hastily arranged; impromptu; spur of the moment; PICKUP : *a scratch jazz ensemble (1851+)* *n* **1** Money; BREAD, DOUGH : *If the mayor doesn't come up with the scratch (1914+)* **2** A loan; an act of borrowing money : *where they are going to make a scratch for tomorrow's operations (1930s+)* **3** : *two scratches in the third race* **4** : *She had found one "scratch," a ticket bet on a horse that had not started (1970s+ Horse racing)* **5** (also **itch**) : *He made a scratch at a crucial juncture/ And when the cue ball goes into the pocket, you call that an itch (Billiards 1909+)* **6** A mention of one's name in the news media, esp when this is useful publicity *(late 1930s+)* *v* **1** To cancel a horse from a race *(1902+ Horse racing)* **2** To cancel a plan, an entrant, someone on a list, etc; SCRUB : *Looks like our tête-à-tête will have to be scratched (1685+)* **3** (also **itch**) To put the cue ball into a pocket inadvertently *(Billiards 1909+) See* FROM SCRATCH, START FROM SCRATCH, UP TO SCRATCH, YOU SCRATCH MY BACK I SCRATCH YOURS

scratch (or **scratch around**) **for** something *v phr* To acquire something, esp something hard to find or get : *I was scratching around for whatever work I could get* [1509+; fr the food-seeking action of chickens]

scratch hit *n phr* A lucky base hit that is nearly an out *(1876+ Baseball)*

scratch sheet *n phr* A daily publication giving betting data, including the cancellations, on races to be run that day : *The first scratch sheet that ever appeared was in 1917 (1939+ Horse racing)*

scrawny *adj* Lean; bony; SCRAGGY, SKINNY *(1833+)*

scream, a *n phr* Someone or something that is hilariously funny; a HOOT, a RIOT : *Isn't this decor a scream? (1903+)*

scream (or **yell**) **bloody murder** *v phr* To make a raucous outcry; complain noisily : *They'll scream bloody murder if we even suggest that (entry form 1882+, variant 1931+)*

screaming *See* DRAG someone KICKING AND SCREAMING INTO THE TWENTY-FIRST CENTURY

screaming meemies, the, or **the meemies** *n phr* A state of nervous hysteria; the HEEBIE-

JEEBIES, the JITTERS : *a town that would give the ordinary thrill-seeker the screaming meemies/ Knowing (a chimpanzee) was on the loose gave him the meemies* [fr WWI Army; apparently fr the soldier's echoic name for a very loud and terrifying German artillery shell, and then the battle fatigue caused by exposure to such matéiel; the name may reflect a soldier's pattern of giving feminine names, here the French *Mimi*, to projectiles and weapons, such as *Betsy, Big Bertha, Moaning Minnie*, etc]

screech *n* Inferior whiskey; PANTHER PISS (1902+), ROTGUT

screeching halt, a *n phr* A sudden and definitive stop : *I'll know when it's coming to a screeching halt/ Let's bring this conversation to a screeching halt* (1970s+)

screenager *n* : *Did you hear about Bobby? He downloaded Windows 95 from his counselor's computer and then sold it to his Dad's accounting firm. What a screenager* (1990s+)

◁**screw**[1]▷ *n* **1** : *She loves a good screw* (1929+) **2** A person regarded merely as a sex object : *She's only a medium screw* (1937+) *v* **1** To do the sex act with or to someone; FUCK • Felt by many to be excusable when *fuck* is the term really intended, and used as an attenuated form in nearly the whole range of *fuck* senses and compounds : *At last people are screwing like minks* (1785+) **2** To take advantage of; swindle; maltreat; FUCK • Rapidly losing all offensive impact : *The city's taxpayers get screwed* (1900+) [*screw*, "strumpet, prostitute," is found by 1725] *See* GOAT FUCK, PUT THE SCREWS TO someone, THROW A FUCK INTO someone

screw[2] *n* A prison guard or warden; turnkey : *a hard-boiled screw* [1812+ Underworld; fr 1700s underworld, "a skeleton key," then *turnkey*, the bearer of such a key]

screw[3] **or screw out** *v* To leave hastily; flee; SCRAM : *Now go on. Screw* [entry 1896+, variant 1908+; perhaps imitative of *scram*; perhaps semantically derived fr *fuck off*, "leave, depart," by way of less taboo *screw off*]

screw around *v phr* **1** To pass one's time idly and pleasantly; potter about; GOOF AROUND **2** To joke and play when one should be serious; FUCK AROUND : *Quit screwing around and take this call* **3** To flirt or dally, esp promiscuously; SWING : *After he met Janet, he stopped screwing around* (1939+)

screw around with something *v phr* To play or tinker with; MESS AROUND WITH : *I told her to stop screwing around with the TV dial* (1970s+)

screwball[1] **or screwhead** *adj* : *screwball antics* *n* **1** An eccentric person; FREAK, ODDBALL : *a*

catchall for screwballs and semi-screwballs from all over/ He's just another screwhead too big for his britches* (1933+) **2** Inferior, commercial jazz played for indifferent faddists (1936+ Jazz musicians) [fr *screwy* and probably based on *screwball*[2]; the *-ball* of this term is the source of the very productive combining word that yields *oddball, nutball*, etc]

screwball[2] *n* A pitched ball that moves to the right from a right-handed pitcher and the left from a left-handed pitcher, unlike a curve ball [1928+ Baseball; said to have been coined by the pitcher Carl Hubbell]

screwed *adj* Drunk (*British & 1980s+ students*) *See* HALF-STEWED

screwed, blued, and tattooed *adj phr* **1** Thoroughly cheated; victimized; maltreated **2** : *In the Pacific Fleet, screwed, blued, and tattooed means that you've hit a foreign port and have done everything of importance in that port—you have gotten laid, had a new set of dress blues hand made, and added to your already prodigious collection of tattoos* (Navy) [1940s+; in the first sense, *blued* is probably fr earlier *blewed*, "robbed"; *tattooed* has the standard sense "struck rapidly and repeatedly"]

screwed up *adj phr* **1** Confused; tangled; spoiled, esp by bungling; BALLED UP, FUCKED UP : *He screwed up the punch line* **2** Mentally and emotionally disturbed; neurotic; FUCKED UP : *Hamlet was a sad, screwed-up type guy* (WWII armed forces)

◁**screwee**▷ *n* A sex partner; a person being screwed : *My screwee was so angry that nothing would distract her* (1970s+)

screw-loose *n* An eccentric person; NUT, SCREWBALL (1940s+)

screw loose, a *See* HAVE A SCREW LOOSE

screw-off *n* A person who evades work; idler; loafer; FUCK-OFF (WWII Army)

◁**screw off**▷ *v phr* **1** To masturbate; JACK OFF (1950s+) **2** FUCK OFF (WWII Army)

screw someone over *v phr* To take advantage of; swindle and victimize; FUCK OVER : *Don't trust the Government. They feel it screwed them over* (1960s+)

screws *See* PUT THE SCREWS TO someone

◁**screw the pooch**▷ *v phr* FUCK THE DOG

screw-up *n* **1** A chronic bungler; a consistently inept person; FUCK-UP (WWII Army) **2** A confused situation; a botch; FUCK-UP : *The program's a total screw-up* (1950s+)

screw up *v phr* **1** To fail by blundering; ruin one's prospects, life, etc; FUCK UP : *I screwed up and got canned* (WWII Army) **2** To confuse; tangle; spoil by bungling; BALL UP, FUCK UP : *It really screws up my sex life* (1938+)

screwy *adj* Very eccentric; crazy; NUTTY, SCREWBALL : *Newspaper guys are mostly screwy*

[1887+; fr the gait of a drunk person suggested by the twistiness of a *screw* thread, whence the various senses of deviation; influenced by the notion of having a *screw loose* in one's head]

◁**screw you**▷ *interj* An exclamation of strong defiance and contempt; FUCK YOU : *Screw you all* (*1940s+*)

script *n* **1** A doctor's prescription, often a forged or stolen one (*1960s+ Narcotics*) **2** Any note written on paper **3** A manuscript (*Theater 1897+, also publishing*)

◁**scrog**▷ *modifier* : *All that scroggin' material out there* v To do the sex act with or to; SCRAG, SCREW : *You guys gotta scrog the sociable cervix* (*1970s+*) [origin uncertain; perhaps fr *scrag*]

scrooch or **scrooge** or **scrouge** *See* SCRUNCH

scrooched *adj* Drunk (*1925+*)

Scrooge *n* **1** A miser; PINCHPENNY, TIGHTWAD **2** A spoiler of Christmas; GRINCH [1940+; fr the Dickens character in the 1843 story *A Christmas Carol*]

scrooge up *v phr* To tense and narrow one's eyelids : *I find myself scrooging up my eyes* (*1909+*)

scrounge or **scrounge up** *n* (also **scrounger**) A person who acquires by begging, borrowing, or pilfering; CADGER, MOOCHER, schnorrer *v* **1** (also **scrounge up**) To acquire by such dubious ways as habitual borrowing, begging, foraging, scavenging, pilfering, etc; CADGE, MOOCH • Popularized by military use during World War I : *eating what little he could scrounge* **2** (also **scrounge up**) To seek and collect; SCRAPE UP : *Let's see what we can scrounge up for supper* [1909+; probably fr British dialect *scrunge*, "squeeze," hence "steal," semantically parallel with *pinch*]

scroungy or **scrounging** or **scrungy** *adj* Inferior; wretched; CRUMMY, GRUNGY : *I'd tell my own children to wear something scroungy/ The musical has a scroungy book/ could have bundled all this scrungy stuff into my car* [1950s+; probably fr the notion of inferior things *scavenged* and *scrounged*, with the form now influenced by *grungy*]

scrub[1] *v* To cancel or eliminate : *They were forced to scrub the whole plan* [1828+; popularized by military use during World War II]

scrub[2] *n* **1** A contemptible person; BUM : *Ed is a scrub* (*1589+*) **2** An athlete who is not on the first or varsity team; a lowly substitute (*1892+*) [ultimately fr *scrub*, "shrub, a low, stunted tree"; the quoted 1990s teenager use is an interesting survival or perhaps a revival based on the second sense]

scrubs *n* Loose-fitting garments, slippers, etc, worn by surgeons, nurses, and others in a sterile environment : *Finally, Bill emerged from the delivery room in green scrubs, cradling a seven-pound baby, saying he was "bonding" with his new daughter* (*1970s+ Medical*)

scruffy *adj* Dirty and unkempt; shabby; slovenly : *The scruffy little city, Knoxville, did it/ one bearded, sad-eyed, scruffy-looking lad* [1871+; fr obsolete British *scruff*, "valueless, contemptible," probably an alteration of *scurf*, "scabbiness of the skin," hence related to *scurvy*]

◁**scrump** or **scromp**▷ *v* To do the sex act; BOFF, JAZZ [1980s+ Students; perhaps a blend of *screw* and *hump*]

scrumptious *adj* Excellent; superior; luxurious : *What a scrumptious dessert!* [1836+; perhaps a humorous alteration of *sumptuous*]

scrunch (also **ooch** or **oonch** or **scooch** or **scrooch** or **scrooge** or **scrouge**) *v* **1** To squeeze oneself into a tighter space : *I scrunched into the corner and covered my ears/ She scrooged over and patted the sofa beside her. Ooch over* (entry form 1844+) **2** To squeeze : *He scrunched the paper into a ball* (*1880+*) [ultimately fr late 16th-century *scruze*, "squeeze," perhaps a blend of *screw* and *squeeze*]

scrunge *n* Dirt; filth; a nasty substance; GRUNGE : *Wipe the scrunge off your shoe* [1970s+ Students; probably fr *grunge*]

scrungy *adj* Dirty; SCUZZY : *and being with a bunch of scrungy addicts* (*1974+*)

scuffle or **scuffle along** *v* or *v phr* **1** To make one's modest living the best one can; struggle along; GET BY, SCRAPE ALONG, SCRUFF (*1939+ Jazz musicians*) **2** To dance (*1950s+ Jive talk*)

◁**scum**▷ *n* **1** Semen; COME (*1960s+*) **2** A despicable person

◁**scumbag**▷ *modifier* : *accused us of practicing scumbag journalism* n **1** A condom; RUBBER **2** (also **scumbucket** or **scummer** or **scumsack** or **scumster** or **scumwad**) A despicable person; ASSHOLE, BASTARD, SLEAZEBAG : *calls Charlton Heston a scumbag/ Everybody says he was a scumbucket/ The scummers were dressed sleeveless now/ And another opportunistic scumsack limps straight to a lawyer* [1960s+; fr *scum*, "semen"]

◁**scumsucker**▷ *n* **1** A person who does fellatio; COCKSUCKER : *strumpet called Tony a scumsucker* **2** A despicable person; SCUMBAG (*1970s+*)

◁**scumsucking**▷ *adj* Despicable; disgusting : *You scum-sucking dog, you think everybody in town doesn't know you keep this whore up here?* (*1970s+*)

scunge *n* A dirty or despicable person or place : *a bit of a scunge* (*1912+*)

scunner *n* Extreme dislike; hostility : *had taken a scunner against the main competitor* [1500+; fr Scots dialect]

scurvy *adj* Gross; repulsive *(College students)*

scut *n* **1** A detestable or contemptible person; CRUMB, LOUSE : *You bloody scut!* *(1873+)* **2** A novice; recruit; neophyte : *The fraternity was famous for treating scuts very roughly (1950s+)* **3** (also **scud** or **scut work**) Menial work such as would be given to a novice : *a detention company doing scut work around the fort (1950s+)* **4** (also **scut dog** or **scut monkey** or **scut puppy**) A junior intern or physician *(1940s+ Medical)* **5** (also **scut work**) Routine and tedious medical procedures usually relegated to the least senior members of the staff *(1940s+ Medical)* [the 1500s slang use, "vulva, cunt," and the standard use "tail of a hare or deer," suggest a core sense "tail, buttocks, ass," reinforced by British dialect *skut*, "crouch down," and perhaps related to Old Norse *skutr*, "stern of a ship"; *scut* meant "little boy," perhaps fr Scots *scudler*, "scullion, kitchen boy," among Scotch-Irish settlers in Pennsylvania]

scuttlebutt *n* Rumors; gossip; presumed confidential information : *worry about a slump, according to business scuttlebutt* [1901+ Navy; fr the chitchat around the *scuttlebutt*, "drinking fountain, water cask," on naval vessels]

scuzz *n* **1** (also **scuzzo**) Dirt; filth; a nasty substance; GRUNGE, MUNG, SCRUNGE : *He has scuzz all over his pants and in his mind* ◁2▷ An unattractive young woman; SCANK, SKAG [1960s+ Teenagers; origin unknown; a blend of *scum* with *fuzzy* has been suggested, but most such suggestions are mere ingenuity]

scuzzbag *n* (also **scuzzball** or **scuzzbucket**) A despicable person; CRUMB, scurve, SLEAZEBAG : *He calls a minister a "scuzzbag"/ As other West Coast scuzzballs are proving (1983+)*

scuzz someone out *v phr* To disgust mightily; nauseate; GROSS someone OUT : *With-it slanguists are scuzzed out at the squared-out weirdos who still use grossed out (1970s+ Teenagers)*

scuzzy or **scuz** *adj* Dirty; filthy; repellent; GRUNGY : *a bunch of scuzzy Moroccan A-rabs* [1960s+ Teenagers; origin unknown] *See* SCUZZ

sea cow *n phr* Milk, esp canned milk *(WWII Navy)*

sealed (up) *adj* Settled; secured : *contract was sealed in January*

seal the deal *v phr* To come to an agreement or reach the point where an agreement is almost certain, often used in reference to sexual relations : *The company sealed the deal with the content provider. / Taking her to a fancy dinner sealed the deal*

seams *See* COME APART AT THE SEAMS

search me *interj* An exclamation or acknowledgment of ignorance; BEATS ME : *Who said it? Search me, I couldn't say (1900+)*

season *See* SILLY SEASON

seas over *See* HALF SEAS OVER

seat *n* The buttocks; ASS *(1607+)* *See* BUDDY SEAT, CATBIRD SEAT, the HOT SEAT, TAKE A BACK SEAT

seat-of-the-pants *adj* Inclined to work by instinct, feel, impulse, etc, rather than by precise rules; practical : *The news had seat-of-the-pants editors who knew their audience (1970s+)* *See* FLY BY THE SEAT OF one's PANTS

sec[1] *n* A second of time : *Come here a sec, Billy (1860+)*

sec[2] *n* A secretary : *His femme secs open the mail (1934+)*

second banana *n phr* A supporting comedian : *Who was second banana, Laurel or Hardy? (1940s+ Show business)* *See* TOP BANANA

second fiddle *adj* : *a sort of second-fiddle appointment* *n* A person or thing that is not the most favored, the best, the leader, etc : *definitely second fiddle before the Convention started (1809+)* *See* PLAY SECOND FIDDLE

seconds *n* **1** A second helping **2** Merchandise that has imperfections *(1792+)*

second sacker *n phr* A second baseman *(1911+ Baseball)*

second-story man *n phr* A cat burglar *(1886+)*

second thought *See* DON'T GIVE IT A SECOND THOUGHT

secret *See* DIRTY LITTLE SECRET

section eight or **section 8** *n phr* **1** A military discharge given for emotional or psychological disability, defective character, or military inaptitude **2** A crazy or eccentric person; a neurotic; NUT [WWII Army; fr *Section VIII*, Army Regulation 615-360]

security blanket *n phr* A thing or person that provides someone with a sense of safety and emotional comfort : *Zeigler instead is Mr Nixon's "security blanket"* [1971+; fr the *blanket* or token fragment of blanket that some small children carry about as a source of comforting familiarity; Charles M Schulz, creator of the comic strip "Peanuts," popularized and may have coined the term]

see *n* **1** Recognition; complimentary notice by a superior : *He was a good cop ten years, but never got a see (1950s+ Police)* **2** A visit of inspection : *numerous "sees" or visits from the sergeant (1930+ Police)* *v* **1** To pay protection money or graft : *doing business without "seeing the cops" (1930+ Police)* **2** To equal a bet or a raise rather than dropping out of the game *(1599+ Gambling)* [first noun sense perhaps an abbreviation of *commendation*] *See* LONG TIME NO SEE, a LOOK-SEE, LOOK SEE

see a man about a horse (or dog) *v phr* To take one's leave for some urgent purpose, esp to go to the bathroom or in earlier times to go have a drink or to meet one's bootlegger • Usu a smiling apology for one's departure; a bland euphemism to conceal one's true purpose *(1927+)*

seed *n* ROACH *(1960s+ Narcotics) See* HAYSEED

see eye to eye *v phr* To hold the same opinion or belief as another person(s) : *We see eye to eye on child-raising*

seen better days *v phr* To be exhausted or worn out; also, to have experienced better times : *skis have seen better days*

see pink elephants *v phr* To have hallucinations from alcoholism [1940+; said to have been originated by P G Wodehouse]

see red *v phr* To become very angry : *Politics make him see red (1897+)*

see stars *v phr* To be knocked unconscious : *boxer seeing stars*

see the light at the end of the tunnel *v phr* To see at last the beginning of the end of a difficult struggle, period, etc : *The Flower People of Saigon invite you to see the light at the end of the tunnel (Vietnam War period)*

see things *v phr* To hallucinate *(1922+)*

see-through *adj* Transparent; made of a very sheer fabric; PEEKABOO : *a see-through blouse (1950+)* *n* : *While empty office buildings (colorfully called "see-throughs") cluttered the skylines, investors did manage to cut their overall tax bills (1990s+)*

see someone's wheels turning *v phr* To observe that someone is thinking, analyzing, etc : *When my dog is in obedience class, I can see his wheels turning (1990s+)*

see-you *n* A customer who always asks to be waited on by a certain person *(1920s+ Salespersons)*

see you *interj* A casual farewell; SO LONG • Often with *around, soon, later,* or another modifier : *the careless "see you's" that people say (1891+)*

see you later, alligator *sentence* See you later • Jocular [1956; first recorded as the title of a song by R C Guidry, which was popularized by Bill Haley and the Comets]

segue or seg (SEHG way or SEHG) *n* 1 Transition from one piece of music, record, etc, to the next without an obvious break *(1937+ Musicians)* 2 A sequel; something that follows or follows up *(1970s+ College students)* *v* 1 To make a "segue" : *Then they segued to "Body and Soul" (1958+ Musicians)* 2 To go smoothly from one thing to another : *His features seg rapidly from fascination to fear (1972+)* [fr Italian, "now follows," an instruction on musical scores, found by 1740]

sell *n* A hoax or swindle; a deception : *The Cardiff Giant was a "sell" (1838+)* *v* 1 To cheat; swindle; hoax : *I've tunneled, hydraulicked, and cradled, and I have been frequently sold (1597+)* 2 To convince someone of the value of something : *But would it sell anybody else? I doubt it (1916+)* [first verb sense said in an article of 1810 to be derived from *sell a bargain*, "the dexterous transfer of any unmarketable commodity for a high price to an unwary customer"] *See* HARD SELL, SOFT SELL, be SOLD ON

sell oneself *v phr* To make oneself appealing and successful with an audience, a potential employer, etc *(1920s+)*

sell someone **down the river** *v phr* To betray someone; take victimizing advantage [1927+; fr slavery days, when a black person or escaped slave *sold down the river* was sent to or returned to the South, a use found by 1851]

sell like hot cakes *v phr* To enjoy very brisk sales : *The General's book sold like hot cakes (1839+)*

sell-out *n* An act or instance of selling out, in either sense : *He disappointed us, but he was honest enough and it was no sell-out/ The new bathing suits should be a quick sell-out (1862+ for betrayal, 1859+ for disposition of tickets, etc)*

sell out[1] *v phr* To become a traitor, esp to prostitute one's ideals, talents, etc, for money or other comforts : *are often labeled Toms and mammies who sold out/ accuse them of selling out Chiang Kai-shek (1888+)*

sell out[2] *v phr* To dispose of entirely by sale : *You can't get that here, we sold out (1796+)*

send *v* To arouse keen admiration, esp as an ecstatic response; excite; TURN someone ON : *Bessie Smith really sent him (1932+ Jazz talk)*

send down *v phr* To send or be sent to prison *(1840+)*

send-off *n* A funeral : *Give a man a classy send-off (1872+)*

send someone **packing** *v phr* To dismiss, get rid of *(1594+)*

send (or take) someone **to the cleaners** *v phr* To defraud of all or most of someone's money *(1907+)*

send someone **to the showers** *v phr* 1 To remove or eject a player, esp a pitcher, from a game *(1940s+ Baseball)* 2 To dismiss or reject someone *(1940s+)*

send-up *n* A mocking, teasing parody; lampoon; SPOOF : *just another stupid soap send-up/ a relentless send-up of attitudes and gestures (1958+ fr British)*

send up *v phr* 1 (also send up the river) To send someone to prison : *He got sent up for grand theft (1901+)* 2 To ridicule, esp by parody;

mock; lampoon; SPOOF : *cracking jokes, sending up everyone and everything in sight* (*1950s+*) [first sense fr or influenced by the course from New York City *up* the Hudson *River* to Sing Sing Prison at Ossining]

send someone **up the wall** *v phr* To make someone furious : *Mention of Picasso sends her up the wall* (*1966+*)

senior moment *n* A momentary lapse of memory, esp in older people; an incident of forgetfulness blamed on aging

sensaysh (sen SAYSH) *adj* Sensational : *I had a sensaysh time* (*1951+*)

separate the men from the boys *v phr* To show who is effective and who is not; separate the sheep from the goats : *Every mayor knows snow can separate the men from the boys, or the two-termers from the one-termers* (*1962+*)

sergeant *See* BUCK SERGEANT

serious *adj* **1** Very commendable; excellent; superb (*1940s+ Black*) **2** Intended to make a good and sober impression; overtly conformistic; sincere : *in a serious suit and striped tie* **3** Impressive; imposing; HEAVY, important : *He pushed a button activating some serious chimes* (*1980s+*) *See* FOR SERIOUS

seriously *adv* Very; extremely (*1981+*)

serve someone **right** *v phr* To be what someone deserves : *serves him right for being mean to her*

session *modifier* : *He used to do a lot of session playing but hardly ever worked for an audience* *n* **1** A dance or party; HOP (*1950s+ Teenagers*) **2** The period of intoxication from a dose of narcotics, esp of LSD; TRIP (*1960s+ Narcotics*) **3** An occasion at which a recording is made in a studio; a studio rehearsal or performance : *Horn is from an earlier session* (*1927+ Musicians*) *See* BITCH SESSION, BULL SESSION, GRIPE SESSION, HASH SESSION, JAM SESSION, RAP SESSION, SKULL SESSION

set *adj* Ready; prepared : *We were all set to go* (*1844+*) *n* **1** The group of pieces musicians perform during about a 45-minute period at a club, show, etc : *Clarinetist Scott opened his set* (*1590+*) **2** An improvisatory musical interchange of about half an hour (*1960s+ Jazz musicians*) **3** A small party or friendly conversational gathering; SCENE : *Don't stop belly rubbing just because we showed on the set* (*1960s+ Black & jazz talk*) **4** A discussion; RAP : *He never said get those Panthers out all through the whole set* (*1960s+ Black*) **5** A narcotic dose of two Seconals® and one amphetamine (*1960s+ Narcotics*) **6** A gang or subgang : *Mr Shakur was initiated into the Eight Trays, a "set" of the Crip gang based in his neighborhood* (*1990s+ Street gang*) [first noun sense in modern use since about 1925] *See* the JET SET

set someone **back** *v phr* To cost : *How much will it set me back if I order a plain steak?/ set us back what was then an astonishing $18 a person* (*1900+*)

set in concrete *See* NOT CARVED IN STONE

set of pipes *See* PIPES

set of wheels *n phr* A car : *if you're feverish for a great set of wheels* (*1940s+*)

set someone or something **straight** *v phr* To determine or specify the truth : *Let me set you straight on that allegation/ I've come to set the whole thing straight* (*1849+*)

settle *v* To imprison, esp for a life sentence : *Foley was "pinched" and "settled" in San Quentin* (*1899+*)

set-to *n* A contention; fight; bout : *Another venomous set-to among the politicians* (*1743+ Boxing*)

setup *n* **1** A person who is easily duped, tricked, etc; PATSY, SUCKER : *a set-up, a tout's dream come true* (*1926+*) **2** A one-day jail sentence (*1920s+ Underworld*) **3** A glass, ice, soda, etc, to be mixed with liquor : *They supplied the set-ups* (*1930+*) **4** Dishes, utensils, etc, constituting a place setting for a meal (*1934+ Lunch counter & restaurant*) **5** Arrangement; organization; situation; mode of operation : *except its size and its co-op set-up* (*1890+*) **6** A house, office, apartment, etc : *He has a very comfy setup in a rehabbed brownstone* (*1940s+*) [most senses apparently fr the setting up of billiard or pool balls to ensure a special or a trick shot]

set up[1] *adj* Gratified; elated; braced : *He looks real set up now that they've published his book* (*1930+*)

set up[2] *v phr* To arrange; prepare for : *set up a meet with the crook* (*1865+*)

set someone **up** *v phr* **1** To prepare and maneuver someone for swindling, tricking, etc; BUILD : *He was so vain it was easy to set him up* (*1875+*) **2** To gratify and encourage; brace : *Finishing first for a change really set me up* (*1526+*) **3** To treat someone; provide food or drink (*1880+*)

set-up pitcher *n phr* A relief pitcher who usually works fairly late in the game and prepares the situation for another relief pitcher known as a "closer" (*1980s+ Baseball*)

Seventh Avenue *n phr* The garment and fashion industry; the RAG TRADE [*1960s+*; fr the fact that New York City's *Seventh Avenue* is the traditional center of the garment industry]

seven-year itch *n* A time of serious dissatisfaction in a relationship or marriage, purportedly after the seventh year

sewer *n* A vein or artery : *if I had put it right in the sewer instead of skin popping* (*1960s+ Narcotics*)

sewermouth *n* A person who uses a lot of foul language

sew something up *v phr* **1** To finish; put the finishing touches on : *They sewed up the contract today* (1904+) **2** To ensure a victory; make a conclusive score, stroke, etc; CLINCH, ICE : *The last-period goal sewed it up for the Drew Rangers* (1960+)

sex *See* UNISEX

sexcapade *n* A sexual escapade (1965+)

sexed up *adj phr* **1** Made sexually more attractive; made more attractive or interesting **2** Sexually aroused

sex goddess *n phr* A woman, usu a movie star, who is a provocative and famous sexual object (1970s+)

sex someone in *v phr* To initiate a woman into a gang by enjoying her sexually : *Given the choice of being "beat in" or "sexed in" she chooses, the former but insists that both are merely ways of showing "love"* (1990s+ Street gang)

sex kitten (or **bunny** or **doll**) *n phr* A young woman who is highly attractive, provocative, and seemingly available sexually (*entry form* 1958+, *variants* 1970s+)

sexpert *n* A sex expert, esp a therapist who treats persons complaining of sexual dysfunction : *The behavioristic sexpert would call this situation homosexuality* (1924+)

sexploitation *modifier* : *a camp sexploitation horror musical n* Commercial exploitation of sex : *Female chauvinist sexploitation will reach a new level* (1940s+)

sexpot *n* A person, esp a woman, who is especially attractive and provocative sexually : *How pitiful the American who cannot command the smile of a sexpot* (1954+)

sex up *v phr* To make more sexy (1942+)

sexy *adj* Very appealing; exciting; desirable; stimulating : *Acid rain is politically sexy, but it hasn't half the allure of jobs* (1970+)

-sey *See* -IE

sez (or **sezz**) **you** *See* SAYS YOU

shack *n* **1** The caboose of a freight train (1899+ Railroad, hoboes & circus) **2** A railroad brake operator, who rode in the caboose (1899+ Railroad, hoboes & circus) **3** SHACK JOB (1940s+) *v* SHACK UP (1940s+) [fr *shack*, "hut, shanty," found by 1878, probably fr earlier *shackle* fr American Spanish *jacal* fr Aztec *xacalli*]

◁**shack job**▷ *n phr* A woman one lives with adulterously; common-law wife; mistress : *This was an early shack-job, not the girl mentioned above* (WWII Army)

shack man (or **rat**) *n phr* A man who lives with or does the sex act with a woman who is not his wife; a man who keeps a mistress (WWII Army)

shack up *v phr* **1** To live with, do the sex act with, and support a woman who is not one's wife; keep a mistress : *The medicine man had shacked up with a half-breed cook/ When I was 13 I shacked up with a Puerto Rican chick of 38* (1935+) **2** To do the sex act; esp, to lead a promiscuous sex life; SLEEP AROUND : *If you drink and shack up with strangers you get old at thirty* (1940s+) **3** To live; reside, esp in a nonpermanent place : *got rid of his home and shacked up in a hotel* (1950+)

shade *n* ◀1▶ A black person (1865+) **2** A receiver of stolen goods; FENCE : *It is sold to a "fence" or "shade"* (1925+ Underworld) *v* To defeat by a narrow margin : *Michigan shaded Iowa. The final score was 98 to 96* (1865+)

shades *n* Sunglasses (1950s+ Bop musicians)

shadow *n* : *They put a shadow on the suspect v* To follow a person secretly; do physical surveillance; TAIL (1872+) [verb sense found by 1602 in an isolated instance]

shaft *v* To treat unfairly or cruelly; victimize : *When do you shaft a pal, when do you hand him the poison cup?/ The oil companies you leased the land to shafted you out of an estimated $650 million* [1950s+; fr the notion of sodomizing a victim]

shaft, the, or a **shafting** *n phr* Unfair or cruel treatment : *Jamaicans have learned from past experience to expect the shaft from foreign journalists* (1950s+) *See* GET THE SHAFT, GIVE someone THE SHAFT

shafted *modifer* Screwed over; cheated : *shafted again by the same airline*

shag *adj* **1** With a date or escort : *Did you go to the party stag or shag?* (1940s+) **2** Excellent; wonderful (1950s+ Teenagers) *n* **1** A party or session where boys and girls experiment sexually (1930s+ Teenagers) **2** A person's date or escort; DRAG : *He didn't have a shag for the prom* (1950s+) *v* **1** To do the sex act; BOFF, SCREW (1788+) **2** To depart; leave, esp quickly; SHAG ASS : *You'd best shag now* (1851+) **3** To chase : *I was allowed to "shag" foul balls/ shagging rabbits* (1912+) **4** To tease and harass; HASSLE, HOUND (1930s+ Teenagers) [origin unknown; perhaps fr *shake* by way of *shack*] *See* GANG BANG

◁**shag ass**▷ *v phr* To depart; leave, esp hurriedly; HAUL ASS, SCRAM (1940s+)

shake *n* **1** RENT PARTY : *charge a few coins and have a shake* (1940s+) **2** A moment; SEC : *Be ready in two shakes* (1839+) **3** Blackmail or extortion; SHAKEDOWN : *This isn't any kind of a shake* (1930+) **4** : *We'd better give the entire house a shake; I know it's here somewhere v* **1** To come to an agreement; shake hands : *Let's shake and call it done* (1873+) **2** : *tried to shake one of the big boys* (1930+) **3** To search a person or place thoroughly; SHAKE DOWN

(*1960s+*) **4** GIVE someone THE SHAKE (*1883+*)
See a FAIR SHAKE, HALF A SHAKE, SKIN-SEARCH, TWO SHAKES

shake a leg *v phr* To hurry; speed up (*1904+*)

shake and bake *v phr* To go very fast : *But we gotta shake and bake through Pennsylvania, down 95, and you can't make time back here/ Roffe-Steinrotter, first among 56 skiers in a giant slalom course, told herself "whoever shakes and bakes the best is going to get the gold"* [*1990s+*; fr the trademark name of a brand of prebaking crumb coating for meats, used by putting the meat and the coating into a bag and shaking; probably referring to the quickness of the operation]

shakedown *n* **1** A night's lodging; an impromptu bed : *I'll get a shakedown on the couch* (*1730+*) **2** An instance of or a demand for blackmail, extortion, etc; victimization by the protection racket : *Listen, I know this is a shakedown* (*1902+ Underworld*) **3** A thorough search of a person or place; SHAKE : *We gave the room a first-class shakedown* (*1914+*) **4** A trying-out or first tentative use, esp of a machine, ship, process, etc : *Let's give this new idea a shakedown and see if it works* (*1930s+*) [final sense fr *shakedown cruise*; all senses fr the notion of a vigorous *shaking* of a person or place to reveal something hidden, a flaw, etc]

shake down *v phr* **1** To blackmail or extort; demand protection money : *shaking down poor peddlers, newsboys* (*1872+*) **2** To search a person or place thoroughly; SHAKE : *a couple of policemen to shake down the neighborhood* (*1915+*)

shake in one's shoes *v phr* To be terrified; fear greatly : *The mere thought has me shaking in my shoes* (*1818+*)

shake it or **shake it up** *v phr* To hurry; SHAKE A LEG : *We've got to shake it* (*1871+*)

shakeout *n* A business upheaval, esp a reduction in the number of competitors in a field; a spate of failures and bankruptcies : *The central event was a major shakeout and contraction of the Eurodollar market/ The recorded-music business is going through a significant shakeout* (*1895+*)

shake out *v phr* To develop; come to fruition; eventuate; COME OUT : *Let's just wait and see how it shakes out* (*1990s+*)

shaker *See* BONE-SHAKER

shakes, the *n phr* An attack of trembling, esp one due to alcoholism or drug abuse; the CLANKS (*1837+*)

shake-up *n* The reorganization of a working group, its methods, etc, usu including some dismissals : *The remedy is a shake-up in the Bureau of the Budget* (*1899+*)

shaking *See* WHAT'S SHAKING

shaky cam *n* A realistic, lower-quality camera effect used originally in advertisements and documentaries to simulate a sense of urgency or excitement : *shaky cam on "NYPD Blue"*

shalump *See* SCHLOOMP

shame *See* a DIRTY SHAME

shamus (SHAH məs, SHAY-) (also **shammus** or **shamos** or **shommus**) *n* **1** A police officer, private detective, security guard, etc; COP : *a British-accented burlesque of the tough American shamus/ Soon a character began to develop: a shamus named Marlowe* (*1925+*) **2** A police informer; STOOL PIGEON (*1940s+*) [fr Yiddish, "sexton of a synagogue," fr Hebrew *shamash*, "servant"; perhaps influenced by the Celtic name *Seamus*, "James," as a typical name of an Irish police officer]

shanghai *v* To put someone into an awkward situation by trickery; to force someone into a situation (*1871+*)

shank *n* **1** A stiletto-like weapon : *We'd yoke him with a shank/ looks like a large screwdriver and is known in prison parlance as a shank* (*1950s+ Prison & street gang*) **2** The end or last part of a period of time, esp of the evening ● Also interpreted as the early or chief part of a period of time : *Let's have one for the road, my friends; it's the shank of the evening* (*1828+*) *v* **1** To stab : *that dude the dicks want for shanking his old lady* **2** To kick : *is shanking punts all over the lot* (*1970s+ Football*) [all senses reflect the basic notion of something long and thin, like a leg bone]

shantytown *n* **1** A poor, dilapidated neighborhood **2** A cluster of makeshift dwellings, often on the edge of a town and inhabited by the vagrant or the very poor; hooverville (*1876+*)

shape up *v phr* **1** To progress; go along : *How are your plans shaping up?* (*1865+*) **2** (also **shape up or ship out**) To correct one's behavior; conform and perform ● Often a firm command or admonition : *From this day on you're going to shape up or ship out. Is that understood? (WWII armed forces, but 1938+*)

shape someone **up** *v phr* To cause someone to conform and perform; correct someone's behavior : *praying for a good depression that could shape these kids up (WWII armed forces)*

shark *n* **1** A confidence man or swindler; HUSTLER, SHARP (*1599+*) **2** A very able student, esp one who does not seem to work hard (*1895+ Students*) **3** An expert, esp a somewhat exploitive or unscrupulous one ● Usually preceded by a modifier showing the field of skill : *the gun-shark's report* (*1920s+*) **4** A lawyer (*1806+*) [all senses fr the predaceous fish, except that the oldest sense may originally have been fr German *schurke,* "rascal"] *See* CARDSHARP. LOAN SHARK

shark-bait *n* A lone or daring swimmer far from the shoreline (*1920+*)

sharp *adj* **1** Stylish; of the latest and most sophisticated sort : *He wore bow ties and sharp suits (1940+ Jive talk)* **2** Good; excellent; admirable; COOL : *I sound like everything was sharp (1940+ Jive talk) n* **1** An expert, esp at card games; PRO : *Hurstwood's a regular sharp* (*1840+*) **2** (also **sharper**) A confidence trickster; a swindler, esp a dishonest card player; CARDSHARP (*1688+*)

sharp as a tack *adj phr* Very intelligent and perceptive (*1922+*) *modifier* : *Becker is a Hollywood type: a driven, sharp-as-a-tack intelligence devoted to a completely second-rate subject* [*sharp as tacks* is found by 1912]

◁**shat on**▷ *v phr* Maltreated; victimized; SHAFTED : *Because women have been shat on for centuries* [1960s+; fr a humorous past-tense form of *shit,* found in the 1700s]

shatting on one's uppers *adj phr* Entirely out of money; BROKE : *She has to blow and she's shatting on her uppers* [1894+; fr *shat,* humorous past-tense form of *shit,* and *uppers,* "shoes so worn they have no soles"]

shave *v* To reduce : *They've shaved the estimate a little* (*1898+*)

shaved *adj* **1** Drunk (*1851+*) **2** Having the ornamental and other nonfunctional parts removed; STRIPPED DOWN (*1950s+ Hot rodders*)

shave points or **shave** *v phr* or *v* To get a gambling or money advantage by failing to score as much as one could; fraudulently lose a game : *Did they think I liked shaving the points? (1971+ Sports & gambling)*

shaver *See* LITTLE SHAVER

shaving *See* POINT-SHAVING

shay *See* GANG BANG

shazam (shə ZAM) *interj* An exclamation of triumphant and delighted announcement, emphasis, etc : *SHAZAM! He was up on the table/ Go ahead and say it, Shazam!, juice it up* [1940+; fr the operative or command word of a magician, similar to *presto change-o*]

shebang, the (shə BANG, shee-) *n* Everything; the WHOLE SHEBANG : *You can have the shebang* [1869+; fr *shebang,* "shanty, hut," found by 1862, of obscure origin; perhaps fr an approximate pronunciation of French *char-à-banc,* "buslike wagon with many seats," in which case the semantics of *the whole shebang* would depend upon the hiring of the whole vehicle rather than one or two seats]

◀**she can sit on my face anytime**▶ *sentence* She attracts me very powerfully in a basic sexual way (*1970s+*)

shed *See* WOODSHED

she-devil *n* A wicked and difficult woman; harridan; harpie : *Hell, I practically had the she-devil cornered* (*1840+*)

◁**shee-it**▷ (SHEE ət) *interj* SHIT [1960s+; humorous imitation of a drawled Southern pronunciation]

sheepskin *n* A college or university diploma [1804+; fr the fact that diplomas were once made of *sheepskin*]

sheesh[1] *interj* An exclamation of disgust, frustration, etc : *Sheesh! I mean, really! You know?* [1970s+; a euphemism for *shit*]

sheesh[2] *n* Hashish (*1960s+ Narcotics*)

sheisty *adj* Like a shyster; unscrupulous : *a sheisty thing to do*

sheive *See* SHIV

shekels (SHEK əls) *n* Money; wealth [1871+; fr the Hebrew name of a unit of weight and money]

shelf *See* ON THE SHELF

shell *v* To pay; SHELL OUT : *to shell at least a buck* (*1948+*) *See* HARD-SHELL

shellac or **shellack** *v* To defeat decisively; trounce; CLOBBER : *The Giants were shellacked again Monday* [1930+ Sports; perhaps fr the use of *shellac* as a finish]

shellacked *adj* Drunk : *One of the boys got beautifully shellacked* (*1922+*)

shellacking *n* **1** A beating : *"Shellacking" and numerous other phrases are employed by the police as euphemisms* **2** A decisive defeat; a drubbing; an utter rout : *Should Black take a shellacking, the National Leaguers are in bad trouble* (*1931+*)

shell game *n phr* A swindle; confidence game; SCAM : *I'm afraid this proposed merger looks like a shell game* [1890+; fr a version of three-card monte played with a pea or other token under walnut *shells*]

shell out *v phr* To pay; put out; contribute; FORK OVER : *get ready to shell out again/ or shell out the enormous amounts of money it takes to market software* (*1801+*)

shemale or **she-male** *n* **1** A female (*1854+*) **2** A tough woman or aggressive lesbian; BULLDYKE (*1972+*) *n* **3** A passive male homosexual **4** A transvestite (*1983+*)

shemozzle (also **shimozzle** or **shlamozzle** or **shlemozzle**) *n* A difficult and confused situation; an uproar; melee; mess. RHUBARB : *It became clear that the whole shlamozzle, introns and exons, are transcribed into RNA* (*1899+*) *v* To depart; POWDER, SCRAM (*1903+*) [ultimately probably fr Yiddish *shlim mazel,* "rotten luck," hence "a difficulty or misfortune," and related to *shlemazel*]

shenanigan or **shenanigans** *n* A trick or bit of foolery; a mild cheat or deception [1855+; origin unknown; perhaps fr Irish *sionnachuighim,* "play tricks, be foxy"]

Sherlock *n* A clever and perceptive person • Often sarcastic : *no shit, Sherlock*

shield *n* A police officer's badge

shift *See* GRAVEYARD SHIFT, LOBSTER SHIFT, SWING SHIFT

shift (or move) into high gear *v phr* To begin to work at top speed; become serious : *although the Senate hearings are just shifting into high gear* (1970+)

shift the goal posts *v phr* To change the rules or conditions disingenuously in order to win (1970s+)

shill *n* **1** (also **shillaber**) An associate of an auctioneer, gambler, hawker, etc, who pretends to be a member of the audience and stimulates it to desired action : *The shill is innocuous-looking* (1916+ *Circus*) **2** A barker, hawker, advertising or public relations person, or anyone else whose job is to stimulate business; FLACK (1940s+) *v* : *That summer he shilled for a sidewalk hawker* (1914+) [origin unknown; perhaps, since it is a shortening of *shillaber*, ultimately fr *Shillibeer*, the name of an early 1800s British owner of a large bus company, the reference being to persons hired as decoys to sit in buses and attract passengers]

shilly-shally *v* To vacillate; be irresolute : *For god sake, stop shilly-shallying and make up your mind* [1782+; found by 1700 in form *shill I shall I*]

shimmy *n* **1** A very energetic vibrational dance and dancing style **2** A flick or flirting of the buttocks : *She calls to the owner, with a little shimmy v* : *I wish that I could shimmy like my sister Kate* (1918+)

shimozzle *See* SHEMOZZLE

shindig *n* A party, reception, festival, etc, esp a noisy dancing party; CLAMBAKE [1871+; probably fr *shin dig*, "a blow on the shin incurred while dancing," found by 1859; perhaps by folk etymology fr the older *shindy*]

shindy *n* An uproar; a confused struggle; DONNYBROOK [1821+ Nautical; origin unknown; perhaps fr Irish *sinteag*, "skip, caper"; perhaps fr *shinny*, the name of a rough hockeylike schoolboy game; perhaps fr Romany *chindi*, "a cut, a cutting up"]

shine *modifier* ◀1▶ : *another shine killing n* ◀1▶ A black person (1908+) **2** Bootleg whiskey; MOONSHINE : *non-blinding shine sold in fruit jars* (1929+) *v* To reject; disregard; avoid; SKIP : *But I always end up shining the rad guys who like me* (1970s+ *Teenagers*) [the racial sense may have originated among blacks, may refer to the glossiness of a very black skin, and hence may reflect the caste system based upon color; among white speakers, this sense was surely influenced by the fact that most *shoeshine* persons were

black; the teenager sense has a black parallel, *shine on*, and the origin may be the poetic notion that when one turns one's back on something, one is letting his "moon (that is, buttocks) *shine on*" it] *See* MONKEYSHINES, STICK IT, TAKE A SHINE TO someone or something, WHERE THE SUN DOESN'T SHINE

shine someone on *v phr* **1** To reject and ignore someone; abandon someone : *I gotta cut this maniac loose. I gotta shine him on* **2** To deceive someone; beguile; BAMBOOZLE, SCAM : *Don't shine me on, buddy boy. I've been yessed by the best* (1970s+) *See* SHINE

shiner *n* **1** A bruise near the eye; BLACK EYE, MOUSE : *a pip of a shiner* (1904+) **2** A shiny table top or other mirrorlike surface a dealer can use to see the faces of the cards he deals (1909+ *Gambling*)

shingle *n* A signboard, esp one designating professional services : *He got him a shingle and started practice last year* (1847+) *See* HANG UP one's SHINGLE, SHIT ON A SHINGLE

shinny or **shinny up** *v* To climb a rope, pole, wall, etc [1888+; fr the use of *shins* and ankles in climbing a rope or pole]

Shinola *See* NO SHINOLA, NOT KNOW SHIT FROM SHINOLA

ship *See* SHAPE UP

shirt *See* BET YOUR BOOTS, GIVE someone THE SHIRT OFF one's BACK, KEEP one's SHIRT ON, LOSE ONE'S SHIRT, SHIMMY, SKIVVY, STUFFED SHIRT

shirtsleeve *adj* Simple and unpretentious; down-to-earth : *Here's what that means in shirtsleeve English* (1908+)

shirttail *adj* Impoverished; mean; paltry : *My brother and I had a pretty shirttail existence as kids* (1929+) *n* An editorial column : *The boss blurbed the story in his shirttail* (1944+ Newspaper office) [both senses depend on the *shirttail* being a short appendage to a shirt; the first sense derives fr the shortness, hence meagerness; the second fr the appendedness, the editor's personal addition]

◁**shit**▷ *interj* An exclamation of disbelief, disgust, disappointment, emphasis, etc : *Oh, shit, I missed the bus!* (1920+) *modifier* : *as well as shit loans to companies like Massey-Ferguson and Turbo Resources n* **1** Feces; excrement; CRAP, POO (by 800s or earlier) **2** Nonsense; pretentious talk; bold and deceitful absurdities; BULLSHIT : *Neighborhood watch, public vigil, shit like that* (1940s+) **3** Offensive and contemptuous treatment; disrespect; insults : *She don't take no shit from nobody* (1903+) **4** Anything of shoddy and inferior quality; pretentious and meretricious trash; CRAP, DRECK : *that ricegrinding piece of shit* (1930+) **5** One's possessions; one's personal effects : *Get your shit, both of you are moving* (1970s+) **6** An obnoxious, disgusting, or contemptible person; a despicable wretch; PRICK. SHITHEEL (*1508+*) **7** Heroin or marijuana; also, other drugs : *insisted on retaining the word "shit" as junkie slang for heroin* (*1940s+ Narcotics*) **8** Nothing; the least quantity; DIDDLY : *of whom I hadn't seen shit/ Engine's froze up, frame's out of line, not worth shit* (*1922+*) **9** Misfortune; hardship; GRIEF : *If you can keep those fucking maggots quiet, you're not going to get any shit from us* (*1937+*) *v* **1** : *They diurnally shit, shave, and shower* (*1308+*) **2** To lie; exaggerate; try to deceive : *"Don't shit me,"* said *Dina/ "You're shitting me, baby," he said/ The sky's the limit, Wilson, I shit you not* (*1934+*) **3** To respond powerfully, esp with alarm, anger, or panic; SHIT A BRICK : *He'll shit when we tell him about this* (*1960s+*) *See* ACT LIKE one's SHIT DOESN'T STINK, ALL THAT KIND OF CRAP, BAD SHIT, BLAZES, BULLSHIT, CHICKEN SHIT, CLEAN UP one's ACT, CROCK, DIDDLY, DOES A BEAR SHIT IN THE WOODS, DOODLE-SHIT, EAT SHIT, FULL OF SHIT, GOOD SHIT, HAVE SHIT FOR BRAINS, HOLY COW, HORSESHIT, HOT SHIT, I'LL BE DAMNED, LIKE HELL, LIKE PIGS IN CLOVER, LIKE SHIT THROUGH A TIN HORN, NO SHIT, NOT GIVE A DAMN, NOT KNOW BEANS, NOT KNOW SHIT FROM SHINOLA, PIECE OF SHIT, PILE OF SHIT, SCARE THE SHIT OUT OF someone, SHOOT THE BULL, SHOVEL THE SHIT, TAKE A DUMP, TAKE SHIT, THINK one's SHIT DOESN'T STINK, TICKLE THE SHIT OUT OF someone, TOUGH SHIT, TREAT someone LIKE A DOORMAT

◁**shit a brick (or bricks)**▷ *v phr* To be very upset and angry; have an emotional crisis; SWEAT BULLETS : *At Cheri's, Mott was shitting a brick/ I had a few scenes where I was really shittin' bricks* (*1961+*)

◁**shit-all**▷ *adj* Not any; none at all; : *Monica, we have shit-all evidence of what the killer looks like* [*1970s+*; related to and perhaps derived from 1930s British *bugger-all* and *fuck-all* in the same sense, used as intensives and based on *not at all;* Dylan Thomas's mythical Welsh village *Llareggub* has a pseudo-Welsh name, which is *bugger-all* spelled backwards]

◁**shit a shitter**▷ *See* DON'T SHIT A SHITTER

◁**shit-ass**▷ *n* **1** An insignificant, contemptible person; JERK, pootbutt **2** SHITHEEL *v* To behave like a despicable or contemptible person, esp by betrayal of a duty or promise : *I don't want anybody shitassing out of it* (*1940s+*)

◁**shit-bag**▷ *n* A completely despised, contemptible person or thing : *Outta my way, shitbag*

◁**shitbox**▷ *n* A worthless, contemptible person : *Get your own candy, shitbox*

◁**shit bullets**▷ *See* SWEAT BULLETS

◁**shitbum**▷ *n* SHITHEEL : *Mooney was a shitbum* (*1980s+*)

◁**shitcan**▷ *v* To discard; throw away; abandon : *If it rained before he entered the tunnel, he would have to shitcan his plans/ I'd already kind of shitcanned the idea* [*1970s+*; fr *shitcan*, "refuse can"]

◁**shit creek**▷ *See* UP SHIT CREEK

◁**shit doesn't stink,** one's▷ *See* THINK one's SHIT DOESN'T STINK

◁**shiteater**▷ *n* A contemptible person; DILDO, JERK, PECKERHEAD : *Those shiteaters accepted the deal. The Communist Party of Cuba was now demanding dues in dollars* (*1940s+*)

◁**shit-eating**▷ *adj* Stupid; self-satisfied : *He has eased himself into a series of chuckling, expansive, shit-eating parts* (*1960s+*)

◁**shit-eating (or turd-eating) grin**▷ *n phr* An expression of smug satisfaction; a stupid gloating look : *Go ahead, sit there with that shit-eating grin on your face/ stood with them, a stupid turd-eating grin on my face* (*1960s+*)

◁**shit-faced**▷ *adj* Drunk : *We'd get totally shitfaced* (*1960s+ Students*)

◁**shit fit**▷ *See* HAVE A SHIT FIT

◁**shit-for-brains**▷ *n* A very stupid person : *What's old Shit-for-brains trying to say?* (*1950s+*) *See* HAVE SHIT FOR BRAINS

◁**shit happens**▷ *sentence* Bad things come to pass in this sad world : *Another shrug. "Shit happens"* (*1980s+*)

◁**shithead or shitface**▷ *n* **1** A stupid, confused, and blundering person; FUCK-UP : *And you'll look like a shithead for backing him in the first place* **2** SHITHEEL : *And this shithead comes sneaking around, asking questions* (*1940s+*)

◁**shitheel**▷ *n* A despicable person; a scoundrel and blackguard; BASTARD, PRICK [*1935+*; probably an intensive form of *heel;* in a tradition of scorn for people who have excrement on their shoes, for example, *shit-shoe,* found by 1903, and *shit-kicker,* by the 1960s]

◁**shit hits the fan,** the▷ *sentence* Trouble breaks out; a fearful crisis ensues; things turn nasty • Often part of a time clause beginning with when or then : *The shit is going to hit the fan, buddy/ The shit didn't hit the fan till this guy, Eddie Jaffe, takes the pad* [*1930s+*; fr the classical joke about the man who, finding no toilet, defecated into a hole in the floor; back downstairs, finding the barroom emptied of its celebrants, he inquired why, and was asked, "Where were you when the shit hit the fan?"]

◁**shithole**▷ *n* **1** The anus; ASSHOLE, POOP CHUTE (*1903+*) **2** A disgusting place; SHITHOUSE : *You must move out of this shithole* (*1960s+*)

◁**shithouse**▷ *n* **1** A toilet : *This ain't no shithouse, man* **2** A filthy, sloppy place; a shambles : *The kid's room was always a shithouse* (*1795+*) *See* BUILT LIKE A BRICK SHITHOUSE

◁shit (or go shit) in your hat▷ *sentence* GO
TO HELL, GO FUCK oneself : *It's unfair, but say so
and people tell you to go shit in your hat*
[1950s+; the similar *shit in your teeth* is
found by 1903]

◁shitkickers or shit stompers▷ *n* or *n phr*
Heavy boots such as farm, cowboy, or hiking boots : *I never see you in anything but those
old shitkickers* (1960s+)

◁shit-kicking▷ *adj* Rough and rural; crude;
stupid : *It's down-home, shit-kickin', ball-
scratchin' country/ gets to carry a piece and
wear that shit-kicking grin*

◁shitless▷ *See* SCARED SHITLESS, SCARE someone
SHITLESS

◁shit (or crap) list▷ *n phr* One's fancied or
real list of persons who are hated, not trusted, to be avoided, etc : *You're going to be on
Professor What's-Her-Face's shit list when she
finds you* (1942+)

◁shitload, a (or shitpot)▷ *n* A very large
number or amount; a shithouse full : *They
sure sell a shitload of them/ make a shitload of
noise/ a whole shitpot of that stuff* (1970s+)

◁shit money▷ *v phr* To be extremely lucrative : *Well, he owns that bakery, which just
shits money* (1980s+)

◁shit on someone or something▷ *interj* An
exclamation of powerful disgust, contempt,
rejection, etc : *Shit on his suggestions!*

◁shit on a shingle▷ *n phr* Creamed chipped
beef on toast, or some similar delicacy
(*WWII Army*)

◁shit on wheels▷ *n phr* HOT SHIT

◁shit or get off the pot▷ *modifier* : *It's shit-
or-get-off-the-pot time* *sentence* (Variation:
piss may replace **shit**) FISH OR CUT BAIT
(1950s+)

◁shit out of luck▷ *adv phr* Having no chance
of success; already too late for what one
wants; very ill-starred; OUT OF LUCK, SOL : *I
guess I'm shit out of luck on this one* (WWI
armed forces)

◁shit one's pants (or in one's pants)▷ *v phr*
(Variations: **drawers** may replace **pants**) To
become frightened; be scared; panic : *Don't
shit your pants, it's only the cat/ Michael was
shitting in his drawers* (1940s+)

◁shits, the▷ *n phr* Diarrhea; the TROTS
(1930+) *See* the GIS

◁shitsky▷ *interj* Oh, shit! : *Shitsky, the cops
are coming n* A despicable person or thing :
ya little shitsky

◁shitstick▷ *n* A contemptible, stupid person;
SHIT-ASS [1903+; the dated form is *shitsticks*]

◁shitstorm▷ *n* A very confused situation or
affair; a crazy jumble : *an artist trying to turn
the shitstorm of his life into music/ Nothing like
a shit storm to improve his mood* [1970s+;
perhaps modeled on *firestorm*]

◁shitsure▷ *adv* Very certainly; definitely :
Shitsure it's gonna be a rough winter [probably
modeled on *sure as shit*]

◁shitter▷ *n* A toilet : *Know where the movie
of the week went? Right in the old shitter*
(1960s+)

◁shitty▷ *adj* 1 Mean; malicious; nasty : *accepted what he characterized as his "shitty
offer"* 2 Tedious and unpleasant; futile; wearing : *a real shitty day* 3 Unwell; ill : *Ralph, I
feel shitty tonight* (1920s+)

◁shitty (or shit) end of the stick, the▷ *See*
GET THE SHITTY END OF THE STICK

◁shitwork▷ *modifier* : *something better than
shitwork jobs n* Menial and tedious work;
degrading routine work; scut work : *the
boredom, the shitwork, the perpetual deadlines*
(1960s+)

shiv (Variations: **chev** or **chib** or **chiv** or **chive**
or **sheive** or **shive**) *n* 1 A knife, esp a clasp
knife or similar weapon : *She gets this anonymous letter sticking the shiv in my back/ The big
knife called the chib* 2 A razor; anything with a
sharp cutting edge *v* : *being shivved by Johnny
Mizzoo* [1912+; fr Romany *chiv*, "blade," by
way of British underworld slang]

shlamozzle *See* SHEMOZZLE

shlang or **shlong** *See* SCHLONG

shlemiel *See* SCHLEMIEL

shlemozzle *See* SCHLEMAZEL, SHEMOZZLE

shlep *See* SCHLEP

shleppy *See* SCHLEPPY

shlock *See* SCHLOCK

shlocky *See* SCHLOCKY

shlontz *See* SCHLONTZ

shloomp or **shlump** *See* SCHLOOMP

shlub or **shlubbo** *See* ZHLUB

shlunk *v* To cover in a viscid and repellent way
: *He dumped the bucket of slime and let it shlunk
all over me* [1970s+; apparently a quasi-
Yiddish echoism]

shmaltz *See* SCHMALTZ

shmaltzy *See* SCHMALTZY

shmatte *See* SCHMATTE

shmear or **shmeer** *See* SCHMEAR[1], the WHOLE
SCHMEAR

shmeck or **shmack** *See* SCHMECK, SMACK

shmegeggy *See* SCHMEGEGGY

shmendrick *See* SCHMENDRICK

shmo or **shmoe** *See* SCHMO

shmooz *See* SCHMOOZ

shmotte *See* SCHMATTE

shmuck *See* SCHMUCK

shnook *See* SCHNOOK

shnozz *See* SCHNOZZ

shocker *n* An unpleasant or disagreeable person or thing, as a bad sporting event : *ran a
shocker of a race* (1958+)

shock jock *n phr* A radio entertainer who
uses vulgar and sensational language : *The*

Federal Communications Commission is warning "shock jocks" that they will be fined if they broadcast indecent material during daylight hours (late 1980s+)

shoe See GUMSHOE

shoehorn v To insinuate by effort; force or fit in : Attorney General Griffin Bell managed to shoehorn an energy pitch into a speech

shoestring adj Tight; low-cost : shoestring budget

shoestring catch n phr A catch made near the ground, usu by an outfielder while running, stooping, and lunging (1912+ Baseball)

shommus See SHAMUS

sho-nuff adv Surely; certainly : but Tip (a peaceful Nubian sho-nuff) settled his beef [1880+; presumed black pronunciation of sure enough]

shoo-in or **shoe-in** modifier : to be a shoe-in candidate n 1 A horse that wins a race by prearrangement (1928+ Horse racing) 2 A person, team, candidate, etc, certain to win; CINCH, SURE THING : The big, powerful Trojans were the shoo-ins (1939+) [shoe-in may simply be a misspelling, but it is probably based on a misunderstanding of the origin of the term; it is a sort of folk etymology]

shoo in v phr To cause a particular horse, esp an inferior one, to win a race [1908+ Horse racing; fr the notion that the beast, not caring to run and not needing to, can be shooed over the finish line and win]

shook up (also **shook** or **all shook** or **all shook up**) adj phr or adj 1 In a state of high excitement or extreme disturbance; very much upset : So Woody kept his voice down, but he was all shook up (entry form 1897+, first variant 1891+) 2 Very happy; exhilarated; HIGH : I expected years in prison; they let me go free, boy was I shook up (1950s+ Teenagers & rock and roll) [revived and popularized in 1950s by Elvis Presley]

shoot interj 1 An invitation to speak, explain, etc : Just a minute. Okay. Shoot (1915+) 2 A mild exclamation of disgust, disappointment, distress, etc•A euphemism for shit : Shoot, it's just the whiskey (late 1800s+) n 1 A photographic or movie-making session : It was not an easy shoot (1970s+) 2 SHOOT THE BREEZE (1940s+) v 1 To photograph, esp to make a movie : They were shooting over in Jersey (1890+) 2 SHOOT UP (1914+ Narcotics) ◁3▷ (also **shoot off**) To ejaculate semen; COME (1922+) 4 To play certain games : watch the flamingos, shoot a little golf, grow a little garden (1926+) [fourth verb sense by 1891 in the case of craps] See TURKEY-SHOOT

shoot (or **fire**) **blanks** v phr To do the sex act without causing pregnancy; suffer male infertility : This guy was shooting blanks. This guy's wad's all dead

shoot bricks v phr To throw the ball ineptly : Especially the free throws. I mean, we were shooting some bricks out there tonight (1990s+ Basketball)

shoot one's **cookies** v phr (Variations: **break-fast** or **dinner** or **lunch** or **supper** may replace **cookies**; **toss** or **lose** may replace **shoot**) To vomit; BARF, RALPH : If I'm any judge of color, you're going to shoot your cookies/ smelled like someone just tossed his cookies (entry form 1920s+)

shoot someone **down** (or **down in flames**) v phr To defeat someone; thwart or ruin someone's efforts; BLOW someone OUT OF THE WATER : Woody, who had been flying along, level and smooth, was shot down in flames (1940s+)

shoot-'em-up modifier : an exaggerated reaction to the male-oriented "shoot-'em-up games" n A movie or TV program with much gunplay and violence : gambled for cigarettes, slurped Tang or watched shoot-'em-ups on TV (1953+)

shooter See PEASHOOTER, SIX-SHOOTER, SQUARE SHOOTER

shoot from the hip v phr To act or respond impulsively and aggressively; be recklessly impetuous; HAVE A SHORT FUSE : A politician should seldom shoot from the hip [1970s+; fr the image of a gunfighter who fires his weapon without aiming, as just drawn from the holster]

shoot hoops v phr To play impromptu basketball; try for baskets : The Boys shoot hoops and zip around on skateboards (1980s+)

shooting gallery n phr 1 A place where a narcotics user can get a dose or injection 2 A party or gathering where narcotics users take injections : in a fellow musician's hotel room during a "shooting gallery" (dope party) (1950s+ Narcotics)

shooting iron n phr A firearm, esp a pistol (1775+)

shooting match See the WHOLE SHOOTING MATCH

shoot oneself in the foot v phr To wound or injure oneself by ineptitude; attack wildly and hurt oneself : Ted Turner has taken to shooting himself in the foot/ a situation, Vance writes, "where we were shooting ourselves in the foot" (1970s+)

◁**shoot** one's **load**▷ v phr To ejaculate semen; have an orgasm; COME (1920s+)

shoot off one's **mouth** v phr (Variations: **bazoo** or **face** or **gab** or **yap** may replace **mouth**) To talk irresponsibly and inappropriately, esp to bluster and brag; TALK BIG : You come busting in here and shoot off your bazoo at me (entry form 1864+)

shoot-out *n* **1** (also **shoot-up**) A gunfight : *the justly famous shoot-out between the Earps and the Clantons in the O-K Corral/ The shoot-up may have been a skirmish between Mafia factions* (*1950s+*) **2** Any fight or violent confrontation; a hotly contested game or issue : *the simple corporate shoot-out reported by the newspapers/ another sociological shoot-out, with men as the heroes this time* (*1970s+*) **3** A form of tiebreaker used in the North American Soccer League, in which five players from each team have five seconds each to attempt goals one-on-one against the goalkeeper (*1978+ Soccer*) **4** An invitational basketball tournament (*1990s+ Basketball*)

shoot the breeze (or **the fat**) *v phr* To chat amiably and casually; CHEW THE FAT : *making transatlantic calls just to shoot the breeze/ enjoying ourselves and shooting the breeze/ sit down on a bench and shoot the fat* (*1941+*)

◁**shoot the bull** (or **crap** or **shit**)▷ *v phr* **1** To lie and exaggerate; talk grandly but emptily; BULLSHIT : *And they weren't just shooting the crap* **2** To chat amiably; SHOOT THE BREEZE : *stand on a corner, shoot the bull/ The basketball guys shoot the shit during timeouts* (*1928+*)

shoot the lights out *v phr* To excel; perform superbly : *These kids will jump right up and shoot the lights out on you/ He shoots the lights out in physics, calculus, biology* [1970s+ Sports; perhaps fr the accuracy of marksmanship implied if one is to hit a small target like a *lightbulb*; certainly influenced by the notion of knocking the *daylights*, or earlier the *liver and lights*, "liver and lungs, innards," out of someone or something]

shoot the works *v phr* To act, give, spend, etc, without limit; GO FOR BROKE : *In whatever pertains to comfort, shoot the works* [1922+; fr the *shooting* of dice in craps, with its extended sense of betting or gambling all one has]

shoot-up *n* A narcotics injection (*1920s+ Narcotics*) See SHOOT-OUT

shoot up *v phr* To take an injection of narcotics; jab a vein, MAINLINE (*1920s+ Narcotics*)

shoot one's wad *v phr* **1** To commit or bet everything one has; GO FOR BROKE, SHOOT THE WORKS **2** To say everything one can on a subject; have one's say **3** To exhaust one's resources; be unable to persist ◁**4**▷ SHOOT one's LOAD [1914+; fr the *wad* of cloth formerly stuffed into a gun barrel to keep the shot and powder in place]

shop *v* To sell; promote; merchandise : *Sid says I need a lawyer to shop me to the non-paying media/ Jacoby has shopped this event around since the day he got here* (*1980s+*) See BUCKET SHOP, CHOP SHOP, HEAD SHOP

shopaholic *n* A person addicted to shopping : *He accuses me of being a shopaholic. I admit that sometimes I spend more than I should* (*1990s+*)

shop around *v phr* **1** To search for something or someone : *I heard he was shopping around for a new Secretary of the Interior* **2** To compare prices, services, etc : *I really wish I had more time to shop around before buying that yacht* (*1922+*)

shopping bag lady *See* BAG LADY

shopping list *See* LAUNDRY LIST

short *n* **1** A prisoner, soldier, etc, near the end of his term (*1925+*) **2** A car; WHEELS (*1932+*) **3** A small drink, esp of hard liquor, or small potent beer *v* **1** To inhale a narcotic in crystal or powder form; SNORT (*1960s+ Narcotics*) **2** To give someone less of something than what was agreed upon : *shorted her on fortune cookies* [automobile sense apparently fr *hot short*, "a stolen car," *short* having come to mean "streetcar" and then "car"; *streetcar* because its runs were *short* compared with those of a train]

short end of the stick *See* GET THE SHITTY END OF THE STICK

short fuse *See* HAVE A SHORT FUSE

short hairs *See* HAVE someone BY THE SHORT HAIRS

short heist *n phr* Petty theft, shoplifting, pursesnatching, etc (*1970s+ Underworld*)

short on *modifier* Having less than desirable (*1922+*)

short one, a *n phr* A single shot of whiskey, often drunk quickly; a small drink (*1859+*)

short-sheet *v* To play a nasty trick; maltreat : *headed for big things until the Reagan crowd short-sheeted you/ England's favorite recreational activity, shortsheeting the royals* [fr a student and barracks practical joke in which a *bedsheet* is folded in half and made to appear as an upper and lower sheet, so when the victim gets into bed the stretching legs and toes are painfully arrested]

shortstop *v* **1** To take food being passed to someone else at the table **2** To wait on another salesperson's customer (*1940s+*)

shorty or **shortie** *n* A very short person; DUSTY BUTT (*1888+*)

shot *adj* **1** Drunk (*1864+*) **2** (also **shot to hell**) Worn out or out of repair : *This old machine is shot* (*1930+*) **3** Exhausted; ill; in bad shape : *Say, am I shot?* (*1939+*) *n* **1** A drink of straight liquor (*1676+*) **2** A glass or other serving of Coca-Cola® (*1950s+ Southern & Western lunch counter*) **3** An injection of narcotics; FIX (*1920s+ Narcotics*) **4** An atomic explosion, a rocket or missile launching, or some other complex sort of military and technological blasting (*1950s+*) **5** A person's particular preference, style, etc; BAG, THING : *That's our shot. That's who we are* (*1960s+*) **6** A try; an attempt, esp at something rather difficult : *He didn't make it, but he gave it a hell of a shot* (*1840+*) **7** A very hard-hit ball, usu a line drive, and often a home run (*1880+ Baseball*) **8** A televison appearance : *But it was the exposure on television that seemed to count most ... with a shot on "Good Morning America" believed to be worth its weight in votes* (*1980s+*) **9** Interpretation; understanding; opinion; guess; TAKE : *Gimme your shot on Leon. You know, tell me about him* (*1980s+*) [the drinking senses are shortenings of an early 1800s expression *shot in the neck*, meaning both "a drink" and "drunk"; *shoot*, "to guess," is found by 1864] *See* BEAVER SHOT, CALL THE SHOTS, CHEAP SHOT, GIVE something A SHOT, GIVE something one's BEST SHOT, GRAB SHOT, HALF-SHOT, HAVE A CRACK AT something, HOT SHOT, LONG SHOT, MUG SHOT, NOT BY A LONG SHOT, ONE-SHOT

shot across the bow, a *n phr* A warning or admonition : *White House dithering led the Republican whip to fire a warning shot across the Administration's bow* [1990s+; fr an old naval practice]

shotgun *interj* I am going to ride in the front passenger seat! : *yelled Shotgun for the test drive modifier* (also **blunderbuss**) Very diffuse and general; indiscriminate; done in haste; SCATTERGUN : *I hate it when the administrators make shotgun accusations/ But this is a blunderbuss technique* (*1930s+*) *n* **1** A machine gun or other rapid-fire gun (*WWII Army*) **2** A type of pipe used for smoking marijuana; BONG (*1960s+ Narcotics*) **3** An offensive formation in which the quarterback lines up well behind instead of immediately behind the center (*1966+ Football*) *See* RIDE SHOTGUN, SIT SHOTGUN

shotgun approach *n phr* A very broad and undiscriminating judgment or action : *It's no good taking a shotgun approach to this matter of addiction* [1960s+; similarly, *shotgun prescription* is found by 1903]

shotgun quiz *See* POP QUIZ

shotgun wedding (or marriage) *n phr* A wedding under duress, esp when the bride is pregnant; a forced marriage; MILITARY WEDDING (*1927+*)

shot in the arm, a *n phr* Something that stimulates and enlivens; an invigorating influence or event : *has given his campaign for the Democratic presidential nomination a shot in the arm* (*1922+*)

shot in the dark *n* A wild guess or try; an attempt that has little chance of success

shoulda coulda woulda *sentence* One ought to have and would have done some-thing • An expression of regret : *"Shoulda, coulda, woulda," the First Lady replied. "We didn't"* (*1970s+*)

shoulder *See* COLD SHOULDER, STRAIGHT FROM THE SHOULDER

shouldn't happen to a dog *See* IT SHOULDN'T HAPPEN TO A DOG

shout *n* **1** A hymn or traditional blues song, esp when sung with a heavily accented beat (*1930s+ Jazz musicians*) **2** An exclamation point (*1950s+ Print shop*) **3** A call, esp on the telephone : *Stradazzi wants you to give him a shout* (*1980s+*) [in the musical sense, *shout*, "a black religious song and dance," is found by 1862]

shout-out *n* A mentioning of a person verbally or in writing, esp to show respect; an acknowledgment given a person during a radio or television show : *The Beatles gave a shout-out to their manager*

shove *v* **1** To pass counterfeit money (*1850+*) **2** To kill; HIT : *Who shoved her?* (*1940s+ Underworld*) **3** SHOVE OFF (*1856+*) *See* KNOW WHAT one CAN DO WITH something, PUSH COMES TO SHOVE, TELL someone WHAT TO DO WITH something

shove it *See* STICK IT

◁**shovel shit (or the shit)**▷ *v phr* To lie and exaggerate; BULLSHIT, SHOOT THE BULL : *I was just fooling, shoveling the shit a little/ no varsity letters for shoveling shit* (*1930s+*)

shove off *v phr* **1** To leave; depart; SCRAM : *when we shoved off* (*1844+*) **2** To kill; murder : *People got shoved off for their money* (*1939+ Underworld*) [fr the boating term for pushing the craft away from a dock, ship's side, etc]

shover *See* PENCIL-PUSHER

show *v* To arrive; appear; SHOW UP : *You suppose he'll show?* (*1300+*) *See* CATTLE SHOW, LET'S GET THE SHOW ON THE ROAD, NO-SHOW, ONE-MAN SHOW, PEEP SHOW

show-and-tell *n* An elaborate display, usu for selling or other persuasion; DOG AND PONY ACT : *There just hasn't been time to arrange the kind of show-and-tell that attracts media attention/ No one seems to have been impressed by the show-and-tell* [1970s+; fr the name of an elementary-school teaching technique of the late 1940s where pupils exhibit and explain things]

show biz *n phr* The entertainment industry; show business (*1940s+*)

showboat *n* (also **showboater**) : *even your most hardassed right wingers had some showboat in them/ Jesse is a showboater, privately* (*1953+*) *v* **1** To behave in a showy, flamboyant way; GRANDSTAND, HOT DOG : *And, please, no showboating, fist-pounding, breast-beating, or blamecasting* (*1951+*) **2** PULL RANK (*1960s+*)

show business *See* THAT'S SHOW BUSINESS

showdown *modifier* : *the opening game of the showdown Yankee–Red Sox series* **n 1** A hand where the cards are dealt face up and the best hand wins at once *(1901+ Poker)* **2** A confrontation, esp a last one *(1904+)*

shower *See* GOLDEN SHOWER, SEND someone TO THE SHOWERS

shower scum *n phr* A completely despised person : *shower scum down the street*

show-off *n* A person who habitually shows off; HOT DOG, SHOWBOAT : *Speedo swimsuit and a globe tied to his shoulder. Show-off*

show off *v phr* To behave in an ostentatiously skilled and assured way in order to impress others; GRANDSTAND, HOT DOG : *He ran a quick eight miles, just showing off (1793+)*

show someone **the door** *v phr* To dismiss someone summarily; eject someone *(1778+)*

showtime, (it's) *interj* It is time to start (esp an exciting activity)

show up *v phr* To arrive; be present; appear : *I had to show up to make a touch (1888+)*

show someone or something **up** *v phr* To reveal; expose : *That slip showed him up for a fraud (1826+)*

shpritz *n* A bit or touch; a dose : *each a free-associational shpritz of surreal hi-de-ho* [1970s+; fr Yiddish, literally, "a squirt"]

shrapnel *n* A meager tip of coins

shriek *n* **1** An exclamation point; BANG, SHOUT *(1864+ Print shop)* **2** Distilled and concentrated heroin; BLACK TAR *(mid-1980s+)*

shrimp *n* A very short or small person; PEANUT *(1386+)*

shrink *n* A psychiatrist, psychoanalyst, or other psychotherapist; HEADSHRINKER *(1960+)*

shrinking violet *n phr* A self-effacing person : *Theodore Roosevelt was no shrinking violet* [1915+; fr the presumed shyness of the *violet*]

shroom or **'shroom** *n* **1** A hallucinogenic mushroom, *Psilocybe mexicana* : *Shroom seekers have bumper crop (1980s+ Narcotics)* **2** Any mushrooms : *shrooms on the pizza*

shtick or **schtick** or **shtik** *n* **1** A small theatrical role or part of a role; a piece of theatrical "business"; BIT : *It turned out to be a nice little "shtick" (1961+ Show business)* **2** A characteristic trait of performance or behavior; a typical personal feature : *To each his own schtick. Chapman performs his with gusto (1968+ Show business)* **3** A clever device; GADGET, GIMMICK : *The "shtick" is that the taped remarks of a number of political figures are tacked onto questions dreamed up by writers (1966+)* **4** One's special area of interest or activity; BAG, SCENE : *Post-post literary theory is not my shtick (1968+)* [fr Yiddish, literally, "piece, bit"]

shtoonk or **shtunk** *See* SCHTOONK

◁**shtup** or **schtup** or **stup**▷ (SHTŌŌP) *n* **1** A person regarded merely as a sex partner; ASS *(1967+)* **2** The sex act; copulation *v* **1** To annoy; pressure *(1952+)* **2** To do the sex act with or to; FUCK : *Why of course he was shtupping her (1967+)* [fr Yiddish, literally, "push, shove"]

shuck *modifier* Deceptive; fake : *All he has to sell is a shuck and jive caricature of Blackness n* A theft or fraud; RIPOFF : *Linear thinking was a total shuck (1950s+ Black) v* **1** To undress; strip oneself *(1848+)* **2** (also **shuck and jive**) To joke; tease; FOOL AROUND : *Twenty-two percent of each trash-truck crew's workday is spent shucking and jiving and shadowboxing/ We ain't got no time for shuckin' (1966+ Black)* **3** (also **shuck and jive**) To swindle; cheat; deceive; esp to bluff verbally and counterfeit total sincerity *(1959+ Black & student)* **4** To improvise chords, esp to a piece of music one does not know; FAKE IT, VAMP *(1957+ Cool musicians)* [black senses probably fr the fact that black slaves sang and shouted gleefully during *corn-shucking* season, and this behavior, along with lying and teasing, became a part of the protective and evasive behavior normally adopted toward white people in "traditional" race relations; the sense of "swindle" is perhaps related to the mid-1800s term *to be shucked out*, "be defeated, be denied victory," which suggests that the notion of stripping someone as an ear of corn is stripped may be basic in the semantics]

shucks *See* AW SHUCKS

shuffle *v* **1** To have a gang fight; RUMBLE *(1960s+ Street gang)* **2** To behave in the stereotypical obsequious way of a black person in "traditional" race relations; TOM : *A lot of brothers and sisters died. So are we just going to shuffle and jive? (1880+ Black)*

shunt *n* An accident; a collision *(1959+ Car racing)*

shush *v* To tell someone to be quiet and stop talking • Very often a command : *"Shush!" he shouted, uselessly, to the large noisy hound* [1905+; the dated form is spelled *sush*]

shut down *v phr* To defeat; outdo; BEAT : *Gore shut down Perot in the debate/ We're gonna shut 'em down (1950s+)*

shut-eye *n* Sleep : *I'll give Betsy the first crack at some shut-eye (1899+)*

shut one's face (or **trap** or **mouth** or **head**) *v phr* To stop talking; SHUT UP • Often an irritated command *(1899+)*

shut it *interj* Enough! Remain silent : *Shut it; you know nothing (1886+)*

shutout *n* A game in which one side is held scoreless *(1940s+ Sports)*

shut out *v phr* To hold an opponent scoreless; BLANK, SCHNEIDER, SKUNK : *The last time Princeton was shut out, Penn did it (1881+ Sports)*

shutterbug *n* A photographer, esp an enthusiastic amateur : *Two of the more prominent Senate-shutterbugs are Sens. Patrick J Leahy and John C Danforth (1940+)*

shut one's trap *v phr* SHUT one's FACE *(1776+)*

shut up *v phr* To be quiet; stop talking • Very often a stern or angry command *(1860+)*

◁**shvantz**▷ (SHVAHNTS) *n* (also **schvantz** or **schvanz** or **schwantz** or **schwanz** or **schvontz** or **shvonce** or **shvuntz**) The penis; SCHLONG [1970s+; fr Yiddish, literally "tail"; hence semantically analogous with *penis,* literally "tail"] *See* STEP ON IT

◀**shvartze** or **shvartzer**▶ *See* SCHVARTZE

shylock or **Shylock** *modifier* : *that were into them for shylock money and couldn't make the payments (1980s+) n* A usurer; LOAN SHARK. **shy** : *In Toronto and Hamilton both, loan sharks ("shylocks") appeared in the gambling clubs (1786+) v* : *the shylocking that went with it as hot dogs go with baseball/ numbers games, shylocking, and other illegal operations (1930+)* [fr the character in Shakespeare's *The Merchant of Venice*]

shy of a load *See* THREE BRICKS SHY OF A LOAD

shyster *n* **1** A dishonest and contemptible lawyer, politician, or businessperson : *You lousy little shyster bastard (1844+)* ◁**2**▷ Any lawyer [origin unknown and hotly disputed; perhaps fr the name of a Mr Sheuster, a New York City lawyer of the early 1800s; perhaps fr German *Scheisse,* "shit," or *Scheisser,* "shitter," by way of anglicized forms *shice* and *shicer* attested fr the mid-1800s, with the addition of the agentive suffix *-ster;* perhaps because prisoners were said and advised to *fight shy of,* "avoid," lawyers who frequented jails, esp the Tombs in New York City; perhaps fr earlier sense of *shy,* "disreputable, not quite honest," and *-ster*]

Siberian Express, the *n phr* A spell of very cold weather *(1980s+)*

sick *adj* **1** (also **sicko** or **sicksicksick**) Mentally twisted; psychopathic, esp in a sadistic vein : *a rapist or a sicko father who abuses his teenage daughters (1551+)* **2** Disgusted; surfeited; FED UP : *Sick to the gills of the Simpson trial? (1853+)* **3** (also **sicko** or **sicksicksick**) Gruesome; morbid; mentally and spiritually unhealthy : *Label it S for Sicko/ He is even better at establishing a sicksicksick atmosphere (1955+)* **4** Needing a dose of narcotics *(1940s+ Narcotics) n* The craving and misery of an addict in need of a narcotic dose *(1940s+ Narcotics)* [modern use of first sense from about 1955 is probably not a survival]

sick him or **sic 'em** *sentence* Attack that person or animal • A command [1845+; fr a dialect pronunciation of *seek*]

sickie or **sicko** *n* A mentally unhealthy person; a psychopath : *It was not considered very kosher to toss out the sickies once they had taken their final vows/ Only sickies get involved with married women (1973+)*

sick joke *n phr* A joke with a grimly morbid tone or point; a nasty sort of jape : *Wouldn't it be a sick joke if I got something without understanding the financial underpinnings (1959+)*

sick someone on someone or something *v phr* To incite someone against someone or something : *They've decided to sick the voters on the whole government (1845+) See* SICK HIM

sick-out *n* A form of job action in which employees declare themselves ill and unable to work; BLUE FLU *(1970+)*

side *n* **1** A sheet containing the lines and cues for one performer *(1933+ Theater)* **2** A phonograph record *(1936+)* **3** The music on one side of a phonograph record, one band of a long-playing record, one segment of a cassette or other tape, etc • Usu plural : *He had never heard these classic sides until recently (1936+) See* ON THE SIDE, STATESIDE, SUNNY SIDE UP, TOPSIDE, the WRONG SIDE OF THE TRACKS

sidebar *adj* Auxiliary; supplementary : *Now he has a side-bar job, hustling beer or sports equipment (1950s+) n* **1** A news or feature story serving as a supplement or background to a main story : *Banner headlines and sidebar after sidebar flashed in front of our eyes/ the wandering sidebars and frivolous frolicking of the Post (1948+ News media)* **2** A conference held between lawyers and a judge unheard by the jury : *Some judges hold these meetings, known as sidebars, in the courtroom at the side of the bench away from the jury (1980s+ Courtroom)* [adjective and first noun senses probably fr the late 1800s use of *sidebar buggy* or *wagon* for a vehicle having longitudinal reinforcements along the *sides;* perhaps fr *side-bar,* "an auxiliary toll-gate on a road leading into a main toll-road"; second noun sense fr auxiliary *bars,* legal or courtroom sites and barriers, formerly found in the Scottish and English parliaments, and so noted by 1708]

sidekick *n* **1** A close friend, partner, associate, etc : *Wayne and his side-kick James Arness (1906+)* **2** A side pocket *(1916+ Pickpockets)* [origin uncertain; *side-pal* in the first sense is found by 1886]

side of a barn, the *See* someone CAN'T HIT THE SIDE OF A BARN

side of one's face *See* LAUGH ON THE OTHER SIDE OF one's FACE

sider *See* PORTSIDER

sides of the street *See* WORK BOTH SIDES OF THE STREET

sideswipe *n* A critical observation, esp an oblique one : *took a sideswipe at "restrictive court decisions"* [1924+; fr *sideswipe*, "a glancing blow," found by 1917]

sidewalks *See* POUND THE PAVEMENTS

sidewalk superintendent *n phr* **1** A person who watches excavation or other construction work, usu through a hole in the surrounding fence **2** Any amateur critic or observer (*1930s+*)

sidewalk surfing *n phr* Skateboarding : *sidewalk surfing not allowed*

sidewinder[1] *n* **1** A wide, looping blow with the fist; ROUNDHOUSE (*1840+*) **2** A tree that does not fall where it was intended to (*1940s+ Loggers*) [both senses literally from a *winding* at or to a *side*, and the second sense probably influenced by *sidewinder*[2]]

sidewinder[2] *n* **1** A dangerous and pugnacious man (*1940s+*) **2** A gangster's bodyguard; GORILLA : *Eddy Prue, Morny's sidewinder* (*1940s+ Underworld*) [fr the dangerous *sidewinder* rattlesnake, so called fr its lateral locomotion, and presumed to be treacherous]

-sie *See* -IE

sieve *n* **1** A leaky boat or ship : *That frog-eating sieve* **2** One who cannot keep a secret *See* HAVE A MIND LIKE A SIEVE

◁**siff** or **the siff**▷ *See* SYPH

sight gag *n phr* A joke or comic turn that depends entirely on what is seen (*1957+*)

sign *See* HIGH SIGN

signify *v* To make provocative comments in a gamelike manner; SNAP, SOUND : *any black kid who has stood in a school yard or on a street corner engaging in the mock-hostile banter that blacks call "signifying"/ In Chicago you still get people doing the old-style rhyming; that's called signifying* (*1932+ Black*)

sign off *v phr* To stop talking; SHUT UP [1928+; fr radio broadcasting, "to end transmission and go off the air"]

sign off on something *v phr* To agree to or approve of a proposal, a legislative bill, etc, esp without actual formal endorsement : *When enough Senators had signed off on the treaty, the President announced it* [1970s+; *sign off*, "to relinquish a right or claim," is found by 1859]

sign on *v phr* To agree to do : *signed on to teach part-time*

sign up *v phr* To join; enroll; enlist : *They signed up for a course in hands-on interpersonal relations* (*1903+*)

silent but deadly or **SBD** *n* A stinky but silent instance of flatulence : *SBDs from the kids*

silk *n* A white person : *So did the silks on the Knapp Commission ever ask about the rate of drug busts?* (*1960s+ Black*)

silk-stocking *adj* Wealthy; affluent : *a silk-stocking neighborhood* (*1812+*)

silly season *n phr* Any period when people do silly things, esp when these are reported in the news media [1861+; fr a term designating the months of August and September, when Parliament was not sitting and valid and useful news was scarce, and the newspapers resorted to reporting frivolities and trivialities]

silver *n* Money : *silver under the mattress*

silver (or **magic**) **bullet** *n phr* A very effective, quasi-magical agent, remedy, etc : *Stokovich looked on Kennedy as his "silver bullet," his absolute best man/ No single silver bullet is going to do the job* [1808+; reflecting an ancient belief that silver weapons can conquer any foe, found, for example, in the Delphic Oracle's advice to Philip of Macedon, "With silver weapons you may conquer the world"]

simmer down *v phr* To become calm and quiet, esp after anger; COOL IT, LIGHTEN UP • Often a command or a bit of advice (*1871+*)

simon-pure *adj* Genuine; unadulterated [1840+; the name of a virtuous Quaker in Susanna Centlivre's 1717 play *A Bold Stroke for a Wife*]

simp *n* A simpleton; a stupid person; KLUTZ : *Simps with mustaches are a menace to society/ I really thought it would be till death do us part. I was such a simp* (*1903+*)

simpatico *adj* Nice; pleasant; sympathetic and congenial *n* Sympathy; affinity : *Alan Keyes has as much simpatico with the Christian right as I do* [1864+; fr Italian or Spanish]

simple *See* STIR-CRAZY

since the year one *adv phr* For a very long time : *They've known each other since the year one/ This is Mozab. I've known him since the Year One* (*1970s+*)

sin city *n* A city or region of a city with attractions that are sinful, such as gambling, prostitution, etc : *Las Vegas, the Sin City* (*1973+*)

sing *v* To inform; incriminate oneself and others; SQUEAL : *Vice Prisoners Ready To Sing* [1710+ Underworld; perhaps related to the expression *a little bird told me*; a variant, *chant*, is found by 1883] *See* HEAR THE BIRDIES SING, the OPERA AIN'T OVER TILL THE FAT LADY SINGS

singer *n* CANARY, STOOL PIGEON (*1935+ Underworld*)

single *n* **1** A dollar bill (*1936+*) **2** A person, esp a criminal, who works alone : *Dillinger now becomes a single* (*1940s+ Underworld*) **3** A solo performer; a one-person act *(1940s+ Show business)* **4** An unmarried person : *The place tried to attract singles (1964+)* **5** A phonograph record having only one piece of music on each side : *The single sold about three million (1949+)* See SWINGING SINGLE

singles *modifier* For unmarried persons : *a singles bar/ a singles party (1960s+)*

sing out *v phr* **1** To speak up; make oneself known and heard; PIPE UP : *If anybody doesn't like it, just sing out (1813+)* **2** To inform; SQUEAL : *and get him to sing out (1815+)*

sink *v* To destroy; ruin; TORPEDO : *I'm afraid we're sunk this time (1613+)*

sinker[1] *n* A biscuit or doughnut [1870+; fr the lead weight used by fishermen to *sink* line and bait, probably an ironic reference to the weight of the biscuit or doughnut] See HOOK, LINE, AND SINKER

sinker[2] or **sinkerball** *n* **1** A pitch that dips downward as it nears home plate **2** A line drive or other batted ball that sinks suddenly toward the ground *(1920s+ Baseball)*

sink-or-swim *adj* Risky; succeed-or-be-ruined : *Playing cornerback in the National Football League, particularly for a young player, is a sink-or-swim proposition (1668+)*

sin tax *n phr* A tax on some activity or product regarded as immoral : *Then there are the always popular so-called sin taxes, which could be slapped on cigarettes and liquor (1963+)*

sis *n* **1** A sister : *That's his sis with him (1656+)* **2** Woman; girl; chick • Used in direct address : *What's up, sis? (1835+)* [a shortening of *sister*]

sissified *adj* Timorous; weak and effeminate; CHICKENHEARTED, PANSIFIED *(1905+)*

sissy *adj* : *wearing sissy clothes (1891+)* *n* **1** A timorous, weak, and effeminate male; daisy, LILY, PANSY *(1887+)* **2** A male homosexual; PANSY : *No more sissies for Jimmy Smith (1970s+)* [fr *sis* fr *sister*]

sissy bar *n phr* A high metal projection at the back of a bicycle to prevent it from rolling over backwards [1969+; fr the fact that someone adopting such a device is timorous]

sister *n* **1** Woman; girl • Used in direct address : *Hey, sister, you'd better leave (1906+)* **2** A black woman *(1926+ Black)* **3** A fellow feminist *(1912+)* See SOB SISTER, WEAK SISTER

sister act *n phr* The sex act between a homosexual man and a heterosexual woman *(1972+ Homosexuals)*

sit *v* To take care of; attend and watch over : *Who'll sit your house while you're gone? (1945+)* See HOUSE-SIT

sitcom *n* A situation comedy series on television : *the new family of sitcoms (1964+)*

sit-down *n* **1** A meal, usu a free one, eaten at a table *(1919+ Hoboes)* **2** A settling for a chat;

meeting; SCHMOOZE : *The voice suggested that we have a little "sit-down" over lunch at Chianti/ Zilber was supposed to go to a sit-down with Pagano in Brooklyn (1861+)* **3** (also **sit-down strike**) A strike in which the workers occupy their job sites but do not work *(1936+)*

sit-in *n* An illegal occupation of a place in order to make a political or philosophical statement [1960s+; the term was popularized during the movement for black civil rights and has many offspring: *be-in, love-in, puke-in,* etc]

sit in *v phr* **1** To join and play with other musicians, esp on one occasion or temporarily : *had the very good fortune of sitting in with him (1936+ Musicians)* **2** To occupy a place as a participant in a sit-in *(1960s+)* [found by 1599 in the first sense "to participate in a game"]

sit in the catbird seat *v phr* To be in the position of advantage; be SITTING PRETTY : *willing to give us a hundred seventy million in preferred notes. We're sitting in the catbird seat* [1930s+; fr a term used by a poker opponent of the late sportscaster Red Barber to explain his situation with two aces in the hole at stud poker; Mr Barber adopted the term, which was afterwards used by James Thurber in a story called "The Catbird Seat" with attribution to Red Barber; probably a Southern dialect term based on a folk notion of the cleverness and masterfulness of *catbirds* and/or their high and superior perch]

sit on *v phr* To fail to act for a long time, usu purposefully; to postpone : *sat on the nomination (1906+)*

sit on someone *v phr* To suppress or squelch someone : *When I opened my mouth they all sat on me (1865+)*

sit on one's ass *v phr* To remain inactive; esp, to fail to cope or deal with a responsibility : *The congressman sat on his ass while the neighborhood hospital deteriorated (1940s+)*

sit on one's hands *v phr* **1** To refrain from applauding; be an unresponsive or adverse audience : *They sat on their hands until he started waving the flag (1926+)* **2** To do nothing; be passive; SIT ON one's ASS : *Even when the thing fell down they just sat on their hands (1950s+)*

sit on my face See SHE CAN SIT ON MY FACE ANYTIME

sit on threes *v phr* To make three-point scores : *But he's out there sitting on threes, and that's all she wrote (1990s+ Basketball)*

sit shotgun *v phr* To sit in the passenger seat of a car; RIDE SHOTGUN : *I sat shotgun in my pop's flower truck (1960s+)*

sit (or stand) still for something *v phr* To accept or condone; tolerate something provocative : *The nation will simply not sit still for the years of slow growth* (1940s+)

sit the pines *v phr* To sit on the bench rather than play : *Of course I'm disappointed. I'm not used to sitting the pines* (1980s+ *Sports*)

◁**sit there with** one's **finger (or thumb) up** one's **ass**▷ *v phr* To be passive and unresponsive; fail to cope; be useless : *I suppose you think I'm just sitting around every day with my thumb up my ass* (1040s+)

sit tight *v phr* **1** To keep one's present position, stance, convictions, etc; refuse to be moved; STAND PAT (1890+) **2** To wait patiently : *Be up as quickly as I can, Vicky. Sit tight* (1903+)

sitting duck *n phr* An easy target; a totally defenseless person (1944+)

sitting pretty, be *v phr* To be in a superior and very pleasant position : *He's just the same genial idiot whether he is out of luck or sitting pretty* (1921+)

situation *n* A bad or suspicious event or happening; a potential crime : *We may have a situation here, Bob (Police)* See ON TOP OF

sit up and take notice *v phr* To pay attention; become aware; WAKE UP AND SMELL THE COFFEE : *Let's do something that'll make him sit up and take notice* (1889+)

six See DEEP SIX, EIGHTY-SIX, HIT ON ALL SIX

six-bit *modifier* Worth or costing seventy-five cents : *a six-bit sandwich* (1840+)

six feet under *adj phr* Dead (1940s+)

six-hundred-pound gorilla *n phr* (also **eight-hundred-pound gorilla** or **nine-hundred-pound gorilla**) A powerful force; a virtually irresistible influence : *She is a 600-pound gorilla. She can intimidate anybody/ likens Spielberg to an "800-pound gorilla," which can be defined as a high-priced Hollywood species that makes its own decisions/ There were no obvious 900-pound gorillas like* Forrest Gump *or* Schindler's List [1970s+; fr a joke in which the question "Where does a *six-hundred-pound gorilla* sleep?" is answered "Anywhere it wants"]

six-pack *n* **1** Three performances a day for two days : *Fridays and Saturdays he has three [shows], the two days' stint known as a six-pack* (1970s+ *Circus*) **2** A set of six photographs from which a witness is asked to identify a suspect (1990s+ *Police*) **3** Any set of six (1970s+) *v* : *elevates in a spray of sand, and "six-packs" her opponents, spiking the ball so savagely that it knocks the defender down* (1990s+ *Beach volleyball*) [fr a set of cans or bottles of beverage, most notably of beer, sold as a unit; the term is found by 1952] See JOE SIX-PACK

six-shooter or **six-gun** *n* A revolver with a cylinder holding six cartridges (1844+)

sixty-four dollar question, the *n phr* The crucial question or issue • The dollar amount has increased over the years : *To flee or not to flee, that's the sixty-four dollar question/ "What will the European Community do?" "Well, that's really the sixty-four-thousand dollar question"/ Are baby boomers going to want a smaller car? That's the $64 million question for Ford* [1942+; fr a radio quiz show where the top prize was $64]

◁**sixty-nine** or **69**▷ *n* Simultaneous oral sex between two persons, whose reciprocally inverse positions suggest the numeral 69 (1888+)

six ways to Sunday See FORTY WAYS TO SUNDAY

size See KING-SIZE

◁**size queen**▷ *n phr* A homosexual who is particularly and nearly exclusively concerned with the length of penises (1972+ *Homosexuals*)

size up *v phr* To estimate or assess : *How do you size up his chances?* (1847+)

sizzle *n* Persuasive pressure; HEAT : *That's the sizzle* (1980s+) *v* FRY

sizzler *n* **1** A very hot day (1901+) **2** A very fast pitch or hard-hit ground ball (1910+ *Baseball*) **3** A cook (1940s+ *Loggers*)

sizzling *adj* Hot, in any sense : *sell some of the sizzling green at a discount* (1845+)

ska (SKAH) *n* An early form of reggae music : *various musical trends, punk, New Wave, power-pop, ska* [1964+; origin unknown]

skag or **scag** *n* **1** A cigarette or cigarette butt (1915+ *Armed forces*) **2** A despicable person or thing; JERK (1960s+ *Teenagers fr black*) **3** An unattractive woman; BAT, SKANK (1920s+ *Black*) **4** Cheap, low-quality heroin (1960s+ *Narcotics*)

skaggy *adj* Ugly; unkempt; nasty; SKANKY : *She's too skaggy for your average john* (1960s+)

skank *n* **1** An unattractive woman; a malodorous woman; SKAG **2** A prostitute; HOOKER : *How long would it take for them to find them f—— skanks (the hookers) again?* (1970s+ *Black*) **3** Copulation; coition; ASS : *how 'bout witnessing some skank* (1980s+) **4** A despicable person; GRUNGE, SLEAZEBAG : *Julie gets used and humiliated by the lens-wielding skank* (1980s+) **5** A slovenly style of dress, possibly imitative of disheveled heroin addicts : *Some teenagers prefer a grungier, if equally tasteless, look known as "skank"* (1990s+ *Teenagers*) *v* To do a sort of reggae dancing in which the body bends forward, the knees are raised, and the hands claw the air : *They move in sympathetic response to the music, skankin' from side to side/ They mosh. They slam. They skank and thrash, too* (1976+)

skanky or **skank-o-rama** *adj* Nasty; repellent; GROTTY, SCUZZY, TRASHY : *The girls were somewhat skanky, with lank hair and rotten posture/*

You moved, the earth moved. Skank-o-rama (1980s+ Teenagers fr black)

skate *n* An inferior horse : *They'd kill that bunch of skates for their hides (1894+)* **v** 1 To default a debt; avoid paying *(1930s+ Black)* 2 To leave; SPLIT *(1915+)* 3 To evade duty; GOLD-BRICK, GOOF OFF : *The gunny accuses you of trying to skate (WWII armed forces)*

skedaddle *v* To run away; flee; fly; depart hastily : *the verb "to skedaddle," which was revived during the war to suggest precipitous flight, and has held its own ever since* [1861+; origin unknown; perhaps fr an attested Scots dialect sense, "spill," which could suggest "scatter, disperse"; the example from 1884 supposes an earlier origin]

skeeter *n* A mosquito *(1839+)*

skeevy *adj* Nasty; repellent; GROTTY, SCUZZY, TRASHY : *How's your skeevy pai? (1990s+ Students)*

skeezer *n* A promiscuous woman; SLUT : *That skeezer has no self-respect/ nice women, those who are neither sluts nor skeezers (women who use men for money), should take no offense (1980s+ Students fr black)*

skell *n* A street derelict who may be a villain : *Perp: also a mutt, a mope, a skid, or a skell* [1980s+ New York City police; ultimately fr Dutch *schelm*, "scoundrel, villain," found in English as *skelum* by 1611]

sketch *See* THUMBNAIL SKETCH

sketchy *adj* Offering little information : *sketchy details*

ski bum *n phr* A person who frequents ski resorts habitually, often doing casual jobs, for the sake of skiing *(1960+)*

ski bunny *See* SNOW BUNNY

skid *n* SKELL *(1980s+ New York City police)*

skid lid *n phr* A motorcyclist's helmet : *suffered severe brain damage while wearing one of the company's skid lids (1970s+ Motorcyclists)*

skid marks *n* Unsightly underwear from excrement : *no laundry wants to see skid marks*

skidoo or **skiddoo** *v* To depart hastily; SCRAM • Often a command or a bit of advice : *We heard the shooting and we skiddooed quick/ Skidoo, skidoo, and quit me* [1905+; perhaps fr *skedaddle*]

skid row or **Skid Row** *n* A street or district frequented by derelicts, hoboes, drifters, etc, such as the Bowery in New York City [1931+; fr *skid road*]

skids, the *See* HIT THE SKIDS, ON THE SKIDS, PUT THE SKIDS UNDER someone or something

skillion or **scillion** *n* An indefinite very large number; BAZILLION, GAZILLION : *I have a scillion things to say (1970s+) See* JILLION

skim *n* Income not reported for tax purposes, esp from the gross earnings of a gambling casino or other such enterprise; BLACK MONEY : *allegedly "cleansed" in the neighborhood of $2 million in "skim," untaxed gambling profits/ Caltronics is in on the skim (1960+ Gambling)* **v** : *"appropriate, conceal, and skim" part of the winnings (1961+ Gambling)*

skimpies *n* Underwear panties : *Once again, Roseanne is pushing the envelope, not to mention the skimpies (1990s+)*

skin *modifier* Featuring nudity; indecently exposing; GIRLIE : *a skin flick (1960s+)* **n** 1 The hand as used in handshaking or hand-slapping as a salutation • Nearly always in the expression *some skin* : *My man! Gimme some skin!/ Slip me some skin (1942+ Black)* 2 An inferior racehorse; BEETLE : *They take the first bunch of skins out to gallop (1923+)* 3 A pocketbook, wallet, etc *(1790+)* 4 One dollar; a dollar bill; frogskin : *One laid out 190 skins (1930+)* ◁5▷ A condom; RUBBER *(1935+)* 6 Drums or bongos *(1938+ Jazz musicians)* **v** 1 To defeat decisively; trounce; SKUNK : *They skinned the Wolverines 20–zip (1862+)* 2 To cheat or swindle; victimize : *You got skinned in that deal (1819+)* 3 To slip away; SKEDADDLE : *and then skin out the window (1876+) See* GET UNDER someone's SKIN, GIVE SOME SKIN, NO SKIN OFF MY ASS, PIGSKIN, PRESS THE FLESH, SHEEPSKIN

skin someone **alive** *v phr* To punish someone severely; castigate roundly : *She'll skin me alive if I'm late again (1975+)*

skin (or **flesh**) **flick** *n phr* A movie featuring nudity and more or less patent sexual activity; BLUE MOVIE, fuck film *(1968+)*

◁**skin flute**▷ *n phr* The penis *(1940s+) See* PLAY THE SKIN FLUTE

skin game *n phr* A confidence game; SCAM *(1868+)*

skinhead *n* 1 A bald person or person with a shaved or cropped head *(1940s+)* 2 A Marine recruit *(1950s+ Marine Corps)* 3 A close-cropped person with neo-Nazi, racist, and other extreme right sentiments : *A mob enraged by the appearance of a nationally known racist chased and beat a group of teenage white supremacist "skinheads" (1960s+ British)*

skin magazine (or **mag**) *modifier* : *Asked whether the skin-mag ban would apply to other magazines in which women are scantily clad or naked n phr* A magazine featuring nudity, more or less explicit sexual activity, etc; NUDIE *(1960+)*

skinny, the *n phr* The truth; the LOWDOWN, the SCOOP : *Are you giving me the straight skinny?/ Here's the skinny: the show's an old-fashioned formula musical* [fr WWII armed forces; origin unknown; perhaps an alteration of *the naked truth*]

skinny-dip *v phr* To swim naked : *Andrew went skinny-dipping in rocky pools (1950s+)*

skin pop *v phr* To inject narcotics into the skin or muscles, rather than into the circulatory system : *I'll have to skin pop (1950s+ Narcotics)*

skins *n* **1** A set of drums *(1938+ Jazz musicians)* **2** Automotive tires : *Protect your present skins (1950s+ Hot rodders & truckers)*

skin-search or **body-shake** *n* A thorough scrutiny of a naked person, esp for hypodermic needle marks, concealed narcotics, etc *(1935+ Police) v* : *They skin-searched both couples (1970+)*

skint *adj* Lacking money; BROKE • Still chiefly British [1925+; fr *skinned*]

skip *n* **1** A person who absconds, esp to avoid paying a bill : *The skip took off with a girl friend* (1915+) **2** SKIPPER (1830+) *v* **1** To fail to attend; absent oneself; SHINE : *if I let you skip school this afternoon* (1905+) **2** (also **skip out**) To depart hastily, escape, abscond, esp to avoid paying a bill, being arrested, etc : *They skipped out of the motel at 2 AM* (1590+)

skip it *v phr* To drop or ignore some matter : *If you can't remember, let's skip it for now* (1934+)

skipper *n* **1** The captain of a ship or boat *(1390+ Nautical)* **2** Any commanding officer; the OLD MAN *(1906+ Army)*

skirt *n* A woman, esp a young woman; BROAD, chick • Regarded by some women as offensive : *a real skirt/ never give any skirt a tumble* (1906+)

skirt-chaser *n* A ladies' man; LOVER-BOY (1942+)

skitch *v* : *some hanging on the sides of the Jeep, "skitching," or dragging their feet through the powder (1990s+ Students)*

skitter *v* To move about rapidly; scamper : *where the poor skitter around the doll's house on the hill like so many rats among garbage* (1845+)

skitz *v* To go crazy; FLIP OUT, SCHIZ OUT : *No, I'm not driving you past Gary's house again. You are skitzin over this guy* [1990s+ Teenagers; see **schizo**]

skiv *n* SHIV

skive *v* To shirk duty : *skive off for a rest* [1919; originally armed forces]

skivvies *n* **1** Underwear; underpants and undershirt • Originally a nautical use : *stripped down to his skivvies and played his harmonica* (1932+) **2** A pair of sandal-like slippers (1945+)

skivvy *n* **1** (also **skivvy shirt**) A man's undershirt, esp a T-shirt : *pants, sneakers, some skivvy shirts* (1932+) **2** A pair of men's underpants, esp of the boxer type (1947+)

skosh or **scosh** (SKOHSH) *n* A little bit; SMIDGEN : *You need a skosh more room here for your*

desk [Korean War armed forces; fr Japanese *sukoshi*]

◁**skull**▷ *n* Fellatio; BLOW JOB *(1970s+ Homosexuals) See* GO OUT OF one's SKULL, OUT OF one's HEAD

skull-buster *n* **1** A police officer *(1930s+ Black)* **2** A very difficult course in school *(1920s+ Students)*

skullcap *n* A helmet; BRAIN DISH *(1980s+ Motorcyclists)*

skullduggery or **skulduggery** *n* Shady behavior; DIRTY WORK, HANKY-PANKY [1867+; a US alteration of Scots *sculduddery*, "bawdry, obscenity," which is attested from the early 18th century]

skull popper *n phr* Liquor; BOOZE, the SAUCE : *His vices are slow horses and fast bookies, rather than 86-proof skull popper (1980s+)*

skull session *n phr* An intensive learning and teaching period, esp a briefing session : *two separate "skull sessions" with six members of the US negotiating team (1959+)*

skunk *n* **1** A despicable person; BASTARD, LOUSE (1840+) **2** Marijuana; POT, GRASS *(1990s+ Narcotics) v* **1** To defeat utterly, esp to hold the opponent scoreless in sports; trounce; CLOBBER : *They're saying I'm going to get skunked in the black community* (1849+) **2** To learn by deduction the signals used by an opposing team telling the quarterback what play to call *(1980s+ Football)* **3** To lack wind for sailing : *We went to Baja last month, but got skunked every day (1990s+ Windsurfers) See* DRUNK AS A SKUNK

skunk someone out of something *v phr* To cheat someone out of something *(1890+ Students)*

sky *v* **1** To hit or kick or throw a ball very high : *See me skying out there?/ This time he skied the punt right over the end zone (1909+ Sports)* **2** To jump high in order to slam-dunk the ball; AIR *(1980s+ Basketball) See* PIE IN THE SKY

sky is the limit, the *sentence* No limits exist : *Yeltsin proudly proclaims that today in Russia the sky is the limit to what a person can earn*

skyjack *n* : *the week's third skyjack to Cuba* (1968+) *v* To take control of an aircraft illegally, usu by claiming to have a weapon or a bomb; commit air piracy (1961+) [modeled on *hijack*]

sky-pilot *n* A member of the clergy; preacher (1883+)

skyrocket *v* To increase rapidly : *Profits are expected to skyrocket after the announcement* (1895+)

skyscraper *n* A very high fly ball, esp near home plate *(1866+ Baseball)*

skywest *See* KNOCK someone or something GALLEY WEST

slab *n* **1** A bed *(1930s+ Jive talk)* **2** One dollar; a dollar bill : *Ten slabs for two days' work!* *(1950s+)* **3** The pitcher's "rubber" at the top of the mound, against which the pitcher braces his foot when throwing *(1919+ Baseball)*

slack *n* A period of inertness or decreased activity : *He'd pulled his weight long enough to get some slack/ a channel surfer trapped in his own den of slack (1851+)* *v* : *Witness the 40,000 or so Americans here now, a lot of them teaching English or just slacking, drinking 50-cent beers in the pubs, grooving to acid jazz at the Roxy*

slacker *modifier* : *this lame "slacker" attitude a la Jeff Spicoli from* Fast Times at Ridgemont High *n* An indolent and detached person; shirker; idler : *The epitome of the slang-slinging, wise-cracking slacker (1898+)* [revived in the 1990s to describe a sort of cultural anomie]

slackmaster *n* Someone who is an expert at slacking off : *don't want to be called a slackmaster*

slag *n* : *its purposeful indie-rock slag at commerciality* *v* (also **slag off**) To denigrate; BADMOUTH, PUT DOWN : *Everybody was getting slagged/ I don't mean to slag the girls at Douglas/ This time I can't give it to you, can't totally slag you off (1971+)* [origin unknown; perhaps fr German *schlagen*, "beat, whip"]

slam *n* An uncomplimentary comment; a jibe; KNOCK : *took a slam at the male stars who dress like "ranch hands" (1884+)* *v* **1** : *Thrifty Slams Riordan on Its Way Out of Town (1916+)* **2** To hit; CLOBBER *(1905+)* ◁▷ To do the sex act with; BOFF, SCREW : *Did you slam her, Jon? (1980s+ Students)* **4** (also **slam-dance**) To do a physically colliding and athletic sort of rock-and-roll dancing, esp in the vein of punk rock : *The music is hardcore, the dance is slamming (1980s+)* **5** To consume or use : *He slammed two beers and then went out on his date/ Did they ever slam heroin? (1980s+ Students) See* GRAND SLAM

slam, the *n phr* the SLAMMER *(1960+)*

slam-bang *adj* Raucous, violent, vigorous, etc : *in climaxes as slam-bang as a four-horse stretch drive/ a couple of slam-bang musical numbers (1823+)* *adv* Violently : *They went at it slam-bang (1840+)* *n* A wild and vicious fight *(1920s+ Prizefighting)*

slam dunk *modifier* : *Welfare reform should have been a slam-dunk issue for the Republicans. But last week they allowed tax cuts to get in the way/ The bombing is not a slam-dunk case. It's going to require a really good presentation by the government to convince the jury n phr* **1** A spectacular success; winner : *Both pro- and antimerger members have been equally taken with the new rabbi. "It's a slam dunk,"* enthuses Corwin *(1990s+)* **2** (also **slam-dunk landing**) : *The safety board said that Flight 2268 didn't need to dive abruptly toward the runway. It contended the pilot elected to quickly slow down the plane for a slam dunk landing by reversing the engines* *v phr* To score a field goal by leaping up and thrusting the ball violently down through the hoop *(1976+ Basketball)*

slammer *n* SLAM DUNK *(1970s+ Basketball) See* GRAND SLAMMER

slammer, the *n phr* **1** A door : *twister to the slammer (1930s+ Jive talk)* **2** (also **the slams**) A jail, prison, etc : *Drunk drivers go to the slammer in this town (1952+ Black)*

slammin' *adj* Excellent; superb; COOL, FUNKY FRESH : *That food was slammin'/ in my opinion the most slammin' song on the album* [1990s+ Teenagers; *slamming* is found in a similar sense, "large, exceptional," by about 1900]

slamming *n* : *Federal regulators plan to adopt tougher rules against switching customers' long-distance companies without their knowledge, a practice known as "slamming" (1990s+)*

slam the door on someone or something *v phr* To put an end to something as if by slamming a dismissive door : *Ray Floyd slammed the door on any would-be challengers with a string of 14 consecutive pars (1786+)*

slang *n* A style or register of language consisting of terms that can be substituted for standard terms of the same conceptual meaning but having stronger emotive impact than the standard terms, in order to express an attitude of self-assertion toward conventional order and moral authority and often an affinity with or membership in occupational, ethnic, or other social groups, and ranging in acceptability from sexual and scatological crudity to audacious wittiness (see *Preface*) [mid-1700s+ British; origin unknown; probably related to *sling*, which has cognates in Norwegian that suggest the abusive nature of slang; the British dialect original term *slang* meant both "a kind of projectile-hurling weapon" and "the language of thieves and vagabonds," reinforcing the connection with "sling"]

slanguage *n* The vocabulary of slang; language employing much slang [1879+; blend of *slang* and *language*]

slant *n* **1** An opinion or point of view; angle : *something about his tone or his "slant" that irritated his contemporaries (1905+)* **2** A look; an ocular inspection : *Take a slant at dat/ The prowl car takes a slant down now and then (1911+)*

slapdash *adj* Hasty and careless; heedless of the fine details; SLOPPY (*1792+*)

slap someone **five** *See* GIVE someone FIVE

slap-happy *adj* **1** Disoriented and stuporous, esp from being hit too often about the head : *a slap-happy bum* (*1936+*) **2** Vertiginous; off balance : *designed to knock philologists slap-happy* **3** Euphoric; intoxicated; HIGH : *He was slap-happy a whole week after the baby came*

slap in the face, a *n phr* An insult or rebuke, esp when unexpected; a rebuff : *His not saying anything is a slap in the face* (*1898+*)

slap something **on** *v phr* To add something, esp increase a price : *slapped on an extra tax*

slap on the wrist, a *n phr* A very mild punishment • Usu said when the punishment is felt to be unjustly lenient (*1914+*) *See* GIVE someone A SLAP ON THE WRIST

slapper *See* KNEE-SLAPPER

slapstick *adj* Featuring rowdy humor, both physical and conceptual; low comedy : *The old burlesque loved slapstick routines* (*1906+ Show business*) *n* : *The Marx Brothers depended a lot on slapstick* (*1926+ Show business*) [fr the *slapstick,* two wooden slats joined at one end, which made a loud splatting noise when used as a comic weapon, the term found by 1907]

slash-and-burn *adj* Crudely violent; irresponsibly vitriolic : *a few years of slash-and-burn expense cutting* [1980s+; fr a type of transitory cultivation in which a forest area is cleared and the undergrowth burned for planting, the term found by 1939]

slasher *n* A gory thriller movie; slice-and-dice film (*1980s+*)

slave away *v phr* To work very hard at something : *slaving away at Thanksgiving dinner*

slay *v* To impress someone powerfully, esp to provoke violent and often derisive laughter : *Pardon me, this will slay you/ The boys who slay me are the ones who have set pieces to recite when they answer the phone* (*1593+*)

sleaze *modifier* : *the sleaze factor n* **1** Anything shabby and disgusting; particularly revolting trash; CRAP, SCHLOCK, SHIT : *a paragon of Dorothy Malone low-fashion sleaze* (*1976+*) **2** SLEAZEBAG (*1976+*) *v* **1** To be sexually promiscuous and disreputable (*1976+*) **2** To scrounge; MOOCH (*1970s+ Students*) [a back formation from *sleazy; sleaze,* "a sleazy quality or appearance," is found by 1954]

sleazebag or **sleazeball** *n* A despicable person; DIRTBAG, SCUZZBAG : *Tartikoff calls the character "a total sleazebag"/ If you're a sleaze-ball, you deserve a recall* (*1970s+*)

sleaze-bucket *adj* Nasty; degradingly repellent : *sleaze-bucket movies* (*1970s+*)

sleazemonger *n* A producer or seller of nasty entertainment : *one of Hollywood's lowlier sleazemongers* (*1970s+*)

sleazy or **sleazo** or **sleazoid** *adj* Disgusting; filthy; nasty; GRUNGY, SCUZZY : *dirty buildings in sleazy sections/ a tremendous evocation of the sleazoid speed-freak scene/ who makes sleazo blood films* [entry form 1941+, second 1972+, third 1970s+; fr the late 1600s British *sleasie,* "thin, flimsy, threadbare," of uncertain origin, whence it came to mean "of inferior workmanship, shoddy"; perhaps fr *Sleasie,* "Silesian," used of linen cloth from that part of Germany]

sleep around *v phr* To be sexually promiscuous; PLAY AROUND (*1928+*)

sleeper *modifier* : *a sleeper play n* **1** Anything, esp a low-budget movie, a show, or a book, which achieves or probably will achieve success after a time of obscurity; DARK HORSE: *My Name is Julia Ross is the first "sleeper" to come to Philadelphia in months/ whose Return of the Secaucus Seven ranked among the more astute sleepers of 1980* (*1892+*) **2** A player who unexpectedly and cunningly gets the ball and runs (*1953+ Football*) **3** A sleeping pill or a sedative (*1960s+ Narcotics*) [the first noun sense may be fr gambling term *sleeper,* found by 1856 and meaning both "an unexpected winning card" and "a pot whose owner has ignored it, and hence is free to anyone who takes it"]

sleep in *v phr* To remain in bed later than usual in the morning (*1888+ Nautical*)

sleep like a top *v phr* To sleep very soundly [1693+; fr the stasis of a spinning *top*]

sleep on something *v phr* To postpone a decision on something until the next day, with the implication that a night's sleep will facilitate judgment (*1519+*)

sleepwalk *n* Advancement without much effort; an easy task or accomplishment : *Getting the contract was a sleepwalk*

sleep with someone *v phr* To do the sex act with someone; GO TO BED WITH someone • A much-needed euphemism : *No girl could love a man unless she had slept with the man over a period of time* (*1400+*)

sleeve *See* ACE UP one's SLEEVE, PUT THE ARM ON someone

sleighride *n* Intoxication from cocaine *v* To use cocaine [1915+ Narcotics; fr the association of *sleighrides* with *snow,* "cocaine"]

slew *n* A large quantity; OODLES, slathers : *a slew of cops* [1839+; probably fr Irish *sluagh,* "host, multitude"]

slewed *adj* Drunk [1801+; fr *slew,* "veer, swing around, hence, walk erratically"]

slice *n* A portion or share; PIECE : *Five grand wouldn't get you a slice of her* (*1550+*)

slice and dice *v phr* To reduce to smaller pieces, inferentially by cutting up : *Congress is the single most unpopular American institution other than the income tax; slicing and dicing its committees will bring the GOP only high praise/ Derivatives allow people to transfer risk, to slice and dice it into little pieces and pass it on/ The Court decided that this broad requirement could be sliced and diced* [1970s+; fr the preparation of cooking ingredients by *slicing and dicing* them]

sliced bread *See* the BEST THING SINCE SLICED BREAD

slick *adj* **1** Smooth and clever; smart : *She's a very slick talker* (1599+) **2** Cunning; crafty : *more than a match for any slick city lawyer* (1807+) **3** Excellent; NIFTY : *The soup was "simply slick"* (1843+) **4** Glib and superficial; without real substance : *They turn out people with slick plastic personalities* (1920+) *n* **1** A magazine printed on glossy paper and usu having some artistic or intellectual pretensions, as distinguished from pulp magazines : *magazines, from top slicks to minor pulps* (1934+) **2** An automobile tire with a very smooth tread : *My Sting Ray is light, the slicks are startin' to spin* (1950s+ Hot rodders) **3** A police bureaucrat regarded as self-serving by the rank and file : *But no way am I hanging around to talk to the slicks on this one* (1980s+ New York City police) [earlier 1800s uses were in comparative phrases like *slick as bear's grease* and *slick as molasses*]

slick as a whistle *adv phr* Very adroitly; cleverly : *She played that horn slick as a whistle* (1830+)

slickster *n* A clever or glib person, esp one who swindles (1965+)

slick someone or something **up** *v phr* To make neat and more attractive; furbish; GUSSY UP : *What are they all slicked up for?* (1828+)

slide *n* **1** A delay in collecting a debt : *How about a slide on my rent?* (1990s+) **2** Something easily done; CINCH, PIECE OF CAKE *v* To depart; SPLIT (1859+)

slim *n* A cigarette (1960s+ Jazz musicians)

slime *n* SLIMEBAG : *"I think he's a slime,"* Louise Hartley said (1950s+) *v* **1** Denigrate harshly and often falsely; SMEAR : *James Earl Jones gets slimed* (1990s+) **2** To speak in an unctuous and cajoling way : *"May I personally take your order, Mr Goodman,"* he slimed (1990s+)

◁**slimebag** or **slimeball** or **slimebucket**▷ *n* A despicable person; a repugnant wretch; GEEK, SCUMBAG, SLEAZEBAG : *I'm a disgusting slime bag, but I don't grovel/ I remember when the slime-balls used to be packed in there so solid/ If* you chill out, those low-life slime buckets will sew your fingers inside your mouth (1970s+)

slim pickings *n phr* Very little to be had or earned; extremely unprofitable returns : *You'll find it's slim pickings there, if you're looking for a fast buck* (1940s+)

sling *v* To sell narcotics; DEAL : *gang-bangers make careers of slingin' 'caine/ I caught my first case for slinging (selling) drugs* (1990s+ Narcotics) *See* HAVE one's ASS IN A SLING

slinger *n* A waiter or waitress; a food server : *Anybody but a California Bar-B-Q slinger would know that* [1934+; fr *sling*, "to pass something from one person to another," found by 1860] *See* GRUB-SLINGER, GUN-SLINGER, HASH-SLINGER, INK-SLINGER

sling hash *v phr* To work as a waiter or waitress : *I used to sling their hash/ She slung hash for a couple of weeks* (1906+)

slinging *See* MUDSLINGING

sling ink *v phr* To write, esp as a newspaper reporter or otherwise professionally (1864+)

slinky *adj* Sinuous and sexy : *one of those slinky glittering females* (1921+)

slip *v* **1** To give; hand : *So I slip him a double Z* (1841+) **2** To lose one's competence or touch; decline : *Only six pages today? I must be slipping* (1914+) *See* PINK SLIP

slip someone **a mickey** (or **a Mickey**) *v phr* To give knockout drops, esp chloral hydrate, secretly in a drink : *He passed out as if someone had slipped him a Mickey* (1951+)

slip between the cracks *See* FALL BETWEEN THE CRACKS

slip (or **give**) **me five** *sentence* Shake hands with me : *Slip me five so I know you're alive* (1926+)

slip something **over on** someone *v phr* To deceive someone; CON, FLIMFLAM : *You can't slip this fraud over on the whole town* [1912+; fr baseball, "to pitch the ball deceptively over the plate"]

slippery slope *n phr* A disastrous course; irrecoverable commitment : *Active euthanasia brings with it many dicey procedural questions, and, ultimately, a slippery slope* (1951+)

slip-up *n* A miscalculation; an accident; GLITCH : *There must have been a hell of a slip-up somewhere along the line* (1874+)

◁**slit**▷ *n* The vulva; CUNT (1648+)

slob *n* **1** A pudgy, generally unattractive, and untidy person : *You great, fat slob!/ a big slob with a chin that stuck out like a shelf* **2** A slovenly and disorderly person; a sloppy and disheveled person : *What a slob! You'd think his room was the town dump* **3** A mediocre person, esp one who is likely to fail or be victimized : *just another poor slob* [1861+; fr Anglo-Irish, used affectionately of a quiet, fat, slow child]

slobby *adj* Like a slob; slovenly (*1961+*)

slog *v* 1 To hit something hard, as a ball 2 To labor; work hard at something : *slogged through the piles of reports*

slo-mo *adj* : *She had a lot of things on her desk top, including a mondo-size slo-mo printer/ chock-full of slo-mo sequences of hunks running along the water adv* In slow motion; slowly : *A man named Ahmed skated slo-mo* (*1970s+*)

slopped *adj* Drunk (*1907+*)

sloppy *adj* 1 Slovenly; disorderly; messy 2 Careless; SLAPDASH (*1825+*)

sloppy joe *n phr* 1 A long, loose pullover sweater worn by women (*1940s+ Students*) 2 A dish made from ground meat cooked in a barbecue sauce and spread on an open bun (*1961+*) 3 A multidecked sandwich served in small thick triangles and filled with meats, cheeses, and mayonnaise, such that it is difficult to eat while keeping the fingers and face clean (*1970s+*)

sloppy seconds *n phr* <1▷ A sex act performed immediately after someone else's act : *Victoria denies having sex in the same bed as Heidi: "I like sex, but who wants sloppy seconds?"* 2 The inferior position; SECOND FIDDLE : *Lowden and Wood argued about who would be the top of the Chicago ticket and who would get sloppy seconds* (*1970s+*)

slops *n* Beer or liquor, esp bad or inferior (*1910+ Hoboes*)

sloshed *adj* Drunk : *a youngish man in a bar, a little sloshed and pouring out his troubles to the bartender/ You'll spend the night getting sloshed on 3.2 salmon piss* [*1900+*; fr *slosh*, "a drink," found by the 1880s]

slot *n* A slot machine; ONE-ARM BANDIT : *The slots are going day and night* (*1950+*)

slouch *See* NO SLOUCH

slough (or **sluff**) (**off**) *v* To waste time; to start to lose momentum or interest in a project : *sloughing off on the homework*

slow burn *modifier* : *Slow-burn resentment gave rise to a flinty local jargon n phr* A gradually increasing anger : *He remembered Edgar Kennedy and his slow burns* (*1930s+*) *See* DO A SLOW BURN

slowly in the wind *See* TWIST SLOWLY IN THE WIND

slow off the mark *adj phr* Late in starting; dilatory; behindhand : *If anything, the Clinton Administration has been a bit slow off the regulatory mark* [*1972+*; fr the *mark* from which foot-racers start]

slow on the draw (or **the uptake**) *adj phr* Dull and dilatory; mentally sluggish [*1940s+*; fr the action of drawing one's pistol, in the classical cowboy context]

slowpoke *n* A slow, sluggish, slothful person : *an old slowpoke* [*1848+*; fr *slow* used for

vowel rhyme with the early 1800s *poke*, "behave dilatorily, potter, saunter," perhaps influenced by 16th-century *slowback*, "sluggard"]

sludd *v* To suffer the terrible effects of chemical attack [Gulf War armed forces; acronym fr *salivate, lachrymate, urinate*, and *defecate*]

sluff *v* To avoid work and responsibility; shirk : *No one accused Bo of sluffing* [*1951+*; fr *slough off*]

slug[1] *n* 1 A bullet : *Doctors said they're still unable to remove the slug* (*1622+*) 2 A dollar : *do the job at 125 slugs a week* (*1887+*) 3 A drink of liquid, esp of whiskey; SNORT : *ordering a slug of Old Stepmother* (*1762+*) *v* (also **slug down**) : *The crowd cheered and jeered and slugged beers* (*1940s+*) [origin uncertain; perhaps fr the resemblance of a lump of metal to the snail-like creature the *slug*; the earliest attested US senses are "gold nugget, lump of crude metal"; the drink and drinking senses appear to be derived fr phrases like *fire a slug* and *cast a slug*, "take a drink of liquor," found as metaphors in late 18th-century British sources, and may be fr Irish *slog*, "a drink, a swallow"]

slug[2] *v* 1 To hit hard, esp with the fist; CLOBBER : *He tried to make peace, but he got slugged* (*1862+*) 2 To make or try for long base hits, esp regularly; GO FOR THE FENCES (*1888+ Baseball*) [fr British dialect *slog*, probably ultimately fr Old English *slagan*, cognate with German *schlagen*]

slugfest *n* 1 A hard and vicious fight, esp a prizefight more marked by powerful blows than by skillful boxing (*1916+*) 2 A baseball game in which many base hits are made (*1930s+ Baseball*)

slugged *adj* Drunk : *I want you really slugged when we shoot the scene* (*1951+*)

slugger *n* 1 A consistent long-ball hitter : *He's no slugger, he likes to place his hits* (*1883+ Baseball*) 2 A boxer more notable for hard hitting than for artistic finesse (*1877+*) *See* CIRCUIT SLUGGER

slug it out *v phr* To fight with powerful blows; try to smash one another; GO TOE TO TOE : *The principals were slugging it out in the alley* (*1943+*)

slug-nutty *adj* Stuporous or uncoordinated mentally and physically from taking too many blows on the head; PUNCH-DRUNK : *"Slug-nutty" fighters are often very talkative* (*1933+*)

slum or **go slumming** *v* or *v phr* To visit places or consort with persons below one's place or dignity; mix with one's inferiors : *So we went slumming over in Philadelphia* [*1884+*; fr *slum*, "wretched poor area," origin unknown]

slum it *v phr* To descend to the level of the lower classes; to endure conditions or accommodations that are worse than what one is accustomed to : *slumming it at the Holiday Inn*

slummy *adj* Inferior; lousy : *slummy conditions*

slump *n* **1** A sudden decline or collapse, esp of economic value or activity : *The stock market is in a dangerous slump* (1888+) **2** A period of bad performance : *The whole team's in a hitting slump* (1895+ Baseball)

slurp or **slup** *n* **1** : *Take a slurp of this soup, it's great!* (1949+) **2** A glissando passage (1940s+ Musicians) *v* To eat or drink with greed : *slurping porridge from a wooden spoon/ The cat slupped up the milk in no time* (1648+) [echoic]

slush *n* Blatant sentimentality; GOO. SCHMALTZ : *He sort of wept and uttered a lot of slush* (1916+)

slush fund *n phr* In politics, money used for shady enterprises like buying votes, bribing officials, etc : *the use of slush funds to defeat selected victims* [1839+; fr the armed forces and especially nautical practice of selling grease and other garbage to accumulate a *fund* to buy little luxuries for the troops or crew]

◁**slut**▷ *n* A sexually promiscuous female, esp one who dresses or acts provocatively (1451+)

smack[1] *adv* (also **smack dab**) Exactly; precisely : *What he said was smack on the mark/ Rosenthal was seated smack-dab next to the Prez in a relatively cozy dinner* (1892+) *n* **1** A blow; a slap : *He gave her a smack on the kisser* (1746+) **2** A kiss; SMACKER (1604+) **3** A try; CRACK : *Let's have a smack at it, shall we?* (1889+) **4** : *Throughout the 45-minute interview, he kept mentioning "smack," which isn't heroin, but a synonym for trash-talking* (1990s+ Sports) *v* **1** Hit; slap: *She smacked him hard* (1835+) **2** To kiss, esp noisily : *She smacked him square on the lips* (1570+) [probably ultimately echoic]

smack[2] or **shmack** or **shmeck** *n* Heroin; HORSE, SHIT : *The cocaine pulled from the front while the smack pushed from the back. It was an incredibly intense high* [1942+ Narcotics; fr Yiddish *shmek*, "a smell, sniff"; an earlier sense was "a small packet of drugs," hence merely a sniff or whiff]

smack[3] *n* : *Smart people who are only interested in school are called "nerds" or "smacks"* (1980s+ Teenagers)

smacker *n* **1** (also **smackeroo**) A dollar; BUCK : *having to cough up a thousand smackers/ That car's not worth a single smackeroo* (entry form 1921+, variant 1940s+) **2** A kiss; SMACK : *Slip me a smacker, sister* (1775+) [the money

sense, attested also of pesos and pounds sterling, may echo the slapping down of a bill on a counter, gambling table, etc, and hence be semantically related to *plank* and *plunk* for coins]

smacky lips *See* PLAY KISSIE

small beer *n* Something or someone insignificant : *that idea is just small beer*

small change *modifier* : *This is small-change stuff n phr* Something of little value : *So I am now small change in Mamie's scorn* (1902+) [fr coins of small value]

small fortune *n* A large amount of money; a higher-than-expected cost : *a small fortune for Valentine's dinner*

small fry *adj* : *small-fry writers like me n phr* **1** Children or a child • Often used as a term of address, either affectionate or derogatory **2** An insignificant person or persons; nonentities : *conveniences not enjoyed by the small fry overhead* [1866+; fr *fry*, "small or immature fish"]

small potatoes *n phr* **1** A trivial amount of money; CHICKEN FEED, PEANUTS : *I received $120,000, which is no small potatoes* **2** An insignificant person, enterprise, etc : *From the tuber is derived the term "small potatoes," applied with more or less humor to anything mean or petty* (1840+)

small (or **fine**) **print,** the *n phr* Unsuspected and possibly injurious conditions or requirements, esp when part of a contract, an insurance policy, etc : *Be sure you look at the small print if you make any deals with that guy/ Does the mayor read the fine print?* (entry form 1944+, variant 1960+)

small talk *n phr* Talk, esp relaxed and idle conversation; phatic communion; CHIN MUSIC, CHITCHAT : *He's very serious and has a hard time making small talk* (1751+)

small-time *adj* Characteristic of the small time; inferior; petty; second-rate; BUSH LEAGUE : *a small-time political power* (1910+ Show business)

small time, the *n phr* Mediocre or inferior businesses, enterprises, entertainment or sports circuits, etc; the BUSH LEAGUES : *After six years in the small time she finally went to Broadway* (1910+ Show business)

smarm *n* The quality of something "smarmy" : *How to write pet stories, then, while skirting the swamps of smarm?* (1937+)

smarmy *adj* **1** Smooth and flattering; unctuously ingratiating; fulsome : *a rather smarmy doctor and a highly officious nurse* **2** Rich and sonorous; orotund and fruity; PLUMMY : *an announcer with a smarmy voice* **3** Smug and self-righteous : *Uncle Sam's Smarmy Look Into Employee Sex Lives* [1924+; origin unknown; since the earliest attested uses have to do with hair oil, it may be a vague blend of *smooth, smear, palm oil, cream,* etc]

smart *adj* **1** Fashionable; stylish; modish (*1718+*) **2** Guided toward a target by laser beams, television signals, etc, rather than simply aimed : *The subs are equipped with smart torpedoes/ the potential accuracy of "smart" bombs and missiles (Armed forces fr Vietnam War)* [the first sense was revived in the 1880s and much reprehended] *See* GET WISE, STREET-SMART

smart aleck or **alec** *modifier* : *I asked you to come here to give us advice, not smart-aleck talk* *n phr* SMART-ASS (*1865+*) [perhaps fr *Aleck* Hoag, a thief whose fate was described in an 1844 book by George Wilkes]

◁**smart-ass** or **wise-ass**▷ *adj* : *That's a smart-ass question* *n* A person who is quick to offer an often-abrasive opinion or comment from a posture of superior intelligence and learning; BIGMOUTH, KNOW-IT-ALL, WISE GUY : *You're a real wiseass sometimes, Mary Anne* (*1960+*)

smart bomb *n phr* **1** An aerial bomb that can be guided directly to its target (*1972+*) **2** Any similarly precise and directed agent : *Researchers experimenting with mice have created a cancer "smart bomb" that attacks and kills leukemia cells without harming normal cells*

smart card *n phr* An identity card that provides extensive information on a person by means of a tiny microchip (*1980+*)

smart cookie *n phr* An intelligent person; sagacious judge : *Joanna was a very smart cookie, and she was apt to put two and two together* (*1948+*)

smart drug *n phr* Any substance alleged to make the user more alert or better able to remember things: *Americans have taken to smart drugs to prepare for tests, prime themselves for business meetings or just burn a little brighter at parties* (*1980s+*)

smart guy *n* SMART-ASS : *Well, I've got news for you, smart guy* (*1940s+*)

smart money, the *n phr* The predictions, expectations, and bets of those who know best : *Try to stick where the smart money is* (*1926+*)

smartmouth *n* An annoyingly impudent, assertive, and critical person; SMART-ASS : *keeps getting beaten up because he's a smartmouth at school* (*1968+*)

smarts *n* Intelligence; BRAINS, SAVVY : *If they had any smarts, they would have put a silencer on a gun and pumped a bullet in his head* [*1970+*; probably on analogy with *brains* and *wits*] *See* STREET SMARTS

smarty or **smartie** *n* smart aleck; SMART-ASS, WISE-ASS • Most often used in address : *I will bid seven on hearts, smarty* (*1861+*)

smarty-pants *n* smart aleck; SMART-ASS, SMARTY : *That smarty-pants always gives a flip answer* (*1930s+*)

smash *n* **1** A total failure; a disaster, esp a financial collapse (*1839+*) **2** (also **smash hit**) A great success; HIT : *Key Largo is an unqualified smash* (*1923+ Show business*) **3** Wine (*1959+ Black*)

smash and grab *modifier* (also **crash and dash**) Crude and violent : *There's a major difference between the smash-and-grab tactics of the tabloids and the relatively sober treatment these stories get on the networks/ Deregulation promoted the casino economy, with its leveraged buyouts and smash-and-grab finance/ The attempted burglary was like scores of other "crash-and-dash" thefts* *n phr* A crude and violent robbery : *The smash and grab guys break through your closed window and grab your valuables, knowing that you're going to be stunned and perhaps blinded by bits of flying glass* (*1927+*)

smashed *adj* Drunk : *I'm really able to go into a bar without getting smashed* (*1962+*)

smashing *adj* Excellent; wonderful • Still chiefly British : *I told her she had a smashing figure* (*1911+*)

smash-mouth *n phr* **1** A particularly violent sort of football : *Smash-mouth was their type of game* **2** Aggression; a condition of confrontation (*1990s+*)

smear[1] *modifier* : *They never stoop to smear tactics* *n* : *His whole campaign was a vile smear of the other party's man* • The current term is "negative campaigning" (*1943+*) *v* **1** To knock unconscious; KAYO (*1920+ Prizefighting*) **2** To defeat decisively; trounce; CLOBBER, SKUNK : *The Rangers got smeared 12–zip* (*1900+*) **3** To attack someone's reputation, esp with false or vague charges of the ad hominem sort; defame : *His technique was always to smear his opponent and avoid talking about issues of substance* (*1847+*) [revived in the 1930s in the political context]

smear[2] *v* SCHMEAR[1] (*1950s+*)

◁**smeg**▷ or ◁**smegma**▷ *n* Something quite yukky or despicable, as the secretion beneath the male foreskin or around the female clitoris

smell *v* **1** To be nasty and contemptible; STINK, SUCK : *The whole damn situation smells* (*1933+*) **2** To take narcotics by inhaling; SNIFF : *You must be smelling the stuff* (*1949+*)

smell a rat *v phr* To be suspicious : *impossible for Schwartz not to have smelled a rat if he had day-to-day contact* (*1550+*)

smell blood *v phr* To be aroused and exhilarated by the imminent destruction of one's prey or opponent : *The Democrats "smelled blood" over the trade issue* [*1970s+*; fr the behavior of predators who attack prey, esp wounded prey]

smeller *n* The nose : *a sock on his smeller* (*1700+*)

smell like a rose *See* COME UP SMELLING LIKE A ROSE

smell to (high) heaven *v phr* To smell very bad and very strongly : *smells to high heaven after nuking the Lean Cuisine*

smidgen or **smidge** or **smitch** *n* A little bit; CUNT-HAIR, SKOSH : *The deck may be stacked a smidgen against Lianna's husband/ I was a smidge stressed as a result of a call from Mother* [1886+; origin unknown; possibly fr Scots Gaelic *smidin*, "small syllable, hence tiny quantity"; found by 1845 as *smitchin* and by 1878 as *smidgeon*]

smile *See* CRACK A SMILE

smiley *See* EMOTICON

smiley face or **smiley** *n phr* A computer "emoticon" (:-), used to express happiness or approval : *messages studded with smiley faces* (*1990s+ Computer*)

-smith *combining word* A person who makes or skillfully uses what is indicated; ARTIST : *jokesmith/ tunesmith/ wordsmith/ wafflesmith* (*1813+*)

smoke *n* **1** A cigarette or cigar : *I mooched a couple of smokes* (*1882+*) **2** Marijuana; POT : *something called smoke or snow* (*1940s+ Narcotics*) **3** Inferior liquor, esp denatured alcohol : *drink that smoke, then pass out petrified* (*1904+ Hoboes*) **4** (also **smoke and mirrors**) Artful lies; talk meant to deceive; BULLSHIT : *Those sections of the article are pure smoke* (*1565+*) ◄**5**► A black person (*1913+*) **6** A very fast fastball : *Has Joe lost his smoke?/ the Yankees' smoke-throwing reliever* (*1912+ Baseball*) **7** A very fast runner, vehicle, etc : *He's no smoke as for speed* (*1980s+*) *v* **1** To shoot someone dead; PLUG : *This wasn't a Jamaican whore got smoked in some vacant lot* (*1926+ Underworld & police*) **2** To be executed in a gas chamber : *still faced death and might one day be smoked* (*1970s+ Underworld and police*) **3** : *pitchers are supposed to be cranked up and smoking* **4** To be very angry; BURN, STEAM : *He was smoking for about an hour after she called him that* (*1548+*) **5** (also **smoke off**) To defeat utterly; trounce; CLOBBER : *He didn't simply beat Carl Lewis. He smoked him/ The dreaded Bostons came to town, and the Brewers smoked 'em on opening day/ For a time we "smoked off" our rivals* (*1980s+*) **6** To hit very hard; CLOBBER : *"Just let me take my jacket off," and bang, the guy from Chicago smokes him/ Alomar smoked a single to left* (*1980s+*) *See* BLOW SMOKE, GO UP IN SMOKE, J

smoke, a *n* Tobacco and a smoking of tobacco (*1882+*)

smoked out *adj phr* Intoxicated by narcotics; HIGH, STONED (*1990s+ Narcotics*)

smoke factory *n phr* An opium den : *a No 9 pill in Hop Lee's smoke factory* (*1905+ Narcotics*)

smoke-filled room *n* A place where intense discussion or negotiation takes place : *the smoke-filled rooms of the Democratic Party*

smoke out *v phr* To find out : *I'll try to smoke out where the bodies are hidden* [1720+; fr the use of *smoke* in order to get bees and other animals *out* of their domiciles]

smoker *n* **1** Something thrown, moving, played, etc, very fast : *a number which is a quartet smoker* **2** (also **smokeball**) A very fast fastball (*entry form 1912+, variant 1940s+*)

Smokey Bear or **Smokey the Bear** or **Smoky** *n phr* or *n* A police officer, esp a state highway patrol officer : *Keep Don advised for the location of "Smokies"* [1970s+ Citizens band & truckers; fr the fact that many state highway patrol police wear a broad-brimmed ranger's hat like that worn by the US Forest Service's ursine symbol]

smokin' *adj* Attractive; good-looking; desirable; COOL, HOT : *What's smokin' in collectibles? Tobacco jars!/ That is a smokin' car* [1980s+; a synonym of *hot*]

smoking *adj* Providing evidence of crime or guilt : *smoking bed/ smoking bimbo/ smoking checkbook* [1980s+; modeled on *smoking gun*]

smoking gun *n phr* Incontestable evidence; the GOODS : *They had discovered the "smoking gun" that would destroy the general's case/ In fact, there may be no "smoking gun," no incontrovertible, black-and-white evidence of wrongdoing* [1970s+; fr the image of a murderer caught with the fatal *smoking* firearm still in hand]

smooch or **smooge** or **smouge** *n* : *I'd rather have hooch, and a bit of a smooch* *v* **1** To steal; pilfer; MOOCH : *Then she went over to the cash box and smooched four $20 bills* (*1941+*) **2** To kiss and caress; NECK, PET : *College kids are still smooching/ a few minutes of torrid hugging and smooching* (*1588+*) [the pilfering sense probably derives from the kissing sense by way of *mooch*; the kissing sense may be fr German *schmutzen*, "to kiss, to smile"; the dated instance is spelled *smouch*; the term was reestablished as *smooch* in the 1930s]

smoosh or **smush** *v* To mash : *The one piece of Spandex flattens the curves as it squashes the bulges, so that your top and bottom weight get smooshed together evenly* (*1914+*)

smooth *adj* Excellent; pleasing; attractive : *Boy, she was smooth* (*1893+ Students*)

smoothie or **smooth article** or **smooth operator** *n* or *n phr* A person who is attractive, pleasant, and full of finesse : *thought of Dr Hugo Barker as a smooth article/ You think* *you're such a smoothie* [1933+ Students; *smoothie* is like *slicker*, but today lacks the connotations of dishonesty and trickiness]

smurf *n* : *The husband and wife were "smurfs," a type of drug-money launderer. A husband-and-wife smurfing team will travel from bank to bank, posing as strangers* v : *To avoid being reported by banks, criminals often make numerous deposits of slightly less than $10,000, a practice known as smurfing* (1980s+)

snaffle *v* To steal; appropriate; SWIPE : *A streetwalker would have snaffled the lot* (1725+)

snafu (SNA FOO) *adj* : *It's a very snafu set-up here* n 1 A very confused situation; FUCK-UP, mess : *The snafu occurred at Markwood Road* 2 A blunder; an egregious mistake; BLOOPER : *My attempt to set things right was a total snafu* v : *He gave it a good shot, but snafued horribly* [WWII armed forces; fr *situation normal, all fucked up*]

snail mail *n phr* Mail sent through regular postal service : *Acrobat has the potential to pay for itself rather quickly by eliminating the need to send documents by courier or even regular mail (snail mail, as it is charmingly called by computer aficionados)* [1980s+ Computer; referring to the slowness of the *snail*]

snake *n* 1 A young woman (WWI Navy) 2 (also **Snake**) A native or resident of West Virginia (1934+) 3 : *US banks, railways, airlines, and some fast-food restaurants have switched over almost entirely to what is known as the "snake," where all stations are served by one single-file line* (1980s+) *v* To depart, esp unobtrusively; sneak : *He snakes out of here without an overcoat* (1848+)

snake-bitten or **snake-bit** *adj* Helplessly incapacitated; ineffective : *O'Neal seems particularly snake-bitten these days/ I suppose when you're snakebit you feel lousy. And I sure feel lousy* (1940s+)

snake eyes *n phr* The point or the roll of two (1929+ Crapshooting)

snake in the grass *n phr* A sneaky, underhanded person

snake oil *modifier* : *Kenosha officials watch out for the "snake-oil salesmen"* n phr A fraudulent remedy : *But I have to admit he sounded sincere, like he really believes in that snake oil he's peddling* (1927+)

snap *n* 1 Energy; vim; dash; PIZZAZZ (1865+) 2 A photograph; snapshot (1894+) 3 An insult, esp a public taunt : *In the relative privacy of the dugout, the quick-tempered wreak havoc with what some teams call "snaps"* (1990s+) *v* 1 : *The photographer snapped him making a rude gesture* 2 To mock or tease; SNAP ON someone (1960s+ Black) 3 To go crazy; FREAK OUT : *that Richard Herrin should have snapped* (1970s+) [the third noun sense is

found by 1648, but the current street and sports use is probably not a survival; the third verb sense is fr the cliché "something *snapped* in his mind"]

snap, a *n phr* Something easily done; BREEZE, CINCH : *Winning next time will be a snap* [1845+; fr mid-1800s *a soft snap*, "something *snapped* up easily, a bargain"]

snap course *n phr* An easy course; CRIP : *His heavily attended snap course is good for a laugh* (1900+ Students)

snap someone's head off *v phr* To make a quick, angry retort : *When I suggested that, she snapped my head off* (1886+)

snap it up *v phr* To hurry; act faster; SNAP TO IT : *Drop over to the main drag and snap it up* (1940s+)

snap on someone *v phr* To insult, esp publicly and in a sort of competitive way : *After Ivey spent five minutes on stage snapping on a white man in the audience, they conducted snapping sessions to get contributions from professionals* [1990s+; the general sense is found by 1578, but the current use is probably not a survival]

snap out of it *v phr* To recover, esp from gloom or sluggardy; become energetic (1928+)

snapping or **snaps** *n* : *Ragging, bagging, snapping, and cracking, these are all word games teens use as a way of competing with one another/ Many blacks regard "snapping," a back-and-forth, can-you-top-this insult contest, as part of their cultural heritage/ I used to think this game was called "playing the dozens," but I recently learned that the '90s term for these insults is "snaps"* (1990s+ Teenagers)

snappy *adj* 1 Quick; brisk; energetic : *Be snappy about it* (1831+) 2 Trim and attractive; fashionable; smart : *wearing a snappy light gray suit* (1881+) *See* MAKE IT SNAPPY

snap to *v phr* To become sharply attentive and responsive : *His soldiers snapped to and did what they were told* [1940s+; fr the quick way a military person *snaps to attention* on command]

snap to (or **into**) **it** *v phr* To hurry; go faster; MAKE IT SNAPPY : *Get that floor clean and snap to it* (1967+)

snarf *v* To take or grab : *How to Keep Bandits From "Snarfing" Your Passwords* (1980s+)

snarf up (or **down**) *v phr* To eat; gobble; SCARF : *We can think of a lot of places we would like to eat chocolate, snarf down a few burgers, and gawk at shiny cars* [1968+; in early 1980s computer slang, defined in the *Hacker's Dictonary* as "to snarf, sometimes with the connotation of absorbing, processing, or understanding"]

snarky *adj* Irritable; touchy : *She's just in a snarky mood, that's all/ a snarky, no-illusions,* but *far-from-hopeless comedy* [1906+; fr British dialect *snark*, "to find fault, complain," fr the basic sense "snort, snore"; of echoic origin, with cognates in many Germanic languages]

snatch *n* **1** : *a $50,000 ransom to get him back from a snatch* **2** : *A piece of paper covering the slit was rolled aside in the course of a snatch* <3> The vulva; CUNT : *Put the goddamned piece up her snatch and pulled the trigger* (1903+) *v* **1** To kidnap : *The kid was snatched as he left school* (1932+) **2** To steal (1765+) *See* PUT THE SNATCH ON someone or something

snazz something **up** *v phr* To make something smarter and more elegant; enhance; GUSSY UP : *and snazzes them up with appliqués/ Install a new loo, or snazz up your current water closet* (1970s+)

snazzy *adj* **1** Elegant; smart and fashionable; clever and desirable; NIFTY, RITZY : *mounted on snazzy mag-type wheels/ While they may appear snazzy now, time will take its toll* (1932+) **2** Gaudy and meretricious; HOKEY, JAZZY : *TV's wittiest, toughest, least snazzy news strip* (1970s+) [perhaps a blend of *snappy* and *jazzy*]

sneak *n* (also **sneak preview**) : *After a sneak in Chicago they decided to shelve it* *v* To show a movie unexpectedly to an audience in order to assess its appeal : *We sneaked it in several cities* (1960s+ Movie studio)

sneakers or **sneaks** *n* Rubber-soled sports shoes : *wearing a sweater, a shirt, short socks, and sneakers/ Anybody see my old sneaks?* [1895+; because one can usually move noiselessly in such footwear]

sneaky *adj* Furtive; shifty; deceptive : *I never trusted that sneaky little weasel* (1833+)

sneaky pete (or **Pete**) *n phr* **1** Inferior liquor, often homemade or bootleg; PANTHER PISS : *discussing the effects of "sneaky-pete"/ piled into the Ritz bar and polished off a whole row of "sneaky pete"* (1940s+) **2** A cheap fortified wine sold in pint bottles called "jugs" : *full of that cheap wine they call "sneaky pete"* (1940s+) **3** Any cheap and inferior wine (1940s+) **4** Marijuana mixed in wine (1950s+)

snide *adj* Contemptible; mean; nasty, esp in an insinuating way • Now used nearly exclusively in reference to remarks and persons who make them : *A woman gets nothing but snide remarks about her driving skills* [1859+; origin unknown]

sniff *v* To inhale a narcotic powder; SNORT (1920s+ Narcotics)

sniffer or **snifter** *n* A cocaine user or addict : *The Baron was "a sniffer" himself* (1920s+ Narcotics)

sniffles or **snuffles** *n* A runny nose from a common cold or allergy : *lots of Kleenex for his sniffles* (1770s+)

sniff (something) **out** *v phr* To seek as if by following a scent : *Mike hopes his kids may sniff out something faster than the police* (1940s+)

sniffy or **snifty** *adj* Disdainful; haughtily fastidious; fault-finding : *even the sniffiest of lexicographers* [1871+; fr the mien of a person who often seems to be smelling something nasty]

snifter *n* **1** A drink of liquor; dram; SLUG, SNORT : *plastered on a couple of snifters* (1844+) **2** A large, bulbous, stemmed glass used for drinking brandy (1937+) [origin uncertain; perhaps fr the common upper-respiratory reaction to taking a strong swallow of liquor, also noted in the earlier term *sneezer* and in *snorter*; *snifter, sneezer,* and *snorter* were all three used to mean "a strong breeze, gale," and all three came to mean "something large and impressive, something very strong," apparently after the drinking senses were established; before the drinking senses, the terms applied to snuff-taking, with its even more pronounced nasal spasms]

snipe *n* **1** A cigarette or cigar butt (1889+) **2** An engine-room hand, aircraft mechanic, or other below-decks crew member : *"Snipes" service and maintain their flying crews' birds* (1920+ Navy) [origin obscure, although apparently these, along with several other slang uses, both British and US, all refer somehow to the long-billed bird and its habits]

snit or **snit-fit** *n* A fit of angry agitation; SWIVET : *He goes into such a snit that he ploughs the car into a wall/ He has a reputation for throwing considerable snits/ And we forget about our little snit-fit in there*

snitch *n* An informer; RAT, STOOL PIGEON : *Maybe some of my old snitches have run across something new* (1785+) *v* **1** To inform; SING, SQUEAL : *The little rat snitched and the little snitch ratted* (1801+) **2** To steal; pilfer; SWIPE : *He snitched a couple of cookies* (1904+) [noun and first verb senses probably fr underworld slang *snitch,* "nose"]

snog *v* To flirt; court; make love; MAKE OUT, NECK • Chiefly British [1945+; origin unknown]

snooker (SNŌŌ kər, SNŌŌ-) *v* To cheat; swindle; SCAM : *The Chinese clearly believe that they snookered Nixon/ I've been snookered before, and it'll happen again/ The simple arithmetic shows that Koch and the city were snookered* [1900s+; fr the pool game called *snooker,* apparently because a novice at the game can easily be tricked and cheated by an expert; compare *euchre*]

snookered *adj* Swindled; cheated : *snookered by the post office again*

snookums *n* Precious one; sweet and dear one • Used to address small dogs, babies, etc : *Yes, you are. You're my little snookums* (*1919+*)

snoop *n* A detective : *Private snoop, hunh?* [ultimately fr Dutch *snoepen*, "pry"]

snoot *n* The nose; snout; SCHNOZZ : *Pokin' him one in the snoot* (*1861+*) *v* To behave haughtily toward; disdain : *people who snoot goat milk* (*1928+*)

snooty *adj* Snobbish; haughty and disdainful; supercilious; HOITY-TOITY, SNIFFY : *the snootiest madame in America/ a generally vain and snooty class of men* [*1919+*; fr the mien of a person who smells something nasty and holds the nose high]

snooze *n* **1** Nap or sleep: *not comfortable enough to suit me for a snooze* **2** Something that induces sleep: a soporific event, person, etc : *The concert was a snooze* (*1960s+*) *v* To sleep; COP ZS, SACK OUT (*1789+*) [origin unknown; perhaps echoic of a snore]

snort *n* **1** A drink of liquor, esp of plain whiskey; HOOKER : *Who's ready for another short snort?/ All hands had another snort* (*1889+*) **2** A dose of narcotic for inhaling; LINE (*1951+ Narcotics*) *v* To inhale narcotics, esp cocaine; SNIFF : *since ma was a viper, and daddy would snort* (*1935+ Narcotics*) [drinking sense fr earlier *snorter* of same purport] *See* SNIFTER

snorter *See* RIPSNORTER, RIP-ROARING

snot *n* **1** Nasal mucus (*1425+*) **2** A despicable person, esp a self-important nonentity : *Tell that little snot to get lost* (*1809+*) *v* To treat someone disdainfully; be haughty : *I should not be "snotted" by an owner, maitre d', or waiter* (*1970s+*) [ultimately fr a common Germanic term for "nose," also represented by *schnozzle, snout, snoot*, etc; the second noun and verb senses probably influenced by *snooty*]

snotnose or **snottynose** *modifier* : *He's just a snotnose kid n* An importunate upstart; a neophyte, esp a knowing one : *some snotnose in New York* (*1941+*)

snot-rag *n* A handkerchief or tissue (*1895+*)

snotty *adj* Supercilious and disdainful : *I won't give that snotty bastard the time of day* [*1926+*; fr *snot* and influenced by *snooty*]

snow *n* **1** Cocaine : *And he was also snorting snow* (*1914+ Narcotics*) **2** : *I thought his rationale was pure snow v* To persuade in a dubious cause, esp by exaggeration, appeals to common sentiment, etc; BLOW SMOKE : *The electorate will not be snowed into supporting that silly measure* (*1945+*) [verb sense fr the idea of snowing someone *under* with articulate reasons] *See* EYES LIKE PISS-HOLES IN THE SNOW

snowball *v* **1** To increase rapidly : *Soon the racket began to snowball* (*1929+*) **2** To dominate and crush; STEAMROLLER : *He's less sensitive to people's feelings. He runs over them, snowballs them* (*1850+*) [first sense fr the fact that a *snowball* rolled downhill becomes larger and larger; second sense fr the notion of attacking someone with *snowballs*]

snowball's chance in hell, a *n phr* No possibility whatever; CHINAMAN'S CHANCE : *He doesn't have a snowball's chance in hell of getting that degree in time* (*1934+*)

snowbird *n* **1** A retired person, usu elderly, who winters in the sunny South : *A Connecticut pharmaceutical firm hires elder "snowbirds" during the warmer months and holds their jobs open while they winter in Florida* (*1980s+*) **2** (also **snowblower**) A cocaine user or addict; COKEHEAD : *Nelly's eyes had a glassy, faraway look. Snowbird, he thought to himself* (*1914+ Narcotics*) **3** Any narcotic addict (*1931+ Narcotics*)

snow (or **ski**) **bunny** *n phr* A young woman who frequents skiing resorts (*1953+*)

snowed in (or **up**) *adj phr* Intoxicated with narcotics; HIGH (*1920s+ Narcotics*)

snow job *n phr* Strong and persistent persuasion, esp in a dubious cause; an overwhelming advocacy : *This is no snow job, either. I wish I had 25 Jerry Koosmans/ Don't let Slattery give you a snow job and get you into trouble* (*WWII armed forces*) *v* : *I was snowjobbed into giving the maximum* [fr the idea of *snowing under* with insistent reasons; now probably reinforced by the narcotics sense of *snow*]

snowman *n* : *Watson took a snowman, as golfers call an 8, here on the fifteenth, ruining what otherwise might have been the low round of the day/ "Whaddya have?" A snowman (an 8 on the hole)* (*1980+ Golf*)

snow someone or something **under** *v phr* To burden or assail with excessive demands, work, etc; overwhelm : *until a frailer man than he would have been snowed under* (*1880+*)

snozzle *See* SCHNOZZ

snuff *modifier* Showing or doing murder, esp the killing of women in sadistic shows or orgies : *the snuff murder of an abused and homeless teenaged girl/ the vogue of the snuff film* (*1975+*) *v* To kill : *more chillingly, STRESS snuffed at least 20 civilians/ Garlic never snuffed me* (*1973+*) [fr the idea of snuffing out a flame; found by 1884 in the form snuff out] *See* UP TO SNUFF

snuff film (or **movie**) *n phr* A movie in which the actual killing of a person is shown • Filmed murder is very likely a lurid idea rather than a fact : *Year Zero has the shock value of a snuff film/ If he'd told them he was* *making a snuff movie he would have been treated better* (1975+)

snuffing *n* A killing, esp a murder : *too eager to put together two unconnected snuffings* (1970s+)

snuffy *adj* Drunk (1823+)

snuggle-bunnies *See* PLAY SNUGGLE-BUNNIES

so *See* SAY-SO

soak *n* A drunkard; LUSH, SOUSE (1820+) *v* **1** To hit; SOCK : *to soak you in the midriff/ Why don't you soak him?* (1896+) **2** To overcharge; make someone pay exorbitantly : *a good case of how soak-the-rich corporation taxes wind up right in the pocketbooks of all of us* (1895+)

soaked *adj* Drunk [1722+; one of Benjamin Franklin's catalog of words for "drunk"]

◁**soak** one's **hose**▷ *v phr* To do the sex act; SCREW : *I think maybe he soaking his hose* (1990s+)

soak yourself *See* GO SOAK YOURSELF

so-and-so *n* A despicable person; BASTARD, JERK : *I think I'll sue the so-and-so See* SON OF A BITCH

soap *n* **1** SOFT SOAP (1854+) **2** SOAP OPERA (1943+) *v* To flatter and cajole; SWEET-TALK : *one of those Republicans who soaped Vivien* (1853+)

soapbox *n* The attitude from which one orates, pontificates, counsels urgently, etc : *Be careful or she'll get on the old soapbox and preach about fiscal iniquity* (1907+)

soap opera *modifier* : *The average man and woman in this country live a soap-opera existence n phr* **1** A radio or television daily dramatic series typically showing the painful, passionate, and riveting amours and disasters of more or less ordinary people : *a new soap opera which threatens to out-misery all the others* **2** A life or incidents in life that resemble such shows : *You want to hear the latest in my never-ending soap opera?* [1939+; fr the fact that in radio days such shows were typically sponsored by *soap* manufacturers]

soaps, the *n phr* Radio or television daily dramatic series collectively (1943+)

◁**sob** or **SOB**▷ (pronounced as separate letters) *n* SON OF A BITCH (1918+)

so bad one **can taste it** *adv phr* Very urgently; very keenly : *She wanted the book so bad she could taste it* [1960s+; fr the earlier expression *I have to piss so bad I can taste it*, implying that the urine had risen in one to the level of the throat and tongue]

sober *See* COLD SOBER, STONE COLD SOBER

sob sister *n phr* A woman news reporter or writer who specializes in sentimental or human-interest material (1912+)

sob story *n phr* A very affecting tale, esp an account of one's disabling troubles; a story

that disingenuously appeals to one's charitable nature : *Do not weep crocodile tears over media sob stories* (1913+)

sock[1] *n* **1** : *To land another sock on Mr Renault's nose* (1700+) **2** A set of mounted cymbals sounded by tramping on a foot pedal; HIGH-HAT (1920+ *Musicians*) *v* To strike; hit hard; CLOBBER, PASTE : *bein' socked to dreamland* (1700+) [probably echoic]

sock[2] *n* **1** A place where money is kept, esp saved; also, savings collectively : *Every dollar that he will receive for the current four-year term will go into the family sock* (1924+) **2** A box, bag, safe, etc, where money is kept (1930s+ *Underworld*) [fr the use of a *sock* as a container; one reference of 1698 indicates that *sock* meant "pocket" in underworld slang]

sock away *v phr* To save or horde; put away as sav-ings : *Last year that group socked away $128 billion in savings bonds/ The American people socked away $3,200,000 in the year's second quarter* [perhaps fr the notion of concealing money in a *sock*; but *sock*, "sew up and conceal," is attested fr the alteration of 1800s *sock* or *sock down*, "pay, dispose of money"]

sockdollager or **socdollager** *n* **1** A decisive blow (1830+) **2** A person or thing that is remarkable, wonderful, superior, etc; HUMDINGER : *his Dauntless Quest to lay his Sockdollager of a Product at the feet of the Public* (1838+) [fr a metathesis of *doxology*, "the finish or finishing part of a religious service," as suggesting something that terminates, like a heavy blow; influenced by *sock*[1]]

socked in *adj phr* Plagued by adverse weather, esp by fog, heavy rain or snow, etc : *You may find yourself partly socked in if you're coming down the Jersey Turnpike this morning* [1953+; probably fr the adverse weather indications given by the *wind sock* at early or small airports; perhaps influenced by the notion of being closed up in a *sock* as money is when it is *socked away*]

sock 'em *See* ROCK 'EM SOCK 'EM

sockeroo *modifier* : *putting some sockeroo catches in the president's plan n* A great success; something with extraordinary power and impact; esp, a lavish and popular film, show, etc; BLOCKBUSTER : *an old-fashioned Hippodrome sockeroo/ with Paramount's "Dear Ruth" the only sockeroo* (1942+)

sock it to someone *v phr* To attack someone vigorously and effectively; LET someone HAVE IT : *Some congressional liberals would like to sock it to business by taking away the tax reductions/ Thanks for socking it to Barbie, that all-American plastic tart* (1877+)

socko *adj* Very powerful; explosively impressive; terrific : *Okay, now a socko surprise/ the socko effect, recorded here by camera* (1939+) *adv* : *find they do socko in their native heath* (1948+) *interj* An exclamation imitating the impact of a hard blow and expressing abrupt force : *Socko! He punches the villain in the jaw* (1924+) *n* A hard punch (1925+)

socks *See* DROP YOUR COCKS AND GRAB YOUR SOCKS, KNOCK someone's SOCKS OFF

socks off, the *adv phr* Very thoroughly • Always used, like the semantically similar *the brains out* and *the pants off*, to intensify a verb : *undressed her and screwed the socks off her/ a theoretical homily on the true meaning of Eros that, I am forced to admit, absolutely bored the socks off me* [1845+; the earliest recorded form is *knock the socks off*, and the usage has been revived recently] *See* BEAT THE SOCKS OFF someone

sod *n* A male; man; GUY • Chiefly British : *Your lodge brother, your neighbor, the guy on the beat who's just a plain good sod* (1818+) *v* To curse and vilify; revile extremely; DAMN, FUCK, PISS ON someone or something : *You do not send the Prime Minister to China to bargain for just an airport. Sod the airport* [fr *sodomite* and *sodomize*]

sodding *modifier* Fucking • A British expression of anger or contempt, or an intensive

sod off *v phr* To leave; depart; FUCK OFF • Often an irritated command : *Well, that's that. If you don't like it, sod off* (1960+ British)

soft *adj* 1 Nonaddictive, as drugs 2 Stupid : *soft in the head*

softball *adj* Trivial and contemptible; nonserious : *a softball question if ever there was one/ This softball performance by Democrats on the Judiciary Committee in the Thomas hearings left many in a huge TV audience wondering what legitimate claim to national power this bumbling crowd could possibly have* [1970s+; based on *hardball*]

soft-core *adj* Somewhat less than extreme; moderated; slightly ameliorated : *The fashion magazine is soft-core pornography/ a softcore picture of a bare-chested woman n* Something that is not extreme, esp a sexually arousing but not carnally explicit movie, magazine, etc : *She doesn't care for X-rated, but enjoys a little soft-core now and then* [1966+; based on *hard-core*]

soft drug *n phr* A narcotic like marijuana and some hallucinogens, thought of as nonaddictive and only slightly damaging to health [1959+; based on *hard drug*]

softie or **softy** *n* A person who is amiably and quickly compliant; someone easy to cajole and victimize : *You are a patsy, a quick push, a big softie* (1886+)

soft in the head *adj phr* Stupid; dim-witted; LAMEBRAINED [1938+; *soft* is found by 1621 in the sense "silly, simple, foolish"]

soft landing *n phr* A slowing of the economy without a crash or recession : *A weakening dollar clearly holds risks for the White House, where prospects of a soft landing after 48 months of economic growth offered some hope* (1980s+)

soft money (or **currency**) *n phr* 1 Currency that is highly inflated or likely to become less and less valuable : *During the first two months of this year, soft money contributions, chiefly from industry, flowed into the coffers of the Republican National Committee* (1940+) 2 Campaign donations that are not regulated by the Federal Election Commission : *raising millions of dollars of what is known in election-financing language as "soft money"/ Clinton is behind in the collection of soft money, funds that are supposed to go for "party-building activities" but can make a big difference in a Presidential contest* (1980s+ Politics) 3 Money from research grants, which may run out if the grant is not renewed (1976+ Universities) [modeled on *hard money*]

soft on *adv phr* Romantically attracted; also, easy on someone : *soft on Kevin Costner/ soft on violators*

soft-pedal *v* To make less prominent; deemphasize; DOWNPLAY : *Even my friends advised me to soft-pedal my criticisms* [1915+; fr the *pedal* on a piano that *softens* the notes played]

soft sell *n phr* Selling or advertising in a nonstrident, noninsistent tone [1955+; modeled on *hard sell*]

soft soap *n phr* Flattery; cajolement; SWEET-TALK : *I won her over finally with a lot of soft soap* (1830+) *v* : *We had to soft-soap the electorate pretty shabbily* (1840+)

soft touch *n phr* 1 A person from whom it is easy to borrow or wheedle something : *You get the reputation of being a soft touch* (1939+) 2 SOFTIE (1940s+) 3 An easy job; a sinecure : *He spent his life seeking the ultimate soft touch* (1955+)

so hot *See* NOT SO HOT

SOL (pronounced as separate letters) *adv* Shit out of luck; ruined; KAPUT : *If the press gets ahold of this, we're SOL* [WWI armed forces; fr *shit out of luck*]

so last year *modifier* Outdated : *jellies are so last year*

sold *adj* Cheated; deceived; EUCHRED, SCREWED : *I've tunneled, hydraulicked, and cradled, and I have been frequently sold* [1876+; one source traces the use to 1597 in Shakespeare]

soldier *n* 1 DEAD SOLDIER (1917+) 2 A low-ranking member of the Mafia; an ordinary thug or gangster *(1963+ Underworld)* *v* To avoid work; idle; shirk; FUCK THE DOG. GOLD-BRICK : *He soldiered on the job and the place was deserted (1840+ Nautical) See* SUNDAY SOLDIER

soldier on *v phr* To persist doggedly : *A little warning bell went off, but I soldiered on (1954+)*

sold on, be *v phr* To be convinced of the value of something or someone; strongly favor or accept : *It took me a half hour to get sold on the job (1928+)*

solid *adj* Wonderful; remarkable; GREAT, GROOVY • Said to have been used regularly by Louis Armstrong : *Man, what solid jive/ That's solid, Willie, let's get together and blow (1920+ Jazz musicians)*

so long *interj* A parting salutation [1865+; origin unknown; perhaps fr German *adieu so lange;* perhaps fr Hebrew *shalom* and related Arabic *salaam,* both greetings meaning "peace"; perhaps fr Irish *slan,* "health," used as a toast and a salutation]

somebody *n* A consequential person : *Leroy was a somebody/ I could have been somebody, Charley. I could have been a contender (1566+)*

some kind of *adj phr* Very good; very effective; some : *God, isn't she some kind of a singer? (1970+)*

some pumpkins *n phr* Something or someone very effective, impressive, etc : *He is some pumpkins (1846+)*

some skin *See* GIVE SOME SKIN, SKIN

something *n* A remarkable person or thing : *Did you see his shirt? It's something! (1582+) See* MAKE SOMETHING OUT OF

something else *n phr* SOMETHING [1909+; an intensive of *something*]

something else again *n phr* Something quite different; something contrasting; DIFFERENT ANIMAL : *The question of wages is something else again (1949+)*

something fierce (or awful) *adv phr* In a harsh and pronounced way; severely : *He cusses her out something fierce/ She came at me something awful (entry form 1909+, variant 1898+)*

something on the ball *n phr* Talent; skill; ability : *a guy with something on the ball* [1912+; fr the curve, speed, etc, that a baseball pitcher puts *on the ball*]

something the cat brought in *n phr* Something or someone bedraggled, perhaps due to weather *(1928+) See* LIKE SOMETHING THE CAT DRAGGED IN

some Zs *See* COP SOME ZS

song *See* TORCH SONG

song and dance or **song** *n phr* or *n* A prepared account or speech aimed at persuasion, apology, advocacy, wheedling, etc : *A flimsy excuse or transparent lie is called "a song and dance"/ Some bum will brace you with a long song of utter inconsequence (1895+) See* GO INTO one's DANCE

◁**son of a bitch** or **sumbitch**▷ (also **son of a b** or **son of a buck** or **son of a gun** or **son of a so-and-so,** all euphemistic) *interj* An exclamation of anger, annoyance, amazement, disappointment, etc : *Son of a bitch! The thing's busted again! n phr* or *n* **1** A despicable person; BASTARD, SHITHEEL : *I told the son of a bitch what I thought of him (entry form 1707+, variants 1975+; gun 1786+)* **2** Something very difficult or vexatious, esp a hard task : *Getting that thing fitted was a son of a bitch* **3** A person or thing that is remarkable, wonderful, superior, etc; BITCH : *Their new album is a son of a bitch, I tell you/ a big son of a buck* [the *son of a gun* variant was said by Admiral Smythe to have been "originally applied to boys born afloat," at a time when women could accompany men to sea, and when children could be born and cradled under a gun or gun carriage, hence have no proper legitimate parentage]

Sooner *modifier* : *the Sooner football team n* A native or resident of Oklahoma *(1930+)* [fr the fact that some settlers entered the public land and staked their claims *sooner* than the legal date and hour in 1889]

SOP or **sop** (pronounced as separate letters) *n* The way things are properly and usually done : *The SOP here is that you ask the chairman first* [WWII armed forces; fr *standard operating procedure*]

soph (SAHF) *n* A sophomore *(1778+ University)*

soppy *adj* Sentimental; maudlin; MUSHY, SCHMALTZY : *the soppy story of a rich-boy dropout (1918+)*

sore *adj* Angry; irritated; PISSED OFF : *I was sore (1738+)*

soreheaded *adj* Angry; resentful; irritable *(1844+)*

sore thumb *See* STICK OUT

sorrow *See* DROWN one's SORROWS

sorry or ◁**sorry-ass**▷ *adj* Wretched; worthless; inferior; HALF-ASSED : *this one kid, and he was a sorry shit/ The reputation of the Barclay has been one of sorry-ass service/ One more sorry-ass useless killing (entry form 1250+, variant 1970s+)*

sorry about that *sentence* I am sorry; please forgive me • Most often an ironic understatement, as when one has been responsible for making a big mistake [1960s+; popularized in the 1960s TV program *Get Smart*]

sort of or **sorta** *adv* Somewhat : *sorta mixed-up (1839+)*

SOS (pronounced as separate letters) *n* The usual tedious exaggerations, pieties,

wretched food, etc [WWII armed forces; fr
same old shit]

so-so *adj* Average; ordinary : *It's a so-so movie*
(1530+)

so's your old man *interj* An exclamation of
contempt and defiance, usu reciprocal : *the
most desperate exercise of so's-your-old-man
since polemics began* (1925+)

soul *adj* **1** Pertaining to a moving form of
popular African-American music : *program
content on soul radio stations/ That's what the
Soul scene taught everybody* **2** : *a soul ballad/
a soul-jazz-blues quintet* *n* **1** An instinctive,
sensitive, humorous, and sympathetic quality felt by black persons to be inherent and to
constitute their essential and valuable attribute : *He's got soul when he dances! I mean
Super Soul!* **2** (also **soul music**) This quality in
music, and music having this quality : *When
Aretha Franklin pours forth a thousand cups
of soul* (1946+ Jazz musicians) *See* BODY AND
SOUL, GRIPE one's ASS

soul brother *n phr* A male black person; BLOOD,
BROTHER (1957+ Black)

soul food *n phr* Food characteristic of and
preferred by black persons, esp of Southern
culture (1957+ Black)

soul kiss *n phr* An intraoral and interlingual
osculation, usu of a steamy sort; FRENCH KISS
(1953+) *v phr* : *The blissful pair soul-kissed
the evening away*

soul sister *n phr* A female black person; SISTER
(1957+ Black)

sound *v* **1** To taunt or provoke; goad; RAZZ **2**
SIGNIFY (1950s+ Street gangs)

sound bite *n phr* A very brief excerpt of speech
or film used esp in political campaigns to
make a quick impression : *They present him
chiefly in a staccato series of sound bites* (late
1980s+)

sound off *v phr* **1** To talk, esp to complain, loud
and long; bluster : *Its leaders have sounded off
on various issues* (WWI Army) **2** To boast;
brag : *He was sounding off again about what a
big shot he is* (WWII Army)

soup *n* **1** Nitroglycerine; NITRO (1902+) **2** Fuel,
esp that used in fast cars, airplanes, etc
(1940s+) **3** The foamy part of a wave : *a big
wave with lots of soup, or white water* (1962+
Surfers) **4** Developing fluid or bath (1929+
Photography) *v* **1** SOUP UP (1940s+) **2** : *I had
the lab soup my test roll normal, and the first
frame was perfect See* DUCK SOUP, IN THE SOUP,
JERKWATER, PEA SOUP

souped up *adj phr* **1** Producing a higher power
or acceleration than the normal : *a Ford with
a souped-up motor/ teen-age infatuation with
souped-up cars in which speed-crazy kids raced*
2 Increased or heightened in value, attraction, production, etc : *the souped-up Premium*

Bonds are also designed to this end [1949+; fr
supercharged, referring to a pump that forces
additional air into the cylinders of an engine
to increase its power; perhaps reinforced
by *soup*, "fuel for a powerful engine," and
"material injected into a horse with a view
to changing its speed or temperament," the
latter attested fr 1911 and earlier]

soup-strainer *n* A mustache, esp a luxuriant
one (1932+)

soup to nuts *n phr* Start to finish; all of the
courses or parts (1950s+)

soup up *v phr* To increase power and speed
above the normal; supercharge : *He souped
up the motors* (1931+) *See* SOUPED UP

soupy *adj* SOPPY (1953+)

sour *See* GO SOUR

sourpuss or **sourpan** *n* A morose person; a
chronic complainer and moaner; PICKLEPUSS
: *the regular assortment of first-night sour-
pusses and professional runners down/ He'd
change into a sour-pan* (entry form 1937+,
variant 1942+)

souse *n* **1** A drunkard; LUSH : *A wonderful thy-
roid substance sobered up the souse in 30
minutes* (1906+) **2** Drunkenness; intoxication : *Economic and religious saviors give a new
kind of emotional souse* (1903+) [fr an extension of *souse*, "pickle brine," something
pickled," hence semantically akin to *soak*,
"drunkard," and *pickled*, "drunk"]

soused *adj* (Variation: **to the gills** may be
added) Drunk [1613+; probably fr the image
of a pickled herring or other pickled fish]

south of the border *adj phr* Failed and ineffective; rejected; ng • The phrase is similar to
and enacted by the thumbs-down sign : *As
performances go, yours was somewhat south of
the border* [1970s+; apparently a blend of
the general notion of *down* as the direction
of failure and rejection with the legendary
significance of the Mexican *border* as the
demarcation *south* of which a hunted or
rejected person may disappear] *See* GO SOUTH

southpaw *modifier* : *switched to a southpaw
stance for his 11th round* *n* **1** A left-handed
player, esp a pitcher; forkhander : *Southpaw
Warren Spahn pitched his 17th victory* (Baseball) **2** Any left-handed person : *Many brilliant persons are southpaws, although perhaps
only coincidentally* (1940s+) [apparently
coined by the humorist Finley Peter Dunne,
"Mr Dooley," when he was a Chicago
sports journalist and baseball diamonds
were regularly oriented with home plate to
the west]

so what *interj* **1** An exclamation of specified
indifference; BIG DEAL : *When she heard the
president was outside, she said, "So what?"* **2**
An exclamation of defiance, reciprocal

challenge, etc : *He told me I had screwed the affair up, and I said, "So what?"* (*1934+*)

so what else is new or **what else is new sentence** Do you have any other startling information? TELL ME ABOUT IT • Always used with heavy irony : *We are told that Stalin's was an exceptionally evil mind. So what else is new?/ Once again, headlines warn of a trade war between the U.S. and Japan. So what else is new?* (*1950s+*)

sozzled *adj* Drunk (*1886+*)

space or **space out** *v* or *v phr* To daydream; woolgather; not attend to what one is doing : *He'd space on calling, break plans with me to hang out with his friends* (*1968+ Teenagers*) See SPACE CADET

space cadet or **space-case** or **space-out** *n phr* or *n* A mad or eccentric person, esp one who seems stuporous or out of touch with reality as if intoxicated by narcotics; NUT, SPACED-OUT : *Alda presents her as such a space cadet that the agony of divorce is tempered/ meant to convince the jury that he is an unreliable space-out, that perhaps he was hallucinating* [*1980s+*; probably fr the 1950s TV program *Tom Corbett, Space Cadet*, which followed the adventures of a group of teenage cadets at a 24th-century space academy, thought of humorously as being *far out, way out,* etc]

spaced-out *adj* **1** (also **spaced** or **spacey** or **spacy**) Stuporous from narcotic intoxication; in a daze : *queerly bashful, shy, respectful, or spaced-out/ with very spaced-out movements, examines the parts of her body/ You get into a trance, spaced, makin' plans* **2** Crazy or eccentric; NUTTY : *the teacher, a spacey and sweetly strange spinster/ He is not spaced-out, a point he makes clear in his new book* [*1968+*; probably fr black usage *space* or *space out,* "go, depart," reinforced by the notion of distance and remoteness in *outer space* and by the notion of blanks, gaps, and *spaces* in an otherwise sane and reasonable train of thought, speech, etc]

space opera *n phr* A movie or show about interplanetary exploration, warfare, sex, etc [*1941+*; coined by Wilson Tucker]

space out *v phr* To become stuporous from narcotic intoxication; be in a daze (*1968+*)

◀**spade**▶ *n* A black person : *The spades inhabited Harlem and let the ofays have Wall Street to themselves* [*1928+*; fr the color of the playing-card symbol and fr the phrase *black as the ace of spades*]

spades See IN SPADES

spag bol *n* Spaghetti bolognese (*1970+*)

spaghetti Western *n phr* A cowboy movie usu made by Italian directors and producers, often in Europe : *reacquaint yourself with films that made the spaghetti Western a grindhouse phenomenon/ The best turkeys, he went on, were spaghetti Westerns, because they earned a lot of bread* (*1969+*)

spam *v* To send a computer message out to myriad people : *the cost to spam an advertisement in thousands of news groups is typically less than $50/ Spamming. Sending out on the Internet the cyberspace equivalent of junk mail* [*1990s+* Computer; fr *Spam,* trademark for a brand of canned meat, which acquired a probably undeserved unsavory reputation among WWII troops]

Spanglish *n* Vocabulary mixing English and Spanish; Spanish characterized by numerous borrowings from English [*1954+*; blend of *Spanish* and *English*]

spanking *adv* Very; extremely, esp in an admirable sense [*1666+*; origin uncertain]

◀**spank the monkey**▶ *v phr* To masturbate; JACK OFF, MILK THE LIZARD (*1990s+*)

spare tire *n phr* **1** Flab about the waist; a certain embonpoint; BULGE (*1925+*) **2** A superfluous and unwelcome person : *I didn't come, because I knew I'd be a spare tire in that crowd* (*1940s+*) **3** A tedious person; a bore (*1940s+*)

spark *v* To initiate and stimulate; trigger : *Willy Mays sparked an eighth inning Giant drive by stealing second* (*1912+*)

sparkler *n* A gem, esp a diamond (*1822+*)

spark plug *n phr* The most stimulating and energetic member of a group, team, etc; LIVE WIRE : *Mr Fadiman himself is a splendid spark-plug* (*1941+*)

spaz or **spastic** (also **spas**) *adj* : *only the spastic twits in competition n* **1** A strange and stupid person; WEIRDO : *The man's a spaz, a total spaz* (*1965+ Teenagers*) **2** A nonathletic person, esp an awkward one (*1977+*) **3** A fit of anger; HISSY FIT : *Well, they threw a spaz and said we can talk on the phone, but I can't see him or have him over* (*1990s+*) [sometimes used cruelly, in reference to the plight of cerebral palsy patients exhibiting constant body *spasms*]

spaz out *v phr* To lose control of oneself; FLIP OUT : *I spazzed out during the Chem final* (*1980s+ Teenagers*)

spazzed out *adj phr* SPACED OUT : *A couple of spazzed out bikers* (*1980s+*)

spazzy *adj* Stupid; WEIRD : *You gotta be spazzy if you think that, just because kids aren't admitted to the casinos, they can't have a great time in Atlantic City* [*1960s+ Teenagers*; fr *spastic*]

speakeasy or **speak** or **speako** *n* A cheap saloon, esp an illegal or after-hours place : *It had been a speakeasy once/ All they give you in these speaks is smoke/ one thing that puts a speako over* [*1889+*; Samuel Hudson, a journalist, says in a 1909 book that he used

the term in Philadelphia in 1889 after
having heard it used in Pittsburgh by an old
Irish woman who sold liquor clandestinely
to her neighbors and enjoined them to
"spake asy"; hence related to early 1800s
Irish and British dialect *spake-aisy* or *speak
softly* shop, "smugglers' den"]

speak someone's (or **the same**) **language** *v
phr* To understand one another very well,
agree with each other

spear carrier *n phr* An unimportant participant; supernumerary : *What helped me most
was having been a catcher and a "spear carrier"
definitely not a star/ like last-minute walk-ons
in the closing scene, spear-carriers in Valhalla*
[1960+; fr the persons who appear on stage,
esp in operas, as soldiers in the background]

◀**spear chucker▶** *n phr* A black person :
*When whites refer to blacks as spear chuckers,
they're not thinking about the Olympics/
Where are the defenders of social stability when
prime-time demagogues like Howard Stern deride African Americans as spear-chuckers?* (late
1960s+)

spec[1] *n* The spectacular opening procession
of a circus : *Mrs Webster rode an elephant in
the "spec"* (*1926+ Circus*)

spec[2] *See* ON SPEC

special *See* the RED-EYE, SATURDAY NIGHT SPECIAL

specs[1] *n* Spectacles; glasses : *Oh Lord, I broke my
new specs* (*1807+*)

specs[2] *n* The specifications of a blueprint, architectural plan, printing order, etc (*1940s+*)

speed *n* An amphetamine, esp Methedrine®
(*1960s+ Narcotics*) *See* BRING someone UP TO
SPEED

speedball *n* A dose of a stimulant and a depressant mixed, esp of heroin and cocaine :
*smack, coke, reefers, acid, speedballs (snorting
cocaine and heroin together), a "luxury"*
(*1909+ Narcotics*) *v* To produce rapidly;
expedite : *I could have the agency speedball you
a nice layout* (*1980s+*)

speed bump *n phr* **1** A transverse hump in a
road made to slow the traffic (*1975+*) **2** :
*Aloe vera extract, fast on its way to becoming
an all-purpose medicinal herb, has run into its
first speed bump: a study suggesting that it delays the healing of some major surgical wounds/
Instead, the drive toward integration has been
stymied by the speedbump of crime* (*1990s+*)

speed demon *n phr* A person who drives fast or
is a fast runner : *speed demon on the court*

speedfreak or **speedo** *n* A habituated user of
amphetamines and other such stimulants :
Well, you know about speedos (*1960s+ Narcotics*)

spell out *v phr* **1** To explain; define : *a commission of distinguished citizens to spell out the
difference between right and wrong* (*1707+*) **2**

To explain very patiently in great detail : *Are
you a schoolboy I have to spell out everything
for you?* (*1940+*)

spender *See* BIG SPENDER

spending money *n* Cash that one is allowed or
able to spend

◀**spick** or **spic▶** *adj* : *Jill don't want anyone to
know she got a spic baby n* **1** A Latino or person of such descent : *female spick, short, fat*
(*1913+*) **2** The Spanish language (*1933+*)
[fr the presumed protestation *"No spick English"*]

spicy *adj* Scandalous; mildly salacious : *a spicy
bit of gossip* (*1886+*)

spiel *n* **1** A barker's or hawker's persuasive talk
(*1896+*) **2** A speech meant to persuade
by force and eloquence; a sales patter; LINE :
I'll give his honor a spiel (*1896+*) **3** An advertising monologue on radio or television
(*1940s+*) [fr German *spielen,* "play"]

spieler *n* A person who makes a persuasively
eloquent speech : *a real accomplished spieler*
(*1894+*)

spiffed *adj* Drunk (*1918+*)

spiffed out *adj phr* Fancily and formally dressed (*1877+*)

spiffed up *modifier* Dressed or fixed up; polished : *spiffed up for a night on the town*

spiffing *adj* SPIFFY (*1872+*)

spifflicated *adj* Drunk : *a slightly spifflicated
gent/ a spifflicated patient entangling himself
in a revolving door* [1906+; fr British dialect
spifflicate, "confound, dumbfound, crush," of
obscure origin, found by 1785]

spiffy *adj* Elegant; excellent; SNAZZY : *They wear
spiffy red-and-gold scarves/ New Model Buggy
for Amish Is Spiffy* (*1853+*) *adv* Well; elegantly : *They don't translate so spiffy* (*1937+*)

spike *n* A hypodermic needle (*1934+ Narcotics*) *v* **1** To strengthen a drink by adding
alcohol or liquor : *He spiked his coffee with
brandy* (*1889+*) **2** To rise to a high level, esp
rapidly : *He also spikes into the upper registers/
push fluids when the patient has spiked a temp*
(*1960s+*) **3** To reject; quash : *The spiking of
Schanberg's column at* The Times *drew hundreds of angry letters from readers/ confident
the man's disbelieving New York editors will
spike the story* (*1908+*) **4** To injure a player,
most often a defending baseman, with the
spikes on one's shoes (*1885+ Baseball*) **5** To
punch a volleyball powerfully and un-
returnably down (*1970s+ Volleyball*) **6** To
slam the ball down, usu done by a player
who has just scored a touchdown (*1970s+
Football*) **7** To shoot : *Figure whoever spiked
Porter probably did us a favor* (*1990s+ Black*)
[all senses fr *spike,* "large nail," hence
"sharp point"; the sense "to reject" may be
fr the earlier phrase *spike a gun,* "render a

cannon useless by driving a spike into the touchhole," or fr the notion of dealing with a paper, bill, manuscript, etc, by impaling it on a spindle or spindle file]

spike up *v phr* To inject narcotics; SHOOT UP : *if he came home and found her spiking up (1960s+ Narcotics)*

spill *v* **1** To upset; down; dump : *I'll spill you in the drink (1731+)* **2** To utter or confess something, esp something damaging; SPILL THE BEANS *(1574+)*

spill one's guts *v phr* To tell everything one knows; be totally and lengthily candid : *"Can I be perfectly frank with you?" "Good. Spill your guts" (1927+)*

spill the beans *v phr* To tell something inadvertently; blurt out a secret *(1919+)*

spin *n* **1** : A distinctive point of view, emphasis, or interpretation; a distinctive character or style : *He put a spin on the facts* [1979+; fr the notion of *spin* on a baseball or pool ball, which gives a deviant rather than a straight track; semantically related to throwing someone a curve]

spinach *n* **1** Nonsense; worthless matter; JUNK : *You could put up with this spinach (1929+)* **2** Money; CABBAGE

spin control *n phr* : *Spin control is the subtle art of massaging reporters' minds after the event has taken place. The "doctors" try to control the interpretation, or "spin," the reporters will put on their stories (mid-1980s+)*

spin doctor or **spinmeister** *n phr* An adviser or agent, esp of a politician, who imparts a partisan analysis or slant to a story for the news media : *Just after the debate, Johnson took his place with the other "spin doctors" (mid-1980s+)*

spin off *n* : *This store is a spin-off from the big one downtown* *v phr* **1** To produce as an entity separated from the whole : *The conglomerate spun off five new companies* **2** To dispose of; rid oneself of; DITCH : *Why didn't he spin off this stupid cunt? (1959+)*

spin one's wheels *v phr* To waste time; work fruitlessly : *Nobody spun his wheels. I'm proud of them/ Stop spinning your wheels, get yourself in gear (1940s+)*

spit *n* Nothing; ZILCH, ZIP : *"What'd she come up with?" "Spit"* [1960s+; a euphemism for *shit*] *See* NOT COUNT FOR SPIT, SWAP SPIT

spit and polish *n phr* Order and precision; orderliness : *spit and polish practiced by the troops*

spitball *n* **1** A pitch thrown using a ball wetted with spit or otherwise illegally besmeared *(1905+ Baseball)* **2** A nasty but feeble attack : *despite the spitballs he keeps getting from the critical liberal media (1970s+)* *v* To speculate; propose conclusions or possibilities : *Well,*

I'm just spit-balling/ You're just spitballing (1955+) [second noun and verb senses fr the mischievous schoolboy's vice of throwing bits of paper soaked in saliva; verb sense fr the notion of tossing such spitballs more or less idly]

spit in someone's eye *v phr* To show extreme contempt and ingratitude : *What I hate is when you pay for it and they spit in your eye (1908+)*

spit it out *v phr* To speak out; reveal; disclose : *If you've got any more to tell me, spit it out right now (1855+)*

spizzerinktum or **spizzerrinctum** *n* Vigor; pep; PIZZAZZ : *the fellow who put foresight, science, and spizzerinktum into their business* [1940s+; origin unknown; since the earliest meaning is "money," perhaps a coinage fr Latin *specie rectum*, "the right sort"]

splash *See* MAKE A SPLASH

splat *n* A slap or smack *(1958+)* *v* To hit with a smacking sound; slap : *I wouldn't be at all concerned that a tomato would splat me in the face (1922+)* [echoic]

splendiferous *adj* Quite splendid [1843+; orig US jocular formation from *splendid*]

splice *v* To marry • Most often in the passive : *crying to be spliced (1751+)*

splinter *See* KNEE-HIGH TO A GRASSHOPPER

split *v* To leave; depart; CUT OUT : *This party is dullsville, let's split (1956+ Jazz musicians) See* LICKETY-SPLIT

◁**split beaver**▷ *n phr* A photograph or view of a woman's vulva between spread legs; SPREAD BEAVER : *I can toss off phrases like "split beaver" with almost devil-may-care abandon (1972+)*

splitsville *n* A parting or dissolution; separation : *teach the little chickadees to fly and then it's splitsville/ Splitsville ... Fergie and Prince Andrew are calling it quits (1980s+)*

split the difference *v phr* To compromise, esp when agreement is near : *We're almost agreed, so let's split the difference/ She may have to realize that the philosophical difference between herself and Rome remains one that finally just can't be split (1750+)*

split the scene *v phr* To leave; depart; CUT OUT, SPLIT : *just as I was about to split the scene (1952+ Black musicians)*

split-up *n* **1** An angry separation : *Me and the old man had a split-up (1908+)* **2** A divorce or legal separation of a married couple *(1975+)*

spoil *v* To kill; WASTE : *You wanted to hate his guts so it would be easier to spoil him? (1980s+)*

spoil someone rotten *v phr* To indulge and pamper someone to an extreme : *Spoiling your kid rotten from the start? (1970+)*

sponge *n* **1** (also **sponger**) A parasite; FREE-LOADER, MOOCHER, schnorrer : *You avoided college boys, sponges* (1598+) **2** A drunkard; SOAK (1900+) *v* : *We were able to sponge lots of meals off his parents* (1676+) *See* THROW IN THE SPONGE

sponge off *v phr* To live off someone else or take advantage of them without offering compensation : *sponged off her for years*

spoof *n* **1** : *Don't take it seriously, it was just a spoof* (1884+) **2** A parody or pastiche; SEND-UP, TAKEOFF : *The show was a spoof of a TV sit-com* (1958+) *v* To fool; hoax; tease : *He was just spoofing* (1889+) [coined by the British comedian Arthur Roberts, born 1852, as the name of a nonsense game he invented]

spoofing *n* To gain access electronically to a computer deceptively and perhaps illegally : *I thought someone might be electronically impersonating him, a practice that is known online as "spoofing"/ The technique is called "spoofing" because it fools a computer into thinking that another, friendly computer is requesting access* (1990s+ Computer)

spook *n* ◄1► A black person : *Some are just spooks by the door, used to give the organization a little color* (1945+) **2** A spy; secret agent : *Mr Wolfson isn't a spook for the CIA* (1942+ Espionage) *v* To put on edge; make apprehensive; frighten : *"It's the first time in my life I've ever been spooked," says a Byrd staffer* (1935+) [fr Dutch]

spooked *adj* Frightened, startled; in a panic (1937+)

spoon *v* **1** NECK, PET **2** To flirt; woo (1831+) *See* GREASY SPOON

spoony *adj* Amorous; romantic : *I guess we got kind of spoony* (1836+) *n* A foolish or silly person : *I don't believe a cock-and-bull story like that. Quiz was no spoony* (1795+)

spork *n* A piece of cutlery combining the features of a spoon, fork, and sometimes, knife (1909+)

sport *n* **1** A stylish and rakish man • Often used as a term of address, sometimes with an ironical tinge : *What did she tell you, sport?* (1923+) **2** GOOD SPORT (1920+) *v* To wear : *He sported a Day-glo necktie* (1778+)

sport a woody *v phr* To have an erection (1980s+ Students)

spot *n* **1** A short commercial or paid political announcement on radio or television : *How do you like the spots, Senator?* (1937+) **2** A nightclub, restaurant, or other such venue of pleasure : *They were often seen in a fashionable spot uptown* (1940s+) *v* **1** To give odds or a handicap; to give an advantage to : *They spotted Pittsburgh five runs before getting down to serious business* (1961+ Sports & gambling) **2** To recognize or identify : *I spot-*

ted her as a phony long ago (1848+) **3** To lend someone something : *spotted her ten bucks* [found by 1718 in the second verb sense as "identify as a wrongdoer"] *See* FIVE-SPOT, HIT THE SPOT, HOT SPOT, JOHNNY-ON-THE-SPOT, NIGHTSPOT, ON THE SPOT, PUT someone ON THE SPOT, SWEET SPOT, TWO-SPOT, X MARKS THE SPOT

spotlight *v* To single out prominently; focus on for emphasis : *He was trying to spotlight the danger of high deficits* (1942+) *See* IN THE SPOTLIGHT

spot-on *adj* Exact; precise; faithful; ON THE BUTTON, ON THE MONEY • Chiefly British : *Elwood's spot-on use of an argot, half G.I. and half cokehead, infuses the book with surprise and a screeching undercurrent of despair* [1956+; found in adverbial use by 1920]

sprawl *n* Spreading overdevelopment of urban areas : *The state can put the brakes on senseless sprawl* (1980s+)

spread *n* **1** Coverage in a newspaper or magazine, esp the full use of facing pages : *Do you know how much a two-page spread in the New York Times costs these days?* (1858+) **2** A copious meal; a feast (1822+)

spread oneself *v phr* To make a great effort; do one's utmost : *You may be sure the staff will spread itself to accommodate you* (1857+)

◁**spread beaver**▷ *n phr* SPLIT BEAVER (1970s+)

◁**spread for** someone▷ *v phr* For a woman, to do or offer to do the sex act with someone; spread her legs for coital access (1950s+)

spread it (on) thick *v phr* To exaggerate; overstate; BULLSHIT : *To say it was for the good of humanity is spreading it a bit thick* (1940s+)

spread oneself thin (or too thin) *v phr* To attempt more than one can do; strain one's resources : *It's a good idea to get involved in a lot of activities, but don't spread yourself too thin* (1960s+)

spring *v* **1** To get out of or be released or escape from prison : *The proprietor knew how to "spring" them, that is, get them out of jail/ When's he springing?* (1900+ Underworld) **2** To reveal or do something as a surprise • Very often used with *on* : *John L Lewis is preparing to spring a dramatic move/ If we spring it on them suddenly they won't know how to react* (1876+)

spring chicken *n phr* A young person, esp a woman : *Maggie Smith is the spring chicken among them* [1906+; fr the market name for a small young chicken] *See* NO SPRING CHICKEN

spring for something *v phr* To pay for, esp a treat of food or drink; POP : *always more than glad to guzzle the pitchers of Michelob you sprung for on payday/ We'll spring for the gas*

spritz *n* **1** A serving of carbonated water, esp an addition of carbonated water to a glass of wine : *She asked for white wine with a spritz* (*1960s+*) **2** A slight rain or shower : *We may get just a wee spritz this afternoon* (*1970s+*) *v* To spray or sprinkle : *the fixative with which he spritzed it so it would not smear/ She spritzed a little scent behind her ear and was ready* (*1976+*) [fr Yiddish, "spray"]

spritzer *n* A glass of wine mixed with carbonated water (*1961+*)

sprout *n* A child, esp an infant : *A girl out your way has married and is coming home with a sprout* (*1934+*)

sprout wings *v phr* To become angelic, before or after death

sprung *adj* Drunk (*1833+*)

spud *n* A potato [1845+; origin unknown; perhaps related to the fact that in British dialect use *spud* means "a weeding instrument" and in US dialect it means "a spade," hence potatoes would be something *spudded* or dug; a relation has been seen between the fact that potatoes are also the nickname of men named Murphy, or indeed of any Irishman]

spunk *n* **1** Energetic courage; mettle; BALLS, GUTS : *little girl's got a lot of spunk* (*1773+*) ◁**2**▷ Semen : *rushing with their hot spunk in their hands to the microscope* (*1888+*) *v* ◁**1**▷ To ejaculate semen; COME : *the filthy pigs spunking into women* (*1970s+*) [apparently fr Celtic *spong*, "tinder, touchwood, punk," fr Latin *spongia*, "sponge"; apparently semantically fr a resemblance between semen and a spongy excrescence found on trees, in which sense the word is found in British dialect]

spunky *adj* Gutsy and enthusiastic; showing courage : *spunky girlfriends*

squad *See* GOON SQUAD, TAXI SQUAD

square *adj* **1** UNCOOL : *You do not try to convert the square world* (*1925+* Jazz musicians) **2** Fair; evenhanded; just : *I'll be square with you* (*1872+*) *n* **1** (also **square meal**) A copious meal : *I've had my three squares every day* (*1882+*) **2** A conventional person, esp one with musical tastes not extending to jazz, swing, bop, etc; clyde : *That GL strictly a square/ I do a little vocal number for the squares* (*1925+* Jazz musicians) **3** (also **square joint**) A tobacco cigarette; SLIM, STRAIGHT (*1960s+* Narcotics) *v* To make things right, just, proper, etc : *He could never square himself with the police after that* (*1859+*) [the sense "conventional person, etc," is said to come fr a jazz musician's and standard conductor's hand gesture that beats out regular and unsyncopated four-beat rhythm, the hand doing so describing a *square* figure in the air]

squared away *adj* Straightened out; settled : *He's all squared away while we go out to dinner*

square deal, a *n phr* Fair and honest treatment : *Don't look for a square deal from them crooks* (*1876+*)

square guy *n phr* An honest and reliable man; right guy : *Trust him; he's a square guy* (*1908+*)

square off *v phr* To put oneself in a fighting posture : *The two biggest companies are squaring off over the microchip market* (*1837+*)

square one *n phr* The place where some process begins or has begun; the original configuration : *So after all this fuss we are at square one again* [1960+; fr board games where a token is moved off the *first square* after the shake of a die, drawing of a card, etc] *See* GO BACK TO SQUARE ONE; BACK TO SQUARE ONE

square peg *n phr* A misfit; an inconvenient and intractable person : *They were square pegs who weren't succeeding* [1901+; fr the earlier expression *put* or *drive a square peg in a round hole*, fr carpentry or joinery]

squares *See* THREE SQUARES

square shooter *n phr* An honest and candid person; STRAIGHT ARROW • Now used nearly always with the conscious irony of archaic sincerity (*1914+*)

Squaresville or **squaresville** *adj* : *on campus, where it once was squaresville to flip for the rock scene n* A putative city inhabited entirely by dull, conventional people : *The Innocent Nihilists Adrift in Squaresville/ Unintimidated by being in the squaresville, which is also the power center of the free world* (*1960s+* Bop talk)

square with *v phr* To be honest with someone; come clean : *You need to square with her about the intrusions*

squat *n* ◁**1**▷ Excrement : *Don't step in the squat* (*1930s+*) **2** Nothing; zero; DIDDLY, ZILCH, ZIP : *She's got squat to do with that kind of shit/ You can't do squat anyway these days* (*1934+*) *v* **1** To sit : *Hey, squat there a minute and I'll be right with you* (*1768+*) ◁**2**▷ To defecate; SHIT, TAKE A DUMP (*1940s+*) *See* NOT GIVE A DAMN, NOT KNOW BEANS, TAKE A DUMP

◁**squaw**▷ *n* A woman, esp one's wife (*1934+*)

squawk *n* : *Okay, what's your squawk this morning?* (*1909+*) *v* **1** To complain; BEEF, BITCH : *Will you stop squawking about the food, please?* (*1875+*) **2** To inform; SQUEAL : *Joe squawked* (*1872+* Underworld) [echoic of an unpleasant sound, esp the grating screech of a bird]

squawk box *n phr* A military public address system; bitch box (*WWII Navy*)

squeak by (or **through**) *v phr* To pass, succeed, achieve a goal, etc, by the narrowest of margins : *He just barely squeaked through his medical boards* (*1938+*)

squeaker *n* **1** A very closely contested and uncertain game, contest, etc : *They met in a squeaker that year* (*1960s+*) **2** Something poised on the edge of one result or another, esp a success versus a disaster : *"It'll be a squeaker," Bartow said. "This is a nervous time for us"* (*1960s+*)

squeaky-clean *adj phr* Perfectly clean; white, sanitary, and untarnished • Sometimes used ironically to emphasize conventionality and unimaginativeness : *this English band, made up of six squeaky-clean men in their early twenties/ one of the most squeaky-clean and buttoned-down of US corporations* [1972+; fr the *squeaky* sound produced by rubbing a finger across chinaware free of grease or dirt]

squeal *n* **1** (also **squeel**) An informer; RAT, SNITCH, STOOL PIGEON : *He was working on a case with a squeal, and he knifed him* (*1750+*) **2** (also **squeak**) A complaint to the police : *cop at stationhouse took the squeal/ The young cops who had caught the squeal didn't know what to do* (*1908+*) *v* To inform; RAT, SING, SQUAWK (*1825+*)

squealer *n* An informer; RAT, SNITCH, SQUEAL (*1865+*)

squeeze *n* **1** A situation of great pressure or peril; CRUNCH : *I'm afraid we're in something of a squeeze just now* **2** One's romantic partner; lover *See* MAIN SQUEEZE, PUT THE SQUEEZE ON someone

squeeze play *n* Pressure or coercion : *a squeeze play over signing the contract* [1916+; fr earlier baseball sense, tactic involving bunting or hitting the ball softly so that the runner at third base can reach home]

squib *n* A brief, sometimes witty piece of material in a newspaper or magazine, usu a space-filler : *A friend of mine, he writes those witty "squibs"* [1739+; fr *squib*, "a small firecracker," of unknown origin]

squid *n* An obnoxious person, esp one who studies too hard; DWEEB, GRIND, LOSER, NERD (*1980s+ Students*)

squiffy or **squiffy-eyed** or **squiffed** *adj* Drunk : *so-and-so's getting "squiffy" at a dance/ one of Frenise's squiffy-eyed nieces* (*entry form 1855+, second variant 1890+*)

squirrel *n* **1** A crazy or eccentric person; NUT, WEIRDO : *I seen some squirrels in my life, but you got 'em all beat* (*1940s+*) **2** A hesitant or confused hot-rod driver (*1950s+ Hot rodders*) *v* **1** (also **squirrel away**) To hoard or cache something; hide and save something for later (*1939+*) **2** To weave about the road while driving, esp a hot rod (*1950s+ Hot rodders*)

squirrel-bait (or **-food**) *n* A crazy or eccentric person; NUT, SQUIRREL : *I'm afraid the old mentor is squirrel-food by now* [first form 1919+, second 1915+; fr the fact that squirrels eat nuts]

squirrelly *adj* Crazy; eccentric; NUTTY : *I tell you, working out alone can make you squirrelly* (*1934+*)

squirt *n* **1** A short or small person, esp an insignificant, contemptible little male; PEANUT : *Ah, what a little squirt is there* (*1839+*) **2** (also **young squirt**) A young man, esp a presumptuous or foppish youth (*1848+*)

squirts *n* Diarrhea

squish *n* : *It wasn't that I was becoming a "squish" (That's a Washington term for a softy)* (*1980s+*) *v* (also **squush** [by 1846] or **squoosh**) To squeeze; compress : *This universe he had built was a Guggenheim and a Toys-R-Us squished into one/ some mondobra engineering breakthrough, to squoosh your breasts together and push them up under your chin* (*1647+*)

squishy *adj* Sentimental; SCHMALTZY, SOPPY : *The sentiment may sound squishy to those who have never been close to him/ the squishy sentimentality attributed to him by most critics* (*1953+*)

squooshy (SKWOO̅ shee) *adj* Soft; yielding and insubstantial : *Support for Reagan is "all very squooshy"* [1970s+; the date should probably be earlier; *sqush*, "to collapse into a soft, pulpy mass," is found by 1884]

SRO (pronounced as separate letters) *n* **1** Standing room only, usu indicating a full house and a successful production (*1890+ Theater*) **2** Single-room-occupancy residence hotel : *They're planning to demolish the SROs on this street* (*1941+*)

stab *n* A try; CRACK, SHOT, WHACK : *Well, I'll have a stab at it* (*1895+*)

stab in the back *n phr* Betrayal; harming someone in a treacherous way • Also verb phrase (*1916+*)

stable *n* The group of people performing similar work, managed by one person : *She's part of his stable of writers* (*1937+*)

stache *See* STASH

'stache *n* A mustache : *If they didn't, Garner would trash his own 'stache* (*1980s+*)

stack *See* BLOW one's TOP

stacked *adj* Very well-built in the sexual sense; having an attractive body, esp a large bosom : *She's well-stacked and sort of young* [1942+; found in the form *stacked up nicely* at Stanford University in 1931]

stack of Bibles *See* SWEAR ON A STACK OF BIBLES

stack the cards (or **the deck**) *v phr* To prearrange something dishonestly; assure one's advantage fraudulently; COLD DECK : *I should have had the job, but they stacked the cards against me* (*1825+*)

stack up *n* A multiple-car wreck *(1950s+ Teenagers)* *v phr* **1** To transpire; go along; succeed : *How are things stacking up for you this year?* *(1911+)* **2** To compare; measure against : *I'd like for somebody to begin stacking up* Native Son *with some of Frank Norris's stuff (1903+)* **3** To wreck a car; RACK UP *(1950s+ Teenagers)* [first two verb-phrase senses fr the *stacking up* of one's poker chips to show winnings or for comparison]

stack Zs *See* COP ZS

stag *adj* For men only; without women : *a stag function/ Several of the brothers were going to the dance stag (1873+) n* **1** A man who goes to a party alone, without a woman partner *(1905+)* **2** (also **stag party**) A party for men only, such as a bachelor party : *as broad as the jokes at a Legion stag (1904+)*

stage *See* UPSTAGE

stagedoor Johnny *n phr* A man who haunts the stagedoor of a theater in order to meet actresses, chorus girls, etc *(1912+)*

stage mother *n phr* A person who is aggressively overzealous in promoting the success of offspring, proteges, etc : *Once there were stage mothers, the legendary behind-the-scenes forces who achieved Broadway immortality as Rose in Gypsy/ Many in the thin Dodger front line were pressed into larger roles, and they were cajoled and hugged and implored and cursed by Lasorda, their loud and unabashedly emotional manager, a stage mother if there ever was one (1919+)*

stagflation *n* A simultaneous stagnation and inflation in the economy *(1965+)*

stairs *See* UPSTAIRS, THE MAN UPSTAIRS

stake *See* GRUBSTAKE

stake-out *n* A police surveillance : *as silently as only a cop on a stake-out knows how to stand/ The stake-outs continued (1942+ Police)*

stake out *v phr* To put someone or something under constant police surveillance : *He's been staked out often enough* [1942+ Police; fr earlier senses, as old as the 1600s, where *stake out* meant "mark off a territory, a line, a track, etc, with stakes"]

stakes *See* PULL UP STAKES

stalk *v* To harass someone, esp a woman, in a menacing way : *During the first week at Wimbledon, a German stalking Steffi Graf had to be expelled/ The clinics have recourse to local laws against blocking an entrance and stalking doctors and nurses/ A 9-year old boy who left a message for a 10-year old girl has been accused of violating the state's anti-stalking law (1980s+)*

stall[1] *n* **1** A pretext or excuse for delaying; a reason for inaction : *His claim of illness is only a stall (1889+)* **2** A pretense or false indication, esp as part of a criminal alibi : *"I'd*

take meals up to him. I think that was just a stall" "You mean the meals were for someone else?" *(1851+) v* **1** To delay; temporize; consume time and delay action; BUY TIME : *I told him to quit stalling and give us a decision (1903+)* **2** (also **stall off**) To subject someone to delay; make excuses for inaction : *You stall her while I try to find her original letter (1906+)* [fr Old English *steall*, "standing, state, place, animal stall," whence the notion of stubbornly holding one's place]

stall[2] *n* **1** A pickpocket's accomplice who in one way or another maneuvers the victim *(1591+)* **2** A criminal's accomplice who primarily diverts attention, obstructs pursuit, keeps watch, etc : *an excellent lookout or "stall" for her male companions (1930+ Underworld)* [fr earlier *stale* or *stall*, "decoy bird," probably fr Anglo-French *estale* or *estal*, "a pigeon used to lure a hawk into a nest"; since delaying and misleading are involved in both, this derivation and that of *stall*[1] have probably intermingled over the centuries, as illustrated by the fact that *stand* meant "a thief's assistant" in the late 16th century]

stallion *n* **1** STUD *(1553+)* **2** A sexually attractive and/or active woman; FOX *(1970s+ Black)*

stamping ground (or **grounds**) *n phr* One's particular domain or territory; one's native heath : *Ann Arbor used to be my stamping ground* [1821+; fr 1700s sense, "a place frequented by animals"]

stand *n* A shop or store; a place of business : *You can get it at the Brooks Brothers stand on Fifth Avenue (1787+) v* **1** To give or pay for as a treat : *She stood him tea and muffins (1821+)* **2** To cost; SET someone BACK : *The suit I got on stood me ten cents (1362+) See* ONE-NIGHT STAND

◁**stand around with** one's **finger up** one's **ass**▷ (or in one's **ear**) *v phr* To be idle and helpless; fail to cope; be useless : *If you're just standing around with your finger up your ass you might as well lend a hand here (1940s+)*

standee *n* A person forced to stand because all seats are sold or occupied : *long lines of standees waiting their turns (1856+)*

stand (or **stand still**) **for** something *v phr* To tolerate or abide something; SWALLOW something • Usu in the negative : *He said he wouldn't stand for being replaced (entry form 1626+, variant 1970s+)*

stand-in *n* **1** A performer who takes the place of another *(1938+)* **2** A substitute or proxy; a deputy : *Naive Stingo, as stand-in for us (1937+)* [perhaps fr the use of a substitute to replace a performer during such tedious procedures as adjusting lights, arranging the stage or set, etc; perhaps also fr the earlier notion of a deputy or place-holder, literally a lieutenant, in French, "a place-holder"]

stand in *v phr* To substitute; act as a proxy : *I'll have to stand in for her and run the meeting* *(1904+ Show business)*

standing O *n phr* A standing ovation : *The audience greeted John Harbison's new cello concerto with a standing O/ Thiede got a standing O (1990s+)*

standing on one's **head** *See* DO something ON TOP OF one's HEAD

standing up *See* DIE STANDING UP

standoff *n* A balanced and static conflict; stalemate; deadlock : *The union and the company are locked in a standoff (1843+) See* MEXICAN STANDOFF

standoffish *adj* Haughty; aloof; reserved and snobbish : *He gave us all a standoffish look (1860+)*

stand-out *n* A person or thing that is extraordinary, usu uncommonly good or talented; an outstanding person or thing : *Her performance of Amanda is the stand-out of the season (1928+)*

stand pat *v phr* **1** To keep one's original five cards in draw poker, without drawing new ones *(1882+ Poker)* **2** To retain one's position; refuse to shift; carry on as one is; SIT TIGHT : *The President stood pat on his decision to cut taxes (1890+)* [fr the adverb *pat*, "exactly, precisely to the purpose"]

stand tall *v phr* To be proud and ready; have an imposing and confident stance *(1970s+ Army)*

stand the heat *See* IF YOU CAN'T STAND THE HEAT STAY OUT OF THE KITCHEN

stand-up *adj* Courageous and personally accountable; bold; GUTSY • Most often in the expression *stand-up guy* : *He handled the humiliating defeat like a stand-up guy/ And he's very, very stand-up (1841+) n* A live interview at the scene of a news event : *I hang a left past the faded Rose law firm and the networks doing evening stand-ups at the entrance (1990s+ Televison)* [adjective sense perhaps fr *stand up and be counted*]

stand someone **up** *v phr* To fail to keep an appointment, esp a date, with someone : *You won't stand me up, now will you?* [late 1800s+; perhaps related to *stand up* in the sense of "go through a wedding ceremony," the image being the forsaken bride or groom left standing alone at the altar]

stand up and be counted *v phr* To announce and be accountable for one's convictions, opinions, etc; not be afraid to speak up : *Maybe a lot agree with you, but they won't stand up and be counted (1900s+)*

stand up for someone *v phr* To defend and support someone; GO TO BAT FOR someone : *Nobody stood up for her, so she had to back off*

starchy *adj* Very stiff or formal in behavior; conventional *(1823+)*

starkers *adj* **1** Naked; stark naked; BARE-ASS : *sitting there at the bar starkers from the waist up/ You jog about, absolutely starkers, and then dive straight into a swimming pool (1923+)* **2** Crazy; BONKERS, NUTS : *The doctor told me I was starkers to do that (1962+)* [fr *stark naked* and *stark, staring mad*, with the British slang suffix *-ers*]

star-struck *adj* Enchanted by entertainment stars; enamored of glamour : *I don't get star-struck (1990s+)*

starters *See* FOR OPENERS

start from scratch *v phr* **1** To begin on an even footing, with no advantage or handicap : *We're gonna have a good life together starting from scratch* **2** To begin with the very first and simplest steps; build from the ground : *So they threw their plans away and started from scratch* [1936+; fr the *scratch-line*, the starting line for races, often scratched in the earth]

stash[1] or **stache** *n* **1** A hoard or cache : *She had a little stash of money in her bureau drawer (1914+)* **2** A hiding place : *if he wasn't home or in his stash/ I have some here, in a stash downstairs (1930+)* **3** A supply of narcotics, esp one's personal supply : *meeting him at the airport with samples of their "special stash" (1960s+ Narcotics)* **4** A place where narcotics and associated paraphernalia are hidden, esp by a dealer *(1960s+ Narcotics) v* (also **stash away**) To hide; hoard; save up : *I had not stashed any dough away/ I'd stash that jug (1797+)* [origin unknown; perhaps a blend of *stow* or *store* with *cache*]

stash[2] *n* A mustache; 'STACHE : *He had a little red stash (1940+)*

state *See* IN A STATE

Stateside or **stateside** *adj* : *a genuine Stateside flavor to the celebration n* The United States itself as distinct from foreign places, overseas possessions, etc *(WWII armed forces)*

static *n* Complaints, BACKTALK, trivial objections, etc : *Here's the policy, and let's not have any static about it* [1953+; fr the atmospheric interference that makes unwanted noise in radio transmissions]

stats *n* Figures or statistics, esp relating to sports; NUMBERS : *They are the kind of stats that a college powerhouse might covet/ An extraordinary cornucopia of mathematical data. Still, the line had to be drawn. No stats (1962+)*

stay *v* To maintain a penile erection *(1960s+)*

stay loose *See* HANG LOOSE

stay out of the kitchen *See* IF YOU CAN'T STAND THE HEAT STAY OUT OF THE KITCHEN

stay put *v phr* To stay where one is; not budge : *No, stay put. I won't be but a minute* (*1843+*)

steady *n* One's constant and only boyfriend or girlfriend (*1897+*) *See* GO STEADY

steak *See* TUBE STEAK

steal *n* A great bargain : *I got that for half price, a real steal* (*1940s+*)

steal someone blind *v phr* To rob someone thoroughly and subtly; strip someone [*1974+*; fr the notion that the person being robbed must or might as well be *blind*]

stealth *adj* Covert; clandestine; SNEAKY : *His piece of stealth journalism was an exercise in character assassination/ The Republicans are turning Dan Quayle into a virtual stealth Vice President; not even any pictures of him on the Bush-Quayle re-election posters* [late 1980s+; fr the US *Stealth* fighter plane, activated in 1983, which, along with a bomber version, was designed to be invisible to radar detection]

steam *v* **1** To anger; make furious : *I steam easily/ It steams me to hear that our fair burg is the Crime Capital of the World* (*1922+*) **2** To make someone hotly amorous : *Be thrilled by, chilled by, and steamed by Gilbert and Garbo* (*1970s+*) *See* LET OFF STEAM

steamed *adj* Angry; PISSED OFF : *I'm too steamed to sleep, Lacey/ O'Neill wasn't the only member of Congress to be steamed* (*1935+*)

steamed up *adj phr* **1** Angry; HOT AND BOTHERED, PISSED OFF : *The first thing she does is get all steamed up about it* (*1923+*) **2** Eager; excited : *He's really steamed up about the new initiative* (*1936+*)

steamroller *v* To dominate and crush; achieve by sheer force; SNOWBALL : *The governor tried to steamroller the bill through* (*1912+*)

steam someone up *v phr* To excite and stimulate; incite enthusiasm (*1930s+*)

steam was (or **is**) **coming out of** someone's **ears** *sentence* He or she was or is very angry : *Houk was red-faced with anger. Steam was coming out of his ears* (*1960s+*)

steamy *adj* Excitingly carnal; sexually arousing; HOT, SEXY : *Hollywood's steamiest starlet* (*1970+*)

steep *adj* Expensive : *steep prices*

steer *n* **1** (also **steerer**) A person who steers patrons and victims : *He is nothing but a steer for a bust-out joint* (*entry form 1939+, variant 1873+*) **2** Advice or information; a bit of useful data (*1899+*) *v* To take or inveigle someone to a place or person where gamblers or confidence men might victimize him : *I been steerin' for Schwiefka all day* (*1889+ Underworld*) *See* BUM STEER

steerer *See* BUNCO-STEERER

stellar *adj* Excellent; great : *stellar character reference*

stem *n* **1** A street, often the main street of a town or city (*1914+ Hoboes*) **2** An opium pipe (*1940s+ Narcotics*) *v* PANHANDLE (*1927+ Hoboes*) *See* MAIN DRAG

stems *n* The legs, esp the attractive legs of a woman (*1891+*)

stephen *See* EVEN-STEPHEN

step off the curb *v phr* To die [fr getting hit by a vehicle by stepping into the street]

step on someone *v phr* To break into a CB or VHF radio transmission : *You'll have to say that again; we're being stepped on* (*1970s+*)

step on it *v phr* **1** (also **step on the gas**) To accelerate; hurry; speed up : *We better step on it; there's only five minutes left* (*entry form 1923+, variant 1920+*) **2** (Variations: one's **dick** or one's **shvantz** may replace **it**) To blunder; make a serious mistake : *It was only a matter of time before he stepped on his cock and another rising star would be looking for a police chief's job in Iowa* (*1970+ Army*)

step out *v phr* **1** To go out socially, esp to a dance or a party : *I haven't stepped out much lately, too busy* (*1907+*) **2** To escort someone socially; date : *Who is she stepping out with these days?* (*1918+*)

step out on someone *v phr* To be romantically or sexually unfaithful to someone; CHEAT, TWO-TIME (*1940s+*)

step up to the plate *v phr* To take responsibility; to step forward to take care of something [reference to baseball]

-ster *suffix used to form nouns* A person involved with, doing, or described by what is indicated : *clubster/ gridster/ mobster/ oldster* [1000+; this Old English suffix, always common, has lately become very popular; for instance, forms like *The Newtster*, "Newt Gingrich," are found]

steven *See* EVEN-STEPHEN

stewed or **stewed to the gills** *adj* or *adj phr* Drunk : *He knew where the colonel lived from the time he'd taken him home stewed/ He came in stewed to the gills* (*entry form 1737+, variant 1922+*) *See* HALF-STEWED

stew in one's **own juice** *v phr* To be left to suffer the consequences of one's actions (*1885+*)

stick *n* **1** A baseball bat (*1868+ Baseball*) **2** A baton or rod of office, now esp a conductor's baton (*1688+*) **3** A golf club : *The golf dudes had their bag of sticks* (*1857+*) **4** A billiard cue : *I lived off the stick three months* (*1674+*) **5** The mast of a ship or boat : *The gale blew the sticks right out of her* (*1802+*) **6** A control lever or handle; JOY-STICK (*1914+*) **7** (also stick shift) A manual gearshift lever, esp one mounted on the floor (*1971+*) **8** A slide rule; slipstick (*1920s+*) **9** A ski pole (*1961+*) **10** A clarinet; LICORICE STICK (*1920+ Jazz musicians*) **11** A marijuana cigarette; JOINT, stick of gage, stick of tea : *Marijuana was easy to get, 25 cents a "stick"* (*1938+ Narcotics*) **12** A tall, thin person; BEANPOLE (*1940s+*) **13** A stiff, awkward person; an overformal person (*1800+*) **14** A dull person; STICK IN THE MUD (*1733+*) **15** A casino croupier (*1940s+ Gambling*) **16** An assistant who poses as an ordinary innocent person; SHILL : *The man who won the $246 was a shill, sometimes referred to as a "stick"/ One operator, known as a "stall" or "stick," distracts or frames the sucker in some way* (*1926+ Carnival & underworld*) *v* To cheat; swindle; esp, to overcharge; SHAFT : *runs the Bowie garage, routinely sticking what customers come his way* (*1699+*) *See* BOOM STICK, DIPSHIT, GET ON THE STICK, GOBSTICK, HAVE A BROOM UP one's ASS, KNOW WHAT one CAN DO WITH something, MAKE something STICK, SHITSTICK, SWIZZLE-STICK, TELL someone WHAT TO DO WITH something

stick around *v phr* To stay at or near a place; HANG AROUND : *I asked the cops to stick around for a few minutes* (*1912+*)

sticker shock *n phr* The nasty impact of a price sticker, esp one on a new car, in inflationary times : *We're seeing more in the way of sticker shock lately/ lawmakers are suffering from "sticker shock" at the potential costs of health reform* (*1970s+*)

stick in the mud *n phr* A dull, conservative person; FOGY : *Be cautious, but don't be a stick in the mud* (*1733+*)

stick it *v phr* ◁1▷ (Variations: **cram** or **ram** or **shove** or **stuff** may replace **stick**; **up** one's **ass** or **in** one's **ear** or **where the sun doesn't shine** may be added) To dispose of or deal with something one vehemently rejects; take back something offered and scorned • Very often used as a rude interjection conveying both rejection and insult : *You can shove your coke up your ass/ Cram it, will you?/ He told them to take the money and ram it/ You can send them to President Carter or stick them in your ear* (*entry form 1922+, shove 1941+, stuff 1955+*) **2** (also **stick it out**) To endure; HANG IN : *It's rough as hell, but I'll stick it* (*1900+, variant 1876+*)

stick it to someone or something *v phr* To assault violently and definitively; SOCK IT TO someone or something : *Pickett has really been sticking it to us in the press* (*1970s+*)

stick one's **neck out** *v phr* To put oneself at risk; invite trouble : *Don't stick your neck out too far* (*1926+*)

stick out *v phr* (Variations: **like a sore thumb** or **a mile** may be added) To be very conspicuous; stand out starkly : *She really sticks out in that bunch/ Low profile? He sticks out like a sore thumb* (*entry form 1842+, sore thumb 1936+, mile 1933+*)

stick something **out** *v phr* To continue to endure something rather unpleasant : *stuck it out until after junior high* (*1882+*)

sticks *n* **1** Drumsticks : *the snare drummer throwing his sticks up* (*1900+ Musicians*) **2** A drummer (*1900+ Musicians*)

sticks, the *n phr* Rural or suburban places; the provinces; the BOONDOCKS, the rhubarbs : *A cop was transferred to the "sticks"/ a revue being tried out in the sticks* [*1905+; fr sticks, "trees," representing the backwoods*]

stick shift *See* STICK

sticktoitiveness *n* Determination; tenacity : *sticktoitiveness over a total of 25 years*

stickum *n* **1** Glue; paste; cement **2** Any viscous fluid; GLOP, GUNK (*1909+*)

stickup *n* **1** An armed robbery; HOLDUP : *a robbery or a "stick-up"* (*1887+*) **2** An armed robber : *Mallory looked at the dark stick-up* (*1905+*)

stick up *v phr* To rob, esp at gunpoint; HOLD UP : *being "stuck up" by highwaymen/ They're liable to go out and stick up a bank if they owe you* [*1846+; apparently fr the command stick 'em up, "hold up your hands"*]

stick up for someone or something *v phr* To defend and support : *If his own family won't, who will stick up for him?* (*1837+*)

stick with *v phr* To continue to carry out : *stuck with it so long* (*1915+*)

sticky *adj* **1** Sentimental; SCHMALTZY, SOPPY : *a sticky little song about a crippled puppy* (*1864+*) **2** Difficult; tricky; nasty : *He considered himself a tap dancer, because he was very agile at gliding away from any sticky situation* (*1915+*) *See* ICKY

sticky-fingered *adj* Prone to steal or pilfer; larcenous; LIGHT-FINGERED : *What are you, sticky-fingered?* (*1890+*)

sticky fingers *n phr* A person inclined to steal; an inclination to steal : *sticky fingers of the neighbors who cat-sit*

sticky wicket *n phr* A very difficult or awkward situation; a nasty affair : *"It's a sticky wicket," he said, but he left open the possibility that it could be orchestrated in a few cases/ It's the original sticky wicket* [*1952+; fr the British phrase bat on (or at) a sticky wicket, "contend with great difficulties," fr the game of cricket*]

stiff *adj* **1** Drunk : *when the regular piano player got stiff and fell from the stool* (*1737+*) **2** Forged; PHONY : *"I put over a couple of stiff* ones" is the way a paper-hanger describes an operation (1940s+ Underworld) n 1 A drunken person : Robbing a drunken man they call "rolling a stiff" (1907+) 2 (also **stiffie**) A corpse : a final chapter narrated by the stiff/ So we scope out the stiffie and everybody says you know, like it was too bad (1859+) 3 A hobo; tramp; vagabond : He bore none of the earmarks of the professional "stiff" (1900+) 4 A migratory worker; OKIE (1899+) 5 A working man or woman; a nonclerical and nonprofessional employee; WORKING STIFF : Coolidge always seemed unreal to the ordinary stiff (1930+) 6 A clandestine letter, esp one passed around among prisoners (1889+ Underworld) 7 A forged check, banknote, etc (1823+ Underworld) 8 A team, fighter, contestant, etc, that is bound to lose; esp, a race horse that will not, cannot, or is not permitted to win : There is also a rumor that Follow You is a stiff in the race (1890+) 9 Any failure; FLOP, TURKEY : gets a million dollars worth of hype, and I hear it's a stiff (1960s+) 10 A person who "stiffs" a waiter : The maitre d', knowing a stiff when he saw one, shrugged v 1 To cause a horse to lose a race : He admitted that he himself had stiffed horses for a fee (1940s+ Horse racing) 2 To fail to tip a waiter or other employee : But he was slow about getting our orders, so we stiffed him/ who not only stiffs waiters and cab drivers, but golf caddies as well (1939+) 3 To cheat, esp out of money, fair wages, etc : The company defends its plan as a business decision and denies it was trying to stiff the women/ which creditors he could stiff, which he could stall, which had to be paid at once (1950+) 4 To swindle; defraud; SCAM : Some of the lessons were not as palatable, though, such as the one about a young woman who stiffed him/ In other words, New York City got stiffed (1950+) 5 To kill; OFF : Nobody was supposed to stiff a member of the family the way Vinnie had stiffed his niece's boy (1974+) 6 (also **stiff-arm**) To treat unfairly and harshly; rebuff or push aside brutally : He had stiffed a Philadelphia charity golf tournament without explanation/ didn't want to stiff him or send him sniffing along false trails/ I'll just stiff-arm them (1973+) [the underworld senses having to do with forged and clandestine papers, cheating, etc, are derived fr an early 1800s British sense, "paper, a document," probably based on the stiffness of official documents and document paper; the senses having to do with failure, etc, are related to the stiffness of a corpse; the sense of harsh snubbing, etc, is fr the stiff-arm in football, where a player, usu a runner, straightens out his arm and pushes it di-

rectly into the face or body of an intending tackler] See BIG STIFF, BORED STIFF, KNOCK someone OUT, SCARED STIFF

stiff upper lip n phr Courage or resolution in the face of fear or danger (1815+)

stiffy n A penile erection

sting n A tricking or entrapment, either in a confidence scheme or as part of a law-enforcement operation : have used sting to describe undercover operations that use a bogus business operation as a front/ Let's contrast Abscam with traditional law-enforcement stings (1975+) v 1 To cheat; swindle; defraud; SCAM (1812+) 2 To overcharge; STICK : He got stung at the corner market (1927+)

stinger n An unpleasant or adverse element; CATCH : Seems like a good proposition, but there's a stinger in it (1950s+)

stink n phr (also **big stink**) An extensive fuss; huge brouhaha; scandal : "I never made a big stink about it," says Righetti (1812+) v (also **stink on ice**) To be deplorable, nasty, totally inept or bungling, disgusting, etc; ROT, SUCK : The whole idea stinks, if you ask me/ The group and its main man stunk on ice (1225+) See ACT LIKE one's SHIT DOESN'T STINK, THINK one's SHIT DOESN'T STINK

stinker n 1 A despicable person; BASTARD : Stop acting like a stinker (1898+) 2 (also **stinkeroo**) Something disgusting, nasty, badly done, etc : If it proves to be a "stinkeroo" leave the theater quietly or suffer in silence (1917+) ◁**stink-finger**▷ See PLAY STINKY-PINKY

stinking adj 1 Despicable; wretched; LOUSY : It was a stinking way to treat her (1926+) 2 (also **stinking rich**) Very wealthy; FILTHY RICH, LOADED : The family, in those years, was stinking (1956+) 3 (also **stinko**) Drunk : and he got pretty stinking (entry form 1887+, variant 1927+)

stinking with modifier With an abundant amount of something : stinking with good luck

stink of money v phr To be rich • Derogatory (1877+)

stink to high heaven v phr To be very disgusting, inept, nasty, etc : filler items that definitely stunk to high heaven (1963+)

stink with v phr To have much of; be oversupplied with : He stinks with confidence, certainly (1960s+)

stinky adj Despicable; nasty; STINKING (1940s+) ◁**stinky-pinky**▷ See PLAY STINKY-PINKY

stir modifier : with the stir haircuts n A jail or prison : John went to stir (1851+) [perhaps fr Romany steriben; the mid-1800s sturaban or sturbin, "state prison," may be a transitional form]

stir-crazy adj (Variations: **bugs** or **daffy** or **simple** may replace **crazy**) Insane, stuporous, hysterical, or otherwise affected mentally by imprisonment : *Any number of others were what we call stir-crazy, going about their routine like punch-drunk boxers* (*1908+*)

stitch, a *n phr* An amusing or hilarious person or thing; a HOOT : *The Gossages were a stitch, playing it very loose/ What a stitch/ Calling this tarty turn an "interpretation" really is a stitch* [*1968+*; fr the expression *in stitches,* "laughing uncontrollably," perhaps fr the notion of laughing so much that it gives one *stitches,* "sudden sharp pains," found by 1601 in Shakespeare]

stocking *See* SILK-STOCKING

stog(ie) (or stogy) *n* A cigar

stoked *adj* Enthusiastic; happily surprised : *Everyone's stoked that he's here and would he do a couple of tunes* [*1963+*; fr surfer talk]

stoked on *adj phr* Enthusiastic over; very much pleased with : *Stoked on cats? If you like catamarans/ I was really stoked on that chick, man* [*1969+*; fr the notion of being fueled and hot like a furnace]

stomach *v* To tolerate : *can't stomach her inaneness*

stomp *n* **1** A jazz number with a heavy rhythmic accent (*1906+ Jazz musicians*) **2** A student who wears cowboy clothing and boots (*1960s+ Students*) *v* To assault viciously; savage; CLOBBER (*1946+*) [fr a dialect pronunciation of *stamp;* verb sense found by 1803 in the sense "stamp on someone"]

stompers *n* Heavy boots [*1899+*; revived in the 1960s] *See* SHITKICKERS, WAFFLE-STOMPERS

stone *adj* Thorough; perfect; total : *Reba's a stone psycho, I tell you/ People think it's a stone groove being a superstar adv* Totally; genuinely : *He is one stone crazy dude* [*1935+* Black; fr earlier adverbial sense "like or as a stone," in phrases like *stone* blind or *stone* deaf] *See* NOT CARVED IN STONE

stone broke *adj phr* Penniless; impoverished : *the money that is made out of stone-broke tramps* (*1886+*)

stone cold sober *adj phr* Totally unintoxicated; COLD SOBER (*1937+*)

stoned or **stoned-out** *adj* Intoxicated with narcotics or liquor; BOMBED OUT, ZONKED : *They get themselves stoned on beer/ The old man was stoned mad/ giggling in that mutually exclusive stoned-out way* (*1940s+ Cool talk*)

stone dead *adj phr* As dead as can be (*1290+*)

stoned to the eyes *adj phr* Completely intoxicated; HIGH : *Under that tree, stoned to the eyes, I wolf down Daybreak, Joan Baez's autobiography* (*1970s+*) *See* TO THE EYES

stoner *adj* An intoxicated or stuporous person : *mumbles a stoner performance that's sidesplittingly funny/ It's different than it was in the '60s because it's not just your obvious stoner*

types. *It's the jocks and the A-plus students. It's just about everybody* (*1960s+*)

stones *n* **1** Testicles; ROCKS • Euphemistic **2** Courage or bravado : *I have the stones to tell her off*

stonewall *n* : *A sustained stonewall, no one's been willing to answer questions for a week* **v** To delay and obstruct, esp by stubbornly keeping silent : *I want you all to stonewall it* [*1914+*; fr a cricket term used of a determined batsman who blocked everything as if he were a *stone wall;* in the US probably influenced by the stolid reputation of the Confederate general Thomas J *"Stonewall"* Jackson; the term became prominent during the early 1970s Watergate scandal]

stooge *n* A servile assistant; a mere flunky or tool : *Whenever Gulliver is not acting as a stooge there is a sort of continuity in his character/ his bail-bond stooges* (*1913+*) *v* : *We're glad to stooge for him* (*1939+*) [origin unknown; perhaps an alteration of *student,* humorously mispronounced as STOO jǝnt, in the sense of an apprentice, especially one unskilled at or learning a theatrical turn of some sort while serving as the underling of a master]

stool *n* (also **stoolie**) A police informer; STOOL PIGEON : *He's nothing but a cop's stool* (*Underworld 1906+, variant 1924+*) *v* : *to make me stool on a friend* (*1911+*) [back formation fr *stool pigeon*]

stool pigeon *n phr* A police informer; SNITCH, SQUEALER : *In New York he is also called a stool-pigeon* [*1930+* Underworld; fr earlier sense "decoy," fr the early 1800s practice of fastening *pigeons* and other birds to *stools* or stands as decoys; this term was applied to the decoy or "hustler" for a faro bank]

stop and smell the roses (or **flowers**) *v phr* To relax from the hurly-burly; enjoy an interval of simple enjoyment : *It's not a total consuming vocation with him as it is with most other members of Congress. So consequently he tends to stop and smell the flowers a lot more*

stop-by *n* A very brief visit, esp by a politician : *Capitol Hill types at this particular bar even include Sen Bill Bradley, who just did a "stop-by," and Rep Richard Gephardt* (*1990s+*)

stop someone or **something dead in** someone's or something's **tracks** *v phr* To stop someone or something very definitely and abruptly : *The economy could be stopped dead in its tracks* [*1950s+*; fr the image of a person or animal dropping straight down on being struck; "to shoot or kill someone dead in his tracks" is found by 1824]

stop on a dime *v phr* To stop quickly and neatly : *The car corners smoothly and stops on a dime* (*1964+*)

stopper *n* A dependable relief pitcher : *I had hoped he'd settle down and be the stopper/ And a bullpen stopper means even more in the confidence he can give the rest of the pitching staff and the entire team (1948+ Baseball)*

storage *See* IN COLD STORAGE

store *See* MIND THE STORE

storm *v* To speed; drive very fast *(1950s+ Hot rodders) See* BLOW UP A STORM, BRAINSTORM, SHITSTORM, UP A STORM

story *See* FISH STORY, SOB STORY, UPPER STORY

story of my life, the *n phr* The sad truth of my earthly career : *Our plans, our hopes, what becomes of them? Nothing ... story of my life (1938+)*

stove *See* HOT STOVE LEAGUE, POTBELLY STOVE

straight *adj* **1** Unmixed; undiluted; NEAT : *He takes his liquor straight (1874+)* **2** Not using narcotics; not addicted; CLEAN *(1950s+ Narcotics)* **3** Having had a narcotics dose, esp the first one of the day : *Once the addict has had his shot and is "straight" he may become industrious (1946+ Narcotics)* **4** Heterosexual; not sexually deviant *(1941+ fr homosexuals)* **5** True; honest and direct : *from straight-poop tough to moral (1530+) n* A tobacco cigarette; SQUARE *(1960s+ Musicians & students) See* GO STRAIGHT

straight and narrow *n phr* Conventionally moral and law-abiding behavior *(1930+)*

straight arrow *adj* : *The distraught heroine murmured to the straight-arrow hero n phr* A person who observes the social norms of decency, honesty, legality, heterosexuality, etc; a nondeviant : *It turns out the boy is a straight arrow underneath his finery/ This is a supervisory job that ordinarily is won by the group Straight Arrow, the Eagle Scout type* [1969+; fr an archetypical upright Native American brave named *Straight Arrow,* mythically associated with a similar Caucasian who is a *straight shooter*]

straight-edge *adj* Not using narcotics; CLEAN, STRAIGHT : *If you're a teenager and you don't do drugs, you're a straight-up, straight-edge (1990s+ Teenagers)*

straighten someone *v phr* To get or administer a narcotic for someone *(1960s+ Narcotics)*

straighten someone out *v phr* To give the correct information, explanation, etc : *First let me straighten you out about where we were when it happened (1894+)*

straighten up *v phr* CLEAN UP one's ACT *(1907+)*

straight face *n phr* A face revealing no ironic amusement or disbelief : *He couldn't tell me that story with a straight face (1897+)*

straight-faced *adj* Maintaining a straight face; POKER-FACED : *It was a big lie, straight-faced, but a lie (1975+)*

straight from the horse's mouth *See* FROM THE HORSE'S MOUTH

straight from the shoulder *adv phr* Honestly and directly; unflinchingly; STRAIGHT : *He gave it to us straight from the shoulder* [1856+; perhaps from the notion of an honest blow delivered *straight from the shoulder* rather than deviously, from the side, etc]

straight goods (or **dope**) *n phr* The truth : *Is all dat straight goods? (1892+)*

straight man *n* A comedian's interlocutor and companion, who acts as the foil; STOOGE : *The late George Burns was the archetypal straight man (1923+ Show business)*

straight shooter *n phr* A direct and honest person; STRAIGHT ARROW : *declares that she is "the straightest shooter you ever saw" (1928+)*

straight talk *n phr* Direct and honest discourse; STRAIGHT GOODS *(1900+)*

straight-up *adj* (or *adv*) **1** Honest; upright; STRAIGHT ARROW : *They were straight-up, nice people/ doesn't believe the women's product can compete with men's volleyball, not straight up, not on the basis of skills or popularity (1910+)* **2** Of cocktails, served without ice cubes; NEAT *(1975+)* **3** Of eggs, sunny side up [*straight-up-and-down* in the first sense is found by 1903]

strain at the leash *v phr* To be impatient or eager *(1910+)*

strap *n* **1** A student interested primarily in sports; JOCK *(1970s+ Students)* **2** A condom; RUBBER *(1990s+)* [first sense fr *jockstrap,* "athletic supporter"]

straphanger *n* A person who rides the subway or bus; a commuter

strapped *adj* **1** Short of money; penniless; BROKE : *He happens to be strapped financially (1857+)* **2** : *We never had a word for carrying a gun. Today, that is what "strapped" means/ They exist in a world of "strapped" (gun-wielding) teenagers (1990s+)* [*strap,* "credit, tick," in the financial sense is found by 1828]

strapper *See* BOOT STRAPPER

strap with *v phr* To stick someone with a responsibility or burden : *16 and strapped with a baby*

strategist *See* ARMCHAIR GENERAL

strawberry *n* A red nose caused by excessive drinking *(1949+)*

straw boss *n phr* **1** The foreman of a work crew **2** Any assistant chief or subordinate director [1894+; said to be fr the arrangement of a threshing crew, where the chief would superintend the grain itself, and the second the straw; perhaps fr Dutch *stroodekkerbaas*]

streak *n* : *The students did a streak across the square v* To run naked in public *(1973+) See* A BLUE STREAK

street *modifier* Having to do with the streets and the street life of a city, esp of a ghetto : *Curtis Sliwa, founder of the street-tough Guardian Angels/ The defendant was not some street punk with a long criminal record* (1967+) *See* ON EASY STREET, TWO-WAY STREET

street, the *See* PUT IT ON THE STREET, WORK BOTH SIDES OF THE STREET

street cred *n phr* Acceptability or popularity, especially among young people in urban areas : *don't want to lose your street cred*

street (or garbage) furniture *n phr* Furniture put in the street for the trash collectors, and sometimes taken for use (1960s+)

street people *n phr* **1** Ghetto dwellers **2** Homeless people such as transient hippies, bag ladies, and the like; drifters (1967+)

streets, the *See* POUND THE PAVEMENT

street-smart or **street-bright** or **street-wise** *adj* Cunning and clever in various practical ways, esp in the street culture of the urban ghetto : *a place for very sophisticated, street-bright people/ supplanting preppie glamour with what's euphemistically called a "streetwise" look. Supertramp is more like it* (1976+)

street smarts *n phr* Cunning and cleverness of a very practical sort, esp that useful in the urban ghetto : *that raging philosophical conflict between street smarts and pinstripes* (1972+)

streetsweeper *n* A kind of shotgun : *a bill that would ban the sale of two kinds of assault weapons—the "streetsweeper" shotgun and the Tec-9 pistol* (1990s+)

street time *n phr* **1** The period when a convict is not imprisoned, but is on parole or probation **2** The time between prison terms (1960s+ Prison)

stressed or **stressed out** *adj* or *adj phr* Suffering from nervous stress : *I'm sorry. I'm just very stressed/ He had to take a two-week leave because he was completely stressed out* (1980s+)

stress out *v phr* To succumb to nervous stress : *Whenever they are at the point of stressing out, inevitably one of them will say to the other, "Want a bugle?"* (1990s+)

stretch *n* **1** A prison term : *a stretch in the Big House* (1821+) **2** STRETCH LIMO (1973+) **3** An unwarranted extension or inference; stretch of the imagination : *Earlier I mentioned Huck Finn and, though it sounds like a stretch, I'm convinced that Pamela Trowel is his direct descendant/ It was not, as they say in Hollywood, a stretch. Throughout those years, Simpson was the good guy* (1990s+) *v* To hang or be hanged (1595+) [prison sense originally "a one-year prison sentence"; third noun sense found by 1710 in the very similar "an exaggerated statement"]

stretch limo *n phr* A limousine that has been lengthened to provide more seating and more luxurious surroundings : *certified designer fashions, eye-popping jewelry, stretch limos/ a bar the length of a few stretch limos* [1973+; probably modeled on the earlier term *stretch* or *stretched* applied to a jetliner with a lengthened fuselage providing more seating]

strictly for the birds or **for the birds** *modifier* Worthless; no good (1944+)

strike *See* SIT-DOWN, WILDCAT

strike it rich *v phr* To have a sudden financial success (1854+)

strike oil *v phr* To succeed : *I worked at the problem eight days before I struck oil* (1866+)

string along *v phr* To agree; follow; join in : *As long as you string along with me, your cafeteria days are over* (1877+)

string someone along *v phr* To deceive; fool, esp into a continuing adherence, cooperation, etc; string : *I'm afraid that he's just stringing me along, trying to encourage me* [1902+; probably fr early 1800s British *string on*, in the same sense]

stringbean *n* A tall, thin person; BEANPOLE (1936+)

strings *See* PULL STRINGS

string someone up *v phr* To hang someone (1872+)

Strip, the *n phr* Any of various main streets in US cities, esp the street in Las Vegas where most of the gambling casinos are found

stripe *See* HASH MARK

striper *See* CANDY STRIPER

stripes *n* Chevrons worn as insignia of noncommissioned rank; crow tracks (1827+)

stripped down *adj phr* **1** Of a car, divested of ornaments and other unnecessary parts; SHAVED (1946+) **2** Reduced to the essentials; disencumbered : *a stripped-down version of the Oedipus myth* (1961+)

stripper or **strippeuse** *n* A striptease dancer : *Norma Vincent Peel, the noted stripper* (entry form 1930+, variant 1939+)

strip-search *n* SKIN-SEARCH (1947+)

stroke *modifier* : *Two things are at stake for employees who parrot their bosses or who always are in stroke mode* (1969+) *n* : *Everybody needs a stroke or two every once in a while* (1969+) *v* **1** To praise and please; caress the ego of; flatter; cosset : *Mr Hoover should be called in privately for a stroking session/ and ads in Rolling Stone were more for the purpose of stroking recording artists* (1561+) ◁**2**▷ To masturbate (1970+) [*stroker*, "flatterer," is found by 1632]

◁**stroke book**▷ *n phr* A lewd or suggestive publication; a pornographic book or magazine; fuck book : *It took a stroke book for me to break the ice* [1970+; fr *stroke*, "masturbate"]

◁stroke house▷ *n phr* A pornographic movie theater [1970+; fr *stroke*, "masturbate"]

stroll *n* An area or route favored by prostitutes for solicitation : *Ms Lopez, a 38-year-old streetwalker, said she had been chased by packs of youngsters who descended at night on the stroll, where prostitutes ply their trade in the industrial park* (*1990s+*)

strong *See* COME ON STRONG

strong-arm *modifier* Using threats of violence; physically brutal : *strong-arm work around election time/ We reprehended his strong-arm tactics* (*1901+*) *v* To use force and intimidation : *We can't strong-arm them into voting our way* (*1903+*)

struggle *v* To have difficulty winning or holding the pace; be in athletic travail : *Mets struggling; Cardinals soaring/ Lendl Struggles to Win* [1970s+ Sports; in the general sense "strive despite difficulties," found by 1597] *See* BUN-STRUGGLE

strung out *adj phr* **1** Using or addicted to narcotics; intoxicated with narcotics : *The entire college population is "strung out" thrice weekly/ got fairly well strung out, fairly well addicted* (*1950s+ Narcotics*) **2** Emotionally disturbed; psychologically tense, brittle, and vulnerable; UPTIGHT : *She got herself strung way out, just one more little push and she was a dead duck/ or slung low and strung-out on drugs or inner tensions* (*1959+*) *adj* **3** Infatuated; in love : *He's strung out on her* (*1960s+ Black*) [apparently by extension fr the black term *on a tight leash*, "in love, addicted," stressing the tethered helplessness of each condition]

strut one's stuff *v phr* To display one's virtuosity, esp in a saucy, provocative way [1926+ Black; fr dances featuring a *strut* like the turkey cock's, popular from around 1900]

stuck on someone or something *adj phr* In love with; infatuated : *That feller was stuck on yuh, Bess* (*1886+*)

stuck-up *adj* Haughty and conceited; snobbish; HINCTY : *We didn't like her at first because we thought she acted stuck-up* (*1839+*)

stuck with *past part phr* Burdened with; saddled with : *Imagine being stuck with a moniker like that all your life* (*1848+*)

stud *n* **1** A man, esp one who is stylish, au courant, etc; DUDE (*1929+*) **2** A sexually prodigious man; COCKSMAN (*1895+*) **3** An attractive man; HUNK : *Everyone knows Mike, he's the total stud of his class* (*1950s+*) **4** A medical student (*1980s+ Medical*) [fr *stud* or *studhorse*, "stallion, esp one kept for breeding," the term found by 1903; first sense popularized by 1940s jive talk]

studly *adj* **1** Masculine; sexually keen; MACHO : *In one episode Ross is flustered when a new girlfriend wants him to talk dirty to her. For advice he goes to studly friend Joey/ Gay men at their pagan-studliest celebrate play, physicality, pretense, not to mention Greco-Roman grappling* **2** Excellent; good; COOL : *It seemed like a studly thing at the time. Microsoft got what it wanted, and I got what I wanted* (*1960s+*)

studmuffin *n* An attractive young man; HUNK, STUD : *The vixen can't stop chasing stud-muffins around the old conference table/ Stud-muffin David Charvet cannot be coaxed from his trailer for a chat* (*1980s+ Students*)

stuff *n* **1** Liquor, esp bootleg liquor : *The stuff is here and it's mellow* (*1920s+ Prohibition era*) **2** Any narcotic : *Where's the stuff?/ He came out and seemed to be off the stuff* (*1920+ Narcotics*) ◁3▷ A woman regarded as a sex object; ASS, COOZ, PUSSY : *classiest stuff this side of Denver* (*1909+*) **4** The various ways a pitcher throws the ball, esp curves, sliders, etc (*1912+ Baseball*) *v* ◁1▷ To do the sex act; FUCK ● Chiefly British and most often heard in the passive imperative form *get stuffed*, a rude insult; used in any sense of *fuck* : *No women, no children, no fun. Stuff this* (*1960+*) **2** To pitch using effective "stuff" : *"He'd stuffed us pretty good before," said Brewers manager Phil Garner* (*1990s+ Baseball*) *See* ALL THAT KIND OF CRAP, the GREEN STUFF, HARD STUFF, HOT STUFF, KID STUFF, KNOW one's ONIONS, KNOW WHAT ONE CAN DO WITH something, ROUGH STUFF, TELL someone WHAT TO DO WITH something, WHITE STUFF

stuffed *See* GET STUFFED

stuffed shirt *n phr* A pompous person; a stiff, self-important bore (*1913+*)

stuff one's face (or **oneself**) *v phr* To eat excessively (*1939+*)

stuff it *See* STICK IT

stuff the ballot box *v phr* To cast or record fraudulent votes in an election (*1854+*)

stuffy *adj* Tediously conventional; pompous and self-righteous : *He was inclined to be a bit stuffy in sexual matters* [1895+; fr *stuffy*, "stale, lacking freshness," influenced by *stuffed shirt*]

stumblebum *n* An alcoholic derelict; a drunken drifter; skid row bum : *to bemoan the lack of charisma and to paint the candidates as a wrangling collection of stumblebums* (*1932+*)

stump *v* **1** To baffle; perplex; nonplus : *The problem's got me stumped* (*1807+*) **2** To make speeches, esp on a political tour : *The candidate is stumping today in Illinois* (*1838+*) **3** A telephone or other wire-carrying pole (*1940s+ Line repairers*) [first sense fr the notion of being blocked by *stumps* in one's way; second sense fr standing up on a *stump* to make a speech]

stump for someone or something *v phr* To advocate or support, esp very actively [1878+; fr the notion of giving speeches from *stumps*]

stumps *n* The legs : *Everybody stir your stumps when Pa calls* (1460+)

stunner *n* Something very attractive or impressive, esp a good-looking woman (1847+)

stunning *adj* Attractive; impressive : *Isn't that a stunning little dress?* (1849+)

stunt *n* Act; bit of behavior; thing to do : *vulgar "stunts" designed to be easily comprehended and greedily relished* (1878+)

◁**stup**▷ *See* SHTUP

stupid or **stupid fresh** *adj* or *adj phr* Excellent; splendid; COOL, RAD : *That's stupid/ Yep. Cool, mellow and stupid fresh* (1980s+ Black)

stupid-assed or **stupid-ass** *adj* Stupid; dumb : *a stupid-assed honor student* (1980s+)

stutter-stepping *n* To run with rapid short steps : *Never mind all that stutter-stepping and looking for daylight* (1970s+ Football)

style *v* To act or play in a showy, flamboyant way; HOT DOG, SHOWBOAT : *You got an A in physics! You're styling!* (1970s+ Black) [*put on style*, "to act in a boastful way," is found by 1871] *See* CRAMP someone's STYLE, DOG FASHION, LIKE IT'S GOING OUT OF STYLE

stylin(g) *adj n* Showing off one's good looks; looking good : *styling in that button-down shirt she's stylin' in her fleece mini boots*

stymie *v* To block or thwart; frustrate : *Instead, the drive toward integration has been stymied by the speedbump of crime* [1857+ Golf; origin uncertain; perhaps fr British dialect *stimey*, "dim-sighted person," fr *stime*, "ray or bit of light"; adopted in golf for situations where the player or, as it were, the ball cannot "see" a clear path ahead]

suave or **swave** *adj* Excellent; fine; COOL *n* Smooth skill; polished adroitness : *He has plenty of suave when it comes to girls v : Then I took her off her feet. I suaved her/ I guess old Buck suaved her off her feet* (1960s+ Teenagers)

sub *n* A substitute of any sort, esp an athlete who replaces another or an athlete not on the first team (1830+) *v : Who'll sub for me when I go on leave?* (1853+)

sub- *prefix for forming adjectives* Inferior to or imitative of what is indicated : *sub–Woody Allen* (1963+)

submarine sandwich or **sub** or **submarine** *n phr* or *n* HERO SANDWICH • Also hoagy, torpedo, grinder, poor boy, etc depending on the locality [1960s+; fr the shape of the bread cut lengthwise for the sandwich]

◁**suck**▷ *n* SUCTION (1960s+) *v* 1 To do fellatio; EAT (1928+) 2 (also **suck rope**, **suck eggs**) To be disgusting or extremely reprehensible; be of wretched quality; ROT, STINK : *A failure as*

an album. It sucks/ Life irretrievably sucks, and what's the use/ Your decision sucks rope/ his own pet phrase, "That sucks eggs," for expressing disdain (1971+) 3 SUCK ASS (1900+) [*Sucks!* as a contemptuous interjection used by British schoolboys is found by 1913]

suckage *n* 1 The worst possible condition or state 2 The amount or degree to which something sucks

suck air *v phr* To be afraid or alarmed, so as to pant; hyperventilate with anxiety : *Were you afraid? I was sucking air a couple of times/* (1970s+)

◁**suck ass**▷ *v phr* To curry favor; flatter and cajole; BROWN-NOSE, POLISH APPLES : *He sucks ass with everybody in the front office* (1940s+)

suck eggs *v phr* 1 To be mean and irritable : *We've sucked on these eggs long enough* (1906+) 2 To do something very nasty, esp when invited to; GO FUCK oneself • A euphemism : *Tell your husband to suck huge eggs* (1970s+)

sucker *n* 1 An easy victim; dupe; MARK, PATSY : *I'm no sucker/ I'm a sucker for a beautiful blonde* (1838+) 2 Any specified object, esp one that is prodigious, troublesome, effective, etc; MOMMA, MOTHERFUCKER • A euphemism for *cocksucker* : *It took me 90 days to get that sucker straightened out* (1978+) *v* To victimize or dupe someone : *if I can sucker him into drawing first* (1939+) [origin uncertain; perhaps fr the *sucker*, a fish supposed to be easily caught; perhaps fr the notion of an unweaned and relatively helpless creature, as suggested by an earlier sense, "greenhorn, simpleton"] *See* COCKSUCKER

sucker for *n* Gullible person; a person who cannot resist something (1960+)

suckerpunch *n* A blow that surprises the recipient, who might have dodged or parried it (1947+) *v* : *He suckerpunched me/ I'll sucker punch a man in a second to get what I want*

suck face *v phr* To kiss and caress; NECK, PET : *You know, kiss. Suck face, kiss* (1970s+)

◁**suck hind tit**▷ *v phr* To be in a disadvantageous situation; get the worst and least of things : *The plum assignments are there. The press coverage is there. We're up here sucking hind tit* [late 1930s+; fr the presumed disadvantage of a *suckling* at the *nethermost teat*]

suck someone **in** *v phr* To deceive; befool or dupe, esp with false promises [1842+; said to be fr the action of quicksand]

sucking *See* COCKSUCKING

suck it up *v phr* To become serious; stop dallying or loafing : *forced the 76ers to suck it up for game four, which they did to beat L.A./ No matter. He'd suck it up and go* [1980s+; fr the military expression *suck up* or *suck in your* *guts,* "pull in your stomach and look trim, as a soldier should"]

◁**suck-off**▷ *adj* Despicable; nasty; SCUZZY : *We did a suck-off thing n* A despicable person, esp a flatterer; BROWN-NOSE *(1950s+)*

◁**suck off**▷ *v phr* To do fellatio or cunnilingus; BLOW, GO DOWN ON someone *(1928+)*

suck up *v phr* To defeat in a speed race; pass in a drag race : *I have also sucked up plenty of cherry red Vettes* [1970s+; fr the notion of drawing the passed car along in one's turbulence behind]

suck (or kiss) up to someone *v phr* To flatter and cajole someone; curry favor with someone; BROWN-NOSE. SUCK ASS : *He gets ahead by sucking up to the mayor/ They are boss kisseruppers. They kiss up to the boss* (*entry form 1860+,* variant *1990s+)*

sucky *adj* Repellent; inferior; LOW-RENT : *I was a real sucky waitress/ "The Tyler Set" can be real sucky, too (1990s+)*

suction *n* Influence; DRAG, PULL *(1940s+)*

sudden death *modifier* : *It's like playing a sudden death inning at the beginning of a game n phr* Any of several arrangements for breaking a tie by playing an extra period during which the first team to score wins the game : *They went into sudden death overtime (1927+ Sports)*

suds *n* Beer *(1904+)*

sugar (or sugar baby, sugar pie) *n* 1 Money; BREAD : *I'd take a trip if I had the requisite sugar* (*1859+)* 2 Dear one; sweetheart • Most often a term of address : *I hear you, sugar (1930+)* 3 Heroin, cocaine, or morphine *(1930s+ Narcotics)* 4 acid, LSD *(1950s+ Narcotics)* [second narcotics sense fr the taking of LSD soaked in a *sugar* cube] *See* HEAVY MONEY

sugar-coat something *v phr* To make something more acceptable or palatable : *We played bad. I'm not going to sugar-coat it (1870+)*

sugar daddy *n phr* A man who provides money, esp one who supports a clandestine sweetheart or a gold-digger : *Mrs Shawsky must have had a sugar daddy on the side/ The Pentagon seems to be playing sugar daddy to a lot of American workers (1926+) See* DADDY

◁**sugar tit**▷ *n phr* Something that gives comfort and security; SECURITY BLANKET [1892+; fr the use of a cloth soaked in *sugar* water to appease a suckling infant; *sugar-teat* is found by 1847]

suicide blonde *n* A woman with hair unprofessionally dyed blonde • Jocular *(1942+)*

suit *n* A serious business or professional person : *some slick suit comes along and sets him free/ turned as the suits from the Housing Authority approached* [1979+; fr the wearing of a suit,

shirt, tie, etc, at work] *See* BIRTHDAY SUIT, MONKEY SUIT, ZOOT SUIT

suitcase *n* A drum *(1935+ Jazz musicians)*

sulks *n* A bout of depression or bad temper *(1818+)*

◁**sumbitch**▷ *See* SON OF A BITCH

sun *See* STICK IT

Sunday *modifier* 1 The best; one's best : *Sunday finest (1794+)* 2 Amateur; occasional : *For a Sunday painter he's not bad (1925+)* [the first date refers to the phrase *Sunday best,* "one's best clothes"] *See* FORTY WAYS TO SUNDAY

Sunday best or **Sunday clothes** or **Sunday-go-to-meeting clothes** *n phr* One's best clothes; BEST BIB AND TUCKER : *both wearing what Delaney descibed as Sunday-go-to-meeting clothes* [entry form 1779+; fr the earlier *Sunday-go-to-meeting clothes*]

Sunday driver *n phr* A slow and careless driver, like one out for a leisurely Sunday drive *(1925+)*

Sunday punch *modifier* : *rockets, the "Sunday punch" weapon of the war n phr* 1 A very hard and effective blow or assault, with the fist or otherwise : *and lay his Sunday punch on your snoot (1929+ Prizefighting)* 2 A strong and effective pitch, esp an overpowering fastball *(1952+ Baseball)*

Sunday soldier or **weekend warrior** *n phr* A military reservist or member of the National Guard, who typically goes on uniformed duty on the weekend *(1950s+)*

sundowner *n* : *A patient who suffers delusions and disorientation at night, but not by daylight (1980s+ Medical)*

sunny side up *adj phr* Of eggs, fried on one side only with the yolk showing yellow *(1900+)*

Sunshine *n* Term of address for a sour person *(1913+)*

sun-worshipper *n* One who likes to sit in the sun, esp to get a tan : *turns sun-worshipper in April (1966+)*

super[1] *n* A superintendent, esp one who is custodian of an apartment building *(1857+)*

super[2] *adj* Wonderful; excellent; very superior : *America's Teenage Girls Speak Language of Their Own That Is Too Divinely Super* [1895+; perhaps fr *superior* or *superfine*; revitalized in the 1960s]

super- *prefix used to form adjectives* Having the indicated quality to an extraordinary degree : *superhappy/ superwonky prefix used to form nouns* A superbly qualified and prodigious specimen of what is indicated : *superjerk/ superjock/ superchick/ Supermom* [1930s+; noun prefix stimulated from 1938 by the comic-book character *Superman*]

super-duper or **sooper-dooper** *adj* Excellent; wonderful; splendid; superb : *this new MGM* *sooper-dooper musical smash* [1940+; rhyming]

superfly *adj* Superior; wonderful; SUPER[2] : *He really thinks he's superfly when he gets into his thing (1971+ Black) See* FLY

superintendent *See* SIDEWALK SUPERINTENDENT

superwoman *n* A woman who successfully undertakes marriage, motherhood, and a full working life all at the same time *(1976+)*

supper *See* SHOOT one's COOKIES

sure *affirmation* Yes; certainly : *Sure, I'll support you (1842+) See* SHITSURE

◀**sure as fuck**▶ *adv phr* Surely; certainly; SURE AS SHOOTING : *Sure as fuck, you didn't tell me you were in there handling her glassware (1980s+)*

sure as God made little green apples *adj phr* Certain; definite : *It's sure as God made little green apples that they'll never get here (1940s+)*

sure as hell *modifier* Absolutely certain : *You sure as hell are not watching TV*

sure as shooting *adj phr* Certain; definite *adv phr* : *Thousands of them are sent by civic leaders and, sure as shooting, by other federal judges affirmation* Yes; certainly *(1847+)*

sure-fire *adj* Unfailing; certain to succeed, happen, etc : *His election is a sure-fire thing (1901+)*

sure thing *affirmation* Yes; certainly; willingly : *Sure thing I'll go with you (1896+)*

sure thing, a *n phr* A certainty, esp a bet that one cannot lose : *His election is a sure thing, right? (1836+)*

surf *v* To move or pass through some range of choices, such as television channels : *I surfed from your show/ They're surfing the same part of the zeitgeist* [1990s+; fr the ease and rapidity of movement while *surfing* on waves] *See* CHANNEL SURF

surface *v* To get up or leave one's room or home : *hasn't surfaced for days since the breakup (1963+)*

surf bunny or **surf bum** *n phr* A person who spends lots of time at the beach; BEACH BUNNY *(1960s+)*

surfer *n* A person who "surfs" : *People are taking the trouble to put the professional sports schedules on line, to be consulted by any surfer of cyberspace (1990s+)*

surf the net *v phr* To browse the Internet *(1992+)*

surprise or **surprise surprise** *interj* An exclamation of feigned astonishment over something perfectly obvious or predictable : *A study conducted by university researchers a year ago found that the Family Support Act was failing to change the welfare culture. Surprise/ There were two favorite spots for tots. Surprise*

surprise. The boys loved the little bosom rose (1953+)

suss out *v phr* To discover by intuition or inquiry; find out; learn : *I sussed out Whoosh was the chief my first time here/ I've got to start sussing out nonscuzzy places to pee all along our most-traveled routes* [1966+; fr *suspect* or *suspicion,* attested as *sus* in British sources by 1930s; perhaps popularized and brought to the US by British rock-and-roll groups]

Suzy Homemaker *n* A woman who fulfills the quintessential housewife role [1960s+; fr children's toy appliance]

-sville or **-ville** *suffix used to form adjectives* Characterized by what is indicated : *dragsville/ splitsville/ squaresville suffix used to form nouns* Place characterized by what is indicated : *Derbyville/ Motorsville (1891+)*

swab or **swabby** or **swabbie** *n* A sailor, esp a Navy seaman : *better fitting dress uniforms for the hard-to-fit doughboy or swabbie* [1798+; probably fr the characteristic activity of using *swabs* for cleaning the decks and other features of a ship]

swacked *adj* Drunk : *Besides, you're swacked all the time (1932+)*

swag *n* 1 Stolen goods, money, etc; loot *(1794+)* 2 Souvenirs, etc, sold at rock-and-roll concerts : *Somehow, these trifling collectibles came to be known as swag (1990s+)* [probably fr the *swag,* "sack," in which loot might be carried]

swagging *n* Getting money or property illegally, esp by pilfering government property or by taking illegal payoffs or tips : *a lack of hard evidence that "swagging" or tipping had actually taken place* [1846+; apparently revived in the 1960s]

swak or **SWAK** (pronounced as separate letters) *sentence* Sealed with a kiss *(1925+)*

swallow something *v* To accept or endure reluctantly; stomach : *What I can't swallow is that he was then promoted (1591+)*

swallow the dictionary *v phr* To develop a great vocabulary

swamped *adj* Overwhelmingly busy : *swamped with projects and tasks*

swank *adj* (also **swanky**) Elegant; stylish; POSH, RITZY : *Carroll's swank office (1913+) n* : *the swank of his riding clothes (1920s+) v* To behave ostentatiously; STRUT : *I saw her swanking up the avenue in furs (1809+)* [origin unknown; perhaps fr Middle English *swanken,* "to sway," cognate with German *schwenken,* "to flourish"]

swap spit *v phr* To kiss *(1938+ College students)*

swat *v* To strike; hit : *He spoke up and got swatted for it (1796+)*

swat (or **SWAT**) **team** *n phr* A police unit wearing military-like uniforms and using military assault weapons on assignments requiring extraordinary coordination and force : *When the terrorists took over the whole building, the commissioner sent in the SWAT team* [1969+; fr acronym of *special weapons and tactics* used as a modifier]

swave *See* SUAVE

swear by *v phr* To have full confidence in something : *swear by Vaseline for makeup removal*

swear like a trooper *v phr* To use a lot of foul language; to use foul language rather expertly

swear off *v phr* To desist from something, with or as if with an abstemious vow : *He swore off cheese and crackers for a whole week* (1898+)

swear (or swear to) on a stack of Bibles *v phr* To affirm with absolute confidence and considerable vehemence : *Don called all those short-term signals for Joe. I'd swear to that on a stack of Bibles* (1866+)

swear up and down *v phr* SWEAR ON A STACK OF BIBLES (1906+)

sweat *v* **1** To suffer; stew; COOK (1610+) **2** To work very hard and meticulously : *Clinton did not sweat buckets to gain a minimum wage increase, fund extensive job training, or stop budget-busting tax breaks for the well-to-do* (1592+) **3** To interrogate a prisoner roughly : *We hauled a bunch of them in, sweated them, nobody would give us anything* (1764+) *See* FLOP SWEAT, IN A SWEAT, NO SWEAT, PANTHER PISS

sweat bullets *v phr* **1** To be very worried; be apprehensive; SHIT A BRICK : *They've been sweating bullets since they heard he was looking for them* (1970s+) **2** (also **sweat blood**) To work very hard : *Their father has to sweat bullets to make a living* (1970s+, variant 1911+)

sweat equity *n phr* An equity or stake earned by hard work rather than purchase : *They've demonstrated with sweat equity that they're team players* (1968+)

sweater (or **pin-up**) **girl** *n phr* A young woman, esp a movie actress or a model, with a notably attractive body, which she features by wearing tight and short clothing (*entry form late 1930s+, variant 1941+*)

sweat hog *n phr* ◁1▷ A heavy and unattractive woman ◁2▷ A sexually promiscuous woman **3** A difficult and incompetent high-school or college student (*1970s+ College students*)

sweat it *v phr* To be apprehensive or uptight • Most often used in the negative : *Well, don't sweat it. Look, is a buck and a quarter okay?* (1963+)

sweat something out *v phr* To endure or suffer, esp with nervous anticipation : *a young*

writer *sweating out the creation of his first short stories* [1876+; revived during WWII]

sweat something out of someone *v phr* To discover by intimidation or harsh questioning (1940s+)

sweats *n* Athletic clothing; warmup suits : *several court reporting firms, a T-shirt and sweats distributor* (1990s+)

sweatshop *n* A factory or workplace with very poor labor conditions

sweep *n* The winning of a tournament, series, etc, without losing a single game : *He took the match in a sweep, straight sets* (1940s+ Sports) *v* : *The Giants swept the World Series that year*

sweeps *modifier* : *a bunch of mealy-mouthed wimps who'd break bread with Adolf fucking Hitler if it meant some kind of rating during sweeps week* *n* Audience ratings and their announcement : *She plans to stay through the May ratings "sweeps"* (1980s+ Television) [perhaps fr *sweepstakes*]

sweep something under the rug *v phr* To avoid or conceal something : *They just swept the whole race matter under the rug* (1961+)

sweet *modifier* Great; excellent : *sweet deal See* BLONDE AND SWEET

sweet ass *See* BET YOUR BOOTS, BUST one's ASS

sweeten *v* To make something more attractive, esp more remunerative : *Then they sweetened the offer by several thousand dollars* (1896+ Cardplaying)

sweetener *n* Something that makes a deal more attractive; encouragement or enhancement, such as a monetary payment : *sweetener was all I needed for the deal*

sweeten someone up *v phr* **1** To bribe or otherwise recompense someone in exchange for something : *He had to sweeten the cops up even after he had the license* **2** To flatter and cajole someone; SUCK UP TO someone : *He sweetened the audience up a little by praising the town* (1950s+)

sweetheart *n* **1** Something excellent; a cherished and valuable object; HONEY : *See that sweetheart of a car?* (1942+) **2** A pleasant person; DOLL : *Wait'll you meet her father, he's a sweetheart* (1940s+)

sweetheart contract (or **agreement**) *n phr* A labor contract that particularly favors the employer and is usually negotiated by a corrupt union official (*1950s+ Labor union*)

sweetheart deal *n phr* A mutually profitable and either unethical or illegal arrangement, usu involving a public agency : *what the cable companies now term a "sweetheart deal." The Port Authority just turned over the whole thing to Merrill Lynch* (1959+)

sweetie *n* A sweetheart, in all senses • Often a term of endearment in address : *And Tom's*

*the first sweetie she ever had/ Ain't my new
computer a sweetie?* [1903+; an isolated instance, *sweet-ee,* is found by 1778]

sweetie-pie *n* A sweetheart, in all senses : *His
sweetie pie came home in the early hours*
(1928+)

sweet mama *n phr* A female lover *(1920s+
Black)*

sweet man (or **papa**) *n phr* A male lover
(1920s+ Black)

sweet nothings *n* Loving remarks or comments : *sweet nothings whispered in her ear*

sweet on someone *adj phr* Enamored of
someone; in love with someone : *He was
never really sweet on Miss Carlisle/ very sweet
on a handsome young man (1740+)*

sweet patootie *See* PATOOTIE

sweet pea *n phr* A sweetheart [1940s+; perhaps a shortening of *sweet patootie,* influenced by the name of the garden plant]

sweet potato *n phr* An ocarina *(1930s+)*

sweets or **sweetums** *n* SWEETHEART, SWEETIE • A
term of endearment : *I'll get it for you, sweets*
(1930+)

Sweet 16 *n phr* The last sixteen teams left in
the annual college basketball playoffs :
Maryland to the Sweet 16 [1990s+ Sports; fr
the traditional phrase for a young girl, found
by 1826, and still much in use]

sweet spot *n phr* The best area on a tennis
racket, hockey stick, golf club, or baseball
bat for contact with the ball or puck : *they
will find the sweet spot with greater frequency
with the Slotz (1974+)*

sweet-talk *n* : *He listened to her sweet-talk very
receptively (1945+)* *v phr* To seek to persuade or soften someone, esp by flattery and
endearments; FAT-MOUTH *(1936+)*

sweet-tooth *n* Narcotic addiction or craving
(1960s+ Narcotics)

swell *adj* Excellent; wonderful; superb : *The
hotels are swell/ He was a hell of a swell fellow*
(1888+) *adv* : *The new owners have treated
me swell (1920s+)* *n* **1** A stylish and well-
groomed person; DUDE *(1786+)* **2** A wealthy,
elegant person; a socialite; nob : *up on the hill
where the swells live (1786+)* [perhaps fr the
late 18th-century phrase *cut a swell,* "swag-
ger," describing the behavior of a person
who *swells* with arrogance]

swelled head *n* Conceit *(1891+)*

swellelegant *adj* SWELL

swift *adj* Smart and clever; intelligent : *Not too
swift, is he*

swig *n* A swallow of liquor; PULL, SLUG [1621+;
origin unknown]

swill *n* Nasty and inferior food or drink; belly-
wash : *What is this swill they've placed before
us? (1570+)*

swim *v* To perform well; succeed; FLY : *I didn't
think the Harptones quite swam last time I saw
them* [1970s+; perhaps fr *sink or swim*]

swimming in or **rolling in** *adv phr* Immersed
in; having a great quantity

swimmingly *adv* Wonderfully; quite nicely :
does swimmingly at illustration

swing *n* **1** A style of white jazz music of the
1930s and '40s, developed from hot jazz and
usu played by big bands : *That pastime was
called Swing, and its king, Benny Goodman, and
most of its greatest exponents and exploiters
were quartered here in New York (1899+)* **2**
An interval between work periods : *with
two hours' swing in the afternoon for lunch
(1943+)* *v* **1** To have a strong but easy and
pleasant impetus : *Chaucer and Jazz are quite
similar; they both swing, they both have the
same punch, vitality, and guts (1935+ Musicians)* **2** To perform very well, as a good jazz
musician does : *It is appropriate that gifted,
gravel-voiced Herschel Bernardi should swing
eight times a week in this particular hit (1918+)*
3 To have a good time; enjoy oneself hugely,
as at a good party *(1957+ Black)* **4** To do the
sex act, esp promiscuously with various partners either seriatim or at once : *The sexual
revolution is not new; people have been swinging as long as they are on this earth (1964+)* **5**
To be stylish, au courant, sophisticated, etc;
be HIP : *"Songs for Swingin' Lovers" (1961+)*
6 To be a member of a teenage street gang
(1960s+ Street gang) **7** To pull off; execute :
Can you swing it

swing (or **go**) **both ways** *v phr* To be bisexual;
be AC-DC : *Do you go both ways? (1960s+)*

swinger *n* A person who "swings," esp in
the mode of sexual promiscuity : *Kissinger,
who enjoyed a reputation as a swinger, was
asked to explain his oft-quoted remark/ Many
swingers even pride themselves on preserving
their marriages through these arrangements*
(1961+)

swing for the fences *v phr* **1** To swing very
hard, trying for a home run : *As the Babe
knew, swinging for the fences often brings more
strikeouts than four-baggers (1970s+ Baseball)* **2** To make a maximum effort; GO FOR
BROKE : *What was striking about Clinton's first
week in office was the way he swung for the
fences on the domestic front/ This stockbroker
prefers to invest his own money in issues more
risky than the ones Morgan Stanley recommends; he is willing to swing for the fences with
his own investments (1980s+)*

swinging single *n phr* A merry and celebra-
tory unmarried person, esp one who is sexually promiscuous as well as au courant :
entertaining other couples every weekend and

making jokes about the "swinging singles" all around them (1967+)

swing shift *n phr* A work shift between the regular day and night shift, typically from four to midnight (1941+)

swipe[1] *n* A stroke or blow, esp a strong one • Most often in the phrase *take a swipe at* : *Let somebody take a swipe at him (1807+)* *v* **1** To steal, esp something small or trivial; pilfer : *nix on swiping anything (1889+)* **2** To run a credit card, identification card, etc, through an electronic detector groove : *Swipe your card there and the door will open (1990s+)* [all senses perhaps fr alterations of *sweep* or *swoop* and the actions of sweeping or swooping up, or of hitting a sweeping blow; noun sense perhaps fr dialect preservation of Old English *swippan*, "beat, scourge"] *See* SIDESWIPE

swipe[2] *n* Inferior liquor, esp of the homemade sort : *the homemade bootleg mess made by the natives out of fruit and called "swipe"* [1960s+; probably related to several late 1780s and early 1800s British senses of *swipe*, "to gulp liquor quickly and deeply," of *swipes*, "small beer," and of *swipey*, "tipsy," all of which may be related to the British nautical *swipes*, "rinsings of the beer barrel," and hence to a sibilation of *wipe*]

swish[1] *adj* Showing the traits of an effeminate male homosexual; mincing; LIMP-WRISTED, NELLIE : *His walk was quite swish (1930s+ Homosexuals)* *n* **1** An effeminate male homosexual; QUEEN : *that fat swish* **2** Elaborate decoration : *place needs more swish* *v* To move, walk, speak, etc, in the manner or presumed manner of effeminate male homosexuals *(fr homosexuals)* [perhaps fr the swinging movements of the hips in a mincing walk; perhaps fr *swish*[2]]

swish[2] *adj* Elegant; fancy; POSH, RITZY, SWANKY : *You can get a very swish version or a very basic version* [1879+; fr British dialect, an apparent variant of *swash*, "a swaggerer," hence semantically related to *swank*]

switch *n* **1** A change, esp a reversal or major alteration : *This is a big switch for the reigning party (1920+)* **2** An exchange, esp an illicit substitution : *He made a switch, giving her the empty purse and taking the valuable one (1935+)* *v* To inform; SNITCH *(1940s+ Underworld) See* ASLEEP AT THE SWITCH

switched *See* I'LL BE DAMNED

switched-off *adj* Not in the current fashion; unconventional; OUT OF SYNC : *responding to his unconventional (at that time), bohemian, "switched-off" quality (1966+)*

switched on *adj phr* **1** Fashionable and admirable; au courant; up-to-date; GEAR : *A larger number of the women were in short, switched-on dresses/ They are among the current drop of switched-on young matrons* **2** Exhilarated; stimulated; HIGH, PLUGGED IN, TURNED ON : *He has powerful friends and you don't, switched-on in-crowd celebrity friends, high-all-the-time-and-getting-away-with-it friends (1964+)*

switcheroo *n* A switch or shift; a reversal : *For people in search of titillating diversion from their daily lives, switcheroos may seem exciting/ We'll use olives instead of cherries (1933+)*

switch-hitter *n* **1** A player who bats both right-handed and left-handed (1930s+ Baseball) **2** A versatile person (1950s+) **3** A bisexual person : *Some people thought he was a switch-hitter. But a nice guy (1956+)*

switch off *v phr* To become disinterested or less interested : *switches off after listening to her for a minute (1921+)*

switch on *v phr* **1** To join the current trends, tastes, etc; become up-to-date (1960s+) **2** To excite and exhilarate; arouse sexually; TURN ON : *He didn't see any girls that switched him on much (1960s+)* **3** To become intoxicated with narcotics; TURN ON *(1960s+ Narcotics)*

swivet *n* A fit of angry agitation; SNIT : *You can't get yourself in a swivet over some isolated instances* [1892+; origin unknown]

swizzled or **swozzled** *adj* Drunk; TIPSY (1843+)

swizzle-stick *n* A stick for stirring a mixed drink [1879+; fr earlier *swizzle*, "stir a drink," fr *swizzle*, "a drink, to drink," perhaps related to *switchel*, "drink of molasses and water, often mixed with rum"]

swoopy *See* ULTRASWOOPY

-sy *See* -IE

sync *n* Synchronism; synchronization (1929+) *v* To synchronize : *Let's sync our plans, okay? (1950s+) See* IN SYNC, LIP-SYNC, OUT OF SYNC

◁**syph** or the **syff**▷ *n* or *n phr* (Variations: **siff** or **the siff**) Syphilis : *syphilis, not siff/ They found out he had the syph while he was doin' time (1914+)*

system *See* OLD BOY NETWORK

T

T *n* A technical foul : *The "T" was absolutely ridiculous (1990s+ Basketball)*

◁**TA** or **T and A**▷ (pronounced as separate letters) *adj phr* : *They turned it into a T and A show n phr* A display of female bosoms and bottoms; a show featuring such display; CHEESECAKE : *the realm of feminine esthetics or, as it is known in the profession, TA/ To enliven their product they call for T and A (1972+)* [fr *tits* plus *ass*]

tab[1] *n phr* **1** The bill or check for something, esp for food or drink : *three- or four-hundred-dollar tabs for unpaid liquor (1942+)* *n* **2** A written acknowledgment of debt; IOU : *They're liable to go out and stick up a bank if they owe you a tab (1950s+)* [origin unknown; perhaps a shortening of *tabulation*] *See* PICK UP THE TAB

tab[2] *n* **1** A tablet **2** A dose of LSD; HIT *(1960s+ Narcotics)*

tab[3] *n* A tabloid newspaper : *just be sure the other tabs and the London papers don't have track pictures either (1990s+)*

tabby *n* PUSSYCAT : *The 348 is a tabby by comparison (1990s+)*

table *See* UNDER THE TABLE

table-hop *v* To go from table to table in a restaurant, nightclub, etc, visiting and chatting : *Linda goes to Elaine's to table-hop, not to eat (1956+)*

tabs *See* KEEP TABS ON

tacky *adj* Inferior; shabby; vulgar; ICKY, RATTY : *She talked in a manner that would be considered a bit countrified, if not slightly tacky/ The girl's hunger for validation, however tacky* [1862+; apparently fr *tacky*, "small, useless horse," and later "hillbilly, cracker"] *See* TICKY-TACKY

taco stand *n phr* A tacky or lousy place : *Let's blow this taco stand*

tad *n adj* **1** A small boy; a child : *I've liked reading since I was just a tad (1877+)* **2** A small amount; CUNT-HAIR, SKOSH, SMIDGEN : *may be taking his new series just a tad too seriously/ seem white to me even if they are a tad deformed (1915+)* [origin uncertain; perhaps a shortening of *tadpole*; perhaps fr British dialect *tadde*, "toad"]

ta-da or **tah-dah** *interj* An exclamation announcing one's arrival or some revelation : *She said "Ta da," and dropped the bath towel, and seduced me/ So, one-oh-two West a Hundred Sixteenth Street is, tah-dah!, Mohammed Temple Number Seven* [1940s+ Show business; originally a two-note musical phrase introducing a performer]

tag *n* **1** A person's name *(1934+)* **2** An arrest warrant : *Is there a tag out for me? (1934+ Underworld)* **3** An automobile license plate : *The Seminoles get special tags (1935+)* *v* **1** To hit; BELT, SOCK *(1940+)* **2** To write graffiti on walls, etc : *tagged with the rebellious urban scrawl of graffiti artists (1980+)* [final sense fr the fact that many such graffiti are the names, or *tags*, of the painter] *See* DOG TAGS

tag along *v phr* To accompany someone, esp when not invited : *If you don't mind, I'll just tag along with you/ Which I can do on my own, or whatever; you want to tag along (1900+)*

tail *n* **1** The buttocks; ASS : *if all of us parked ourselves on our tails/ I hadn't tossed him out on his tail (1303+)* ◁**2**▷ A woman regarded solely as a sex partner, object, or organ; ASS : *a nice piece of tail (1933+)* ◁**3**▷ Sexual activity or gratification; ASS, FUCKING : *It was said that the freshmen up at Yale got no tail (1920+)* **4** A person who follows another for surveillance; SHADOW : *The security officer was even going to put a tail on the children (1914+)* *v* : *tailing a jewelry salesman (1907+)* [in the second noun sense, *tail*, "sex organ," is found by 1362] *See* one's ASS OFF, DRAG one's TAIL, GET one's TAIL IN A GATE, HAVE A BROOM UP one's ASS, HAVE A TIGER BY THE TAIL, HAVE someone or something BY THE TAIL, PIECE OF ASS, RINGTAIL, WORK one's ASS OFF

tailbone *n phr* The buttocks; ASS *(1940s+)*

tailgate *v* **1** To follow another car, truck, etc, dangerously closely; HIGHTAIL : *drove her car behind him, tailgating him between red walls of dead brick* **2** To watch girls go by *(College students)* **3** To join what one says closely to what has just been said; DOVETAIL *(Army)*

tailgate party *n phr* **1** An outdoor party or picnic, typically in the parking lot of a sports stadium, and served on the tailgates of station wagons **2** A style of jazz said to resemble the early New Orleans sort *(Jazz musicians)* [musical sense fr the fact that the *tailgate* of the band's wagon was left down to give slide-room for the trombone]

tailor-made *adj* **1** Exactly fitting or appropriate : *a situation tailor-made for that sort of intervention* **2** Made especially for someone or something; custom-made : *He had his own tailor-made piano stool n* A ready-made cigarette, as distinct from a hand-rolled one; pimp stick

tailpipe *See* BLOW IT OUT

tails *n* Men's formal dress

tailspin *See* IN A TAILSPIN

481

take *n* **1** The money taken in for a sporting event, at a gambling casino, etc; GROSS : *Nevada's take has been hit by a recession* (*1931+*) **2** An acceptable portion of movie or TV recording, musical recording, taping, etc : *The director said okay, it was a take* (*1922+*) **3** A portion; extract; bit; OUTTAKE : *fast takes from the latest research that may change your life* (*1847+*) **4** One's interpretation or reaction : *What's your take? You think he was telling the truth or was it just drunken bragging?* (*1980s+*) *v* **1** To cheat or defraud someone; swindle; SCAM : *The old couple got taken for their life savings* (*1920+*) **2** (also **take** someone **into camp** or **take** someone **downtown**) To defeat someone utterly; trounce; CLOBBER : *UCLA took Illinois in the Rose Bowl/ Last year Tanner took Borg downtown in the same round/ In his heart, Gingrich thinks, "I can take them all"* (*1939+*) **3** To succeed; COME OFF, CUT IT : *I tried to apologize, but I guess it didn't take* (*1633+*) [the third noun sense's dated example refers to a portion of reporter's copy set in type] *See* DOUBLE-TAKE, ON THE TAKE

take a back seat *v phr* To assume or accept a subordinate position; demote or degrade oneself : *He said he wouldn't take a back seat to anybody but the president himself* (*1888+*)

take a bath *v phr* To suffer a financial or other loss; go to the cleaners, TAKE A BEATING : *Is it possible to take a bath on items previously thought to be incapable of depreciation?/ Though the Republicans didn't take a bath, they did not end up breaking even in this election* [1940s+; fr Yiddish, where *er haut mikh gefirt in bod arayn,* literally "he led me to the bath," means "he tricked me"; the sense is derived fr the deception of persons reluctant to take a steam bath and have their clothing decontaminated and who hence had to be tricked; probably reinforced by *cleaned out* and *taken to the cleaners* as terms for loss of money in gambling or business]

take a beating *v phr* **1** TAKE A BATH (*1940s+*) **2** To be bested in a transaction; pay too much : *You really took a beating if you paid $2 a pound* (*1970s+*)

take a break *v phr* To rest or cease temporarily from working; caulk off, KNOCK OFF : *Why don't you guys take a break while I figure this out?* (*1940s+*)

take a bye *v phr* To decline; choose not to take; PASS something UP : *The kid took a bye on breakfast* [1880s+; fr the term *bye* used when a participant in a tournament passes to the next level without playing, since he or she has drawn no opponent]

take a chill pill *v phr* To calm down or relax; CHILL OUT

take a crack at something *See* HAVE A CRACK AT something

take a dig at someone *v phr* To make an irritating or contemptuous comment; BADMOUTH : *When he took a dig at his mother, his brother decked him* (*1970s+*)

take a dim view of something or someone *v phr* To regard as not especially hopeful, delightful, etc; greet with less than buoyant enthusiasm : *Her parents take a decidedly dim view of me* (*1941+*)

take a dive *v phr* To fall in a feigned knockdown or knockout; lose a fight, game, etc, dishonestly; TANK : *He refused to take a dive, so they took him out* (*1942+ Sports*)

◁**take a dump**▷ *v phr* (Variations: **crap** or **shit** or **squat** may replace **dump**) To defecate; SHIT : *two dogs taking a dump on a restaurant lawn/ like taking a dump on Mom's apple pie* (*1940s+*)

take a fall *v phr* To be arrested; FALL : *He took a fall, Duke/ who had already taken two falls for burglary* (*1940s+ Underworld*)

take a flyer (or **flier**) *v phr* To take an ambitious gamble; take a risky chance or chancy risk, esp financially : *I don't believe you, but what the hell, I'll take a flyer* [1885+; fr *flyer,* "jump, leap"]

◀**take a flying fuck**▶ *v phr* (Variations: **frig** may replace **fuck**; **at a rubber duck** or **at a rolling doughnut** may be added) May you be accursed, confounded, humiliated, rejected, etc; GO FUCK oneself, GO TO HELL : *about four guys who could really tell me to go take a flying frig and make it stick/ And if I was to tell you to go take a flying fuck at a rolling doughnut, what would be your reaction, Sid? [flying fuck* is explained in a source of about 1800 as "copulation done on horseback," found in a broadside ballad *New Feats of Horsemanship*]

take a gander *v phr* To have a look; scrutinize; inspect : *I go over and take a gander into it* (*1914+*)

take a hike *sentence* Leave me alone; go away; GET LOST : *He took one look at my clothes and told me to take a hike* (*1960s+*)

take a (or **the**) **hit** (or **chop**) *v phr* To be punished, damaged, etc, esp when not solely responsible; be the scapegoat : *Your standard of living will take a big hit over the short term/ Those accounts aren't even insured; the fund can't keep taking hits like that/ The Government winds up taking the hit for Resolution Trust/ I was vice president of the institute, so he thought I should take the chop for those demonstrations* (*1990s+*)

take a hosing *v phr* To be cheated or duped; be unfairly used : *The average worker and his family think they're taking a hosing* (*1940s+*)

◁**take a leak**▷ *v phr* To urinate; PISS, WHIZ : *fella has to take a leak/ You worry you'd miss it if you took a leak and went to the refrigerator* (*1934+*)

take a load off (or **off your feet**) *v phr* To sit down; rest; relax : *He waved Vito into a chair, "Take a load off. You take anything in your coffee?"* (*1945+*)

take a meet *v phr* To meet; collogue : *Get down here, Babe! I need you to take a meet* [1990s+; *meet*, "meeting," is found by 1879; it often refers to a clandestine or criminal activity]

take a nosedive *v phr* To decline or collapse; to go into a sudden rapid drop or decline : *Her popularity took a nosedive*

take a number *sentence* Don't be impatient; take your place in line : *"Tall enough to kick you in the balls," he said. "Take a number," I said* [1980s+; fr the practice at a busy shop or office, where petitioners are invited to *take* a printed *number* card to ensure their serial priority]

take a page from someone's **book** *v phr* To imitate or emulate someone : *I think I'll take a page from Castro's book and grow a beard and cigar* (*1970s+*)

take someone or something **apart** *v phr* **1** To criticize severely and in a detailed way; defame **2** To defeat; thrash : *mugger took them apart* (*1942+*) **3** To dismantle : *took the Legos apart*

take a peek *v phr* To look; examine : *Shall we just take a peek at that sore?* (*1836+*)

take a pop at (or **whack**) *v phr* To throw a punch at; hit : *took a pop at me and I flattened him*

take a potshot at someone *v phr* To criticize harshly; assault critically : *I don't want to take potshots at Frank* [1927+; fr the notion of a *shot* taken merely to put game in the cooking *pot*, hence not sportsmanlike or punctilious but crudely practical]

take a powder *v phr* To leave; depart hastily, esp to avoid arrest or detection; POWDER : *and take a powder out of here that day/ that goddamned Matthews, who took a powder to Florida* [1930s+; fr the magical *powder* of a magician or sorcerer, capable of making a person disappear or change form, a use found by 1688]

take a rain check *v phr* To arrange postponement or delay of some occasion that one cannot attend at the invited time : *Thanks awfully, Syl, but we're booked that night and will have to take a rain check* (*1950s+*) *See* RAIN CHECK

take a run at someone *v phr* To approach or assault with a view to capture or seduction : *I wouldn't take a client of mine into the place, unless he was such a close associate that* nobody was going to take a run at him (*1970s+*)

take a shine to someone or something *v phr* To incur a liking for; like : *May Venus take such a shine to you both* (*1839+*)

◁**take a shit** (or **a crap, a dump, a squat**)▷ *See* TAKE A DUMP

take a shot (or **whack**) (**at**) *v phr* To make an attempt; to try to do something : *take a shot at culinary school*

take a walk *v phr* To leave; absent oneself; abscond (*1871+*)

take care of *v phr* To kill : *boys took care of Willie in the basement of the warehouse*

take care of business *v phr* To perform stylishly and effectively; deal well with what one needs to : *I got up and took care of business* (*1950s+* Black fr *take care of business,* found by 1955 among jazz musicians, apparently originally meaning "to copulate")

take care of Numero Uno *v phr* To devote oneself to one's own profit and well-being; see to oneself; FEATHER one's NEST : *The Lord helps them that take care of Numero Uno* (*1970s+*) *See* NUMERO UNO

take someone **down a peg** *v phr* To deflate or reduce someone; esp, to humiliate someone pompous or vainglorious; CUT someone OFF AT THE KNEES : *Somebody ought to take that cocky bastard down a peg* [1664+; said to be fr the fact that a ship's flag or ensign was belayed on pegs, hence a lower peg meant less dignity in a salute; *take a peg lower* is found by 1589]

take someone **downtown** *See* TAKE

take one's finger out *v phr* A request or demand for effort from a lazy person [1941+; fr the notion of idleness characterized by having one's finger inserted in a body orifice]

take five *v phr* To take a short respite from work; TAKE A BREAK [1929+; about the time it takes to smoke a cigarette]

take someone **for a ride** *v phr* **1** To murder by kidnapping and disposing of the body in a remote place, in gangster fashion (*1927+*) **2** To cheat or swindle someone (*1929+*)

take heat *v phr* To endure punishment, complaints, etc : *I took a lot of heat and I stayed in the kitchen/ They think they're taking the heat for being unaware and not doing anything* [1940s+; fr *if you can't stand the heat stay out of the kitchen,* attributed to President Harry S Truman]

take in *v phr* To perceive and understand : *I can't quite take in what he's saying* (*1727+*)

take (or **rope**) someone **in** *v phr* **1** To let someone stay with one; offer shelter : *took in the stray cat* **2** To deceive or cheat someone : *might try to take you in*

take it *v phr* To endure pain, violent attack, the buffets of fate, etc; HANG TOUGH, TOUGH IT OUT : *Valley Forge proved the Continentals could take it* (1920+)

take it easy *v phr* 1 To keep one's anger and excitement under check; be calm : *Take it easy, Mac, nobody's hurt* 2 To work slowly and smoothly : *Hurry and you're dead, take it easy and you survive* 3 To stop working; relax; loaf : *I got to take it easy for a few minutes* [1880+; *take it easy* is most often used as a parting salutation or a bit of advice for living, in each case intending all senses at once]

take it hard (or **big**) *v phr* To react very strongly to something : *I thought she'd ignore it, but she took it big/ We were surprised he took the news so hard* (1894+)

take it on the chin *v phr* To be soundly defeated; be trounced : *They took it on the chin badly in the last period* (1928+)

take it on the lam *v phr* To leave, esp hastily; escape; LIGHT OUT : *The girl "took it on the lam"* (1897+ Underworld)

take it or leave it *interj* This is your only choice : *Spaghetti for dinner. Take it or leave it*

take it out of someone's **hide** *v phr* To exact the harshest kind of compensation, even physical punishment, usu in place of a gentler or a monetary one : *He'll pay up, by God, or I'll take it out of his hide!* (1940s+)

take it out on someone or something *v phr* To punish or mistreat an innocent subject for wrongs one has suffered : *Whenever his boss yells at him, he takes it out on his secretary* [1903+; perhaps fr *take it out of* someone's *hide*]

take it to the street *v phr* To make something public; to blather : *taking her misery to the street*

take one's **lumps** *v phr* To accept and endure severe treatment; TAKE IT : *The boys were taking their lumps trying to stay on wild Brahma bulls* [1949+; *get the lumps*, "to be beaten up," is found by 1935]

take something **lying down** *v phr* To accept something submissively (1860s+)

take one's **medicine** *v phr* To accept and endure what one has deserved; FACE THE MUSIC (1903+)

taken *See* be HAD

take names *See* KICK ASS AND TAKE NAMES

take-no-prisoners *modifier* Ruthless; uncompromising : *Ciarelli's take-no-prisoners approach earned her fifty-five thousand dollars on the sand last year* [1990s+; fr the putative command of a combat officer that all enemies be killed, none captured]

take no shit *See* TAKE SHIT

taken to the cleaners, be *See* GO TO THE CLEANERS

takeoff *modifier* : *and if it comes to a take-off thing in the street n* 1 An imitation, esp of a famous person, actor, etc; an impression : *You should hear her takeoff of Liz Taylor* (1846+) 2 A robbery, and armed street robbery or mugging : *He always uses the mugger's jargon for a street robbery: "take-off"* (1960s+)

take off *v phr* 1 To leave; depart; SPLIT : *They all took off for Houston* (1813+) 2 To have a sudden success, spurt of activity, etc; take fire : *but nonsense that doesn't take off can be a trial/ Phase 2 of PAC face lift is taking off with a bang* (1963+) 3 To rob; commit burglary; HOLD UP, RIP OFF : *We took off a bar/ They want to keep dealing, not just take off two dudes for a little cash* (1970+) 4 To kill; WASTE, ZAP (1970s+ Black) 5 To give oneself a narcotic injection; SHOOT UP (1960s+ Narcotics) 6 To leave work for a time : *I'm going to take off without pay for a week or so* (1940s+) 7 To imitate; mimic; parody : *She takes off a drunk hilariously* (1750+) [first sense based on the rising and departure of an airplane]

takeoff artist *See* RIPOFF

take off like a bat out of hell (or **like a bigass bird**) *v phr* To depart hastily; leave in a hurry; CUT OUT (WWII armed forces)

take on *v phr* 1 To behave angrily; make a fuss : *How you do take on!* (1430+) 2 To stop and search someone, demand identification, question harshly, etc; JACK UP, ROUST : *We were also taught that good cops take on a lot of people* (1970s+ Police)

take someone or something **on** *v phr* 1 To accept an assignment, job, role, etc : *I'm a bit diffident about my qualifications, but I'll take the chairmanship on* (1300+) 2 To accept combat or confrontation with someone or something : *The Knights took over the Philadelphia Inquirer and later took on the Morning Journal head-to-head* (1885+)

takeout *modifier* Having to do with food bought to be eaten away from the place where it is prepared : *pies she hoped to sell to the "take-out" trade* (1940s+)

take someone or something **out** *v phr* To kill; destroy; totally disable : *They asked Col Beckwith what he intended to do with the Iranian guards. "Take them out." The Brits were just seeking to reassure themselves that we were not planning to take out a country* [1939+; perhaps fr the football term *take out*, "block an opponent decisively"]

takeover *n* The buying of the control of one company by another, usu by the wooing and rewarding of stockholders and often against the wishes of the acquired company's management : *a popular means of conducting corporate takeovers* (1958+)

take something **public** *v phr* **1** To make something known in general : *took their romance public* **2** To sell shares in a company to the general public : *took Ask Jeeves public and then it tanked*

taker *n* A person who accepts a bet, challenge, offer, etc : *I dared them all but got no takers* (1810+)

◁**take (or eat) shit**▷ *v phr* To accept or endure humiliation, victimization, bullying, etc; EAT DIRT • Often in the negative : *Yeah, but at least you don't take any shit from anybody/ Do I have to take this shit from my own partner?* (1940s+)

take some doing *v phr* To be very difficult; be arduous : *It took some doing, but they got there inside an hour* (1891+)

takes two to tango, it *See* IT TAKES TWO TO TANGO

take the cake *v phr* To win or deserve the highest award and admiration : *His new sonnets quite take the cake* [1847+; fr the prize awarded in a *cakewalk* dancing contest]

take the cure *v phr* To submit to a treatment program or enter a treatment facility : *wanted to take the cure*

take the fifth (or **five it**) *v phr* To refuse to testify in court on the basis of the protection of the Fifth Amendment of the US Constitution; to refuse to answer any questions : *took the Fifth on every question*

take the (or **some**) **heat** *v phr* To incur and endure heavy censure or criticism; to take a punishment : *took the heat for letting the cat out the door*

take the heat off *v phr* To relieve someone from scrutiny or criticism; also, to take the punishment in place of another : *The appearance of other suspects took the heat off him for a while*

take the money and run *sentence* If a chance for profit comes, legally or not, accept it : *An objective person would say, if you can get the state out for 73 million, take the money and run!* [1960s+; the title of a 1969 Woody Allen movie]

take the pledge *v phr* To promise not to drink alcohol : *ready to take the pledge* [fr the Alcoholics Anonymous pledge]

take the plunge *v phr* To act decisively, despite prior apprehension : *He took the plunge and bought a new computer* (1876+)

take the rap (or **the fall** or **the jump**) *v phr* To accept or suffer the punishment for something, esp for something one did not do : *If she gets caught, I'll take the rap for her/ Make*

sure *Brewster doesn't come unglued. He has to take the fall right along with Beck/ Marcus got to take the jump for it* (1930+)

take the starch out of *v phr* To reduce or deflate someone's ego or conceit : *took the starch out of her when she didn't win*

take the wind out of someone's **sails** *v phr* To reduce someone's initiative or momentum; to rob of an advantage : *hate to take the wind out of your sails*

take things easy *v phr* To relax and make slow or little progress, esp to recover and recuperate : *take things easy now you are sick/ taking things easy in retirement*

take to *v phr* **1** To have a fancy or particular liking or desire for : *took to doing yoga every morning* **2** To develop a habit or apply oneself to a pursuit : *took to begging*

take someone **to the cleaners** *v phr* To win or otherwise acquire all or very much of someone's money, esp at gambling, in a lawsuit or business deal, etc; CLEAN someone OUT : *Smarten up, Chrystie, take him to the cleaners/ Ephron did not take him to the cleaners in the divorce* (1949+)

tale *See* FISH STORY

talk *v* **1** To inform; confess and implicate others; SQUEAL : *Socks would never never talk* (1924+) **2** To talk about; have as one's topic • Always in the progressive tenses : *The administrators aren't talking toga parties/ What we're talking here is seventy-five a key See* BACK TALK, BIG TALK, FAST TALK, HAPPY TALK, PEP TALK, PILLOW TALK, STRAIGHT TALK, SWEET-TALK

talk a blue streak *v phr* To talk rapidly and copiously : *I left him talking a blue streak about his persecution* (1895+)

talk a good game *v phr* To speak, if not to perform, impressively : *These political embarrassments helped to establish that the Clinton people talked a good game but weren't up to the grownup job of governing* (1973+)

talk someone's **arm** (or **ear** or **head**) **off** *v phr* To address someone at very great length; GAS : *Donna talked his ear off* (entry form 1833+, variant 1935+)

talk big *v phr* To boast and exaggerate; be self-aggrandizing; SHOOT OFF ONE'S MOUTH : *He was talking pretty big about how they treated him* (1584+)

talkie *n* A talking movie (1913+)

talking head (or **hairdo**) *n phr* A person, esp a news reporter, an interviewer, an expert, etc, who appears on television in a close-up, hence essentially as a bodiless head : *using the medium as something more than a static platform for talking heads/ what the TV experts term a talking head, just Ronnie in an easy* *chair/ one of those plays for which talking hairdos go to the videotape (1968+)*

talk jockey *n phr* The "host" of a radio talk show [1972+; modeled on *disc jockey*]

talk out of turn *v phr* To speak too candidly; be too bold verbally; SHOOT OFF one's MOUTH : *I may be talking out of turn, but I think you ought to make the decision right now, and live with it (1934+)*

talk radio *n phr* Radio programs on which callers speak with a "host" : *QVC is talk radio taken to its most shallow, most comforting limits* [1985+; *talk show* is found by 1965]

◁**talk shit**▷ *v phr* **1** To say very rude or untruthful things in order to offend or hurt : *Why do you let your child talk shit to you* **2** To make empty threats : *You don't scare me. I know you are talking shit*

talk shop *v phr* To discuss work or business rather than have social conversation (1854+)

talk-talk or **talky-talk** *n* Mere talk, esp bombast or idle chatter (1902+)

talk the talk and walk the walk *v phr* To be both sincere and effective : *They Talk the Talk and Walk the Walk/ In the end Perot could talk the talk, but he couldn't walk the walk (1990s+)*

talk through one's **hat** *v phr* To lie and exaggerate; talk nonsense; BULLSHIT [1887+; said to be fr the deceptive demeanor of men who hold their *hats* over their faces on entering church, and are supposed to be praying]

talk to the hand (or **tell it to the hand**) *sentence* Don't bother me as I am not listening to you; I'm ignoring you • said with the hand raised, palm facing out toward the adversary's face : *Complaining again? Talk to the hand (1990s+)*

talk turkey *v phr* To speak candidly and cogently; LAY IT ON THE LINE, LEVEL : *Do you want to talk turkey, or just bullshit?* [1824+; fr a story of the white man who said to the Native American, Wampum, that in dividing the game he would give him the choice: "You take the crow and I'll take the turkey, or I'll take the turkey and you take the crow," whereupon Wampum declared that the white man was not *talking turkey* to him]

talk until one **is blue in the face** *v phr* To talk forever, but with nobody listening : *talk till you are blue in the face, but no one is changing their mind*

talk up a storm *v phr* To talk loud, long, impressively, incessantly, etc; CHEW someone's EAR OFF : *City Teen-Agers Talking Up a "Say What?" Storm (1970s+)*

tall *See* STAND TALL

tall can of corn *See* CAN OF CORN

tall one *n phr* A large alcoholic drink : *Make it a Long Island iced tea, a tall one*

tall order *n* A difficult assignment or task : *a tall order for a newbie*

tall timbers, the *n phr* Rural areas; the BOONDOCKS, the rhubarbs (1920+ Show business)

tan someone's **hide** *v* or *v phr* To beat someone severely; thrash : *Fetch me my gin, son, 'fore I tan your hide* [1670+; fr the making of a hide into leather by *tanning*] *See* BLACK AND TAN

◁**T and A**▷ *See* TA

tang *See* POON TANG

tangle *v* To fight; MIX IT UP (1928+)

◁**tangle assholes**▷ *v phr* To come into conflict; disagree; quarrel; fight : *Remind them how it was the first time we tangled assholes (1970s+)*

tango *See* IT TAKES TWO TO TANGO

tang out *v phr* To cease; make an end of; BAG : *I'm going to tang out on studying (1980s+ Students)*

tank *n* (also **fish tank, fish bowl, holding tank**) A detention cell; a jail cell : *when he goes into the tank as a prisoner/ I'm in the fish tank. There are forty of us in the diagnostic center* (entry form 1912+) *v* **1** (also **tank up**) To drink liquor, esp heavily : *I think he'd tanked up a good deal at luncheon* (1902+) **2** To lose a game, match, etc, deliberately; THROW : *He lost so implausibly they were sure he had tanked/ the "tanking" of unlucrative doubles matches merely to catch a plane* (1976+ Sports) **3** To fall precipitately; collapse : *At FBI headquarters, morale has tanked after the Idaho investigation/ Analysts say Texaco shares could tank to $25–$30 in bankruptcy* (1980s+) *See* DRUNK TANK, GO IN THE TANK, THINK TANK

tanked or **tanked up** *adj* or *adj phr* **1** Drunk (1893+) **2** Defeated; outscored : *team was tanked again* **3** Dead; out of service : *the tanked clunker sat in the garage*

tanker *n* A competitive swimmer : *The Lady Hawk tankers sprinted to nine first-place finishes (1990s+)*

tap *n* : *Tap, also tap-off and tip-off. A jump ball. The center jump which begins the game* (1980s+ Basketball) *v* **1** To rob; burgle : *Only chicks this guy taps?* (1879+) **2** To select; designate : *When she was tapped for the job, Reno in her 15th year as State Attorney for Dade County* (1952+) *See* HEEL-TAP

Tap City *adj* Lacking money; penniless; BROKE : *You're Tap City? No problem (1970s+)*

tap dance *v phr* To improvise, tergiversate, etc, in order to hide one's ignorance : *I didn't read the poop sheet, so I had to tap dance when the question came (1970s+ Army)*

tape *See* RED TAPE

tap someone for something *v phr* To solicit money from; beg or borrow from; HIT someone. TOUCH : *I tapped my brother for another two hundred* (*1940s+*)

tap out *v phr* To lose all one's money, esp in a gambling game : *"It's tapping me out,"* he *says* [1940s+ Gambling; perhaps fr having *tapped* everyone available for a loan and found none]

tapped out *adj phr* **1** Penniless; BROKE, TAP CITY : *Tapped out, a bank goes under/ the tapped-out underdog he is supposed to be* (*1940s+ Gambling*) **2** Exhausted; FRAZZLED, POOPED : *thought he looked terrible, haggard, pale, tapped out* (*1940s+*)

tar *n* A sailor [1676+; fr the *tarpaulin* garments they made and wore]

◁**tard** or **'tard**▷ *n* RETARD : *The stupid shit. What a 'tard* (*1983+*)

tarnation *n* Damnation [1790+; a euphemistic alteration of *damnation*, apparently influenced by obsolete US slang *tarnal damned*, an alteration of *eternal*]

tart *n* A promiscuous woman, esp a prostitute; harlot; HOOKER : *nothing cheap for us like the grimy tarts on Mercury Street* [1887+; fr *tart*, the pastry confection, esp the English *jam-tart*; in original early 1800s use it meant any pleasant or attractive woman and only specialized at the end of the century]

tart up *v phr* To decorate; prettify; bedizen; GUSSY UP : *go the glam route or tart it up or punk it down/ American directors feel obliged to tart up Shakespeare* (*1938+*)

taste *n* **1** A share or percentage of profits; a PIECE OF THE ACTION (*1960s+ Theater*) **2** A dose of a narcotic; HIT (*1960s+ Narcotics*) **3** Liquor in general; a drink of liquor (*1919+*) *See* SO BAD one CAN TASTE IT

tat *n* A skin tattoo : *There were two favorite spots for tats* (*1990s+*)

ta-ta *interj* A parting salutation; a farewell [1823+; fr nursery talk]

◁**tatas**▷ *n* A woman's breasts • Often with *bodacious* : *bodacious tatas of Victoria's Secret commercials*

tater *n* **1** A home run : *the man who hit all those long taters in the American League/ Bolton insisted the outfield fences be moved in, thus allowing his own team's heavy hitters to launch their taters* **2** A potato : *meat and taters/ Fry up some taters for lunch* [1960s+ Baseball; perhaps fr earlier Negro League use revived by George "Boomer" Scott when he joined the Boston Red Sox in 1966]

tattooed *See* SCREWED, BLUED, AND TATTOOED

taxi dancer *n phr* A woman at a public dance hall who dances for hire (*1941+*)

taxi squad *n phr* A group of professional football players who are not officially members of a team, although they may be paid to be available as a reserve [1966+ Football; fr the fact that a former owner of the Cleveland Browns would give such players jobs with his *taxicab* company to support them and keep them available]

TCB (pronounced as separate letters) *v* To perform very well what one needs to do : *where he is always to be found TCBing* [1970s+ Black; fr *take care of business*, found by 1955 among jazz musicians, apparently originally meaning "to copulate"]

tchotchke (CHACH kə, TSAHTS kə) (Variations: **tchatchka** or **tchotzke** or **tsatske** or **chotchke** or **chatchke**) *n* **1** Something trivial, esp a gewgaw or decorative trifle; bagatelle; plaything : *little rainbows and neon tchatchkas found in California neon boutiques/ you know, the tchotzkes, the jewelry/ his job at the mall vending Watusi chatchkes* **2** A precious or adorable person, usu a child : *The baby is a tchotchke* **3** A woman considered as a plaything : *She's Harry's tsatske* [1964+; fr Yiddish *tsatske* fr Slavic]

TD or **Tee Dee** (pronounced as separate letters) *n* A touchdown (*1940s+ Football*)

t'd off *See* TEE'D OFF

teacups *See* ASS OVER TINCUPS

teakettle *See* ASS OVER TINCUPS

team *See* SWAT TEAM

team up *v phr* To join together in some effort; BUDDY UP (*1956+*)

tea party *n phr* **1** A gathering where marijuana is smoked : *Marijuana "tea parties" are little things* (*1940s+ Narcotics*) **2** An easy, pleasant, safe occasion • Most often used in the negative : *It wasn't exactly a brawl, but the meeting was no tea party either* (*1960s+*)

tear[1] (TAIR) *n* A drinking spree; BENDER, BINGE : *Fred wanted to go on a little tear in the big town* (*1869+*) *See* ON A TEAR

tear[2] or **tear-ass** *v* To go very fast; rush around rapidly : *McAllister had no inclination to go tear-assing up the slope and into the hills* (*entry form 1599+, variant 1940s+*)

◁**tear someone a new asshole** (or **one**)▷ *v phr* To completely and severely criticize or chastise someone : *tear you a new one if you get in one more accident*

tear someone or something apart *v phr* To criticize severely; to express a completely negative opinion : *tore him apart for being late*

tear someone or something down *v phr* To speak or write critically or disparagingly of; to criticize (*1978+*)

tear one's hair (out) *v phr* To behave frenziedly, expressing grief, rage, frustration, desperation, or anxiety : *tearing her hair over the SATs* (*1600+*)

tear into *v phr* **1** To attack, criticize, or scold severely : *tore into him for losing the keys* **2** To start eating voraciously : *tore into that steak after the hike*

tear-jerker *n* **1** A sentimental story, movie, song, etc : *See the old tear-jerker* **2** A person who appeals to sentimentality; a fomenter of pathos : *a magniloquent tear-jerker named Delmas (1921+)*

tearoom or **t-room** *n* A public toilet *(1970s+ Homosexuals)*

teaser *n* **1** A woman who invites or offers sexual activity but refuses to do the sex act; COCK-TEASER : *Maybe Bella was right in calling his "uptown lady" a "teaser" (1895+)* **2** Anything offered as a sample and intended to increase appetite or desire : *He showed them one chapter as a teaser (1934+)*

techie *n* A computer enthusiast, expert, etc : *But nerds these days aren't what they used to be. Many of these techies who grew up with computers have gotten older and gotten a life/ Or maybe it was when Conde Nast invested in the glossy techies' magazine* Wired *(1980s+)*

Technicolor yawn *n phr* The act and product of vomiting [1963+; fr *Technicolor*, trademark for a color-film process]

techno- *prefix used to form nouns* Having the indicated knowledge of, involvement with, or attitude toward technology, esp advanced and computer technology : *technobuddy/ technofreak/ technogood/ technopeasant*

technopop or **techno** *n* Popular music using much technical equipment : *manages to hammer enough melody into the wall of technopop he has erected (1990s+)*

teddy *n* A one-piece women's undergarment serving as both chemise and panties [1924+; perhaps fr *teddy bear*]

tee'd (or teed or t'd) off *adj phr* Angry; PISSED OFF : *When people get teed off they want to march* [1950s+; perhaps fr *ticked off*; perhaps a euphemism for *pee'd off*, "pissed off"]

teed up *adj phr* Drunk [1928+; probably fr 1920s black *teed*, "drunk," probably related to marijuana or *tea* intoxication, and to *tea*, "whiskey," a use attested fr the 17th century]

teensy-weensy or **teeny-weeny** *adj* Very small; tiny : *the teensy-weensy kind that small-town dailies like (entry form 1906+, variant 1894+)*

teenybopper *n* (also **teenie bopper** or **teenybop** or **teeny-rocker**) A teenager or preteenager, esp one who undertakes the hippie or rock-and-roll culture and way of life : *Teenyboppers opt for zodiac signs/ attract shady record promoters like rock stars attract teenyboppers (1966+)*

tee off *v phr* To hit someone or something very hard : *He hit a homer, really teed off* [1953+;

fr the opening shot of each hole in golf, *off the tee*]

tee someone off *v phr* To make angry; PISS someone OFF : *This moping is teeing me off* [1961+; probably a euphemism for *pee* or *piss* someone *off*, influenced by *tee off on* someone, fr golf]

tee off on someone or something *v phr* **1** To verbally assault someone, esp to reprimand : *The critic really teed off on my book, alas (1955+)* **2** To hit the ball very hard : *He teed off on it and it went right over the wall (1932+ Baseball)*

teeth *See* DRESSED TO THE TEETH, DROP one's TEETH

Teflon *modifier* Immune to criticism; sacrosanct or elusive : *They called Reagan the Teflon president* [fr a trademark brand of plastic coating]

telegraph *v* To signal one's intentions, often inadvertently : *The tone of her voice telegraphed it (1925+)*

telegraph one's **punches** *v phr* To let an opponent know one's intentions inadvertently : *never get to the top, he telegraphs his punches (1936+ Prizefighting)*

telephone (or phone) tag *n phr* The repeated exchange of recorded telephone messages : *I don't feel like playing telephone tag with her/ "Having computers in our volunteers' homes has eliminated phone tag," says Power, referring to the pervasive round-robin of messages left and phone calls missed (1990s+)*

tell *See* SHOW-AND-TELL

tell it like it is *v phr* To be candid and cogent; tell the truth, even though it be unpleasant; GIVE IT TO someone : *by Negro psychiatrists William H Grier and Price M Cobbs, who tell it like it is (1964+ Black)*

tell it to the Marines *sentence* I do not believe what you have just told me; what you say is false and fu-tile [1806+; the usage, esp in the form "tell it to the marines, but the sailors won't believe him," reflects the contempt in which *marines* were held by naval seamen]

tell me about it *sentence* What you are saying is obvious; SO WHAT ELSE IS NEW : *"Put the water on while I shower. I smell like a goat." "Tell me about it" (1980s+)*

tell someone off *v phr* To reprimand; CHEW someone OUT : *The man had just been told off, and told off plenty (1919+)*

tell someone what to do with something *v phr* (Variations: **where to put** [or **shove** or **stick** or **stuff**] may replace **what to do with**) To reject something vehemently and defiantly • A euphemism for *stick it up your ass* : *She told me rudely what to do with my proffered assistance/ The first thing I did when I got* *home was to tell my old boss where to stick my old job (entry form 1946+)*

tell someone where to get off (or **to go**) *v phr* To rebuke, rebuff, or deflate firmly; LET someone HAVE IT • A euphemism for *go to hell* : *I advised Alice to tell him where to get off when he tries that big-shot stuff (1900+)*

temp *n* A temporary employee : *Instead of a full-time secretary he kept hiring temps (1923+)*

ten *See* HANG TEN

ten, a *n phr* A young woman who is maximally sexually attractive; a perfect female specimen [1980s+; perhaps fr *ten-carat;* perhaps fr the conventional question "Where would you put her (him, it) on a scale of one to *ten?"*]

ten-carat *adj* Big; impressive; imposing : *No more ten-carat heels were going to tell me sorry*

tenderfoot *n* A newcomer; neophyte; callow person; GREENHORN (*1881+*)

tenderloin *n* A district of a city where vice and corruption are rife [1887+; fr earlier sense of undercut of a sirloin steak; orig applied specifically to a district of New York City, fr the notion that the proceeds from corruption made it a juicy morsel for the local police]

ten feet tall *adj phr* Hugely impressive; menacing : *Iraq had an extremely large military force, and we gave them credit for being ten feet tall in certain areas (1962+)*

ten-foot pole *See* NOT TOUCH someone or something WITH A TEN-FOOT POLE

ten-four or **10-4** *affirmation* That is correct; okay : *That's a ten four, you have it just right (fr citizens band) n phr* The signal that a message has been received, the equivalent of the earlier and military "roger" (*1962+ Citizens band*) [fr a code of conventional procedure signals used esp by the police, where *ten* was a sort of prefix, and the numeral following bore the message; *ten seven,* for example, meant "transmissions finished"]

tense up *phr* To become stiff, ineffective, and semiparalyzed from nervous tension (*1973+*)

ten-spot *n* **1** A ten-dollar bill; ten dollars; dime-note, tenner : *A ten-spot can't get you past two counters in a grocery store without limping (1848+)* **2** A ten-year prison sentence : *after having served a ten-spot (1928+ Prison)*

tent *See* PUP TENT

-teria *See* -ATERIA

terminal *adj* Extreme; unmitigated : *Terminal cuteness is the dread disease of too much Southern writing* [1990s+; based on the medical sense "fatal, incurable"]

terminally *adv* Intractably; hopelessly : *All but the terminally high-minded should try to get to see the Blue Man Group (1990s+)*

terrific *adj* **1** Excellent; wonderful; GREAT : *The script is apt to be terrific* **2** Prodigious; extreme; amazing : *Times Square hotel biz is on the terrific fritz (1888+)*

territory *See* GO WITH THE TERRITORY

terror *See* HOLY TERROR

test *See* POP QUIZ

test the waters *v phr* To make a preliminary assessment : *I've tested the waters, and this product works! One sign of this is the number of vice presidents who are testing the union's political waters* [1970s+; an example from 1888 may refer to such an assessment or may refer to an actual testing of well-water]

tetchy *adj* Irritable; irascible; testy : *the days when tetchy film crews invaded the center of soporific conferences* [1592+; fr dialect *tetched,* "crazy, touched in the head"]

Texas leaguer *n phr* A hit that falls out of reach between the infielders and the outfielders; BANJO HIT, BLOOPER [1905+ Baseball; fr the fact that such hits were used in minor-league baseball's *Texas League* as trick plays]

Tex-Mex *adj* Texan-Mexican *n* **1** A native of the Texas-Mexico border region : *Fender, who calls himself a Tex-Mex, was born in the south Texas valley border town of San Benito* **2** A style of cooking characteristic of the Texas-Mexico border region : *exemplars of Tex-Mex, the mongrel cuisine that has grown up along America's southern border (1949+)*

TGIF (pronounced as separate letters) *sentence* Thank God it's Friday : *When I came out of the Wheaton Liquor Store I didn't see a cruiser. TGIF (1970s+)*

thang *n* Thing • Jocular mispronunciation : *doing my thang*

thanks a lot (or **a bunch** or **a million**) *sentence* Thank you very much • Often used ironically : *Well thanks a lot; that kick in the face was just what I needed! Thanks a bunch (entry form 1940s+, variant 1980s+)*

thanks for nothing *sentence* Thank you very much for what you have not done for me : *Willie has an assortment of bumper stickers: To All You Virgins, Thanks For Nothing (1960s+)*

thank you ma'am *n phr* A bump or hole in the road [1849+; because riders bounce up and down as if they were bowing thanks] *See* WHAM-BAM THANK YOU MA'AM

that ain't (or **isn't**) **hay** *sentence* That is a large sum; that is not insignificant • *Chopped liver* is very commonly used analogously; *cornflakes* and *zucchini* are also found, but rarely : *And what they pay me in addition ain't hay (1943+)*

◁**thatch**▷ *n* Pubic hair : *love to get under her thatch (1933+)*

that does (or **tears**) **it** *sentence* That ruins things; that's the last straw [entry form 1968+, variant 1909+; by 1837 in the form "Now you have done it"]

that'll hold you *sentence* That will care for your needs; that will keep you from being troublesome : *So I gave him the ten thou and said "That'll hold you"* (*1900+*)

that's all someone **needs** *sentence* That is precisely what someone does not need; that is excessive, fatal, very ill timed, etc : *Another tax increase is all I need right now/ A speeding ticket? Brother, that's all you needed* [1930s+; perhaps fr a translation of the ironical Yiddish lament *Dos felt mir nokh*, "I still lack that"]

that's all she wrote *sentence* That is the sum and end of it; that is the bitter end : *Tell him that's it, brother, that's all she wrote* [1940s+; fr the sad case of someone, esp a World War II soldier, who got a *Dear John* letter from his sweetheart, ending the affair]

that's big of you *sentence* Your behavior is very generous • Often used ironically : *That's big of you, to help him up after you knock him down* (*1920+*)

that's my boy (or **girl**) *sentence* You have done very well; I'm proud of you; WAY TO GO (*1930s+*)

that's show business (or **show biz**) *sentence* Such is the unpredictable or grim nature of things; THAT'S THE WAY THE BALL BOUNCES : *We didn't get invited, but that's show business* (*1947+*)

that's that *interj* That is final. That is the way it is going to be : *I'm going to finish this and that's that*

that's the ball game *sentence* That's the end of the affair • Usu spoken by the loser

that's the ticket *sentence* That's just what is needed : *You have a spare blanket? That's just the ticket* [1838+; origin uncertain]

that's the way the ball bounces (or **the cookie crumbles**) *sentence* Such is life; such are the buffetings of fate; c'est la vie : *Guess that's the way the ball bounces* (entry form *1951+, variant 1956+*)

the goods *n phr* **1** Competent and genuine; the REAL CHEESE : *They told me she was the goods, and I believed them* (*1904+*) **2** Convincing evidence against someone : *He turned himself in when he knew the cops had the goods on him* (*1913+*) [second sense fr *goods*, "stolen property"]

the hang *n phr* A useful knowledge and command of something : *He fired me just when I was getting the hang of the operation* (*1845+*)

the limit *n phr* As much as one can tolerate : *He's the limit in this town* (*1885+*)

them apples *See* HOW DO YOU LIKE THEM APPLES

the pits *n phr* The most loathsome place or situation imaginable : *The Soviet "government is the pits"* [1953+; fr *armpits*]

there or **right there** *adj* or *adj phr* Very competent; very well informed; WITH IT (*1849+*)

there ain't no such animal *sentence* No such person or thing exists : *Those looking for New Jersey farm-raised certified organic turkeys are out of luck. There ain't no such animal* (*1922+*)

there's no (or **no such thing as a**) **free lunch** *sentence* The world is a hard place and one must work for what one gets (and even then one may not get it) : *Rep David Obey believes there is no such thing as a free lunch* [1980s+; fr the memory of old-time saloons, where one could eat from a copious *free lunch* on the bar, even with a minimal liquor purchase]

there's no way *adv phr* Under no conceivable circumstances : *There's no way I'll ever see it your way* (*1975+*)

there you are or **there you go** *sentence* **1** That is, unfortunately, the way things happen; THAT'S THE WAY THE BALL BOUNCES : *Beau started to laugh softly, at the absurdity of everything. "Well, there you go," said Beau* **2** Things happen as expected; results follow actions : *You push this one, see? There you go, it turned on* **3** You have done something wrong again, of your habitual sort : *There you go, meddling again* (entry form *1883+, variant 1897+*)

thick *adj* **1** (also **thickheaded**) Stupid; dull-witted (*1597+, variant 1801+*) **2** (also **thick as thieves**) Intimate; very well acquainted : *The two of them are very thick* (*1756+, variant 1833+*) **3** Shapely; CURVACEOUS (*1980s+ Teenagers*) *See* SPREAD IT THICK

thieving *adj* Inclined to steal : *thieving piece of crap* (*1598+*)

thighs *See* THUNDER THIGHS

thin dime, a or one *n phr* **1** The least amount of money; a RED CENT : *He was stony broke, not a thin dime could he produce* **2** A dime; ten cents : *which sells old-fashioned ice cream sundaes for one thin dime* [1918+; fr the fact that the *dime* is the *thinnest* and smallest of US coins]

thing *n* One's particular predilection, skill, way of living or perceiving, etc : *He ignored the world and stuck to his thing* [1841+; revived in the 1960s] *See* the BEST THING SINCE SLICED BREAD, HAVE A THING ABOUT, JUST ONE OF THOSE THINGS, SURE THING, a SURE THING

thing, a *n phr* An amorous couple : *I just found out you and he are a thing* (*1943+*)

thingamajig *n* (also **thingumabob** or **thingumadoodle** or **thingummy** or **thingamadoger** or **thingamadudgeon** or **thingumbob** or **thingamananny**) An unspecified or unspecifiable object; something one does not know the name of or does not wish to name; DINGUS, DOODAD, GADGET : *When you want to go down you push this thingamajig up as high as it will go/ a thingummy so addicted to lethal violence* (*entry form 1824+, first variant 1832+, others late 1700s+ or 1800s+*)

thingy or **thingie** *n* A thing; GIZMO, THINGAMAJIG : *one of those thingies on the roofs of churches that the water spouts through* (*1968+*)

think *See* DEEP-THINK

think something *v phr* To concentrate on; aspire to; desire : *A fashion magazine could tell its readers to "think pink" one season, because they'd been thinking navy blue or yellow or aqua the season before* (*1980s+*)

think-piece *n* A newspaper or magazine article of intellectual virtue or pretension; a thoughtful essay : *The Knightly Quest drifts off into a think-piece on the nature of romantics and the state of the nation* (*1947+*)

◁**think** one's **shit doesn't stink**▷ *v phr* To be very conceited; be stuck up and self-impressed : *The way she looks down her nose you know she thinks her shit doesn't stink* (*1940s+*)

think tank *n phr* An institute or institution that specializes in the custody of interpretive intellectuals, esp in the social sciences, and usu caters to and is financed by a government in return for studies, prognostications, etc : *A peace academy would be part graduate school, part think tank* [*1959+; think-tank, "the brain," is found by 1905*]

thin-skinned *adj* Overly sensitive to criticism or insult : *can't be thin-skinned and expect all the neighbors to like you*

third base *See* GET TO FIRST BASE

third degree or **third** *n phr* or *n* Long and harsh, even brutal, questioning, esp by the police : *The Third Degree, A Detailed and Appalling Exposé of Police Brutality/ He's giving me a third about some gun he says I had* [*1900+; origin uncertain*]

third sacker *n phr* A third baseman (*1911+ Baseball*)

third wheel *n* An extra person in a social venue, esp one that interferes or gets in the way : *He was a third wheel when they went to the fair*

this *n* My penis • Accompanied by a gesture toward the indicated part : *Hey Vanessa, how about the bailiffs seize this?/ "Mom said to go walk the dogs" "Walk this, John! You walk the dogs!"* (*1940s+*)

this is it *sentence* The final crisis is here; the unavoidable has come; prepare for the worst : *He held her hand fast and said "This is it, kid"* (*1942+*)

thoroughbred *n* An underworld figure who is loyal and trustworthy to cohorts (*Underworld*)

thou (THOU) *n* A thousand, esp a thousand dollars; GRAND : *A hundred and fifty thou is business* (*1867+*)

thought *See* DON'T GIVE IT A SECOND THOUGHT

thrashing *n* A thorough or sound defeat : *thrashing by their rival* (*1815+*)

threads *n* Clothes, esp a suit of clothes; DUDS (*1926+*)

three-alarm (or **five-alarm**) **fire** *n* A very exciting or overwhelming event; a crisis

three-bagger *n* A three-base hit; a triple (*1940s+ Baseball*)

three bricks shy of a load *adj phr* Stupid; NOT ALL THERE : *A fine man, all right. It's too bad he was three bricks shy of a load* (*1970s+*)

three-dollar bill *See* PHONY AS A THREE-DOLLAR BILL

three-letter man *n phr* A homosexual [*1930s+ College students; fr the fact that fag has three letters, and based on the custom of gauging athletic distinction by the number of varsity letters*]

three-peat *n* The third repetition of a feat; something like a "hat trick" : *won the match and with it a chance for the rare three-peat/ Streisand's return to Broadway leaves one hungry for yet another album, a three-peat* [*1990s+; modeled on repeat*]

three sheets to (or **in**) **the wind** *adj phr* Drunk [*1821+; fr the fact that a drunken person is as helpless and disorganized as a sailboat with its sheets, that is, with its sails, flying, and hence its course and movement entirely out of control*]

three squares or **three hots and a cot** *n phr* Enough to eat; an acceptable standard of living : *He isn't rich, but he gets his three squares every day/ homeless men do break the law to get "three hots and a cot"* (*1899+*)

three-time loser *n phr* A criminal who has been convicted several times and is in jeopardy of an automatic life sentence in some states if convicted again; hence a hardened and perhaps dangerous criminal (*1914+*)

thriller *n* An exciting movie, play, etc, esp a horror show; CHILLER (*1889+*)

thriller-diller *n* A very effective thriller; CHILLER-DILLER (*1950s+*)

throb *See* HEARTTHROB

throne *n* A toilet; JOHN, SHITTER (*1922+*)

through a tin horn *See* LIKE SHIT THROUGH A TIN HORN

through one's **hat** *See* TALK THROUGH ONE'S HAT

through the mill *adv phr* By the course of hard experience; where the most difficult and practical experience is to be had : *He knows just where it's at; he's been through the mill* (*1818+*) *See* GO THROUGH THE MILL, PUT someone THROUGH THE MILL

throw *v* **1** To confuse and incapacitate; amaze; confound; FLABBERGAST : *When he called me that it just about threw me* (1844+) **2** To lose a game, race, etc, deliberately; TANK : *Basketball players confess that they have accepted bribes to "throw" games* (1868+) **3** (also **pitch** or **toss**) To be host or hostess at; arrange for : *The president has to throw him a luncheon/ One of his assistants actually pitched a party for me/ Kendall tossed a cocktail party for a group of us visiting writers* (1922+)

throw, a *adv phr* For each; apiece; PER EACH : *The meetings were a dollar "a throw"* [1896+; probably fr carnival games where the customer pays so much for several *throws* of a ball, a ring, etc, trying to win a prize]

throw someone a curve *v phr* To do something quite unexpected; deceive by the unpredicted : *But Spicoli threw him a curve* (1940s+)

throw a fit (or spaz) *v phr* To behave or react very angrily; HAVE KITTENS : *She just about threw a fit when I told her we weren't going/ Well, they threw a spaz and said I can't see him or have him over* (*entry form* 1896+, *variant* 1990s+)

◄**throw a fuck into someone►** *v phr* (Variations: **bop** or **boff** or **screw** may replace **fuck**) To do the sex act with someone; FUCK : *It's inevitable that someone is going to want to throw a bop into someone else's wife* (*entry form* 1940s+)

throw a monkey wrench into something *v phr* To confuse or disable something : *Hot-eyed radicals eager to throw a monkey wrench into the social machinery* (1920+)

throw something **at** something *v phr* To cover or pelt a problem with some usu futile remedy : *Experience with throwing bureaucrats at such problems does not presage success* (1970s+)

throwaway *modifier* **1** : *He had a sort of throwaway casualness about him* **2** Designed to be thrown away; disposable : *It came in throwaway bottles* (1928+) **3** Useless; superfluous; cruelly neglected : *a three-times convicted killer, a throwaway man now/ Haiti has always been a throwaway nation* (1970s+) *n* A line, joke, etc, deliberately spoken unemphatically, thus increasing its effect (1955+ *Show business*)

throwback *n* A retro thing, person, etc; a reversion to a technique or method of an earlier period : *That guy tries so hard to be a throwback to the 60s* (1888+)

throw something **back** *v phr* To drink something; also, to eat something : *threw back a few beers*

throw down *v phr* **1** To threaten or challenge; start trouble : *I told him about Sam throwing*

down on me with a gun/ irate macho mesomorphs about to throw down (1950s+) **2** To challenge a rival break dancer by performing a particularly difficult feat or gyration (1980s+ *Black teenagers*) **3** To have fun; GET DOWN, PARTY : *I'm going to throw down at the party Saturday night* (1980s+ *Teenagers*) **4** To eat, esp voraciously : *threw down some burgers* [first two senses perhaps fr late 1800s *throw down on*, "aim one's pistol at"; perhaps fr *throw down the gauntlet*, "issue a challenge," found by 1548]

throw someone or something for a loop *See* KNOCK someone or something FOR A LOOP

throw one's hat in the ring *v phr* To issue a challenge, esp to announce one's candidacy in an election, for an appointment, etc (1917+)

throw in the towel (or the sponge) *v phr* To concede defeat; give up; FOLD [1940s+; fr the signal of surrender given by a defeated boxer's manager or associate when he tosses a *sponge* or a *towel* in the air or into the ring; found by 1960 in the form *throw up the sponge*]

throw money at something *v phr* To spend extravagant amounts of money in the hope of solving some problem : *The answer to the quality of schools is not just to throw money at the problem* (1970s+)

throw someone out on someone's ass (or ear) *v phr* To eject someone, esp violently; BUM-RUSH : *I just raised a little question and they threw me out on my ass*

throw the book at someone *v phr* To impose a severe punishment, esp to assign a maximum sentence to a criminal; treat mercilessly : *If he catches you one more time he'll throw the book at you* [1932+; fr the image of a judge *throwing the* whole *lawbook* full of punishment indiscriminately at the convicted person]

throw the bull *v phr* SHOOT THE BULL

throw together *See* KNOCK TOGETHER

throw one's weight around *v phr* To use one's influence, esp in a crude way; exploit one's authority : *You'll never get picked if you start throwing your weight around* (1916+)

thumb *n* A marijuana cigarette; JOINT (1960s+ *Narcotics*) *v* (also **thumb a ride**) To solicit rides along a highway by pointing with one's thumb in the direction one wishes to travel; HITCHHIKE (1939+) [narcotics sense fr the fact that one sucks the cigarette as a baby does its *thumb*] *See* a GREEN THUMB, STICK OUT

thumbnail sketch *n phr* A very brief account; esp, a quick biography [1852+; so brief, that is, as to be written on a *thumbnail*]

thumbs See ALL THUMBS, TWIDDLE one's THUMBS

thumbs down *n phr* A negative response; a negation : *It's thumbs down on his promotion this year* [1906+; fr the *pollice verso* gesture of the audience at a Roman gladiatorial show, indicating that a defeated gladiator was to be killed rather than spared]

thumbs up *n phr* A positive response; an affirmation; the NOD : *We go, the answer is thumbs up* [1887+; the opposite of *thumbs down*] See THUMBS DOWN

thumping *adj* Especially great; also, large : *thumping good time* (1576+)

thunder thighs *n phr* Heavy thighs, esp when regarded as ugly and undesirable : *Bye-bye thunder thighs. You can have slimmer legs in 30 days/ the sinewy thunder thighs of marathoner Gayle Olinekova* (1970s+)

thusly *adv* Thus : *content to sum up his contribution thusly: "It was the toughest thing I ever attempted"* (1865+)

tick[1] *n* Credit : *plenty of canned goods and plenty of tick at the store* [1642+; fr *ticket*]

tick[2] *n* **1** A degree, esp of upward motion or increase; a discrete amount : *if the price would have stayed where it was or skipped up a few more ticks* (1970+) **2** A second; a JIFFY : *I'll be there in a couple of ticks* (1879+) See RICKY-TICK, UPTICK, WHAT MAKES someone TICK

tick[3] See TIGHT AS A TICK

ticked off or **ticked** *adj phr* or *adj* Angry; PISSED OFF, TEE'D OFF : *Steve Kemp is ticked off* (1959+)

ticker *n* **1** A telegraphic printing machine for stock quotations, news reports, etc : *It's just coming in on the AP ticker* (1883+) **2** The heart : *He tapped the left side of his chest. "Ticker," he said* (1930+)

ticket *n* An official license or certificate, esp one for a ship's officer, a radio operator, etc (late 1800s+) See BIG TICKET, HAVE one's TICKET PUNCHED, MEAL TICKET, WALKING PAPERS

ticket, the *n phr* Exactly what is wanted : *That's the ticket, my dear, at last* [1838+; perhaps fr *the winning ticket* in a lottery, a race, etc]

tickety-boo *adj* : *The sergeant reported that all was tickety-boo* *adv* Very well; splendidly : *Weitz's report just after liftoff that "everything's going tickety-boo so far"* (WWII British armed forces) [origin uncertain; perhaps fr *the ticket*; more likely fr the slightly earlier Royal Air Force *tiggerty boo* in the same sense, fr Hindi *teega* plus unexplained but euphonious *boo*]

tickled *adj* Pleased; happy : *She says she's tickled to be off her soap in New York* (1586+)

tickled to death (or **pink**) *adj phr* Very much pleased; happy as can be : *They were tickled to death with the suggestion/ I am tickled pink to have been asked* (entry form 1834+, variant 1922+)

tickler See FRENCH TICKLER, RIB-TICKLER

tickle the ivories *v phr* To play the piano, esp to play it well (1906+)

◁**tickle the shit** (or **piss**) **out of** someone▷ *v phr* To please someone very much; overjoy someone (1940s+)

ticklish *adj* Difficult because it requires sensitive handling : *ticklish question* (1591+)

tick someone off *v phr* To anger someone; PISS someone OFF : *Just the slightest thing could tick off Harold* (1915+)

tick-tock *n* A clock; also, by extension, the human heart : *wind the tick-tock/ tick-tock is going strong at 70*

ticky-tacky *adj* (also **ticky-tack**) Inferior; shabbily made or done; TACKY : *oil rigs and ticky-tack motels/ draw their energy from the ticky-tacky-taco style of curio shops* (1969+) *n* Shabby materials; insubstantial and inferior goods : *little houses made of ticky-tacky* (1962+) [coined by Malvina Reynolds and used in "Little Boxes," a 1960s satirical song about California housing tracts where the houses are described as little boxes made of *ticky-tacky*]

tiddly or **tiddled** *adj* Drunk, esp slightly drunk : *a little tiddly, which is to say, shot or blind* (1905+)

tiddy See TOUGH SHIT

tied up *modifier* Busy : *tied up with a conference call*

tie-in *n* **1** A connection : *I wonder if there's any tie-in with organized crime* (1934+) **2** An item sold because of the existence of another item : *The book is a movie tie-in* (1943+)

tie someone or something **in knots** *v phr* To immobilize or paralyze with complications : *Lobbyists had helped tie the Energy and Commerce Committee in knots* (1957+)

tie it up *v phr* WRAP UP (1954+)

tie one on *v phr* To get drunk; go on a spree (1940s+)

tie the knot *v phr* To get married; also, to marry two people

tie up *v phr* To inject narcotics into a vein, or tie a rubber tubing around one's arm in order to find a vein; SHOOT UP : *pop a handful of bennies, then tie up, smoking a joint at the same time* (1960s+ Narcotics)

tiff *n* A minor quarrel or fight (1754+)

tiger *n* A strong, virile man; a dangerous man • Often used in direct address, either admiringly or ironically : *He's switched from being a pussycat to being a regular tiger* (1940s+) See HAVE A TIGER BY THE TAIL

tight *adj* **1** Parsimonious; tight-fisted; stingy : *He is tight in his dealings (1805+)* **2** (Variations: **as a drum** [or **a lord** or **a mink**] may be added) Drunk : *Little tight, honey?/ I wasn't especially tight (1830+)* **3** Close; sympathetic : *John and Mary are very tight (1956+)* **4** Attractive; COOL : *Renee's wig is tight (1980s+ Students) See* SIT TIGHT

tight as a tick *adj phr* Very drunk [1927+; fr the inflated tightness of an engorged *tick*, found in reference to fullness by 1678]

◁**tight-ass**▷ *adj* : *That is Dr Nathan Schlemmer, very uptight, very tight-ass n* A tense and morally rigid person : *I know that one, a real tight-ass (1970+)*

◁**tight-assed**▷ *adj* **1** Not disposed to sexual promiscuity; chaste : *Washington, I saw, was full of tight-assed women (1903+)* **2** Tense; overly formal : *tightassed British film critic (1967+)*

tighten one's belt *v phr* To prepare for an economic recession or depression : *tightening our belts due to gas prices*

tighten someone up *v phr* To discipline someone; rectify someone's life : *There were actually men on the block that if you did something wrong they were going to catch you and tighten you up (1980s+ Black)*

tight money *n phr* Money when the supply is scarce, esp during a period of high interest rates *(1866+)*

tight spot *n phr* A difficult situation; JAM : *I'm in a tight spot and would appreciate your help (1852+)*

tightwad *adj* : *Don't be so tightwad with that hootch n* A parsimonious person; a stingy person; a miser : *the "tightwads" who have saved money (1900+)* [fr the forbidding tightness of his *wad* of money]

till *See* WITH one's HAND IN THE TILL

till hell freezes over or **till kingdom come** *adv* Forever

till (or until) one is blue in the face *adv phr* Until one is able to do no more; to the point of helpless exhaustion : *Hail and beware the dead who will talk life until you are blue in the face* [1864+; fr the *facial blueness* or darkening symptomatic of choking]

till the fat lady sings *See* the OPERA AIN'T OVER TILL THE FAT LADY SINGS

timber *interj* An exclamation of triumph, achievement, etc [1912+; fr the cry of loggers as a tree begins to fall] *See* the TALL TIMBERS

time *See* BAD TIME, the BIG TIME, DOUBLE-TIME, GIVE someone A HARD TIME, GOOD TIME, HAVE oneself A TIME, MAKE TIME, MAKE TIME WITH someone, the SMALL TIME, STREET TIME

time (out) *interj* Wait; stop talking or doing something : *Time out. It's my turn*

time of day, the *See* NOT GIVE someone THE TIME OF DAY

timer *See* OLD TIMER

times *See* HARD TIMES

time warp *n phr* A blank, an inordinate rapidity or slowness, a blatant discontinuity, a seeming anachronism, or some other anomaly of time : *The case of five people indicted more than four years ago has been "lost in a time warp" of delays, state prosecutors say* [1954+; fr science-fiction notions of instantaneous eons and the like, devised to legitimize travel over enormous distances within conceivable and dramatically useful periods of time, and based on Albert Einstein's concept of "curved space"]

tin can *n phr* **1** A depth charge *(WWII Navy)* **2** A naval warship, esp a destroyer *(1937+ Navy)* **3** A car, esp a Model T Ford *(1923+)*

tin ear *n phr* Unselective and unmusical hearing; auditory tastelessness : *He sometimes has a tin ear for dialogue/ I have a tin ear (1909+)*

tinkle *n* A telephone call • Chiefly in the expression *give someone a tinkle (1938+) v* To urinate; PEE • A nursery use *(1950+)*

Tinseltown *modifier* : *With familiar Tinseltown inventiveness, the new film has been entitled Grease 2 n* Hollywood; the Los Angeles–Hollywood movie and TV area and culture : *if he couldn't nab a ride to Tinsel Town in an hour's time/ It sometimes seems that the whole society has spiritually decamped for Tinseltown (1975+)* [fr *tinsel*, "gaudy, glittering decoration," plus *town*]

tip *n* : *our tip to him would be to behave (1845+) v* (also **tip off**) To give useful information or advice, esp advance information that gives an advantage of some sort : *The room clerk tipped him/ Who tipped Larkin off? (1749+, variant 1891+)* [origin uncertain; perhaps fr the notion of *tipping*, that is, tilting something in someone's direction]

tip one's hand (or mitt) *v phr* To disclose one's plans, secrets, etc, esp inadvertently : *That would be tipping her mitt too much/ somehow, even with the best intentions, you'd tip my hand* [entry form 1917+; fr the revealing of one's *hand*, that is, *mitt*, in a card game; *tip*, "give, exhibit," is found in underworld slang by 1610]

tip-off *n* A revealing, esp a warning; a particularly useful clue : *the tip-off on what's ahead (1901+)*

tip over *v phr* To rob; HEIST, KNOCK OVER : *Ya wanta help us tip over this bank? (1935+ Underworld)*

tipple *n* **1** Liquor, esp strong; also, a drink of strong liquor • Also can be a verb **2** A drinking bout

tippler *n* A relatively restrained drinker of alcohol [1580+; orig a tavernkeeper]

tippy-toe *v* To walk silently : *God-damn it, Hubert! Don't tippy-toe around like that (1901+)*

tipster *n* A person who gives tips, esp on horse races (1862+)

tipsy *adj* Mildly drunk (1577+)

tip the elbow *See* BEND THE ELBOW

tip-top *adj* Excellent; first-rate : *He assured me his health was tip-top (1722+)*

tire *See* SPARE TIRE

◁**tired-ass**▷ *adj* Tedious; overused; tired : *thinking in tired-ass racial cliches (1970s+)*

◁**tit**▷ *n* A woman's breast : *She couldn't make it out there. No tits* [1928+; a respelling of *teat*] *See* COLD AS HELL, GET one's TAIL IN A GATE, SUCK HIND TIT, SUGAR TIT

◁**tit art**▷ *n phr* Appealing photographs of young women; CHEESECAKE (1970s+ Newspaper office)

◁**titless wonder**▷ *n phr* A stupid or inane person; JERK

◁**tit man**▷ *n phr* A man whose favorite part of the female body is the breasts (1940s+)

◁**tits**▷ *adj* **1** Excellent; wonderful; GREAT, NEAT : *What a tits car she's got! (1960s+)* **2** Easy; simple : *a real tits quiz (1960s+ College students) See* WITH BELLS ON

◁**tits and ass**▷ *modifier* : *The magazine had a tits-and-ass section purporting to be a review of bathing-suit styles n phr* A display of female bosoms and bottoms; also, a show, dance, etc, featuring such a display; CHEESECAKE, TA : *Tits and ass, that's what the attraction is. An Apache team and tits and ass (1972+)*

◁**tits up**▷ *modifier* Upside down; on one's back : *buttered bread fell tits up*

◁**titty**▷ *n* A breast; TIT : *His dipping titties touched the floor before his chin did (1746+) See* TOUGH SHIT

tizzy *See* IN A TIZZY

TKO (pronounced as separate letters) *n* A technical knockout, declared when one fighter is judged unfit to continue, although still conscious (1940s+ Prizefighting) *v* : *He was TKO'd in the fourth round*

TLC (pronounced as separate letters) *n* Tender loving care : *some TLC for the sick boy*

toad *n* A repellent person; ASSHOLE : *The only time you want the guy to ask first is if he's a toad (1568+) See* KNEE-HIGH TO A GRASSHOPPER

toast *adj* **1** Excellent; wonderful; COOL, TITS, TUBULAR : *She told me my clothes were real toast (1970s+ Teenagers fr black)* **2** Ruined; actually or occupationally destroyed; KAPUT : *finished in one's career, as in "He's toast"/ Much of the punditocracy that once embraced Clinton is declaring him dead. Buried. Toast (1980s+) v* To talk or chant in the reggae music mode : *not exactly toasting, it was a kind of primitive rapping, consisting mainly of new slang words and an occasional joke (1970s+ Musicians)*

to a T (or **tee**) *adv* Precisely; in the smallest detail : *job fits her to a tee*

to beat the band (or **the Dutch**) *adv phr* In an unrestrained way; to the highest pitch; very much; ALL-OUT : *I hollered to beat the band/ We ran to beat the Dutch* [entry form 1897+, variant 1775+; fr the notion that such extreme effort could even drown out *the band*, or, in the mid-1700s version, *this beats the Dutch*, could convince even a stolid, phlegmatic *Dutch* man]

to boot *adv phr* In addition; in extra measure : *She has lots of talent and more to boot* [1000+; fr Old English, "as profit, to the good"]

toddle off *v phr* To walk away : *toddled off to clean out the bookcases*

to-die-for *adj* Very desirable; extremely attractive; DISHY : *constant companion of the to-die-for Marilyn Montgomery (1990s+)*

to-do *n* A disturbance; fuss; FLAP : *What's all the to-do? (1827+)*

toe *See* GO TOE TO TOE, TURN UP one's TOES

toehold *See* GET A TOEHOLD

toe jam *n phr* Malodorous matter and filth under and around the toenails (1934+)

◁**toe-jam queen**▷ *n phr* A male homosexual foot-fetishist (1972+ Homosexuals)

toe-tag *v phr* To kill

toe the mark (or **the line**) *v phr* To behave properly; KEEP one's NOSE CLEAN : *If he doesn't toe the mark, fire him* [entry form 1813+, variant 1895+; fr the *mark* or *line* indicating the starting point of a race]

toe to toe *See* GO TOE TO TOE

toffee-nose or **toffee-nosed** *adj* Snobbish or pretentious (1925+)

together *adj* **1** Composed and effective; free of tension and anxiety : *Now they're together, unless they're strung out (1960s+ Counterculture fr black)* **2** Stylish and au courant; socially adept (1960s+ Black) *See* GET IT TOGETHER, HAVE IT ALL TOGETHER

to go *modifier* Packaged up for taking home or off the premises : *want that order to go*

tog out (or **up**) *v phr* To get dressed, esp in nice clothes (1790s+)

togs *n* Clothing, esp that worn for a specific purpose : *riding togs* [1779+; fr *tog*, "coat," ultimately fr Latin *toga*]

to hell *adv phr* **1** (also **to hell and gone**) Thoroughly; irretrievably : *This thing's busted to hell/ The plan's wrecked to hell and gone* **2** (also **to heaven** or **to high heaven**) Very strongly; fervently; sincerely : *He swore to hell he'd never do it again/ I wish to heaven she'd leave (1912+)*

toity *See* HOITY-TOITY

toke[1] *n* **1** A puff or drag at a cigarette, cigar, etc, esp a marijuana cigarette : *He still took a toke of marijuana from time to time* **2** A cigarette, esp a marijuana cigarette : *Elaborately, I lit a toke* **v** : *to toke vigorously on an oversize cigar* [1950s+; probably fr Spanish *tocar* in its sense "touch," or "tap, hit," or "get a shave or part," or a combination of these]

toke[2] *n* **1** A gambling chip or token, esp one given to a dealer as a tip *(1961+ Gambling)* **2** A gratuity given by a gambling casino, brothel, or other business to cabdrivers for bringing in clients : *Cab drivers have long been paid "tokes" when they deliver customers to a long list of varied business establishments (1971+ Gambling)*

tokus (TOH kəs, TŌŌ kəs) *n* (also **tokis** or **tuchis** or **tuckus** or **tush** or **tushie** or **tushy**) The buttocks; ASS, BOTTOM • A frequent euphemism for *ass* : *knocked him right square on his tokus/ He shakes his tushie with elegant languor/ bumps her tush gently along* [1914+; fr Yiddish; *tush* forms are affectionate, used esp with children]

told *See* FUCKING WELL TOLD

◁**Tom** or **tom**▷ *n* A black person who emulates or truckles to the white majority taste and culture; OREO, UNCLE TOM *(1959+ Black)* **v** : *sleeping, resisting, tomming, killing the enemy/ You too young to be Tomming*

tomato *n* An attractive young woman; BABE, chick : *I was telling you about this kraut and the English tomato* [1922+; fr the connotations of lusciousness, tautness, full color, etc]

tomboy or **tomgirl** *n* A young girl who prefers boyish pursuits, looks, etc, to the presumed feminine ones *(1592+)*

tomcat *n* : *In his younger days he was a notorious tomcat* **v** To pursue male sexual activity avidly [1927+; fr the common name for a male cat, popularized by the 1760 book *The Life and Adventures of a Cat*, in which the creature was named *Tom*]

Tom, Dick, and Harry *See* EVERY TOM, DICK, AND HARRY

tomfool *adj* Stupid; foolish; NUTTY : *some tomfool scientist* [1762+; found by 1356 as the actual name of a man, also called Thomas fatuus, "foolish Tom"]

Tommy (or **tommy**) **gun** *n phr* A handheld automatic repeating firearm; a submachine gun; BURP GUN, CHOPPER [1929+; fr the name of the .45-caliber *Thompson* submachine gun, the earliest well-known weapon of this sort, and a favorite arm of the gangster era]

tommyrot *n* Nonsense; balderdash; BALONEY, BULLSHIT [1884+; origin unknown; perhaps fr British *tommy*, "goods, esp food, supplied to workers in lieu of wages"]

tonic *n* Liquor : *tonic will settle you down*

tonk *n* HONKY-TONK

ton of bricks *See* HIT someone LIKE A TON OF BRICKS

tonsil hockey *n phr* **1** Fellatio; oral sex • Euphemistic **2** French or other intimate kissing

tons of *modifier* A lot of something : *tons of fan mail*

too big for one's breeches (or **britches** or **boots**) *modifier* Conceited *(1830s+)*

toodle-oo *interj* A parting salutation • Thought of as a humorous affectation, like "cheerio" [1907+; perhaps an alteration of French *à tout à l'heure*, "see you soon, so long"]

too hot to handle *adj phr* Very delicate or explosive; very controversial : *The March was rejected by PBS as "not suitable to their programming" (nobody actually said it was too hot to handle)* [1940s+; found in baseball by 1932, designating a very hard-hit ball]

took *See* be HAD

tool *n* ◁1▷ The penis *(1553+)* **2** A pickpocket *(1920+ Underworld)* **3** (also **dull tool**) An incompetent person; also, someone who can be duped or victimized easily *(1700+)* **4** A diligent student; greasy grind, NERD : *Nerds can also be "goobs" or "tools" (Students)* **v** **1** To do the sex act with or to; BOFF, BOP, SCREW : *Hit the man in the ass with a board while he was tooling your old lady (1980s+)* **2** (also **tool along**) To speed; BARREL : *I climbed into the Buick and tooled it down the ramp (1853+)* [underworld sense perhaps fr the practice of using a small boy as a sort of *tool* in pickpocketing, or perhaps fr Romany *tool*, "handle, take"; second verb sense fr earlier tool, "a whip"]

tool around *v phr* To drive around, esp recreationally : *tooling around with the top down*

too many *See* ONE TOO MANY

too many chiefs and not enough Indians *sentence* Nobody wants to work around here, though everybody wants to be a boss; the project suffers from a surplus of directors and advisers

too much *adj phr* **1** Wonderful; superb; the MOST : *The way she blows that horn is too much* **2** Excessively good, bad, wonderful, incredible, etc; prodigious; overwhelming : *You ate 23 hot dogs in one sitting? Man, you're too much* n FAR OUT *(1930s+ Jazz musicians)*

toon *n* A cartoon : *"What are you, man, some kind of visionary?" "No, no, I'm just an ordinary toon" (1990s+) See* LOONY-TUNE

too rich for someone's blood *adj phr* Exceeding someone's capabilities, purse, desires, etc; too much : *I don't go out with them anymore; it's too rich for my blood (1884+)*

toot *n* **1** A spree, esp of drinking; BENDER, BINGE, KICK • A tooter is a person on a drinking spree : *It gave me an excuse to go off on a four-day toot/ He got a bonus and went on a shopping toot* (*1790+*) **2** Cocaine : *Am I witnessing mere incompetence or too much toot?/ made it easier for the press to imagine him doing a little toot in the basement of Studio 54* (*1960s+ Narcotics*) **3** A whiff of cocaine into the nose; SNORT : *I don't suppose you have a toot till payday?* (*1977+ Narcotics*) **4** A flatulation; FART (*1930s+*) *v* **1** : *He was himself tooting cocaine on a daily basis* (*1975+ Narcotics*) **2** To flatulate; LAY A FART : *"What's that smell?" "Oh, Andrea tooted again"* (*1930s+*) [the drinking sense is probably fr the image of someone tooting on a drinking horn, that is, holding a glass up as if it were a horn one were blowing; *toot* or *tout*, "drink deeply, quaff," are attested fr the 1600s; narcotics sense probably related to *honker*, "horn, nose," as something to be *tooted*]

tooth *See* CLEAN AS A WHISTLE, LONG IN THE TOOTH, SWEET-TOOTH

tootie fruitie *n phr* A weak and ineffective male; SISSY, WIMP : *We're all a bunch of God-damned tootie fruities* [1970s+; fr *tutti-frutti*, "ice cream containing candied fruit," fr Italian, literally "all fruits," with a punning on *fruity*, "homosexual, gay"]

tootin' *See* ROOTIN'-TOOTIN', YOU'RE DAMN TOOTIN'

too too *adj phr* Excessive, esp in social elegance, fastidiousness, affectation, etc : *Well, isn't his caring just too too!* (*1881+*)

toot (or **blow**) **one's own horn** (or **trumpet**) *v phr* To praise and flatter oneself; advertise one's virtues; boast : *I am not ashamed of the text, but of being thought to "toot my own horn"* [entry form 1940+, *blow* 1859+, *trumpet* 1854+; the phrase *sound the trumpet of mine own merits* is found by 1576]

toots (TOOTS) *n* (also **tootsie** or **tootsy** or **tootsie-wootsie** or **tootsy-wootsy**) A woman; DOLL • Often used in address, often disparagingly, and as a nickname : *Not any more, toots, not any more, my precious darling angel/ How about one of those tootsie-wootsies?/ He was also paying for a penthouse apartment on Park Avenue for his tootsie* [entry form 1936+, *tootsie-wootsie* 1895+; perhaps fr *tootsie*]

tootsie *n* A foot • A nursery use : *Pull up a chair and warm your tootsies* (*1854+*)

top *modifier* : *He got the top recommendation* (*1714+*) *n* **1** TOP SERGEANT (*WWI Army*) **2** The best; most superior : *You're the top, you're the Louvre Museum* (*1593+*) *v* **1** To hang someone : *A colleague sent to the gallows has been topped* (*1718+*) **2** To kill; BUMP OFF someone, HIT (*1930s+*) **3** To surpass; better; CAP : *I'll top that story with one of my own*

(*1586+*) **4** To be executed for a capital crime (*1960s+ Black*) *See* BLOW one's TOP, COME OUT AHEAD, FROM THE TOP, GO someone or something ONE BETTER, MUTTONHEAD, OFF THE TOP, ON TOP OF, POP-TOP, RAG-TOP, TIP-TOP

top banana *n phr* **1** The leading or featured comedian in a burlesque show; the chief comic (*1950s+ Show business*) **2** The leader, president, manager, etc; BOSS, BIG ENCHILADA : *refuses its members opportunity to become top banana* (*1970s+*) [said to have originated fr a burlesque routine having to do with a bunch of *bananas*]

top brass, the *n phr* **1** The highest of military officers : *They went to the top brass at the Pentagon* (*1940s+*) **2** The highest executives, managers, etc : *The top brass at Xerox liked the idea* (*1949+*)

top dog *n phr* The most important person; the chief; BOSS : *Who's top dog around this place?* (*1900+*)

top dollar *n phr* The highest sum of money offered or given : *They pay top dollar over there* (*1970+*)

top-drawer *adj* Of the highest quality; most superior; TOPS : *The drinks they serve are absolutely top-drawer* [1920+; fr a British expression *out of the top drawer*, "upper-class, well-bred"]

topline *v* To feature as the main attraction : *bio-pic that was expected to topline Elizabeth Taylor and Lauren Bacall* [1980s+]

top-notch *adj phr* Superior; of the highest quality; TOP-DRAWER : *She's a top-notch racquetball player* [1900+; fr *notch* as representing position, rank, etc; found as a noun phrase, "the highest degree of excellence," by 1833]

top of one's **head** *See* OFF THE TOP OF one's HEAD

tops *adj* Best; most superior; absolutely first-rate; the TOPS : *I wish you could print Mencken every month; he's tops/ Sanitation Service Is Tops* (*1935+*)

tops, the *n phr* The best; the acme : *The English department is the tops here* (*1937+*)

top sergeant *n phr* **1** A first sergeant; top-kick (*1898+*) **2** A lesbian who takes the dominant, masculine role; BUTCH, DYKE (*1950s+ Homosexuals*)

topsy-turvy *adj* Disordered; upside down (*1528+*)

torch *n* An arsonist; an incendiary; FIREBUG : *If your suspicions are right, the torch will be close by* (*1938+*) *v* To set a fire deliberately; burn a building : *The lumberyard at 12th and C was torched, for the insurance* (*1931+*) *See* CARRY THE TORCH

torch job *n phr* An instance of arson : *mob-linked torch jobs for a 10 percent cut of insurance proceeds* (*1970s+*)

torch song *n phr* A popular song bemoaning one's unrequited love : *If it is unrequited, the song is a torch song* (1927+) *See* CARRY THE TORCH

torchy *adj* In love with someone who does not reciprocate; hopelessly enamored : *Junie, still torchy for the Ragtime Kid* [1941+; fr *carry the torch*]

-torium *See* -ATORIUM

torpedo *n* 1 A gunman, esp a hired killer; HIT MAN : *the torpedoes who worked for Ciro Terranova* (1929+ *Underworld*) 2 HERO SANDWICH (1970s+) *v* To destroy; annihilate; SINK : *in an offensive that torpedoed cease-fire talks* (1895+)

toss *v* 1 To search, esp a person for weapons, drugs, etc; SHAKE DOWN : *How do you think Leo will react to getting tossed in the apartment?* (1939+) 2 To determine by throwing up a coin for "heads or tails" : *I'll toss you for the drinks* (1833+) 3 To vomit : *tossed after drinking so much* 4 To throw something away : *tossed those old paperbacks* 5 To drink some liquor; take a drink : *tossed a beer and got back to work See* THROW

toss one's cookies (or **lunch**) *See* SHOOT one's COOKIES

toss in the sponge *v phr* THROW IN THE TOWEL

toss off *v phr* 1 To do something easily and casually : *They sat down and tossed off a couple of limericks* (1874+) 2 To drink, esp at one gulp; KNOCK BACK : *She tossed off three double Scotches* (1590+)

toss-up, a *n* An even matter; a case of even probabilities, values, etc : *It's a toss-up between those two candidates/ I don't know which way to bet; it's a toss-up* [1809+; fr the fact that the choice might as well be made by *tossing up* a coin]

total *v* 1 To destroy; totally wreck, esp a car : *It didn't look like much of a wreck, but his car was totaled* (1954+) 2 To maim or kill; grievously injure; WASTE : *Mightn't a tile have fallen off a roof and totaled us by dinnertime?* (1895+) [first sense fr the phrase *a total loss,* having to do with something insured]

totaled *adj* 1 Destroyed; wrecked completely : *The totaled car made you wonder how they survived the wreck* (1954+) 2 Stuporous from narcotics, liquor, etc; STONED, WASTED (1960s+)

total loss, a *n phr* A person or thing that is hopelessly futile; LOSER (1940s+)

totally *modifier* Completely; unquestionably : *totally his fault/ totally awesome*

totally clueless *adj phr* Uninformed; ignorant; in the dark [1970s+ Teenagers; *Clueless* is a late 1930s Royal Air Force term]

to the eyes (or **the eyeballs**) *adv phr* Entirely; thoroughly; UP TO HERE : *Carlotta keeps her doped to the eyeballs on Thorazine all her adult life* (1778+) *See* STONED TO THE EYES

to the gills *See* SOUSED, STEWED

to the ground *See* BEAT TO THE GROUND

to the mark *See* UP TO SCRATCH

to the max *adv phr* To the highest degree; utterly; totally : *Many of these were obscure to the max* [1970s+ Teenagers & Army; fr a shortening of *to the maximum*] *See* GROTTY

to the nines *See* DRESSED TO THE TEETH

to the salt mines *See* BACK TO THE SALT MINES

to the teeth *See* DRESSED TO THE TEETH

to the tune of *adv phr* In the amount of; to the extent of : *It'll cost him a bundle, to the tune of sixty grand or so* (1716+)

to the wall *See* BALLS TO THE WALL

totsie *See* HOTSIE-TOTSIE

touch *n* 1 : *a quick ten- or twenty-dollar touch* (1846+) 2 A small serving of food or drink *v* 1 (also **touch up**) To get or borrow money, a loan, etc; HIT : *Who better to touch up than the richest guys in town?* (1760+) 2 To deal with or handle something or someone• Usu in the negative : *won't touch that one* [*touch up* variant may be influenced by British *touch up*, "to grope a woman"] *See* SOFT TOUCH

touch all bases *v phr* 1 To be thorough; leave nothing undone, esp in matters of consultation, communication, etc : *The plan flopped because you didn't touch all bases on the way* 2 To be very versatile; be apt for various experiences : *Humphrey is a man to touch all bases* [1980s+; fr the necessity of *touching all bases* in baseball when one makes a home run]

touch and go *modifier* Possible but very uncertain; precarious : *touch and go for a while, until she saw the doctor*

touch base with someone *v phr* To consult with or inform as to an impending matter : *Before you sign it you'd better touch base with your lawyer* [1980s+; fr *touch all bases*]

touched *adj* 1 Honored or flattered : *touched that you would think of us* 2 Slightly crazy; eccentric : *Emeril seems a bit touched*

touchie-feelie or **touchy-feely** *adj* Having to do with sensitivity training and other such goings-on where people touch and feel each other : *They're all part of the touchie-feelie movement/ It's not going to be a touchy-feely thing* (1970s+)

touch someone or something **with a ten-foot pole,** not *See* NOT TOUCH someone or something WITH A TEN-FOOT POLE

tough *adj* 1 Difficult; regrettable; unfortunate : *That's a tough break, pardner* (1883+) 2 Physically menacing; vicious : *Don't act tough with me, you little jerk* (1906+) 3 Excellent; superb; the MOST • Sometimes spelled *tuff* : *That's a really tough set of wheels*

(1937+ Black) n A hard and menacing person *(1866+) See* TOUGH IT OUT

tough (or hard) act to follow, a *n phr* A challenging or daunting prelude : *her portrayal of Catwoman was a tough act for Michelle Pfeiffer to follow* [1980s+; fr the vaudeville ambiance where one performer succeeded another; one truism was "Never follow a dog act"]

tough call *n phr* A hard decision or prediction : *This next election is bound to be a tough call* [1990s+; fr the decisions made by sports officials and football quarterbacks]

tough cookie *n phr* **1** TOUGH GUY **2** A stubborn and durable person : *He's a tough cookie. He isn't going to talk, threats or no threats* *(1928+)*

tough cop *See* GOOD COP BAD COP

tough customer *n phr* A difficult person to deal with : *known as a tough customer*

tough guy (or baby) *n phr* A menacing man; BIMBO, HOODLUM, ROUGHNECK, TOUGHIE : *Bogart used to play tough guys a lot (entry form and baby 1932+)*

toughie or toughy *n* **1** A menacing person, esp a man; TOUGH, TOUGH GUY : *getting the toughies off the streets/ That servant will talk her out of it. She's a toughie* *(1929+)* **2** Something difficult; a severe test : *This is a toughie/ has 3 toughies barring its way to a perfect season* *(1945+)*

tough it out *v phr* To endure something doggedly and bravely; persist and survive against rigors; HANG TOUGH : *He's never really had to tough it out in this world of ours/ He is toughing out a feeling that since Mom divorced he is essentially homeless (1830+)*

tough nut (or egg) to crack, a *n phr* A difficult problem; BITCH, TOUGHIE : *Getting them all here on time will be a tough nut to crack (1970s+)*

tough row to hoe, a *See* a HARD ROW TO HOE

tough sell *n phr* Something difficult to advocate or "sell" : *High-tech warehousing a tough sell (1990s+)*

◁**tough shit**▷ *interj* (Variations: **luck** or **nibs** or **noogies** or **patootie** or **rocks** or **teabags** or **tiddy** or **titty** or **titties** may replace **shit**) That's too bad; that's a terrible shame ● Often ironical and mocking : *Lord, what tough luck/ "Tough tiddy," the Boss said/ to which one has to say, with whatever empathy, "tough nibs"/ "And guess what they had the nerve to tell me." "Tough patootie"/ That's tough shit, man, my heart really bleeds/ Well, tough titty* [entry form 1940s+, luck 1886+, noogies 1960s+, tiddy 1934+; most forms probably fr black or Southern; the mammary forms seem based on a black folksaying, "It's tough titty, but the milk is good"]

tourist trap *n phr* A a place that attracts and exploits tourists : *Manchester, Vermont, is a tourist trap (1939+)*

tout *n* **1** A person who sells betting advice at a racetrack; TIPSTER *(1865+)* **2** : *He makes a slender living with his touting at Belmont v* To advocate aggressively; publicize; ballyhoo. FLACK : *He's now touting acupuncture (1920+)* [ultimately fr Middle English *tuten,* "look around, peer," by way of *tout,* "be on the lookout"]

towel *See* THROW IN THE TOWEL

◁**towelhead**▷ *n* Any person who wears a turban, esp a person from the Middle East *(1985+)*

town *See* GO TO TOWN, HICK TOWN, MAN-ABOUT-TOWN, ONE-HORSE TOWN, ON THE TOWN, PAINT THE TOWN, SHANTY-TOWN, TINSELTOWN

Town *See* BEAN TOWN

townie or towny *n* A permanent resident of the town one grew up in or went to school in; also, a resident of a college town not affiliated with the college : *townies that graduated from Valley*

toxic waste dump *n* An extremely horrible person or place

toy boy *n phr* Male lover of an older woman or man *(1981+)*

TP *n* Toilet paper : *need a roll of TP v* To decorate with toilet paper : *got TP'd on Halloween*

track *v* **1** To agree with other information; chime : *What you say doesn't track with what I know (1970s+ Army)* **2** To make sense; be plausible; FIGURE : *It does not necessarily track that because Son of Sam sells papers in New York he will sell books in Seattle/ She's practically out of her mind. Like, she isn't even tracking (1970s+)* [probably fr *track,* "the groove of a phonograph record, a continuous line or passage of a tape recording," influenced by earlier *track,* "follow, come closely and directly behind"] *See* FAST LANE, GO ON TRACK, HAVE THE INSIDE TRACK, ONE-TRACK MIND

track, the *See* the TURF

track record *n phr* Any record of performance, esp of success; CHART, FOOTPRINT, form : *I have a lot of relevant experience and a good track record/ Voluntary organizations have a much better track record in the third world* [1965+; fr the *record* of performance of a racehorse on the racetrack]

tracks *n* **1** railroad tracks *(WWII Army)* **2** The scars or puncture marks caused by narcotics injections : *wear long sleeves (to cover their "tracks," needle marks) (1960s+ Narcotics) See* HEN TRACKS, STOP someone DEAD IN someone's or something's TRACKS, the WRONG SIDE OF THE TRACKS

trade *n* : *Most White gay men use it to mean a heterosexual male who has sex with men for* *money or other consideration ("He can be done for trade"; "Watch out for him; he's rough trade")/ flashy, precise, and humpy as decidedly sexy trade in a Czardas with six girls (1935+ Homosexuals) See the* RAG TRADE, ROUGH TRADE

trademark *n* A person's particular trait or strong point; someone's MIDDLE NAME : *Shyness is not my trademark* (1869+)

◁**trailer trash**▷ *n* A poor, lower-class white person, esp one living in a mobile home with trash in the vicinity • Used in singular or plural : *She's just plain trailer trash*

train *n* : *popularly known as gang bangs or trains* *v* To do the sex act on a woman serially, man after man, in a gang; GANG-BANG : *announced that they were going to train her* (1970s+) [related to *pull a train*; perhaps influenced by earlier *train*, "romp, carry on wildly"] *See the* GRAVY TRAIN, ON THE GRAVY TRAIN, PULL A TRAIN, RIDE THE GRAVY TRAIN

train wreck *n phr* **1** (also **crump**) A person with many medical problems and in failing condition (1980s+ *Medical*) **2** An extremely harrowing situation or condition : *The special prosecutor's office is a worthy institution, but it will leave behind a legal train wreck/ Demographers refer to collisions between rising demand and diminishing resources as train wrecks* (1980s+)

tramp *n* A promiscuous woman; a harlot; punchboard (1922+)

trank *n* A tranquilizer; a tranquilizer tablet or capsule (1967+) *v* (also **trank out**) : *Last I heard, still at some pricey Rambler's Retreat, tranked to the tits/ The idea was to keep me tranked out so that everything would sort of stabilize* (1972+)

trannie or **tranny** *n* **1** A transvestite or transgendered person; CROSS-DRESSER, tv : *A slicked-back platinumed, pirouetting trannie takes over the dance floor* (1983+) **2** An automobile transmission

trap *modifier* : *to figure out why my trap money was shitty* (1970s+ *Black*) *n* **1** The mouth; YAP : *When she opens her trap she has an accent that is British* (1776+) **2** A nightclub : *a pretty good East Side trap* (1932+) **3** An amount of money earned by a prostitute, and usu given to her pimp : *Ray's woman got in the car. Her trap was fat* (1970s+ *Black*) *See* BEAR TRAP, BLOW OFF one's MOUTH, BOOBY TRAP, FLEABAG, FLY TRAP, SHUT one's TRAP, TOURIST TRAP

traps *n* The trapezius muscles : *Billitzer's lats, delts, traps and quads are ready for anything. Three or four days a week he runs through a 90-minute workout that has left him tuned and tough* (1990s+)

trash *n* A despicable, ill-bred person or group : *Don't mind them, they're just trash* (1604+) *v*

1 To vandalize; mutilate or destroy, sometimes as an act of political protest; WASTE : *They have also made it a practice to "trash" (wreck) restaurants, publishing houses, and other businesses that discriminate against the third world of sex/ One year we were trashed three times* (1970+) **2** To vilify; excoriate; BAD-MOUTH, DUMP ON : *the other mayoralty that Koch likes to trash whenever he gets the chance/ Much given to the rave-pan approach to her craft, she can trash in a flash* (1975+) **3** To scavenge discarded furniture and other items that have been thrown away (1960s+) [noun sense fr *white trash*, a black term of opprobrium] *See* WHITE TRASH

trashed *adj* **1** Drunk; intoxicated by alcohol or drugs : *got trashed on Friday night* (1981+) **2** Wrecked or ruined; messed up on purpose : *trashed hotel room of the rockers* (1926+)

trashing *n* The act or an act of those who trash in the senses of wrecking and vilification : *the Weathermen favoring of trashing was a ridiculous concept/ In my experience the public contributes every bit as much to the trashing of our presidents as we grimy ones do* (late 1960s+)

trash talk (or **talking**) *n phr* Provocative insults addressed by one athlete to others : *They learn about intimidation, bullying, bad call, trash talk, and that ends justify means/ Trash talking is littering the air at NBA stadiums* (1990s+ *Sports*)

trash talker *n phr* A person who does "trash talk" : *If Muhammad Ali was the first trash-talker in boxing, Floyd Patterson was the last gentleman* (1990s+ *Sports*)

trashy *adj* Despicable; inferior; LOW-RENT, LOW-RIDE (1620+)

traveler *See* FELLOW TRAVELER

trawler *n* CHANNEL SURFER, GRAZER (1990s+)

treat someone like a doormat (or ◁**like shit**▷) *v phr* To deal with in a humiliating, haughty, or oppressive manner : *We treated poor old Uncle Bob like a doormat/ and is also a fucking nitwit imbecile who treats me like shit and makes me talk about vultures* (1970s+)

tree *See* LIT UP, OUT OF one's TREE, UP A TREE

tree-hugger *n* An environmentalist; duck-squeezer : *TBS owner Ted Turner is a tree-hugger from way back* [late 1980s+; said to have been used of Celia Harbeck, a Chicago woman who actually hugged trees in Jackson Park to prevent their being cut down]

Trekkie or **Trekker** *n* A devotee of the television science-fiction series *Star Trek* : *Star Trek II. The Wrath of Khan. Come, all ye Trekkers/ Trekkies hate being called Trekkers. They call themselves "Trekkers"* (1976+)

trenches *See* IN THE TRENCHES

trendy *adj* (also **trendacious** or **trendoid**) Following new trends in fashion, art, literature, etc; anxiously au courant : *Fetch a tumbril for these fellows, or at least a trendy tailor/ A trendacious couple wear head-to-toe charcoal black/ Your trendoid older sister gives you all her hand-me-downs on the 5th* (1962+) *n* (also **trendoid**) : *That will undoubtedly have great appeal to all you trendies out there/ and even a few tough trendoids from the East Village and Soho* (1968+)

trial balloon *n* A test of how someone will react : *set up a trial balloon and got the expected outcome*

tribe *n* One's group of friends or relatives : *dreading the tribe coming for New Year's*

trick *n* 1 A prostitute's client or sexual transaction : *woman walking the streets for tricks to take to her room* (1915+) 2 A casual homosexual partner; NUMBER *(1970s+ Homosexuals)* 3 A shift or duty period : *She doesn't require any breaks at her eight-hour trick* (1669+ *Nautical*) *v* 1 To serve a customer : *She had tricked a john from Macon* (1965+ *Prostitutes*) 2 (also **trick out**) To do the sex act, either hetero- or homosexually; FUCK : *They can go "tricking out" with other gay people* (1970s+) *See* HAT TRICK, LOBSTER SHIFT, TURN A TRICK

trickledown *modifier* : *The planners counted on a trickledown effect when they relieved the rich of all taxation n* The stimulation of a whole economic system by the enrichment and encouragement of those in the upper reaches (1944+)

trick out *v phr* To ornament or adorn, often garishly • Also **tricked-out** as an adjective : *He tricked out his ride*

tricks *See* DIRTY TRICKS, GO DOWN AND DO TRICKS, HOW'S TRICKS

trigger *n* A gunman; HIT MAN, TRIGGER MAN : *He's a trigger* (1935+ *Underworld*) *v* 1 To commit a robbery : *Police said Sims has triggered dozens of holdups* (1950s+) 2 To initiate something; provoke something : *My innocent remark triggered a strange reaction* (1938+) *See* QUICK ON THE DRAW

trigger-happy *adj* Irresponsible in the use of firearms; eager to fire a gun

trigger man *n phr* A gunman; HIT MAN, TRIGGER *(1920s+ Underworld)*

trim *n* 1 A woman, esp one regarded as an object of sexual conquest (1955+) ◁2▷ The sex act with a woman; ASS, CUNT, gash : *Uou looking for some trim* (1960s+) *v* To defeat utterly; trounce; CLOBBER : *They got trimmed 8–zip* (1950s+)

trip[1] *n* An arrest; a prison sentence; FALL [1920s+ *Underworld*; fr *trip*, "stumble, fall"]

trip[2] *n* 1 A psychedelic narcotics experience : *users like beat poet Allen Ginsberg (30 trips)* (1959+ *Narcotics*) 2 Any experience com-

parable with a psychedelic experience : *The park is an icon. A nostalgia trip back into a youth/ I've known Chuck for many years and he's a trip. He's fun to be around* (1966+) 3 A truly amazing person or thing : *She's such a trip v* 1 (also **trip out**) To have a psychedelic narcotics experience or comparable experience : *That film really tripped me out* (1959+ *Narcotics*) 2 To act stupidly : *He was trippin' at the party/ If you're crazy, east side teens may say you're "trippin'," "postal," or "gerpin'"* (1980s+ *Teenagers*) *See* BAD TRIP, EGO TRIP, HEAD TRIP, LAY A TRIP ON someone, POWER TRIP

tripe *n* Contemptible material; nonsense, worthless stuff; CRAP, JUNK : *What the hell do they have to give us that tripe for?/ anyone who could make money on "such tripe"* [1895+; fr *tripe*, "animal stomach used as food," because it is held in low regard]

triple whammy *n phr* A three-part attack, difficulty, threat, etc : *Triple Whammy on the Farm* (1940s+)

tripped out *adj phr* Having or symptomatic of a psychedelic narcotics experience : *a tripped-out laughing jag* (1960s+ *Narcotics*)

tripper *n* 1 An excursionist; a tourist : *the tripper class* (1813+) 2 A person who takes psychedelic narcotics (1960s+ *Narcotics*) *See* ROUND-TRIPPER

trippy *adj* 1 Intoxicated with narcotics; dazed; SPACED-OUT, STONED : *allowing the band to be tagged as a "trippy" band* 2 Bizarre; phantasmal; surreal : *a trippy fantasy, the Harvard University Press version of Instant Wingo* (1960s+ *Narcotics*)

troll[1] *n* A stupid person; a dullard [1970s+ *Army*; probably fr the dwarf or demon of Norse mythology]

troll[2] *v* 1 To go about looking for sexual encounters; CRUISE : *Women who are out trolling bars do not deserve the protection of the law* (1967+) 2 To seek respondents on the Internet; SURF : *The firm was trolling for green card applicants in need of legal help* (1990s+ *Computers*) [fr the action of fishing by trolling]

trophy child *n* A child whose accomplishments or other attributes are used by the parents to impress others : *The star athlete became the trophy child for the stepfather*

trophy wife (or **husband**) *n phr* A mate, often a younger person, chosen for decorative and prestige value : *Apparently the Senator and she have a private vision that might make him as much a trophy husband as she a trophy wife* [1984+; said to have been coined by Julie Connelly of *Fortune*]

trot out *v phr* To produce and display for admiration : *Oh Lord, he's trotting out his war record again* (1845+)

trots, the *n phr* Diarrhea; the SHITS (*1904+*)

trouble *See* DOUBLE-TROUBLE, DROWN one's SOR-ROWS

trough *See* GREASE TROUGH

truck *v* **1** To carry; haul; lug : *Why are you trucking all that weight around?* (*1681+*) **2** To leave; go along (*1925+ Jazz musicians*) **3** To dance the jitterbug; esp, to do a jitterbug dance called "Truckin" (*1930s+ Jive talk*) *See* MACK TRUCK

trucking *See* KEEP ON TRUCKING

trumped up *adj phr* **1** False; concocted; fabricated; PHONY : *The indictment was trumped up for revenge* (*1728+*) **2** Heavily promoted or overly praised : *backfired that it was trumped up*

try *See* the OLD COLLEGE TRY

try it on for size *v phr* To accept or attempt something tentatively : *Let's try this scenario on for size and see if it binds in the crotch* (*1956+*)

tsk-tsk *v* To use a mildly deprecating tone : *Editorial writers have been tsk-tsking over the fact that there are fewer and fewer union members* (*1967+*)

tsuris or **tsoris** or **tzuris** (TSOOR əs, TSAWR əs) *n* Troubles; tribulations; anxieties; sufferings : *if Samuels, with all his tsuris, wins the Democratic nomination/ There is a tsoris, which is a kind of trouble spot/ during a long streak of tzuris* [*1960s+*; fr Yiddish fr Hebrew *tsarah*, "trouble"]

tubby or **tubbo** *n* A fat person : *the ex-tubbies trying to live on lettuce leaves/ Hey, you're kind of a tubbo, ain't you?* (*entry form 1891+, variant 1980s+*)

tube, the *n phr* **1** Television, as an industry, a medium, a television set, etc : *making a name for herself as a singer on the tube/ not a chance, unless you were back at the hotel watching on the tube* (*1959+*) **2** A police shotgun (*1990s+ Los Angeles police*) **3** The inner curve of a big wave **4** A can of beer [first sense a shortening of *cathode ray tube* or *picture tube*] *See* the BOOB TUBE, DOWN THE TUBE

tube steak *n phr* **1** A frankfurter; HOT DOG (*1963+*) ◁2▷ (also **tubesteak of love**) The penis; WEENIE (*1980s+*)

tub of guts (or **lard**) *n phr* A fat person, esp a repulsive one : *that tub-o'-guts* (*1940+*)

tubular *adj* Wonderful; excellent; AWESOME, GREAT [*1970s+ Teenagers*; fr surfing term describing a wave like a *tube,* that is, a cylindrical space around which the crest is curling as the wave breaks, and inside which the surfer happily rides]

tuchis or **tuckus** *See* TOKUS

tuck *See* NIP AND TUCK

tucker *See* BEST BIB AND TUCKER

tuckered (out) *adj* Tired (*1840s+*)

'tude *n* Attitude; view of things; typical reaction • Usually negative, sour, or surly [*1970s+ Teenagers* fr black; fr *attitude*]

tuff *See* TOUGH

tumble *n* A response indicating interest, affection, etc *v* To be arrested; FALL, TRIP (*1901+ Underworld*) *See* GIVE someone A TUMBLE

◁**tuna** or **tuna fish**▷ *n* or *n phr* **1** The vulva; CUNT **2** A woman; a female [*1970s+ Black*; fr the similarity, recognized esp in black slang, between the odor of the vulva and that of fish or other seafood; perhaps somehow influenced by *Tiny Tuna*, homosexual slang for a sailor as a sex object]

tune *See* FINE-TUNE, LOONY-TUNE, TO THE TUNE OF

tuned *past part* Possessed or practiced upon sexually; be had [*1970s+ Canadian teenagers*; perhaps related to earlier British and Australian *tune*, "beat, hit," hence semantically to *bang*]

tune in *v phr* To become aware, au courant, involved, etc : *Tune in, turn on, drop out* (*1960s+ Counterculture*)

tune out *v phr* To cease being aware, au courant, etc; the opposite of "tune in" (*1960s+ Counterculture*)

tunes *n* Music, esp popular : *new tunes on my iPod*

tune up *v phr* To bring something, esp a car motor, to its best state of effectiveness; tinker with to improve : *tuning up for the race at Santa Ana* [*1901+*; fr the process of *tuning* a musical instrument, suggested by the fact that the performance of motors can be gauged by their sound]

tunnel vision *n phr* Very narrow and restricted vision or perception; the inability to see anything except what is directly in front (*1949+*)

T someone **up** *v phr* To call the maximum permissible number of technical fouls : *He had already T'd Barkley up for a technical foul. Now he did the same for Oakley, and summarily threw him out of the arena* (*1990s+ Basketball*)

◁**turd**▷ *n* **1** A piece of excrement (*1000+*) **2** A despicable person; PRICK, SHIT (*1518+*)

◁**turd face**▷ *n phr* A thoroughly despised person; creep; TURD

◁**turd in the punchbowl**▷ *See* GO OVER LIKE A LEAD BALLOON

turf *n* **1** The sidewalk; the street (*1930s+ Jive talk*) **2** The territory claimed or controlled by a street gang : *I tried to imagine my Deacons pacing the turf or talking about me* (*1953+ Street gang*) **3** A particular specialized concern; THING : *Counterterrorism is not their exclusive turf/ I never thought of myself as* *pretty, that was my sister's turf* (1970+) *v* To transfer a patient to another ward or service in order to evade responsibility, decisions, irritations, etc *(1970s+ Medical)* [*turf,* "the road," in the first sense is found in hobo use by 1899]

turf (or **track**), the *n phr* The work and venue of a prostitute; the street : *During early years "on the turf," as the saying went, she was thrifty and ambitious/ I didn't want to lose her, now that she was ready for the track* [1860+; fr an analogy between the prostitute's work and that of a racehorse]

turf war (or **battle**) *n phr* A contention over the rights to a certain activity, location, etc : *We get eye-glazing accounts of turf wars between the Council on Economic Policy and the Commission on International Trade and Economic Policy/ Faget suspected a turf battle for control of the Mercury program* (1950s+)

turista *n* Diarrhea; AZTEC TWO-STEP, MONTEZUMA'S REVENGE [1970+; fr Spanish, "tourist"]

turk *See* YOUNG TURK

turkey *n* **1** An inferior show, esp a failure; BOMB, FLOP : *Management prudently kept the turkey out of town* (1927+ *Show business*) **2** Anything inferior, stupid, or futile; LEMON, LOSER : *For all ordinary purposes it was simply a turkey/ calling the bill a turkey, said it would send the wrong signal* (1941+) **3** A stupid, ineffectual person; JERK : *You'd be stuck with that turkey practically until he died* (1951+) **4** The victim of a mugging or street robbery : *On an average night, they attacked eight victims or "turkeys," taking a total of about $300* (1970s+ *Underworld & teenagers*) **5** Three consecutive strikes (1940s+ *Bowling*) [fr the common and perhaps accurate perception of the *turkey* as a stupid creature, an avian loser; the bowling sense is exceptional] *See* FULL OF SHIT, TALK TURKEY

turkey-shoot *n phr* Something very easy; CINCH, PIECE OF CAKE : *Getting a job is no turkey-shoot anymore* [1970s+; fr the marksman-ship contests where *turkeys* are tied behind a log with their heads showing as targets]

turn someone *v* To cause a suspect to change his testimony and implicate others : *We tried to turn Rowe, but he was too scared. He said he'd do life before he'd hand up his associates* (1980s+ *Police*) *See* TALK OUT OF TURN

turn someone **around** *v phr* To change someone's attitude, behavior, etc : *You fuck it up, that's turning me around* (1970s+)

turn a trick *v phr* To do the sex act for profit; do one piece of work as a prostitute; TRICK : *Many of the prostitutes were students, models, or would-be actresses who turned tricks part-time* (1946+)

turned off *adj phr* **1** No longer using narcotics; CLEAN *(1960s+ Narcotics)* **2** Indifferent; bored (1960s+) **3** Tired; FED UP (1960s+)

turned on *adj phr* **1** Intoxicated, esp from narcotics; HIGH : *I'm really turned on, man. I'm higher than a giraffe's toupee* (1950s+ *Narcotics*) **2** Stimulated; aroused; excited; switched on : *You are so sexualized, and so turned on* (1960s+) **3** Aware and up-to-date; au courant; HIP, PLUGGED IN : *flower children who flock to New York's turned-on Macdougal Street/ an outlaw lobbyist, a turned-on Nader* (1960s+)

turner *See* PAGE TURNER

turn in *v phr* To go to bed; HIT THE SACK (1833+)

turn (or **knock**) someone's **lights out** *v phr* To punish someone severely; incapacitate someone : *Man, if I sued every guy who ever turned my lights out, I wouldn't have time to do anything else/ It looked like we started out with a bang, but then the kid turned our lights out* (1980s+)

turn-off *n* Something that damps one's spirits; a sexual or emotional depressant; WET BLANKET : *The film is in fact a sexual turnoff* (1975+)

turn off *v phr* To become indifferent; lose concern : *When he found he couldn't hack it, he just turned off* (1970s+)

turn someone **off** *v phr* To depress someone; be a deterrent to someone's spirits : *It seems like everybody turns you off/ Policies and practices that are not "relevant," to use his language, "turn him off"* (1950s+ *Beat talk*)

turn off someone's **water** *See* CUT OFF someone's WATER

turn-on *n* **1** Something that arouses and excites; a sexual or emotional stimulant : *which physical attributes of men are a turn-on for women/ Reluctance is often a turn-on* **2** Excitement; ecstasy; elation : *He'd never felt a turn-on like that* (1960s+)

turn on *v phr* **1** To use narcotics, esp to begin to do so : *Tune in, turn on, drop out* **2** To take or inject narcotics : *Do you turn on with any of the local heads?* (1960s+ *Counterculture & narcotics*)

turn someone **on** *v phr* **1** To excite or stimu-late someone; arouse someone : *The professor was trying to find out what turns women on* (1903+) **2** To introduce someone to some-thing; pique someone's curiosity : *He turned me on to Zen* (1960s+)

turn on a dime *v phr* To be able to turn around in a very short radius : *That car corners very sweetly, and turns on a dime* (1970s+)

turn on the waterworks *v phr* To weep; begin to cry; BLUBBER : *I turned on the waterworks* (1885+)

turnout *n* **1** An audience, the participants at a meeting, etc : *We always get a good turnout for the council sessions* (*1816+*) **2** Clothing; dress; GET-UP, TOGS (*1859+*) **3** A heterosexual man who turns homosexual : *A Navy turnout is one who went in heterosexual but came out dreaming of pecker* (*1970s+ Homosexuals*)

turn someone **out** *v phr* To introduce someone to something; initiate someone, esp to narcotics, sex, prostitution, etc : *He takes a "square broad" (a nonprostitute) and "turns her out"* (*1970s+*)

turnover *n* The eve of one's release from prison : *He told me next Sunday was his turnover and I should meet him at the gate* (*1934+ Prison*)

turn something or someone **over** *v phr* To ransack or rifle, esp to steal : *turned over the tavern after closing* (*1859+*)

turn tail (and run) *v phr* To run away in fear : *turned tail at the first sign of trouble*

turn turtle *v phr* To turn upside down; capsize : *in the heavier puffs, they thought she would turn turtle* [*1860+*; fr earlier *turn the turtle*, found by 1818, referring to making a turtle helpless by turning it on its back]

turn someone **up** *v phr* To inform; in effect, to turn someone over to the police; HAND UP : *Maybe you better turn me up/ Somebody turned him up* (*1872+ Underworld*)

turn up one's **nose** *v phr* To regard or treat with contempt : *turned up his nose at the new recipe* (*1818+*)

turn up one's **toes** *v phr* To die (*1950s+*)

turtle *See* TURN TURTLE

turtleneck *n* The foreskin of the penis • Euphemistic : *may get rid of the turtleneck*

tush or **tushie** or **tushy** *See* TOKUS

tux *n* A tuxedo (*1922+*)

twaddle *n* Idle talk; blathering (*1782+*)

◁**twat**▷ (TWAHT) *n* **1** The vulva; CUNT. **2** A woman considered merely as a sex object or organ; ASS, PIECE OF ASS (*1656+*)

tweenager *n* A preteenager, generally aged 10–12; also, a youth who has just become a teenager [*1949+*; blend of *(be)tween* and *(teen)ager*]

twenty-five *n* LSD [*1960s+* Narcotics; fr the fact that *25* is part of its chemical designation]

twenty-four seven or **24/7** or **24-7** *adv phr* Twenty-four hours a day seven days a week; always : *they founded 24-7: Notes from the Inside. (The title, if you have been living under a rock, refers to being locked up 24 hours a day, 7 days a week)/ If I could I would stay on vacation twenty-four-seven* [late 1980s+; said to have been initiated by street gangs selling crack cocaine, available always]

twentysomething *See* GEN-X

twenty-twenty (or **20-20**) **hindsight** *n phr* Perfect foresight of what has already been seen : *observers empowered with 20-20 hindsight wanted to know* (*1962+*)

twerp or **twirp** *n* A contemptible person; JERK, NERD : *ill-mannered, foul-mouthed little twirp/ Wrangel may have been a pretentious twerp* [*1874+*; origin uncertain]

twiddle one's **thumbs** *v phr* To waste time; be forced to sit idly and perhaps rotate one's thumbs about one another : *I was anxious to help, but all I could do was twiddle my thumbs while they debated* (*1846+*)

twink or **twinkie** or **twinky** *adj* : *Quentin Crisp croaks in a nasal monotone like a twinkie Mr Magoo modifier* : *I found this gorgeous twink carpenter in the Mission n* **1** A young, sexually attractive person; tempting teenager : *You know, the twink who used to be Fielding's lover/ The Weemawee twinkies troop out to the kickoff line* **2** A weird or deviant person, esp a homosexual; a social outcast : *They think "twinky" or sissy or something like that/ Rafi comes on strong, but he's a twink at heart* [*1963+*; origin uncertain]

twist someone's **arm** *v phr* To induce or persuade someone very strongly; importune someone powerfully, as if by physical force : *You grab this opportunity to twist my arm* (*1940s+*)

twisted *adj* **1** Very much intoxicated with narcotics; HIGH : *twisted, so high he doesn't know where the hell he is* (*1960s+ Narcotics*) **2** Unusual; perverted : *My Twisted World of Convoluted Music*

twister *n* **1** A tornado (*1897+*) **2** A key (*1930s+* Jive talk) **3** A spree; BENDER : *their periods of sobriety between twisters* (*1940s+*) *See* BRONCO BUSTER

twist slowly (or **twist**) **in the wind** *v phr* To suffer protracted humiliation, obloquy, regret, etc : *The second mistake was to let Sherrill twist slowly in the wind/ just letting you twist slowly, slowly in the wind* [*1973+*; perhaps coined by John Ehrlichman, an aide of President Richard Nixon, fr the gruesome image of a hanging body]

twisty *adj* Attractively feminine; SEXY : *Most female doctors aren't as, uh, young. No, ah, say twisty might be more like it* (*1970s+*)

twit *n* A contemptible and insignificant person; a trivial idiot : *Craig Stevens as her twit of a husband/ I've got the authorization, you fucking twit* [*1934+*; origin unknown; rapidly adopted in the 1970s, perhaps because of the popularity of the British television series *Monty Python's Flying Circus*, on which the term was often employed]

two *See* NUMBER TWO, ONE-TWO

two-bagger *n* **1** A two-base hit; a double *(1880+ Baseball)* **2** A very ugly person; DOUBLE-BAGGER : *two-bagger, a girl who needs exactly that to cover her ugliness (1970s+)*

two-bit *adj* Cheap; tawdry; trivial; TACKY : *the two-bit bureaucrats/ Congressmen were panic-stricken, running around like two-bit whores* [1929+; literally, worth only *two bits*]

two bits *n phr* A quarter; twenty-five cents [1730+; fr the quarter part of a Mexican *real*, which had eight *bits*]

two cents *See* PUT one's TWO CENTS IN

two cents' worth *n phr* A little; a trivial amount : *I'll give you two cents' worth of advice about that (1942+)*

twofer (TOO fər) *n* **1** A cheap cigar *(1911+)* **2** A theater ticket sold at half the normal price *(1948+)* [fr the phrase *two for*, in these cases *two for a nickel* and *two for the price of one*]

two-fisted drinker *n* A heavy drinker

two hats *See* WEAR TWO HATS

two hoots *n* Anything at all : *don't give two hoots about them (1925+)*

two shakes or **two shakes of a lamb's tail** *n phr* A moment; a wink; a JIFFY : *Hold it, I'll just be two shakes* [1883+; by 1840 in the form *a couple of shakes*]

two-spot *n* A two-dollar bill *(1904+)*

two-step *See* AZTEC TWO-STEP

two-time *v* To deceive and betray someone; esp, to betray one's proper sweetheart by consorting with someone else : *Two-Timing Boy Wrecks Girl's Dream* [1924+; perhaps fr *two at a time*; perhaps fr *making time with two at once*]

two-time loser *n phr* **1** A person who has been convicted twice and therefore risks a higher sentence another time *(1931+ Underworld)* **2** A person who has been divorced twice : *Nora Ephron, funny two-time loser (1970s+)*

two-timer *n* A person who double-crosses or is unfaithful to another *(1927+)*

two-topper *n* A table for two in a restaurant : *only two-toppers at 5 p.m.*

two to tango *See* IT TAKES TWO TO TANGO

two ways *See* WORK BOTH WAYS

two-way street *n phr* A situation that cannot or should not be handled by only one person : *After all, Sam, keeping a marriage happy is a two-way street (1951+)*

tzuris *See* TSURIS

U

ugly *See* PLUG-UGLY

ugly as sin *adj phr* (Variations: **galvanized sin** or **catshit** may replace **sin**) Very ugly; extremely repellent (*entry form 1821+*)

uie or **u-ey** *n* A U-turn (*1976+*)

ultraswoopy *adj* Very fast : *a down-sized, hitech, ultraswoopy model next year* (*1970s+*)

umpteen *modifier* Of any large unspecified number : *exhausted all the encomia in your vocabulary on umpteen reviews* [fr WWI; said to have been first used by British military signalers during World War I to disguise the number designations of units]

umpteenth *modifier* The ordinal form of "umpteen" : *Here's the umpteenth development in the battle* (*fr WWI*)

uncle *n* **1** A pawnbroker (*1756+*) **2** A receiver of stolen goods; FENCE (*1924+ Underworld*) **3** A federal narcotics agent; NARC (*1920+ Underworld & narcotics*) [last sense fr *Uncle Sam*] *See* SAY UNCLE

Uncle Dudley *See* YOUR UNCLE DUDLEY

Uncle Sam *n phr* **1** The US government; the US as a nation (*1813+*) **2** A federal agent or agency; FED (*1940s+ Underworld*) [said to have originated during the War of 1812 when Samuel Wilson of Troy, New York, locally known as *Uncle Sam*, stamped US on supplies he provided for the government, and this was jocularly taken to be his own initials]

Uncle Tom *n phr* A black man who emulates or adopts the behavior of the white majority; a servile black man; AFRO-SAXON, OREO [1922+ Black; fr the title character of Harriet Beecher Stowe's novel *Uncle Tom's Cabin*, who was stigmatized as a dishonorably submissive black]

uncool *adj* Not cool; wrong, excited, rude, etc (*1953+ Cool talk*)

under *See* GET OUT FROM UNDER

under one's belt *adj phr* Successfully achieved or survived : *Get a couple more months' experience under your belt and we'll talk about a promotion* (*1954+*)

underground *adj* **1** Apart from and opposed to conventional society; esp, advocating and representing the hippie and narcotics subculture : *The Voice started as a sort of underground newspaper* (*1953+*) **2** In hiding; concealing one's identity and whereabouts, esp to escape arrest (*1820+*)

underground, the *n phr* Political or cultural dissenters collectively who lead a partly or wholly clandestine life and resist the dominant regime; also, their arena of life and operations [WWII & 1960s+ counterculture; term first applied to the various resistance movements against German occupation in World War II and then adopted by the 1960s counterculture, which saw the US government and culture as analogous with the Hitlerian]

under one's hat *adj phr* Secret; in confidence : *Here it is, but it's strictly under the hat, see?* (*1885+*)

under one's nose *adv phr* In plain sight, although unnoticed : *I'm afraid I may be missing something that's right under my nose* (*1548+*)

under one's own steam *modifier* Acting independently (*1912+*)

underpinnings *n* Legs (*1912+*)

under the collar *See* HOT UNDER THE COLLAR

under the gun *adj phr* In a position of danger; urgently called on to take action : *Under the economic gun* [1940s+; fr a poker term for the player called upon to open, bet, fold, raise, etc]

under the table *adj phr* **1** Very drunk (*1921+*) **2** : *What was the best under-the-table offer you got? adv phr* Illegal; secret and illicit; unethical : *He would never make any deals under the table* (*1940s+*)

under the weather *modifier* **1** Not feeling well; ill **2** Intoxicated with alcohol

under the wire *adv* Done just before deadline; at the last minute : *turned in under the wire*

under someone's thumb *adj phr* Entirely in someone's control : *Our boss likes to keep us under his thumb* (*1754+*)

under wraps *adv phr* In secrecy; in obscurity : *We had better keep this under wraps for a while* (*1939+*)

undies *n* Underwear, esp women's panties : *a glimpse of her undies* (*1906+*)

unflappable *adj* Calm; imperturbable; cool : *They admired Mrs Thatcher's unflappable mien* (*1958+*) *See* FLAP

◄**unfuckingbelieveable**► *adj* Unbelievable • A fairly common use of the "fucking" infix : *"Totally unfuckingbelieveable," said Duffy* (*1940s+*)

unglued *See* COME UNGLUED

ungodly *modifier* Horrendous; outrageous : *got in at an ungodly hour*

unisex *adj* Intended for or fitting for both sexes : *The unisex trend was launched by the era's pacesetters, the teenagers* (*1968+*)

unit *n* The penis

unleaded coffee *n phr* Decaffeinated coffee : *Feel like having a big decaffeinated espresso with* *lots of milk and no foam? In java jive, that's an unleaded grande latte without (1980s+)*

unmentionables *n* Underwear; undergarments : *required to don upper and lower unmentionables (1910+)*

uno *See* NUMERO UNO

unreal *adj* Excellent; wonderful; GREAT : *Like great. She's real unreal (1965+)*

unstuck *See* COME UNGLUED

until one is blue in the face *See* TILL one IS BLUE IN THE FACE

until kingdom come *adv* Forever (1898+)

until the cows come home *adv* Until a long time in the future (1610+)

up *adj* **1** Exhilarated; happy; sparkling; hopeful : *I was feeling up. I thought it had been a very successful evening (1815+)* **2** Encouraging; hopeful; UPBEAT : *I don't like down movies, I like up movies (1970s+)* **3** Ready and effective; keyed up; in one's best form : *Obviously, Kennedy wanted to be "up" for the meeting (1972+)* **4** Intoxicated by narcotics, esp amphetamines; HIGH : *as it does when you're up on bennie (1960s+ Narcotics)* **5** (also **up and rolling** or **up and running**) Functioning; in operation; active : *English-only a is a phony issue raised only to get folks' bile up and running in time for the presidential race (1980s+ Computer)* *n* **1** A source of excitement; a pleasurable thrill; LIFT : *Her words gave me a huge up (1966+)* **2** An amphetamine dose, capsule, etc; UPPER : *Let's do some ups tonight (1960s+ Narcotics)* *v* To raise; increase : *My confidence has upped itself (1925+)* [first adjective sense is based on *up*, "effervescent, bubbling," used of beer and other drinks; later similar uses, from the 1940s, are based on the "high" produced by narcotics]

up against it *adj phr* In a difficult situation; in serious trouble : *When they saw the gap they knew they were really up against it (1896+)*

up against the wall *sentence* Prepare to be humiliated, attacked, robbed, despised, etc; GO FUCK oneself : *our commune motto, "Up against the wall, motherfuckers"/ Up against the wall, IBM and General Electric and Xerox and Procter & Gamble and American Express* [1960s+ Counterculture; fr a line in a poem by LeRoi Jones (Amiri Baraka), "Up against the wall, motherfuckers," fr the command of a holdup man to his victim, or of the police to a person being arrested, forcing him to immobilize himself by leaning forward arched with hands against a wall; probably influenced by the fact that people are executed by being shot against a wall]

up someone's alley *See* DOWN someone's ALLEY

up-and-coming *adj* Promising and energetic : *I gathered a few up-and-coming young writers for my staff (1848+)*

up-and-down *n* A close look; scrutiny : *The tray-toter gave me the slow up-and-down* [1924+; found by 1820 in Byron's *Don Juan*, "a survey up and down"]

up and up or **on the up and up** *adj phr* Honest; reliable; STRAIGHT-UP : *It's an up and up place/ I almost wonder if the whole bunch of 'em are on the up and up (1863+)*

◁**up** one's **ass**▷ *See* SIT THERE WITH one's FINGER UP one's ASS, STICK IT

up a storm *adv phr* Very intensively; very diligently; very competently : *and they're really dancing up a storm (1953+)*

up a tree *adj phr* In a predicament; faced with a dilemma; helpless (1825+)

upbeat *adj* Optimistic; encouraging; positive : *They use catchy, upbeat phrases/ A triumph of upbeat pictures over the downbeat* [1947+; apparently fr the musical term *upbeat*, "a beat on which a conductor raises his baton," but since such beats have no emotional connotations, the coiner must have seized on the general positive notion of *up* and taken *beat* to mean "stroke, movement"]

upchuck *v* To vomit; throw up; BARF, RALPH : *It is enough to make one upchuck* [1925+; fr *up* plus *chuck*, "throw"]

up for *modifier* Ready to participate; eager to do : *up for Chinese food*

up for grabs *adj phr* **1** Available, esp newly available : *"High Haven," Luke repeated sonorously, "is up for grabs"/ I got two doozies up for grabs* **2** Problematical or undecided, esp newly so : *The whole question of one-man-one-vote is up for grabs again (1940s+)*

up front *adj phr* **1** From the beginning; first; at once : *we knew right up front that if I did the film, I'd be rich (1980+)* **2** Honest; open; truthful : *very up-front about who she is and what she thinks/ "These people are not being up-front and honest," the Mayor said (1972+)* *adv phr* (also **in front**) In advance; before any deductions : *His twin wasn't getting enough cash (something like $1,000) up front/ Don't pay your money up front (1972+)*

up in the air *adj phr* Unsettled; undecided; uncertain : *When he left, the whole project was up in the air for a while (1933+)*

upmanship *See* ONE-UPMANSHIP

upmarket *adj* Appealing to or created for wealthy people : *a daily newspaper which would make even the Sun look up-market (1972+)*

upper or **uppie** *n* **1** An amphetamine; a stimulant narcotic; : *the effect of mixing "uppers" and "downers" (1960s+ Narcotics)* **2** A source of excitement; a pleasurable thrill; UP : *It may not be the same kind of thrill as winning a hand of poker at a casino, but it's definitely an upper (1973+) See* PEPPER-UPPER, PICKER-UPPER

upper crust (or **drawer**), the *adj phr* (also **upper-drawer**): *His manners were silkily upper-crust/ the upper-drawer voters n phr* The social aristocracy; the elite (*1835+*) *See* ON one's UPPERS, SHATTING ON one's UPPERS

upper story *n phr* The brain; the mind : *definite shortcomings in the upper story (1699+)*

uppity *adj* Conceited; arrogant; snobbish; HINCTY : *the most uppity colored fellow I ever ran into in my life/ to estimate if this reporter was going to give her any sass or put on any uppity airs (1880+ Black)*

◁**up shit** (or **shit's**) **creek**▷ or **up the creek** *adj phr* (Variation: **without a paddle** may be added) In serious difficulty; very unfortunate; ruined : *Then you guys'll be up the creek for good* [entry form 1937+, perhaps related to the early 1800s term *up Salt River*, of much the same meaning, and which may refer to the Salt River in Kentucky, a legendary abode of violent and brutal people; but the term is attested in British armed forces use without US attribution fr the early 1900s]

upside or **upside of** *prep* On the side of; in : *He got whacked upside the head with a board (1970+ Black)*

upside, the *n phr* The hopeful aspect; the good news : *The upside is that she's still conscious* [1980s+; both *upside* and *downside* originally referred to the fluctuations of the stock market]

upside one's **face** *See* GO UPSIDE one's FACE

up one's **sleeve** *See* ACE UP one's SLEEVE

up-South *n* The North, esp with respect to its racism (*1970s+ Black*)

upstage *adj* Haughty; aloof; snobbish : *"Upstage" has taken on the additional meaning of "ritzy," that is, arrogantly proud and vain (1918+)* *v* **1** To attract attention to oneself and away from other performers, esp by standing upstage so that they must look at you and turn their backs to the audience (*1933+ Theater*) **2** To demand and receive inordinate attention at the cost of others : *The secretary was trying to upstage the president on this, so he had to act at once (1921+)*

upstairs *adv* In the brain; mentally : *became a little balmy upstairs (1932+)* *See* KICK someone UPSTAIRS, THE MAN UPSTAIRS

upstate *modifier* In prison • Euphemistic [*1934+*; fr the placement of prisons in remote areas far from large cities]

uptake *See* QUICK ON THE DRAW, SLOW ON THE DRAW

up the ante *v phr* To raise the price, offer, sum in question, etc; increase; make a higher demand : *I think I may up the ante to a cool fifty/ The trader decides to up the ante* [1970s+; fr the *ante* in poker, which gives one the right to take part]

◁**up the ass**▷ *adv phr* **1** Thoroughly; perfectly well : *I know country music up the ass on the guitar* **2** (Variations: **butt** or **kazoo** or **gazoo** or **gazool** may replace **ass**) To a very great extent; in excess; UP TO HERE : *They want vision? Vision up the kazoo!/ Bob Gottlieb has class up the gazoo/ I've got lawsuits up the gazool, which is one thing that disillusions me about writing (1971+) See* KAZOO

up the flagpole *See* RUN something UP THE FLAGPOLE

up the river *adv phr* In prison [*1924+*; fr the fact that Ossining Correctional Facility, formerly called Sing Sing, is *up the Hudson River* from New York City; from 1891 the term referred only to Sing Sing] *See* SEND UP

up the wall *adj phr* Crazy; wild; NUTTY : *It doesn't drive us crazy. At least, I don't know anybody who is up the wall about it* [*1951+*; fr the image of insane persons, frantic and deprived drug addicts, wild animals, etc, trying to climb a wall to escape] *See* DRIVE someone UP THE WALL

uptick *n* **1** A rise, esp in stock prices; an increase of value : *the strongest and broadest uptick in the history of the company/ Another 10 percent uptick and you double up again* **2** Improvement; raising : *His apparent uptick in spirit was contagious* [*1970+*; fr the use, on boards above stock-market stations, of a plus sign (compare British *tick*, "check mark") beside a stock of which the last sale represented a rise in price; a minus sign represents a *down tick*; probably influenced by the *tick*, like *click*, or *notch*, representing one degree of change; compare *ratchet up*]

uptight *adj* **1** Tense; anxious : *He was all uptight about student plagiarism (1934+)* **2** Excellent; COOL, GREAT (*1962+*)

up to one's **ass** *See* one HAS HAD IT

◁**up to** one's **ass** (or **neck**) in something▷ *adj phr* (Variations: **in alligators** or **in rattlesnakes** may be added for emphasis) Deeply involved; overwhelmed : *Every time I turn around we're up to our asses in something/ You're up to your ass in alligators, get a bigger alligator/ We're going to be up to our necks in soccer (1940s+)*

up to one's **eyeballs** (or **eyebrows**) *adv phr* To a very great extent; totally; UP TO HERE : *one smaller outfit which is in farm equipment smack up to its corporate eyeballs (1940s+) See* one HAS HAD IT

up to here *adj phr* Surfeited; disgusted; FED UP : *I'm so up-to-here with the primaries and the TV news interviews adv phr* To the utmost; excessively; in great quantity : *Look, my friend, I've had it up to here with your bitching*

[1940s+; fr the notion of being fed to excess, fed up, and with the implicit gesture of indicating one's throat as the place up to which one has had it] *See* one HAS HAD IT

up to par *modifier* Average; standard : *pizza up to par for the area (1899+)*

up to scratch (or **the mark**) *adj phr* Satisfactory; acceptable; qualified : *I'm afraid this story isn't quite up to scratch* [1911+; fr the early custom of drawing a line across a boxing ring and requiring that the able and willing fighter stand with his toe touching the *mark* or *scratch-line*]

up to snuff *adj phr* 1 Satisfactory; acceptable; UP TO SCRATCH : *His work doesn't come anywhere near up to snuff* 2 In good health; feeling well : *I don't feel quite up to snuff this morning* [1811+; origin uncertain; the original British sense was "shrewd, not gullible," apparently referring to the fact that one could be blinded with *snuff* in the eyes and victimized; the early 1800s US phrases *in high* (or *great*) *snuff,* "in good form, high fettle, etc," perhaps having to do with *snuff* as an aristocratic commodity and symbol, may also be related]

up to speed *adj phr* Informed; au courant; aware of the situation : *Ballard was up to speed now (1980s+) See* BRING someone UP TO SPEED

up to the wire *See* COME UP TO THE WIRE

uptown *n* Cocaine; the lady [1960s+ Narcotics; fr the aristocratic and wealthy overtones of cocaine as compared with other narcotics, fr the earlier sense of *uptown,*

"affluent, swanky," as distinct fr *downtown;* the topography and demography of Manhattan Island underlie these senses] *See* the BOYS UPTOWN

◁**up yours**▷ *interj* (Variations: **you** or **your ass** or **your butt** or **your gig** or **your giggy** or any other synonym of **ass** may replace **yours**) An exclamation of strong defiance, contempt, rejection, etc : *Up yours, sister, he thought tardily as the barbs quivered home* [1950s+; a shortening of *stick it up your ass*]

use *v* To use narcotics; take a dose or injection of a narcotic : *I used this morning and I'm still nice (1950s+ Narcotics)*

use one's **head** (or one's **bean**) *v phr* To think; reason out one's actions : *teaches a man to use his head and to do the best he can/ You certainly used the old bean (1828+)*

user *n* A person who uses narcotics, esp an addict *(1950s+ Narcotics)*

usual *See* AS PER USUAL

usual suspects, the *n phr* The persons one would expect : *The amusing Rossini concert was well executed by the usual suspects (Hampson, Marilyn Horne, Samuel Ramey, June Anderson)/ We are given new perspectives on those who are the usual suspects in any consideration of modern lesbian writing: Willa Cather, Virginia Woolf, H.D. and Djuna Barnes* [1943+; fr an order given by Claude Rains as the French police official in the 1943 movie *Casablanca*]

UVs *n* Ultraviolet rays; sunshine : *catch some UVs on the deck*

V

vac *n* A vacuum cleaner : *Bring a vac to clean up the apartment* *v* To use a vacuum cleaner : *vac the apartment*

vamoose or **vamose** (va MOOS) *v* To leave; depart, esp hastily; LAM, SCRAM, SPLIT : *We better vamoose, Moose* [1834+; fr Spanish *vamos*, "let us depart"]

vamp[1] *v* To improvise, esp an accompaniment; play casually and extemporaneously; fake. SHUCK [1789+ Musicians; probably fr 1500s *vamp*, "provide with a new (shoe) vamp, renovate," ultimately fr conjectured Anglo-French *vampé* fr Old French *avant-pié*, "foot-sock"; a refooted sock or a *revamped* shoe were felt to be in a way false, or improvised, hence the sense of "fake"]

vamp[2] *n* A seductive, sexually aggressive woman; a temptress : *The flirt had become the "baby vamp"* (1911+) *v* : *I haven't tried to vamp Sam* (1904+) [fr *vampire*, and esp fr the 1914 movie *A Fool There Was*, in which Theda Bara played a seductive woman, the title and concept coming fr Rudyard Kipling's poem "The Vampire"]

vamp[3] or **vamp on** *v* or *v phr* 1 To assault; trounce; BEAT someone UP, CLOBBER : *They knew that he'd vamp on them if they got wrong/ Chairman, chairman wake up, the Pigs are vampin'* 2 To arrest; BUST [1970s+ Black; perhaps related to black English *vamp* someone, "come at someone suddenly and aggressively"; perhaps fr *vamp*[2] reinforced by the murderous aggression of Count Dracula, a genuine and popular *vampire* in Bram Stoker's novel and the movies made from it]

vanilla *adj* 1 Conventional; usual; bland; WHITE BREADY (1970s+) 2 : *As a self-confessed vanilla-sexual* (1970s+) 3 PLAIN VANILLA (1970s+) *n* 1 A white person, esp a white woman (1970s+ Black) 2 A person of ordinary sexual preferences; a usual heterosexual; STRAIGHT : *They called women who did not proclaim joy at being chained to the bedposts or chaining someone else "vanilla"* (1970s+) [fr the white color and the perhaps unimaginative choice of *vanilla* ice cream]

varoom *See* VROOM

Vatican roulette *n phr* The rhythm method of birth control (1962+)

va-voom or **va-va-voom** *adj* (also **voomy**) : *pressing the tits of this va-va-voom sophomore and shtupping her pussy/ Under that icky mask, I think you're the voomiest* *interj* An exclamation of delight, esp of excited sexual interest [1960s+; probably fr *vroom* and *varoom*]

V-ball *n* Volleyball : *intramural V-ball*

VC *n* The Vietcong or a member of the Vietcong; victor charlie [Vietnam War armed forces; fr *Vietcong*]

veejay or **VJ** *n* A person who presents a program of music videos, esp on television [1982+; fr the pronunciation of the initial letters of *video jockey*, after *DJ* (disc jockey)]

veeno *See* VINO

veep *n* A vice president : *Veep Fresco Thomas, Coach Jake Pitler, and Dressen* [1949+; fr pronunciation of *vp*]

veg[1] (VEJ) *n* 1 A vegetable (1918+) 2 A person lacking normal senses, responses, intelligence, etc. (1970s+)

veg[2] (VEJ) *v* (also **vedge** or **veg out**) To relax luxuriously and do nothing; vegetate; GOOF OFF, MELLOW OUT : *I'm going to vanish up to someplace beautiful and just veg for two solid days/ when you could escape from the world by vegging out in front of the tube* [1980s+ College students; fr *vegetate*]

vegetable *n* A person lacking normal senses, responses, intelligence, etc; BASKET CASE, GOMER, GORK, RETARD : *He was fine the first couple of years of marriage, but then he turned into a vegetable*

veggie *modifier* : *a veggie pal of ours* *n* 1 A vegetarian (1975+) 2 A person who relaxes and does nothing : *When I finish this paper, I'm just going to be a veggie* (1980s+ College)

veggies or **vegies** *n* Vegetables (1955+)

velvet *n* Profit, esp an easy and unexpected profit; gambler's winnings; money in general : *There are substantial money returns, "velvet," for those who secure places* (1901+)

vent *v* (also **ventilate**) To relieve one's feelings by vehement expression; LET IT ALL HANG OUT : *Last year the critics vented madly about all the great shows the networks killed/ Alvin ventilated, complaining about the prosecutors, his business partners, the intolerance of his wife* (1990s+)

ventilate *v* To shoot; PLUG [1875+; fr the notion of letting air into someone]

verbal (or oral) diarrhea *n phr* (also **diarrhea of the mouth**) Logorrhea; uncontrollable loquaciousness : *You've got verbal diarrhea* (1940s+)

verse *See* CHAPTER AND VERSE

vet[1] *modifier* : *the vet producer of scouting plays* *n* A veteran, esp a former member of the armed forces : *I'm a combat vet* (1869+)

vet[2] *modifier* Veterinary : *the vet school* *n* A veterinarian (1862+) *v* To examine closely; scrutinize critically : *Random House plans a* review of its procedures for "vetting" or checking a book prior to publication/ The hosts are a carefully vetted collection of bubble brains (1904+) [verb sense fr the close examination of an animal by a *veterinarian*]

vette or **'vette** *n* A Corvette® car (1960s+)

vibes[1] *n* A vibraphone or vibraharp *(1937+ Jazz musicians)*

vibes[2] or **vibrations** *n* What emanates from or inheres in a person, situation, place, etc, and is sensed; CHEMISTRY, Karma : *The vibes were good that morning for our reunion* (1967+)

vicious *adj* Excellent; superb; wonderfully attractive *(1970s+ Teenagers)*

vidiot *n* A person addicted to television; vidaholic : *Daytime? That's when you give America's vidiots pure junk food* (1980s+)

vidkid *n* : *Even preadolescent vidkids fused like Krazy Glue to their Super Nintendo and Sega Genesis games, the training wheels of cyberpunk* (1990s+)

vig or **vigorish** or **viggerish** *n* Profits of a bookmaker, a usurer, a criminal conspirator, a casino, etc : *I'm not nailing you no vig for last week/ About 180 percent a year in interest, known in the trade as vigorish, vig, or juice* [1908+ fr gambling; probably fr Yiddish fr Russian *vyigrysh*, "profit, winnings"]

-ville *See* -SVILLE

vinegar *See* FULL OF PISS AND VINEGAR

vino or **veeno** (VEE noh) *n* Wine, esp red jug wine [1919+; fr Italian, "wine"]

vinyl *modifier* **1** : *woman who rides the vinyl grooves* **2** Having to do with discotheques, the dancing done there, etc : *The only vinyl junkies were the nattily-suited variety n* Phonograph records; recording : *Now this disco graffiti has found its way to vinyl and created quite a bit of excitement* [1976+; fr the chemical material used for phonograph records, semantically analogous with earlier *wax*]

VIP (pronounced as separate letters) *n* A very important person; BIG SHOT (1933+)

vision *See* TUNNEL VISION

visit from Flo or **visitor** *n* The menstrual period (1980+)

visit from the stork *n phr* The birth of a baby

VJ *See* VEEJAY

vogueing *n* To do a dance involving poses similar to glamour magazine models : *Vogueing, an unusual dance fad popular in New York's underground clubs* (1980s+)

volume *n* A dose or capsule of Valium®, a tranquilizer : *I'd take maybe five volumes in the morning* (1970s+)

vote *v* To suggest what one wants : *I vote for BLTs for dinner* (1814+)

vroom or **varoom** *modifier* (also **vroom-vroom**) : *if you drive a sporty, vroom-vroom model n* The noise of a powerful car *v* To speed, esp in a roaring car : *as we vroomed up and down the Watchung Mountains* (1967+)

W

wack or **whack** *adj* Worthless; stupid; "wimpish" : *You'll have to deal with some really wack people n* **1** A crazy or eccentric person; NUT, SCREWBALL, WEIRDO : *Two wacks if I ever saw one/ a father who was so abrasive and married now to such a wack (1938+)* **2** A drink of liquor **3** A blow or hit made at someone or something

wack off *See* WHACK OFF

-wacky *combining word* CRAZY, NUTTY : *car-wacky/ chick-wacky (mid-1940s+)*

wad *n* **1** A roll of money : *My grandmother'd just sent me this wad about a week before (1864+)* <2> An amount of semen : *shoot one's wad See* SHOOT one's LOAD, SHOOT one's WAD

-wad *combining word* A disgusting or unpleasant person ● Used as second formative in *dickwad, dipwad, dripwad, phlegmwad, jerkwad, scumwad,* and *tightwad;* -*wad* joins -*bag,* -*ball* and -*head* as very productive elements for forming insults [1980s+ & '90s teenagers; fr several sources: *wad* as defined above; *wad,* "an unattractive or unpopular person," in late 1800s college slang; *wad,* "a quantum of semen," fr 1920s; *wad,* "a mass or lump of something"; *wad,* "the male genitals," recently attested but not widespread]

wader *See* HIGH WATERS

waffle *n* : *I was tired of all the candidates' waffle v* To speak or behave evasively; tergiversate; equivocate : *When asked for specifics, I demur, I waffle/ unlike the windy, waffling, anonymous editorial writers (1803+)* [fr northern British dialect, "waver, fluctuate," perhaps related to another dialect sense, "yelp, yap"]

waffle-stompers *n* Heavy hiking boots; SHITKICKERS [1970s+; fr the pattern of the soles, which make a *wafflelike* print]

wag *See* CHIN-WAG

wag one's **chin** *v phr* To talk : *to be seen waggin' your chin with a sleuth (1920+)*

wagon *n* A naval vessel *(Navy fr WWI) See* FALL OFF THE WAGON, FIX someone's WAGON, MEAT WAGON, OFF THE WAGON, ON THE WAGON, PADDY WAGON

wail *v* **1** To play jazz well and feelingly : *We were wailing, but nobody had a tape machine (1930s+ Jazz musicians)* **2** (also *whale*) To do very well; perform well *(1950s+ College students fr cool talk fr jazz musicians)* [fr the notion of a well-performed blues number, with its melodious lamentations]

wailing or **whaling** *adj* Excellent; wonderful; GREAT *(1954+ Black musicians)*

waist *See* PANTYWAIST

wait up *v phr* To pause, when well ahead, for someone to overtake one ● Often a panting request *(1920s+)*

wake up and smell the coffee (or something else) *sentence* Become aware before it's too late : *The legislators had better wake up and smell the coffee/ Why Bond Bulls Need to Wake Up, Smell the Coffee/ Wake up and smell where the money's going (1990s+)*

wake-up call *n phr* A summons to action; clarion call : *The vote should be taken as a wake-up call to the civil rights movement that it better reinvigorate its leadership/ I sure hope this hurricane is a wake-up call (1970s+)*

walk *v* **1** (also, earlier, **walk free**) To be released from prison *(1970s+)* **2** To be acquitted of or otherwise freed from a criminal indictment : *more killers walk because of the incompetence of arresting officers/ Actually, I'm gonna cop a plea. A $15 fine and I'll walk (late 1950s+)* **3** (also, fr 1890s, **walk out**) To go out on strike : *Several more Caterpillar locals have decided to walk (1970s+ Labor unions)* **4** To leave someone, esp a spouse or lover; GET LOST, TAKE A HIKE : *She said if he didn't straighten out he could walk See* FRENCH WALK, TAKE A WALK, WIN IN A WALK

walk all over someone *v phr* To intimidate and maltreat someone [1890s+ College students; based on mid-1800s *walk over*]

walkaway or **walkover** *n* An easy victory; CINCH, PUSHOVER : *It looked like a walkover for Clarence/ The odds were on the Redskins in a walkaway*

walk away from *v phr* To turn one's back on; fail to respond to when needed : *The offer promises motorists who switch to a Ford that they can walk away from the lease, no questions asked, after trying the car for six months (1960s+)*

walk away with *v phr* To win easily : *That year the Tigers walked away with the pennant (1899+)*

walking papers (or **ticket**) *n phr* A dismissal or discharge; esp, a rejection; PINK SLIP : *Two baseball veterans got their walking papers today (1820s+) See* GIVE someone HIS WALKING PAPERS

walking timebomb *n phr* A person who is likely to explode into violence [fr *timebomb,* an explosive device with the detonator set to go off]

walking wounded *n phr* Persons who are injured, esp in a psychological or spiritual way, but still functional; depressed people : *by the end of the year the salesmen are "walking* *wounded", just plain going bonkers* [1960s+; fr a WWI military medical term for a *wounded* person who is ambulatory]

walk off with *v phr* To appropriate to oneself something lent or entrusted by another (*1727+*)

walk-on *modifier* : *Since antiquity the figure of the black has played far more than a walk-on part in Western culture* **n** A very minor, usu nonspeaking, role; an insignificant or minimal sort of participation : *looking like last-minute walk-ons in the closing scene of "Götterdammerung"* (*1900+ Theater*)

walk on air *v phr* To be ecstatic : *for a week after the promotion she was walking on air* (*1887+*)

walk on eggs or **thin ice** *v phr* To proceed very carefully; go gingerly and warily : *I always feel as if I'm walking on eggs around her/ walking on thin ice to criticize the government* (*1859+*)

walk on water *v phr* To do miraculous things; emulate Jesus Christ : *Not everybody thinks Colin Powell walks on water* (*1970s+*)

walkout *n* A strike : *There's a walkout at the supermarkets right now* (late *1880s+ Labor union*)

walk out on someone or something *v phr* To abandon; TAKE A WALK : *She was fed up, and just walked out on the whole deal* (*1890s+*)

walkover *See* WALKAWAY

walk the plank *v phr* To be destroyed or sacrificed; be fired : *Rostow's Deputy Walks the Plank; Rostow Hangs In/ If you don't have the votes, you don't make your friends walk the plank* [1835+; fr the pirate practice of forcing unwanted persons to *walk* out on a *plank* and plunge into the sea]

walk the walk *v phr* walk the talk : *the department is "walking the walk" of reengineering government* (*1980s+*)

walk-through *n* A rehearsal, in the theater, sports, etc; DRY RUN (*1959+*)

walk through *v phr* To explain something carefully and gradually; learn something by going slowly through the steps : *I'll walk you through it one more time; you nearly have it right* [mid-1800s+ Theater; fr the practice of learning a role partly by moving about onstage without speaking the lines]

walk-up *n* A room, apartment, building, etc, without an elevator : *second-floor walk-ups above stores* (*1919+*)

wall *See* BALLS TO THE WALL, BOUNCE OFF THE WALLS, CLIMB THE WALL, DRIVE someone UP THE WALL, GO TO THE WALL, HOLE IN THE WALL, NAIL someone TO THE CROSS, OFF THE WALL, UP AGAINST THE WALL, UP THE WALL

wallbanger *n phr* **1** A dose or capsule of methaqualone; LUDE : *called wall bangers by*

the kids (*1950s+ Teenagers & narcotics*) *n* **2** (also **Harvey Wallbanger**) A drink made of vodka or gin and juice (late *1960s+*) [presumably fr the effect of the drug or potion on the consumer]

wall-eyed *adj* Drunk (*1920s+*)

wallflower *n* A person, esp a woman, who is peripheral and uncourted at a dance, party, etc : *the homely and ugly girls who were called wall-flowers* (*1820+*)

wallop *n* **1** A hard blow; a severe and resounding stroke : *She gave him a wallop on the chin* **2** Power; CLOUT, MOXIE : *She'd be good if she had a little more wallop* *v* **1** : *He walloped the ball right over the wall* **2** To defeat utterly; CLOBBER [1823+; fr British dialect, "beat, thrash," apparently fr Old Norman French *walop*, "gallop"] *See* CIRCUIT CLOUT

walloping *adj* Extreme; large : *walloping amount of chili*

wall-to-wall *adj* Total; all-encompassing : *a wall-to-wall nightmare in which society dissolves/ wall-to-wall hookers, niggers, and junkies/ It was wall-to-wall people* [1967+; fr the phrase *wall-to-wall carpeting*, found by 1953]

wally or **Wally** or **wallie** *n* **1** Stupid person; moron **2** An awkward person; KLUTZ **3** An unfashionable person : *The Arnolds call anyone who wears conventional clothes, a Wally* ◁**4**▷ The penis; DORK, PRICK : *No wonder men are in awe of their wallies. First thing in the morning, a penis is a pretty magnificent sight* [1990s+ Students fr British rock groups; origin unknown; perhaps fr the nickname for Walter or Wallace, suggesting, as Clyde does, someone like a wally; perhaps, improbably, fr British *wally*, "pickle"; *wally* in current senses appears to be borrowed from British use; however, it is attested in the US in the early 1900s meaning "A small-town sport," and in 1915–22 in college (Bryn Mawr) and flapper slang meaning "a goof with patent-leather hair"]

walsy *See* PALSY-WALSY

waltz *n* Something easily accomplished; CINCH, PIECE OF CAKE (*1968+*) *v* To move in a smooth, unhurried, yet sprightly manner : *Jesse James could have waltzed in there and carted off the patio furniture/ someone waltzing into that wreck that we've grown old with searching* (*1862+*)

waltz someone **around** *v phr* To evade or deceive : *Have you been waltzing me around for three months* (*1950s+*)

waltz off with *v phr* To take something away nonchalantly or with ease : *waltzed off with the grand prize*

wambulance *n* A hypothetical rescue vehicle to spirit away someone who whines and complains : *I'm calling the wambulance for that brat*

wampum *n* Money; cash; BREAD [1897+; short for Algonquian *wampumpeag,* "beads made from quahog shells and used as money"]

◁**wang** or **whang** or **whanger**▷ *n* The penis; COCK, PRICK : *I can see your whang. Your dong is visible/ a trigger that was bigger than an elephant's proboscis or the whanger of a whale* [1935+; probably fr *whangdoodle,* "something of uncertain name, gadget"; many such terms, like *diddlywhacker, dingus, doodle,* and *thingy,* are euphemisms for the penis] *See* PULL one's PUD

wang chung *n phr* Going out on the town; going out to have fun [1983+; fr song "Everybody Wang Chung Tonight" by the British group Wang Chung]

wangdoodle *See* WHANGDOODLE

wangle *n* : *made a precise science out of the wangle* *v* To get or arrange by shrewd maneuvering; contrive cunningly : *President Truman has given Ching a free hand in trying to wangle agreements (1880s+ British printers' slang)* [origin unknown; perhaps a form of *waggle,* "overcome, get the better of"; popularized by WWI soldiers]

wank *n* 1 : *He had a good wank as he watched her* 2 A contemptible person; GEEK, JERK, DORK : *He got what he wanted needed. Which was a little badoom-badoom. Ugh. Complete wank (1970+)* *v* ◁1▷ (also **wank off**) To fondle one's own penis; JACK OFF, BEAT one's MEAT *(late 1940s+ British)* 2 To have fun; PARTY, HAVE A BALL *(1990s+ Canadian students)*

wanker *n* ◁1▷ A masturbator, either literally or figuratively; JERK-OFF : *There I was, this clubfooted wanker sitting on the organ seat/ all manner of artsy bubbleheads and academic wankers/ It was just wankers (late 1940s+ chiefly British)* 2 A fun-loving person; PARTY ANIMAL *(1990s+ Canadian students)* ◁3▷ The penis *(1990s+ Students)* [origin unknown; perhaps fr British dialect *wank,* "a violent blow," and semantically analogous with *beat* one's *meat, whack off, pound* one's *peenie,* etc]

wanna *v phr* Want to : *I wanna get some ice cream* • Purposely mispronounced

wannabe or **wannabee** or **wanna-be** or **wanta be** (WAW nuh bee) *n* Someone who aspires to be someone else, esp a star or hero : *Rambo Wanna-be's/ A "poser" or a "wanta be" is someone who tries to be like someone else* [1980s+ California surfers & black street gangs; fr imprecise or dialectal pronunciation of "want to be"]

want list *See* WISH LIST

want out *v phr* To want no association or involvement with : *want out of this stupid town*

war *See* HOT WAR, PSYWAR

warbler *n* A woman singer; CANARY [1946+; found by 1633 as "singer"]

war chest *n* A political campaign's funding; also, an amount saved for a planned purchase or venture

wardrobe malfunction *n phr* An embarrassing display of a body part when clothing droops, falls, or is torn • Euphemistic : *Janet Jackson's infamous wardrobe malfunction (2004+)*

wardrobing *n* The practice of purchasing clothing to be worn once and then returned for a refund : *finding ways to discourage wardrobing through the Internet*

warehouse *n* Any large, impersonal institution : *a warehouse for the elds (1970+)*

warhorse *n* A seasoned and reliable veteran; a grizzled doyen *(1837+)*

warm body *n phr* A person regarded as merely such, without individual qualities, virtues, vices, etc; an animate person who occupies space; CHAIR-WARMER : *I'll look you up if all I need is a warm body (1960s+)*

warmed over *adj phr* Derivative and only slightly changed; revived unimaginatively : *The president, he wrote, had "offered the poor the Protestant Ethic warmed over"/ out of the mouths of bunnies and gulls, some warmed-over Gibran (1970+)* *See* LOOK LIKE DEATH WARMED OVER

warmer *See* BENCHWARMER, CHAIR-WARMER

warm fuzzy *n phr* 1 A compliment; a word of praise; also, such praise collectively; STROKE : *You need some warm fuzzy* 2 Pleasant feelings, esp when tinged with nostalgia : *This was the sort of evening that gave you the warm fuzzies, cherished memories, funny lines/ Although foster parenting can provide plenty of warm fuzzies, the job is always challenging* [1970s+; probably fr the notion of a snuggling small animal, like Charles Schulz's *warm puppy*]

warm the bench *v phr* To be held in reserve *(1907+ Sports)*

warm up *v phr* To do exercises and preparatory maneuvers before some activity, esp some sports effort *(1868+ Sports)*

warm someone up *v phr* To induce a receptive and approving attitude in someone, esp by joking and cajoling : *The second banana warmed the audience up before the star appeared (1950s+)*

warp *See* TIME WARP

war paint *n phr* Cosmetics [1869+; fr the facial paint worn by Native American warriors]

warped *adj* 1 Very odd; eccentric : *warped sense of humor* 2 Intoxicated by drugs; BENT

warrior *See* SUNDAY SOLDIER

wart 516

wart *n* A flaw; an imperfection : *The new format has some warts, but no integrity warts* [probably from *warts and all*] *See* WORRYWART

warts and all *n phr* The accurate totality of someone or something, including the imperfections : *Audiences hearing the local orchestra week after week hear it with warts and all/ Your friends see Doherty, warts and all/ Lyndon Johnson, warts and all* [1763+; fr the putative remark of Oliver Cromwell to his portraitist Peter Lely: "Remark all these roughnesses, pimples, warts, and everything as you see me"]

war zone *n* A situation or place where there is fighting or crime, such as a rough neighborhood : *the war zone of Bridgeport*

was *See* BE NEVER-WAS

wash *n* **1** A drink to follow another, to wash it down; CHASER : *What for a wash? (1950s+)* **2** An elaborate justification; WHITEWASH : *It looked like a wash to me (1950s+)* **3** A balance between opposing values, cases, effects, etc; a moot situation; STANDOFF, a TOSS-UP : *The net effect of the medical testimony was a wash/ I'd have to go to bed at the same time as my 6-year-old. So it's pretty much a wash/ the Ferraro factor. Was it a political plus, a minus, a wash? (1870s+ Stock market)* v To prove acceptable; bear testing • Usually in the negative : *Well, it just won't wash/ The stereotype of gay males as child molesters just doesn't wash any more/ That washes. I'll buy it (1849+)* [verb sense said to be fr a defective printed calico that could not be *washed*; third noun sense perhaps fr the notion that equal opposing elements *wash* each other out or away, or *wipe the slate clean*] *See* HANG OUT THE WASH, WHITEWASH

wash (or air) one's dirty linen *v phr* (Variation: **in public** may be added) To talk or argue about intimate matters in public [1867+; probably a translation of earlier French *Il faut laver ton linge sale en famille*]

washed out *modifier* Extremely tired; exhausted : *washed out from all this work*

washed up or **all washed up** *adj phr* No longer valid or active as a performer, competitor, worker, etc; ausgespielt, FINISHED : *I'm all washed up/ Borden is all washed up* [1923+ Theater; fr the notion of *washing up* one's hands at the finish of a job or a day's work]

washing *n* A technique of evading surveillance by taking an absurdly indirect route from one place to another *(1990s+ Police)*

wash someone's mouth out with soap *v phr* To punish someone for using offensive language : *Ma Gingrich ought to wash Newtie's mouth out with soap. He owes the First Lady big time (1920s+)*

washout *n* **1** A failure; a total fiasco; FLOP : *I'm afraid our big birthday bash was a washout* **2** A student pilot or aviation cadet who fails to complete the course and become a qualified pilot : *the major cause for the large number of "washouts"* [WWI British military; origin unknown; perhaps because the student's name was *washed* or scrubbed from the roster]

wash out *v phr* **1** To fail, esp to fail to finish a pilot-training course and be qualified : *Then I was washed out on a slight technicality (WWI flyers)* **2** To eliminate or cancel; SCRATCH, SCRUB **3** To lose all one's money; TAP OUT : *hustlers who really knew how to gamble. I always got washed out (1900s+)*

WASP or **wasp** *adj* : *Westchester and Darien and places like that, WASP country* *n* A person of nonminority or nonethnic background, ancestry, etc, as conceived in the United States; a White Anglo-Saxon Protestant : *The Republican Party is run largely by "wasps" (1962+ Sociologists)* [said to have been coined by the Philadelphia author E Digby Baltzell]

waspish *adj* Dominated by and characteristic of WASPs : *This town is naughty and waspish and expensive*

waste *v* **1** To defeat utterly; trounce, beat up; CLOBBER *(Teenagers fr 1950s+ Street gang)* **2** To wreck; destroy; mutilate; TRASH : *Stallone wastes everything in his path (1450+)* **3** To kill; BLOW someone AWAY, TAKE someone or something OUT *(1964+)*

wasted *adj* **1** Penniless; BROKE *(1950s+ Cool talk)* **2** Intoxicated by narcotics or alcohol; STRUNG OUT : *Everybody was getting kind of high on acid, wasted, in fact (1950s+ Narcotics & cool talk)* **3** Exhausted; POOPED *(mid-1950s+)* **4** Wrecked; ruined; destroyed : *Like, I'm wasted. I can't lose no more (late 1950s+)*

watch *See* GRAVEYARD WATCH, ON someone's WATCH

watcher *See* CLOCK-WATCHER

watch it *interj* Be careful; look out *(1916+)*

watch one's mouth *v phr* To be careful of what one says, esp to stop being provocative, obscene, presumptuous, etc • Often an irritated command : *Watch your mouth, white boy (1970s+)*

watch or **read my lips** *sentence* **1** Listen very carefully to me : *Hey, watch my lips. You. Me. Her. That's it (1970s+ Army)* **2** Do you read lips? [second sense is a euphemism for a silently spoken obscenity or insult]

watch the submarine races *v phr* To do sex play in a parked car [1980s+ Teenagers; fr the fact that no submarine races are in progress to be watched]

watch this space *sentence* Wait for further developments to be announced [1917+; orig a note to look regularly at a particular portion of a newspaper for future announcements]

water *See* COME HELL or HIGH WATER, CUT OFF someone's WATER, DEAD IN THE WATER, FIREWATER, HIGH WATERS, HOLD one's WATER, HOT WATER, IN DEEP WATER, IN HOT WATER, JERKWATER, LONG DRINK OF WATER, ON THE WAGON, TEST THE WATERS

water-cooler story *n phr* A piece of gossip; latrine rumor (*1990s+*)

watering hole (or **spot**) or **waterhole** *n phr* or *n* A bar; a saloon; a drinking place : *That place is the waterhole of choice for aspiring actors/ a posh watering hole on Madison Avenue/ gathering for the school's alums and their friends at selected watering spots* (*1960s+*)

water wagon *See* ON THE WAGON

waterworks *See* TURN ON THE WATERWORKS

wave, the *n phr* A stadium demonstration in which sections of spectators successively stand up and sit in synchronism, for no apparent reason (*1980s+ Sports fans*)

wavelength *See* ON THE SAME WAVELENGTH

wave-maker *n* A person who raises questions, imposes difficulties and objections, etc : *said that he is a wave-maker whose troubles arose from his insistence on injecting moral values* [1960s+; perhaps from an old joke in which a set of persons in hell, immersed up to their mouths in feces, are heard to chant "Don't make waves," very melodiously]

wax *n* : *Play the tune and cut a wax of it* *v* **1** To defeat; outdo; BEAT, CLOBBER, ZAP (*1884+*) **2** To assault and maul; injure or kill : *I've always got a few bucks to wax Red Gs* (*1884+*) **3** (also **put on wax**) To make a phonograph recording; record : *Louis Armstrong waxed "Beale Street Blues"/ put the Stone Age stuff of jazz on wax* (*1920s+ Jazz musicians*) [the origin of the violent senses is unknown; perhaps semantically analogous with *polish off*, referring to wax as a polish; recording senses fr the material used, as *vinyl* was used later] *See* the WHOLE BALL OF WAX

way *adv* Very; extremely; absolutely; TO THE MAX : *one of the way coolest in the US* (*1980s+*) *affirmation* Yes; on the contrary • Used as a response to the negative "No way!" (*1990s+*) [the intensifier may have developed from *all the way*, attested along with *way*, both meaning "very" in prison slang of the 1980s] *See* BEAT one's WAY, the FRENCH WAY, GO OUT OF one's WAY, GO THE LIMIT, the GREEK WAY, the HARD WAY, IN A BIG WAY, KNOW one's WAY AROUND, NO WAY, RUB someone THE WRONG WAY, THERE'S NO WAY

way it plays, the *adv phr* According to the usual pattern : *The way it plays in there, you can't plead the Fifth* *n phr* The usual pattern; what is to be expected : *Well, I guess that's the way it plays when you get old*

way off (base) *modifier* Not even close to correct; on the wrong path : *way off on your account of what happened*

way out *adj phr* **1** Imaginative; original and bold, esp successfully and admirably so (*1940s+ Jazz musicians*) **2** Excellent; wonderful; FAR OUT, GREAT, OUT OF SIGHT (*1950s+ Cool talk fr jazz musicians*) **3** Intoxicated with narcotics; HIGH, OUT OF IT (*1960s+ Narcotics*) [probably fr earlier *out of this world* or *out of sight*]

ways *See* FORTY WAYS TO SUNDAY, HAVE IT BOTH WAYS, SWING BOTH WAYS, WORK BOTH WAYS

way the ball bounces (or **the cookie crumbles**) *See* THAT'S THE WAY THE BALL BOUNCES

way to go *sentence* You are doing extremely well; that is splendid • An exclamation of praise and encouragement : *Ron, stick that old hand out. Way to go, Prez* [a shortening of *that's the way to go*]

way to run a railroad, the wrong *n phr* (Variations: **a hell of a** or **a stupid** or **what a** or other deprecative modifiers may precede **way**) Not the best way to do something : *Mfune blasted the White House for not including the Black Caucus in the formulation of policy: "This isn't any way to run a railroad"/ Arafat's flawed technique in governing Jericho and Gaza is an awful way to run a railroad* (*1980s+*)

wazoo *n* The buttocks; anus; ASS [1970s+; perhaps a variant of *kazoo*]

weak sister *n phr* An unreliable person, esp a male (*1857+*)

◁**weapon**▷ *n* The penis (*1000+*)

wear a wire *v phr* To be fitted with a concealed listening or recording device : *And wear a hidden tape recorder, what do they call it? Wear a wire* (*1950s+*)

wear cement shoes *v phr* To be killed and disposed of by the crime syndicate, esp by being sunk in the water (*1990s+*)

wear the pants (or **trousers** or **britches**) *v phr* To be the dominant one in a marriage, household, etc • Nearly always said of a woman [1931+; *wear the breeches* can be traced to the 1400s in a French version (*braies*) and to the 1500s in English]

wear two hats *v phr* To have two separate jobs or functions • The phrase may specify more than two hats: *three hats, several hats* : *Each of these men wears two hats: one as topbraid officer, the other as a member of the Joint Chiefs/ Rockefeller to Wear Two Hats* (*1966+*)

weasel *n* : *Little Joe turned weasel* **v 1** To evade and equivocate; use deceptive language; deceive : *They told the candidate to stop weaseling and get to the substance/ I was trying to weasel some bank from you* (1956+) **2** To inform; SING, SQUEAL *(1920s+ Underworld)* [the first verb sense is said to be based on the *weasel's* habit of sucking the meat or substance from an egg, leaving only the shell; the other senses reflect the more general nasty reputation of the *weasel*, which has meant "contemptible person" since at least the 1500s]

weasel out *v phr* To withdraw from or evade, esp a promise or obligation, in a sneaky, underhanded way : *I coulda cut them loose, coulda made some excuse, even coulda weaseled out* (1956+)

weasel words *n phr* Language designed to deceive; empty talk; self-serving verbiage [1900+; words as empty as an eggshell that a *weasel* has sucked]

wedding *See* SHOTGUN WEDDING

wedgie or **wedgy** *n* The prank of pulling the underwear upward from behind by the waistband; melvin. MURPHY : *the impression of leaping through the camera lens and giving the viewers a wedgie/ by pulling up their underpants to give them "wedgies"* [1970s+ Children; presumably fr *wedging* the underpants between the buttocks]

weed *n* **1** (also **the weed**) Tobacco (1606+) **2** A cigar, esp an inferior one : *Throw that weed away and have a good one* (1847+) **3** (also **the weed**) A marijuana cigarette; JOINT *(1920s+ Narcotics) See* REEFER

weeder *n* A difficult college course that weeds out weaker students

weedhead *n* A user of marijuana; POTHEAD *(1960s+ Narcotics)*

weeds *n* Clothing, esp for mourning (1362+)

wee hours *n phr* The hours just after midnight : *the story of what happened in the wee hours of Dec 2, 1985* [1890s+ fr Scottish; Scottish *wee sma' hours* is attested in the late 1700s]

week *See* KNOCK someone INTO THE MIDDLE OF NEXT WEEK

weekend warrior *See* SUNDAY SOLDIER

weenie (also **weeny** or **weinie** or **weeney** or **wienie**) *modifier* : *You'd never know that weenie voice belonged to a gorilla* **n 1** (also **wiener** or **weener**) A frankfurter; HOT DOG : *this wienie and kraut combination* (1911+) ◁**2**▷ (also **wiener** or **weener**) The penis; esp, the relaxed penis **3** (also **weeniehead** or **weiner-head**) An ineffectual, despised person; JERK, WIMP : *She plans to be a weenie, is a weenie, asks to be loved anyway, and is loved anyway/ Anybody who zips their coat when the temperature is higher than zero is an automatic*

weenie (1960s+) **4** (also **ween**) A very serious student; greasy grind, throat : *Premeds known to their less pressurized campus colleagues as throats and weenies/ Weens are strange creatures with pallid faces, glassy eyes, and calculators strapped to their belts* (1970s+ College students) [fr German *Wienerwurst*, "Vienna sausage," with pejorative senses developing fr its penile shape] *See* PLAY HIDE THE WEENIE

weensy *See* TEENSY-WEENSY

weep *See* READ 'EM AND WEEP

wee-wee *modifier* : *the Cuomo family dog and her controversial weewee pads* **n 1** : *specimen of wee-wee* **2** The penis *v* To urinate [1930+; perhaps a euphemism for the euphemism *pee-pee* for *piss*, used in talking to small children]

weigh in *v phr* To make a contribution to something, esp to a debate, quarrel, etc; present an addition : *Ellen Goodman and Meg Greenfield also weighed in with women's rights polemics* [1909+; perhaps fr the formal *weighing in* of a prizefighter before a match; perhaps fr the notion of bringing weight to bear]

weight *n* The amount of narcotics an addict needs for a week : *I'm going up there to give her her weight for the week, you know* (1960s+ Narcotics) *See* CARRY A LOT OF WEIGHT, THROW one's WEIGHT AROUND

weird *adj* Excellent; wonderful; COOL [1940s+ Bop talk & cool talk; also attested as 1920s British upper-class use]

weirdo or **weirdie** or **weirdy** *n* A very strange, eccentric, repellent person; BIRD, CREEP, GEEK : *He's a weirdy, all right* [1955+; *weirdie* is attested from 1894, but was probably Scots dialect]

weird out *v phr* To become or make hallucinatory or intoxicated; to feel a loss of reality because of a strange experience : *Talk to me. I'm weirding out/ You're weirding me out already, Dag*

welcome to the club *sentence* Now you have joined me in adversity; now you see how badly things turn out : *So you've been fired? Welcome to the club, old buddy* (1970s+)

◁**welldigger's ass**▷ *See* COLD AS HELL

well-heeled *adj* **1** Having much money; rich : *the average, fairly well-heeled, middle-aged American male* (1897+) **2** Well-armed : *He's always well-heeled* (1873+)

◁**well-hung**▷ *adj* Having large genitals : *Death takes the innocent young. And those who are very well hung/ A guy with 640K of RAM is the electronic equivalent of well-hung* (1611+)

well-oiled *adj* Drunk : *He happened to be well-oiled, as was usually the case* (1900s+)

well told *See* FUCKING WELL TOLD

welsh or **welch** *n* : *Link can't take a welsh, so he looks around for a way to get his dough* *v* To default on or evade an obligation, esp paying a gambling debt : *Say, are you going to welsh on me?/ Some American officials feel that the Syrians welshed on their promise* (1857+) [apparently fr the same bigoted stereotype of the *Welsh* reflected in the English nursery rhyme "Taffy was a Welshman, Taffy was a thief," although perhaps a borrowing of German *Welsch*, "foreigner"]

West *See* MAE WEST

western or **Western** *n* A book, movie, etc, about the Old West (1909+) *See* SPAGHETTI WESTERN

wet *adj* **1** Permitting or advocating the sale of liquor : *This is a wet county* (1870+) **2** Inferior, feeble; stupid and unappealing; WIMPISH : *A man is "wet" if he isn't a regular guy* (1916+) **3** Bloody; gory : *He's criminally liable even if Willoughby did the wet work* (1970s+ *Police*) **4** Sexually aroused : *Simon is a smoothie who likes to woo women with fast rides: "The 'vette gets 'em wet"/ Elvis dreamed of belting "All Shook Up" for strange, wet women* (1940s+) *See* ALL WET, GET one's FEET WET

◁**wetback**▷ *n* A Mexican who enters the US illegally, esp as a migratory worker • The term may be generalizing to include all illegal immigrants : *An American's as good as a wetback, who is a Mexican whom we don't know how he got here* [1929+; fr the fact that they get their *backs* wet in wading across the Rio Grande; the terms *wet pony, wet cow,* etc, were used earlier for animals brought illegally across the border]

wet blanket *n phr* A person who dampens and smothers all enthusiasm; a person who prevents fun; a pessimist; KILLJOY, PARTY-POOPER (1879+)

wet dream *n phr* A male's erotic dream during which he has an orgasm (1851+)

wet hen *See* MAD AS A WET HEN

wet noodle *n* A naysayer; WIMP : *being a wet noodle about the concert*

wet one *n* A cold beer : *could use a wet one after the dig*

wetware *n* The human brain : *Slip a microchip into snug contact with your gray matter (a.k.a. wetware)/ wetware: the human brain and its DNA code* (1980s+ *Computer*)

wet one's **whistle** *v phr* To have a drink, esp of liquor [late 1300s+; Chaucer says of a drunken miller's comely wife: "Her pretty whistle was well wetted"]

whack *n* **1** A hit; blow : *to explore their manhood and give and take a few whacks* (1737+) **2** A try; BASH, CRACK, SHOT : *He was given a whack at drama reviewing* (1891+) **3** WACK *v* **1** To strike; hit (1721+) **2** (also **whack out**) To kill; execute, gangland style : *the lieutenant took it personal when they whacked the witness* (1980s+ *Mobsters*) **3** (also **wack**) To dilute a narcotic; cut a narcotic (1960s+ *Narcotics*) [probably echoic; in second verb sense, the use of *whacks*, "any form of force," is attested among Chicago gunmen in 1932] *See* HAVE A CRACK AT something, OUT OF WHACK, WACK

whacked or **whacked out** *adj* Exhausted; tired out; BEAT, BUSHED, POOPED : *You were whacked-out. Want to take a hot shower?* (1919+)

◁**whack** (or **wack**) **off**▷ *v phr* To masturbate; JERK OFF [1960s+; one of the many terms equating masturbation with *banging, beating,* or *pounding*]

whale[1] *n* A large or fat person; BEACHED WHALE (1900+)

whale[2] *n* A heavy blow : *She gave him a hard whale to the nose* *v* **1** To hit; thrash; trounce : *They whaled us six-zip/ She hauled off and whaled him a shrewd blow* (1790+) **2** (also **wail**) To do extremely well; excel (1980s+ *Students*) [fr British dialect spelling of *wale*, "strike, beat," perhaps related to Old English *wæl*, "slaughter, carnage, death"]

whale away *v phr* To attack or do something vigorously and persistently : *I was whaling away at the cleaning job/ He's best when he's whaling away at the other candidates* (1897+)

whale into (or **on**) someone or something *v phr* To attack vigorously : *He'd barely met me when he whaled into me for not answering his letter/ Instead of whaling on the ball, Agassi should hit low, dipping topspin returns* (1790+)

whale of a someone or something, a *n phr* An excellent or large example; a very superior specimen : *That woman is a whale of a politician* [1900+ *Students*; fr the prodigious size of the *whale*]

whale (or **wail**) **on** something or someone *v phr* **1** To perform extremely well **2** To criticize severely; denigrate; CLOBBER : *and he just wailed on a chunk of code Michael had written* (1980s+ *Students*)

whaling *n* A beating (1852+) *See* WAILING

wham *interj* (also **whammo**) An exclamation signaling the suddenness, violence, surprise, etc, of a quick, sharp blow : *Wham! suddenly the meaning hit me/ And then—whammo—she was blindsided* (1932+) *v* To hit; strike; SOCK : *And the whamming continues* [1925+; echoic, and related in sound symbolism to *whip, whale, whack, whomp, whop,* and other wh-words denoting blows]

wham-bam (or **ram-bam** or **slam-bam**) **thank you ma'am** *n phr* A very quick sex

act, esp a casual coupling : *And short it was:
a regular "wham, bam, thank you, Ma'am"/
He's not a wham bam thank you ma'am, he's
a thriller/ They're more slam-bam-thank-you-
ma'am type guys (WWII armed forces)*

whambang *adj* Huge; loud and vigorous;
WHOPPING (*1950s+*)

whammy, the *n phr* The evil eye; a crippling
curse; HEX, the indian sign : *with a whammy
of ordinary indebtedness over his head* [1932+;
origin unknown; popularized in the comic
strip "Li'l Abner" by Al Capp, beginning in
1941, where a character named Evil-Eye
Fleegle can paralyze with a stare; the dated
example is spelled *wami*] *See* DOUBLE
WHAMMY, TRIPLE WHAMMY

whams *See* the WHIM-WHAMS

whangdoodle or **wangdoodle** or **wingdoodle**
n An unspecified or unspecifiable object;
something one does not know the name of or
does not wish to name; GIZMO, THINGAMAJIG :
Push in this dingus, step on this wingdoodle
[1931+; fr mid-1800s sense, "a mythical
beast of strange but indefinite traits"]

whanger *See* WANG

whankster (also **wankster, whangster, wang-
ster**) *n* A pretend or wannabee gangster
[probably fr *white* and *gangster*]

whassit *n* An unnamed or unspecified thing
[1931+; casual pronunciation of *whatsit*
(what is it)]

what *See* SAY WHAT

what are you giving me? *sentence* What kind
of nonsense are you asking me to believe? :
*What are you giving me? Don't try to bullshit a
bullshitter (1880s+ Western)*

whatchamacallit or **what-you-may-call-it** or
what-d'ye-call-it (WHUT chə mə CAWL it)
n An unspecified or unspecifiable object;
something one does not know the name of
or does not wish to name; GIZMO, THINGAMA-
JIG : *lady in a robe and a white whatchamacallit
around her head appeared* [1920+; *what-d'ye-
call-it* is attested from 1573, and *what-ye-
call-'em* as London slang in 1710]

what crawled up your ass or **what crawled
up your ass and died** *sentence* What is
troubling you? *(1990s+ Students)*

what do you say *sentence* How are you? how
have things been? : *What do you say, Ed?
Long time no see (1900s+ Western)*

what else is new *See* SO WHAT ELSE IS NEW

whatever *adv* Perhaps; possibly ● Often a reply
to an unanswerable question, with the force
of "Could be" or "We'll see" : *Well, whatever.
The point was, he was dead/ Which I can do
on my own, or whatever* [1900+; perhaps a
shortening of *whatever's fair*, attested in
1960 student use]

whatever turns you on or **whatever floats
your boat** *sentence* Enjoy whatever you
enjoy; *chacun à son goût* : *You listen to Russ
Limburger? Whatever turns you on/ So do I,
but there isn't a wrong way or a right way to do
either. Whatever floats your boat, Anatole*
(*1980s+*)

what for *n phr* A drubbing, either physical or
verbal; a thrashing; severe punishment : *a
sadistic desire to watch the big shots get what
for* [1873+; fr the startled question *what for?
why?* asked by someone being assaulted] *See*
GIVE someone WHAT FOR

what gives *sentence* **1** What is going on?
WHAT'S UP : *What gives, I asked her* **2** How are
you? how have things been with you? WHAT
DO YOU SAY **3** What is wrong? I do not understand : *"What gives?" he croaked in an
annoyed tone* ● Since the early 1960s, this
sense is often referred to a person: "What
gives with Joe?"; and is often an exasperated
inquiry: "What's bothering you? Why are
you behaving this way?" [1940+; a translation of Yiddish or German *was gibt,*
"what's going on"]

what goes around comes around *sentence* **1**
Retribution follows wrongdoing; justice may
take time, but it will prevail : *"What goes
around comes around," Young said/ Always
remember this, what goes around comes around*
2 Things have a tendency to recur : *So once
again in the world of music, everything that
goes around comes around (1970s+ Black)*

what one is driving at *n phr* What one means;
what one is trying to say : *The persons may
know what you are driving at (1762+)*

what it takes *n phr* The desirable strength,
character, appeal, etc : *I wonder if he has what
it takes to get this job done (1929+)*

what makes someone **tick** (or **run**) *n phr*
Someone's motives, inner psychology, system
of principles, etc : *It's the gambling instinct
that makes me tick/ What Makes Sammy Run?*
[1947+; fr the analogy of human motiva-
tion with the mechanism of a clock]

whatnot *n* An unnamed or unspecified thing
(*1964+*)

what say *sentence* SAY WHAT, WHAT DO YOU SAY
(*1825+*)

what's been shaking *See* WHAT'S SHAKING

what's buzzin', cousin *sentence* What is happening? WHAT'S COOKING (*1930s+ Jive talk*)

what's cooking or **what cooks** *sentence* **1**
What is happening? WHAT'S GOING DOWN :
*What cooks, Jimmy?/ "What's cooking?," I
asked Cardoza (1930s+ Jive talk)* **2** How have
you been? WHAT DO YOU SAY

what's eating (or **what's got into**) someone
sentence What is troubling someone; why is

someone behaving this way; WHAT'S WITH someone : *What's eating you today? I can't get a civil word from you* (first form *1893+*, second *1876+*)

what's going down *sentence* What is happening? WHAT'S COOKING *(1940s+ Black)*

what she wrote *See* THAT'S ALL SHE WROTE

what's-his-name *n* (Variations: **her** or **its** or **your** may replace **his; face** or ◁**ass**▷ may replace **name**) An unspecified or unspecifiable person or thing; someone or something one does not know or remember the name of or does not wish to name; WHOOZIS : *What did old what's-his-face have to tell you?/ But aren't you afraid you're going to get on Professor What's-Her-Face's shit list* (first form *1757+*)

what's-it or **whatsis** or **whatzis** (WHUT sit, -sǝs) *n* An unspecified or unspecifiable object; something one does not know the name of or does not wish to name; DINGUS, THING-AMAJIG : *the world's tallest free-standing what's-it/ What's that whatsis he's playing with?* (*1882+*)

what's it to you *sentence* It's none of your business; don't butt in : *What's it to you if I want to go?* (*1896+*)

what's shaking or **what's been shaking** *sentence* What is happening? WHAT'S GOING DOWN : *Hello, what's shakin'?* [*1950s+* Jazz musicians; perhaps fr an analogy between *shaking* and being vigorously alive; the *shake* was a jazz dance known fr about 1900]

what's the big idea *sentence* Why are you being so presumptuous, aggressive, etc? account for your behavior at once (*1917+*)

what's the good word *sentence* How are things going with you? what have you to tell me about yourself? • A cordial greeting (*1920s+*)

what's the haps *sentence* What is happening? WHAT'S GOING DOWN, what's the scam (*1990s+ Teenagers*)

what's up or **wass up** *sentence* What is happening? what is the matter, question, problem, etc? (*1881+*)

what's what *n phr* The current state of reality; basic truth (*1553+*)

what's with someone or something *sentence* **1** What is the problem, difficulty, etc? : *What's with this guy? All I did was say hello* **2** What is the explanation? why is this? : *What's with the free food? Explain* [late 1930s+; fr Yiddish *vos iz mit*, "what is with"]

what (in) the devil? *interj* What has happened? What is going on?

what the doctor ordered *See* JUST WHAT THE DOCTOR ORDERED

what the hell (or **hey**) *interj* **1** (also ◁**what the fuck**▷) An exclamation of surprise,

puzzlement, resentment, etc : *What the hell! Who does this clown think he is, anyhow?/ Is five successive base hits enough? Let's make it seven, what the hey/ What the fuck, Boyce!* (*1872+*) **2** (also **what the hay**) An exclamation of resignation, acceptance, etc : *What the hell, it isn't the greatest, but it'll do* (*1872+*) *n phr* (also ◁**what the fuck**▷ or **what in hell**) What? • Lengthened for emphasis and euphony : *What the hell do you think you're doing?/ So what the fuck is this about?* (*1836+*)

what the Sam Hill *interj* WHAT THE HELL • A euphemistic form (*1927+*)

what-you-may-call-it *See* WHATCHAMACALLIT

what you see is what you get *sentence* The situation, thing, person, etc, is precisely as it appears to be; no trickery, decoration, glowing promises, etc, are involved here [*1980s+*; probably fr the supposed statement of a salesperson both assuring and warning a customer about the wares]

whatzis *See* WHAT'S-IT

whee *n* Urine; PISS, WHIZZ : *that will scare the whee out of you* [*1980s+*; probably fr *wee-wee*]

wheel *See* BIG WHEEL, INVENT THE WHEEL, REINVENT THE WHEEL

wheel and deal *v phr* To make many and frequent arrangements and agreements, esp in business and aggressively [*1950s+*; perhaps fr the baseball phrase describing a pitcher's windup and throw]

wheeler *See* EIGHTEEN-WHEELER, FOUR-WHEELER

wheeler-dealer *n* A person who wheels and deals; BIG-TIME OPERATOR, ganze macher (*1950s+*)

wheelhouse *n* A batter's preferred hitting zone over the plate; KITCHEN [*1959+* Baseball; probably fr the controlling prominence of the *wheelhouse* on a riverboat or a ship]

wheelie *n* **1** A riding on the rear wheel only, with the front wheel raised off the ground (*1960s+ Motorcyclists & bicyclists*) **2** To ride a skateboard on one pair of wheels (*1970s+ Skateboarders*) *See* POP A WHEELIE

wheeling *See* FREE-WHEELING

wheel man *n phr* The driver of a car used in a robbery or other criminal endeavor : *Like, I'm a pretty good wheel man, you know what I mean?* (*1930s+ Underworld*)

wheels *n* **1** The legs : *His wheels are good. His arm is probably better than it was/ even the veiny old wheels* (*1940s+*) **2** A car : *He tried to convince them that their wheels belonged to someone else* (*1950s+ Hot rodders*) *See* SET OF WHEELS, SHIT ON WHEELS

wheels fall off, the *sentence* Trouble breaks out; a fearful crisis ensues; things turn nasty; the SHIT HITS THE FAN : *We were in good shape until that play, and then the wheels kind of fell off (1990s+)*

when (or **if**) **push comes to shove** *modifier* At a time when a situation worsens or intensifies : *if push comes to shove, I will help out*

when the bell rings *adv phr* At the beginning; when the time comes : *When the bell rings, we'll work hard and let the chips fall where they may (1990s+)*

when the chips are down *modifier* At a crucial or decisive moment; when an important point is reached (1945+)

when the hammer comes down *adv phr* When the decision is made; when all is said and done : *I just hope that when the hammer comes down, that they will look at my performance on the field* [1990s+; probably fr the terminating blow of the auctioneer's *hammer*]

where does one **get off** doing something *sentence* How does he or she dare? what right has he or she? : *Where does she get off being so snotty?/ Where does he get off, saying I'd do that?* [1900+; fr *get off*, "cease, stop," probably fr the notion of getting off a train; so the question is "When does one desist?"]

where someone's **head is at** *adv phr* One's mental condition; one's attitudes, thoughts, aberrations, etc : *They have the maturity to understand where a freak's head is at (1960s+)*

where someone **is at** *n phr* Someone's essential nature, current value system, attitudes, etc : *might make sense in evaluating where you are all at/ everything from Woody Guthrie to the country blues. That's where I was at (1960s+ Black)*

where someone **is coming from** *n phr* 1 What someone means; what someone is saying (1977+) 2 WHERE someone IS AT

where I sit *See* FROM WHERE I SIT

where it's at *adv phr* At the site of stimulating and modish events, trends, etc; WHERE THE ACTION IS : *Where the important stuff is going on. This is where it's at/ Why should only book writers write books? They're not where it's at/ TV is where it's at n phr* The essential locus of the truth; the core of things : *A lot of cats are finding out where it's at in the joint (1960+) See* KNOW WHERE IT'S AT

where someone **lives** *adv phr* At a vital or crucial place; in one's most essential nature, feelings, etc; profoundly : *Let them hear the click when you cock it. And point it right where they live/ an ability to capture the moment and zap you where you live/ Her appeal hit me where I live (1860+) See* HIT someone WHERE HE LIVES

where the action is *adv phr* : *Do you want to live where the action is? n phr* The site of

stimulating and modish events, trends, etc; a place of excitement; WHERE IT'S AT : *Don't come here if you're looking for where the action is* [1970s+; probably fr *action*, "gambling"]

where the bodies are buried *See* KNOW WHERE THE BODIES ARE BURIED

where the rubber meets the road *n phr* Where the action is most immediate; the place of the nitty-gritty : *Assembly lines like this one at Northrop are like living things. This is where the rubber meets the road (1980s+ Army)*

where the sun doesn't shine *adv phr* : *Put it and all his other contributions where the sun doesn't shine/ Give you a hickey where the sun doesn't shine n phr* One's anus; ASS, ASSHOLE (1980s+) *See* STICK IT

where to get off (or **to go**) *See* TELL someone WHERE TO GET OFF

where to put (or **shove** or **stick** or **stuff**) something *See* KNOW WHAT one CAN DO WITH something, TELL someone WHAT TO DO WITH something

wherewithal, the *n phr* Money; the NEEDFUL (1833+)

whew or **whooee** (hw EE OO) *interj* An exclamation of astonishment, relief, incredulity, etc : *It faces ABC's not-nearly-so-formidable Ellen. Whew/ "Wooooeee!" says Dahl in mock terror* [1890+; probably echoic fr the whistling exhalation of a relieved person]

whiff *n* 1 A swing at and miss of a baseball; also, a strikeout 2 Cocaine; SNOW : *Hey, man, know where I can score some whiff? (1970s+ Narcotics) v* 1 To strike at a ball and miss (1916+ Baseball) 2 To strike out : *surpassed Sandy Koufax's single-season strikeout record, whiffing 383 batters (1916+ Baseball)* 3 To inhale cocaine into the nose; SNORT, TOOT (1970s+ Narcotics)

whingding *See* WINGDING

whipped *See* PUSSY-WHIPPED

whipped up *adj phr* (also **whipped**) Exhausted; BEAT, POOPED : *found the controllers dangerously whipped up/ Leading one of those late-night bands, I'm whipped when I get off that bandstand (late 1930s+ Jazz musicians)*

whip up *v phr* To make hurriedly : *Let's whip up a new policy on this/ Just relax while I whip up dinner*

whirlybird *n* A helicopter; CHOPPER • Along with *egg-beater*, nearly obsolete (1951+)

whiskers *See* BET YOUR BOOTS, the CAT'S MEOW

whistle *v* To move very rapidly, as if with a whistling sound; BARREL : *Two bills whistled through the Montana legislature (1813+) See* BELLS AND WHISTLES, BLOW THE WHISTLE, DOO-DAD, NOT JUST WHISTLING DIXIE, WET one's WHISTLE, WHISTLE DIXIE, WOLF WHISTLE

whistle blower *n* A person who makes an accusation of wrongdoing, illegality, etc : *Thanks to yet another whistle blower, it is now known that even the cost of the one-inch square plastic caps has flown as high as the planes/ trading inside information with whistle-blowers and publicity seekers* (1970+)

whistle Dixie *v phr* **1** To say something of no consequence in order to make a positive impression **2** To engage in wishful thinking [1940s+; fr the effect of Dan Emmett's 1859 minstrel song "Dixie," which became the favorite of the Confederates]

whistle in the dark *v phr* To speculate or take a wild guess

white *n* Cocaine (1940s+ Narcotics) *See* BLACK AND WHITE, BLEED someone WHITE, LILY WHITE

white bready or **white bread** or **white-bread** *adj phr* or *adj* Conventional; bourgeois; PLASTIC, SQUARE : *Some of the sequences are Middle American. Evans calls them white bready/ two normal white bread all-American boys/ He taught them to give up the safe, white-bread types* [1980s+; fr the marketing fact that most Americans prefer soft, factory-baked *white bread*]

white-collar *modifier* **1** Employed as clerks, office workers, etc : *The white collar workers don't strike very often/ As early as the 1920s they were called white-collar slaves and by the 1950s nine-to-fivers* **2** Performed by people who work in offices, esp by managers, high executives, etc : *White-collar crime has become a serious problem* (1919+)

white elephant *n phr* Something putatively valuable, often a gift, that one does not want; an embarrassing piece of bric-a-brac : *a wonderful collection of white elephants, trash, treasures* [1851+; fr the *white elephant* of Thailand, which, although it is sacred and royal, is also a clumsy sort of possession for one's house]

white-haired boy *See* FAIR-HAIRED BOY

white hat *modifier* : *I told them they were the white-hat guys* *n phr* A law-abiding, morally upright, and heroic person, as distinct from the villainous black hat [1970s+; fr the conventional dress of heroes in cowboy movies]

white hope or **great white hope** *n* A person or thing on which hopes are based [1911+; fr a white boxer who might beat Jack Johnson, the first black boxer to be world heavyweight champion (1908–15)]

white knight *n phr* A person or company that intervenes to thwart a hostile takeover bid : *Miami firm calls $1.6 billion bid "inadequate"; seeks white knight for rescue* [1981+; fr the *White Knight* in Lewis Carroll's *Through the Looking Glass*]

white-knuckle *adj* Marked by tension, suspense, fear, etc : *Invocations of a Soviet threat have become so common. He calls it "the white-knuckle show"/ A genuine white-knuckle road* (1980s+)

white knuckle *n phr* Something tense, uncertain, frightening, very suspenseful, etc; CLIFFHANGER : *It was a white knuckle* (1980s+) *v* : *"Just plain folks" can white knuckle it around Mugello's tight curves* [fr the pallor of knuckles on an anxiously clenched hand]

white knuckler *n phr* **1** An airplane flight, esp an anxious one on a commuter airline : *You take a white-knuckler. Smilin' Jack at the controls* (1980s+) **2** A tense and anxious person; someone or something frightened : *A list of companies in trouble: The white knucklers*

white lightning *n phr* **1** Inferior whiskey; PANTHER PISS, ROTGUT : *He had a pint of bootleg white lightning* (1921+) **2** acid, LSD (1970s+ Narcotics)

white man's disease *n* In sports, a white person's inability to jump high

◁**white meat**▷ *n phr* A white person, esp a woman, regarded solely as a sex partner [immediately fr the *white meat* and *dark meat* of cooked fowl; *meat*, "the vulva," is attested fr the late 1500s]

white picket fence *n phr* A comfortable, peaceful, and affluent sort of life; rural paradise : *What do I want after this rat-race? The white picket fence* [fr the frequent depiction of such life in such dwellings by filmmakers of the 1930s and '40s]

white stuff *n phr* **1** Grain alcohol used for making bootleg liquor (1920+) **2** Cocaine or morphine; SNOW (1908+ Narcotics)

◁**white trash**▷ *n phr* (often **poor white trash**) PECKERWOOD, REDNECK (1855+ Black)

whitewash *n* : *Several Republican senators reported that the report was a "whitewash" of McCarthy's charges* *v* **1** To win decisively, esp not permitting the opponent to score; SKUNK (1851+) **2** To make something unsavory, damaging, etc, seem to be legitimate and acceptable, usu by falsification or concealment; decontaminate someone's actions or reputation (1762+)

whitewater *n* Frequent changes in the structure and environment of a company, like mergers, cutbacks, and reengineering : *Some whitewater is fun, but it takes a lot out of you* [1990s+ Corporate; fr rafting or kayaking in turbulent and dangerous *white water*]

Whitey or **whitey** *n* A white person; mister charlie, OFAY (1940s+ Black)

whiz[1] *n* A very successful performer; an outstanding expert; HUMDINGER : *the town's most promising high school football whiz/ a whiz at exterior (as opposed to psychological)* *characterization* [1914+; perhaps a shortened form of *wizard*]

whiz² or **whizz** *n* : *I just came down for a whizz* (*1971+*) *v* To urinate; PISS : *exactly twenty-five minutes after whizzing in his pants for the last time/ I gotta whiz. Will you just cover me at the register for a minute?* (*1929+*) [perhaps echoic; perhaps related to late 1800s British *hold your whiz,* "be quiet, shut up," similar to *hold your water*]

whiz³ *v* To pick pockets [1925+ Underworld; apparently fr the *whizzing* speed with which an expert pickpocket works]

whiz⁴ *See* GEE WHIZ²

whizbang *modifier* : *definitely has been a whizbang franchise-winning tool n* **1** A person or thing that is remarkable, wonderful, superior, etc; BEAUT, HUMDINGER : *It's a whizbang of an idea* (*1915+*) **2** A very successful performer; an outstanding expert; WHIZ¹ : *In time we'll all be varsity whizbangs/ The TV whizbangs were sweating through their pancake makeup* (*1915+*) **3** A mixture of cocaine and morphine; an injection of this mixture (*1920s+ Narcotics*) [fr an intensification of *whiz* either due to or influenced by the echoic use of *whizbang* to designate an artillery shell in World War I]

whiz kid *modifier* : *Then the whiz-kid lawyers collided with a tougher adversary n phr* A very clever young person; a youthful prodigy : *the physics whiz kid* (*1930s+*) [fr *whiz¹* blended with *quiz kid,* "very bright child or young person," used of participants in a 1930s radio quiz program]

whizzer *n* A pickpocket; WHIZ (*1925+ Underworld*)

who *See* SAYS YOU

whoa or **woah** *interj* **1** An exclamation of surprise and delight; WOW • This interjection appears to be replacing the very popular *wow* of the 1960s : *Unsolicited confession: woah!* (*1980s+*) **2** (also **whoa there** or **whoa Nelly**) An exhortation to wait, go slow, not be hasty : *Whoa, Nelly. Two aliens are heading this way* (*1940s+*) [fr *whoa!* "Stop, horse!" attested fr the 1840s]

who died and made someone something *sentence* Where did you get your authority? what makes you presume? : *Who died and made Louis Farrakhan the judge of every other black person's racial loyalty?/ Who died and made you marriage counselor to the Broncos?* (*1990s+*)

whodunit *n* A mystery or detective story, play, movie, etc, esp a novel : *a conventional whodunit* [1937+; fr *who done it,* "who committed the crime?"; claimed as a coinage by and of various persons]

whole bag (or **box**) **of tricks,** the *n* Every possible thing; everything (*1960s+*)

whole ball of wax, the *n phr* The totality; everything; the whole thing; the WHOLE SHEBANG : *For that price you get the whole ball of wax* [1950s+; origin unknown; perhaps fr a manner of distributing the land of an estate to heirs, described in the early 1600s, in which the amount of each portion is concealed in a *ball of wax* that is drawn out of a hat in a sort of lottery. If so, the term went unrecorded for a very long time]

whole enchilada, the *n phr* The totality; everything; the whole thing : *We're talking best seller, mini-series, the whole enchilada*

whole famn damily *n phr* The whole family • An amusing euphemism : *I hate him and his whole famn damily* (*1940s+*) *See* FARLEY

whole hog *adv phr* Utterly; without reservation : *He believed me whole hog* [fr early 1800s *go the whole hog,* "act, give, etc, without reservation," explained in 1852 as fr the butcher's question whether the customer wants the whole slaughtered animal, at a cheaper price than the prime parts only]

whole kit and caboodle, the (also **whole caboodle, whole kit and boodle**) *n phr* Everything (*1880s+*)

whole lot *n* Everything (*1805+*)

whole megillah, the *See* the MEGILLAH

whole new ball game, a *n phr* A totally new situation; something completely different from what has been the case : *Since the government got into it this has been a whole new ball game* (*1960s+*)

whole nine yards, the *n phr* The totality; everything; the whole thing; the WHOLE SHEBANG : *went with the odd-looking ship, built a press platform in front of it, had power brought in for press lights, "the whole nine yards"/ guys in black tie passing champagne and the whole nine yards/ Floods. Fires. The whole nine yards* [1960s+ Army & Air Force; origin unknown; perhaps based on the load of a concrete mixing and hauling truck, which normally comes in a *nine-yard* and a ten-yard size; perhaps based on *yard,* "one hundred dollars," rather than on the linear or cubic measure]

whole 'nother, a *adj phr* Completely different; new : *getting in would be a whole nother thing/ That's a whole 'nother question; we'll get to it later* (*1980s+*)

whole schmear, the *n phr* (Variations: **schmier** or **schmeer** or **shmear** or **shmeer** or **shmier smear** may replace **schmear**) The totality; everything; the whole thing; the WHOLE SHEBANG : *names, ages, business they're in, daily schedules, the whole schmear/ the* *whole fucking schmeer* [1940s+; fr Yiddish *shmeer* fr *shmeeren*, "spread"; probably immediately fr the spreading out of the hand in a pinochle or rummy game]

whole shebang, the *n phr* The totality; everything; the whole thing; the WHOLE SCHMEAR : *We could move the whole shebang/ The whole shebang is festive, pleasantly show-offy and communal* [1895+; fr mid-1800s *shebang*, "hut, hovel," perhaps fr Irish *shebeen*, "cheap saloon," hence "the house and everything in it"]

whole shooting match, the *n phr* The totality; everything; the whole thing; the WHOLE SCHMEAR [1896+; probably fr the crowd that would gather at a frontier *shooting match*, hence, "the whole crowd"; perhaps influenced by earlier British *the whole shoot* of the same meaning, fr *the whole shot*, "the whole cost or price"; noted in 1900 as a favorite expression of children]

whole works, the *See* the WORKS

wholly owned subsidiary *n phr* Someone or something in the complete control of another person or entity : *Public transportation in Boston is practically a wholly owned subsidiary of Bill Bulger's/ We must put on a happy face and embrace George Pataki, a wholly owned subsidiary of Alfonse D'Amato* [1990s+; fr the phrase used to describe one company owned by another]

whomp or **whump** *v* **1** To defeat utterly; CLOBBER : *The Tigers got badly whomped* (1952+) **2** To hit; BASH : *sturdily whumped at the New Deal's "insane deficit policy"* (1973+) [echoic fr the sound of a blow, perhaps influenced by dialect *whup* and *whop*, "whip"]

whomp up *v phr* To make; devise or build : *I whomped me up one heck of a nightmare* (1950+)

whoop-de-do (HOOP dee dōō) (also **hooptydoo** or **hoopty-do** or **hoop-de-doo** or **hoop-a-doop** or **hoop-de-doop** or **whoop-de-doo** or **whoop-de-doodle**) *adj* : *The racketeering, gossiping, whoop-de-doodle thing, it is a piece of stinking fish* (1920s+) *n* **1** Raucous confusion; noisy celebration; jolly fuss : *a gay sense of flossy whoop-de-doo/ but, in spite of this whoop-de-doo/ Cowboys and soldiers created a deafening hoop-a-doop* (1929+) **2** A series of ruts or bumps in a road : *A department analysis of the ripples, called whoopdedoos by engineers* (1980s+ *Motorcyclists & highway engineers*) [echoic]

whoopee (WHOO pee) *interj* An exclamation of joy and approval; hurrah (1862+) *n* Exuberant merriment; wild celebration; WHOOP-DE-DO : *"Whoopee" seems to have entered New York with the accent on the first*

syllable (1928+) [based on *whoop*, which is found fr late 1300s; popularized and perhaps coined by the colmnist Walter Winchell]

whoopee (or **whoopie**) **cushion** *n phr* A bladder that makes a loud flatulating sound when sat upon : *It's Grandma's whoopie cushion. I thought you'd like that, you little fart* (late 1950s+)

whoop it up *v phr* To celebrate; carouse; have raucous fun : *It's natural the Boys should whoop it up for so huge a phallic triumph* (1884+)

whoopla *See* HOOPLA

whoops (HOOPS) *n* A blunder; serious mistake; GOOF, OOPS : *"I think we got a whoops," said a police inspector* (1980s+) *v* (also **whoops up**) To vomit; OOPS : *A man had whoopsed into his National Observer* (1980s+)

whoozis or **whozis** or **whoozit** (HOO zəs) *n* An unspecified or unspecifiable object; something one does not know the name of or does not wish to name; THINGAMAJIG : *Is impotence in the whoozis?/ There should be a whozis over the first n/ What do you call this whoozis on top here?* (1929+)

whoozit (HOO zət) *n* A person whose name one does not know; what's-his-face : *Hello to Fred and Whoozit* (1931+)

whop *n* **1** : *Give a good whop this time* (1440+) **2** A try or chance; CRACK, POP, SHOT : *politicians, judges, people from out of town, $50 to $100 a whop* (1980s+) *v* To hit; WHACK (1575+) [echoic]

whopper *n* **1** Something huge and powerful : *The Mauritius tortoise must have been a whopper/ You know, come up with the whopper before Election Day* **2** A very bold lie : *He told a whopper and got away with it* [1785+; fr *whop*]

whopping *adj* Huge; very impressive : *It was a whopping idea she had* (1706+)

◁**whorehouse**▷ *adj* Of a gaudiness or bad taste befitting a cheap brothel; HONKY-TONK : *The room is painted a sort of whorehouse pink* (1940s+)

whosis (also **whoosis, whosit, whoosit, whoozit**) *n* Used for referring to someone whose name is not known or remembered [1923+; casual pronunciation of "who is this" or "who is it"]

who's on first *n phr* The most basic facts; WHAT'S WHAT : *With the energy tax seemingly changing every few minutes, many corporate executives say they don't know who's on first* [1950s+; fr a confusing comedy baseball routine of Bud Abbott and Lou Costello]

who's your daddy *interj* Who is your friend or caregiver? I am that person

whump *See* WHOMP

wicked *adj* **1** Impressive; prodigious; MEAN : *He can shake a wicked spatula/ Look at the wicked bat he swings!* **2** Excellent; wonderful; BAD, GREAT *(1920+)*

wicked bad *adj* Extremely good : *wicked bad cheese fries*

wicket *See* STICKY WICKET

wickey *See* ICKY

wide *See* HIGH, WIDE, AND HANDSOME

wide ones *See* FOUR WIDE ONES

wide open *adj phr* **1** Free of police hindrance; hospitable to profitable vice : *Phoenix City was a famous wide-open town (1892+)* **2** Vulnerable; open to attack *(1915+ Boxing)* **3** Going at full speed; FLAT OUT, like sixty *adv phr* : *He always drove his bike wide open* [third sense from *wide-open throttle*, probably fr railroading]

widget or **widgit** *modifier* : *as though it were read aloud from the press release of a widget manufacturer* *n* A mechanical, electrical, or electronic device; GADGET, GIZMO : *It's three floors of sights, sounds, illusions, movements, gadgets, widgets, and gizmos/ not an activity I would recommend to anyone daunted by a widgit more complicated than a stapler (1920+)* [an alteration of *gadget*, perhaps based on hypothetical *which it* on the model of *whatzit* and *whoozis*]

widow-maker *n* Anything that is lethally dangerous, esp a falling bough or a dead tree *(1945+ Loggers)*

wiener *See* WEENIE

wiener dog *n phr* A dachshund; SAUSAGE HOUND : *For wiener dogs across Wisconsin (1990s+)*

wife *n* **1** A member of a pimp's group of prostitutes : *She is his favorite "wife" at the moment (1900+ Prostitutes)* **2** The more passive of a homosexual couple *(1883+)*

◁**wife-beater**▷ *n* A sleeveless undershirt worn by men • Fr regarding this as the attire of a male who would do this

wiff or **wif** (WIF) *n* **1** A wife **2** WHIFF

wig *adj* Excellent; wonderful; GREAT, NEAT : *a real wig rock trio (1960s+ Teenagers)* *n* **1** One's head; one's mind *(1930s+ Jive talk)* **2** A cool jazz musician *(1950s+ Jazz musicians)* *v* **1** To talk, esp casually and freely; RAP : *We stood around wigging (1930s+ Jive talk)* **2** To annoy someone; BUG : *She ordered me to stop wigging her (1930s+ Jive talk)* **3** To play cool or progressive jazz *(1950s+ Jazz musicians)* **4** To behave more or less hysterically; FLIP, FREAK OUT, WIG OUT : *I realized my goddamn father wasn't there, again, and I wigged (1950s+ Cool talk)* **5** To be happy and in harmony; DIG *(1950s+ Cool talk)* *See* BLOW ONE'S TOP, FLIP ONE'S LID

wigged out or **wigged** *adj phr* **1** Out of touch with reality; deluded; OUT OF IT : *one of whom is comically wigged out on cleanliness and ecology/ if you're really feeling wigged out by any and all contact (1950s+ Students)* **2** Intoxicated with narcotics; HIGH *(1950s+ Narcotics)*

wigging *modifier* Crazed; out of control : *wigging over the big spider*

wiggle *See* GET A MOVE ON

wiggle room *n phr* Space, either real or figurative, in which to maneuver; ELBOW ROOM : *Clinton's health plan gives Congress wiggle room (mid-1980s+)*

wiggle one's way out *v phr* To extricate oneself from difficulty, often by devious means : *men who are just trying to wiggle their way out of their obligations (1685+)*

wiggy *adj* **1** Exciting and up-to-date; COOL, FAR OUT : *But I have some really wiggy experiences (1960s+ Cool talk)* **2** Intoxicated on or using narcotics; OUT OF IT, SPACED-OUT, WIGGED OUT : *one of whom is so wiggy that she got fired from her job* **3** Crazy; weird; strange : *Things were wiggy/ neither a wiggy sexual penitent, nor a kohl-eyed tough cookie See* WIG OUT

wig out *n phr* To become mentally unbalanced; lose one's sanity : *whose guiding genius, Brian Wilson, spent years wigging out in a sandbox* *v phr* To become ecstatic; enjoy oneself hugely; FLIP, FREAK OUT, WIG : *The first time I read* The Collected Stories *I wigged out* [1950s+ Cool talk fr jazz musicians; fr a complex set of jazz uses, mostly based on the idea of *flipping* one's *wig*, "losing one's head"]

wild *adj* Excellent; exciting; wonderful; COOL *(1950s+ Cool talk)*

wild about (or **over**) *adj phr* **1** Enthusiastically approbatory of; CRAZY ABOUT : *the new lemon flavored cough drop everyone's wild about (1879+)* **2** In love with

wild and woolly *adj phr* Crude and raucous; untamed; uncouth : *a couple of good old country boys having a wild and woolly time* [1884+; fr an alliterating phrase *wild and woolly* West, the *woolly* perhaps referring to range steers, to range horses, or to the unkempt heads of cowboys and frontiersmen]

◁**wild-ass** or **wild-assed**▷ *adj* Madly exuberant; untamed; CRAZY, WILD : *Shepard tops himself as a wild-ass country boy/ and for goddamned sure a wild-assed warrior/ Ijah was a kind of wild-ass type* [1960s+; an example of the use of *ass*, "the whole person"]

wild card *modifier* : *the wild-card slot/ last year's wild-card team* *n phr* **1** Something outside of the normal rules, category, etc; an unpredictable thing, event, etc : *Being from Princeton wasn't like being from Jersey, it was* *a wild card (1920s+ Card games)* **2** A team picked for a playoff by some more or less arbitrary method, not having won its championship during the season : *We can always hope the Lions will be the wild card (1950s+ Sports)* [fr poker and other games, where in some cases one or more *wild cards*, having any value the player desires, may be designated]

wildcat *modifier* Done or ventured individually, apart from ordinary corporate structures : *a wildcat well/ a wildcat cab (1883+)* *n* **1** A mixture of the drugs cat (metcathenone) and cocaine *(1990s+ Narcotics)* **2** (also **wildcat strike**) A strike not authorized by the union authorities *(1937+ Labor union)* *v* To drill for oil, esp without strong corporate and financial backing *(1877+)* [fr the independent behavior of feral felines; in the 1840s a Western bank issued banknotes picturing a *wildcat* and then suspended payment; in early 1900s show business, to *wild-cat* meant to book a theater tour day-by-day]

wilding *n* Concerted violent behavior by groups of usu black teenagers : *A pack of 33 teenagers swept out of Harlem for a night of wilding, attacking anyone who looks vulnerable* [late 1980s+ Urban black; the word became widespread after a particular attack in April 1989]

willie or **willy** *n* ◁1▷ The penis; WEENIE • Adopted in US slang fairly recently : *The notion that some small part of the cosmic order hung on our teenage willies was a heavy load for us young soldiers in St. Ignatius' Army of Christ/ The plethysmograph, basically a strain gauge wrapped around the willy, electronically registers the pulls and tugs of arousal and then draws them as jagged peaks and valleys on a line graph (1905+)* **2** corn willie *See* DOODAD

willies, the *n phr* Acute nervousness; a spell of uneasiness; the JITTERS : *The thought of an intense daily association with this troglodyte gave me the willies/ The willies or the creeps. Call it what you like/ For years her friends' shoptalk gave him the willies* [1896+; perhaps fr *the woollies*, a dialect term for nervousness and uneasiness, perhaps suggested by the itchy sensation of wool on the skin]

willikers *See* GEE WHIZ

will the real someone **please stand up** *question* May the actual claimant now be identified : *After listening to Mr. Brown and Mr. Christopher, it was tempting to ask: Would the real Secretary of Commerce please stand up?* [1950s+; fr a television panel show, *To Tell the Truth*, where three different people claimed to have a certain identity, and the real one was finally asked to stand up]

wimp or **whimp** *n* An ineffectual person; a soft, silly person; a weakling; DRIP, NEBBISH : *Unmacho. Short hair, glasses, awkward, uncertain. WIMP/ his unfortunate and unfounded charge that Thompson portrayed him as a "wimp"/ Apparently whimps complained it was too hot* [1960s+ College students; origin unknown; perhaps fr J Wellington *Wimpy*, a relatively unaggressive character in the comic strip "Popeye"; perhaps fr the early 1900s British university *wimp* "young woman," perhaps fr *whimper*; occurs in a 1920 George Ade story, which may be the source of the term, used more in intervening years in the adjective form *wimpish*]

wimpish or **wimpy** or **wimpo** or **wimpoid** *adj* Having the traits of a wimp; soft; weak : *less wimpy version of the husband she leaves/ seats that go wimpo during cornering/ a wimpoid ballad with the refrain "the doggone girl is mine" (entry form 1925+, first variant 1967+, others 1960s+ and later)*

wimp out or **wimp** *v phr* To cancel or withdraw from an action or place because of fear; CHICKEN OUT : *I could feel for my friend because I've wimped out on the assertive front/ "I know it seems disrespectful to you," I wimped (1980s+)*

win a few lose a few or **win some lose some** *sentence* One cannot always be victorious or successful; YOU CAN'T WIN 'EM ALL : *Manning fought from within Luce's empire against the Republicanizing of the news, and as Theodore White predicted in urging him to take the job, he won some and lost some*

wind *See* BREAK WIND, PISS AND WIND, TWIST SLOWLY IN THE WIND

windage *See* KENTUCKY WINDAGE

windbag *n* A person who talks too much, esp a pompous prater; bag of wind, GASBAG : *a windbag who shoots the gab (1827+)*

wind down *v phr* **1** To come or bring to a gradual halt or conclusion : *The campaign has begun to wind down/ Shall we wind down our collection drive? (1952+)* **2** To relax gradually : *Let me sit here for a few minutes, to wind down (1958+)* [modeled on the *winding down* of a clock or other machine]

winder *See* SIDEWINDER

window *n* A time period when something may be accomplished; a critical period : *We now have a window of opportunity to try for peace in Bosnia again/ They're worried about a window of vulnerability* [1967+; fr the 1960s astronautics term for the exact time and directional limits governing the launching of a rocket to achieve a certain orbit or destination, which were pictured as a *window* through which the rocket must be shot] *See* BAY WINDOW, OUT THE WINDOW

wind up *v phr* To finish : *We wind up learning less* (*1825+*)

wind something up *v phr* To finish; bring to a conclusion : *I suggest we wind this discussion up and go home* (*1825+*)

windy *adj* Given to talking too much; overly garrulous, esp pompously so : *It's another one of his windy orations* (*1513+*)

Windy City *n* Chicago (*1887+*)

wine *See* JUG WINE

win for losing *See* someone CAN'T WIN FOR LOSING

wing *n* An arm, esp a baseball pitcher's throwing arm (*1297+*) *v* **1** To shoot someone, not necessarily in the arm : *You were winged by something big, 45 maybe* (*mid-1800s+*) **2** WING IT (*1885+*)

wingding or **whingding** *n* **1** An epileptic or drug-induced fit, esp as counterfeited to attract sympathy (*1927+ Hoboes, prison, and narcotics*) **2** A fit of anger; a violent outburst of feeling : *going to throw a wingding they'll hear in Detroit* (*1933+*) **3** (also **wingdinger**) An energetic celebration or commotion; a noisy party; RUCKUS : *Then they did their wingding out in front of the West Wing* (*1949+*)

wingdoodle *See* WHANGDOODLE

wing it or **wing** *v phr* To improvise; extemporize; act without sufficient preparation; FAKE IT : *Winging It, Coping Without Controllers/ He was confident of his ability to wing it, adjusting to counter her responses* [first form 1933+, second 1885+; fr the notion that an actor could learn his lines in the stage's *wings*, or be coached while standing there; *wing the part* is found by 1886]

wingman *n* Someone who backs up or supports a friend, esp in a social setting : *I'll be your wingman tonight*

wingnut *n* A weird or insane person; WEIRDO, nutcase : *Too weird for me. You guys are wingnuts* [1980s+; probably fr *wingy* and *nut*]

win going away *v phr* To win easily, increasing one's lead to the end; WIN IN A WALK : *We saw the results in Pennsylvania—the Democrat won going away* (*1840s+ Horse racing*)

win hands down *v phr* To win easily [1880s+; orig referring to a jockey dropping his hands and relaxing the reins when victory appears certain] *See* HANDS DOWN

win in a walk *v phr* To win easily; be a confident victor (*1896+*)

winkie *n* **1** (also **winky, winkle**) The penis : *Had Kaufman discovered a bump on his winkie, he probably would have shared that with us, too* (*1970s+*) **2** (also **winker**) The vulva (*1916+*) [both the penis and vulva have

been likened to eyes: *upright wink* is recorded as a fanciful term for the vulva, and *one-eyed snake* for the penis]

winks *See* FORTY WINKS

winner *n* A very promising and successful person or thing; HOT SHOT : *Your new poem is a winner/ Hire this guy, he looks like a winner/ That passing shot was a winner*

wino *n* A habitual drunkard, esp a derelict who drinks cheap wine; STUMBLEBUM : *a couple of "winos" who had been drinking cheap sherry in the bar/ patronized largely by vagrants, winos, dehorns, grifters* (*1900s+ Hoboes*)

win out *v phr* To win; prevail : *De Bird of Time will win out in a walk* (*1896+*)

win-win *modifier* A success for both sides : *win-win situation*

wipe *n* A killing, murder

wiped *adj* Exhausted; POOPED, BEAT (*1950s+*)

wiped out *adj phr* **1** Drunk : *Everybody had been too wiped out to watch* **2** Tired; exhausted : *At the end of that hearing she felt wiped out*

wiped out, be *v phr* To be wrecked, ruined, finished; GET IT IN THE NECK, SHOOT someone DOWN

wipe it off *v phr* To force oneself to stop smirking or joking; stop larking • Very often a stern command : *Wipe it off, Mister, this is no comic routine* (*WWII armed forces*)

wipeout *n* **1** A fall from the surfboard, esp a spectacular one (*1960s+ Surfers*) **2** (also **wipe**) A killing, esp a gangland execution; RUBOUT : *I don't know a goddam thing about this goddam Covino wipe* (*1925+*)

wipe out *v phr* To lose control of the surfboard during a ride and be thrown off into the water : *About six of them wiped out on one big wave* (*1960s+ Surfers*)

wipe someone out *v phr* To kill; ICE, OFF, RUB OUT (*1577+*)

wipe the slate clean *v phr* To cancel or ignore what has gone before; begin anew; GO BACK TO SQUARE ONE : *Let's just wipe the slate clean and pretend it never happened* (*1921+*)

wipe (or clean or mop) up the floor with someone *v phr* To defeat utterly and abjectly; trounce easily; CLOBBER (*first form 1875+*)

wire *n* **1** : *Send me a wire if you get the job* **2** : *They checked to see whether she was wearing a wire* **3** An overstimulated person; an anxious, excitable person : *You know I'm a natural wire. What I need is a drink to calm me down* *v* **1** To send a telegram : *Wire me when you get there* (*1859+*) **2** To place eavesdropping devices in a room, office, etc, or concealed on someone's body; BUG : *She quietly checked to see if her bedroom was wired/ The FBI wired me before they sent me to see the suspect* (*1950s+*) *See* COME UP TO THE WIRE.

DOWN TO THE WIRE, GO TO THE WIRE, HAYWIRE, HOT-WIRE

wired *adj* **1** (also **wired up**) Intoxicated by narcotics, esp cocaine or amphetamines; HIGH, SPACED-OUT : *"If you're wired, you're fired,"* is how Willie Nelson warns band members about cocaine usage/ That night Elvis was wired for speed (1970s+ Narcotics) **2** (also **wired up**) Eagerly excited; overstimulated; HIGH, HYPER, JACKED UP : *Keeping the people wired with a mix of Sixties vines and Eighties technology/ They have him wired up tight with the slogans of TV and the World Series* (1970s+) **3** Anxious; nervous; UPTIGHT : *I got wired when Myrt was sneaking a break and Jerry showed up* (1970s+) **4** (also **wired up**) Certain and secure; totally under control; assured; RACKED, taped : *Mention of all those other top contenders is just a smokescreen and Brown's got it wired/ Then I get this wired up and I think, well* (1950s+ fr poker) **5** Wearing an eavesdropping device; having such a device planted; BUGGED : *He's wired. He's wearing a tape recorder* (1957+) [fr *wire* as conducting an electrical charge or stimulus, or as used for binding; *wired up* is recorded as a US term for "irritated, provoked" in the late 1800s and may be related to the sense "anxious, nervous"] *See* HAVE something CINCHED

wired into *adj* Intimately involved in; closely and sympathetically connected with; INTO : *"I'm wired into Marin Transit right now." "That's cool if you get off on buses"/ for the first time, I really felt wired into that poem* [1970s+; fr *wire* as creating a close connection]

wires *See* PULL STRINGS

wise *adj* Aware; cunningly knowing; HEP : *Get wise, son!/ He's close-mouthed and wise, stir-wise* (1896+) *See* GET WISE, STREET-SMART

◁**wise-ass**▷ *modifier* : *And I don't need any big-deal Boston wiseass dick to come out here and piss all over my town, you understand* n SMART-ASS (1970s+) *See* NOBODY LIKES A WISE-ASS

wisecrack *n* A witty remark, esp one with a knowing, sarcastic edge; a joke; GAG, ONE-LINER : *at least two wisecracks in the first paragraph/ makers of wars and wise-cracks, a rum creature* [1924+; perhaps fr the theatrical term *crack a wheeze*, "tell a joke"]

wise guy or **wiseguy** *n phr* **1** (also **wise apple**) A person who is ostentatiously and smugly knowing; smart aleck, SMART-ASS : *My little brother is an irrepressible wise guy* (1896+) **2** (also **wise hombre**) A shrewd and knowing person; a person who is "wised up" : *The wise guys said Frank didn't stand a chance* (1896+) **3** A professional criminal, esp a mob member : *The wiseguys like places they're*

known/ *Hanging out at a neighborhood restaurant in the Italian section of Queens, the first thing he learned is that the wiseguys never talk about what they do* (1970s+ Underworld)

wisenheimer (WĪ zən hī mər) *n* A person who is ostentatiously and smugly knowing; smart aleck, SMART-ASS : *the way an old-time carny handles a tough wisenheimer with the aid of a hammer* [1904+; fr *wise* plus the German or Yiddish element *-enheimer* found in surnames based on German place names ending in *-heim;* the coinage may be motivated by the humorous attempt to add weight to the term and is perhaps tinged with anti-Semitism]

wise to *adj phr* Aware of, esp of something shady or forbidden : *They soon became wise to his little deceptions* (1915+)

wise up *v phr* To become shrewdly aware; GET SMART, GET WITH IT • Often an exhortation : *Wise up or you'll lose this opportunity/ Now, however, the industry is wising up* (1914+)

wise someone **up** *v phr* To give useful and usu covert particulars; put someone wise : *My adviser was a good scout and wised me up* (1905+)

wish (or want) list *n phr* A presumed list of things one wants : *intent on buying every weapon the generals and admirals put on their wish lists*

wishy-washy *adj* Marked by imprecision and vacillation; inconstant; uncertain : *The wishy-washy player keeps putting off the evil day/ It's not overpowering like Opium and not wishy-washy* [1873+; fr a rhythmic reduplication of *washy*, "weak, diluted, watered-down," probably influenced by *wishy* as suggesting vacillating desires; the original sense was "weak, insubstantial, trashy," found by 1703]

wit *See* NITWIT

witch *n* A vicious woman • A euphemism for *bitch* : *She's being very nasty about it, a real witch* (1940s+)

witch's tit *See* COLD AS HELL

with *adj phr* Having the usual accompaniment, that is, onions with hamburger, cream with coffee, etc : *We ordered two coffees with, to go* (1930s+ Lunch counter)

with something **and a dime I can get a cup of coffee** *sentence* The honor, award, compliment, etc I have received is not worth much : *She likes me? With that and a dime I can get a cup of coffee* (1970s+)

with a ten-foot pole *See* NOT TOUCH someone or something WITH A TEN-FOOT POLE

with bells on *adv phr* (Variations: **on** may be dropped; **knobs** or **tits** may replace **bells**) Very definitely; without any doubt; emphatically • Used especially in affirming that one will be present at a certain time and place : *Don't worry, I'll be there with bells on/ I'll be here Thursday. With bells* [1900s+ Theater; perhaps the suggestion is that one will be very conspicuous, like a train or a fire engine *with bells*]

with (one's) eyes (wide) open *modifier* Fully aware : *went into the project with eyes wide open*

◁**with** one's **finger up** one's **ass**▷ *See* SIT THERE WITH one's FINGER UP one's ASS

with flying colors *adv phr* In a bold and assured way; grandly; HIGH, WIDE, AND HANDSOME : *She won nicely, in fact with flying colors* [1706+; probably fr the image of a naval vessel with the national flag bravely *flying*]

with one's **hand in the till (or the cookie jar)** *adv phr* With no possibility of escape or evasion; in flagrante delicto; DEAD TO RIGHTS : *Most people think all members of Congress have their hands in the till. Last week's indictment of Rostenkowski simply confirms it/ I got caught with my hand in the cookie jar* [1970s+; fr the situation of a thief caught *with his hand in the money-box* or *cash register*]

within an ace *See* COME WITHIN AN ACE

with it *adj phr* **1** Coolly cognizant; absolutely in touch; stylish and au courant; HEP : *He affects clothes that carefully cultivate the "with-it" image/ to spend less time attempting to be "with it" and to exert greater effort to communicate with our deprived and our outcast/ Shadows of course there are, Porn-Ads, with-it clergy (1930s+ Black)* **2** Working in a carnival as a full-time professional : *had previous short experiences traveling with carnivals before becoming fully "with it" (as carnival workers describe the fully-initiated member) (1920s+ Carnival & circus) See* GET WITH IT

with one's **left hand** *adv phr* At less than full efficiency; more or less casually : *Talese said, "The Frank Sinatra piece is something I dashed off with my left hand"* [the *Oxford English Dictionary* in the 1903 volume lists *work with the left hand,* "implying inefficiency of performance," as obsolete, without dates or examples]

with one hand tied behind one's **back (or behind** one) *adv phr* **1** Very easily; readily and neatly : *I can do that job with one hand tied behind my back*•The phrase originally referred to fistfights (1890+) **2** At a great disadvantage; under a handicap : *This is what Lord Owen calls "negotiating with one hand tied behind your back" (1990s+)*

◁**without a pot to piss in**▷ *See* NOT HAVE A POT TO PISS IN

without skipping (or missing) a beat *adv phr* With no pause or discontinuity; smoothly :

She segued to the tricky point without skipping a beat/ Without missing a beat, she plucked the pipe from Dolan's mouth [1940s+; fr *heartbeat* and musical *beat*]

with the punches *See* ROLL WITH THE PUNCHES

with the territory *See* GO WITH THE TERRITORY

witless *See* SCARE someone SHITLESS

wolf *n* **1** A sexually aggressive man; an ardent womanizer; COCKSMAN : *Mary considered him quite a wolf (1847+)* **2** An aggressive male homosexual; a homosexual rapist : *the sodomist, the degenerate, the homosexual "wolf" (1915+ Prison & hoboes)* *v* : *I give with the vocals and wolf around in a nite club*

wolf something down *v phr* To eat voraciously; gobble : *wolfed down the grilled cheese*

wolf whistle *n phr* A two-note whistled expression, esp of male appreciation for the sexual attributes of a woman *(1940s+)*

woman *See* BAG LADY, the LITTLE WOMAN, OLD WOMAN

woman-chaser *n* A womanizer; LADIES' MAN, SKIRT-CHASER, WOLF *(1890s+)*

wombat *n* An eccentric person; FREAK, NUT [1980s+ Teenagers; probably fr the inherently amusing name of the *wombat,* a pudgy Australian marsupial, and the occurrence of *bat,* "crazy person, nut," as an element of the name]

Wonder Bread *adj phr* Conventional; WHITE BREADY : *Of course, the president's a little too Wonder Bread* [1980s+; fr the trademark of a popular brand of white bread]

wonk *n* **1** An overstudious student; an intellectual; greasy grind : *I had a real wonk of a roommate. The guy drove me bats/ Along come these wonks with slide rules sewn into their sports jackets* **2** A flunky; a stupid person [1990s+ College students; origin unknown; perhaps fr British *wanker,* "masturbator"; in British sailor slang, *wonk* meant "midshipman"; the term became suddenly common in the phrase *policy wonk* during the first year of the Clinton administration, 1993]

wonkish *adj* Redolent of policy, theory, discussion, etc : *Greenberg felt that a wonkish tone had pervaded the transition (1990s+)*

wonky[1] *adj* **1** Badly done or made; ineffective; weird; COCKEYED : *the wonky clutter of a Victorian parlor/ Only the steering feels wonky to me (1923+)* **2** Out of order; needing repair; DOWN *(1990s+ Computer)* [fr British dialect *wanky* or *wankle,* "weak, unsteady"; perhaps related to *wanky,* "spurious, doubtful," said of coins and attested by 1913]

wonky[2] *adj* Tedious and serious, esp anxious and overstudious in an academic situation : *"Jenny Cavilleri," answered Ray. "Wonky music type"/ a class which I have long dismissed* *as hopelessly wonky* [1970s+ Students; fr *wonk*]

won't eat you, someone *sentence* Don't worry, that person will not harm you : *Answer the question; we won't eat you* (*1738+*)

woo *See* PITCH WOO

◁**wood**[1]▷ *n* A white person; PECKERWOOD, REDNECK : *just because they find some cum in that wood's ass* [1970s+ Black; fr a shortening of *peckerwood*]

◁**wood**[2] or **woody**▷ *n* An erect penis; BLUE-VEINER, HARD-ON (*1980s+ Prison*) *See* SAW WOOD

◁**woodchuck**▷ *n* CRACKER, REDNECK (*1980s+*)

woodenhead *n* A stupid person; BLOCKHEAD, KLUTZ

wooden kimono *n phr* PINE OVERCOAT (*1926+*)

wooden nickels *See* DON'T TAKE ANY WOODEN NICKELS

wooden overcoat *n phr* PINE OVERCOAT (*1903+*)

wood-pusher *n* A chess player, esp an unskilled one; patzer : *enough to make any parlor wood-pusher loosen his collar and roll up his sleeves* (*1950s+*)

woods are full of someones or somethings, the *sentence* The named things or persons are in plentiful supply; these things are cheap and available : *Look, the woods are full of computer programmers; I want one that's a real whiz* (*1940s+*)

woodshed or **shed** *v* To rehearse; practice one's part, role, etc, esp to do so alone and rigorously : *Bix did plenty of woodshedding, playing alone/ I just learned a new technique and I've got to shed on it* [1930s+ Jazz musicians; fr the *woodshed* as the traditional place where one could be alone to work, think, smoke, etc]

woodwork *See* CRAWL OUT OF THE WOODWORK

woody *n* **1** A station wagon with wooden outside trim : *Get your woody working* (*1950s+ Surfers, orig a wooden surfboard*) ◁**2**▷ An erect penis

woof *v* **1** To talk idly; chatter meaninglessly : *I ain't woofin'. I'm not fooling* (*1934+ Black*) **2** To boast, esp menacingly; bluff : *The extreme of arguing is "woofing," like Ali and Frazier* (*1934+ Black*) **3** To vomit : *woofed in the backroom* [echoic fr the idle or menacing barking of a dog]

wool *See* PULL THE WOOL OVER someone's EYES

wool hat *n phr* A rural person; a bumpkin; REDNECK (*1828+*)

woolies or **woollies** *n* Long woolen underwear; LONG JOHNS (*1940s+*)

woolly *See* WILD AND WOOLLY

woolly-headed *adj* Inclined to idealism and hopeful fantasy; impractical : *She dismissed it*

as another woolly-headed scheme of mine (*1883+*)

wootsie or **wootsy** *See* TOOTS

woozily *adv* In a woozy manner : *I balanced myself woozily on the flats of my hands/ tottered woozily off a plane from Tripoli* (*1911+*)

woozy *adj* **1** Not fully alert and conscious; half-asleep; befuddled : *You'll just get woozy if you stay up any longer/ some woozy tourist* **2** Dizzy; faint; unwell [1897+; origin unknown; perhaps fr *oozy*, suggesting the insolidity and limpness of mud]

◀**wop** or **Wop**▶ *adj* : *big wop tenor n* An Italian or a person of Italian extraction; DAGO (*1912+*) [apparently fr southern Italian dialect *guappo*, "dandy, dude, stud," used as a greeting by male Neapolitans]

word *interj* **1** An exclamation of agreement and appreciation, used when someone has said something important or profound : *If it's really meaningful, "Word, man, word" should be used* (*1980s+ Black teenagers*) **2** WORD UP *See* EAT one's WORDS, FIGHTIN' WORDS, FROM THE WORD GO, WEASEL WORDS, WHAT'S THE GOOD WORD

-word *combining word* Used in real or mock euphemisms to avoid saying a taboo or repulsive word : *C-word, "cancer"/ F-word, "fuck"/ L-word, "liberal"/ T-word, "taxes"* (*1980s+*)

word hole (or **cake hole** or **pie hole**) *n* The mouth

word up *interj* An exhortation to listen, to pay attention : *Word up, fool. We be fresh tonight* [1980s+ Black; probably based on *listen up*]

work *v* **1** To go about a place begging, selling, stealing, etc; ply one's often-dishonest trade : *She did not deserve charity. She worked the town* (*1851+*) **2** To exert one's charm, power, persuasiveness, etc, esp on an audience; manipulate : *To watch Dick Engberg work the crowd and Al McGuire tossing peanuts to the spectators/ We watched him work the room a bit* (*1851+*) *See* BULLWORK, DIRTY WORK, DONKEYWORK, GRUNT WORK, NICE WORK IF YOU CAN GET IT, SCUT

workaholic *modifier* : *I made a hardy attempt to suppress my workaholic tendency n* A person whose primary and obsessive interest is work; a compulsive worker : *This type of person is a work freak, a workaholic* (*1968+*) [coined fr *work* plus *-aholic* (fr *alcoholic*) by the pastoral counselor W E Oates]

◁**work** one's **ass** (or **buns** or **tail**) **off**▷ *v phr* To work very hard; BUST one's ASS : *They work their ass off all year/ The dead acoustics of the room force the students to work their tails off/ Complains one Apple staffer, "People are working their buns off"* (*1940s+*)

work both sides of the street *v phr* To take two contrary positions at once; HAVE IT BOTH WAYS : *Most politicians have a good instinct for working both sides of the street* [1930s+ Politics; probably fr the notion of a hoboes' or beggars' agreement to parcel out the territory]

work both ways or **cut two ways** *v phr* To suggest or entail a necessary contrary; have double and opposite application : *Most often the claim of mental cruelty works both ways in a marriage/ I see your point, but don't you see it cuts two ways?* [originally fr the notion of a two-edged sword]

worked up *adj phr* Angry; excited; distraught : *The whole town was worked up over the shooting incident (1883+)*

working *See* HAVE something GOING FOR someone or something

working girl *n phr* A prostitute; HOOKER : *an old white pimp named Tony Roland who was known to handle the best-looking "working" girls in New York/ The customer was a working girl just like Jenny (1960s+ Prostitutes)*

working stiff *n phr* A common working man; an ordinary worker : *made good cars cheap and paid working stiffs $5 a day/ The author has been a novelist. He has also been a movie and TV working stiff (1930+)*

work it *v phr* To behave in a blatantly seductive way; engage in high-pressure salesmanship : *Meanwhile, De Luca and Saperstein are working it hard from the conference room* [1980s+; propagated from a scene in the 1990 movie *Pretty Woman*, in which one prostitute urges another to *Work it, girl*, "activate your derriere," as she approaches a possible client]

work it into the ground *See* RUN something INTO THE GROUND

work like a charm *v phr* To achieve the objective with perfect success (1880+)

work out *v phr* **1** To end; eventuate; PLAY OUT, RUN, SHAKE OUT : *How's this plan going to work out? (1885+)* **2** To do strenuous exercises; have a hard session of physical conditioning : *The president works out every day in the palace gym (1909+)*

work something out *v phr* To achieve an agreement, esp by compromise : *We'll just stay at it until we work something out* [1970s+; found by 1849 in the sense "to solve"]

work someone over *v phr* To beat someone, esp cruelly and systematically; MESS someone UP : *He tells me to work this guy over, do a number on him (1927+)*

works, the, or **the whole works** *n phr* Everything; the totality of resources; the WHOLE SCHMEAR, the WHOLE NINE YARDS : *the works, shave, haircut, massage, and tonic* [1912+; perhaps like *kit and caboodle* in referring to an entire outfit of equipment, conceived as a *works*, "factory, workplace and equipment"; perhaps referring to the entirety of a mechanism like that in *gum up the works*] *See* GIVE someone THE WORKS, GUM UP, IN THE PIPELINE, SHOOT THE WORKS

work up *v phr* To devise; WHOMP UP : *We'll have to work up a good story to explain this one (mid-1800s+)*

work oneself up *v phr* To allow oneself to get very upset : *worked herself up for nothing*

world *See* DEAD TO THE WORLD, FREEWORLD, GO AROUND THE WORLD, HAVE THE WORLD BY THE BALLS, OUT OF THIS WORLD

world-beater *n* A very effective person; a winner; a champion : *Sometimes I think you're a world-beater (1893+)*

world-class *adj* Very superior; outstanding; superexcellent : *a few of the nasties are scenery-chomping world-class scum/ took one look at me and bolted off in world-class time!* [1950+; fr the superiority of an athlete who competes successfully in the Olympic Games or other worldwide events]

world is one's oyster, the *sentence* The person referred to is doing very well, is prosperous, is happy, has great prospects, etc : *Before the crash his rich grandfather figured the world was his oyster*

worm *n* ◁1▷ A despicable person; BASTARD, JERK : *Cut that out, you little worm (fr 800s)* **2** (also **tapeworm**) A program that copies itself from one computer to another in a network, does not destroy data, but can clutter up a system : *which is now classified as a "worm" because the writer of the program did not mean to do damage/ A worm, in computerese, is one of the many varieties of viruses that infect computers (late 1980s+ Computer) See* CAN OF WORMS

worm-burner *n* A fast-moving ground ball in baseball, golf, etc

worm-food *n* A dead body; corpse

worm out of something *v phr* To evade or avoid an unpleasant situation, esp by ignominious means : *This time we have him dead to rights, and he won't worm out of it (1893+)*

worm one's way *v phr* To enter or penetrate stealthily, like a worm or snake : *has used his sophisticated skill to worm his way into many of the nation's telephone networks (1845+)*

worry *See* NOT TO WORRY

worrywart *n phr* A person who worries excessively; a constantly apprehensive person [1956+; fr the designation of such a person in the comic strip "Out Our Way" by J R Williams]

worship the porcelain god(dess) *v phr* To vomit, esp in the toilet *See* HUG THE PORCELAIN GOD(DESS), PRAY TO THE PORCELAIN GOD

worst-case scenario *n phr* A speculation or prediction as to what would happen if everything turned out as badly as possible : *our worst-case scenario in Western Europe (1960s+ Armed forces)*

worth *See* TWO CENTS' WORTH

worth one's salt *adv* Worth what it costs to keep : *anyone worth their salt will be kept*

would you buy a used car from this man *question* Can this person really be trusted; is this an honest face [1960s+; fr the belief that used-car salesmen are notoriously dishonest; popularized as applied to President Richard M Nixon]

wound or **wound up** *adj phr* Tense; anxious; on edge : *She was a tall, angular woman, tightly wound, with a Nefertiti profile and hands made for scratching (1788+)*

wounded *See* WALKING WOUNDED

wounded duck *n phr* **1** In baseball, a short looping fly that falls for a hit; TEXAS LEAGUER **2** In football, a wobbling forward pass, which might be intercepted *(1980s+ Sports)*

wow[1] *interj* (also **wowee-kazowee** or **wowie-kazowie**) An exclamation of pleasure, wonder, admiration, surprise, etc • This old interjection had a new popularity in the early 1900s and again during the 1960s and later : *Wow, what a nice voice you have!/ Oh, wow, far out!/ Hey, wow!/ I have a PhD in communications from UCLA. Well, wowee-kazowee!/ Big rock-'n'-roll concerts are often as much about wowie-kazowie production values, video, neon, fireworks, suggestively costumed young men and women, as music* (entry form 1513+, variants 1990s+) *n* **1** Something very exciting and successful; a sensation : *It would be a wow of a scrap/ a wow of a line! (1920+)* **2** A theatrical success; boffola, HIT *(1920s+ Show business) v* To impress someone powerfully and favorably; KNOCK SOMEONE DEAD, LAY THEM IN THE AISLES : *wondering whether he'll make a fraternity and whether or not he'll wow the girls/ all self-proclaimed poets who, to wow an audience, utter some resonant line (1920s+ Show business)* [echoic of a bark or howl of approval] *See* POWWOW

wow[2] *n* An intrusive wavering sound from a record player, usu caused by uneven running of the turntable [1930s+ Electronics; echoic of a howl or yowl]

wowser[1] *n* Something very successful and impressive; a sensation; WOW[1] : *It would make a wowser of a movie/ The four-beat peroration is a wowser* [1928+; fr *wow*, perhaps influenced by *rouser*]

wowser[2] *n* A stiff and puritanical person; a prude and prig; KILLJOY, PARTY POOPER • Now outdated and sure to be confused with *wowser*[1] : *men of letters, who would swoon at the sight of a split infinitive, such wowsers they are in regard to pure English* [1899+; origin unknown; claimed in 1899 by John Norton, an Australian muckraking publisher, as his coined acronym for the name of his organization *We Only Want Social Evils Righted*]

wrap *n* : *Well, it's a wrap on the squash v* To complete; finish; WRAP UP : *Filming, based on Bob Randall's 1977 thriller, wrapped last summer/ Because when it wraps, they strike the sets and you're stuck (1970s+ Movies and television)* [possibly fr the shrouding of a corpse]

wrapped *adj* Under control; in hand; TOGETHER : *got everything wrapped, whole fuckin' world on the half-shell (1980s+)*

wrapped up *adj* Busy with someone or something : *wrapped up with a customer*

wrapper *See* PLAIN WRAPPER

wraps *See* UNDER WRAPS

wrap-up *n* A completion; a final treatment, summary, etc; RECAP : *This is the 11:30 pm wrap-up of the news (1950s+)*

wrap up *v phr* To complete; finish : *Let's wrap the matter up now and call it a day (1926+)*

wreck *n* **1** An old car or other vehicle; HEAP, JALOPY *(1930s+)* **2** An exhausted or dissipated person; a human ruin : *He's pretty smart, but physically a wreck (1795+)*

wrecked *adj* Intoxicated with or addicted to narcotics *(1960s+ Narcotics)*

wriggle out *v phr* To avoid or evade something (1848+)

wringer *See* GET one's TAIL IN A GATE, PUT someone THROUGH THE WRINGER

wrinkle *n* **1** An idea, device, trick, notion, style, etc, esp a new one : *Wearing that thing sideways is a nice wrinkle (1817+)* **2** A defect or problem, esp a minor one; BUG : *The plan's still got a few wrinkles, nothing we can't handle (1643+)* [origin of first sense unknown; perhaps fr the same semantic impulse as *twist* in a similar sense, referring to a quick shift in course; perhaps a reference to a lack of plain simplicity in dress or decoration, and the prevalence of stylish pleats, folds, etc, since the earliest form is *without all wrinkles*; second sense fr the notion of *ironing the wrinkles out* of something]

wrist *See* GIVE someone A SLAP ON THE WRIST, LIMP WRIST

write someone a blank check *See* GIVE someone A BLANK CHECK

write home about *See* NOTHING TO WRITE HOME ABOUT

write the book *v phr* To be very authoritative or seasoned; be an expert • Usu in the past tense : *Can she sing? Hell, she wrote the book* (*1980s+*)

write-up *n* A written article, news story, etc : *I figure you have seen the write-ups/ The papers gave his book a good write-up* (*1885+*)

wrongo *adj* 1 Prone to error; inept : *an almost endearingly wrong-o, sloppily managed outfit* 2 Undesirable : *That's the wrongo car for her n* 1 A wicked or criminal person; a villain 2 An undesirable person or thing; a person of the wrong sort : *a "closet for wrongos" on the second floor that "looks like an attic decorated by a cross-eyed paper hanger in a hurry"* 3 Something wrong or improper; an error, lie, misstatement, etc : *They haven't hit me with a wrongo yet, although they did miss a whopper this morning* (*1937+*)

wrong side of the bed *See* GOT UP ON THE WRONG SIDE OF THE BED

wrong side of the tracks, the *adv phr* A socially and economically inferior neighborhood; the slums : *He did very well for a boy from the wrong side of the tracks/ I was born on the wrong side of the tracks* [fr the fact that poor and industrial areas were often located on one side of the railroad *tracks*, partly because prevailing wind patterns would carry smoke into them and away from the better-off neighborhoods]

wrong way, the *See* RUB someone THE WRONG WAY

wrote *See* THAT'S ALL SHE WROTE

wuffo *n* A person who annoyingly asks "why" or "what for" questions

wuss or **wussy** (WOO see) *n* A weak person; PUSSYCAT. WIMP : *6 Ways Not to be a Wuss/ "Wussy" was a particularly expressive word, the handy combination of wimp and pussy* [1960s+ Teenagers; perhaps a shortening of hypothetical *pussy-wussy*]

X

X^1 *n* A person's signature : *Just put your X on this and we're in business* [fr the custom of an illiterate person to make an *X* in place of a written signature]

X^2 *n* Ecstasy, a variety of amphetamine narcotic *(1990s+ Narcotics) v* To use the narcotic ecstasy : *Many of us have had the experience of being around someone who is X-ing*

X amount *n phr* An indefinite number : *There's always X amount of people out there laughing and talking* [1970s+; fr the algebraic symbol *X*]

X'd out *modifier* Eliminated; crossed-out : *X'd out items on the to-do list*

X-er *n* A member of Generation X : *a 25-year-old self-proclaimed champion of the X-ers (1990s+)*

X marks the spot *sentence* This is the place; here is the exact location : *I pointed to the map and told her "X marks the spot"* [1813+; fr the graphic convention of designating a precise location on a picture, map, etc, with an *X*; the date refers to the earliest example found where a particular place is marked with an *X*]

X-rated *adj* Lewd; obscene; pornographic; BLUE, DIRTY : *He uttered a few well-chosen X-rated words* [fr the now-superseded early 1950s system of rating movies according to the amount of sex, verbal obscenity, violence, etc, they contain, *X* being the most censorious rating]

Xs and Os *n phr* Symbols used to chart plays with Xs and Os representing players : *He gets the job done; he's a great "X" and "O" guy/ "You coach a mentality," Kotite said before today's game. "It's not just Xs and Os"* *(1990s+ Sports)*

XYZ *interj* Examine one's zipper; make certain one's fly is zipped up

Y

yada, yada, yada *n phr* Talk, talk, talk : *the BS of her yada, yada, yada*

yadda yadda *adv phr* And so on; so they say repeatedly : *Snyder is too old, too abrasive, yadda yadda, on and on* (1990s+)

yahoo *n* An oaf; an uncultivated or boorish person; JERK : *look, you yahoo, take a seat*

yak (also yack or yack-yack or yack-yack-yack or yackety-yack or yackety-yak or yak-yak or yak-yak-yak or yakitty-yack or yakkity-yak or yock or yock-yock or yock-yock-yock or yok or yok-yok or yok-yok-yok or yuck or yuck-yuck or yuck-yuck-yuck or yuk or yuk-yuk or yuk-yuk-yuk) *n* 1 Talk, esp idle or empty chatter; mere babbling : *All they can talk about, yack-yack-yack, is their own specialty/ I don't care how owlish you look, how convincing you sound, this is just yak yak yak until you do it/ in the midst of all the political yuk-yuk that dins around us/ if the State Department would stop its incessant yakitty-yak* (1958+) 2 A laugh; a guffaw : *"Take off your clothes." Pause for audience yuks/ It makes me furious when I have a corny line and it gets a yock* (1938+) *v* 1 (also yack it up or yak it up or yock it up or yuk it up) : *Everybody is yakking out an opinion on whether he should now reconsider his candidacy/ sparing the rod and yak-yakking and explaining all the time/ The students were seated on the floor, still yocking away/ I'll be 75 and hanging around bars yocking it up* (1950+) 2 (also yack it up or yak it up or yock it up or yuk it up) : *Ken Gaul is yukking, tugging at his pointy satyr's beard/ There'd be Don, yockin' it up like crazy. He's so hysterical with laughter/ former senator George McGovern, yukking it up with Paul Volcker* (1938+) [echoic, perhaps of Yiddish origin]

yammer *n* Talking : *He kept up his tedious yammer* (1500+) *v* 1 To talk loudly; YAK : *They were yammering away about taxes* (1513+) 2 To complain; whine and nag; BITCH : *They are always yammering about mere details* (1786+) [fr Scots dialect, related to German *Jammer*, "lamentation, misery"]

yang or yang-yang *n* The penis; jang, WANG : *A macho machine, a celebration of the yang, bang, whang/ Like I need a three-foot yang-yang* (1970s+) *See* YING-YANG

yank *v* To victimize or harass; dupe; mislead : *The detective uses expressions like "You gotta be yankin' me"* [1970s+; an alteration and shortening of yank someone's chain or jerk someone *around* or jack someone *around*]

Yank *n* 1 A US citizen; an American : *inquiring after the "Yank" and swearing to have his life* (1778+) 2 A US soldier : *Some Tommies resented the Yanks for being overpaid (WWI British army)* [a shortening fr *Yankee* for both senses]

yank someone's **chain** *See* JERK someone's CHAIN

yantsy *adj* Excited; nervous; aroused; ANTSY [1970s+; probably an alteration of *antsy*]

yap[1] *n* 1 A stupid person; a half-wit; BOOB : *just a no-account yap* (1894+) 2 A rural person; HICK, YOKEL (1900+ Hoboes) 3 A criminal's victim; MARK, PATSY (1912+ Underworld) [probably fr British dialect, "half-wit"]

yap[2] *n* The mouth; BAZOO : *every time you open your yap to say something* (1900+) *v* To talk, esp idly or naggingly; YAMMER : *You've been yapping away* (1886+) [probably echoic, and similar to the sense "yelp," esp as a small dog does] *See* BLOW OFF one's MOUTH, OPEN one's YAP

YAP (pronounced as separate letters) *n* A young person in one of the learned and well-paid professions [1970s+; fr *Young American Professional*]

yard[1] *n* A hundred dollars; a $100 bill : *"Mac, what you payin' for this?" Stony looked around the room. "A yard and a half"* [1926+; fr the unit of measure] *See* HALF A YARD

yard[2] *v* To be sexually unfaithful; CHEAT : *She told him she didn't like to yard on her man* [1960+ Black; said to be fr the phrase *backyard woman*, "mistress, illicit sex partner"]

yardbird *n* 1 A convict (1956+) 2 A recruit; a basic trainee (WWII armed forces) 3 A soldier who because of ineptitude or misdemeanor is confined to a certain area, and often ordered to keep it clean and neat (WWII armed forces) [fr the fact that convicts exercise in the yard of the prison, and that neophyte soldiers are confined to the grounds of the training post during their first weeks; the basic metaphor is probably based on the behavior of urban pigeons]

yard dog *n* A disgusting or despicable person whom one does not want around

yards *See* the WHOLE NINE YARDS

yatata (YA tə tæe) *n* Talk, esp idle talk and chatter; YAK *v* : *Mustn't yatata yatata yatata in the public library* [1940s+; echoic]

yawn *See* TECHNICOLOR YAWN

yawner *n* Something boring; a tedious account : *Most of the time, stories about child care are a snooze, total yawners* (1940s+)

yawn in Technicolor *v phr* To vomit; BARF, RALPH : *John was sick. He yawned in Technicolor all over Mary's lap* (1980s+)

yay or **yea** (YAY) *adv* To this extent; this; so•A sort of demonstrative adverb used with adjectives of size, height, extent, etc, and often accompanied by a hand gesture indicating size : *Dorsey almost did him in yea years ago/ Helen Venable said she'd swear on a stack of Bibles yea high* [1950s+; perhaps fr *yea*, "yes," specialized fr an earlier sense "even, truly, verily" to something like "even so, truly so, verily so"; perhaps fr Pennsylvania German, based on German *je*]

yazzihamper *n* An obnoxious person

yea big *modifier* About this big•Said with a hand gesture to explain size : *been here since he was yea big*

yeah (YE, YE ə) *affirmation* Yes; certainly; right : *Don't say "yeah." It's common* (1905+) *See* OH YEAH

yeah man *interj* An exclamation of agreement, pleasure, affirmation, etc (1934+)

yeah, right *interj* I don't think so•Said with complete disbelief and sarcasm : *You'll clean the house? Yeah, right*

yecch or **yech** *See* YUCK

yell bloody (or **blue**) **murder** *v phr* To shout and complain loudly : *The crowd in the kitchen was yelling bloody murder* [entry form 1931+, variant 1859+; *scream bloody murder* is found by 1882]

yell one's head off *v phr* To complain loudly and persistently; express oneself forcefully (1940s+)

yellow *adj* **1** Cowardly; faint-hearted; CHICKEN : *Don't get into this race if you're yellow* (1856+) **2** Having light skin for a black person : *You know that baker we hired. The yellow boy* (1808+) *n* Cowardice; poltroonery; excessive timidity•Most often in the expression "yellow streak" or "streak of yellow" : *I'm afraid he has a streak of yellow in him* (1896+) [the origin of the coward sense is unknown; perhaps it is derived fr the traditional symbolic meanings of *yellow*, among which were "deceitfulness, treachery, degradation, the light of hell"] *See* HIGH YELLOW

yellow-bellied *adj* Cowardly; YELLOW : *You yellow-bellied jerk* (1924+)

yellow-belly *n* A coward; a poltroon : *He is a contemptible yellow-belly, scared of his own shadow* [1930+; probably a rhyming expansion of *yellow*; influenced by the early 1800s sense, "a Mexican, esp a Mexican soldier," perhaps fr the color of their uniforms]

yellow-card *v phr* To punish someone for a stupid action : *We yellow-carded him for*

leaving the beer in his drunk where we could find it [*fr a soccer penalty*]

yellow dog *n phr* **1** A contemptible person; scoundrel; cur; BASTARD (1881+) **2** An informer; RAT (1980s+ Underworld)

yen *n* A strong craving; a keen desire; a passion : *He's got a yen for faro/ a yen to put on paper what I was saying in class* (1906+) *v* : *I yenned to own a Rolls Royce* (1919+) [fr a Peking dialect Chinese word, "smoke," hence opium, perhaps reinforced by *yearn*; found by 1876 as "the craving of a narcotic addict"]

yenta or **yente** (YEN tə) *n* A garrulous and gossipy person, usu a woman; BLABBERMOUTH : *Terrible Tom and Rampaging Rona stopped talking to each other, which is something small-screen yentas should never do* [1923+; fr a Jewish woman's given name perhaps derived fr Italian *Gentile* or French *Gentille*, degraded by its association with a humorous character *Yente* Telebende in a regular column of the New York Yiddish newspaper the *Jewish Daily Forward*]

yep *affirmation* Yes; certainly; sure; YEAH (1891+) *See* NOPE

yes-man *n* An obsequious and flattering subordinate; ASS-KISSER : *Joe Davies, Roosevelt's yes-man at the Kremlin/ This president doesn't want yes-men* [1913+; said to have appeared first in a 1913 drawing by the sports cartoonist T A Dorgan, showing a group of newspaper assistants, each labeled *yes-man*, all firmly agreeing with their chief; perhaps fr German *Jaherr*, cited in 1941 as "long current"]

yes siree or **yes siree bob** *affirmation* : *I'll take that, yes siree bob, I'll take that any day of the week* (1846+)

yike or **yikes** *interj* An exclamation of alarm or surprise : *"There are people next door," she said. "Yikes,"* *Hawk said* (first form 1940s+, variant 1971+)

ying-yang or **yin-yang** *n* **1** The anus; ASS, ASSHOLE, WHERE THE SUN DOESN'T SHINE•Nearly always in the expression *up the ying-yang*, "in great abundance" : *A mother-jumper of a winter. Snow up the yin-yang* (1970s+) **2** The penis; PRICK : *a peek at one of my troopers with tubes up his ying-yang* (1960s+) **3** A stupid or foolish person (1970s+ Army) [origin uncertain; perhaps coined because of the increasing currency of the Chinese term *yin* and *yang*, "the female and male principles in nature," influenced by *wang*, "penis"; perhaps fr Louisiana French *yan-yan*, "ass"]

yin-yang or **ying-yang** *n* Nonsense; cant; BULLSHIT : *talking all this yin-yang about us women* (1990s+)

yip *v* To talk in an insistent, petulant, and annoying way : *Will you please stop yipping* *about your rights?* [1907+; echoic of the high-pitched bark of a small dog]

yipe or **yipes** or **yikes** *interj* An exclamation of dismay, alarm, emphatic response, etc : *Yipes, it's a rattlesnake! Yipe, that hurt!* [esp teenagers; probably fr the spontaneous interjection *yi*, a cry of pain or dismay, with the *p* or *k* stop intruding after lip closure, as it does in *nope* and *yep*]

yippee (yip EE) *interj* An exclamation of pleasure, approval, triumph, etc : *Yippee, all my candidates won!* (*1920+*)

yippie *n* A member of the Youth International Party, a left-wing group espousing values of the counterculture movement of the 1960s and early '70s [1969+; fr the acronym of the name of the group, reinforced by the rhyme with *hippie*]

YM *v* To send a message via Yahoo Messenger : *He YMed me* (*1990s+ Computer*)

yo *interj* A greeting or said to get someone's attention; HEY : *Yo, dudes and babes!* [1859+; even though *yo* and *yoho* are very old utterances, found by 1420, the recent revival of *yo* as a primarily black interjection has spawned comment; Ernest Paolino of Philadelphia, indignant because a New York writer had claimed the syllable for New York, recalls it from the 1930s as shortening of *walyo*; in the WWII Army it was the common form of *here!* used in responding to roll-calls]

yo-boy *See* WIGGER

yock *See* YAK

yok *See* YAK

yokel *n* A rural person; a bumpkin; HAYSEED, HICK [1812+; perhaps fr a dialect name for a woodpecker, hence semantically similar to British dialect *gowk*, "cuckoo, simpleton"] *See* LOCAL YOKEL

yo mama *interj* **1** Hey, you **2** So you say

yonder *See* DOWN YONDER

you *See* SAYS YOU

you ain't seen nothing yet *sentence* What follows is much better than what you have had before : *put her mouth lightly against mine and said "You ain't seen nothing yet"* [1920s+; this was a catch-line of the singer and comedian Al Jolson, and the first words in his 1927 movie *The Jazz Singer*]

you and what army or **you and who else** *interj* Who is daring to threaten me?

you bet (or **betcha**) *affirmation* Yes; certainly; surely; BET YOUR BOOTS [1857+; *betcha* form fr *you bet you* or *you bet your life*]

you (or **you'd**) **better believe** something *sentence* Something is absolutely certain; something is assured; you are absolutely right : *Am I ready to try? You better believe it/ You'd better believe she's the best* (*1856+*)

you can say that again *sentence* That is absolutely right; I totally agree with you (*1941+*)

you can't fight city hall *sentence* It is futile to pit yourself against the political or other chiefs and their establishment; it is foolish to take on a battle you cannot possibly win (*1970s+*)

you can't get there from here *sentence* **1** The place referred to is very remote and the route hard to describe (*1930s+*) **2** The problem described is insoluble

you can't take it with you *sentence* You'd better use it because after you die it's not useable

you can't win *interj* It is hopeless (*1926+*)

you can't win 'em all *sentence* One cannot always be successful; WIN A FEW LOSE A FEW • Often said ruefully after one has failed, or comfortingly to someone else who has failed [1910+ Sports; attributed to a pitcher named Clifton G Curtis after losing his 23rd game of the season]

you don't have to be a brain surgeon *sentence* (Variations: It **doesn't take** or **You don't need** may replace **you don't have to be;** **Harvard MBA** or **rocket scientist** may replace **brain surgeon**) This problem is not very difficult; superintelligence is not required : *It doesn't take a brain surgeon to realize that some viewers might be uncomfortable with this subject/ You don't need an MBA from Harvard to understand the long-term consequences/ We didn't have to be rocket scientists to understand that this would put us on the leading edge* (*1990s+*)

you go *See* THERE YOU ARE

you got a problem with that *question* Does something about my true and useful statement bother you • A very truculent response : *So she's not Mother Teresa in a tut, you got a problem with that?/ Evander Holyfield, who'll defend his heavyweight title this week, loosens up with ballet exercises. You got a problem with that?* (*1990s+*)

you got it *interj* **1** I agree; I will give you what you requested : *Double order of fries? You got it* **2** You are right : *You got it. I'm finished*

you-know-what (or **-who**) *n* Something or someone one does not wish to name, usu because it is both obvious and indelicate or taboo; WHATSIS : *They were knocked on their you-know-what/ A Rhodes scholar, he earned his law degree at Yale (like you-know-who)* (*1605+*)

◁**you must have mistaken me for someone who gives a shit**▷ *sentence* I do not care at all and you know that; what makes you think I care

you name it *sentence* You cannot designate anything not included here; the WHOLE SCHMEAR : *Casinos, giant water slides, aquariums, old-time steam engines, wine tasting, you* *name it: attracting tourists has become the gold rush of the '90s* [1962+; fr the retailing locution *you name it, we got it*]

young squirt *See* SQUIRT

Young Turk *n phr* A person, usu a young one, who threatens to overthrow an established system or order; an active rebel or reformer : *He scrutinizes the new staff very carefully, and is dreadfully fearful of potential Young Turks* [1908+; originally, a member of *Young Turkey,* a revolutionary party of late 1800s Turkey, which finally established constitutional government in 1908]

you pays your money and you takes your choice *sentence* The proposition is very uncertain; take a good guess : *How many shots were fired at the OK Corral? No one knows. Just pay your money and take your choice* (*1883+*)

your basic *adj phr* Definite; unquestionable • Used with a negating irony or slight sense of disbelief : *Now that would be your basic clue, right?/ He had your basic heart of gold* (*1980s+*)

you're damn (or **darn**) **tootin'** *affirmation* That is emphatically true; you are absolutely right : *Did I run? You're damn tootin' I did* (*1932+*)

you're telling me *interj* I strongly agree (*1932+*)

you're (or **you**) **the man** *interj* Congratulations : *Good work. You the man*

your money is no good here *sentence* You are our guest; you get everything free • Modified to a clause in the example : *The FBI agents began to discover that their money was no good in Wright City, and this made them uncomfortable* (*1900+*)

yours truly *pron phr* I; me; myself : *Both of whom are repped by yours truly* [1844+; fr the conventional parting salutation of a letter]

you said it *affirmation* You are absolutely right; that is correct; DEF, RIGHT ON (*1919+*)

you scratch my back, I scratch yours *sentence* Let us cooperate; let us be reciprocally and mutually helpful : *I'd love the whole country to get a good gander at how a labor union's supposed to run! You scratch my back, I'll scratch yours!* [1858+; *scratch me and I'll scratch thee* is found by 1704]

yowza or **yowsah** *affirmation* Yes, sir; certainly : *Recycling tax. Camping fees. State park fees. License plate renewal tax. Yowza* [1934+; popularized by the band leader Ben Bernie]

yo-yo *n* **1** A vacillating person; one who has no firm convictions : *Feldstein's sudden turnaround makes the president look like a yo-yo* (*1958+*) **2** A stupid and obnoxious person;

JERK, NERD : *Some yo-yo yells "What happened, you bum?"* (*1970+ Teenagers*)

yuck (also **ech** or **yecch** or **yech**) *interj* An exclamation of disgust : *"Those women on the PBS specials seem to love it." "Yuck,"* Connie mugged (*1969+*) *n* A disgusting substance, person, or thing; someone or something nasty : *precipitation in the form of rain, snow, and assorted other atmospheric yuck/ clean all the yecch out of her system/ Mario is an intellectually dishonest person. He's just yecch* (*1943+*) [perhaps echoic of gagging or vomiting] *See* YAK

yucky or **yecchy** or **yucko** *adj* Disgusting, esp in a filthy and viscous way; thoroughly nasty : *Some of it is awful yucky/ Cripes, what's that yucko bulging overhead object?* (*1970+*)

yuk *See* YAK

yummy *adj* Pleasant, esp sensually; delicious; delightful : *What a yummy cake!/ a yummy prospect* (*1899+*)

Yumpie *n* YUPPIE : *the highly desirable "Yumpies," young, upwardly mobile professionals* [1984+; fr *young upwardly mobile professional*]

yum-yum *interj* An exclamation of pleasure, esp of sensual delight (*1878+*) *n* Something sweet or pleasant, esp to eat (*1889+*) [perhaps fr a locution used with children, hence contextually as well as phonetically related to *tummy* or *tum-tum*]

yup *affirmation* YEP (*1906+*)

Yuppie *n* (also **Yup** or **yuppoid** or **yupster**) An affluent, usu city-dwelling, professional in his or her 20s and 30s; a prosperous and ambitious young professional : *Yuppies are dedicated to the twin goals of making piles of money and achieving perfection through physical fitness and therapy/ The narrow dance floor is soon crammed with "Yuppies," young urban professionals taking time out from social climbing/ The Yups discover that the locals have been putting up with this for years/ His death must have made more than a few Madison yupsters check their calendars/ photos of two generically cheerful yuppoids holding scotch glasses* [1984+; fr *young urban professional,* and modeled on *yippie;* perhaps coined for a 1983 book called *The Yuppie Handbook,* which was modeled on the earlier book *The Official Preppy Handbook*]

yuppify *v* To change a place, clothing, etc, to be characteristic of or welcoming to yuppies (*1984+*)

◁**yutz**▷ *n* **1** The penis; COCK, PRICK, SCHLONG : *as I was sticking my yutz into her Dark Place* (*1980s+*) **2** (also **yotz**) A fool; LOSER : *My ex-boyfriend was such a yutz/ some sweaty, exhausted, dignity-free yutz in a grotesquely unnatural pose* (*1980s+ Students*) [origin unknown]

Z

Z or **Zee** *n* Some sleep; a nap : *If he wants a few zees we can go on automatic* *v* To sleep; snooze; COP ZS : *Gotta Z a little while* [1960s+; fr the conventional sibilant or buzzing sound attributed to a sleeping or snoring person]

za or **'za** (ZAH) *n* Pizza : *Rents are parents. Za is pizza* [1968+ Teenagers; a shortening of *pizza*]

zaftig *See* ZOFTIG

zany *adj* Amusingly or ridiculously strange (1918+)

zap *interj* An exclamation imitating sudden impact; WHAM : *It's a gradual thing. It ain't zap, you're healed* (1929+) *n* Vitality; force; PIZZAZZ, ZIP (1968+) *v* **1** To kill or disable; strike violently; CLOBBER, WASTE : *Sitcom Zaps Boardroom Bozos* (1942+) **2** To administer electroshock therapy (1980s+ *Medical*) **3** To cook or heat in a microwave oven; NUKE : *Zap one minute, open the microwave door, stir and break up the meat pieces with a fork* (1990s+) [fr the echoic word used to convey the sound of a ray gun in the comic strip "Buck Rogers in the Twenty-Fifth Century"]

zapper *n* A remote control, esp for a television (1981+)

zarf *n* A repulsive person, esp male

zebra *n* **1** A referee or other sports official who wears a striped shirt on the playing field : *Pro football zebras point immediately toward the offending team/ a crooked Zebra (also known as an umpire)* (1978+ *Sports*) **2** An unlikely, arcane, or obscure diagnosis (1980s+ *Medical*) **3** A person of mixed black and white race : *I've been called a "zebra" and an "Oreo"* (1980s+) [the medical sense is fr the saying "If you hear horse's hoofbeats going by outside, don't look for *zebras*"]

zero *n* A truly insignificant person : *That zero will never get her to go to the dance*

zero cool *adj phr* Extremely aware, alert, up-to-date, relaxed, etc; COOL [1980s+; probably fr the concept of *absolute zero*]

zero in *v phr* To aim at or concentrate on a specific person, thing, etc; single out : *We're trying to zero in on the problem* [1944+; fr the zeroing of the sights of a rifle, that is, adjusting the sights so that the round hits the exact point aimed at and the shooter needs to make no, or *zero*, estimated correction in aiming]

zero out *v phr* To eliminate; reduce to nothing : *When Gingrich threatens to zero out all funding for public broadcasting, there's every reason to believe he can make good on the threat* (1990s+)

zero-tolerance *adj* Allowing no exceptions to a rule or law : *His parents have zero-tolerance policy on drugs* *n* Extreme intolerance of anti-social behavior; a policy of no exceptions to a rule or law : *The schools urge zero tolerance of smoking among minors*

zhlub *n* (also **schlub** or **shlub** or **shlubbo** or **zhlob** or **zshlub**) A coarse person; a boorish man; JERK, SLOB : *the presence of fine wines and the absence of shlubs/ replied Angela as she glided off to cut the poor schlub out of her will/ Lieberman was the worst. Lieberman was a real zshlub* [1964+; fr Yiddish fr Slavic, "coarse fellow"]

◄**zig** or **zigabo** or **zigaboo**► *See* JIGABOO

ziggety *See* HOT DIGGETY

zig-zig *See* JIG-JIG

zilch *modifier* : *York has close to zilch industry* *n* **1** Nothing; zero; ZIP : *The city has turned its smaller islands into zilch/ got the jeep for practically zilch* (1960s+) **2** storch (1970s+ *Teenagers*) **3** A minor skin lesion; ZIT (1970s+ *Teenagers*) *v* To hold an opponent scoreless; BLANK, SKUNK (1960s+ *Sports*) [probably fr *zero*, and like *zip*[1], primarily a variant coined from a familiar word beginning with *z*; notice, in this regard, how *zilch* has become a variant of *zit*; in British use, but not US, *zilch* might be reinforced by *nil*, "zero"; all senses may derive fr the early 1900s US college use *Joe Zilsch*, "any insignificant person," popularized during the 1930s by ubiquitous use in the humor magazine *Ballyhoo* with the spelling *Zilch*, an actual German surname of Slavic origin] *See* JOE BLOW, NOT KNOW BEANS

zillion *See* JILLION

zillionaire *n* An enormously rich person; a supertycoon : *and Larry Dunlap will become an instant zillionaire/ his earlier piece about how the Hong Kong zillionaires are buying up San Francisco* (1940+)

-zine (ZEEN) *suffix used to form nouns* Magazine : *teenzine/ fanzine* (1949+)

zing *n* Energetic vitality; power; vigor; OOMPH, PEP, PIZZAZZ, ZIP : *Rock adds zing/ with plenty of zing in both the V-8 engine and the powerful Six* (1918+) *v* **1** (also **zing along**) To move rapidly and strongly; ZIP : *The movie zings right along* (1961+) **2** To throw; inject, esp rapidly and strongly : *like the Beatles every once in a while can zing it in there* (1960s+) **3** To insult; assault verbally, esp with bitter humor : *King Caen, who zings everyone, gets a taste of his own medicine/ A woman on the editorial board merrily zinged the winking* *minister (1974+)* [probably echoic of the whishing sound of rapid movement, like *zip* and *zoom*]

zinger *n* **1** A quip, esp one that is somewhat cruel and aggressive; a funny crack or punch line : *Watt's off-the-cuff zingers have been a frequent source of pain for the Reagan Administration/ The plump little actor is polished and funny; his zingers stay zung* **2** A quick and sharp response; a sturdy retort : *get right in there with Williams, stand eyeball to eyeball, and plant the zinger on him, bang, or else you would be dismissed (1950+)*

zingy *adj* Full of energy and vigor; PEPPY, ZIPPY : *written by no less than the zingy Nora Ephron/ Zingy Zeroes, Wall Street's hot bonds (1948+)*

zip[1] or **zippo** *n* **1** A mark or grade of zero **2** Zero; nothing; a score of zero; ZILCH : *People aren't exactly beating down the doors to buy California port. "The market is zip, zero, and not too much"/ dipped into your moneybag and found zippo* [1900+ Students; like *zilch*, probably coined from a familiar word beginning with z] *See* NOT GIVE A DAMN, NOT KNOW BEANS

zip[2] or **zippo** *n* Energy; vitality; vim; PIZZAZZ, ZING : *There is a zip and a zing here/ bounced back with the real zippo* [1900+; echoic of the sound of something swishing rapidly through the air, giving an impression of force, and also of the tearing of cloth; such a use is attested fr 1875]

◀**zip**[3]▶ *n* A Vietnamese; DINK [Vietnam War; said to be fr *zero intelligence*]

zip gun *n phr* A homemade pistol : *a zip gun, the kind kids make themselves (1950+)*

zipless *adj* Denoting a sexual encounter that is brief and passionate [1973+; coined by Erica Jong, "because when you came together, zippers fell away like petals"]

zip one's lip (or one's **mouth**) *v phr* To stop talking, esp abruptly and completely; SHUT UP : *I just had to zip my mouth and do what I could* [1942+; fr the notion that one has a *zipper* fastener *on one's mouth*]

zippy *adj* Energetic; PEPPY, ZINGY : *the zippy pacing by Russell* [1904+; fr *zip*[2]]

zit *n* **1** A minor skin lesion; a pimple; a blackhead : *First Arnie's zits mysteriously clear up* **2** A mark left by a love-bite, a strong kiss, etc; HICKEY : *She tried to conceal the big zit on her neck* [1966+ Teenagers; origin unknown; perhaps echoic of the squishy pop made when the pus is squeezed from a blackhead]

zizz *n* : *She stretched out for a short zizz* *v* To sleep; snooze; nap; COP ZS *(1920s+ British armed forces)* [echoic of the sibilance or buzzing of one who sleeps, hence semantically akin to the notion of *sawing wood*]

zoftig or **zaftig** (ZAWF tik, ZAHF-) *adj* Sexually appealing or arousing to males, esp in a plump and well-rounded way; curvaceous; BUILT LIKE A BRICK SHITHOUSE : *zoftig, pleasantly plump and pretty/ The legs of the Red Suit are cut so high and deep, even the leanest female bum looks like a zaftig peach* [1937+; fr Yiddish, literally "juicy"]

zombie (ZAHM bee) *n* **1** A very strange person, esp one with a vacant, corpselike manner; WEIRDO *(1930s+ Students)* **2** An unresponsive person; a mentally numb or dead person : *My students are all zombies this term (1936+)* [origin uncertain; perhaps fr an African word akin to *nzambi*, "god"; perhaps fr Louisiana Creole, "phantom, ghost," fr Spanish *sombra*, "shade, ghost"; popularized by horror stories and movies featuring the walking dead persons of voodoo belief]

zombie someone **out** *v phr* To make someone stuporous like a zombie : *The medication I received for a couple of years "zombied me out" so bad I couldn't work (1980s+)*

zone[1] *See* IN A ZONE

zone[2] *n* (also **zoner**) A person intoxicated with narcotics, esp habitually so; SPACE CADET *(1960s+ Narcotics)* *v* To be inattentive; be hazily preoccupied : *He zoned so bad he didn't even hear the teacher call his name/ I was kind of zonin', checking things out (1980s+)* [fr *ozone*, "a very high level of the atmosphere"]

zoned or **zoned out** *adj* or *adj phr* Intoxicated with narcotics; HIGH [1960s+ Narcotics; fr *zone*; influenced by *spaced out*]

zone something **out** or **zone out** *v phr* To omit from consciousness; shut out of the mind : *I can just zone everything out and keep going (1960s+)*

zonk or **zonk out** *v* or *v phr* **1** To lose consciousness, esp from alcohol or narcotics; fall asleep; become stuporous : *He suddenly zonked and went rigid (1968+)* **2** To strike a stupefying blow; CLOBBER : *"We've been zonked," said Jim Robbins (1950+)* [fr *zonked*]

zonked or **zonked out** or **zonkers** *adj* or *adj phr* **1** Intoxicated by narcotics or alcohol; HIGH, STONED : *zonked, one step past being stoned/ Either while I was still zonked out or in the shower (1960s+ Narcotics)* **2** Very enthusiastic; excited; HIGH : *Rene Carpenter remembers Gilruth as "a kindly, wonderful man who was zonked on this project" (1970s+)* **3** Exhausted; BEAT, POOPED : *After just an hour of that I was zonked (1972+)* [echoic of a heavy blow; a 1929 *Bookman* article on sound effects is entitled "Socko, Whamo, and Sonk!"]

zoo *n* A crowded and chaotic place : *Opening Day is always a zoo/ The emergency room at Bellevue was usually a zoo (1935+)*

zoom in (on) *v phr* To concentrate or focus on something or someone to the exclusion of other things : *zooming in on the question of decency*

zoot suit *n phr* A man's suit with a jacket having very wide lapels, heavily padded shoulders, and many-buttoned sleeves, with very high-waisted trousers full in the leg and tapering to narrow cuffs • Such garments were worn as symbols of status and defiance, esp by urban black hipsters and Los Angeles Chicanos : *Some were garbed in short sleeve shirts, others in zoot suits/ Jelly got into his zoot suit with the reet pleats* [1942+; origin unknown; probably in essence a rhyming phrase of the sort common in black English and slang; perhaps related to other jive and cool-talk terms like *vootie*]

zowie *interj* An exclamation imitating sudden impact; POW, WHAM : *I ducked, but zowie, it caught me on the nose* (1913+) *n* Energy; vitality; vim; ZING, ZIP : *full of zing, full of zest, full of zowie* (1940s+)

Zs, some *See* COP ZS

zshlub *See* ZHLUB

APPENDIX A
Words for "Drunk,"
Intoxicated," and
"Intoxicated by Drugs"

Words in SMALL CAPITAL LETTERS are defined in the book.

Drunk

activated
alkied (up)
ALKIED, ALKEYED
annihilated
antifreezed
aped
apeshit
BAGGED
baked
balmed
balmy
bamboozled
banjaxed
barreled (up)
bashed
BASTED
bats
batted
battered
batty
belly up
belted
bent

bent out of
   shape
bewottled
binged
bladdered
blimped
BLIND
BLIND DRUNK
blind(ed)
blissed (out)
BLITZED
blitzed (out)
BLOATED
blocked
blooey
BLOTTO
blowed (away)
blown (out)
blown (up)
blown away
BLUE
blue around
   the gills
bobo
BOILED
BOMBED

bombed (out)
BONGO, BONGOED
bonkers
BOOZED, BOOZED UP
BOOZY
boozy-woozy
both sheets in
   the wind
bowzed
BOXED
boxed (up)
brewed
bruised
bunked
BUNNED
busted
BUZZIN'
buzzing
BUZZY
CANNED
carrying a (heavy)
   load
chucked
clear
CLOBBERED
COCKED
COCKEYED

comboozelated
commode-hugging
   drunk
cooked
CORKED
corked (up)
corky
CORNED
country drunk
CRASHED
creamed
CROCKED
CRONK
cross-eyed
   (drunk)
crumped (out)
crunk
crying drunk
cut
DAGGED
DAMAGED
DEAD DRUNK
DEAD TO THE WORLD
DECKS AWASH
dinged out
DIPSY
discombobulated

545

discomboobulated
down
DRUNK
DRUNK AS A SKUNK
drunk back
EDGED
electrified
ELEVATED
eliminated
EMBALMED
faced
faded
FALLING-DOWN DRUNK
far gone
far out
feel groovy
feeling no pain
feshnushkied
FIRED UP
fitshaced
fixed
flaked
flaked out
flako
flaky
flash
FLATLINED
FLOATING
flooey
floored
folded
foozlified
four sheets (to the wind)
four sheets in the wind
foxy
FRACTURED
FRAZZLED
FRIED
FULL
funked out
funky-drunk
fuzzed
FUZZLED
fuzzy
GAGED
gargler
GASSED
gassed (up)

GEEZED, GEEZED UP
giffed
GINNED, GINNED UP
glad
glass(y)-eyed
glazed (drunk)
glazed (over)
glued
goggle-eyed
gone
goofy
googly-eyed
gooned
grape shot
greased
GROGGED
groggified
groggy
guyed out
guzzled
HALF CROCKED
HALF IN THE BAG
HALF SEAS OVER
half up the pole
HALF-BAGGED
half-baked
half-blind
half-canned
half-cocked
half-corned
half-crocked
half-lit
HALF-SHOT
half-sprung
HALF-STEWED
half-under
HAMMERED
HAPPY
hard up
heeled
heister
hepped (up)
HIGH
hit under the wing
hoary-eyed, orie-eyed, orry-eyed
honked
honkers
hooched (up)

hooted
hootered
horizontal
hot
howling (drunk)
illuminated
impaired
in a bad way
in a heap
in one's cups
in orbit
in rare form
in the bag
in the grip of the grape
in the gun
in the ozone
in the pink
in the suds
inside out
JAGGED
jambled
JAMMED
jazzed (up)
jiggered
jingled
jolly
jugged (up)
juicy
jungled
Kentucky fried
keyed (up)
keyed up to the roof
killed (off)
kited
KNOCKED OUT
knocked up
KOed
laid
laid back
LAID OUT
laid to the bone
lathered
layed
lifted
light
liquefied
LIQUORED UP
LIT

LIT TO THE GILLS
LIT UP, LIT UP LIKE A CHRISTMAS TREE
LOADED
loaded for bear
loaded to the barrel
loaded to the gills
loony
LOOPED, LOOPING
loop-legged
loopy
loose
lost in the sauce
LUBRICATED
LUSHED, LUSHED UP
maggot(ty)
mashed
maxed out
MELLOW
messed up
Mickey finished
milled
mixed (up)
moist around the edges
moonlit
mopped
moppy
muddled (up)
muggy
nipped
non compos
non compos poopoo
obliterated
off
OILED
on the blink
on the fritz
on the sauce
OSSIFIED
Otis
out
out cold
out like a light
out of it
out of one's skull
out of sight
out of the way
overserved

packaged
pafisticated
paid
PARALYZED
PARBOILED
pee'd
peonied
pepped (up)
perked (up)
perking
perma-fried
PETRIFIED
phfft
PICKLED
PIE-EYED
PIFFED, PIFFLED
PIFFLICATED
pigeon-eyed
pilfered
pinked
pipped (up)
pissed
PIXILATED
pixolated
PLASTERED
plastered to the
    wall
pleasantly plastered
PLONKED
plonked (up)
plootered
PLOTZED
plowed (under)
polished (up)
POLLUTED
pooped (out)
poopied
pop-eyed
popped
POTTED, POTTED UP
powdered (up)
preserved
primed
psyched (out)
puggled
pummelled
pushed
put to bed with a
    shovel
putrid

quartzed
queer
queered
racked (up)
ratted
rattled
raunchy
riffed
ripe
ripped
ripped (off)
ripped (up)
roasted
ROCKY
ROSY
rotten
RUM-DUM
rummed (up)
rummy
SATURATED
sauced
sawed
scammered
schicker
schickered
SCHNOCKERED, SNOCK-
    ERED
schnoggered
scorched
screeching (drunk)
SCREWED
screwed tight
screwy
scronched
SCROOCHED
seeing pink
    elephants
sent
sewed up
SF
shagged
shammered
SHAVED
SHELLACKED
shicker
shikker, shicker
shined
SHIT-FACED
shitty
shnockered

SHOT
shot in the neck
shot-away
shot-up
shredded
sizzled
skulled
skunk-drunk
skunked
slaughtered
SLEWED
slewy
slightly rattled
SLOPPED
SLOSHED
sloshed (to the
    ears)
sloughed (up)
slued
SLUGGED
slushed (up)
SMASHED
smeared
snapped (up)
snoggered
snooted
snoozamorooed
snotted
snozzled
SNUFFY
snuffy
SOAKED
socked
soft
soggy
sopping (wet)
soppy
so-so
sossled
soupy
SOUSED
southern-fried
SOZZLED
sozzly
spanked
SPIFFED
SPIFFLICATED
spificated
spiked
SPRUNG

squiffed
SQUIFFY, SQUIFFY-EYED,
    SQUIFFED
stale drunk
starched
starchy
steamed (up)
stew
STEWED, STEWED TO THE
    GILLS
stewed (up)
stewed to the ears
STIFF
stiffed
stinking
STINKING, STINKO
stinking (drunk)
stone blind
stoned (out)
stoned out of one's
    squash
stoned silly
stonkered
stozzled
stuccoed
stung
stunned
stupid
SWACKED
swamped
swigged
swiggled
SWIZZLED, SWOZZLED
swoozled
tacky
TANKED, TANKED UP
tanky
tanned
TEED UP
that way
thawed
THREE SHEETS TO THE
    WIND, THREE SHEETS
    IN THE WIND
tiddled
TIDDLY
tiffled
TIGHT
TIGHT AS A TICK
tipply
tipsy

top-heavy
tore (up)
tore down
torn (up)
torqued
totalled
touched
toxicated
toxy
trammeled
trashed
tubed
tuned
tweased
tweeked
twisted
two sheets to the wind
under the affluence of incohol
UNDER THE TABLE
under the weather
up the pole
upholstered
varnished
vegetable
vomatose
w(h)acked
w(h)acked (out)
waa-zooed
walking on rocky socks
WALL-EYED
waxed
way out
well-fixed
WELL-OILED
wet
whack
whazood
whiffled
whittled
whooshed
wigged (out)
wiggy
wing heavy
WIPED OUT
wiped over
wired

wired up
woofled
woozy
wrecked
zagged
zissified
zoned (out)
zonked (out)
zonker
zoobang
zooed
zooted
zootied
zorked
zosted
zounked (out)
zozzled
zunked

Intoxicated

BENT
BENT OUT OF SHAPE
BLASTED
BUZZED
HIGH AS A KITE
JUICED, JUICED UP
OUT, OUT COLD
RIPPED
SLAP-HAPPY
STONED TO THE EYES
STONED, STONED-OUT
TOTALED
WASTED
ZONKED, ZONKED OUT, ZONKERS

Intoxicated by Drugs

amped
backed up
BAKED
beaming
beaned up
belted
bent
bent out of shape
blind(ed)
blissed (out)
blitzed (out)

blixed
blocked
blowed (away)
blown (out)
blown away
BLOWN-OUT
BOMBED OUT
bonged
BONGED-OUT
BOOTED
boxed (up)
boxed out
CHARGED UP
CHOKED OUT
COKED, COKED-UP, COKED-OUT
cooked
CRANKED UP
crisp
destroyed
DOPEY, DOPY
edged
enhanced
faded
far out
feel groovy
fixed
flaked out
FLOATING
FOGGED OUT
foxy
fried
FUCKED UP
funked out
GAGE, GAGED
gassed (up)
GBed
GEED, G'D
GEEZED, GEEZED UP
girked
GONE
GONGED
GOOFED
goofed (up)
GOONED, GOONED OUT
gowed up
groovy
HIGH
HOPPED UP
horsed

hurt
hyped (up)
in orbit
in the ozone
IN THE POCKET
jacked
jacked up
jazzed (up)
keyed (up)
keyed up to the roof
killed (off)
KNOCKED OUT
KOed
laid
laid back
laid out
layed
LIFTED
LIT UP, LIT UP LIKE A CHRISTMAS TREE
LOADED
luded out
MAXED
mellow
messed up
mohasky
monolithic
numbed out
off
oiled
OSSIFIED
out
out of it
out of sight
out of this world
over the hump
overamped
perking
perma-fried
PETRIFIED
phased
phazed
phumfed
plowed (under)
plugged in
polluted
popped
POTTED, POTTED UP
primed

psyched (out)
racked (up)
red
riffed
ripped
ripped (off)
ripped (up)
scattered
schnockered
schnoggered
scorched
sent
shot-up
skagged out
skating

skulled
smashed
smeared
SMOKED OUT
snaved in
SNOWED IN, SNOWED UP
SPACED-OUT, SPACED,
    SPACEY, SPACY
spiked
stoned (out)
stoned out of one's
    gourd
stoned out of one's
    head
stoned out of one's
    squash

stoned silly
strung (up)
STRUNG OUT
taken
tea'd up
teed (up)
trashed
TRIPPY
TURNED ON
TWISTED
UP
w(h)acked
w(h)acked (out)
warped
WAY OUT

wide
WIGGED OUT, WIGGED
wiggy
wingy
wiped over
wired up
WIRED, WIRED UP
WRECKED
zerked (out)
zipped
ZONED, ZONED OUT
zonked (out)
zootied
zounked (out)
zunked

APPENDIX B
Guide to Text Messaging Abbreviations

404	I don't know	ATM	At the moment
411	Info	ATST	At the same time
86	Out of, Over	AWOL	Absent without leave
@TEOTD	At the end of the Day	AYEC	At your earliest
2NITE	Tonight		convenience
4EVER	Forever	AYK	As you know
A or S or L	Age or sex or location	AYOR	At your own risk
A3	Anytime, anywhere,	B or C	Because
	anyplace	B or F	Boyfriend
AAF	As a friend	B4	Before
AAP	Always a pleasure	B4N	Bye for now
AAR	At any rate	BAK	Back at keyboard
AAR8	At any rate	BAU	Business as usual
AAS	Alive and smiling	BBIAF	Be back in a few
ABT2	About to	BBIAM	Be back in a minute
ACK	Acknowledgment	BBL	Be back later
ADBB	All done bye-bye	BBS	Be back soon
ADD	Address	BBT	Be back tomorrow
ADN	Any day now	BC	Because
ADR	Address	BCNU	Be seein' you
AEAP	As early as possible	BCOZ	Because
AFAIK	As far as I know	BD	Big deal
AFC	Away from computer	BF	Best friend
AFK	Away from keyboard	BFD	Big f***ing deal
AIMB	As I mentioned before	BFF	Best friends forever
AISB	As it should be	BFG	Big f***ing grin
AKA	Also known as	BFN	Bye for now
ALAP	As late as possible	BG	Big grin
AMAP	As many as possible	BGWM	Be gentle with me
AML	All my love	BLNT	Better luck next time
AOTA	All of the above	BM&Y	Between me and you
ASAP	As soon as possible	BOL	Best of luck
ASL	Age or sex or location	BR	Bathroom
ASLMH	Age or Sex or Location or	BRB	Be right back
	Music or Hobbies	BRT	Be right there
AT	At your terminal	BTA	But then again

BTDT	Been there, done that	FAB	Features, attributes, benefits
BTHOOM	Beats the hell out of me		
BTSOOM	Beats the sh*t out of me	FAWC	For anyone who cares
BTW	By the way	FBM	Fine by me
BW	Best wishes	FC	Fingers crossed
C or P	Cross post	FF	Friends forever
CID	Consider it done	FICCL	Frankly I couldn't care a less
CMIIW	Correct me if I'm wrong		
CMON	Come on	FISH	First in, still here
COB	Close of business	FITB	Fill in the blank
COS	Because	FO	F*** off
CR8	Create	FOAF	Friend of a friend
CRAT	Can't remember a thing	FOFL	Falling on floor laughing
CRB	Come right back	FOMCL	Falling off my chair laughing
CRBT	Crying really big tears		
CSL	Can't stop laughing	FRT	For real though
CU	See you	FTTB	For the time being
CUA	See you around	FUD	Fear, uncertainty, disinformation
CUL	See you later		
CUL8ER	See you later	FWIW	For what it's worth
CUL8R	See you later	FYA	For your amusement
CUNS	See you in school	FYEO	For your eyes only
CWYL	Chat with you later	FYI	For your information
CYA	See ya	G	Grin
CYL	See you later	G or F	Girlfriend
CYO	See you online	G2CU	Good to see you
CYT	See you tomorrow	G2G	Got to go
D or L	Download	G2R	Got to run
DEGT	Don't even go there	G9	Genius
DGA	Don't go anywhere	GA	Go ahead
DGT	Don't go there	GAL	Get a life
DIKU	Do I know you?	GB	Goodbye
DIY	Do it yourself	GBH	Great big hug
DKDC	Don't know don't care	GBU	God bless you
DL	Download	GD or R	Grinning, ducking, and running
DMI	Don't mention it		
DNC	Does not compute	GDR	Grinning, ducking, and running
DQMOT	Don't quote me on this		
DRIB	Don't read if busy	GFI	Go for it
DTS	Don't think so	GG	Gotta Go or Good Game
DUST	Did you see that?	GGN	Gotta go now
DV8	Deviate	GIAR	Give it a rest
E123	Easy as one two three	GIGO	Garbage in, garbage out
EAK	Eating at keyboard	GL	Good luck
EBKAC	Error between keyboard and chair	GLHF	Good luck, have fun
		GLNG	Good luck next game
EG	Evil grin	GMTA	Great minds think alike
EL	Evil laugh	GOI	Get over it
EM?	Excuse me?	GOK	God only knows
EMA	E-mail address	GOL	Giggling out loud
EMFBI	Excuse me for butting in	GR&D	Grinning, running and ducking
EOD	End of day		
EOM	End of message	GR8	Great
EWI	E-mailing while in-toxicated	GT	Good try
		GTG	Got to go
EZ	Easy	GTH	Go to hell
EZY	Easy	GTRM	Going to read mail
F2F	Face to face	H&K	Hugs & kisses
F2T	Free to talk	H2CUS	Hope to see you soon

H8	Hate	ISTM	It seems to me
HAGD	Have a good day	ISWYM	I see what you mean
HAGN	Have a good night	ITM	In the money
HAGO	Have a good one	IUSS	If you say so
HAK	Hugs & kisses	IYKWIM	If you know what I mean
HAND	Have a nice day	IYO	In your opinion
HB	Hurry back	IYSS	If you say so
HD	Hold	IYSWIM	If you see what I mean
HF	Have fun or Hello friend	J or C	Just checking
HHIS	Head hanging in shame	J or K	Just kidding
HIH	Hope it helps	J or W	Just wondering
HOAS	Hold on a second	j00r	Your
HRU	How are you?	JAC	Just a sec
HTH	Hope this helps	JAM	Just a minute
HUGZ	Hugs	JIC	Just in case
HV	Have	JJA	Just joking around
IAC	In any case	JK	Just kidding
IAE	In any event	JM2C	Just my two cents
IANAE	I am not an expert	JMO	Just my opinion
IANAL	I am not a lawyer	JOOTT	Just one of those things
IAT	I am tired	JP	Just playing
IB	I'm back	JT	Just teasing
IBRB	I'll be right back	K	Okay or All right
IBTD	I beg to differ	k or b	keyboard
IC	I see or In character	KBD	keyboard
ICBW	It could be worse or I could be wrong	KEWL	Cool
		KFY	Kiss for you
ID10T	Idiot	KIR	Keep it real
IDGAF	I don't give a f***	KISS	Keep it simple, stupid
IDK	I don't know	KIT	Keep in touch
I-D-L	Ideal	KMA	Kiss my a**
IDM	It doesn't matter	KNIM	Know what I mean?
IDTS	I don't think so	KOTC	Kiss on the cheek
IDUNNO	I don't know	KOTL	Kiss on the lips
IFU	I f***ed up	KPC	Keeping parents clueless
IG2R	I got to run	KWIM	Know what I mean?
IGGP	I gotta go pee	KYPO	Keep your pants on
IGTP	I get the point	L8R	Later
IHNO	I have no opinion	LD	Later, dude or Long distance
IIRC	If I remember correctly		
ILBL8	I'll be late	LMAO	Laughing my a** off
ILU	I love you	LMK	Let me know
ILY	I love you	LOL	Laughing out loud
IM	Instant message, Instant messaging	LTM	Laugh to myself
		LTNS	Long time no see
IMHO	In my humble opinion	LYL	Love you lots
IMNSHO	In my not so humble opinion	LYLAB	Love you like a brother
		LYLAS	Love you like a sister
IMO	In my opinion	M8	Mate
IMS	I am sorry	MFI	Mad for it
INAL	I'm not a lawyer	MIHAP	May I have your attention please
INMP	It's not my problem		
INNW	If not now, when?	MOMPL	One moment please
INPO	In no particular order	MOOS	Member of opposite sex
IOH	I'm outta here	MorF	Male or female?
IOW	In other words	MoS	Mother over shoulder
IRL	In real life	MOSS	Member of same sex
IRMC	I rest my case	MSG	Message
ISS	I said so	MTF	More to follow

MTFBWU	May the force be with you	P&C	Private and confidential
MTFBWY	May the force be with you	PCM	Please call me
MUSM	Miss you so much	PDQ	Pretty darn quick
MWBRL	More will be revealed later	PITA	Pain in the a**
		PLMK	Please let me know
MYOB	Mind your own business	PLS	Please
N or A	Not applicable or Not affiliated	PLZ	Please
		PM	Private Message or Personal message
n00b	Newbie		
N1	Nice one		
N2M	Not to mention	PMFI	Pardon me for interrupting
N-A-Y-L	In a while		
NBD	No big deal	PMFJI	Pardon me for jumping in
NBIF	No basis in fact	PO	P*ss off
NE	Any	POAHF	Put on a happy face
NE1	Anyone	PONA	Person of no account
N-E-1	Anyone	POOF	Goodbye
NFI	No f***ing idea	POS	Parent over shoulder
NFM	None for me or Not for me	POV	Point of view
NFW	No f***ing way	PPL	People
NG	New game	PROLLY	Probably
NIMBY	Not in my back yard	PRT	Party
NLT	No later than	PRW	People or parents are watching
NM	Nothing much or Never mind	PTL	Praise the Lord
NMH	Not much here	PTMM	Please tell me more
NMP	Not my problem	PU	That stinks!
NO1	No one	PXT	Please explain that
NOYB	None of your business	P-ZA	Pizza
NP	No problem	Q	Queue
NRN	No response or reply necessary	QIK	Quick
		QL	Quit laughing!
NTK	Nice to know	QT	Cutie
NTYMI	Now that you mention it	R&R	Rest and relaxation
NUFF	Enough said	RBAY	Right back at ya
NVM	Never mind	RBTL	Read between the lines
NW	No way	RE	Regards or Hello again
OBTW	Oh by the way	RFD	Request for discussion
OIC	Oh, I see	RFS	Real f***ing soon
OMDB	Over my dead body	RL	Real life
OMG	Oh my God	RME	Rolling my eyes
OMIK	Open mouth insert keyboard	RML	Read my lips
		RMMM	Read my mail, man!
OMW	On my way	RN	Right now
ONNA	Oh no not again	ROFL	Rolling on floor laughing
OO	Over and out	ROTFL	Rolling on the floor laughing
OOH	Out of here		
OOI	Out of interest	ROTFLUTS	Rolling on the floor laughing unable to speak
OOTD	One of these days		
OP	On phone		
OT	Off topic	ROTM	Right on the money
OTB	Off to bed	RSN	Real soon now
OTL	Out to lunch	RTFM	Read the f***ing manual
OTOH	On the other hand	RTK	Return to keyboard
OTP	On the phone	RTM	Read the manual
OTT	Over the top	RU	Are you...
OTTOMH	Off the top of my head	RUMOF	Are you male or female?
OTW	Off to work	RUOK	Are you okay?
OVA	Over	RUUP4IT	Are you up for it?
OWTTE	Or words to that effect	RX	Regards

SAL	Such a laugh	TFDS	That's for darn sure
SC	Stay cool	TFN	Thanks for nothing
SCNR	Sorry, could not resist	TFW	Too freakin' weird
SEP	Somebody else's problem	TGIF	Thank God it's Friday
SETE	Smiling Ear-to-Ear	THKS	Thanks
SH	Sh** happens	THNQ	Thank-you
SICNR	Sorry, I could not resist	THNX	Thanks
SIG2R	Sorry, I got to run	THX	Thanks
SIS	Snickering in silence	TIA	Thanks in advance
SIT	Stay in touch	TIAD	Tomorrow is another day
SITD	Still in the dark	TIC	Tongue in cheek
SLAP	Sounds like a plan	TK	To come
SMAIM	Send me an instant message	TLK2UL8R	Talk to you later
		TM	Trust me
SMEM	Send me e-mail	TMB	Text me back
SMHID	Scratching my head in disbelief	TMI	Too much information
		TMOT	Trust me on this
SNAFU	Situation normal all fouled up	TMWFI	Take my word for it
		TNA	Temporarily not available
SO	Significant other	TNC	Tongue in cheek
SOL	Sh** out of luck	TNSTAAFL	There's no such thing as a free lunch
SOL	Sooner or later		
SOMY	Sick of me yet?	TNX	Thanks
SOP	Standard operating procedure	TOM	Tomorrow
		TP	Team player
SorG	Straight or gay?	TPML	Tomorrow p.m.
SOTMG	Short of time, must go	TPTB	The powers that be
SPK	Speak	TSIA	This says it all
SPST	Same place, same time	TSTB	The sooner, the better
SRY	Sorry	TTFN	Ta ta for now
SS	So sorry	TTG	Time to go
SSDD	Same stuff, different day	TTTT	These things take time
SSINF	So stupid it's not funny	TTUL	Talk to you later
STFU	Shut the f*** up	TTYL	Talk to you later
STR8	Straight	TTYS	Talk to you soon
STW	Search the Web	TU	Thank you
STYS	Speak to you soon	TVN	Thank you very much
SUITM	See you in the morning	TWIMC	To whom it may concern
SUL	See you later	TX	Thanks
SUP	What's up?	TXS	Thanks
SWAK	Sent with a kiss	TY	Thank you
SWDYT	So what do you think?	TYT	Take your time
SYL	See you later	TYVM	Thank you very much
SYS	See you soon	U2	You too?
T+	Think positive	UGTBK	You've got to be kidding
TA	Thanks a lot	UKTR	You know that's right
TAFN	That's all for now	UL	Upload
TAH	Take a hike	U-L	You will...
TAM	Tomorrow a.m.	UR	Your or You're
TANSTAAFL	There ain't no such thing as a free lunch	U-R	You are...
		UV	Unpleasant visual
TAS	Taking a shower	UW	You're welcome
TBC	To be continued	VBG	Very big grin
TBD	To be determined	VBS	Very big smile
TBH	To be honest	VM	Voice mail
TC	Take care	VSF	Very sad face
TCB	The trouble came back!	W/O	Without
TDTM	Talk dirty to me	WAD	Without a doubt
TEOTWAWKI	The end of the world as we know it	WAG	Wild ass guess
		WAM	Wait a minute

WAN2TLK	Want to talk	WYCM?	Will you call me?
WAYF	Where are you from?	WYLEI	When you least expect it
WB	Welcome back	WYP	What's your problem?
WB	Write back	WYRN	What's your real name?
WBS	Write back soon	WYS	Whatever you say
WC	Who cares?	WYSIWYG	What you see is what you get
WDYS	What did you say?		
WDYT	What do you think?	WYT	Whatever you think
WE	Whatever	WYWH	Wish you were here
WF	Way fun	X	Kiss
WFM	Works for me	X-I-10	Exciting
WG	Wicked grin	XLNT	Excellent
WIIFM	What's in it for me?	XME	Excuse me
WK	Week	XOXO	Hugs and kisses
WKD	Weekend	YA	Your or Yet another
WOMBAT	Waste of money, brains and time	YBS	You'll be sorry
		YDKM	You don't know me
WRK	Work	YGBK	You gotta be kidding
WRT	With regard or respect to	YGBKM	You've got to be kidding me
WRUD	What are you doing?		
WT	Without thinking	YHM	You have mail
WTB	Want to buy	YKW?	You know what?
WTF	What the f*ck	YKWYCD	You know what you can do
WTG	Way to go!		
WTH	What the heck?!	YMMV	Your mileage may vary
WU?	What's up?	YNK	You never know
WUCIWUG	What you see is what you get	YOYO	You're on your own
		YR	You're right or Yeah right
WUF?	Where are you from?	YTTT	You telling the truth?
WWJD	What would Jesus do?	YW	You're welcome
WWY?	Where were you?	YWIA	You're welcome in advance
WWYC	Write when you can		
WX	Weather	ZZZZ	Sleeping